The Westminster
Theological Wordbook
of the Bible

The Westminster Theological Wordbook of the Bible

Edited by DONALD E. GOWAN

Westminster John Knox Press
LOUISVILLE • LONDON

Book design by Sharon Adams
Cover design by Eric Handel, LMNOP
Cover art: Adam is tempted by Eve in the Garden of Eden in a stained glass panel designed by John Thornton as part of the Great East Window (ca. 1405–1408) in York Minster. © Angelo Hornak/CORBIS

First edition
Published by Westminster John Knox Press
Louisville, Kentucky

This book is printed on acid-free paper that meets the American National Standards Institute Z39.48 standard. ∞

PRINTED IN THE UNITED STATES OF AMERICA

03 04 05 06 07 08 09 10 11 12 — 10 9 8 7 6 5 4 3 2 1

Library of Congress Cataloging-in-Publication Data

The Westminster theological wordbook of the Bible / edited
      by Donald E. Gowan.—1st ed.
      p. cm.
   Includes bibliographical references.
   ISBN 0-664-22394-X (case)
   1. Bible—Theology—Dictionaries.   I. Gowan, Donald E.

   BS543.W47 2003
   220.3—dc21   2003041179

To my grandchildren
Joshua and Jennifer Hannan

Preface

Although a study of the vocabulary of the Bible is only the first step in interpretation, it is an essential step. The words of Scripture are heavy with meaning, carried from generation to generation by tradition, and from time to time filled with new insights by inspired writers. The aim of this book is to provide for serious students of the Bible essays on its theological vocabulary by a carefully selected group of scholars, chosen because of their fields of specialization. Scholarship and readability have been essential criteria in planning the book, thinking of two groups of potential readers: those without much theological training who seek a reference book they can use with ease and those who may be able to use more technical works, but either do not have ready access to them or do not need, for their immediate purpose, all the details those books provide.

Many Bible dictionaries, of varying sizes, are now available, containing a wide range of information concerning Scripture and the ancient Near East. This book is distinguished from them by its focus on theology, for it has been defined so that in a volume of modest size theological articles of some depth could be offered. The words *theological wordbook* define it exactly. It is a "wordbook," and as such it does not offer articles on broad and general theological topics. It is based on the vocabulary of the NRSV and intends to offer the reader help in understanding all the English words of any theological significance in that translation, with reference to the original Hebrew, Aramaic, and Greek terms that those words translate. So, for example, the articles on "authority" and "atonement" discuss the ways those words are used in the Bible and do not enter into general discussions of the authority of Scripture, or of the theories of atonement developed in Christian history. These may be found in other types of books. Proper names are included only when the writers of Scripture use them for a theological purpose. So "Adam" is included because of Paul's comparison of Adam and Christ, but "Paul" is not, for no writer uses him as a theological topic. The intention has been to offer, in the midst of an abundance of recent and voluminous reference books intended to inform serious study of the Bible, a reference whose pages are focused very carefully on theology, discussing history and sociology and literary criticism only to the extent that they are needed to explain what these words mean.

The book has been written so that it can be used by readers who do not know the biblical languages. For those who have access to and can use more technical resources, three lengthy works are recommended:

G. J. Botterweck and H. Ringgren, eds., *Theological Dictionary of the Old Testament* (Grand Rapids: Wm. B. Eerdmans Publishing Co., 1974–2002); 12 volumes, as yet incomplete.

E. Jenni, C. Spicq, and C. Westermann, eds., *Theological Lexicon of the Old Testament*, and *Theological Lexicon of the New Testament* (Peabody, Mass.: Hendrickson Publishers, 1997); 3 volumes each.

G. Kittel and G. Friedrich, eds., *Theological Dictionary of the New Testament* (Grand Rapids: Wm. B. Eerdmans Publishing Co., 1964–1974); 10 volumes.

Lengthy articles on some of the words in this book also appear in two large Bible dictionaries:

G. A. Buttrick, ed., *Interpreter's Dictionary of the Bible* (Nashville: Abingdon Press, 1962, 1976); 5 volumes.

David Noel Freedman, ed., *Anchor Bible Dictionary* (New York: Doubleday, 1992); 6 volumes.

The five works listed above will not be cited in the bibliographies except where an author has made explicit reference to one of them in an article. The bibliographies have been provided partly by the authors and partly by the editor, who has also supplied articles where assignments could not otherwise be completed. The simplest possible form of Hebrew transliteration has been used, aiming at an approximate pronunciation without the use of diacritical marks, except for ʾaleph and ʿayin. Those who know Hebrew will be aware of its inaccuracy, but they will recognize the words.

I thank Dr. Donald K. McKim, Academic and Reference Editor at Westminster John Knox Press, for originating the idea for this book and for asking me to be its editor, as well as for many helpful words of advice along the way. I also thank the authors, who have contributed such excellent articles, and especially those who agreed to take an extra one late in the process.

DONALD E. GOWAN

Contributors

Dale C. Allison Jr.
Errett M. Grable Professor of New
  Testament and Early Christianity
Pittsburgh Theological Seminary
Pittsburgh, Pennsylvania

Samuel E. Balentine
Russell T. Cherry Professor of Old
  Testament
Baptist Theological Seminary
Richmond, Virginia

Ronald E. Clements
Emeritus Professor of Old Testament
  Studies
King's College, University of London
London, United Kingdom

L. William Countryman
Sherman E. Johnson Professor in Biblical
  Studies
Church Divinity School of the Pacific
Berkeley, California

Jerome F. D. Creach
Associate Professor of Old Testament
Pittsburgh Theological Seminary
Pittsburgh, Pennsylvania

Carol J. Dempsey, OP
Associate Professor of Theology
University of Portland
Portland, Oregon

Thomas B. Dozeman
Professor of Old Testament
United Theological Seminary
Dayton, Ohio

James A. Durlesser
Senior Pastor
Stone United Methodist Church
Meadville, Pennsylvania

Kathleen Anne Farmer
Professor of Old Testament
United Theological Seminary
Dayton, Ohio

Stephen Farris
Professor of Preaching and
  Worship
Knox College, Toronto School of
  Theology
Toronto, Ontario, Canada

Terence E. Fretheim
Elva B. Lovell Professor of Old Testament
Luther Seminary
St. Paul, Minnesota

Frances Taylor Gench
Professor of New Testament
Union Theological Seminary &
  Presbyterian School of Christian
  Education
Richmond, Virginia

John Goldingay
David Allan Hubbard Professor of Old
  Testament
Fuller Theological Seminary
Pasadena, California

Donald E. Gowan
Emeritus Robert Cleveland Holland
  Professor of Old Testament
Pittsburgh Theological Seminary
Pittsburgh, Pennsylvania

Douglas R. A. Hare
Emeritus William F. Orr Professor of
  New Testament
Pittsburgh Theological Seminary
Pittsburgh, Pennsylvania

Craig Keener
Professor of New Testament
Eastern Baptist Seminary
Wynnewood, Pennsylvania

Richard N. Longenecker
Distinguished Professor of New Testa-
  ment, Bethel Seminary, St. Paul,
  Minnesota
Professor Emeritus of New Testament,
  Wycliffe College, University of
  Toronto, Toronto, Ontario, Canada

I. Howard Marshall
Honorary Research Professor of New
  Testament
University of Aberdeen, Scotland
United Kingdom

Christopher R. Matthews
Co-editor of *New Testament Abstracts*
Adjunct Professor of New Testament
Weston School of Theology
Cambridge, Massachusetts

Ulrich W. Mauser
Otto A. Piper Professor of Biblical
  Theology Emeritus
Princeton Theological Seminary
Princeton, New Jersey

J. Clinton McCann Jr.
Evangelical Professor of Biblical
  Interpretation
Eden Theological Seminary
St. Louis, Missouri

Margaret S. Odell
Associate Professor of Religion
St. Olaf College
Northfield, Minnesota

Graham S. Ogden
Translation Consultant
United Bible Societies
Daylesford, Australia

Dale Patrick
Professor of Bible; Endowment
  Professor of the Humanities
Drake University
Des Moines, Iowa

David L. Petersen
Professor of Old Testament
Candler School of Theology, Emory
  University
Atlanta, Georgia

John J. Pilch
Adjunct Assistant Professor, Georgetown University, Washington, D.C.
Research Associate, University
  of Pretoria, Pretoria, South Africa

Paul L. Redditt
Professor of Old Testament
Georgetown College
Georgetown, Kentucky

John Reumann
Professor Emeritus of New Testament
  and Greek
Lutheran Theological Seminary
Philadelphia, Pennsylvania

Willard M. Swartley
Professor of New Testament
Associated Mennonite Biblical Seminary
Elkhart, Indiana

W. Sibley Towner
Professor Emeritus of Biblical
  Interpretation
Union Theological Seminary &
  Presbyterian School of Christian
  Education
Richmond, Virginia

Stephen Westerholm
Associate Professor of Biblical Studies
McMaster University
Hamilton, Ontario, Canada

Abbreviations

AB	Anchor Bible	*Int*	*Interpretation*
ABD	*Anchor Bible Dictionary*, ed. D. N. Freedman	ITC	International Theological Commentary
AnBib	*Analecta biblica*	*j.*	*The Jerusalem Talmud*
ANESTP	*The Ancient Near East: Supplementary Texts and Pictures Relating to the Old Testament*, ed. J. B. Pritchard	*JBL*	*Journal of Biblical Literature*
		JETS	*Journal of the Evangelical Theological Society*
		JNES	*Journal of Near Eastern Studies*
ANET	*Ancient Near Eastern Texts*, ed. J. B. Pritchard	*JSJ*	*Journal for the Study of Judaism in the Persian, Hellenistic, and Roman Periods*
AV	Authorized Version of the Bible	*JSNT*	*Journal for the Study of the New Testament*
b.	*The Babylonian Talmud*		
BJRL	*Bulletin of the John Rylands University Library of Manchester*	JSNTSup	Journal for the Study of the New Testament: Supplement Series
BTB	*Biblical Theology Bulletin*	*JSOT*	*Journal for the Study of the Old Testament*
CBQ	*Catholic Biblical Quarterly*		
CBQMS	Catholic Biblical Quarterly Monograph Series	JSOTSup	Journal for the Study of the Old Testament: Supplement Series
CEV	Contemporary English Version	*JSP*	*Journal for the Study of the Pseudepigrapha*
ConBOT	Coniectanea biblica: Old Testament Series	*JTS*	*Journal of Theological Studies*
EvQ	*Evangelical Quarterly*	KJV	King James Version of the Bible
EVV	English Versions		
ExpTim	*Expository Times*	LXX	Septuagint Version of the Old Testament
HBT	*Horizons in Biblical Theology*		
HTR	*Harvard Theological Review*	*m.*	*The Mishnah*
HUCA	*Hebrew Union College Annual*	Mg	References to variant readings in the margin of a translation
ICC	International Critical Commentary		
		MT	Masoretic (Hebrew) Text of the Old Testament
IDB	*The Interpreter's Dictionary of the Bible*, ed. G. A. Buttrick	NAB	New American Bible

NCB	New Century Bible	SNTSMS	Society for New Testament
NEB	New English Bible		Studies Monograph
NIB	*The New Interpreter's Bible,*		Series
	ed. Leander E. Keck	*SNTW*	*Studies of the New Testament*
NIV	New International Version		*and Its World*
	of the Bible	SPS	Studies in Peace and
NovT	*Novum Testamentum*		Scripture
NRSV	New Revised Standard	*ST*	*Studia theologica*
	Version of the Bible	*STDJ*	*Studies on the Texts of the*
NT	New Testament		*Desert of Judah*
NTS	*New Testament Studies*	t.	*Tosephtah*
OT	Old Testament	TDNT	*Theological Dictionary of the*
OTL	Old Testament Library		*New Testament,* ed. G. Kittel
OtSt	*Oudtestamentische Studiën*		and G. Friedrich
par.	Parallels in the other	TDOT	*Theological Dictionary of the*
	Synoptic Gospels		*Old Testament,* ed. G. J. Bot-
REB	Revised English Bible		terweck and H. Ringgren
RefJ	*Reformed Journal*	TEV	Today's English Version
RSV	Revised Standard Version	TLOT	*Theological Lexicon of the Old*
	of the Bible		*Testament,* ed. E. Jenni and
RV	Revised Version of the		C. Westermann
	Bible	*TynBul*	*Tyndale Bulletin*
SBLDS	Society of Biblical Literature	WBC	Word Biblical Commentary
	Dissertation Series	WUNT	Wissenschaftliche Unter-
SBLMS	Society of Biblical Literature		suchungen zum Neuen
	Monograph Series		Testament
SBT	Studies in Biblical Theology	ZAW	*Zeitschrift für die alttesta-*
SJT	*Scottish Journal of Theology*		*mentliche Wissenschaft*

Abaddon   see Grave

Abba   An Aramaic form of the Hebrew and Aramaic word for "father" (ᵓab). The Aramaic form is "emphatic" and may make the word determinative ("the father") or vocative ("O father!"). It is quoted three times in the Greek NT, each time followed by the Greek translation: *abba ho pater* (Mark 14:36; Rom 8:15; Gal 4:6). Both the Aramaic and the Greek are to be understood as vocatives ("Father!"), since all three occurrences are addresses to God in prayer.

From Gal 4:6 and Rom 8:15 it is clear Paul knew that early Greek-speaking churches used in prayer what would be for them a foreign word, as they experienced a special relationship with God. Paul calls this relationship *adoption*, as children of God, and *heirs* (see *inherit*) with Christ, a gift of the *spirit* that makes it possible for them to address God in this way. For the Galatian church, which was struggling with questions concerning obedience to Jewish ceremonial law, Paul speaks of the gift of childhood as a sign of freedom from slavery to law (4:1–7). The slavery of which he speaks in Romans is slavery to sin (8:12–17).

That these churches, far-removed from Aramaic-speaking regions, sensed a special power in the word ᵓabbaᵓ must have been the result of learning that it had a regular and impressive place in the worship of the Palestinian churches. Recent discussion of the use of the word has focused on Joachim Jeremias's extensive development of the idea proposed by earlier scholars, that Jesus constantly used it in prayer and that his practice of addressing God as ᵓabbaᵓ was unprecedented in Judaism. Hence it must reveal "the heart of Jesus' relationship with God" (Jeremias, 62). A misunderstanding of Jeremias has led some to claim that ᵓabbaᵓ was "baby talk," as if Jesus addressed God as "Daddy," a view Jeremias himself called "inadmissible naivety" (p. 62). Critiques of his work have shown that although the form ᵓabbaᵓ has not been found as an address to God other than in the three NT

passages, God was addressed in Jewish prayer as "Father" (ᵓab), "my Father" (ᵓabi), and "our Father" (ᵓabinu) prior to and during the NT period. Jewish prayer typically appealed to the fatherhood of God in times of distress when the help of the one who rules the world was needed.

It cannot be proved that Jesus was unique in using ᵓabbaᵓ to address God, or even that he always used it, as Jeremias claimed. Mark chose to include the word in his quotation of the prayer in Gethsemane (unlike Matt 26:39 and Luke 22:42), however; this, plus the use of the word in the worship of Greek-speaking churches, suggests that early Christians remembered that Jesus typically prayed in this way. (For his other uses of "Father," see *family*.)

The word did not continue to be used in Christian worship beyond the first century, unlike the Hebrew words *amen*, *hallelujah*, and *hosanna*, which also appeared in transliterated form in the NT. This was in spite of the fact that the fatherhood of God became a subject of great importance in Christian theology. From Paul's uses of *abba* it would appear that its distinctive theological sense for the early church had to do with the change of status for converts, from slavery to childhood—involving both its privileges ("heirs with Christ") and responsibilities ("you are not in the flesh; you are in the Spirit" Rom 8:9; "do not use your freedom as an opportunity for self-indulgence" Gal 5:13). Paul took the cry "Abba" in prayer to be a sign that the Holy Spirit was at work in believers to bring them into something like the same intimate relationship with God experienced by Jesus Christ.

Mary Rose D'Angelo, "Abba and 'Father': Imperial Theology and the Jesus Traditions," *JBL* 111 (1992): 611–30; James Barr, "*Abba* Isn't 'Daddy,'" *JTS* 39 (1988): 28–47; Joseph Fitzmyer, "*Abba* and Jesus' Relation to God," in *À Cause de L'Évangile* (Études sur les Synoptiques et les Acts; Paris: Cerf, 1985), 15–38; Joachim Jeremias, *The Prayers of Jesus*, SBT² 6 (Naperville, Ill.: Allenson,

1967), 11–65; Marianne Meye Thompson, "Joachim Jeremias and the Debate about *Abba*," in *The Promise of the Father: Jesus and God in the New Testament* (Louisville, Ky.: Westminster John Knox Press, 2000), 21–34.

DONALD E. GOWAN

Abhorrence, Abhorrent, Abomination, Abominable

Just as the English language offers several words for the bad deed—error, sin, evil, harm, and each with its own set of connotations—so too does the Hebrew language. One of those Hebrew words, to ʿebah, is regularly translated "abomination," though other English words are sometimes used, e.g., "abhorrence, abhorrent." As these two English words suggest, to ʿebah is a "strong" word for the bad deed. It does not typically refer to unintended malfeasance, but some truly detestable act, often with ritual, religious, or cultural implications. Other Hebrew words, e.g., *shiqquts*, may also be translated as "abomination" (1 Kgs 11:5).

An abomination regularly represents a judgment by one group—whether cultural or religious—that some other group's behavior is inappropriate. Genesis 43:32 makes clear that Egyptians deem eating with Hebrews to be an abomination. In a similar vein, Israelites viewed deities of other nations to be abominations, a judgment presumably not shared by those other peoples. So the judgment that something was an abomination was not that of an individual, but rather represented mores and beliefs of a culture.

"Abomination" appears with special prominence in three OT books: Deuteronomy, Ezekiel, and Proverbs. Put another way, it pervades all three portions of the Hebrew canon: Torah, Prophets, and Writings. In Deuteronomy, the Hebrew noun, regularly translated as "abhorrent," refers to practices that may be identified with those of other peoples, but that are forbidden to Israel. Making images of a deity is abhorrent (Deut 7:26; 27:15) as are worship of strange or foreign gods (Deut 12:31; 13:14; 32:16) and inappropri-

ate forms of divination (18:10). Abhorrent things also can include improper dietary practices (14:3) and scandalous remarriage (24:4). Rarely does Deuteronomy include ethical indictments of the sort found in Proverbs.

In Ezekiel, the noun is embedded in that prophet's indictments of Israel for, especially, religious infractions, particularly those that defame the purity of Yahwistic ritual. For Ezekiel, to venerate an idol is to commit an abomination (Ezek 18:12). The vision report in Ezek 8 lists a number of non-Yahwistic religious practices, which are summarily labeled as "abominations." The term also appears prominently in chap. 16, which details the misdeeds of Jerusalem, personified as a woman. In that metaphor, Jerusalem's sexual misdeeds are construed as abominations.

In Proverbs, the usage broadens and is shared by wisdom literature in other cultures. For example, the language of "abomination" appears in the Egyptian text, the Wisdom of Amenemope, a document that lies behind Prov 22:17–24:22. Amenemope judges negatively certain forms of behavior in the following manner: "Do not converse with false men, because it is an abomination of God." Proverbs 12:22 is very similar: "Lying lips are an abomination to the LORD." Though Proverbs often uses the term "abomination" in a very general way ("The way of the wicked is an abomination to the LORD" [Prov 15:9]), it often refers to misdeeds in the public realm, especially the business world ("A false balance is an abomination to the LORD" [Prov 11:1]).

Both Deuteronomy and Proverbs frequently utilize the expression "abomination of/to Yahweh." This phrase does not bear the same explicit ritual connotations as those in Ezekiel. "A false balance is an abomination to the LORD" (Prov 11:1) might mean: inappropriate mercantile transactions are not simply violations of moral norms. These misbehaviors also constitute a religious offense, since Yahweh authorizes moral norms such as justice and beneficence.

In sum, individual streams of OT tradition used "abomination" in diverse ways. When one reads about the sorts of actions labeled as abominable, one senses that such misdeeds strike at the core of the existence of the covenant community. To worship other gods, to lie, to steal are, of course, proscribed by the Ten Commandments. Abominations are those actions that violate Israel's core ethic as represented by the Decalogue.

DAVID L. PETERSEN

Abraham   *see* **Covenant; Promise**

Accomplish   *see* **Fulfill**

Adam   The name of the first male human being. In Hebrew the name means "man," that is, either a male individual or humankind. The English versions of the Bible differ concerning where the name first appears. In NSRV "Adam" does not occur until Gen 4:25, where *ʾadam* is found without the definite article. Up to this point Adam is referred to as "the man." In KJV, however, the name appears at 2:19, and in NIV at 2:20. Adam is mentioned in the OT only in Gen 1–5 and 1 Chr 1:1, but he becomes theologically significant in the NT.

In Rom 5:12–21 Paul contrasts Adam and Christ. Sin and death spread to all from Adam's disobedience, but through Christ's obedience many will be justified and obtain life. In Rom 3:25 Paul had employed the sacrificial metaphor for the atonement, but here the Adam motif prompts the proposal that the atonement results from Jesus' obedience. It is possible that Adam's disobedience is implicit in other passages that stress the saving power of Christ's obedience (Heb 5:8–9; 10:5–9), but this must remain speculative.

Adam appears again in 1 Cor 15:22: "For as in Adam all die, so all will be made alive in Christ." "In Adam" and "in Christ" express Paul's fascination with the corporate aspect of human existence. "In Adam" refers to humanity's collective life apart from God. "In Christ" designates the new humanity that has come into existence through the death and resurrection of Jesus. When he contrasts the physical body and the "spiritual body," Paul again refers to Adam: "The first man, Adam, became a living being [citing Gen 2:7, adding "Adam"]; the last Adam became a life-giving spirit. . . . The first man was from the earth, a man of dust; the second man is from heaven" (1 Cor 15:45, 47). Here "life-giving spirit" refers to the power of the risen Christ to impart eternal life to those who believe: "Just as we have borne the image of the man of dust, we will also bear the image of the man of heaven" (1 Cor 15:49). It is noteworthy that this contrast suggests to Paul a new christological title, found nowhere else in NT: "the last Adam." This title emphasizes Christ's role as head of the new humanity.

Two other passages deserve brief attention. In the reverse genealogy provided for Jesus by Luke, the final item is "Adam, son of God" (Luke 3:38). In the Greek, "son" does not appear (hence the use of italics in KJV). Throughout the genealogy (except for v. 23) the relationship between generations is indicated simply by the genitive case, used with the meaning "of" or "from." Adam is of or from God, but is not here called God's son. This idea would be repugnant to Luke, since it would diminish the significance of Jesus' sonship. In a genealogy it might even remind Gentile readers of the pagan stories of demigods procreated by Zeus.

The late-first-century author of 1 Timothy sought to suppress the praying of women in church services countenanced by Paul (1 Cor 11:5). "I desire, then, that in every place the men [using the term for male human beings] pray. . . . Let a woman learn in silence with full submission" (1 Tim 2:8, 11). He justified this policy on the basis of Genesis 2–3: "For Adam was formed first, then Eve; and Adam was not deceived, but the woman was deceived and became a transgressor" (1 Tim 2:13–14).

DOUGLAS R. A. HARE

Adopt, Adoption   While various formulas appear in the ancient Near East for legal transfer of a person from one family or slavery to a new family, sometimes making the adoptee heir (see *inherit*), such a practice and specific examples are difficult to document in Israel and are generally not of theological importance (see *family*). Possible examples are Abraham's proposal to make the slave Eliezer his heir (Gen 15:2–3) and Abraham's use of Hagar as a surrogate mother (Gen. 16:1–4; cf. 30:1–13, "Bear upon my knee" [v. 3] may be an adoption rite). Others are Gen 48:5–6, adoption of grandchildren; and Ruth 4:16, after levirate marriage (Deut 25:5–10; Ruth 4:7–15). At Esth 2:7 and 15 NRSV uses "adopt" for Mordecai taking Esther as his own daughter. Acts 7:21 says of Moses that "Pharaoh's daughter adopted him" (Exod 2:10 "she took him as her son"; cf. 1 Kgs 11:20). These examples occur outside Israel or involve non-Israelites.

More significant are adoption formulas for a king in Israel such as Ps 2:7, "You are my son," with the response to God, "You are my Father" (Ps 89:26–27; 2 Sam 7:14). This language appears with regard to Jesus at his baptism (Mark 1:11 par. Luke 3:22; cf. Matt 3:17); and his transfiguration (Mark 9:7 and par. Matt 17:5; Luke 9:35). Acts 13:33 applies Ps 2:7 to the resurrection (cf. Heb 1:5; 5:5). If at an early stage an "adoptionist Christology" was involved, NT estimates about Christ readily moved on beyond ideas of a man adopted by God.

Quite significant theologically is the inclusion at Rom 9:4 of "the adoption" in Paul's list of privileges that belong to Israel. This is the one of five instances in the Pauline corpus of a word that literally means "sonship," acceptance of ancient Israel as, like the king, "son of God." Hebrew lacks any term for adoption, just as later rabbinic laws seem to know no such category. But a number of OT passages lie behind Paul's term, which he drew from the Greco-Roman world. Exodus 4:22–23 has Moses say to Pharaoh, "Thus says the LORD: Israel is my first-born son. . . . Let my son go that he may worship me." The same idea appears in Exod 6:6b–7, "I shall adopt you as my people" (REB); Deut 14:1, "You are children of the LORD your God" (cf. Jer 31:9); and Hos 11:1, "out of Egypt I called my son" (applied to Jesus at Matt 2:15). "The adoption" at Rom 9:4 suggests fatherly affection and hoped-for filial obedience. Romans 9:26 picks up language from Hosea (2:23; 1:10) saying that "not my people" will become again "children of the living God." In 1 Pet 2:10, along with other NT phrases in 2:9, Hos 2:23 is applied to converts to Christ in contrast to their former status.

Paul applies the adoption metaphor, from a practice well known from Roman law, in a chiastically structured sentence at Gal 4:4–5: "God sent his Son,

(A) born of a woman,   (B) born under the law,
(B′) in order to redeem those who were under the law,   (A′) so that we might receive adoption as children."

This "sending formula" is then paralleled by the statement "and because you are children (literally "sons"), God has sent the Spirit of his Son into our hearts, crying 'Abba! Father!' So you are no longer a slave but a child, and if a child then also an heir, through God" (vv. 6–7). Note the progression from "under the law" to adoption as an heir through the work of Christ and gift of the Spirit, and personalization in the move from the plural "you" to the singular in v. 7. Romans 8:14–16 presents a similar picture of children of God led by the Spirit of God. There is movement from "a spirit of slavery" (life enslaved to sin, death, law, the flesh) to a "spirit of adoption," heralded by the cry "Abba! Father!" (8:15). They are children, heirs, but with the provisos that we face "the sufferings of this present time" or age (8:18) and still "wait for adoption" to be complete, at the "redemption of our bodies" in the resurrection (8:23). As adoptees we have "the first fruits of the Spirit" (8:23) but live in hope, not fulfillment. Ephesians 1:5 grounds "adoption as (God's) children" in God's will and choice "before the foundation of the world." Revelation 21:7 applies the old promise to Israel's king, now in the plural, "I will be their God and they will be my children," a status achieved through faith and baptism (Gal 3:25–29), but eschatologically completed only in God's future.

J. M. Scott, *Adoption as Sons of God, WUNT²* 48 (Tübingen: J. C. B. Mohr, 1992).

JOHN REUMANN

Adultery, Adulterer, Adulteress, Adulterous *see* **Marriage**

Adversary *see* **Satan**

Advocate *see* **Spirit**

Afflict, Affliction, Afflicted *see* **Suffer**

Afraid *see* **Fear**

Age *see* **Time**

Alien, Foreigner, Stranger, Orphan, Widow Central to Israel's life as a community is covenant that calls people to be in right relationship with God, with one another, and, ultimately, with all creation. Part of being in right relationship with one another meant caring for the alien, the orphan, and the widow—the most vulnerable and, to some extent, the most powerless of people with respect to economic, social, and political status.

Alien. The "alien" (*ger*, often translated "sojourner") was a person who had come to live in a place away from his or her district and social group, putting himself or herself under the protection of another clan or family (so "resident alien"; now often called "client status"). Aliens were thus dependent upon the goodwill of those with full status as citizens. The book of Genesis sets the stage

for Israel's care for the alien. The first time the word appears in the OT is in Gen 12:10. Here Abraham is described as going down to Egypt to reside there as an alien because of the famine in his own homeland. The memory that Abraham's descendants lived for years in Egypt as aliens led Israel in later times to insist that those who come into their land as sojourners must be treated as they would have wished to be treated in Egypt. In Exod 22:21, the Israelites are given a divine command: "You shall not wrong or oppress a resident alien, for you were aliens in the land of Egypt." This command is reinforced in Exod 23:9: "You shall not oppress a resident alien; you know the heart of an alien, for you were aliens in the land of Egypt." Significant here is the phrase, "you know the heart of an alien." Israel has had the lived experience of how it feels to be an alien, which is cause for compassion.

In addition to being protected by Israelite law, aliens also enjoyed certain benefits as outlined in the Torah. Like the Israelites, they shared in Sabbath rest, along with the animals, the slaves, and the land (Exod 20:10; 23:12; Lev 16:29). As long as they were circumcised, aliens could partake in the Passover meal (Exod 12:48–49) and were permitted to offer sacrifices as well (Num 15:14–16, 26, 29). With the Israelites, they were to observe both the law of unleavened bread (Exod 12:19) and the Day of Atonement (Lev 16:29) and were required to abstain from eating or drinking the blood of animals (Lev 17:10, 12–13). Because they were usually economically disenfranchised, they had the right to glean in fields (Lev 19:10; 23:22). Finally, aliens were forbidden to worship Molech (Lev 20:2) and had to pay honor to God's name (Lev 24:16). Anyone who deprived an alien of his or her due would be cursed (Deut 27:19). Thus, the Pentateuch provides an insight into the laws that govern the Israelites' actions toward aliens, and offers a perspective on what the responsibilities were for an alien residing in Israel.

In the writings of the prophets, Jeremiah warns the Israelites not to oppress the alien (Jer 7:6; 22:3; cf. Zech 7:10), while Ezekiel rails against community members for their despicable treatment of the alien: "Father and mother are treated with contempt in you; the alien residing within you suffers extortion; the orphan and the widow are wronged in you" (Ezek 22:7; see also 22:29). For those guilty of oppressing and mistreating aliens, God's judgment looms large: "Then I will draw near to you for judgment; I will be swift to bear witness against the sorcerers, against the adulterers, against those who swear falsely, against those who oppress the hired workers in their wages, the widow and the orphan, against those who thrust aside the alien, and do not fear me, says the LORD of hosts" (Mal 3:5).

In the Psalms, "alien" assumes a different nuance, particularly in the lament psalms where the psalmist equates his experience with the experience of the alien (Pss 119:19; 120:5).

In the NT, Stephen speaks of Moses as a "resident alien" (*paroikos*) during his sojourn in Midian (Acts 7:29), but 1 Pet 2:11 uses the word in a more significant way. The early Christians thought of themselves as "aliens and exiles" in the world, set apart from their environment by their new beliefs and way of life (cf. Heb 11:13).

Foreigner. Closely associated with, yet distinguished from, the "alien" is the "foreigner" (the most common translation of *neker, nokri*). The foreigner is defined in 1 Kgs 8:41 as one who is "not of your people Israel [and] comes from a distant land."

A "foreigner" did not enjoy the same status as an alien and could not share in the Passover (Exod 12:43), was subject to being charged interest by others (Deut 23:21), could not be chosen king (Deut 17:15), and did not have debts forgiven even in the sabbatical year (Deut 15:2–3). The book of Ruth, however, holds up Ruth as a model foreigner—a woman who becomes an ancestor of David. In Third Isaiah, foreigners are key participants in the restoration of Israel (Isa 60:10; 61:5) and are considered to be a part of "God's people" (Isa 56:3–8): "Do not let the foreigner joined to the LORD say, 'The LORD will surely separate me from his people'; and do not let the eunuch say, 'I am just a dry tree'" (v. 3).

In the NT, the "foreigner" (*allophylos*) appears in only one significant passage. In Luke 17:18, the foreigner is the recipient of Jesus' praise because he is the only one of ten lepers cured by Jesus who returns to say thank-you and to offer praise to God. Significant here is the fact that Jesus cared not only for the members of the house of Israel but also those who were non-Israelites. The divine plan of salvation and liberation, then, is all-encompassing as Luke's story foreshadows.

Stranger. The word *zar* denotes otherness, illegitimacy, and even danger to an extent that *ger* and *neker/nokri* do not. Job said in his misery, "My serving girls count me as a stranger" (Job 19:15). The psalmist also lamented, "I have become a stranger to my kindred, an alien (*nokri*) to my mother's children" (Ps 69:8). Proverbs 11:15 advises one not to guarantee a loan to a stranger, as one likely to be untrustworthy. The prophets use *zar* to refer to the enemy nations (e.g., Ezek 7:21; 28:7; Joel 3:17; Obad 11). There is thus a significant difference of attitude toward the resident alien, who is to be loved as oneself (Lev 19:34); the foreigner, with whom one may have restricted, friendly relationships; and the stranger, who is likely to be suspected and even feared.

Jesus' instruction on the judgment of the nations speaks of welcoming the stranger in a context that suggests he refers to Jewish traditions of hospitality (Matt 25:31–46; Matthew uses the Greek *xenos*; we do not know what Aramaic word Jesus may have used). Here Jesus equates himself with the stranger and clarifies for his listeners the point that anytime they have welcomed and cared for the stranger among them, they have welcomed and cared for Jesus himself. In Jesus' eyes, suspicion, fear, or qualified acceptance have no place; the stranger may be the "least" within society, but more important, the stranger is also a member of his family (v. 40). Jesus' understanding of family, then, includes both Jews and non-Jews and paradoxically, although Jesus is a Jew himself, he is often treated like a stranger among his own people. Hence, his self-identification with the stranger is self-revealing. The entire passage calls people then and now to a largeness of heart that is foundational to the Jewish and Christian traditions.

Widow and orphan. Two other groups of people considered to be among the most vulnerable within society were widows and orphans. In a social climate that was predominantly patrilineal and patriarchal, a woman whose husband had died and who had no sons or brothers was a "widow." A fatherless child was an "orphan." Both the widow and the orphan were at the mercy of the community for care and protection. Israelite law protected the widow and the orphan and called the community to this responsibility (see, e.g., Exod 22:22; Deut 10:18; 24:19–21; 27:19). Both widows and orphans were subject to injustice, especially since neither had a male family member to speak on their behalf and to safeguard their property, which was frequently the object of theft and another's greed: "They drive away the donkey of the orphan; they take the widow's ox for a pledge" (Job 24:3). Israel's prophets reminded the community of its obligation toward the orphan and the widow. Isaiah cried out: "Learn to do good; seek justice, rescue the oppressed, defend the orphan, plead for the widow" (Isa 1:17). Jeremiah proclaimed: "Thus says the LORD: Act with justice and righteousness, and deliver from the hand of the oppressor anyone who has been robbed. And do no wrong or violence to the alien, the orphan, and the widow, or shed innocent blood in this place" (Jer 22:3; see also Zech 7:10). The prophets also upbraided various community members who exploited the widow and the orphan. Isaiah delivered a direct invective against Israel's leadership: "Your princes are rebels and companions of thieves. Everyone loves a bribe and runs

after gifts. They do not defend the orphan, and the widow's cause does not come before them" (Isa 1:23). Ezekiel exposed the injustices of his people: "Father and mother are treated with contempt in you; the alien residing within you suffers extortion; the orphan and the widow are wronged in you" (Ezek 22:7; see also Jer 5:28). In the course of their life in the land, many of the Israelites and Judahites fell prey to apostasy and idolatry that resulted in their forgetfulness of God and God's ways. Unfaithful to both covenant and Torah, they had fallen out of "right relationship" with their God and God's people, and hence the most vulnerable among them become their prey. As noted earlier, the prophet Malachi makes clear that the community's waywardness and wickedness, particularly in relation to the widow and orphan, will not be tolerated by God (see Mal 3:5). Widows were often identified with the *poor* (Isa 10:2; Job 24:3–4, 9; 31:16; Zech 7:10), but Ben Sirach reminds the community that God does not show partiality to the poor. Rather, God listens to the prayer of those who have been wronged and is especially attentive in this regard to the supplication of the widow and the orphan (Sir 35:16–17; cf. Ps 146:9).

In the NT, the orphan is mentioned once. James reaffirms the spirit of the OT ethic by defining "religion that is pure and undefiled" as "to care for orphans and widows in their distress, and to keep oneself unstained by the world" (Jas 1:27). The widow, however, plays a prominent role in the Gospels and in 1 Timothy, one of the Pastoral Epistles. In Mark's Gospel, Jesus holds up the poor widow as a model of generosity who made an offering not from her own financial abundance but, instead, from her own economic poverty (Mark 12:41–44; cf. Luke 21:1–4). Luke portrays Jesus responding repeatedly to the needs of widows; he raises a widow's son from the dead (Luke 7:11–17) and makes a widow the central character of one of his parables that instructs his listeners of the justice that is to be afforded to widows

(Luke 18:1–8). Finally, 1 Tim 5:3–16 establishes various stipulations that are to be carried out with respect to the Christian community's responsibility toward widows and, reciprocally, offers instruction on how widows are to conduct themselves within the community. This passage in Timothy reflects a much more calculated treatment of widows, not found in either the OT or the Gospels, and thus, one is given to surmise that there was some sort of unrest in the community being caused by some of the widows, particularly by the younger ones. First Timothy 5:3–16 suggests that there is to be mutual respect on the part of both the community extending care and the widow who is the recipient of the community's goodwill.

In sum, alien, foreigner, stranger, orphan, and widow are five distinct yet related terms that have as their common denominator a sense of vulnerability to which the Jewish and Christians communities are called to respond.

F. C. Fensham, "Widow, Orphan, and the Poor in Ancient Near Eastern Legal and Wisdom Literature," *JNES* 21 (1962): 129–39; Donald E. Gowan, "Wealth and Poverty in the Old Testament: The Case of the Widow, the Orphan, and the Sojourner," *Int* 41 (1987): 341–53; Christiana van Houten, *The Alien in Israelite Law*, JSOTSup 107 (Sheffield: JSOT Press, 1991); Patrick D. Miller, "Israel as Host to Strangers," in *Today's Immigrants and Refugees: A Christian Understanding* (Washington: U.S. Catholic Conference, 1988), 1–19.

CAROL J. DEMPSEY

Almighty   see Power; God

Amaze   see Sign

Amen

A Hebrew word used as an affirmative response in both Testaments. The root meaning concerns that which is trustworthy, thus both faithful and true. As used in the OT, it may indicate (a) agreement with an oath or announcement (1 Kgs 1:36; Neh 5:13; Jer 28:6), (b)

willingness to accept the consequences of a statement (the curses in Deut 27:15–26), or (c) a response to a blessing (Ps 106:48). It is used once as a substantive in Isa 65:16: " . . . by the God of '*amen*.'" Either the RSV and NAB ("truth") or the NRSV ("faithfulness") would be appropriate translations, but REB paraphrases, ". . . by God whose name is Amen."

The LXX sometimes transliterated the word, showing that it was used in worship in Greek-speaking Jewish congregations, but elsewhere provided the appropriate translations, *genoito* ("so be it") and *alethos* ("truly"). Since early Christian congregations obviously used the Hebrew word as a response in worship, it appears in the NT as an affirmation (Rom 1:25; 11:36), and as the conclusion to a blessing (Heb 13:25). It appears as a substantive clearly referring to Christ in Rev 3:14: "the words of the Amen, the faithful and true witness." This may be an echo of Isa 65:16.

NRSV transliterates *amen* everywhere it occurs in the NT except in the words of Jesus, who used it in an unusual way, to introduce a statement rather than as a response: "*Amen*, I say to you . . ." (e.g., Matt 6:16; in John, *amen amen*, e.g., John 3:5). This is the familiar "Verily" of KJV; now rendered "Truly" by NRSV. There are a few possible examples of the use of the word in this way in Judaism, but there are no parallels to its prominence in Jesus' speech, so this may be a reflection of the church's memory of his claims to authority, documented elsewhere (e.g., Matt 7:29; Luke 4:36).

J. M. Ross, "Amen," *ExpTim* 102 (1991): 166–71.

DONALD E. GOWAN

Ancestors   see Promise

Angel

Angels, heavenly beings who serve as God's agents in the world and model the praise of God, frequent the pages of both Testaments. In the OT they are also called "sons of God" = heavenly beings (Ps 29:1), "holy ones" (Ps 89:5–7; Zech 14:5), heavenly "hosts" (1 Kgs 22:19; see *hosts, lord of*), and possibly simply "gods" (Ps 82:1; cf. Ps 8:5; Deut 32:8). In view of their role they are also called "watchers" (Dan 4:13), "ministers" (Ps 103:21), and "the army of the LORD" (Josh 5:13–15). In both Testaments, angels are referred to as "men" (Gen 18:1–2; Dan 10:5; Mark 16:5; cf. Heb 13:2), since the human form is often assumed in their appearances. Tradition has identified *seraphim* and *cherubim*, winged creatures, as angels (see Isa 6:2–3; cf. Dan 9:21); if so, they are an extension of the iconography of the sanctuary (Exod 25:18–20; Ps 80:1) The Hebrew and Greek words (*maʾak; angelos*) also refer to human messengers, especially prophets (Hag 1:13; Luke 9:52).

No undue speculative interest in angels is evident, except both Testaments report the names of two angels (Gabriel; Michael), and the NT associates them with light and white garments (Matt 28:2–3) and speaks of angelic ranks (1 Thess 4:16). The latter descriptions probably reflect the considerable interest in angels in the postexilic period (see Zech 1–6; Dan 10:5–6) and, in more speculative ways, in apocryphal and pseudepigraphical literature (see Tobit; *Jubilees; 1 Enoch*). This heightened interest in divine beings that mediate the work of God may reflect an increased distancing of God from the world during the late postexilic period. Given this heritage, the NT is remarkably restrained in its frequent speaking of angels.

Both Testaments also refer more specifically to the "angel of the Lord" (Gen 16:7; Matt 1:20). But in OT theophanic texts this figure refers to God in embodied human form (e.g., Exod 3:2) and is to be distinguished from other angels (though not in actual appearance, Gen 18:1–2). The activities of the "angel of the Lord" include birth announcements (Gen 16:11–12), commissions (Judg 6:11–24), "interruptions" (Gen 22:11–12), and prophetic communications (2 Kgs 1:3).

These innumerable (Deut 33:2) spiritual beings are members of the divine council, within which they interact with God regarding what is happening in the world (1 Kgs 22:19–22; Jer 23:18–22). Their wisdom and insight (2 Sam 14:17, though limited, Matt 24:36) is taken seriously by God (see Gen 1:26). Created by (Neh 9:6) and subordinate to God, they serve at God's bidding (Ps 103:20–21), as "spirits in the divine service" (Heb 1:14).

Angels function similarly in both Testaments, most fundamentally as messengers between God and world, bearing a word that is not their own, by means of dreams (Gen 31:11; Matt 2:13, 19–20) and visions (Zech 1:7–17; Acts 10:3–6) as well as more directly (Num 22:32–35; Matt 28:5–7). They also serve as God's agents in various nonverbal activities, from judgment, both historical (2 Sam 24:16; Acts 12:23) and eschatological (Matt 13:49–50; 2 Thess 1:7–8), to blessing (Pss 34:7; 91:11; Heb 1:14), protection (Gen 24:7; Matt 18:10), and deliverance (2 Kgs 6:15–17; Acts 12:7–11), even answering prayers (Dan 9:21–23). Angels assume this role at key points in the life of Jesus, from annunciation to resurrection (Luke 1:26–28; 2:9–15; 22:43; Matt 4:11; 28:1–7). The NT even considers the law to have been mediated by an angel (Gal 3:19).

Angels can get caught up in the affairs of earth and act wickedly (Gen 6:1–4; Jude 6; cf. Ps 82), and *Satan* can come as an "angel of light" (2 Cor 11:14), and so God will pass judgment on them (Isa 24:21).

Angels offer praise to God in an exemplary way (Ps 148:2) and rejoice over the repentance of sinners (Luke 15:10). But angels are not to be worshiped (Col 2:18), though they often were in Israel (2 Kgs 21:3–5). Such practices are condemned as idolatry, for Yahweh alone is God and is Lord of the "hosts."

———

TERENCE E. FRETHEIM

Anger, Angry   see Wrath

Animals (Beast, Dragon, Lamb, Leviathan, Rahab, Sheep and Goats)   The Bible mentions many different kinds of animals. Some of them are

common animals of the field, farm, and forest. Others exist only in the world of myth. When the biblical writers spoke of common animals of creation, sometimes they did so in a straightforward and literal manner. At other times they spoke of the animals of creation in figurative ways to make theological statements and religious affirmations. Similarly, the biblical writers used the mythical animals to make theological statements.

Beast. Hebrew *hayyah* and Aramaic (Dan 4:12; 7:3, 5, 6, 7, 11, 19, 23) *haywah*, "living creature"; also Hebrew *behema*, *be'ir;* Greek *zoon*, living being; *therion*, wild animal.

From the Hebrew word *behema*, "beast," "animal," "cattle," is derived the name "Behemoth." Behemoth's primary appearance in Scripture is in the second speech of God in Job 40:15–24. Here Behemoth and Leviathan (Job 41) are paired as two beasts of God's creation. While many commentators have seen a hippopotamus in the description of Behemoth in Job 40:15–24 and a crocodile in the description of Leviathan in Job 41, it is probably best to see Behemoth and Leviathan as imaginary or mythic beasts.

The term "beast" is used in the book of Daniel and in the Revelation to John to refer to mythical or symbolic creatures. In Dan 7, "four great beasts came up out of the sea, different from one another" (v. 3). These "four great beasts" symbolized four great kingdoms of the earth, probably the Babylonian, Median, Persian, and Macedonian or Greek kingdoms.

In Rev 13, John reports having seen two beasts, the first "rising out of the sea" (v. 1) and the second emerging "out of the earth" (v. 11). These two beasts served the dragon (see Rev 12). The dragon gave the first beast "his power and his throne and great authority" (13:2). This first beast represents Rome and the Roman Empire. See Rev 17:9, where the beast's seven heads are interpreted as "seven mountains"; Rome was built on "seven mountains" or seven hills.

The second beast, the beast that rises out of the earth in Rev 13:11, "exercises all the authority of the first beast on its behalf, and it makes the earth and its inhabitants worship the first beast" (13:12). So, while the first beast represents Rome and the Roman Empire, the second beast represents the officials of Rome who carry out the blasphemous, wicked policies of the emperor.

John observes in Rev 13:11 that the second beast has "two horns like a lamb" but speaks "like a dragon." The second beast, representing the local officials who force people to worship the emperor, is deceptive. The local officials seem innocent enough, even messianic, "like a lamb" (13:11). The words that they speak, though, are the words of the dragon. Indeed, this second beast is extremely deadly; for he is given the authority to order that "those who [will] not worship the . . . [first] beast . . . be killed" (13:15).

Dragon. Hebrew *tannin* (Isa 27:1; 51:9; Job 7:12; Neh 2:13; plural *tanninim* in Ps 74:13) or *tannim* (Ezek 29:3; 32:2). In Exod 7:9, 10; Deut 32:33; Ps 91:13, *tannin* refers to a snake or a serpent. Greek *drakon* (Rev 12:3, 4, 7, 9, 13, 16, 17; 13:2, 4, 11; 16:13; 20:2).

The dragon was well known in ancient Near Eastern mythology. In the Babylonian creation myth, the *Enuma Elish*, the dragon Tiamat is killed by the deity Marduk. The Ugaritic myths from Ras Shamra in Syria tell of Baal's defeat of the sea god Yam, "Prince Sea," in order to establish order out of chaos. In the Ugaritic myths, Baal also vanquishes Lotan, the seven-headed serpent, and the sea dragon Tannun (= Hebrew *tannin*, *tannim*). The writers of the Hebrew Bible borrowed this myth from the Canaanites and transformed it into a story of how Yahweh, not Baal, brought order out of chaos and established divine rule in the world by defeating the dragon (see *water*). The affirmation that it was Yahweh who vanquished the dragon can be seen in numerous passages in OT. See for example Pss 74:13–14; 89:10; Isa 27:1; 51:9; Job 26:12–13.

The idea that Yahweh will defeat the

dragon surfaces anew in the Revelation to John. Echoing the early myths that tell of the slaying of the dragon at creation, John's vision tells of the defeat of the dragon at the time of the new creation. The dragon, identified in Rev 20:2 as "that ancient serpent, who is the Devil and Satan," is vanquished in the climactic battle.

In the Hebrew myth, the dragon is known by several names:

1. *Leviathan.* Hebrew *liwyathan*, equivalent to the Ugaritic *lotan.* The dragon that Yahweh vanquishes in the Hebrew myth is referred to by the name "Leviathan" in Job 3:8; 41:1; Pss 74:14; 104:26; Isa 27:1; 2 Esd 6:49, 51–52 (also mentions "Behemoth"). Isaiah 27:1 describes the sea dragon as "Leviathan the fleeing serpent, Leviathan the twisting serpent." Similarly, a myth about Baal from Ugarit describes the dragon as "Leviathan the slippery serpent . . . the wriggling serpent" (Baal I.i.1–3; Driver, 103).

2. *Rahab.* Hebrew *rahab.* The dragon that Yahweh vanquishes in the Hebrew myth is referred to by the name "Rahab" in Job 9:13; 26:12; Ps 89:10; Isa 51:9. The name is also used as a title for Egypt, presumably recalling the dragon myth in Ps 87:4; Isa 30:7.

The dragon is also known as "Yam," meaning "Sea." This name corresponds to the Canaanite sea god of the same name. See Job 7:12: "Am I the Sea (Heb *yam*), or the Dragon (*tannin*), that you set a guard over me?" See also Hab 3:8.

Lamb. The most common Hebrew words translated "lamb" are *kebes*, which is used to denote a "male lamb" (e.g., Gen 30:32, 35; Lev 14:13, 21, 24, 25; 17:3; Num 6:12, 14; 7:15, 21, 27, 33, 39, 45, 51, 57, 63, 69, 75, 81; Isa 11:6; Jer 11:19; Ezek 46:13), and *kebsa*, which signifies a "female lamb" or "ewe lamb" (e.g., Lev 14:10; 2 Sam 12:3, 4, 6). The Hebrew word *seh* is also translated "lamb" (e.g., Exod 12:3, 4, 5; 34:20; 1 Sam 17:34; Isa 53:7; 66:3). *Talah* is used for "lamb" in 1 Sam 7:9 and Isa 65:25. Greek: *amnos* (John 1:29, 36; Acts 8:32), *aren* (Luke 10:3), *arnion* (more than twenty times in Revelation, e.g., 5:6, 8, 12,

13; 13:11). The Hebrew word *pesah* and the Greek word *pascha*, words that refer to the festival of Passover, are used to refer to the Passover lamb (2 Chr 30:15, 17; 35:1, 6, 11, 13; Ezek 6:20; Mark 14:12; Luke 2:7; 1 Cor 5:7).

In the Bible, lambs are animals that are slain. They were vulnerable to attack by "a lion or a bear" (1 Sam 17:34–35). When people were suffering from brutal conflict and were facing death, they were described as being like "a (gentle) lamb that is led to the slaughter" (Isa 53:7; Jer 11:19).

Lambs are among the most common sacrificial animals in Scripture. In Gen 22:7, Isaac innocently asks his father Abraham, "Where is the lamb for a burnt offering?" In the law codes of Exodus, Leviticus, and Numbers (Exod 29:38–42; Lev 9:3; 12:6; 14:10–13, 21–25; 23:12; Num 6:9–15; 7:15, 21, 27, 33, 39, 45, 51, 57, 63, 69, 75, 81; 28:1–8, 11–14), lambs are the required or prescribed sacrifice for many different rituals.

Probably the most important use of the lamb was in the Passover ritual. In Exod 12, the Hebrews were instructed by God to kill a lamb and to smear some of its blood on the doorposts of their homes. They were to roast the lamb and eat it with unleavened bread and bitter herbs. The blood of the lamb smeared on the doorpost was to be a sign that would protect the people of God during the tenth plague, the plague of the death of the firstborn.

These passages from OT in which lambs are described as vulnerable, gentle, and helpless, and in which they are the required sacrifice in many different liturgical rites, helped to shape one of the most meaningful images of Jesus in NT—that of the Lamb of God. Although the Synoptic Gospels and the Gospel of John differ on the chronology of the week Jesus died, all four Gospels agree that Jesus was crucified at the time of the observance of Passover when the Passover lamb was slain (see, e.g., Mark 14:12; Luke 22:7). The apostle Paul commented in 1 Cor 5:7 that "our paschal (that is,

Passover) lamb, Christ, has been sacrificed." In the same way, 1 Pet 1:19 says that "the precious blood of Christ" is "like that of a lamb without defect or blemish."

It is in the Johannine literature, however, that the idea of Jesus as the Lamb of God is most fully developed. Twice in the Gospel of John, John the Baptist is said to refer to Jesus as the "Lamb of God" (John 1:29, 36). In one passage, John goes so far as to declare that Jesus is "the Lamb of God who takes away the sin of the world" (1:29). Repeatedly in the Revelation to John, the risen Christ is referred to as the "Lamb." Note that in the Revelation, the Lamb, the risen Christ, bears the marks of having been slain (Rev 5:6; see also 5:12).

Sheep and goats. Sheep: Greek *probaton.* Goat: Greek *erithos.* Two kinds of animals that are used by Jesus in Matt 25:31–33 as symbols for different kinds of people. In his discussion of the judgment of the nations, Jesus creates an analogy in which the Son of Man, seated "on the throne of his glory," "will separate people one from another as a shepherd separates the sheep from the goats." The imagery in Jesus' analogy is drawn from Ezek 34:17–19 and is based on common shepherding and goat-herding practices in the ancient Near East. During the daytime, the sheep and the goats were allowed to graze together. But at night, since goats needed to be kept warmer than sheep, the goats were separated from the sheep and were sheltered in a cave.

In Jesus' discussion of the judgment, the sheep will be placed at the right hand of the divine judge, and the goats will be place on the left. The sheep, therefore, are given the position of honor. Matthew 25:46 makes it clear that the sheep symbolize "the righteous" who will enter "into eternal life" while the goats represent people who "will go away into eternal punishment."

G. R. Driver, *Canaanite Myths and Legends* (Edinburgh: T. & T. Clark, 1956, 1976).

JAMES A. DURLESSER

Anoint, Anointed, Anointing, King, Messiah, Christ   In the OT the Hebrew verb *mashah,* "anoint," is used of the application of oil to the body. Nontechnically, it can refer to the use of oil after bathing (2 Sam 12:20; Ezek 16:9, figuratively, of God's treatment of Israel). Anointing the head with oil was one of the ways of welcoming a guest (Ps 23:5; see also Luke 7:46). Most occurrences of the verb, however, refer to the setting apart for special service of persons (kings, priests, and, in one instance, a prophet) and sacred things.

In Exod 40:9–11 God instructs Moses to take the anointing oil and anoint the tabernacle, its furniture, the altar and its utensils, the basin and its stand. In the same passage he is told to anoint Aaron and consecrate him as priest, and also his sons, for "a perpetual priesthood" (Exod 40:12–15). In the act of anointing special oil was poured from a horn or vial onto the head of the candidate. A graphic picture of the event is presented by Ps 133:2, "It is like the precious oil on the head, running down upon the beard, on the beard of Aaron, running down over the collar of his robes." The phrase "the anointed priest" (Lev 4:3, 5, 16) refers to the high priest, "the priest who is exalted above his fellows, on whose head the anointing oil has been poured and who has been consecrated to wear the vestments" (Lev 21:10).

There is only one reference to the anointing of a prophet. In 1 Kgs 19:16 Elijah is told to anoint Elisha as prophet in his place.

Most instances of the verb "anoint" refer to a king.

King and kingship in Israel. The biblical record retains the tradition that the kings of Israel and Judah derived their right to rule from the people. In 1 Sam 11:15 we read, "So all the people went to Gilgal, and there they made Saul king before the LORD in Gilgal" (see also 1 Kgs 16:16). Similarly, it is the people who anoint David as king over Judah (2 Sam 2:4), and Israel (2 Sam 5:3; see also 2 Kgs 11:12). Accompanying this tradition was the notion of a limited monarchy: "Samuel told the people the rights and duties of the kingship; and he wrote them in a book" (1 Sam 10:25). Deuteronomy 17:14–20 sets forth "the law of the king." There is also mention of a covenant of the king with the people (2 Sam 5:3; 2 Kgs 11:12).

Somewhat in tension with this understanding of the kingship is the view that the king is selected and appointed by God and anointed by God's representative. Thus Samuel can say to Saul, after he has poured oil on his head, "The LORD has anointed you ruler over his people Israel" (1 Sam 10:1; see also 2 Sam 12:7). Samuel anoints David, at God's command, before the representatives of Judah and Israel do (1 Sam 16:12–13). Hence the phrase "the Lord's anointed" (1 Sam 24:6 and often). Derivatives of this expression are "my anointed" (1 Sam 2:35; Ps 132:17), "his anointed" (Pss 2:2; 18:50; see also Rev 11:15; 12:10), "your anointed" (Pss 89:20; 132:10). Since the king is celebrated in the psalms as David's descendant, one of these phrases sometimes occurs in parallel with a reference to David (Pss 18:50; 132:10, 17). None of these expressions is used with reference to the high priest. It must also be noted that the expression "the Anointed" ("the Messiah") never occurs in the Hebrew Scriptures or the Apocrypha.

Because of the use of "his anointed" as a designation of the political ruler, it can be used figuratively of Cyrus, the Persian conqueror, in Isa 45:1: "Thus says the LORD to his anointed, to Cyrus, whose right hand I have grasped to subdue nations before him." A figurative use is found also in Isa 61:1, "The spirit of the Lord GOD is upon me, because the LORD has anointed me." From the context it appears that the speaker is a prophetic rather than a royal figure (see also Luke 4:16–27).

Despite the fact that some nations deified their kings as a way of strengthening their rule, Israel's monotheism prohibited this practice. There are passages that appear to succumb to it. In Ps 45, addressed to the king (v. 1), we read,

"Your throne, O God, endures forever and ever. . . . Therefore God, your God, has anointed you" (vv. 6–7; these verses are quoted in Heb 1:8–9). It is almost certain that the psalmist did not intend his exuberant language to be taken literally; here "God" is used metaphorically as a way of describing the glory of the king's rule, just as is the phrase "forever and ever." The same must be said of Isaiah's prophecy of a successor to David, who will be called "Wonderful Counselor, Mighty God, Everlasting Father, Prince of Peace" (Isa 9:6). Because of belief in the incarnation, Christians can apply this prophecy to Jesus, but it is improbable that the Hebrew poet himself intended his phrase "Mighty God" to be taken literally. Certainly there is not the slightest hint in these passages or elsewhere in the Hebrew Scriptures of king worship. So some translators read the two words as "divine hero," and REB takes that to mean simply "mighty hero."

Alongside veneration of the king and celebration of his might in the coronation hymns (e.g., Pss 2; 45) there was an antimonarchical strain in Israelite thought. When Samuel reports to God that the elders of Israel have asked him to appoint a king, God responds, "they have rejected me from being king over them" (1 Sam 8:7). After Samuel has warned them about all the evils of monarchy, the people answer, "No! but we are determined to have a king over us, so that we also may be like other nations" (1 Sam 8:19–20). Deeply imbedded in Israelite piety was the conviction that God alone was truly king, God alone was the mighty warrior defending his people, as expressed in Ps 24:8: "Who is the King of glory? The LORD strong and mighty, the LORD, mighty in battle." Several psalms begin with the cry "The LORD is king!" (Pss 93, 97, 99). Although God was king of Israel in a special sense, monotheism dictated the belief that God's kingship extended over all the earth (Ps 47).

Disillusionment with the rule of actual kings led Israelite thought in two directions. On the one hand, the hope for an ideal king, who would truly represent God's rule, never died out. One of its finest expressions is found in Isa 11:1–5. In Ezek 34:20–24 God promises to act as saving shepherd of his flock through his servant David. On the other hand, resistance to the idea of a human monarchy produced hope for the manifestation of God's rule without any earthly king. This may or may not be true of Daniel, depending on the meaning of Dan 7:13–14. These verses may refer to an individual royal figure, but this is not certain, since the interpretation of the vision in v. 27 takes the "one like a human being" as a symbol for "the people of the holy ones of the Most High." There is no mention in Daniel of a king as a future deliverer of Israel (the two anointed ones mentioned in 9:25–26 are not deliverers; neither is the prince of the covenant of 11:22). This task is assigned rather to the archangel Michael (Dan 12:1).

Anointed in the Greek OT. In the LXX, the Greek translation of OT, *mashah* is represented by *chrio,* a verb normally used with the meaning rub or smear ointment, oil, or perfume on the body. This could include medicinal applications and the preparation of a corpse for burial. Hellenistic culture had no tradition of pouring oil on a person's head as an act of consecration. The participle *mashiah,* "anointed," was translated in most passages not by a participle but by the adjective *christos,* "smeared." To the ears of uninitiated Greek readers the expression "the Lord's anointed" must have sounded very strange indeed—"the smeared one of the Lord." There were many Hebrew expressions for which the translators had to give Greek words new meanings, producing "Jewish Greek." *Christos* is a prime example. In a number of passages *christos* has no article, which could give it the appearance of a name.

Pre-Christian Judaism. Christians have long assumed that Jews uniformly expected God to send his anointed, "the messiah," to establish a golden age of peace and righteousness by force of arms. The Jewish literature written between 200 B.C. and A.D. 100 contains remarkably little evidence of this belief. Indeed, some scholars have bluntly declared that "the messiah" was not a title in Judaism in this era. The lack of interest in the messiah can be explained in part by a generally negative reaction to the Hasmonean rulers, and the feeling that the power of Rome was too overwhelming to be defeated by any earthly king.

Nevertheless, there is evidence that some Jews believed that God would rescue Israel by means of a royal deliverer, "the anointed." This phrase appears in the Psalms of Solomon, a Pharisaic work from the first century B.C. After praying that God raise up the son of David to purge Jerusalem from Gentiles, smash the arrogance of sinners, and destroy unlawful nations with the word of his mouth, the psalmist prophesies, "their king shall be the Lord Messiah" (*Ps Sol* 17:26–32). There are a number of passages in the Dead Sea Scrolls that refer to the anointed of Israel and to the shoot of David, with allusions to other OT passages about a future king, such as 2 Sam 7:14. Scholars are quite correct in reminding us that Judaism was very diverse at the time of Jesus; we may even speak of "judaisms." It appears probable that the expectation of "the Lord's anointed" was unimportant to many Jews. Nonetheless, we should assume that this hope was well known, and thus available to any who wished to cherish it. The role and functions of the anticipated "anointed" were vague, and therefore individuals and groups could develop their own "job description" for the messiah. Thus, if a prophet like John the Baptist had announced the advent of the anointed, his hearers would have recognized the term, but they would have wanted to know what he understood by it.

Paul's letters. The epithet *christos* had already been applied to Jesus before Paul's conversion. In 1 Cor 15:3 the apostle reminds his readers of the tradition he had received and had transmitted to them, "that Christ died for our sins in accordance with the scriptures." Here there is no definite article, suggesting that "Christ" has already become a proper name like "Jesus," as in the frequent combination "Jesus Christ." Scholars incline to the view that the word means "Messiah" in Paul's writings only when it is accompanied by the definite article, as in Rom 9:5, where NRSV has "the Messiah." It seems unlikely, however, that *christos* had already become a name without meaning prior to Paul's conversion. Although the evidence is admittedly slim, it appears that the Hebrew *mashiah* and the corresponding Aramaic word had already become a name with content, that is, a name designating the eschatological deliverer. In John 4:25 the Samaritan woman declares, "I know that Messiah is coming." The Gospel writer here uses *messias*, a grecized form of the Hebrew or Aramaic term, and includes no definite article, suggesting that *messias* is not a title ("the anointed") but a name. He then adds an interpretation of this foreign name for his Greek readers, "who is called Christ" (there is no article with "Christ").

Even if the name "Christ" had lost much of its messianic force for his Gentile readers, it seems likely that Paul had this meaning in mind in the line "we proclaim Christ crucified, a stumbling block to Jews and foolishness to Gentiles" (1 Cor 1:23). It is probable that Christian preaching of a crucified Messiah was an immense stumbling block for Paul himself prior to his conversion. The proclamation of a crucified Jesus would not have been so offensive; he would have regarded it merely as foolishness.

If it is true that *christos* remained for Paul a name with content, this helps to explain why Paul can so frequently reverse "Jesus Christ" to "Christ Jesus," that is, "Messiah Jesus." One suspects that the word retained some of its messianic force even when used alone, as in 2 Cor 5:10, "for all of us must appear before the judgment seat of Christ," where a royal function is in mind. Since the definite article precedes *christos* in this verse, it would also be possible to translate the phrase as "the judgment seat of the Messiah."

Opposed to this hypothesis, however, is the fact that Paul never uses the phrase "Jesus the Christ." He finds no reason in his letters to declare "Jesus is the Christ," or to borrow "the Lord's Christ" from the LXX. It was possible for Paul's original readers—and today's readers also—to read all the statements in which "Christ" appears (except for Rom 9:5) without thinking "Messiah." While it is probable that for Paul himself "Christ" retained a messianic connotation, it is clear that traditional Jewish ideas about the messiah contribute little to his understanding of what God did for the world through Jesus. For Paul, messiahship does not tell us who Jesus is; Jesus redefines messiahship.

One of Paul's most important contributions to Christology is the idea of Christians being "in Christ" or "in Christ Jesus," as in Rom 8:1, "There is therefore now no condemnation for those who are in Christ Jesus." Sometimes this motif is attributed to Paul's "Christ mysticism." This may be helpful in understanding certain passages, for example, 2 Cor 12:2, "I know a person in Christ who . . . was caught up to the third heaven," but here "in Christ" may mean simply "a member of the church" (see also Rom 16:3; Phil 4:21). It is important not to ignore the corporate dimension of "in Christ," as in Rom 12:5, "so we, who are many, are one body in Christ" (see also Gal 3:26, 28). Perhaps underlying Paul's use of "in Christ" is the notion of the Messiah as the head of God's people, but this would hardly explain the idiom. In 1 Cor 15:22 "in Adam" and "in Christ" identify two different kinds of humanity. Transfer to the new humanity "in Christ" is accomplished by faith (Rom 5:1, 12–21).

Two other special uses of "Christ" in Paul's letters deserve brief notice. In Gal 2:20 the apostle writes, "It is no longer I who live, but it is Christ who lives in me" (see also Rom 8:10). He also uses the metaphor of putting on new clothes: "As many of you as were baptized into Christ have clothed yourselves with Christ" (Gal 3:27; see also Rom 13:14).

"Christ" in the Synoptic Gospels and Acts. In Mark, the earliest Gospel, *christos* appears only seven times. In 1:1 and 9:41 NRSV takes the word to be a name, "Christ," but in all other instances renders the word as "the Messiah." All the instances in Matthew and Luke are translated "the Messiah." At the dramatic center of the Gospel, Peter confesses, "You are the Messiah" (Matt 16:16). Jesus immediately announces that he must be killed. When Peter rebukes him, he is sternly rebuked by Jesus for setting his mind on human things. In this narrative Jesus does not reject Peter's confession, but radically redefines the Messiah's role. Luke omits the dialogue with Peter, but retains the idea of the suffering Messiah (Luke 9:20–22). Matthew amplifies Peter's confession, "You are the Messiah, the Son of the living God," and includes Jesus' blessing of Peter (Matt 16:16–20).

All three Gospels include the anecdote in which Jesus asks his opponents in the temple, "How can the scribes say that the Messiah is the son of David?" After quoting Ps 110:1, in which David the psalmist wrote, "The LORD said to my lord, 'Sit at my right hand,'" Jesus says, "David himself calls him Lord; so how can he be his son?" (Mark 12:35–37; see also Matt 22:41–45; Luke 20:41–43). This psalm text reappears in the trial scene. After the high priest asks, "Are you the Messiah, the Son of the Blessed One?" Jesus replies, "I am; and 'you will see the Son of Man seated at the right hand of Power,'" (Mark 14:61–62; compare Matt 26:63–64; Luke 22:67–69). Psalm 110:1 was the most important proof text for interpreting Jesus' resurrection as his exaltation to the right hand of God (Acts 2:32–36). In this way the idea of the messiah was reshaped again to include waiting at God's side until his rule was fully established.

Both Matthew and Luke associate the notion of messiah with Jesus' birth (Matt 1:18; 2:4; Luke 2:11, 26). Matthew emphasizes the teaching role of the messiah (23:10; compare 28:18–20). Luke displays a special interest in the suffering of the messiah, which he finds prophesied in Scripture (Luke 24:26, 46; Acts 3:18; 26:22–23). In Acts the missionaries, whether Peter, Paul, or someone else, attempt to convince Jews by means of Scripture that Jesus is the messiah (e.g., 2:14–36; 9:22; 18:28).

"Christ" in John and 1 John. In the Gospel according to John, *messias*, a grecized form of *mashiah* and its Aramaic equivalent, appears twice (and nowhere else in the NT). In both cases it seems to be a name rather than a title ("the Anointed"). Andrew tells Peter, "We have found the Messiah," and the author then renders this name into the more familiar name "Christ" (John 1:41). Similarly, the Samaritan woman declares, "I know that Messiah is coming," and the author adds "who is called Christ" (John 4:25). "Christ" is also used as a name twice in the familiar combination "Jesus Christ" (John 1:17; 17:3).

In all other instances "Christ" is preceded by the definite article and is correctly rendered in NRSV as "the Messiah." Twice John the Baptist asserts "I am not the Messiah" (1:20; 3:28). Messengers from the Pharisees ask him, "Why then are you baptizing if you are neither the Messiah, nor Elijah, nor the prophet?" (1:25). This is a strange question, since there is no evidence of the expectation that any of these end-time figures would baptize. John's use of the question indicates that Christians regarded baptism as an end-time rite.

"The Messiah" occurs five times in John 7. The setting is the temple during the Festival of Booths. The crowd wonders whether Jesus is the messiah, and whether the authorities know his identity (John 7:26). Some insist that he cannot be the messiah, since his place of origin is known, whereas no one knows where the messiah is from (v. 27). Many, however, believe in Jesus, saying, "When the Messiah comes, will he do more signs [John's word for miracles] than this man has done?" (v. 31). Jewish sources do not attribute healing miracles to the messiah, but David is credited with driving an evil spirit out of Saul (1 Sam 16:23), and it was expected that the messiah would be empowered by the spirit of God (Isa 11:1–3). A few verses later the issue of Jesus' origin is taken up again. To those who say "This is the Messiah" the skeptics respond, "Surely the Messiah does not come from Galilee, does he?" Scripture asserts that the Messiah comes from David's town, Bethlehem (7:41–42). There is great irony here, since from the beginning of the Gospel the author has presented Jesus as the Word that became flesh (John 1:14). The crowd's ideas about the messiah are thus totally inadequate for a proper understanding of Jesus.

In light of John's incarnational theology it is rather surprising to find this statement near the end of the Gospel: "Now Jesus did many other signs. . . . But these are written so that you may come to believe that Jesus is the Messiah, the Son of God, and that through believing you may have life in his name" (John 20:30–31). Apparently "messiah" has been redefined by attachment to "Son of God," which for John is an incarnational title. This modification of "messiah" can be seen also in Martha's confession, "I believe that you are the Messiah, the Son of God, the one coming into the world" (John 11:27), where "coming into the world" refers to the incarnation (see John 1:9; 6:38, 51).

In the Johannine letters "Christ" appears most frequently in the double name "Jesus Christ," but twice it has the article and can be translated as "the Messiah": "Everyone who believes that Jesus is the Christ has been born of God" (1 John 5:1; see also 2:22). What he means by "Messiah" becomes clearer when we read a few verses later, "Who is it that conquers the world but the one who believes that Jesus is the Son of God?" (1 John 5:5).

Jesus. Did Jesus regard himself as the messiah? Did others during his lifetime view him as the messiah? These two questions are vigorously debated by scholars. Some argue that Jesus' life and ministry were so unmessianic that no one would have regarded him messiah; this was first proposed after his resurrection. Others insist that it is unlikely that the resurrec-

tion experience would have convinced his followers that he was the messiah unless there was some preresurrection experience in support of this claim.

The least contested item in historical Jesus research is that he was crucified by the Romans. Since crucifixion was the form of execution reserved primarily for rebellious slaves, brigands, and political rebels, there is little reason to doubt the historicity of the *titulus,* the charge against him that, according to Roman custom, was placed above his head on the cross. It is mentioned in all four Gospels: "The King of the Jews" (Matt 27:37; Mark 15:26; Luke 23:38; John 19:19). In view of Jesus' opposition to anti-Roman violence (Matt 5:41 was aimed specifically at people who deeply resented the right of Roman soldiers to commandeer their services), it seems extremely unlikely that this charge would have been brought against him unless at least some of his supporters were intimating that he was the promised messiah.

Did Jesus openly and vigorously reject this suggestion? The cross provides the surest evidence that he did not. Did he himself publicly claim to be the messiah? Assuredly not, because only God could identify the messiah. Such a claim would have provided the surest evidence of its falsity. Jesus obeyed the rule he taught others: "For whoever exalts himself will be humbled, and whoever humbles himself will be exalted" (Matt 23:12 NIV; in different contexts, Luke 14:11; 18:14).

John J. Collins, *The Scepter and the Star: The Messiahs of the Dead Sea Scrolls and Other Ancient Literature* (New York: Doubleday, 1995); John Day, ed., *King and Messiah in Israel and the Ancient Near East: Proceedings of the Oxford Old Testament Seminar,* JSOT-Sup 270 (Sheffield: Sheffield Academic Press, 1998); Sigmund Mowinckel, *He That Cometh* (Nashville: Abingdon Press, 1954); J. Neusner, W. S. Green, and J. Z. Smith, eds., *Judaisms and Their Messiahs at the Turn of the Christian Era* (Cambridge: Cambridge University Press, 1987).

DOUGLAS R. A. HARE

Antichrist   The real theological development of this concept actually takes place in the teaching of the church, but the term originates in the Bible. Obviously there could be no antichrist until a christ had appeared, so the idea is strictly a NT one (see *anoint*). It is not a very important one there, either. The term occurs only five times, all within the Johannine epistles. Most of the meager evidence we have about that author's understanding of the concept can be deduced from 1 John 2:18: "Children, it is the last hour! As you have heard that antichrist is coming, so now many antichrists have come" (see also 1 John 2:22; 4:3; 2 John 7). From this we learn that (a) the antichrist is a harbinger of end times; (b) he was a known figure of early Christian tradition; but, surprisingly, (c) the title can be applied to many. Fuller discussion by the author discloses that the many are people, not demons, who "went out from us" (2:19). They are "those who do not confess that Jesus Christ has come in the flesh" (2 John 7). Evidently an antichrist was a heretic, one who was against ("anti-") the orthodox view of Christ, perhaps one whose Christology underestimated the humanity of Jesus (in short, a Docetist).

We cannot know whether or not the antichrist of the end time who makes his literary debut in 1 John was none other than "the lawless one" or "the man of sin" of 2 Thess 2:3–12. We do know, however, that the church soon made that identification, and linked the antichrist with the beasts of Rev 13:2–18 as well. Over the centuries, the antichrist has been located in past, present, and future. He has been portrayed variously as Papist, Anglican, Jew, Arab, and Communist. In spite of his obscure scriptural origins, he lives on today in the preaching of television evangelists and millenarians of all sorts.

W. SIBLEY TOWNER

Apostle   In early, secular Greek usage, the term "apostle" (*apostolos*) was espe-cially associated with maritime commerce and military expeditions. It typically functioned in a passive sense and connoted the quality of being sent, apart from any notion of authorization. The absence of the latter nuance holds even in those few cases where it denotes an individual (e.g., Herodotus, 1.21; 5.38). Although the term "apostle" is all but absent in the LXX (see 1 Kgs 14:6), forms of the cognate verb "to send forth" (*apostello*) occur over 700 times, most frequently to render the Hebrew root *shalah*, especially where it connotes an instance of a commission of some sort. Thus the use of *apostello* in a technical sense to indicate the sending of an envoy with a particular task (e.g., Isa 6:8) furnishes the meaning of the noun "apostle."

The first occurrence of the word "apostle" in the Gospels is found at Mark 3:14 (unless this is an interpolation from Luke 6:13) where it designates the select group of twelve *disciples* singled out by Jesus "to be with him, and to be sent out to proclaim the message." They also receive authority to cast out demons (3:15). That they perform these specific duties is reported in connection with the only other occurrence of the term apostle in Mark at 6:30, where the disciples inform Jesus about the results of their earlier commissioned activities (6:7–13). Thus the term is attested for Mark regardless of how the textual evidence for its occurrence in 3:14 is evaluated. Matthew's sole use of the term is at Matt 10:2, where the names of the Twelve are listed in the account parallel to Mark 6:7–13. Luke offers parallels to both Markan occurrences (Luke 6:13; 9:10) as well as four additional instances. In three of these references "apostles" functions as a synonym for the Twelve (17:5; 22:14; 24:10), and the fourth may refer to the Twelve but could also simply be an example of the generic use of the term. That the Lukan conception of the apostles is much more developed than its Synoptic counterparts becomes clear in the Acts of the Apostles, where the connection between the Twelve and the apostles is emphasized and solidified. References to the apostles, that is, the Twelve or various members of that group, occur some two dozen times. The significance of the apostles in Acts lies especially in their collective function as the essential witnesses (1:8, 22; 2:32; 3:15; 5:32; 10:39, 41; 13:31) who undergird the proclamation of the church. The episode of the replacement of Judas by Matthias in Acts 1:21–26 spells out what is essential in the Lukan understanding of an apostle, namely, that such persons must have participated in all the activities of the earthly Jesus. At the other extreme, the single use of "apostle" in the Fourth Gospel is a generic reference to "messengers" not being greater than the one who sent them (John 13:16). That verse well illustrates the sense of authorization or commission that derives from the OT verbal complex *shalah/apostello* that is key for the meaning of the noun "apostle" in the NT. Rabbinic usage of *shaliah* may offer the closest analogue to the NT use of apostle (e.g., *m. Berakhot* 5:5: "the one sent by a man is as the man himself"), but further specifying the precise relation among these sources is complicated by the uncertainty about the date of the rabbinic evidence.

In comparison with the usage of "apostle" in the Gospels, particularly that of Luke-Acts, Paul's employment of the term is distinctive for its wider range of meanings. Paul makes clear reference to those who were apostles before him (Gal 1:17; 1 Cor 15:7). But the fact that he can mention the Twelve (15:5) and the apostles (15:7) separately in the same context, as well as include himself among the apostles as the last of their number (1 Cor 15:8–9), shows that Paul does not restrict membership in the group of apostles to the Twelve. Paul's statements about his own status as an apostle (Rom 1:1; 11:13; 1 Cor 1:1; 2 Cor 1:1; Gal 1:1) underline its import as a designation for someone specially chosen and commissioned by God. Paul seems to view an appearance of the risen Christ as one prerequisite among the credentials needed for membership in the apostolic circle (1 Cor 9:1; 15:7). This

distinction, however, apparently did little to secure the designation apostle for the female eyewitnesses in the Gospel tradition. Apart from Paul's solemn and often emphatic technical usage of "apostle," he can also employ the word in a rather generic sense when he refers to various "church envoys." Thus in the discussion about arrangements for the collection, Paul refers to certain brothers as "messengers of the churches" (*apostoloi ekklesion*, 2 Cor 8:23). In Phil 2:25 Epaphroditus appears as Paul's "brother and co-worker and fellow soldier" and as the "apostle" (NRSV: "messenger") of the Philippians. A further discrete use is found in those places where apostle appears to function as a designation for itinerant preachers and missionaries (Rom 16:7; 1 Cor 9:5; 12:28; cf. Eph 2:20; 3:5; 4:11), a connotation that in some cases seems fitting for Paul himself and his companions (e.g., 1 Cor 4:9; 1 Thess 2:7). A certain tension arises among the various senses of the word as it is employed by Paul insofar as Paul's own reference to himself as the last apostle in chronological terms implies a select group that was in fact limited and closed.

That the word was considered available for use by others is evident in Paul's dispute with the so-called "super-apostles" in 2 Cor 10–13 (see 11:5; 12:11). Paul considers that these individuals can only be classified as "false apostles" (*pseudapostoloi*) who masquerade as apostles of Christ (11:13; cf. Rev 2:2), and that they are the equivalent to ministers of Satan (11:15). It is in the face of this unprecedented "apostolic" challenge that Paul uncharacteristically insists that he performed the signs of a true apostle among the Corinthians, namely "signs and wonders and mighty works" (2 Cor 12:12).

Ironically the narrow conception of the term as an exclusive designation for the Twelve favored by Luke-Acts seems to have meant that in Luke's second volume it was necessary to withhold from Paul the title that to him was fundamental for his vocation as the one sent to the Gentiles (Rom 11:13). The fact that "apostles" occurs at Acts 14:4, 14 in reference to Barnabas and Paul in contradiction to Luke's normal usage is sometimes taken as evidence of a source in which the meaning is akin to the usage in 2 Cor 8:23 and Phil 2:25. It is just possible, however, given the obviously heroic status of Paul in the second half of Acts, that the discrepancy is an all but tacit admission that Paul also ranked alongside the Twelve as an apostle. To be sure, the Pauline tradition developed an image of Paul as the apostle par excellence. By the end of the NT period the primary significance of the term "apostle" was increasingly in line with the Lukan notion of the twelve apostles, or individual members of the group, in both "orthodox" and "heterodox" usage. The apostle Paul stands out as the exception that proves the rule.

CHRISTOPHER R. MATTHEWS

Appear, Appearance   *see* **Presence**

Ark of the Covenant   *see* **Presence**

Arm of God   *see* **God**

Armageddon (RSV), Harmagedon (NRSV)   A term used once in the Bible (Rev 16:16) to denote the place where the kings of the earth will assemble for battle "on the great day of God the Almighty" (16:14). It is identified by the author as Hebrew, but its origin remains uncertain. It resembles most closely the Hebrew words *har megiddo* "Mount Megiddo," and most interpreters read it that way. The city of Megiddo had been the site of famous battles, since it lay near the north-south road through the Mount Carmel ridge (Judg 5:19; 2 Kgs 23:29–30; 2 Chron 35:22; Zech 12:11) and for that reason might have been projected as the location of another great battle. The term Mount Megiddo never occurs in the OT, however, and the tradition of a gathering of the nations that will lead to their destruction always focuses on Jerusalem (Pss 2; 46; 48; Joel 3:1–3, 11–17; Zech 12; 14; and

also Rev 20:7–10). This has led to the suggestion that the term is derived from the Hebrew *har midgo*, "mountain of his fruitfulness," and thus does refer to Jerusalem (*IDB* 1:227). Other suggestions seem less likely than these two.

More has been made of Armageddon in later interpretations than the text justifies. A battle is alluded to in Rev 16:14, but it is never described. The author moves immediately to the pouring out of the seventh bowl, which leads to terrible natural phenomena that destroy the cities of the nations and Babylon. There remain several more acts in the great drama of Revelation, including a battle at an unnamed place in 19:19–21, until the powers of evil are finally destroyed at the "beloved city," in 20:7–10, so Armageddon is not the great, final battle that it has become in the popular uses of the term.

DONALD E. GOWAN

Ascend   In addition to its normal meaning of "go up" (e.g., a mountain), there are several religious uses, all referring to movement from earth to heaven. Prayers ascend to heaven (Acts 10:4). Angels ascend after completing their mission on earth (Judg 13:20; Tobit 12:20). Elijah ascended in a whirlwind (2 Kgs 2:11).

The verb is used several times in John with reference to the ascension of the risen Jesus. In 20:17 Jesus tells Mary Magdalene to tell his disciples, "I am ascending to my Father and your Father" (see also 3:13; 6:62).

Surprisingly, "ascend" is not found in the ascension narrative in Acts 1, where "taken up" (vv. 2, 11) and "lifted up" (v. 9) are used. Similar language is used by Luke at the conclusion of his Gospel: "While he was blessing them, he withdrew from them and was carried up into heaven" (Luke 24:51). The passive verb is also used in John 12:32, "And I, when I am lifted up from the earth, will draw all people to myself" (here John is probably referring both to the crucifixion and to the ascension). A passive verb is found also in

1 Tim 3:16 ("taken up in glory"). These are all "divine passives"—they imply that God is responsible for raising Jesus to heaven. This is made explicit in Phil 2:9, "Therefore God also highly exalted him." The verb "ascend" is used of Christ's ascension in Eph 4:8–10, but in some passages another verb is used: "who has passed through the heavens" (Heb 4:14), "who has gone into heaven" (1 Pet 3:22). In many passages the ascension is simply assumed, as in Heb 1:3: "When he had made purification for sins, he sat down at the right hand of the Majesty on high." This verse alludes to Ps 110:1, "The LORD says to my lord, 'Sit at my right hand until I make your enemies your footstool.'" Psalm 110:1 is quoted or alluded to in the NT more often than any other OT text; it was a fundamental tool for early Christian understanding of the postmortem existence of Jesus. The conviction that the risen Jesus is seated at God's right hand lies behind all the allusions to the ascension. Whether explicit or implicit, the ascension is the logical link between the resurrection of Jesus and his exalted position at God's right hand. The same, of course, is true of all those texts that refer simply to Jesus being in heaven or coming from heaven (e.g., Acts 3:21; Phil 3:20; 1 Thess 4:16).

Significantly, the verb is not used for the postmortem experience of believers. In sharp contrast to the gnostics, the NT authors have no interest in the ascent of the soul. The explanation lies in the belief in the resurrection of the body. Believers expected to sleep in the ground until Christ's coming in glory (1 Cor 15:52; 1 Thess 4:13–17). There is no consistency on this issue, however. In Phil 1:23 Paul writes, "My desire is to depart and be with Christ, for that is far better," suggesting that he expects to be in heaven immediately after his death. This implies an ascent of some kind, but Paul might prefer to think of being "caught up" (see 2 Cor 12:2, 4) rather than "ascending," in order to give credit to God.

DOUGLAS R. A. HARE

Astonish *see* **Sign**

Atone, Atonement, Cover The language of "atonement" has been very important in the history of Christian theology—a somewhat surprising development, given that it is not common in the NT. While there has never been a single orthodox definition on the subject, some Christian traditions have been insistent on one or another explanation of it. As a result, the contemporary Western Christian may find it difficult to avoid approaching the Scriptures without already "knowing" what atonement is all about. Part of the work of biblical theology is to shed such preconceptions at least long enough to let the texts themselves speak to us—and perhaps contradict us.

The English word "atonement" derives from the prepositional phrase "at one." Its original meaning was something like "reconciliation." The verb "atone" seems to be derived from the noun; it did not appear in KJV, though the noun was used broadly there. In subsequent theological usage, however, atonement has come to mean something more like expiation or propitiation. Theories of the atonement developed in the West have often borrowed the topic of satisfaction from Western law (Roman and Germanic) and combined it with biblical elements.

The Hebrew (*kipper, kippurim*) and Greek terms (various forms and derivatives of *hilaskomai*) commonly translated "atone, atonement" tend to have somewhat different sets of connections and connotations. The Hebrew terminology is used, in the OT, primarily in the context of the sacrificial cultus of the tabernacle and temple, where it expresses what happens in the relationship of God and humanity as a result of the sacrifices offered. (**"Sacrifice"** here should be understood somewhat broadly, since the language of atonement also appears in connection with such associated materials as the half-shekel levy [Exod 30:13–16] and the use of incense [Num 16:46–47].)

The etymological root of the Hebrew terms may originally have meant "cover." If so, it is no longer used in that sense in the Scriptures of Israel. Still, we may see a basic metaphor of "covering" at work. Other terms for covering (particularly *kasah*) also appear in general statements about the ways in which the distance between God and humanity is overcome or at least rendered harmless (e.g., "Happy are those . . . whose sin is covered," Ps 32:1, quoted in Rom 4:7). While language of "covering" can appear with a purely practical meaning in the Scriptures, it also has sacred significance, being associated with matters either holy or the opposite thereof. The various parts of the tabernacle all had their covers, which were particularly important when it was being prepared for the breaking of camp; they served, in transit, to protect the sacred and the profane from coming into contact with each other (Num 4:5–15). The blood of game animals was to be drained out and covered with earth (Lev 17:13). Vessels without coverings could allow impurity to enter their contents under certain circumstances (Num 19:14–15). God's own presence in the tabernacle is both manifested and veiled by a covering of cloud (Exod 40:34–38). And God's hand covers Moses so that Moses will not see God's face and die (Exod 33:20–23).

Covering, in other words, takes certain things "out of circulation," as it were. They are separated from what is immediately around them. The tabernacle and ark can be moved without fear either of their being contaminated or of their presenting a danger to their handlers of the kind narrated in the story of Uzzah and Ahio (2 Sam 6:1–11). The contents of a covered vessel remain pure. The blood of a game animal, even though it cannot be sacrificed on the altar, is placed beyond reach of any human misuse or disrespect. In contrast, when Job calls on the earth *not* to cover his blood, he is thereby asserting it as an ongoing issue between God and humanity—something *not* to be set aside (Job 16:18).

We are perhaps most familiar with the idea of atonement as a way of dealing with sin. It was also important in dealing with another issue that imposed distance between humanity and God: impurity. (See *clean*.) Certain sacrifices and rites prescribed for women after childbirth and for lepers and for those healed of sexual discharges—all unclean persons—are specifically described as making atonement (Lev 12:7–8; 14:18–21, 30–31; 15:15, 30). Atonement is even made for houses that have been afflicted with "leprosy" (Lev 14:53).

All of these rites are highly public. The idea of "covering" sins or impurity and thereby producing "atonement" is not, to borrow another English usage, a cover-up. The transaction is public. Both the offended (God) and the offender (the human sinner or unclean person) are part of it. It is a mutual arrangement by which the old offense is placed, quite deliberately, out of consideration. The relationship is no longer determined by it.

Exactly how sacrifice accomplishes this is never really clear. It is a truism of liturgical studies that rites are typically older than their explanation. We do know that some Israelites regarded sacrifice as a kind of gift to God, much as one might offer tribute to a king (e.g., Ps 68:29). The cultic language of the "pleasing odor" expresses a similar idea; the aroma is the form in which the sacrifice reaches God (e.g., Lev 1:9). On the other hand, some OT writers cast scorn on this idea: since God owns all the cattle on a thousand hills, why would God need a sacrifice from humanity (Ps 50:7–15)?

The imagery and language of "covering" and "atonement" should be taken not as an explanation (at least, not one of the sort expected by later theologians), but rather as a pervasive metaphor for the restoration of broken relationships between God and humanity, particularly, though not exclusively, as this was accomplished by sacrificial means.

At some points, "atonement" and "covering" function still more directly as apotropaic measures, intended to prevent or halt disaster when humanity brushes up against the forbidden. A census was one such dangerous moment. Although God commands the taking of a census in Num 26, David's census evokes a plague as punishment (2 Sam 24; 1 Chr 21). This sense of danger explains why Exodus specifies a half-shekel offering by each registrant as *"ransom"* or "atonement" (30:11–16).

Incense could serve the same function. Aaron uses it as "atonement" to halt a plague sent as punishment for the people's questioning of Moses and Aaron (Num 16:46–47). Similarly, incense serves to "cover the mercy seat" when the high priest enters the Holy of Holies on the Day of Atonement and so to protect the priest from seeing God and dying (Lev 16:11–13).

Blood plays a particularly important role in atonement. For example, the high priest was to perform atonement for the high altar once a year with sacrificial blood (Exod 30:10). And the most common single context for atonement language is in reference to sin offerings (e.g., Lev 4–6). Atonement, however, does not always involve blood. Not only can the half-shekel payment and incense serve the purpose of atonement; so does the goat for Azazel, which was not slaughtered, in the Day of Atonement rites (Lev 16:10).

Atonement is available, through sin or guilt offerings, for individuals, for public, sacral figures (such as priests and ruler), and for community as a whole (Lev 4). In particular, the solemn annual rites of the Day of Atonement (Lev 16) serve to restore the connection of the whole nation with God. They involve the sacrifice of a bull in atonement for the priest's own sins and those of his household, of a goat for the sins of the whole people, and the sending of the scapegoat into the wilderness. The high priest is to enter the Holy of Holies only on this one day of the year and there sprinkle blood from these sacrifices before the mercy seat (the Hebrew name of which, *kapporeth,* is related to the language of atonement). The high priest also anoints the altar itself with blood in order to atone for it and cleanse it from the sins of the preceding year.

Some later Israelite Wisdom writings move outside the realm of the sacrificial cultus to identify other means of atonement or covering. Sirach has a high interest in the priesthood and its atoning role (45:16, 23), but he can also write that "to forsake unrighteousness is an atonement" (35:5). Other atoning acts include the honoring of one's father (Sir 3:3), pleasing the great (!) (20:28), and almsgiving (3:30). Proverbs mentions "loyalty and faithfulness" (16:6). Indeed, "love covers all offenses" (Prov 10:12, quoted in 1 Pet 4:8 and adapted in Jas 5:20).

This broadening of the means of atonement continues in early Judaism and Christianity (as already suggested by the reuse of Prov 10:12 in James and 1 Peter). With the destruction of the temple in A.D. 70, this becomes a vital move for Judaism. It does not, however, necessarily involve the rejection of the sacrificial cultus, whether literally in the context of the temple or, for Christians, as reinterpreted in terms of the life and death of Jesus. Rather, it uses the language of the sacrificial cultus to give new dignity and meaning to what might otherwise have seemed like isolated personal pieties, such as prayer, fasting, and almsgiving.

The ancient Greek translators of the Scriptures of Israel tended to choose their translations of *kipper* from various compounds of *hilaskomai.* (They also, at times, spoke of the priest's atoning action in terms of "praying for" the worshiper, which seems to separate it from the sacrificial act and place it more in the power of the priest. This usage appears in the Vulgate as well.) *Hilaskomai* would not have awakened for the Greek reader the connotations of covering that seem to have been associated with *kipper.* This did not mean the disappearance of the covering metaphor, since it also appeared in ways that were easier to translate directly (e.g., Prov 10:12). But it did shift the basic metaphor for what was happening in the sacrificial cultus.

For the Greek terminology suggested not so much a "covering" of the offense as a restoration of the goodwill of the offended party. The sacrificial cultus serves to render God *hileos,* "kind, merciful." In ancient Greek texts outside the Scriptures, one might be inclined to translate it "propitiate" in relation to the gods, "appease" in relation to human beings. In other words, where the Hebrew *kipper* seems to have focused more on what happens to the offense in the process of atonement, the Greek terminology focuses more on what happens to the offended party, who is rendered more amenable, kindly, forgiving, and conciliatory.

The idea that a human death (not a deliberate human sacrifice, but a death occurring in other ways) might function like a sacrificial atonement was not unknown in ancient Israelite religion. It is one of the themes (though the word itself does not appear) in the Servant Songs of Second Isaiah, where the Suffering Servant becomes "an offering for sin" (Isa 53:10). It appears, too, in 4 Macc 17:22 as a theological explanation of the value of martyrdom: "And through the blood of those devout ones and their death as an atoning sacrifice, divine Providence preserved Israel."

This is a particularly important transition for early Christians, who conceive the execution of Jesus as having changed the relationship of God with humanity. Invariably, this death is seen not as a sacrifice offered by humans to God, but as a sacrifice generously offered by God on behalf of humans. The point is made twice in 1 John, first to emphasize its universal effectiveness ("the atoning sacrifice for our sins, and not for ours only but also for the sins of the whole world" [2:2]), and second to emphasize the divine initiative in the matter ("In this is love, not that we loved God but that he loved us and sent his Son to be the atoning sacrifice for our sins" [4:10]).

Alongside the initiative of God, NT writers emphasize the voluntary acceptance of this mission by Jesus, whether in the Garden of Gethsemane (Matt 26:39;

Mark 14:36; Luke 22:42; cf. John 12:27–28) or in a preincarnational act of self-emptying (Phil 2:6–11). For God as well as Jesus, it is an act of self-giving in ways that the modern reader may have difficulty perceiving. Since the household, not the individual, was the basic social unit of antiquity, the child was an extension of the father and the continuation of the family's identity, the same identity presently incorporated in the father. The divine *family,* so to speak, devotes its full resources to this purpose.

But what exactly is this act to achieve? As noted above, the Scriptures have no single explanation of how atonement "worked." It was, above all, a cultic reality. The effectiveness of the sacrifice did not depend on one's theological analysis of it. It depended on the correct performance of the ritual—correct not only in the sense that it proceeded according to form, but in the sense that the participant was rightly disposed. Indeed, Num 15:22–31 holds that sacrificial atonement was available only for unwitting, unintended sins. Accordingly, one must bring to the sacrifice not only good intentions for the future but the same, however fallible, for the past.

Later Christian theology has expanded substantially on the question of what "happened" in the crucifixion and resurrection of Jesus. Among the metaphors available already in the NT are conquest of an enemy (e.g., Col 2:15), *redemption* or ransoming of sinners, and salvation from the *wrath* of God (e.g., Rom 5:9). A good many Christians understand the generalized language of sacrificial atonement as identical with the last: the death of Jesus appeases God's anger at human sinfulness. Does this in fact hold?

When 1 John describes Jesus as the "atoning sacrifice (*hilasmos*) for our sins," does it mean to say that Jesus' death somehow satisfies God's anger? Terms for "anger" or "wrath" do not appear in 1 John and only once in the Gospel of John (3:36). It is, accordingly, difficult to see the wrath of God as the critical focus of atonement in Johannine theology.

Indeed, the whole emphasis is on God's initiative in creating and restoring relationship with humanity. It is easier and imposes less on the text simply to assume that sacrifice does what it does without further explanation.

Sacrifice is a public act shaping the relationship of humanity and God. Whether it is thought of metaphorically in the more particularly Greek terms of appeasing an offended party or in the more Hebrew terms of "covering" what offends, it reestablishes the "at-one-ment" of the parties involved. The point that 1 John is making is only obscured by insisting on God as the object of the atoning act. For this author, God is the subject of it, the offerer of the sacrifice.

The same point is to be found in other NT writers interested in the atonement model for interpreting Jesus' death. In Rom 3:23–26, Paul describes Jesus' atoning death as demonstrating God's righteousness after having passed over previous sins; it demonstrates "at the present time" that God is righteous and makes (or deems) righteous those who associate themselves with what Jesus has done. Has God "put [Jesus] forward as a sacrifice of atonement" to satisfy God's own anger? This is a possible reading, but it neglects the main point, which is that *God* has provided the public rite that can reconcile God and humanity.

The Epistle to the Hebrews offers the longest and most complex account of Jesus in terms of the temple cultus (though the author actually refers only to the tabernacle, never to its stationary successor). Here Jesus is both priest and sacrifice (9:11–14). He is the eternal Son who becomes authentically human, for a true priest must have standing with both parties in order to effect atonement (2:14–18; 4:14–5:2). And his priesthood, named after the Gentile Melchizedek, not the Israelite Aaron, is the only really conclusive means of such atonement (5:8–10; 7:1–9).

Jesus' sacrificial work, according to Hebrews, is superior in several ways. It is unique and eternal, occurring only once and without need of repetition. It moves from this lower world (as Platonically understood) of shadows and copies into the higher world of the real and singular, until Jesus enters the heavenly tent, not made with hands, (the original of which the tabernacle in the wilderness was only a reproduction), there to present his sacrifice in the very presence of God. The author draws on the rites of the Day of Atonement for the culminating part of this imagery. Only once, in all this, does the author use the actual language of atonement (Heb 2:17).

Other NT writings contain what appear to be allusions to a sacrificial interpretation of Jesus' death. Jesus is the "Lamb of God" in John 1:29, 36 and the "Lamb that was slaughtered" in Rev 5:12. But, apart from Hebrews, the theology remains relatively little elaborated.

The same has not been true of subsequent Christian theology, which has become far more precise and definite on this point than that of the biblical writers. One will understand the scriptural use of this language of atonement best by allowing the texts to remain somewhat ambiguous rather than forcing them into complete systematic consistency. The fundamental thing in sacrificial atonement is the rite itself, not the explanations of it. By approaching God in worship, human beings seek to overcome whatever separates us from the Holy. It is the understanding of the Scriptures that God not only welcomes our approach but has created particular cultic means to facilitate it.

The practice of atonement through the sacrificial cultus poses a problem for postbiblical Christianity and Judaism. Since sacrifice has long been out of use, we tend to treat it as an idea rather than a practice. It becomes an unknown something that we try to reason our way "into" rather than a common, accepted practice that can be used to explain other things. A particular difficulty for many modern readers of the Bible is the fact that the Israelite sacrificial cultus involved the death of animals. Its use by early Christians as a way of understanding the execution of

Jesus extends this problem to a human death.

Is the death of the animal (and, by extension, of Jesus) the critical feature in atonement? As we have seen, it is not the only way to bring about atonement; but it is undoubtedly the primary one in the religion of Israel. The problem that arises for many is the sense that God therefore seems bloodthirsty, insistent on death as a principal condition of human approach. But this may be to understand sacrifice in excessively instrumental terms. Death is readily associated with the Holy because both death and the Holy testify to the human encounter with the ultimate limits of our power and control. Does sacrificial cultus arise from a divine demand to be fed (an idea rejected, as we have seen, in Ps 50 and parodied, in the ancient Greek world, by Aristophanes' *Birds*)? Or is the context of death simply a place where humans have repeatedly encountered the Holy and expect to encounter it again?

The idea that sacrifice makes atonement by "purchasing" God's goodwill, satisfying God's anger, or paying a penalty is an inadequate interpretation of our texts. Indeed, God's goodwill is already abundantly evident in God's provision of worship as a way of approach to the Holy. Atonement is rather a formal process of reconnecting what has come to be separated, whether by impurity or by sin. If we think of this in terms of the metaphor of "covering," we are suggesting that past offenses are being excluded from consideration and therefore no longer impose a separation. If we think of it in terms of propitiation or appeasement, there may be more danger of our piety turning into a means of changing God's mind; and yet the point of the process remains that any sense of alienation is being brought to an end. As the author of 1 John insists, this is God's doing, not that of human beings.

The role of death or blood in this process is very prominent in the sacrificial cultus of ancient Israel. The general development, however, in the Wisdom books of the OT, the Apocrypha, and the NT is to extend the atoning value of sacrifice to other significant acts of good: almsgiving, faithfulness, acts of love. These do not replace ritual atonement, but draw new theological value from their association with it. In the NT, the death of Jesus takes the central place in this reworking of the sacrificial cultus. It makes atonement fully and eternally available as an act in which the divine and the human reaching out to each other is fully effective. As a result, it calls for a new kind of life on the part of Jesus' followers. "Since we have confidence to enter the sanctuary by the blood of Jesus, . . . let us approach with a true heart in full assurance of faith" (Heb 10:19–22).

Hartmut Gese, *Essays in Biblical Theology* (Minneapolis: Augsburg Publishing House, 1981), 93–116.
L. WILLIAM COUNTRYMAN

Authority A conferred ability or capacity to act. Authority is the translation of Gk. *exousia*, which is used 102 times in the NT, with the most frequent occurrences in Revelation (21 times) and Luke (16 times). In ordinary usage, the term often appears in legal contexts and can therefore connote rights. Authority does not primarily denote intrinsic power, but rather the externally recognized right to exercise power. Even so, authority and power are so closely related that authority is often understood to be power. NRSV translates *exousia* as "rights" in the following contexts: Paul and other apostles have certain "rights" (*exousiai*, 1 Cor 9:4–6; 2 Thess 3:9); believers who remain steadfast have the "right" to eat from the tree of life (Rev 22:14). In John 10:18; Acts 26:18; Rev 9:19; and elsewhere, NRSV translates *exousia* as power. While the concept of authority is certainly evident in the OT, NRSV does not often use the word "authority" (see *call, power*). The present discussion focuses on the use of authority in the NT, where the word is used primarily in connection with the work of Jesus Christ, Satan's arrogation of power to himself, and the disciples' responsibility to use their authority in the service of the gospel.

Even though only three NT texts refer to God's authority (Luke 12:5; Acts 1:7; Jude 25), it is presumed that the source of all genuine authority is God. The story of Jesus revolves around his claim to authority that has been given to him by God (Matt 28:18). Jesus' authority is evident in early and immediate responses to his works of healing, which are clearly contrasted with human power and teaching (e.g., Mark 1:22, 27). Indeed, divinely conferred authority gives Jesus the power and the right to do what God does: to forgive sins (Mark 2:10, and par. Matt 9:6 and Luke 5:24), to perform his works of healing and expulsion of demons (Mark 1:27 and par. Luke 4:36), even to cleanse the temple (Mark 11:15–19, 27–33; cf. Ezek 8–11). While such authority should be easy to understand (Matt 8:9 and par. Luke 7:8), the scribes refuse to acknowledge that Jesus' authority is from God (Matt 21:23–27 and par Mark 11:28–29 and Luke 20:2–8). The rejection of Jesus' authority leads to his crucifixion. In Luke's account, the implication is that the leaders thereby put themselves under the authority of Satan (Luke 20:20, cf. 4:6; 22:3–5).

Luke's portrayal of Satan is reminiscent of that of Revelation, where Satan confers authority to earthly agents and thus appears to have power equal to God's. However, in Revelation, Satan has been rejected from heaven and has no authority of his own to give (cf. 12:7–9). The authority that he confers on the beast and his successors is therefore a counterfeit authority. Although it would appear that the serpent's arrogation of authority to himself undercuts the sovereignty of God, God remains in control by "allowing" those who have received authority from the serpent to exercise it, but only for a short period of time. In addition, God confers authority on certain natural and supernatural agents (death, 6:8; locusts, 9:3, 10, 19; the angel in charge of fire, 14:18). Thus, despite appearances to the contrary, all earthly manifestations of cosmic and supernatural authority remain under the control of God.

Having been given all authority (Matt 28:18), Jesus confers it on his disciples, who continue to do the works of Jesus in his name (Matt 10:1 and par. Mark 3:15 and Luke 9:1). Because it is conferred, the disciples' use of their authority must follow Jesus' model of service and resist earthly models of rank and privilege (Luke 22:24–27). Paul similarly advises the Corinthians to follow his example. Although he has certain "rights" (Gk. *exousiai*) as an apostle, yet for the sake of the gospel he willingly gives them up out of concern for the well-being of others in the church (1 Cor 9).

MARGARET S. ODELL

Avenge, Avenger, Vengeance

The concept of revenge builds upon the idea that it is appropriate to return harm for harm. In the Bible, the limits of revenge— if any—are debated, as are the agents of revenge, but the concept itself is not challenged except in the teachings of Jesus in the Sermon on the Mount.

Old Testament. The primary Hebrew word for "avenge" is *naqam* (see Num 31:2; Deut 32:35; 2 Kgs 9:7). It appears in its fullest savagery in Gen 4:24, where Lamech tells his two wives that he killed a man for wounding him. His revenge thereby exceeded the damage he had suffered "seventy-sevenfold." In evaluating his action, Lamech alluded to God's earlier promise to Cain that if anyone killed Cain, God would punish him sevenfold (Gen 4:15). God's threat seems to have been intended to reassure Cain that no harm would come to him and to deter Cain's enemies, but even a sevenfold revenge is excessive by the typical standard of the OT. That standard is the so-called *lex talionis* or law of retribution, which requires that retribution be no more than equivalent to the crime, that is, an eye for an eye, a tooth for a tooth, and so on. Cases included such acts as murder (Gen 9:6; Exod 21:12; Lev 24:17, 21), killing an animal, and injuring another human (Lev 24:19–20). Modern readers often assume that these laws demand exact retribution, when they do not. For example, in the case of injury to a pregnant woman that results in a miscarriage, the method of settling the dispute is a lawsuit (Exod 21:22). Or, if a master injures his slave, the slave is to be set free (Exod 21:26–27). It is probably better, then, to understand these laws as establishing *limits* on revenge rather than demanding exact retribution. Ultimately, of course, the OT counseled leaving revenge to God (Deut 32:35; Lev 19:18; Prov 20:22). Mendenhall has argued that *naqam* is associated mostly with God because the term normally fits cases where judicial process is unavailable, and one must appeal to God for redress. Thus he would usually translate the word as "deliver" or "rescue" (Mendenhall, 69–104).

However, except for two places (Ps 149: 7 and Ezek 25:15) where the Hebrew word is *tokehah* (which normally means "rebuke," "correction"), NRSV translates as "vengeance" some form of the root *naqam*. In three places the reference is to humans taking vengeance (Lev 19:18; Josh 10:13; 1 Sam 25:26); everywhere else (thirty-two times, unless Gen 4:15 is an exception) it is God that takes vengeance. In Lev 19:18, God instructs Israel not to take vengeance on other Israelites, but to love their neighbors as they loved themselves, while Jer 50:15 announces the vengeance of the Lord upon Babylon and directs the Israelites to take part by doing unto the Babylonians what they have done to the Israelites. Psalm 94:1 makes this point as bluntly as possible: "O LORD, you God of vengeance, you God of vengeance, shine forth!"

In other cases NRSV offers more interpretive translations. One example is "avenge" for *darash* (seek, study, care for) in 2 Chr 24:22. Zechariah, the son of the priest Jehoida, was stoned for opposing the apostasy of the people of Israel. With his dying breath, he implored God to see

and inquire into such a miscarriage of justice (i.e., requite; cf. Ps 9:12). In another case NRSV translates the verb *sum* (put, place, set) as "avenge." In Judg 9:24, God sends an evil spirit on Abimelech and the men of Shechem for slaughtering the sons of Jerubbaal (Gideon). This was done, says the author, so that the violence done to the sons of Jerubbaal might "be placed" upon Abimelech. In 2 Sam 16:8, Shimei son of Gera curses David and his men for the death of Saul, predicting that the Lord would "avenge" (*shub*, "return") the blood of Saul. Finally, Jer 51:35 contains two nominal sentences, the first of which may be translated: "my violence and my torn flesh (are about to be) upon Babylon." NRSV supplies the verb "avenge" in that sentence and in the second as well.

NRSV translates two nominal forms of *naqam* by the term "avenger" (Ps 8:2 and 99:8). More frequently word *go'el* is so translated (cf. Deut 19:6, 12; 2 Sam 14:11). A *go'el* is a kinsperson who loans money when a family is about to lose its land (Lev 25:25; see **redeem**) and who exacts revenge for harm done to a kinsperson. Numbers 35:12–25 and Josh 20:3–9 establish cities of refuge. These cities were places to which people charged with a crime could flee for protection from persons seeking revenge until a trial could be held (Num 35:12). In cases where a person kills another and is convicted of murder, the *go'el* actually performs the execution (35:19, 21). If the defendant is found innocent (35:22–25a), however, the *go'el* must leave and the defendant must remain in the city until the high priest dies. Then he is free to leave. If he departs the city early, for any reason, the *go'el* may take revenge.

New Testament. The NT differs from the OT in its presentation of the teachings of Jesus, who challenges the *lex talionis* by instructing his disciples not to resist someone doing them evil, but to turn the other cheek if they were struck (Matt 5:38–39). Paul admonishes Christians not to take vengeance (*ekdikesis*), even on enemies. They are to leave it to God:

"Vengeance is mine, I will repay, says the Lord" (Rom 12:19). In doing so, Paul reverted to the OT by quoting Deut 32:35. Christians too were in danger of confronting God as an avenger (*ekdikos*), so he exhorts them not to sin (1 Thess 4:6). The ungodly are in even more danger. Second Thessalonians warns that God will inflict vengeance through Jesus on those who do not know or obey God (1:8), and Heb 10:30 threatens vengeance on those who spurn Jesus. That warning is followed by the chilling remark: "It is a fearful thing to fall into the hands of the living God" (10:31). In Rev 6:10, martyrs cry out to God to avenge (*ekdikeo*) them, and Rev 19:2 insists that God's judgments are just and true, so God will avenge the death of the martyrs.

G. E. Mendenhall, *The Tenth Generation: The Origins of the Biblical Tradition* (Baltimore: Johns Hopkins Press, 1973), 69–104.

PAUL L. REDDITT

Awe, Awesome   *see* **Fear**

Babylon   *see* **City**

Baptism, Baptize   Washing with *water* is essentially a means of removing physical dirt from the body; but we can readily understand how it can be seen as something more. When Pilate washed his hands at the trial of Jesus, it was a symbolic way of cleansing himself from any guilt attached to his condemnation of a man who was perhaps innocent (Matt 27:24). In the OT we have a variety of occasions on which people were washed to remove whatever defilement could prevent them from coming before God, as when priests prepared for their service in the tabernacle or the temple (Exod 29:4). Bodily emissions were regarded as defiling the person (not just as dirtying the body) and had to be washed away (Lev 15). Such washings would have a deeper significance and indicate some kind of spiritual cleansing even though there was an obvious temptation to think that the outward act and the outward cleansing were what really mattered; the washing in Isa 1:16 is clearly metaphorical.

By NT times there was a tendency to extend the range of such washings. The Pharisees promoted the extension of priestly cleanliness to include ordinary, lay people and were punctilious about washing themselves and the domestic vessels that they used for eating (Mark 7:4 uses the term "baptism" to refer to this). The Qumran sect, which saw itself as a priestly group, practiced frequent washings, and there are references to this in their writings. Other individuals and groups performed regular washings as an important rite.

Against this background it is not surprising that there should appear a latter-day prophet who called his audience to confess their sins and undergo a rite that symbolized and expressed *repentance* that would lead to divine *forgiveness* (Mark 1:4). John, nicknamed the Baptizer, believed in the imminence of divine *judgment* upon the Jews for their sins and called them to a baptism with water in the River Jordan. Whether he immersed them in a sufficient depth of water or poured water (lavishly) over them is uncertain; the normal usage of the Greek verb elsewhere to refer to immersion points more to the former possibility, but the verb could be used in an extended sense (e.g., of people being deluged by a flood or "drowned" in alcohol), and some of the symbolical language used of baptism definitely points to the latter (cf. Ezek 36:25; 1 Cor 12:13b, where the imagery is of pouring water on crops). The fact that John was called "the Baptizer" suggests that he himself carried out the rite, whereas elsewhere people probably baptized themselves.

John drew a contrast between what he was doing with water and what would be done by the "Stronger One" whom he expected to come as God's agent: he would baptize with the Holy *spirit* and with *fire* (Matt 3:11; Luke 3:16; Mark 1:8 omits "and with fire"). This description suggests the performance of some action akin to baptism with water but effected by the Holy Spirit. This could be a purging or judgment with the Spirit, and the mention of fire reinforces this kind of interpretation. But does it mean cleansing or judgment? And does it affect different people in different ways? These are not easy questions to answer. They also bring out the inherent difficulty of finding an alternative English word or phrase to replace "baptize." Manifestly "baptize" means something rather more than simply "immerse" or "deluge"; for John it referred to a religious ritual, that is, to an immersion with religious significance, and this significance is that the action is one of "cleansing," which is tantamount to the washing away of sin and removal of the threat of judgment. Applied to baptism with the Spirit and fire, the term must indicate something analogous to washing with water, but infinitely more effective.

Among the people who came to John was Jesus; he was baptized, and as he came up out of the water, the Holy Spirit came upon him and he heard the voice of God affirming him as God's Son and Servant (Mark 1:9–11). Are we to understand this as a baptism with the Spirit, in which case the meaning has shifted to indicate something more like "being gifted with the Spirit"? It is certainly tempting to do so. This would then open up the significance of baptism to indicate reception of the Spirit as divine empowering for service rather than simply as cleansing from sin (which for the Evangelists would have been inappropriate in the case of Jesus). Thus the term "baptism" shifts in reference from "washing" to "religious washing" to "a spiritual analogue to washing (symbolized by the physical action)" to "a spiritual action that includes the motif of cleansing as one part of its significance."

Did Jesus follow the example of John and baptize other people? The only references to his doing so are in John 3:22 and 4:1, where baptism by Jesus is mentioned alongside baptism by John, but the comment is added that it was not Jesus himself who did the baptizing but his disciples. If we assume that this statement is historical, then it is likely that Jesus (perhaps especially at this early point) saw his activity as similar to that of John and as fulfilling John's prophecy, and therefore acted in continuation of what John was doing.

Development in the use and significance of baptism does not come until after Easter; baptism becomes the universally recognized outward form of initiation into the Christian faith and church (Eph 4:5). In Acts 1:4 Jesus is represented as telling his disciples not to leave Jerusalem but to wait for the promise of the Father that they had received from him (Luke 24:49), which he backs up with a reference to John's prophecy: before many days this would be fulfilled when they would be baptized with the Holy Spirit. The promise is repeated to the effect that the disciples would receive power when the Holy Spirit came upon them (Acts 1:8). In the light of these statements, the baptism with the Spirit prophesied by John is interpreted not just as a cleansing by the Spirit (although that is certainly included: Acts 2:38) but primarily as the reception of the Spirit as a source of spiritual power, rather like the way in which the Spirit could come upon people in some OT stories to give them a "more than human" power (it is helpful to use this phrase rather than "supernatural" to avoid the impression that it is essentially or only the power to do miracles that is in mind). Understood in this way, Jesus was baptized with the Spirit in the sense that he received the Spirit as the source of divine power and direction for his work. Then the experience of the disciples at *Pentecost* is to be understood in the same way; Luke's description of the event with its "tongues of fire" resting on each of the recipients and the imagery of wind indicates that he saw this as the fulfilment of John's prophecy of baptism with the Spirit and with fire. He says here that the disciples were filled with the Spirit (Acts 2:4).

Peter explains the event in terms of the fulfilment of Joel's prophecy that God would pour out his Spirit on all flesh, so that they would prophesy and see visions. Then at the end of his public explanation, he calls the audience to be baptized for the forgiveness of sins and says that they will receive the gift of the Spirit (Acts 2:38). Here there is a combination of baptism with water (nothing else can be meant in Acts 2:41) and the reception of the Spirit; it is true that Luke does not mention the latter specifically, but it is quite inconceivable that he regarded Peter's promise as being unfulfilled. Admittedly some scholars have argued that the reception of the Spirit by the baptized people took place on a later occasion, but such an explanation would not have occurred to anybody who was not convinced on other grounds that baptism with the Spirit is an experience subsequent to conversion and water baptism. For no such later occasion is recorded by Luke; it is a classic example of an unconvincing argument from silence. The important point is that we can say that baptism with the Spirit is the same thing as reception of the Spirit, and is the same again as being filled with the Spirit (although "filling" was a repeatable experience).

The actual phrase "to baptize with the Spirit" is surprisingly mentioned only in one other place in the NT, in 1 Cor 12:13, where Paul reminds his readers that all were baptized into one *body* by one Spirit and all were made to drink of one Spirit. The imagery in the latter phrase is that of plants in a field being irrigated with water poured upon them (and points to baptism by affusion rather than by immersion).

Reception of the Spirit at or in close conjunction with baptism is assumed to be normal (Acts 9:17f.). Nevertheless, Acts draws attention to a number of odd cases. In the case of Cornelius and his family, the Spirit comes upon them before they have been baptized, and this is taken as an indication that, even though they are Gentiles, they should forthwith be baptized with water (Acts 10:44–48). Elsewhere being baptized but not having received the Spirit is seen as something

that must be remedied. So when the Samaritan converts have been baptized but have not received the Spirit, Peter and John pray and lay hands on them, and the Spirit comes (Acts 8:14–17). Apollos had received the baptism of John rather than Christian baptism, but he was "full of spirit and fervour" (Acts 18:25 REB), and therefore he was not baptized again with water. However, the twelve men at Ephesus who had received John's baptism but had not received the Spirit were baptized in the name of Jesus and had hands laid on them, at which point the Spirit came on them (Acts 19:1–7). Whether the *laying on of hands* normally accompanied baptism (cf. the linking in Heb 6:2) is not clear; it is certainly far less prominent and theologically significant. It is curious that Acts shows so much interest in these "exceptions" to the "normal" practice.

In all of the cases so far, we see that baptism with the Spirit, that is, the reception of the Spirit, is the expected accompaniment of Christian baptism with water. In at least some of the cases those who receive the Spirit display some kind of evidence of the coming of the Spirit, speaking in tongues, praising God, and prophesying being mentioned (Acts 10:46; 19:6).

Our survey so far has shown that baptism with water was expressive of forgiveness of sins (cf. Acts 22:16) and of the reception of the Spirit. At the same time willingness to undergo baptism expressed repentance and faith on the part of the baptized. Certainly baptism was preceded by some kind of explanation of what was happening. John the Baptist preached about its significance. In the same way, every reference to baptism in Acts indicates that it was preceded by Christian teaching; thus it was seen as a response to the message with its warnings of judgment on the unrepentant and its promises of salvation to those who repented and believed (Acts 8:12 is typical).

We have seen a distinction between John's baptism and Christian baptism. The latter was distinguished by phraseology that spoke of baptism "into Christ"

(Rom 6:3; Gal 3:27; contrast 1 Cor 1:13, where the possibility of "baptism in the name of Paul" is mentioned, and 1 Cor 10:2, which speaks by analogy of baptism into Moses) or "in the name of Jesus Christ" (Acts 2:38; 8:16; 10:48; 19:5). How is this phraseology to be understood?

We have two separate phrases, rather than one being shorthand for the other. An action which is done in the *name* of Christ is usually one where the power of Christ is invoked to enable it, such as a miraculous healing (Acts 3:6). Therefore a baptism in the name of Christ is one where the power or authority of Christ is invoked so that what takes place is not an empty, weak human act but is an action in which Christ is active (so probably also in Jas 2:7). This ties in with the prophecy of John the Baptist where Christ is the baptizer with the Spirit, but the human baptizer acts as Christ's agent with his authorization and claiming his power to be effective. Moreover, since Christ has received the Spirit from the Father to pour out on his people (Acts 2:33), it is appropriate to pray for him to do so. There is, then, nothing particularly difficult about this phrase.

In Rom 6 Paul is attempting to show that to continue sinning is incompatible with the new status of those who have been justified by grace through faith (and are no longer under necessity to keep the law in order to be justified). He asks his readers whether they are unaware that people who have been baptized "into" Christ have also been baptized "into his death." Through baptism into his death they were buried with him, with the intention that just as he rose from the dead, so they too might live a new life. For Paul, who assumes that his readers would share this understanding, baptism signifies some kind of relationship to the death of Jesus, effecting a death and burial of the baptized person that will be followed by a new *life*. Now baptism "into death" is hardly parallel to baptism "into water." Consequently, it is left uncertain just how the thought of Paul is moving at this point. Sometimes light has been

sought from the mystery religions, but this explanation is flawed for numerous reasons. The same point is made in Col 2:12, where the readers are described as having been "buried with him in baptism" and "also raised (see *resurrection*) with him through faith in the power of God, who raised him from the dead" (cf. Eph 2:5 for the same thought but without mention of baptism). This understanding of baptism is peculiar to Paul in these two passages. It is conceivable that Paul is saying that if a person is baptized into Christ, it is into a crucified and risen Christ, and that he is simply taking an existing understanding of union with Christ as involving union with him in his death, burial, and resurrection and then understanding baptism as the point at which this union takes place. Since plunging into water could certainly be understood as potentially fatal, it may well be that baptism could be understood as death. We have the statement of Jesus in which he spoke of his forthcoming death as a baptism that he had to undergo (Mark 10:38–39; Luke 12:50), employing this imagery of drowning in the water. That may be enough to account for Paul's language, granted his creative mind. Could it then be that knowledge of the resurrection of Jesus, coupled with the fact that people were only temporarily under or in the water of baptism, led to his further statement that they were temporarily buried and then raised back to life? Thus the action in baptism "submersion into the water and coming up out of it" is symbolical of being buried and then rising again. This explanation assumes that baptism was by immersion in water but does not necessarily imply that this was the only mode that was practiced.

In 1 Pet 3:20 Peter notes that Noah and his family were saved "through water"; he sees the water of the flood (that destroyed the wicked) as saving them by supporting the floating ark. Then he comments that, in a way corresponding to this, baptism now saves his readers. There is probably nothing more than a loose parallel here between two functions of water. (As has been wryly noted, the point of the ark was precisely that the occupants were not submerged in the water!) To say that baptism "saves" could be open to the interpretation that the rite has become the means of salvation and even that it is efficacious in itself. In view of all that Peter says about Christ dying for sins and the faith of his readers, he cannot mean that, but rather that the act of baptism is the way in which the act of salvation is symbolized and becomes effective: it is a concrete expression of faith. This is confirmed by the further explanation he gives that baptism is the pledge or request of the baptized for a good conscience to God; they want to have the assurance that their sins are not counted against them.

It is obviously presumed that baptism is preceded by the making known of the gospel, is received by people who are responding to the gospel with faith, and is followed by spiritual effects in their lives as they begin to live by the power of the Holy Spirit. The practice in many churches of extending baptism to infants (as opposed to older children), who cannot hear the gospel and respond with conscious expression of faith, and where any spiritual effects are conjectural, is a matter of much controversy. Appeal has been made to the baptism of whole households in the New Testament (Acts 11:14; 16:15, 31), but infants are not expressly mentioned, and Acts 18:8 indicates that, in the particular case of Crispus, his whole household shared his faith. Certainly where a person has been baptized with water in infancy and then baptized with the Spirit after responding to the gospel, it would seem that a genuine Christian initiation has been completed and there is no need for a further rite of "believer's baptism," but whether this separation of the water and the Spirit is desirable remains debatable.

G. R. Beasley-Murray, *Baptism in the New Testament* (Carlisle: Paternoster, 1972); J. D. G. Dunn, *Baptism in the Holy Spirit* (London: SCM Press, 1970); W. F. Fleming-ton, *The New Testament Doctrine of Baptism* (London: SPCK, 1948); I. Howard Marshall, "The Meaning of the Verb 'Baptize'," in S. E. Porter and A. R. Cross, eds., *Dimensions of Baptism* (Sheffield: Sheffield Academic Press, 2002), 8–24.

I. HOWARD MARSHALL

Beast *see* **Animals**

Believe, Believer, Unbelief, Doubt, Faith, Faithful, Faithfulness, Trust God's faithfulness and the need for human beings to respond to him with faith (both belief and trust) and faithfulness are important themes in both the Old and New Testaments; in the NT, however, faith in God takes expression in faith in his Son, Jesus Christ, sent by God to be the Savior of humankind.

Within the OT, three themes call for attention: the faithfulness of God, the need for humans to trust God, and the persistent unbelief of God's people.

God's faithfulness (Hebrew *'emeth* or *'emunah*) is his trustworthiness, constancy, and dependability. It is demonstrated when he keeps his word to those to whom he has made commitments (Ps 89:33–34) and particularly when he acts on behalf of his covenant people (Pss 25:10; 98:3; Mic 7:20). They in turn appeal to God's faithfulness in their prayers for his help (Ps 143:1; see also 2 Sam 2:6; 15:20) and express confidence that he, in his faithfulness, will defend them (Ps 61:7; 91:4). They may see an example of his faithfulness even in the afflictions that he sends to discipline them for their good (Ps 119:75) as well as in the fresh mercies that encounter them each new day (Lam 3:22–23). God shows himself slow to anger but great in his devotion and faithfulness to his people (Exod 34:6; Ps 86:15). Frequently God's faithfulness involves his vindicating the righteous and punishing those who oppress them (Pss 54:5; 57:3). This faithfulness in upholding justice is seen, not simply among his covenant people, but throughout the earth (Pss 33:4–5; 36:5–6; 89:14), as is his faithfulness in caring for and preserving what he has created (Pss 36:5–6; 119:90). So characteristic of God is his faithfulness that he is said to be surrounded by it (Ps 89:8). It goes before him (Ps 89:14), and reaches to the clouds (Pss 36:5; 57:10; 108:4). It endures, moreover, to all generations (Pss 100:5; 117:2; 119:90).

Because God is great and God is good, it is appropriate and right for human beings to *trust* God (Hebrew usually *batah*), looking confidently to him to meet their every need (Ps 4:5). Rather than attempting to secure their own well-being ("rely[ing]" on their "own insight," Prov 3:5; foolishly "trust[ing] in their own wits," 28:26), they should "trust in the LORD with all [their] heart" (Prov 3:5). Whereas those who fend for themselves may be tempted to do wrong to achieve their ends, those who "trust in the LORD" (or "commit [their] way to the LORD") can simply "do good," knowing that God will act on their behalf (Ps 37:3, 5–6). In times of crisis and fear, those who have the Lord as their God will put their trust in him (Ps 25:2; 31:6, 14; 56:3). As they do so, they will find that his steadfast love surrounds them (Ps 32:10; Prov 29:25) and that he delivers them (Ps 22:4; Dan 3:28; 6:23). Isaiah in particular called on his people to trust God when they were under attack, rather than seek the help of other nations (Isa 30:15; see also 7:9); and he denounced their folly in relying on the Egyptians, who were mere mortals, and on horses and chariots, rather than "look[ing] to the Holy One of Israel" (Isa 31:1, 3). Elsewhere, too, the foolishness of putting one's trust in people (Jer 17:5; even in princes, Ps 146:3), in wealth (Ps 49:6; Prov 11:28; see also Job 31:24), in instruments of war (Ps 44:6), or in false gods (Ps 115:4–8; Isa 42:17) is contrasted with the blessedness of those who make the Lord their trust (Ps 115:9; Jer 17:7; see also Ps 40:4; 84:12). On the other hand, those who live in open defiance of God's commands should not presumptuously trust in his protection, even if they are his people and his sanctuary is in their midst (Jer 7:4).

The OT contains occasional notes indicating that Israel *believed* God (Hebrew usually *heʾemin*) or believed his servant, when something miraculous took place in their midst (Exod 4:30–31; 14:31; Ps 106:12; see also Exod 4:1–9; 19:9). More commonly, God's people are denounced for their persistent unbelief and faithlessness in spite of repeated demonstrations of God's power and his love toward Israel (Deut 1:32; 32:20; Pss 78:22, 32; 106:24). Such unbelief is never portrayed as an intellectual problem; rather it demonstrates Israel's stubborn *refusal* to believe (Num 14:11; see also 2 Kgs 17:14), its disobedience and innate rebelliousness (Deut 9:23). Conversely, life is promised to those who show faith in (or faithfulness to) God (Hab 2:4); and prophets can anticipate a day when a transformed Israel will itself be acknowledged as "the righteous nation that keeps faith" (Isa 26:2; see also Jer 3:22).

The Synoptic Gospels call for a faith (Greek *pistis,* verb *pisteuein*) in God as the heavenly Father who knows and will surely provide for the needs of his children (Matt 6:30). Nor should any doubts be entertained, by those who turn to God in prayer, of his ability or willingness to grant what they request (Matt 21:21–22; see also Jas 1:6–8). Such faith need not in itself be great: if directed toward God, even faith "the size of a mustard seed" will be rewarded (Matt 17:20). Trust in God takes natural expression in belief in his word (Luke 1:45; contrast 1:20) and, most importantly, in faith in those whom he has sent. The ministry of John the Baptist was divinely authorized and called his listeners to repentance and righteousness. Those who believed John, Jesus said, would enter God's kingdom; those who did not respond in faith would not (Matt 21:31–32). Jesus himself, as the herald of God's kingdom, called for faith in the gospel (Mark 1:15; see also Luke 8:12–13). As the one in whom the power of God's kingdom was present, he repeatedly and miraculously met the needs of those who turned to him in faith (Matt 9:2, 22, etc.). Indeed, it was "according to [their] faith" that their requests were granted (Matt 8:13; 9:29; see, conversely, 13:58); "all things can be done for the one who believes" (Mark 9:23). Astonishing faith was shown at times by non-Jews: by a centurion who, himself empowered by the authority of his superiors, recognized in Jesus the power of a divine commission and, hence, the adequacy of Jesus' mere word to cure his servant (Matt 8:5–13); and by a Canaanite woman who would not be denied in her request that Jesus heal her daughter (Matt 15:21–28). On the other hand, Jesus dealt graciously even with one who cried desperately for his help not simply to heal his son but also to give him the faith that would overcome his lingering unbelief (Mark 9:24). Jesus' disciples, however, were repeatedly rebuked for the lack of faith (Mark 4:40), the "little faith" (Matt 14:31; 16:8; 17:20), or the slowness of faith (Luke 24:25). They demonstrated their panic in danger (Matt 14:31), their anxiety in need (Matt 16:8), their failure to cure a demoniac (Matt 17:19–20), and their inability to grasp and believe all that the prophets said about Jesus (Luke 24:25). Even Jesus' resurrection was met with initial doubt on the part of some of his disciples (Matt 28:17; Luke 24:11, 38, 41). Those for whom the Gospels were written, who knew that these same disciples would become the leaders of the early church, were thus reminded not only of the shortcomings of Jesus' followers but also of the forgiving grace of their Lord.

In John's Gospel, "God the only Son, who is close to the Father's heart," became incarnate to make known the God whom no one has ever seen (John 1:14, 18). People's response to Jesus, the Son of God, is thus in reality their response to God, and the same trust that ought to be placed in God should be placed in his Son as well (14:1). According to Jesus, "Whoever believes in me believes not [simply] in me but in him who sent me" (12:44). Such faith involves, in the first place, a recognition that Jesus was sent by God (11:42; 16:27, 30; 17:8) as the Messiah, God's own Son and Holy

One (6:69; 11:27; 20:31); it entails, secondly, a looking to him for true and eternal life (6:68–69). Note the metaphors John uses of "light" (1:7–9), the "drink" and "bread" that satisfies (4:14; 6:35), and so forth. Those who believe in God's Son become themselves God's children (1:12) and are given eternal life (3:15, 16, 36; 5:24; 6:40; 11:25). Such faith is by no means restricted to those who personally witnessed Jesus' activity; the Gospel speaks of people who believe through the testimony of others as well (4:39; 17:20; 19:35; 20:31) and pronounces a special blessing on those who believe without the benefit of sight (20:29). Those who do *not* believe, however, are under God's condemnation (3:18, 36) and will die in their sins (8:24).

John's Gospel devotes much attention to reasons why people should believe in Jesus and to reasons why many do not. *Testimony* was borne to Christ as the true "light" by John the Baptist—"so that all might believe through him" (1:7). The works that Jesus was given by his Father to complete were themselves a reason to believe (10:37–38; 14:11). The Father's own testimony—a divinely granted assurance of the heart—is given to those who believe in Christ (5:32, 37–38; 8:18). On the other hand, an unwillingness to believe in him (3:18) follows inevitably from an unwillingness to "come to the light" and have one's evil deeds exposed (3:19–21). Nor is faith possible among those who place higher stock in the approval of human beings than in that of God (5:44; see also 12:42–43). On a different level, unbelief itself finds a place in the Father's mysterious plan and characterizes those who are not Christ's "sheep" (John 10:26; 12:38–40). Unbelief may itself be masked by a demand for a *sign* (2:18; 6:30; see also 4:48). Jesus refused to comply with such demands, responding to those who made them with a challenge to further insight rather than meeting their requests (2:18–22; 6:30–40). True and lasting faith must in any case be distinguished from the temporary or superficial belief that was impressed by signs but did not penetrate to their true significance (2:23; 8:30–31).

The healing of a lame man in Acts is an example of what can be done through faith in the name of Jesus (Acts 3:16) and is reminiscent of healings done by Jesus himself in the Gospels. The reference in Acts 14:9 to a crippled man who "had faith to be healed" is similarly reminiscent of references in the Synoptic Gospels to those who were healed "according to [their] faith." And when Paul speaks of his "faith in God," meaning his confidence that what God through his angel has told him will take place (Acts 27:24–25), we are reminded of the similar response by Mary recorded in Luke's Gospel (Luke 1:45). Since all Christians have believed in the gospel, those singled out as "full of faith" in Acts (Stephen, in 6:5; Barnabas, in 11:24) were presumably those characterized by a remarkably strong and unwavering faith that expressed itself in effective, powerful witness. Here we may see a further development of the issue of the measure of one's faith and of what faith can achieve, a discussion that was introduced in Luke 17:5–6. In each of these respects, then, Acts—volume two of Luke's narrative of Christian beginnings—retains aspects of the depiction of faith found in the Gospel with which that history began.

Elsewhere in Acts, belief is frequently indicated as the appropriate response to the message of the apostles and signals the entry of the one who believes into the Christian community (the community of *believers*, Acts 5:14; 13:48, etc.). The object of such faith is at times specified ("Believe on the Lord Jesus," 16:31; see also 9:42; 14:23; 20:21; 22:19; the prophets, as those who foretold what Christ would do, are referred to as the object of faith in 26:27), though at other times it is simply understood (2:44; 4:32; 17:12). Since faith in Christ is what distinguished these "believers" from others, "the faith" comes to stand for that to which they owe their allegiance: they are said to be "obedient to the faith" (Acts 6:7), to "continue in the faith" (14:22), or to be "strengthened

in the faith" (16:5). Through their faith, moreover, they are saved (16:31) and sanctified (26:18).

Paul's usage of "faith" terminology, like that in Acts, is fundamentally determined by his Christian *mission*; as an apostle, he took the message of the gospel to listeners who otherwise faced the outpouring of God's wrath (1 Thess 1:10; 5:2–3). Faith in the gospel thus transferred its listeners from the numbers of those who are "perishing" to the community of those "who are being saved" (1 Cor 1:18, 21). As in Acts, the latter group could simply be referred to as the "believers" (1 Thess 1:7; 2:10, 13). Paul's own mission was directed primarily toward a Gentile world that he saw as characterized by idolatry as well as by unrighteousness (see Rom 1:18–23). For such believers, coming to "faith in God" (1 Thess 1:8) meant turning away from idols "to serve a living and true God" (1 Thess 1:9–10) as well as belief in the gospel of Christ's death and resurrection (1 Thess 4:14; cf. 1 Cor 15:1–4). But the two are not, in Paul's mind, to be distinguished. The message of the gospel is itself the "word," not of human beings, but of God (1 Thess 2:13). Hence true faith in *God* is necessarily shown by faith in *God's word* in the gospel. Those who respond in faith to the gospel are at the same time those who are "called" by God through the proclamation of the gospel "into his own kingdom and glory" (1 Thess 2:12; see also Rom 10:17): in those who believe the "word of God" is thus effectively "at work" (1 Thess 2:13).

Though Paul's own vocation was as an apostle to the Gentiles (Rom 15:16; Gal 2:7–9), the message of the gospel itself is universal and requires the same response of faith from all who hear it: "it is the power of God for salvation to everyone who has faith, to the Jew first and also to the Greek" (Rom 1:16; see also Rom 3:30). But whereas for Gentiles such faith meant turning from a life of idolatry and unrighteousness, for Jews it meant turning from the pursuit of righteousness through the (Mosaic) law (Rom 9:31;

10:3–4). Paul had himself pursued such righteousness before his Damascus encounter with the resurrected Lord (Phil 3:6); as a result of that encounter, however, he renounced his former pursuit in order to "gain Christ," to be "found in him," having "the righteousness from God based on faith" (Phil 3:8–9). Later, when Jewish-Christian missionaries attempted to impose the requirements of the Mosaic law on Paul's Gentile converts, Paul found himself compelled to articulate the difference between the "righteousness of faith" and that based on the law and to show why the former, but not the latter, led to justification and life.

Paul's Jewish-Christian opponents would not have seen any tension between Christian faith and a requirement to observe all the prescriptions imposed by the Mosaic law. In their minds, Messiah had indeed come—Jesus *was* the Messiah—and he had died for human sins; but this divine provision for human sinfulness still operated within the context of the Mosaic covenant. For Paul, however, the law and its covenant operated on a different principle from that of faith (Gal 3:12). The fundamental principle of the Mosaic covenant was that "the person who does these things [that is, what the law commands] will live by them" (Rom 10:5; Gal 3:12; see also Rom 2:13). Moreover, the practical *effect* of the law was not only that Gentile sinners— who neither possessed the law nor practiced the righteousness it required—were condemned, but also that Jews themselves, though possessing the law, were exposed no less than the Gentiles as culpable before God (Rom 3:19–20). "There is no distinction, since all have sinned and fall short of the glory of God" (Rom 3:22–23). The law thus serves to demonstrate human sinfulness, but it cannot overcome it (Rom 3:20; 5:20; 7:7; 8:3) or bring life to the dead (Gal 3:21). Hence "no one will be justified by the works of the law" (Gal 2:16; see also 2:21; Rom 3:20, 28). The "righteousness of faith" made possible through the gospel is thus not to be combined with observance of the law

as the path to God's approval, but is rather the divine solution to the dilemma created by humanity's failure to observe God's requirements spelled out in the law.

The "righteousness of faith" is made possible through the death of Christ, atoning for human sins (Rom 3:24–26). Those who believe in Christ are forgiven of their sins (Rom 4:6–8; their "trespasses" are not counted "against them," 2 Cor 5:19) and restored to good terms with God: they are "reconciled" to him (2 Cor 5:18–20); "justified by faith," they have "peace with God through [the] Lord Jesus Christ" (Rom 5:1). The righteousness that is now theirs is a gift that they receive (Rom 5:17) from God *by faith* (Phil 3:9), *apart from* the righteous works that normally would be required of those to be deemed righteous (Rom 4:4–8; see 2:13). Hence Paul repeatedly stresses the gratuity characteristic of the righteousness of faith (Rom 3:24; 4:4–8, 16; 5:1–2, 6–8, 15–17; see also Eph 2:8–9; 2 Tim 1:9; Titus 3:4–5) and its exclusion of human boasting (Rom 3:27–28; 4:2–3). That faith is required as a human response does not, for Paul, compromise the gratuity of the gift: partly because he sees faith as a turning to God to *receive* help by those who are themselves helpless (here Paul sees a model in Abraham's faith that he would be a father of many nations, though his own procreative powers and the womb of his wife were "already as good as dead," Rom 4:18–22); partly because faith itself is a gift (Phil 1:29), called into being (as noted above) by the effective proclamation of the gospel.

The faith by which Paul's converts initially became "believers" was of course to be maintained throughout their lives: in several letters Paul expressed the concern he felt lest his converts should abandon their faith and his work prove in vain (1 Cor 15:2; 2 Cor 13:5; Col 1:22–23; 1 Thess 3:5; see also 1 Tim 6:10). Here his solicitude is similar to that shown by the author of the Letter to the Hebrews, who warns his readers against the consequences of abandoning the faith in which they had made a good beginning (Heb 3:14; 6:9–12). To do so would be to follow the disastrous example of Moses' contemporaries who perished in the wilderness because of their unbelief (Heb 3:7–19; 4:2). Rather they should follow in the footsteps of those OT witnesses who persisted in faith in what they could not see (Heb 11:1, 7, 8, 26, 27; cf. 2 Cor 5:7) in the face of all manner of hardship and temptation (11:4–38; 12:1). The ultimate example, however, is Jesus himself, "the pioneer and perfecter of our faith," who endured both the pain and the shame of the cross "for the sake of the joy that was set before him" (Heb 12:2).

If Christian faith is not to be confused with an initial belief that is abandoned when confronted by the trials and temptations of life (note the reference to *temporary* faith in Luke 8:13), neither is it to be confused with a mere belief (such as demons themselves may hold, Jas 2:19) that is not accompanied by appropriate works of obedience and righteousness: such "faith without works," James reminds us, is "dead" (Jas 2:17) and cannot justify (2:24). The terminology is not Pauline— Paul insists precisely that one *is* justified by faith apart from works (Rom 4:2–8; see also 9:11–12; 11:6; Eph 2:8–9)—but the essential conviction is shared by Paul no less than by other NT authors (see, for example, Matt 7:17–27; 1 John 3:7). Paul too warns his communities that those who persist in sin have no place in God's kingdom (Rom 8:13; 1 Cor 6:9–10; Gal 5:19–21). He too summons his readers to lives of goodness and holiness (Gal 6:10; 1 Thess 4:3, 7). For Paul, however, the practice of Christian righteousness is not a requirement added to that of (a merely intellectual) belief; it is rather the inevitable outworking of a faith that has turned from a life of disobedience to God to one that is lived in his service (Rom 6:17–18; 1 Thess 1:8–9). Living in a way that pleases God is a natural expression of such faith, and Paul rejoices when he sees his converts' faith in action (1 Thess 1:3; 2 Thess 1:11; see also Gal 5:6). That their faith can still be deficient (1 Thess 3:10)

and have room to grow (2 Thess 1:3) does not imply that his converts still harbor doubts of the truth of their convictions; rather there is still—and throughout their earthly lives there will be (see 1 Thess 3:12–13; 4:1, 10; 5:23)—a need to express more consistently and completely the practical implications of their faith.

Finally, it should be noted that Paul can speak of a faith that is not the possession of every believer but a special gift of the Spirit to certain believers, just as some believers (but not all) possess special gifts of wisdom, knowledge, or healing (1 Cor 12:4–11). Extraordinary things may be done by those with such faith—though they should remember that, in spite of whatever faith they may possess, they amount to nothing without love (1 Cor 13:2).

Brevard S. Childs, *Biblical Theology of the Old and New Testaments* (Minneapolis: Fortress Press, 1993), 595–623.

STEPHEN WESTERHOLM

Birthright   *see* Firstborn

Blameless   *see* Innocent

Blaspheme, Blasphemer

In secular Greek sources, "blasphemy" (verbal form, *blasphemeo*) has the connotation of "abusive speech" or the misuse of words (see Beyer, *TDNT* 1:621; Wis 1:6). This general meaning is evident in biblical texts where the word means "slander" (Luke 22:65; 2 Pet 2:10, 12). However, NRSV mainly uses the term "blasphemy" for the more specific offense of speaking against God's will and character. The particular nuance of blasphemy as inappropriate speech appears in Lev 24:10–23, which reports that a foreigner in Israel's midst blasphemed (Hebrew root, *naqab*) the name (of God) "in a curse" (v. 11). However, NRSV rightly does not limit its use of the term to offenses of the tongue. The word in Neh 9:18 identifies casting an image as blasphemy, and later in 9:26 it denotes the killing of the prophets as a sign of rejecting Torah. In the Nehemiah texts the Hebrew term is *naᵓats,* which means "contemn." Hence, NRSV appropriately recognizes the curse of God's name in Lev 24:11 as a quite concrete and specific example of the more general offense of defying the power and authority of God. In an extension of this idea, Jas 2:7 labels injustice and denial of Christian unity as blasphemous.

The notion of blasphemy as a negation of divine prerogative has two chief theological nuances in the Bible. First, blasphemy is tantamount to *usurpation* of divine authority. This is the charge against Jesus in Mark 2:7. Second Maccabees 8–10 also seems to imply that Antiochus IV is guilty of such an offense. Antiochus is said to have committed blasphemies against the divine name (2 Macc 8:4) and is labeled a blasphemer (2 Macc 9:28). However, this characterization of him and his actions is not related to a specific curse of the Lord. Rather, the account describes his overall repudiation of Yahweh's authority by profaning the temple and punishing God's people. In sum, Antiochus places himself above God. This is evident in his self-imposed title, Epiphanes, meaning (God) "manifest." This foreign ruler stands in contrast to Nebuchadnezzar, who, upon recognizing the power of Israel's God, decreed that any nation that "utters blasphemy against the God of Shadrach, Meshach, and Abednego shall be torn limb from limb, and their houses laid in ruins; for there is no other god who is able to deliver in this way" (Dan 3:29).

Second, in some theological usage blasphemy has the general sense of defamation. Disparaging the divine name in a curse would be an example (Lev 24:10–23). This is also the case with the famous saying of Jesus concerning blasphemy against the Holy *Spirit* (Matt 12:31–32; Mark 3:28–30; Luke 12:10). Jesus' statement comes as a response to religious officials who say he cast out demons because he had a demonic source of power. In response, Jesus declares that slandering him could be forgiven, but casting aspersion on the Holy Spirit at work in him was another matter (Gundry, *Mark,* 175–77). This may also be the implication of blasphemy in Acts 13:45, which refers to the Jews disparaging Paul's message; whether this is merely slander or speech against God's intentions as expressed in Paul's gospel is difficult to judge, but probably the latter is intended. The use of *blasphemeo* in 1 Pet 4:4 is similarly difficult. The connection of blasphemy to eternal judgment (v. 5) seems to indicate that defamation of Jesus' followers is indirectly slander against their God (see Achtemeier, *1 Peter,* 283–85 and the alternate translation he offers).

Although blasphemy in such contexts has stronger connotations than "disrespect" (in the typical English use of that term), that word may be appropriate for Josephus's comments that Jews were not to blaspheme the gods of others (*Antiquities of the Jews* 4.207; *Against Apion* 2.237). That is, whether blasphemy is mere lack of tolerance for another faith or a more serious offense that brings divine wrath depends on one's perspective and belief in the efficacy of the deity offended (see Acts 19:37). However, the Josephus references are consistent with other biblical texts in that they pair blasphemy with the destruction of idols. It confirms again that blasphemy, in almost every context, involves the denial or abrogation of a deity's authority.

Paul J. Achtemeier, *1 Peter,* Hermeneia (Minneapolis: Fortress, 1996); Robert H. Gundry, *Mark: A Commentary on His Apology for the Cross* (Grand Rapids: Eerdmans, 1993).

JEROME F. D. CREACH

Bless, Blessed, Blessing In the biblical world a blessing was a set of "power-laden words" thought to have ability to create or maintain the well being of a person or community (Harrelson, *IDB* 1:446). It was much more than a kind or encouraging word. Indeed, the blessing should be understood as a performed utterance, sometimes spoken as a formal element of worship and accompanied by other gestures and ritual acts (Gen 48:13–16; Lev 9:22). To comprehend the role of the blessing in the ancient Near East, one must appreciate the assumption that forces of good and evil were constantly impacting human life and that certain individuals had ability to access those forces with carefully chosen words. Hence, the blessing is related to, and represents the antithesis of, the *curse*. Scholarly discussion of this issue has often focused on the use of the blessing or curse in magic, in which the speaker uses certain formulae to gain an advantage or accomplish his or her own agenda. This is sometimes distinguished from the genuine religious context, in which the spoken word brings about God's purpose. However, it is impossible to draw a clear line between the two uses of blessings, for even its legitimate employment assumed the reality of magic (1 Cor 12:1–3; Gal 1:8).

That certain individuals were thought to have special power to bring good (blessing) or ill (curse) through the spoken word is clear in the story of Balaam (Num 22–24). However, it also explains the dread of individuals like Samuel, whom the elders of Bethlehem greeted with trembling when they saw him enter their town (1 Sam 16:4).

Pronouncement of blessing. NRSV uses the verb "to bless" in its various modulations to indicate the act of conferring a blessing (Gen 1:22, 28; Lev 9:22, 23). When the word applies to a human who offers a blessing to another person or persons, it typically denotes a spoken word with an inherent force that participates in the reality of what is wished for. In the OT, this is communicated by the Hebrew root *berak*. The verb can simply report that a blessing was offered (X blessed Y; Gen 14:19; 27:23), or it can take an imperative form (or a second-person imperfect with similar force) to order that a blessing be given (Num 6:23). The Greek equivalent of *berak* is *eulogeo*. Like its Hebrew counterpart, the active form of this verb

connotes the conferral of a blessing (Mark 10:16), while imperative forms instruct that a blessing be offered (Luke 6:28; Rom 12:14; 1 Cor 4:12).

Two special uses of the verb deserve notation. One is the imperative, *baraki*, which occurs in certain poetic texts. It calls the worshiper to "bless the LORD" (Ps 103:1). This expression is theologically peculiar because it seems pretentious for a person to bless God as one would bless another person (see further below). Another special case is the third-person form (known as a jussive) of *berak* in the priestly blessing in Num 6:24b–26 that indicates a wish for God to bless the Israelites. It might seem odd to find a request for a blessing within a blessing. However, it indicates that God is the source of all good fortune and the task of the priest was to petition God on behalf of the people for God's favor.

The patriarchal narratives in Genesis contain fine examples of the pronouncement of blessings. Isaac gave Jacob a blessing that rightly belonged to the eldest son, Esau, after being tricked by Jacob and Rebekah (Gen 27:23). This story reveals at least two important features of the ancient blessing. First, it shows what was surely one important context of this spoken word, namely, a patriarch's investiture of his children. The father was one person thought to have special authority to bless, at least in this situation. Second, the story reveals the power a blessing was thought to contain. Its tangible value was such that it was, in effect, part of the oldest son's inheritance. Thus this story is paired with the account of Jacob purchasing Esau's birthright, that is, his right to inherit half the father's property (Deut 21:15–17) (see *firstborn*). The story is also illustrative in that it includes the actual words of the blessing Isaac offered (Gen 27:27b–29). The blessing pertains to prosperity such as would be recognized in the ancient Near East: fertility of the earth (v. 28a), abundance of crops (v. 28b), dominance over potential enemies (v. 29a), and chief place among siblings, as expected of an eldest son (v.

29b). The blessing concludes with a general pronouncement of blessing on those who bless Jacob, and curses on those who curse him (v. 29c). The contents of the blessing are strikingly similar to the blessing of Rebekah in Gen 24:60. There the wish is conferred that she produce many offspring (v. 60b) and that her descendants rule over their foes (v. 60b). Given the similar nature of other occurrences of blessings in OT (Gen 1:22, 28), these elements may be taken as typical, particularly in a family or clan setting.

The Aaronic blessing in Num 6:22–26 is another text that reveals much about the role of the blessing in the biblical world. It shows that the priest was another person with inherent authority and, indeed, duty to bless others. The literary context of the blessing is informative. It is introduced by a command to Aaron and his sons to bless the Israelites with the prescribed words (Num 6:23). Hence, the blessing is presented as a regular duty of the priest as a regular part of worship. The content of the priestly blessing is more generalized than the examples from family settings, but nevertheless it is parallel in its wish for protection and prosperity, expressed as *shalom* (v. 26). The order to bless concludes by saying that the blessing is tantamount to putting God's name on Israel. It states further that the priest's words precipitate the Lord's blessing. The latter statement again links the priestly blessing with the wish for God to bless (Gen 28:3; Deut 14:29; Ruth 2:4). The text assumes that God brings about the effects of blessing formulae. In other words, when one human blesses another, he or she merely taps the essence of God's character and action that is to ensure *shalom* and bring prosperity.

David's blessing of Israel in 2 Sam 6 is further evidence that the blessing had an official place in worship. The blessing David offered comes after the ark has been placed in the tent prepared for it and after David has offered sacrifices. There is no indication of the content of the blessing except that it was offered "in the

name of the LORD of hosts" (v. 18), an indication that David, like the Aaronic priests in Num 6:22–24, sought God's favor for the people. The account says that David then turned to bless his own house. The ensuing scene is suggestive of the contents of that part of the ceremony. Namely, the conflict with Michal, and the concluding statement that she "had no child to the day of her death," suggests the blessing had to do with royal offspring and the strength of the Davidic line. Hence, we might imagine David's blessing of his household as a version of the blessings known from Gen 24:28–29 and 27:27b–29, shaped to fit the royal context.

Deuteronomy 27–28 presents yet another circumstance for the blessing in the context of public worship. In this case blessings are paired with complementary curses as a conclusion to the covenant agreement between God and Israel. Moses makes provision for the covenant to be renewed in the land in a ceremony in which these blessings and curses are recited antiphonally (Deut 27:11–13). The specific blessings (28:3–14) are said to come if Israel is obedient to the Lord's torah given through Moses (28:2). The presence of blessings and curses in this type of text is common in the ancient Near East as a conclusion to formal agreements, particularly treaties between nations or city-states.

A unique type of pronouncement of blessing is the phrase "bless the Lord," which appears frequently in the Psalms and dominates other poetic texts such as the apocryphal Prayer of Azariah (see also Jas 3:9; Tob 12:6, 17, 18; 13:6, 10; 14:8, 9; Sir 32:13; 39:35; 45:26; 50:22; 51:12; cf. 1 Pet 1:3). It is possible that the phrase originated in the belief that the human could enhance the deity's power by offering a blessing. However, it came to be virtually synonymous with phrases like *"praise* the Lord" and "give *thanks* to the Lord." Nevertheless, the wish for God to be "blessed," and similar statements like "blessed be the Lord" (1 Pet 1:3; Tob 3:11; Jdt 13:17; 2 Macc 1:17) carry an important theological idea about God's character. Namely, God is the source of and primary bearer of *shalom*. All blessings ultimately proceed from God. Hence, if the phrase "bless the Lord" is heard as an ascription of praise, it must be understood as homage specifically for God's provision of blessings to humankind.

Scripture contains some important guidelines for the proper use of the blessing in relation to the curse. Proverbs 30:11 identifies the blessing of one's parents as a filial responsibility, noting that one who curses his or her parent, or fails to bless them, is reprehensible. The NT contains instructions for blessings with great theological import. Namely, Jesus instructs his disciples to "bless those who curse you" (Luke 6:28). This statement occurs in a larger section of teaching that encourages action contrary to expected practice. In a possible allusion to these words of Jesus, Paul instructs, "Bless those who persecute you; bless and do not curse them" (Rom 12:14). Furthermore, Paul characterizes the apostles' action according to this countercultural response to aggression (1 Cor 4:12). These features of the early Christian community are all the more remarkable, given the seriousness of the speaking of blessings and curses, with their magical forces that were thought to bring good or evil.

Numerous times in the OT God is said to bless. God blessed humankind (Gen 1:22, 28), God blessed the Sabbath (Gen 2:3; Exod 20:11), God blessed Noah (Gen 9:1), and so on. To be blessed by God was to have divine favor, not necessarily to be spoken to by God. God's blessing upon a person is sometimes simply reported in a narrative, as in the examples above. At other times, the declaration of God's blessings comes within a blessing itself. For example, Melchizedek blesses Abram by saying, "Blessed be Abram by God Most High" (Gen 14:19). This use of the blessing illustrates further the belief that God is the ultimate source of all good fortune. It also shows that the one offering a blessing could invoke the name of God as part of the blessing formula.

The effects of blessing. Blessing refers not only to the spoken formula that is thought to bring *shalom*, but also to the effects of the words uttered. The blessing itself is described by use of nominal forms of roots already discussed (Hebrew *beraka* and Greek *eulogia*). The noun forms are translated "blessing" because they indicate the favor that results from a blessing having been spoken or the benefits of divine favor (Gen 12:2; Rom 15:29; 1 Cor 10:16). In other words, blessing can refer to the divine favor itself, borne out in tangible expressions of prosperity or protection. In this sense, the blessing is what is bestowed by God (Sir 47:6). An important part of the tradition of God's blessing of Abraham is God's assurance that the Lord makes the name of Abraham great "so that you will be a blessing" (Gen 12:2). Abraham's life has a force capable of bringing fullness of life to others, since his life is endowed with God's grace.

The state of blessedness. A final use of these words is to pronounce the state of a person who has received divine favor. In such usage, the adjective "blessed" describes a favored status. In the OT, this is sometimes communicated by a passive form, *baruk*, such as in the line, "Blessed is the one who comes in the name of the LORD" (Ps 118:26). The NT contains the Greek equivalent in a passive form of *eulogeo* (Luke 1:42; John 12:13). "Blessed" can refer to a human state, as in the examples just cited. However, the word can also refer more ambiguously to God. This is quite common in the Psalms and other poetic literature, as in the phrase, "Blessed be the LORD" or similar expressions (for example, Pss 18:46; 72:18; 124:6; see the Greek equivalent in Tob 3:11; Jdt 13:17).

Another important pair of terms lie behind the English "blessed": Hebrew *'ashre* and Greek *makarios*. Perhaps the best-known example of the Greek word is in the Beatitudes of Jesus (Matt 5:3–11; Luke 6:20–22; see also the eight occurrences in Rev 1:3 [2x]; 14:13; 16:15; 19:9; 20:6; 22:7, 14). But there is some debate about whether *makarios* indicates the state of one who has received a blessing or simply communicates an observation of reality. NRSV translates the Hebrew equivalent as "happy" because it has been determined that *ashre merely describes a fortunate circumstance (Ps 1:1). The question is made difficult by the fact that Luke 6:24–25 matches the blessings with parallel woes. This indicates to some scholars that Jesus' words have a force to bring about the circumstances of which he speaks. In other words, they see in this text an example of blessings and curses like those in Deut 27–28. However, the Greek terms *makarios* (blessed) and *ouai* ("woe") probably have their origins in the wisdom tradition and the funeral dirge respectively, both representing observations about how life is, rather than pronouncements of how life will be.

F. Charles Fensham, "Malediction and Benediction in Ancient Near Eastern Vassal-Treaties and the Old Testament," *ZAW* 74 (1962): 1–9; W. J. Harrelson, "Blessings and Cursings," *IDB* 1:446–48; Waldemar Janzen, "*ashre* in the Old Testament," *HTR* 58 (1965): 1–12; Claus Westermann, *Blessing: in the Bible and the Life of the Church* (Philadelphia: Fortress, 1978).

JEROME F. D. CREACH

Blood Throughout the Scriptures, blood is a significant medium religiously, morally, and theologically. Like breath (see *spirit*), it stands *pars pro toto* for life itself (Gen. 9:4). Accordingly, it figures strongly in relationships among human beings and between human beings and God. For convenience, we will look at its theological meaning under three basic headings: kinship and vengeance, purity, and sacrifice. But we shall find that the three are not completely separate.

Kinship and vengeance. Blood serves to express and ground the relatedness of family. In a cultural setting where the household was the basic social unit, the sense of common "flesh and blood" establishes each family's tight-knit character. On the one hand, the next of kin is responsible for *redeeming* lost land and family members. On the other, kin are also expected to exact vengeance for harm done to a family member.

When human blood is shed, it cries, almost literally, for vengeance, as in the case of the blood of Abel (Gen 4:10–14). It is the duty of the "*avenger* of blood" to kill a murderer (Num 35:16–21). But even the unintentional killing of another is seen in early Israel as demanding such response, and the Torah sets limits and provides alternatives to this practice. In particular, it institutes "cities of refuge," where the accidental slayer is protected from vengeance (Num 35:22–28; Deut 19:4–10).

God thus appears primarily as the limiter of vengeance, first in the case of Cain, to whom he gives a protective sign and a guarantee of overwhelming response as deterrent to anyone who would take vengeance on him (Gen 4:13–16). Again, even though vengeance remains in force for murder, the person who has killed another accidentally can flee to a city of refuge and must remain there until the death of the current high priest (Num 35:28). In some unspecified way, this sacral figure's death released the killer from the burden of bloodguilt.

The concern here is not for justice alone, though that is certainly present, but for the pollution of the land occasioned by bloodshed (Num 35:30–34). This is why ritual concerns are involved in cases of murder and involuntary homicide. And if a corpse is found without any clues as to the murderer, the elders of the nearby towns have to undertake a process to decide responsibility and a rite to rid their territory of bloodguilt (Deut 21:1–9).

God also appears as the executer of vengeance (e.g., Deut 32:43; Judg 11:36; Rev. 19:2). Whether as avenger or restrainer of vengeance, it is impossible to think of God, the creator of life, as indifferent to its violation. Either God takes vengeance directly for shed blood or intervenes to stop the endless spiral of vengeance. Human revenge is thus discouraged: "Vengeance is mine, I will repay, says the Lord" (Rom 12:19, referring to Deut 32:35).

In the NT, blood continues to be an important symbol of kinship. Hebrews takes it in an incarnational direction: "Since, therefore, the children share flesh and blood, [the Son] himself likewise shared the same things" (2:14). Only so could he serve human beings as priest (2:17–18). Given this relationship, Jesus can fulfill the role of next of kin and be the redeemer of all humanity, using his own blood for this purpose: "by your blood you ransomed for God saints from every tribe and language and people and nation" (Rev 5:9). God can equally be the avenger of his family, the faithful: "Sovereign Lord, holy and true, how long will it be before you judge and avenge our blood on the inhabitants of the earth?" (Rev 6:10).

Purity. We have already seen that shed blood pollutes the land. Blood could also violate the purity code in other ways (see *clean*). The menstruating woman, for example, is seen as unclean in a rather serious way, in that she can render unclean any who come into contact with her, even indirectly (Lev 15:19–24). No rationale is given for this in Torah. We can speculate that menstrual blood was understood as a loss of procreative potential, a grave issue in a world that was constantly struggling to maintain population levels; but this remains speculative. And in fact the blood of childbirth has the same effect (Lev 12).

The other context where blood becomes a source of impurity is in relation to food. Even in the case of game animals, the draining of the blood was considered of highest priority. The Torah reiterates that "the life of the flesh is in the blood" (Lev 17:11; cf. Gen 9:4). Improperly slaughtered animals, whose blood has not been returned, as it were, to God, whether in formal sacrifice or by emptying it onto the ground and covering it, are not fit for Israelite consumption. The slaughterer who does not handle the blood properly is "guilty of bloodshed" (Lev 17:4).

Ironically, from the modern reader's perspective, blood is a key ingredient in purification as well as a source of impurity. Certain sacrifices *atone* for impurity, and the blood is used directly for this purpose. For example, in the rite of cleansing a leper, the priest takes two birds, sacrifices one, dips the other (with some additional items) in the blood of the first, and sprinkles the leper who is being cleansed. Then the second bird is released (Lev 14:1–9). On the eighth day, another sacrifice takes place, and the priest uses some of the blood to anoint the former leper on the right ear, thumb, and big toe (Lev 14:14). Blood is potent for both purity and impurity.

This purity dimension of blood is necessarily caught up in the larger conflict about purity in the NT. In Israelite usage, to be impure is not intrinsically sinful, but it does impose certain barriers between the impure person and any approach to God in the sanctuary. Although purity requirements may serve as a way of connecting the worshiper to the Holy, they have an inevitable side effect of excluding some people. Menstruating women, for example, are not to approach the sanctuary (Lev 15:31).

The Gospels suggest that Jesus made a point of ministering to and including people who were presumed unclean ("tax collectors and sinners"). One miracle story makes a particular point of this in relation to menstruation. A woman with a hemorrhage (and therefore continuously unclean, Lev 15:25–30) touches the hem of his garment and is healed. Jesus does not rebuke her for contaminating the other people in the crowd—or himself—but instead commends her faith (Matt 9:20–22; Mark 5:25–34; Luke 8:43–48).

Mark's Gospel also insists that Jesus rejected the significance of food purity (7:14–23; less strongly in Matt 15:10–14). The theme of Jesus' table fellowship with "tax collectors and sinners" is recurrent in the Synoptic Gospels. And the Gentile mission necessitated at least some accommodation in the matter, since one of the principal expressions of early Christian life was that the community ate together. Much Gentile food would be impure, some of it because of the presence of blood.

In Acts, the apostolic council issues a decision that places minimal restrictions on Gentile Christians (no food offered to idols, blood, or things "strangled" [Acts 15:28–29]). Paul, on the other hand, never mentions these restrictions but has his own way of dealing with the issue. He insists that "nothing is unclean in and of itself" (Rom 14:14) but goes on to say that if anyone is inwardly insecure about the violation of purity law, that person must indeed observe it (Rom 14:22–23). He counsels the "strong," who agree with him in principle, not to place temptation in the way of the "weak," who are still committed to the keeping of purity (Rom 14:15–21; 1 Cor 8).

At the same time, the blood of Jesus can be spoken of as purifying the faithful. Hebrews regards purification as one consequence of Jesus' sacrifice, even making the rather overstated claim, as precedent, that "under the law almost everything is purified with blood" (9:22). In a vivid image of purification, Revelation speaks of the garments of the saints as having been made "white in the blood of the Lamb" (7:14).

Sacrifice. The acme of the religious and theological importance of blood in Scripture is its role in various rites of *sacrifice.* The blood of sacrificial victims is used in a variety of ways, particularly by splashing it against the altar (e.g., Lev 1:5), daubing it on things and people in acts of consecration or purification (e.g., Lev 4:7; 8:23), and dashing it over the sacrificial assembly (Exod 24:8).

Sacrificial blood has an apotropaic function in the story of the first Passover (Exod 12:7, 13). It serves to bind God and the people together in covenant sacrifices (e.g., Exod 24:3–8). And it serves to reestablish this bond, through sin and guilt offerings, when the bond has been weakened by the sin or impurity of the people or to celebrate it in sacrifices of thanksgiving and "well-being" (e.g., Lev 3:1–11).

This sacrificial use of blood ceased with the destruction of the Jerusalem temple in A.D. 70. Judaism found a substitute for it in prayer, fasting, and almsgiving. Christianity had already begun to make use of the language and imagery of sacrificial blood as a way of talking about the meaning of Jesus' life and work.

Christian sacrificial discourse typically follows the pattern of sin offering or of covenant offering. As regards sin offerings, there was no particular need to explain how the shedding of blood could effect atonement for sin. It was simply a fact of religious life. The need for theological explanation became more acute among Christians only as the actual practice of animal sacrifice disappeared. Paul, accordingly, can simply speak of Jesus as "a sacrifice of atonement by his blood" (Rom 3:25). First John says that "the blood of Jesus [God's] Son cleanses us from all sin" (1:7). Hebrews asserts that "under the law . . . without the shedding of blood there is no forgiveness of sins" (9:22), and that is enough to show why the author feels a need to interpret Jesus' death in sacrificial terms.

The tradition of the Last Supper, on the other hand, is shaped not by the sin offering, but by the covenant offering. This is apparent in language about the "blood of the covenant" (Matt 26:28; Mark 14:24) or "the new covenant in my blood" (Luke 22:20; 1 Cor 11:25). It departs, however, from the tradition of the covenant sacrifice in that the blood is not sprinkled or dashed over the worshipers but drunk by them. This, of course, represents a scandalous violation of food purity, a point that John's Gospel actually emphasizes. When John's Jesus says, "Unless you eat the flesh of the Son of Man and drink his blood, you have no life in you," his hearers respond with "This teaching is difficult; who can accept it?" (John 6:53, 60).

Hebrews draws on both sin offering and covenant sacrifice in its treatment of the meaning of Jesus' death. It presents Jesus' blood as the only truly effective means of removing sin (10:1–24). Indeed, the author is not quite clear whether there is any possibility of further forgiveness for those who sin again after having been "enlightened" (probably a metaphor for baptism [6:1–8; cf. 12:16–17]). At the same time, the author argues that Jesus' followers are participants in a new covenant with God, one that is sealed by the "blood of the eternal covenant" (9:11–22; 13:20).

While this essay has sought to disentangle three strands in the theological significance of blood, it is clear that the three are never entirely independent of each other. There was a very strong sense of the importance and power of blood in divine-human interactions. This power resided on the plane of religion, particularly of worship. It did not depend on the intellectual understanding of a concept but on the ability of rites and metaphors to shape and express the human grasp of the ungraspable.

Thus John's Gospel seems to be using sacrificial motifs in Jesus' discourse about his body and his blood (6:25–65). The purifying and covenant-making powers of blood are at least alluded to here. Yet John brings the discourse to its climax in terms of an act absolutely forbidden by Torah—the drinking of blood. It both draws on and subverts the religious tradition, thus producing something that is both old and new.

Again, Hebrews is able to move easily between the purifying and atoning functions of blood—and to create a model of sacrifice that freely combines the rites of the Day of Atonement with other sacrificial practices. All this suggests that, for first-century authors, the theological importance of blood was simply beyond question. There was no need to explain it. Indeed one could "strike sparks" off the language by violating existing expectations about usage and so create new possibilities of theological insight.

For the Johannine tradition, the importance of this is summed up in the sight of water and blood flowing together from the wound in Jesus' side (John 19:34–35). The author of 1 John, thinking along the same lines, insists on Jesus as the one who came "not with water only but with the

water and the blood" (5:6). Even the Spirit can only witness alongside these, not replace them (5:7–8).

While the language of blood is sometimes difficult for modern readers, distanced as we tend to be from any actual practice of animal sacrifice, there may still be no better language for capturing the high stakes implicit in the biblical narrative. Blood is important not because it represents death, but because it represents life. It therefore points to what can be accomplished by the creative and faithful disposition of life. In the death and life of Jesus, it captures the extent of God's own risk in pursuing intimate relationship with humankind.

Leon Morris, "The Biblical Use of the Term 'Blood,'" *JTS* n.s. 3 (1952): 216–27; 6 (1955): 77–82.

L. WILLIAM COUNTRYMAN

Boast, Boastful   *see* Pride

Body   The main NT word is *soma*. The main OT term, *basar,* is usually translated "flesh," so for the body in the OT, see *flesh.*

Body and person. The human person comprises body or flesh or outer person, and *soul* or *spirit* or heart (see *mind*) or inner person. The two are mutually dependent and equally indispensable to being human, and any of the words for them can stand for the whole person. Yet the inner and outer person are distinguishable and partially separable. Believers are committed to being holy in body and spirit (1 Cor 7:34; cf. 2 Cor 7:1). We have cleansed our heart from a wicked conscience and washed our body with pure water (Heb 10:22). Another human being can destroy body but not soul, though both can be destroyed in hell (Matt 10:28). It is possible to be absent in body but present in spirit (1 Cor 5:3). A journey to heaven may happen "in the body or out of the body" (2 Cor 12:2–3).

First Thessalonians 5:23 implies a threefold division into spirit, soul, and body, but given the twofold picture elsewhere, more likely Paul is speaking loosely of the inner person relating to God, the inner person in itself, and the outer person. Psalm 16:9–10 similarly speaks of heart, soul (*kabod*), body, and person (*nephesh*—NRSV "me").

The body in itself is a whole combined of various parts, all of which affect the whole. An eye or a hand can lead the whole body to disaster, but an eye that sees well suffuses the whole body with light (Matt 5:29–30; 6:22–23). It is tempting but stupid to worry about provision for the body (6:25). Having the body in common with other people gives us the capacity to empathize with people imprisoned or oppressed (Heb 13:3: see NRSV Mg).

Body and holiness. We are called to glorify Christ in our bodies (1 Cor 6:20). Christ can be exalted in our bodies, by life and by death (Phil 1:20). Through the attacks that come to our bodies because we serve Christ, we can carry and exhibit the death of Jesus that came about through people's attacks on him—and in our bodies we can also then exhibit his resurrection life (2 Cor 4:10). No believers should make trouble for people who so bear Jesus' marks branded on their bodies (Gal 6:17).

Sin is first a matter of the mind, but it does lead to the degrading of the body (Rom 1:18–25). The body therefore requires disciplining, though regulations concerning what can be handled, tasted, or touched have only a superficial value in this connection (Col 2:21–23). But Paul does speak of pummeling his body and making it serve him, rather than serving it (1 Cor 9:27). Human maturity can be defined in terms of the capacity to keep the body under control and clean, to which the key is the tongue (Jas 3:1–6).

So while Christians are free, this does not mean they are free to do anything, and specifically to do anything with their bodies. Indeed, when we are judged, it will be on the basis of what we have done in our bodies (2 Cor 5:10). We must cleanse ourselves of all defilement of body or spirit: it is here that holiness, moral maturity, and reverence must be realized (2 Cor 7:1; body here is *sarx*, usually translated "flesh"). For instance, our commitment to Christ requires us to pay attention to what we eat—overeating or eating what is bad for us ignores the body's spiritual significance (cf. 1 Cor 6:13a). The body is not a morally insignificant thing, like (say) a rock (if a rock is morally insignificant). Likewise the body is not meant for sexual *immorality* (1 Cor 6:13b). That emerges from a number of facts: see 1 Cor 6:14–20. (a) God raised Jesus' body and will raise ours (v. 14). (b) Christians have come to cleave to Christ in their inner being like a man and woman cleaving to each other in their bodily sexual union, as happens even in "casual sex." The link of inner and outer person means it is as if our bodies become Christ's limbs. That makes it impossible to undertake an immoral sexual union as if this did not affect that other union (vv. 15–17). (c) Sexual union is a particularly profound form of human act that affects the whole person in a way other acts do not, because of that link between inner and outward person (v. 18). (d) Indeed, the link means our bodies become sanctuaries of the Holy Spirit (v. 19), as Jesus' body was (John 2:21). Sexual immorality defiles this sanctuary. (e) Christ paid a price for us to buy us out of our slavery, and our bodies as much as our spirits are part of the persons for whom Christ paid this price (vv. 19–20). It is striking that Paul's next words argue for proper sexual expression between husband and wife, and see them as having authority over each other's bodies (1 Cor 7:4).

Paul's exposition of the dynamics of human life in Rom 6–8 shows how the body can both be identified with the person and distinguished from it. On the one hand, we have died to sin—that is, we have associated ourselves with Christ as one who historically did die to sin (i.e., he let sin exact its final demands of him), even though sin of course had no claim on him. Our association with him then means that in effect we died to sin. Thus "our old self [lit. "our old human being"] was crucified with him." The aim of this was that "the body of sin [or "the sinful body" RSV] might be destroyed." The verb is not the usual one for "destroy"; it suggests something like "overthrown." Thus we are no longer enslaved to sin: the sinful body has been robbed of its power (6:6). To put it another way, Christ died to the law, letting it exact its demands of him, and our association with him means his body's dying to the law also counts for us (7:4). To put it yet another way, our body is dead because of sin (8:10).

We are thus in a position to prevent sin exercising authority in our mortal bodies and thereby making us obey their passions (6:12). Here the idea that sin starts in the mind is complemented by awareness of the body's power. But we can present the different parts of our body to God as means for doing what is upright, rather than presenting them to sin as means for doing what is wicked (6:13). God gives new life to our bodies through the Spirit, so that by the Spirit we can put to death the body's deeds and follow the Spirit's moral leading (8:11–14). We can present our bodies to God as a living sacrifice (12:1), following the pattern Christ set (Heb 10:5–10). Perhaps this exhortation is a further sign that the body, far from being a dispensable part of the self, *is* the self. We present our *selves* to God as a sacrifice.

Dead body. Most OT occurrences of "body" refer to corpses, the words being *gewiyyah, guphah, meth, nebelah, nephesh,* or *peger*; the NT equivalent is *ptoma*. Most of these words can be used for animal as well as human carcasses, which draws attention to the commonality of humans and animals.

The first two words refer especially to the bodies of Saul and his sons (1 Sam 31:10–12; 1 Chr 10:12). The story emphasizes the appropriateness of giving bodies a proper burial, for only then do the people find their rest. The same implication emerges from the use of the more common words *nebelah* and *peger* (etymologically they link with words for "lan-

guish" and "faint," which is suggestive). It is a terrible fate if bodies are given to the birds (Ps 79:2). It is grievous that the body of the man of God in 1 Kgs 13 will never reach his family tomb, though at least the prophet who warned him this would happen ensures that the body reaches his own tomb. Dead bodies deserve to be treated with care, respect, and honor. Thus John's disciples fetch John's corpse in order to bury it (Mark 6:29), and Joseph and Nicodemus do the same for Jesus (John 19:38–42). The woman who pours her perfume on Jesus' head anoints his living body for burial (Mark 14:8).

When someone is executed and the body is hanged on a tree to make it a public spectacle, it must be taken down and buried before nightfall, otherwise it would defile the land (Deut 21:22–23; Josh 8:29). Senior priests and Nazirites must therefore avoid contact with dead bodies (Lev 21:11; Num 6:6), because they will be disqualified from their ministry for a while or their vow will be invalidated (see *clean*). Ordinary people who have contact with dead bodies similarly contract defilement and must go through a rite of cleansing (Num 19:11–20; Hag 2:13).

One assumption underlying the concern with burial and the possibility of defilement is that sense that the body is intrinsic to the person. Indeed *nephesh,* which usually means the person or self or soul, can refer to a dead body (e.g., Lev 21:11). The body *is* the person, even when it is dead. At the same time, a dead body is therefore an odd or paradoxical thing. It looks just like a person, but it behaves like an inanimate thing. A living person came into being when God breathed life into a body, so the body without the spirit is dead (Gen 2:7; Jas 2:26). A dead body fits no categories. It confuses the distinction between life and death. Perhaps it is this that makes it defiling.

Jesus bore our sins in his body on the tree (1 Pet 2:24). We were reconciled in his fleshly body by his death (Col 1:22). The conviction that Jesus' death is the means of salvation is the more remarkable in light of the defiling nature of a dead body. So is Jesus' invitation to eat bread that stands for his body that was about to be broken (Mark 14:22; cf. 1 Cor 11:24). The paradoxical link of defilement and power also underlies the conviction that people who eat the bread or drink the wine unworthily, without examining themselves, are guilty of the Lord's body and blood and eat and drink judgment against themselves (1 Cor 11:27–29). They fail to discern the body—perhaps the Christian body, or perhaps the Lord's body (see NRSV Mg).

Renewing of the body. A sign that the whole person of Jesus has come back to life is that his body is no longer in its tomb (Luke 24:3). The new life people receive through Christ comes both to soul and body, sometimes first to the body and then to the soul, sometimes the opposite. Thus Jesus healed people's bodies ("she felt in her body . . ." Mark 5:29—then later Jesus bade the woman go in peace), while Peter addressed the dead body of a disciple and bade her rise (Acts 9:40). Some dead bodies were raised when Jesus died, in anticipation of the complete new life this heralded (Matt 27:52). The fact that inner and the outer belong integrally together makes it inevitable that eternal life involves both inner and outer, as Jesus' resurrection did. We thus await the redemption of our bodies (Rom 8:23). It is not surprising that Michael and the devil fought over Moses' body (Jude 9).

The raising of our bodies is difficult to imagine, as it would be difficult to work out from a seed what will be the nature of the wheat or flower or vegetable that will come from it once it has "died." This comparison provides a way of thinking about the difference between the natural body and the *resurrection* body. One is perishable, physical, made of dirt, derived from Adam; the other is imperishable, spiritual, made from heaven, derived from Christ (1 Cor 15:35–49). Christ's resurrection body gives some indication what ours will be like. It is, of course, material—Christ is visible and visibly identical with the person who was executed, and

he can speak, eat, and drink. But it is not subject to the limitations of an ordinary body. It can appear and disappear at will. It is wholly subject to the leading of the Spirit, as our present bodies are not. But Christ will transform our lowly bodies to make them like his splendid body (Phil 3:21).

To put it another way, our body is the home we live in (2 Cor 5:1–10). Our present home is a flimsy and vulnerable tent (in 2 Pet 1:13 the word for "body" is *skenoma,* which literally means a movable dwelling such as a tent). But God has prepared a solid house for us. It would be nice to be rid of this insecure tent, not so as to live in the open, but so as to move to that more substantial dwelling. It would be nice for the mortal to be replaced by the everlasting. And the presence of the Spirit in us both makes us more certain that God will eventually give us that new home, and also thus makes us long for it more deeply. After all, being at home in the body means being away from the Lord—it means walking by faith, not by sight. But because of that Spirit-inspired certainty, we can face *death* and leaving the body with equanimity, even with enthusiasm, because it means being at home with the Lord.

Body as a metaphor. The body's diversity in unity provides an image for understanding the believing community. Sharing in the fellowship meal and partaking of one loaf means the congregation is one body (1 Cor 10:17). Its meetings must take place in such a way as to discern the unity of the body, which excludes some people eating and drinking to excess while others go hungry (11:29).

Like the body's different limbs, the community of the baptized has different members (1 Cor 12:1–31; Rom 12:4–8). As well as coming from different classes, they have different *gifts.* Their task is to fulfill their individual functions aware of doing so for the sake of the body as a whole. They are neither to undervalue their contribution, as if the ear thought it did not count because it was not an eye, nor to overvalue it, as if the ear thought it could fulfill the functions of all the body's parts. Indeed human beings make a point of covering some humbler (but indispensable) body parts with splendid clothing—so that the humbler has greater honor. As the different body parts work together, irrespective of their degree of honor or apparent importance, so God designs the believing community to care for one another so that all share in everyone's honor or hurt.

Ephesians extends this idea in seeing the whole worldwide church as the body of which Christ is the head (1:22–23), a body uniting Jews and Gentiles (2:16). Under Christ's headship this body manifests its diversity of gifts in a unity of purpose on that larger canvas (4:1–16; cf. Col 1:18, 24; 2:19). It is the different parts' relationship to the head that helps them function properly in relation to one another, so that the one body functions as one body.

Ephesians 5 takes the image further again. As Christ is the body's head and the church submits to him, so a husband is his wife's head and she submits to him. How does that work out? Christ acts as head of the church by loving it and dying for it, and the church submits to him by accepting his doing that. A husband acts as head of his wife by loving her and giving himself for her, nourishing and caring for her as he would for his own body, and she submits to him by letting him do that. (There is thus no suggestion that the head-body image implies the husband making decisions for the wife, except in requiring her to accept his self-sacrifice.)

Rudolf Bultmann, *Theology of the New Testament* (New York: Charles Scribners' Sons, 1951), 1:192–203; R. H. Gundry, Soma *in Biblical Theology, with Emphasis on Pauline Anthropology* (Cambridge: Cambridge University Press, 1976); John A. T. Robinson, *The Body: A Study in Pauline Theology*, SBT 5 (London: SCM Press, 1952); Hans Walter Wolff, *Anthropology of the Old Testament* (Philadelphia: Fortress Press, 1974).

JOHN GOLDINGAY

Bond, Bondage   *see* **Slavery**

Book   *see* **Write**

Bow, Rainbow   *see* **Noah**

Bread   In an agricultural economy based on grain rather than rice or potatoes, it is natural that bread is the staple food, whereas meat tends to be more of a luxury and the slaying of an animal is a sacrificial action. "Bread and water" thus represent the minimum sustenance required for survival. On occasion the manna supplied miraculously by God in the wilderness can be referred to as "bread" (Ps 105:40 RSV). There was an important distinction between bread made with leaven (that functioned like yeast in making the dough rise) and the unleavened bread that was prepared and eaten at the time of the combined festivals of Passover and Unleavened Bread (Exod 12:14–15). The "bread of the Presence" (or "shewbread") was kept in the tabernacle or temple (Exod 25:30; Lev 24:5–9); whatever their origins, the twelve loaves, consumed weekly by the priests and then replaced, symbolized the covenant between Yahweh and his people.

Bread accordingly stands for the food that people need in order to live. The Lord's Prayer is concerned with the basic needs of God's people. They pray first for God to be given his rightful place in their lives. Then they pray for themselves, and first of all for the bread that they need today (Matt 6:11) or daily (Luke 11:3). The bread is qualified as *epiousios,* a Greek word of uncertain meaning traditionally translated as "daily," but more probably either "necessary for existence" or "belonging to this coming day." Most likely the reference is to material bread, but a reference to spiritual food cannot be certainly excluded.

Although bread is essential, nevertheless the comment of Jesus after his forty-day fast in the wilderness relativizes its importance. Citing Deut 8:3, he affirmed that people do not live only by bread but also by every word that comes from the mouth of God. The thought may simply be that God's words nourish a person spiritually or that obedience to them is more important than the satisfaction of bodily requirements.

In the Gospels there is a significant series of incidents and teaching centered around bread. All the Gospels describe the presence of a large crowd with Jesus in the wilderness, that is, an uninhabited area with no immediate resources for replenishing their supplies (Matt 14:13–20 and par.). For whatever reason, they had no food at the end of a long day, and the only apparent solution was for them to make their way back to the neighboring villages. Jesus took the initiative and found that there was nothing more than five small loaves (more akin to rolls) and a couple of (small) fish available. Having given thanks to God for them, that is, the normal "grace" before a meal, he distributed them, and miraculously they multiplied to feed the crowd with plenty over and to spare. A second, similar incident involving different numbers of people and amounts of food is reported later by Mark (8:1–10) and Matthew (15:32–39).

The story could be nothing more than an account of a miracle attesting that the power of the kingdom of God is at work through Jesus. Specifically Jesus showed a compassionate response to human need (Mark 8:2). Some modern readers have reinterpreted the story to the effect that the example of Jesus sharing the food encouraged other people who had food in their bags to bring it out and share it with those around them, but that is certainly not the understanding of the storytellers.

Much more relevant is the way in which the story is reminiscent of a similar action by the prophet Elisha, who fed a hundred men with a small quantity of food and had some left over (2 Kgs 4:42–44), and thus establishes a parallel between Jesus and a revered prophet. The wilderness setting also suggests a parallel with Moses feeding the people with bread (manna). The two feedings have been understood as symbolizing provision for the Jews and the Gentiles respectively (the second appears to take place in Gentile territory, but the location of the first is debatable). The feedings thus testify to the compassionate power of God through Jesus to care for human need as he had done in the past through Moses and Elisha.

A strange incident follows in Mark 8:11–21, where the disciples were in a boat on the sea without any food with them. When Jesus warned them against "the yeast of the Pharisees" (yeast being an ingredient in bread), they curiously replied, "We have no bread." Jesus chided them for this and reminded them of the feeding miracles and the leftovers on each occasion. It seems that he was warning them against unbelief, since the Pharisees had been pestering him for a sign, even though he had just fed the crowds, and suggesting to them that with him in the boat they should not be worried about where they were going to get food.

At his last meal with his disciples the evangelists record deliberately and precisely how Jesus took the bread, said the blessing to God, broke it, and distributed it to the disciples with the words "Take; this is my body" (Mark 14:22 and par.). The wording is very similar to that used at the feeding miracles. This could be inevitable, since on all three occasions Jesus was following the standard Jewish religious practice. However, the distribution of the bread is perhaps significant. If so, it can be argued that the incidents fall into a series, so that they may illuminate one another. Jesus' last meal is obviously one of close fellowship with his disciples, and the sharing of the bread is a means of binding them together. However, the sharing of the bread is given a fuller significance, since it means that they receive a symbol of his body. In the context of the sharing of the cup and the reference to his blood, this must also refer to his self-giving in death, and thus the bread symbolizes Jesus himself as he gives himself in death for his disciples. The meal is thus a visible, physical symbol of a spiritual reality.

In the light of this, some scholars want to argue that the earlier feeding miracle should be understood as "the Galilean Lord's Supper." Quite what is meant by this is not certain. The essential points that distinguished the Jerusalem Lord's Supper are not present in the earlier narrative(s); there are no context of the impending death of Jesus and no interpretative saying. Restraint in interpretation is therefore advisable. Certainly all the meals can be seen as occasions of fellowship with Jesus, although this element is not marked in the miracle stories, which are much more concerned with the remarkable provision that Jesus is able to give.

However, the situation is different in the Gospel of John. John is remarkable in that the account of the Last Supper of Jesus is altogether silent about the actual meal and the attention is focused instead on the preceding footwashing. By contrast, after Jesus had fed the crowd in John 6, there was an extended exposition of its significance (John 6:25–71). The people themselves recognized in Jesus the prophet who was to come into the world and the king of God's people: the analogy with Moses and Elisha is recognized, and the intended lesson is drawn (John 6:14). However, the comments of Jesus himself moved in a different direction. He accused the crowds who came after him of wanting more physical food when they should rather have been looking for the food that nourishes eternal life. They questioned whether he could provide this, pointing out that Moses gave the people bread from heaven. Jesus responded that it was really God who gave it to them, and what he gives is "true bread," that is, the "real bread," of which physical bread is only a symbol. When they asked for this bread, Jesus replied that he himself is the bread. We can readily see how the saying at the Last Supper, where Jesus gives himself under the symbolism of bread to the disciples, leads to this identification of Jesus as himself the true bread that nourishes eternal life. Jesus then went even further by identifying the bread more closely as his flesh

that he would give for the life of the world; in plain words, he functions as the bread through his self-giving in death. Taking this point literally leads to the absurd suggestion that Jesus wants people to eat his physical flesh. Jesus seized on this wording to insist that people must eat his flesh and drink his blood in order to gain eternal life. The language would have been repulsive, especially to Jews with their abhorrence of meat that still had the blood in it. Christian readers recognize more easily that the language of Jesus alludes directly to the bread and cup of the Lord's Supper, that he is speaking metaphorically, and that he is insisting that eternal life is to be gained only through his self-giving in death and a relationship of faith in him, which is so close that it can be described metaphorically as feeding on him.

Here, then, the feeding miracle becomes the occasion for teaching about the significance of what Jesus said at the Last Supper. It may be that John has the teaching in this setting in order that it may be understood that it is the spiritual relationship with Jesus that matters and not the physical eating and drinking; as is made clear at the end of the discussion, it is not the "flesh," that is, the physical, that matters but the spiritual, namely, the words that Jesus has spoken.

The Last Supper was taken up in the early church as the Lord's Supper. However the one arose out of the other, Paul makes it clear that what the believers did when they met together was intended to follow the pattern established by Jesus (1 Cor 11:23–26). In his teaching here it is clear that the purpose of the meal is to proclaim the death of Jesus, in that the broken bread represents the body of Jesus that was (given) for his people.

Elsewhere Paul can refer to this same event as the breaking of bread. He insists that the bread which believers break when they come together is a participation in the body of Christ. And he adds that because they partake of one bread, those who eat it are one **body** (1 Cor 10:16–17). This comment makes it clear that the pattern established by Jesus of using one loaf that was broken into small pieces was continued in the Pauline congregations. But Paul attaches importance to the fact that by sharing together in one loaf the believers manifest that they form one "body," just as the fact that they are all baptized by one Spirit means that they constitute one body. The common comparison of a community to a body is here taken over and understood spiritually of the church, which is the body of Christ. To share in the one loaf, therefore, is a sign of belonging and a sign of commitment. To the present writer, that is all there is to it. Suggestions by some theologians that the bread at the Christian meal is somehow to be identified with the church go beyond what the language implies. But there is a stronger belief that somehow the bread becomes or is to be identified with the personal body of Christ, so that to take the bread is to participate in the body of Christ, which was put to death on the cross for our salvation. The problem is whether the "is" in the saying of Jesus, "This is my body," is to be taken of symbolization ("represents") or identification ("is actually"). The former is more probable.

In Luke 24:28–31 Cleopas and his companion invite the unknown traveler who is walking along the road with them into their dwelling for the night; at the meal he takes bread, blesses God for it, and gives it to them. Immediately they recognize him, and simultaneously he disappears from sight. They know that it is the risen Jesus. They naturally refer to what happened as "the breaking of bread." Subsequently Luke speaks of the early Christians meeting to break bread (Acts 2:42, 46; 20:7, 11); the same language is used in Acts 27:35, where we may assume that Paul broke the bread for himself (and presumably for his Christian companion, the narrator of the story), but not for the others on board who "ate some food themselves." The coincidence of Luke's language with Paul's requires that the reference is to the same kind of meal as he describes, although there is some scholarly debate as to whether Luke's phrase may have originally referred to a meal with a somewhat different character and focus, specifically a meal without wine which was more in the nature of a joyful meal with the risen Lord present than a solemn memorial of his death. Whatever be the history behind this phraseology, Luke's story indicates that the breaking of bread was understood in the early church as an occasion at which the risen Lord was present as the host. Believers, therefore, experienced fellowship with him as a person; and his role as host makes it the less likely that they thought of themselves as actually feeding on his flesh. Nevertheless, John's language speaks of Jesus as both the dispenser of living bread (John 6:27) and as himself the bread that came down from heaven (John 6:35). In such a case, it is probable that the personal must have priority over the impersonal; Jesus compares himself and the salvation that he bestows to bread, but this really means that he is the Savior, all the more so since salvation or eternal life is essentially a relationship to him rather than a "thing" that he gives.

I. H. Marshall, *Last Supper and Lord's Supper* (Grand Rapids: Eerdmans, 1981).

I. HOWARD MARSHALL

Breath, Breathe *see* **Spirit**

Bride, Bridegroom *see* **Marriage**

Brother *see* **Family**

Burn *see* **Fire**

Call In both the OT and the NT "to call" (Hebrew: *qaraʾ*; Greek: *kaleo*) is a common verb whose basic meanings include to make contact with another by voice, to name, to summon, and to invite. The word takes on the distinctive senses of salvation and vocation when it is God who calls, in which case it comprises such notions as divine initiative, election, sanction, and guidance (see *choose*).

In the Hebrew idiom, naming is done by *calling* the **name**: At creation God calls the light Day and the darkness Night (Gen 1:5), the dome Sky (1:8), and the dry land Earth (1:10). Adam called (NRSV: "named") his wife Eve (3:20) and the son after his likeness Seth (5:3). An angel instructs Hagar to call her son Ishmael (16:11), and the Lord instructs Abraham to call his son with Sarah, Isaac (17:19), with whom the everlasting covenant will be established. The angel Gabriel informs Mary that her son "will be called *Son of God*" (Luke 1:35). In a dream an angel instructs Joseph to call (NRSV: "name") the son Mary bears "Jesus" (1:21; cf. 1:25), who shall be called Emmanuel (1:23). In 1 John 3:1 the love of God is demonstrated by virtue of the fact "that we should be called children of God."

The expression "to call upon the name of the Lord," however, means to worship. According to Gen 4:26, people began to call upon (NRSV: "invoke") the name of the Lord during the time of Seth and Enosh. Seth's descendant Abraham calls upon the same Lord (12:8; 13:4).

God's initiative is often expressed in terms of calling. God calls Abraham (Isa 51:2; Heb 11:8; see Gen 12), Moses (Exod 3:4; 19:20), Samuel (1 Sam 3:4–14), the prophets (Isa 49:1), and Israel (Isa 48:12; Hos 11:1). God calls through Wisdom to people who pay no heed (Prov 1:24; cf. Isa 50:2), who then call upon God too late (Prov 1:28). God calls Israel by name (Isa 43:1; 45:3). The call to Israel at Isa 41:9 is closely connected with the vocabulary of election ("I have chosen you"). The Lord calls Israel in righteousness to be a light to the nations (42:6).

The operation of God's call in the course of salvation history is emphasized by the quotation of Hos 11:1 in Matt 2:15: "Out of Egypt I have called my son." Jesus calls *disciples* (Mark 1:20 and par.) who immediately follow him. His entire activity can be characterized as having come to call sinners (Mark 2:17 and par.). As the good shepherd Jesus calls his own sheep by name (John 10:3).

Paul's discussion of those called by God in Rom 8:28–30 juxtaposes the verb "call" with others that serve to illustrate its depth of meaning: "foreknow," "predestine," "justify," and "glorify." As Paul explains in 9:11–12, God's purpose of election comes about through his call. Those called by God are both Jews and Gentiles (9:24). The God who calls people into fellowship with his Son is faithful (1 Cor 1:9; 1 Thess 5:24). His call is to peace (1 Cor 7:15; cf. Col 3:15) and freedom (Gal 5:13) and comes to people notwithstanding the circumstances of their lives (1 Cor 7:17–24). Paul chastises the Galatians for deserting the one who called them in the grace of Christ (Gal 1:6), even as Paul himself was called through grace (1:15). To be the recipient of God's call obligates one to live a life worthy of that calling (1 Thess 2:12; cf. Eph 4:1), especially since God calls to holiness (1 Thess 4:7; cf. 1 Pet 1:15). In the later Pauline writings God's call is specified to include eternal life (1 Tim 6:12); it is a call based on grace from before time (2 Tim 1:9). In Hebrews, Christ as high priest mediates a new covenant so that those called may receive an eternal inheritance (Heb 9:15). God has called a people "out of darkness into his marvelous light" (1 Pet 2:9). Although those who are called experience suffering (2:20–21), they will also inherit a blessing (3:9) and be restored (5:10). The salvific sense of "invited," meaning "called," is well illustrated by Rev 19:9.

The Greek verbal noun "call" or "calling" (*klesis*) corresponds to the special sense of the verb in the OT. It appears in the NT primarily as a Pauline technical term. Paul can use it with reference to his own summons by God in Christ (Phil 3:14), and it stands as a fundamental point of reference in the lives of Christian believers (1 Cor 1:26; 7:20). Despite outward circumstances, such as Israel's resistance to the gospel, "the gifts and the calling of God are irrevocable" (Rom 11:29). Apart from the remaining Pauline references (Eph 1:18; 4:1, 4; 2 Thess 1:11; 2 Tim 1:9), elsewhere in the NT this noun appears only in a reference to the "heavenly calling" of Heb 3:1 and the "call and election" of 2 Pet 1:10.

The Greek verbal adjective "called" (*kletos*) participates in the same technical senses that have been identified for *kaleo* and *klesis*. It serves to define succinctly the nature of Paul's apostleship in both Rom 1:1 and 1 Cor 1:1. In the former passage its import is elucidated in the immediately following phrase "set apart for the gospel of God," which in turn is explicated in the verses that follow. In the latter passage the aspect of divine initiative is accented in the phrase "by the will of God." To be called is not an attribute for *apostles* alone, however, since all those who love God are "called according to his purpose" (Rom 8:28). Thus "called" can be employed to refer to believers in Paul's letters (Rom 1:6, 7; 1 Cor 1:2, 24) and elsewhere (Jude 1; Rev 17:14). Note that while in Rev 17:14 "called" is equivalent to "chosen" and "faithful," in Matt 22:14 "called" or perhaps "invited" is opposed to "chosen."

Of course the call of God in both Testaments is often illustrated in narratives that may or may not explicitly use or emphasize the literal vocabulary of calling reviewed here. When God calls to Moses out of the burning bush (Exod 3:4), the word functions in its most ordinary sense of an audible sound to gain someone's attention. But as the larger story (3:5–4:17) makes clear, this call has the most profound theological implications. Later God again calls Moses to the top of Sinai to receive the Ten Commandments (19:20). Other instructive examples of God's initiative in calling human beings in the OT to fulfill particular roles according to his purpose concern Gideon (Judg 6:11–24), Samuel (1 Sam 3:1–21), Elisha (1 Kgs 19:19–21, in which Elijah is the intermediary), Isaiah (Isa 6:1–13), Jeremiah (Jer 1:1–19), and Ezekiel (Ezek 1:1–3:27). In the various call stories of the disciples in the Gospels (Mark 1:16–20; 2:14–17; Luke 5:1–11; John 1:35–51), the initiative is now found with Jesus. The personal *authority* of Jesus becomes a factor for those who answer his call (Luke 5:1–11; John 1:47–49). Out of the larger group of disciples Jesus calls twelve to be his close associates (Mark 3:13–19). The Johannine

account in particular highlights connections with OT expectations. The importance of the call/conversion of Paul is underlined by its threefold narration in Acts (Acts 9:1–19a; 22:1–21; 26:1–23). In these NT call accounts not only does the summons come from Jesus, but the call is to a vocation associated with his mission and for which, since the resurrection, he serves as the object.

As Peter assures those who respond favorably at the conclusion of his Pentecost discourse in Acts, the promise of God's salvation is for "everyone whom the Lord our God calls to him" (Acts 2:39).

———

CHRISTOPHER R. MATTHEWS

Chasten, Chastise   *see* **Correct**

Cherub (plural **Cherubim**)   A winged creature usually associated with the presence of God. Other than having wings, cherubim are not described, except for the elaborate and difficult passages in Ezek 1:5–12; 10:7–22; 41:19, where they are composite beings with a human form, four wings, and four faces (only two in 41:19). Since Ezekiel had great difficulty in describing the cherubim he saw, it should not be assumed that those on the ark of the covenant and in the temple looked like those in his vision. All of the mentions of cherubim represent assumptions that there was a "spiritual" realm inhabited by creatures who were unlike those on earth. God did not dwell in isolation in heaven, it was believed (cf. 1 Kgs 22:19; Isa 6:2–7), but was accompanied by other beings, usually simply called the host of heaven (see *hosts, angel, seraph*). The composite creatures of Ezekiel's visions are reflections of the widespread practice in ancient Near Eastern art of attempting to depict supernatural beings or forces by combining parts of earthly creatures, especially of the lion, the bull, the eagle, and human forms. Deities were frequently shown enthroned above composite beings. Israel shared some of those tendencies, but wisely refrained from much speculation about the heavenly realms.

Two golden cherubim rested on the cover of the ark of the covenant (see *presence*), which was understood to be a movable throne for the invisible God (Exod 25; 37; esp. 25:22; Num 7:89; 1 Sam 4:4; 2 Sam 6:2). Cherubim also decorated the curtains of the tabernacle (Exod 36:8) and the walls of the temple (1 Kgs 6:29, 32). Within the Holy of Holies of Solomon's temple were two large cherubim made of olive wood and covered with gold, whose wings overshadowed the ark (1 Kgs 6:23–28). In each case they served as symbols that this was a place where God might choose to be present. In Ezekiel's vision the cherubim are associated with the unlimited freedom of movement of the throne chariot, and this corresponds to some extent with the poetic reference: "He rode on a cherub, and flew; he came swiftly upon the wings of the wind" (Ps 18:10 = 2 Sam 22:11).

The word is used differently in two texts. After Adam and Eve were expelled from Eden, God placed cherubim to the east of the garden, and they are associated with a flaming sword that guarded the way to the tree of life (Gen 3:24). In a difficult text, the king of Tyre is either identified with or associated with a "guardian cherub" (Ezek 28:14, cf. v. 16). In both cases the cherub serves as a guardian associated with the garden of God.

DONALD E. GOWAN

Child   see **Family**

Choose, Chosen, Elect, Election
The verb *bahar* in the OT is used frequently when human choosing is involved, but its theological significance resides primarily in those occurrences in which God is the subject of the verb. In many instances, the object of God's choice is the *people* of Israel (see Deut. 7:6–7; 10:15; 14:2). The fact that several of the clearest and most striking articulations of Israel's divine chosenness occur

in the book of Deuteronomy is revealing, because Deuteronomy is the covenant document par excellence. In short, the vocabulary of chosenness or election is fundamentally about God's will to establish a relationship between God and humanity (see *covenant*); or, in a word, this vocabulary is essentially about love.

Indeed, in reflecting on its chosenness, Israel realized that it possessed no inherent merit that would explain God's choice. Rather, the only "explanation" is that "the LORD loved you" (Deut 7:8; see 10:15). Hence, Israel's chosenness is a matter of *grace* as well as love. God's choice of a particular people is related to another object of God's choice that is also featured prominently in the book of Deuteronomy—that is, God's choice of a particular place, the temple in Jerusalem, "as a dwelling for his name" (Deut 12:11; see 12:14, 18, 21, 26; 14:23–25; 15:20; 16:6–7, 11, 15; 17:10; 18:6; 26:2; see also 1 Kgs 8:44, 48; 11:13, 22, 36; 14:21). This divine choice also articulates God's will for relatedness to people, because the temple in Jerusalem served essentially as God's "house," to which God's people were invited to come to encounter God's presence, including the sharing of sacrificial meals that symbolized the communion between God and those gathered in God's chosen place.

A further object of chosenness within the book of Deuteronomy is "a king whom the LORD your God will choose" (17:15). To be sure, the positive view of the monarchy articulated in Deut 17:14–20 is not unanimous among OT traditions. Even within the so-called Deuteronomistic History (the books of Joshua through 2 Kings that seem largely to reflect the theology found in the book of Deuteronomy), the controversy surrounding the initiation of a monarchy is preserved (see especially 1 Sam 8–12, including 1 Sam 8:18, which suggests that the people eventually "will cry out because of your king, whom you have chosen for yourselves"). Even so, amid opposition that included Samuel himself, God agreed to the people's request for a king; and elsewhere, the divine choice of David and his descendants is articulated (see 1 Sam 16:1–13; 2 Chr 6:6; Ps 89:1, 19). Like God's choosing of a particular people and place, the divine choice of a king was intended to serve the purpose of relationship. The king is viewed as nothing less than God's "son" (see 2 Sam 7:14; Ps 2:7 and *adopt*); and the king is entrusted with the implementation of the divine will for justice and righteousness (see Ps 72:1–7, 12–14). Thus, the concept of vocation or mission is an inextricable element of being chosen.

To be sure, all this sounds scandalously particularistic. Hence it is crucially important to do what interpreters of the OT have not always done—namely, to realize that the divine chosenness of a particular people, of a particular place, and of particular persons to implement the divine is set within the context of a God who creates the whole world and who ultimately desires relatedness to all humanity, all creatures, and all creation.

In other words, it is critically important to recognize that the Bible begins with creation. Although the verb *bahar* is not present, Gen 1 relates that humanity as a whole is given the mission of "dominion" (Gen 1:28). The first covenant mentioned in the Bible confirms God's will to be related to the whole creation. In addition to God, parties to the covenant include not only Noah and his descendants (see Gen 6:18; 9:9), but also "every living creature" (Gen 9:10, 12, 15, 16) and even "the earth" itself (Gen 9:13).

When the story appears to narrow to Abraham and his descendants, the scope of God's concern actually continues to be creationwide. God's relationship with Abraham, which is several times described as a "covenant" (Gen 15:18; 17:1–14), is meant not only for the benefit or blessing of Abraham, but God also intends that "in you all the families of the earth shall be blessed" (Gen 12:3). Although the verb *bahar* does not appear in the Abraham narratives, NRSV interpretively translates the verb *yada'* in Gen 18:19 as "chosen" (more literally, "known"),

describing the relationship between God and Abraham (see Neh 9:7, where the verb *bahar* is used to indicate that "God . . . chose Abram"). Interestingly, Abraham's mission in Gen 18:19 is described as "doing righteousness and justice."

As suggested above, righteousness and justice are precisely what the kings, as chosen ones, were supposed to do. Their failure to exercise leadership toward the enactment and embodiment of righteousness and justice among the people called forth the criticism of the prophets (see Amos 3:1–2); and eventually the prophetic verdict is that the exile is the result of the repeated failures of kings and people. But beyond the despair of exile arose a renewed sense of hope, articulated especially in the book of Isaiah and explicitly utilizing the root *bahar*. Israel is "chosen" (Isa 41:8–9; 43:10, 20; 44:1–2; 45:4) and given the vocation or mission of *servant*. Among other things, this mission involves the establishment of "justice" on a universal scale (Isa 42:1–4; see "chosen" in v. 1). To be sure, there is an ongoing debate over the identity of the "servant," which at times seems to be Israel and at times seems to be some unidentified individual. In any case, the beneficiaries of God's work are to be not only "the survivors of Israel" (Isa 49:6), but also the servant's role is "as a light to the nations, that my salvation may reach to the end of the earth" (Isa 49:6; see 42:6).

The mission of the chosen servant, along with the vision of many peoples gathering in Jerusalem (Isa 2:2–4), recalls the divine promise that "all the families of the earth shall be blessed" in Abraham (Gen 12:3), and it coheres with the Bible's initial portrayal of a God who chooses to create and chooses to be related to all humankind, and indeed to all creatures and all creation. As Dale Patrick concludes, "the very logic of election tends toward universalism" (*ABD* 2:439).

At the same time, even within the book of Isaiah, there is evidence of division within God's people. The "chosen" (Isa 65:9, 15, 22) will experience God's favor, but others God "will destine . . . to the sword" (Isa 65:12). The final chapters of the book of Isaiah (chaps. 56–66) are sometimes labeled as proto-apocalyptic; so perhaps not surprisingly, the full-blown apocalypticism of the book of Daniel also suggests a sharp distinction between those who will experience "everlasting life" and those who will experience "everlasting contempt" (12:3). The same tension is evident in the NT as well.

Given the prominence of royal titles from the OT that are applied to Jesus—especially "anointed one" (Hebrew *mashiah*; Greek *christos*; see Ps 2:2; Matt 1:1) and "son of God" (see 2 Sam 7:14; Ps 2:7; Mark 1:1, 11)—it is not surprising that Jesus, like David and his descendants, is known as God's "chosen" or "chosen one" (Luke 9:35; 23:35). In what Matt 12:17 identifies as a fulfillment of prophecy, the servant song of Isa 42:1–4 is quoted and applied to Jesus, suggesting that Jesus is the fullest expression of the "servant, whom I have chosen" (Matt 12:18; see Isa 42:1). All this is part of the biblical recasting of royalty or messiahship as loving servanthood rather than enforcing power.

As God's "chosen one," Jesus chooses others. He "called his disciples and chose twelve of them, whom he also named apostles" (Luke 6:13; see John 6:70; Acts 1:2). Although not one of the Twelve, Paul laid claim to apostleship; and the Lord's speech to Ananias in Acts 9:15 designates Paul as "chosen" (see also Acts 22:15). The divine initiative is especially clear in John, where Jesus says to the disciples, "You did not choose me but I chose you" (John 15:16).

But chosenness is not limited to the apostles. Like Jesus, these chosen ones chose others (see Acts 15:22, 25, 40). In the Pauline letters (and those attributed to Paul), it is suggested that other individuals and indeed the whole church are divinely chosen or "elect" (see 1 Cor 1:27–28; Eph 1:4; Col 1:27; 3:12; 1 Thess 1:4; 2 Thess 2:13; 2 Tim 2:10; Titus 1:1). This perspective is echoed elsewhere as well (see Jas 2:5; 1 Pet 1:2; 2:4, 9; 2 Pet 1:10; Rev 17:14).

As in the OT, God's choice does not involve worthiness or merit. According to 1 Cor 1:27–28, "God chose what is foolish . . . weak . . . low and despised in the world" (see also Jas 2:5). Grace and love are of the essence. As in the OT, chosenness means vocation or mission. Paul, aptly known as the apostle to the Gentiles or nations, is to be a "witness to all the world" (Acts 22:15); and the risen Christ sends the eleven disciples to "make disciples of all nations" (Matt 28:19; see Luke 24:47). The same tendency towards universalism that can be found in the OT is present in the NT as well (see above).

But as also in the OT, the NT reflects a tension between the tendency toward universalism and the conclusion that some may be lost. The saying of Jesus in Matt 22:14 suggests that "many are called, but few are chosen." The Greek word underlying "chosen" is a form of the verb *eklegomai*. NRSV often translates this verb and its derivatives as "choose, chose, chosen"; but the tendency is to translate them as "elect, election" in those contexts that suggest that God's universal intent will not be realized. For instance, in those sections of the Gospels of Matthew and Mark that are often labeled as "apocalyptic," the NRSV translation is "elect" (see Matt 24:22, 24, 31; Mark 13:20, 22, 27).

The tension that exists in both Testaments seems to be the result of attempts to explain why certain persons seem to respond to God and others do not. This struggle is particularly evident in Rom 9–11, where Paul attempts to come to terms with Israel's unbelief (see Rom 9:11, 18; 11:5, 7, 28). On the one hand, Paul says: "What then? Israel failed to obtain what it was seeking. The elect obtained it, but the rest were hardened" (11:7). But, on the other hand, Paul concludes that "all Israel will be saved. . . . As regards election they are beloved. . . . For God has imprisoned all in disobedience so that he may be merciful to all" (Rom 11:26, 28, 32).

Given that the apostle Paul himself seems ambivalent, perhaps the best counsel for theological appropriation of the biblical language and conceptuality of chosenness and election is to consider it, as Paul suggests, a "mystery" (Rom 11:25; see *mystery*). In the face of this mystery, Paul advises humility for those who consider themselves among the elect: "So do not become proud, but stand in awe" (Rom 11:20).

Given too the importance of the biblical language of chosenness and election in the history of doctrine, including Reformed doctrines of predestination and double predestination, it is worth noting too that the Hebrew verb *bahar* is used not only to describe God's choice of persons but also to invite persons to choose God (see Deut 30:20; Josh 24:15). To be sure, this does not resolve the tension between the tendency toward universalism and the conclusion that some will be lost; but it does offer a biblical basis for suggesting that the rupture of relationship between God and humankind happens only because of the human failure to choose God rather than God's failure to choose humanity (see *determine*).

Horst Dietrich Preuss, *Old Testament Theology* (Louisville, Ky.: Westminster John Knox Press, 1995), 1:27–39; Seock-Tae Sohn, *The Divine Election of Israel* (Grand Rapids: Eerdmans, 1991).

J. CLINTON McCANN

Christ   *see* Anoint

Christian   The term occurs three times in the Bible, in Acts 11:26; 26:28; and 1 Pet 4:16. According to Acts 11, early in the ministry of Paul he spent a year with Barnabas in Antioch of Syria, and Luke adds the comment, "and it was in Antioch that the disciples were first called 'Christians.'" The second reference in Acts occurs near the end of Paul's ministry, and according to Luke the term was then known in Palestine, since Agrippa could use it familiarly: "Are you so quickly persuading me to become a Christian?" Writing to believers who face the possibility of persecution for their faith, Peter speaks of two kinds of suffering: that which is deserved because of sin (4:15) and suffering "as a Christian," that is, simply because one is a Christian. The term next occurs in the letters of Ignatius (martyred in A.D. 108), who used it regularly, both as noun and adjective (e.g., *Magnesians* IV.1; X.1; *Romans* III.2). He also spoke of "Christianity" (*Christianismos*) as the name of his religion (*Romans* III.3; *Philadelphians* VI.1).

The form *Christianos* is not proper Greek, but is a Latinism that had become a common way of denoting the adherents of a given person, such as the "Herodians" in Matt 22:16; Mark 3:6; 12:13. The primary question concerning the word is whether it was created by the disciples in Antioch as a way of identifying themselves to the pagan world (Bickerman), or whether it originated with nonbelievers, either as an official way of distinguishing the followers of Christ from the Jews of the synagogues, or as a derisive term (Gealy, and most scholars). Bickerman argued that since the verb in Acts 11:26 is active, the sentence must be translated "disciples for the first time called themselves Christians." Within the community they called themselves by other terms, as the NT documents reveal, such as believers, brothers, disciples, and saints. They knew Paul's term "slaves of Christ," that is, those who belong to Christ (e.g., 1 Cor 7:22; Gal 1:10; see *serve* and *slave*). That term, with its origins in the OT concept of "servant of the Lord," would have been misunderstood outside the church, so believers began to identify themselves to outsiders as *christianoi*, "those who belong to Christ."

Bickerman made a good case for his position, but the majority of scholars argue that since Christian writers seldom used the term until late in the second century (only the three mentioned above did so), it was more likely to have been created by non-Christians. Confusing the matter are the variant spellings of Christ and Christian used by Christian and non-Christian writers alike (cf. Tacitus, *Annals*

XV.44.3). The variants *Chrestos, Chrestus,* and *Chrestianoi* often appear, and Chrestus was a familiar proper name, meaning "good, useful." So it is argued that non-Christians heard *christos* and converted it to the understandable *Chrestos*, then created the form *chrestianoi*, which was thus the original form of the word they used to identify believers. But epsilon and iota were frequently interchanged in the same words in ancient spelling, so caution should be used in drawing conclusions from such variants.

The significance of the appearance of the term is to be found in the evidence it supplies for the changing meaning of the word "Christ." It was the Greek translation of the Hebrew *mashiah*, "Messiah," "**Anointed** One." Outside the Jewish world "anointed one" would have been virtually meaningless, and "Christ" thus became thought of as a name more than a title. In the church it functioned as the most important title for Jesus, but even in Paul's letters it began to be used partly as a name (e.g., Rom 8:17, 35). Beginning at Antioch, it was the name Christ rather than the name Jesus that came to be the primary term used to identify his followers.

E. J. Bickerman, "The Name of Christians" *HTR* 42 (1949): 108–24; F. D. Gealy, "Christian" *IDB* 1:571–72.

DONALD E. GOWAN

Church   After the resurrection and ascension of Jesus, his followers met regularly for prayer and apparently for the study of Scripture (Acts 1:14, 16). Evidently they intended to continue as a community dedicated to the claim that the resurrection proved that Jesus was the Messiah (Acts 1:22; 2:22–24, 32). From the day of Pentecost on, the preaching of the apostles significantly enlarged that community, and Luke twice describes its distinctive features. They held all things in common, attended the temple together, ate and prayed together, and were instructed by the apostles (Acts 2:42–47; 4:32–37). The reference to "break-

ing of **bread**" in Acts 2:42 may indicate that they already were commemorating the Last Supper. Eventually (Acts 5:11) Luke calls this community of believers the *ekklesia,* translated "church" everywhere in the NT except Acts 7:38; Heb 2:12 (congregation), and Acts 19:32, 39, 41; Heb 12:23 (assembly). The English word "church" (cf. Scottish *kirk* and German *Kirche*) is of uncertain origin but is commonly thought to come from the Greek *kyriakon* (belonging to the Lord), not a term used of Christian groups in the NT.

We cannot be sure what the Aramaic-speaking Christians of Palestine called their group(s), but *ekklesia* is most likely a translation of *kᵉnishtaʾ*, which also means assembly. The Hellenistic communities may have chosen *ekklesia* because they found it regularly used in the LXX to translated the Hebrew *qahal*, which sometimes denoted assemblies of Israelites. Discussion of Hebrew terms for assembly, and LXX translations of them, has ensued because of the question whether Christians were claiming continuity with Israel by their choice of *ekklesia*. They made that claim in other ways (see *people of God*), but the Hebrew terms *qahal* and ʿ*edah*, both meaning "assembly," are not theologically freighted (they are used of all sorts of groups), and what the NT says of the *ekklesia* seems to have developed from Christian experience rather than having been carried over from the OT (Marshall, 363; Schnackenburg, 57–60). The effort to use etymology to support the idea that Christians thought themselves to be "called out" of the world has been shown to be unsupported by anything in the NT. It may be significant that of the various ways the movement was designated (e.g., the *way; Christians*—those belonging to Christ), the word that became the standard term was a word that simply meant "assembly, gathering, group." From the first, to belong to Christ meant to belong to his group, and this idea was developed theologically later, in the concept of the church as the *body* of Christ. Ernest Best emphasized this in a striking way: "It is impossible to conceive of a Christian who is not a member of the Church, which is related to Christ as in him and as his Body. . . . Individual Christians consequently do not exist" (Best, 190).

As Luke uses the word in Acts, it can refer to a single congregation and thus appear in the plural when several are referred to, but can also be used as a collective reference to all Christians: "Meanwhile the church throughout Judea, Galilee, and Samaria had peace and was built up" (Acts 9:31). See also 1 Cor 15:9; Gal 1:13; Phil 3:6; and the concept of the body of Christ.

The ekklesia *as described in Acts and the epistles.* In 1 Thessalonians, which is generally considered to be the earliest document of the NT, Paul has a double way of addressing the Christians in Thessalonica (1:1). They are "the church of the Thessalonians," and this way of identifying churches by location is commonplace. Churches in cities such as Jerusalem (Acts 8:1; 11:22), Antioch (13:1), and Corinth (1 Cor 1:2; 2 Cor 1:1) are mentioned, as well as groups of churches in given areas (Judea, Galilee, and Samaria [Acts 9:31], Galatia [Gal 1:2]). There is no indication in the NT that Christians had buildings set aside for their meetings, for the only other designation of place that appears is the reference to someone's house; e.g., "Aquila and Prisca, together with the church in their house, greet you warmly in the Lord" (1 Cor 16:19; cf. Rom 16:3–5; Col 4:15; Phlm 2).

Any sort of group(s) meeting regularly might have been identified in these ways, but for Paul, Thessalonian Christians are the church "in God the Father and the Lord Jesus Christ." The common word *ekklesia* has been given theological significance by the statement that it belongs to God and Christ (using either "in" or "of"; cf. Acts 20:28; Gal 1:2, 13; 1 Thess 2:14).

The uniqueness of the *ekklesia* is described in various ways. God "obtained [the church] with the blood of his own Son" (Acts 20:28). The Holy *Spirit* dwells in the church, which is thus God's temple

(1 Cor 3:16). The Spirit works powerfully within the church, bestowing special gifts on its members (1 Cor 12) for the building up of the church (1 Cor 14:12; see *gifts*). More than once, Paul used the idea of a building as a metaphor for the church, with Christ as its foundation or cornerstone (1 Cor 3:11; Eph 2:20–22; also 1 Pet 2:4–6). He uses that imagery as one of the ways to determine appropriate behavior in the church; right behavior is what builds up (Rom 14:19; 1 Cor 3:10–15; 10:23; 14:26).

No single image was adequate to describe the uniqueness of the experience the first Christians found in their "assembly." The OT concept of God's people as a family reappeared. Christians are members of the "household of God" (1 Tim 3:15; Eph 2:19). It may have been Jesus' reference to himself as "bridegroom" (Matt 9:15) that suggested comparing the relationship of husband and wife to that of Christ and the church in Eph 5:23–32. The love of husband for wife should be like that of Christ for the church, which led him to give himself up for it (v. 25) and nourish and tenderly care for it (v. 29). Another way of expressing this sense of nearness to God within the church made use of the concept of holiness, which originally denoted that which uniquely belonged to God (see *holy*). So Paul referred to "the churches of the saints" (1 Cor 14:33), that is, those who have been made holy, set apart as God's own possessions (cf. Acts 9:13, 32, 41; Rom 1:7; 1 Cor 1:2; Heb 13:24; etc.).

The remarkable sense of unity of all Christians, in spite of the geographical distance that separated them and the fact that the early church already included people of various backgrounds, is expressed not only in the use of *ekklesia* both for individual congregations and for Christians as a whole but especially in the image of the church as the body of Christ. The Pauline authorship of Ephesians and Colossians, where the concept appears most prominently, is challenged—and defended—but it is clearly a Pauline *idea*, at any rate. In his discussion of the issue of spiritual gifts in the church at Corinth, he spoke of the church as an organism, the body of Christ, and of Christians as parts of the body, differing, but all necessary (1 Cor 12:12–27). He repeated the same idea more briefly in Rom 12:4–8. This was a remarkable development of the belief in the continuing presence and activity of the risen Christ in the world. Christ became not only spiritually but also physically present in the world in the form of these groups of ordinary people, who felt themselves to be transformed, not only individually, but as a group. The church can thus become a part of the glorious description of the "cosmic Christ" in Col 1:15–20. "He himself is before all things, and in him all things hold together. He is the head of the body, the church; he is the beginning, the firstborn from the dead, so that he might come to have first place in everything" (vv. 17–18; cf. Eph 1:22–23; 5:27).

The letters of the NT show no interest in establishing a proper form of organization for the church. Leadership seems to have arisen spontaneously at first (as they would say: by the leading of the Holy Spirit), in order to meet the needs of the new communities. Luke reports that there were prophets and teachers in the church at Antioch (Acts 13:1). General oversight of the affairs of congregations was entrusted to elders, who would have been literally the older men who were respected for their faith, likely a carryover from the organization of the synagogue (Acts 14:23; 20:17, 28; 1 Tim 5:17; Titus 1:5; Jas 5:14; 1 Pet 5:1–5). Both men and women served as deacons (Rom 16:1; Phil 1:1; 1 Tim 3:8–13). (See *minister*.) Congregations found themselves moved by the Holy Spirit to commission certain people to travel to other parts of the world on special assignments. So the Jerusalem church sent Barnabas to Antioch to provide leadership as that church began to grow (Acts 11:22). Later the Antioch church commissioned Barnabas and Saul for mission work in Cyprus (Acts 13:2–3) and still later sent them to Jerusalem for a different reason, to discuss the question of the admission of Gentiles into the church (Acts 15).

Paul's list of spiritual gifts in 1 Cor 12 offers hints of the activities of the early congregations. They seem to have been essentially places of prayer (Acts 12:5; 14:23; Jas 5:14) and of instruction (Acts 11:26; 1 Cor 4:17; cf. 1 Cor 14:19). The Lord's Supper had become a regular part of worship (1 Cor 11:17–34). Congregations seem to have had little influence on the communities in which they lived except for their effect on the lives of those who became believers, although note the concern for hospitality and for those in prison in Heb 13:2–3. "Social action" became a significant part of church life soon after the NT period, especially as the church saw itself responsible for continuing the gracious work of Christ, in caring for the sick and the poor.

The ekklesia *in Matthew 16:18–19 and 18:15–20.* In the Gospels, the word *ekklesia* occurs only in these two passages. Jesus' message ordinarily concerned the **kingdom of God,** which is not identified with the church in the NT. For various reasons, questions have been raised about whether these two texts could have come from Jesus: (1) It is strange that Mark and Luke also record the confession of Peter (Mark 8:27–29; Luke 9:18–20) without including "you are Peter, and on this rock I will build my church," and so on. This has led to the suggestion that Matthew has added a tradition that first appeared in the early church. (2) Jesus' message focused on the coming, or presence, of the kingdom of God, an eschatological subject, about which he said nothing in terms of human organization. Matthew 16:18–19 and 18:15–20 seem to be incompatible with his real concerns. (3) In the early Palestinian church Peter did not have the exalted authority that he should have had if Matt 16:18–19 were known to that church as words of Jesus.

1. There has been a long debate over these issues, which cannot be resolved to everyone's satisfaction (for a survey, see Davies and Allison, 602–15), but several considerations make the words seem not

as out of place as the above three statements make them appear to be: (1) There is no easy explanation of why these verses appear only in Matthew, but the claim that the word *ekklesia* reveals that they were created in the Hellenistic churches is not well founded. There is general agreement about the strongly Semitic coloring of 16:17–19. Jesus began with a beatitude ("Blessed are you"), used Peter's father's name ("Simon son of Jonah"), spoke of struggle with the powers of the netherworld ("the gates of Hades"), and used a typical rabbinic expression (binding and loosing). These features do not prove that Jesus originally spoke these words, but they make a Palestinian origin more likely than an origin in the Hellenistic churches.

2. Jesus' message certainly emphasized the kingdom of God, but he also began to create a new community around himself during his ministry. In order not to misunderstand the sayings in Matt 16 and 18, it is necessary to bracket out every overtone of the English word "church" and the Greek word *ekklesia*. We cannot be sure of the Aramaic word Jesus might have used, but it may have been *kᵉnishtaʾ*, another completely neutral word, also meaning "assembly, gathering, group," and it could have referred simply to his followers. He was accompanied, at least during parts of his ministry, by more than the Twelve. According to Luke 10:1 he sent out seventy of them to preach the kingdom (10:9). A group of women went with Jesus and the Twelve, supporting them from their own resources (Luke 8:1–3). John says that at a turning point in Jesus' ministry many of his disciples deserted him (John 6:66), and it should be noted that "disciple" in the Gospels is not a word used only of the Twelve. There were about 120 who remained faithful in Jerusalem after the resurrection (Acts 1:15). The kind of issue Jesus dealt with in Matt 18:15–20 is thus one that he could anticipate during his own earthly ministry, within the "Jesus movement" (his *ekklesia*, in Matthew's Greek). There was sometimes tension within the Twelve, as when James and

John sought special places for themselves (Mark 10:35–45), and any group of seventy or one hundred people will need some provision for decision making. Since Jesus expected the kingdom to be imminent, the question remains, however, whether he would have spoken of any "organization" beyond his lifetime.

3. The question of Peter's role cannot be discussed at length here, except for brief comments on the three debated parts of Matt 16:18: "on this rock I will build my church"; "keys of the kingdom"; "whatever you bind on earth will be bound in heaven, and whatever you loose on earth will be loosed in heaven." The metaphor of building on a rock was used in another way by Jesus in Matt 7:24–25. The concept of the church as a building (noted above) led to rather free use of ideas about foundations in the Epistles. Paul could claim that he laid a foundation, and the foundation was Jesus Christ (1 Cor 3:10–11). In Ephesians, the foundation is the apostles and prophets, with Christ Jesus as the cornerstone (Eph 2:20), and 1 Pet 2:4–8 also speaks of Christ as cornerstone.

The "keys of the kingdom of heaven" do not refer to church life, since there is no NT support for equating the *ekklesia* with the kingdom. Since the keys are associated with binding and loosing, the meaning of that phrase in Jesus' time may be decisive. It referred to authoritative rabbinic teaching concerning what was forbidden (bound) and what was permitted (loosed). Later in Matthew, Jesus accused the scribes and Pharisees of locking people out of the kingdom of heaven by their teaching (Matt 23:13), and he spoke of the "key of knowledge" (Luke 11:52). Jesus affirmed that the Father in heaven had revealed to Peter the truth that he was the Messiah, the Son of the living God, and what follows may then be the promise that Peter's (and the other apostles') teaching will be confirmed in heaven (cf. 18:18–19) (Flew, 95–97).

The texts in Matthew 16 and 18 may thus have originated with Jesus, but as teaching concerning the group that followed him during his earthly ministry. If so, they need not conflict with what he said about the kingdom of God. It is very likely that Matthew used *ekklesia* in his Greek text because he took these words to be applicable to the church he knew, but it seems less likely that Jesus originally intended them that way.

Ernest Best, *One Body in Christ: A Study in the Relationship of the Church to Christ in the Epistles of the Apostle Paul* (London: SPCK, 1955); W. D. Davies and Dale C. Allison Jr., *A Critical and Exegetical Commentary on the Gospel according to Saint Matthew*, vol. 2, ICC (Edinburgh: T & T Clark, 1991); R. Newton Flew, *Jesus and His Church: A Study of the Idea of the Ecclesia in the New Testament* (London: Epworth Press, 1938); I. Howard Marshall, "New Wine in Old Wineskins: V. The Biblical Use of the Word 'Ecclesia,'" *ExpTim* 84 (1973): 359–64; Rudolf Schnackenburg, *The Church in the New Testament* (New York: Herder & Herder, 1965).

DONALD E. GOWAN

Circumcise, Circumcision

This article deals with the origins of circumcision and its meaning in the OT, the Hellenistic Jewish world, and the NT.

Etymology and meaning. The Hebrew verb for "to circumcise" is *mul* (so especially Gen 17:10), which carries the meaning "to cut, cut round," and the corresponding noun for "circumcision" is *muloth* (a feminine abstract plural; cf. Exod 4:26). The Greek (LXX) translation of this is *peritemno*, which provides the usual word in the NT for the custom of circumcision, with the corresponding noun being *peritemnos*. The Hebrew has a direct antonym for the custom in its use of the noun *'arel*, "one who is uncircumcised." This is the term used to describe Philistines in Judg 14:3 and 15:18; We should note also 1 Sam 18:25–27, where the mutilation of the corpses of David's Philistine enemies reveals the deep cultural and ethnic distinction that the custom of circumcision entailed.

In OT times the Hebrew people, as also the Egyptians and most eastern Semites, circumcised their male children (see below, on the origin of the rite), and this remains the case among many Semitic peoples up to the present day. Those, like the Philistines, who did not adopt this practice were consequently regarded as ritually and hygienically unclean. Accordingly it is noteworthy that the Greek translation of Deut 30:6 translates the Hebrew verb "to circumcise" by one meaning "to make clean," whereas in Esth 8:17 the Greek translation of a Hebrew verb meaning "to join the community" introduces a reference to circumcision as a sign of such membership.

The origin of the custom. The custom of cutting off the foreskin of young boys was practiced by many ancient African and Semitic peoples, though not without some notable exceptions. It appears to have been more prevalent among western Semites than those more eastern peoples and was certainly the custom among ancient Egyptians. The Philistines, who probably originated in the eastern Mediterranean (cf. Amos 9:7), provide the most notable biblical exception to the custom, although later Greek and Roman aversion to it served to shape subsequent Jewish and Christian attitudes. It appears originally to have been carried out before marriage and the Hebrew word for "father-in-law" suggests it was his duty to perform this action. It prepared a youth for marriage and was associated with entering puberty (a so-called rite of passage). Among some ancient and modern African communities a comparable rite is performed on girl infants, though this is never the case in the OT.

The most striking biblical instance of the carrying out of circumcision in adulthood and of its relationship to marriage, is found in Exod 4:24–27. When Moses set out to flee from Egypt, with his wife and sons (Exod 4:20), his life was threatened by no less a figure than the Lord God: "But Zipporah [Moses' wife] took a flint and cut off her son's foreskin, and touched Moses' feet with it, and said, 'Truly you are a bridegroom of blood to me!' So he [God] let him alone. It was then she said, 'A bridegroom of blood by circumcision'" (Exod 4:25–26). The action, with all its strangeness, shows every indication of retaining a very ancient custom (note the use of a flint knife) and an original link with marriage and the birth of a first child. That Zipporah acts in place of the subject's father-in-law (an Arabic word for "father-in-law" suggests this) is noteworthy, as also is the feature that a failure to perform circumcision (originally prior to marriage?) was regarded as life-threatening. The assumption that underlies the practice is that, before a new marriage could bring forth new life, the token of submission to the Lord God as the giver of life was made through circumcision. Comparable acts of submission to God before the fruits of new life could be enjoyed are indicated by regarding newly planted fruit trees as "uncircumcised" until the fourth year (Lev 19:23–25). If part of the purpose of circumcision was the concern to protect the ability of male youths to bring forth new life, it can be related to other attitudes and laws aimed at protecting male sexual potency (cf. the laws of Deut 23:1; 25:11–12).

The sign of the covenant between God and Abraham's descendants. Genesis 17:10–14, 23–27 provides the central OT passage explaining the purpose of the custom of circumcision. It is prescribed to be carried out on every male child on the eighth day after birth as a sign of his incorporation into the *covenant* made by God with Abraham and his descendants. This practice remains a central feature of Jewish life to the present day.

It seems likely that the custom is very ancient, as the use of flint knives indicates, and the age at which circumcision was carried out probably varied in different communities. It is also probable that there were variations in the interpretation placed upon it as a necessary step toward marriage and the protection of new life and safe childbirth. That there existed at one period different customs in regard to the practice of circumcision between local tribal and urban communi-

ties provides the setting for the narrative of betrayal in Gen 34:1–31. The family of Jacob refuse to permit their daughter Dinah to marry Shechem, a member of the family of Hamor, until all the male members of this family are circumcised. When this is done, and these men are still recovering from its effects, they were treacherously killed and their property taken.

According to the prescribed Jewish custom circumcision was carried out only on male children on the eighth day after birth. It is interpreted as a covenant sign of incorporation into the Jewish community, relating each male child to the heritage of Abraham and the promise of God made to this ancestral figure. Its hygienic and life-protecting concerns were largely ignored once it had become a badge of membership of the Jewish religious community. It carried significance as a physical mark of commitment to a spiritual and moral obedience to the faith of Abraham.

In the later OT period an increasing number of Jews found themselves living among Gentile neighbors who did not practice circumcision, and this experience reinforced its importance as a mark of loyalty to "the God of Abraham." The fact that its origin could be traced back to the great ancestor, even before the covenant laws given to Moses, gave to it a special significance. In consequence it acquired quite unique importance as a fundamental sign of membership of a Jewish community. This feature is highlighted in Esth 8:17 (LXX) and Jdt 14:10.

The fact that circumcision was customarily carried out in infancy, soon after birth, meant that the infant subject became aware only in later years of its religious and personal implications. If it were truly to serve as a mark of commitment to the faith of Abraham, the outward, physical sign was required to be confirmed by an inward commitment to the Jewish way of life. The OT itself contains some significant assertions that circumcision could be of no importance as a sign of membership of God's

66   Circumcise

covenant community unless it was matched by conduct demonstrating wholehearted commitment to the law of Moses. Without this inward commitment the outward sign became meaningless. Accordingly, in the course of Israel's religious development in biblical times, the physical sign, which had originated as a hygienic and social act in a Middle Eastern world, came to be regarded somewhat differently in the more western Mediterranean world, where it was not a widespread custom. It became a badge of religious loyalty and commitment to the Jewish community and exemplified adherence to a way of life shaped by obedience to the law of Moses. Its purely hygienic and anthropological origins were therefore largely left aside. The fact that it could be physically painful when carried out in adult years, and could evoke hostile responses by Gentile neighbors, made it a difficult issue for potential converts to Judaism. For these people, the unwillingness to undergo its painful demand frequently became a serious barrier to full identification with Jews and the Jewish way of life.

The spiritual meaning of circumcision. The distinctiveness of circumcision as a mark of religious loyalty made it a useful metaphor for wholeheartedness in worshiping the Lord as God. Foreigners could be described in Ezek 44:7, 9 as "uncircumcised in heart and flesh." The lack of the physical mark of covenant loyalty was taken to reveal a lack of regard for the religious and moral laws of Israel. More strikingly and enduringly important was Jeremiah's appeal to the people of Israel to "circumcise" their hearts (see *mind*), implying that, even though the outward mark was present, the inward commitment that it expressed was not (cf. also Deut 10:16)! Similarly Jer 6:10 refers to Israel's "uncircumcised" ear (NRSV Mg; see *hear*). A similar call for an inward spiritual commitment and loyalty to match the outward sign is found at Qumran in the 1QS 5.5. The implication is that, even when the outward sign of loyalty is present, the inward commitment may not

be. Whether the reverse is also true—that the inward commitment to God and the covenant may be present even when the outward sign is lacking—was later to become a major matter of controversy. It divided Jews from each other, but most especially it reflected directly on the question whether male Gentile converts to Judaism, who had not been circumcised as infants, could be admitted to the Jewish community and regarded as equal to fellow Jews who had been circumcised.

Circumcision in the Hellenistic Jewish world. In general the Greek (LXX) translation of the Hebrew OT highlights quite strongly the issue of circumcision in order to draw attention to the point that, for men, membership in the Jewish community involved its acceptance. In the Hellenistic world of late OT times, this feature of Jewish community life was regarded with suspicion by Gentile neighbors among whom the practice was not customary. As a result, when conflicts arose in which Jewish religious observance was opposed and ruthlessly attacked, the mark of circumcision was readily used as a test of Jewish loyalty (so esp. 1 Macc 1:48, 60–61). Since the physical mark of circumcision stood out as a sign of a man's commitment to the covenant that God had made with the patriarch Abraham, it was also understandable that, in a world where such religious signs of dedication could be regarded with suspicion, the practice could be ignored. In response, the Jewish rebels led by Mattathias forcibly imposed circumcision on male boys in Judea (1 Macc 2:46). Against such a background the custom had become a sign of personal commitment to Judaism and its religious laws. Conversely, attempts by some Jewish youths to eradicate the effects of circumcision, in order to demonstrate their adoption of Hellenistic culture, displayed their anxiety to throw off this badge of their traditional religion.

The issue of circumcision continued to enjoy prominence in Hellenistic and Roman times for another reason. A significant number of serious-minded Gentile men strongly admired Jewish faith and morality and wished to associate themselves with the synagogue and its worship. For them the question of whether or not they should accept circumcision in order to convert fully to Judaism became a major issue. Many would not go this far, since it was a feature of Jewish life that was painful and had no moral attraction. The custom therefore gave rise to two classes of Gentile adherents of Judaism: those who accepted circumcision and those who did not. By following the latter course, Gentile men were regarded as holding back from a full incorporation into the Jewish community. Some Jewish women married Greek (uncircumcised) men, and the question of whether to circumcise their male children then arose (cf. the case of Timothy in Acts 16:1–3). As a religious badge, therefore, the practice of circumcision took on a far wider significance than that relating to its hygienic usefulness, drawing attention to itself as a primary, but controversial, feature of Jewish allegiance. Access to the central, most sacred court of the Jewish (Herodian) temple in Jerusalem was denied to those who had not been circumcised (cf. Acts 21:28–29).

With the rise of Christianity and its spread among Gentile communities of diverse religious and ethnic origins, the question of whether converts to this greatly modified version of Jewish faith and custom should be expected to adopt circumcision became a matter of dispute. Should they follow previous Jewish practice in regard to converts, or did the "Law of Christ" set such followers of the new movement free from the need to adopt such a physical badge?

Circumcision in New Testament times. The earliest Christians were Jews; all Jewish male persons would certainly have received the sign of circumcision in infancy. This was certainly the case in regard to Jesus, and the story of his circumcision is recorded in Luke 1:59 and 2:21. The apostle Paul too had been circumcised on the eighth day after his birth, precisely as the rule of Genesis pre-

scribes (Phil 3:2). It was not until Paul's missionary endeavors had brought large numbers of Gentile converts into the new faith that the question of circumcision arose afresh to became a major issue for the early Christian church. Converts to the Christian faith who had a Jewish background would, in almost all cases, have been circumcised in infancy. But most Gentile converts would not. Many of the Gentile admirers of Jewish life and worship, who formed a group of God-fearing adherents without full membership of synagogue life, now joined the Christian church. For them the issue of circumcision would already have taken on great importance.

It appears that originally the earliest Christian communities simply perpetuated the previous Jewish practice regarding the requirement of circumcision for new converts, but very soon a firm ruling over such matters on the part of all churches became a necessity. Where the custom for new converts had varied between different Christian churches, it became essential to establish uniformity. This made it the central issue when the leading early Christian apostles and elders met at a council in Jerusalem (Acts 15:1–29). The ruling arrived at was that circumcision was not required of Christian converts, although some other aspects of Jewish customary law regarding food and personal morality were upheld as necessary (Acts 15:20, 29).

However, this meeting of church leaders held in Jerusalem did not finally settle the matter for the emerging Christian church, and dissension continued between "the circumcision faction" (cf. Gal 2:12–24) and the other group, who insisted that it was not necessary for Christians to be circumcised. It is evident that other questions concerning a wide-ranging list of obligations associated with Jewish interpretation of the law of Moses were also involved. These concerned dietary laws, the avoidance of showing respect to idols, and rigid abstention from work on the Sabbath day. Circumcision, however, was the most striking feature among those who wished to retain their observance of "Jewish" law.

The issue of circumcision and the true nature of "the Law of Christ" that it was important for Christians to follow is dealt with extensively in Paul's letter to the Galatian Christians (esp. Gal 5:2–12). The background is evidently that, after having accepted Paul's assurance that circumcision was not necessary for Gentile converts to Christianity, an influential group of Jewish Christians had taught the contrary view, with deeply disturbing consequences for the church. The firm rebuttal of the activities of these people by Paul, and the confident reaffirmation that Christians were free from the restraints and limitations of such a continuing adherence to the purely formal and customary demands of Jewish law, have made this epistle one of the foremost expositions of Christian faith. The requirement of circumcision summarized an understanding of *law* as a set of formal rules and regulations that could never, in their entirety, be fully complied with. In its place Jesus had, by his atoning sacrifice, brought Christians freedom from such a threatening law and had given a new law of love, which enabled Christians to serve both God and humanity with confidence and assurance of God's acceptance.

In this way the issue of circumcision came to represent, in the rise of the early church, a powerful test case of the nature of Christian freedom and the new power of the law of love, which Christ had brought by his sacrifice. Alongside it many other issues relating to food regulations, Sabbath observance, and the avoidance of paying respect to idolatry and idolatrous practices all came to be linked together. Faith in Jesus was not simply a road by which Gentiles were to be brought under the dominance of Jewish law, as it had developed in the Hellenistic-Roman age. In its place the new law of love spelt freedom from an understanding of faith based on the observance of a host of regulations.

Paul's refusal to accede to the demands of the early Jewish Christians in respect of the practice of circumcision also drew heavily upon a further aspect of OT teaching that was related to it. As there had already emerged in the books of Jeremiah and Deuteronomy a contrast between circumcision as a purely physical sign and a "circumcision of the heart" that expressed a true wholehearted commitment to Abraham and the Jewish way of life, so it highlighted the distinction between a religious observance of the *"flesh"* and one that embraced the *"spirit."* It was a contrast between an outward formal observance of religion and one that embraced the whole personality of a human being. Accordingly Paul's exhortation to live by the Spirit, and not to follow the way of the "flesh" (Gal 5:13–26) could also find in the different attitudes that had emerged over circumcision an exemplary feature that summarized the Christian way of life.

It is evident, from the continuing conflicts that beset the early Christian church in the first two centuries of its growth, that the problems encountered by Paul remained a matter of contention for a long time (cf. Eph 2:11–16; Col 3:11). They eventually resulted in two different expressions of Christian life, one essentially Jewish and tied to continued observance of Jewish law, and one resolutely Gentile and committed to the new freedom from such a pattern of Jewish law (cf. Col 4:11). The issue of circumcision remained a major point of conflict between Christians, as shown by the *Epistle of Barnabas* 9, and eventually resulted in the disappearance of a distinctive "Jewish Christianity" in which circumcision was regarded as necessary, whereas in Gentile churches it was not.

RONALD E. CLEMENTS

City, Jerusalem, Zion, Babylon

This article deals with the biblical treatment of cities generally and of the special cities Jerusalem and Babylon.

City. Usually in Hebrew ʿir, signifying a permanent settlement, a walled, fortified area, in contrast to temporary, unwalled settlements; occasionally in Hebrew *qiryah*; in Aramaic *qirya(h)*; in Greek *polis.*

The OT displays a certain degree of ambivalence regarding cities and city life. The biblical record of the development of the city begins in Gen 4:17 with the observation that Cain, son of Adam and Eve, a murderer (4:8), a human cursed by Yahweh (4:10–12), "built a city, and named it Enoch after his son Enoch." That the biblical writer wanted to make clear to the reader that Cain was responsible for urban ways of life is to be seen in the name "Cain." The name plays on the Hebrew word *qayin*, meaning "metalworker" or "smith." This correspondence between the name Cain (Heb. *qayin*) and the Hebrew word for "metalworker" or "smith" is developed in the genealogy at the end of Gen 4. Here Cain is portrayed as the ancestor of those who pioneered urban technology and guilds. In Gen 4:20–22, we are introduced to the descendants of Cain who were the founders of the guilds of metalworkers and smiths, musicians and tent dwellers and herders. Rather than thinking of these last two categories of individuals as groups of nomadic shepherds, it is perhaps better to think of them as individuals who lived outside the city and raised animals in support of urban populations (Frick, 205–6).

While Cain and his descendants are portrayed in Genesis as being the founders of urban culture, of positive things like metalworking and music, they are also portrayed as being very violent. The story of Cain's murder of his brother Abel in Gen 4:1–16 and the observation in Gen 4:17 that Cain "built" a city are soon followed by a song of vengeance in 4:23–24, which escalates the violence far beyond the murder of one's brother. The message is that the spread of urban culture has also brought about the spread of violence. The problem of the murder of one person's brother has become the problem of limitless vengeance and violence (see *numbers: seven*). On a more positive note, far from seeing the city as

something inherently evil, Deuteronomy saw "fine, large cities that you did not build" as part of the gift of the land that God gave to the Israelites (Deut 6:10). Two cities in particular play significant theological roles in the Bible. These two cities are Jerusalem, or Zion, and Babylon.

Jerusalem, Zion. The name "Jerusalem" has traditionally been taken to mean "city of peace" (Heb. ʿir shalom). There are difficulties with this interpretation, however. The first component of the name "Jerusalem" (Heb. *yeru*) is not the word for "city" (ʿir). It is more likely that the name "Jerusalem" goes back to pre-Israelite days and means "foundation of (the Canaanite god) Shalem." A shortened form of the name "Jerusalem" appears in Ps 76:2, where the name "Salem" (Heb. *shalem*) is used in parallel with the name "Zion." It is likely that the mention of "Salem" (Heb. *shalem*) in Gen 14:18 also refers to Jerusalem. It is perhaps due to the tradition that the city of Jerusalem was the "foundation of (the god) Shalem" that the prophet Isaiah insisted that "The LORD has founded Zion" (14:32; see also Pss 87:1; 48:8).

The derivation and meaning of the name "Zion" (Heb. *tsiyyon*) are not at all certain. Among the suggestions for the name's derivation and meaning are the following: from *tsayon*, "waterless land," "parched ground," and from *tsin*, "to protect," thus meaning "fortress."

Originally the name Zion referred to the old section of Jerusalem that was the pre-Israelite (Jebusite) city, then later to the "city of David" (2 Sam 5:7). In the Psalter, though, the name "Zion" is often used to refer to the Temple Mount, God's "holy hill" (Ps 2:6), the location that Yahweh "has desired . . . for his habitation" (Ps 132:13). Eventually, the name "Zion" came to be used synonymously with the name "Jerusalem." While the name "Jerusalem" appears in the OT in both poetic and prose texts, with prose texts predominating, "Zion" is found most frequently in poetry.

After David became king over Judah (2 Sam 2:4), then of Israel (5:1–5), he realized the need for a capital that would unify the various tribes that had entered into alliance under his leadership. He found such a capital in Jerusalem. Second Samuel 5:6–10 recounts David's capture of Jerusalem from the Jebusites. It is a difficult text to understand. What is clear is that David and his mercenaries captured the Jebusite "stronghold of Zion" in a commando-style raid and renamed it "the city of David." With the assistance of Hiram, king of Tyre, David erected a house for himself at Jerusalem and made Jerusalem the royal center for the kingdom (5:11–12).

Soon thereafter, David brought the ark of the covenant (see *presence*) to Jerusalem (6:1–23). David's son and successor Solomon erected a temple that would serve as an enduring resting place for the ark (1 Kgs 6–7). Since all of the tribes in the confederation revered the ark and viewed it as the presence of God among the people of God, the presence of the ark in Jerusalem strengthened Jerusalem's position as the center of the kingdom. Jerusalem became not just the "city of David," the city where the king dwelt. With the arrival of the ark of the covenant, Jerusalem also became the "city of (our) God" (Pss 46:4; 48:1, 8; 87:3), the "city of the LORD of hosts" (Ps 48:8), the city where God dwelt (Pss 9:11; 76:2; 132:13–14; 135:21; Isa 8:18). In fact, it was presence of the ark of the covenant in Jerusalem and the erection of the temple as a resting place for the ark that secured Jerusalem's unique status among the cities of Israel and Judah. Jerusalem's theological significance was grounded in the presence of the ark in Jerusalem and in the belief that the ark was the representation of the presence of God among the people of God (Noth).

The presence of the ark of the covenant in Jerusalem and the unique status of Jerusalem as the city of God did not prevent Jerusalem from becoming corrupted by human sin, though. Several prophets uttered oracles of judgment against Judah as a nation and against Jerusalem specifically as the capital city

where the religious and political leaders established policy. The prophets indicted Jerusalem and its leaders for rebellion against God, for ethical and social sins against the poor and the disenfranchised, and for political sin in which the leaders in Jerusalem courted the favor of pagan nations. Oracles of judgment against Judah and Jerusalem can be found throughout Isa 1–12; Jer 2–25; Ezek 1–24; and in Mic 3:9–12 and Zeph 1.

Several key themes developed as a part of the theology that centered on Jerusalem (the five themes discussed below are adapted from King, 764).

1. *God chose Jerusalem as the place where the divine presence would dwell.* As noted above, the Psalter heralded Jerusalem as the city that God had chosen for the divine presence to dwell (Pss 9:11; 76:2; 132:13–14; 135:21; see also Isa 8:18). Deuteronomy 12:5 came to be understood as the definitive statement declaring Yahweh's choice of Jerusalem as the place where the divine presence would dwell. Even though Jerusalem is not named in Deut 12:5, this verse came to be understood as sanctioning Jerusalem— and only Jerusalem—as a place of worship. God chose Jerusalem "out of all your tribes as his habitation to put his name there. You shall go there." According to this verse, God's *name* will dwell as the manifestation of the presence and power of God at the place that God chooses.

Using language borrowed from Deuteronomy, the books of Kings speak of Jerusalem as the city that God has chosen as the dwelling for the divine name out of all the tribes of Israel (1 Kgs 11:13, 32, 36; 14:21; 2 Kgs 21:4, 7; see also 2 Chr 6:6; 7:16; 12:13; 33:7).

2. *Jerusalem is a holy city and Zion is a holy mountain, the spiritual center of the earth.* Isaiah 45:13; 48:2; 52:1; 60:14; Pss 46:4; 48:1, 8; 101:8 all proclaim Jerusalem to be the city of God. Zion, the Temple Mount, is identified as the mountain or hill of Yahweh in Ps 24:3; Isa 2:3; 30:29; Mic 4:2; Zech 8:3. In Ps 87:1; Isa 27:13; Zech 8:3, Zion is referred to as "the holy

mountain," in Ps 2:6 God refers to Zion as "my holy hill," and in Pss 48:1; 99:9 the designation is "his [i.e., God's] holy mountain."

The geography of theology does not need to correspond to the geography of mapmaking. The Temple Mount is not the highest mountain in the region. Yet in the theology of the Zion tradition, Zion is exalted as "the high mount" (Pss 68:18; 87:1). The eschatological poem in Isa 2:2–4 and Mic 4:1–4 goes beyond the affirmation that Zion is "the high mount" and looks for a day when, "the mountain of the LORD's house shall be established as the highest of the mountains, and shall be raised above the hills" (Isa 2:2; Mic 4:1).

Just as in theological geography Zion was a "high mount" or even "the highest of the mountains," so in theological geography Jerusalem was "in the center of the nations, with countries all around her" (Ezek 5:5). And Jerusalem was "at the center (literally, "navel") of the earth" (Ezek 38:12).

3. *Since God founded Jerusalem and chose Jerusalem as the place where the divine name should dwell, and since Jerusalem was holy and exalted as God's holy hill, the city was invulnerable and could not be touched by enemy armies.* Some of the psalms announced that God would protect Jerusalem from powerful foes (Pss 46; 48; 76). Undoubtedly, the mysterious deliverance of Jerusalem from the Assyrian assault of 701 B.C. (2 Kgs 18:13–19:37; Isa 36:1–37:38) would have contributed to the development of the idea that Jerusalem was unconquerable. All of the other towns in Judah fell to the mighty army of Assyria. But not Jerusalem! When faced with the dire threat of the Assyrian assault on Jerusalem in 701 B.C., the prophet Isaiah confidently prophesied the word of God: "I will defend this city to save it, for my own sake and for the sake of my servant David" (Isa 37:35; see all of 37:33–35; see also 38:6).

Isaiah's contemporary Micah, however, did not accept the idea that Jerusalem was invulnerable. In fact, when Micah looked at the sin of Jerusalem

(3:9–11) and listened to the affirmations of false security from corrupt leaders (3:11b), his only conclusion was that "Zion shall be plowed as a field; Jerusalem shall become a heap of ruins, and the mountain of the house a wooded height" (3:12).

But Jerusalem was not destroyed as Micah had prophesied. It seemed as if the belief in the invulnerability of Jerusalem had won the day. A century after Micah's time, however, the prophet Jeremiah began to warn that, contrary to the popular belief that Jerusalem was indestructible, the city was, in fact, going to be destroyed. In his famous temple sermon, Jeremiah urged the people to amend their ways and warned the people not to listen to "deceptive words" that falsely assured them of the safety of the temple of the Lord (7:1–15). It is interesting to note that Mic 3:12 was quoted at Jeremiah's trial (Jer 26:18–19).

In 587/6 B.C., the Babylonians proved that Jerusalem could indeed be destroyed. In January of 587 B.C., Nebuchadnezzar, king of Babylon, laid siege to Jerusalem. The siege dragged on for a year and a half, and eventually all the food in Jerusalem ran out. In July of 586 B.C., Jerusalem's fortifications were breached and the city fell to Babylon (2 Kgs 25:1–7; Jer 52:3b–11; see also the book of Lamentations). A month later, in August of 586 B.C., the Babylonians destroyed the city walls and burned the temple, the palace, and the houses of the most influential people. The residents of Jerusalem, individuals who somehow survived the lengthy siege, were exiled to Babylon.

After the destruction of Jerusalem, the prophets began to look forward to the building of a new city of Jerusalem and a new temple of God (Jer 30:18–22; 31:38–40; Hag 2:6–9; Zech 8:3–8; Isa 40:1–2; 52:1–2, 7–10). In a poignant vision Ezekiel saw God leave Jerusalem and the temple because of the sinfulness of the city (9:3; 10:18–19; 11:22–25). But then, in his final vision (chaps. 40–48), Ezekiel saw the glorious return of God to a new temple and a new Jerusalem (43:1–9).

Similarly, in Zech 8:3 God promises to return to Zion to "dwell in the midst of Jerusalem."

4. *A wonderfully miraculous stream (of healing* **water**) *will flow from God's mountain.* The prophetic vision for a new Jerusalem included the image of a river or spring that flows from the Temple Mount (Ezek 47:1–12; Joel 3:18; Zech 14:8; Ps 46:4).

5. *All nations will make pilgrimage to Jerusalem as a way of affirming the sovereignty of God.* The eschatological poem in Isa 2:2–4 and Mic 4:1–4 announces that "all the nations shall stream" to Jerusalem and that "many peoples" will want to come to Jerusalem to receive instruction in the ways and word of God. The most complete elaboration of the theme is in Isa 60. Psalm 87 develops the theme in such a way that Zion becomes everyone's spiritual home. See also Isa 11:12; Jer 3:17; Zech 2:11; 8:22.

Jerusalem is frequently mentioned in the Gospel narratives. It is, however, mentioned only a few times by Jesus in his recorded teachings. In his third passion prediction in the Synoptic Gospels, Jesus declares, "See, we are going up to Jerusalem" (Matt 20:18; Mark 10:33; Luke 18:31). Jerusalem is also mentioned in Matthew's record of the first passion prediction (16:21). Jesus offers a lament over Jerusalem in Matt 23:37–39, and Luke 13:34–35; in Luke 13:33 Jesus comments that "it is impossible for a prophet to be killed outside of Jerusalem." Jesus also mentions Jerusalem in Matt 5:35; Luke 10:30; 13:4. In the Gospel of John, Jesus tells a Samaritan woman that "the hour is coming when you will worship the Father neither on this mountain [meaning Mount Gerizim] nor in Jerusalem" (4:21).

Jerusalem is most prominent in the Gospel according to Luke. In 2:22–23, Luke tells of the presentation of Jesus at the temple in Jerusalem, and in 2:41–50 he reports Jesus' pilgrimage to the temple at age twelve.

Luke gives an account of Jesus' Galilean ministry in 4:14–9:50. Near the end of this record of Jesus' Galilean ministry, Luke, in his report of the transfiguration of Jesus, refers to what Jesus was "about to accomplish at Jerusalem" (9:31). Matthew and Luke do not mention Jerusalem in their reports of the transfiguration.

After narrating the events of Jesus' Galilean ministry, Luke devotes a sizable section of his Gospel to a travel narrative in which Jesus resolutely travels to Jerusalem in order to fulfill his messianic destiny. Luke begins his story of Jesus' journey to Jerusalem in 9:51: "When the days drew near for him to be taken up, he set his face to go to Jerusalem" (see also 9:53). To remind his readers of Jesus' final destination, Luke makes further references to Jerusalem in the course of Jesus' journey in 13:22; 17:11; 19:11.

The important role of Jerusalem in the Gospel of Luke is also apparent in chapter 24. Here Luke reports Jesus' postresurrection appearances, and in the Gospel of Luke (as opposed to Matthew), all of the appearances take place in and around the city of Jerusalem.

Jerusalem serves as a geographical hinge between the Gospel of Luke and the Acts of the Apostles. In Acts 1:8, which serves as the program for ministry and the verse around which the rest of the book of Acts is structured, Jerusalem is the center of ministry, the starting point from which the message of the gospel will spread into "all Judea and Samaria, and to the ends of the earth."

Matthew twice refers to Jerusalem as "the holy city" (4:5; 27:53). In John's Gospel, Jesus makes three trips to Jerusalem in the course of his ministry.

In his allegory of Hagar and Sarah, Paul created a polarity between "the present Jerusalem," the Jerusalem that is here on earth, and "the Jerusalem above," a heavenly perfect Jerusalem (Gal 4:25–26). The writer of the letter to the Hebrews mentions this "heavenly Jerusalem" in 12:22 and alludes to it in 11:10, 16. Early in the Revelation to John (3:12), mention is made of "the new Jerusalem that comes down from my God out of heaven." In Rev 14:1, John sees "the Lamb, standing on Mount Zion," and with him were the

144,000 (see *numbers*). Here, as in the OT, Jerusalem is the gathering place of the faithful, the spiritual center to which the people of God come. The reference to "the new Jerusalem" in Rev 3:12 sets the stage for the more complete description of "the holy city, the new Jerusalem," in 21:1–22:5.

Babylon. Hebrew *babel;* Greek *babylon.* Genesis 11:9 plays on the name of the city Babel by deriving the name from the Hebrew root *balal,* "to mix," "to confuse," "to confound." The Babylonians commonly understood the name of their city to mean "gate of God."

The story in Gen 11:1–9 recounts the building of "a city, and a tower with its top in the heavens" (v. 4a). The reference to "a tower with its top in the heavens" fits well the common Babylonian understanding of the meaning of the name of their city, "gate of God." Undoubtedly, the tower of Babel in the story in Gen 11:1–9 reflects a memory of the great temple towers known as ziggurats that were an important feature in the cities of ancient Mesopotamia.

Clearly the building of this city and tower in Gen 11:1–9 was something that disturbed God. With the building of the "city, and a tower with its top in the heavens," the boundary between the divine and humans was being threatened. Verse 6 records God's concern that the building of the city and tower was "only the beginning of what they will do; nothing that they propose to do will now be impossible for them." Thus the story of the building of the city and tower in Gen 11:1–9 has been interpreted as a return to the concern that first surfaced in Gen 3:5, 22 that people might become like God. The story has been interpreted as a story of human presumption and pride. But the story in Gen 11:1–9 also functions as a critique of the accumulation of godlike power in cities, power that can be used for destructive purposes, power that has to be stopped by divine intervention.

Several prophetic oracles announce God's judgment on Babylon (see Isa 13–14; 47; Jer 50–51). Yet Jeremiah wrote a letter to the exiles in Babylon (chap. 29) urging them to build homes, plant gardens, and have families in Babylon. He explained that the exile was not going to end any time soon, so they would do well to establish lives for themselves in their city of captivity.

The judgment that was prophesied against Babylon in the OT finds significant development in the Revelation to John in the NT. Except for statements about the Babylonian exile in Matt 1:11, 12, 17, a quotation of Amos 5:25–27 in Acts 7:42–43, and a mention in 1 Pet 5:13, the only other references to Babylon in the NT are in Revelation (14:8; 16:19; 17:5; 18:2, 10, 21). Babylon is the name given to the evil power of the end time. It is described as "the great city that rules over the kings of the earth" (17:18), "the great city" (18:10, 16, 18, 19, 21), and "the mighty city" (18:10). An angel announces the fall of Babylon in 14:8: "Fallen, fallen is Babylon the great!" In 17:1–19:10, John vividly reports a vision of Babylon and its fall. Babylon is portrayed as "the great whore" (17:1; 19:2) on whose forehead "was written a name, a mystery: 'Babylon the great, mother of whores and of earth's abominations'" (17:5). The whore was "sitting on a scarlet beast (see *animals*) . . . and it had seven heads and ten horns" (17:3). This beast is the same beast that John described in 13:1 as "having ten horns and seven heads." Revelation 17:9 explains that the "seven heads" represent "seven mountains." Rome was built on seven hills. We can conclude therefore that John saw Babylon, the wicked city of the OT, as a symbol for Rome, the wicked city of the NT. It is likely that the reference to "Babylon" in 1 Pet 5:13 is also a symbolic reference to Rome.

Frank S. Frick, *The City in Ancient Israel* (Missoula, Mont.: Scholars Press, 1977; Donald E. Gowan, *Eschatology in the Old Testament* (Philadelphia: Fortress Press, 1986; Edinburgh: T. & T. Clark, 2000), 4–20; Leslie J. Hoppe, *The Holy City: Jerusalem in the Theology of the Old Testament* (Collegeville, Minn.: Liturgical Press, 2000); Philip J. King, "Jerusalem," *ABD* 3:747–66;

Martin Noth, "Jerusalem and the Israelite Tradition," in *The Laws in the Pentateuch and Other Essays* (Philadelphia: Fortress Press, 1967), 132–44.

JAMES A. DURLESSER

Clean, Cleanse, Defile, Impure, Profane, Pure, Unclean

Leviticus 10:10 charges priests "to distinguish between the holy and the common, and between the unclean and the clean." That mandate presents two related but distinct oppositions. The world of the *holy* includes, of course, the deity: "Holy, holy, holy is the LORD of hosts" (Isa 6:3). However, many things other than the deity may be holy. There are holy times, holy places, holy people, and holy objects. The world of cleanness is quite different, since it focuses on the world of humanity and life on earth and does not regularly involve the world of the deity. One does not normally speak of clean time or clean places (see, however, Lev 10:14), though on occasion a text may refer to an unclean object (e.g., a clay pot, Lev 11:33). Normally, the language of cleanness refers to the world of animal and human life, especially humans as clean or unclean. The sphere of clean/unclean is, therefore, more limited in scale than is that of holy/common.

The binary opposition between clean and unclean is regularly expressed in Hebrew by the terms *tahor* and *tame᾽* respectively. *Tahor*, normally translated "clean," can, however, bear other meanings. For example, when biblical texts speak of solid gold, they use the adjective *tahor*, which in that case means "pure gold" (e.g., Exod 25:11). Similarly, undiluted olive oil may also be "pure" (Lev 24:2). When used to describe people, and apart from the ritual sphere, *tahor* may also signify a morally blameless individual. The term stands in parallelism with words or phrases such as "right" (Prov 20:11), "gracious in speech" (Prov 22:11), "upright" (Job 8:6), "no iniquity" (Job 33:9), "clean hands." Here, in Psalms and Wisdom literature, the notion of purity involves an ethical rather than an essentially ritual character.

The Hebrew adjective *tame᾽* is routinely translated as "unclean" or "defiled." The verbal forms differ in nuance. The Qal conjugation seems to focus on ritual uncleanness, whereas the Niphal and Piel forms also include reference to sexual misdeeds (e.g., Gen 34:5).

Uncleanness is probably best viewed as a condition or situation into which a human might enter. Uncleanness is also a condition to be avoided and a status that, when incurred, is to be reversed. A person might become unclean through a natural process, such as emitting a liquid, touching something unclean, or eating unclean food. Menstruation would be an example of the first, touching a lizard of the second, eating shrimp of the third. In addition, an individual might be defiled by committing an egregious moral or religious misdeed, for example, by worshiping a deity other than Yahweh or by murdering someone. One has a sense that the OT attests to quite different types of uncleanness.

The OT, especially the book of Leviticus, invests considerable attention to describing at least five ways by means of which a person might become unclean: by eating an unclean animal or touching its corpse (Lev 11), by giving birth (Lev 12), by having a skin disease (Lev 13–14), by generating a bodily discharge (Lev 15), and by touching a human corpse (Num 19). These five forms of uncleanness involve, for the most part, "natural" uncleanness, that is, things unavoidable in typical human life. In each instance, the text also describes the manner in which the uncleanness may be removed. If one touches the carcass of an unclean animal, that uncleanness will wear off by evening. However, if the carcass touched clothing, it must be washed. (Simply touching an unclean animal that is alive apparently does not make a person unclean.) The uncleanness that results from childbirth lasts longer. A woman must wait thirty-three days after giving birth to a son before making a purificatory sacrifice and sixty-six days if she bears a daughter. Here both time and a burnt offering are required. Skin disease involves both detailed diagnosis (Lev 13) and complex purification (Lev 14). As with childbirth, both time and ritual are involved. Once the disease has passed, a complex set of rituals takes place over a period of eight days. Bodily discharges of men (e.g., semen) and women (e.g., blood) may also create a state of uncleanness. The biblical text addresses ejaculations of various types. That of normal sexual intercourse requires bathing and involves a state of uncleanness of less than one day, whereas seminal emission of a diseased type demands a period of eight days and further bathing. A woman's discharge of blood is similarly parsed according to its normalcy or abnormality and with differing purifications. Finally, contact with a human corpse creates a form of uncleanness that lasts for seven days. Such corpse defilement requires acts of ritual ablution.

According to the priestly authors, thoroughgoing concern with such contamination is designed to "keep the people of Israel separate from their uncleanness, so that they do not die in their uncleanness by defiling my tabernacle that is in their midst" (Lev 15:31). Such a formulation implies that there will always be uncleanness, but that it must be kept under control so that it does not ultimately desecrate the deity's holy space. However, the requirements for cleanness seem to involve far more than the risk of defiling the tabernacle. The home—rather than the tabernacle—is the primary place where most uncleanness would occur. Hence concern for remaining clean was something germane to everyday life—eating, bodily functions, sexuality. Moreover, decisions about whether or not something is unclean were, finally, left to the priests as arbiters over these areas of personal life. (A priest has the power to pronounce someone clean; so Lev 13:6, 13, 17, 23, 28, 34.) To that extent, laws involving cleanness are more "invasive" than are those involving

holiness, which focus primarily on the world of sacral places and acts.

Various objects can engender uncleanness. Contemporary readers are probably not surprised that a human corpse is viewed as unclean. However, the reasons why certain animals are deemed clean or unclean are less obvious. In several places, the OT offers a list of those animals that are appropriate and inappropriate for human consumption (Lev 11; Deut 14). The basic conception is fourfold: animals, aquatic creatures, birds, and insects. In each instance, the category is parsed in a binary fashion. Animals have a cloven hoof or not; they do or do not chew their cud. Clean animals are those with cloven hoofs and those who chew their cud. Aquatic creatures may have fins or not; scales or not. Clean "fish" have fins and scales. The situation with birds is less clear, since neither list offers comparable binary categories. Instead the lists stipulate only those birds that are unclean—many of which either are raptors or eat carrion. Finally, insects are categorized according to whether or not they walk on all fours and whether they have "jointed legs." Those that walk and have such legs may be consumed. One looks in vain for some common denominator among those four categories deemed permissible for human consumption. The list clearly includes domestic land animals, "typical" fish, birds that do not consume flesh (e.g., by implication, the dove or quail), and locusts or grasshoppers. In all four cases, such foods, especially the first three, were characteristic of the Israelite diet. Hence, to a certain extent, these laws regarding food items may be less of a prohibition and more of a ratification of ancient Israelite dietary practice, a social mode that distinguished that culture from certain of its neighbors. (N.B., vegetable life is not classified as either clean or unclean. The absence of such classification presumably reflects the importance of blood, which was absent from flora but not fauna. Grain might become unclean only if it is contaminated by the corpse of an unclean animal.)

A person might become unclean in a surprising way, namely, through contact with the world of the holy. For example, the priest who officiates at the ceremony by means of which corpse contamination is removed becomes unclean. That uncleanness results not from the corpse contamination but from contact with the ritual materials (ash, water) used to remove the contamination. Similarly, the priest who sends the goat into the wilderness on the Day of Atonement becomes unclean and requires cleansing (Lev 16). Here it becomes clear that holiness can create uncleanness, a phenomenon no doubt related to the dangerous quality of the holy.

The world of uncleanness or defilement (tame') is far broader than these lists in the Tetrateuch. Other forms of behavior could result in uncleanness. The world of sexuality was especially important. For example, according to Gen 34, an Israelite author viewed Dinah to have been made unclean by her sexual intercourse with Shechem. In a similar vein, a married woman who has sexual intercourse with a man other than her husband is "defiled" (Num 5:11–31; Ezek 18:6). So too, non-Yahwistic religious practices could create radical uncleanness (so Ezek 5:11, which surely refers to the acts of religious impropriety described in Ezek 8).

Leviticus 18:19–30, part of the Holiness Code, is also concerned with cleanness/uncleanness in the area of sexuality and religious malpractice. These verses are unusual in the Holiness Code to the extent that they utilize the vocabulary of defilement, language infrequent elsewhere in the Code. (In the book of Leviticus, moral infractions apart from the world of sexual mores are rarely construed to create uncleanness; cf. Isa 59:3.)

The forms of defilement just described focus on the behavior of individuals. However, ancient Israelite authors also address uncleanness or defilement created by the community at large. Such acts could result in the defilement of more than a person. Ezekiel, using the metaphoric Oholah and Oholibah can speak of

Israel defiling the temple (Ezek 23:38; see also Jer 32:34). Hosea refers to the whorish behavior that defiles all of Israel (5:3; 6:10). Jeremiah charges Israel with "defiling my land" (Jer 2:7) due to the veneration of Baal. One senses a certain theology at work in these judgments. Whereas an individual might engage in inappropriate religious, sexual, or other behavior and become unclean as a result, if the community as a whole undertakes such activity, the temple, the land, or the community as a whole becomes defiled and subject to punishment by the deity.

As noted above, the OT knows various types of uncleanness. Scholars have attempted to conceptualize this variety. For example, David Wright has classified uncleanness into two basic categories: permitted and prohibited impurities. This useful disjunction differentiates permitted impurities, which belong to natural or innate human behaviors or bodily functions, and prohibited impurities, which derive from voluntary or willful activities that are primarily immoral. Most forms of permitted uncleanness are cited in Lev 11–16 and Numbers 19. They share an ability to have the uncleanness removed. Prohibited uncleanness is attested more broadly in the OT, that is, well beyond the books of Leviticus and Numbers.

In a move beyond Wright, Klawans has maintained that the Hebrew Bible contains reference to two quite distinct forms of defilement: ritual impurity and moral impurity. Klawans has identified five essential differences between these two types of defilement. (1) Ritual impurity does not stem from sin, whereas moral impurity derives from terrible deeds, especially sexual misdeeds (e.g., adultery), idolatry, and homicide. (2) Ritual impurity involves a contagious quality, whereas moral impurity does not. (3) Ritual impurity is temporary, subject to erosion by time, whereas moral impurity is permanent. (4) Rites of purification can help remove ritual impurity, whereas only punishment or atonement can remove moral impurity, if in fact the defilement can be absolved. Often, there is no way for the impurity to be removed, apart from the death or banishment of the responsible party. (5) The OT uses different vocabulary for these concepts. The discourse of *"abomination"* and "pollution" belongs to the world of moral impurity, but not to that of ritual impurity. In sum, the OT attests two essentially different forms of uncleanness.

Attention to the variable of gender offers an interesting perspective on the world of cleanness and uncleanness. Being a female or giving birth to a female involves a greater propensity toward uncleanness. Menstruation would mean that a woman is automatically unclean on a monthly basis. There is nothing comparable for males. Further, a woman who bears a son is unclean for seven days, whereas if she bears a girl, she is unclean for fourteen days. The reason for the female gender to have a greater proclivity toward uncleanness may betray the gender identity of those who created the strictures regarding cleanness.

This gender variable has affected the lexicography of uncleanness. For example, the Hebrew noun *niddah* bears a root meaning of menstrual blood, though it has in many recent English translations been translated as "impurity." Leviticus 15:24 offers a clear case. "If any man lies with her [i.e., a woman who is having a period], and her *niddah* falls on him, he shall be unclean seven days." There can be little question that *niddah* here simply means menstrual blood. However, since menstrual blood creates a ritual state of uncleanness, modern translators have linked the two notions. So did ancient Israelite writers. For them, *niddah* came to mean not only uncleanness quite apart from menstrual blood; it also was used to describe acts of moral impurity, such as improper sexual intercourse (Lev 20:21) or acts of religious turpitude (2 Chr 29:5) —here the noun is translated as "filth." Of course, once such a semantic extension took place, it connoted these meanings back onto the natural uncleanness of menstrual blood.

One might wonder why life in the world that God created should be deemed "unclean." The priestly theology found in Gen 1 deemed the world to be good, and the world of humanity to be "very good" (Gen 1:31). This is the same religious tradition that is elsewhere so concerned about uncleanness. How is it then that innate human activity, such as childbirth, should result in uncleanness? Children are good, as is motherhood. If one builds on the distinction between ritual and moral impurity, then one may say that although childbirth—probably because of the presence of blood—creates ritual impurity, it does not involve sin or immorality. Uncleanness in the OT need not connote something that is evil or wrong.

Cleanness was a special requirement of God's people, not of all humanity. As such a requirement, cleanness distinguished Israel from other communities. Mary Douglas has argued that the (clean) body symbolizes the (clean) community. And Israel, during the time that many of the stipulations regarding cleanness were formulated, was a community concerned with its identity, with defining who did and did not belong to that religious community. Porosity—places where the community or the body was open to the outside, for example, through either ingestion or egestion—required special attention. Laws about diet were analogous to laws about marriage, since both involved similar issues: who might enter the community and what might enter the body.

New Testament authors were concerned about the categories of unclean and clean, especially with regard to the consumption of food. However, both postbiblical Jewish and Greco-Roman literature addressed notions of defilement. One may, therefore, not simply "jump" from the Hebrew Bible to the NT, without recognizing the significant evidence from the Dead Sea Scrolls and the Hebrew Bible Apocrypha, among other literature. Klawans has argued that one leitmotif in the literature deriving from this period was the question of the relation between moral and ritual impurity. Did sin make one impure? Did impurity bear a moral connotation? The categories were biblical, but the answers were charted after the Torah achieved canonical force. At Qumran, for example, some writers maintained that ritual and moral impurity were part of a single system. For them, impurity was sinful. This view was not shared by all Jewish writers.

For early Christians, a central question was whether or not the requirements of Jewish Torah observance were mandatory for early Christians. Pauline literature appears to offer a principle by means of which to structure the debate: "Nothing is unclean in itself" (Rom 14:14), which affirms the just-stated motif in Gen 1. However, Paul goes on to maintain that concern for another person's well-being should guide how one deals with food and drink. Paul here includes in his reflection the consumption of wine as something potentially hurtful, though not expressly unclean. (Wine, of course, was never viewed as unclean in the OT.) In a similar vein (1 Cor 8), Paul appears to believe that eating food that had been part of a sacrifice to idols, though in principle not problematic, may cause the fall of someone who is less sophisticated. Here again, the pragmatics of communal concern are more important than the observance of ritual purity.

The situation in the Gospels is somewhat different. There are two key texts: Mark 7:15 and Matt 5:8. In the first, Jesus is quoted: "There is nothing outside a person that by going in can defile, but the things that come out are what defile." In the ensuing verses, this somewhat enigmatic saying, called a "parable," is spelled out for the disciples. "The things that come out" are understood to be vices, not physical matter. This interpretation construes Jesus as addressing moral issues, not those involving dietary practice. Of course, it is possible that Mark 7:15 originally referred to dietary practice (or was even linked to debates about eating with "defiled hands," so 7:1)

but has later been edited in order to move the conversation in another direction. Matthew 5:8, one of the Beatitudes, reads as follows: "Blessed are the pure in heart, for they will see God." Here again, proper character, exemplified by the image of a pure heart, rather than the consumption of clean food, is at stake for one of the Gospel writers or redactors. Concern for moral purity seems to have taken priority over concern for ritual purity.

Luke-Acts offers a parade text, Acts 10:10–16, concerning an even broader issue involving the world of the unclean. In a trance, Peter experiences a number of unclean animals, which the deity commands Peter to kill and eat. When Peter demurs, he is admonished, "What God has made clean, you must not call profane." Later in that same chapter, we learn that what at first appears to be an issue involving dietary practice involves instead the conversion of Gentiles. Peter then says, "I truly understand that God shows no partiality, but in every nation anyone who fears him and does what is right is acceptable to him" (Acts 10:34–35). The Gentile is not to be viewed as impure, but is, rather, eligible to be part of the church.

The NT, then, deploys the language of cleanness and defilement in ways understandable within the debates about these issues in postbiblical Jewish literature. In addition, some NT writers used this discourse to argue on behalf of redefining those who are eligible to become its members, namely, those who might otherwise have been deemed to be unclean—whether as Jewish tax collectors or Gentiles.

In conclusion, the notions of cleanness and uncleanness encompass different worlds, including both ritual and moral issues. In the OT both are important, though one tradition may highlight ritual issues (e.g., the "priestly" portions of Leviticus), and another may highlight moral issues (e.g., the Holiness Code in Leviticus). Concerns for ritual cleanness, as exemplified by the dietary laws, seems to have several functions, one of which was to create an Israelite identity. Concern for moral cleanness involved broader moral norms, such as concern for the sanctity of a family or for human life. Here Israel affirmed values shared by other cultures. After the formation of the Hebrew Bible, those who lived out of its ethos wrestled with the relationship between these two worlds of cleanness. In some cases, they were merged; in others, one was given greater priority than another. In the NT, most writers deemed moral cleanness to be more important than ritual purity.

G. Anderson and S. Olyan, eds., *Priesthood and Cult in Ancient Israel*, JSOTSup 125 (Sheffield: Sheffield Academic Press, 1991); Mary Douglas, *Purity and Danger: An Analysis of the Concepts of Pollution and Taboo* (London: Routledge & Kegan Paul, 1966); Frank Gorman, *Divine Presence and Community: A Commentary on the Book of Leviticus*, ITC (Grand Rapids: Eerdmans, 1997); Frank Gorman, *The Ideology of Ritual: Space, Time, and Status in the Priestly Theology*, JSOTSup 91 (Sheffield: Sheffield Academic Press, 1990); P. Jenson, *Graded Holiness: A Key to the Priestly Conception of the World*, JSOTSup 106 (Sheffield: Sheffield Academic Press, 1992); Joseph Klawans, *Purity and Sin in Ancient Judaism* (New York: Oxford University Press, 2000); I. Knohl, *The Sanctuary of Silence: The Priestly Torah and the Holiness School* (Minneapolis: Fortress, 1995); B. Levine, *Leviticus*, JPS Torah Commentary (Philadelphia: Jewish Publication Society, 1989); B. Levine, *Numbers 1–20*, AB 4A (New York: Doubleday, 1993); J. Milgrom, *Leviticus 1–16*, AB 3 (New York: Doubleday, 1991).

DAVID L. PETERSEN

Cloud, Pillar of   *see* **Presence**

Command, Commandment   *see* **Law**

Compassion   Several Hebrew words are translated "compassion" in the NRSV without a clear pattern emerging. *Raham/rehum* (*"mercy"*), *hanan/hannun* (*"grace"*), *hamal* (*"pity"*), and *naham* ("console," *"repent"*) are all translated "compassion" in selective texts. God states, "If your neighbor cries out to me, I will listen, for I am compassionate" (*hannun*; Exod 22:27). Moses exhorts the Israelites to avoid contact with objects devoted to God under the ban "so that the LORD may turn from his fierce anger and show you compassion (*rahamim*), and in his compassion (*raham*) multiply you" (Deut 13:17). Yahweh warns the city of Jerusalem, "No eye pitied you, to do any of these things for you out of compassion (*hamal*) for you" (Ezek 16:5). And God proclaims judgment against the northern kingdom with the words "Compassion (*noham*) is hidden from my eyes" (Hos 13:14). The translations indicate that the English word "compassion" is used to convey a range of meanings about the concern of God for the oppressed, divine and human pity, the avoidance of punishment, and even fertility.

The Hebrew phrase consisting of the verb *kamar* (to grow hot, excited) with either the noun *raham* (mercy) or *noham* (console) provides definition for compassion in the Hebrew Bible. The phrase first appears in the story of Joseph, who, upon seeing his brother Benjamin after many years of separation, runs out of the room weeping, because he "was overcome with affection" (*nikmeru rahamayw* = "his mercy/compassion was hot," Gen 43:30). The phrase returns in the story of Solomon and the two prostitutes, each of whom claim the same baby. When Solomon suggests cutting the baby in half to satisfy the competing claims of the two women, the genuine mother offers to give away her child, "because compassion for her son burned within her" (*nikmeru rahameha* = "her mercy/compassion was hot," 1 Kgs 3:26). God shares the same emotion toward Israel in the book of Hosea, stating, "How can I give you up Ephraim? . . . My heart recoils within me; my compassion grows warm and tender (*nikmeru nihumay* = "my sorrow is hot," 11:8). Compassion in each instance is such an intense identification with another that the passion of the relationship dictates the action (in this sense compassion is similar to *love*). Joseph is unable to maintain the charade with his brothers upon seeing Benjamin, a mother is willing to give up her child for its life, and God is willing to act against divinely established justice to preserve Israel.

Several Greek words are also translated "compassion" in the NRSV of the NT. The emotional identification with another continues to be the root idea in the different words. The author of Hebrews reminds his audience of their past "compassion for those who were in prison" (Heb 10:34), using the Greek word "sympathy" (*sympatheo*). The author of James (5:11) describes God as "compassionate (*polysplanchnos*) and merciful (*hypomeinantas*), using language that also describes divine pity and *patience*. The apostle Paul exhorts the Christians at Colossae to have "compassion" (*splanchna oiktirmou*) in their mutual interactions. And the ministry of Jesus is also characterized by compassion for humans in the Gospel tradition. Mark writes that Jesus had compassion (*splanchnizomai*) on the crowd because they were like sheep without a shepherd (Mark 6:34). And again, in Mark 8:2 Jesus declares his compassion (*splanchnizomai*) for the crowd.

THOMAS B. DOZEMAN

Condemn, Condemnation   *see* Judge

Confess, Confession   We confess (or make a confession) when we acknowledge, before another or before others, something as true. In English, truth that is "confessed" is generally painful or embarrassing to the one making confession. The Hebrew and Greek words translated "confession" in the NRSV (usually *hodah* and *homologein*, respectively, and their related forms) may, but need not, have the same implication.

Several different types of confession are worth noting here. First, sin needs to be confessed, not hidden, if the sinner is to find mercy and forgiveness (Ps 32:5). Such confession is to be made to the God against whom, ultimately, sin is committed; it clearly implies a willingness on the part of the confessor to forsake what is wrong (Prov 28:13). It may be made in private prayer (Dan 9:4), but commonly it is publicly expressed (Matt 3:6; Acts 19:18), at times (in the OT) in a cultic setting accompanied by a rite of atonement (Lev 5:5–6; cf. Num 5:7). Personal sins are of course to be confessed, but in several texts a representative figure confesses the sins of his people (Aaron on the Day of Atonement, Lev 16:21; Daniel and Nehemiah in exile, Dan 9:20 and Neh 1:6; Ezra at a time of crisis in the postexilic community, Ezra 10:1). A communal confession of sin is envisaged in Lev 26:40 and Ezra 10:11 (see also Neh 9:2–3). In a judicial setting, confession may precede the punishment of the wrongdoer. Here the confession involves an acknowledgment not only of the wrong committed but also of the justice of God in causing the wrong to be brought to light and punished (Josh 7:19). Elsewhere, however, God's willingness and faithfulness to forgive are constantly and gratefully affirmed (1 John 1:9).

A second type of confession involves the open acknowledgment, rather than the denial, that one belongs to Christ, in a context where such an acknowledgment exposes the confessor to danger. Jesus declared that (at the day of judgment) he will "acknowledge" (that is, recognize as his own) those who have "acknowledged" him before others (the Greek word is the same as that elsewhere translated "confess" [Matt 10:32]; note also Rev 3:5). Christ's own boldness in speaking the truth when on trial is referred to as his "confession" in 1 Tim 6:13. Though Peter's threefold denial of Christ represents the most obvious failure to acknowledge Christ in this way, John speaks of many "even of the authorities" who believed in Jesus but would not openly "confess" allegiance to him because of their fear of the consequences (John 12:42–43; see also 9:22).

An initial confession of faith (in the words "Jesus is Lord," according to Rom 10:9–10) was required of those who would enter the Christian community; presumably it accompanied the baptism of the confessor. Such an initial confession was of course to be followed by appropriate Christian behavior (2 Cor 9:13; also 1 Tim 6:12, unless the reference here is to a confession that accompanied Timothy's "ordination"). The writer of the Epistle to the Hebrews stresses the importance of maintaining throughout life the faith that was then confessed (4:14; 10:23; cf. 3:1). But the worship of the church appears to have involved other occasions in which confession was made, both of God's name in praise (Rom 15:9; Heb 13:15) and of the substance of one's faith. The Epistles of John stress the importance of the latter confessions for distinguishing between those who adhere to true Christian faith and those who have departed from it (1 John 2:23; 4:2, 3, 15; 2 John 1:7). The later creeds of the church represent a further development along these lines.

God's universal rule is not yet acknowledged by all, but Israelite faith looked forward to the day when it would be (Isa 45:23). The early church believed that the coming universal confession would involve the acknowledgment, redounding to God's glory, that "Jesus Christ is Lord" (Phil 2:11).

STEPHEN WESTERHOLM

Conscience   Consciousness or awareness, especially of right and wrong. The distribution of this word in Scripture is surprising. It appears only once in the NRSV translation of the OT (1 Sam 25:31), as a free rendering of the Hebrew *leb*, "heart" (see **mind**). The phrase in which it appears is "pangs of conscience," literally, a "stumbling block of the heart." Since the phrase could as easily have been rendered using one of the more common translations of *leb*, this solitary instance need not detain us long. It need

only be said that some of the functions that the NT and contemporary thought attribute to the conscience belong to the heart in the OT. In this connection, note 1 Tim 1:5, where a "pure heart" and a "good conscience" appear in parallel.

The word does appear more frequently in the NT, though never in the Gospels or in Revelation. It appears most frequently in Paul, in the Deutero-Pauline and other epistles, and twice in Acts, both in speeches of Paul. NRSV commonly uses it to render the Greek *syneidesis*, "consciousness" or "awareness." One could, for example, be aware of God, as in 1 Pet 2:19. Where this awareness appears to relate to matters of right and wrong, however, NRSV renders the word as "conscience."

The conscience can bear witness (Rom 2:15) or act as a testimony (2 Cor 1:12; cf. Rom 9:1; 13:5). Romans 2:15 is a particularly interesting text. Some Gentiles, says Paul, do what the law requires because of "the law . . . written on their hearts." Their conscience bears witness to this law; that is, God has implanted even in Gentiles an equivalent to the written Torah. That this is the case is evidenced by their conscience, that is, their awareness of right and wrong. The key reality here, however, is not the conscience but rather the law implanted or written by God. The conscience only demonstrates the existence of the law.

The conscience can be kept clear, though effort is required to do so (Acts 24:16; 1 Pet 3:16). As is the case with all human faculties, the conscience can, however, be weak (1 Cor 8:7, 10, 12) or corrupted (Titus 1:15). It is even possible for the conscience to be "seared with a hot iron" (1 Tim 4:2). Interestingly, those whose conscience is "seared" in that text are not obvious evildoers but religious people who reject the true faith in favor of excessive asceticism. They have what we might call an overactive conscience rather than an inactive one. Bad religion as well as wicked deeds can vitiate the conscience. The conscience can also be perfected (Heb 9:9), purified (Heb 9:14), and sprinkled clean (Heb 10:22), a reference to priestly purification and perhaps even to baptism.

Sometimes Paul's language about conscience sounds very contemporary. Questions of conscience can be raised or not raised and a course of action undertaken for the sake of conscience (1 Cor 10:25–27). Paul distinguishes between one's own conscience and the consciences of others (1 Cor 10:28–29). It is vital not to read references to conscience in the NT with contemporary understandings in mind. The conscience does not function as an independent and sovereign arbiter of right and wrong, as it does in contemporary popular thought. Paul would not say, for example, "Let your conscience be your guide." Rather, conscience in the NT is that facility of the inward person on which right or wrong makes an impression. The conscience does not determine right and wrong. Right and wrong are determined by God, and the human person may display an awareness of it. The awareness is the conscience, which bears much the same relation to right and wrong that film does to light.

STEPHEN FARRIS

Consecrate   *see* **Holy**

Cornerstone   In the Bible "cornerstone" is always used figuratively. Its use in two OT passages is important for early Christian thought about Jesus.

In Ps 118:22 NRSV reads, "The stone that the builders rejected has become the chief cornerstone." The KJV gives a more literal translation of the Hebrew: "The stone which the builders refused is become the head *stone* of the corner" (the Hebrew does not contain the word "stone," so KJV puts the word in italics). The LXX follows the Hebrew closely in the phrase "head of a corner." But what does "head" mean here? NIV understands "head" as referring to the top of the building rather than to the foundation: "The stone the builders rejected has become the capstone."

The psalm text is quoted five times in the NT, always with the words of the LXX, "head of a corner" (Matt 21:42; Mark 12:10; Luke 20:17; Acts 4:11; 1 Pet 2:7). In all five texts the NRSV has "cornerstone" and NIV has "capstone." Both translations are possible, because of the inherent ambiguity of the Greek phrase. "Head" implies the top of a building, whereas "corner" suggests a position in or near the foundation. Whatever the precise meaning, the phrase points to a position of special prominence. In the Gospels the psalm is quoted by Jesus after the parable of the Wicked Tenants. From the context it is clear that the builders who have rejected the stone are Jesus' enemies, and he is the stone, whom God places in a key position in his building.

Isaiah 28:16 NRSV reads, "Therefore thus says the Lord GOD, See, I am laying in Zion a foundation stone, a tested stone, a precious cornerstone, a sure foundation: 'One who trusts will not panic.'" Here there is little room for argument, since Isaiah so clearly refers to the foundation. The text is quoted in 1 Pet 2:6, in a passage that also cites Ps 118:22. This passage develops the stone analogy to include Christian believers: "Come to him, a living stone, . . . and like living stones, let yourselves be built into a spiritual house" (1 Pet 2:4–5). The image of the church as a stone edifice is also found in Eph 2:20, where Gentile believers are assured that they have been "built upon the foundation of the apostles and prophets, with Christ Jesus himself as the cornerstone."

DOUGLAS R. A. HARE

Correct, Chasten, Discipline, Reprove, Rebuke   A group of five words concerned with instruction. Such instruction may be perceived positively ("Happy are those whom you discipline, O LORD," Ps 94:12) or negatively ("For you hate discipline," Ps 50:17). The words can also carry the connotation of "judge" or "punish" (see *judge*), when instruction carries with it penalties for wrong thought or behavior ("O LORD, do not rebuke me in your anger, or discipline me in your wrath," Ps 6:1; cf. Prov 15:10 "severe discipline").

Old Testament

Correct. NRSV translates two verbs as "correct." The first, *yakah* (Ps 141:5), means "decide, appoint, prove, correct, rebuke," and the second, *yasar* (Jer 10:24; Prov 9:7), means "discipline, chasten, admonish." A nominal form of the latter (*musar*), which means "instruction (see *wisdom*), discipline, chastening, correction," is translated "correction" six times (Job 37:13; Jer 2:30; 5:3; 32:33; Zeph 3:2, 7). The particular force of the English word "correction" is to point out errors. Of these texts, Jer 5:3 exhibits that meaning most clearly. There the prophet affirms that God seeks truth, but the inhabitants of Jerusalem have refused to accept God's correction (cf. Zeph 3:2, 7). Moreover, correction may be invited (Ps 141:5) or rejected (Prov 9:7). The prophet Jeremiah invokes God's correction but in just measure, lest it destroy him (10:24)! Clearly he views correction, even by God, as punitive and potentially excessive.

Chastise. The root *yakah* also can be translated "chastise" (Ps 39:11; 94:10) or "chasten" (Job 33:19), with no apparent difference in meaning. The same is true for forms of *yasar*, translated "chastise" twice (Jer 30:11; 46:28) and "chasten" once (Isa 26:16). The connection between chastising (*yakah*) and punishing is clear in Ps 39:11: "You chastise mortals in punishment (*yasar*) for sin, consuming like a moth what is dear to them." The connection of *yasar* and *yakah* to "teaching" is made clear in Ps 94:10 (which is quoted in Heb 12:6): "He who disciplines (*yasar*) the nations, he who teaches (*lamad*) knowledge to humankind, does he not chastise (*yakah*)?"

Discipline. NRSV translates only the verb *yasar* and the nominal form of that root *musar* as "discipline." Discipline was first and foremost the responsibility of

parents (Prov 19:18; 23:13; 29:17). At times it was administered through bodily punishment ("the rod of discipline drives [folly] far away," Prov 22:15; cf. Prov 29:19). King Rehoboam threatened to enforce his discipline (i.e., compliance with his directives) through force (1 Kgs 12:11, 14; 2 Chr 10:11, 14). The ultimate source of discipline, however, was God ("Know then in your heart that as a parent disciplines a child so the LORD disciplines you," Deut 8:5). God would discipline Israel with punishment in accordance with what they deserved (Hos 7:12), and God would punish other nations as well (Ps 94:10). Jeremiah said that Ephraim accepted God's discipline (Jer 31:18).

Reprove. In English, the word "reprove" (or "reproof") often means "correct gently or kindly," while "rebuke" carries a harsher connotation. That distinction is sometimes blurred in the OT, where different forms of the word *yakah* are translated both ways (e.g., "reprove" in Lev 19:17 and "rebuke" in Ps 6:1, even though the contexts suggest a harsh meaning). However, texts like Prov 19:25 ("reprove the intelligent, and they will gain knowledge") do carry the kinder connotation of "reprove," and even "instruct" as well (cf. Job 5:17; Prov 1:23; 3:12).

Rebuke. The word most frequently translated "rebuke" (i.e., correct harshly) is the verb *ga 'ar*. It can be used either of human (Gen 37:10; Ruth 2:16; Jer 29:27) or of divine rebuke (Pss 9:5; 68:30; 106:9; 119:21; Prov 10:17; Isa 17:13; 54:9; Zech 3:2; Mal 2:3; 3:11). A feminine noun (*ge 'arah*) derived from *ga 'ar* likewise refers to human rebuke in places (Prov 13:1; 17:10; Eccl 7:5), divine in others (Job 26:11; Ps 18:15 = 2 Sam 22:16; Pss 76:6; 80:16; 104:7; Isa 50:2; 51:20; 66:15).

Wisdom literature. The word *yakah* is used frequently in Wisdom literature. In Job 5:17; 6:25, 26; 22:4; Prov 1:23, 25, 30; 3:11, 12; 5:12; 6:23; 13:18; 19:25; 29:15, NRSV translates it "reprove." Elsewhere NRSV renders it "rebuke" (cf. Prov 10:17; 15:10; 24:25; 25:12; 27:5; 30:6). The word *yasar* also appears in Wisdom literature with the meaning "discipline" (Prov 19:18; 29:17), as does a noun formed from it: *musar* (Prov 5:23; 6:23; 12:1; 13:1, 24; 15:10). In light of this usage, some attention will be directed to such instruction as it was conceived of in the Wisdom literature (see *wisdom*).

The introduction to the book of Proverbs (1:2–7) broaches this issue. At the outset (1:2) it invites the reader to attain wisdom and discipline (*musar* NRSV: "instruction") and (in 1:3a) to acquire the "discipline of prudence" or "instruction in wise dealing" (*musar haskel*). This discipline or instruction would issue in the virtues of righteousness, justice, equity, sagacity, knowledge, and discretion (1:3b–4). The author of the prologue is clearly a scribe and teacher, someone that today would be called a tutor. Still, he assumes the posture of a parent instructing a child, warning the child against forgetting the instruction (*musar*) of his father or the teaching (*torah*, see below) of his mother (1:8). Such instruction perhaps consisted of an apprenticeship in the father's craft and socialization into family and society by the mother. The tutelage of the scholar could build on the earlier education of the child and prepare him for public service.

Torah. The term *torah*, which appears in Prov 1:8, means "direction, instruction, law," so its relationship to these terms also needs mentioning. *Torah* could refer to instructions from parents, priests, prophets, and the wise. It could be oral or written. It could be human or divine in origin. It could be familial, political, ritual, or ethical in purpose. Regardless, it seems to instruct or point someone in the right direction.

New Testament

Correct. NRSV uses all of these words in the NT also, though not as interchangeably as in the OT. The first, "correct," appears in 2 Tim 3:16, which is notable for its statement of the purpose of inspired Scripture: to teach. It uses four Greek words (translated "teaching," "reproof," "correction," and "training") with simi-

lar meanings. The word translated "correction" is *epanorthosis*, which also means "improvement" or "restoration."

Chasten. The only instance of chasten or chastise is Heb 12:6 ("the Lord disciplines those whom he loves, and chastises every child whom he accepts"), which quotes Prov 3:11–12. The word translated "chastises" is *mastigoo*. Its range of meanings include whip, flog, scourge, punish, chastise, afflict, torment, and mistreat. KJV translates the verb "scourge," presumably in a figurative sense. It is used in parallelism with the verb "to discipline" (*paideuo*), suggesting that a gentler translation is preferable.

Discipline. Discipline, which is closely associated with instruction, is first the responsibility of parents in the NT, also. Hebrews 12:8 simply presupposes that parents will discipline their children: "If you do not have that discipline in which all children share, then you are illegitimate." Ephesians 6:4 directs fathers to rear their children "in the discipline (*paideia*) and instruction (*nouthesia*) of the Lord." For Christians, such instruction is the foundation for further discipline by God. Hebrews 12:9 and 11 argue that if Christians received the discipline of their human parents, they should be even more willing to receive the discipline of God. Such discipline might seem unpleasant at first, but will yield the "peaceful fruit of righteousness" later on (12:11; cf. 1 Cor 11:32). Similarly Heb 12:5–6 quotes Prov 3:11–12, which affirms that God disciplines those whom God loves (cf. Rev 3:19).

First Peter employs a different word for "discipline": *nepho*, "to be sober or self-controlled." Extrabiblical literature uses it in reference to the self-discipline or self-control exercised by athletes. This word describes one who has received training or instruction and benefited from it. It presupposes persons in the congregation who instructed new converts. (Cf. Titus 2:1–8, which describes mature Christians' modeling self-control and teaching the same to newer Christians.) *Nepho* appears three times. In light of the imminent end of all things, the author admonished the readers to "be serious and discipline (*nepho*) yourselves for the sake of your prayers" (1 Pet 4:7). Similarly, they were to discipline themselves and be alert, because the devil was on the prowl for someone to devour (5:8). The third occurrence (1 Pet 1:13) sandwiches a present participle of *nepho* between injunctions to prepare for action and to set one's hope on the grace that Jesus would bring at the second coming. The disciplined Christian would be "sober-minded," choosing the rewards of fidelity over anything paganism had to offer.

Reprove. The aforementioned 2 Tim 3:16 mentions "reproof" (*elenchos*) in the sense of "correct gently" as one of the functions of Scripture, and 1 Cor 14:24 probably enjoins the same with respect to an unbeliever or outsider who enters a church. Titus 2:15, by contrast, seems to imply the meaning "correct harshly," when it instructs the preacher to speak, exhort, and "rebuke" (KJV) with full authority. Revelation 3:19 speaks of God's correcting (whether gently or harshly) and disciplining all those whom God loves.

Rebuke. NRSV translates *elencho* "rebuke" only once, and that in a context where the primary NT word for rebuke (*epitimao*) appears in the same verse (2 Tim 4:2). *Epitimao* means "rebuke, reprove, censure, speak seriously, warn." The verb could conceivably have the meaning "warn" instead of "rebuke" when Peter takes Jesus aside to discuss Jesus' disclosure of his death and resurrection (Matt 16:22; Mark 8:32), but the context suggests otherwise. Matthew uses it in regard to Jesus' rebuking the winds over the Sea of Galilee (8:26; Mark 4:39; Luke 8:24) and a demon he was exorcising from a boy (17:18; Mark 9:25; Luke 9:42). Luke adds another narrative in which Jesus rebuked his disciples for wanting to call down fire from heaven on a Samaritan village (9:55). In addition to these two narratives, Mark adds an earlier incident when Jesus rebuked, silenced, and exorcised a demon from a man in Capernaum (1:25;

Luke 4:35). In the Lukan parallel to this narrative (4:35), Jesus next rebuked a fever affecting Simon Peter's mother-in-law and also demons he exorcised from people in a crowd (4:36–41). Luke also uses the term in describing John the Baptist's rebuke of Herod (3:19) and the rebuke of one of the thieves crucified with Jesus by the other (23:40). The practice of public rebuke in churches (cf. 1 Tim 5:20; 2 Tim 4:2; Titus 1:13; Jude 9) is traced to Jesus' own instructions in Luke 17:3.

PAUL L. REDDITT

Counsel, Counselor   *see* **Wise**

Countenance   *see* **Presence**

Covenant   The primary term used in the OT to describe a covenant is *berith*, which appears to have been derived from a noun meaning "bond" or "fetter." Alternatively, it is suggested that it has been drawn from a word meaning "between," since the purpose of a covenant was to establish an agreement or understanding between two persons or groups. The noun is often used with a verb meaning "to cut"; hence to make a covenant is (in Hebrew) literally "to cut a covenant." This possibly originated with the custom of dismembering an animal, as in the strange ritual described in Gen 15:9–11, in which a solemn covenant between God and Abraham was inaugurated. Such a ritual may have been some form of "blood" ceremony of the kind frequently found where persons undertake solemn and binding agreements "on their life!" A second noun frequently used to describe a covenant, most especially that between God and Israel as a religious community, is *'eduth*, usually translated in KJV as "testimony," and "decree" in NRSV (e.g., Deut. 4:45; Ps 25:10) but which appears as a close synonym of *berith*.

Three fundamental features of the making of a covenant are the declaration of a solemn *promise,* or oath, in which the parties entering into the covenant agreement give firm and explicit assurances to the other party or parties concerning what they will do as a result of the covenant. In addition to this giving of promises, certain conditions are laid down which form the terms, or "rules" of the covenant. What these are, and what punishments, or forfeits, may be demanded if they are not kept, can then vary from case to case. A third feature of the covenant is that some formal oath, usually involving the summoning of God to be a witness or overseer of the covenant, is made. This was frequently, and probably usually, accompanied by a ritual involving animal sacrifice, establishing the binding nature of what had been declared and agreed. Other features were undoubtedly often added to these three, but they explain essentially what a biblical covenant was.

From a social and ethical perspective it is evident that covenants formed a very basic and widely practiced feature of life in the ancient world. In earliest social groups the extended family, drawing on ties of kinship across several generations, gave rise to large clan or tribal units. In these the bonds of kinship were of primary importance, and the authority of the senior heads of families was paramount in resolving disputes and punishing wrongdoing. Peace was maintained through a strong sense of kinship loyalty. Covenants became essential where these kinship bonds either did not exist or had become weak and fragmented. By means of such covenants new understandings could be reached to maintain peace and to prevent feuds and disagreements causing prolonged conflict.

Forms of covenant. It is clear from what has been noted above that covenants could take a variety of forms and could be established at many different levels. At the simplest level a covenant could be established between two persons who were, or who were likely to be, serious rivals. The most obvious example is that of the covenant made between Jonathan and David (1 Sam 20:13–17), through which they declared their perpetual friendship and mutual trust. This was to have important consequences once David rose to become the king of Israel. At a much wider level, international treaties between nations were elaborate forms of covenant. These could be treaties of mutual self-defense, reflecting a policy that became necessary for the many smaller nations that were threatened by Egypt and the Mesopotamian powers of Assyria and Babylon. Israel was either repeatedly involved in such treaties or was strongly pressured to join them. Variations of this were the detailed imperial or suzerainty treaties that were imposed by the ancient great powers on smaller kingdoms and cities. In these the superior power offered protection in exchange for payments of tribute and the renunciation of all commitments to any rival kingdom. In general, politics in the ancient world was largely a case of making covenants, sometimes openly between several smaller nations and sometimes secretly, with families, tribes, and cities all seeking to strengthen and maintain themselves against the real or potential threats posed by rivals.

Two issues have especially dominated discussion of the different forms of covenant in regard to their relevance to OT ideas. The first relates to the involvement of God in such covenant-making arrangements. Usually a deity became involved as the Guardian or Overseer of a covenant between human groups. Any breach of the terms of the covenant was punished by the aggrieved partner, who could claim support from the deity who had been invoked as guarantor of the covenant. The oaths that usually formed a feature of a covenant could even be supported by curses, which threatened failure to honor the covenant conditions. Variations were possible as to whether the punishments for breaking the covenant were carefully spelled out or were left to the overseeing deity to administer. If the parties to the covenant worshiped different gods or acknowledged several gods, then appropriate adaptations would accommodate this.

Against such a background it becomes evident that it was unusual for a covenant to be made directly between a God and a people, as in the case of ancient Israel. It is possible that the roots of such an understanding are to be traced to a period when the twelve tribes that constituted Israel were effectively in a mutual covenant with each other, under the authority of the one Lord God. In this case God was both guardian and author of the covenant, which itself was a mutual agreement between the tribes.

The second major issue concerning the forms of covenant in the OT concerns the status of the various parties to any such covenant. It is evident to serious theological reflection that God cannot be regarded as bound to a covenant in the same way that human beings are bound. This would savor too much of a bargain in which God relinquished a measure of sovereignty in order to grant certain powers and entitlements to human beings. In the course of Christian history the issue has given rise to wide-ranging theological discussions concerning the sovereignty of God. Yet it is not one that can be settled simply on the basis of OT usage. It is clear from the wide variety of forms of covenant in the ancient biblical world that no one single form predominated. All kinds of variations and adaptations were possible. In any case, the idea of God's covenant with Israel, or with human beings generally (the promise to *Noah* in Gen 8:20–9:7 is sometimes described as the Noachic "covenant"), inevitably requires recognition that the idea of covenant can be no more than a limited metaphor of the way in which God is related to human beings.

The point has been widely noted among scholars that the vocabulary of covenant is spread surprisingly unevenly throughout the OT. For so central a concept, this occasions surprise and has called for explanation. Central to the entire Hebrew Bible are the assertions that "The LORD is the God of Israel," and "Israel is the people of the LORD" (see *people of God*). The issue is then how this

mutual relationship is understood and defined. Covenant is clearly only one of several ways by which such a relationship can be described and interpreted. Fatherhood (cf. Hos 11:1), motherhood (cf. Isa 54:1), and *marriage* (cf. Isa 54:6) are other such descriptions and serve to show that such language creates word pictures that are in themselves partial and incomplete ways of asserting how God is related to human beings. The idea of covenant should not therefore be emphasized as necessarily more important than these other metaphors, which are all analogies, based on different kinds of human relationship. In referring to the bond between God and Israel the great prophets seldom refer to it as a covenant, and it is in the book of Deuteronomy and the other literature influenced by this book (especially 1 and 2 Kings and Jeremiah) that it is employed very frequently.

International treaties. A major feature of biblical scholarship since 1950 has been the recovery of documents from the ancient Near East detailing the treaties that were made between the great powers of Egypt, Asia Minor, Mesopotamia, and the lesser cities and kingdoms that lay between them (*ANET* 199–206; *ANESTP* 531–41). From the time of Moses to Judas Maccabeus, the great powers sought to impose their will over the lesser ones by imposing treaties upon them. In turn these lesser powers endeavored to protect themselves as best they could by negotiating covenants among themselves. In the politics of the time much effort was spent in plotting to break free from the painful consequences of submitting to the superior powers, but usually at the cost of relying on untrustworthy human partners. All the major prophets of the OT reflect extensively the dangers and dilemmas that faced Judah and Israel in pursuit of such policies. After the death of King Solomon, the rift that divided Judah from Israel was deepened by the different choices of treaty partners made by these two sister kingdoms.

Literary records of such international treaties serve to highlight their complexity and have illuminated the biblical history in a remarkable fashion. Furthermore such documentation also serves to shed fresh light on the reasons why the idea of a covenant between the Lord God and Israel remained an important feature of the biblical worldview. Only by submitting to the sole absolute authority and supremacy of the Lord God could Israel feel that it was wholly free from the tyranny and exploitation represented by the endless negotiations and conflicts that human covenant- (treaty-) making brought.

The covenant with Israel. In the biblical narratives there are two primary covenants made between God and a community of human beings. Both are of the greatest importance for the biblical message as a whole. The first is the covenant made between God and Abraham and his descendants, which is described in Gen 15:1–21, repeated in Gen 17:1–22, and anticipated in a promise made to Abraham in Gen 12:1–9. The sign of this covenant was the practice of *circumcision* in infancy upon all the male children of Abraham's family (Gen 17:9–14).

This covenant is usually described as the covenant with Abraham, or the patriarchal covenant. The OT frequently spells out more fully the names of Abraham, Isaac, and Jacob, marking three generations of the human partners to the covenant. The divine promises it embodies are that Abraham's descendants will become a great nation (Gen 12:2) and that they will take possession of the *land* shown to Abraham (Gen 12:7; 15:7), the extent of which is defined very broadly (Gen 15:18–21). Much of the remainder of the book of Genesis shows how this promise began to be fulfilled through three generations that grew into a large, extended family, with many complex internal family feuds and rivalries.

The second of the covenants between the Lord God and a human community is described as having been revealed and ratified by God through Moses to all Israel on Mount Sinai (otherwise called Mount Horeb). It is affirmed in Exod

19:5–6, but effectively the entire report of God's revelation on Mount Sinai described in Exod 19:1–40:38 is concerned with this Sinai covenant. It is the central covenant of the OT.

One of the most memorable and influential features of this covenant is that it includes the Ten Commandments among the conditions that its human partners are to observe (Exod 20:1–17; Deut 5:6–21; see *law*). It is this covenant that establishes the formal basis for Israel's existence as a nation (so esp. Exod 19:5–6). Since the covenant with Abraham and that made on Mount Sinai are both concerned with Israel's existence as a nation, it is evident that they overlap. The first was in the form of a promise made to Abraham by the Lord God that his descendants would become a nation, whereas the Sinai covenant was a formal declaration that this promise was soon to be fulfilled. However, the inclusion of the Ten Commandments as the conditions that Israel must obey for the covenant to continue inevitably drew the issues of law and obedience into the interpretation of it. In what circumstances could Israel, or parts of it, be said to have broken the covenant? The question of loyalty and obedience was drawn more fully into the understanding of the Sinai covenant than had been the case for the earlier covenant with Abraham. Saint Paul reflected extensively on this issue in the NT Epistle to the Galatians. Overall the relationship between law and promise (or "grace") has remained a point of primary reflection about the meaning of covenant among both Jews and Christians.

God's covenant with the royal dynasty of David. We have noted that the covenant between God and Israel revealed on Mount Sinai through Moses was akin to a national constitution. It declared Israel to be "a priestly kingdom and a holy nation" (Exod 19:6). However, for Israel to exist as a nation like other nations, it was essential that it should have a form of central government and natural that this should take the form of kingship, the common pattern among Israel's neighbors. It was also natural that such kingship should rest in the hands of a royal dynasty of kings; such, at least, was the customary pattern in the ancient Near Eastern world. Although Israel's first royal family was that of King Saul, which continued briefly after Saul's death with his son Ishbaal (Ishbosheth), this dynasty's rule was brief and unsuccessful. It was quickly surpassed and replaced by that of King David. In the OT, therefore, a central expression of the belief in a divine covenant is found in the claim that the Lord God had declared to king David that his sons and heirs would forever possess the right to rule over Israel (2 Sam 7:1–17). This commitment to the Davidic dynasty is made the most basic feature concerning the future government of Israel as a nation. It is sometimes described as an "everlasting covenant" (2 Sam 23:5; Ps 132:12; Isa 55:3). It is noteworthy that internal conflicts over the authority and permanence of this covenant formed a major point of dissension, which caused the breakup of the kingdom of David after the death of Solomon (1 Kgs 12:16–19).

We find therefore that the belief that ancient Israel was the human partner in a covenant relationship involving the Lord God is actually described as a series of covenant relationships. Each of them is focused on one of the three great founding fathers of Israel as a people: Abraham, Moses, and David. Undoubtedly the covenant made on Mount Sinai for which Moses acted as the human mediator occupies the central place, but it is nevertheless of significance that two other covenant mediators, Abraham and David, also play an important part. In the book of Deuteronomy these three strands of covenant theology are related to each other by emphasizing the centrality of the Sinai (Horeb) covenant mediated through Moses (Deut 5:2). The covenant with Abraham is presented as merely preliminary and promissory to this (Deut 5:3–5). The covenant of kingship with the royal figure of David is left out almost altogether, reduced to the demand that Israel's king should obey the law of Moses and be one whom "the LORD your God will choose" (17:15). The institution of kingship is thereby made wholly subordinate to Moses and the law given through him (Deut 17:14–20).

The Old Testament as a covenant literature. The focus upon Moses and the revelation at Mount Sinai as central to the covenant theology of the OT provides its many varied writings with their central coordinating theme. Alongside those of promise and law, the idea of a divine covenant enables writings from very diverse periods to be linked together. It provides a focal point and goal affirming that the involvement of the Lord God in ancient Israel's history is to be understood in a manner analogous to that of human covenants and treaties. It shows how human events reveal a spiritual and theological purpose.

Covenant implies a people and a community in a special relationship to God. The Greek translation of the OT (LXX) reflects this more fully than does the familiar English of KJV by translating the Hebrew word for "assembly, congregation" as *synagoge* = "assembly, congregation, and hence synagogue." In this way the OT idea of a people in covenant with God prepares for the NT belief in a church, which is itself a "covenant community" (Greek *ekklesia*, "assembly").

It should also be borne in mind that, although in the OT the Sinai covenant is linked directly to Israel's existence as a nation (so esp. Exod 19:6), this political state of affairs lasted historically for only a relatively short period. It effectively ceased with the destruction of the Jerusalem temple in 587 B.C. and the ending of the rule of the Davidic line of kings. Jerusalem lay in ruins, its temple destroyed and its royal family deposed and living in exile. Little was left that could be described as a viable nation. Under the cruel pressure of Assyrian and Babylonian imperial demands and punitive attacks, such total ruin had been the fate of several of the nations that had once been Israel's neighbors. All that remained to the survivors of Israel, who now increasingly found themselves scattered in many lands, was the hope of their nation's rebirth. This situation has given rise to Jeremiah's important prophecy that there would, at some future time, be a "new covenant" between God and Israel in which the law that had once been written on tablets of stone would be written on the heart of every member of the people of God (Jer 31:31–34).

As a consequence, by the time of the birth of Jesus the "covenant community" of the OT extended across both the small community of Jews living in ancient Judea and a far larger number of Jews living in Egypt, Mesopotamia, and other lands. The word "covenant" implied much more than "nation." It demanded faith and obedience, rather than race and territory, as its essential conditions of membership. It highlighted an awareness that the Lord God had shown through history how a great variety of men and women had been called into a covenant relationship that gave them the birthright to be the "people of God."

The centrality of the idea of covenant in the formation of the Hebrew Bible serves to show why, for the Christian, its many writings fit together to form an "Old Testament," in which the very title "Testament" is (through the Latin *testamentum*) a conventional translation of the biblical word for covenant.

The covenant in the New Testament. The central passage for the NT's understanding that a new people of God has been created by the life, death, and resurrection of Jesus is to be found in Luke 22:20. The words of Jesus at the Last Supper mark the beginning of a new era in the story of Israel: "This cup that is poured out for you is the new covenant in my blood." By his death, anticipated by this action of sharing a cup of wine, Jesus inaugurated a new order, which parallels and replaces the old order begun by Moses on Mount Sinai (Exod 19:5–6). The old sacrificial system was now replaced by the death of Jesus at Calvary, in which the human offering of the life of the Son of God, wholly given back to God, replaces the inadequacies of animal offerings.

It is also of significance that the three-fold pattern of covenant mediators in the OT—Abraham, Moses, and David—is given a new focus and unity through the person of Jesus of Nazareth. The genealogy of Saint Matthew's Gospel traces his ancestry back to Abraham and David (Matt 1:2, 6), whereas the new Sermon on the Mount (Matt 5:1–7:27) presents the new covenant law of Christian obedience as a new law "written on the hearts of men and women" precisely in the manner of the new covenant foretold by the prophet Jeremiah (Jer 31:33). The new covenant by which the Christian church was brought into being through Jesus is therefore the full and eternal covenant, which fulfils and replaces all three of the great divine covenants of the OT.

This theme of the fullness and adequacy of the new covenant brought into being through the death of Jesus gives rise to several fundamental features of the new order of the Christian community. The first of these is found in the claim that the Christian church is fully continuous with the community of God in the OT. In line with this claim lies the further claim that the new covenant mediated through the obedience of Jesus on the cross completely displaces and supersedes the rituals and sacrifices of the old covenant order (cf. Heb 9:15–28). So also the new law of grace written on the heart of every Christian supersedes the complexity and many-sided rules and formalities of the old covenant law declared through Moses and written on tablets of stone (see *law*). Finally, it is important for the interpretation of the Bible as a work comprising two "Testaments" (i.e., covenants) that they are related to each other in a scheme of promise and fulfillment. The covenant order of the OT is shown to be provisional and preparatory, since the full universality and wholeness of the revelation of God becomes a reality only with the new covenant inaugurated at the Last Supper by Jesus. The theme of promise and anticipation passes over into realization and fulfillment.

David Noel Freedman, "Divine Commitment and Human Obligation: The Covenant Theme," *Int* 18 (1964): 419–31; reprinted in *Divine Commitment and Human Obligation: Selected Writings of David Noel Freedman*, vol. 1, ed. John R. Huddleston (Grand Rapids: Eerdmans, 1997), 168–78; D. R. Hillers, *Covenant: The History of a Biblical Idea* (Baltimore: John Hopkins Press, 1969); Dennis J. McCarthy, S.J., *Treaty and Covenant: A Study in Form in the Ancient Oriental Documents and in the Old Testament*, 3d ed., AnBib 21A (Rome: Biblical Institute Press, 1981); Steven L. McKenzie, *Covenant* (St. Louis: Chalice Press, 2000); E. W. Nicholson, *God and His People: Covenant and Theology in the Old Testament* (Oxford: Oxford University Press, 1986).

RONALD E. CLEMENTS

Cover *see* **Atone**

Covet *see* **Desire**

Create, Creation, Creator, Creature

The theme of creation pervades the biblical narrative and has three interrelated points of reference: the beginning and the end of the world and the times in between.

1. Most fundamentally, creation is an act of God whereby "heaven and earth" are originally brought into being. The creation accounts in Gen 1–2 are the primary witness to this creative activity and provide *a universal frame of reference* in terms of which the entire Bible is to be interpreted. Several other texts witness to this originating creative action of God (Pss 33; 104; Wis 9:1–2; Heb 11:3). Still others link Wisdom and the Logos to this creative act (Prov 8:22–31; John 1:1–5).

2. Creation refers to the ongoing activity of God in every sphere of life whereby the world, often threatened by the presence of sin and evil, is ordered and maintained (Ps 104:30; the theme of blessing).

This focus of creational activity has to do, not only with God's continuing work in nature, but also with the ordering of families and nations (Gen 4–11), including the development of law (Gen 9:1–7). That Isa 40–55 can so readily use the language of creation for God's salvific action in the return from exile is a signal of God's continuing creative work between the beginning and the end (e.g., Isa 41:20). But, while creation language can be used to interpret God's ongoing work in the historical sphere, it would be a mistake to reverse this link and understand the original creation as a salvific event; that would collapse creation and fall. The promise of a new heart and spirit (Ezek 11:19–20; 35:26–27) is another instance of God's continuing creative work.

3. Creation is that divine eschatological action whereby a new heaven and a new earth are brought into being (Isa 65:17; Rev 21:1–5); this consummation reveals the direction of all of God's prior work, whether in creation or redemption. The books of Genesis and Revelation provide a creational bracket for the Bible, and texts in between are a continuing witness to the purposive work of God the Creator toward a new creation.

The importance of creation theology in biblical-theological reflection has been slow in taking hold, as a survey of recent OT theologies will show. The causes are many and complex, but an anthropocentrism has certainly been at work. One could also cite an emphasis on (salvation) history, the history/nature split, an existentialism that tends to see all of reality from the perspective of human existence, a political theology centered on the liberation of the human, and a theology of the word, sharply focused on the human. End-of-the-world scenarios have also played a role: God will soon blow everything up, so why bother to care about creation?

The Genesis creation accounts. The classical consensus in the study of Gen 1–2 spoke of the contiguous placement of two creation accounts, 1:1–2:4a (Priestly) and 2:4b–25 (Yahwist). The differences between these texts are often noted. For example, the Priestly account orders the creation of the entire cosmos into a seven-day sequence, climaxing in the Sabbath rest. Its rhythmic cadences have a doxological character and may have been honed through the regular round of the community's praise of God the Creator. This highly structured account speaks of creation in terms of order and stability, of separations and boundaries. The Yahwistic text, on the other hand, narrates a story that is focused on the creation of the earth and its creatures, bespeaking creation in more interactive terms, involving the human being in the creative process (2:5, 18–23).

That said, it is now common to think of the Priestly writer as the redactor of older materials, including the Yahwist. And so, the Priestly understanding of creation is to be found in Gen 1–2 as a whole. From a canonical perspective, a coherent understanding of creation is presented in the interaction of these chapters with each other. One effect of such a reading highlights the similarities in the two accounts. Hence, not everything in the first account is so structured and static, as readers have noted the asymmetry in the portrayal of creation. For example, eight creative acts occur over six days; "it was so" is missing from day five and "and God saw that it was good" is missing from day two; both of these phrases are missing from day six. Moreover, not unlike the second account, God involves creatures in the creative process (earth in 1:11, 24; waters in 1:20), and human beings are given responsibilities regarding the ongoingness of the created order (1:28). These features give to the first account a more open, dynamic character than is often allowed. The second account as well, for all its narrative ambiguities, also speaks of boundaries (esp. the law, 2:16–17) and separations (2:22–23). And so both accounts, each in its own way and in interaction with each other, witness to the "ordered freedom" of the creation.

Genesis 1–2 as a whole speaks of the modes of creation from several (overlapping) perspectives. (1) God creates by means of the word (Gen 1:9; Ps 148:5; Heb 11:3). (2) God creates by means of the word, followed by deeds of separation or other creative actions (Gen 1:6–7; Ps 33:6). (3) God speaks with others (divine beings or creatures) and invites their participation in the creative process (Gen 1:11, 26). (4) God uses that which has already been created as "raw material" to bring still other creatures into being (Gen 2:7). (5) God creates some creatures out of nothing (Gen 1:14–16). Later texts will extend this point to encompass all of God's creative activity (2 Macc 7:28; Rom 4:17; Heb 11:3). (6) God and humans name creatures, thereby bringing further order to the creation (Gen 1:5–10; 2:20). (7) God evaluates what has been created, the results of which could entail further creative work on the part of either God or creatures (Gen 1:4–31; 2:18).

Some scholars would add still another mode of creation: God creates through combat with chaotic forces and victory over them. This conclusion is drawn with an eye to ancient Near Eastern parallels as well as biblical texts that seem to portray creation in these terms (Pss 74:12–17; 77:12–21; 89:10–15). But this view is unlikely. Genesis 1–2 are remarkably free of opposition, and Gen 1:2 refers not to evil forces but to an earth that is empty and formless, a starting point for further creations. Moreover, the "chaos" of Gen 1:2 is not an ongoing ontological reality, persisting beyond God's ordering activity and constituting a potential (evil or other) threat to God's creation. Rather, this "chaos" should be understood as that to which the creation could revert because of the adverse effects of *creaturely* activity. In addition, the supportive texts noted are allusive and present only in poetry. To assume that Israel understood such poetic imagery in a literal way may be as profound a mistake as to think of these Genesis chapters as journalistic prose.

A relational model of creation. Two important conclusions may be drawn regarding these accounts:

1. The creation is not presented as a finished product; rather, a certain

open-endedness characterizes the created order that leaves room for further developments. At least since Augustine the absence of a seventh-day formula in Gen 2:1–3 has been noted, leaving the future open-ended for further creative activity. Even more, God gives the command to humans to "subdue the earth" (Gen 1:28), implying that God's evaluation of the creation as "good" does not carry the sense of "perfect." For humans to subdue the earth means that, in time, creation would look other than the way it did on the seventh day. Ironically, God gives humans this "natural law" so that the created order would *not* remain the same. For the created order to have remained fixed just as God originally created it would be a failure of the divine design! Development and change are what God intends for creation. God creates a paradise, but that garden is not a static place. Genesis 1–2 presents readers with a dynamic situation in which the future is open to a number of possibilities and in which creaturely activity is crucial for the proper becoming of the creation.

2. God is not the only subject of creating activity; rather, God involves already created beings in further acts of creating and in the ongoing process of creational development. Genesis 1–2 does not present God's creating as a unilateral act. Rather, God at times speaks with that which has already been created and involves them in further creative activity (Gen 1:11–12, 20, 24). Moreover, in Gen 1:26 God is imaged as one who shares the creative process with that which is not God; the "us" is usually identified with the divine council (see Jer 23:18–22). The "let us make" signals that a relationship of mutuality exists within the divine realm; when humans are created in the *image* of this kind of God—and *male and female* are made equal here and in 2:23—this implicitly entails a sharing of the creative process with them. The texts that follow report this kind of human involvement.

Initially, God's sharing of power with the human takes the form of a command, "Be fruitful and multiply . . . have domin-

ion" (Gen 1:28). God thereby chooses not to retain all creative power. This theme is explicitly developed regarding humans in Gen 2:5 (cf. 2:15), where the presence of a human to till the ground is considered just as indispensable as the rain for the development of the creation. Humans are thereby given responsibility for intracreational development, bringing the world along in ways that are attuned to God's purpose. This theme is developed still more sharply in Gen 2:18–25. God here evaluates the creational situation and announces that it is "not good" that the man should be alone. In the action that follows, God invites the human to participate in the move from a "not good" to a "good" creation. God creates the birds and animals and brings them to the human and invites a response. Notably, the human does not simply acquiesce to what God initially offers, which in turn sends God back to the drawing board. In other words, the human decision regarding the created order is honored by God and is taken into account in moving into new stages of creaturely development. To expand on this point, the human, in the process of determining that the animals would not satisfy the creational need, named the animals. Inasmuch as it was *God* who did the naming of several creatures in Gen 1:5–10, this human naming comparably entails a process of discernment regarding the nature of intracreaturely relationships and hence is a creative act. Remarkably, Gen 2:19 states: "whatever the human being called every living creature, that was its name." Without qualification God relinquishes dominion to the human within the process of creation. The decision of the human, initially deciding against the animals and then positively for the woman, has shaped the future of the created order in a decisive way. God did "split the Adam," but it was the human decision that led to that divine action.

These texts thus witness to a relational model of creation, wherein both God and creatures participate in the becoming of creation. God is not simply independent and the creatures simply dependent; God has chosen to enter into an interdependent creative process. Amid all the order of the creative process, God builds in a degree of open-endedness and unpredictability, leaving room for genuine creaturely decisions and actions regarding developments in the created order. This is a risky move for God, for the creatures may misuse their God-given power; yet, even when they do, God exercises constraint and restraint and continues to engage humans in this process (see Ps 8).

What emerges from these texts is not a static or mechanistic world. To be sure, there are the consistent rhythms of the creation: seedtime and harvest, cold and heat, summer and winter, day and night (Gen 8:22; Jer 31:35–37). But God has built an openness into the created order that waits not only upon God but also upon creaturely activity, not least decisions that humans make. Another point would be that God does not have a final will in place from the beginning regarding how the created order will develop. God makes adjustments in the divine will for the world in view of God's ongoing interaction with a created order that is still in the process of becoming and in view of God's ultimate purposes for all creatures.

Representative creation texts beyond Genesis. This relational understanding of creation is supported by many other biblical texts; more generally, creational themes decisively inform the ongoing story of Israel. We note Gen 12–50, Exodus, and the Wisdom literature as representative.

Genesis 12–50 is replete with such creational perspectives. Abram is called by God for a universal purpose—to extend blessing to "all the families of the earth" (Gen 12:3; see *"families"* in Gen 10). This theme can be tracked through Gen 12–50, with particular attention not only to its verbal repetition (18:18; 22:18; 26:4; 28:14), but also to the numerous contacts between Israel's ancestors and "nonchosen" families. *Blessing* includes not only the continuity of life through struggles of barrenness and birth (see the recurrent genealogies) but the pervasive concern

for kinship and family, an order of creation. From another perspective, the Joseph story reveals a concern for the nation, an order of creation, raising issues of economics, agriculture, and the dynamics of political and governmental life, through which God is at work for blessing (41:53–57; 47:13–26). Blessing is also evident in the concern for the fertility of the land and animals. The effect of human wickedness upon the created order (for example, Sodom and Gomorrah) raises environmental considerations. Positively, the divine valuing of human words and deeds reveals the important role of the human in the ongoing creative process.

The book of Exodus is also decisively shaped by creational themes. Most basically, it is the Creator God who delivers Israel from Egypt, evident not least in the creational themes in Exod 15. God's work in creation is initially seen in the life-giving, life-preserving realities in Exod 1:7, 12, 20 and continues apace in the plague narratives—environmental havoc wreaked by Pharaoh's genocidal, anticreational behaviors (Exod 7–12). God's use of the nonhuman creation as instruments of blessing and redemption (via judgment) is evident in the plagues, the sea crossing, the wilderness wanderings, and the Sinai theophany. The valuing of human leadership is especially evident in the figure of Moses. What God does in Israel's redemption stands in the service of endangered divine goals for life in creation. Moreover, God's purpose in Israel's redemption is ultimately for the sake of all creation (9:16), for "the earth is the LORD's" (9:29). The creationwide scope of God's purpose in and through the calling of Israel (19:5) is revealing of an initially exclusive move for the sake of a maximally inclusive end. The law given at Sinai, given for the sake of the good order of society (with inevitable effects on the natural order), is a creational reality, dependent on ancient Near Eastern law and giving greater specification to already existing law (e.g., Gen 9:1–7). Finally to be lifted up are the long-noted links between tabernacle and creation (Exod 25–31; 35–40).

Wisdom literature has a comparable contribution to make to reflections on creation, with its own twists. In the speeches of the Lord in Job 38–41, God takes Job out into the wilds of the creation, revealing a cosmos more complex than either Job or his friends imagined. Images are used that portray a well-ordered world, with accompanying themes of care and nurture. At the same time, readers get wild and strange images—the wildness of sea and weather, the uncertainties of the night, the unusual animals, and Behemoth and Leviathan, Job's own Jurassic Park. God's world does not run like a machine; it cannot be reduced to a world so ordered that there is no room for irregularities or for randomness. As Eccl 9:11 puts it: "time and chance happen to them all." God's creation is highly complex, wherein diversity reigns supreme, the regular and the unexpected occur, the clear and the ambiguous reside side by side, and the beautiful plays with the bizarre. Both eagles and ostriches!? These chapters are God's own imaging of the creation, and everything doesn't fit into a nice, neat little schoolroom of nature. Recent learnings from the scientific community demonstrate the rightness of this vision, revealing a cosmos of great complexity, remarkable openness, and a genuine interplay of law and chance. Such a perspective is reinforced by the book of Proverbs, which is best characterized as a creation theology, teaching that observations of life in creation are important in discovering the truth about God, the human, and the world (e.g., Prov 30:18–33).

The most basic NT perspective on creation is essentially continuous with that of the OT (Mark 10:6–8; 1 Tim 4:4; Rev 4:11; 10:6; 21:1). At the same time, christological reflections occasion newly shaped formulations on matters creational. These include Christ's involvement in the original creation (John 1:1–5; 1 Cor 8:6; Col 1:15; Heb 1:2), his stature as a new *Adam* (1 Cor 15:21–22; Heb 2:5–9),

his regular use of creational motifs in his parables (Luke 8:4–15; 15:3–7), the reconciliation of all things through the blood of his cross (Eph 1:9–10; Col 1:15–20; 2 Cor 5:17–19), the firstfruits of the resurrection (1 Cor 15:12–57), and his coming again on the clouds of heaven to usher in the new heaven and new earth (Matt 24:30–31; Rev 1:7) and to be its sun and moon (Rev 21:23; see Isa 60:19–20). Renewed images of the creation stories in Genesis shape the vision of the new heaven and earth (Rev 22:1–2; see *heaven*). Paul witnesses to the present groaning of all creation and articulates the promise that it will be redeemed and set free along with human beings (Rom 8:19–22). God's ultimate goal for the cosmos is not redemption; it is new creation.

Ancient and modern parallel interests in creation. Creation literature is not unique to the Bible. Sumerian, Mesopotamian, Egyptian, and Canaanite creation accounts (or remnants thereof) have been unearthed in recent centuries. Scholarly efforts initially focused on the Babylonian *Enuma Elish* following its appearance in 1876. More recent work has concentrated on the Babylonian Epic of Atrahasis (about 1600 B.C.), published in 1969, with its creation-disruption-flood-repopulation sequence. Special attention has also been given to Egyptian parallels, for example, the great hymn to the sun-god Aten and Ps 104. Creational language and themes in Canaanite (Ugaritic) writings also have their parallels in the biblical writings.

In comparing these extrabiblical texts with biblical literature, it is apparent that Israel participated in a culture with a lively interest in questions of creation. While some have claimed that Israel depended directly on this literature, it is now more common to speak of a widespread fund of images and ideas upon which Israel (and, less directly, the NT community) drew that helped shape both its stories of creation and reflections related thereto. Included among those parallels are the primordial waters, divine rest, creation as separation, images of creator as potter, farmer, and speaker of the word, as well as the textual sequence in Gen 1–9. Dissimilarities include the lack of a theogony and a conflict among the gods, the prevailing monotheism, and the high value given human beings. These elements should not be overly interpreted in polemical terms so that the genuine contribution of this literature to Israel's reflection on creation is diminished. For Israel, God the Creator had long been at work in the life and thought of these other cultures, enabling insight into matters regarding creation.

The postbiblical world has continued to explore the topic of creation, with scientific inquiries dominating the last several centuries. Much energy has been expended in seeking to relate the biblical understanding of creation and the results of scientific research. To claim that God created the world and all that exists is a confession of faith, grounded in God's self-revelation (Heb 11:3), and not the result of scientific investigation. That said, the biblical writers made use of available knowledge of the natural world in developing their reflections; creation is not collapsed into a theological or confessional framework. Israel recognized that insight about creation must be generated from many perspectives to speak the full truth about the world. The creation accounts are prescientific in that they predate modern science, but not in the sense that they betray no interest in "scientific" issues (1 Kgs 4:33). Israel reflected on issues of "how" as well as "who" and "why." Such knowledge is evident in God's use of the earth and waters in mediating creation (Gen 1:11–12, 20, 24), the classification of plants and animals into certain kinds (Gen 1:11–12, 21–25), as well as the ordering of each day's creation. These accounts integrate theological reflection with knowledge from various fields of inquiry. Their observations may differ from modern understandings (e.g., the age of the world and its development), but the biblical writers would have welcomed that and, implicitly, invited every generation to engage in

the same integrative task with the ever-changing knowledge about the world that becomes available.

William Brown, *The Ethos of the Cosmos: the Genesis of the Moral Imagination in the Bible* (Grand Rapids: Eerdmans, 1999); T. Fretheim, "The Book of Genesis," *NIB*, 1 (1994): 319–674; J. D. Levenson, *Creation and the Persistence of Evil* (San Francisco: Harper, 1988); R. A. Simkins, *Creator and Creation: Nature in the Worldview of Ancient Israel* (Peabody, Mass.: Hendrickson, 1994); P. Trible, *God and the Rhetoric of Sexuality* (Philadelphia: Fortress, 1978).

TERENCE E. FRETHEIM

Cross, Crucify The verb and noun do not appear in the OT, because crucifixion was not a punishment used in Israel. Deuteronomy 21:22–23 speaks of hanging a person on a tree, but only after execution, apparently for deterrence. Paul quotes from this passage in Gal 3:13, "Christ redeemed us from the curse of the law by becoming a curse for us—for it is written, 'Cursed is everyone who hangs on a tree.'" "Tree" is used instead of "cross" in Acts 5:30; 10:39; 13:29; 1 Pet 2:24.

Crucifixion, one of the most brutal forms of capital punishment ever devised, was borrowed by Alexander the Great from the Persians and taken over from his successors by the Romans. It was used by Rome primarily for the execution of rebellious slaves, brigands, and political insurgents. Jesus' crucifixion clearly belongs in the third category: he was executed as "the King of the Jews" (Matt 27:37; Mark 15:26; Luke 23:38; John 19:19).

In each of the Gospels the passion of Jesus, culminating in his death on a cross, takes up a large amount of space (almost a third of Mark's Gospel), yet the crucifixion itself receives very little attention. In Matthew, for example, the act is reported laconically by a single Greek word, "having crucified" (Matt 27:35). None of the Gospels report the pounding of nails into his hands (which can be inferred from the resurrection appearance to Thomas, John 20:27) and feet, the use of ropes, the nakedness of the victim (perhaps a loincloth was supplied because of Jewish sensibility), and the excruciating agony. Strangely, more attention is paid to various groups of onlookers than to Jesus. Only in Luke is Jesus presented as a "noble martyr" (23:34, 43, 46, but v. 34 is missing in a number of the best manuscripts).

It is difficult for modern people to appreciate the immense shame attached to this public humiliation. Roman crosses were usually placed near well-used thoroughfares, on elevated locations. Only Heb 12:2 explicitly refers to the shame, "endured the cross, disregarding the shame," but it may be implicit in Paul's declaration, "we proclaim Christ crucified, a stumbling block to Jews and foolishness to Gentiles" (1 Cor 1:23). The claim that a dead prophet was the Messiah was utter foolishness, but far more offensive to Jews was the notion that a crucified man was the Lord's anointed (see *anoint*). Undoubtedly Paul himself had been immensely offended by Christian preaching before his Damascus experience. Thereafter the crucified Messiah became the center of his gospel (1 Cor 2:2; Gal 3:1). The saving death of Jesus on the cross was for Paul the supreme manifestation of God's love (1 Cor 15:3; Rom 5:8). Paul used the crucifixion figuratively of the transformation of believers, as in Gal 5:24, "And those who belong to Christ Jesus have crucified the flesh with its passions and desires" (see also Rom 6:6; Gal 2:19; 6:14).

A very different figurative use is found in Jesus' saying, "If any want to become my followers, let them deny themselves and take up their cross and follow me" (Mark 8:34; Matt 16:24; another form of the saying appears in Matt 10:38; Luke 14:27). Some take this reference literally; Jesus is inviting his followers to accept crucifixion. It seems far more likely that the reference to the cross is figurative. His audience was very aware of the fact that many Jewish freedom fighters were being crucified (see

Mark 15:7). Jesus told his hearers, "If you wish to become my followers, you must be just as brave, just as committed as these freedom fighters, who are willing to risk crucifixion." Luke indicates that he understands the saying figuratively by adding one word: "let them deny themselves and take up their cross *daily* and follow me" (Luke 9:23).

Martin Hengel, *Crucifixion in the Ancient World and the Folly of the Message of the Cross* (London: SCM Press, 1977).

DOUGLAS R. A. HARE

Curse A curse is a speech meant to create or bring malevolence to the one(s) who receive(s) it. Or the word can refer to the act of uttering such ill-intentioned formulae (to curse). In the ancient Near East the curse, like the *blessing,* was taken with utmost seriousness because of the belief in the power of the spoken *word.* A curse was usually a public proclamation, as evinced by the qualifications in Eccl 10:20: "Do not curse the king, even in your thoughts, or curse the rich, even in your bedroom." Certain persons were thought to have potentiality to speak the curse effectively so as to bring ill on others. The holy man was one such person. Second Kings 2:23–24 reports that Elisha cursed a group of boys in response to their taunting him, and two she-bears came from the woods and mauled forty-two of the lads. This probably also explains why the elders of Bethlehem trembled when Samuel entered their town (1 Sam 16:4). They knew him to have ability to curse (or bless), and they feared that the reason for his visit was to bring disaster upon them.

NRSV translates a variety of Hebrew and Greek words with the English, to curse: Hebrew verbs *'arar, qalal, 'ala, naqab, qabab;* Greek verbs *kataraomai, anathematizo, katanathematizo, kataraomai, katalaleo.* Nominal forms of these words, as well as the Hebrew *herem* (Mal 4:6), are likewise translated with the noun "curse" in NRSV. A special case is the Hebrew term *berak*, "to bless," which is sometimes used as a euphemism in place of one of these terms (1 Kgs 21:10, 13; Job 2:9).

The curse was closely connected to magic in that it was assumed to have a force of its own and it could be used for selfish purposes. However, the extensiveness of such evil forces in the mind of biblical authors is debated. Sigmund Mowinckel theorized that references to "evildoers" in the Psalms (34:16; 94:4, 16; 125:5) refer to those who have ability and desire to utilize magical powers to bring harm (Mowinckel, 1:199–200; 2:6–7). Whether or not all such references have these types of people in mind, the Balaam story is a parade illustration of their existence (Num 22–24). Balaam was summoned by Baalak of Moab to curse Israel. He obviously had a reputation as a "hired gun" who could use the curse against anyone he chose. This background of magic and evil intent, however, sets up the real theological point of the story, namely, that Israel's God stands above all such powers. Balaam goes through ritual acts meant to direct the curse against Israel, but each time God forbids the curse to be uttered. Balaam speaks a blessing instead. Hence, the OT addresses the problem of evil as misused in the curse by giving assurance that evildoers and their curses could not do their work unless God permitted it.

A widespread, legitimate use of the curse in the ancient Near East was in legal documents such as treaties (see *ANET*, 203–5). They served in such texts as prohibitive elements that ensured loyalty to the agreement. For example, Judg 9:15 shows a curse being placed on those who rebuffed the authority of a newly elected ruler. But the fullest and best illustration of this use of the curse is in Deuteronomy. This book, which bears striking resemblance to Hittite treaties from the fourteenth century, is conceived in part at least as a covenant between God and Israel. The agreement is sealed by blessings and curses. As Moses declares, "See,

I am setting before you today a blessing and a curse: the blessing, if you obey the commandment of the LORD your God that I am commanding you today; and the curse, if you do not obey the commandments of the LORD your God" (Deut 11:26–28). The specific curses in Deut 27:15–26; 28:16–19 then lay out the implications of breaking the agreement. They are comprehensive, declaring misfortune on all aspects of life in the present ("Cursed shall be your basket and your kneading bowl," Deut 28:17) and making the future uncertain ("Cursed shall be the fruit of your womb," Deut 28:18). This use of the curse acknowledges that there are dire consequences for breaking covenant. However, this feature of Deuteronomy has meaning because of the assumptions concerning the power of the curse. It was almost palpably present in the document as an enforcer of the agreement. Similar use of the curse is Joshua's word against anyone who would rebuild Jericho (Josh 6:26). It intended to prohibit the action and set ahead of time the consequences for anyone who violated the command.

In addition to the formal use of curses in legal texts, curses were self-imposed in order to add weight to or to guarantee the reliability of a statement. This is the case in Peter's denial of Jesus in Matthew and Mark (Matt 26:74; Mark 14:71). He says on *oath* that he does not know Jesus and he utters a curse. The nature of the oath Peter takes is unclear, but perhaps he invoked God's name, as the high priest asks Jesus to do (Matt 26:63). Likewise, the content of Peter's curse is not certain. However, it likely contained some wish for misfortune if his statements prove untrue.

Certain curses were restricted or prohibited. Cursing God was considered blasphemy (see *blaspheme*) and punishable by death (Lev 24:10–23). Also, cursing one's father or mother was considered a capital crime. Both of these cases, in different ways, show the seriousness of the curse and the potential harm it could do to the Israelite community, either undermining the authority of God or weakening the structure of the patriarchal family unit. Further, cursing the king was forbidden, because to curse the Lord's anointed was to deny divine authority (2 Sam 16). It was also not permitted to curse the blind or deaf, because such would be unjust (Lev 19:14).

Numbers 5:11–31, which presents the law of jealousy, is a theologically difficult text that presents a different conception of the curse than discussed heretofore. It makes provisions for a trial of a woman who is accused of marital infidelity when there is no evidence except her husband's suspicions. The trial takes place through an ordeal in which the priest writes curses on a surface that can be erased. Then they are washed off into a container of water. The woman drinks the "water of bitterness," and the water "brings the curse" (Num 5:24). Although the exact effect upon the woman is unclear, what is certain is that the curse results from ingesting the words, not hearing them. Hence, the notion that a curse consisted of powerful words remains, but the means by which those words are received is quite different from any other text.

Malachi 4:6 is unique in the NRSV in that it uses the term "curse" to translate the Hebrew *herem*, a word that is normally rendered *"devoted* to destruction" (cf. Josh 6:17). This word appears most often in the context of holy war to refer to that which is banned, or declared off-limits to human contact. Items designated *herem* are typically destroyed, like a sacrifice, to show that they belong to God. The "curse" of Mal 4:6 seems to be the destruction of the residents of the land if they refuse to heed Elijah (Stuart, *ABD* 1:1219).

The concept of cursing assumes that some person or object is its target so that the effect can be observed. So Jesus' disciples note that the fig tree he cursed subsequently withered (Mark 11:21). But Job 3 uses the word figuratively to speak of Job cursing the day of his birth. This poetic text is a lament by one who thinks his existence is meaningless. Therefore, he "curses" the very notion of procreation, of bringing another person to life, only to experience pain (Job 3:11–19).

This terminology appears only six times in Paul's letters, but Paul uses it to address a key theological topic, namely, the relationship between Jesus and the law. Paul declares that Jesus "redeemed us from the curse of the law by becoming a curse for us" (Gal 3:13a). Here Paul draws upon Deut 21:23: "anyone hung on a tree is under God's curse" (Gal 3:13b), taking "hung on a tree" to refer to crucifixion. This combination of ideas is important for Paul's theology because it allows him to expound his understanding of the Mosaic covenant as an interim, punitive agreement between God and Israel. Paul perceives the curses in Deut 27–28 as the primary feature of the law, in contrast to the covenant with Abraham, presented in terms of blessing (Gen 12:2). For Paul, the Abrahamic pact is God's ultimate plan for humankind, and Jesus is the seed of Abraham through whom the promise is fulfilled (Gen 12:2–3; 15:5; Gal 3:16). But Paul defends the historical importance of the law by arguing that Jesus' deliverance of humanity from its curse is anticipated in the law itself. That is, recognizing Jesus as the bearer of the law's curse clarifies the role of the law in God's salvific work. It is contrary neither to the Abrahamic covenant nor to the gospel but serves as a necessary bridge between the two. When Jesus embodies the law's curse, the law's role as disciplinarian (Gal 3:24) ends, and the era of God's blessing, as pledged to Abraham, begins.

S. H. Blank, "The Curse, Blasphemy, the Spell, and the Oath," *HUCA* 23 (1950–51): 73–95; F. Charles Fensham, "Malediction and Benediction in Ancient Near Eastern Vassal-Treaties and the Old Testament," *ZAW* 74 (1962): 1–9; Sigmund Mowinckel, *The Psalms in Israel's Worship* (Oxford: Basil Blackwell, 1962).

JEROME F. D. CREACH

Dark, Darkness   *see* **Light**

Daughter (of Babylon, of Jerusalem, of Zion)   *see* **Family**

David   *see* **Anoint; Covenant**

Day   *see* **Time**

Day of the Lord   The phrase "day of the Lord" refers to a time at which Yahweh will act. It is used twenty-one times in the OT and appears only within prophetic writings, mostly in Joel and Zephaniah. The noun "day" is a figurative use of the term and refers to a period of time. That time is future, but it is never specified as to exactly how far in the future it might lie. However, it is often spoken of as being "near" (Isa 13:6; Joel 1:15; 2:1; Obad 15; Zeph 1:14), so that when the phrase is used, it is generally as a warning of some impending divine action. The day is an inescapable reality (Zeph 1:18).

The overriding theme associated with the phrase is that it will be a time of judgment on God's people as well as on their enemies. It is compared with a time of destruction in which Yahweh's anger is expressed in judgment. That judgment will rid the earth of sinners (Isa 13:9), and rid Judah of its enemies (Jer 46:10). It will also be a time of judgment for all nations (Obad 15). Ezekiel uses the phrase (13:5) to refer to the way in which Yahweh will bring judgment on the prophets and leaders of Judah for their failure to defend the city (see also Zeph 1:8). Cosmic imagery is used in Joel 2:2–11 to describe what will happen on that day. He describes it in terms of darkness and gloom (2:31), as does Amos (5:18, 20), in which the sun and moon will cease shining and there will be darkness and no light. These cosmic images are extended in Zeph 1:14–18 to include destruction of the entire world and its inhabitants.

The reason for this impending judgment is the sin of Judah and the other nations. People have been very religious, but their daily lives have failed to demonstrate justice (Amos 5:18–20), so just

requital will be carried out (Obad 15). For many, therefore, the day is going to be a terrifying and bitter moment (Isa 13:9; Joel 2:11–12, 31; Zeph 1:14), and so people are called upon to turn to Yahweh. For those who heed the prophets' call to humility and a new life, the day has the potential to be a time of rescue or salvation (Isa 58:13; Joel 2:12–17; Zeph 2:1–3).

Yahweh's means of judgment is usually through the agency of a foreign power, though that is often "hidden," as it were, under the figurative language of a cosmic meltdown. Joel 2 employs the figure of a locust plague to refer to the invading enemy as the divine agent of judgment.

In the NT there are six references to the day of the Lord (Jesus Christ). The OT themes carry over into these usages so that it is also spoken of as a future moment in which God in Christ will bring judgment upon the world. Its coming is certain, but its timing is unknown. Both 1 Thess 5:2 and 2 Pet 3:10 use the imagery of a thief coming in the night to express that unknown timing. Their purpose is similar to that of the prophets, in the sense that they call the believers to be always circumspect in their way of life and to live so that if the day were to come at any moment, they would be ready. The day is therefore a time in which sinners will be judged and the righteous will be saved (1 Cor 1:8; 5:5; 1 Thess 5:2; 2 Thess 2:2). The NT development of the theme is linked with the reappearance of Christ as judge. The *day* will be preceded by a period of rebellion in which forces opposing God will claim power (2 Thess 2:3–12). However, the appearance of Christ will put an end to that exercise of power, and Christ will slay those powers. Cosmic imagery used by the OT prophets is also adopted in the NT (2 Pet 3:10).

GRAHAM S. OGDEN

Deacon   *see* **Ministry**

Death, Die, Perish (*see also* **Grave**)
Death is the great enigma of life—indeed,

the ultimate frustration. For many, in fact, it is the fundamental crime that makes all of life ultimately futile. The Bible is principally concerned with life—physical and spiritual *life*, as well as *eternal life*. Life, however, is always lived out in the face of death, and so the Scriptures also deal with issues having to do with death, dying, and the state of the dead.

In the Old Testament

The Hebrew noun *maweth* ("death"), its verb *muth* ("to die"), and their derivatives occur more than a thousand times in the OT. "Perish" translates several Hebrew verbs used the same ways as "die." Death (*maweth*) came into human experience as a punishment for sin (Gen 3:19, 22). Every person in OT times died, with the apparent exceptions of Enoch (Gen 5:22–24) and Elijah (2 Kgs 2:1–12). The estimation of death remains constant and unitary throughout the whole of the OT, even though there were variations on other matters within the religion of Israel and many developments regarding death took place later in Second Temple Judaism.

The inevitability of death. The hope of the righteous in Israel was not that they would never die or somehow escape Sheol (see *grave*). Death and Sheol were as much a part of every person's experience as birth and family. Nor did they think of what would later be called *immortality*, or *resurrection*. These concepts were rooted in what they felt about divine justice and covenantal relationships with God, but they did not come to expression in Jewish thought until later. Rather, the thought of the righteous with regard to death and dying in ancient Israel was simple and realistic. "I am about to die," said Joseph to his brothers (Gen 50:24). "I am about to go the way of all the earth," said Joshua in his final words to the people (Josh 23:14) and David on his deathbed to Solomon (1 Kgs 2:2). Death and Sheol were as undeniable and unavoidable as that.

The standard view of death in the OT is that it is ordained by God as the inevitable, final event in every person's life (2 Sam 14:14a; Job 7:9–10; Ps 89:48). People were understood as having a "soul" (*nephesh*) and as being imbued with "spirit" (*ruah*). But they were always viewed as holistic creatures, not as composed of separable parts and able to exist as "souls" or "spirits" apart from their "bodies" (as in Greek anthropology). So when their life force (*nephesh*) ebbed away (Gen 35:18) or their body (*basar*) was destroyed, people died. They were then viewed as being either with their ancestors in the family sepulchre (Gen 50:13; Josh 24:32; 1 Kgs 2:10; 11:43) or in Sheol among princes, classes, and nations (Isa 14:9–11; Ezek 32:21–30); in either case, existing as vague entities in a monotonous netherworld, without the powers associated with human life and apart from communion with God (Eccl 9:5–6).

So the repeated lament of God's people in the OT is epitomized in the words of Job to his companions: "Are not the days of my life few? Let me alone, that I may find a little comfort before I go, never to return, to the land of gloom and deep darkness, the land of gloom and chaos, where light is like darkness" (Job 10:20–22; cf. Pss 88:3–5, 10–12; 115:17). For while God looks tenderly on the death of his faithful ones (Ps 116:15), death nonetheless ends all human experiences and all relationships with the ongoing life of the nation. What was desired by God's people was simply (1) a long life, (2) a good death, (3) the carrying on of one's ideals in the lives of one's posterity, and (4) the continued welfare of the nation, all, somehow, as ordained by God and under his blessing.

The real horror to the genuinely religious Israelite, however, was that death ends all personal relations with God. For in Sheol the dead are forsaken and remembered no more by God; they experience no longer God's steadfast love, faithfulness, or saving help (Ps 88:3–5, 10–12). Furthermore, they themselves no longer remember God or are able to give God praise (Pss 6:5; 115:17; Isa 38:18).

In Second Temple Judaism

During the period of Second Temple Judaism (ca. 200 B.C.–A.D. 120) there arose within Judaism a number of further developments in the conceptualization of death and the state of the dead. Some of these came about as Jews were forced by national calamities and personal catastrophes to rethink issues having to do with theodicy (i.e., the vindication of God's justice). Others were due to the impact of Greek ideas on Jewish thought regarding persons and their experiences after death. Still others may be explained as Jewish responses to widespread Greek attempts to gain an encyclopedic knowledge that, among Jewish thinkers, encouraged new analyses of previously held beliefs and various attempts to work out in a more intellectualized manner Judaism's traditional piety.

Developments in many of the Jewish writings of this period include these: (1) that the dead, both righteous and wicked, continue to exist as disembodied spirits or souls, who possess personal qualities despite their disembodiment (1 Enoch 9:3, 10; 2 Esd 7:78–101); (2) that there is a separation of the righteous and the wicked at death, as based on their moral characters during their earthly lives (1 Enoch 22:5–13; 25:4–6; 2 Esd 7:113; 14:35); (3) that Sheol (Greek: "Hades") is compartmentalized, with its two major compartments being Gehenna for the wicked and Paradise (see *heaven*) for the righteous (1 Enoch 22:1–14; 2 Esd 4:41–42; 7:36); (4) that Sheol (or "Hades") is an intermediate state with preliminary rewards and punishments, though with all of its inhabitants awaiting a future resurrection and final judgment (1 Enoch 22:1–13; 2 Esd 7:75–101; 2 Baruch 21:23; 23:4; 30:2; 59:10); and (5) that on the day of judgment the righteous will be vindicated and transformed (1 Enoch 37:4; 39:4–5; 40:9; 45:4–5; 51:1–5; 58:3–6; 61:5; 62:13–16; 100:5; 102:4–5; 103:3–4; 108:11–15; Jubilees 23:31; 2 Esd 2:39, 45; 7:32–38, 125; 8:51–54; 2 Baruch 51:1–13), whereas the wicked will be judged and condemned (2 Esd 7:32–38; 2 Baruch 51:1–13).

Furthermore, there is a repeated emphasis in these writings on death as God's punishment for human sin. Representative of this development on the theme "You shall die!" of Gen 2:17 and 3:3 are Sir 25:24 ("From a woman sin had its beginning, and because of her we all die"), 2 Esd 7:116–126 ("It would have been better if the earth had not produced Adam, or else, when it had produced him, had restrained him from sinning. For what good is it to all that they live in sorrow now and expect punishment after death?"), and 2 Baruch 23:4 ("Because when Adam sinned, death was decreed against those who should be born"). This emphasis also appears in such major passages as the *Manual of Discipline* (1QS), col. 11; the *Psalms of Thanksgiving* (1QH), col. 4; 2 Esd 3:7–8, 21–22; and 2 Baruch 48:42–43; 54:15; 56:5–6.

In the New Testament

The Greek noun for "death" is *thanatos*, with the noun *teleute* ("the end") also used once as a euphemism for death (Matt 2:15). The verbs *apothneskein* ("to die") and *teleutan* ("to come to an end") mean "to be dying" (present tense), "to die" (aorist tense), and "to be dead" (perfect tense).

Conceptions regarding death and the state of the dead in the NT are based on the Jewish Scriptures. They also often parallel speculative developments spelled out in the writings of Second Temple Judaism. Particularly in the realm of the popular piety of Jews in the time of Jesus, the writings of the Jewish apocalyptic writers seem to have had more of an impact than either the OT or the various schools of Pharisaic thought (as later codified in the Talmud). It is important, therefore, when analyzing NT statements about death and the state of the dead, to treat them in terms of both basic convictions expressed in the OT and developments in the writings of Second Temple Judaism.

Death as a tyrant and the last enemy. Death in the NT, as in the OT, is the divinely ordained lot of all people (Heb 9:27). Yet it is a dreadful thing (Rev 6:8), which is feared (Rom 8:13–15; Heb 2:15) and to be sought only in the most terrible of circumstances (Rev 9:6). It is never portrayed in heroic terms (not Christ's death; Mark 8:31; 9:31; 10:33–34, par.), nor is an apostle's death on behalf of others (2 Cor 4:12) or the faithfulness of Christian martyrs unto death (Rev 2:10; 12:11). It is always the antithesis of life. It is, in fact, the "last enemy" (*eschatos echthros*), whose tyranny Christ has condemned on the cross (Col 2:13–15; 2 Tim 1:10) and whose existence he will destroy when he comes again (1 Cor 15:26; Rev 20:14).

Death as the consequence and punishment of sin. While Gen 3:3 identifies death as the punishment for sin, the relationship between sin and death is not explicitly detailed in the rest of the OT, though, of course, it may be inferred throughout the narratives of God's dealing with his people and their frequent rebellion. Paul, however, spells out that relationship in Rom 5:12–21 (cf. 1 Cor 15:21–22). In so doing, he not only speaks of sin as a responsible act and death as its consequence, as did the Jewish apocalyptic writers, but also emphasizes the divine grace that Christ has brought for all, in contradistinction and in order to counteract the condemnation that Adam brought on all.

The destruction of death. The tyrannical power of death has been destroyed by Christ's death on the cross (Col 2:13–15); its effects are nullified by the proclamation and acceptance of the gospel (1 Tim 1:10); and its very existence will be obliterated at "the end" or final culmination of Christ's redemptive work "when he hands over the kingdom to God the Father" (1 Cor 15:24–26). In that Christ's death dealt with sin, it also dealt with death (Rom 6:7–10; 8:3). Death is overcome for those who make Christ's death their own in faith. So Christ is called "the firstborn from the dead" (Col 1:18; Rev 1:5; cf. Rom 8:29), for he is the one who has made the destruction of death possible for all who are committed to him.

Exactly how all this will work out for believers in Christ, who are still subject to physical death until its final destruction at "the end," is not spelled out in the NT. Believers will not "perish" (usually *apollymi*), a word used by some NT writers to refer to one's ultimate destiny after death, without further explanation (John 3:16; 10:28; and contrast 2 Thess 2:10). Jesus himself used a great deal of the imagery that developed during Second Temple Judaism about life after death in his parable of the Rich Man and Lazarus in Hades (Luke 16:19–31). And there appear a number of other figures of speech elsewhere in the NT for the situation of the righteous after death, such as "with the Lord" (2 Cor 5:8), "with Christ" (Phil 1:23; cf. Acts 7:59; John 12:26), in "his heavenly kingdom" (2 Tim 4:18), in "the heavenly Jerusalem" (Heb 12:22), and in the "dwelling places" prepared by Christ for his own in the Father's house (John 14:2). Indeed, as the prophet Isaiah has generally said and Paul repeats: "No eye has seen, nor ear heard, nor the human heart conceived, what God has prepared for those who love him" (1 Cor 2:9, quoting Isa 64:4).

Richard Longenecker, ed., *Life in the Face of Death: The Resurrection Message of the New Testament* (Grand Rapids: Eerdmans, 1998); Robert Martin-Achard, *From Death to Life: A Study of the Development of the Doctrine of the Resurrection in the Old Testament* (Edinburgh and London: Oliver & Boyd, 1960); Karl Rahner, *On the Theology of Death* (New York: Seabury, 1973).

RICHARD N. LONGENECKER

Deceit, Deceive *see* **True**

Dedicate, Dedication *see* **Holy**

Defile *see* **Clean**

Deliver, Deliverance, Deliverer *see* **Save**

Demon *see* **Evil**

Deride, Derision *see* **Laugh**

Desire, Covet, Envy, Lust These terms overlap in meaning but are not synonymous. The Bible always treats envy and lust as evil realities. With one exception, NRSV always uses the verb "covet" negatively. Desire in itself is not condemned, however, though many particular desires are evil. In certain philosophical systems, it is considered that perfection necessarily involves the absence of desire. This is certainly not the case in the Bible. God desires "steadfast love and not sacrifice, the knowledge of God rather than burnt offerings" (Hos 6:6; cf. Matt 9:13; 12:7; Heb 10:5, 8). Similarly God desires "truth in the inward being" (Ps 51:6; cf. Ps 68:16). Indeed our salvation rests in the profoundest sense upon divine desire. God "desires everyone to be saved and to come to the knowledge of the truth" (1 Tim 2:4). God's desires, it should be noted, are relational: "When God desired to show even more clearly to the heirs of the promise the unchangeable character of his purpose, he guaranteed it by an oath" (Heb 6:17). The God of covenant desires Zion as a habitation (Ps 132:13–14), and "godly offspring" (Mal 2:15). These divine desires are no less strong, yearning, and passionate than our own evil desires.

Jesus also displays this desire for our salvation: "Jerusalem, Jerusalem . . . How often have I desired to gather your children together as a hen gathers her brood under her wings!" (Matt 23:37; Luke 13:34). "Father, I desire that those also, whom you have given me, may be with me where I am" (John 17:24). We see here that Jesus' desires also are relational. It is characteristic of him that he wishes to sit at table with his friends (Luke 22:15).

Furthermore, the Bible never suggests that the righteous must vanquish desire or banish it from their natures. Humans are beings who, by nature, desire. This may even be a consequence of being created in the image of God. Just as God yearns for us, so also humans may desire God: "Whom have I in heaven but you? And there is nothing on earth that I desire other than you" (Ps 73:25; cf. Isa 26:8).

There are many right desires. We may desire to "be with Christ" (Phil 1:23), desire a "better country, that is, a heavenly one" (Heb 11:16), or desire "to act honorably in all things" (Heb 13:18). Such godly desires may cause us to turn to God for the first time or more completely. We may also desire freedom (Jer 34:16) or to understand (Dan 2:3). Particularly striking is the desire, described in richly sensuous terms, for the commandments of God: "More to be desired are they than gold, even much fine gold; sweeter also than honey, and drippings of the honeycomb" (Ps 19:10). Humans may share in the divine desire for the welfare of others. Paul prays for the people of Israel, desiring "that they may be saved" (Rom 10:1). He encourages the Corinthians in their expressed, though incomplete, desire to help the poor in Jerusalem (2 Cor 8:10).

Right desires are not only those we can easily identity as "spiritual," however. It is proper—indeed nearly the Lord's command—to wish for "oxen, sheep, wine, strong drink, or whatever you desire" (Deut 14:26). It is right to "desire life and desire to see good days" (1 Pet 3:10). God fulfills right desires: "O LORD, you will hear the desire of the meek" (Ps 10:17; cf. Pss 20:4; 21:2; 145:19 and many other examples). Indeed, God fulfills the desires of all living creatures (Ps 145:16). "A desire fulfilled is a tree of life" (Prov 13:12).

In a society of fallen beings, devoted too often to self-aggrandizement, however, many desires are inevitably wrong. The word "desire" appears more often negatively than positively in the Bible. Wrong desire is pervasive: "for all that is in the world—the desire of the flesh, the desire of the eyes, the pride in riches—comes not from the Father but from the world. And the world and its desire are passing away, but those who do the will of God live forever" (1 John 2:16–17). Giving in to desire is dangerous, beginning even in the garden (Gen 3:6) and continuing through Scripture. In Paul in particular, desire belongs to the *flesh*, a spiritual principle utterly opposed to God's will. Such desire must be resisted:

"Instead, put on the Lord Jesus Christ, and make no provision for the flesh, to gratify its desires" (Rom 13:14 and many examples).

One common form of evil desire is sexual. "Lust" is wrong sexual desire. The word is also used metaphorically, of spiritual unfaithfulness. Though evil desires are often sexual, sexual desire itself is not evil. It is permissible to desire a woman for a wife, even a foreign woman (Deut 21:11; cf. Ps 45:11). The Song of Songs rejoices in sexual desire: "I am my beloved's, and his desire is for me" (Song 7:10). In the curse pronounced upon Eve, the curse is not, as might be supposed, sexual desire for the husband, but rather the lack of reciprocity in the response—"he shall rule over you"—and the connection to the increased pains of childbirth. Lust is wrong because it turns away from or actively threatens relationships within which sexual desire is a blessing. This raises a key point. As we have seen, God's desires are relational, seeking always wholeness in relationships. Evil desires such as lust, envy, and coveting, by contrast, threaten relationships.

Aside from Ps 34:12, the word "covet" is used negatively by NRSV. (The Hebrew verb behind "covet" is sometimes used positively, but NRSV renders it in those cases by some form of "desire.") Coveting is expressly forbidden in the tenth commandment: "You shall not covet your neighbor's house . . . your neighbor's wife, or male or female slave, or ox, or donkey, or anything that belongs to your neighbor" (Exod 20:17; cf. Deut 5:21). Two of the four NT occurrences of the word (Rom 7:7; 13:9) are direct allusions to this commandment and a third (Jas 4:2) may be an indirect allusion. It differs from the commandments that precede it ("You shall not murder . . . commit adultery . . . steal") in that it appears to deal not simply with actions but with an internal disposition. Coveting that which belongs to the neighbor will, however, often lead to action. The verbs "covet" and "take" sometimes appear together (e.g., Deut 7:25; Josh 6:18; 7:21; cf. Mic 2:2). In this respect it might be compared to the commandment to honor one's father and mother, which also refers to an internal disposition that issues in courses of action. However, the attitude itself may be wrong, apart from any action, because it is always a threat to the relationships within which humans live. That the disposition itself is wrong is reinforced by the constant negative use in both testaments of the word "envy." This is very nearly a synonym of "covet," though one may chiefly covet or envy the possessions of others but may also envy their position or status. Envy too must be overcome (1 Pet 2:1 and many other examples).

In this world of broken relationships, desires are very often wrong, emerging as envy, lust, or the coveting of that which belongs to the neighbor. If a right relationship with God were restored, however, desires themselves might become righteous. It might then even be safe to say with Augustine, "Love God and do what you want."

STEPHEN FARRIS

Determine, Predestine The word "predestine" does not occur in the NRSV translation of the OT; and several words or phrases underlie NRSV's translation of "determine" in the OT. For instance, "I have determined to make an end of all flesh" (Gen 6:13) is more literally "An end to all flesh has come to my face." Other words or phrases translated "determined" would more literally be "counsel(ed)" (2 Chr 25:16) "decide(d)" (Job 14:5; Dan 11:36), "set" (Job 38:5), "set my face" (Jer 44:11), and "do/did" (Isa 37:26).

Of these instances, Dan 11:36 most clearly suggests that God has foreordained or predestined an event or series of events: "for what is determined shall be done" (see also Isa 37:26). Of course, other OT texts suggest God's direction of events before they unfold, or at least as they unfold (see Gen 50:20; Jer 1:1–5). Offering a different perspective, however, are several OT texts that indicate God's genuine surprise at a particular turn of events. For instance, what God "thought" or intended, according to Jer 3:19–20, does not occur. God intended and prepared for a fruitful relationship between God's own self and the people; but despite God's intent and preparations, the people prove to be faithless. Furthermore, Jer 3:22 suggests that the future is genuinely open, dependent not simply upon God's intent or determination but rather upon the people's response to God.

Then too, several texts indicate that God sometimes changes God's mind or announced intention—not arbitrarily, but as a manifestation of divine compassion. In Exod 32:7–14, for example, Moses persuades God *not* to do what God had already determined to do and announced to Moses. Instead of destroying the disobedient people and starting over with Moses, as God had announced, "The LORD changed his mind about the disaster that he planned to bring on his people" (Exod 32:14; see also Amos 7:3, 7, where God changed God's mind or "relented" concerning something that God had apparently already determined to do).

In the NT, Luke 22:22 indicates that the unfolding of Jesus' life and death is "as it has been determined" (Gk. *horizo*; see Acts 2:23; 10:42; 17:31). Using a related verb (*proorizo*), Acts 4:28 also suggests that circumstances surrounding Jesus' death had been "predestined to take place" (see also 1 Cor 2:7).

The other four occurrences of the verb *proorizo* are used not in relation to Jesus but rather to members of the church in Rome, who are "predestined to be conformed to the image of his Son" (Rom 8:29; see 8:30), as well as members of the church in Ephesus (Eph 1:5, 11; NRSV "destined"). Both Romans and Ephesians associate this predestination with God's foreknowledge (see "those whom he foreknew" in Rom 8:29 and "before the foundation of the world" in Eph 1:4).

The theological purpose of the vocabulary of predestination is to claim that persons really do belong to God as a result of God's initiative; that is, they are part of God's "large family" (Rom 8:29) or "household" (Eph 2:19), as a result of the reconciling work of Jesus Christ. The Bible does not speak with a single voice concerning the details of divine determination or predestination (see above). For instance, does God choose all people to be God's own? Are people able to reject God's offer of relationship? The church, of course, and especially the Reformed churches have long wrestled and are still wrestling with these and related questions (see *choose*). J. K. S. Reid's conclusion is helpful: "If any fail to come to the enjoyment of this blessedness, it will not be because by the p.[redestination] of God they have been assigned another fate, but because they have turned their face away from the determined means of salvation proffered in Jesus Christ. That it should be possible for this to occur within the d.[etermination] of all things by God is as finally mysterious as the existence of evil" (*Theological Wordbook*, 68).

J. K. S. Reid, "Determinate, Determine, Predestinate (AV), Foreordain (RV)," *A Theological Wordbook of the Bible*, ed. Alan Richardson (New York: MacMillan, 1950), 64–68.

J. CLINTON MCCANN JR.

Devil   *see* **Satan**

Devote, Devoted   The idea of devoting something to the deity or devoting oneself to certain modes of behavior belongs to the worlds of many religions. In this regard, the English word "devote" is used to translate a variety of Hebrew and Greek words and phrases. One may devote oneself to God (Ps 86:2), to keeping the commandments (1 Kgs 8:61), to prayer (1 Cor 7:5), to good works (Titus 3:14).

According to Leviticus 27, there is a special form of dedication, signified by the Hebrew word *herem*. A field may be "devoted" to the Lord and through such dedication become holy (Lev 27:21). Once land or an animal is so devoted, it must remain in that status (Lev 27:28). Humans who have been devoted to the Lord must "be put to death" (Lev 27:29). This requirement probably reflects a stipulation in the Deuteronomic law code, namely, that nothing "devoted to destruction" should remain in Israel's possession (Deut 13:17).

This idea—that those things which are totally devoted to Yahweh must be destroyed—appears with greatest vigor in descriptions of Israel's holy wars. Again, the Deuteronomic law code stipulates: "You shall annihilate (herem) them—the Hittites and the Amorites, the Canaanites and the Perizzites, the Hivites and the Jebusites—just as the LORD your God has commanded" (Deut 20:17). Anything that breathes—whether animal or human—is to be killed. This mandate appears within the chapter, Deut 17, that prescribes the ways in which Israel shall conduct its warfare.

Narrative depictions of Israel's early wars confirm this notion of the "ban" or total destruction. Towns are to be utterly destroyed (Num 21:2). All that live in the city, "both men and women, young and old, oxen, sheep, and donkeys," are put to the sword (Josh 6:21, cf. 8:26). Two biblical texts in particular exemplify the requirement of "total devotion" to Yahweh. The first begins by stating, "But the Israelites broke faith in regard to the devoted things" (Josh 7:1). During an attack on Ai, Achan took some of the devoted things. Later in the story, we learn that such booty included "silver, the mantle, and the bar of gold." Such a violation of the "ban" eventuated in the stoning to death not only of Achan but all those alive with him, a punishment similar in its radicality to the requirement of the total destruction of the "devoted things." A second and similar story involves Saul and Samuel. In the aftermath of Israel's defeat of Amalekites: "Saul and the people spared Agag [the Amalekite king], and the best of the sheep and of the cattle and of the fatlings, and the lambs, and all that was valuable, and would not utterly destroy them; all

that was despised and worthless they utterly destroyed (heherimu)" (1 Sam 15:9). Samuel deems this act to violate Israel's norms of holy war, even though Saul claims that the people had spared "the best of the sheep and the cattle to sacrifice to the LORD your God" (1 Sam 15:15). Therefore, Samuel, in a divine oracle, rejects Saul from being king and proceeds to kill Agag. Clearly, even the appearance of personal gain was deemed to be a violation of the holy war "ban."

Such utter violence against both animal and human life strikes many contemporary readers as repugnant. Whether such practice was a religious ideal that was never practiced is, in some ways, beside the point. The ethos it engenders is one that does not encourage respect for life. To explain the notion of such total annihilation as a sacrifice to the deity is, potentially, to offer religious grounds for genocide.

DAVID L. PETERSEN

Disciple In Greek the word disciple (*mathetes*), derived from the verb "to learn," carries the basic sense of dependence upon a superior for instruction (Matt 10:24–25; Luke 6:40). Any student, whether training for a craft or some intellectual pursuit, may be termed a disciple. Adherents of particular philosophical schools in the classical and Greco-Roman periods are often known as the disciples of a certain master. In such cases the emphasis is primarily on the intellectual bond that connects the disciple to the master through generations rather than the idea of direct instruction. In addition to the sphere of philosophy in a strict sense (e.g., Plato and the Academy), the ancient world knew of master-disciple relationships where a "religious" dimension was present (e.g., Pythagoras, Epicurus) and where one meets the relationship between mystagogue and adept (e.g., the mystery religions).

The OT does not offer anything that clearly corresponds to the Greek world's notion of master-disciple relationships. The word *mathetes* does not appear in the LXX (except as a variant reading in codex A at Jer 13:21 and 20:11) and its usual Hebrew equivalent *talmid* (derived from *lamad*, "to learn") appears only at 1 Chr 25:8, where it refers to students among the musicians of the temple. Another Hebrew noun (also from *lamad*) is once rendered "disciples" in English at Isa 8:16. In the OT the people of God learn from God (e.g., Deut 4:10; see **preach**), and accordingly in a general sense there is no room apart from the divine teaching for an individual to serve in the role of an instructor for a limited group of disciples. Moses, the priests, and the prophets all serve as God's representatives, and they do so as commissioned agents of God who pass on what they receive. Nevertheless, even though the terminology of "disciple" is virtually absent in the OT, there are analogous social formations in groups such as the schools of the prophets, an example of which many scholars see behind Isa 8:16. Similarly the production of the Wisdom literature is often associated with the existence of scribal schools. In both cases, the maintenance of a prophetic tradition or an intellectual tradition must have at least required teachers and students, if not disciples per se.

In the NT the word "disciple" occurs only in the Gospels and Acts, where it appears 261 times. In the vast majority of cases it refers either explicitly or implicitly to those attached to Jesus as their master. It also occurs a number of times to designate those attached to John the Baptist (Matt 9:14; 11:2; 14:12; Mark 2:18; 6:29; Luke 5:33; 7:18; 11:1; John 1:35, 37; 3:25). According to the Fourth Gospel Jesus' first disciples had originally been disciples of John who then transferred their allegiance to Jesus (John 1:35–37). That they do so, however, is consistent with the witness of John himself (1:36; 3:30). In one of the more curious episodes in Acts, Paul finds some disciples at Ephesus who still know nothing other than the baptism of John (Acts 19:1–7). Several

of the NT instances of the term "disciple" refer to adherents of the Pharisaic party (Mark 2:18 and par.; Matt 22:16) or more generally of Moses (John 9:28). At Acts 9:25 there may be a reference to disciples of Paul, although some suspect that the personal pronoun "his" there was added later by a scribe, especially since such a use of "disciple" goes against the practice of Acts elsewhere. In contrast to the use of the word in the Hellenistic world to denote relationships of formal dependence (e.g., in the philosophical schools), in the NT "disciple" signifies a life-guiding and comprehensive personal attachment. Differences between Jesus and John the Baptist with respect to fasting are illustrated in the way that their stances are reflected in the practices of their respective disciples (Mark 2:18 and par.). That a master would typically provide instruction in so important a realm as prayer furnishes a natural setting for the request of Jesus' disciples that he teach them to pray, just as John had taught his disciples (Luke 11:1). While in the Gospels the disciples are ordinarily the personal followers of Jesus as he pursues his ministry, in Acts the term is extended and is used as the normal designation to refer to all Christians (Acts 6:1–2, 7; 9:1, 10, 19; 11:26, 29; 13:52; 15:10; 21:16). Thus by preaching the gospel, Paul and Barnabas "make disciples" (Acts 14:21).

The Gospels emphasize the initiative of Jesus in calling disciples to attach themselves to him (Mark 1:17; 2:14; par.; John 1:43). Inquirers who approach him on their own volition are not portrayed as successful in joining the disciples (Luke 9:57–58, 61–62). Insofar as the act of following Jesus constitutes the action of a disciple, the verb "to follow" (*akoloutheo*) often appears in the Gospels to mark the distinctive dependent connection of the disciple to Jesus (Mark 1:18 and par.; 2:14 and par.; 2:15; 10:28 and par.; 15:40–41 and par.). The **call** of Jesus can be as brief as "Follow me" (Matt 8:22 and par.; Mark 1:17 and par.; 2:14 and par.; 10:21 and par.). In John, Jesus declares, "Whoever serves me must follow me" (John 12:26). The relation between Jesus and his disciples is personal from the start, illustrated by the manner in which Jesus makes an overwhelming impression on those who accept his call (see esp. Luke 5:1–11; John 1:47–49). It is comprehensive insofar as the disciple renounces ordinary social relations and self-interest to be devoted exclusively to the relationship of discipleship (Luke 14:26–27 and par.). Unlike an apprentice, the disciple is not in training to succeed the master, even though an essential part of being a disciple involves replicating the master's activity. Rather, the disciple can be equated with a servant (Matt 10:24–25; John 13:16; 15:20). Moreover, the alignment of disciples with Jesus also entails suffering: "If any want to become my followers, let them deny themselves and take up their cross and follow me" (Mark 8:34 and par.).

Out of the larger group of disciples, Jesus chose twelve to work more closely with him (Mark 3:13–19). Luke in particular highlights the identity of these twelve disciples as the twelve *apostles* (Luke 6:13), while also continuing references to a larger circle of followers (Luke 6:17; 19:37; cf. John 4:1; 6:60–71; 8:31). During the ministry of Jesus one important function of the disciples is to enable Jesus to extend his proclamation to a wider circle (Mark 6:7–13 and par.). According to Luke, Jesus not only sends out *the Twelve* two by two for this purpose but also a larger group of 70 (or 72) "in pairs to every town and place where he himself intended to go" (Luke 10:1). Although the latter are not explicitly termed "disciples," the commission they receive and the results of their mission are comparable with the activity of the Twelve (Luke 10:2–12, 17–20). After the resurrection the eleven disciples are commissioned to "make disciples of all nations" (Matt 28:19). Even as the Father has sent Jesus into the world, so he sends those given him by the Father into the world (John 17:18).

The appearance of the disciples in the Gospels cannot simply be considered as an attempt to give an actual portrayal of their historical roles during the time of Jesus. In the Gospel of Mark, for instance, the disciples can function as foils (e.g., 6:35; 8:27; 14:12) who elicit some corrective teaching or activity by Jesus. This is particularly the case in those instances in which the disciples misunderstand Jesus' words or actions (e.g., 5:31; 6:37; 8:4), fail in their own actions (9:18), or are rebuked by Jesus (8:33; 9:33–37; 9:38–39; 10:13–16). In these and other cases the Gospel writer is able to use the example of the disciples to instruct and encourage other believers insofar as the failures of the disciples in Mark are met with the sustaining love of God. Thus even Mark's treatment of the Twelve pertains in many cases not so much to the particular historical individuals who made up this group as to the portrait of disciples and discipleship in general. While Matthew and Luke tend to mitigate the harshness of the Markan portrayal of the disciples, their own narratives can use them in literary ways comparable to Mark's treatment for the instruction of their readers. For example, Matthew's account of the stilling of the storm (Matt 8:23–27) is uniquely placed after several would-be disciples seek to "follow" Jesus (Matt 8:18–22). Next the disciples "follow" Jesus into a boat (8:23), which as early as Tertullian has been interpreted to represent the church. When the boat is imperiled by a great storm, only in Matthew do the disciples cry out the Christian prayer, "Lord, save" (8:25), after which they are rescued by Jesus.

The usage of "disciples" in the Gospels and Acts may be compared and contrasted with the rabbinic *talmidim*, who devote themselves to the study of Scripture and tradition under the guidance of a rabbi. Basic here is the teacher-student relationship, in which the student, subject to the authority of the teacher, acquires knowledge by listening to what the rabbi says. Questions and discussion round out the process. The gathering of circles of *talmidim* around rabbis gives rise to schools that represent particular traditions (e.g., the house of Hillel and the house of Shammai). There are certain similarities here to education as found in the Greek and Hellenistic philosophical schools. Although reference can be found in the Talmud to the *talmidim* of Jesus (*b. Sanh.* 43a), unlike the rabbinic model, where the student seeks out the teacher, in the Gospels Jesus takes the initiative in establishing the circle of his disciples. Furthermore, while it was possible for students of the rabbis to become rabbis themselves, a similar progression is not available for the disciple of Jesus, who always remains a disciple. In addition, the disciples of Jesus come from various social locations and do not form the profile of a school in the restricted sense of a group devoted to formal learning. Moreover, there are women among those who follow Jesus along the way (Luke 8:1–3) and to the end (Mark 15:40–41 and par.).

A special use of "disciple" in the singular occurs in the Fourth Gospel where "the disciple whom Jesus loved," never identified by name, appears at key moments in the latter part of the Gospel (John 13:23–25; 19:26–27; 20:2–10; 21:7; 21:20–23) and is put forward by 21:24 as the guarantor of the narrative. In Acts this function of authenticating the testimony of the Christian account of the life, death, and resurrection of Jesus belongs to the select group of twelve disciples known as the apostles. They are the "witnesses" (Acts 1:8, 22; 2:32; 3:15; 5:32; 10:39, 41; 13:31) who guarantee the church's tradition.

Given the pervasive use of the word "disciple" in the Gospels and Acts, it is surprising that it is absent in the rest of the NT documents. Apart from any linguistic connection, other terms such as "believers" or "saints" function in a synonymous way to indicate those who have devoted themselves to following Christ.

CHRISTOPHER R. MATTHEWS

Discipline *see* **Correct**

Dishonor *see* **Shame**

Dome *see* **Heaven**

Doubt *see* **Believe**

Dragon *see* **Animals**

Dread, Dreadful *see* **Fear**

Dream *see* **Reveal**

Drink *see* **Water**

Ear *see* **Hear**

Eat Since eating is a fundamental human necessity, it is not surprising that the term occurs frequently in the Bible, often with no particular theological significance. Hunger, starvation, and famine due to natural causes or to warfare were common experiences, sometimes understood as divine chastisement for idolatry and sin.

Nevertheless, there is some truth in the affirmation that for the Jews every meal was a religious occasion, at least in theory. This reflected the recognition that God was the provider of all food (Ps 104:14–15, 27–28; Matt 6:25–34), and it was appropriate both to thank him for it and to pray for his continuing provision (Deut 8:1–10; Matt 6:11). Religious festivals included cultic meals; the sacrifices that were offered to God were mostly of foodstuffs, some of which was burnt as an offering to God, while other portions were for the priests or for the worshipers.

By NT times it was customary for Jews to give thanks to God at mealtimes; whether or not this was an invariable custom for all Jews, it was at least the ideal. When Jesus fed the crowds at the feeding miracles, he gave thanks for the food in the normal way (Mark 6:41; 8:6–7), and there is no indication that the thanksgiving was a prayer for God to act in multiplying the loaves and fishes. Sometimes the verb used is "to give thanks" (e.g., Mark 8:6; 14:23) and sometimes "to bless" (Mark 8:7; 14:22). Although "to bless" can have the food as its object, the alternation between the verbs indicates that the meaning is rather "to bless (i.e., thank) God in respect of the food" and does not mean that the person praying is asking God to do something to the bread; one may of course pray to God that the food will nourish the partakers, but this is not to consecrate the food in any kind of way. The fact that one can give thanks to God for the food may have been important in respect of suggestions that some foods were "unclean" or inappropriate for believers to eat. First Timothy 4:3–5 indicates that if God has created food to be eaten with thanksgiving to God for his provision, then believers should not reject foods; rather they are sanctified through the word of God and prayer. They do not defile the partakers.

Because food provides both nourishment and pleasure, it is not surprising that heaven can be portrayed under the imagery of a banquet (Matt 8:11; Luke 13:29; Rev 19:9; cf. Isa 25:6). To be deprived of food is considered a hardship that may be unavoidable or that may be accepted voluntarily as part of the self-denial entailed in being a disciple or missionary (2 Cor 11:27). On the general question of abstinence from eating, see *fast*.

Eating together has significance as an expression of belonging together as a family, as friends, or as sharers in the same religious fellowship. The action of Jesus in eating with tax collectors and sinners was strongly condemned by his opponents, who recognized the significance of what he was doing (Mark 2:15–17; Matt 11:19; Luke 15:2). Paul vigorously attacked the way in which social divisions surfaced in the congregational meals at Corinth (1 Cor 11:17–34).

Certainly there were theological problems with resulting practical consequences in the early church over the matter of eating. Law-abiding Jews considered certain foods to be unclean because they were listed as forbidden in the Torah (Lev 11). These included the reptiles and other creatures that appeared in Peter's dream (Acts 10). The dream assured Peter that these had now been made clean by God. Pharisaic Jews believed that foods prepared by Gentiles were unclean, either because the Gentiles had not observed the kosher regulations in the law regarding the draining off of blood, or because anything touched by a Gentile could be assumed to be unclean. This led to the Pharisaic practice of washing before meals (Mark 7:2–5). Peter's vision likewise asserted that such foods were not unclean; Mark 7:14–23 contains the Evangelist's conclusion that the statement of Jesus to the effect that what enters a person from outside cannot defile them had the effect of making all foods clean. It followed that eating with Gentiles was not defiling (cf. Acts 11:12).

Nevertheless there was a significant body of opinion in the early church that did not share this insight and insisted that Jewish Christians should not eat with Gentile Christians; for those with this view, it was necessary for Gentile Christians to be circumcised and to keep the other requirements of the law for such table fellowship to be possible (Acts 15:5). The discussions between Paul and Barnabas and the leaders of the church in Jerusalem reached agreement that Gentile believers did not have to be circumcised. In Paul's account of the matter in Galatians, nothing is said about food (Gal 2:1–10), but in the following paragraph we learn that in Antioch the Jewish and Gentile believers had been eating together (and, it is implied, sharing the same food) until some people came from James and persuaded them to eat separately (Gal 2:11–14). In the account in Acts 15, it was agreed that circumcision was not required, but that Gentile believers should be asked to abstain from food sacrificed to idols (i.e., eaten in a pagan temple), from blood, and from animals that had been strangled rather than slaughtered in the approved Jewish manner (Acts 15:20, 29). Thus the Gentiles were being required to eat and provide food that would not offend Jewish scruples. Presumably in Luke's eyes this represented a compromise, although it was one for which the meeting claimed the authority of the Holy Spirit (Acts

15:28–29). It established a basis on which fellowship was possible, but we do not know for certain how long it continued and where it was in force. The only other reference to it is in Rev 2:14, 20, where the eating of idol food is condemned. The gist of the agreement is confirmed by 1 Cor 10:14–22, where Paul also forbids believers to eat in temples and so to have fellowship with demons.

In the accounts of Jesus sending out his disciples on mission, they are commanded to eat whatever is set before them (Luke 10:7–8). This seems to suggest both that they are entitled to such provision from the people to whom they bring the gospel and also that they are to be content with the fare provided without looking for better quarters; it may be that later missionaries could have seen in this command a hint that they were not to ask questions about whether the food was "clean."

Further associated problems about eating arose in the early church. In 1 Cor 8–10 there is reflected the controversy at Corinth over whether believers might eat food that had been offered to idols. Paul's answer is that since idols do not exist, such offering cannot make any difference to the food; therefore believers are free to eat meat when it is sold in the marketplace or in an unbeliever's home. He recognizes that some believers may not have this insight, so that to eat the food would be for them to go against their conscience, and going against your conscience is sinful; in such a situation, personal liberty may need to be curtailed so as not to tempt these "weak" believers to partake against their consciences. However, Paul makes a distinction between eating food bought in the market and sharing in a meal in a pagan temple, where the meal implies some kind of worship of the idol; he strongly forbids the latter, because to participate in idolatry is to have some kind of link with the demons who are behind idolatry (1 Cor 10:14–22).

The problem reappears in a somewhat different form in Rom 14, where a distinction is made between believers who eat anything and those who eat only veg-etables. Probably "everything" includes meat, and the problem is again that of the offering of the meat to idols or possibly whether the meat has been slaughtered in a way acceptable to Jews. Paul is insistent that believers should not condemn one another for different practices, although he again insists that it is wrong to do what may cause a fellow believer to stumble.

In 2 Thess 3 we have echoes of a situation where some believers were living in idleness and expecting other people to provide for their needs. Paul protests that although the apostles were entitled to provision from the congregations, he personally had not used this privilege so that he might set a good example to others. He comments that anybody who is not willing to work should not eat (2 Thess 3:10); voluntary idleness is not to be encouraged, although elsewhere those who are poor and cannot find work are to be cared for.

It is not surprising that the language of eating and drinking furnished an important metaphor for the reception of spiritual provision. The exhortation "O taste and see that the LORD is good" (Ps 34:8) is picked up in 1 Pet 2:3, where believers are encouraged to long for the word of God to nourish them, as newborn infants crave for milk. Especially in John salvation is compared to *bread* and acceptance of salvation to eating the bread of life (and drinking the living water offered by Jesus); Jesus speaks of himself as not only the dispenser of this bread but also as being himself the bread (John 6:27, 35, 51). Consequently he can talk of "eating his flesh," which is true food. Yet he also makes it clear that it is his words that are spirit and life, and this should rule out any misunderstanding of what he says (John 6:63; compare other references to "eating" words: Ps 119:103; Ezek 3:1–3; Rev 10:8–11).

———

I. HOWARD MARSHALL

El Elyon   *see* **Most High**

Elder   *see* **Ministry**

Elect, Election   *see* **Choose**

Emmanuel   *see* **Immanuel**

End   *see* **Time**

Enemy   *see* **Satan**

Enjoy   *see* **Joy**

Envy, Envious   *see* **Desire; Jealous**

Eternal   *see* **Time**

Eternal Life (*see also* **Life**)   "Eternal life" (Greek *zoe aionios*), an expression that builds on the Israelite understanding of life, came to indicate during Second Temple Judaism the eschatological life of the future and was used by early believers in Jesus in both futuristic and realized ways. It connotes for the lives of believers "unending duration" (i.e., "everlasting") and "God-given quality" (i.e., "eternal") —sometimes the one; sometimes the other; and sometimes both.

In Judaism

Among the ancient Israelites, human *life* was considered a gift from God and dependent on God for not only its creation but also its sustenance, direction, and fulfillment. God was understood to be the Lord of both life and death (Deut 32:39; Job 12:10) and to control human destiny (Exod 32:32; Ps 69:28; Isa 4:3; Mal 3:16). So there was a lively realization within the Israelite nation that life is more than mere physical existence (Deut 8:3; Prov 19:23). Furthermore, there was a consciousness among many of the more godly Israelites that somehow fellowship with God cannot be broken, even by death, for God has established an eternal covenant with his people (Ps 16:10–11; Prov 12:28).

Such an understanding blossomed during the period of Second Temple Judaism (ca. 200 B.C. to A.D. 120) into a conception of a future, eschatological life—that is, "eternal life" or life in "the Age to Come." There can be little doubt that the events and pressures of the day acted as catalysts for a rethinking of Jewish theology during this time. The disastrous wars of the Greeks and the Romans against the Jews caused many Jews to ask about the validity of God's eternal covenant with his people, and Grecian ways of analytical and individual thought caused many Jews to ask not only about the situation of their nation but also about the present circumstances and ultimate fate of pious individuals. Israelite thought had been rooted in convictions about God, but without always analyzing those convictions or spelling them out in terms of the issues of the day. When faced with military and political oppression and foreign ideological pressures, Jewish thinkers reached back into their revealed heritage and came up with an extension of that heritage that spoke of "eternal life" or "the life of the age"— which came to mean life in "the Age to Come."

The Hebrew phrase "everlasting" or "eternal life" (*hayyim ʿolam*) first appears in Dan 12:2 to describe the reward of the righteous in future, eschatological days: "Many of those who sleep in the dust of the earth shall awake, some to everlasting life, and some to shame and everlasting contempt." And this theme of everlasting or eternal life was picked up by many Jewish writers during the Second Temple period in speaking of the fate of the righteous. For example, in *Psalms of Solomon*, written about the middle of the first century B.C., there appear such statements as: "They that fear the Lord shall rise to life eternal (*zoe aionion*) and their life (*he zoe auton*) shall be in the light of the Lord and shall come to an end no more" (3:12); "The life (*zoe*) of the righteous shall be for ever (*eis ton aiona*), but sinners shall be taken away into destruction" (13:11); "The saints of the Lord shall inherit life (*zoen*) in gladness" (14:10).

Likewise 2 Maccabees, in detailing the martyrdom of seven brothers at the hands of the Seleucids during the Maccabean rebellion, depicts the second brother as saying, as he was dying: "The

King of the universe will raise us up to an everlasting renewal of life (*aionion zoes*), because we have died for his laws" (7:9). It further presents the fourth brother as proclaiming to his tormentor: "For you there will be no resurrection to life (*anastasis eis zoen*)" (7:14); and it portrays the youngest brother as declaring: "Our brothers . . . have drunk of ever-flowing life (*aenaou zoes*) under God's covenant" (7:36). The author of 4 Maccabees, reflecting back on that gruesome scene, describes the mother of the seven martyred brothers as follows: "She loved religion . . . that preserves them for eternal life (*eis aionion zoen*) according to God's promise" (15:3). And in *1 Enoch* 37–71 (the Parables or Similitudes), probably written sometime during the first century A.D., there is a frequent use of the expression "everlasting" or "eternal life" (*zoe aionios*)—as, for example, in Enoch's claim that "the lot of eternal life has been given to me by the Lord of Spirits" (37:4); in the description of the angel Phanuel who has jurisdiction over "those who inherit eternal life" (40:9); and in the declaration that "the righteous shall be in the light of the sun and the elect in the light of eternal life: the days of their life shall be unending" (58:3; cf. 91:10; 103:4).

This emphasis on everlasting or eternal life can also be found at many other places in the apocalyptic and nonconformist writings of Second Temple Judaism. Furthermore, it appears in early rabbinic materials that reflect much of the language of an earlier time. For example, it can be seen in the early Aramaic Targums (ca. first century A.D.) when dealing with such passages as Lev 18:5 and Deut 33:6, where in the Hebrew Scriptures "life" is referred to (cf. *Targum Onkelos* and *Pseudo-Jonathan*, loc. cit.). And in the codifications of the later Talmud it is found in the criticism of Rabbi Eliezer (ca. A.D. 90–100) concerning those who set aside eternal life and occupy themselves only with transitory life (*b. Betzah* 15b), as well as in similar discussions ascribed to Rabbi Simeon ben Gamaliel (ca. A.D. 140; *j. Moed Katan* 82b) and Rabbi Simeon ben Jochai

(ca. A.D. 150; *b. Shabbath* 33b)—though in these latter statements there is, perhaps, more of an emphasis on the duration of human life (i.e., "everlasting") than its God-given quality (i.e., "eternal").

Concurrent with this stress on "everlasting" or "eternal" life, there also arose within Jewish apocalyptic circles of the Second Temple period a doctrine of two "ages" (*ʿolamim*): "This Age" and "the Age to Come." The doctrine of the Two Ages is expressed most explicitly in 2 Esd 7:50: "The Most High has made not one world but two." But it is alluded to at a number of other places in the Jewish apocalyptic materials as well, and often in a manner suggesting that it had been for some time a feature of Jewish thought (cf. 2 Esd 6:7–10; 7:29; 2 Baruch 14:13; 15:7–8; 44:15; 48:50). It seems also to have entered rabbinic circles, as expressed, for example, in the statement of the great teacher Rabbi Hillel in *Mishnah Aboth* 2:7b: "If a man has gained a good name he has gained [something] for himself; if he has gained for himself words of the Law he has gained for himself life in 'the Age to Come.'" In line with this usage, Rabbi Johanan ben Zakkai, who about A.D. 80 reconstituted Judaism at Jabneh, declared that "God revealed to Abraham 'this Age,' but not 'the Age to Come'" (*Genesis Rabbah* 44; cf. *Tosephta Peah* 4:18).

Two features in the Jewish discussions of the Two Ages are present: (1) that "the Age to Come" is eternally existent, being always in the heavens even as "This Age" works itself out on earth; and (2) that "the Age to Come" expresses itself on earth after the general resurrection. Sometimes, however, "the Age to Come" was understood as being equivalent to "the Messianic Age" (cf. Davies, *Torah in the Messianic Age*).

In Early Christianity

The Pauline letters. Paul uses the term "life" (*zoe*) in the sense of (1) physical life, whose antithesis is death (Rom 8:38; 1 Cor 3:22; Phil 1:20), and (2) a new quality of human existence, which results from the active presence of God's Spirit in the human personality (Rom 6:4; 8:2, 6, 10; 2 Cor 4:10–12). But he also uses "life" (*zoe*) in the sense of the future, eschatological possession of the believer (Rom 8:11)—which future life he relates inseparably to the believer's present life. Both the present life and the future life of the believer, however, are grounded not only on the concept of a living God, who gives life and promises life (as in Judaism and expressed in Titus 1:2) but preeminently on the work of Jesus Christ and his **resurrection** from the dead (Rom 5:10, 17; 6:23; 8:2; 2 Cor 4:10–11; Titus 3:7).

The expression "eternal life" (*zoe aionios*) appears in the Pauline letters eight or nine times (depending on whether 1 Tim 6:19 should be read as "true [*ontos*] life" or "eternal [*aionios*] life"). Once or twice in the Pastoral Epistles it refers to the believer's present life (1 Tim 6:12; possibly also 6:19). But Paul's usual use of "eternal life," as witnessed by his major missionary letters, is with reference to the believer's future, eschatological life—as in Rom 2:7, which speaks of it as the reward "to those who by patiently doing good seek for glory and honor and immortality"; Rom 5:21, which depicts it as the final goal of divine grace in a believer's life; Rom 6:22–23 (twice), which presents it as the ultimate result of freedom from sin and servitude to God; and Gal 6:8, which portrays it as the harvest reaped by a life dominated by the Spirit (cf. also "the hope of eternal life" in Titus 1:2 and 3:7).

In such a futuristic usage Paul seems to be reflecting the developing Jewish doctrine of life in "the Age to Come"—though, again, as with his teaching on new life generally, grounding that future expectation not only in the living God, who has "promised before the ages began" and "never lies" (Titus 1:2), but also in the work of Jesus Christ and his resurrection from the dead (Rom 6:23; Titus 3:7). And in some sense that eternal life, which will have its full expression only in the future, is present already by the working of God in the life of believers through his Spirit, who is the "first fruits," "first installment," "guarantee," or earnest of the future (Rom 8:23; 2 Cor 1:22; 5:5; Gal 4:6; 5:5).

The Synoptic Gospels. The term "life" (*zoe*) appears fifteen times in the Synoptic Gospels, with the adjective "eternal" (*aionios*) being added in eight of these occurrences. "Life" and "eternal life" are often used equivalently—as, for example, in the rich man's question "Teacher, what good deed must I do to have eternal life?" and Jesus' response: "If you wish to enter into life, keep the commandments" (Matt 19:16–17). The expression "eternal life" in the Synoptic Gospels, however, most often refers to future, eschatological blessings—that is, the inheritance promised to the righteous in "the Age to Come" of Jewish expectation (Matt 19:29; 25:46; Mark 10:30; Luke 18:30). And the two terms are used at times interchangeably with the expression "the kingdom of God"—or, as in Matthew's Gospel, "the kingdom of heaven" (Matt 19:23–29; Mark 9:43–47; 10:17–30; Luke 18:24–30).

The Fourth Gospel. "Eternal life" (*zoe aionios*) is a major and pervasive theme in the Fourth Gospel. Like the evangelist's use of "life" in an absolute sense, "eternal life" signifies not simply duration. Rather, it takes up the notion that "the Age to Come" has been inaugurated by Jesus' resurrection, and so denotes the quality of life that is appropriate to believers now living in that inaugurated age.

The Fourth Gospel expressly uses "eternal life" eighteen times, with another six occurrences appearing in 1 John. What distinguishes the Fourth Gospel from the Synoptic Gospels in its use of "eternal life," however, is, first of all, its more "realized" emphasis in highlighting the present actualization of the life of the Age to Come (cf. 3:15, 36; 5:24, 40; 6:40, 47, 54; 10:28; 17:3), without denying that such actualizations will come to full culmination in the future. As Raymond Brown points out: "For the Synoptics 'eternal life' is something that one receives at the final judgment or in a future age (Mark x 30; Matt xviii 8–9), but for John it is a present possibility for men [i.e., 'people,' citing John 5:24]" (*The Gospel according to John*, cxviii). Furthermore, John's Gospel is to be distinguished from the Synoptic Gospels in its more intense focus on Jesus as the mediator of "eternal life" (6:68; 17:2–3), and its express calls for a believing response to the person and work of Jesus in order to receive this new life (3:36; 5:24; 6:40, 47, 53–54).

The present experience of eternal life in John's Gospel is an anticipation of—but not a substitute for—the believer's future physical resurrection to the full enjoyment of eternal life. This means that eternal life for humans, while at present not simply the same as creaturely existence, cannot be viewed as divorced from physical life and so existing on some totally separate "spiritual" level. The Logos of the Fourth Gospel mediates divine life to a world that is alienated from its Creator and so under the domination of death—both spiritually and physically. Therefore the experience of the present renewal of life, which is conceptualized as "eternal life" in the present, will lead to a fully restored relationship with God the Creator and Redeemer in the future, which will be "eternal life" completely fulfilled and include in that relationship everything that is truly human.

Raymond E. Brown, S.S., *The Gospel according to John (I–XII)*, AB (Garden City, N.Y.: Doubleday, 1966); W. D. Davies, *Torah in the Messianic Age and/or the Age to Come*, JBL Monograph Series 7 (Philadelphia: Society of Biblical Literature, 1952); David Hill, *Greek Words and Hebrew Meanings: Studies in the Semantics of Soteriological Terms* (Cambridge: Cambridge University Press, 1967), 163–201; Xavier Léon-Dufour, *Life and Death in the New Testament: The Teachings of Jesus and Paul*, trans. T. Prendergast (San Francisco: Harper & Row, 1986); Richard N. Longenecker, ed., *Life in the Face of Death: The Resurrection Message of the New Testament* (Grand Rapids: Eerdmans, 1998); Marianne Meye Thompson, "Eternal Life in the Gospel of John," *Ex Auditu* 5 (1989): 35–55.

RICHARD N. LONGENECKER

Everlasting   *see* **Time**

Evil, Demon   English dictionaries use words such as "bad, wicked, injurious" to define "evil" as an adjective, and "distress, calamity, suffering, misfortune" to define it as a noun. These rather bland, secular definitions pale in comparison with the meaning that gathers around the terms in the Bible.

The primary terms to be considered here are the very common noun *ra*ᶜ in the Hebrew Bible and the Greek noun *ho poneros* and adjective *kakos/on* in the NT. All of these can on occasion mean simply "bad," as a dread disease is bad (Deut 7:15) or rotten fruit is bad (Matt 7:17). However, the majority of the uses of these terms refer to evil in its malevolent sense.

Philosophy and common experience alike distinguish at least four categories of evil: *sin* or moral evil, natural evil (chance or bad luck), *suffering*, and finitude or imperfection. In the Bible, "evil" most often carries the first of these senses. True, the Bible knows about the other three aspects of evil as well. The storm that threatened the ship on which Jonah was riding to Tarshish was called by the sailors a "calamity" (Jonah 1:7–8), by which they meant a *natural evil* or disaster. The plague that struck Israel after David took a census (2 Sam 24; 1 Chr 21) was a natural evil (2 Sam 24:16). Under the heading of *suffering* as evil, the entire book of Job is an exploration of the unmerited suffering of a righteous man that Job and his friends could only construe as evil (Job 30:26; 42:11). As for *finitude or imperfection* as evil, death stands as the prime example—that persistent and inescapable evil that inheres in mortal experience (Ps 23:4; Eccl 9:3). However, it is remarkable how often in the Bible these latter three senses of evil are affiliated and even subordinated to the first. That is to say, at least by the characters in the narratives or the writers themselves, they are perceived to be evils inflicted by God as retribution for moral evil. It is noteworthy that the Hebrew word for punishment, ᶜ*awon*, is also a word for sin. This implies that little distinction existed in the biblical view between moral evil committed by an individual or nation and the inevitable outcome, itself experienced as an evil. (Cain exemplifies this in his cry "My punishment is greater than I can bear!" [Gen 4:13]—that could also be translated "My sin is unforgivable.")

Our focus must be on moral evil or sin, therefore, because this is the primary sense of the term in the Bible and the one to which other senses are often subordinated.

Components of the biblical view of moral evil include the violation of the will of God expressed in torah, transgression of the limits set by God, and destruction of the works of God. Moral evil is something that belongs to human beings. Only human beings make the conscious choice to sin, and morality is bound up in choice. Evil, then, is not simply the absence of good but the active power of human choice. True, in biblical narratives tinged with folklore, evil comes to be understood as a malevolent, spiritual power of superhuman dimensions, often personified with the face of Satan, the devil, or demons. However, moral evil is typically thought of in terms of specific sins such as those enumerated in the legal codes and in such moral teachings asthe Sermon on the Mount. Even today people tend to think of more mundane sins when they contemplate the vast theological issue of evil. (The more than eight million topics listed on the Web under the heading of "evil," for example, range from Harry Potter through vampires to capital punishment and ghostwritten term papers.)

Theology and philosophy want to treat a topic like evil systematically, beginning from first principles. An initial question appropriately addressed in a systematic discussion of evil would be "If God is the good and all-powerful creator of all things, why does evil exist in the world?" The Bible, however, does not think or speak systematically. To this burning question of the ages, it offers no answer at all. Genesis 3 never says where evil comes from. The serpent is not Satan or the devil, making a sneaky entry into a previously

unspoiled Eden. It is simply an extraordinarily intelligent creature who raises the inevitable question "Why would you not want to eat of the tree of the knowledge of good and evil?" Indeed, one could say that for the sake of the plot of the Bible—humankind moving out of the garden, filling the earth, and having dominion here—the "fall" was a necessity. (In Eastern Christian thought, especially in that of the patristic writer Irenaeus [ca. A.D. 120–202], Gen 3 was construed as a fall upward from childish innocence to sadder but wiser maturity—the story of everyone.) It also sets up the great Christian drama of redemption, in which the solidarity of humankind in the sin of Adam is overmatched by the solidarity of humankind in the grace and salvation that come from the new Adam, Jesus Christ (Rom 5:12–21; 1 Cor 15:21–22). Speaking reflectively upon the story of creation and of the fall, one might say that the "dust of the ground" (Gen 2:7) of which we are made is our ticket to freedom. Any creature who is wholly other than God inevitably has the freedom to engage in evil, apart from and in opposition to the will of God.

As for evil itself, it just is, even as God just is.

Beside the burning question "How can evil exist in a world made by a good God?" stands another fundamental one: "Is it possible that God is the author of evil?"

Certain biblical texts do in fact hint at a shadow side of God. (The Lord's inexplicable attempt to kill Moses in Exod 4:24 is an example. So is Job's charge in Job 9:22 that "he destroys both the blameless and the wicked," not to mention the Lord's assertion in Isa 45:7 that "I make weal and create woe.") However, the whole witness of Scripture is clear. God is not the author of evil. Indeed, interpreters have asserted that Christianity is theologically *monistic* and ethically *dualistic*. That means that God is one and God is good. Neither a shadow side of God nor an anti-God, Satan, rises to the level of parity with God. Human beings have the dual nature, capable, whether through defect or necessity, of both good and evil. Though it is true that Scripture speaks of "principalities and powers" of evil, evil on the cosmic scale is not really the worry. Human behavior is. As the Preacher says, "The hearts of all are full of evil" (Eccl 9:3; see also Jer 17:9; Matt 7:11). The need for theodicy (justification of God's way with evil) remains, for sure—if God is all good and all-powerful, why does God put up with evil? Unsystematic answers may emerge from the text, but an evil side of God will not be among them.

God is portrayed, of course, especially in the OT, as having a judging side. To the extent that judgment entails suffering and is experienced as that kind of evil (the third category mentioned at the beginning of this article), the biblical prophets and theologians are willing to say that evil comes from God. "Does disaster befall a city, unless the LORD has done it?" (Amos 3:6). The elaborate list of sanctions that follows the covenant code in the book of Deuteronomy (Deut 27–28) enumerates the rewards and punishments that accompany obedience and disobedience respectively. Some are administered by God directly, but many flow forth as destinies of blessing or curse produced by the deeds themselves. This retributional theology is played out in the Deuteronomistic history of the kings of Judah and Israel (1–2 Samuel, 1–2 Kings), is endorsed in the Psalms of the Two Ways (e.g., Pss 1, 37, 49, 73, 112), and is projected on to the big screen of apocalyptic victory of good over evil in Dan 7–12 and in the NT book of Revelation. In short, moral evil calls forth the punitive evils of suffering and death.

Yet the system is not closed. Even in Deuteronomy, in which evil and its inevitable consequences seem most closely tied together, the Torah and its sanctions conclude with this famous divine affidavit: "I call heaven and earth to witness against you today that I have set before you life and death, blessings and curses. Choose life . . ." (Deut 30:19).

This does not say, "You have made your choice against good (= life) and for evil (= death), and you are therefore condemned." Instead, the choice of good or life is set forth as an abiding option, and God remains ready to bless rather than curse. Nowhere is the power and permanence of the divine intention to overcome evil with good more dramatically displayed than on the cross and in Jesus' words there: "Father, forgive them; for they do not know what they are doing" (Luke 23:34). The judgment that produces suffering, which itself is perceived as evil, is in the full message of Scripture embraced by God's grace.

Perhaps, then, God is powerless to prevent evil, given the fact that imperfection and finitude are built into the very fabric of the created order. If human beings are created partly out of the earthly clay of freedom, they will certainly sin unless God somehow alters their essential humanity, and they must certainly suffer the evil fate of mortal creatures. This line of thinking about evil is very much in the mind of the Preacher who wrote the book of Ecclesiastes: "This is an evil in all that happens under the sun, that the same fate comes to everyone" (Eccl 9:3). He believes that there is no point in trying to do good, because suffering and death come to all equally. Though rooted in certain indisputable facts of human experience, that pessimistic view does not prevail in Scripture. How does God deal with evil? God works in and through it to advance the cause of good and the reign of God. Joseph puts it succinctly to his brothers in summing up the story of their treachery and ultimate reconciliation with him: "As for you, you meant evil against me; but God meant it for good" (Gen 50:20 RSV). He speaks not of double causality but of God working within the same human finitude and moral evil that yield suffering and death to move people and events in the direction of life. Perhaps Paul had this picture in mind when he wrote his stirring assurance to the church in Rome, "We know that all things work together for good for those who love God" (Rom 8:28).

To sum up, evil and good are not on a par in Scripture. Evil's power is far more profound than any personification of it, be it in the form of Satan, the devil, or demons. It is ubiquitous and can even be thought of as cosmic in scope, as the writer of Ephesians does when he speaks of "spiritual forces of evil in the heavenly places" (Eph 6:12). And yet God wins in the struggle. Evil is encompassed by good. God has no rival from the side of the satanic. That is why in the end, the psalmist can say in perfect trust, "Even though I walk through the darkest valley, I fear no evil; for you are with me" (Ps 23:4). That is why Jesus offers us words with which to express trust even as we petition God, "Lead us not into temptation, but deliver us from evil" (Matt 6:13 RSV).

Demon. The folk of the ancient world found it helpful to personify the profound and ubiquitous reality of evil in various ways (see *Satan*). Demons were one such localization of evil. Like Satan and the devil, demons make little appearance in the OT, perhaps because of the abhorrence felt by OT writers toward anything that smacked of the old polytheism. We hear of goat-demons or satyrs, twice as objects of idolatrous worship (Lev 17:7, 2 Chr 11:15) and twice simply as denizens of the howling wilderness that follows God's destruction of enemies (Isa 13:21; 34:14). The rare Hebrew word *shedim*, taken to refer to foreign deities to whom Israel sacrificed children, is also translated "demons" by the NRSV (Deut 32:17; Ps 106:37).

In the NT a demon is a generic evil spirit under the command of a ruler of demons (e.g., Beelzebul in Matt 12:24) who may infest a person or an animal (see, for example, Matt 8:31, where the demons affecting the Gadarene demoniacs are cast into a herd of swine). The noun demon (Greek: *daimon*) is used sixty-nine times, preponderantly in the Synoptic Gospels. (The KJV never uses the word "demon," preferring "devil"

instead. Guided by the distinction in Greek terminology, NRSV rightly separates these lesser spirits from the more powerful figure of the devil, who is often equated with Satan himself.) They manifest themselves primarily in physical and mental illness of human beings. In Matt 4:24, demoniacs are listed under the heading "the sick" along with epileptics and paralytics. Much of Jesus' healing ministry consisted of casting demons out of stricken people, and his power of exorcism is one of the gifts of the Spirit he passed on to his disciples (Matt 10:8; Mark 3:15; Luke 9:1). Only twice in the NT is there mention of demons being worshiped by sinful human beings (1 Cor 10:20–21; Rev 9:20).

It is evident that the Gospel writers and even Jesus himself believed in the existence and reality of demons. Traditional believers, especially in the rapidly growing churches of the southern hemisphere, continue to do so today and to invoke powerful spiritual weapons against them. Nevertheless, in the older churches of the Northern and Western worlds, demons are now widely viewed as elements of folklore. They are understood to be means whereby ancient peoples could grasp and even manage the reality of evil more readily. As ciphers for madness, they stand in for rage, hate, physical disease, and all else that leads to mental illness and dysfunction. In this view, however, the problem of evil is much bigger than demons. To say that Hitler had a demon would be to trivialize him. It is far more frightening to say that he was a human being like the rest of us, who engaged himself to evil on the largest scale possible.

John Hick, *Evil and the God of Love* (New York: Harper, 1966); C. S. Lewis, *The Problem of Pain* (New York: Macmillan, 1940); Paul Ricoeur, "Evil," *The Encyclopedia of Religion* (New York: Macmillan, 1987), 5:199–208; W. Sibley Towner, *How God Deals with Evil* (Philadelphia: Westminster Press, 1976).

W. SIBLEY TOWNER

Exile The destruction of the holy city of Jerusalem by Nebuchadnezzar's Babylonian army in 587/586 B.C. and the ensuing mass deportation we know as the Babylonian exile posed the biggest crisis of faith ever to confront the theologians of the OT. The stark fact that it happened and the ideological framework that grew up around it have continued to shape both Judaism and Christianity. Although the exile as such is specifically mentioned in NT only as a place marker in the genealogy of Matt 1:11–12, 17, the reality of the Jewish Diaspora (begun in Babylon, renewed by Rome) was the essential matrix for the growth of Christianity (e.g., Jas 1:1; 1 Pet 1:1). The reality of *galuth* (exile) has given Judaism the context in which to exercise its vocation to be a light to the nations of the world (Isa 42:6).

History. The people of the Bible experienced an exile earlier than the Babylonian one, of course. In 721 B.C., the Assyrian king Sargon II seized Samaria, the capital of the rebellious vassal northern kingdom of Israel. True to Assyrian policy, he then engaged in a massive transfer of populations. The kingdom's cities were resettled with foreigners (2 Kgs 17:24), while the ten northern tribes of Israel disappeared forever by assimilation into the lands and peoples of their captivity. The prophets Amos and Hosea interpreted this tragedy as the judgment of God upon an apostate people.

The surviving southern kingdom of Judah played politics shrewdly during the century that followed. In a period of transition between the decline of Assyria and the rise of the new Mesopotamian superpower, Babylon, the good King Josiah (640–609 B.C.) was able to effect in Judah the religious reform so ardently desired by the Deuteronomists and by the contemporary prophet, Jeremiah. After Josiah's death at the hands of Pharaoh Neco, the Egyptians installed his son Jehoiakim as a puppet ruler (609–598). Egyptian domination of the region was giving way to that of Babylon, however, and Judah found itself on the losing side in the struggle. In a punitive raid, Nebuchadnezzar besieged Jerusalem. Jehoiakim died during the siege and was succeeded by his son, Jehoiachin. After a reign of only three months, he chose surrender over total destruction; according to the Babylonian Chronicles, Jerusalem fell to Nebuchadnezzar on March 15/16, 597 B.C. We are told in 2 Kgs 24:10–17 that the conqueror carried away the temple valuables, together with the king, his mother, his wives, and eight to ten thousand of the nobility and the soldiers; "no one remained except the poorest people of the land" (2 Kgs 24:14).

In less than a decade the flag of rebellion was raised again. Nebuchadnezzar had installed another son of Josiah, Zedekiah, in 597 to rule Judah as a vassal. Sometime after 592 B.C. this puppet king began an alliance with Egypt, a bad decision that led to another Babylonian campaign in Judea. At the end of an eighteen-month siege, Jerusalem fell in 587/586 B.C. Zedekiah's sons were slaughtered before his eyes, and then his eyes were put out (2 Kgs 25:7). Nebuchadnezzar seized the temple treasures, burned the temple and the city, and deported the populace to Babylon, leaving only "some of the poorest people of the land to be vinedressers and tillers of the soil" (2 Kgs 25:12).

Jeremiah 52:30 even speaks of a third deportation about 582 B.C.—inflicted as punishment for the assassination by Judean superpatriots of the Babylonian appointed governor, Gedaliah—and sets the total number of exiles from all three deportations at 4,600.

We know little about life as it continued in Judah during the years 587–538 B.C. Psalm 79 is a communal lament over the destruction of the city of Jerusalem. Jeremiah 41:4 pictures men from the former northern kingdom coming to engage in mourning rituals at the temple site. The book of Lamentations as a whole may preserve the genuine voice of the Judeans as they gathered at the site of the temple for worship. That voice continues to be heard on the ninth of Ab, the Jewish fast day devoted to ritual mourning of the destruction of the first and second temples and other tragedies that befell the Jews (see *Mishnah Ta'anit* 4:6).

Regarding life in the community of the exiles in Babylon itself, we have evidence from both in and out of the Bible. The fifth century B.C. cuneiform Murashu Texts from Nippur mention Jews involved in commerce and economic life. Evidently some of the exiles took the advice of Jeremiah to "build houses and live in them. . . . take wives and have sons and daughters. . . . seek the welfare of the city where I have sent you into exile, and pray to the LORD on its behalf" (Jer 29:5–7). In the Bible we have the prophecy of Ezekiel, who was carried away in 597 and dwelt among the Jewish exiles at Tel-Aviv on the River Chebar in Babylon (Ezek 1:1; 3:15), as well as the thrilling songs of Isaiah of the Exile (Isa 40–55). We also have the account of the favorable treatment accorded to King Jehoiachin, scion of the house of David, who preferred surrender to destruction. According to 2 Kgs 25:27–30 and Jer 52:31–34, he was released from prison and given a place at the royal table, a status of respect that is confirmed in Babylonian archives.

There is reason to believe that the great priestly codification of law and custom incorporated into the final edition of the Pentateuch may have been done in scribal circles in Babylon. The tales of Dan 1–6 offer idealized pictures of gifted young Jews rising to high positions in the royal courts of Babylonian kings. Many also believe that the characteristic Jewish institutions of Sabbath observance and dietary law received new emphasis among the Jewish minority in Babylon, partly as ways of maintaining sharp religious and ethnic identity. On the other hand, the exiles adopted much from their conquerors, including the Aramaic language and alphabet that continued in use among the Jews even after the exile.

In short, for all of its trauma and tragedy, the exile also fructified Jewish life.

The exile came to an end shortly after Cyrus, the king of the new megapower,

Persia, conquered Babylon on the night of October 11, 539. Ezra 1:2–4 and 2 Chr 36:22–23 preserve the text of the so-called edict of Cyrus, authorizing Jews to return to Jerusalem from exile and to rebuild the temple. He even made restitution of temple treasures (Ezra 1:7–11). Not all did return, of course, and a large and vibrant Jewish community remained in Mesopotamia until the twentieth century A.D. However, after 538 B.C. many (Ezra 2:64 says 42,360!) of the priestly and royal elites returned from Babylon and reclaimed their leading positions in the homeland. Led by the grandson of Jehoiachin, Zerubbabel, and spurred on by the prophetic exhortations of Haggai and Zechariah, these returnees led the reconstruction of the temple until it was dedicated in March 12, 515 B.C. (Ezra 6:15).

Theological significance. The exile was a major theological problem, because it demanded vindication of God. Not only did a God who allowed an elect people to be driven out of a promised land look like a traitor, but that God also looked weak compared with rival national deities. The embarrassed question was inevitable: "Why should the nations say, 'Where is their God?'" (Ps 79:10; see also Ps 115:2; Joel 2:17). To the degree that a theological explanation of the exile had credibility, the faith of Israel and the exilic community itself could survive. Indeed, such an account could prepare Jews and Christians for life in Diaspora in ages to come.

The interpretation that prevailed was that the exile was the consequence of the nation's apostasy. Yahweh was justified not only in allowing the destruction of Israel and then Judah but also in using Assyria and Babylon as instruments of the divine wrath. Thus were God's justice and power vindicated, but so was God's graciousness in allowing the survival of a remnant both in exile and in the homeland.

The task of making this theological sense fell above all to the prophets, and to the Deuteronomists who wrote the history of the kings of Israel and Judah in a way that reflected the prophetic judgment. In their final edition of the

Former Prophets (Joshua–2 Kings), probably issued during the exile, we hear twin themes: the condemnation of the apostasy and covenant violation of nearly every king of Israel and Judah, and the gracious promise by Yahweh of an ongoing dynasty. The latter is enunciated by the Lord through the prophet Nathan to David in the dynastic oracle of 2 Sam 7:16: "Your house and your kingdom shall be made sure forever before me; your throne shall be established forever." Depending on which of these two themes one emphasizes, the great historiographic center of the Hebrew Bible can be read either as an obituary for the chosen people, culminating in the destruction of Jerusalem and the exile, or—pairing the dynastic oracle with the concluding notice of the restoration to a place of dignity of the last of the Davidic monarchs in 2 Kgs 25:27–30—as a testimony of hope. In either case, it helped provide a theological rationale for the exile.

The prophet Jeremiah was active during the deportations of 597 and 587. He was uncompromising in his interpretation of these events as the curse that inevitably flowed from the sin of kings and people. His scathing temple sermon (Jer 7:3–15) typifies his preaching prior to the destruction of Jerusalem. He answers those who mumble the mantra "This is the temple of the LORD" with these words: "If you do not oppress the alien, the orphan, and the widow . . . then I will dwell with you in this place." But if you persist in your sin, "I will do to the house that is called by my name . . . what I did to Shiloh. And I will cast you out of my sight" (Jer 7:6–7, 14–15). Punishment for sin was not a pleasant way of looking at the tragedy of the exile, but it at least made it intelligible. Jeremiah was willing to accept as inevitable the yoke of Babylonian conquest (Jer 27). In his letter to the exiles he was willing to lay the groundwork for a near future life far removed from the old institutions of ark, temple, kingship, and Jerusalem itself (Jer 29:4–23), even as he hoped for a distant future of faithful obedience (31:31–34).

The same dialogue between present faithlessness accompanied by inevitable sanctions and promise of a future restoration also describes the preaching of the prophet Ezekiel. In fact, his entire book pivots on the announcement to the exiles in Babylon that Jerusalem had fallen (Ezek 33:34). Before that point he had foreseen disaster and spoken of the desolating abandonment of the temple and holy city by the glory of the Lord (e.g., Ezek 10:4–5, 18–19; 11:22–23). From this point on, he begins to prepare the way for restoration with oracles of promise and a detailed vision of the new temple in a rebuilt Jerusalem (Ezek 40–48), to which the glory returns for good (Ezek 43:1–5).

Another theological development in the book of Ezekiel is affiliated with the *glory* of the Lord as well. His call to be a prophet occurred not in the temple but in Babylonian exile, when he had a vision of the glory of the Lord seated on a heavenly chariot (Ezek 1–3). In reporting this, he offered an enlarged theological understanding of the sphere of Yahweh's dominion. Unlike a tribal deity, the God of Israel could speak outside the temple and the *land* of Israel.

No discussion of the theological understanding of the exile would be complete without reference to the work of Deutero-Isaiah (Isa 40–55). Preaching in Babylon as the exile neared its end, this greatest of all prophetic lyricists begins his message with the words "Comfort, O comfort my people, says your God. Speak tenderly to Jerusalem, and cry to her that . . . she has received from the LORD's hand double for all her sins" (Isa 40:1–2). After just retribution for sin comes gracious restoration. His exilic monotheism is more radical and becomes more normative than that of any of his predecessors: Yahweh has no competitors (44:6), and Israel is answerable to none but Yahweh. Most of this prophet's message is the announcement of the end of the exile and a return to the land under the metaphor of a new exodus.

He also invokes the image of a *servant* of the Lord. In one of the four passages that are termed the Servant Songs, this figure seems to be an individual (Isa 52:13–53:12), but in another he is identified as the collective entity of Israel (49:1–6). To this servant Israel, God says, "I will give you as a light to the nations, that my salvation may reach to the end of the earth" (49:6). As in Ezekiel, the theological impact of the exile here is to make the vocation of God's chosen people far more sweeping than could be exercised within the confines of a chosen land.

Though in the restoration after the exile much will be salvaged from the pre-exilic polity of Judah, including the temple itself, priesthood, Torah, and prayer, thanks to the preaching of these powerful and inspired interpreters of events, Israel's vocation is enlarged to worldwide dimensions. Far from being weaker than the other gods, Yahweh proves to be stronger, manifesting the reign of God in the uttermost parts of the earth. From now on, people of God will move into that extended sphere. Indeed, they will embrace diaspora as a permanent part of the life of God's people.

Ralph W. Klein, *Israel in Exile: A Theological Interpretation* (Philadelphia: Fortress Press, 1979); James D. Newsome Jr., *By the Waters of Babylon: An Introduction to the History and Theology of the Exile* (Atlanta: John Knox Press, 1979); Daniel Smith-Christopher, *A Biblical Theology of Exile* (Minneapolis: Fortress Press, 2002).

W. SIBLEY TOWNER

Eye *see* **See**

Face *see* **Presence**

Faith, Faithful *see* **Believe**

False, Falsehood *see* **True**

Family, Household, Father, Mother, Son, Daughter, Child, Brother, Sister Kinship language figures prominently in the OT and NT. Much of the OT narrative recounts family

history, and in both testaments family terminology is a central matrix of theological reflection and discourse. It provides much of the language and imagery by which Israel articulated its covenant commitment with Yahweh and by which early Christians conveyed their understanding of both the God revealed in Jesus Christ and the church.

Old Testament

"Family" and "household." The word "family" is used to translate several Hebrew words denoting kinship groups. Most frequently, it represents one of two kinship groups that can be distinguished, the *mishpahah* or the *beth ʾab*. The *mishpahah*, the larger of the two, was comprised of a number of families, bound by common ancestry and heritage. Living in close proximity in a village setting and sharing common settled space, they worked cooperatively in the farmlands surrounding the village to subsist and to sustain each other. The *mishpahah* has been described as a "residential kinship group" or "protective association of families." The closest English equivalent is probably the word "clan" (though "clan" does not necessarily convey its coresident nature), and in fact *mishpahah* is frequently translated in this way in the NRSV. In Israel's tribal society, the *mishpahah* was an intermediate kinship group, smaller than the "tribe" (*shebet, matteh*), but larger than the *beth ʾab* (literally, "father's house"). These concentric groups (tribe, clan, and family household) were the three primary units of social organization based on kinship (see Josh 6:15 for clear differentiation between them).

The most important of these kinship groups, the *beth ʾab*, is also rendered in modern English translation as "family." Sometimes the word *bayith* (literally, "house") appears alone in reference to this group and is translated as either "family" or "household." In order to capture both the social and economic dimensions of the *beth ʾab*, a better translation would be "family household."

Though the smallest of the kinship groups, the *beth ʾab* was considerably larger than the two-generational group referred to in modern parlance as the "nuclear family." It was a multigenerational kinship group, an extended family, comprised of all the descendants of a single living ancestor (with the exception of married daughters). It included the head of the household and his wife, any sons along with their wives and children, any wives and children of grandsons, and any unmarried daughters. (When a daughter married, she became a member of her husband's family household.) The *beth ʾab* also included the family's residential compound of linked dwellings, land, tools, livestock, and any unrelated persons attached to the household, such as resident workers or slaves. It was thus the basic unit not only of Israel's social structure but of its economic life. Within Israel's agrarian culture, it functioned as a self-sufficient economic unit in which all household members played integral roles. The *beth ʾab* also preserved the faith, memory, law, and traditions of the nation, passing them on to each generation. It thereby played a central role in the Israelites' religious experience of covenant life with God.

Though much of the authority of the *beth ʾab* was lodged with the male head of household, the group was profoundly interdependent. The fact that it was referred to as "the father's house" reflects both its patrilineal and patrilocal nature (i.e., descent was reckoned through the male line, and a female left her father's household to join her husband's upon marriage). But interestingly, four references to a "mother's house" (*beth ʾem*) also appear in the OT (Gen 24:28; Ruth 1:8; Song 3:4; 8:2) and serve as a reminder of the mother's integral and influential role within the life of the family household.

The word "family" is used to convey both *mishpahah* and *beth ʾab* in modern English translation, because in many texts the lines between the two are indistinct. Translators have had to decide on a case-by-case basis which group is in view. The word "family" also appears, upon occasion, as a translation of other Hebrew words such as *ben* and *ʾah*, which, translated literally, refer respectively to "sons" and "brothers." In patriarchal cultures, references to men are often intended as generic references to both men and women. Thus in these cases, the word "family" is employed for more inclusive and accurate translation.

In short, kinship terminology, in both Hebrew and English, is fluid and decidedly elastic. In some cases, it is difficult to make hard and fast distinctions between words, for the family metaphor often extends beyond the *beth ʾab* and *mishpahah* to include the tribe and even the nation. The word *bayith* or "house," for example, can refer not only to the *beth ʾab*, but in some instances to the *mishpahah*, as well as to descendants of a person far removed in time (e.g., "the house of Isaac"). It is attached, in particular, to the royal household and the development of the Davidic dynasty ("house of David"), yet also extends to embrace the entire nation, the "house of Israel."

Whatever its reach, kinship language consistently bears witness to a reality of central importance in the OT world: that of collective family identity. Ancient Israelites and early Jews did not think of themselves as autonomous individuals. Instead, they were embedded in a family household that served as the primary locus of identity, responsibility, and security within the national covenant relationship with Yahweh. Indeed, it is striking that even the nation is described in kinship terms as the "house (*bayith*) of Israel" and in several instances as the "house of Yahweh" (Num 12:7; Jer 12:7; Hos 8:1). Such language reflects Israel's understanding of itself as the nation formed from chosen ancestral households. Moreover, throughout the OT both Yahweh and the nation are cast metaphorically in the roles of various members of the family household (see below). Kinship language thereby becomes a primary signifier of covenant life with Yahweh. The family household was, in fact, one of two major social institutions that shaped Israel's self-understanding and its articulation of the character and activity of God. The other was the monarchy.

Members of the family household. Given the importance of collective family identity in the OT world, persons are always identified in relation to others, as someone's father or mother, son or daughter, sister or brother. A variety of Hebrew words specify various members of the family household. Though the terms are straightforward, usually designating blood relatives, they are also employed in metaphorical ways, often to convey theological realities.

The Hebrew word ʾab, translated as "father," usually designates a blood relative, a male parent. The father was the head of the family household, which, as we have noted, was both patrilineal and patrilocal in nature. For these reasons, it was designated by the phrase beth ʾab (literally, "the father's house," though this phrase appears in the NRSV translation as "family").

Even in reference to blood relatives, however, the word ʾab or "father" can have a broader frame of reference. It can be used, for example, in reference to a grandfather (as in 1 Kgs 15:15), and to ancestors in general, particularly in its plural form (ʾaboth). Indeed, the plural form of the word (literally, "the fathers") can collectively evoke the ancestors of Israel, such as Abraham, Isaac, and Jacob, the patriarchs of the faith (Deut 4:37; 10:15), or the whole exodus generation, which experienced the decisive event in Israel's history of salvation (Lev 26:45; Josh 24:6, 17). However, because women too were among those forebears, and because biblical references to men are often intended as generic references to both women and men, this use of ʾab and ʾaboth appears consistently, and appropriately, in the NRSV translation as "ancestor(s)."

The word ʾab or "father" has metaphorical uses as well, sometimes designating men who appear in the biblical narrative

in authoritative or guardian roles. Joseph, for example, is referred to as a "father to Pharaoh" (Gen 45:8), and Job speaks of himself as a "father to the needy" (Job 29:12–16). A prophet can be referred to as "father" (2 Kgs 6:21) as can a priest (Judg 18:19) or a king (1 Sam 24:11).

The most striking use of ʾab, however, is as a theological metaphor, descriptive of God's relationship with Israel. Upon occasion, God is referred to quite specifically as "father" (Deut 32:6; Jer 31:9), compared to a "father" (Ps 103:13; Prov 3:12), or identified as the "father" of the Davidic king (2 Sam 7:14; Ps 89:26). In a number of instances, father imagery is at play, though the word "father" itself does not appear. By means of this imagery, God is conveyed in a variety of parental roles, loving, pitying, teaching, disciplining, longing, and caring for Israel, God's "son" (e.g., Hos 11:1–11). Parental language or imagery for God is by no means as central to OT theological reflection as it is in the NT. Nevertheless the idea of the fatherhood of God was clearly embedded in Israel's consciousness and undoubtedly influenced the presentation of God and of sonship in the NT.

The word "mother" (ʾem) appears far less frequently than "father" (ʾab) in the OT and usually designates a blood relative, a female parent. As noted above, though the family household is usually referred to as the "father's house" (beth ʾab; "family" in the NRSV), in four striking instances it is referred to as the "mother's house" (beth ʾem; see Gen 24:28; Ruth 1:8; Song 3:4; 8:2), and there may be no doubt about the mother's integral and influential role within the family. The words "father and mother" appear together more than forty times in the OT, and both parents were to be honored (Exod 20:12; Deut 5:6) and obeyed (e.g., Prov 1:8; 19:26; 20:20; 23:22–25).

The word ʾem or "mother" is also employed metaphorically. Deborah's leadership as a judge is honored by the designation of her as a "mother in Israel" (Judg 5:7). In a few instances, cities are identified as "mothers" (Babylon, for example, in Jer 50:12 and Abel in 2 Sam 20:19) and thus as guardians and nurturers of their inhabitants. Jerusalem too is described with maternal imagery as one who gave birth to her sons and daughters (Isa 49:18–21; Ezek 16:20). Though God is never referred to specifically as "mother" (*'em*) in the OT, maternal imagery is used to convey God's maternal creativity and abiding love, care, and compassion. For example, God is described as one who births and suckles Israel (Deut 32:11, 18–19; Isa 46:3–4; 49:15) and performs maternal tasks, providing comfort, food and water, clothing, and instruction (Exod 16:8, 15; Num 11:18; Neh 9:20–21; Hos 11:3–4). Moreover, the word for "compassion" in Hebrew (*rahamim*) is closely related to the Hebrew word for "womb" (*rehem*). Both words are used in reference to God far more often than in reference to humans in the OT, thereby evoking the intensity of God's maternal love for Israel. In sum, both paternal and maternal metaphors give expression to Israel's understanding of God's character and activity.

Of all the members of the family household, the "son" is most visible in the OT narrative, for the language of sonship is pervasive. The word "son" (*ben* in Hebrew) has a wide range of meaning, and is used in literal, metaphorical, and theological ways. While it usually designates a mother or father's male offspring, it can convey other family relationships, such as grandson (Gen 31:28, 55). It can also refer more generally to any male descendant in the same lineage and thus plays a central role in OT genealogies. The phrase "my son," used repeatedly throughout the book of Proverbs in direct address, may well be used literally, as the words of a father to a biological son, but it also evolves into a technical designation for a student.

The word *ben* or "son" is used more broadly and metaphorically to establish a variety of connections. In fact, the expression "son of" came to be a standard way to describe a characteristic feature of someone or something. For example, the expression "son(s) of" can be attached to the name of a place to designate the people or inhabitants of that place. Thus "sons of Israel" frequently appears as a name for the nation, as in Exod 2:25 ("Israelites" in the NRSV; see also the "sons of Zion" and the "sons of Greece" in Zech 9:13). The expression "son of" can also designate a professional group; for example, "sons of the prophets" in 2 Kgs 4:38 and Amos 7:14 ("the company of prophets" in the NRSV) describes professional membership in the prophetic guild, just as "sons of Aaron" (Lev 3:2) designates the priestly guild. Alternatively, the expression can connect someone with a particular social class or circumstance, a particular quality, or a particular fate: for example, "sons of affliction" in Prov 31:5 ("the afflicted" in the NRSV); "sons of valor" in Judg 18:2 ("valiant men" in the NRSV); or "son of death" in 1 Sam 20:31 ("he shall surely die" in the NRSV). As these examples indicate, in the interest of inclusive language, modern English translations such as the NRSV find a variety of suitable means by which to convey the nature of the connection or characteristic being established.

Finally, two uses of *ben* or "son" bear decidedly theological connotations: "son(s) of man" and "son(s) of God." The expression "son(s) of man" (*ben/bene 'adam, ben 'ish,* or *ben 'enosh*) basically designates the human being (as distinct from other living creatures). This phrase makes its first appearance in the OT in the story of the tower of Babel (Gen 11:5) and from there on characteristically conveys human alienation from God. The "*Son of Man*," however, is also a focus of God's grace and redemption (e.g., Ps 8:4; 144:3, "human beings" and "mortals" in the NRSV). The much-discussed appearance of the Aramaic phrase "son of man" in Dan 7:13 (*kebar 'enash*) is in a class by itself, and scholars continue to debate both its meaning and its relationship to the NT "Son of Man" tradition.

Three different parties are associated with the notion of divine sonship. In a few instances the phrase "sons of God" (*bene ha'elohim*) designates divine beings, and may be related to the idea of a heavenly court. In Gen 6:1–4, for example, male divine beings have relations with human women. This strange story is undoubtedly influenced by Near Eastern mythological tradition, and given Israel's strict monotheism, reflection on a divine council of any sort is limited (but see Job 1:6; 2:1; 38:7; and Ps 29:1). Divine sonship was more clearly associated with the Davidic king, who was "adopted" as son of God at his enthronement and reigned as Yahweh's representative (see Ps 2:7; 2 Sam 7:14; see *adopt; son of God*). Finally, the nation of Israel itself is described with language and imagery of divine sonship. The prophet Hosea, in particular, makes memorable use of this metaphor, describing Ephraim/Israel as a beloved son (*ben* and *na'ar*) and Yahweh as Israel's compassionate father (Hos 11:1–11; see also Exod 4:22–23; Deut 1:31; Jer 31:9).

The word *bath* or "daughter" appears far less frequently in the OT than the word *ben* or "son" and usually designates a mother or father's female offspring, a blood relative. It is sometimes used more generally to designate the women of a people or city (e.g., "daughters of Moab" in Isa 16:2 or "daughters of Jerusalem" throughout the Song of Songs). It can also be linked to the name of a city or country and as such functions as a personification of that place or its inhabitants (e.g., "daughter Egypt" in Jer 46:11, 19, 24 and "daughter Babylon" in Jer 50:42; 51:33). It is most frequently linked to Zion ("daughter Zion") or Jerusalem ("daughter Jerusalem"), often as a term of endearment, and thereby emphasizes the special relationship between God and the chosen city: Zion or Jerusalem is the very daughter of God.

The vocabulary of childhood is vague and elastic. The two most common Hebrew words translated as "child" are *yeled* and *na'ar*. Both can reference any of the stages of life between the womb and marriage. Thus both *yeled* and *na'ar* are used of the unborn and newborn, the unweaned and weaned, youths and

young men. With but one exception (Ruth 1:5), the terms refer to unmarried children. When referencing family relationships, both designate male children. Feminine forms of these terms (*yalda* and *na'ar*) occasionally appear in reference to female children. Throughout the OT, children are clearly regarded as a gift of God and a great blessing, and barrenness or loss of children as a great tragedy.

However, *na'ar* is also used in nonfamilial ways to designate a servant or employee under the authority of a superior. In these instances, status and office is in view, rather than age, and other language is employed in translation to convey the nature of the relationship (such as "servant" or "young man," or language of military or civil service; e.g., Gen 18:7; Josh 6:22–23; 1 Kgs 20:14–15; Isa 37:6).

Finally, sibling vocabulary is employed to describe a range of kinship relations. The word "brother" (*'ah*) figures prominently in OT narratives (particularly those of Genesis), which feature an unusual number of conflicted fraternal relationships. It usually designates an immediate family relationship—that of blood brother or half brother—but can be used with reference to a wider circle of relatives, as well as to members of the same tribe. Legal materials in Deuteronomy also specify appropriate treatment of one's "brother," and in this case the reference is clearly to other members of the broader covenant community—to fellow Israelites. A "brother" is thus a fellow countryman and a fellow believer.

The word "sister" (*'ahoth*) bears the same wide range of meaning, for it too can denote a blood sister, a relative from the wider kinship circle, or, less frequently, a fellow citizen. It also has further uses. Throughout the Song of Songs, "sister" is used as a term of endearment in reference to the beloved (though "brother" is not used in a similar way; see Song 4:9–12; 5:1–2; 8:8). It is also used occasionally to refer to faithless kingdoms or cities. Thus the northern kingdom of Israel and the southern kingdom of Judah are referred to as sisters in Jer

3:7–10, and the wicked cities of Jerusalem, Samaria, and Sodom are described as sisters in Ezek 16:46–61. In these instances, feminine imagery is associated with transgression.

New Testament

"Family" and "household." In the NT, the word "family" is used to translate two Greek words, *patria* and *oikos*. The word *patria*, which appears only three times in the NT (Luke. 2:4; Acts 3:25; Eph 3:14), specifically denotes lineage or "family tree." The far more common word, *oikos* (literally, "house"), designates the family as household, and so appears in the NRSV translation as both "family" and "household." Thus "family" in the NT world does not correspond exactly to our modern sense of the word as a nuclear group of persons related by blood, marriage, or adoption. It corresponds more closely to the Israelite *beth ʾab* (literally, "father's house") discussed above, in that it includes not only persons related by blood or marriage but also unrelated persons attached to and dependent on the household such as slaves, employees, and clients. (In the Greco-Roman world, "clients" were free persons obligated and loyal to a patron, the head of the household, who provided protection and assistance of various sorts out of his resources.) It also included the household's material goods. The family household was thus the basic social and economic unit of Greco-Roman society, just as the *beth ʾab* was the basic unit of Israelite society. Moreover, it too was the locus of the individual's identity and allegiance. In the NT world, as in the OT world, persons did not think of themselves as autonomous individuals. They saw themselves as members of a family group in which they were inextricably embedded.

In light of this, the NT sounds a profoundly countercultural note when it subordinates family loyalty to loyalty to the gospel (Mark 3:31–35 and par.). To be sure, in the Gospels Jesus urges disciples to honor their parents, according to the fifth commandment, thereby supporting the traditional Jewish family structure (Matt 19:16–22; Luke 18:18–20). However, his first disciples leave home and parents behind to follow him (Mark 1:14–20; Luke 18:28–30). Moreover, Jesus openly acknowledges that discipleship can generate family conflict and disruption, and he relativizes loyalty to the family whenever it conflicts with loyalty to the gospel (e.g., Luke 12:51–53; 14:25–33; Mark 13:12). In the NT epistles, it is evident that some believers lived in households that did not share their Christian commitment (e.g., 1 Pet 3:1; 1 Cor 7:12–16), yet they are not expected to give up their faith for that of the head of household to ensure domestic stability, as would have been the norm. Clearly the claims of the gospel and the new reality it represents are of ultimate importance in the lives of believers and take precedence over family loyalty if they are forced to choose.

Moreover, the Christian community itself becomes a new locus of collective identity—a new family for believers. Thus, any who find their family ties disrupted find a new home in the "family of faith" (Gal 6:10). In the Gospels, Jesus is represented as redefining the family: "Whoever does the will of God is my brother and sister and mother" (Mark 3:35). And in the NT epistles, the church is described as the very "household of God" (Eph 2:19; Heb 3:2–6; 1 Tim 3:15; 1 Pet 4:17).

During the first two centuries of the Common Era, Christians held all their meetings in private households, for church-owned buildings and land did not exist before the third or fourth centuries. Indeed the importance of the private household for the growth and character of the early Christian movement cannot be overemphasized. In short, early churches were "house churches," and thus household language and imagery became a central matrix for theological, ecclesiological, and ethical reflection. By means of it, early Christians articulated their understanding of the God revealed in Jesus Christ and their life together in the church.

Members of the family household. Language denoting various members of the family household appears throughout the NT. While it can be used literally to denote blood relations, it more frequently conveys theological realities.

The word "father" (*pater*) for example, can refer to a male progenitor or ancestor. It can also be used metaphorically, as when Paul describes himself as the "father" of persons he has evangelized (1 Cor. 4:15; Phlm 10). Abraham is designated as the father of all who believe in Christ, who follow him in his faith (Rom 4:11–12; Gal 3:7). But throughout the NT "father" is used most frequently with reference to God. The point of the NT's father language and imagery is not that God is male but rather that God is intimately related to us in Jesus Christ—as a father, or parent. In short, "father" language is language of intimacy, family, and relationship. While God is spoken of as "father" in the OT (see above), the NT speaks of the intimacy of God's relationship to humanity with unparalleled emphasis.

Christian description of God as "father" probably derives from Jesus' own reported practice of addressing God as "father" (*pater*; *abba* in Aramaic, Mark 14:36; see also Rom 8:15; Gal 4:6; and see *abba*). And with the Lord's Prayer, Jesus instructs disciples to pray to God as "Our Father" (Matt 6:9). Interestingly, father-language for God appears far more frequently in later Gospels than in the earliest one. Mark, the earliest Gospel, presents Jesus as referring to God as "father" 4 times. God appears as "father" 15 times in Luke and 49 times in Matthew (both of which use Mark as a source), while John, regarded by many as the last Gospel to be written, speaks of God as "father" no less than 109 times. More than any other NT witness, the Gospel of John employs family imagery of father and son to describe the very life of God. What this suggests is that the early church employed father-language with increasing frequency as it developed its theological reflection. However, the parenthood of God is also a basic assumption throughout Paul's letters, the earliest of Christian documents. Paul speaks of God as the father of Christians, the father of all creation, and above all, as the father of Jesus Christ. As "father," God is the very source of spiritual and material life. As "father," God pours out love and forgiveness upon believers (Matt 6:12, 15; Luke 15) and cares deeply about their welfare (Rom 8:28; Matt 6:8, 26, 32; Luke 11:11–13) as well as their growth in grace and holiness of life (1 Thess 2:12; 4:7, 9; see also Col 1:12; Eph 5:1). And as "father," God acts above all to reconcile the world to God's own self through Jesus Christ, God's "son."

The word "son" (*huios* in Greek) can be used literally in the NT to designate a physical descendant (e.g., Matt 21:28; Mark 13:12; Luke 15:31). It also has figurative uses, denoting other relationships, memberships, or associations, for example, "sons [NRSV, heirs] of the kingdom" (Matt 8:12), "sons [NRSV, children] of light" (Luke 16:8), "son of the devil" (Acts 13:10), "son of perdition [NRSV, one destined to be lost]" (John 17:12). In Acts, Paul refers to himself as a "son of Pharisees" (Acts 23:6). Paul also employs *huios* metaphorically when he refers to persons or groups with whom he has a close relationship in the Christian faith as "sons" ("children" in the NRSV translation; 1 Cor 4:14, 17; Phil 2:22; Phlm 10).

However, given the centrality of "fatherhood" in the NT's conception of God, the role of "son" (*huios*) in the NT belongs preeminently to Jesus Christ. The designation of him as "son" throughout the NT conveys the unique filial relationship of intimacy, love, knowledge, oneness, and obedience that binds him to his heavenly Father. As son, he is the revealer of his heavenly Father (John 10:15). Those who accept Jesus Christ as God's gift of reconciling grace share in his filial relation to God and receive the identity and status of "sons of God" or "children of God" (Gal 3:26; Rom 8:14–29; 9:4; John 1:12; 1 John 3:1–2). Paul speaks of this in terms of the Christian's *adoption* (*huiothesia*) by

God (see Rom 8:14–17; Gal 4:1–7) in order to underline the fact that the sonship of believers is not a natural one but rather conferred by divine grace. As adopted sons (and daughters) of God, believers are "heirs" of life and glory (Gal 4:1–7). Paul uses the terms "sons of God" (*huioi tou theou*) and "children of God" (*tekna tou theou*) interchangeably (e.g., Rom 8:14, 16, 17, 19). (In the interest of inclusive language, the NRSV often renders the phrase "sons (*huioi*) of God" as "children of God," for male references are frequently generic, and both women and men are included in the notion of divine sonship.) However, in order to preserve the unique nature of Jesus' divine sonship, the Gospel of John reserves the word "son" (*huios*) for Jesus, and employs a different word, *tekna*, when he refers to believers as "children (*tekna*) of God." Moreover, in John one becomes a child of God by rebirth (rather than adoption), or by being "begotten" or "born of God" (John 1:13; 3:3, 7).

The word *tekna* is a gender-neutral word. It refers to a child, regardless of gender, in relationship to its parents. Another word for "child" (*pais*) appears occasionally in the NT, but only in Matthew, Luke, and Acts. In a number of instances, both of these words refer literally to children. Jesus himself appears as a child in the infancy narratives of Matthew and Luke, and during his ministry, as represented in the Synoptic Gospels, he insists that the God's kingdom or reign belongs to children. Indeed he maintains that "whoever does not receive the kingdom of God as a little child will never enter it" (Mark 10:13–16; Matt 19:13–15; Luke 18:15–17). This saying conveys our total dependence on God for salvation. In a culture that was deeply ambivalent about children, the most marginal members of society, an affirmation such as this was astonishing. Nevertheless childhood terminology is relatively infrequent in the NT, for the recognition of childhood as an important developmental stage in the life cycle is a modern phenomenon.

Interestingly, child language in the NT is more often metaphorical than literal, used as an appellation for disciples or believers. Indeed, those referred to as "children" in the NT are most often adults. Believers are sometimes addressed as "children" by church authorities (Gal 4:19; 2 Tim 1:2; Phlm 10; 1 John 2:1, 12, 18, 28). In the Gospels, Jesus himself addresses disciples as "children" (Matt 9:2; Mark 2:5; 10:24), and in the Johannine community Christians may have been commonly designated as "children of God" (John 1:12; 1 John 3:1, 2, 10; 5:2).

The word "brother" (*adelphos*) is used in the NT to designate both physical brothers and spiritual brothers. In the Gospels, it most often refers to physical brothers, while the figurative sense prevails in other NT writings. Paul uses the term more frequently than any other NT writer, usually in reference to fellow Christians. In the NRSV, the frequently generic sense of *adelphos* is appropriately conveyed by the translation "brother *and sister*." In the NT the community of brothers and sisters has its origins in rebirth or adoption rather than natural birth (John 3:1–15; Rom 8:14–17; Gal 4:1–7), and is established by Christ's death (Eph 2:11–18). Its most visible characteristic is the love that unites Christians to each other and to God (John 14:34–35; 1 John 1:9–11; 4:7–21; 1 Pet 1:22–23). Indeed, an adjective frequently attached to *adelphos* is *agapetos* or *egapemenos* ("beloved").

Male terminology for members of the family household (such as father, son, and brother) appears with far more frequency in the NT than terminology for female members of the household. This is largely a reflection of the patriarchal culture in which the NT emerged, as well as the patriarchal structure of the Greco-Roman household. Nevertheless, vocabulary for female members of the family household surfaces occasionally in the NT and should be noted. The word "sister" (*adelphe*) appears only twenty-six times in the NT. Like "brother," it can refer to physical kinship (Mark 6:3; Luke 10:39–40) or spiritual kinship within the community of faith (Rom 16:1; Mark 3:35; Phlm 2). In 2 John 13 the church itself is referred to as an "elect sister." The word "daughter" (*thugater*), which appears twenty-eight times, usually refers to a daughter in relation to her father or mother, regardless of age (e.g., Mark 5:35; Matt 15:22, 28; Luke 2:36), though it can also be used in a figurative sense to denote a fellow Christian, membership in a particular community, or the inhabitants of a particular place (Mark 5:34; Luke 13:16; Matt 21:5). Finally, "mother" (*meter* in Greek) appears eighty-three times in the NT, primarily in the Gospels (seventy-one times) where the bulk of the references are to Mary, the mother of Jesus. "Mother" is used elsewhere in both literal and figurative ways, denoting biological mothers (e.g., Matt 20:20; Mark 7:10) as well as fictive kinship relationships within the Christian community (e.g., Rom 16:13; 1 Tim 5:2). Upon occasion, "mother" is also used metaphorically of cities: for example, Paul refers to Jerusalem as "our mother" in Gal 4:26; and Babylon (Rome) is referred to as the "mother of whores and of earth's abominations" in the book of Revelation (Rev 17:5).

In sum, terminology for the family household and its members plays a significant role in NT reflection and discourse. It provided categories for articulating early Christian understanding of the church, "the family of faith" or "household of God," and of life together within it. It also provided essential insight into the character and activity of God.

Peter Lampe, "'Family' in Church and Society of New Testament Times," *Affirmation* 5 (spring 1992): 1–20; Carolyn Osiek and David L. Balch, *Families in the New Testament World: Households and House Churches* (Louisville, Ky.: Westminster John Knox Press, 1997); Leo G. Perdue, Joseph Blenkinsopp, John J. Collins, and Carol Meyers, *Families in Ancient Israel* (Louisville, Ky.: Westminster John Knox Press, 1997); Marianne Meye Thompson, *The Promise of the Father: Jesus and God in the New Testament* (Louisville, Ky.: Westminster John Knox Press, 2000).

FRANCES TAYLOR GENCH

Fast Fasting is a voluntary practice usually carried out for religious reasons; it consists in abstinence from food and drink (Exod 34:28) in whole or part for a period of time, whether as a one-time event or as a regular practice. It is to be distinguished from specific forms of abstinence, such as the abstinence from alcohol practiced by Nazirites and Rechabites or abstinence from specific kinds of food (such as meat, Rom 14:6).

The specific reasons for the practice varied. Fasting could be an expression of sorrow and an accompaniment of mourning (1 Sam 31:13). Sometimes it was in response to divine command (Joel 1:14). Or it could be carried out in conjunction with prayer, in the belief that this made the prayer more effective (Jonah 3:7–10). If the people praying were prepared to afflict themselves and deny themselves, this indicated the fervency of their prayer or was a kind of service to God in return for which they expected something from him.

Fasting accompanied some religious rituals (Zech 8:19). The Jews fasted on the Day of Atonement as an indication of penitence for sin (Lev 16:29 NRSV Mg). However, giving to the poor and social righteousness generally were more important than fasting as a religious ritual, particularly when the latter was no more than a ritual accompanied by selfish behavior (Isa 58:1–8; Jer 14:12; Zech 7).

By NT times fasting twice a week was a part of Pharisaic religious practice (Luke 18:12). Voluntary fasts were also undertaken by individuals. Anna served God in the temple with prayers and fasting by night and day (Luke 2:37). She is an example of acceptable piety, a woman completely dedicated to God and longing for the coming of the redemption of God's people.

Jesus ate nothing for forty days while he was in the wilderness and facing temptation from Satan (Matt 4:2; Luke 4:2). No reason is given; the implication, however, is that he did it in obedience to God. At the end of the ordeal he refused to create food at the tempter's instigation and commented that people do not live solely by bread but also by God's words (Deut 8:3). Taken literally, this response would allow the taking of food so long as the need to feed on God's words was also fulfilled. Jesus was suggesting that obedience to God's words is primary; he may have been implying that to do so eliminated the need for food at least temporarily, that in this case God had told him not to take food. Or again the point may be that obeying God and being nourished by his words are more important and necessary than food—and, by natural extension, the satisfaction of other, normal human desires and requirements.

In the parable of the Pharisee and the Tax Collector, the Pharisee recounted to God how he fasted twice weekly, naming this along with other acts that he regarded as evidence of his fulfillment of his religious duties (Luke 18:10–14). Jesus condemned the attitude of self-righteousness that accompanied the piety, rather than necessarily the piety itself.

Jesus also criticized people who fasted publicly so that other people would see them and admire them for their religious practices, just as they might also say their prayers publicly or give charitable gifts openly (Matt 6:16–18). For Jesus, fasting, prayer, and charitable giving were things to be done in private, and then God would reward them. If anything, the persons fasting should disguise the fact, so that they could not be accused of trying to get public recognition for their piety.

The evangelists also describe an occasion when the followers of John and the Pharisees were fasting, but Jesus' disciples and presumably Jesus himself were not (Mark 2:18–20 and par.). The incident generated a question to Jesus, which he answered by using the analogy of the wedding where the guests will not fast while the ceremony is in progress. This would be inappropriate while the bridegroom is with them. Here fasting is associated with sadness that would be out of keeping with joyous festivity. Yet Jesus prophesied that the time would come when the bridegroom would no longer be with them. The Jewish book of Tobit (6:13–14) furnishes a parallel to this in a story of a bridegroom who suddenly died on his wedding night. In the context of the Gospel as a whole Jesus was referring to his own death. That would be an occasion for sadness and fasting would then be appropriate. Yet his death was swiftly followed by his resurrection, and we have no record of his followers either then or subsequently mourning and fasting because of his death. It is unlikely, then, that Jesus was either prophesying that his disciples would fast for this reason or instructing them to do so. Rather the emphasis lies on the joy of the new era brought about by the presence of Jesus (cf. the parabolic sayings that immediately follow about the new cloth and the new wine and John 16:16–24).

These are the only certain references to fasting in the Gospels. When the disciples were unable to cast a demon out of a boy, Jesus commented that their failure was because this kind could not be cast out except by prayer (Mark 9:29); a considerable number of MS(S) add "and by fasting," but this addition is generally regarded as a later assimilation of the wording to a well-known formula (Luke 2:37). Matthew's version of the story (17:20) emphasizes rather the disciples' lack of faith and their need for even a tiny amount. The saying in Mark 9:29 is not found here, although later MS(S) assimilated the text to Mark.

Fasting is mentioned in two places in Acts. In Acts 13:2–3 the leaders of the church in Antioch were gathered together "worshiping the Lord and fasting" when they heard the Spirit telling them to set apart Barnabas and Saul for a task to which God was calling them. They responded by fasting and praying and laying hands on the missionaries and then sending them off. Here fasting was the accompaniment of prayer. Similarly, in Acts 14:23 the missionaries appointed elders for each congregation; then they prayed with fasting and committed them to the Lord. These passages show that the association of fasting with prayer is a stable one and suggest that fasting was considered appropriate. Possibly sessions of prayer lasted for a long enough time to dignify the period as a fast from food.

During Paul's voyage to Rome the ship ran into a serious storm; the people on board did not take food for fourteen days (Acts 27:21, 33–36), until Paul urged them to do so with the promise that they were not going to perish. This was clearly a fast in the hope of influencing the gods to protect them. Although Paul set an example of eating to them, it is not clear whether he had shared in the fast up to that point; probably he considered it unnecessary because from the outset he was convinced that God would protect them all.

Paul himself referred to occasions of going without food in 2 Cor 6:5 and 11:27 as part of the privations of being a traveling missionary; the latter reference fairly clearly and the former very probably are to involuntary deprivation of food and drink. We have, therefore, no reference outside Acts to early Christians voluntarily fasting.

The paucity of mention suggests that fasting was marginal to the congregational and personal life of the early Christians. There is no evidence that asceticism was seen as something important for its own sake. Its significance is expressed in terms of obedience to God being more important than the satisfaction of normal, human desires. It is also on occasion an accompaniment to prayer, the implication being perhaps that normal human activities may distract a person from giving full commitment to God in prayer (cf. 1 Cor. 7:5 with reference to physical sexual relationships). I have used this phrase "normal human activities" to indicate that the principle extends to more than food. That is to say, if food or anything else comes between people and their relationship to God, then they must get their priorities right. It is interesting that in some contemporary church circles a "prayer breakfast" (rather than "praying and fasting") can be an effective practice.

———————

I. HOWARD MARSHALL

Father (God) *see* **Abba; God**

Father (Human) *see* **Family**

Fault *see* **Sin**

Favor

The Hebrew nouns *hen* and *ratson* are frequently translated "favor" in the NRSV. The noun *hen* derives from the verb *hanan,* "to show **grace**," and *ratson* is from the verb *ratsah,* "to be pleased with." Although the two terms often overlap in meaning, they convey a slightly different perspective. *Hen* indicates a positive attitude between persons or between God and humans, usually requiring some form of action as a demonstration of favor. *Ratson* conveys a more passive meaning, indicating the reception of an act of grace.

The noun *hen* is often used in the idiom "to find favor in the eyes of." The meeting of Jacob and Esau in Gen 32–33, long after Jacob had stolen the birthright from Esau, illustrates the meaning of the phrase and also demonstrates the difference between *hen* and *ratson.* At the outset of Gen 32, Jacob directs his servant to lavish gifts upon Esau with the following message, "in order that I may find favor in your sight" (Gen 32:5). When the two brothers finally meet, Esau inquires about the purpose of the gifts. Jacob responds, "to find favor with my lord" (Gen 33:8). But Esau refuses the gifts out of friendship, prompting Jacob to repeat the phrase, this time as a condition of friendship, "If I find favor (*hen*) with you, then accept my present from my hand; for truly to see your face is like seeing the face of God—since you have received me with such favor (*ratson*)" (Gen 33:10). The statement of Jacob indicates that the word *hen* in the phrase "to find favor in the eyes" carries an active meaning, requiring more than Esau's positive attitude toward Jacob. The conditional statement requires an action by Esau to demonstrate his "favor" toward Jacob. The verb *ratsah* occurs at the end of the statement with a passive meaning of attitude. Esau has received Jacob with "favor."

Other examples of the phrase "to find favor in the eyes of" reinforce the meaning in Gen 33:8–10. Abraham invites the three divine travelers into his tent with the conditional statement, "if I find favor with you, do not pass by your servant" (Gen 18:3). Jacob uses the phrase on his deathbed, requiring an oath from Joseph, "If I have found favor with you, put your hand under my thigh and promise to deal loyally (*hesed*, **steadfast love**) and truly (*?emeth*, **true**) with me" (Gen 47:29). God tells Moses that gifts from the Egyptians will indicate that the Israelites have favor in their eyes (Exod 3:21; 11:3; 12:36). Ruth has favor in the eyes of Boaz (Ruth 2:2, 10, 13). "Favor" in each of these instances requires some form of action, a visit from the travelers, an oath of loyalty from Joseph, Egyptian gifts to the Israelites, and food from Boaz to Ruth.

Individuals can also have "favor in the sight of the LORD," which is signaled by divine action toward them. Noah is saved from the flood because of divine favor (Gen 6:8). Moses is able to dissuade God from punishing the Israelites after the golden calf because of his favor in the eyes of the Lord (Exod 33:12, 16; see also Num 11:11, 15). But, more often, the divine favor toward humans is indicated more passively with the noun *ratson*, usually in the context of cultic worship and sacrifice, where the word is translated "acceptable." Proper sacrifices are "acceptable" to God, meaning that God receives them with favor (Lev 1:3; 19:5; 22:19). Aaron, the high priest, is directed to wear a rosette stone in the sanctuary when he is in presence of God so that "they [the Israelites] may find favor (*ratson*) before the LORD" (Exod 28:38).

The Greek *charis* (grace) is infrequently translated "favor" in the New Testament. The story of Joseph's slavery in Egypt is recounted in Acts 7:10 as a divine rescue in which God "enabled him to win favor (*charin*) . . . before Pharaoh." Acts 24:27 states that Porcius Festus "wanted to grant the Jews a favor (*charin*)." And Acts 25:3 states that the Jews requested Festus to transfer Paul to Jerusalem "as a favor." When *charis* conveys the more theological meaning of *hen* and *ratson* it tends to be translated "grace" or "*mercy*."

THOMAS B. DOZEMAN

Fear, Fearful, Awe, Awesome, Dread, Dreadful, Afraid The Greek verb most frequently translated in NRSV as "to fear" or "to be afraid" is derived from the verb "to flee." This gives us a basic meaning of the word "fear," which we understand at an instinctual level. Fear is that which makes us want to run away. When faced by a being or a force strong enough to take away our lives, we are afraid. It is natural for humans to fear the "terror of the night, or the arrow that flies by day" (Ps 91:5). Both testaments are full of this kind of fear. There is fear of other people who might kill (Gen 20:1), of being stoned by a mob (Acts 5:26), shipwreck (Acts 27:17, 29), a king's edict (Heb 11:23). All of these can in the end be reduced to the most basic human fear, the fear of death. On a slightly less immediate level, one might fear a former persecutor perhaps turned Christian (Acts 9:26) or the effect of bad news on an aged father (Gen 44:34). Here fear is simply a negative apprehension of the future and thus the opposite of *hope*. All this is so fundamental and familiar to humans that it needs little explanation. To be human is to be afraid, at least at times.

The good news is that God relieves this kind of fear, as we are told in some of the most loved verses of Scripture: "Even though I walk through the darkest valley,

I fear no evil; for you are with me; your rod and your staff—they comfort me" (Ps 23:4; cf. Ps 91:5; Isa 35:4 and numerous other examples). But God does not only remove fear. God is also the proper object of fear. This brings us to a concept in Scripture that is almost uniquely difficult for moderns, the "fear of God." Part of the concept is quite simple. It is obviously right for evildoers to fear God. An uneasy conscience distances people from God and may make an encounter with God a matter of fear. This begins dramatically even in Eden. So Adam in the garden, newly conscious of right and wrong, is filled with fear. "I heard the sound of you in the garden, and I was afraid" (Gen 3:10). This fear is more than an internal unease in the presence of God. The witness of Scripture is that God judges and punishes evil. It is therefore a "fearful thing to fall into the hands of the living God" (Heb 10:31). It is probably the fear of judgment that is cast out by perfect love (1 John 4:18), for elsewhere love is not the opposite of fear, nor does it remove from the faithful the duty of fearing God.

The Scriptures as a whole think it right and proper that the righteous should fear God. The righteous fear God, and God acts to save those who do so. See Luke 1:50 and many other examples. Indeed "the fear of the LORD is the beginning of wisdom" (Ps 111:10; cf. Prov 1:7; 9:10). It "prolongs life" (Prov 10:27), is "pure, enduring forever" (Ps 19:9), and is "Zion's treasure" (Isa 33:6). In early texts, "Fear" may even become a name of God as, for example, in Gen 31:53. Nor is the fear of God merely an OT concept, See, for example, 1 Pet 2:17: "Honor everyone. Love the family of believers. Fear God. Honor the emperor." In Acts, those Gentiles who yearn after the God of Israel and who receive the gospel when it is proclaimed "fear God" (Acts 13:16, 26; cf. the description of Cornelius in Acts 10:22). Sometimes NRSV handles this aspect of the concept by using the word "awe," but in many cases the original is the same as the word elsewhere translated simply as

"fear." By contrast, the wicked do not fear God. See for example, Pharaoh and his court (Exod 9:30), or the unjust judge in Jesus' parable who has "no fear of God and no respect for anyone" (Luke 18:4).

Despite our discomfort, it is vital to retain the concept of a righteous fear. First, it is right to recognize that God is indeed dangerous. Life and death are in God's hands before they are in the hands of any other. God's power is far greater than that of the minor powers whom we sometimes fear greatly. The fear of God is a proper recognition of God's sovereignty.

Second, a right fear of God is closely related to obedience and even to love. The use of the word "fear" in Deuteronomy is particularly interesting. The Deuteronomist's frequent use of parallelism helps us to understand more clearly the meaning of the word "fear." Deuteronomy 13:4 is a typical example: "The LORD your God you shall follow, him alone you shall fear, his commandments you shall keep, his voice you shall obey, him you shall serve, and to him you shall hold fast." To fear, it appears, is also to follow, to observe the commandments, to serve, and to hold fast to God. It is to worship God and to swear by God's name (Deut 10:20), and even to love and serve God wholeheartedly: "So now, O Israel, what does the LORD your God require of you? Only to fear the LORD your God, to walk in all his ways, to love him, to serve the LORD your God with all your heart and with all your soul" (Deut 10:12). This fear of God must be learned (Deut. 14:23; 31:13), and it is for the good of those who fear God, preserving them alive (Deut 6:24).

There is a specific kind of fear in both Testaments that is related to an epiphany of God or a messenger of God. It ought not be supposed that it is wrong to experience fear on such an occasion. Nevertheless the response to this fear is "Do not be afraid," surely one of the most characteristic and significant phrases in Scripture. The pattern occurs repeatedly, from Genesis (Gen 15:1) to Revelation (Rev 1:17). Perhaps nowhere are the words more familiar than in the Christmas story: "But the angel said to them, 'Do not be afraid; for see—I am bringing you good news of great joy for all the people'" (Luke 2:10). That verse reminds us that the command not to fear is part of an announcement or oracle of salvation. The saying prepares us to hear good news. As such it is very close to the heart of the gospel. It should be no surprise, therefore, to find this language in Matthew's account of the resurrection (Matt 28:4, 10).

Because of God's saving presence, assured ultimately by the resurrection of Jesus Christ, all lesser fears can pass away. The faithful of both Testaments can say, "The Lord is my helper; I will not be afraid. What can anyone do to me?" (Heb 13:6; quoting Ps 118:6). There is no need even to fear those who can slay only the body, for their authority is no longer ultimate (Matt 10:28). We need no longer fear for our lives, for those lives are in the hands of one who has conquered death and says to us, "Do not be afraid."

Contemporary Christians will hear this language of salvation and reassurance more easily than a command to fear God. Nevertheless both understandings of the word "fear" are necessary. It is the task of Christian proclamation to declare both the freedom from fear that comes to those who are in Christ and also the summons to fear God. Only if both words are preached and heard will the Christian experience assurance but not complacency.

STEPHEN FARRIS

Female *see* **Man and Woman**

Fight, Fighting *see* **War**

Fire, Flame, Burn Fire: Hebrew primarily ꜣesh; Aramaic *nur*; Greek: *pyr*. Flame: Hebrew *lahab, lahat*; Greek *phlox*. Burn: Hebrew *baꜣar, saraph*; Greek *kaio*.

The Bible speaks of fire in the context of common household and industrial use (Exod 32:24; Isa 44:12, 15; Jer 36:22; John 18:18; 21:9; Acts 28:2). The potential for fire to consume anything in its path led to its symbolic use, especially in Wisdom literature, as a way of describing human emotions (Job 31:9–12; Prov 26:20–21; Sir 9:8; 23:16; 28:10–11).

The most significant use of fire in Scripture is as a symbol of the presence of God. In Gen 15:17, when God entered into covenant with Abram, the presence of God is seen as "a smoking fire pot and a flaming torch" passing between the pieces of the animals that had been slaughtered for the ceremony. Exodus 3:2 reports that "the angel of the LORD appeared" to Moses "in a flame of fire out of a bush" and that "the bush was blazing, yet it was not consumed." Verse 4 makes it clear that it was God who was communicating with Moses from the burning bush.

The Sinai revelation of God in Exod 19 is paradigmatic for the understanding of fire as a symbol for the holiness, mystery, and glory of God (see esp. v. 18).

The pillar of smoke by day and the pillar of fire by night symbolized the presence of God leading the Hebrews through the wilderness (Exod 13:21–22; Num 14:14; Deut 1:33; see also Ps 78:14).

Fire can be seen in the Psalms as a symbol for the revelation of God (Pss 18:8, 12, 14; 50:3). Similarly in prophetic visions God's self-revelation is seen in fire (Isa 66:15; Ezek 1:27; Mal 3:2). The "perpetual fire" on the altar symbolized the continual presence of God (Lev 6:12–13).

Given the strong association of fire with the revelation of God, it is somewhat surprising to read in 1 Kgs 19:12 that, when God was revealed to Elijah on the holy mountain, "the LORD was not in the fire."

John's vision in Rev 1 sees the risen Christ as having eyes "like a flame of fire" (1:14; 2:18), and the Spirit of God was revealed at Pentecost in tongues as of fire (Acts 2:3).

Fire was often thought of as manifesting the divine presence in judgment. See the stories of Sodom and Gomorrah (Gen 19:24), Nadab and Abihu (Lev 10:2), and Korah and his followers (Num 16:35).

Fire frequently appears in prophetic texts as an instrument of divine judgment (Jer 11:16; 17:27; 21:14; 22:7; Ezek 15:7; 16:41; 24:10–11; Hos 8:14; Amos 1:4, 7, 10, 12, 14; 2:2, 5; Nah 3:13). In the NT, images of divine judgment by fire were often linked with agricultural imagery, creating ideas of burning chaff (Matt 3:12; Luke 3:17), tares (Matt 13:40), trees that do not bear fruit (Matt 3:10; 7:19; Luke 3:9), and branches on the vine that do not bear fruit (John 15:6). Fire is seen in Revelation as a symbol of judgment (8:7–8; 9:17–18; 14:10; 16:8; 18:8; 19:20; 20:9–10, 14–15).

Besides judgment, the fire of God's presence is also thought of as a purifying, refining fire (Ps 66:12; Isa 43:2; Zech 13:9; 1 Cor 3:13–15). A *seraph* (the word "seraph" is derived from the Hebrew word for "burn") used a burning coal from the heavenly altar to purify the lips of the prophet Isaiah at the time of the prophet's call (Isa 6:6–7).

In sum, "God is a devouring fire" (Deut 4:24), "a consuming fire" (Heb 12:29).

JAMES A. DURLESSER

Firstborn, Birthright The traditional rules of *inheritance* in Israel are nowhere spelled out in detail, but it is clear that to be the firstborn child involved special privileges (Gen 27:19; 29:26). According to Deut 21:15–17, even the son of a disliked wife must be afforded the privilege of a "double portion," when he is the father's firstborn. The importance of being the firstborn in Israel's family structure is revealed by the frequency with which OT characters are so identified. The privilege did not always pass as custom would indicate, however, and OT authors show a considerable interest in the exceptions. That Esau sold his birthright to his younger twin Jacob is related at some length in Gen 25 and is recalled in Heb 12:16. Other cases where younger sons take precedence over their elders include Isaac and Ishmael (Gen 21:1–21), Joseph's sons and

Reuben and Judah (1 Chr 5:1–2), Ephraim and Manasseh (Gen 48:8–20), and Solomon and Adonijah (1 Kgs 1–2). It is likely that the authors saw in these examples evidence of God's freedom to *choose* whom he would, without regard to human plans and systems.

When God declared Israel to be his firstborn son (Exod 4:22), it was his gracious choice to treat the Hebrew slaves in Egypt as a father would treat an oldest son (cf. Jer 31:9). He once calls the king his firstborn, in Ps 89:27, as evidence of his intention to pour out the fullness of his blessings.

An important part of the sacrificial system may have originated in early practices of animal husbandry that are lost to us, but OT authors found its explanation in the exodus theme of "firstborn." Since Pharaoh slaughtered the children of God's firstborn, Israel, God slaughtered all the firstborn of Egypt, in the last plague (Exod 4:22–23; 12:29). Israelite law then declared that every firstborn, of people and animals, belongs to God. All were to be sacrificed to him, except for the offspring of donkeys and humans (Exod 13:2, 11–16). The latter were to be redeemed (Exod 34:20; Num 18:15). The special place of the Levites in Israelite society was also explained as a form of redemption of the firstborn (Num 3:12–13, 45–46; 8:16–18). Micah referred to a horrible misunderstanding of God's claim on the firstborn, as he had a hypothetical worshiper ask whether human sacrifice was called for: "Shall I give my firstborn for my transgression, the fruit of my body for the sin of my soul?" The prophet's answer was what every Israelite should know God wanted: "to do justice, and to love kindness, and to walk humbly with your God" (Mic 6:7b–8).

New Testament authors used the traditional favored role of the firstborn as one of their ways of emphasizing the exaltation of the risen Christ, alluding to the resurrection as a new birth, first experienced by Christ: "He is the head of the body, the church; he is the beginning, the firstborn from the dead, so that he might come to have first place in everything" (Col 1:18); "And again, when he brings the firstborn into the world, he says, 'Let all God's angels worship him'" (Heb 1:6); "Jesus Christ, the faithful witness, the firstborn of the dead, and the ruler of the kings of the earth" (Rev 1:5). Paul offered a vivid image of Christians' relationship with Christ when he spoke of him as the elder brother, the "firstborn within a large family" (Rom 8:29 NRSV; Greek: "among many brothers"). Hebrews even extends the privilege of being firstborn to all those who are enrolled in heaven (Heb 12:23).

DONALD E. GOWAN

Flame   *see* Fire

Flesh   The main OT word is *basar*, which also covers much of the meaning of "body." The NT word is usually *sarx*.

Flesh as physical reality. "Flesh" denotes body tissue, such as the muscle and fat lying between skin and bones (e.g., Gen 2:21, 23). It is a painful place to have a thorn (2 Cor 12:7). By its nature flesh is thus soft, pliable, and lively, so it provides a positive image for personal renewal: Israel has a heart of stone, an inflexible mind, but God promises it a heart or mind of flesh. This is another way of saying that God's spirit will be put within the people, so that they are inspired to do what God says (Ezek 11:19; 36:26–27). "My flesh faints" in its longing for God, the way it faints in a land "where there is no water" (Ps 63:1).

"Flesh" often refers to an animal's body tissue, much of which can be eaten, though not with the *blood* in it (Gen 9:4). But human beings cannot eat human flesh—to have to do so, at times of severe need, is a terrible thing (Deut 28:53–55). For animals to eat human flesh is likewise a terrible fate for the person (e.g., 2 Kgs 9:36) and the consuming of the flesh is a final act of degradation and punishment (Jas 5:3; Rev 17:16; 19:18, 21). The background is that the flesh or body is an inte-

gral part of the person. It is having flesh and bones that distinguishes human beings, and therefore the risen Jesus, from a spirit (Luke 24:39; cf. 1 Tim 3:16). It is thus a serious matter when the flesh is defiled, for example, by skin disease (Lev 13, NRSV "body"), though purification rites do avail for the flesh (Heb 9:13). For circumcision to be "in your flesh" suggests it has solid grounds in the physical—it is not merely "spiritual" (Gen 17:13). A sign in the flesh matters. Jews were Jews in the flesh; Gentiles were Gentiles in the flesh—and therefore outside the people of God (Eph 2:11, see NRSV Mg; cf. Col 2:13). To be one with other human beings in a family is to be one in bone and flesh (e.g., Gen 29:14). In or from his flesh Job expects to see God (Job 19:26). Yet Paul has come to see that what he has in Christ far exceeds the value of what he has in the flesh (Phil 3:3–4). It is therefore odd to insist on fleshly observances for people who were outside God's people and have come into it by another route (Gal 3:3; cf. 4:21–31; 6:12–13; Col 2:11–23).

By extension, the flesh can suggest the visible body as a whole (Lev 17:16; Job 21:6). No one hates their own flesh—that is, their own body (Eph 5:29). In sexual intercourse two people become one flesh (Gen 2:24)—their intermingling makes it as if they are now one body (1 Cor 6:16). In danger, one's flesh can live in hope (Ps 16:9; cf. Acts 2:26). Although Jesus died, his flesh did not experience corruption (Acts 2:31). Jesus can be manifested in our mortal flesh (2 Cor 4:11). I live my life in the flesh by faith in Christ (Gal 2:20; cf. Phil 1:22, 24). In his flesh Paul accepts the persecution that comes to him as a servant of Christ and completes the suffering that Christ did not undergo (Col 1:24). Death means being judged in the flesh (1 Pet 4:6).

Human beings thus integrally and essentially combine an outer and an inner person, flesh or body, and *soul* or *spirit* or heart (see *mind*), which affect each other (Pss 84:2; 73:25–26; Eccl 12:12; Ezek 37:8–10). The degeneration of the flesh is a sign of the dissolution of the person, and thus its restoration is a sign of the whole person's healing (2 Kgs 5:10–14). But there may be a disjunction between flesh and heart or spirit (Ezek 44:7, 9; Mark 14:38). Paul envisages delivering an immoral person to Satan for the destruction of the flesh, so that his spirit may be saved on the day of the Lord (1 Cor 5:5). Christ was put to death in the flesh but made alive in the spirit (1 Pet 3:18; cf. 4:1).

Flesh as the whole person. As flesh can thus stand for the physicality essential to being human, it can stand for the human person as a whole. It must be wrong that people of the same flesh include slave owners and slaves (Neh 5:5). When people are without food, home, or clothing, it must be wrong to hide yourself from your own flesh (Isa 58:7, NRSV "kin"). "Flesh and blood" simply means human beings (Gal 1:16; Eph 6:12; cf. Heb 2:14). Flesh and blood did not reveal Jesus' significance to Peter (Matt 16:17). Mere flesh and blood cannot share in God's reign—it is perishable and needs to put on immortality (1 Cor 15:50–53). People who become God's children are born "not of blood or of the will of the flesh or of the will of man, but of God" or "of the Spirit" (John 1:13; 3:6; cf. 6:63). It is no use judging according to the flesh (John 8:15; see NRSV Mg).

The Word became flesh (John 1:14) when Jesus was born of David according to the flesh (Rom 1:3; cf. 1 John 4:2; 2 John 7). Jewish believers are similarly descendants of Abraham according to the flesh (Rom 4:1). Being one with the Jewish people according to the flesh gives Paul a deep concern for them to come to acknowledge Jesus (Rom 9:3). According to the flesh the messiah comes from the Jewish people, but it is the children of the promise who are God's children, not the children of the flesh (Rom 9:5, 8). Flesh is the antithesis of spirit or promise here, though not as if to dismiss flesh. Jesus' earthly life is the days of his flesh (Heb 5:7). His flesh opens up the way into God's presence (10:20). He gives his flesh (i.e., himself as a physical human being)

for the life of the world and gives his flesh to his followers to eat (John 6:51–56)—that is, gives himself (6:57). Here "flesh" has the same meaning as "body" in other NT passages referring to the Last Supper or the Lord's Supper and denoting the whole person.

"All flesh" can mean "everybody" (e.g., Num 16:22; Deut 5:26; Pss 65:1–3; 145:21; Jer 32:27; Joel 2:28–29; Luke 3:6; John 17:2). By further extension flesh can refer to both human beings and animals in their bodiliness (e.g., Gen 6:17, 19). God is in covenant relationship with all flesh—all that lives (Gen 9:17). It is sometimes difficult to tell whether passages refer to all living things, all human beings, or all Israel (e.g., Gen 6:12, 13; 9:15–17; Isa 40:5–6).

Flesh as weak and as sinful. Flesh also stands for physical humanity in its weakness (Gen 6:3). God does not give full vent to wrath when we deserve it but keeps in mind that we are flesh, a passing breath (Ps 78:38–39). After long years of exile, "all flesh is grass" (NRSV "all people are grass"), withered by the searing desert wind (Isa 40:6; cf. 1 Pet 1:24). God can be described as having or being a heart, a soul, or a spirit, but not as having or being flesh. The gods' dwelling is not with flesh (NRSV "with mortals"), Babylonian theologians lament (Dan 2:11). Flesh can thus suggest feeble humanity over against God's dynamic power. Egyptian forces are human not divine, their horses flesh not spirit (Isa 31:3; cf. 2 Chr 32:8; Jer 17:5–8). If I have God to trust in, "I am not afraid; what can flesh do to me?" (Ps 56:4). God does not have fleshly eyes, so as to be limited to seeing what human beings can see (Job 10:4).

The negative connotation of flesh is heightened in passages where flesh denotes not so much an aspect of the individual human person but the human person in its moral weakness and resistance to God, or a broader fleshly realm distinct from the realm of the Spirit, a realm people trust in and live by independently of the realm of the Spirit (cf. the antithesis in Gal 5:13–26). We used to be living in the flesh, and our sinful passions, aroused by the law, then worked death in our bodies (Rom 7:5; cf. 8:6; Eph 2:3). By nature our minds are thus set on the flesh and are hostile rather than submissive to God (Rom 8:7–8). Indeed, as people who are of the flesh, we are under sin's domination (7:14). In this sense, nothing good dwells in our flesh—we could want to do what was right but not actually do it (7:18). With our minds we serve the law of God, but with our flesh we serve the law of sin (7:25b). Because of the flesh, then, law is weak, even at its best. It can tell us what to do but not help us do it, and it thus leaves us in a worse place than we were before (8:3).

But God sent Jesus "in the likeness of sinful flesh" (Rom 8:3). Jesus' humanity was not only apparent—he really was a son of David according to the flesh (1:3). But he was never a slave of sin as we are, even though he submitted to the law's authority so as to be able to terminate its authority over anyone. His flesh was sinless. So he was born "in the *likeness* of *sinful* flesh"—his flesh was in one sense exactly the same as ours, but in another sense vitally different.

In dying he terminated any claim of the law on him and thus condemned sin in the flesh (8:3; cf. 1 Pet 4:1). When we identify with him and let his death count for us, the law's claim on us is likewise terminated. In his fleshly body he thus reconciled us to God by freeing us from living sinful lives (Col 1:22). In his flesh he annulled the law and brought into being one new people, not divided by whether or not they adhere to the law (Eph 2:14–15). The law thus no longer has the power to arouse our sinful passions, as it could when we lived in the flesh (Rom 7:5). Because Christ's death counts for us, we have crucified the flesh with its passions and desires (Gal 5:24). To put it another way, in Christ we have been circumcised inwardly by putting off the body of flesh in Christ's "circumcision" (Col 2:11). This is the sense in which we are no longer living in the flesh (Rom 8:9), because we are no longer living under the law's authority. We carry on living in the

flesh in the sense of living in the body, but we no longer live by human desires (1 Pet 4:2; see NRSV Mg). We no longer walk according to the flesh or set our minds on the things of the flesh (Rom 8:4–5).

This does not happen automatically or invariably. It is a possibility now opened up to us, or rather an obligation now placed on us. Because Christ died for us, we can and must take up the opportunity to follow the Spirit's moral leading rather than living according to the flesh (Rom 8:12–14). We must put on Christ and make no provision for the flesh, to gratify its desires (Rom 13:14; cf. 1 Pet 2:11). But it is entirely possible for people who could be spiritual to be fleshly—for instance, to indulge in jealousy, quarrelsomeness, sexual sin, idolatry, drunkenness, or greed (1 Cor 3:1–3; cf. Gal 5:13–21, see NRSV v. 13 Mg; 2 Pet 2:18; 1 John 2:16; Jude 8). And if we sow to the flesh, we reap corruption in the flesh (Gal 6:8). But if we try outward disciplinary practices as a means of controlling the flesh, we will see they are of no value compared with relying on what Christ achieved for us (Col 2:23).

Rudolf Bultmann, *Theology of the New Testament* (New York: Charles Scribner's Sons, 1951), 1:232–49.

JOHN GOLDINGAY

Folly, Fool, Foolish, Simple

These terms are a part of the wisdom tradition of the Bible. Generally they were taken more seriously in the cultures of the Bible than in modern English.

Old Testament. Several Hebrew words have been translated "folly," "fool," "foolish," "foolishness" (*ᵉewiyl, ᵓiwweleth, kasal, kesel, kᵉsiyl, kᵉsiyluth, sakal, sikluht, pᵉthiy, nabal, nᵉbalah*), but "simple" in NRSV consistently translates only the Hebrew word *pᵉthiy*.

In English, the words "fool," "foolish," "foolishness," and "folly" all seem to come from the same root. An English reader might assume that a phrase such as "the fool displays folly" (Prov 13:16) contains two uses of the same root. In fact, however, the Hebrew often uses two entirely unrelated words for fool (*k^esiyl*) and folly (*'iwweleth*) in a single sentence (e.g., Prov 12:23; 13:16; 14:8, 24; 15:2, 14; 17:12). Modern English is not able to distinguish between the finer nuances of meaning that probably accompanied the different Hebrew words when they were first used to describe unwise behavior.

However, we can deduce from the contexts in which the various words occur that almost all the terms translated "fool," "foolish," "foolishness," and "folly" have stronger negative connotations in Hebrew than they ordinarily do in English. In American usage these terms may have playful associations, connoting something closer to absurdity than to sin. But in Hebrew these words often carry with them overtones of sinful, willful misbehavior (ranging from lack of forethought to sexual immorality and blasphemy). The negative connotations of foolishness and folly may have originated in the Wisdom literature: where true *wisdom* is identified with "the *fear* of the LORD" and the *knowledge* of God (e.g. Prov 1:7, 29; 2:5; 9:10), folly (understood as the opposite of wisdom) must be considered ungodly, impious, and sinful. But folly's association with sinfulness prevails in the prophetic, poetic, and narrative texts as well.

The Hebrew *k^esiyl* (fool) is used almost exclusively in Proverbs and Ecclesiastes (sixty-seven times), appearing elsewhere only three times in Psalms (where NRSV translates "fool" in Ps 49:10, "fools" in 94:8, and "stupid" in 92:6). In Proverbs the foolish are not thought to be merely lacking in native intelligence. Rather the fool is pictured as one who hates to turn away from evil (13:19). The fool (*k^esiyl*) is a complacent person (Prov 1:32) who actively refuses to appreciate or properly utilize wisdom teachings (23:9; 26:7, 9). The fool "utters slander" (10:18), enjoys doing wrong (10:23), "throws off restraint and is careless" (14:16), does not conserve precious resources (21:20), is unreliable (26:6), and "gives full vent to anger"

(29:11). Fools engage in self-deception (14:8) and are more interested in expressing an opinion than in understanding a subject (18:2).

In Proverbs folly is the opposite of wisdom, and fools are put in stark contrast to the wise. But when Wisdom and Folly (*k^esiyluth*) are personified in Prov 9, NRSV makes the personification of Wisdom obvious (9:1–6) and hides the personification of Folly (9:13–17). Nevertheless, it is still clear that Wisdom personified and Folly personified use identical language to address the simple and that Folly's lure is counter to morally justifiable behavior. In NRSV "simple" consistently translates *p^ethiy*, which seems to connote either open-mindedness or empty-mindedness. The LORD can be good to the simple (Ps 116:6), but in most cases (in the Wisdom literature) "simple" is not considered a complimentary term. The simple are naive or gullible (14:15) and easily misled (Prov 1:32), as Folly personified tries to do in Prov 9:16–17. The simple, however, are not portrayed as deliberately obtuse. While they lack foresight, they can learn from others' experiences, though perhaps not as easily as the "intelligent" (Prov 19:25; 21:11).

The words fool (*'ewiyl*) and folly (*'iwweleth*) are used far more frequently in Proverbs than in any other section of the OT, but their occasional uses in the Prophets and Psalms are also instructive. In Proverbs a fool (*'ewiyl*) is one who despises wisdom and instruction and thus shows contempt for the religious attitude called "fear of the LORD" (Prov 1:7). Fools engage in all sorts of unproductive speech (10:8, 14, 21, etc.), mock religious practices (14:9), and are quick to quarrel or show anger (12:16; 20:3). In Wisdom literature folly (*'iwweleth*) is synonymous with lack of discipline (Prov 5:23) and lack of foresight (Prov 14:8), but in non-Wisdom texts folly is more specifically associated with morally culpable behavior. The speaker in Ps 69:5 equates folly (*'iwweleth*) with wrongdoing and Jeremiah says God's people show themselves to be foolish (*'ewiy*) when they do not know God, when they are "skilled in doing evil, but do not know how to do good" (Jer 4:22). The related root *ya'al* is used in Num 12:11 in connection with *hata'* (to sin) and in Isa 19:13 as a synonym for being deluded or led astray.

If knowledge allows the wise to make plans or decisions that are in accord with God's intentions (and are therefore effective or productive), then folly or foolishness (*sakal*, *sikluth*) can be used to describe any kind of decision making that goes counter to the will of the Lord (and is therefore ineffective and nonproductive). Thus foolishness is the opposite of knowledge (Isa 44:25) and the reverse of good *counsel* (2 Sam 15:31). Samuel says Saul has acted "foolishly" by not keeping the commandment of the Lord (1 Sam 13:13) and David describes his numbering of the people as both sinful and foolish (2 Sam 24:10 = 1 Chr 21:8). When King Asa relies on human allies rather than on Yahweh for help in a military crisis, he is said to have acted "foolishly" (2 Chr 16:9). Such wrong-headed decision making is not merely a matter of bad judgment. Foolish people (*sakal*) are those who are deliberately blind to the consequences of their actions, "who have eyes, but do not see, who have ears, but do not hear" (Jer 5:21). In contrast to the prophetic viewpoint, Ecclesiastes suggests that the height of foolishness (*sikluth*) is to talk unproductively (to the point of "wicked madness" and exhaustion) about what the future might hold (Eccl 10:12–15).

While all of the terms commonly translated "fool," and so on have morally reprehensible overtones (to one degree or another), the words *nabal* and *n^ebalah* carry by far the most negative freight. Fools (*nabal*) and their folly (*n^ebalah*) are connected with all sorts of godless behavior. "Fools say in their hearts, 'There is no God'" (Ps 14:1 = 53:1). They "leave the craving of the hungry unsatisfied" and "deprive the thirsty of drink" (Isa 32:6). They exalt themselves (Prov 30:32) and "utter error concerning the LORD" (Isa 32:6; see Job 42:8). Translating *nabal* and

n^ebalah with words like "fool" and "folly" may lead readers to minimize the offensive nature of the acts that are labeled in this way. It may be misleading for NRSV to suggest that the stubborn and rebellious behavior of the Israelites in the wilderness was merely foolish (Deut 32:6). When the same word is used elsewhere in the OT to describe punishable behavior (such as sex outside of marriage, the "sin of Achan," or the rape of Dinah), NRSV calls it "an outrage" (Gen 34:7), "a disgraceful act" (Deut 22:21), or "an outrageous thing" (Josh 7:15). Thus in Isa 9:17 the behavior referred to as *n^ebalah* (which is said to merit punishment and provoke God's anger) is closer to wickedness than to folly in ordinary English usage.

New Testament. The Greek words that are translated "fool," "foolish," "foolishness," "folly" include *aphron/aphrosyne*; *moraino/moros/moria*; *anoia/anoetos*; and *asynetos*. Words translated this way in the Gospels carry approximately the same negative overtones as the corresponding words had in OT texts. Luke uses *anoetos* once in the Emmaus story, when Jesus calls the disciples "foolish" for not believing "all that the prophets have declared" (Luke 24:25). Otherwise, only words based on *moros* and *aphron/aphrosyne* are used to describe "foolish" (willfully disobedient) behavior in the Gospel accounts. Thus Mark lists folly (*aphrosyne*) at the end of a long list of "evil things" that "come from within" and "defile a person" (7:21–23). Luke uses *aphron* and Matthew uses *moros* in accusations: "You fool" (Luke 12:20; Matt 5:22) and "You fools" (Luke 11:40) or "You blind fools" (Matt 23:17). The context makes it clear that the "scribes and Pharisees" addressed here are blind by choice (as in Jer 5:21). Matthew uses *moros* four more times in two parables. The person who refuses to act on Jesus' words is said to be like "a foolish man who built his house on sand" (Matt 7:26) and the foolish bridesmaids who did not prepare themselves for a long wait apparently miss out on their chance to enter the kingdom of heaven (Matt 25:1–13), indicating that their behavior is blameworthy.

Paul uses "foolish" (*asynetos*) once in Rom 1:31 (in the midst of an extensive list of examples of the kinds of "wickedness" that come from refusing to acknowledge God) and again in Rom 10:19, when he quotes from Deut 32:21 (where it translates the Hebrew word *nabal*). But in Rom 1:14 (where "foolish" seems synonymous with "barbarians") and again in Gal 3:1, 3 (where Paul chastises those who seem to be backsliding), "foolish" translates *anoetos*. In Titus 3:3 *anoetos* ("foolish") appears again, in a list of vices including "disobedient, led astray . . . despicable, hating one another."

The remaining occurrences of the English words "fool," "foolish," and "foolishness" in the Epistles translate either *aphron/aphrosyne* or *moraino/moros/moria*. While the Gospel writers use these terms more or less interchangeably, Paul seems to make a distinction between the associative meaning attached to these two word families. When Paul intends for his audience to hear the OT overtones of sin attached to the concept of foolishness, he uses *aphron* or *aphrosyne* (as do Mark, Luke, and 1 Pet 2:15). In Eph 5:17 "foolish" is clearly opposed to "understand[ing] what the will of the Lord is." In Rom 2:19–20 foolishness is parallel to being blind and in darkness. And in 2 Cor 11–12 Paul repeatedly uses *aphron* and *aphrosyne* to describe what he sees to be the unfaithful behavior of boasting about one's own accomplishments.

Paul knows that it is foolishness (*aphrosyne*) to try to point out the ways in which he is equal (or superior) to the "super-apostles" with whom the Corinthians are enthralled (2 Cor 11:1–6). Boasting "according to human standards" (2 Cor. 11:18) is the essence of foolishness and Paul says he would rather not be thought of as a fool (*aphron*) in this sense. But the Corinthians have forced him into it by comparing him unfavorably to the "super-apostles" (2 Cor 12:11).

On the one hand, Paul says, if people are already calling him a fool, he might as well go ahead and promote himself as fools do (2 Cor 11:16–18). So when he begins to list his qualifications as an apostle, he admits that he is "speaking as a fool" would speak (11:21). On the other hand, Paul comforts himself with the thought that he will not truly be a fool when he boasts, because he is speaking the truth, as most fools do not (2 Cor 12:6). In keeping with the major narrative thread of the OT (in which God consistently chooses those whom the world would consider least qualified to carry out God's intentions), Paul lists as his qualifications for ministry a wide variety of tribulations and weaknesses (2 Cor 11:23–29; 12:7–10). Thus Paul concludes that if he must boast like a fool (*aphron*), he will boast of the things that show his weakness (11:30) in order better to prove that it is the power of God, not the power of the apostle, that truly matters (see Judg 7:2).

In an earlier argument with the Corinthians, Paul had arrived at a similar theological conclusion using an entirely different group of words. While Paul's use of *aphron* and *aphrosyne* in 2 Corinthians recalls the OT association between foolishness and sin or disobedience, his use of *moraino, moros,* and *moria* in 1 Cor 1–4 calls up images of the mimic fool (the buffoon or clownlike character who was so widely known from Greco-Roman theater productions). L. L. Welborn makes a convincing case for understanding Paul's use of "fool" in these chapters as Paul's appropriation and reinterpretation of a derogatory label that the well-educated, elegant, and sophisticated speakers in Corinth used to mock Paul's appearance and manner of speaking. Paul's detractors (who themselves embodied the types of wisdom and strength most admired in the Greco-Roman world) have called him a *moros* (a buffoon-type fool), and he has accepted that role (for the moment) in order to take advantage of the traditional freedom such a fool was allowed to have in speaking truth to power (Welborn, 53). Paul turns the tables on those who consider themselves either wise or strong by reminding them that "God's foolishness is wiser than human wisdom, and God's weakness is stronger than human strength" (1 Cor 1:25). God has chosen to work through events that seem (by human standards) to epitomize weakness and failure ("the cross," v. 18), and God has chosen to "call" people who seem unqualified by human standards (v. 26), "so that no one might boast in the presence of God" (v. 29). Thus Paul argues that those who think they are wise are merely fooling themselves, because "the wisdom of this world is foolishness with God" (1 Cor 3:18–19). Since God's self-revelation is mediated by those who seem laughably weak in the eyes of the world, faithful apostles like Paul are "fools for the sake of Christ" (1 Cor 4:10).

L. L. Welborn, "Paul's Appropriation of the Role of the Fool in 1 Corinthians 1–4," *Journal of Theology* 106 (2002): 39–54.

KATHLEEN ANNE FARMER

Foreign, Foreigner *see* Alien

Forever *see* Time

Forget *see* Remember

Forgive, Forgiveness, Pardon

"Forgive" and "pardon" may seem to have slightly different connotations in English, but in the usage of NRSV (where "pardon" appears only in the OT and Apocrypha) both English word groups represent the same range of vocabulary in the original languages. Together their meaning is somewhat different from what might normally be attached to them in the modern Western world.

Both "forgive" and "pardon" refer, in Scripture, to public, social acts. Where the modern reader, being more psychologically oriented, may at first think of forgiveness primarily as an interior act or process, the tendency of ancient Mediterranean cultures was to focus on public actions more than private motivations. That does not mean a complete lack of interest in the latter. Jesus' admonition

that forgiveness must be "from the heart" (Matt 18:35) implies that there must be deliberate, intentional commitment to the public act; it is not enough to feign forgiveness for the convenience of the moment.

In scriptural context, "forgiveness" means the public removal of a past offense from further consideration. It will no longer affect the relationship of the parties concerned. The forgiver will no longer bring it to mind (Jer 31:34). Those forgiven, however, should indeed remember the event, since it places them in a new kind of relationship—even, one might say, a certain indebtedness—to the one who has forgiven them. One psalm, for example, attributes the later misfortunes of Israel to the breaching of this relationship (Ps 78:32–66).

The Scriptures of Israel occasionally mention forgiveness as a transaction among human beings (e.g., Joseph and his brothers, Gen 50:15–21). But God's forgiveness of human sin is the principal point of interest. God is sometimes portrayed as reluctant to forgive sin, for example, when Joshua solemnly warns the Israelites about the gravity of their covenant with God (Josh 24:19). More often, God is portrayed as eager to forgive, actively offering forgiveness in the hope that the people will respond to it and their relationship can be restored: "You are a God ready to forgive, gracious and merciful, slow to anger and abounding in steadfast love, and you did not forsake them" (Neh 9:17).

At times, God is portrayed in both ways at once: "forgiving iniquity and transgression and sin, yet by no means clearing the guilty" (Exod 34:7; cf. Num 14:18; Ps 99:8). God forgives sin, but still punishes it. This is not as contradictory as it at first seems. It means that the punishment inflicted stops short of a complete severing of the relationship. God remains open to the restoration of the relationship and, in effect, allows a limited punishment to erase the offense. Forgiveness does not simply usher the forgiven person into a world without consequences.

God's anger (see *wrath*) at sin may become known in the form of political reversals (e.g., Dan 9:15–19), natural disasters (e.g., the locusts of Amos 7:1–3), or perhaps ill health (e.g., Jer 33:6–8). All these signal a need to appeal to God for forgiveness. Part of the work of prophets, from Moses onward, is both to proclaim the need for forgiveness and to intercede with God for the people (e.g., Exod 32:32). In the process, the prophets may remind God of the divine propensity to forgive (e.g., Dan 9:9). They may even encourage this result, much as one might with a human king, by pointing out that it is in God's own interest to maintain relationship with the people God liberated from Egypt (e.g., Num 14:13–19).

Jeremiah describes the effects of God's forgiveness as a renewal of relationship with God, a new sense of responsibility on the part of the people, a new and internalized grasp of God's commandments, and a willingness to obey them. In short, God's forgiveness will lead ultimately to a new covenant, written on the people's hearts rather than on tablets of stone (Jer 31:31–34).

Humanity can help bring the process of divine forgiveness into play in two ways. One is through the sacrificial cultus, where sin offerings have the effect of "covering" or "making *atonement* for" at least some past offenses. (Numbers 15:22–31 limits this process to unintentional offenses, but this is not always the case.) What is "covered" is no longer a factor in the ongoing relationship. Another common metaphor of forgiveness is that of "setting aside" or "taking away" the offense (Heb. *nasaʾ*, which NRSV translates "forgive" in Gen 18:24 and elsewhere).

For the most part, it is the priest who, by offering the prescribed sacrifice, "covers" the offense. In a few texts, however, God is said to "cover" sins, at which point NRSV translates the Hebrew verb with "forgive" or "pardon" (e.g., Pss 65:3; 79:9; Jer 18:23). In either case, the results are the same.

The other way in which humanity helps bring about forgiveness is through

"turning" or *repentance*. By turning back to God and seeking renewal of the relationship, the people are able to take advantage of God's predisposition to forgive. So strong is this predisposition that in one passage God actually directs Isaiah to obscure the message given him so as to *prevent* such "turning" (Isa 6:9–10). God's only "defense" is to keep the people from repenting. Otherwise, God will certainly "heal" (as in the Hebrew Bible) or "forgive" them (as in the quotation of the passage in Mark 4:12).

In the NT these same themes all reappear, along with a new insistence on the relationship between God's forgiveness of humanity and our forgiveness of one another. The concern for mutual forgiveness does not begin with the NT. Proverbs 17:9 recommends forgiveness as a way of maintaining friendship, and Joseph's act of forgiveness serves as a model for the reader in Genesis. Sirach 28:2 even makes the point that forgiving one's neighbor will lead to one's own prayer for forgiveness being heard. But the subject is less prominent in the earlier Scriptures.

As in the OT, the disruption of our relationship with God may be recognized in the NT partly by the lack of prosperity and health in the community. Forgiveness can counter these. In Zechariah's song at the birth of John the Baptist, God's forgiveness serves as prelude to the redemption of Israel (Luke 1:68–79). Again, when healing the paralytic who is let down through the roof, Jesus begins by forgiving his sins (Matt 9:2–8; Mark 2:1–12; Luke 5:17–26).

Despite this connection, there is a certain ambivalence in the NT about attributing all ill health to the influence of sin. In John's Gospel, Jesus heals a paralytic at the pool of Bethzatha and then warns him not to sin again, lest something worse happen to him (5:14). Yet, in the same Gospel, Jesus rejects the assumption that sin is responsible for another man's blindness (9:2–5). James 5:15 mentions healing and forgiveness together; but the point of the passage is to celebrate the power of the prayer of faith. Even earlier, Jeremiah's references to this issue seem to be celebrating the power of forgiveness more than offering an explanation of the sources of illness. The point then seems to be that forgiveness, in restoring right relationship with God, is replete with beneficial effects.

Humanity can seek forgiveness, in the NT as in the Scriptures of Israel, by repentance and also through sacrificial means. References to repentance and forgiveness often appear together. John the Baptist is presented as preaching a "baptism of repentance for the forgiveness of sins" (Mark 1:4; Luke 3:3). Acts presents early Christian preachers as doing much the same (2:38). In the sermons of Acts, however, the key offense to be repented of is specifically the rejection and execution of Jesus (5:29–32; 8:22). Accordingly, the same point can be made by describing belief as the necessary prelude to forgiveness (10:43). Belief in Jesus, since it reverses the earlier rejection, is effectively a kind of repentance in this case.

Many readers are troubled by the citation of Isa 6:9–10 in Mark 4:10–12, implying that God is not eager to forgive and that Jesus formulated his message in such a way as to keep outsiders from understanding it. No doubt the widespread use of this passage from Isaiah reflects the early Christians' perplexity as to why some people "got" the message and others did not. (The passage is also quoted in Matt 13:14–15, Luke 8:9–10, and Acts 28:26–27, though in these instances the final verb is given as "heal" rather than "forgive.")

In Mark's version, however, the treatment is more complex than this. Jesus' speech to his disciples (4:10–20) seems to indicate that they are now complete insiders, who understand everything that he will say—or at least can expect to understand it. But in the following chapters of the Gospel, this turns out to be very far from the case. It is typically outsiders such as the Syrophoenician woman (7:24–30) who grasp Jesus' meaning in life-giving ways, while the disciples all wind up betraying Jesus to one degree or another. Rather than a straightforward assertion of God's unwillingness to forgive, this text must be read as embodying Mark's use of irony to remind the faithful of his own time not to presume arrogantly on their own intimacy with Jesus.

In another case, however, the refusal of forgiveness is straightforward and does not appear to be at all ironic—the case of blasphemy against the Holy *Spirit* (Matt 12:31–32; Mark 3:28–29; Luke 12:10). This difficult passage makes a sharp distinction between rejection of Jesus and rejection of the Spirit. Rejection of Jesus can be forgiven; rejection of the Spirit cannot. In the context that Matthew and Mark give it, the saying is a response to the refusal of the religious authorities to admit that Jesus' exorcisms bring about good. To deny the goodness of an act that gives life and health is so to skew one's own sense of values that one can no longer recognize the goodness of God, the source of forgiveness.

To the degree that such a stance rejects the very basis of all relationship between humanity and God, it cuts itself decisively off from renewal of that relationship through divine forgiveness. Indeed, the one who blasphemes against the Spirit will not be able to recognize God's forgiveness when it is extended. In this offense, one is no longer able to distinguish good from evil; and this is why it lies beyond forgiveness. One must note that religious leaders are identified here as particularly susceptible to it.

The ritual approach to forgiveness through sacrifice also appears in the NT, where it now takes the form of associating forgiveness with Jesus' *blood*. The Synoptic evangelists use the language of covenant *sacrifice* in their accounts of the Last Supper (Matt 26:28; Mark 14:24; Luke 22:20). By describing the cup as Jesus' blood "poured out for many for the forgiveness of sins," Matthew also links it with the sin offerings and the idea of atonement. Sacrifice, as noted above, had the particular function of "covering" offenses so that they no longer played a role in the relationship.

This draws together a number of threads in the Israelite tradition about forgiveness. Since Jesus is seen as fulfilling God's will, God is intimately involved here in creating the opportunity of forgiveness. God, of course, was already the provider of the sacrificial avenue of approach, having graciously prescribed it in the Torah. Now, given Jesus' particular intimacy with God as Son, God is also intimately involved in the performing of the sacrifice. God's readiness to forgive thus becomes evident in a variety of ways.

What is distinctive in the NT, as compared with the earlier Scriptures, is an insistence on forgiveness among human beings as well as from God. This works out in two ways. First, the NT writers attribute to Jesus (and through him to his followers) the power to forgive sins. There was always, of course, a recognition that human beings have the power to forgive offenses against themselves. Indeed, without such a perception, we would have no language for describing God's forgiveness of us. But Jesus claims authority to forgive offenses against God or, to put it another way, to forgive in the absolute sense (Matt. 9:2–3; Mark 2:5–7; Luke 5:20–21).

The Gospels present this as an occasion of scandal for the religious leadership of Jesus' time. It does indeed go well beyond the prophetic role of interceding with God for forgiveness. In the story of the paralytic let down through the roof, Jesus goes on to verify his pronouncement of forgiveness by showing that it has the healing, life-giving effect expected by Jeremiah (Matt. 9:4–7; Mark 2:8–12; Luke 5:22–25).

NT writers assume that this power to forgive sins continues with Jesus in his death and resurrection and that those who trust in him can avail themselves of it. The authority to forgive also continues in the body of Jesus' followers. John's Gospel tells of the risen Jesus breathing the Spirit on them and specifically con-

ferring on them the power to forgive and to withhold forgiveness (20:22–23). The power to withhold forgiveness is simply the reverse side of the power to extend it. This means that, like Jesus, Jesus' followers hold the same authority exercised by God in the Scriptures of Israel: to forgive or not to forgive. Since the followers have this power through their association with Jesus and with the Spirit, it must be exercised not willfully but in accordance with Jesus' own practice of generosity. It must also follow the principle of truth (see *true*) that is central to John's Gospel and is exemplified, negatively, in the Synoptics in the account of the unforgivable sin and in Jesus' repeated attacks on hypocrisy.

If we remember the point made above, that forgiveness in the ancient Mediterranean world was not primarily an interior act but a public and social one, we will not be surprised to find Paul exercising the power to forgive in a relatively formal manner in cooperation with the congregation at Corinth (2 Cor 2:10). The later Pauline tradition continued to insist on the importance of forgiveness for the life of the community: "just as the Lord has forgiven you, so you also must forgive" (Col 3:13; cf. Eph 4:32).

Second, forgiveness within the human community is directly related to God's forgiveness of humanity. The tradition of Jesus' teaching insists that to receive God's forgiveness for ourselves implies an obligation to extend forgiveness to others. This is integral to both versions of the Lord's Prayer, which connect our request for forgiveness from God with our willingness to forgive others (Matt 6:12; Luke 11:4). Matthew puts it in still more trenchant form when Jesus says that if we do not forgive others, God will not forgive us (Matt 6:14–15). Jesus tells Peter that the obligation to forgive is inexhaustible and that God, like the master of the unforgiving slave in the parable, will punish those who do not forgive (Matt 18:21–35).

We appropriate God's forgiveness of us in our willingness to forgive others and also in a general response of love. In

Luke's version of the anointing story (7:36–50), Jesus draws a sharp distinction between the behavior of his very respectable host and the woman of ill repute who bathes and anoints his feet. It may be that the host, being devout, does not experience the need for forgiveness. Jesus does not necessarily deny that in the story. The point rather is that forgiveness produces a new abundance of love, generosity, and hospitality—of a sort that may perhaps be missing among more strictly correct people.

In sum, the whole biblical story hangs on God's willingness—even eagerness—to forgive. Forgiveness removes the offense from the public "space" between God and erring humanity. It does not, however, mean that we thereby enter a world without consequence. Sin always has consequences. It means rather that sin is not the final determinant of the relationship between humanity and God. God's generosity is the final determinant.

Humanity can "put itself in the way" of God's forgiveness by approaching God in rites of worship (themselves a divine gift) and by turning back toward God in repentance. These are not so much ways of persuading God to relent—though they may at times be spoken of in those terms—as they are ways of availing ourselves of a forgiveness that is already prepared.

Repentance represents the human acknowledgment of failure and responsibility for damage to the relationship. Worship is a way of acknowledging the reality of God's forgiveness. Worshipers could have confidence in the sacrificial cultus of the temple only because it was put in place by command of God in the Torah. When Christians affirm that forgiveness is connected with the blood of Jesus, we are saying that God participates with us in this worship and is willing to suffer any cost in order to extend forgiveness to us.

Humanity can frustrate God's willingness to forgive but not erase it. The only point at which we place ourselves beyond God's forgiveness is through the sin against the Spirit, the moment when

we begin to call good evil and evil good and lose our moral compass entirely. At that point we can no longer recognize God's love even when it is available to us. The devout must be constantly reminded that we are the people most in danger of doing exactly this.

According to the NT, genuine acceptance of forgiveness implies the willingness to extend it to others as well. A core element in Jesus' teaching is that we cannot receive forgiveness for ourselves without doing this. To accept God's forgiveness for ourselves means to participate in a vast project of *reconciliation,* by which God is restoring the whole creation to friendship with God and with one another. This gives faithful disciples the power and obligation to forgive sins, both in God's name and in our own. Indeed, the Christian community exists through and for the constant widening of the circle of forgiveness and the new kind of human unity this makes possible.

Walther Eichrodt, *Theology of the Old Testament* (Philadelphia: Westminster Press, 1967), 2:443–483; Vincent Taylor, *Forgiveness and Reconciliation* (London: Macmillan, 1941).

L. WILLIAM COUNTRYMAN

Fornication   *see* **Immorality**

Forty   *see* **Numbers**

Fountain   *see* **Water**

Four   *see* **Numbers**

Free, Freedom, Liberty   In a very general and abstract way, freedom might be defined as the ability of individuals and groups to choose to remove obstacles effectively in order to pursue or achieve some goal or end. The three main aspects of freedom are ability to choose; effective removal of obstructions to goals; and pursuit or attainment of some goal or value. The word "freedom" can mean any of these elements alone, or some combination of two, or even all three together. Further, each of these usages is capable of various degrees of ambivalence. For instance, in the United States, freedom practically always involves the idea of freedom from obstacles that Americans view chiefly as arbitrary and external constraints of personal freedom. The obstacles are identified either in other individuals or groups. Removing the external obstacles facilitates self-realization and is called "freeing" or "liberation." In contrast, Europeans in general focus on internal obstacles that inhibit freedom, such as various mental states like ignorance, falsehood, stupidity, and mental illness, and self-destructive habits like vice. The Bible in general recognizes that human beings have the ability to make free choices (e.g., Gen 2:16), but the overriding understanding of freedom is "liberation from slavery." The prime example, of course, is the exodus. God led the Israelites out of slavery in Egypt to freedom (from obstacles in making choices). However, as the biblical tradition makes quite clear, the exodus was not liberation so much as it was acquisition by a new owner. "I will free you from the burdens of the Egyptians and deliver you from slavery to them. I will redeem you. . . . I will take you as my people, and I will be your God" (Exod 6:6–7). This aspect of freedom is the attainment of a new goal or end in life, namely, to serve God. Liberation is better understood as *redemption,* that is, acquisition by a new owner or master, God. In effect, then, "freed" people remain *slaves* or servants, but to a new lord or master.

The social institution of slavery, in fact, provides Paul—whose letters contain extended treatments of freedom—with images and analogies for his reflections on freedom. For Paul, Christ is central. Christ is the dividing line between two periods. Prior to Christ, all in Israel were slaves (Gal 5:1). They were slaves to "elemental spirits" (Gal 4:9; celestial entities that determined the calendar and annual cosmic cycles, such as those in astral forecasts called *dodeka-*

eterides), which for Paul had counterparts in sin (a determinative active force functioning through the "flesh"), in flesh (that aspect of the human person that is opposed to and alienates itself from God), in death (physical, to be sure, but also conduct that squelches human growth or life), and in law (an approach to pleasing God based on doing "works" of the law). This was human existence in a world without Jesus Messiah.

Despite a shameful death, Jesus was raised by God and therefore must have been pleasing to God. What did Jesus accomplish for human beings? He redeemed them, that is, he removed the aforementioned obstacles to pleasing God, allowing human beings to serve God faithfully. Paul's argument with the Galatians is rooted in his amazement (Gal 1:6) that they who once were slaves in a Gentile way now want to be slaves in an Israelite way by accepting circumcision and the rest. This decision would effectively nullify the freedom from obstacles attained by Christ and reintroduce those obstacles.

Yet just as in the exodus, those who are freed through Jesus' redemptive act actually accept a new master. The freedom for humans worked out by God in Christ implies subjection to Christ (Rom 14:18; 1 Cor 3:23; 7:22; Eph 6:6; Col 3:11) or to the "law of Christ" (Gal 6:2; 1 Cor 9:21). This freedom ought not to be self-serving (1 Cor 6:12; 10:23) but rather express itself in service of one's neighbor (Gal 5:13).

In the present experience of freedom, Christians can also freely choose to return to the slavery of sin (Rom 6:12–13). Paul exhorts Christians to choose and continue to choose to be "slaves to righteousness for sanctification" (Rom 6:19). One cannot hold both options simultaneously. Slave service to sin leads to death; slave service to God leads to life eternal (Rom 6:22–23). Fidelity to freedom in the present will blossom into even greater liberty yet to come (Rom 8:21, 23–25; 2 Cor 1:22; 5:5; Eph 1:14). What we possess at the moment is the down payment.

The slave service owed by believers to God is to be paid by service to neighbor:

"For you were called to freedom, brothers and sisters; only do not use your freedom as an opportunity for self-indulgence, but through love become slaves to one another" (Gal 5:13). The phrase translated by the NRSV as "become slaves" literally is a verb: "render slave service." The present tense of this verb emphasizes an enduring behavior rather than a single deed or action. It is to be a lifestyle, a way of life. And this service requires love (Gal 5:13) as the necessary context.

The concrete dimensions of this slave service are determined by the Spirit (Rom 7:6; 12:11). In Rom 12–15, Paul presents a program for such service. First (Rom 12–13), he offers general principles that should guide Christians in meeting the requirements of God's righteousness. Slave service extended to neighbor should be rooted in *agape*, that is, in reciprocal caring and concern (Rom 12:9–13). While ordinarily translated "love," *agape* means group attachment, behavior that reveals one adheres to a group, hence "caring for, consideration toward, considerateness of" fellow group members. To "serve the Lord" (Rom 12:11) ordinarily means much more than keeping individual commands of God. It describes total dependence upon and submission toward God because of how God relates to human beings (Judg 10:13, 16; Pss 2:11–12; 99:4; 102:18–22). If human beings render slave service to God as God expects, God will accept such not as slaves, but as Paul indicates, as adopted children (Gal 4:1–7; Rom 8:12–17). Serving the Lord is accomplished by serving one's neighbor.

Paul makes this point with even greater clarity when he applies his general principles (Rom 12–13) to the "weak" members of the community (Rom 14–15). Slave service rendered to Christians must be rooted in righteousness, peace, and joy in the Spirit (Rom 14:17). This service is directed to Christ, who is plainly one's Christian neighbor (Rom 14:18). One ought to treat the neighbor justly, in a conciliatory fashion, with sensitive care rather than insisting on expressing one's own freedom to the hurt of neighbor. This is "the will of God—what is good and acceptable and perfect" (Rom 12:2). Thus, speaking within a context familiar from first-century slavery, Paul describes Christian freedom not simply as complete unrestraint or freedom from constraint but rather a switch of masters. Because we have been redeemed or "freed" by God in Christ, we must render slave service rooted in love to our neighbor. Paul's understanding of freedom helps believers grasp the significance of the verses Jesus read from Isaiah (61:1ff.) in the synagogue at Nazareth: "[The Lord] has sent me to proclaim release to the captives" and Jesus' comment: "Today this scripture has been fulfilled in your hearing" (Luke 4:18, 21).

Bruce J. Malina, "Freedom: A Theological Inquiry into the Dimensions of a Symbol," *BTB* 8 (1978): 62–76.

JOHN J. PILCH

Fulfill, Fulfillment, Accomplish

A total of fifteen different Hebrew verbs and five Greek verbs are rendered by these English terms in NRSV. Additionally, several noun or verb phrases are used. Together they provide some 140 instances of the concept of fulfillment or completion.

By far the greatest number of these examples identify God as the expressed subject or as the implied subject. It is God who will accomplish his purposes. He will fulfill what was spoken by the prophets, what was promised in the past in the Scriptures, or the covenant commitment that God made to his people. The rest of the examples have human subjects, though in Ps 148:8 it is the natural world that fulfills God's commands. The verb forms are usually active forms, but there are also numerous examples that use the somewhat impersonal passive form of the verb—certain things or promises "will be fulfilled." The implication is that God will be the one to bring about his purpose or will.

In the OT, the most frequent Hebrew verb used in these contexts is the general verb *ʿasah*, "do, make." It can be used with God or humans as the subject: Esth 5:6, 8; 7:2; 9:12; Isa 46:10; Ezek 12:25 (2x).

The verb *maleʾ*, "fill," is also frequently rendered "fulfill" in NRSV. This verb refers basically to the action of filling a container. In 2 Sam 7:12; 1 Chr 17:11; 2 Chr 36:21; Job 39:2; Dan 9:2 it is applied to the completion of a given time. Elsewhere it seems to overlap with other verbs applied to the fulfillment of divine promises (2 Chr 6:4, 15) or plans (Ps 20:4–5).

The verb *qum*, literally "establish, set up," is also frequently rendered "fulfill" in these contexts. In Gen 26:3, for example, the idea would seem to be that God's oath or promise to Abraham, to bless his descendants, becomes a reality when Isaac obeys God and rejects Egypt as a destination during a famine. In Num 23:19 the carrying out of promises made beforehand is a mark of the divine nature. In this verb is the sense that without realization, intention remains incomplete.

Another verb that denotes completion or bringing to a final resolution is *shillem*. It appears in Deut 23:21 and Eccl 5:4–5 in the context of individuals carrying out or fulfilling vows and religious commitments they have made. In Isa 44:26 it speaks of God implementing the message of God's prophetic messengers.

What is to be fulfilled or accomplished is most often some word spoken at an earlier time. These may be God's promises, his words or commands, or those of human agents. When God is subject, the object of these verbs is most often "promises," "words," or related terms. In the case of human agents, what are fulfilled are also promises and vows made. We have noted above that the Hebrew verb *maleʾ* is frequently connected with time and so what is fulfilled or completed in those contexts is a set period of time.

In Ps 119:123 and Ezek 12:23 we have examples of verbless phrases, both rendered in NRSV by the verb "fulfill" in view of a parallel expression. In Ps 119:123 it is

the Hebrew verb *kalah*, "be complete." In Ezek 12:23 it is the verb *qarab*, "come near," used with the time phrase and implying the coming to fruition of a vision.

Completion or finalization is the sense of the verb *tamam*, found in Lam 4:22.

Although NRSV uses the verb "accomplish" in rendering the final Hebrew phrase in Isa 60:22, the actual sense is "do something quickly." The focus of the Hebrew verb is the speed with which something is done rather than the accomplishing of the task.

As we move to the NT, we find fewer Greek verbs rendered by English "fulfill" or "accomplish." Essentially there are only two verbs used, *pleroo* and *teleo*.

Matthew's Gospel on fifteen occasions uses the verb *pleroo* to speak of the many fulfillments of OT sayings or events that it associates with Jesus' ministry. For the most part these are words spoken by the prophets. On one occasion it refers to the fulfillment of the "scriptures of the prophets" (Matt 26:56) and once (5:17) to the fulfillment of the law. Both active forms, "to fulfill," and passive forms, "to be fulfilled," are used in this Gospel without any apparent distinction. In 3:15 a purpose phrase is used when Jesus says that his being baptized by John is "to fulfill all righteousness." This means Jesus accepted that by being baptized he was bound to "fulfill" or live out the demands of a righteous life. The link that Matthew makes between Jesus' life and ministry and the prophetic word expresses that Gospel writer's view that Jesus fulfills all the hopes of OT faith.

Elsewhere in the Gospels we note a similar use of the verb rendered as "fulfill." While Luke and John frequently use the verb *pleroo*—eighteen times in all—Mark uses it only twice. In 1:15 Mark speaks of the "time" being fulfilled, in the sense of its reaching its climactic moment, the breaking in of God's kingdom. In 14:49 Jesus' arrest is linked to the fulfillment of Scripture. Acts records four uses of the verb, and on one occasion NRSV so renders a verbless clause (7:17). In

John 3:29 John the Baptist employs the notion of fulfillment when he states that his joy or delight has been made complete by knowing that he has played the role of the one who announced the arrival of the Christ.

In the Epistles, the concept of fulfillment is not so prominent, with only ten uses noted, mainly in Romans and James. Once again, however, we see that the link to the completion or bringing to reality of words spoken beforehand in Scripture is uppermost.

The second Greek verb that features in these expressions is the verb *teleo*, with its strong connection to the notion of finality, bringing something to a conclusion. There are only five examples of this verb, notably two of them in Revelation. It is the only verb given this rendering in Revelation (10:7; 17:17). There are also two examples in Luke, 1:45 and 22:37. However, in each of these examples there is the same connection to the bringing to completion of what was spoken earlier.

NRSV has rendered several other Greek verbs by the verb "accomplish." Apart from *pleroo* and *teleo*, Matt 5:18 has the verb *ginomai*, "become, happen." In the context of the Law and Prophets being fulfilled, Jesus states that nothing there written will be done away with before "all is accomplished." Although there are interpretational differences over this phrase's exact meaning, it clearly sees some future time when the purpose of Christ's coming would complete what the Law and Prophets pointed to.

Romans 15:18 provides an example of the verb *katergazo*, in which Paul speaks of his ministry as the means God has used to accomplish a following among the Gentiles. Similarly, in Eph 1:11 the verb *energeo*, "to achieve, accomplish," describes God as achieving what God intends, in this case, through Paul's ministry.

GRAHAM S. OGDEN

Full, Fullness   In the OT the adjective "full" (Hebrew *male*) describes contain-

ers or other objects that can be filled with material of any kind. Examples are things that are full of choice flour and incense (Num 7:13–86), of horses (2 Kgs 6:17), of water (Ps 65:9). It also is used to describe objects or people that are filled with abstract qualities such as wisdom or skill (Deut 34:9; 1 Kgs 7:14), youth (Job 20:11), trouble (Job 14:1), steadfast love (Pss 33:5; 119:64), and knowledge (Isa 11:9). It may refer to communities that are full of violence and crime (Ezek 7:23), of bloodshed and perversity (Ezek 9:9).

This same root can also be applied to something that is fully grown, complete in itself or mature. Crops or harvest are so described in Gen 41:7 and Exod 22:29.

The sense of something being complete, and in that sense full, is found in an example such as Gen 23:9, where the full price is paid, or Lev 25:30, which notes the passing of a full year. There is an overlap here with the several examples in which the noun "all" (*kol*) describes the complete or full measure of something, for example, Deut 14:28 ("full tithe").

The noun "fullness" (Hebrew *mele'ah*) appears on only three occasions, Exod 22:29; Num 18:27; Deut 33:16. In each it describes the bounty of the harvest or of the earth's produce.

Another Hebrew root that serves this semantic range is *saba*, often rendered as "satisfied" or "sated," full in the sense of having an adequate amount of something (Lev 26:5; Prov 30:9). This root is frequently found in the phrase "full of days," describing a person who has lived a long time, for example, Gen 25:8; 35:29; 2 Chr 24:15; Job 42:17. In Job 14:1 it is applied to human life, describing it as full of trouble. Probably the root here suggests that people have to endure a great deal of pain during their lives, rather than implying that life is so full of pain that there is nothing but trouble. See also Ps 88:3.

Less frequently we note the Hebrew root *shalam* rendered in this manner. In Deut 25:15 weights and measures are described as full in association with the adjective "honest." The meaning is that these objects should conform to a standard and not be deficient in any way. This same sense is found in Ruth 2:12, where Naomi wishes Ruth a full reward for her faithfulness. Similarly in 1 Chr 12:38 the warriors came to Hebron "with full intent" to make David king, implying that none of them disagreed with that decision. Other examples in Prov 19:17 and Jer 51:56 indicate that "lacking nothing" is the emphasis provided by this root: full payment or reward is to be made.

One other verb that requires noting is the Hebrew verb *kalah*, used some seven times (Isa 10:23; Jer 5:10, 18; Lam 4:11; Ezek 11:13; Nah 1:8; Zeph 1:18) in the phrase "make a full end." The adjective "full" refers to the completeness of the destruction.

On three occasions NRSV uses the expression "full of rage/wrath," expressed by the root *'abar*, "become furious." Psalms 78:21, 59; 89:38 suggest that these are poetic uses of the root. We note that each example has Yahweh as the subject.

In the NT the basic terms *pleroma* (noun "fullness") and *pleres* (adjective "full") dominate. The noun form suggests completeness (as in Rom 11:12, 25) in which the full extent (Rom 15:29) or all the attendant qualities (Eph 1:23; 4:3) or the essence of the object is referred to (Eph 3:19; Col 1:19). In 1 Cor 10:26 it speaks of the bounty of the earth, everything that the earth produces, while in Gal 4:4 it points to the appropriateness of a time determined by God, the fruition of the divine plan (Eph 1:10). Where the adjective "full" is used, it may describe a container filled with material (Matt 14:20; 15:37) or persons filled with spiritual qualities such as the Holy Spirit (Luke 4:1; Acts 6:3, 5, 8) and grace (John 1:14). Forms of the verb *pleroo* describe persons being satisfied (Luke 6:25; Phil 4:18–19) and the action of filling a person with happiness (Acts 2:28) or knowledge (Col 1:25).

The adjective *mestos* may also be used to describe the quality of having been filled with some material (John 19:29; 21:11; Jas 3:8) or quality (Matt 23:28; Acts 13:10; Jas 3:17). Those who are full of greed (Luke 11:39) or cursing (Rom 3:14), of blasphemy (Rev 17:3) and abomination (Rev 17:4) can be described with the verb *gemo*. It is probable that this is a term preferred by individual writers rather than one with a special semantic value, since it seems to occur mostly, though not exclusively, in Revelation.

The adjective "full," denoting a thing completed, in Jas 1:4 translates *teleios*. As we noted in OT, the totality is often rendered as "full," though the original text may have used the adjective "all." See Phil 1:9; Col 1:10; 1 Tim 1:15; 2:11; 4:9.

GRAHAM S. OGDEN

Gehenna *see* **Grave**

Gentiles The word is derived from the Latin *gens*, "nation," as it is used in the Vulgate. The Greek word in the NT is *ethnos*, used as Jews of the first century A.D. used the Hebrew word *goy*. *Goy* was originally a strictly political term meaning *nation*, but by the NT period it had come to be used to designate an individual from any of the foreign nations, thus any non-Jew. So the NT divides humanity into Jews and Gentiles. Since circumcision was the physical mark of membership in the covenant people, Gentiles are also designated "the uncircumcised" (Acts 11:3; Rom 3:29–30; Eph 2:11).

In the Gospels, "Gentiles" is used in Matt 4:15 in the context of the inauguration of Jesus' public ministry that commences with the arrest of John the Baptist (Matt 4:12–17). Here Matthew rereads a reference in Isa 9:1–2 to "Galilee of the nations" (v. 1); in Matthew, it is "Galilee of the Gentiles" (v. 15). Jesus' proclamation is simple: "Repent, for the kingdom of heaven has come near" (Matt 4:17). Matthew echoes this vision of salvation in 12:18–21: "and he will proclaim justice to the Gentiles." Here Matthew again rereads a passage from Isa 42:1–3, which states that "he will bring forth justice to the nations" (Isa 42:1b). To the Isaiah passage Matthew adds, "And in his name the Gentiles will hope" (Matt 12:21; cf. Luke 2:32).

The Gentiles become an object of comparison for the Jews with respect to prayer. Matthew depicts Jesus instructing his disciples not to pray as the Gentiles do: "When you are praying, do not heap up empty phrases as the Gentiles do; for they think that they will be heard because of their many words" (Matt 6:7). Additionally, the disciples' virtue is to exceed the Gentiles': "And if you greet only your brothers and sisters, what more are you doing than others? Do not even the Gentiles do the same?" (Matt 5:47). Together these two references shed light on the Gentiles' piety: they do pray and they are virtuous. The prayer and virtue of Jesus' disciples, however, must become more than that of the Gentiles; their prayer and virtue must bear fruit through virtuous action done on behalf of "the least," "the outcast," "the sinner," the one who has "offended." The disciples are to be a people of reconciliation who embody a hospitality of heart toward all.

Finally, Matthew portrays Jesus' persecutors as the Gentiles: "Then they will hand him over to the Gentiles to be mocked and flogged and crucified; and on the third day he will be raised" (Matt 20:19; cf. Mark 10:33; Luke 18:32). Luke features Jesus foretelling the fall of Jerusalem, which he attributes to the Gentiles: "They will fall by the edge of the sword and be taken as captives among all nations; and Jerusalem will be trampled on by the Gentiles, until the times of the Gentiles are fulfilled" (Luke 21:24).

In the Acts of the Apostles, the Gentiles are acknowledged as the recipients of the Holy *Spirit* even though they are not circumcised: "The circumcised believers who had come with Peter were astounded that the gift of the Holy Spirit had been poured out even on the Gentiles" (Acts 10:45), an event that appears to have created surprise and wonder among the Jews. The Gentiles are a people who accepted the word of God (Acts 11:1). They are recognized as having been given by God "the repentance that leads to life"

(Acts 11:18). Paul and Barnabas, frustrated by the rejection of the Jewish people, turn the focus of their preaching and attention to the Gentiles, who rejoice in and praise the word of God (Acts 13:44–48). Finally, Paul understands clearly that Jesus' mission of God's salvation was meant for both the Jews and the Gentiles (Acts 26:23), and thus he urges them to "repent and turn to God and do deeds consistent with repentance" (Acts 26:20).

The Gentiles are central to Paul's preaching to the people of Rome, Galatia, and Ephesus. They are mentioned only once in his second letter to the Corinthians, where they are viewed as a possible source of danger (2 Cor 11:26). They are also mentioned only once in Colossians and Thessalonians, where they are lauded as partakers in God's divine plan of salvation. Throughout Paul's letter to the Romans, Paul stresses his ministry as an apostle to the Gentiles, and he repeatedly preaches that God and salvation are for the Gentiles and the Jews: "Or is God the God of the Jews only? Is he not the God of the Gentiles also? Yes, of Gentiles also" (Rom 3:29). For Paul, faith is foundational to salvation; *circumcision* is not. Faith is what the Jews and Gentiles have in common; faith binds them together in their relationship to God and God's inclusive divine plan for both (see Rom 3:21–31). In his letter to the Galatians, Paul continues to acknowledge his work among the Gentiles (Gal 1:16; 2:2, 8, 9; 3:8, 14; Eph 3:1, 8) and challenges the Jews to set a positive example for the Gentiles to follow (Gal 2:14).

Finally, the letters to Timothy reiterate the focus of Paul's mission and message: "For there is one God; there is also one mediator between God and humankind, Christ Jesus, himself human, who gave himself as a ransom for all—this was attested at the right time. For this I was appointed a herald and an apostle (I am telling the truth, I am not lying), a teacher of the Gentiles in faith and truth" (1 Tim 2:5–7; cf. 2 Tim 4:17).

CAROL J. DEMPSEY

Gifts (Spiritual) The biblical conception of "gifts of the Spirit" is both broader and narrower than our common usage of the phrase today. It is broader in that the Spirit empowers people for a much wider range of tasks in the Bible than the samples Paul lists in the texts to which we traditionally look. God gives both the Spirit and many signs of the Spirit's work as gifts to the church. It is narrower in the sense that most of Paul's lists emphasize God imparting special "grace" (*charis*) for particular gifts (Rom 12:6; Eph 4:7–8, 11; *charismata* in Rom 12:6; 1 Cor 12:4, 9, 28, 30–31; cf. 1 Tim 4:14; 2 Tim 1:6; 1 Pet 4:10), more than they emphasize the Spirit, except where the context requires an emphasis on the Spirit (1 Cor 12:4–11), though in light of Paul's whole theology the Spirit's activity should be assumed throughout.

"Gifts of the Spirit" outside Pauline literature. Many texts in the Bible speak of the Spirit empowering God's people for various activities. The Spirit could provide people with wisdom in skilled design to glorify God (Exod 28:3; 31:3; 35:31), with wisdom for leadership (Num 11:17, 25; Deut 34:9; Judg 3:10; 6:34; 11:29), and with physical strength (Judg 14:6, 19; 15:14; perhaps 1 Sam 11:6–7). In the vast majority of cases, however, the Spirit reveals God's message or empowers people to prophesy (e.g., Num 11:25, 29; 1 Sam 19:20, 23; see *spirit*).

In Acts, Luke refers to the Spirit itself as a "gift" (*dorea*; Acts 2:38; 8:20; 10:45; 11:17), especially for witness (1:8); he defines it by the biblical spirit of prophecy (2:17–18). Accompanying this gift even at its initial reception at times are empowerments that would be called "gifts" by Paul: prophecy (19:6), praise (2:11; 10:46), and speaking in tongues (2:4; 10:46; 19:6; some obvious manifestation is implied by Acts 8:18, but Luke does not specify its nature). Because Luke's emphasis in Acts is on cross-cultural witness, it is not surprising that Luke highlights, as a sign of the Spirit's empowerment for this witness, the manifestation of speaking in tongues (2:4;

10:46; 19:6), perhaps mentioning it whenever his sources note it.

Scholars frequently debate whether Luke understands tongues-speaking the same way that Paul does. Certainly in Acts 2:4–11 he understands them as genuine languages that may be understood by bystanders familiar with other languages, although the languages appear unknown to the speakers. Some have proposed that in other passages, however, Luke has in mind a form of ecstatic babbling, a form of glossolalia they also find in Paul (1 Cor 12–14).

Because "tongues" in 2:4 clearly refers to genuine human languages, however, it seems unnatural to distinguish its sense in 10:46 and 19:6. "Languages" is, after all, what "tongues" means. Yet clearly they are languages unknown to (or at least unlearned by) the speakers, or there would be no need to specify that some under the Spirit's inspiration spoke "in languages"—since in fact everyone in Acts spoke in languages of some sort! Nor would Luke specify the tongues as "other"; nor would he expect his audience to suppose Galileans had naturally mastered the diverse languages indicated in 2:8 (though some postulate a miracle of hearing, though Luke does not specifically indicate this).

Some have argued that Luke misunderstood an early Christian phenomenon reported elsewhere by Paul. This must be regarded as less than certain, however. Paul also calls the phenomenon "languages" (*glossai*). That Paul expects the mind to be "unfruitful" during this activity (1 Cor 14:14) might suggest that he believes that inspiration temporarily displaces rational thought ecstatically, as in Philo (cf. 2 Cor 12:1–4). Then again, Paul may simply mean that the mind does not directly produce this prayer, just as the human spirit does not directly produce the interpretation (1 Cor 14:13–15). In either case, it seems likely that Paul understood the phenomenon as genuine languages unknown to the speaker, though many interpreters today would disagree with this assessment (and it is not clear that all the Corinthians would have agreed). Contrary to some earlier interpreters, the phenomenon of tongues has few early parallels outside Christianity, especially if it was understood as genuine languages (see Forbes).

Apart from its usage in Pauline literature, however, only 1 Peter uses the term *charisma*, but in a sense very similar to Paul's (1 Pet 4:10). Like Rom 12:4–6, this passage occurs in a paranetic context (a string of brief exhortations) related to how to treat one another (1 Pet 4:7–11). Believers should employ their various gifts to serve one another (4:10; cf. Rom 12:3) as good managers of God's *charis*, or grace (Rom 12:6; Eph 4:7; cf. 1 Cor 4:1–2). Examples of particular gifts here (in 1 Pet 4:11) are speaking as if inspired and serving, both of which appear in Pauline lists (e.g., Rom 12:6–7).

Hebrews speaks of "gifts" (literally "dividings" or "distributions") of the Spirit according to God's will, along with (or rhetorically amplifying) miracles confirming the apostolic testimony (Heb 2:3–4), but the specific meaning is unclear. Whether Hebrews refers to distributing the Spirit in various ways that confirm the apostolic message (cf. Acts 8:17) or distributing particular manifestations of the Spirit in the Pauline sense depends on which background we presuppose the writer had in mind.

The meaning of gifts (charismata) *in Paul. Charisma*, the term most often associated with spiritual gifts today (though absent in the key passage Eph 4:7–13), is a favorite Pauline term with a much wider usage than what we usually mean when we say "charismatic." It can apply (most frequently) to the gift of salvation by Christ (Rom 5:15–16; 6:23) and also to God's promises to Israel (Rom 11:29), as well as to divine enabling for celibacy (1 Cor 7:7).

Some other passages, however, do refer to spiritual gifts in probably the same sense as the gift-list passages (1 Cor 1:7). Sometimes such passages refer to spiritual gifts as somehow available through the ministry of Christian leaders

(Rom 1:11), including empowerment for a ministry of public teaching (1 Tim 4:14; 2 Tim 1:6).

Charisma is, in usage as well as etymology, an expression of *charis*, generally translated *"grace"* in the New Testament (cf. 2 Cor 1:12). In the context of the first-century Roman world, where patronage played a prominent role, much of Paul's audience may have understood *charis* in terms of God's benevolence or generosity, given freely but inviting a generous response of thanks that would honor him. As expressions of such, *charismata* properly should invite not pride but the sort of humility and gratitude expected of a patron's client. Paul's predilection for the term implies a perspective that underlies his critique of the abuses of gifts in the Corinthian churches.

Some of the passages most often consulted concerning spiritual gifts refer more explicitly to this concept of "gracing" than to the Spirit (Rom 12:6–8; Eph 4:7–13; cf. also 1 Pet 4:10–11). Yet even in the passages where Paul does not explicitly link these divine enablements with the Spirit, his larger theology implies dependence on the Spirit as the agent of gracing (e.g., Rom 8:2–16; 15:13, 19; Eph 2:22; 3:5; 4:4; cf. 1 Pet 4:14). In another passage Paul refers to gracings as "spiritual gifts," a phrase that (given Paul's usage of "spiritual" elsewhere) undoubtedly means "gifts of the Spirit" (Rom 1:11; cf. 1 Cor 14:12, where the NRSV understands "gifts" as implied by the context, probably correctly).

Three key passages in Pauline letters address the matter of these grace-gifts or benevolences in the context of diverse members of Christ's *body* (Rom 12:4–8; 1 Cor 12:12–27; Eph 4:4–13). Discussions of human members of a corporate body are a regular topic in Greco-Roman literature from the time of Menenius Agrippa forward (e.g., Livy 2.32.9–12; Dion. Hal. 6.83.2–6.86.5; Dio Cass. 4.17.10–13), often referring to the value of each individual to the state. Such discussions emphasize how each part, though with a different and sometimes lower status role to play, is essential to the welfare of the whole. That Paul so frequently connects God's "gracings" to this body image therefore reveals his emphasis on the value of diverse kinds of abilities among Christians: each has equal worth and should focus on doing best what God has gifted him or her to do, not seeking to match what others can do more skillfully. This means that their areas of benefit are typically determined more by God's empowerments than by external "job descriptions"—though Paul also indicates that Christians can seek for further gifts that will meet known needs (Rom 12:1–3; 1 Cor 12:31; 14:1, 39).

Romans 12 provides one important example of these gracings. Though Paul's emphasis in much of Romans is on unity between Jewish and Gentile Christians, Rom 12 focuses on all individual Christians working to serve one another. Some today would consider Paul's examples here, except for prophecy, as "natural abilities," but this sort of distinction violates Paul's pattern of thought. Each of these gifts must be exercised according to divinely inspired "faith" (12:3–8), which God has parceled out to different members for different gifts (12:3; here "measuring" seems to imply not so much "amount" as direction).

1. First Corinthians 12–14. Although Paul's individual lists are not much longer in 1 Corinthians (12:8–10, 28–30; 13:1–2; 14:26) than elsewhere, Paul addresses the Spirit's gifts at much greater length here, over the course of chapters 12–14. Because Paul's treatment of gifts is most extensive here (albeit due to the abuses in Corinth), it will constitute our largest focus in this article. Most churches taught by Paul seem to have had supernatural experiences (1 Cor 14:13, 37, 39; 2 Cor 12:12; Gal 3:5; 1 Thess 5:20; cf. Rom 15:18), and he expected them elsewhere, even before his arrival (Rom 1:11–12; 12:6–8).

But the partisan spirit that permeated the rest of the Corinthian Christians' relationships (e.g., 1 Cor 1:10–12) had also extended to their abuse of God's gifts as a tool of pride, requiring his more extensive comment here. It is important for us to recognize, however, that Paul denigrates not their gifts (1:4–7) but their pride (4:7). Gifts in which they prided themselves include knowledge and speaking (rhetorical) prowess, inviting several comments (1:5, 19–27; 8:1, 7, 10–11). Their pride in their use of tongues (on which gift, see comments above) seems to have been so excessive that it required an even more lengthy response (14:1–39).

Paul begins his case in 1 Corinthians by arguing that spiritual inspiration does not necessarily indicate spiritual maturity (12:1–3; cf. also 1 Sam 18:10; 19:20–21). He reminds them that many of them had experienced some form of inspiration in Greek religion before their conversion (12:2), so content is important in determining the source of inspiration (12:3; the examples here are probably hypothetical and extreme, as in 13:1–3). Paul then points out that the same God, Lord, and Spirit provide a variety of gifts, so that all believers play a vital role—and none dare exalt themselves over others (12:4–6). That Paul wishes to underline this point is clear from his anaphora, an emphatic rhetorical figure, in his threefold repetition of *diaireseis* ("varieties," "kinds," "distributions") beginning these verses. Although the Spirit grants these graces to each member of Christ's body (hence the potential, in their hands, for their abuse), the purpose is not to serve the individual recipient but to serve all Christ's body through that recipient (12:7).

Paul goes on to list individual gifts in 12:8–10, using another form of emphatic repetition ("to another . . . to another," though varying the Greek term). The first four examples repeat "by the Spirit" (12:8–9), implying this source for the gifts in the rest of the list (explicitly stated in 12:11, which reinforces 12:4–6 and hence forms a literary frame around this list of gifts). These gracings are thus expressions of God's power in believers' lives, as Paul's list of the Spirit's "fruit" elsewhere expresses God's character (Gal 5:22–23). Although modern readers often focus on this list, it is one of several lists in this section (12:28, 29; 13:1–2, 8–9; 14:6, 26).

Although this list, like other Pauline gift lists, provides merely examples of God's gracious enablements, it does use the Corinthian situation as a criterion for selection. Perhaps because the Corinthians emphasized knowledge and speech (1:5, 17–25), Paul begins with "utterance of wisdom" and "of knowledge," which could be translated "wise speech" and "knowledgeable speech." As a Greco-Roman city, Corinth highly valued philosophy and especially rhetoric; Paul emphasizes speech for a different purpose and focuses on a different kind of *wisdom* and *knowledge* (1:17–2:16; 3:19; 8:1; 13:2, 8; 14:6). These gifts probably therefore refer to ability to communicate divine wisdom (perhaps especially the *gospel*, 2:6–7) and knowledge (probably something like teaching, cf. 14:6; Rom 12:7).

Although Paul elsewhere speaks of faith's operation in all the gifts (Rom 12:3, 6), many think that 1 Cor 12:9 refers to a special expression of faith (see *believe*), the sort that can move mountains (13:2; a hyperbole used by Jesus and other Jewish teachers for what was virtually impossible). Some suggest that "gifts of healings" in the same verse implies that many have faith to deal with particular kinds of illnesses or on particular occasions; the Gospels and Acts abundantly illustrate this emphasis in early Christianity. *Miracles* (12:10) in early Christian usage probably overlaps with "gifts of healings" (e.g., Acts 19:11–12, noting both healings and exorcisms), but because Paul simply lists samples, it is doubtful that he would be concerned about overlapping ranges of meaning among designations on his list.

Prophecy (12:10; see *prophet*) appears regularly in lists of gracings, usually near the top when any ranking could be inferred (Rom 12:6; 1 Cor 13:2, 8; 14:6; Eph 4:11); this priority becomes most explicit in 1 Cor 12:28–29. This ranking is not surprising, given the range of ministry subsumed under this title in Israel's history, where it is the most frequently mentioned ministry of God's message

(on prophecy, see esp. Aune). The biblical tradition of prophecy is more diverse than our usual understanding of it today, although it always implies divine inspiration (see more fully the brief discussion on OT prophecy under *spirit*). What is most remarkable is that Paul could expect at least several prophets, and potentially more, in house churches that probably rarely held more than fifty persons (14:5, 29, 31). However much the churches resembled local religious associations, philosophic lectures, or synagogues, such prophecies clearly distinguished them and would prove amenable to visitors only if the prophecies provided clear evidence of divine activity, as Paul seems to expect (14:24–25).

In some periods in ancient Israel, master prophets mentored younger disciples, apparently overseeing their maturation in the gift (1 Sam 19:20; 2 Kgs 2:3, 5, 7; 4:38). First-generation prophets in Pauline churches, conversely, had to oversee each other (1 Cor 14:29). "Discernment" (*diakrisis*) "of spirits" (12:10) may emphasize such evaluation of prophecy. Although all the prophets in a congregation were to evaluate (*diakrino*) prophecies (14:29), Paul may mention this gift in addition to the broader category of prophecy to stress their need for discernment (see 1 Thess 5:19–22).

Although Paul clearly does not oppose the gift of tongues (14:5, 18, 39), many suggest that he lists it last (both in 12:10 and 28–29; cf. 12:30) because of its abuse in Corinth (cf. 14:1–39; on tongues, see discussion above). That Paul speaks of various kinds of tongues in 12:10 might suggest that not all are recognizable human languages (cf. 13:1) or simply that the Spirit distributes different languages for different individuals (cf. the plural gifts of healings in 12:9). That he mentions "interpretations" here (as in 12:30; 14:5, 13, 26–28), in contrast to Luke's reports about initial experiences with tongues in Acts, may fit his emphasis on the value of intelligible speech (e.g., 14:6, 16–19; see below).

In contrast to some modern interpreters who sharply distinguish "gifts" from "offices," Paul mixes them freely in 12:28–30. Here he adds *apostles*, a designation frequently used but never defined in the NT. Many scholars think that the term evokes the Jewish concept of *shaliah*, a commissioned messenger or agent backed by the full authority of the sender, provided one functioned within one's commission. Jewish texts often portrayed the prophets as God's agents; but early Christian texts generally rank apostles higher than prophets, as having a special authority (something like prophetic judges such as Moses, Samuel, and Deborah; cf. 2 Cor 3:5–6). Although Luke restricts the title almost entirely to the Twelve (except in Acts 14:4, 14), Paul employs the title much more widely (Rom 16:7; 1 Cor 15:5–9; Gal 1:19; 1 Thess 1:1 with 2:6–7). "Forms of leadership" (12:28; other translations have "administrations" or similar titles) represents a Greek term literally meaning "helmsman" but often applied figuratively; we may think of those offering direction the way a helmsman would steer a ship. Although Paul here emphasizes the importance of every member of the body, he does not reject leadership (Phil 1:1; 1 Thess 5:12). Nor do later Pauline writings, which emphasize leadership, ignore what we consider more "charismatic" gifts (1 Tim 1:18; 4:14; 2 Tim 1:6–7).

Paul's two lists of gifts in this chapter (12:8–10, 28–30) frame his discussion of the diverse members of Christ's body in 12:12–27. This suggests that edifying the church is the entire reason Christians have diverse gifts, and that this is their primary public goal (14:4–6, 12–19, 26). After the second list, Paul speaks about being "zealous for" the "greater" gifts (12:31). Interpreters differ as to whether he merely describes their zeal (cf. 14:12) or encourages it, but in view of similar expressions in 14:1 and 14:39, he likely encourages it. Which then are the "greater gifts"? In 14:1 and 14:39, he specifies prophecy, because it builds up the church, God's temple (see 14:1–40). But just as Paul's list of gifts frames his discussion of the body in 12:8–30, so also his

exhortations to pursue the greater gifts (12:31; 14:1) frame his discussion of love (13:1–13). Just as the body of Christ is the purpose for the gifts of its different members, love is the proper motivation for seeking the "greater" gifts, that is, those that will edify the church.

Paul's rhetorically polished discussion of *love* (1 Cor 13) is inseparable from the surrounding context of gifts. Paul first addresses the value of such gifts without love: one who has all gifts without love is useless (13:1–3). Some of the depictions are probably hyperbolic (moving mountains; perhaps angelic languages), but the overstatement reinforces the point.

In the sort of description of a virtue often found in rhetorical exercises, Paul then defines the character of love (13:4–7). Jarringly (for its implied audience), its characteristics are what the Corinthians are not: love is not jealous (13:4), in contrast to them (3:3); love is not boastful (13:4), in contrast to them (1:29, 31; 3:21; 4:7); love is not puffed up (13:4), in contrast to them (4:6, 18–19; 5:2; 8:1); love does not seek its own things (13:5), in contrast to them (cf. 10:24, 33); love does not count a wrong against oneself (13:5), in contrast to them (6:7–8); and love does not celebrate injustice (13:6), in contrast to them (5:2).

Finally Paul argues that whereas the gifts are temporary, love is eternal (13:8–13). Paul is not denigrating the gifts per se; the implied time of their passing is Jesus' future coming, when they will be supplanted by the greater fulfillment to which they merely point (13:10, 12). Love, however, will never be supplanted but is the "greatest" virtue (13:13), which guides believers in seeking the truly "greatest" gifts for strengthening the body (12:31).

Paul goes on to specify that prophecy is a "greater" gift than tongues, precisely because prophecy edifies not only oneself but the entire church (14:5). He is careful to note that inspired, unknown languages should not be forbidden even in the public assembly (14:39), but when used there they should be interpreted so everyone present can benefit from them (14:5, 13, 27–28). By extension, all gifts should be employed only in the public assembly in ways that benefit all those present; they should never be abused merely to draw attention to the user.

Individuals could pray in tongues privately for their own edification (1 Cor 14:4–5); Paul apparently approves of such usage and prayed in tongues regularly himself (14:18–19). Most texts that speak about tongues imply that they are a form of inspired prayer or praise (Acts 2:11; 10:46; 1 Cor 14:14–17). Some argue plausibly that they could also sometimes function as prophecy or teaching if interpreted (1 Cor 14:6); used privately, one might speak in inspired tongues "to oneself" as well as to God (if 14:28 should be understood thus, which is open to debate). Paul defines prayer in an (unknown) language as prayer with one's spirit rather than with one's mind, apparently referring to one's affective as opposed to rational dimension (14:2, 14). Paul at least envisions Christians praying with their spirit and interpreting with their mind in the house churches (14:15–17) and singing the same way (14:15; cf. "Spirit-inspired songs" in Eph 5:19; Col 3:16).

Paul wants each Christian to contribute something spiritually useful in the meeting (14:26)—an ideal genuinely realistic in interactive house fellowships but impossible in many more massive, modern church meetings. Likewise, Paul's regulations for prophecy and tongues (14:27–33) make sense for meetings of a particular size and duration, not for those much smaller or longer on the one hand, or for those much larger or shorter on the other hand.

The general principle behind these instructions is order (14:40), which was also blended with inspired praise in ancient Israel (1 Chr 25:1–8). The comments about women in 14:34–35 interrupt the flow of thought and may be a later addition (see Fee, *Presence*, 272–81); if original, they may be a brief digression regarding another matter of order in the meetings. Ancient lectures often included questions, but women speaking out publicly, especially if they were less educated, could be seen by outsiders as a breach of propriety (Keener, *Paul*, 70–100). In either case, Paul would not be prohibiting women's involvement in the gifts mentioned elsewhere in the chapter; he permits their activity in these gifts earlier in the same letter (11:5).

2. Ephesians 4:7–13. As lists of gifts framed a mention of Christ's body in 1 Cor 12:8–30, the unity of Christ's body frames a discussion of some gifts in Ephesians 4:4–16. The passage described one gift (*dorea*) of Christ, perhaps referring to Christ himself as the gift, or to the Spirit given by or in Christ, or to all the grace that Christians receive in him (4:7; cf. 3:2, 7–8). Any of these interpretations would fit Pauline theology (though the first interpretation might be more emphatic than the others that by these gifts members of Christ's body are extensions of his own ministry to his body).

But this one gift involves diverse gifts (4:8, *doma*), because each one receives grace for a different sort of ministry (cf. 3:2, 7–8). In keeping with the letter's emphasis on Christ's triumphant exaltation (1:20–23; 2:6), the passage borrows the military image of a general who has taken plunder and distributes it among his troops (this may help account for the rewording of Ps 68:18 both here and in targumic tradition). Verse 11 lists the gifts Christ gave (*didomi*).

The specific gifts listed, however, differ from Paul's earlier lists in Romans and 1 Corinthians (just as the foci of the lists in Romans and 1 Corinthians differ from each other). This passage focuses on specific gifts that involve direct ministry of God's message: apostles and prophets (treated above), evangelists (those who bring the good news of Christ, as in Acts 21:8; 2 Tim 4:5; perhaps in this context they may also help equip other Christians to do so), and pastors and teachers. The structure in Greek is parallel for the first four gifts, but changes for the fifth, apparently linking the fifth and the fourth

Glory 161

together as pastor-teachers. Pastors are literally "shepherds," and early Christians seem to have expected those who shepherded their fellow Christians to teach and lead (John 21:16; Acts 20:28; 1 Pet 5:2; cf. Jer 3:15; 23:1–40; 50:6; Ezek 34:1–16).

While this passage thus focuses on church leaders as gifts, it retains the emphasis on the ministry of all Christians. The ministers of God's message are gifts to all the saints, for the purpose of equipping all of them for the work of service and building up Christ's body, the new temple (4:11–12). The text seems to imply that these gifts will remain necessary as long as saints need to be brought to mature unity in trusting and knowing Christ (4:13).

While focus on particular gifts waxed and waned in subsequent history, Christians in the following centuries not only recognized them in Scripture but continued to testify of miracles, prophecies, and other supernatural activity. After the radical Enlightenment, such claims became less common in mainstream Western Christianity but today have come to characterize the faith of a growing segment of Christendom, especially in the Two-Thirds World and among Pentecostal and charismatic renewal movements in the West.

———

David E. Aune, *Prophecy in Early Christianity and the Ancient Mediterranean World* (Grand Rapids: Eerdmans, 1983); D. A. Carson, *Showing the Spirit: A Theological Exposition of 1 Corinthians 12–14* (Grand Rapids: Baker, 1987); Gordon D. Fee, *God's Empowering Presence: The Holy Spirit in the Letters of Paul* (Peabody, Mass.: Hendrickson, 1994); Gordon D. Fee, *Paul, the Spirit, and the People of God* (Peabody, Mass.: Hendrickson, 1996); Christopher Forbes, *Prophecy and Inspired Speech in Early Christianity and Its Hellenistic Environment* (Peabody, Mass.: Hendrickson, 1997); Craig S. Keener, *Gift and Giver: The Holy Spirit for Today* (Grand Rapids: Baker, 2001); Craig S. Keener, *Paul, Women, and Wives: Marriage and Women's Ministry in the Letters of Paul* (Peabody, Mass.: Hendrickson,

1992); Craig S. Keener, *The Spirit in the Gospels and Acts: Divine Purity and Power* (Peabody, Mass.: Hendrickson, 1997); Siegfried Schatzmann, *A Pauline Theology of Charismata* (Peabody, Mass.: Hendrickson, 1987); Max Turner, *The Holy Spirit and Spiritual Gifts in the New Testament Church and Today*, rev. ed. (Peabody, Mass.: Hendrickson, 1998).

CRAIG S. KEENER

Glad, Gladness *see* **Joy**

Glory, Glorious, Glorify The English word "glory" derives from the Latin *gloria*. The term denotes admiration won by doing something significant or by possessing attributes held in high esteem. It is more than fame, because it is experienced as a quality of something or someone, the aura emanating from the person or being. Glory overlaps in meaning with majesty, that quality of rulers intrinsic to their authority. Glory also overlaps with the aesthetic attributes splendor and grandeur, peculiar kinds of beauty associated with light, color, and magnitude. The rhetoric of the sublime is designed to evoke the experience of these in audiences.

Old Testament

The NRSV employs "glory," "glorious," and "glorify" to translate the noun, adjective, and verb formed on the Hebrew root *kabed*. The Hebrew words have a broader range of meanings, including "heavy, burdensome; great in number; weighty," as well as glory. This exposition is limited to cases translated by "glory," "glorious," and "glorify."

The verb "glorify" is used as an equivalent of praise (e.g., Ps 22:23). When Hebrew *kabed* has a human object, NRSV uses "honor" (e.g., Exod 20:12).

The adjective "glorious" is rarely used of creatures (Isa 28:1, 4, Jer 48:17) and then in statements about what is lost; however, objects associated with God can be so described, for example, "city of God" (Ps 87:3). The most common use of the adjective is of some attribute of God, for example, "right hand" (Exod 15:6), the Lord's "name" (Deut 28:58).

The noun is by far the most common. Occasionally it is used of humans. In Prov 19:11; 20:29; 25:2, it designates a particular human virtue. Job so describes his prosperity (29:20). Glory is often ascribed to humans when it is lost (2 Sam 1:19). The natural grandeur of the mountains of Lebanon is their glory (Isa 35:2). The human species itself has been crowned with glory by God (Ps 8:5).

The vast majority of the uses of "glory" in Hebrew Scripture refer to God. Glory characterizes God's unique being, mirrored in the heavens (Ps 19:1; Hab 3:3), and pervading the earth (Isa 6:3); it is one of God's attributes (e.g., Ps 63:2), and can be used as a circumlocution for God (1 Sam 4:21). The expressions "God of glory" (Ps 29:3) and "King of glory" (Ps 24:7) could be translated as "glorious God/King."

The appropriate response to experiencing God's glory is to ascribe glory to God (e.g., Ps 96:3, 8). It is Israel's calling to declare the Lord's glory (e.g., Isa 66:19). God's glory is communicated to the community that glorifies him (e.g., Ps 149:9; an individual in Ps 3:3). Giving glory to other gods is sinful and results in the loss of glory (Ps 106:20; Jer 2:11; Hos 4:7).

Rather surprisingly, "glory" is not found in Genesis. One might well have expected it in creation accounts, but neither Gen 1 nor Gen 2 has it. Indeed, the term is fairly rare in the hymnic celebrations of creation; it is missing in, for example, Pss 33; 74; 89; Isa 40:12–26; Job 26; 38–39. It does show up in praises of God's manifestations in nature (Ps 19:1; throughout Ps 29).

In the Pentateuch, "glory" is reserved for the exodus from Egypt, theophany at Mount Sinai, and wilderness wandering. At the climax of the exodus, when the Israelites are pinned between sea and army, the Lord hardens Pharaoh's heart so that God may "gain glory for myself" over Pharaoh (Exod 14:4, 17, 18). Israel's God appears on the world historical stage for the first time by overthrowing this great imperial army. A few chapters later God appears theophanically as he introduces Israelites to manna (16:7, 10). The cloud manifests divine glory for the rest of the Israelite sojourn.

At Mount Sinai the Lord signaled his presence in cloud, fire, earthquake, and thunder. While "glory" is not used in Ex 19, it appears in Deut 5:24 and Exod 24:16–17. After the golden calf rebellion (Ex 32), Moses returns to the mountain. There he asks to see the Lord's glory (33:18); the request is denied or modified for Moses' protection. It is as if there are levels of intensity to divine glory, like the sun that blinds one who looks at it directly.

The sanctuary became the repository of God's glory revealed at Mount Sinai (Exod 29:43; 40:34); the Jerusalem temple became its residence upon dedication (1 Kgs 8:10–11; 2 Chr 5:14).

Divine glory appears during the wilderness sojourn to exercise judgment. Toward the end of the spies' story (Num 14), God commutes the death sentence but adds: "[A]s I live, and as all the earth shall be filled with the glory of the LORD—none of the people who have seen my glory and the signs that I did in Egypt and in the wilderness . . . shall see the land" (14:21–23). On the one hand, an oath looks forward to universal revelation of God's glory; on the other, accountability is imposed upon witnesses to the glory. The events of this sacred time are an earnest of the denouement of history.

The language of glory virtually disappears from the narrative from the time of the conquest through the era of the monarchy. When the ark is captured, "the glory is departed from Israel" (1 Sam 4:21–22). The temple is filled with the Lord's glory (1 Kgs 8:11), but nothing is said about God's glorification of kings (though one psalm ascribes glory to the king: 45:3).

Among prophets, "glory" is found frequently in the books of Isaiah and Ezekiel but is otherwise rare. In Isaiah's call vision, seraphim cry out that God's glory fills the earth (Isa 6:3). The theme of God's revelation of his glory throughout the world appears in Isa 24:14–16; 40:5; and 66:18–19 (also Pss 97:6; 102:16; 108:5). Inhabitants of the earth are expected to respond by glorifying God (Isa 42:12); God will give his glory "to no other [god]" (Isa 42:8; 48:11). Israel has been "created for my glory" (43:7), an election theme recalling Deut 26:19.

Ezekiel's use of "glory" reminds us of his priestly lineage; it is a visible manifestation of God in the temple that leaves before its destruction (Ezek 8–11) and will return after reconstruction (chaps. 43–44). Zechariah foresees a restored Jerusalem in which the Lord will be "the glory within it" (2:5).

The messianic passages of Hebrew Scripture do not speak of the ideal king's glory, but the poetic description of "one like a son of man" (Dan 7:13 NRSV Mg) speaks of his investment with "dominion and glory and kingship" (Dan 7:14).

New Testament

"Glory" translates the Greek word *doxa* (retained in our word "doxology"). In Hellenistic Greek, this word has a much broader range of meanings than in the NT: "opinion," even "delusion"; "judgment" and "reputation" as well as "honor, splendor, glory." *Doxa* occurs in the NT only for the last of these meanings. While the verb, *doxazo*, could mean "believe," "suppose" in Hellenistic Greek, it means "praise," "glorify," or "clothe in splendor" in the NT.

"Glory" is occasionally used for the physical phenomenon of brightness (Luke 9:31; 1 Cor 15:40–41) and regal attire (Matt 6:29; Luke 12:27). Applied to humans, it most often means "honor" (e.g., John 5:44; 12:43), in contrast to the glory God bestows. The majority of NT occurrences ascribe glory to God or Christ or to the salvation given by God. The verb means "praise"—giving due credit to God—when humans (or angels) are subjects. When God is subject and humans the object, it means communication of the divine attribute to humans.

The Gospels. In Matthew and Mark, "glory" is used theologically only of Christ's second coming (Matt 16:27; 25:31; Mark 13:26). These derive from Dan 7:13–14. The verb is used frequently for the crowd's response to Jesus' miracles (e.g., Matt 9:8; Mark 2:12). In Matthew Jesus urges his audience to "let your light shine before others, so that they may see your good works and give glory to your Father in heaven" (5:16). Luke passes on second coming sayings (9:26; 21:27) and uses glory to underscore the theophanic character of Jesus' birth (2:9, 20, 32) and transfiguration (9:31–32).

John makes no reference to Jesus' apocalyptic glory, but applies the term strategically to the incarnate and crucified/risen Son of God, beginning with John 1:14. Jesus' task on earth is to reveal God's glory (John 2:11; 5:41; 12:43). In Jesus' high priestly prayer, he asks the Father to "glorify me in your presence with the glory that I had in your presence before the world existed" (17:5). Glorification occurs in his crucifixion/resurrection (12:23) and is communicated to his followers (17:22).

Pauline letters. The Pauline corpus uses "glory" frequently and distinctively. Doxologies running through these letters have their roots in OT hymnody, for example, Rom 16:27, "the only wise God, through Jesus Christ, to whom be the glory forever" (similarly Eph 3:21; Phil 2:11; 4:20; Gal 1:5; etc.). Honoring the saving God incorporates Christ as the crowning achievement of God's saving activity.

The salvation accomplished by Jesus Christ is the act of God that brings God glory, of which the most explicit statement is the Christ hymn, Phil 2:6–11. Also, "in him every one of God's promises is a 'Yes.' For this reason it is through him that we say the 'Amen,' to the glory of God" (2 Cor 1:20); the reception of God's "yes" is to the glory of God. The people of God "live for the praise of his glory" (Eph 1:12); their power to praise God's glory is an earnest of redemption (1:14). The believing community is the vanguard of the submission of all to Christ, bringing glory to God.

Only once in the Pauline corpus, 2 Thess 1:9–10, does the second coming elicit the term glory. However, once Christ is named "the Lord of glory," who was foolishly crucified by "the rulers of this age" (1 Cor 2:8). The proper response to the glory of God is to glorify God. This comes to expression in praises, of which Paul's own doxologies are representative. Giving glory to God, as Abraham did (Rom 4:20–21), means more than uttering words of praise; it must be the orientation of Abraham's will. Elsewhere, glory is to be the motive and guide for all action (1 Cor 10:31; 2 Cor 8:19).

One of the most frequent and distinctive uses of "glory" in Pauline letters is as a cipher for the state of salvation. The present entails suffering, but this is more than made up for by "the glory about to be revealed to us" (Rom 8:18; also Rom 5:2; 9:23; 2 Cor 4:17; Col 1:27; 3:4; 1 Thess 2:12; 2 Thess 2:14; 2 Tim 2:10).

The future state of glory can even be applied to the body. Paul draws an analogy between bodies with various kinds or degrees of glory (1 Cor 15:40–41), then contrasts the state of the body that dies to the one raised (15:42–43). A similar contrast is made more briefly in Phil 3:21.

In Rom 1–3, Paul twice accords "the glory of God" the status of norm or measure (1:23; 3:23). Idolatry is a deliberate distortion of the Creator's glory (1:23); not only have all humans sinned, they "fall short of the glory of God" (3:23).

In 2 Cor 3:7–11, Paul compares the glory of the old covenant to the greater glory of the new, indulging in a rather fanciful allegory in which Moses' bright face that must be veiled (3:7, 12–13) becomes the veil over Scripture removed by Christ, in whose face the glory of God shines (4:4, 6).

General Epistles. "Glory" is used fairly frequently in Hebrews, the Petrine letters, and the Revelation to John. In Hebrews, glory is apportioned according to a hierarchy of being (1:3; 5:5). Though Christ's glory is derivative, when he is compared to other humans, he can be said to possess or emanate glory (2:9).

The benediction concluding the letter ascribes glory either to Christ or to the God of peace (13:21).

First Peter shares with Pauline letters the formula that God is glorified "through Jesus Christ" (4:11; cf. Rom 16:11, etc.). Distinctive to 1 Peter is the application of glory to Christ in his resurrection and exaltation (1:11, 21; 4:13; 5:1). Humans have only a fading glory (1:24); faith, however, will result in glory (1 Pet 1:7; 5:4, 10). Second Peter says that God already glorified Jesus at the transfiguration (2 Pet 1:17) and ascribes glory to Christ (1:3; 3:18) as does Jas 2:1.

In the Revelation to John, "glory" is most often one in a series of divine attributes, formulated in hymnic language (1:5b–6; 4:9, 11; 5:12, 13; 7:12; 19:1, 6–8a). While glory tends to lose any distinctive meaning in these lists, it does stand out in a description of the new Jerusalem, lit by the glory that emanates from God (21:11, 23). In the symbolism of this book, divine glory has absorbed the symbol of light so salient in Johannine literature (cf. John 1:4, 5, etc.; 1 John 1:5, 7).

Glorifying is the appropriate human comportment toward God (Rev 14:7; 16:9). At the time of salvation, kings and nations bring their glory into the city (21:24–26). Perhaps John is affirming that the achievements of historical life are preserved as well as transcended in the ultimate denouement.

DALE PATRICK

Goats   *see* **Animals**

God, Gods   This article deals with the names and nature of God and of the foreign gods mentioned in the Bible.

Names of God

In polytheistic cultures the divine has many names. For communities venerating a multitude of gods, it is natural to identify different manifestations of divinity by giving them individual names that distinguish them from one another. Even individual gods and goddesses embrace a wealth of powers that suggest to their devotees a plethora of names. Nowhere is this more evident than in ancient Egypt. Hymns to the Egyptian god Osiris praise him "in all his names," the Egyptian Amun is given the epithet "with many names whose number is unknown," and Osiris's sister-wife Isis is called "the one with many names."

In contrast to this multiplicity of names in polytheistic religions, the God of the OT and NT is known by only a few names. These names have their history in which the nature of the biblical God is reflected. The effort to understand the names of God in the Bible is therefore at the same time an effort to grasp the reality of the biblical God (see *name*).

Yahweh. NRSV uses the word "lord" to translate two different Hebrew expressions designating God. Where the divine name Yahweh appears in the Hebrew text, NRSV substitutes LORD in capital letters, following an old tradition in English Bibles. When the initial letter alone is capitalized as "Lord," NRSV represents the Hebrew ʾadon. "LORD" (*yhwh*) is exclusively a proper name for the God of Israel, which distinguishes Israel's God from the gods of other peoples: "For all the peoples walk, each in the name of its god, but we will walk in the name of the LORD (*yhwh*) our God (ʾelohenu) forever and ever" (Mic 4:5). "Lord" as rendition of ʾadon is a general noun, meaning "master," "ruler." Both words referring to the same divine subject can occur in a single sentence: "For the LORD (*yhwh*) your God is God of gods and Lord (ʾadon) of lords, the great God (ʾel), mighty and awesome" (Deut 10:17). The name Yahweh is found more than 6,800 times in the Hebrew OT, by far the most frequent designation of God. In addition to the long form of the name, *yhwh*, there are several shorter forms, like *yo* or *yahu*, that are found especially in personal names (e.g., *yonathan* = Jonathan; *yeshayahu* = Isaiah). The existence of the long form alongside the shorter forms does not seem to indicate changes in meaning.

The book of Exodus preserves traditions that link the revelation of the name Yahweh to Moses. According to the Priestly account, God introduces himself by that name to Moses before the beginning of the liberation from the Egyptian bondage: "God also spoke to Moses and said to him: 'I am the LORD (*yhwh*). I appeared to Abraham, Isaac, and Jacob as God Almighty (ʾel shaddai), but by my name "The LORD" I did not make myself known to them'" (Exod 6:2). The introduction distinguishes a period of ancestors, during which the name Yahweh was not known, from the disclosure of the name to Moses, but the identity of "God Almighty" (see *power*) with "Yahweh" is maintained. The memory of this name change is also found in Exod 3:9–15, a passage commonly identified as a composite of the Yahwistic and Elohistic traditions. In that account Moses requests of God to be given a name so that he can identify the God who promises liberation to the enslaved Israelites: "Moses said to God: 'If I come to the Israelites and say to them, "The God of your ancestors has sent me to you," and they ask me, "What is his name?" what shall I say to them?' God said to Moses, 'I AM WHO I AM.' He said further, 'Thus you shall say to the Israelites, "I AM has sent me to you."'" God also said to Moses, 'Thus you shall say to the Israelites, "The LORD (*yhwh*), the God of your ancestors, the God of Abraham, the God of Isaac, and the God of Jacob, has sent me to you"': This is my name forever, and this my title for all generations'" (Exod 3:13–15). In this section also the identity of the ancestral God with Yahweh is preserved, but the name Yahweh is assumed to be unknown to the Israelites in Egypt, and the meaning of the name is explained in a word play connecting the name Yahweh to the Hebrew verb *hayah* "to be."

While there is widespread agreement that Exod 3:13–15 explains the name Yahweh by connecting it with the root *hayah*, no consensus has yet been reached about what that connection implies. One group of scholars derives the name *yhwh* from the causative form of the word *hayah*, suggesting that the divine name means "the one who causes to be, the creator." Another group of experts links the name to the basic form of the same verb, leading to the understanding of Yahweh as "the one who is," or "the one who will be." In this writer's view the second alternative is to be preferred, because the adoption of a causative form of *hayah* necessitates an emendation in the wording of Exod 3:14, and it would have to disregard the fact that a causative stem of *hayah* cannot be found in the OT.

The immediate context of Exod 3:14 throws some light on the cryptic expression "I AM WHO I AM (*ʾehyeh ʾasher ʾehyeh*)." Directly preceding the explanation of the name Yahweh, the fearful Moses, insisting on his inadequacy to confront Pharaoh and lead Israel to freedom, is answered by God, "I will be (*ʾehyeh*) with you" (Exod 3:12). A similar promise is given twice in Exod 4. Moses, pleading his lack of eloquence, is answered by God, "I will be (*ʾehyeh*) with your mouth" (4:12); the same pledge is repeated when Aaron and Moses are designated as joint speakers, "I will be with your mouth and with his mouth" (4:15). The translation of Exod 3:14 that is most consonant with the close context of the verse is, therefore, the phrase "I will be whoever I will be." The verse expresses the divine promise to be present with, and to be active on behalf of, those whom God chooses to be his partners and his messengers. But it cannot be overlooked that the phrase gives the promise in a form that avoids all specificity, guarding the divine freedom to act for the benefit of Yahweh's people in a way that is solely determined by God's own decision.

In the Priestly tradition that is parallel to the J and E version in Exod 3, Yahweh introduces himself three times, with great emphasis, as "I am the LORD (*yhwh*)" (Exod 6:2, 6, 7). Moses' introduction to the new name of the God of the ancestors is connected to two notions that are theologically of supreme importance. Yahweh is the liberator from the Egyptian

bondage ("I will free you from the burden of the Egyptians and deliver you from slavery to them," 6:6), and he is initiating a bond with Israel that is expressed in the covenant formula "I will take you as my people, and I will be your God" (6:7, see *covenant*). In this way the name Yahweh is linked to a historical act of liberation and to the history of a particular people (see *people of God*), which is indissolubly connected with the divine name. Both affirmations run like a broad stream through many parts of the OT. The opening declaration of the Decalogue states: "I am the LORD your God, who brought you up out of the land of Egypt, out of the house of slavery" (Exod 20:2; Deut 5:6). In Israel's prayers to Yahweh, he is remembered in words almost identical to the preamble of the Decalogue (Ps 81:10), and earliest prophecy invokes his memory as the God who led Israel from Egypt, besides whom the people knew no other god (Hosea 12:9; 13:4). The fascinatingly archaic cycle of narratives about the ten plagues of Egypt that set the exodus of Israel in motion is the longest sustained composition of miracle stories in the entire Bible (Exod 7–12). More or less expanded summaries of the exodus are found in several types of OT literature written for different occasions and for different purposes (Deut 6:20–25; 26:5–11; Josh 24:5–7; Pss 105:26–38; 106:6–12; 136:10–15; Ezek 20:5–10). The covenant formula, Yahweh is Israel's God and Israel is Yahweh's people, occurs, in various wordings, so frequently in the OT that it has been called its theological center. One of its most elaborate forms is found in Deut 26:18–19: "Today the LORD has obtained your agreement: to be his treasured people, as he promised you, and to keep his commandments; for him to set you high above all nations that he has made, in praise and in fame and in honor; and for you to be a people holy to the LORD your God, as he promised."

In Exod 3:13–15 and 6:2–8 the name Yahweh is linked to God's promise to be with his people and to the divine self-introduction in the statement "I am Yahweh," the liberator from the Egyptian bondage. The two motifs "God with us (you, me)" and "I am Yahweh" are not only frequent in OT traditions. They have also served as leading ideas in the NT, where they provide theological continuity to the OT and at the same time achieve a strikingly new specificity. The Gospel of Matthew incorporates the theme of "God with us" at the beginning and at the end of its story line, providing a thematic bracket that enfolds the whole narrative of Jesus' life. Adopting the name Emmanuel from Isa 7:14, Matthew puts the birth of Jesus under the heading of the promise "God with us" (see **Immanuel**). Although Mary's child will be called Jesus, "all this took place to fulfill what had been spoken by the Lord through the prophet: 'Look, the virgin shall conceive and bear a son, and they shall name him Emmanuel,' which means 'God with us'" (Matt 1:22–23). The child Jesus is wrapped in the cloth of promise that in his life it will become manifest that "God is with us." And when the story of this life has been told, the same promise will be reaffirmed. In the last scene of the Gospel, when the risen Christ appears to his disciples, the parting words of the risen are the declaration "I am with you always, to the end of the age" (Matt 28:20). The promise of Yahweh, "I will be with you," is now transformed into Jesus' promise "I am with you always." The risen Jesus speaks in the place, and with the authority, of Yahweh. But this change does not invalidate the old promise of Yahweh's presence; rather it consolidates it.

Similarly, the OT phrase "I am Yahweh" lends its distinctive tone to the Gospel of John. The statement "I am Yahweh" is sometimes abbreviated in Deutero-Isaiah to "I am he" or "it is I" (ʾani hu; LXX ego eimi; Isa 41:4; 43:10; 43:25; 46:4). This declaration of the divine presence is sometimes found in the mouth of Jesus in some narratives of John's Gospel. When Jesus appears before terrified disciples who see him walking on the sea, he addresses them, "It is I; do not be afraid" (Greek: "I am";

John 6:20). The encouragement "do not be afraid" is often found in OT scenes of theophanies and is here attached to the phrase "It is I," which is characteristic of OT self-introductions of God. The same language of divine identification is employed in Jesus' words: "I told you that you would die in your sins, for you will die in your sins unless you believe that I am he" (ego eimi, 8:24) and "when you have lifted up the Son of Man, then you will realize that I am he" (ego eimi, 8:28). The claim "I am he" gives the Johannine Jesus participation in God's presence that transcends the boundaries of time: "Very truly, I tell you, before Abraham was, I am" (8:58). It is this claim that is expressed in the famous "I am" words of Jesus in the Gospel of John. Jesus says of himself that he is "the bread of life" (6:35, 41, 48, 51); "the light of the world" (8:12); the door to the sheepfold and "the good shepherd" (10:7, 11); "the way, and the truth, and the life" (14:6); and "the true vine" (15:1).

Yahweh Tsebaʿoth. The Hebrew noun *tsebaʿoth* is used exclusively as a divine epithet. It occurs in the OT 285 times in combination with the name Yahweh and with quite a number of other titles and designations of God. By far the most frequent combination (240 times) is the phrase *yhwh tsebaʿoth*, generally translated by NRSV as "LORD of hosts" (see **hosts**). Attempts to understand the meaning of the phrase "Lord of hosts" have noted that the phrase is connected with two different concepts. Since the related verb *tsabaʿ* means "to go to war, to fight in battle," *tsebaʿoth* sometimes seems to refer to Israel's army, as in 1 Sam 17:45, where David says to Goliath, "You come to me with sword and spear and javelin; but I come to you in the name of the LORD of hosts, the God of the armies of Israel." In other contexts the Lord of hosts is portrayed as the ruler over heavenly beings who are in Yahweh's company. The acclamation "O LORD God of hosts" (*yhwh ʾelohe tsebaʿoth*) is echoed in heaven by "the assembly of the holy ones," the "heavenly beings," the "council of the holy ones," who surround Yahweh's throne in heaven like a cabinet of ministers (Ps 89:5–8). A variation of the understanding of *tsebaʿoth* as heavenly beings saw in the phrase "Lord of hosts" a summation of God as universal ruler over everything, including the astral powers of sun, moon, and stars, which were venerated as gods not only by non-Israelites but also by kings, officials, priests, prophets, and people of Jerusalem (Jer 8:1–2).

The first mention of the Lord of hosts in the OT occurs in 1 Sam 1:3, 11; 4:4. In the old Israelite town of Shiloh the Lord of hosts is invoked, and he is attached to the ark, where he is enthroned on the cherubim, sphinxlike figures whose wings serve as the seat of the invisible Yahweh (see *cherub*). After the transfer of the ark to Jerusalem, the temple on Mount Zion becomes the home of the Lord of hosts (Isa 8:18). The concept of the Lord of hosts serves as vehicle to express Yahweh as king over all that is in heaven and on earth. In Isaiah's inaugural vision Yahweh appears "sitting on a throne, high and lofty," and six seraphs shout his praise: "Holy, holy, holy is the LORD of hosts; the whole earth is full of his glory," a vision of which Isaiah says, "My eyes have seen the King, the LORD of hosts" (Isa 6:2–5). As Lord of hosts Yahweh is the assurance that Jerusalem will be inviolable from harm through enemies: "God is in the midst of the city; it shall not be moved. . . . The LORD of hosts is with us; the God of Jacob is our refuge" (Ps 46:5, 7).

ʾElohim (ʾEloha, ʾEl). Yahweh, the God of Israel, is by this name distinguished from the other gods. Other nations have their own gods. There are "all the gods of Egypt" on whom Yahweh will execute his judgment (Exod 12:12). Sometimes the fact that many peoples have their own gods is acknowledged as a divine decree as in Deut 32:8: "When the Most High apportioned the nations, when he divided humankind, he fixed the boundaries of the peoples according to the number of the gods." Sometimes it is portrayed negatively as human arrogance that fashions

the gods according to each nation's whims: "Every nation still made gods of its own. . . . the people of Babylon made Succoth-benoth, the people of Cuth made Nergal, the people of Hamath made Ashima; the Avvites made Nibhaz and Tartak; the Sepharvites burned their children in the fire to Adrammelech and Anammelech, the gods of the Sepharvaim" (2 Kgs 17:29–31). As different countries have their own gods (2 Kings 18:35), so can important cities have their own distinct divinities: Baal-zebub resides in Ekron (2 Kgs 1:2), and in his distress even the Judean king Ahaz sacrifices to the gods of Damascus (2 Chr 28:23).

Besides using the personal name Yahweh in referring to Israel's God, the OT also employs the noun *ʾElohim* and without perceptible change in meaning, the words *ʾEl* and *ʾEloha* to signify the same divine subject. In contrast to Yahweh, *ʾElohim* is not a personal name but a generic noun that means "divine being." However, a linguistic oddity needs to be noted. *ʾElohim* is in its grammatical form a plural, which can, and occasionally does, mean "gods" as well as "God," depending on the context. Without question, gods are meant in the first prohibition of the Decalogue, "You shall have no other gods (*ʾelohim*) before me" (Exod 20:3; Deut 5:7). The phrase "other gods (*ʾelohim*)" occurs sixty-three times in the OT, in each case referring to a plurality of gods. But in the overwhelming majority of cases, more than two thousand times, the grammatical form denotes the one God who is identical with Yahweh, the God of Israel. The identity of Yahweh with *ʾElohim* is expressed in Deuteronomy by the constantly repeated phrase "Yahweh your (our) God (*ʾElohim*)." Two examples of this language may stand for more than 250 instances in the book. Israel remembers that "the LORD our God made a covenant with us at Horeb" (5:2), and because of this covenant Israel "must therefore be careful to do as the LORD your God has commanded you" (5:32). Outside the book of Deuteronomy individual leaders of Israel are frequently mentioned as persons of particular authority and power because of their special attachment to Yahweh their God. The people ask Samuel to "pray to the LORD your God . . . so that we may not die" (1 Sam 12:19), and King Jeroboam requests help by a man of God with the words "entreat now the favor of the LORD your God, and pray for me" (1 Kgs 13:6).

A special note is necessary with regard to the patriarchal stories in Gen 12–50. In those narratives the identity of Yahweh with God (*ʾElohim*) is also preserved (Gen 16:13; 21:33; 28:13). But a close investigation of the names associated with divine appearances in these chapters of Genesis shows a considerable number of texts in which *ʾEl* seems to be the name for an individual god. Melchizedek is the priest of God Most High (*ʾEl ʾelyon*, 14:18); Hagar names Yahweh *ʾEl Roi* (El who sees?, 16:13); Abraham calls on "the LORD, the Everlasting God" (*ʾEl ʿolam*, 21:33); an altar in Shechem is called "God, the God of Israel" (*ʾEl ʾelohe yisrael*, 33:20 NRSV Mg); there is a "God of Bethel" (*ʾEl bethel*, 31:13; 35:7); God identifies himself to Jacob in a dream saying, "I am God (*haʾel*), the God (*ʾelohe*) of your father" (46:3); and the summary designation of the God of Abraham, Isaac, and Jacob as God Almighty (*ʾEl shaddai*) in Exod 6:3 is also used in Gen 17:1; 28:3; 35:11; 43:14; and 49:25. This evidence suggests the conclusion that the "God of the fathers" in the patriarchal period was either assimilated to, or was identical with, the god *ʾEl* who was a deity commonly worshiped among Semitic peoples. At the time of the literary fixation of the patriarchal traditions in the narratives as we now have them, however, the identity of Yahweh with the "God of the fathers" was taken for granted. Therefore, the revelation of the name Yahweh to Moses, described as an innovation in Exod 3 and Exod 6, stands beside the use of the name Yahweh in the Yahwistic strand of the narrative from the creation story on (Gen 2:4b–3:25) to the continued invocation of Yahweh's name in the time of Enosh (Gen 4:6), by Noah (Gen 9:26) and Abraham (Gen 12:8).

The ancestral traditions in Gen 12–50 speak of God as giver of promises to those who are the recipients of the divine communication (see *promise*). The promises of progeny, of the possession of land, and of God's presence accompany the narratives from beginning to end. Abraham's move into a new land is set in motion by the promise of numerous children: "I will make you a great nation" (Gen 12:2), a promise that is repeated to the old Jacob as he prepares to go to Egypt: "Do not be afraid to go down to Egypt, for I will make you a great nation there" (Gen 46:3). Under this arch of promises, the commitment of God to give progeny to Israel's ancestors is reiterated several times (Gen 15:5; 17:2–5; 22:17; 26:4). Connected to this is the promise of land, which is also repeated several times over as the story unfolds (Gen 12:7; 13:14–18; 15:7; 17:8; 26:3–4). And the promise that God will be with Abraham and his descendants puts the hope for children and land into the framework of divine presence (Gen 28:15; 46:4).

The threefold promise, however, is subjected to the most severe tests. From Abraham to Moses the divine promise is consistently in danger of being contradicted by facts. The future mother of the promised children is in danger of being lost to foreign rulers (Gen 12:10–20; 20; 26:6–11). Sarah remains childless well past the age of childbearing (Gen 18:9–15), and when her son Isaac is finally born, he is threatened with extinction by the command of the same God who had sworn that Isaac should become the carrier of the promise (Gen 22). As to the land, the picture is no more encouraging. The ancestors of Israel remain aliens in the land, Abraham is buried with his wife Sarah in the cave of Machpelah in a field Abraham had purchased from the Hittites who owned the land (Gen 25:7–11), and the entire family of Jacob is driven from the country by a famine so that, at the beginning of Moses' time, Israel is away from its promised land under the yoke of Egyptian slavery (Exod 1).

Only once in Gen 12–50 is God as the giver of promises coordinated with the believer whose faith honors the promise: Genesis 15:6 says of Abraham that "he believed the LORD; and the LORD reckoned it to him as righteousness" (see *believe* and *just*). Faith and promise belong together, and their unity has become a powerful theme in the NT. To the writer of Hebrews, faith is "the assurance of things hoped for, the conviction of things not seen" (Heb 11:1). Among the "cloud of witnesses" for faith (12:1) stands Abraham, who left his home for an unknown destiny (11:8), disregarding the fact that his body was "as good as dead" (11:12), and offered up the child of the promise (11:17–18). To the apostle Paul, Abraham has become the primary figure of faith, whose story is used to illumine the nature of trust in God's promises. The correspondence between promise and faith is emphasized in both Gal 3–4 and in Rom 4. In both letters the figure of Abraham is absorbed into the Christian message of Christ as the one in whom all promises of God are affirmed (2 Cor 1:20). In Gal 3–4 Christ is seen as the offspring that is promised to Abraham (Gal 3:16), and in this fulfillment of God's promise Gentiles and Jews together will be justified as the ancient promise to Abraham had stated: "All the Gentiles shall be blessed in you" (3:8). In Rom 4 Paul has drawn Abraham, the father of faith (Rom 4:11–12), as energetically as in Galatians, into the force field of his faith in Christ. Abraham's faith, which defies his biological deficiencies, becomes to Paul faith in the God "who gives life to the dead and calls into existence the things that do not exist" (4:17), so that the narrative of Abraham's faith is written for the Christian hearers and readers as evidence of the God "who raised Jesus our Lord from the dead" (4:24).

ʾAdon (ʾAdonai). As already mentioned above, Hebrew ʾadon is rendered in NRSV by the spelling Lord, in distinction from LORD, which stands for *yhwh*. ʾAdon is, strictly speaking, not a name of God but a title of honor. It is used in the OT in secular contexts of human beings who exercise power over others. Joseph's brothers address him as the high administrator in Egypt with "my lord" (Gen 44:18–20) because Joseph is "lord (ʾadon) of all his [i.e., Pharaoh's] house and ruler over all the land of Egypt" (Gen 45:8). Frequently a king is called ʾadon, as in 1 Kgs 1:2 where David is addressed by his servants with "my lord the king."

In application to God, ʾadon functions as one of the many titles that can be given to God. "Lord" is one of a long list of attributes that are associated with God, who is called "the Holy One of Israel" (Isa 1:4, and frequently in Isaiah), the "God Most High" (Gen 14:19), the "God merciful and gracious" (Exod 34:6), the "God of glory" (Ps 29:3), to cite only a few. But the special form ʾadonai became a substitute for the name Yahweh and in that way advanced from being an attribute of God to becoming a name of God. In consequence of the third commandment of the Decalogue, "You shall not make wrongful use of the name of Yahweh (NRSV the LORD) your God" (Exod 20:7; Deut 5:11), a reluctance to use the holy name *yhwh* at all became more and more pervasive. The tendency to avoid pronouncing the holy name of the tetragram led finally to the adoption of the reading ʾadonai in place of the name *yhwh* throughout the OT. When the Masoretes, the rabbinical editors of the Hebrew Bible during the ninth century A.D., provided vocalization signs to the four consonants of the tetragram, they indicated that Yahweh should always be pronounced as Adonai. This led to the longstanding misconception that the divine name was to be pronounced as "Jehovah," a misunderstanding produced by the addition of the vowels of ʾadonai to the consonants of the tetragram *yhwh*.

The substitution of the word "Lord" for the name "Yahweh" in rabbinical usage is of great significance. It is witness to the dominant concept associated with the divine name Yahweh. Yahweh is awesome and totally superior to all human thought and act. Yahweh's is the sole command over heaven and earth. He is the peerless and undisputed ruler of history, the creator of the cosmos, and the power who determines the destiny of all. He is, therefore, not only the God of Israel, but at the same time the God of the universe. He is The Ruler by definition. This aspect of his name was expressed in the substitution of the word 'adonai for yhwh in the Masoretic instructions for the reading and pronunciation of the Hebrew Bible.

Names of foreign gods

In a passage reminiscent of legislative provisions in the OT, Ps 81:9–10 declares, "There shall be no strange god among you; you shall not bow down to a foreign god. I am the LORD your God, who brought you up out of the land of Egypt." Yet, in violation of that injunction, Israel's history is replete with efforts to search for strange gods, deities "they had never known" who are "abhorrent things" that act as "demons" (Deut 32:16–17; Jer 5:19). Generally OT polemics against foreign gods do not identify them by name. But the presence of divinities other than the God who established a covenant with Israel is felt in many parts of the OT, and there are enough occasions at which their names are mentioned to give us some concrete data about the foreign gods who are addressed in the texts.

The classification as "foreign gods," distinct from the God of Israel, is called into question by some recent researchers who have sought to explore the early history of Israel's religion and claim that early Israel, deep into the monarchic period, was itself a form of Canaanite culture, in its religious life as well as in its social and economic structures. Especially the relationship of Yahweh to the Canaanite deities El and Baal is described in a way that renders the term "foreign gods" misleading. Yahweh is said to have emerged from an El worship, and even the god Baal is seen to have provided material concepts to the developing Yahwism in Israel's history. It is pointed out that the individual high god El is not mentioned in passages critical of non-Israelite deities in the OT and that some characteristics of the nature of Yahweh

are shared with the Canaanite El. With regard to Baal it is noted that titles attached to him are adopted in some OT passages as titles of Yahweh. For example, Baal as the god of weather and storm is represented as the "rider on the clouds," as is Yahweh in Ps 68:4, 33. Even the key concept of the kingship of God in the OT (see *kingdom of God*) may well be an adaptation of Canaanite ideas of the divine. Both El and Baal are venerated as "king of the gods," and so is Yahweh praised as king of the divine assembly in passages like Ps 95:3: "the LORD is a great God, and a great King above all gods" (similar: Pss 96:4; 97:7, 9). If there is good reason to assume that Israel's worship of Yahweh grew out of, and continued for a long time to live within, the religious soil of Canaanite cults, the choice of the phrase "foreign gods" as an antonym of Yahweh would seem to be inappropriate.

However, this reconstruction of the history of Israel's religion is not synonymous with the message of the OT about Israel's God. For instance, the discovery of certain similarities of the West Semitic El with Yahweh cannot explain the formation of the patriarchal narratives that depict Yahweh as the God of promise whose words guide the lives of generations of his elect, who live under the arch of Yahweh's governance in the face of seemingly insurmountable obstacles. There are no stories of this kind about El, but Yahweh lives in those stories. No matter what dependencies on other divinities may have existed, and no matter how much the actual religion of Israel may have been part and parcel of the general cultic surroundings, the OT traditions about Israel's encounters with Yahweh speak of a God who is distinct from other divinities. The distinctness of Yahweh from other gods belongs to his nature, according to constant OT claims. Therefore, a theological understanding of this God requires the readiness to hear what OT traditions have to communicate about gods other than Yahweh/Elohim.

Information about foreign deities in the OT can be arranged in three groups:

tribal gods, Cannanite deities, and Egyptian and Mesopotamian divinities.

Tribal gods. First Kings 11 narrates the decline of the reign of Solomon. The aging king, under the influence of his numerous foreign wives, allows the worship of foreign gods and goddesses in his kingdom. He builds high places, open-air sanctuaries, for his wives from neighboring peoples in the immediate vicinity of Jerusalem. Some of these divinities are mentioned by name: Astarte, the goddess of the Sidonians; Milcom, the "abomination of the Ammonites"(11:5); Chemosh, the "abomination of Moab," and Molech, the "abomination of the Ammonites" (11:7, see *abomination*). Not all of these gods are tribal gods; Astarte and Molech are major divinities that will be discussed later. But Milcom and Chemosh are associated exclusively with two eastern neighbors of Israel.

The Moabites are twice in the OT called the "people of Chemosh" (Num 21:29; Jer 48:46). Chemosh is the god in charge of protecting the territory belonging to Moab (Judg 11:24). The god is mentioned repeatedly, once with the name Ashtar-Chemosh, on a stone bearing the inscription of King Mesha of Moab (around 830 B.C.), on which Mesha records his military success against Israelite forces. Mesha calls himself the son of Chemosh, under whose leadership the victorious campaigns are waged, including the slaughter of seven thousand inhabitants of the Israelite town of Nebo, who were devoted to destruction "as satiation for Chemosh and Moab." The character of Chemosh as a protector deity for a tribe is also reflected, from the standpoint of an Israelite, in an oracle against Moab in Jer 48. In the oracle, Chemosh will share the fate of the people who are put under his protection. Moab will be taken into captivity, and so will Chemosh with his priests and attendants (48:7), so that Moab will become ashamed of its god (48:13).

First Kings 11 speaks of two "abominations of the Ammonites," the gods Milcom (11:5, 33) and Molech (11:7). Are the two gods identical, are two distinct sanctuaries meant, dedicated to separate gods, or is the name Molech due to scribal error? The answer to these questions is uncertain. Milcom appears in the entire OT only in 1 Kgs 11:5, 33, while Molech is a much more frequently mentioned and powerful god who is, however, linked to the Ammonites only in 1 Kgs 11:7. Moreover, Molech has traits in common with a Phoenician-Punic deity by the same name that will be discussed in the class of Canaanite gods.

Canaanite gods. The term "Canaan" has in the OT a variety of geographical, genealogical, and theological meanings. In conformity with the most widely employed connotation in the OT, the word is used here as a summary designation of a non-Israelite population in the geographical area of Syro-Palestine, bordering Mesopotamia in the north and Egypt in the south. This meaning of the words "Canaan" and "Canaanite" is already determined by a theological decision, assumed in many OT texts, that transcends purely historical evidence because it posits the existence of "Israel" as a distinct community whose membership is determined by its allegiance to the covenant with Yahweh. Historical evidence favors strongly the assumption that both the early confederacy of tribes and the later monarchic structure of Israel were permeated by Canaaanite culture to a degree that makes a clean distinction between "Israel" and "Canaan" tenuous. The religious life of the early tribes and the Israelite kingdoms was deeply affected by this state of affairs. In spite of that, the sketch of Canaanite divinities that follows is based on the acceptance of the decision made by the Yahwism expressed in the canonical tradition of the OT, in which the faith of Israel is sharply set apart from, indeed set against—the gods of Canaan. The reconstruction of a theology of Canaanite deities can only in part depend on statements found in the OT. Textual and archaeological material from outside the OT evidence needs to be considered, especially the large amount of mythological texts from the ancient city of Ugarit that dates from the early fourteenth century B.C.

The head of the Canaanite pantheon is the god El. El is not the oldest of the gods, but he is the patriarch of the family of deities who, in a struggle against the primal gods, emasculates his father Shamem and so establishes the rule of the gods who reign over the present world order. El is the father of the gods venerated in the cult and the creator of the world. In the OT there is no polemic against El. He is not characterized as a Canaanite divinity but is identified with Yahweh in the patriarchal narratives of Genesis (see pp. 168–170 above). Answers to the intricate historical and theological questions arising from this identification remain, at present, controversial.

By far the most important Canaanite deity in the OT is Baal. "Baal" is a general noun meaning "lord, owner," but it is also used in application to the divine denoting either "divinity," since all divinity implies some form of lordship, or a specific god by the proper name Baal. The epics of Ugarit tell of Baal's fights against other gods, his victory over his divine opponents, and the confirmation of his rule in which he is given the title king and the palace from where he exercises his dominion. The two enemies among the gods over whom he prevails are Yam ("Sea") and Mot ("Death"). In the epic relating Baal's struggle with Mot, both Baal and Mot become victims of the other's power. Baal must surrender to Mot's temporarily superior strength. Baal, the god of wind and rain, storm and the clouds, is banished to the netherworld by the force of Death, at which time it is announced to the council of the gods that Baal is dead. But the goddess Anath, the ally of Baal, avenges Baal's imprisonment in the underworld by reducing Mot to impotence, splitting him up into pieces and grinding him to powder. Somehow—the epic does not tell us in what way—both Baal and Mot are revived to stand up against each other in a final battle. The ending of the epic is

lost, but it is clear that Baal emerges victorious and the power of Death is tamed.

The goddess Anath, Baal's warriorlike companion, is not known from the OT. Instead, Baal is in the OT associated with two other goddesses, Astarte and Asherah. Astarte is widely venerated in many ancient Near Eastern religions as the goddess of love and war. She is presented in Ugarit as the wife of El, but in the OT she is placed at the side of Baal. In some OT passages the two goddesses Asherah and Astarte are not clearly distinguished from each other. The plurals ʾasheroth (and ʾasherim) and ʾashtharoth are sometimes combined with the plural baʿalim. In passages of this kind they mean not so much individual deities as the general designation "goddesses" and "gods." Baals and Asherahs are coupled in verdicts of Israel's apostasy in Judg 3:7; the combination of Baals and Astartes is used in Judg 10:6 and 1 Sam 7:3–4. In other instances, the singular of both Baal and Asherah can be linked (1 Kgs 18:19), but the coordination of Baal (singular) and Astartes (plural) is also used (Judg 2:13). It appears that OT language does not intend terminological clarity about these deities. There is Baal as the power of fruitful vegetation, whose winds and rains bless the earth with life; but there are also many local manifestations of Baal that may well differ from each other in details, as the Baal-zebub of Ekron in 2 Kgs 1:2, without losing the essential unity with the concept of the god of the fertile nature of sky and earth. By the same token, Asherah and Astarte have in most OT contexts virtually been blended into one. Since Hebrew has no word for "goddess," Asherah and Astarte are employed as substitutes for a missing term and function to represent the "female deity."

Asherah is, however, in a significant number of contexts more concretely described. "Asherah" is the individual name for a goddess of the Canaanite pantheon. But she is also represented in a cultic image, and the degree of relatedness between goddess and image is so great that "Asherah" becomes the word for an object used in her cult. NRSV translates *ʾasherah* in those instances with "sacred pole," noting only in a footnote that the Hebrew word thus rendered is *ʾasherah* (e.g., 2 Kgs 17:10, 16). The "sacred pole," Asherah as image, is never described in the OT, but it is made clear that it is a "carved image" (2 Kgs 21:7) that must be "set up" (2 Kgs 17:10). The Asherah as image appears to have been a stylized tree, or a wooden pole, that represents the goddess. It is often mentioned in assocation with "high places, pillars, and sacred poles (*ʾasherim*) on every high hill and under every green tree" (1 Kgs 14:23). In these open-air sanctuaries the wooden pole stood for the female deity, and the pillars of stone symbolized the male aspect of divinity represented by Baal (2 Kgs 3:2; 10:26–27). Some comments in the history of Israel's kings seem to suggest that the cult of Asherah in Israel was particularly popular with women. King Asa of Judah removed his mother Maacah from the official status of "queen mother" because she "made an abominable image for Asherah" (1 Kgs 15:13), and the reform measures of Josiah included the demolition of the houses of male prostitutes in the Jerusalem temple "where the women did weaving for Asherah" (2 Kgs 23:7).

The so-called Deuteronomistic History (Joshua–2 Kings) presents Israel's religious life as a constant, and more often than not as an unsuccessful, struggle with Canaanite cults. Baal—sometimes together with Asherah and Astarte, sometimes by himself—is Yahweh's antagonist in the claim for Israel's allegiance. In the worship practices of Israelite homes and communities there was a high degree of commingling of Yahwistic and Baalistic elements. Yahweh put on characteristics of Baal, and the sense of Israelite culture being separate from Canaanite culture was often at least blurred, if not altogether unknown. Already before the time of Israel's settlement the people yearn for their own gods. The stories of the golden calf (Exod 32) and the incident of the veneration of the Baal of Peor (Num 25:1–5) during the

wanderings in the wilderness exemplify this tendency. In spite of the solemn affirmation of exclusive allegiance to Yahweh, the God of Moses, at the end of Joshua's leadership (Josh 24), Israel gets enthralled by the lure of the gods of the land: "Then the Israelites did what was evil in the sight of the LORD and worshiped the Baals; and they abandoned the LORD, the God of their ancestors, who had brought them out of the land of Egypt; they followed other gods, from among the gods of the peoples who were all around them, and bowed down to them" (Judg 2:11–12). There are episodes of protest, in the description of the Deuteronomistic historians, when the awareness of Yahweh's exclusive claim on Israel breaks out in reforms: Gideon destroys an altar of Baal and the accompanying Asherah (Judg 6:25–32); Elijah eliminates in a horrific contest the Baal priests of the royal family of Ahab and Jezebel (1 Kgs 18); Jehu eradicates the royal house of Ahab, together with the worshipers of Baal, in one of the bloodiest scenes of the OT (2 Kgs 10, esp. vv. 18–27). The purging of Jerusalem's worship under Hezekiah (2 Kgs 18) and Josiah (2 Kgs 23) sets these kings apart as models of a dedication to Yahweh alone that is the source of life and blessing for the people of the covenant (Deut 28:1–14).

The OT narratives from the period of the judges and from the time of Samuel tell of encounters of Yahweh with the god Dagon. In these stories the aim of the storyteller is concentrated on the superiority of Yahweh over Dagon, whose nature and competency remain unclear. The blinded and bound Samson is brought by the Philistine leaders to be displayed at "a great sacrifice to their god Dagon" as proof of Dagon's superiority over Samson and his God (Judg 16:23–24), but the almost incapacitated Samson still manages to bring down the house upon Dagon's devotees. In a similar vein, Dagon is rendered defenseless against Yahweh's power in the scene of 1 Sam 5:1–7. The Philistines manage to capture the ark of the covenant and deposit it in

Dagon's temple in Ashdod. But in the night the invisible Yahweh, enthroned on the cherubim of the ark, topples the image of Dagon, who is left mutilated after the encounter. The god Dagon, who is in the OT identified as god of the Philistines (Judg 16:23; 1 Chr 10:10), was known and venerated in West Semitic and Mesopotamian areas. In the Ugaritic texts he appears only in the phrase "Baal the son of Dagon," although as a rule El is considered Baal's father in the epic. The name Dagon has been connected to the Hebrew word *dagan* (grain) or to *gan* (fish). The derivation of the name remains uncertain, but Phoenician traditions testify to the connection of Dagon with grain. Although OT traditions allocate Dagon in Philistine territory, it may well be that names of two Israelite towns indicate that Dagon worship was not restricted to Philistine lands. A list of towns belonging to the tribe of Judah mentions Beth-dagon ("house of Dagon"), and the area of the tribe of Asher also contained a place called Beth-dagon (Josh 15:41; 19:27). As late as the time of the Maccabees, there is still a temple of Dagon in Azotus, the old city of Ashdod (1 Macc 10:83; 11:4).

The god Molech is in 1 Kgs 11:7 said to be associated with the Ammonites, perhaps by scribal error (cf. 11:5). But Molech is not a tribal god. The seven OT passages that mention him are all connected to rites of child sacrifice. Most explicit is Lev 20:2–5, where Molech appears four times. The sacrificing of a child is condemned in this law in most relentless tones, Yahweh personally expressing determination to root out offenders if human society will not do so. But in spite of the strictest condemnation, child sacrifice to Molech continued in Israelite society down to the time of the late monarchy and the exile. Second Kings 23:10 reports Josiah's measures to prevent the murderous rite in Jerusalem, and Jer 32:35 chastises the same act in words that seem to indicate that there were circles in Jerusalem who justified the practice as having divine approval.

Egyptian and Mesopotamian divinities. The conquest of Samaria by the Assyrians (722/21 B.C.) and the destruction of Jerusalem and its temple at the hands of the Babylonians (586 B.C.) resulted in the exposure to new sets of gods for the people of Yahweh who had, until the middle of the eighth century B.C., lived alongside or within a religious culture dominated by tribal and Canaanite deities. The two national catastrophes required of the remnants of the northern and southern kingdoms of Israel and Judah to face the question whether the gods of the victorious powers had not been proven dominant over Yahweh, whose people had suffered a disastrous humiliation. Much of the OT literature from the exilic and postexilic period is written in answer to this question (see pp. 177–78 below). One would expect that, in this literature, the Akkadian gods would play a major role and that their names would appear as frequently as the names of Baal, Asherah, and Astarte in the preexilic tradition. That is, however, not the case. Only very infrequently are individual foreign deities named in OT sections of exilic and postexilic origin. This silence is part of the OT answer to the problem of Yahweh's seeming defeat by Mesopotamian gods. But very rarely a named foreign deity surfaces, almost like a lone representative of a whole family of gods who remain wrapped in obscurity.

The only Egyptian god whose name appears in the OT is the god Amun, although Egyptian gods in general are mentioned in the narrative of Yahweh's liberation of Israel from Egypt. In a solemn statement of self-determination Yahweh declares: "On all the gods of Egypt I will execute judgments: I am the LORD" (Exod 12:12). This declaration is the only instance in which the account of the plagues in Egypt dignifies Egyptian gods with as much as a general reference. In an oracle of Jeremiah the gods of Egypt are mentioned again, but this time at least one of them is deemed deserving to be named. In Jer 46:25 Yahweh says: "See, I am bringing punishment upon Amon of

Thebes, and Pharaoh, and Egypt and her gods and her kings." Amon (Egyptian Amun), situated in Thebes, was since 2000 B.C. equated with the sun god Re, and in this combination he became the state god of upper and lower Egypt. In this status he was chief of the Egyptian pantheon, identified later by the Greeks with Zeus, and it is in this role as supreme god of Egypt that the oracle in Jer 46:25 uses his name.

In comparison to the sparsity of references to Egyptian gods in the OT, the references to named deities of Mesopotamia are a little more frequent. In a picture of the practice of idol worship in Jerusalem, Jeremiah speaks of women who "knead dough, to make cakes for the queen of heaven" (7:18), a practice that according to the same prophet was defiantly continued in Egypt by Jerusalemite women who had managed to flee after the destruction of the city (44:17–19, 25). Although this queen of heaven is not identified by name, many interpreters see in her Ishtar, a major Mesopotamian goddess of love and war, who was associated with the planet Venus. In the list of obscure Akkadian deities in 2 Kgs 17:30–31, Nergal stands out as a major god who is known from Mesopotamian texts. He is like Ishtar a planetary god who is placed together with the planet Mars, a god of war and hunting. More frequently introduced in OT sayings are the Babylonian gods Bel and Nebo; they are named together in Isa 46:1, and Bel alone appears in Jer 50:2 and 51:44. Bel, linguistically related to Baal, is used either as a byname or as a substitute name for Marduk, who since the time of Hammurabi in the eighteenth century B.C. had become city god of Babylon and who had in that capacity advanced to being the national god of Babylonia. Nebo (Akkadian Nabu) was closely associated with Bel/Marduk as the god of wisdom and the art of writing. The association of the two gods had become so close that Nabu was styled to be the son of Bel/Marduk. Finally, the book of Ezekiel speaks of Tammuz. In a vision of

abominations that are committed in the very temple of Jerusalem, Ezekiel sees women "sitting there weeping for Tammuz" (8:14). The god Tammuz is a dying and rising deity, similar in this capacity to Baal, whose relegation to the underworld and consequent drying up of the vegetation on earth were ritually lamented by women devotees. Ezekiel 8:14 is a particularly striking flash of light illuminating the degree of syncretistic practices in Jerusalem even in the precincts of the temple dedicated to Yahweh.

One God without idols

The first and the second commandments of the Decalogue prohibit acknowledgment of gods other than Yahweh, and the manufacture of images: "You shall have no other gods before me," and "You shall not make for yourself an idol" (Exod 20:3–4; Deut 5:7–8). These two commandments not only regulate cultic practice in Israel in the OT period, but they state fundamental principles that describe faith in the biblical God in both OT and NT.

One God alone. Dictionaries of religion are virtually agreed on the thesis that there are three major world religions that have in common a monotheistic faith: Christianity, Judaism, and Islam. The OT is seen as the most significant stepping stone on the way to expressing a strict monotheism, which is understood to be the conviction of the existence of one single deity, denying the reality of any other gods. It is, further, widely understood that the NT had adopted the monotheistic stance from Judaism: the faith of the NT in one God is one of the most fundamental tenets of this inheritance from the OT and from the Judaism of the NT period. In the past few decades, however, views have been presented that question the legitimacy of this assumption from a variety of different approaches. It is impossible to provide here even an outline of the discussions, which have by no means reached a viable consensus, but it is necessary to state the point of departure that is chosen in this presentation of the OT and NT confession of one single

God without idols (see *confess*). This point of departure is the understanding that the faith in a single God is woven into the fabric of the community whose response to the covenant God is itself a part of the singularity of the community's deity. The gift of God to the community and the claim of God on the community are the ground from which the confession of God's oneness arises. The proclamation of God's act of liberation and the ordering of life in response to this act are the preconditions to which the faith in one God belong. Therefore, the loyalty to the God of the covenant—rather than answers to ontological problems about the first cause of being—is of paramount significance for the first commandment.

Sometimes the existence of private or tribal gods is mentioned without polemic. Rachel is said to have taken her father's household gods (Gen 31:34); Jephthah suggests that the god Chemosh has given their territory to the Ammonites (Judg 11:24); David fears Saul's persecution will drive him from the land of Israel into Philistine territory, where he will have to "serve other gods" (1 Sam 26:19); and the Syrian Naaman wants to ship two mule-loads of Israel's earth to his own land of Aram because it is Yahweh's earth, while back in his own country one has to bow down to the local god Rimmon (2 Kgs 5:17–19). No book in the OT insists more urgently on the exclusive service of Yahweh than the book of Deuteronomy, but Deuteronomy has not expurgated the notion that the worship of "all the host of heaven," while forbidden to Israel, is "allotted to all the peoples everywhere under heaven" (4:19), and that the population on earth was apportioned land in accordance to the number of gods (32:8). Psalms praising the kingship of Yahweh speak of divine beings that are in the company of the God of Israel. The heavenly beings (lit. "sons of gods") are called upon to ascribe glory and strength to Yahweh who is enthroned as king (29:1, 10), "all gods bow down before him" (97:7), Yahweh is "a great God, and a great King above all gods"

(95:3), who "has taken his place in the divine council," and "in the midst of the gods . . . holds judgment" (82:1), which will even include a sentence of death on the gods for their lack of justice and understanding (82:2, 5–7). In these psalms the gods are nameless and voiceless, they do not own some portfolio independent of Yahweh, their king, and they are subjected entirely to Yahweh's judgment.

It has often been claimed that Deutero-Isaiah (Isa 40–55), an unknown prophet of the exile, has achieved the triumphant breakthrough to a strict monotheism. Indeed, many of his oracles extol Yahweh's exclusive claim to be God beyond all gods: "I am the LORD, and there is no other; besides me there is no god" (45:5; very similar 45:6, 18, 21–22). With a pointed challenge to the other gods, Yahweh says: "I am the first and I am the last; besides me there is no god. Who is like me? Let them proclaim it, let them declare and set it forth before me. . . . Is there any god besides me? There is no other rock; I know not one" (44:6–8). There is no question: the superiority, incomparability, and ultimacy of Yahweh, the God of Israel, cannot be more strongly affirmed. But Deutero-Isaiah's proud oracles are not statements of an ontological monotheism. The divine status of other gods is denied by the use of three different Hebrew words of negation. The same negations are employed in Isa 40–55 in reference to nations, to princes and rulers, and to people waging war against Yahweh's nation. Before Israel's God "all the nations are as nothing" (40:17); Yahweh "brings princes to naught, and makes the rulers of the earth as nothing" (40:23); and those who war against Israel "shall be as nothing at all" (41:12). Obviously the nations oppressing Israel, their princes and rulers, and their military are not meant to be declared ontologically nonexistent. On the contrary, they are the most painful realities the exiled Israelites have to contend with. But confronted with the power of Yahweh—who will act on behalf of his people in the second exodus and in his return to Zion for the establishment of his reign as king (52:7–8)—enemy nations, their princes and rulers, and their war machine will be reduced to impotence. In like manner, face to face with Israel's God, the gods will be outclassed. They are summoned to account for themselves in the court of Yahweh, to present their insight into the future "that we may know that you are gods" (41:23). But, as in the psalms of Yahweh's kingship, the gods have no answers, they remain nameless shadows. Compared to Yahweh, they are powerless nongods whose spell over human life is broken.

In the NT, the missionary practice of the apostle Paul displays an attitude to pagan gods that is in essential aspects continuous with the OT insistence on the exclusive claim and the incomparable power of Yahweh. The proclamation of the gospel, the message of God's grace through the work of God's Son, only confirms for Paul the confession of the OT that God is one (Deut 6:4). In the preaching and teaching of Paul, the confession of one single God places Jews and non-Jews into the same position. Jews and non-Jews alike are equally dependent on God's undeserved grace, and equally entitled to benefit from this grace, because "God is one" (Rom 3:29–30). The missionary Paul brings this message of the one God to a society in which the worship of many gods had shaped the lives of individuals and institutions. When the first Christian communities were founded, the step to becoming a member of the body of Christ meant, first and foremost, a turning away from the idols to the only true and living God (1 Thess 1:9–10). Life under the spell of pagan cults amounts to ignorance about the true God and to enslavement under the yoke of powers who parade as gods but are, in reality, compared to the Father of Jesus Christ, not worthy of the title (Gal 4:8; see *abba* and *family*). To state, however, that the gods of pagan religion are not worth the name "god" does not imply that these gods are purely the figments of religious

fantasy. They may be unable to speak, but they have enough force to entice and lead astray (1 Cor 12:2). Paul was confronted in Corinth with a group of Christian enthusiasts who had propagated the slogan: "no idol in the world really exists" because "there is no God but one" (1 Cor 8:4). Paul agrees with the statement: "For us there is one God, the Father, from whom are all things and for whom we exist, and one Lord, Jesus Christ, through whom are all things and through whom we exist" (8:6). But the Christian enthusiasts transform the Christian confession of God's oneness in Christ into a general principle of religious enlightenment. The Christian confession of the one God is true. But it is effective in the body of the community ("for us") that is continually nourished and rejuvenated through the gospel. Outside of this force, the truth of the confession of one God becomes a dangerous slogan that Paul counters by the warning "there may be so-called gods—as in fact there are many gods and many lords" (8:5). The power of the gods cannot be ignored by relegating them simply to nonexistence. Outside of the power of God's rule in Christ, they remain virulent enticements that the Christian community must "flee" (1 Cor 10:14) because pagan sacrifice is an act of worship of demons (1 Cor 10:20). In continuity with the approach of the OT, Paul's missionary thought and practice is governed by the demand of loyalty to the God of the covenant, not by a general metaphysic culmination in an abstract theory of monotheism.

The central affirmation of Deut 6:4–5—"Hear, O Israel: The LORD is our God, the LORD alone"—is not only the twice-repeated daily confession of every Jew at the time of the NT but also the unquestioned affirmation of the NT tradition (Mark 12:29–30; Rom 3:29–30; 1 Cor 8:6; Eph 4:5–6; 1 Tim 2:5; Jas 2:19). However, the NT has elaborated the OT and Jewish confession of the one God through the addition of a christological statement. Paul commends the Thessalonians for their turning from idols to serve the true and living God and for expecting God's Son from heaven as the savior from the wrath to come (1Thess 1:9–10; see *son of God*). The affirmation of the oneness of God together with the oneness of Christ is most obvious in 1 Cor 8:6, where the sentence "there is one God" is immediately followed by the corresponding sentence "and one Lord, Jesus Christ." The "and" that connects the two sentences is to be understood, not as an addition to, but as an explanation of, the first affirmation through the second. That God is one becomes, in the gospel of Jesus Christ, manifest and concrete through the life, death, and resurrection of Christ. The Son of God shares in the unique status and power of the Father. The incomparability of Yahweh is reflected in the incomparability of Jesus Christ. The exclusive loyalty owed to God is made concrete in the exclusive loyalty to Christ owed by every member of Christ's body. For this reason the confessional tone of the OT sentence "Yahweh is our God, Yahweh alone" is echoed in christological confessions of the NT. The disciples are told that they have only one Father in heaven but, by the same token, they also have one teacher, the Christ (Matt 23:9–10). The promise of God given to Abraham, that the divine blessing would be given to the Gentiles, is extended "to one person, who is Christ" (Gal 3:16). The one Lord who rules through faith and baptism shares in the distinction of the "one God and Father of all" (Eph 4:5–6), and the same participation in the distinction of singularity is stated in 1 Tim 2:5: "there is one God; there is also one mediator between God and humankind, Christ Jesus." In the language of the book of Acts, speaking of the crucified and raised Jesus Christ: "There is salvation in no one else, for there is no other name under heaven given among mortals by which we must be saved" (4:12).

Without idols. Ancient Near Eastern religions were not unacquainted with tendencies to concentrate divine powers in one supreme god, but Yahweh's demand of exclusive loyalty was a novelty in the surroundings of these religions. The prohibition of images in the OT is also not entirely without parallels in the cultures around Israel. A practical lack of images existed in several cults among Israel's neighbors, but the insistence, on principle, to worship Yahweh without the representation in an image was a revolutionary innovation.

Injunctions against representations of God in the form of an image are found in all collections of law in the OT (Decalogue: Exod 20:4–6; Deut 5:8–10; other collections: Exod 20:23; 34:17; Lev 19:4; Deut 27:15; see *idol*). The prohibition of images expanded in Israel's history to include cultic representations that had originally not been held to be idolatrous: the serpent of bronze from the time of Moses (Num 21:4–9) had been kept in the temple in Jerusalem during the monarchic period until the image was destroyed in the course of Hezekiah's reforms when it was deemed to be an idol (2 Kgs 18:4). Over the course of time ideas changed as to what constituted idolatry. The aniconic legislation in the OT usually gives no reason why the figurative representation of Yahweh was to be outlawed. There are, however, two exceptions. The prohibition of idols in the Decalogue adds the explanatory comment: "whether in the form of anything that is in heaven above, or that is on the earth beneath, or that is in the water under the earth" (Exod 20:4; Deut 5:8), and Deut 4 offers a reference to the reception of the law at Sinai that is to bind Israel to God's voice as the medium of Yahweh's presence: "Since you saw no form when the LORD spoke to you at Horeb out of the fire, take care and watch yourselves closely, so that you do not act corruptly by making an idol for yourselves" (Deut 4: 15–16). Israel heard Yahweh's voice at the event of the giving of the law, but it had no vision that could provide a sight capable of capturing Yahweh's presence (see *hear* and *see*). Therefore it is not to bow down to anything that is either male or female (Deut 4:16), or that is like animals, birds, or reptiles (4:17), or that belongs to the visible forces of the sky (4:19). Heaven, earth, and netherworld are the totality of the world in which human life is lived, the arena of our experience that we call nature. None of the forces of nature lend analogies to the God who speaks in initiating the covenant and in announcing the order of life in which the covenant is preserved. God's presence is in a living voice, not in a sight of what nature provides. Seeing God is a dangerous, even life-threatening experience. Israel, about to receive the law, is warned "not to break through to the LORD to look; otherwise many of them will perish" (Exod 19:21). Even the appearance of the angel of Yahweh strikes terror in Gideon and Manoah, because they know that "we shall surely die, for we have seen God" (Judg 13:22; 6:22–23). Isaiah is shaken in terror when he has the vision of God enthroned as king (Isa 6:5). Moses and Elijah have to hide their faces when Yahweh appears to them (Exod 3:6; 1 Kgs 19:13). The burning bush that is not consumed awakens Moses' curiosity (Exod 3:2–3), but what is emphasized at great length in the chapter of Moses' call is not the natural marvel but the continuous verbal communication of God to Moses, which fills almost the entire chapter. Yahweh cannot be compared to any power of nature, because no power in nature is capable of providing a true analogy to him. Israel's God, the God without images, is experienced through his voice as the personal will who communicates himself freely and ever anew in his *word*.

The impossibility and illegitimacy of picturing Yahweh in an image of nature is connected to the fact that Israel's God is almost entirely free of mythological traits. Some mythological concepts, like Yahweh's fight with the sea monsters (Isa 27:1), remain fragments. Yahweh has no commerce with other divinities. Light and night, solar and stellar forces, sea and land—all divinities in pagan religions—are wonderful but secular realities, created by God (Gen 1). Yahweh does not share in the history of the gods. He has no

birth and suffers no death, and is not drawn into the conflict of the gods with each other, like Baal, Mot, and Yam—not even as arbitrator among them, like El. Yahweh is removed from polarities that are characteristic of the society of divine beings in pagan religions. Yahweh does not participate in the gender differentiation that sets gods and goddesses apart from each other. Israel's God is neither male nor female, and the fact that OT texts present him as a husband confirms this: Yahweh is always depicted as a consort of a human community and never as the partner of a goddess (Hos 2; Jer 2:2; Ezek 16; 23). Popular religion in Israel accommodated Yahweh to sexually differentiated roles of Canaanite deities (Hos 4:14; Deut 23:17–18; 2 Kgs 23:7), but the canonical texts of the OT stand firm in their opposition to this acculturation: Yahweh is transcendent to the world of sexuality. Of equal importance is the insistence of some OT traditions that Yahweh is the "living God." Canaanite divinities incorporate the cycle of nature that is at work in the constant process of renewal and rebirth and of decay and death. Yahweh, on the other hand, cannot be imaged in analogy to these natural movements. To Yahweh's people death spreads ritual impurity (Num 19:11–13), cults of the dead are prohibited (Deut 18:11), death cuts off from the experience of God's acts with his community (Ps 88:10–11). God belongs to life that he gives from the beginning (Gen 2:7), and hymns extol him as the living God (Pss 18:46; 42:2; 84:2). On this basis Jesus utters the bold assertion that Abraham, Isaac, and Jacob are not dead, because their God "is God not of the dead, but of the living" (Mark 12:27), and Paul moves close to a definition of God by stating that God "gives life to the dead and calls into existence the things that do not exist" (Rom 4:17).

The prohibition of images expresses a concept of God that separates God from all forces of the universe. The God of Israel and the God of the NT transcends nature to a degree foreign to the religions around the biblical community. Taken by itself, however, this observation could become misleading. Israel's cult tolerates no idols, but Israel's language of God is replete with pictures. What is illegitimate in the form of manufactured objects is found in great profusion in many biblical documents. Idols of animal shape have no place in Israel's worship, but in some of Hosea's oracles God compares himself to animal life: "I am like maggots to Ephraim, and like rottenness to the house of Judah. . . . I will be like a lion to Ephraim, and like a young lion to the house of Judah" (5:12, 14); other sayings have Yahweh speak of himself as a leopard and a bear (13:7–8). Comparisons of God to animals are, however, rare in the OT. Exceedingly frequent are, on the other hand, figures of speech that manifest God in human form (anthropomorphism) and with human emotions (anthropopathism). He acts and speaks like a human and has a mouth (Jer 9:12), eyes (Amos 9:4), and ears (Hos 8:18). Like a human he possesses arms (Jer 52:10), hands (Amos 9:2), fingers (Deut 9:10), and feet (Isa 66:1). He can walk in the garden (Gen 3:8) and shut with his own hands the ark on Noah and his family (Gen 7:16), as he can come down from heaven to take a look at the city of Babel and its tower (Gen 11:5). God is said to share with humans emotions like joy (Zeph 3:17) and delight (Jer 9:24), but also anger and passion (Deut 29:20) and even regret (Gen 6:6). In these anthropomorphic and anthropopathic descriptions of God, God appears very much in the image of a man—and occasionally of a woman (e.g., Isa 49:15)—in spite of his superiority over the processes of nature. This God is open to the worshiper, ready to engage in dialogue, near enough to care, and close enough to help. The teaching of Jesus in the NT picks up the OT's presentation of God in human form and leads it to new heights. Jesus' parables proclaim the kingship of God by telling stories of human conduct. God is understandable, in Jesus' parables, through the acts that demonstrate God's rule, and this action is intelligible because it happens in language telling about Galilean farmers and landowners, judges and homemakers. Jesus was, and is, empowered to speak of God in human terms because he is himself in human life the image of God (2 Cor 4:4; Col 1:15; Heb 1:3; see *image*). In his life, death, and resurrection is demonstrated the dominion of the only true and living God, who is the master of nature, transcendent above all powers of the universe, and also the faithful companion to humans who hear his voice. God, at one and the same time far above us and closest to us, will lead history to its consummation when all things will be subjected to him "so that God may be all in all" (1 Cor 15:28).

Donald E. Gowan, *Theology in Exodus: Biblical Theology in the Form of a Commentary* (Louisville, Ky.: Westminster John Knox Press, 1994); Trygve N. D. Mettinger, *In Search of God: The Meaning and Message of the Everlasting Names* (Philadelphia: Fortress Press, 1988); Patrick D. Miller, *The Religion of Ancient Israel* (London: SPCK and Louisville, Ky.: Westminster John Knox Press, 2000); Neil Richardson, *Paul's Language about God* (Sheffield: Academic Press, 1994); Werner H. Schmidt, *The Faith of the Old Testament: A History* (Philadelphia: Westminster Press, 1983).

ULRICH W. MAUSER

Good "Good" in Heb. (*tob*) and Gk. (*agathos, kalos, arete*) occurs frequently in Scripture (827 times in NRSV). Linked to sensory and moral perception, the term comprises practical value, performance, moral, and aesthetic dimensions. God declares creation good (Gen 1:4, 12, 18, 21, 25); indeed, "everything . . . was very good" (1:31). While these uses are aesthetic and practical, the testing of Adam and Eve is moral, knowing "good and evil" (Gen 2:9; 3:5; cf. appraisal of events concerning Joseph in 44:4; 50:20).

"Good" is God-oriented, for God the Lord is good (2 Chr 6:41; 7:3; Pss 16:2; 25:8; 34:8; 54:6; 100:5; 106:1; 107:1; 118:1, 29; 145:9; Jer 33:11; 1 Pet 2:3) and does good (Ps 84:11; 103:5; 107:9; 119:68). God's goodness is manifest to the covenant people in redemption from slavery, wilderness provisions, and giving the land (Pss 106–7; Josh 24:20) and in teaching and law (Jer 6:16; Rom 7:12), forgiveness (Hos 3:5), and the promise of restoration and a new covenant (Jer 32:40; Zech 8:15). No human is good (Pss 14:1, 3; 50:3; cf. Rom 7:18–20); only God is good (Mark 10:18 and par. Matt 19:17).

"Good" means "practical value," with reference to trees (Gen 2:9), ears of grain (41:5), and "the good and broad land, a land flowing with milk and honey" (Exod 3:8; cf. Deut 8:7–10). In "All things work together for good" (Rom 8:28; Mg "God works for good"), "good" embraces possibly all levels of meaning. Many of the eighteen occurrences of "good" in Proverbs and seven in Ecclesiastes combine the practical and moral. The aesthetic quality occurs in sensuous pleasures of sweetness (Jer 6:20), fragrance (Song 1:3), and beauty (Gen 24:16). "How very good and pleasant it is when kindred live together in unity" (Ps 133:1) combines the aesthetic and moral. Similarly, "I am the good (kalos) shepherd" (John 10:11, 14) connotes quality, the noble shepherd who lays down his life for the sheep.

The moral meaning is linked to hospitality (Gen 26:29), loyalty (1 Sam 29:9— "blameless" in NRSV), and the recurring call to do, seek, or discern the good (Pss 34:14; 37:27; Hos 14:2; Rom 12:2; 16:19; Heb 5:14; 13:16; 1 Pet 3:11; 1 Tim 6:18). This moral sense, denoted usually by agathos, is expressed in commands to do good even "to those who hate you" (kalos in Luke 6:27; agathopoeite in v. 35) and to fellow believers (agatho, Rom 12:9; 1 Pet 4:10; cf. 3:6). Agathos often contrasts to evil. Believers are to "overcome evil with good," rather than repay evil for evil (Rom 12:21; 1 Thess 5:15; 1 Pet 3:9). Believers are to "hold fast to what is good" (kalos, 1 Thess 5:21).

While the moral may imply performance use, such terms as "good works" and "the good fight of the faith" (1 Tim 6:12) emphasize that one has done well. When one is persecuted, good conduct and a good conscience fortify amid suffering (1 Pet 3:13–22; Heb 11:39; cf. Rom 13:3–4). Good works testify to God (Matt 5:16; 1 Tim 6:18) and evidence salvation through God's grace by faith in Christ (Eph 2:10).

Jesus reveals God's goodness. Luke sums up Jesus' mission as going "about doing good and healing" (Acts 10:38). Proclaiming the gospel is good tidings of peace (Isa 52:7; Luke 2:10, 14; Acts 10:36; Rom 10:15; Eph 6:15). "Good news" and "gospel" (seven nominal uses in Mark, twenty-five verbal in Luke-Acts, and often in Paul in both forms) describe Jesus' kingdom message.

The Holy Spirit is God's good gift (Luke 11:11–13). Goodness (agathosyne, RSV; NRSV translates "generosity") manifests the fruit of the Spirit (Gal 5:22–23); goodness (arete; RSV translates "virtue") is a formational virtue enabling believers to "become participants of the divine nature" (2 Pet 1:3–5).

WILLARD M. SWARTLEY

Gospel The English word "gospel" renders the Greek word euangelion, which meant originally "a reward for good news" and then simply "good news" or "news." Mark summarizes the initial public activity of Jesus as "proclaiming the good news of God" (1:14). This is immediately defined in eschatological terms, "The time is fulfilled, and the *kingdom of God* has come near," and followed by the summons "believe in the good news" (1:15). Apart from these two instances, the noun occurs six more times in Mark (1:1; 8:35; 10:29; 13:10; 14:9; 16:15) and four times in Matthew (4:23; 9:35; 24:14; 26:13) but is absent from Luke (although it appears twice in Acts, at 15:7 and 20:24). Luke instead employs the verb "to announce good news" (euangelizomai) ten times in his Gospel and fifteen times in Acts (elsewhere in the Gospels the verb appears only at Matt 11:5). The verb is especially prominent in Jesus' reading of Isa 61:1–2 at the Nazareth synagogue in Luke 4:18, where it serves to distinguish the focus of Jesus' ministry. Jesus' proclamation of the gospel is characterized by the message about the approaching kingdom of God, *healing*, and exorcism. Thus when disciples are sent out to share in his activity, they are commissioned to do these same things (Matt 10:7–8).

In the OT the Hebrew word *besorah* has the general meaning of "proclaiming good news" or "tidings" (1 Kgs 1:42), used, for example, in connection with military victory or the death of an opponent (1 Sam 31:9; 2 Sam 4:10; 18:19, 20, 31). The use in 2 Kgs 7:9 more closely approximates the sense of the term "good news" as a reference to God's salvation when it refers to the discovery that the Arameans who had been besieging Samaria had fled. While a religious sense appears in several Psalms (40:9; 68:11), it is especially in the second part of Isaiah, with its references to the victory of God and the start of a new age (Isa 52:7 [cited at Rom 10:15]; cf. 40:9; 41:27), that significant conceptual parallels to the NT usage centering on the message of God's salvation may be found. While the ideas of victory and liberation are also associated with the Greek verb in secular usage, the Lukan citation of Isa 61:1–2 indicates the formative influence of the Greek OT on the NT.

Paul understands his call to be an apostle as equivalent to being "set apart for the gospel of God" (Rom 1:1). He explicitly connects this gospel concerning Jesus (the Son) with the promises announced in Scripture by the prophets (1:2). Most basically the gospel is "the power of God for salvation" for all who have faith, both Jew and Gentile (1:16). But in Paul's view it is especially the justification (see *just*) of the *Gentiles* that lies at the heart of the gospel. In fact, the declaration to Abraham that "all the Gentiles shall be blessed in you" can be designated "the gospel" (Gal 3:8). Paul is anxious that the gospel he proclaims not be perceived as merely a matter of teaching and emphasizes that it is not of

human origin but has been revealed by Jesus Christ (Gal 1:11–12). It is "veiled to those who are perishing" (2 Cor 4:3; cf. Eph 6:19: "the mystery of the gospel"). The gospel also may be described as the basic message that, in accordance with the Scriptures, Christ died for our sins and was raised, and that he appeared to many (1 Cor 15:1, 3–8). Although the emphasis is usually on the "good news," the gospel also includes an eschatological day of judgment (Rom 2:16).

It is significant that the noun "good news" is employed in publicizing the imperial cult in the Greco-Roman world. One of the best-known illustrations of this usage is found in an inscription from Priene dated to 9 B.C., which celebrates Augustus as a "savior" (*soter*) for humankind who has surpassed all previous benefactors by ending war and arranging all things. The inscription proclaims the birthday of the god Augustus as marking a new age, which is "good news" (*euangelion*) for all the world. Similar inscriptions show that such propaganda was widespread. It is likely that Christians, fully aware of the imperialistic uses of the term, made use of it in part to challenge the dominant interpretation of the ordering of the world and to declare their own understanding of the onset of a new age brought in by another savior. Thus in various NT contexts the appearance of the term "good news" may not so subtly convey the conviction that the salvation of God will replace the salvation promoted by the emperor. For example, in the Lukan infancy narrative of Jesus, an angel brings "good news (*euangelion*) of great joy for all the people," namely the birth of Jesus as a "savior" (*soter*) who is also the Messiah (Luke 2:10–11). In the immediately preceding context the emperor Augustus himself had been mentioned (2:1) in connection with a decree that turns out to work according to biblical expectations. The praise of God by a multitude of angels contrasts with that of the human ruler insofar as both are lauded for bringing peace to the earth (2:13–14).

In Acts the noun "gospel" (NRSV "good news") appears only twice, on the lips first of Peter (Acts 15:7) and then of Paul (20:24). But Acts also employs a variety of objects for verbs of preaching that are virtually synonymous with the gospel, such as "the word" (e.g., 6:2, 4, 7; 8:4, 14, 25; 13:5; 15:36; 18:5). The verb "to announce good news" (*euangelizomai*) is used among others (e.g., "*preach*, proclaim" *kerysso*) to mark the preaching activity of the early church. Thus it denotes the daily proclamation of the apostles (5:42), Philip's activity (8:4, 12, 35, 40; note that at 21:8 Philip is described with a cognate word as "the evangelist"), that of Peter and John (8:25), the dispersed Hellenists (11:20), and especially Paul (13:32; 14:7, 15, 21; 15:35; 16:10; 17:18). At 10:36 God is said to preach peace through Jesus Christ. A comparison of the use of the verb in Acts with that in Luke's Gospel shows that the preachers in Acts are consciously portrayed as the successors of Jesus, insofar as they do what he had done.

The use of the term "gospel" in early postbiblical texts to refer to the details of the life and activity of Jesus (e.g., *Did.* 8:2; 15:3–4) led to the sense of a Gospel as an account or genre. Some see this meaning already present in Mark 1:1. The proliferation of Gospels already in the second century beyond those that eventually found their way into the NT canon shows how popular the conception of a Gospel book was for the early Christians. This led to Irenaeus's argument for the fourfold Gospel (see *Adv. haer.* 3.11.8), in which he sought to defend the unity of the gospel message in light of what he saw as the danger of heretical deviations owing to the confusing multiplicity of Gospels.

CHRISTOPHER R. MATTHEWS

Grace, Gracious Both OT and NT treat grace as both a gift and a quality.

In the Old Testament
The Hebrew verb *hanan* means "to be gracious." The NRSV translates the Hebrew with a range of English words, including "to show *mercy*" (Deut 7:2), "to be kind" (Prov 14:21), "to seek *favor*" (Hos 12:4), "to plead" (1 Kgs 8:33), "to entreat" (Deut 3:23), "to be generous" (Judg 21:22), and even "to charm" (Prov 31:30). The adjective *hanun* is usually translated "gracious" (Exod 34:6–7), although it can also be rendered by the English "compassionate" (Exod 22:27; see *compassion*). The adjective is restricted, for the most part, to descriptions of God.

Grace as a gift. The most prominent use of "grace" in the Hebrew Bible is to describe relationships. Relationships built on grace issue from the quality of a person's character, when one has affection for another, prompting the spontaneous bestowal of a gift. The gift of grace is a free act of generosity (Judg 21:22), and it can exist only in the relationship between persons or between God and humans. It is not a possession or a commodity. "Favor," states the proverb, "is better than silver or gold" (Prov 22:1).

The story of Jacob and Esau provides a clear illustration of the relational quality of grace between humans. Upon returning to Canaan, Jacob seeks the favor of Esau by giving him goods and possessions (Gen 32:5). When the brothers meet, Esau embraces Jacob and asks about the meaning of the gifts, indicating his disinterest in them. And it is only in the moment of mutual affection without ulterior motive that the gifts become acts of grace, and not a means of manipulating the behavior of another. Jacob says to Esau, "'Please accept my gift that is brought to you, because God has dealt graciously with me, and because I have everything I want.' So he urged him, and he took it" (Gen 33:11).

The story of Jacob and Esau is unusual in that the characters are brothers, sharing a similar social status. The relationship created by grace is more often between unequal parties in the Hebrew Bible. A person of superior rank bestows grace on a subordinate. The book of Proverbs reflects the social hierarchy between the elite wisdom teachers and the poor by repeatedly urging the pupil to be gracious to the poor. "Those who despise their neighbors are sinners, but happy are those who are kind (Hebrew, show grace) to the poor" (Prov 14:21; see also 14:31; 28:8). Such acts of grace are grounded theologically. "Whoever is kind to the poor lends to the LORD, and will be repaid in full" (Prov 19:17). Kings also disperse grace to their subjects. Their subordinates often request the gift of grace through forms of entreaty. When a subordinate requests an act of grace from a king, it is often translated "to entreat" or "to plead." When Jeremiah makes such a request of King Zedekiah, he states, "Now please hear me, my lord king: be good enough to listen to my plea, and do not send me back to the house of the secretary Jonathan to die there" (Jer 37:20). Esther addresses King Ahasuerus with similar language, "If I have won the king's favor, and if it pleases the king to grant my petition and fulfill my request . . ." (Esth 5:8; see also 4:8; 7:3; 8:3, 5). The messenger of Ahab "fell on his knees before Elijah, and entreated him, 'O man of God, please let my life, and the life of these fifty servants of yours, be precious in your sight'" (2 Kgs 1:13).

The most common use of grace as a gift occurs between God and humans. God embodies grace (Exod 34:6–7; see *"Grace as a quality"* below) and states to Moses, "I will be gracious to whom I will be gracious" (Exod 33:19). God wishes to dispense grace to the Israelites. The prophet Isaiah declares to the leaders of Judah, "the LORD waits to be gracious to you; therefore he will rise up to show mercy to you. For the LORD is a God of justice; blessed are all those who wait for him" (Isa 30:18). One reason for God's affection toward Israel is the covenant with the ancestors (2 Kgs 13:23). The gracious attitude of God to Israel is the foundation for humans to entreat God in the lament psalms. Repeatedly the psalmist states, "Be gracious to me, O LORD" (Pss 4:1; 6:2; 9:13; 25:16; 31:9; 56:1; 57:2; 123:2, etc.). The call for grace in the lament Psalms also implies a relationship between unequal

parties. It is a plea, in which the worshiper is in the subordinate position, bowing, falling on their knees, and making supplication (Ps 30:8–10; Mal 1:9). The gift of grace bestowed by God upon the worshiper may be rescue from an enemy (Ps 6:3), healing (Ps 41:4), forgiveness including deliverance from divine punishment (Neh 9:17, 31; Joel 2:13), or an act of justice (Amos 5:15). God's grace may even extend beyond the Israelite community to include an act of forgiveness toward the nations (Jonah 4:2).

Grace as a quality. Grace can indicate a charismatic quality, especially in God, and less commonly in humans. Grace as a quality possessed by a human is some feature of the person that is noteworthy or beyond what might be expected. Beauty in a woman may be a grace (Prov 5:19), which brings her honor (Prov 11:16). Eloquent and persuasive speech is a grace (Prov 22:11). The ability of the king to speak persuasively is described as a grace (Ps 45:2). The Preacher also states that the grace of eloquent speech is important for the ruling elite, "words spoken by the wise bring them favor" (Eccl 10:12). But grace in humans may also be dangerous. Eloquent speech can be deceptive: "when an enemy speaks graciously, do not believe it" (Prov 26:25). And the same is true with feminine beauty: "Charm (Hebrew, grace) is deceitful, and beauty is vain" (Prov 31:30). Even the charismatic allure of an entire culture can deceive. The prophet condemns Assyria, "because of the countless debaucheries of the prostitute, gracefully alluring, mistress of sorcery, who enslaves nations through her debaucheries, and peoples through her sorcery" (Nah 3:4).

The quality of grace is most often associated with God in the Hebrew Bible. In fact, only God is described as being "gracious" (*hanun*) in the Hebrew Bible. It is an attribute or quality of the deity indicating compassion (Exod 22:27) and goodness (Ps 86:16). The revelation and initial bestowing of divine grace occurs in a liturgical formula, first revealed to Moses after the sin of the golden calf (Exod 32). God wishes to destroy the Israelites for breach of covenant, but Moses successfully intercedes for the people on the basis of his own favor with God (Exod 33:12–23). God is persuaded to renew the covenant with the Israelites and calls Moses to the summit of the mountain to reissue the stone tablets, the legal document of the covenant. On the mountain God passes before Moses and reveals a new dimension of deity, proclaiming, "The LORD, the LORD, a God merciful and gracious, slow to anger (*patient*), and abounding in **steadfast love** and faithfulness" (Exod 34:6). The divine attributes overlap in meaning, aiding in the interpretation of grace. Divine grace embodies compassion and patience beyond the expectations of the covenant law, allowing the deity to forgive sin as an act of free will (v. 7). The priestly benediction in Num 6:24–26 adds further definition to the content of divine grace by linking it with the qualities of blessing and peace: "The LORD bless you and keep you; the LORD make his face to shine upon you, and be gracious to you; the LORD lift up his countenance upon you, and give you peace." Divine blessing is the source of health and well-being for humans. Peace is the utopian environment in creation and community that results from blessing. Grace is neither blessing nor peace. It is, rather, the divine quality that makes blessing and peace concrete within the community and world. Grace results from God turning God's face toward the Israelites.

In the New Testament

The LXX often translates the Hebrew *hen* (favor), *hanan* ("to be generous; to give grace"), and *hanun* ("gracious") with the Greek *charis*. In classical Greek, *charis* describes the quality of something that delights. It may be an object, such as wine, or the characteristic of a person, their speech, beauty, or intellect. *Charis* could also describe ethical acts of grace, such as benevolence to inferiors. According to Aristotle, the gods bestow *charis* on individuals, who in turn bestow the gift

on others by helping them (*Rhetoric* ii.7). *Charis*, moreover, is mutual and reciprocal. Acts of *charis* (grace) prompt thanks (*charis*) in the one receiving the gift. Both the act and the response of thanks are the same word, *charis*, in Greek. The NT writers in general also employ the term *charis* to convey the act of grace, qualities of grace, and thankfulness, but the term takes on special significance in the writings of the apostle Paul.

Grace as a gift. Grace as a gift is not a central term in the Gospels to describe the relationship between persons or between God and humans. It is absent in Mark and Matthew, and occurs only sparingly in Luke-Acts and John. The term is limited to the Prologue of John, where the gift of grace in the form of the incarnate Word derives from God. "And the Word became flesh and lived among us, and we have seen his glory, the glory as of a father's only son, full of grace and truth" (John 1:14). The result of God's gift of grace is that humans receive "grace upon grace" (John 1:16), meaning a new relationship with God as divine children (John 1:12–13). In the Gospel of Luke, God's special relationship with Mary (Luke 1:30) and with Jesus (Luke 2:40, 52) is also a gift of grace, which influences the relationship of Christians. The book of Acts states that "with great power the apostles gave their testimony to the resurrection of the Lord Jesus, and great grace was upon them all," meaning they were generous to the poor (Acts 4:33–34; see Prov 14:21, 31; 28:8). Grace as a divine gift that transforms relationships is developed further in 1 Peter, where it also states that God's gift of grace must be used in service for others (4:10).

The grace of God as gift is a central feature in the teaching of the apostle Paul. He repeatedly refers to his call as an act of divine grace. In Galatians, Paul states, "God, who had set me apart before I was born and called me through his grace, was pleased to reveal his Son to me" (Gal 1:15–16). "I am what I am, " declares Paul, "by the grace of God" (1 Cor 15:10). In Romans Paul provides theological reflection on how divine grace is a gift that creates a relationship between God and humans. Grace is the peace of God (see the Priestly Benediction in Num 6:22–24) made available to humans through Jesus Christ, "though whom we have obtained access to this grace in which we stand" (Rom 5:2). Humans now live in the grace of God. "For by grace you have been saved through faith, and this is not your own doing; it is the gift of God" (Eph 2:8). The grace of God in Christ has ethical implications for human relationships. Paul outlines for the Corinthians the ethics of grace. First, he anchors them in Christ: "For you know the generous act (grace) of our Lord Jesus Christ, that though he was rich, yet for your sakes he became poor, so that by his poverty you might become rich" (2 Cor 8:9). The grace of God in Christ replicates itself in humans. Thus Paul states his expectation that the Corinthian Christians will exhibit the same grace through acts of generosity to the needy (2 Cor 8:1–7). Such grace will call forth more generosity (*charis*) from God and thanksgiving (*charis*) to God from Paul (2 Cor 9:6–15).

Grace as a quality. The New Testament expands the role of grace as a quality in God and in humans. Grace finds its source in God, and it is uniquely God's to give. The quality of divine grace is evident in Jesus. The Prologue to John suggests this, when it states that the divine Word was enfleshed in Jesus (John 1:14–16). The incarnation embodies grace in a person, making Jesus the first human in a new age, in which grace is now abundantly available. Paul's analogy between Adam and Jesus provides illustration. Death reigned in the world through the sin of Adam, states Paul, but through Christ grace now rules the world (Rom 5:12–21). And the new age of Jesus is rich in grace, exceeding human expectations (Rom 5:15; Eph 2:7). Paul dispenses it freely in his greetings, "Grace to you and peace from God our Father and the Lord Jesus Christ" (Rom 1:7; 1 Cor 1:3; 2 Thess 1:12), and in his closing benedictions, "The grace of the Lord Jesus Christ, and the love of God, and the communion of the Holy Spirit be with all of you" (2 Cor 13:13; Rom 16:20; Gal 6:18; Phil 4:23; see the Priestly Benediction in Num 6:22–24).

The quality of grace in the new age surrounds humans and is also evident in them. Humans are saved through grace. The apostle Paul also describes the salvation of God as grace (Rom 3:24; Gal 2:17–21; see also Acts 20:32). Acts 18:27 describes the work of Apollos as greatly helping "those who through grace had become believers." And once saved, Christians must stand in grace (Rom 5:2), grow in grace (2 Pet 3:18), be strong in grace (2 Tim 2:1). They must guard themselves lest they fall from grace (Gal 5:4), fail to obtain grace (Heb 12:15), or even insult the Spirit of grace (Heb 10:29).

The quality of grace in humans is evident in special powers. Miracles, for example, are signs of the abundant quality of grace in the world. Acts 14:3 states that Paul and Barnabas "remained for a long time [in Iconium], speaking boldly for the Lord, who testified to the word of his grace by granting signs and wonders to be done through them." The apostle Paul further describes charismatic *gifts* of grace (*charisma* and *pneumatikos*) bestowed upon the Christian community in general and to individuals. Paul describes the nature and quality of the charismatic gifts of grace in 1 Cor 12. All Christians receive "spiritual gifts (*pneumatikos*)," according to Paul, "for in the one Spirit we were all baptized into one body—Jews or Greeks, slaves or free—and we were all made to drink of one Spirit" (1 Cor 12:13; see also Rom 15:27). But just as the body has different members, so individual Christians receive distinct gifts of grace (*charismata*), including apostleship, prophecy, teaching, healing, leadership, inspired interpretation, and speaking in tongues. Each "grace gift" is a manifestation of the one Spirit (1 Cor 12:7). The different gifts are intended to work in consort for the common good to build up the body of the community.

THOMAS B. DOZEMAN

Grave, Sheol, Pit, Hades, Gehenna, Abaddon, Hell (*see also* Death)

Several terms are used in the OT and NT for "the place of the dead," "the netherworld," or what has commonly been called "hell." Many of these biblical terms overlap in meaning, yet each carries its own particular nuance.

The grave. The common term for a grave or tomb in Hebrew is *qeber*, which appears repeatedly throughout the OT (or *qeburah* in Gen 35:20 and Ezek 32:23–24). In the NT the Greek terms *mnemeion* and *mnema* are widely used. Burial in family tombs, which were cut into exposed rock or in caves, was the normal practice. Because of Egyptian influence, Jacob was embalmed (Gen 50:2). Saul and his sons, however, were cremated by the people of Jabesh Gilead because their bodies had been mutilated by the Philistines (1 Sam 31:12). Even criminals were to be buried (Deut 21:22–23). To be left unburied and eaten by dogs was the terrible fate of Jeroboam I and Jezebel (1 Kgs 14:11; 21:23; cf. 2 Kgs 9:35).

Sheol. The most common word in the OT for the place of the dead is *she'ol*, which occurs sixty-five times—all but fifteen in poetical passages. The etymology of the word is disputed. Some argue it derives from a Hebrew noun meaning "hollow place"; others, from a Hebrew verb meaning "to be desolate"; and still others from an Assyrian verb that means "to sink." More likely it comes from the Hebrew verb "to ask" (*sha'al*) and connotes a place where only questions and uncertainty abound. The dead descend to Sheol, which was thought to be located somewhere below the earth (Ps 139:8; Isa 14:9).

Sheol was a place of darkness (Ps 143:3; Lam 3:6)—so dark that even its light was darkness (Job 10:22). It was a place of dismal silence (Pss 94:17; 115:17) to which all people were consigned (Ps 89:48) and would exist forever (Job 7:9–10; 16:22; Eccl 12:5–8). Its inhabitants were called "shades" (*repha'im*), who existed as shadowy and nonpersonal entities, whatever their previous status in life (Isa 14:9–11; 38:10–13). The term "shades" does not denote ghosts or spirits, as in Greek thought, but shadowy entities that reflected only a semblance of their former selves. Being bereft of all personality and strength, they merely existed in a monotonous underworld—without the powers associated with human life and apart from communion with God. They were, in fact, not even able to remember God or offer him praise (Pss 6:5; 115:17; Isa 38:18).

So we find the various laments of God's people recorded in the Hebrew Scriptures, as, for example, that of Job 10:20–22: "Are not the days of my life few? Let me alone, that I may find a little comfort before I go, never to return, to the land of gloom and deep darkness, the land of gloom and chaos, where light is like darkness."

Or the lament of Ps 88, where the writer cries out in verses 3–5 and 10–12: "My soul is full of troubles, and my life draws near to Sheol. I am counted among those who go down to the Pit; I am like those who have no help, like those forsaken among the dead, like the slain that lie in the grave, like those whom you remember no more, for they are cut off from your hand. . . . Do you work wonders for the dead? Do the shades rise up to praise you? Is your steadfast love declared in the grave, or your faithfulness in Abaddon? Are your wonders known in the darkness, or your saving help in the land of forgetfulness?"

Since in some OT passages (cf., e.g., Ps 88 quoted above) "Sheol" is used in parallel with "the grave" (*qeber*), it has been argued that Sheol should be understood as only a Semitic locution for the grave, and so translated (as in the KJV and NIV) simply "the grave" (cf. R. L. Harris, *JTS*). But in light of parallels with ancient Near Eastern concepts of the afterlife and the detailed portrayals of Sheol in the literature of Second Temple Judaism (cf. esp. *1 Enoch* 22:1–13; *2 Esd* 7:75–101), few scholars today find this position persuasive.

During the period of Second Temple Judaism, there were various developments in the Jewish understanding of Sheol. One such development had to do with Sheol as an intermediate state for the dead. For while the OT and the earlier Second Temple writings highlight the finality of Sheol, at least for the wicked (1 En. 94–104; Jub. 7:29; 22:22; 24:31), in later writings from this period Sheol is depicted as an intermediate state, with its rewards and punishments being only preliminary to the eternal bliss and final judgment to follow—both for the righteous and the wicked dead (1 En. 22:1–14; 2 Esd 7:75–101). Also, as influenced by the Greek concept of "the *immortality* of the soul," there arose during this time the idea that the souls of the righteous proceeded immediately to heaven at their deaths, there to await the resurrection of their bodies, while the souls of the wicked remained in Sheol (cf. Josephus, *War* 3.375).

During this period, in fact, there seem to have coexisted among the Jews two somewhat diverse understandings of Sheol: (1) that it was the habitation of both the wicked and the righteous dead, whether eternal or intermediate, who were separated into their respective compartments (1 En. 22:1–14; 51:1; 102:5; 103:7; 2 Macc 6:23; Josephus, *Antiquities* 18.14; *War* 2.163; 2 Esd 4:41; 7:32; 2 Bar. 11:6; 21:23); and (2) that it was the place of punishment, whether final or temporary, for only the wicked dead (1 En. 63:10; *Pss. of Sol.* 14:6; 15:11; Wis 2:1; 17:14, 21; Philo, *Som* ("Dreams") 1.151; Josephus, *War* 3.375; 2 En. 40:12–42:2).

The Pit. A synonym for *she'ol* is the Hebrew word *bor*, which appears sixty-five times in the OT and is usually translated "the Pit" (e.g., Isa 14:15; Ps 28:1). The word *shahath*, "corruption," is also used at times in synonymous fashion (Job 33:22). In Greek, the noun *phrear*, "bottomless pit," appears three times in Rev 9:1–3 as a synonym for Sheol or the Greek term *hades*.

The abode of the dead was viewed by the Hebrews as being dusty, for death is a return to the dirt. So the dead are portrayed as having descended into Sheol, which was a descent into "the dust" or "the Pit" (Job 17:16; 21:26). Correlating other images of Sheol that arose during the period of Second Temple Judaism, 2 Esd 7:36 contrasts "the Pit" or "place of torment" and "the furnace of Gehenna," on the one hand, with "the place of rest" and "the Paradise of delight," on the other. And Rev 9:2–3 speaks of smoke "like the smoke of a great furnace" arising from the "bottomless pit," which darkened the sky, polluted the air, and spawned locusts throughout the earth.

Hades. Hades is the Greek term (*hades*) for the netherworld and the name of the god of the netherworld. In the Septuagint it uniformly renders the Hebrew term *she'ol* (e.g., Job 38:17; Isa 14:11, 15; 28:15; 38:10). And it appears in this manner, together with all that is ascribed to Sheol, in all sorts of Jewish writings composed in Greek during the period of Second Temple Judaism (e.g., Philo, *Life of Moses* 1.195; Tob 3:10; Wis 16:13; 3 Macc 5:51; *Pss. Sol.* 16:2; Josephus, *War* 1.596; *Antiquities* 6.332).

In the NT it is the place of the dead, the netherworld (Matt 11:23 and par. Luke 10:15; 16:23; Acts 2:31; Rev 1:18). It is also the power expressed by that netherworld (Matt 16:18; Acts 2:24 [as in the Western text and many Latin Fathers]) and the personification of the evil of that netherworld (1 Cor 15:55 [as in some manuscripts]; Rev 6:8; 20:13–14).

Gehenna. The Greek name *Gehenna* derives from the Aramaic *Gehinnam* (b. *Erubin* 19a), which in turn derives from the Hebrew *Ge-Hinnom* or "Valley of Hinnom" (Josh 15:8; 18:16). The lower half of the Wadi er-Rababi, or Valley of Hinnom, which lies south of Jerusalem, acquired a very bad reputation because of the worship of Molech and the child sacrifices that took place on the high places of Topheth located there during the days of Ahaz and Manasseh (2 Kgs 16:3; 23:10; 2 Chr 28:3; 33:6). With Josiah's reforms, however, idolatry was suppressed (2 Chr 34:32–33), and the Valley of Hinnom became a garbage dump for the city of

Jerusalem. It was viewed as an appropriate place for the city's garbage, not only because of its location outside the city and the prevailing wind currents, but also because of its past history, which was poignantly brought to mind by its constantly smoldering fire that consumed its decaying contents. Jeremiah symbolically pronounced judgment over this corrupt ravine, calling it the "valley of Slaughter" (Jer 7:31–33; 19:6).

In the apocalyptic writings of Second Temple Judaism, the punishments and final judgment of the wicked dead are depicted in terms of the imagery of this sinister valley, with its contents of decay, corruption, and smoldering fire (*1 En.* 54:1–2; 108:3–6; *2 En.* 10:1–6). Sometimes Gehenna is identified with Sheol itself (*Pss. Sol.* 14:6; 15:11; 16:2; *1 En.* 54:1–2; 63:10); sometimes as a compartment of Sheol (*1 En.* 51:1 [Ethiop. mss. B and C]; 56:8; 90:26); and sometimes as a place of endless torment to which the wicked are consigned at the final judgment (*1 En.* 48:9; *2 Bar.* 85:12–13; *2 En.* 10:1–6). In some passages, however, no such distinctions are readily discernible (*1 En.* 108:3–6; *2 Esd* 7:36). Sometimes it is located in the middle of the earth (*1 En.* 26:1; 90:26); sometimes in heaven, whether a "third heaven" (as in *3 Bar.* 4:4–5) or a "northern heaven" (as in *2 En.* 10:1, Recension A); and sometimes its location is stated as being known only to God (2 Esd 4:7).

In the NT Gehenna is portrayed as an abyss of unquenchable and everlasting fire, to which the wicked who come under divine judgment at the last day will be consigned (Matt 5:22; 13:42, 50; 23:33; Mark 9:43). The ungodly are called children of Gehenna (Matt 23:15), who will dwell in the place prepared for Satan and his demons (Matt 25:41; Rev 19:20; 20:10, 14–15). There are, however, two rather clear distinctions made in the NT between Hades and Gehenna, as Joachim Jeremias (*TDNT* 1:658) has pointed out: (1) "Hades receives the ungodly only for the intervening period between death and resurrection, whereas Gehenna is

their place of punishment in the last judgment; the judgment of the former is thus provisional but the torment of the latter eternal (Mk. 9:43 and par.; 9:48)," and (2) "the souls of the ungodly are outside the body in Hades, whereas in Gehenna both body and soul, reunited at the resurrection, are destroyed by eternal fire (Mk. 9:43 and par., 45, 47 and par., 48; Mt. 10:28 and par.)."

Abaddon. Another synonym used in the OT for Sheol is the word *Abaddon,* which connotes "destruction." It is found only in Job 26:6; 28:22; 31:12; Ps 88:11; Prov 15:11, usually in parallel with Sheol or Death. It may be not only a term for netherworld but also the name of the king or angel guarding the abyss of Sheol or Gehenna. For that is how it is used in its one appearance in the NT, in Rev 9:11: "They [the destroying locusts] have as king over them the angel of the bottomless pit; his name in Hebrew is Abaddon, and in Greek he is called Apollyon."

Hell. "Hell" is our contemporary term for the netherworld, which arises from the Old High German and Old English verb *helan,* meaning "to conceal." It appears in many modern translations of the Bible for Sheol, Hades, and Gehenna.

R. L. Harris, "The Meaning of the Word Sheol as Shown by Parallels in Poetic Texts," *JTS* 4 (1961): 129–35; Joachim Jeremias, "*hades,*" *TDNT* 1:146–49; Joachim Jeremias, "*geenna,*" *TDNT* 1:657–58.

RICHARD N. LONGENECKER

Guilt, Guilty   *see* Sin

Hades   *see* Grave

Hallelujah   A Hebrew expression, used four times in the Greek NT (Rev 19:1, 3, 4, 6). It is composed of two words, "Praise!" (plural imperative) and the short form of the divine name Yahweh. (NRSV preserves the traditional spelling, -*jah,* although the correct pronunciation is *yah.*) The term occurs frequently in the Psalms, where English versions always

translate it as "Praise the LORD!" (e.g., Pss 111–13; 146–50). Revelation alludes to typical reasons for the praise of God in the OT: his sovereignty (Rev 19:6), his truth and justice (19:2), and his "salvation, glory, and power" (19:1). Compare Pss 111:7–9 and 113:4–5.

The *praise* of God in the worship of the Jerusalem temple frequently took the form of song (e.g., Pss 146:2; 149:1; 150; 2 Chr 29:30; Ezra 3:10–11). The use of the Hebrew word in music may explain why it became a fixed liturgical term even among Greek-speaking Jews, and then in the early church. The LXX transliterates it rather than translating, evidence for its use in worship. So the author of Revelation could use it in new hymns of triumph, assuming his readers understood it. Note that two Hebrew loan words that came into Christian worship appear together in Rev 19:4: "Amen. Hallelujah!" The oldest Greek mss. had no way of representing the *h*-sound, so the term was written *ALLELUIAH,* resulting in the mispronunciation frequently encountered today, especially in hymnody.

DONALD E. GOWAN

Hand of the Lord   *see* **God**

Hands   *see* **Laying on of Hands**

Hardening of the Heart   *see* **Mind**

Harmagedon   *see* **Armageddon**

Hate

The Hebrew verb *sane'* means "to hate." The noun *sina'* translates as "hatred." Another verb, *satam,* can also carry the meaning of "to hate" in the sense of "bearing a grudge" (Gen 50:15). The LXX translates the Hebrew *sane'* as *miseo,* which is also the word for hate in the NT. Hatred carries a range of meanings in the Bible to describe human relationships, the disposition of one human toward another, and the attitude of God toward unethical behavior and certain forms of worship.

The root meaning of "to hate" in the Hebrew Bible suggests a forced separation. The story of Abimelech and Isaac in Gen 26 provides an example. The chapter recounts the increased wealth of Isaac while a resident alien in the territory of King Abimelech. Abimelech is threatened by Isaac's change of status and drives him out of his territory, stating in v. 16, "Go away from us; you have become too powerful for us." But after Isaac resettles outside of the territory of Abimelech in Gerar, the king has a change of mind and offers to make a covenant with Isaac, prompting Isaac's response in v. 27, "Why have you come to me, seeing that you hate me and have sent me away from you?" The hatred of Abimelech toward Isaac certainly includes hostility (the king is threatened by Isaac's wealth and power), but the focus of Isaac's statement is the forced separation of having been sent out of Abimelech's land.

The root meaning of forced separation in the act of hating is developed in a number of different ways in the Hebrew Bible. Hatred as banishment from land and kindred continues. Jephthah is hated by his brothers and thus driven away (Judg 11:7). Hate is also used in the context of polygamous marriage. It describes the unequal love of a husband for one wife over another. Genesis 29:30–31 states that Jacob "loved Rachel more than Leah." Although the text does not state that Jacob hated Leah, she is described as the "hated one" (v. 33) because of Jacob's preference for Rachel. The meaning of "hate" in this story suggest less the hostile passion usually associated with hatred than the separation or distance between Jacob and Leah as a result of his preference for Rachel. Here as elsewhere it carries the sense of rejection in contrast to choice. Inheritance laws regulating polygamous marriages in Deut 21:15–17 use the same language of the "loved" and the "disliked" wife to describe the unequal affection of the husband.

Divorce laws in Deut 22:13–16 and 24:3 reinforce the meaning of hate as separation when they describe the act of divorce as a man's hatred toward his wife. But the focus of the law to protect the wife from slander indicates that the use of hatred to describe divorce includes hostile passion (see also the story of Samson's divorce in Judg 14–15). The story of Joseph and his brothers reinforces the hostile passion involved in hating. Genesis 37:4–8 begins by recalling the story of Rachel and Leah. The narrator states that Jacob loved Joseph more than his brothers. But the story moves in a different direction. The brothers are not described passively as the "hated ones" as was the case with Leah. Rather they become the subject of the action. They hate Joseph, which is defined more clearly as not being able to maintain peace with him. The laws pertaining to murder accentuate the hostility associated with hating. Deuteronomy 19:4–11 describes the unintentional killing of another human as lacking hate, as compared to premeditated murder, in which there is hate.

God also hates in the Hebrew Bible, indicating both hostile passion and separation from certain acts of worship and unethical behavior. God hates abhorrent things: child sacrifice (Deut 12:31), stone pillars (Deut 16:22), violence (Ps 11:5), and evildoers (Ps 5:5). The psalmist often identifies with God by hating the same forms of worship or evil persons (Pss 101:3; 139:22). The godly in general are also commanded to hate evil (Prov 8:13), but not to hate the members of their community (Lev 19:17). The perception that God hates Israel and that the act of salvation from Egypt was motivated by hate and destruction is so abhorrent to the deity that it can influence divine behavior. Thus Moses persuades God not to punish the Israelites in the wilderness with the argument that the other nations would say that their God hated them (Deut 9:28). Malachi's way of saying God chose Jacob rather than Esau was "I have loved Jacob but I have hated Esau" (Mal 1:2–3).

The NT characterizes the conflict against God in the world as hatred. Those who hate Jesus ("the light") are evildoers (John 3:20). They are ungrounded, living in unbelief (John 15:25) and darkness (1 John 2:9–11). In contrast to this, Jesus commands his disciples not to hate their enemies (Matt 5:43; Luke 6:27). But disciples are commanded in following Jesus to hate their families (Luke 14:26; Matt 10:37) and even their own life (John 12:25), that is, to make a choice in favor of him. The command recalls the use of hate in polygamous marriage (Deut 21:15–17), indicating unequal love.

Hate is attributed to God or Jesus in a number of texts. Jesus hates evil in general (Heb 1:9) and the immoral worship of the Nicolaitans at Ephesus (Rev 2:6). And the apostle Paul uses the contrast between *love* and hate from Mal 1:2–3 to describe divine election (Rom 9:13).

The NT writers idealize the hatred disciples experienced in a way that is not evident in the Hebrew Bible. Jesus in Luke 6:22 commends his disciples for being hated: "Blessed are you when people hate you, and when they exclude you, revile you, and defame you on account of the Son of Man." When disciples are hated on account of their faith in Jesus, they participate in the passion of Jesus, according to Mark 13:13. And the hatred of the world toward the disciples of Jesus even has eschatological significance. According to Matt 10:16–23, that disciples will be hated is a sign of the end time.

THOMAS B. DOZEMAN

Heal, Health, Ill, Illness, Sick, Sickness

In contemporary societies such as the United States, average citizens possess an incredible amount of knowledge about health, sickness, and related questions. Newspapers, magazines, and television regularly report scientific breakthroughs in the field of medicine, using technical, scientific language. Pharmaceutical companies run full-page advertisements in popular magazines for new medicines to treat allergies, high blood pressure, cholesterol, and many other ailments. These advertisements contain the same technical information used by physicians and pharmacists. While such knowledge among ordinary lay people is important and impressive, it leaves the mistaken impression that scientific perspectives are the only way to interpret health and sickness concerns in all places and at all times, whether in antiquity or the present. An important lesson was learned and perhaps too soon forgotten in the West, particularly in the United States after World War II. Efforts to spread the benefits of Western medicine to other cultures at that time met with disinterest, resistance, and outright rejection. Gradually practitioners realized how deeply ethnocentric and biomedically reductionistic was the medical science they were enthusiastically and diligently attempting to share. They also began to appreciate how other cultures address the universal human issues of health and sickness. This experience contributed to the development of a new anthropological subdiscipline: medical anthropology. Because reading the Bible is a challenge in cross-cultural communication, understanding, and interpretation, basic definitions from this cross-cultural discipline can be very helpful in understanding what the authors of Scripture wrote and what they intended to express.

From a cross-cultural point of view, the "normal" human condition is called well-being. That is the kind of answer anyone gives in any language and in any culture to the question: "How are you?" Typically the response will be "fine," "well," "o.k.," or some culturally colloquial equivalent (e.g., in colloquial Polish: *wszystko w porzadku*, "everything is in order"). Health is just one element of well-being. In the West, having a job, a family, a home, and much more are also part of well-being. The loss of well-being is a misfortune of which there exists a wide variety: failing a course in school, losing a job, declaring bankruptcy, getting a divorce, losing a loved one to substance abuse or death, losing one's health, and so forth. The misfortunes are real, and the description of them is frequently itself an interpretation or a metaphor.

Medical anthropologists have refined a vocabulary for interpreting the loss of one's health. Two key words describe the loss, each from a different perspective; for this reason, they are not realities but rather explanatory concepts. (1) The explanatory concept "disease" adopts a scientific, Western, biomedical perspective of the event. It describes departures from the "normal" in the structure and/or functions of human organs and organ systems. A disease may well be present even if a given culture does not recognize it as a disease. The majority of one South American tribe clearly suffers from a facial skin problem, yet these are considered "normal and healthy" in contrast to the minority with clear and normal skin, who are considered sick. When faced with a disease, biomedicine first seeks to correlate constellations of signs and symptoms for the purpose of explaining, predicting, and controlling the condition. Technically, this is called diagnosis, prognosis, and therapy. (2) The explanatory concept "illness" adopts a sociocultural perspective and accordingly labels the *human* and cultural (not biomedical) perceptions, experience, and interpretation of certain socially disvalued states, including but not limited to "disease." Illness represents the personal and social interpretation of sickness (the reality). In addition to the individual, his or her entire social network is afflicted and involved. Illness is largely a cultural construct: culture dictates what to perceive, value, and express, and then how to live with the illness. Metropolitan Opera star Denyce Graves took a German colleague to her Pentecostal church. The visitor was baffled when some members of the congregation began "falling out." In African American and related cultures, "falling out" is a phenomenon that biomedicine might diagnosis as a fainting spell. While "fainting" might be part of that reality, the explanatory concept "falling out" includes and describes much more. Further, "falling out" is not a sickness at all!

Biomedicine seeks to identify the single cause of the disease so that it might search for the single remedy or "cure" that can destroy the cause or help regain effective control over disordered biomedical and/or psychological processes. Cure is also an explanatory concept. Science admits that cures are relatively rare. Cancer patients must be in remission for five years before the oncologist will use the word "cure." In contrast, "healing" is an explanatory concept describing a strategy or process directed toward illness in order to provide personal and social meaning for the life problems caused by sickness, whether it be a disease or an illness. Healing is social and communal. The therapist interacts with and affects the community as well as the sick person. Anthropologists admit that healing in any culture is as basic as the gift relationship or the exchange relationship. Healing is one of the primary forms of symbolic action (see the Gospel of John, below). It occurs more often than cure, because the sick person may eventually come to grips with the sickness and discover or create new meaning in life. Others might not agree with that meaning, but the answer selected by the sick person is meaningful to her/him.

Reading the Bible with these definitions in mind (sickness, disease, illness, curing, healing) helps a reader to avoid imposing contemporary biomedical interpretations on the ancient Mediterranean text. This is a distinct form of ethnocentrism at its worst: medicocentrism. Further, the definitions help a reader to make respectful sense of the Bible where translations might actually be confusing the problem. The NRSV note on Naaman, who "suffered from leprosy" (2 Kgs 5:1–14), explains leprosy as "a term for several skin diseases; precise meaning uncertain" (v. 1 Mg). Not only is the reality described by that Hebrew word uncertain, but it is also uncertain whether this was a "disease" at all! Since paleopathologists have not yet discovered any bones in Israel with evidence of true leprosy (Hansen's disease), his condition was probably not leprosy and may not even have been a disease in the modern understanding of this word.

A related and equally important question is, did Elijah "cure" Naaman? Did anyone in the Bible "cure" anyone? Without scientific evidence to support that judgment, it is best to admit that we have no way of knowing. One cannot deny that physical amelioration may indeed have occurred, but one cannot prove it or say exactly what it was. Those, however, who wanted to be healed (to find meaning in life) certainly were healed (Matt 13:58). Certainly Naaman did, and was.

Finally, ancient Israelite culture, like all peasant cultures, believed that no human being could master or control nature. One could only "suffer" it or try to live in harmony with it. Any person who seemed capable of controlling nature was extraordinary (e.g., Matt 8:27; 14:26). No one would deny what happened. The question is how did it happen: "By what *authority* [or power] are you doing these things, and who gave you this authority [or power]?" (Matt 21:23).

Old Testament. Since in the biblical world only God has power over all creation, God is the source of sickness and healing (Exod 15:26), life and death (2 Kgs 5:7). Even though Satan afflicts Job in his well-being, including his health, that happens only by God's permission (Job 1:12; 2:6–7; God restores total well-being in 42:10). Sometimes prophets are associated with God in healing (1 Kgs 14:1–13; 17:18–24; 2 Kgs 4:22–37; 8:9–10; Isa 38:1), but God is the healer (2 Kgs 5:15). The prophet is simply the broker, God's instrument. Prayer was the primary vehicle people used for seeking healing from God (Num 12:13; 1 Kgs 17:21; Isa 38:3; Jer 17:14).

Loss of well-being or "wholeness" included wounds (Isa 53:5), which could be severe (Jer 10:19) or even incurable (Jer 15:18) and quite extensive (Isa 1:6, which also indicates remedies for wounds). Broken bones (fractures: Ps 34:20; Ps 37:17; Ezek 29:7, etc.) were treated by binding in a splint (Ezek 30:21). Often broken bones are a metaphor describing the destruction of an enemy's power or might (Jer 48:25). Deformities in an Israelite precluded participation in worship (Lev 21:18–20), because lack of physical integrity or wholeness was considered offensive to God's holiness and wholeness (Lev 21:16–24). Nevertheless people who suffered physical deformities or handicaps were not necessarily considered as cursed by God or punished for the sins of ancestors. To the contrary, recent research indicates that they were frequently considered blessed and channels of divine blessing to others. They were protected by the Torah (Lev 19:14; Deut 27:18).

It is possible that the Israelites were familiar with contagious diseases, though it is impossible to identify from symptoms reported exactly what these were. Experts hypothesize that only some contagious health problem can explain the sudden or quick death of large numbers of people. For example, while laying siege to Jerusalem, King Sennacherib of Assyria found 185,000 of his soldiers dead one morning. The Deuteronomic Historian explains that they were slain by an angel of the lord (2 Kgs 19:35). Exegetes recognize that the number is surely exaggerated and that the total report itself is contrary to plausible historical reconstruction of the event. But some significant loss of military personnel probably did occur, and it may well have been the consequences of some sanitation (in modern terms, "public health") problem, namely, a rapidly spreading contagious and fatal condition.

We must not lose sight of the obvious theological interpretation of this and other events reported in the Bible. That perspective is always uppermost in the minds of the authors of Scripture. In the case of Sennacherib's army, the foremost concern is God's redeeming activity, rather than the fact of or reason behind the sudden demise of that military force. This is also true in the case of so-called leprosy in Bible. In the most extended discussion of this problem (Lev 13–14), the Hebrew Bible's description of what is translated "leprosy" simply is not Hansen's disease. None of the symptoms reported is representative. No traces of leprosy have been found in extant bones

analyzed. Scholars argue that Hansen's disease was unknown and perhaps nonexistent in biblical lands. Closer examination of the text, however, reveals the real concern prompted by this serious skin disorder (preferable to "disease"). Those who suffer this problem are declared unclean and are ejected from the clean or holy community (Lev 13:46). For a collectivistic person to be cast out of the community from which his/her identity derives and upon which his/her survival depends is the equivalent of a death sentence. It is similar if not equivalent to the modern experience of suffering from a fatal and irremediable disease. People can and have actually died from the experience, even in the absence of any fatal disease. The concern for God's chosen community and its individual members was to be *holy*, as the Lord is holy (Lev 11:44–45; 19:2; 20:26; 21:18; etc.). Individual members of the community suffering from this skin problem were unclean (see *clean*). It was their uncleanness that could be spread, not necessarily their physical condition. (Even real leprosy, Hansen's disease, is minimally contagious and takes ten years to incubate after infection.) The concern was not contagion but rather pollution. The fear was not of "catching" a physical problem but of becoming unclean, unholy, and therefore unfit for further association with the holy community.

To be unclean is to be "dirty," and dirt by definition is matter out of its proper place. Boundaries determine the proper place. "Here" it is dirt; "there," across this boundary, is where it belongs. Just as the holy community needs to protect inviolable boundaries (unclean or unholy people should not be present), the individual member needs to maintain his or her boundary (the skin of the human body) inviolable. Nothing "dirty" should enter the human body through any orifice, natural or unusual, like a wound penetrating the skin. Anthropologist Mary Douglas observed that there the human body replicates the social body, and vice versa. Threats to the one boundary (skin of the human body) are also threats to the other (the integrity of the social body). In her analysis of Lev 13–14, she pointed out the significance of the concerns for skin, clothing, and walls of the house. These represent a series of boundaries, each one of which in its turn seeks to safeguard the next one and ultimately the integrity of the individual. The issue of biblical leprosy and its amelioration is perhaps the clearest illustration of healing in the Bible. Declaring an afflicted person clean and allowing that person to rejoin the holy community most certainly restores meaning to that person's life. That is what healing by definition accomplishes.

New Testament. Like the OT, the NT does not provide sufficient information for a reader to identify the health problems, their causes, their remedies, or even exactly how therapies worked. Even when the English words are familiar (blind, leper, paralytic), the reader does not know the social system realities to which these words refer. Hence it is impossible to tell whether the words accurately render the cultural meaning of the original Hebrew or Greek words or are an interpretation of them. Matthew describes one category of people whom Jesus healed literally as "moonstruck" (4:24; 17:14–18). English versions report "epileptic" (NRSV) or "lunatic." The former is an anachronistic "scientific" interpretation. The latter is closer to the native understanding, since the ancients believed that the moon was a living being that could exert a deleterious effect on human beings (Ps 121:6). Indeed some worshiped the moon as a deity (Job 31:26–27). That Jesus could help these people demonstrated that he did not consider the moon to be a deity and that he was immune to and even stronger than the moon's power.

A currently popular hypothesis among medicocentric researchers is that the majority of, if not all, the health problems in the NT can be described as conversion or somatiform disorders. This is technical jargon that describes the "presence of symptoms or deficits affecting voluntary motor or sensory function that suggest a neurological or other general medical condition." In other words, ailments of the people who approached Jesus (and others) for help were in reality a pattern of illness reproduced by them in order to escape from some unpleasant or demanding situation. While this explanation might make plausible, contemporary, Western sense, it does not reflect the ancient understanding. True enough, to this day circum-Mediterranean cultures in general are not only nonintrospective but anti-introspective (see 1 Sam 16:7). People in such cultures will normally tend to somatize their fears, concerns, or other mental states. But they did not perceive human beings in this fashion; hence to impose such an interpretation on their reports is to misunderstand and misrepresent them. The explanatory concept "conversion disorder" serves no useful purpose for interpreting the reports in the Bible. It is not biomedicine but medical anthropology that helps us keep the key question in mind: how did sick and possessed people presented in New Testament reports lose meaning in life? By what means was that meaning restored?

Mark presents Jesus as a "holy man," who teaches and heals (1:21–27; 2:11; 4:1; 5:2–20, 30). Who would be better qualified than a teacher to help rediscover meaning in life? At the outset of his career, the teaching of Jesus impresses those in the synagogue (1:22). Immediately he frees a possessed person from an unclean spirit (1:25–26) and dispels the fever of Simon's mother-in-law (1:30–31). This scenario concludes with the first of six statements that capture the heart of Jesus' ministry: he heals the sick and casts out demons (1:32–34; see also 1:30; 3:10–11; 6:5, 7–13, 56). Here is someone not only keenly intent on restoring meaning to people's lives but capable of doing so effectively.

The illnesses Jesus heals in Mark include a fever (1:29–31); a serious skin condition (1:40–45); inability to walk (2:1–12); nonfunctioning ("withered") hands (3:1–6); death (5:21–24, 35–43); acute menstrual irregularity (5:25–34); hearing loss or defective hearing and speech impediment (7:31–37); and sight loss or serious eye problems (8:22–26; 10:46–52).

It is nearly impossible to determine with certitude what each of these illnesses was to contemporary scientific satisfaction, because the descriptions are sometimes no more than a single word or verse. On the other hand, no one in any report ever denied what happened: an afflicted ("unclean") person was restored to wholeness. This restoration permitted that person to resume full membership and participation in God's holy ("clean") community. The ensuing discussion between Jesus and his opponents invariably centered on the source of his power for effecting such changes. Since the result was beyond normal human ability, the power must derive from some other person, either demonic or divine (Mark 3:20–30 and par. Matt 12:22–37). The ancients had no concept of significant impersonal causality. Jesus' power did not come from a demonic source. It is clearly stronger than demonic power.

Matthew also presents Jesus as teacher (Matt 5–7) and follows this immediately with a cluster of ten mighty deeds (Matt 8–9). In addition to healing and exorcism stories, the cluster includes Jesus' calming of a storm while at sea with his disciples (8:23–27; Mark 4:36–41; Luke 8:22–24). Matthew's complete picture of Jesus shows one who wields extraordinary power over nature in many dimensions. This is most unusual in ancient culture. Jesus however is perceived by others and presented by the evangelists as a "holy man" (Mark 1:24) after the pattern and tradition common to holy men in all the world's cultures, typically called shamans by anthropologists. Because of ready access to the divine realm, Jesus participates in that divine power and mediates well-being for fellow human beings in need. (The passive voice in these deeds—called the theological or divine passive—points to God as the real agent with Jesus as the channel, intermediary, or broker.)

In Luke's presentation of Jesus as healer (the Gospel and Acts of the Apostles), blindness plays a central role. The *inclusio* constituted by citations from Isaiah (61:1, 2; 6:9–10) in Luke 4:18–19 and Acts 28:26–27 highlights blindness as focal. Though Jesus says of himself, "the blind receive their sight" (Luke 7:22), Luke reports only one healing of a blind person (Luke 18:35–43). His two-volume work makes it clear that while physical restoration of sight was welcome, of much greater importance was it to see, understand, and interpret what one sees, especially concerning the person and deeds of Jesus (Luke 10:21–24; contrast Luke 11:29–32). Indeed, given the resistance Jesus experienced, it was easier for a physically blind person than for sighted persons to truly understand Jesus and his works (Luke 18:35–43). Luke develops this theme further in Acts but sadly concludes that many still do not see, understand, believe (Acts 28:24). This is Luke's picture of Jesus as an authorized, Spirit-filled prophet who vanquished unclean spirits and illnesses associated with them (Luke 7:16; 9:8, 19; 24:19), but also all misfortunes.

John's Gospel requires special attention and careful interpretation because it is a document produced by an antisociety in its antilanguage. An antisociety is one that is set up within another as a conscious alternative. It is a type of resistance that can express itself as passive symbiosis or as active hostility and destruction. The purpose of its distinctive antilanguage characterized by overlexicalization is to bond members closer together and befuddle outsiders. John reports only three healings: a boy healed at a distance (4:46–54), a man crippled for thirty-eight years (5:1–20), and a man born blind (9:1–41). In each instance, Jesus' healing restores meaning to the sick person's life.

The case of the man born blind (9:1–41) yields important insight when interpreted with the aid of a medical anthropological model of symbolic healing. People interpret reality within their cultural contexts, and the interpretation is largely metaphorical but identified with the realities they interpret. Westerners tend to adopt military imagery. They wage war against disease, poverty, terrorism, and other misfortunes. Middle Easterners adopt a different view. But in all cases, experts agree that the metaphorical structure of a culture is as decisive in healing as physiological or pharmacological elements.

As a first step in symbolic healing, Jesus builds a symbolic bridge to link the blind man's experience, his social relations (family, neighbors, Pharisees), and cultural meanings (sin, *light*, life). The dialogue in this story builds the bridge. This blindness is not the result of anyone's sin (v. 3). Light, a key symbol in John, is central. Light in creation didn't need the sun to exist. Light in the human person is alive, deriving from the heart and emerging from the eyes in the seeing process. A blind person is filled with darkness and needs light to become whole again.

In the next step, Jesus links the blind person to this mythic world through the dialogue. Jesus is the Light of the world whose works give life (John 4:46–54; 6:1–14; 11:1–44) and restore meaning to life (John 2:1–12; 5:1–20; 6:16–21; 9). After putting mud on the man's eyes, Jesus sends him to the pool of Siloam. The next time they meet, the man professes loyalty to Jesus ("Lord, I believe!" 9:38). The man has accepted the connections made by Jesus in the mythic world. This is evident in his dialogues with Jesus, just as Jesus' discussion with the parents, neighbors, Pharisees, and hostile Judeans indicates that some have accepted while others have rejected these connections.

Finally, Jesus uses spittle and mud as a transactional symbol that guides the blind man's emotional reactions. Jesus generalizes the man's blindness (which is a personal experience equivalent to death) into a therapeutic meaning system (living light). The blind man particularizes this symbolic meaning into his own life: Jesus, the Light of the world, gives sight, life, and insight to him. The healing

is effective because all participants in the process share the mutual expectations that shape, name, and remedy the illness—blindness. Setting aside scientific understanding helps a reader understand the Bible on its own terms and helps its theology to stand out more clearly.

As for early Jesus groups, Paul notes that healing was one of the *charismata* (*favors*) bestowed on some members by God through the Spirit present in the churches (1 Cor 12:9). James too speaks of Jesus-group healings using means widely familiar in antiquity: anointing and transferring healing power through touch (James 5:14–16).

D. C. Duling, "The Therapeutic Son of David: An Element in Matthew's Christological Apologetic," NTS 24 (1978): 392–410; John J. Pilch, *Healing in the New Testament: Insights from Medical and Mediterranean Anthropology* (Minneapolis: Fortress Press, 2000); John J. Pilch, "Improving Bible Translations: The Example of Sickness and Healing," BTB 30 (2000): 129–34; Harold Remus, *Jesus as Healer* (Cambridge: Cambridge University Press, 1997); K. Seybold and U. B. Mueller, *Sickness and Healing* (Nashville: Abingdon Press, 1981).

JOHN J. PILCH

Hear, Ear, Voice of the Lord   The human ear and the capacity to hear are gifts of God's creation (Ps 94:9; Prov 20:12; Sir 17:6). Their restoration to those who have lost them marks the return of God's favor to his people (Isa 35:5) and, in the NT, the power and grace of Jesus' mission (Luke 7:22; 22:50–51). Important as the gift of hearing may be, however, the Bible places much more emphasis on *proper* human hearing. It also has much to say about what *God* hears—and refuses to hear.

Proper human hearing includes that given to the cries of the needy; people who close their ears to such cries can expect to have their own cries for help ignored (Prov 21:13). Conversely, it is characteristic of the righteous that they refuse to hear (or take part in) the plots of the wicked (Isa 33:15). Part of the point of inflicting punishment on wrongdoers is that others may hear and take warning (Deut 13:11; 17:13; 19:20; Acts 5:5). Reports of what the Lord has done are to be passed on so that each new generation may hear them with their own ears and celebrate his goodness (Pss 44:1; 78:3–4). Even those who do not belong to his people may hear of the Lord's greatness and come to acknowledge him (Exod 18:1, 8–12; 1 Kgs 8:41–42).

Most important, people need to hear—and heed—the word of God. To Job in his suffering, God seemed distant, and all he had heard of God was but a "whisper" (Job 26:14); later, however, he himself heard God speak to him "out of the whirlwind" (38:1; 42:4). The people of Israel saw no form when they encountered the Lord at Mount Sinai; but they heard a voice that declared to them God's commandments (Deut 4:12–13). Throughout the biblical text, God commands human attention by *speaking* what people must *hear*.

In some texts, God speaks to people directly in an audible voice, as to Job and to Israel when he gave the Ten Commandments (Deut 5:22, following 5:6–21; see also Num 7:89; 1 Sam 3:10; Isa 6:8; 30:21; Acts 10:13). The people of Israel responded (not unlike Job) in terror: "If we hear the voice of the LORD our God any longer, we shall die" (Deut 5:25). They asked that henceforth Moses would receive and pass on God's messages rather than that they should hear God's voice themselves (5:27). This was agreed to (5:31). Moses' intermediary role is seen as the model for that of Israel's prophets (18:15–19). God's *word* was pictured as spoken directly in the prophets' "ears"; they were to pass it on (Isa 22:14; 50:4–5; Ezek 3:10–11, 17), and their listeners were to heed what the prophet said as they would heed the very word of God (Deut 18:19). When God's commandments in the law and his word through the prophets were recorded, then the reading of these texts was to be heard carefully (Deut 31:10–12; Neh 8:3; see also Rev 1:3).

In Proverbs, the "wise" invite their "children" to "hear" their words and to be attentive to their teaching, or to "wisdom" and "understanding" in general (2:1–2; 4:20; 5:1; etc.). Encouragement is frequently given to "hear" (that is, heed) wholesome admonitions and rebukes (15:31; 25:12; see also Eccl 7:5). Though the words and rebukes of the wise are not designated the "word of the Lord," they do summon their hearers to a life in pursuit of true wisdom—the wisdom by which the universe itself was made (Prov 3:19–20; 8:22–36). The life of *wisdom* is thus a life that conforms to God the Creator's purposes and is pleasing to God (8:35).

In the NT, the ears of Jesus' followers are said to be blessed inasmuch as they heard the message of the inbreaking kingdom of God, a message that God's people earlier had longed to hear (Matt 13:16–17). But heavy responsibility came with the hearing of Jesus' words: to those willing to hear and receive what Jesus said, more would be given; but those who would not hear it would lose whatever insight they already possessed (Mark 4:24–25). Jesus repeatedly urged those with "ears" to "hear" (and heed) what he said (Mark 4:9, 23, etc.; the same appeal accompanies the letters to the churches in the book of Revelation [2:7, 11, etc.]). He identified as his (spiritual) kin those who hear God's word and do it and pronounced his blessing on them (Luke 8:21; 11:28). When John's Gospel speaks of the "dead" who "hear the voice of the Son of God" and come to life (5:25), the statement is true on three levels: it anticipates the physical raising of Lazarus at Jesus' command (11:1–44); it points to the end-time resurrection, at the voice of God's Son, of all who have died—some to life, others to condemnation (5:28–29); but it also indicates that even now the spiritually dead who hear Jesus' word and believe will find life (5:24). Faith in the early Christian gospel necessarily presupposed the hearing of its proclamation (Acts 4:4; Rom 10:17; 1 Thess 2:13); those who had themselves heard the word of life now declared it for others (1 John 1:1–3).

At times references in the Bible to "hearing" include the idea of heeding and obeying what is said; at other times "hearing" God's word is sharply contrasted with "doing" or "obeying" it, and warnings are directed at those who only "hear" (Ezek 33:30–32; Matt 7:24–27; Rom 2:13; Jas 1:22–25). NRSV largely avoids the ambiguity by translating the Hebrew verb *shamaᶜ* and the Greek *akouo* as "hear" when the words mean *merely* "hear," but as "listen" or even "obey" (Exod 19:5; Jer 7:23–24) when they mean more. Note, for example, that the same Hebrew word is rendered "hear" in Ps 81:8a, but "listen" in 81:8b, 11, 13; and the same Greek word is translated both "hear" and "listen" in Mark 4:9: "Let anyone with ears to hear listen!" As a result, a failure to heed the word of God may at times be spoken of as a failure to "hear" it (i.e., heed and obey; Deut 30:17), whereas at other times it will be referred to as *mere* "hearing" without understanding or obeying (Matt 13:13). A common play on the two senses in which the word is used speaks of those who "hear" but do not (*really*) "hear" (NRSV "listen," Matt 13:13); alternatively, such people may be said to have "ears" but not to "hear" (Jer 5:21; Ezek 12:2; see also Isa 42:20; 43:8), or even to have "uncircumcised" ears (Jer 6:10, NRSV Mg; Acts 7:51). Israel is characteristically portrayed in these terms; its refusal to listen to the voice of the Lord or the word of his servants is frequently lamented (Deut 8:20; Josh 5:6; 2 Kgs 18:12; Ps 106:25; Jer 3:25; 7:28; 25:4; 35:15; Zech 7:11–12). At times, Israel's obtuseness is itself attributed to divine judgment (Isa 6:10; see also Deut 29:4); elsewhere a day is foreseen when God's favor will return to Israel and his people will be enabled to (truly) "hear" (Isa 32:3; Bar 2:31). In the meantime, the prophetic word must be spoken— whether or not people are inclined to hear it (Ezek 2:5, 7; 3:11, 27).

Though other nations worship false gods and idols that cannot hear their prayers (Deut 4:28; Pss 115:6; 135:17; Wis 15:15), the Lord's "ear" is said to be "open" to the cries of the righteous and the needy (Pss 10:17–18; 34:15; Sir 21:5). Many prayers in the Bible begin with a request that God will "incline" his ear, or let his ear "be attentive" to his servants' pleas (2 Kgs 19:16; Neh 1:6; Ps 5:1, etc.; see also Lam 3:56). Many prayers of thanksgiving express gratitude that God has so "inclined" his ear and listened, and has granted requests that were made (Pss 18:6; 40:1; 116:1–2). He heard the groaning of his oppressed people in Egypt and acted to deliver them (Exod 2:24; 3:7; see also Gen 21:17; 29:33). At times God is requested to act because of the justice of the petitioner's cause or in light of the petitioner's trust in God (Pss 17:1; 86:1–3). Often the appeal is based on God's own righteousness, faithfulness, or mercy (Pss 71:2; 143:1; Dan 9:18). Since God knows what his children need before they even ask him, they are not to imagine that God hears them because they "heap up empty phrases" in their prayers (Matt 6:7–8; see also Isa 65:24); those who ask according to his will may be assured that he will hear them (1 John 5:14). On the other hand, the Lord hears his people's complaining (Exod 16:8; Num 11:1), unbelief (Deut 1:32–34), and rebellion (Ps 78:17–22, 56–59) as well; none is to imagine that the God who made the ear is himself unaware of what they do (Ps 94:4–9; also 1 Kgs 19:28; Ps 59:7; Jas 5:4). Though his "ear" is never "too dull to hear," the sins of those who pray may keep God from heeding their prayers (Isa 59:1–2; also Job 27:8–9; 35:12–13). Indeed, he refused even to hear the prayers of Jeremiah on behalf of his sinful compatriots (Jer 7:16; 14:11–12).

STEPHEN WESTERHOLM

Heart *see* **Mind**

Heaven(s), Dome/Firmament, Paradise

The term "heaven(s)" (Heb. pl. *shamayim*; Gk. *ouranos*) denotes: a physical component of the cosmos, the dwelling place of God and, in apocryphal, pseudepigraphical, and NT literature, the abode of the righteous dead

(= paradise). Heaven is also referred to as "height" (Ps 148:1; Rom 8:39), "on high" (Ps 92:8; Luke 1:78), and "high(est) heaven" (1 Kgs 8:27; Sir 16:18; Luke 19:38). The last (and the plural "heavens") may have led post-OT interpreters to claim that heaven had multiple levels, most commonly seven (cf. "third heaven" in 2 Cor 12:2–4, identified with "paradise"). The phrase "heaven and earth" refers to the entire universe that God has created (Gen 1:1; Acts 17:24). Both heaven and earth are thus creatures of God and together they refer to the cosmos as a unity in which everything has its proper place and function. At the same time, this phrase testifies to a bipartite structure, two realms, within this unified created order (see Ps 135:6).

Heaven as sky. In its literal usage, heaven is named "Sky" in Gen 1:8, where it is identified with the "dome" (*raqia^c*; Gen 1:6–20; also called "firmament" in Pss 19:1; 150:1), the solid (Job 37:18) canopy that God created to separate the waters above from those beneath (seas). Windows for the flow of precipitation (and wind), stored above the dome (Job 38:22; Jer 10:13), are built into the expanse (Gen 7:11; 8:2). The dome was supported by pillars, anchored deep within the earth (Job 26:11; 2 Sam 22:8). Lights are placed "in" the dome to give light (Gen 1:14–17).

The splendor of the heaven/firmament is revealing of the artistry of the Creator (Pss 19:1; 50:6; 97:6). Heaven is called upon to praise the Lord (Ps 148:4), understood as its functioning in the way that God intended in its creation. The heaven may also be the "bulletin board" for "signs and wonders" (Dan 6:27) from God, including the rainbow and various meteorological phenomena (Gen 9:12–17; Luke 21:11, 25), probably understood in hyperbolic terms (Acts 2:19–20).

Human wickedness may have negative effects upon the environment, including heaven. These effects are seen especially in prophetic announcements of judgment (Isa 13:10–13; 34:4; Jer 3:3; 4:23; Ezek 32:7–8). God's judgmental activity does not introduce anything new (that is, a penalty) but mediates the natural effects of human sinfulness. The NT uses this language to portray judgments associated with the Parousia (Mark 13:24–26; Rev 6:12–14; 8:12). In the context of those cataclysmic events, the creation of a new heaven and earth is promised (Isa 65:17; 66:22). This is an act of renewal, not the replacement of one cosmos by another (cf. Pss 78:69; 93:1; Jer 31:35–36). While a few texts may imply the latter (Isa 34:4; 51:6; 2 Pet 3:10; Rev 21:1), they probably refer to a purging of the universe from all the effects of human wickedness.

Heaven as divine dwelling place. For both testaments, heaven is God's dwelling place (Ps 103:19; Matt 6:9; 23:9), but God is not alone in heaven; it is also the abode of the angelic hosts (I Kgs 22:19; Matt 18:10; see **hosts**). In creating heaven, God builds God's own abode into the structures of the created order (Ps 104:1–3). Heaven thus becomes a shorthand way of referring to God's dwelling place *within the world.* From this "lofty abode" God looks down, hears, and speaks (Exod 20:22; Ps 102:19; Jer 25:30), though suffering persons may wonder whether God has ceased doing so (Lam 3:44; Isa 64:1–3). God is commonly said to come/go down from God's own realm to earth (Gen 11:5–7), but this is a movement *from within* the created order, not from outside the world. God, who is *other than world,* has made this world God's own home. In God's own words, "Heaven is my throne and the earth is my footstool" (Isa 66:1). Yes, "heaven and the highest heaven cannot contain" God (1 Kgs 8:27), but this probably coheres with Jer 23:23–24: God is both near and far, filling heaven and earth. That is, no *specific place* within the world, including God's own heavenly abode, has the capacity to contain God.

At the same time, the distinction between heaven and earth is important. "The heavens are the LORD's heavens, but the earth he has given to human beings" (Ps 115:16). God can be said to dwell on earth in divinely chosen spaces, including tabernacle, temple, Zion, and the church and its individual members (Exod 29:45–46; 1 Kgs 8:12–13; Ps 74:2; 1 Cor 3:16; Eph 2:22). But heaven is God's own realm, and therein God's presence is especially intense and unmediated; indeed God's will is done in heaven in a way that cannot be said of the earth (Matt 6:10). Heaven is unreachable by human beings, though exceptions are made, at least in vision (1 Kgs 22:19; Isa 6; Ezek 1; 1 Cor 12:2–3). But unreachability does not entail unaffectability. Heaven and its hosts can be affected by human actions, both positively (Luke 15:7) and negatively (Gen 6:1–4; see *angel*). And hence there is need for a new creation of both heaven and earth.

Heaven is thus not simply a symbol of God's exaltedness or transcendence; it constitutes a theological claim regarding God's choice to make this dimension of the created order the very dwelling place of God.

Heaven as abode of the righteous dead (paradise). God's dwelling place also becomes the source of God's gifts (Deut 33:13; Ps 78:23–25; John 6:32–33). Indeed, heaven in itself can be a gift, and so in time it becomes the destination of the righteous dead. The OT gives only intimations of such an view, from Elijah's assumption into heaven (2 Kgs 2:11) to the promise of *resurrection* and *eternal life* in Dan 12:2–3 (see *grave*). The idea is more fully developed in later Jewish literature (2 Esdras), wherein considerable speculation about heaven is generated, including visions of heaven and ascents to heaven (*1–2 En.;* cf. Rev 4–5, 21–22). But it is especially in the NT where heaven — from which the Christ descended (John 6:38–58) and to which he ascended to be with the Father (Acts 1:10–11; Eph 1:20)— becomes the eternal home of the righteous (John 14:2–4; 2 Cor 5:1; Eph 2:6; Phil 3:20; Heb 11:13–16; Rev 11:12). At the same time, the vision of the New Jerusalem, which comes "down out of heaven from God" (Rev 21:1; cf. Matt 24:30–31), suggests that heaven comes to

earth, so that, finally, heaven and earth are one. This kind of future is proleptically experienced by Christians on earth, as seen in the language of *kingdom of heaven,* present in the person and work of Christ and hence those who believe in him (Matt 18:1–4; 19:14).

Heaven is also called paradise (related to Heb. *pardes,* "park, garden," Eccl 2:5). The Greek *paradeisos* is used in the LXX for the garden of Eden (Gen 2:8–10). This identification led later Jewish literature and the NT to an understanding of paradise as a coalescence of the garden of Eden and the abode of the righteous dead (*1–2 En.;* 4 Esd). Hence heaven is finally seen in terms of a new garden of Eden (Rev 2:7), to which the righteous are gathered, apparently at death (Luke 23:43; 2 Cor 12:4).

R. Knierim, "Cosmos and History in Israel's Theology," *HBT* 3 (1981): 59–123; T. Fretheim, *The Suffering of God: An Old Testament Perspective* (Philadelphia: Fortress, 1984), 37–39.

TERENCE E. FRETHEIM

Heir   *see* **Inherit**

Hell   *see* **Grave**

High   *see* **Most High**

Holy, Holiness, Consecrate, Dedicate, Holy Place, Holy of Holies, Saint, Sanctify

The notion of the holy, present in most religions, involves the conviction that certain objects, places, and times have a numinous quality. In his classic study *The Idea of the Holy,* Rudolf Otto thought that the holy embodied at least five qualities: awfulness, overpoweringness, urgency, the wholly other, and fascination. For Otto, to encounter the holy was to encounter a terrible but fascinating mysteriousness (*mysterium tremendum et fascinans*). He deemed Moses' confrontation with Yahweh in Exod 4:24 to be just such a moment. In ancient Israel, the holy is often part of an equation that may be expressed by a binary opposition: the sacred and the profane or "the holy (*qadosh*) and the common (*hol*)" (see Lev 10:10). In the OT, the deity is, of course, holy: "Holy, holy, holy is the LORD of hosts" (Isa 6:3). However, other things can also be holy; these include times, places, buildings, communities, persons, and food.

Although the holy is akin to a religious universal, each culture creates its own ways of expressing holiness. In ancient Israel, ideas of the sacred and the profane (or common) are related to another important binary code: the pure and the impure or, to use the language of Lev 10:10, "the *clean* and the unclean." Interestingly, purity and holiness are not identical; the same may be said for the profane and the impure. For example, it is possible for something to be pure and profane. The various combinations of these four categories elicit much reflection and stipulation in the OT. The binary category—holy and common—makes it sound as if the holy is absolute. However, there are different levels or gradations of holiness. For example, objects can be "holy" or "most holy" (Lev 7:6). Similar, there are zones of holiness. As one moves away from the Holy of Holies in the temple, one encounters lower levels of holiness.

Holy things are often dangerous. When he was taunted, Elisha, a holy man, killed those who were not honoring him (2 Kgs 2:23–25). The ark, a holy object, was, when touched by a common person, lethal (2 Sam 6:6–7). And the deity was so holy that simply to see God was to endanger one's life (Exod 19:21). In many cases, the "holy" does not involve the "ethical." To understand that the ark can kill simply because it is holy is at the same time to obviate the question of whether it was "bad" for Uzzah to die when he touched the ark.

God. The deity is utterly holy. Exodus 15:11 affirms the deity as one "majestic in holiness, awesome in splendor, doing wonders." Holiness primarily and ultimately refers to God. "I am God and no mortal, the Holy One in your midst" (Hos

11:9b). The book of Isaiah offers consistent testimony to God's holiness by using the appellation "the Holy One of Israel" (e.g., Isa 12:6).

The notion of Yahweh's holiness is associated with several motifs in the OT. God may appear in a theophany, which often includes *fire*. (If the root meaning of holy in Hebrew is cognate with Akkadian *qadashu* [which means "to shine" or "to be clean"], then Yahweh's holiness would naturally involve light and fire.) Moses' experience with the burning bush would be paradigmatic (Exod 3:1–6), as would poetic expressions such as Ps 18:8, 14, in which fire imagery figures prominently. The notion of Yahweh giving light to worshipers—"the LORD make his face to shine upon you," Num 6:25 (cf. Ps 31:16) with its solar implication—is consistent with this broader motif.

In addition to fire and light, the holiness of the deity connotes majesty like that of a king. Exodus 15:11 speaks of the deity: "Who is like you, O LORD, among the gods? Who is like you, majestic in holiness?" Such majesty is that befitting a royal figure, as the final line of this poem demonstrates: "The LORD will reign forever and ever" (Exod 15:18).

Israel affirms that God dwells with them, whether that presence is depicted using the object of the tent of meeting, the tabernacle, or the temple. This conviction that the deity is physically present with the people—as opposed simply to dwelling in the heavens or on a mountain—creates problems. The people must be protected from the deity, and the deity must be protected from the people. In order to protect God from the people and the people from God, the deity dwells in a holy place, to which only the priests have immediate access. The priests, as holy people, protect commoners from being endangered by the deity; and they, as holy people, do not threaten the deity by contact with the profane or impure world.

Israel knew about the existence of minor deities, who were inferior to Yahweh. These members of the divine council are also holy; for example, see

Ps 89:5. When a human joins in its deliberations, that person must be purified, so Isa 6.

People. In both the OT and the NT, individual humans such as priests could be holy if they were set apart in some sense in order to belong to the Holy One. Exodus 29 (cf. Lev 8–9 for a description of the process) prescribes the process for the consecration, literally, the making holy, of a priest. It involves various rites (washing, animal sacrifices, anointing with oil and blood, clothing, vegetable sacrifice, eating). Even though an individual must be born into a priestly lineage, that individual becomes a priest only through this process of consecration. Nonpriests can also be holy. The Nazirite is an obvious case. According to Num 6, the Nazirites "separate themselves to the Lord" and in so doing become "holy" (Num 6:5). An individual becomes a Nazirite by means of "a special vow"—that the person will not drink wine, cut his hair, and so forth. Moreover, there is a ritual process for the desacralization of that individual (Num 6:13–20). Another type of individual may be viewed as holy, as is suggested by the phrase "a holy man of God" (2 Kgs 4:9). Elijah and Elisha are each labeled as a "man of God" (1 Kgs 17:18; 2 Kgs 4:7, respectively). These persons possess the power of the holy such that they can act with godlike power. However, these individuals do not appear to become holy men through a process of consecration (cf. 2 Kgs 2:13–14).

Scholars have observed that the temple includes different levels of holiness, the highest occurring at the Holy of Holies. The same is true for holy people. The Aaronide high priest, who has access to the Holy of Holies, is the holiest individual. Thereafter comes the lineage of the Aaronid priests. And behind them stand the Levites. Nonlineage groups such as Nazirites and "holy men," though they may possess great power, are at an even further remove from the physical loci of holiness. Different levels of holiness among people typically reflect a different status in the human community.

"Saints" (derived from the Latin *sanctus*) is used in English to refer to holy individuals. The word appears only once in the OT (NRSV), Ps 31:23. There it translates the noun *hasid* (faithful) rather than *qadosh* (holy). The phrase "holy ones," which might have been translated "saints" (e.g., Dan 7:27), seems to refer to religiously loyal Jews. In the NT, "saints" regularly translates the Greek word for "holy ones" (*hagioi*, 1 Cor 6:2). There "saints" refers to early Christians. Various literatures use the word with different nuances. The word is rare in the Gospels (appearing only in Matt 27:52). In Revelation, "saints" are those who suffer at the hands of others, whereas in the Pauline literature, "saints" refers to groups of early Christians, often defined by their place of residence. For example, Rom 15:25–26 speaks of the "saints" in Jerusalem.

The OT testifies to the notion that the entire community can be viewed as "a holy people" (*'am qodesh*), thus set apart for a special relationship with God (Deut 7:6; cf. Exod 19:6). This judgment is characteristic of the Deuteronomist and the Holiness Code (Lev 17–26), but not of the Priestly school. For the Deuteronomist, the people are already holy. Their election by Yahweh has apparently secured the status of holiness, though that status is presumably contingent upon their keeping the torah found in Deuteronomy. According to the Holiness Code, the people must follow the ordinances found therein: "*Consecrate* yourselves therefore, and be *holy*; for I am the LORD your God. Keep my statutes, and observe them; I am the LORD; I *sanctify* you" (Lev 20:7–8). (The Hebrew root *qadash* appears in "consecrate," "holy," and "sanctify.") In the Holiness Code, the demand that the people be holy is coupled with the notion of admonitions for ethical behavior, a combination also found in Isaiah. Here "religious" categories are integrated with "ethical" ideals.

Holy space/place. Various types of places are or can become holy because of the presence of God. Humans can encounter an area that is sacred. For example, while acting as shepherd, Moses found himself on "the mountain of God," part of which was described as "holy ground" (Exod 3:1–6; cf. Jacob's comparable experience at Bethel, Gen 28:10–22). Since the Holiness Code construes "the land" of Israel to be holy, there is minimal reference to the temple (*mishkan*, "dwelling") (Lev 26:11). In the utopian torah of Ezek 40–48, only a portion of the land is deemed to be a "holy district" (Ezek 45:1). These claims about the holiness of the entire land or parts thereof appear to function more as theological affirmations than as experiential judgments about the numinous in all portions of the land. Many cultures testify to the sacrality of certain places, whether or not they involve structures built by humans.

The OT attests that humans can construct objects or buildings that symbolize holiness or become holy. In the family stories, Jacob reacts to his sense of Luz's holiness—"How awesome is this place!" (Gen 28:17)—by erecting a stone pillar and pouring oil on it (Gen 28:18). Here the act of building derives from a prior sense of holiness. The building of a temple represents a different dynamic, namely, creating something out of profane materials, which then become holy through a process of consecration. The tabernacle in the wilderness and the temple in Jerusalem are parade examples (see *presence*).

Though the tabernacle and the Solomonic temple are, of course, holy, those structures present gradations of the holy. When describing the function and placement of the curtain in the tabernacle, Exod 26:33 states that "the curtain shall separate for you the holy place from the most holy." The holy is not a monolithic entity but can be parsed, based in part in proximity to the deity. The Holy of Holies is where the deity is most manifest; as one moves away from the Holy of Holies, the intensity of the sacred diminishes. The nave is less holy than the Holy of Holies, the courtyard is less holy than the nave, and the city beyond walls of the temple is less holy than the temple complex.

The Holy of Holies or most holy place is also known as "the inner sanctuary" or *debir*. It is described as a cube, twenty cubits to a side. The most complete description occurs in 1 Kgs 6:15–28. This symmetry no doubt offers a geometric sense of wholeness, which complements that space's holiness. Like much of the rest of the temple, it is adorned with gold.

Two objects were placed in the Holy of Holies: two *cherubim*, with their wings touching, and "the ark of the Lord." The former were apparently built in, whereas the ark was placed inside the Holy of Holies on the day that the temple was dedicated. This combination of "perfect" space, cherubim, and ark creates an interesting amalgam, testifying that Yahweh is present in the *debir*. The deity could appear above them, a motif consistent with an affirmation that occurs in both prose and poetic texts, Yahweh as one "enthroned above the cherubim" (2 Kgs 19:15; Ps 80:1). (Cf. the description of the departure of the Lord from the temple, "Now the glory of the God of Israel had gone up from the cherub on which it rested" [Ezek 9:3].) The ark confirms the notion that the deity was present in the Holy of Holies. In the so-called ark narrative (1 Sam 4:3) Israelites offer the following proposal: "Let us bring the ark of the covenant of the LORD here from Shiloh, so that he may come among us and save us from the power of our enemies." Clearly the ark here and elsewhere functions as a symbol of divine immanence. (In addition, over time the ark became a container for "the two tablets of stone.") In sum, from a simple architectural perspective, the *debir* is the most protected and sacral space in the temple. And with the cherubim and ark in it the *debir* becomes truly "the most holy place." Only the Aaronid priest can enter the Holy of Holies and only on the Day of Atonement (Lev 16), when the priest sprinkles blood upon the covering of the ark and near it onto the floor (Lev 16:15).

Holy time. The OT testifies that time can become holy: "So God blessed the seventh day and hallowed it" (literally, "made it holy") (Gen 2:3). Special though the Sabbath was, other times were also holy. "These are the appointed festivals of the LORD, which you shall celebrate at the time appointed for them" (Lev 23:4). The subsequent list of such holy convocations includes: Sabbath, the festivals of Passover, unleavened bread, first fruits, Weeks, trumpets, Booths, and the Day of Atonement. When one explores the notion of holiness, as it was associated with some of these days, a dialectic emerges. For example, on the one hand, God has made the Sabbath holy (Lev 23:3). On the other hand, God commands the people to "remember the sabbath day and keep it holy." The Decalogue requires certain behavior in order to create the sacral Sabbath, whereas the Holiness Code views the sacrality of the Sabbath as a given. The tension is between holiness as contingent and holiness as absolute.

Gradations of holiness appear in time, as well as with place and people. Of the moments prescribed in Lev 23, one should probably view the Day of Atonement as the most holy of days. Unlike the Sabbath, it occurs only once a year, but like the Sabbath, it requires that the people do "no work." The distinction between the Sabbath and the Day of Atonement is even stronger in the ritual prescriptions of Num 28–29, where the requirement of "no work" is not stipulated for the Sabbath (Num 28:9–10), whereas it is present for the Day of Atonement (Num 29:7).

Consecration/sanctification as action/ inaction. Both humans and the deity can make something holy, and they can do this in several ways. It should be no surprise that the deity, as a holy being, can sanctify or consecrate something. When establishing the daily offerings, Yahweh states: "I will consecrate the tent of meeting and the altar; Aaron also and his sons I will consecrate" (Exod 29:44). Clearly Yahweh is able to make both objects and people holy.

Israelites too have that power, a power in the hands of both priests and nonpriests. Certain acts of consecration are reserved for priests, for example, "Aaron was set apart to consecrate the most holy things" (1 Chr 23:13). However, stipulations such as "Every firstling male born of your herd and flock you shall consecrate to the LORD" (Deut 15:19) make clear that nonpriests were also able to undertake acts of consecration. Though some acts of consecration confer a state of perpetual or permanent holiness (1 Kgs 9:3), the law of the Nazirite, which involves acts of consecration by nonpriests, creates temporary states of holiness (Num 6:8). The command that early Christians greet one another with "a holy kiss" belongs to this same type of behavior, that is, acts of consecration by nonpriests.

Consecration/sanctification occurred in a number of ways. *Anointing* with oil was used in acts of consecration (Lev 8:12). In addition, *blood* could be deployed in making things holy (Lev 8:30). Priests typically manipulated these liquids. Sacrifices too were involved in acts of consecration, but it is less clear how the sacrifice, as such, actually instilled holiness. Sacrifices clearly took place at the time when a temple was dedicated or consecrated; for example, innumerable sheep and oxen were sacrificed at the dedication of Solomon's temple (1 Kgs 8:5). And yet the nature of sacrifice as such and the creation of the state of holiness is less overt than is the manipulation of the aforementioned liquids—blood and oil.

In the cases just mentioned, consecration occurred because someone had intended it. However, the power of the holy is such that simple contact with a holy object can consecrate an individual. The altar had that power (Exod 29:37). In a similar fashion, any object that touches the grain offering (Lev 6:18) or sin offering (Lev 6:27) will become holy (cf. Hag 2:12–13.) This power of holy objects to make other things holy is directly related to the power of the holy to kill.

Consecration often involves making something holy, something that had hitherto been profane. However, other acts of consecration appear to be more of a dedication—or even change in ownership—

rather than a change in status, that is, from the profane to the holy. For example, the final chapter of the Holiness Code (Lev 27) presents a number of cases according to which property could be "consecrated." The case in Lev 27:14 is instructive. An Israelite could "consecrate" a house, in which case a priest would assess the value of the house. The consecrating of the house apparently meant that the individual would receive that assessed value from the temple. If the person wanted to regain ownership of the house, he would have to return that amount of silver, plus 20 percent. If, however, he did not want to resume ownership, the temple could sell the property (or retain ownership). Consecration here seems to involve the passage of property from the nonpriest to the priest, even though the house itself would not have become "holy" through some ritual act.

The absence of normal activity could also eventuate in consecration. Keeping the Sabbath "holy" is achieved by the absence of "any work" (Deut 5:12–14). The act of fasting belongs to the same category, since fasting is really negative activity, not eating as one normally does. It is no accident that "denying oneself" or fasting is required on the most holy day, the Day of Atonement (Lev 16:29). Holiness can be achieved either by extraordinary deeds, that is, activity beyond the quotidian, or by the absence of ordinary behavior.

One might think that acts of consecration or sanctification result in a state of holiness. That can be true, but sanctification, particularly in the NT, is also an ongoing process. On the one hand, early Christians might view themselves as sanctified due to the action of Christ (2 Thess 2:13; Heb 9:11–14). On the other hand, sanctification is contingent upon living in appropriate ways. In Romans, Paul challenges his audience to "present your members as slaves to righteousness for sanctification" (Rom 6:19; cf. Heb 12:14 "holiness"). Early Christians viewed themselves as both already sanctified (1 Cor 1:2; 6:11) and challenged to be sanctified (1 Thess 4:3).

Just as things can be made holy, they can be removed from that status. Specific rituals existed to permit the Nazirite to move from holy to normal/profane existence (Num 6:13–20). However, in the OT far more attention is devoted to the instance in which improper or intended desacralization occurs. Such desacralization happens when, for example, a blemished priest comes near the altar. In such a case, a holy place is profaned. This kind of behavior is prohibited so that "he may not profane my sanctuaries" (Lev 21:23). Similarly, a holy person may be profaned, even as may be the holy people of Israel. Surprisingly even God's name can be profaned: "You shall not give any of your offspring to sacrifice them to Molech, and so profane the name of your God" (Lev 18:21). Obviously God remains holy, but an act in which Israel worships another deity affronts the very name of Yahweh. Ezekiel, as is often the case, makes an even more radical claim. The deity can be profaned by acts of impiety (Ezek 13:19; cf. Deut 32:51).

The language of dedication is related to that of consecration. In fact, in certain NRSV texts, the same Hebrew word (*qaddesh*) that elsewhere is rendered "consecrate" is translated "dedicate/dedication." However, another Hebrew word, apparently involving some kind of anointing practice (*hanak*), is also translated as "dedicate" (Deut 20:5; 1 Kgs 8:63; 2 Chr 7:5). Interestingly these three texts all refer to dedicating a building, whether a person's house or the deity's abode. Other more general Hebrew words are also translated by the English word "dedicate," for example, Num 18:6 (*nathan*).

Holy objects. Apart from time, places, and people, different kinds of things could become holy. The list is a long one, including a holy linen tunic (Lev 16:4), holy bread (1 Sam 21:6), holy incense (Exod 30:35), holy anointing oil (Exod 30:25), and holy water (Num 5:17). In most cases, these are objects found in the profane world—such as clothing, food, water—that have been devoted to use in

Israelite religious ritual. The same is true for the furnishings of the temple. Tables and lamps, which could be found in homes, were, when created for and used in the temple, holy (Exod 40:9).

However, a special class of objects could become especially holy: food used in ritual. Just as there are higher levels of holy places and peoples, so too some sacrifices are "holy of holies." These are valued as "a most holy part of the offerings by fire to the LORD" (Lev 2:3, 10). "A most holy part" echoes the notion of "the holy of holies." These sacrifices and these sacrifices alone were (a) eaten by holy people, the Aaronide priests, and (b) eaten within the temple court. In contrast, the sacrifice of well-being, which is also part of the list of standard offerings (Lev 3:1–17), can be eaten by all Israelites and "in all [their] settlements" (Lev 3:17).

Conclusions. In sum, holiness is a category of many facets. The universe of the OT could be divided between the sacred and the profane. However, neither the world of the sacred nor the world of the common is uniform. There are the holiest of holy things, for example, the Holy of Holies in the temple and certain sacrifices, and this in contrast to things that exemplify lesser levels of holiness. And there are profane or simply common things, as exemplified by much in human life. Finally, those things that profane the sacred, for example, veneration of foreign gods, are the truly profane possibilities in life. Humans—holy and common—are charged with manifesting holiness in their lives. To do such, especially according to the Holiness Code and the book of Isaiah, involves not only avoiding profane actions, but also loving "your neighbor as yourself" (Lev 19:18).

Mircea Eliade, *The Sacred and the Profane* (New York: Harper, 1959); John Gammie, *Holiness in Israel* (Minneapolis: Fortress, 1989); Frank Gorman, *The Ideology of Ritual: Space, Time, and Status in the Priestly Theology,* JSOTSup 91 (Sheffield: JSOT Press, 1990); J. Jenson, *Graded Holiness: A Key to the Conception of the World,* JSOTSup 106 (Sheffield: JSOT Press, 1992); Jacob Milgrom, *Leviticus 1–16,* AB 3 (New York: Doubleday, 1993); Rudolf Otto, *The Idea of the Holy* (New York: Oxford, 1958).

DAVID L. PETERSEN

Holy Spirit   *see* Spirit

Hope   Hope appears in NRSV, as in the Greek and Hebrew originals, both as a noun and a verb. As a noun, it means confident expectation of good in the future, almost always dependent on the goodness of God. As a verb, it means to display or to live by that confident expectation.

For the most part NRSV uses "hope" in the OT to render Hebrew verbs, especially *kawah* and *yahal,* whose primary meaning is "to wait for," and nouns derived from those verbs. In the NT, NRSV renders the noun *elpis* and the verb *elpizein* as "hope." In secular Greek, the word *elpis* could simply mean "expectation," whether of good or ill. What we might call hope was simply an expectation of the good, which, it was recognized, might be little more than wishful thinking. In biblical literature, however, *elpis* is not a neutral expectation; it is almost always expectation of good. The one exception is the LXX's translation of Isa 28:19, where NRSV reads the relevant phrase as "sheer terror." An excessively literal reading of the LXX at that point would be "a bad hope." An expectation of evil would normally be *fear.* Hope is thus the opposite of one meaning of the very complicated word "fear." Moreover, hope is not wishful thinking. It is, rather, a reasonable and confident expectation of good, because it is based upon a knowledge of the nature and mighty deeds of God.

Hope in the Old Testament. The distribution of the word in the OT is interesting. It does not appear in the Torah. It appears frequently, however, in the Writings, the third division of the OT in the Hebrew Bible. It is found particularly often in the book of Job, especially in the first half, and in the Psalms. The word also appears from time to time in the Prophets. A more theologically significant observation would be that hope is most likely to appear in theological reflection, worship, or prophecy amid troubles. Hope is discussed frequently in Job, both by Job and his comforters. Beautiful statements of hope appear in Lamentations and in psalms in which the psalmist struggles with difficulties of every sort. It would be fair to say that trouble lurks somewhere in the context wherever hope is mentioned.

Some form of the verb "to wait for" could replace most instances of the verb "hope" in the OT. "Truly the eye of the LORD is on those who fear him, on those who hope in his steadfast love" (Ps 33:18) could easily become " . . . on those who wait for his steadfast love." With very little literary or theological difficulty, the same could be done with respect to the noun "hope" also. Indeed, sometimes the words appear in parallel: "I wait for the LORD, my soul waits, and in his word I hope" (Ps 130:5). "And now, O Lord, what do I wait for? My hope is in you" (Ps 39:7).

We place our hope in that which we are willing to wait for. In contemporary English we might say "hang on" for. Hope is that which keeps us "hanging on." So, for example, Job says, "See, he will kill me; I have no hope" (Job 13:15). It is as if he were saying, "I have nothing worth waiting for," or "I have nothing to keep me hanging on." By contrast, to hope in the Lord is to "hang on" because of God. Without hope, life is worthless and indeed may well end soon.

Because hope is most necessary to the human spirit amid troubles and yet is inevitably challenged by those troubles, it is always problematic and cannot be grasped or maintained easily. Troubles and sorrow can overwhelm hope. The failure of hope is a terrible thing, a fit subject matter for a curse. Job, referring to the day of his birth, says, "Let the stars of its dawn be dark; let it hope for light, but have none; may it not see the eyelids of the morning" (Job 3:9). It is possible even for faithful individuals or for God's people to experience the loss of hope: "My days are swifter than a weaver's shuttle, and come to their end without hope" (Job

7:6). "Our bones are dried up, and our hope is lost; we are cut off completely" (Ezek 37:11). One might almost say that to live is to hope and to hope is to live. Without hope, an individual or a people are little more than dry bones.

All this has been substantiated in the profoundest way by the observations of the great psychiatrist Viktor Frankl. Frankl, a captive in a Nazi death camp in World War II, noted that those of his fellow prisoners who had a structure of meaning in their lives, dedicated Communists or practicing Jews and believing Christians, were more likely to have hope than their fellow prisoners. Because they possessed a hope amid all the brutalities of the death camp, they were more likely to continue living. But, observed Frankl, if they ever lost their hope, these prisoners died almost immediately. There is an old saying, "Where there's life, there's hope." (This is almost a paraphrase of Eccl 9:4.) It would be at least as true to say, "Where there's hope, there's life."

This loss of hope ought not to be rebuked easily. Ironically, some of the most moving and poetic OT statements about hope are found in the mouths of Job's comforters. These statements are not necessarily false. Most of them can be paralleled elsewhere in Scripture. But words of hope must not be used as cheap or sentimental nostrums whose only purpose is to deny the reality of the depth of life's pain and sorrow.

The phrase "hanging on" might suggest passivity to some ears. Though in some troubles "hanging on" is all one can do for a time and, indeed, may constitute a triumph, hope at its best issues in action. It can issue, for example, in praise: "Why are you cast down, O my soul, and why are you disquieted within me? Hope in God; for I shall again praise him, my help" (Pss 42:5, 11; 43:5).

Very occasionally, the OT uses the word "hope" in a manner similar to the ordinary, nontheological language of our time. So one might hope, or rather give up hope, for a husband and children, as in Ruth 1:12. Caravans hope for water in the desert (Job 6:19). No one could be foolish enough to hope to capture Leviathan (Job 41:9). This observation also holds true for the NT. So, for example, slave owners hope to make money from the abilities of their slave (Acts 16:19). A corrupt governor can hope for a bribe (Acts 24:26). Or we read "I hope to see you soon" (3 John 14).

Normally, however, hope is a strictly theological term. The ultimate source of hope is God and God's love and power to save. We read therefore: "Let your steadfast love, O LORD, be upon us, even as we hope in you" (Ps 33:22). "O Israel, hope in the LORD! For with the LORD there is steadfast love, and with him is great power to redeem" (Ps 130:7). "Can any idols of the nations bring rain? Or can the heavens give showers? Is it not you, O LORD our God? We set our hope on you, for it is you who do all this" (Jer 14:22). It is clear from these examples and others that the ground of Israel's hope is God's love and God's power to save. Sometimes Israel hopes in God's word (Ps 119:49, 74, 81, 114, 147) or in God's ordinances (Ps 119:43). Ultimately, of course, to trust in God's word is to trust in God. So certain is Israel that hope comes from God, that the Lord is sometimes even named "hope": "O hope of Israel! O LORD!" (Jer 17:13; cf. Jer 50:7).

This expectation for the future might rest not precisely on God or God's goodness but on one's own relationship to God: "Is not your fear of God your confidence, and the integrity of your ways your hope?" (Job 4:6). Significantly, the words are those of Eliphaz, one of Job's comforters. It may well be that hope in one's integrity before God is subtly but significantly different from hope in God.

It is possible, of course, to place one's trust in a vain hope. It is characteristic of the wicked that they do just this: "Such are the paths of all who forget God; the hope of the godless shall perish" (Job 8:13; cf. Job 11:20). (The words are spoken by Bildad and Zophar, Job's comforters, but they may represent Israel's understanding rightly at this point.) Israel may also

be tempted to hope wrongly, in the power of Egypt, for example, Isa 20:5. Even when Israel does wrong, however, God may still give reason to hope (Ezra 10:2; Hos 2:15). Hope is thus a gift of *grace* and a rich sign of the *goodness* of God. That is to say, those who are faithful both hope in the goodness of God and experience hope as a sign of or gift of that goodness.

There are also some significant instances in which NRSV uses "hope" to translate words derived from the verb *batah*, "to trust" (see *believe*); for example, "O God of our salvation; you are the hope of all the ends of the earth and of the farthest seas" (Ps 65:5). This will be particularly significant for the NT usage of hope. It should be noted that the LXX frequently used the Greek *elpis* and *elpizein*, the words almost invariably rendered as "hope" in NRSV and other English versions, to translate *batah* and its derivatives. Two key elements in the meaning of hope are carried forward from the OT to the NT: hope as waiting and hope as trust. And, of course, in the NT as in the OT, it is in God alone that the faithful may rightly hope.

Hope in the New Testament. The word "hope" appears more frequently in the NT than the OT but not dramatically so. As was the case with the OT, the word is not evenly distributed throughout the NT. It is rare in the Gospels and, surprisingly, not found in Revelation but is used frequently in the Epistles and in Paul's speeches in Acts. Nevertheless, though it is a word and a concept of considerable importance in the OT, in the NT it acquires an even greater significance. It is, together with faith and love, one of the three great realities that abide (1 Cor 13:13).

There is a considerable continuity between the Testaments with respect to hope. Trouble often continues to lurk in the context when hope is mentioned. A classic example of this might be Paul's word to the Romans: "Suffering produces endurance, and endurance produces character, and character produces hope, and hope does not disappoint us, because God's love has been poured into our hearts through the Holy Spirit that has been given to us" (Rom 5:3–5). Hope remains a matter of patient waiting even in the midst of troubles: "Rejoice in hope, be patient in suffering, persevere in prayer" (Rom 12:12). As in the OT, moreover, hope is not a matter of waiting in passivity. Hope leads to action: "Since, then, we have such a hope, we act with great boldness" (2 Cor 3:12). Once again, as in the OT, hope issues in praise, "so that we, who were the first to set our hope on Christ, might live for the praise of his glory" (Eph 1:12).

Hope is also intimately connected to trust: "Through him you have come to trust in God, who raised him from the dead and gave him glory, so that your faith and hope are set on God" (1 Pet 1:21). That verse leads to an important observation: the meaning of hope overlaps with many other key NT concepts. In 1 Pet 1:21, we note that hope is paired with faith. This linkage is not accidental. Indeed, the closest thing to a definition of faith in the NT explains that word in connection with hope: "Now faith is the assurance of things hoped for, the conviction of things not seen" (Heb 11:1). According to Paul, Abraham, the model of faith, is also a paragon of hope: "Hoping against hope, he believed that he would become 'the father of many nations'" (Rom 4:18). Trust is the common element of faith and hope. Indeed, it might be suggested that faith is trust in its present aspect and hope is trust turned to the future.

A particularly interesting verse in this connection is Rom 8:24: "For in hope we were saved. Now hope that is seen is not hope. For who hopes for what is seen?" Hope has to do with that which is not yet seen, the "hope of glory" (Col 1:27), a hope "laid up . . . in heaven" (Col 1:5), the hope of the return of Christ (Titus 2:13). Moreover, it is in this hope that we are "saved." It is interesting to remember that according to Eph 2:8, we are saved "by grace . . . through faith." Perhaps we could say that Christians are saved by grace, through faith and in hope.

It is time to be more precise about the defining characteristic of hope in the NT. Let us return for a moment to the OT to begin the task of specifying this defining characteristic. A particularly interesting verse is 1 Chr 29:15, part of David's prayer for the people of Israel: "For we are aliens and transients before you, as were all our ancestors; our days on the earth are like a shadow, and there is no hope." It is as if the natural state of humanity is to have no hope or useless and empty hopes. (This thought is echoed in the NT; see Eph 2:12, "having no hope and without God in the world.") But David is not speaking only of the godless; the prayer is offered on behalf of *Israel*. Though the remainder of the prayer is quite beautiful in its expressions of praise, the particular problem raised here, the hopelessness of people whose lives pass away like shadows, is never answered. "But whoever is joined with all the living has hope, for a living dog is better than a dead lion" (Eccl 9:4). In the end, however, even the dog dies and all of us with it. The ultimate challenge to hope is not trouble in this life. Rather, it is death. That challenge is addressed only fitfully in the OT itself. At some point, in the centuries before Christ, however, some of the faithful in Israel came to believe in and hope for a general resurrection. This leads us to the NT.

Paul repeatedly claims in the speeches in Acts that he is being persecuted for the "hope of Israel" (Acts 24:15, 26:6, 7; 28:20). It is clear that this hope is the hope of the resurrection (Acts 24:15). The resurrection is actually a hope of only part of Israel, a fact Paul uses cleverly in a difficult moment: "When Paul noticed that some were Sadducees and others were Pharisees, he called out in the council, 'Brothers, I am a Pharisee, a son of Pharisees. I am on trial concerning the hope of the resurrection of the dead'" (Acts 23:6). Christians shared at least with Pharisees a hope of a general resurrection. The distinctively Christian hope is more specific, however. The distinctive and indeed the constitutive emphasis of Christianity was to ground that hope on the resurrection of Jesus Christ.

It appears that Jesus raised hopes among his followers, but these hopes were dashed by his death on the cross. Cleopas says on the road to Emmaus, "But we had hoped that he was the one to redeem Israel" (Luke 24:21). Those original hopes are triumphantly vindicated, however, by the resurrection. Now Christian hope depends on the resurrection and is defined by it: "Blessed be the God and Father of our Lord Jesus Christ! By his great mercy he has given us a new birth into a living hope through the resurrection of Jesus Christ from the dead" (1 Pet 1:3). Because of the resurrection, Christians have a hope for the future. Christians are not limited by death and ought not suppose that their hope is limited to this life as we know it: "If for this life only we have hoped in Christ, we are of all people most to be pitied" (1 Cor 15:19). The remainder of 1 Cor 15 makes it clear that the Christian hope lies in the resurrection of Christ. On a personal level, this hope is to share in Christ's resurrection. On a cosmic level, the hope is for the return or the manifestation of the crucified and resurrected one. In some evangelical circles, the second coming is called "the blessed hope," a phrase taken from Titus 2:13: "We wait for the blessed hope and the manifestation of the glory of our great God and Savior, Jesus Christ."

That brings us to a final observation: hope is in the NT a thoroughly eschatological reality. That is why, along with faith and love, it abides when other, lesser things pass away. Hope stretches forward to the consummation that God will bring. The church trusts that there will be such a consummation and that it will be good, because the faithful have already seen its inauguration in the resurrection of Jesus Christ.

In the meantime, because of that hope Paul can say, "Therefore, my beloved, be steadfast, immovable, always excelling in the work of the Lord, because you know that in the Lord your labor is not in vain" (1 Cor 15:58). Those who can say "Amen" to the apostle's words know hope already.

STEPHEN FARRIS

Hosanna   An appeal, composed of two Hebrew words: *hoshiʿah*, "save!" and the particle *naʾ*, "please!" It occurs in Matt 21:9, 15; Mark 11:9, 10; and John 12:13, in the context of Jesus' entry into Jerusalem the Sunday before his death. In Jewish literature the term was always an appeal for help, but very early in Christian history it was misunderstood and thought to be a cry of praise. (So the hymn, "Hosanna, loud hosanna, the little children sang; through pillared court and temple the joyful anthem rang.") It should be noted that only Luke describes Palm Sunday as a joyous occasion (19:37), and he does not quote the word. John's use, "Hosanna! Blessed is the one who comes in the name of the Lord—the King of Israel!" (12:13), may be understood as containing the actual meaning of the word as an appeal for help, but the ways Matthew and Mark use it, with "son of David" and especially with "the highest" have led to much scholarly discussion. All three Gospels clearly contain partial quotations of Ps 118:25–26: "Save us, we beseech you, O LORD (*ʾannaʾ YHWH hoshiʿah-nnaʾ*). . . . Blessed is the one who comes in the name of the LORD." Matthew adds "to the son of David" after "Hosanna," and both Matthew and Mark add "in the highest heaven," and these expressions cannot logically follow "Please save!"

Various efforts have been made to explain the apparent discontinuity: (1) It is claimed that the use of Ps 118 in temple worship had led Jews to overlook the literal meaning of "hosanna," and it had become a joyous cry; but there is no evidence to support this. (2) Others say that Matthew and Mark did not know Hebrew or Aramaic and thus used the word incorrectly. This is doubtful, and hardly explains why they would have quoted a word they did not understand. (3) The

Greek datives very likely are efforts to translate the Hebrew particle *l-*, which often means "to." Because of the discovery of a particle *l-* in ancient Ugaritic that has a vocative sense, however, it has been proposed that the people were really saying, "O Son of David" and "O Most High." But this assumes that a particle that was a vocative in 1200 B.C. was still understood that way by the people of Jerusalem in the first century A.D., although misunderstood by the Gospel writers.

Although not well accepted, C. C. Torrey's explanation seems to be as helpful as any. He pointed out that the Hebrew particle *l-* can be used to indicate the direct object of the verb *yashaʿ* "save," as in Pss 72:4; 86:16; 116:6; 1 Chr 18:6. He then proposed that Matthew and Mark provided an overly literal translation of what he assumed to be the original Hebrew: "Save the Son of David!" (*hoshaʿnaʾ lᵉben dawid*) and "O give thy help from on high" (*hoshaʿnaʾ bimᵉromim*). But the use of the dative in Greek led readers in the early church, who knew no Semitic languages, to think the two phrases should be understood as "Hosanna *to . . . ,*" and so they thought the Hebrew term must be a cry of praise (Torrey, 77–78).

If the meaning "Please save!" or "Please help!" is taken to represent what the people really cried out on Palm Sunday, it puts the events of that day in a different light from what is traditional and suggests that Luke has already made it "brighter" than it originally was. Jesus' ride into Jerusalem, probably intended as a deliberate fulfillment of Zech 9:9 (cf. Matt 21:4–5), would have been taken as a very serious occasion by those who accompanied and greeted him, and this appeal, "Hosanna," would have been a prayer for divine help for the one they hoped would become their king (Mark 11:10; John 12:13).

Eric Werner, "'Hosanna' in the Gospels," *JBL* 65 (1946): 97–122; Charles C. Torrey, *Documents of the Primitive Church* (New York: Harper & Bros., 1941).

DONALD E. GOWAN

Hosts (Lord of)

This frequent epithet or name (Isa 47:4) for the God of Israel is often expanded: "LORD, God of (the) hosts"; "LORD, the God of hosts, the God of Israel"; "LORD of hosts, the God of Israel"; "Lord, LORD of hosts." The word "hosts" (*tsebaʿoth*) is a plural of the noun *tsabaʿ*, often translated as "army" (Judg 4:2, 7) or a "host" of human or nonhuman, earthly or heavenly creatures (Gen 2:1). More abstractly, it can refer to service assigned or undertaken, military or cultic.

The uneven distribution of this epithet for God is striking. It does not occur in the Pentateuch, Joshua, or Judges (and is rare in Kings and Chronicles); nor does it appear in Ezekiel or Isa 56–66 (only six times in Isa 40–55 and in only eight psalms, especially Zion psalms). The epithet is rare in the NT (only Rom 9:29; James 5:4). On the other hand, it is common in Isa 1–39, Jeremiah, Haggai, Zechariah, and Malachi. That 90 percent of its occurrences are in prophetic literature qualifies its earlier military and royal connotations.

The identification of the "hosts" in the epithet is a complex issue; they include Israel's armies, the angelic host, and celestial bodies. It is common to understand the "hosts" in military terms; see, for example, 1 Sam 17:45, where the "LORD of hosts" is apposite to "the God of the armies of Israel" (cf. 1 Sam 15:2). It may have been first associated with the early Israelite sanctuary at Shiloh, where the ark of the covenant was initially housed (see 1 Sam 1:3, 11). The ark, on which the Lord was believed to be enthroned (1 Sam 4:4), is "called by the name of the LORD of hosts" (2 Sam 6:2). This enthronement motif and the use of the ark in Israel's battles (1 Sam 4) suggest that the Lord of hosts was understood as the royal commander of Israel's armies (see Ps 24:7–10). When David transferred the ark to Jerusalem, the "LORD, the God of hosts, was with him" and he offered sacrifices in that name (2 Sam 5:10; 6:18). Such events probably account for the sometime association of the epithet with Zion (see 2 Sam 7:26; Ps 46; Isa 6:3; 31:4–5). At the same time, God is not necessarily linked to such cultic places or military activities. The Lord of hosts may not go forth with Israel's armies (1 Sam 4; Ps 44:9; 60:10) and indeed may fight against them through the use of the armies of other nations (Jer 28:14).

The "hosts" may also be the heavenly host, referring either to angelic messengers or celestial bodies. Regarding the latter, God created the luminaries (Isa 40:26; 45:12) and involved them in battle against Israel's enemies (Judg 5:20). In view of Job 38:7, this heavenly host *symbolized* the other heavenly host, namely, the angelic messengers (or divine council; see *angel*) that God "recruited" for divine service in the world (Ps 103:20–21). All "the host of heaven" is explicitly identified in terms of this divine council in 1 Kgs 22:19; other texts refer to these figures as "heavenly beings" (Ps 29:1; Mg: "sons of God") and "holy ones" (Ps 89:5–7).

The predominance of the epithet in prophetic texts suggests a specific linkage between this divine council and the prophet's role as a messenger of the word of the Lord (see Jer 23:18, 22; 1 Kgs 22:19). The prophet is understood to be a member of the heavenly host, whose responsibility it is to speak the word of God. The military/royal sense of the term is sharply diminished in the prophets (though not entirely absent, Isa 13:4; 31:4). Instead, it focuses on the God-Israel relationship, with the "hosts" (including angelic figures and prophets) being those who mediated the word of God. Jeremiah speaks of this connection most directly ("Thus says the LORD of hosts," 6:6 and often). Isaiah 21:10 makes the prophetic point well: "What I have heard from the LORD of hosts, the God of Israel, I announce to you" (cf. Luke 2:13).

TERENCE E. FRETHEIM

Hour   *see* **Time**

Household   *see* **Family**

Human, Human Beings, Humanity, Humankind   These expressions mainly translate Hebrew *ʾadam* and Greek *anthropos*. Hebrew *ʾish* and Greek *aner* denote a man as opposed to a woman, but also an individual human being, like traditional English "man." (See *man and woman*.) Other Hebrew words for human beings are *ʾenosh* and *geber*, which are similar to words for "frail" and "strong," but the contexts do not usually suggest that the words have these specific connotations. NRSV sometimes renders the various words by expressions such as "mortal," "one," "person," "people," "those," "others," "everyone," and "those who live."

Humanity before God. Humanity was created in the *image of God* after a special act of reflection on God's part (Gen 1:26–28). Scripture has various ways of describing God's subsequent ongoing involvement with all humanity. God made from one (NRSV, "from one ancestor") every nation of human beings (Acts 17:26). All human beings gain their light from the life that has always resided in God's word, which enlightens them (John 1:4, 9). If the divine breath or *spirit* were withdrawn, all human beings would die (Job 34:14–15). It is the spirit in a human being, God's breath, that makes for understanding (Job 32:8; cf. Ps 94:10–11). Wisdom delighted in humanity when it was created and is calling to it now (Prov 8:4, 33). God has done mighty deeds and earned renown among all humanity (Jer 32:20).

When God is so gloriously majestic, what are human beings, that God pays attention to them? But God made them a little lower or less than God/angels, but/and crowned them with splendor and honor, and gave them authority over the animal world (Ps 8; cf. 144:3; Job 22:2; also 7:17–20, with irony). So human beings can illustrate how things are when God rules (e.g., Matt 13:24, 31, 44; 18:12; 21:28). The duty and blessing of human beings is then to revere God and keep God's commands, do the right thing, love commitment, and walk humbly with God (Eccl 12:13; Mic 6:8). It is by the word

God speaks and by keeping God's commands that human beings live (Lev 18:5; Deut 8:3; Neh 9:29; Ezek 20:11, 13, 21; Matt 4:4; Acts 5:29).

Admittedly, "we do not yet see everything in subjection to [humanity], but we do see Jesus, who for a while was made lower than the angels, now crowned with glory" (Heb 2:6–9). He was born in human likeness or human form (Phil 2:7). When people saw him act, they glorified God for giving "such authority to human beings" (Matt 9:8). The human Christ acts as mediator between God and humanity to pursue God's desire for all human beings to be saved (1 Tim 2:4–5; cf. 4:10; Titus 2:11). Resurrection comes through a human being, as life and then death did (1 Cor 15:21, 45–49).

Human beings are dependent on God to make their steps firm when God delights in their way (Ps 37:23). God directs human steps and we may not be able to understand them; it is God's purpose that will be established through them (Prov 16:9; 19:21; 20:24; Jer 10:23). Likewise God made the mouth for humanity, so God can do things with and through any individual human mouth (Exod 4:11; Prov 16:1). Human wrath serves only to praise Yahweh (Ps 76:10). So human insight and planning must not be confused with or allowed to rival God's insight or planning (e.g., Isa 29:13; Matt 15:9; cf. Job 28:13; 28:28; 1 Cor 1:25; 2 Cor 5:16; Col 2:8–9, 18, 22). The gospel is not of human origin, and neither is Paul's preaching and teaching (Gal 1:1, 11–12; 1 Thess 2:13; 4:8). Human beings cannot take God on or do what they like and need to recognize that they are just human beings and be wise enough to revere God for the greatness that creation reflects to us (Job 33:12; 37:20–24; Ps 9:19–20; Rom 9:20). God's weakness is stronger than human strength and wisdom; God can do what human beings cannot (Matt 19:26; 1 Cor 1:25; 2:5).

In particular, the Most High rules over human kingship, and as creator of humanity makes the decisions about how to use human beings such as Cyrus in working out a purpose, decisions that depend on God's mercy, not on human will and exertion (Isa 45:11–13; Dan 4:25, 32; 5:21; Rom 9:16). So I can and must trust in God, not worry what human beings can do to me, and not put confidence in human beings (Pss 56:11; 60:11; 108:12; 118:6, 8; 146:3–4; Jer 17:5–8; Heb 13:6). If a plan or undertaking is of human origin, it will fail (Acts 5:38). It is foolish to fear human beings who die, and not to keep in mind Yahweh their creator (Isa 51:12–13). The Egyptians are human beings, not God; their horses are flesh, not spirit (Isa 31:3). Human beings who are of the earth must not pretend to divine standing or tyrannize other human beings (Ps 10:18; Ezek 28:2).

Israel and the church are particular embodiments of humanity. In Christ God created one new humanity in place of the two (Jews and Gentiles; Eph 2:15). In Israel, human beings eat angels' bread (Ps 78:25), experience wondrous expressions of steadfast love from God (Ps 107:8, 15, 21, 31), and hear God heed a human voice (Josh 10:14). God can give a human being an experience of heaven (2 Cor 12:2–5). But servants of God are human beings, not God, so people should not bow down to them (Acts 14:15). The trouble is that human majesty and power can make human beings rivals to God, so that they must be put down, to show they are only creatures with breath (Isa 2:9–22; 5:15; 13:7). But when God thus afflicts or grieves human beings, this does not come from God's heart (Lam 3:33, NRSV "willingly").

In some sense it is possible for human beings to *see* God and stay alive (Exod 24:9–11; Isa 6:5; Amos 9:1), but in another sense this is impossible (Exod 33:20; John 1:18; 1 Tim 6:16). No human being is to be present in the sanctuary while the priest is making the Day of Atonement offerings (Lev 16:17). But human beings can find shelter in the shade of Yahweh's wings—that is, in the temple (Ps 36:7). God dwelt among human beings, though then withdrew that presence (Ps 78:60). But God does not dwell in the wooden and stone images made by human hands, art, and imagination (Deut 4:28; 2 Kgs 19:18; 2 Chr 32:19; Pss 115:4; 135:15; Isa 37:19; 44:11; Jer 10:1–16; 16:20; Acts 17:29). Nor does God live in houses made by human hands, nor is God served by human hands (Acts 7:48; 17:24–25). Yet the descent of the new Jerusalem means God makes a home among human beings (Rev 21:3).

God writes letters on human hearts as well as on stone, letters that can be read by all human beings (2 Cor 3:2–3). Human words can be deep waters, and human beings get great satisfaction out of what they say; they sharpen each other, and praise tests them (Prov 18:4, 20; 27:17, 21). It is good to do what is right in the eyes of other human beings as well as in God's eyes, and walking in love gives us human approval (Rom 14:18; 2 Cor 8:21); but if it comes to a choice, we must choose God's approval (Gal 1:10). Likewise, extraordinary human beings can inspire us (Jas 5:17), but human words are not enough to explain God's truth, so why boast about human leaders? (1 Cor 2:13; 3:21).

Humanity and the world. Humanity is part of the animate world. Like sea creatures and birds, humanity was blessed by God and thereby given the encouragement and commission to multiply and fill the earth (Gen 1:28). God gives animals grass to eat and gives human beings a place that grows fruit and the means of making wine, oil, and bread (Gen 1:29; 2:15–16; Ps 104:15–16). God's ideal for human beings is for all to sit under their own vines and fig trees (Mic 4:4). Yet God cares about the animate world, independently of its relevance to humanity (Job 38:26–27). We should not cut down trees in wartime as if they were human beings (i.e., enemies, Deut 20:19).

But God puts both human beings and animals under a king's authority (Jer 27:5; Dan 2:38). The fate of humanity and animals is often bound up together. Both perish, but God delivers both (Pss 36:6; 49:12, 20). Both suffer from the plagues in Egypt (Exod 8:17, 18; 9:9, 10, 19, 22, 25; 12:12; 13:15; Ps 135:8). Both can become tainted and convey taint (Lev 5:2–3; 7:21;

1 Kgs 13:2; 2 Kgs 23:14, 20). Humanity can drag animals down with them, but God will also restore both (Jer 7:20; 31:27; 32:43; 33:10, 12; 36:29; 50:3; 51:62; Ezek 14:13–21; 29:8; 36:11; 38:20; Zeph 1:3; Hag 1:11; Zech 2:4; 8:10). Both can join in penitence (Jonah 3:7–8). The *firstborn* of both are owed to God (Exod 13:2; Num 3:13; 8:17; 18:15), though the firstborn of human beings are to be bought back with a sheep (13:13, 15; Num 18:15) and/or are replaced by the consecration of the Levites (Num 3:12; 8:18). But you cannot buy back something "devoted to destruction," whether human or animal (Lev 27:28–29).

Yet there are differences between human beings and animals. While the first man's naming of the animals may indicate his exercise of authority over them, more directly it suggests a recognition that they are different from him. Indeed, there are different bodies for human beings, animals, birds, and fish (1 Cor 15:39). Human beings are made in the image of God as God's final act of creation. A human being can offer compensation for killing an animal, but must be killed for killing a human being (Lev 24:21). A human being is worth much more than a sheep (Matt 12:12).

Humanity is created *male and female* (Gen 1:27). So are other creatures, but Genesis does not note this, so presumably it has some special significance for human beings. As is the case with other creatures, being male and female makes it possible for human beings to multiply and fill the earth, but its distinctive significance for human beings is that they are thus in a position to fulfill the task of subduing the earth, exercising authority over other creatures on God's behalf. The second creation story spells this out. Here the background to God's making of human beings is the need for someone to serve (i.e., work) the ground. On his own, the man cannot do this; creation is "not good" until God brings into being a second human being who complements the first (2:18). The woman provides the man with the help he needs.

While the first story emphasizes humanity's links with the animate world and its differentiation from it, the second emphasizes humanity's analogous relationship with the ground. The man is shaped out of dirt from the ground and brought into being to serve it (2:5, 7). The similarity of the words for "man" and "ground" (*ha'adam, ha'adamah*) underlines humanity's common origin with the ground and its task in relation to it. The basic features of being human are thus to look after the other creatures and to grow things. The heavens belong to Yahweh, but the earth is given to human beings (Ps 115:16).

But the first human being comprises more than merely something shaped like a form (or an image) from the dirt. He comes into proper existence and becomes a living being (*nephesh hayyah*) only when God breathes into him "the breath of life" or "living breath" (*nishmat hayyim*, 2:7). Here, human beings thus comprise **body** plus breath of **life**, a different, complementary analysis to the one elsewhere that distinguishes between outer person (body) and inner person (spirit or self or personality). While animals also have the breath of life (1:30), that "breath of life" is a different expression. Humanity has *neshamah*; animals have *nephesh*. It may be coincidence that we do not have an instance of the former term applied to animals; but as we have it, the terminology marks a difference between human beings and animals, which are simply "formed from the ground" (2:19).

Alongside the general permission to eat of the fruit trees in the garden is a prohibition on eating from the good-and-bad-knowledge tree. In Western terms, having access to this tree and being able to decide to disobey God suggests that human beings had free will, but the emphasis of the story lies elsewhere. It sees human beings as having free will to decide which of the rest of the trees to eat, but God did not leave them to decide whether to eat of the knowledge tree. God gave them no choice on that matter. They could ignore God's instructions, but this did not constitute the exercise of freedom of choice but an act of disobedience.

Human life's shortcomings. From the beginning, human life was characterized by constraint and pressure. Human beings had the task of subduing a resistant world, they were forbidden access to a key resource (the tree that could enable them to distinguish between good and bad), and one of God's creatures tried to beguile them to do the opposite of what God said (Gen 1–3).

Their falling for this enticement made their situation worse. Henceforth the troubles of human beings lie heavily upon them (Eccl 8:6; Job 5:7; 7:1). There are times when divine beings or mighty ones make unfair decisions for human beings (Ps 58:1). Divine beings get involved with the daughters of humans (Gen 6:1–4). The human spirit can endure sickness, but when the spirit is broken—who can bear it? (Prov 18:14). Human beings resemble very feeble members of God's creation, rather than masters of it (Job 25:6; Ps 22:6). They can think they see the right way to go but find it leads to death (Prov 14:12; 16:25). They cannot discover what is good to do or what is going on in the world or what is going to happen (Eccl 2:3; 7:14; 8:17; 9:1; 10:14). As human beings they can feel they understand nothing (Prov 30:2–3). They can dream but not know what they dreamt (Dan 2:10). The human heart has not conceived what God has prepared for those who love God (1 Cor 2:9).

Like death, human eyes are never satisfied (Prov 27:20). All human toil is for the mouth, but the appetite is never satisfied. Human beings can gain all that they desire but not have chance to enjoy it. They gain nothing from their toil; they cannot even express how wearisome things are. It is an unhappy business that God has given human beings to be weary with. Yet the best thing for human beings is to enjoy work, food, and drink as gifts from God (Eccl 1:3, 8, 13; 2:22, 24: 6:1–3, 7; 8:15).

The most important fact about being human is that we are going to die (Eccl 7:2). This distinguishes human beings from God (Ezek 28:9). No human beings can stop *death,* evade it, reverse it, or ransom themselves or anyone else from it (Job 14:10, 14; Pss 49:7–9; 89:48; Eccl 8:8; 12:5; Ezek 31:14; Heb 9:27). Human beings cannot abide in honor; they perish (Ps 49:12). At the human level, one looks forward only to death (1 Cor 15:32).

Was humanity mortal when created? The man is told that death will result from eating from the good-and-bad-knowledge tree, which suggests human beings would be immortal if they refrained. But the presence of the life-tree suggests it was this tree's fruit that would convey a life lasting longer than the familiar threescore years and ten; thus God later denies access to this tree by means of which human beings might live forever. What is clear is that, one way or another, humanity was designed to enjoy lasting life, but decisions that were taken back at the beginning of humanity's story mean we no longer have that opportunity. Death is an act of judgment on our human sinfulness.

In addition, the days of a human life are few (Eccl 2:3). This is a comfort in light of human inclination to transgression and violence—the opportunity to indulge in these is short-lived (Ps 17:3–4, 14). Yet in light of it, for what emptiness has God created all humanity! (Ps 89:47). The point is underlined when God determines, "My spirit shall not abide in mortals [the ordinary word for humankind in NRSV] forever" (Gen 6:3). God sets a limit of 120 years, which may be the longest imaginable human lifespan or may be the time that is to pass before the calamity of the great flood.

Not only is human life short: it is vulnerable and unpredictable. We never know when it may suddenly be terminated (Ps 39:5–6; Eccl 9:12). Under the oppression of other people, human beings can be as helpless as fish caught in a net (Hab 1:14). Israel's periodic experience of God's wrath provides it with a focused experience of the general limitedness of human life, which contrasts with God's eternity; when God determines it is time

for us to return to dirt, that decides the matter (Ps 90). Human beings flourish and then die as quickly as wildflowers, a breath, or a passing shadow (Job 14:1; Pss 103:15–16; 144:3–4).

After the unraveling of God's creation project, the disastrous flood came about because human wickedness was so great in the earth. Indeed, in Noah's day "every inclination of the thoughts of their hearts was only evil continually" (Gen 6:5). By means of the flood God sought to give humanity a new start, while recognizing that things could get that way again— "for the inclination of the human heart is evil from youth" (Gen 8:21). This makes it pointless to bring another flood. Rather, God seeks to place some constraints on humanity that may restrain its evil inclination or place a limit on its negative results.

There are times when the conditions in Gen 6 seem to have recurred, when the faithful quite disappear from humankind and baseness is exalted among them (Ps 12:1, 8), when God looks down from heaven on humankind to see if there are any wise, any who have recourse to God, and finds there are not (Ps 14:2), when it seems that every human being is false (Ps 116:11), when it is hard to find a trustworthy human being (Prov 20:6), when there is no human being who acts justly and seeks truth (Jer 5:1–5) or repents (Jer 8:6) or has any insight (Jer 51:17) or is faithful and upright (Mic 7:2). In situations like that, God may send affliction to human beings to draw them back to God (Job 33:29–30). God promises to chastise David's successors by human means rather than by abandoning them; David prefers to fall into the hands of God than those of human beings (2 Sam 7:14; 24:14; 1 Chr 21:13).

There are human beings to whom God imputes no iniquity in the sense that there is no deceit in them—no mismatch between appearance and inner attitude (Ps 32:2). There are good and bad human beings; on judgment day they will give account for their lives (Matt 12:35–36). Human beings are justified by their deeds (Jas 2:24). But elsewhere Scripture declares that there is no human being who is righteous or pure in God's eyes and wholly lives by God's standards (1 Kgs 8:46; Job 4:17; 9:2; 15:14; 25:4, 6; Eccl 7:20; Rom 3:20). Indeed the minds of human beings are full of evil; God made human beings "straightforward, but they have devised many schemes" (Eccl 7:29; 9:3). Unlike God, human beings are inclined to lie and change their minds (Num 23:19; 1 Sam 15:29). Human beings act in anger, whereas God does not (Hos 11:9). They act with jealousy and quarreling and designate themselves by one Christian teacher or another (1 Cor 3:3–4). They can tame animals, but not the tongue, and human anger does not effect God's righteous purpose (Jas 1:19–20; 3:7). They can gain the world but forfeit their life (Matt 16:26).

It is what comes out of human mouths and hearts or minds that defiles (Matt 15:11, 18, 20). The human heart and mind are cunningly deceptive, but God sees and examines or tests human beings so as to see who is righteous and wicked and deals with them appropriately (Job 13:9; Pss 11:4–7; 14:2; 33:13; 53:2; 64:6–7; Prov 5:21–23; 15:11; 24:12; Jer 32:19; Lam 3:35). Whereas human beings have to rely on outward appearances, God can look into the inner person and relate to people on that basis (1 Sam 16:7; 1 Kgs 8:39; 2 Chr 6:30; Job 13:9; Acts 15:8). Human beings can think they are pure, but God weighs the spirit (Prov 16:2; cf. 21:2). But why then does God test Job so hard, as if God were subject to human limitations (Job 10:4–7)?

Walter Brueggemann, *Theology of the Old Testament* (Minneapolis: Fortress Press, 1997), 450–91; Brevard S. Childs, *Biblical Theology of the Old and New Testaments* (Minneapolis: Fortress Press, 1993), 566–94; Aubrey R. Johnson, *The Vitality of the Individual in the Thought of Ancient Israel* (Cardiff: University of Wales Press, 1964).

JOHN GOLDINGAY

Humble, Humility see **Pride**

Husband see **Marriage**

Hypocrisy, Hypocrite The Greek word *hypokrisis* originally meant "acting," and so it has come to be used in English for pretending or claiming to be better than one really is. In the Greek literature of Hellenistic Judaism, however, the word was almost never used that way. It almost always referred to lying and deceit, condemned as wicked. The contexts of its uses in the NT also show that for those authors *hypokrisis* did not mean "hypocrisy" exactly as we understand it. The word was a favorite of Matthew's; he used the noun "hypocrite" fourteen times and "hypocrisy" once. Mark uses the words only twice, Luke four times. *Hypokrisis* also appears in Gal 2:13, 1 Tim 4:2, and 1 Pet 2:1 ("insincerity" in NRSV). The verb *hypokrinomai* is used once in the sense of pretending to be what one is not, in Luke 20:20, but the nouns more accurately refer to contradictory behavior, which need not be deliberately deceptive.

In Matt 7:5, "hypocrites" are those who can see their neighbor's faults but cannot see their own. Matthew 15:3–9 condemns scribes and Pharisees for teachings that nullified the commandment to honor father and mother; not "hypocrisy" as we use the word. In Luke 12:54–56 "hypocrites" are those who can interpret signs in nature, but not the "present time," and in Luke 13:15–16 they cannot see a parallel between the need to care for cattle on the Sabbath and relieving a woman from a burden she had borne for eighteen years. These texts help to explain why "blind guides" is a parallel to "hypocrites" in Matt 23:16. Matthew 23 addresses those who are convinced of their righteousness (thus, not pretending) but are in fact far short of it in their behavior. Paul also does not so much accuse Peter and the others of insincerity or pretense as of committing a serious breach of faith (Gal 2:13). In 1 Tim 4:2 the word is used of "liars" who promote false teaching in the church, and in 1 Pet 2:1 it is associated with malice, guile, envy, and slander.

DONALD E. GOWAN

Idol, Idolatry

The English term "idol" descends from the Greek *eidolon*, "image, phantom." When it is applied to an object of worship, the term quickly turns pejorative. Though it portrays a god, it lacks any reality beyond itself. What it represents is, in short, a figment of the imagination, a false god.

Old Testament

From the beginning, in its official religion Israel chose to uphold an austere religion of aniconic monotheism. This is an amazing fact, considering that tiny Israel lived in the midst of giant cultures with rich polytheistic traditions in which the gods were worshiped in physical forms (humans, animals, abstract objects such as obelisks or blocks). At least until after the Babylonian exile, Israel struggled against the challenge presented by idols in its environment and in its very midst. This helps account for the rich semantic assemblage of Hebrew terms that lies behind the word "idol" and its synonyms in our English versions. More than fifteen in number, these terms descend from root meanings that range over all aspects of idols: their physical nature (carved or cast image, representational picture, and the word *gillul[im]*—used thirty-seven times in Ezekiel alone—that has something to do with rolling, perhaps as a log or a cylinder); their moral status (things of sin, horror, grief; detestable things); the term *ʾelil*, especially common in Isaiah, which carries the sense of "nothingness, worthlessness." These Hebrew terms and our English definition of the word "idol" connect in various ways to several theological themes tied to the phenomenon of idolatry in the OT.

The dangers of holiness. Ancient Israel believed deeply in the potency of holiness. *Holy* things were off limits at peril of life. The inner sanctums of the tabernacle and the temple could be entered only by the high priest. The ark of the covenant (see *presence*), the very seat of their God, Yahweh, posed a peril to the unauthorized in Israel (1 Sam 6:19; 2 Sam 6:8). It also had power against hostile gods.

When the Philistines stole the ark from Israel (1 Sam 4:11), their first impulse was to place it in the temple of their god, Dagon, in their temple in Ashdod. But when they arrived there the next day, they found Dagon lying flat on his face before the ark. Holiness, the near presence of deity, could, it was widely believed even in Israel, exert immense power.

But the ark was not an idol, nor were the other holy things in Israel. To the objects that other peoples deliberately set out to make foci of divine presence, Israel gave no credence at all. Babylonians, Egyptians, and Canaanites were serious about the construction, care, and feeding of their representations of their gods, for in these cultures an idol was a literal manifestation of deity, a physical point of encounter with the god. Many cult idols and their sanctuaries, together with the associated texts, have been preserved in Egypt and Mesopotamia. From Canaan no large cult statues remain, but numerous small, popular figurines of the Canaanite pantheon—the high god El; Baal, his son, "the cloud rider"; and Baal's sister-consort, Anat/Asherah—have come to light. A god would enter into the body of a properly manufactured image with the help of cultic ceremonies. The Israelite tradition itself depicts such practices going on, as, for example, in the late apocryphal addition to Daniel called "Bel and the Dragon." When Daniel questioned the vitality of the god Bel, before whose cult statue the Babylonians daily spread a large repast of meat, bread, and wine, the priests asked him, "Do you not think that Bel is a living god? Do you not see how much he eats and drinks every day?" (v. 6).

We know from the material remains of ancient Israel that some of the people sometimes succumbed to the temptations of idolatry. Figurines of fertility goddesses bespeak popular superstition. Altars, pillars, and even inscriptions hint at cult practices not in tune with the radical monotheism of Deuteronomy and the prophets. Old Testament literature confirms the struggle to reject the putative power of the objects of popular holiness. Reformers like Gideon had no compunction about smashing altars and pulling down the sacred poles (= asherah) that belonged to their own people (Judg 6:25–32). The prophets called for the purging of idolatry (e.g., Hos 8:4–6; Mic 1:7), and good King Josiah did it wholesale, even destroying the idols and temples to foreign gods erected by his predecessor kings from Solomon through Manasseh (2 Kgs 23:4–25). Nor did the OT writers view with favor making cast images of Yahweh, such as was done by the Ephraimite Micah (Judg 17) and probably by Jeroboam I when he put golden calves (representations or at least steeds of Yahweh) in Dan and Bethel (1 Kgs 12:25–33). The prohibition against image making, which the OT places among the ten categorical imperatives that stand before all the rest of the law, says, "You shall not make for yourself an idol" (Exod 20:4; Deut 5:8). Taken in connection with the preceding verse, "You shall have no other gods before me," this seems to prohibit worship of more than one God. But taken in connection with the succeeding commandment, "You shall not make wrongful use of the name of the LORD your God," this points toward the danger of manipulating God ("wrongful use"), getting God in a box, bringing the power of God under the control of the individual. That is always the danger and fallacy of an idol.

Undivided loyalty. Israel's most basic confession of faith is the famously ambiguous *Shemaᶜ*, which begins either this way: "Hear, O Israel: The LORD is our God, the LORD alone," or this way: "Hear, O Israel: the LORD our God is one LORD" (Deut 6:4). (The Hebrew permits both readings.) Either way, the stress is on unity. Either the Lord has a total claim on the people's allegiance, to the exclusion of all other sovereign claims; or the Lord is one, not to be worshiped in many and diverse local manifestations, including idols. The first of these understandings is consistent with the first commandment in the Decalogue, "You shall have no

other gods before me" (Exod 20:3; see also Deut 5:7). When no other gods are placed between the Lord and the worshiping people, so that that people can love the Lord with *all* their heart, soul, and might, a bond of loyalty comes into being that cannot be diverted by the tempting sight of images. Idolatry and adultery share the common feature of divided loyalty. That is why both Hosea (chaps. 1–3) and Ezekiel (chaps. 16; 23) variously represent idolatrous Israel, Judah, and Jerusalem as whores offering themselves to strangers. Consistent with the second reading of the *Shemaᶜ* is the command "You shall not make for yourself an idol" (Exod 20:4–6; Deut 5:8–10; cf. Exod 34:17). As noted above, this ban on constructing any "graven image" in the form of any living thing and making it an object of worship was taken to include any representation whatever of Yahweh.

The folly of worshiping something that has no objective reality. The OT offers no evidence to suggest that the writers thought that an idol had any actual spiritual potency, even a demonic one. No writer pours more contempt on idols and their makers than the prophet of the exile, Isa 40–55. In a sustained prose essay in 44:9–20, Isaiah, who must have lived in a culture in which encounters with idols were a fact of daily life, pictures a craftsman using half of a block of wood to make a cooking fire and carving an idol from the other half. Such a person is too deluded to free himself from this trap of his own making and to say, "Is not this thing in my right hand a fraud?" (44:20; see also Isa 41:21–29; 45:20–25; 46:1–13).

How the Lord wills to be worshiped. When all is said and done, the best case made for imageless worship in the OT is simply that God wills to be known and obeyed through the medium of words, not forms. Deuteronomy 4:9–20 relates this to the event at Horeb, when God's foundational disclosure of torah was effected by voice only (see v. 12). Revelation without the medium of form established the norm; idols are a corruption (v. 16).

New Testament. Thanks in part perhaps to the withering contempt of the prophets, idolatry seems to have ceased to be a major problem in Judah after exile. With the intense contact with Hellenistic culture, where a more aesthetic idolatry was practiced, the issue reasserts itself in the NT. The semantic repertoire is much more limited, however, centering largely upon the Greek word *eidolon.* In Acts 7:41 Stephen flatly brands Aaron's golden calf as an idol. Paul makes the idols of Athens serve his own purpose (Acts 17:16–31), contrasting the true authority of the unknown God whom he proclaims with the merely imaginative images of gold, silver, or stone (v. 29). Sometimes Paul gives idols the status of demons (1 Cor 10:20–21; Rev 9:20 also seems to make the equation). Yet generally he denies that they have any reality (1 Cor 8:4).

In Acts 15:20 James includes abstention "from things polluted by idols" in his minimal list of regulations incumbent upon Gentile converts to Christianity. Presumably this alludes to meat sacrificed to idols, whether eaten in the cultic ceremony itself or purchased later in the market. Much of Paul's discussion about idols also centers on this question (1 Cor 8; 10). If idols are not really gods, such meat should not be harmful to believers. However, believers should take great care not to participate in any cultic meal other than that provided by God (the Eucharist), lest they cause another person to fall (1 Cor 8:13) or become partners with demons (1 Cor 10:20).

W. SIBLEY TOWNER

Ill, Illness   *see* Heal

Image, Likeness (of God)

"Image" most often represents Hebrew/Aramaic *tselem* and Greek *eikon.* "Likeness" most often represents Hebrew *demut* and Greek *homoioma.* In each language the first word is more concrete, the second more abstract. "Image" thus most often refers to a material representation of something—notably, the visible representation of a deity that symbolizes the presence of the deity for worshipers. When Israelites make such images, it is not always clear whether these represent Yahweh or other deities. In the latter case they suggest unfaithfulness to Yahweh. In the former case the OT's fundamental objection is not that God is spirit but that images fall fatally short of adequately representing Yahweh as one who is alive and who acts and speaks. Images have no life and cannot represent these key aspects of Yahweh's character (see, e.g., Deut 4; Isa 40:18–20; 44:9–20; Jer 10:1–16).

The OT uses the expression "image of God" in a positive sense only in reference to the creation of humanity (Gen 1:26–27; cf. 5:3; 9:6). On the assumption that the image of God must link with something that humanity has in common with God, over the centuries it has usually been located in human beings' intellectual, moral, or spiritual nature. But elsewhere "image" always denotes something concrete, and one would expect the divine image in humanity to lie in something more outward. That polemic in Deuteronomy might suggest it lies in humanity's capacity to act and speak. The polemic in passages such as Jer 10 might suggest it lies in humanity's having the breath of life—Gen 1 would then be anticipating the account in Gen 2. Or perhaps we should link the phrase to what follows in Gen 1:26: being made in God's image means that humanity represents God as it takes up the task of subduing the world on God's behalf. Subsequently Gen 1:27 follows up reference to the image by alluding to humanity's being male and female, but animals also have this characteristic, so it is hardly the case that this defines the image—as if its point was that being male and female meant being relational (see **man and woman**). More likely the link is that being male and female makes it possible for humanity to fill the earth and thus fulfill the task of subduing the world. Egyptian thinking saw only the king as in God's image, while Paul associates the image only with men (1 Cor 11:7).

Since "likeness" is more abstract than "image," the addition of the second word as a qualifier in the phrase "in our image, according to our likeness" may be designed to safeguard against too crass an understanding of the first word. It may then be significant that Ezekiel prefers the term "likeness" in his description of his vision of God's glory (Ezek 1). The psalmist expects to wake up with excitement and see God's likeness (Ps 17:15)—here the word is *temunah*, the likeness or form that Moses saw (Num 12:8). In Gen 5:1–3 the words are used in the reverse configuration.

In isolation, Gen 5 might imply that only the first two human beings were created in God's image, and one might infer that the divine image disappeared through their act of disobedience. But Gen 9:6 implies that humanity continues to bear God's image (cf. Jas 3:9). There the significance of the point lies in the fact that one human being must not kill or assault another, because that is in effect to attack God.

The fact that human beings image God makes it possible to speak of God in human terms. It gives anthropomorphism a theological basis. God is a humanlike person, not (e.g.) an abstract force or the ground of our being or an entity so transcendently different from us as to make relationship impossible. It is now possible to speak of God as having human qualities and feelings such as love, compassion, faithfulness, hatred, and anger, and possible for God to appear in humanlike form, as God often does in the OT (e.g., Gen 18). There is no difficulty in speaking of God becoming a human being; the inherent link between God and human beings makes this possible. Thus the NT speaks of Christ as the image of the invisible God (Col 1:15; cf. 2 Cor 4:4); in becoming a human being he makes the invisible God visible. The NT means more than that Christ is a perfect human being, a human being who fully realizes the human destiny to image God. As often happens when the NT uses OT words and ideas, the NT uses the idea of

the image in a new way. "Image" now suggests identity rather than mere similarity (cf. Heb 10:1, where NRSV translates *eikon* "true form"). Christ as God's image is God's true reflection.

Paul uses the idea of "image" in another distinctive way to describe what Christ achieved. He implies that God's image in humanity became tarnished, but in Christ it can be renewed (Col 3:10). We are being transformed into the image of Christ, who is the image of God (2 Cor 3:18; 4:4). Our new selves are "created according to the likeness of God in true righteousness and holiness"—literally, "created according to the likeness of God" (Eph 4:24).

Walter Harrelson, in "The Second Commandment," *The Ten Commandments and Human Rights* (Philadelphia: Fortress Press, 1980), 61–72; Claus Westermann, *Genesis 1–11* (Minneapolis: Augsburg Publishing House, 1984), 142–61.

JOHN GOLDINGAY

Immanuel, Emmanuel
A symbolic name, meaning "God is with us," used four times in the Bible (Isa 7:14; 8:8; Matt 1:23; translated by NRSV in Isa 8:10). It is used in different ways by Isaiah and Matthew. Isaiah was sent to King Ahaz to assure him that the threat from Syria and the northern kingdom of Israel would soon come to nothing. As confirmation that his promise was true, Isaiah predicted that a child would soon be born (the text literally reads "a young woman is pregnant") and given the symbolic name Immanuel, and that before the child would be old enough to distinguish good from evil, the danger threatening Judah would have passed. For the sign to have any meaning, Isaiah must have been speaking of a child to be born soon. The promise in the name was in fact fulfilled, for Assyria soon broke the power of Syria and the northern kingdom.

It is not completely clear whether the other two uses of Immanuel in Isaiah are to be taken as names or as sentences. The threatening passage in 8:5–8 may be understood as a follow-up to Ahaz's refusal to accept Isaiah's advice. A promise, "God is with us," would be an inappropriate conclusion to such a threat, so this is probably addressed to that child with the symbolic name, and NRSV so renders it. The next unit (8:9–10) is bad news for the "peoples" and "countries," however, and ʿimmanu-ʾel is introduced by ki "for," so it seems to function as a sentence rather than a name, and NRSV has accordingly translated it "God is with us."

The "young woman" (ʿalmah) of Isaiah's Hebrew (7:14) became more specifically a "virgin" (parthenos) in the Greek of the LXX, which Matthew quotes in 1:23. It has been suggested that Matthew claimed Jesus was born of a virgin because of what he found in this verse, but it seems more likely that the *virgin birth* was already part of the tradition he had been taught. The occurrence of parthenos in Isa 7:14 then led him to connect Jesus with the potent promise in the name Immanuel (transliterated "Emmanuel" in the Greek). Although much has been made of the virgin birth in later Christian theology, it was the symbolic name that was most meaningful for Matthew, for he translated it to be sure those reading his Greek text would know what it means. Mary's child was not in fact named Emmanuel, but Jesus, another name with a meaning important for Matthew (1:21). But "God is with us" has been identified as a major theme of his Gospel, for it begins and ends with it. Jesus' last words are the promise, "And remember, I am with you always, to the end of the age" (28:20). The promise now specifically involves the presence of Jesus.

The divine promise, "I will be with you," and the resulting expressions of confidence, "God is with us," appear in various forms 104 times in the OT. They primarily appear as a promise of divine presence to help when one faced a dangerous or uncertain task. Matthew thus made a highly significant claim when he said that this potent promise was fulfilled

in the person of Jesus. The concept of incarnation does not yet appear in Matthew, but his use of Immanuel at the beginning of his Gospel may already be a move in the direction of incarnational theology.

Donald E. Gowan, "I Will Be With You," in *Theology in Exodus: Biblical Theology in the Form of a Commentary* (Louisville, Ky.: Westminster John Knox Press, 1994), 54–75.

DONALD E. GOWAN

Immorality, Immoral, Fornication, Fornicator

These are words frequently used in NRSV to denote sexual activity that NT authors declare to be completely unacceptable for Christians (other common words are "adultery" and "impurity"). The English words are translations of the Greek *porneia* (also rendered "unchastity" in Matt 5:32; 19:9). The verb *porneuo* is translated "indulge in sexual immorality" (1 Cor 10:8) or "practice [commit] fornication (Rev 2:14, 20; 17:2; 18:3, 9), and the noun *porne* is translated "prostitute" (e.g., Matt 21:31–32) or "whore" (e.g., Rev 17:1). The noun *pornos* is variously rendered as "sexually immoral person" (1 Cor 5:9), "immoral" (1 Cor 5:10), and "fornicator" (1 Cor 6:9). As the NT writers use these words, they clearly include any form of sexual activity outside of *marriage*. They are associated with *aselgeia*, "licentiousness" (Mark 7:21–22; 2 Cor 12:21; Gal 5:19), and with *akatharsia*, "impurity" (2 Cor 12:21; Gal 5:19; Eph 5:3; Col 3:5). The latter is clearly moral, and not the ritual impurity that concerned Judaism. The NT not only reaffirmed the OT's condemnation of adultery but also speaks frequently in these more general terms of the need to resist the temptations of sexual promiscuity (see *body*). In the lists of the kinds of behavior that will be destructive of self and of the Christian community, sexual misdeeds play a prominent place, very likely because the Hellenistic culture in which most of the early Christians lived permitted a great deal that Judaism, and then Christian leaders, called unacceptable (1 Thess 4:5; 1 Pet 4:3–4).

Jesus offered a moral definition of "defilement" in contrast to the Pharisaic emphasis on laws of ritual cleanness with reference to food: "It is what comes out of a person that defiles. For it is from within, from the human heart, that evil intentions come: fornication, theft, murder, adultery, avarice, wickedness, deceit, licentiousness, envy, slander, pride, folly" (Mark 7:20–22; cf. the shorter list in Matt 15:19). The lists of behavior not fit for citizens of the coming kingdom of God in the Epistles put sexual misbehavior in a similar prominent place. Galatians 5:19–23 begins with fornication, impurity, and licentiousness; 1 Cor 6:9–10 with fornicators, idolaters, adulterers, male prostitutes, sodomites; and Col 3:5–8 with fornication, impurity, passion, and evil desire. Another list concludes instead with "impurity, sexual immorality, and licentiousness" (2 Cor 12:20–21). In each case, the sexual irregularities are associated with antisocial behavior, such as anger, jealously, and gossip, so one's sex life was considered to be not a purely personal matter but something that contributed to the health or dis-ease of the Christian community. The inclusion of idolatry in immediate association with sexual sins should also be noted (Gal 5:20; Col 3:5; 1 Cor 5:11; cf. Rev 2:14, 20). Paul went beyond the negative practical effects of promiscuous sexual activity in 1 Cor 6:15–20, where he cited Gen 2:24, "they become one flesh," claiming that God intended the sexual relationship to be that which physically unites one man with one woman. Relations outside of marriage would thus disrupt the very order of creation (cf. Matt 19:4–6; Eph 5:31).

James D. G. Dunn, *The Epistle to the Galatians* (Peabody, Mass.: Hendrickson Publishers, 1995), 301–15; Brendan Byrne, S.J., "Sinning against One's Own Body: Paul's Understanding of the Sexual Relationship in 1 Corinthians 6:18," *CBQ* 45 (1983): 608–16.

DONALD E. GOWAN

Immortality, Immortal (*see also* Resurrection) "Immortality" is the translation of two nouns that appear ten times in the New Testament: *athanasia* ("deathlessness"), which occurs three times and denotes the immunity from death enjoyed by God (1 Tim 6:16) and resurrected believers (1 Cor 15:53–54); and *aphtharsia* ("incorruptibility" or "imperishability"), which occurs seven times and signifies the immunity from decay that characterizes the divine state (Eph 6:24) and the resurrection state (1 Cor 15:42, 50, 53–54). The adjective *aphthartos* ("immortal," "incorruptible," or "imperishable") occurs four times and describes the quality of the divine nature (Rom 1:23; 1 Tim 1:17), the Christian's reward (1 Cor 9:25), and the future state of resurrected believers (1 Cor 15:52). All these terms occur only in the Pauline letters—mostly in 1 Cor 15.

The immortality of the soul. The idea of "the immortality of the soul" arose in the sixth century B.C. within the Greek Orphic cult, which claimed as its founder the legendary Thracian poet and musician Orpheus, and was formalized as the basic anthropological concept of Greek philosophy by Plato (ca. 428/27–348/47 B.C.). It held that a person is a soul, an immortal being enclosed in a mortal case, and that the body is the soul's prison (Greek: *soma sema,* "the body is a tomb"), from which it may not emerge until the divinely allotted time of death (cf., e.g., Plato, *Cratylus* 400; *Phaedrus* 250; *Gorgias* 493; *Axiochus* 365; Aristotle, *On the Soul* 1.5, 411b; *Nicomachean Ethics* 1.12.6, 1102a).

Inherent human immortality, however, is an idea alien to the Jewish Scriptures, and there is no equivalent term in the OT to *athanasia* ("deathlessness"). Only God is "living" (Deut 5:26; Josh 3:10; Pss 42:2; 84:2; Jer 10:10) and the possessor of "life" (Ps 36:9). In fact, in the OT, as in all ancient Near East literature, it is the mortality of humans that separates them from deity or the gods. Though some mortals may have been thought to have crossed that boundary, and so admitted directly into the divine world (e.g.,

Utnapishtim in the Gilgamesh Epic; apparently also Enoch of Gen 5:24 and Elijah of 2 Kgs 2:3–12), such instances were considered exceptions and the intrinsic immortality of humans rejected.

It was only during the period of Second Temple Judaism (ca. 200 B.C.–A.D. 120), when the Greek concept of immortality was fused with the Hebrew concept of humans having been created in "the image of God" (Gen 1:27), that Jews began to distinguish between body and soul (1 En. 22:7; l02:5; Wis 9:15; 2 Macc 7:37; 14:38; Let. Aris. 139; 236; Josephus, Contra Apionem 2.203) and to regard the soul as inherently immortal (Josephus, Jewish War 1.84; 2.154–55, 163; 6.46; 7.341–48; Jewish Antiquities 17:354; 18.14, 18). Some of these Jewish immortality concepts were clothed in resurrection language, others in astral imagery, others in terminology drawn from ideas about reincarnation and the transmigration of souls, and still others in distinctly Grecian anthropological forms of expression.

Likewise, a Greek understanding of the immortality of the soul is alien to the NT. It is only God who possesses life in himself (John 5:26; 6:57) and is inherently immortal (1 Tim 6:16). He makes alive through his spirit, and so his spirit is called "life giving" (John 6:63; 1 Cor 15:45). It was Christian writers of the late first and second centuries who, attempting to make the gospel palatable to the Greek mind and defend it against false accusations, took up again the thesis that the human soul (psyche) is inherently immortal (athanatos, "deathless"), comparing it, for example, to the mythological phoenix, a bird that every five hundred years died but reconstituted itself from its decomposed material remains to continue for another five-hundred-year period, ad infinitum (1 Clement 24–27; Justin Martyr, First Apology 44:9; Dialogue with Trypho 4:5; 124:4; Tatian, Address to the Greeks 13:1; 15:4; and the anonymous Epistle to Diognetus 6). And though these early apologists used such analogies to support a Christian doctrine of resurrection, they failed to distinguish between Christian teaching on immortality, which is given to believers by God at their resurrection, and Greco-Roman beliefs in the natural immortality of the soul.

Immortality and resurrection. The terms for immortality in the NT—whether *athanasia* ("deathlessness"), *aphtharsia* ("incorruptibility" or "imperishability"), or *aphthartos* ("immortal," "incorruptible," or "imperishable")—are never used in connection with the word "soul" (*psyche*), but always associated only with the **resurrection** and transformation of persons (eight times, all in 1 Cor 15). And never do we find Paul (or any other NT writer) using the noun *athanatos* ("immortal") or the verb *athanatizo* ("I make immortal" or, in the passive voice, "I become immortal"), which were the common terms for immortality in the Greek world—even though the verb would have been suitable in such passages as Rom 8:11 and 2 Cor 5:4. It may plausibly be argued that these latter terms were avoided by Paul and other NT writers because they could so easily have been misunderstood as implying that immortality was natural to the human condition and existed apart from resurrection.

In speaking of the uniqueness of God, 1 Tim 6:16 states, "It is he alone who has immortality." The corollary of God being the only one inherently immortal is that any immortality ascribed to humans must be seen as a gracious gift of the divine will (Rom 2:7; 6:23). Humans can be immortal only derivatively. Their immortality is not essential or intrinsic, but derived or extrinsic.

First Corinthians 15 clearly places the reception of immortality at the time of the resurrection, for it juxtaposes resurrection and immortality in such phrases as "what is raised is imperishable" (v. 42) and "the dead will be raised imperishable" (v. 52). This does not mean that the dead will be raised and thus be seen to be already immortal, but that the dead will be raised and thus become immortal. Far from already possessing immortality, believers in Christ Jesus are described as those who "seek" for immortality (Rom 2:7) and receive it at the time of their resurrection (1 Cor 15:20–23, 42–53).

From a Christian perspective, the doctrines of "immortality" and "resurrection" stand or fall together. It is a case of "resurrection to immortality" and "immortality through resurrection"—or, as expressed by Paul and rephrased by Murray Harris, "raised immortal." To deny resurrection is to deny immortality, since the embodiment involved in the event of resurrection is necessary for the enjoyment of the meaningful existence implied by immortality. On the other hand, to deny immortality is to deny resurrection, since the permanent supply of the divine life pledged by immortality is necessary to sustain the resurrection life of transformed persons. Each involves the other, so that choosing between them is not only unnecessary but also impossible.

Pierre Benoit and Roland E. Murphy, eds. *Immortality and Resurrection* (New York: Herder, 1970); Oscar Cullmann, *Immortality of the Soul or Resurrection of the Dead?* (New York: Macmillan, 1958); Murray J. Harris, *Raised Immortal: Resurrection and Immortality in the New Testament* (Grand Rapids: Eerdmans, 1985); Murray J. Harris, "Resurrection and Immortality in the Pauline Corpus," in *Life in the Face of Death: The Resurrection Message of the New Testament*, ed. R. N. Longenecker (Grand Rapids: Eerdmans, 1998), 147–70; George W. E. Nickelsburg Jr., *Resurrection, Immortality, and Eternal Life in Intertestamental Judaism* (Cambridge: Harvard University Press, 1972; London: Oxford University Press, 1992); Krister Stendahl, ed., *Immortality and Resurrection* (New York: Macmillan, 1965).

RICHARD N. LONGENECKER

Impure, Impurity   *see* **Clean**

Indignation   *see* **Wrath**

Inherit, Inheritance, Heir

Old Testament. The concept of inheritance in the OT appears frequently in contexts of family custom where the issue is distribution of property to surviving heirs. But the more theologically significant occurrences of the concept involve Israel's conviction that the land of Canaan/Palestine/Israel was God's possession, which God had allotted to Israel as an inheritance. This belief had and has tremendous theological consequence, but it also has been and is subject to deadly misunderstanding and abuse.

In what is presented as divine speech to Moses on Mount Sinai, God says in Lev 25:23 that "the land is mine; with me you are but aliens and tenants" (see also Josh 22:19; 2 Chr 20:11; Jer 2:7). Solomon's prayer in 1 Kgs 8 also affirms divine ownership of the land, but it puts a slightly different perspective on the matter, referring to "your [God's] land, which you have given to your people as an inheritance" (v. 36). This perspective is congruent with the one voiced frequently in the Pentateuch and elsewhere, that is, the land of Canaan/Palestine/Israel is the land promised to Abraham and his descendants as a possession or inheritance (see Gen 12:7; Exod 3:7–8; 32:13; Lev 20:24; Deut 19:10; 34:4; Ps 105:7–11; Jer 12:14).

The Pentateuch anticipates Israel's possession of the land, but Israel's receiving of the land as an inheritance is not narrated until the book of Joshua (thus suggesting to some scholars an original Hexateuch, consisting of the books of Genesis through Joshua). According to Josh 11:23, "Joshua took the whole land, according to all that the LORD had spoken to Moses [see Deut 1:38]; and Joshua gave it for an inheritance to Israel according to their tribal allotments." The subsequent chapters in the book of Joshua recount the tribal allotments in great detail; and in fact, chapters 13–19 contain no less than forty-four occurrences of the word "inheritance."

Although chapters 13–19 of the book of Joshua seem to make for tedious reading, they suggest the theological potential of viewing the land as an inheritance, as well as the possible dangers. These chapters go to great lengths to point out that each clan or family of every tribe (except Levi; see 13:14) receives a portion of land. This is so important because in an agrarian society land represents the ability to make a living. To have a piece of land means to have a future; indeed, to have land means *life*.

This is why it was so grievous for land to be lost, as reflected in the story of Naboth's vineyard in 1 Kings 21. Naboth insists that King Ahab not take his land, saying, "The LORD forbid that I should give you my ancestral inheritance" (v. 3). Even though King Ahab agrees to compensate him, Naboth refuses to give up the inheritance. He apparently is well aware that to be without land is to be consigned to poverty and even death (see Mic 2:1–5), so Naboth does not want to set any deadly precedents.

The crucial significance of land is highlighted also by the jubilee material in Lev 25, which seeks to address the dangerous situation of loss of land. Every fifty years, persons who have lost their land are to "return to their ancestral property" (v. 41; see v. 13). The immediately accompanying rationale cites the exodus from Egypt (v. 42; see v. 55).

When taken together, the preceding texts suggest a theological construal of inheritance, the point of which is not land per se, but rather life. The completion of God's liberating work in the exodus is found in the gift of land to persons whose lives were threatened, originally by landlessness, then by enslavement in Egypt, and later by landlessness again. The divine ownership of the land, along with the insistence on land for everyone, suggests the theological conclusion that God wills life for all people.

But of course this conclusion seems to be compromised by the preceding texts, especially the book of Joshua, which reports that in order for the Israelite tribes to possess the land, other peoples had to be displaced or destroyed or disinherited (see Josh 11:21–23; 21:43–45; 23:4). What about God's will for life for these persons?

It is precisely at this point that the shape of the OT canon is of paramount importance. The story of Abraham and his descendants is set in the context of a story that *begins* with creation and that portrays a God who wills life for *all humankind* (Gen 1–11). Even when the story appears to narrow its focus to Abraham and his family, the ultimate divine purpose is to effect a blessing for "all the families of the earth" (Gen 12:3). The subsequent material in the Pentateuch and in the Former Prophets (Joshua–2 Kings) must be heard *in this context*, as well as in the context of the Latter Prophets (Isaiah, Jeremiah, Ezekiel, the Book of the Twelve). Isaiah, the first book of the Latter Prophets, suggests that Jerusalem (representing the land Israel inherited from God) is to become a gathering place for all nations (Isa 2:2–4) and that Israel's mission is to be "a light to the nations" (Isa 42:6; 49:6). Nothing in the book of Joshua (or Judges or any other book) should be interpreted to contradict this portrayal of God's will or the portrayal of the purpose of Israel's election (see *choose*). In short, *in this canonical context*, the language of inheritance serves to affirm that God wills for all people to "inherit" land/future/life and that God chooses to use the people of God to effect this blessing.

This interpretive direction is reinforced by those texts that do not link the concept of inheritance with land. Not only can the people of Israel be called God's inheritance or "possession" (see Deut 4:20; 9:26, 29; and often) or "heritage" (see 1 Kgs 8:51, 53; Ps 33:12; Isa 19:25, which also calls Egypt "my people" and Assyria "the work of my hands"!), but God's own self can be viewed as the "portion" of God's people (see Pss 16:5–6; 73:26; 119:57; 142:5; Lam 3:24; the Hebrew word is used in conjunction with "inheritance" in Joshua to indicate a particular tract of land). This latter usage may be patterned after the experience of the tribe of Levi, which was given no land as an inheritance, but rather about whom it was said, "the LORD God of Israel is their inheritance" (Josh 13:33). In any case, by not connecting inheritance with land, these texts serve to affirm that God is the ultimate source of future and life. Rather than viewing these texts as "spiritualizations" of the texts that link inheritance and land, as is traditionally the case, it would be better to view them as canonical invitations to interpret more wholistically the texts that do link land and inheritance. In short, God's gift of land to Israel was not an instance of divine favoritism at the expense of the Canaanites. Rather, it exemplifies God's will that dispossessed people threatened with death be given access to life.

From this perspective, the land is not to be protected as a right but shared as a gift. In other words, the mission of the people of God is to use the gifts that they have received in the service of "all the families of the earth" (Gen 12:3). The failure to discern the canonical clues to interpret wholistically the inheritance of the land of Canaan/Palestine/Israel has led to deadly hostilities that have persisted from ancient times to the present, both within and beyond the actual land of Canaan/Palestine/Israel. Some Jews, with the support of some Christians, have viewed and continue to view the land of Canaan/Palestine/Israel as an inherited right to be defended at the expense of other people, rather than as a divine gift to be shared for the benefit of all people. Some Christians—for instance, English settlers of the North America continent—have historically viewed themselves as the New Israel and have concluded that this designation gave or gives them the right to take other people's land and resources for their own benefit. The results have been and are deadly; but they illustrate powerfully the theological import assigned to biblical words and concepts!

New Testament. While portions of the NT show an awareness of the OT connection between inheritance and the promise of land to Abraham and his descendants (see Acts 7:5; 13:19; Heb 11:8), the NT generally has followed the interpretive direction of understanding inheritance more wholistically (see above). Not surprisingly,

of course, the understanding of inheritance in the NT is grounded christologically.

A key text is Mark 12:1–12, which suggests that as Son of God, Jesus is "the heir" to "the inheritance" that God confers (see v. 7; see Heb 1:2, 4). Since inheritance in the OT was linked to land or place, it is not surprising that the Gospels have also transferred the OT theology of place to Jesus. In the OT, the land of Canaan/Israel/Palestine was God's place, focused on God's house, the temple, in Jerusalem. In the NT, Jesus himself is the locus of God's presence and power (see Matt 26:61; Mark 14:58; John 2:19–20). This is especially evident in the Gospel of Luke, where the risen Christ meets the disciples not in Galilee (as in Matthew and Mark) but rather in Jerusalem; and from Jerusalem the disciples are sent "to all nations" (Luke 24:47). The inheritance Jesus offers is not tied to any particular land, but rather involves what land represented in the OT (see above)—that is, life.

The parallel to Mark 12:1–12 in Matt 21:33–44 specifically names the inheritance as "the kingdom of God" (v. 43; see also Matt 25:34; 1 Cor 6:9; 15:50; Gal 5:21; Eph 5:5; James 2:5). As Foerster concludes, "The kingdom or inheritance is the new world in which God reigns alone and supreme" (782). In other words, the inheritance is the gift of life as God intends human life to be.

Life as God intends it can also be called "eternal life," and several texts suggest that this is the inheritance (see Matt 19:29; Mark 10:30; Luke 10:25; 18:18; see also Titus 3:7; 1 Pet 3:7; and Rev 21:7, where "these things" includes "the water of life"). Other words name the inheritance differently, but they communicate essentially the same thing—for instance, "salvation" (Heb 1:14) and "blessing" (Heb 12:17; 1 Pet 3:9).

The logic of inheritance is simple, and it is communicated clearly by Paul: "In Christ Jesus you are all children of God through faith" (Gal 3:26). This makes all people—"Jew or Greek . . . slave or free . . . male and female" (Gal 3:28)—"Abraham's offspring, heirs according to the promise"

(Gal 3:29; see Rom 4:13). The concept of inheritance, of course, revolves around what children of a parent receive. So it is crucial that Paul again makes the case in Romans "that we are children of God, and if children, then heirs, heirs of God and joint heirs with Christ" (Rom 8:16–17). Because Christ fully embodied the life that God intends, the inheritance will mean to "suffer with him [Christ] . . . so that we may also be glorified with him" (Rom 8:17).

The same reality is articulated in the Beatitudes, which are essentially a portrait of life in God's realm (see "kingdom of heaven" in Matt 5:3, 10). Included among the "blessed" or "happy" are "the meek, for they will inherit the earth" (Matt 5:5; cf. Ps 37:9, 11, 22, 29, 34). This inheritance does not come without suffering and persecution (see Matt 5:11), but its "reward" (Matt 5:12) is the reality of living life fully under the claim of God.

Just as the kingdom of God is both a present reality and one still to be fully consummated, so the inheritance is both "now" and "not yet." This is at least implicit in the Gospels and Paul (see Paul's discussion of hope in Rom 8:18–25, immediately following the three occurrences of "heirs" in 8:17; and it is explicit in Eph 1, where the "inheritance" (vv. 11, 14, 18) of God's "children" (v. 5) involves a "hope" (vv. 12, 18) that points toward "a plan for the fullness of time" when God will "gather up all things in him [Christ], things in heaven and things on earth" (v. 10; see *mystery* and *plan*). This future cosmic unity is, however, already anticipated and embodied by the reality that "the Gentiles have become fellow heirs, members of the same body, and sharers in the promise in Christ Jesus though the gospel" (Eph 3:6). In short, as suggested in the OT as well (see above), God wills that all people ("Gentiles" mean "nations") share in the divine inheritance, the fullness of life that God intends for all humankind and all creation.

W. Foerster and J. Herrmann, "*kleros*, . . . *kleronomeo*, . . . *kleronomia*," *TDNT* 3: 758–85.

J. CLINTON MCCANN JR.

Iniquity   *see* **Sin**

Innocent, Blameless   In the OT the word most often translated "innocent" is *naqi*, from a root meaning "to be free," hence, free of responsibility or guilt. Forms of the root *tamam—tam, tom, and tamim*—are the words most frequently translated "blameless." The root has the basic sense of "completeness." In the NT no single Greek word prevails. Seven different negatives occur, each only a few times, all with the sense of "blameless" or "faultless."

Innocent. This is primarily a legal term, affirming that a person is not guilty of a crime, although it sometimes (esp. in Job) has a broadly moral sense. The person most often declared "innocent" is the one who might have been executed for a crime, but was acquitted, or the person who had been killed for no valid reason. It thus usually refers to specific cases. The term "innocent *blood*" occurs frequently, as do verbs of killing, since "innocence" and death (delivered from, or unjustly experienced) were so closely related (Deut 19:10, 13; 21:8, 9; 1 Sam 19:5; Jer 22:3; etc.).

The book of Job uses forms of *naqah* several times as one of its terms for Job's claim that he does not deserve his sufferings. So it is a virtual synonym for "righteous, blameless, and upright," as used in this book (e.g., Job 4:7; 17:8). The word also refers in general to the moral life in Pss 15:5; 19:13.

In the NT, the reference to innocent blood reappears in Matt 23:35; 27:4, 24; and Acts 20:26 (NRSV, "not responsible for").

Blameless. The most striking occurrences of "blameless" (*tamim, tam*) are in the descriptions of the character of Noah and of Job, who seem to be called almost perfect: "Noah was a righteous man, blameless in his generation. Noah walked with God" (Gen 6:9). "There was once a man in the land of Uz, whose name was Job. That man was blameless and upright, one who feared God and turned away from evil" (Job 1:1; also 1:8; 2:3).

Even these men, honored for their righteousness (cf. Ezek 14:12–29), were not depicted as perfect, given the drunkenness of Noah (Gen 9:20–27) and Job's challenges to God's justice. "Blameless," like "innocent," sometimes means not deserving of punishment in a specific situation (e.g., Gen 44:10; Judg 15:3), but it is usually a general term of approval for the moral character of one's life. Abraham was to be an example: "The LORD appeared to Abram, and said to him, 'I am God Almighty; walk before me, and be blameless'" (Gen 17:1). In the texts cited above the word is parallel with "righteous (see *just*)," *"upright,"* and *"fear* of God." Elsewhere, it is used with "loyal" (2 Sam 22:26 = Ps 18:23, 25) and "faithful" (Ps 101:6).

Old Testament writers tended to be more optimistic about human potential for good than Paul, and certainly more so than Reformed theologians. In the OT usually people can obey God if only they exercise the will to do so: "Surely, this commandment that I am commanding you today is not too hard for you, nor is it too far away. . . . No, the word is very near to you; it is in your mouth and in your heart for you to observe" (Deut 30:11, 14; and see vv. 11–20). Only Jeremiah and Ezekiel expressed serious doubts concerning the present ability of people to obey God: "Can Ethiopians change their skin or leopards their spots? Then also you can do good who are accustomed to do evil" (Jer 13:23; cf. 2:30; 5:1; 6:10; 17:9; and Ezekiel's promise of a new heart and new spirit, to replace the heart of stone; Ezek 36). Elsewhere, in spite of the long record of disobedience to God's will in the OT, the writers will use words such as blameless and righteous, not only to describe God's ideal for humanity, but also to identify those whose lives were relatively pleasing in God's sight (e.g., 2 Chr 15:17; Ps 37:37; Prov 11:20). The psalmists might include themselves in that group (e.g., Pss 18:23; 19:13).

Another form of the root *tamam, tom* is translated "integrity" and appears in parallel with "innocence" (Gen 20:5),

"uprightness" (1 Kgs 9:4), "fear of God" (Job 4:6), "righteousness" (Ps 7:8), and trust in God (Ps 26:1).

The word *tamim* is used of God in several texts where NRSV translates it *"perfect."* The translation is understandable, since "blameless" would suggest God's innocence might be questioned. It is used in wholehearted praise of God, as in Deut 32:4: "The Rock, his work is perfect (*tamim*), and all his ways are just. A faithful God, without deceit, just and upright is he" (cf. 2 Sam 22:31 = Ps 18:30; Job 37:16). In Ps 19:7 it is the law of the Lord that is perfect, and the word is used in parallel with "sure," "right," "clear," "true," and "righteous." These uses show that "blameless" can involve qualities that go beyond the question of guilt or innocence.

Luke describes the parents of John the Baptist the way an OT author would have done: "Both of them were righteous before God, living blamelessly according to all the commandments and regulations of the Lord" (Luke 1:6). Paul uses "blameless" in the sense of "innocent" with reference to his earlier life (Phil 3:6), and his treatment of the Thessalonian Christians (1 Thess 2:10). But elsewhere in the NT the ideal of blamelessness is directly connected with God's saving work in Jesus Christ, "so that you may be blameless and innocent, children of God without blemish in the midst of a crooked and perverse generation, in which you shine like stars in the world" (Phil 2:15; cf. Eph 1:4; 1 Tim 3:10; Titus 1:6, 7). It is an ideal for the present life, but its fulfillment is expected in the last day (Phil 1:10; Col 1:22; 1 Thess 5:23).

DONALD E. GOWAN

Insight   *see* **Wisdom**

Inspire   *see* **Prophet**

Instruct, Instruction   *see* **Wisdom**

Integrity   *see* **Innocent**

Intelligence   *see* **Wisdom**

Intercede, Intercession   *see* **Pray**

Israel   The word appears more than two thousand times in the Bible, mostly in the OT, with only some seventy examples in the NT. In general terms, we note that "Israel" can denote an individual, the descendants of that individual, or Israel as the northern kingdom with Samaria as its capital. However, further investigation reveals the name as a reference to a given geographical area and as a collective noun that can apply to those who left Egypt at the exodus, as well as those who later entered Canaan. In the NT further refinements are noted.

The first and foundational reference is Gen 32:28–29, in which Jacob has his name changed to "Israel." The name is explained as meaning someone who has striven with or contended against God. The same statement of name change is found in Gen 35:10, but lacks the explanation for the name. Thus an individual is named Israel, though the name Jacob is remembered and used in a variety of contexts as a parallel term (cf. Gen 35:20–22). Genesis 42:5 brings us to the first mention in OT of the "sons of Israel" (see also 45:21; 46:5; Exod 1:1). This collective use leads to the use of the name as a reference to the people as a whole. In Gen 47:27 "Israel" refers to those who left Canaan and settled in Egypt and "gained possessions in it." In this context, "Israel" refers to the growing community of Jacob's descendants and in this case to those who consist of the immediate family of Jacob. This principle of referring to all Jacob's descendants by means of the collective term "Israel" was applied to the generations who were born in Canaan prior to the descent into Egypt, as well as to those who later left Egypt under Moses (Hos 11:1). This latter group included those who were not physically descended from Jacob but who joined the Israelites as they left Egypt and so by choice became part of the community. It could apply also to subsequent generations who formed the community living

in Canaan. Phrases such as "all Israel" (Judg 8:27), "the tribes/people of Israel," "the congregation of Israel" (Exod 12:3) are ways of speaking about all the people who were descended from Jacob. An interesting example of the name is found in Exod 4:22, where Israel is described as Yahweh's "firstborn son" in an apparent reference to the individual Jacob. However, the clear sense is that this is a reference to Jacob's descendants. This particular expression would seem to rest on literary grounds—it opens the way to a mention of the firstborn of Egypt.

When "Israel" appears in the phrase "in Israel," we are confronted by an ambiguity. The phrase has two possible meanings: it can refer to a geographical area or to the community of Israelites. In Gen 34:7 "in Israel" may refer to the land or territory occupied by the Israelites. Similarly, Deut 18:1, 6 and 1 Sam 13:19; 18:6; 27:1 are examples in which the name refers to the territory occupied by the Israelites, territory that encompassed the whole of Canaan. On the other hand, in 2 Sam 13:12–13 we have examples in which the phrase "in Israel" could be territorial or a reference to the community of Israelites. The context here allows both interpretations.

Israel as a community is the focus of references such as Exod 12:3, 6, 19, where it is described as "the congregation of Israel." The additional point of interest here is that the community is not confined to those physically descended from Jacob, but includes those who are "alien" or "a native of the land." Thus "Israel" as the community gathered to celebrate the Passover was wider than those with a blood relationship to Jacob. Circumcision of alien males incorporated them into the community of Israel (12:47–48). This community may be described as the "house of Israel" (Exod 40:38; Lev 10:6; 17:8; etc.) or the "congregation of Israel" (Exod 12:3). One rather special use of the name "Israel" is found in 1 Sam 31:1, where the name refers not to all the people but only to those males who fought in the army as representatives of the nation.

These various uses of the name "Israel" incorporated the larger community who left Egypt and entered the land of Canaan. The name continues to have this sense throughout the early days of the monarchy under Saul, then David and Solomon. Thus "the kingdom of Israel" was the term applied to all people within the territory ruled by these kings. First Samuel 24:20 is an example of this. However, we note that the intertribal tensions that were present from early days are reflected in the rise of David to prominence. While David is anointed king at Hebron over the "house of Judah," that is, over the southern tribes of Judah and Benjamin, it is not until more than seven years later that he is made king over the entire nation. This is described as being a kingship "over Israel and over Judah, from Dan to Beer-sheba" (2 Sam 3:10; 1 Kgs 1:35). This distinction between the nation of Israelites and the group of ten tribes making up the northern kingdom, called "Israel," marks a development in the use of the name. In 1 Kgs 12:19 we see clear reference to this division, with "Israel" in rebellion against the house of David. In this context (12:18) we also note the phrase "all Israel" but with a circumscribed meaning—it refers only to some representatives of the people from the northern alliance of tribes, not to the entire nation. Likewise in 12:20 "all Israel" refers only to the northern kingdom. "All Israel" is a phrase first found in Exod 18:25, in which Moses appoints judges from among the people. However, we note that the semantic range of this phrase depends on the context in which it occurs. It may refer to the entire community prior to entering Canaan, but it may also refer to a limited number of people within the community.

Throughout the records of the divided monarchy, "Israel" refers to the northern kingdom with its capital in Samaria. It is also known as "Ephraim," the name of Joseph's younger son (Gen 48:8–22).

In Psalms the references would appear to point to the entire community of Israelites. The term is frequently used as a parallel to "Jacob." Similarly, in Isaiah the term is inclusive, as is reflected in phrases like "both houses of Israel" in 8:14. Yahweh, the nation's God, is referred to as "the light of Israel" and the peculiarly Isaianic phrase "the Holy One of Israel" indicates that "Israel" is essentially a term for the entire nation (10:17; 17:7; 30:15; 41:14; etc.). "Ephraim" is used as an alternative term for specific reference to the northern kingdom in passages like 7:8–9, 17; 9:9; 28:1–3; etc., as it is in other prophetic writing (see Jer 31:9; Hos 5:3 for examples). Hosea 11:1 refers to the descendents of Jacob in Egypt as "Israel," while 12:12 looks back to the individual Jacob/Israel.

Territorial reference in the term "Israel" is noted in Ezek 6:2–3; 36:1, 4; 37:21–22; etc. Here the "mountains of Israel" includes the land and its peoples and clearly refers to the entire territory occupied by the Israelites. In 11:10 the prophet speaks of "the border of Israel" in another geographical use of the term, while in 20:40 he refers to Jerusalem, the holy mountain, as "the mountain height of Israel." Similarly, in Mal 2:11 "Israel" is a term parallel to "Judah" and "Jerusalem," all of which seem to be geographical references. Zechariah 12 is called an oracle concerning Israel, while the details of the chapter indicate that the focus is on Judah, Jerusalem, and the house of David. See also Zeph 3:14. Thus the name is applied to both the northern kingdom and the entire nation, including Judah.

In the NT we note the use of the name "Israel" following lines similar to those of OT, though there is no reference to Israel as the northern kingdom. There are territorial references in Matt 2:20–21; 9:33. Ambiguous uses are found in Mark 15:32, in which both territorial and community sense are present. The Jewish nation as a whole is clearly referred to in John 1:31; Acts 2:36; etc.. The primary sense in NT is that of the Jewish people as a whole.

Special attention needs to be given to the use of the name in Romans, where Paul refers to his own people, the Jews, as

"Israelites," but then goes on to say that not all Israelites "truly belong to Israel" (9:6). That is because Paul is making a distinction between those who are physically descended from Abraham and those who are "children of the promise" (9:8). These latter may be what he in Gal 6:16 calls "the Israel of God," those who have faith in Christ (see *people of God*).

G. A. Danell, *Studies in the Name Israel in the Old Testament* (Uppsala: Appelbergs boktrykeri, 1946).

GRAHAM S. OGDEN

Jealous, Zealous   The words translated "jealous, zealous" (Heb. *qinaʾ*; Gk., *zelos; phthonos*) carry two basic senses, each of which carries an emotional dimension. Most basically, the words specify "a single-minded devotion, which when turned upon the self, produces envy or hatred for others; or when turned beyond the self, produces overpowering zeal leading to total selflessness" (Good).

When used of humans, this word can have the negative sense of envy and suspicion of others (hence, "jealous": Joseph's brothers, Gen 37:11; Jesus' accusers, Matt 27:18), which can be personally or relationally destructive (Job 5:2; Prov 6:34; Sir 30:24). Jealousy is inimical to a spirit-filled community (Num 11:29; Rom 13:13; Gal 5:20, 26, "works of the flesh"; 1 Tim 6:4) and is not characteristic of love (1 Cor 13:4) or wisdom (Jas 3:14). Yet jealousy in a negative sense may be used for positive ends; Israel's jealousy of God's work among the Gentiles may lead to their salvation (Rom 11:11, 14).

On the other hand, the words are used positively in the sense of fervor and devotion in advancing a just cause or in rendering service (hence, "zealous"; Elijah, 1 Kgs 19:10; the psalmist, Ps 69:9) or in expressing the love between a man and woman ("passion," Song 8:6). Zeal is also (to be) exercised on behalf of the gospel (2 Cor 9:2), the good (1 Pet 3:13), spiritual gifts ("strive for" 1 Cor 14:1), good deeds

(Titus 2:14), the law (1 Macc 2:26–27; Acts 21:20), the sanctuary (Ps 69:9; quoted of Jesus, John 2:17), or repentance ("be earnest" Rev 3:19). Zeal can be unenlightened (Rom 10:2), however, or misplaced (Saul's violence, 2 Sam 21:2; Paul's persecution of Christians, Phil 3:6; cf. Acts 5:17).

When used of God (rarely in the NT), its sense is to be fiercely protective of (the relationship with Israel; Isa 26:11) or to fervently yearn for it (Jas 4:5). God twice names the divine self as "jealous" in Exod 34:14 (cf. Exod 20:5; Deut 5:9). The language for God, a metaphor drawn from the sphere of marriage, by definition has both an inner and outer reference, but the inner reference is the prior one. Because God cares deeply about Israel, God cares about what Israel does with its allegiances. The language of jealousy indicates how close this issue is to the divine heart (cf. the "divine jealousy" of the apostle Paul toward the Corinthians, 2 Cor 11:2). Faithfulness is not a formal matter with God; it touches God's inner life. Faithfulness is not only something that God expects but also, with an inescapable reference to the divine inwardness, what *God feels* with respect to this people. Yet, while having emotional content, the language focuses on commitment within a relationship and emphasizes the seriousness with which God takes Israel's undivided loyalty to its marriage partner.

This language is linked to the prohibition of the worship of other gods (Deut 6:14–15; 32:21). Divine jealousy means that God will not, indeed cannot (given the commitment), remain unmoved by a violation of the marriage on Israel's part; it will entail both pain and anger for God ("provoked to jealousy," 1 Kgs 14:22; Ps 78:58). That may be exercised against the unfaithful (Ps 79:5; Heb 10:27, "fury of fire"; Zeph 1:18, "the fire of his passion"; Deut 4:24, "a devouring fire"; 29:20, "passion will smoke"), other nations (Isa 26:11; Nah 1:2), and the church because of idolatry (1 Cor 10:22). Human zeal on behalf of God, however, could ameliorate the effects of divine anger (Num 25:11). Or jealousy may include a divine ardor on Israel's behalf, for God's own sake (Ezek 39:25), either positively (Isa 9:7; Joel 2:18; Zech 1:14; 8:2) or negatively ("fury" against the nations, Isa 42:13; Ezek 36:5; 38:19). The use of the fire metaphor signifies a fervent divine passion that expresses itself as either protectiveness or anger.

E. M. Good, "Jealousy," *IDB* 2:806–7.

TERENCE E. FRETHEIM

Jerusalem   *see* City

Jesus   The name "Jesus," popular with Jews before the advent of Christianity, comes from a Hebrew root meaning "to help" or "to save." This explains Matt 1:21: "You are to name him Jesus, for he will save his people from their sins." The NT often adds "Christ" before or after "Jesus." The former, which means *"anointed* one" or "messiah," was originally a title indicating that Jesus was the Davidic (see *son of David*) king of Israel, the fulfillment of royal prophecies and eschatological expectations. The titular force, however, soon faded, and "Jesus Christ" became a personal name. This is already true in the Pauline epistles.

Method
Before the Public Ministry
The Beginning of the Public Ministry
  The Baptist and Jesus
  The Baptism and the Temptation
The Teaching of Jesus
  The Kingdom of God and Eschatology
  Salvation and Judgment
  Scripture
  Torah and Ethics
  Jesus' Rhetoric
The Deeds of Jesus
  Ministry to the Marginal
  Moral Model
  Miracles
Self-Conception
  Prophet
  The Son of Man
  Messiah

Disciples
  The Twelve
  Itinerants
  Women
Final Days
  Anticipation of Death
  Jerusalem and the Temple
  Arrest and Interrogation
After Death
  Burial
  Resurrection
Final Remarks

Method

Scholars disagree on the reliability of the extant sources—the canonical Gospels and Paul, extracanonical texts, reconstructed sources such as the hypothetical sayings source known as Q—and so they do not concur on how much we can know about the historical Jesus. Discussions of method have led to no consensus. Many attempt to reconstruct Jesus by passing individual units through various criteria of authenticity. Yet those criteria are not particularly reliable, and it seems safer to base one's major conclusions upon the larger patterns and themes that run throughout the various sources. It is in such patterns and themes if anywhere that the Jesus of history has been remembered.

Before the Public Ministry

Aside from Matt 1–2 and Luke 1–2, first-century Christian writings have next to nothing to say about Jesus before his public ministry, and the Matthean and Lukan texts are problematic for the historian. This is not just because they are so full of supernatural elements, including the virginal conception, but also because they are so colored by biblical texts. Matthew cites the OT fully five times in his first two chapters, which also introduce an extensive Moses typology that orders the first part of his book: Israel's deliverer is born; a wicked king sits upon the throne; that king slaughters Jewish infants; the hero's years after infancy go unrecorded; he passes through the waters; he goes into the desert; he stays there for a period of time marked by forty units; temptation comes in the form of hunger and idolatry; the deliverer goes up on a mountain; he issues the commandments. As for Luke 1–2, it is equally intertextually dense. Particularly heavy is the influence of 1 Sam 1–2 (note especially the parallels between Luke 1:46–55 and 1 Sam 2:1–10). Furthermore, much in Matthew's infancy narrative is missing from Luke, and vice versa. Only Luke, in which Mary is the main character, has the stories about John the Baptist's infancy, about the shepherds and the angels, and about the presentation in the temple; and only Matthew, in which Joseph is the main character, tells of the guiding star, the *magi*, and the slaughter of the infants. And then there are the conflicting details, the most obvious being the differences between the genealogies in Matt 1:1–18 and Luke 3:23–38.

All of this cannot but discourage the quest for Jesus' beginnings. There are, however, some areas of agreement between Matt 1–2 and Luke 1–2 that must be certainly historical. Jesus' parents were named Mary and Joseph, and whether or not he was born in Bethlehem (so Matt 2:6, citing Mic 5:1–3), he did, as the tag "Jesus of Nazareth" proves, later live in Nazareth (Matt 2:23; Luke 2:39). One can also plausibly defend Jesus' Davidic descent, his birth before the death of Herod the Great in 4 B.C., and (whatever one makes of the virginal conception) the possibility that Mary became pregnant before Joseph and Mary began to live together.

Regarding Jesus' upbringing, we have only one story, that of Jesus in the temple (Luke 2:41–52). For the rest, the tradition says that he was a carpenter (Mark 6:3), from which we cannot infer much of anything. Certainly it is hazardous to insist that he must have worked on building projects in nearby Sepphoris and so imbibed Greco-Roman culture while there. Joseph's absence from the accounts of the public ministry implies that he was by then dead. Some have guessed, from the invariably positive connotations of "father" (see *abba*) in his teaching, that Jesus had very good feelings about Joseph, which he naturally transferred to God. Others have surmised, on the basis of Mark 3:21 (Jesus' family seeks to restrain him) and 31–35 ("Whoever does the will of God is my brother and sister and mother"), as well as from the paucity of maternal imagery in his sayings, that Jesus' relationship with Mary was less positive.

The Beginning of the Public Ministry

The Baptist and Jesus. The canonical Gospels associate Jesus' public appearance with John the Baptist, about whom we know less than often thought. Apart from a passing summary in Josephus (*Antiquities* 18:116–19) and a handful of pertinent passages in the Jesus tradition, there is very little to go on. But several generalizations seem safe. One is that John was some sort of ascetic who lived an austere existence. He dwelt in the desert (Mark 1:4; John 1:23, 28). His clothing was made of camel's hair (Mark 1:6). He had an odd diet of locusts and wild honey (Mark 1:6); and his followers' fasting called attention to itself (Mark 2:18). Matthew 11:18 = Luke 7:33 (Q) characterizes him as neither eating nor drinking.

We also know that the Baptist was a preacher of *repentance* and dispenser of ethical instruction (Matt 3:7–10 = Luke 3:7–9 [Q]; Mark 1:4; Luke 3:10–14, 18). This fact is closely related to another, namely, that eschatology preoccupied him. For John the imminence of the consummation mandated change. In Matt 3:7–12 = Luke 3:7–9, 15–17 (Q), he combats complacency by warning of the *wrath* to come; he sees an ax being at the root of trees that are then thrown into fire; and he announces a coming one who will *baptize* with fire and *spirit*, in whose hand is a winnowing fork for *judgment*.

John opposed the notion that all Israel has a place in the world to come. More than a few Jews hoped that descent from Abraham would, as long as they did not abandon the Torah, gain them entry into the world to come (*m. Sanhedrin* 10:1). John thought otherwise: "Do not presume to say to yourselves, 'We have

Abraham as our ancestor'; for I tell you, God is able from these stones to raise up children to Abraham" (Matt 3:9 = Luke 3:8 [Q]). This is a straightforward rejection of the idea that to be born into the *covenant* with Abraham is to be saved. Perhaps the same demurral lies behind John's baptism. Perhaps his ritual was a transmutation of Jewish proselyte immersion, so that in calling for baptism he was asking Jews to think of themselves as *Gentiles*, as people outside the covenant community.

That Jesus submitted to John's baptism shows his essential agreement with him on many if not most matters, and this is confirmed by sayings that explicitly praise the Baptist; see especially the collection in Matt 11:7–19 = Luke 7:24–35 (Q). John 3:22 even claims that Jesus himself baptized for a time. It is natural then that the Gospels depict Jesus as being, like John, a preacher of repentance, as being preoccupied with eschatology, and as being convinced that membership in the covenant guarantees nothing. There is not even fundamental discontinuity in the matter of asceticism, for the missionary discourses depict a very harsh lifestyle (Matt 10:1–16 = Luke 10:1–16 [Q]; Mark 6:8–11), and some of Jesus' *disciples* abandoned families and business (Matt 8:18–22 = Luke 9:57–60 [Q]; Matt 10:34–36 = Luke 12:51–53 [Q]; Matt 10:37 = Luke 14:26 [Q]; Mark 1:16–20; 2:14; 10:28–31; Luke 9:61–62). Jesus himself was almost certainly unmarried (presumably Matt 19:12 was originally a riposte to the slander that he was a eunuch). He demanded the guarding of sexual desire (Matt 5:27–28; see "Women," pp. 249–50). He issued strident warnings about money and property, and he and his followers lived, at least some of the time, as itinerants (Matt 8:19–20 = Luke 9:57–58 [Q]; Matt 10:9–10, 13 = Luke 10:4, 7–8 [Q]; Mark 1:16–20; 2:13–14). The tradition found no difficulty depicting Jesus fasting and seeking to be alone (Mark 1:12, 35, 45; 6:31–44; 8:1–10; John 3:22). Although he joyously celebrated the presence of the *kingdom* (see pp. 239–40),

Jesus nonetheless lived and demanded self-discipline and rigorous self-denial (Matt 10:38 = Luke 14:27 [Q]; Matt 10:39 = Luke 17:33 [Q]; Matt 23:12 = Luke 14:11 [Q]; Mark 8:34; 9:43–48; John 12:25).

Not only were Jesus' teaching and lifestyle congruent with much of what John said and did, but his predecessor's vision of a coming eschatological figure probably contributed to Jesus' very self-conception. John had, according to Matt 3:11–12 = Luke 3:16–17 (Q), prophesied: "I baptize you with water; but one who is more powerful than I is coming; I am not worthy to untie the thong of his sandals. He will baptize you with the Holy Spirit and fire. His winnowing fork is in his hand, to clear his threshing floor and to gather the wheat into his granary, but the chaff he will burn with unquenchable fire" (Luke). Matthew 11:2–6 = Luke 7:18–23 (Q) purports that, when John sent disciples to ask Jesus whether he might be this coming one, the answer he received was indirect yet clearly affirmative.

In line with this, Luke 12:49–50 ("I came to bring fire upon the earth, and how I wish that it were already kindled! I have a baptism with which to be baptized, and what stress I am under until it is completed"; cf. *Gos. Thom.* 10) not only implies that Jesus anticipated going through the eschatological baptism of fire that the Baptist predicted—something submission to John's prophylactic baptism independently attests (cf. Mark 9:49)—but it also makes Jesus himself the dispenser of that fire. Here then Jesus makes the same equation as he does in Matt 11:2–6 = Luke 7:18–23 (Q). If Jesus has come in order to cast fire upon the earth, then he is the eschatological figure of judgment John prophesied. "I came to cast fire on the earth" is exegesis of "he will baptize you with fire."

Most of the disjunctions scholars typically draw between Jesus and John presuppose that we know more about the latter than we do. To claim, for instance, as so many have, that Jesus had proportionally much more to say about salvation (see *save*) than John makes the unwarranted assumption that the few extant lines of John's preaching mirror exactly the whole of his message. It remains very telling that our sources, in various ways, make the two out to be similar. In Mark's Gospel, Herod Antipas supposes that Jesus might be John the Baptist risen from the dead (6:14), and the populace at large has the same supposition (8:28). Mark himself, in his editorial work, makes the ends of John and Jesus parallel: both are arrested, both are bound, both are executed, and both are laid in a tomb (6:17–29; 14–15). Q offers something similar, for Matt 11:16–19 = Luke 7:31–35 suggests that Jesus and John had similar goals and proclamations and even that their differences were more in the delivery than in the substance. Parallels between John and Jesus likewise appear in Luke 1:5–25, 26–38, 57–80; 2:1–52 (the infancy narratives for John and Jesus mirror each other) and in Matt 3:2 and 4:17 (John and Jesus proclaim the very same message). This tradition of likening John and Jesus is striking in view of the Christian tendency to exalt the one over the other, and surely it originated because Jesus so much reminded people of John and because Jesus related himself to John's ministry and expectations in positive ways.

The baptism and the temptation. As they stand, the baptismal narratives communicate the theology of the early church. The descent of the dove (Mark 1:10; John 1:32) is likely a new creation motif: the Spirit of God hovers over the waters as in Gen 1:2; the end is as the beginning (cf. 4Q521, which uses the language of Gen 1:2 to describe the eschatological community). The voice that declares Jesus to be God's Son (see *son of God*) conflates Ps 2:7 and Isa 42:1 and so proclaims him both Davidic Messiah and suffering *servant.* One should not doubt, however, that Jesus did in fact submit to John's baptism, for this is not the sort of event the early church would have invented. It is moreover altogether likely that Jesus experienced his baptism as a prophetic call. This explains both why his public

ministry began shortly thereafter and why his followers remembered the event even though it involved Jesus submitting to John (cf. Matt 3:14–15).

The accounts of Jesus' temptation also express the theology of the community. Mark 1:12–13, so strikingly brief, probably depicts Jesus as the antithesis of the first man, *Adam* (cf. Rom 5:12–21; 1 Cor 15:21–23, 45–49). Before his disobedience, Adam lived in peace with the animals (Gen 2:18–20), and angels honored and fed him (*Life of Adam and Eve* 4:2; 13:3–15:3; *Aboth of Rabbi Nathan* A 1). After succumbing to temptation, he was cast out. Mark reverses this sequence: Jesus is first cast out. Then he is tempted. Then he gains companionship with the animals and the service of angels.

Matt 4:1–11 = Luke 4:1–13 (Q), in which the devil (see *Satan*) tempts Jesus three times, promotes a different Christology. Q depicts Jesus not as the antithesis of Adam but as the antithesis of Israel. It quotes Deut 8:3; 6:16; and 6:13, all texts having to do with the exodus, and it makes Jesus repeat Israel's history in the desert: there is temptation from hunger (cf. Exod 16:2–8), temptation to put God to the test (cf. Exod. 17:1–3), and temptation to *idolatry* (cf. Exod 32). And Jesus' forty days in the wilderness correspond to Israel's forty years in the desert (Exod 16:35).

The theology of the temptation narratives and their fairy-tale-like quality—Satan shows Jesus the whole world in Mathew and Luke, and angels appear in Mark—raise acute questions about their historicity. Perhaps Jesus engaged in prayer and fasting in solitude before his public ministry, and later the church elaborated upon this theologically. Some have thought that Mark 3:27 (Jesus binds the strong man) and Luke 10:18 (Jesus saw Satan fall from heaven) might be figurative ways of referring to a personal victory Jesus had while wrestling with Satan in the wilderness.

Even if one denies that Jesus, near the beginning of his ministry, went into the wilderness and there experienced a time of spiritual testing, this does not empty the temptation texts of all authentic memory. Stories that do not reproduce history may nevertheless convey it, and the temptation narratives highlight several themes that appear elsewhere in the sources. That Jesus beats Satan coheres with the many stories of successful exorcism, as well as with sayings such as Matt 12:28 = Luke 11:20 (Q): "But if it is by the finger of God that I cast out demons, then the kingdom of God has come to you." That Jesus is, as the devil's challenges in Q assume, a miracle worker, clearly harmonizes with the rest of the tradition (see p. 246); and that he does not perform miracles on demand matches Mark 8:11–13, where he refuses to grant a *sign* (cf. Matt 12:38–42 = Luke 11:29–30 [Q]; Luke 11:16; 17:20). That the Spirit leads Jesus (Matt 4:1 = Luke 4:1 [Q]; Mark 1:12) fits his self-perception as the eschatological prophet of Isaiah 61, upon whom the Spirit of God rests (see pp. 246–48). That he can cite Scripture when he rebuffs the devil is consistent with his habit elsewhere of quoting from and otherwise creatively engaging biblical texts (see pp. 241–44). That Jesus is a man of great faith who, in need, waits upon God appears throughout the tradition: he goes not just without amenities but without necessities and trusts his Father to take care of him and his followers (Matt 6:11 = Luke 11:3 [Q]; Matt 6:25–34 = Luke 12:22–32 [Q]; Matt 7:7–11 = Luke 11:9–13 [Q]). That he refuses the devil's offer of the kingdoms of the world correlates with the likely circumstance that Jesus, who died as a messianic pretender, expected to become king in Jerusalem yet waited upon God to make him so (cf. John 6:15). Finally, that Jesus spends time alone in the desert and there fasts is consistent with his having practiced a mild form of asceticism (see pp. 236–38).

The Teaching of Jesus

The kingdom of God and eschatology. Against the traditional equation of the kingdom of God (or of heaven; there is no difference in meaning) with the church and the once popular view of the kingdom as an evolving society, J. Weiss and A. Schweitzer argued a century ago that Jesus preached repentance in the face of the impending eschatological judgment. Largely in response to the latter's picture of Jesus as an apocalyptic visionary, C. H. Dodd developed his theory of "realized eschatology." According to Dodd, Jesus believed that the prophecies of the OT had already met fulfillment, that the *"day of the Lord"* had arrived. Most contemporary scholars now think of Weiss and Schweitzer on the one hand and of Dodd on the other as representing two extremes, between which a third position commends itself. If Jesus announced that the kingdom of God had, in some sense, already come, he likewise spoke of eschatological events still to unfold. The phrase "already and not yet" is now a commonplace of scholarship.

Jesus' future expectations were drawn from the well of OT and Jewish tradition. He anticipated the *resurrection* of the dead (Matt 8:11–12 = Luke 13:28–29 [Q]; Matt 12:38–42 = Luke 11:29–32 [Q]; Mark 12:18–27) and a great judgment (see pp. 240–41). He thought in terms of rewards for the righteous and recompense for the wicked (Matt 10:32–33 = Luke 12:8–9 [Q]; Mark 8:35; 9:41–48; Matt 25:14–30, 31–46). And he prophesies trouble for the saints (Matt 10:14–15 = Luke 10:11–12 [Q]; Matt 10:16 = Luke 10:3 [Q]; Mark 10:35–40; Matt 10:23, 25). There is no evidence that Jesus shared some of his contemporaries' expectation that the Gentiles would suffer destruction at the end (*Jub* 24:29–30; *1 En.* 90:19), and the existence of an early Christian mission to Gentiles confirms that he did not anticipate their eschatological annihilation.

Jesus expected not the utter destruction and replacement of this world but rather a revolutionary change, not another earth but this earth made new— a revised, second edition with the earlier deficiencies corrected. The story of the flood in Genesis is analogous: this world is first destroyed before it—the same world—is recreated. Presumably he knew and accepted the biblical prophecies of a desert in bloom (Isa 35:1–2), unprecedented fertility (Amos 9:13–15), and the taming of wild animals (Isa 11:6–9). For Jesus, the differences between heaven and earth became indistinct in the eschaton, that is, the two things in effect merged and became one. "Heaven on earth," one might say.

Jesus did not relegate God's reign to the future. He explicitly announced its presence (Matt 12:28 = Luke 11:20 [Q]; Luke 17:20) and otherwise indicated its arrival by speaking of the defeat of Satan (Matt 12:28 = Luke 11:20 [Q]; Mark 13:27; Luke 10:18), a secret presence (Mark 4:11–12, 26–29), and new wine (see *vine*) (Mark 2:22). Although controversial, it is probable that Luke 17:20–21, in which the kingdom is "among you," refers to Jesus himself. His presence means the presence of the kingdom.

Traditionally Christians have thought that the OT foretells two messianic advents and that Jesus fulfilled certain prophecies at his first coming and will fulfill others at his second coming. The distinction between two advents cannot, however, be found in the OT and is foreign to Jewish eschatology. It is not likely that Jesus himself thought in terms of or spoke about two messianic advents. More probably the end time was for him constituted by a sequence of events, some of which had already occurred. Much had come to fulfillment, but not to fulfillment without remainder.

Jesus taught that eschatological judgment was near. Recent attempts to deny this do not persuade. It must nonetheless be emphasized that he probably confessed his ignorance of the end's precise date (Mark 13:32). Further, Matt 6:10 = Luke 11:2 ("Your kingdom come") and Luke 13:6–9 (the fig tree is given another year to bear fruit) assume that the day or hour of the consummation is not set in concrete, that its arrival is partly contingent upon divine **grace** and human response (an idea common in ancient Jewish and Christian literature; cf. Acts 3:19–20; 2 Pet 3:11–12; *b. Sanhedrin* 97b-98a; *b. Shabbath* 118b). In addition, Matt

11:20–24 = Luke 10:13–15 (Q) and other texts reflect bitter disappointment over Jesus' failure to win more converts. How such disappointment affected his eschatological convictions we do not know; but the general failure of many to welcome God's final messenger might well have made for second thoughts about what the future held. Jesus' expectations were probably more contingent and indeterminate than many have supposed.

Salvation and judgment. The tradition nowhere leaves the impression that good Jews are saved because they are good Jews, that is, because they are descended from the patriarchs. From beginning to end it presupposes, rather, that the question of salvation is open and that Jesus' audience, notwithstanding their heritage, should fret about their fate in the coming kingdom. They should not presume to be safely in as opposed to out. When Mark 1:15 summarizes Jesus' message with words that include "repent," this rightly catches the spirit of his message.

Mark 10:15 has Jesus saying, "Truly I tell you, whoever does not receive the kingdom of God as a little child will never enter it" (see **family**). Although some have thought that Jesus was here calling for trust or humility, or for the ability to say "*Abba*," it is far more likely that when he urged people to become children, he was, like the Baptist in Matt 3:8–10 = Luke 3:8–9 (Q), telling them to start their religious lives over, telling them to go back to the beginning. In later Judaism, the convert is "like a new-born child" (*b. Yebamot* 22a; *b. Berakhot* 47a), and John 3:3 clearly takes our saying to mean that one must undergo a second birth. Jesus' saying about becoming children is, then, akin to the Baptist's call for repentance and baptism; one has to start from scratch.

The context for Jesus' call to begin one's religious life anew was the same as that of the Baptist, namely, eschatological judgment. Both prophets were looking to the future judgment. Both believed its arrival would be sooner rather than later. And both believed that some or many of their Jewish contemporaries might flunk the coming assize (for Jesus see Matt 7:24–27 = Luke 6:46–49 [Q]; Matt 10:15; 11:20–24 = Luke 10:12–15 [Q]; Matt 12:41–42 = Luke 11:31–32 [Q]; Mark 3:29; 8:35, 38; 9:42–48; Matt 25:14–30, 31–46; Luke 16:19–31).

If descent from Abraham does not get one in, what does? Part of the answer lies in Matt 10:32–33 = Luke 12:8–9 (Q), which probably goes back to something close to the following: "Truly I say to you, he who acknowledges me before men, the *Son of Man* will acknowledge before the angels of God; but he who denies me before men, the Son of Man will deny him before the angels of God" (cf. Mark 8:38). Whatever the meaning one gives to "Son of Man" (see pp. 247–48), the saying makes the fate of at least some human beings at the eschatological judgment hinge upon their response to Jesus. Although this link between Christology and salvation is remarkable, it is only to be expected. Jesus conceives of himself as the leader-to-be of the restored *people of God* (see p. 248), and it would not make sense for those who do not acknowledge God's chosen leader to share in God's kingdom.

The declaration that blasphemy (see *blaspheme*) against the Spirit is unforgivable (Matt 12:31–32 = Luke 12:10 [Q]; Mark 3:28–30) tells the same story. Both the Beatitudes (Matt 5:3, 5–6 = Luke 6:20–21 [Q]) and the answer to the Baptist (Matt 11:2–6 = Luke 7:18–23 [Q]) make Jesus the anointed prophet of Isa 61:1–2 who bears the Spirit of God (see pp. 246–47), and it follows that to reject Jesus is to reject the Spirit, which is precisely the one great sin. Similarly, Matt 11:20–24 = Luke 10:12–15 (Q), where Jesus pronounces woes on Galilean cities, and Matt 12:41–42 = Luke 31–32 (Q), where he denounces his generation, plainly presuppose that some will suffer loss because they have not embraced his proclamation of the kingdom. So these sayings also illustrate Matt 10:32–33 = Luke 12.8–9: to reject Jesus or what he stands for is to invite eschatological calamity. It is only natural that Paul and

other early Christians make acceptance of Jesus the criterion of salvation. This is already a pre-Easter theme.

Scripture. Most intertestamental Jewish literature is intertextual literature; that is, it is in dialogue with the OT. One anticipates then that a Palestinian teacher such as Jesus might engage the Bible. In line with this, the Gospels have him quote, refer to, or allude to the OT on many occasions. Examples include the Beatitudes (Matt 5:3–4, 6, 11–12 = Luke 6:20–23 [Q]), which draw upon the prophetic oracle in Isa 61:1–2 (see below); Luke 9:62, the call to put hand to the plow and not look at the things behind, which alludes both to the call of Elisha in 1 Kgs 19:19–21 and to the fatal error of Lot's wife in Gen 19; Matt 12:28 = Luke 11:20 (Q), Jesus' declaration that he casts out demons by the finger of God, which depends upon Exod 8:19 and traditions about the contest between Moses and the magicians of Egypt; Matt 6:28–29 = Luke 12:27 (Q), which demotes Solomon in all his glory below the lilies of the field; and Matt 10:34–35 = Luke 12:51–53 (Q), which appends a paraphrase of Mic 7:6 to the declaration that Jesus has come to bring a sword.

Jesus uses Scripture in several ways. Above all, he lives in the conviction that his own time is witnessing the fulfillment of eschatological prophecies: "Blessed are the eyes that see what you see! For I tell you that many prophets and kings desired to see what you see, but did not see it, and to hear what you hear, but did not hear it" (Matt 13:16–17 = Luke 10:23–24 [Q]). In his answer to John the Baptist, Matt 11:2–6 = Luke 7:18–23 (Q), Jesus alludes to a series of passages from Isaiah: the blind see (cf. Isa 29:18; 35:5; 42:18; 61:1), the lame walk (cf. Isa 35:6), the deaf hear (cf. Isa 29:18; 35:5; 42:18), the dead are raised (cf. Isa 26:19), and the *poor* have good news preached to them (Isa 29:19; 61:1). The clear implication is that Jesus' ministry is the fulfillment of Isaiah's oracles. Matters are the same in Matt 10:35–36 = Luke 12:53 (Q): "They will be divided: father against son and son against father, mother against daughter and daughter against mother, mother-in-law against her daughter-in-law, and daughter-in-law against mother-in-law." This is, as noted above, a clear paraphrase of the eschatological prophecy in Mic 7:6. So once again Jesus' ministry fulfills an eschatological oracle. In this case, however, it is not the saving miracles of the end time that are entering the present but the tribulation of the latter days.

In addition to interpreting his ministry as the fulfillment of eschatological prophecies, Jesus also uses the Bible in order to startle and generate reflection. Luke 6:27–45, for instance, contains several imperatives that reverse commandments of Lev 19. Leviticus 19:2 demands holiness because God is *holy.* Jesus demands *mercy* because God is merciful. Leviticus 19:17 commands one to judge one's neighbor. Jesus commands one not to judge others. Leviticus 19:18 says "*love* your neighbor." Jesus says "Love your enemy." Leviticus 19:17–18 offers instructions for repairing relations with "brothers." Jesus says it is not enough to do good just to "brothers" (Matt 5:47). Similarly provocative uses of the OT occur in Matt 10:37 = Luke 14:26 (Q), where "Whoever comes to me and does not hate his own father and mother . . . cannot be my *disciple*" reverses the imperative to love father and mother. In Matt 5:32 = Luke 16:18 (Q) and Mark 10:11 (cf. 1 Cor 7:10–11), Jesus prohibits divorce, a ruling that begs for clarification in the light of Deut 24:1–4. In Matt 5:21–22, he cites Exod 20:13 = Deut 5:17, the prohibition of murder (see *kill*), not in order to agree or disagree with it, but in order to transcend it. In Matt 5:27–28, he quotes Exod 20:14 = Deut 5:18, the command not to commit *adultery,* and then goes beyond it to demand more (see *marriage*). In these last two examples, Scripture is not the last word but the first word only: Moses is not enough. Similar is Mark 12:35–37, where Jesus sets Ps 110:1 against itself. Often then he quotes Scripture neither to illumine a point nor to support an argument but rather to go his own way. Jesus says

the unexpected and contradicts what everyone knows, including the writers of Scripture.

Torah and ethics. Despite the previous paragraph, the tradition remembers Jesus upholding torah. In Mark 7:8–13 he rebuts opponents by accusing them of not honoring father and mother. A few verses later, he composes a list of vices that includes theft, murder, adultery, so here again he endorses the Decalogue (Mark 7:21–23). Something similar happens in chapter 10, where Jesus answers the rich man with "You know the commandments: 'You shall not murder; You shall not commit adultery; You shall not steal; You shall not bear false witness; You shall not defraud; Honor your father and mother'" (Mark 10:19). Jesus also commends the Decalogue in Mark 12:28–31, for the double commandment to love is a summary of the Ten Commandments: to love God is to fulfill the first table, to love ones's neighbor is to fulfill the second table (cf. Philo, *Decalogue* 106, 121, 108–10; Rom 13:9; Irenaeus, *Against Heresies* 4.16.3).

Jesus appears as a defender of Torah even in the *Sabbath* controversies. He does not say, in Mark 2:23–28, that the Sabbath has been abolished, as do some later Christians. Nor does he say that the true God did not institute the Sabbath. Instead of attacking the Sabbath, Jesus appeals to David and to the hunger of David's men in 1 Sam 21. Jesus is saying that one imperative can trump another, that human need can, in some cases, overrule Sabbath-keeping, which, it is assumed, remains intact. There is nothing revolutionary in this: Jewish law certainly knows that Sabbath observance might be the lesser of two goods (the law-observant Maccabees decided to take up arms on the Sabbath; 1 Macc 2:29–41). In Mark 3:1–6, where Jesus heals a man with only a few words—"Stretch out your hand"—he again makes no general declaration encouraging Sabbath breaking. He rather appeals to compassion as raising an exception to the rule of Sabbath law: "Is it lawful to do good or to do harm on the Sabbath, to save life or to kill?" (v. 4). The idea that humanitarian concern can interfere with Sabbath observance is at home in Judaism. Few if any would have disputed the principle, only (perhaps) its applicability to the present case. Jesus himself implies that what he has done is "lawful." So when Matt 5:17 has him pronounce that he has not come "to abolish the law and the prophets," and when Luke 16:17 (Q) has him observe that "it is easier for heaven and earth to pass away, than for one stroke of a letter in the law to be dropped," they are clearly in harmony with much of the tradition.

Yet if Jesus extols the Decalogue and repudiates antinomianism, there is another side to him. Jesus hardly honors his mother when he asks, in Mark 3:33, "Who are my mother and my brothers?" Even more radical is the little call story in Matt 8:21–22 = Luke 9:59–60 (Q), where Jesus responds to the reasonable "Lord, first let me go and bury my father" with the scandalous "Follow me, and let the dead bury their own dead." To bury parents is to honor them, and Jesus here dismisses that duty. Closely related is Matt 10:37 = Luke 14:26 (Q): "Whoever comes to me and does not hate his own father and mother . . . cannot be my disciple." This is a deliberate contrast to Exod 20:12 = Deut 5:16, "Honor your father and your mother." Jesus also appears as a radical in Matt 5:21–26 and 27–30, where he bans anger and attacks lust. While the torah is not here broken—the one who observes Jesus will necessarily observe Moses all the more—Jesus formulates his own imperatives in contrast with Moses. He is clearly signaling that Moses does not suffice, that the law is not wholly adequate. Jesus demands more than the torah demands.

Other texts are even more far-reaching. In Matt 5:31–32 = Luke 16:18 (Q) and Mark 10:2–12 (cf. 1 Cor 7:10–11), Jesus prohibits divorce, which Moses permits (Deut 24:1–4). And then there is Matt 5:33–37, which disallows swearing altogether (cf. Jas 5:12) and does so by paraphrasing Moses, who does not forbid it

(cf. Exod 20:7; Lev 19:12; Num 30:3–15). To say that *oaths* are not needed seems a plain rejection of Scripture, especially as God and the saints swear in the Bible (Gen 14:22; 22:16; Exod 6:8; Isa 45:23). One understands why Theophylact, in his commentary on Mathew, could offer nothing more than this lame line: "At the time of Moses, it was not evil to swear. But after Christ, it is evil."

How do we reconcile the law-observant Jesus who teaches the Decalogue and even upholds the torah in its entirety with one who at other times plays fast and loose with the commandment to honor one's parents, finds multiple occasions on which to depart from Sabbath law, uses a formula that starkly contrasts his own words with those of Moses, and disallows oath taking and divorce, which the torah allows?

Jesus sometimes turns Scripture upside down and inside out in order to startle, to drive home a point, and to find permanent lodging in memories. This is certainly the effect of transforming "Honor father and mother" into "Hate father and mother," or of putting instruction into the form "You have heard that it was said to those of old. . . . But I say to you."

There is, however, much more to Jesus' radicalism than rhetoric. Something more is going on in the saying that the dead should bury their own dead or in the Sabbath controversies, where Jesus deliberately brings two commandments into conflict so that one must choose between them. The Gospels, with their several Sabbath conflicts, create the impression that Jesus is much interested in the problem of competing moral imperatives. Although he nowhere extols breaking the Sabbath, he breaks it if doing so restores a human body to wholeness or feeds the hungry. Again, parents should be honored, as the Decalogue enjoins and as Jesus repeats in Mark 7 and 10; yet if showing such honor hinders obedience to the call to discipleship, then it must suffer neglect. Compassion prevails over the Sabbath; discipleship outweighs filial obligation.

Jesus' treatment of the law cannot be isolated from eschatology. If the kingdom is at hand, then the renewal of the world is nigh; and if the renewal of the world is nigh, then paradise is about to be restored; and if paradise is about to be restored, then concessions to sin are no longer needed. This is the implicit logic of Mark 10:1–12. Because the last things will be as the first and because, for Jesus, the last things have come, so have the first. Hence Jesus requires a prelapsarian ethic: "From the beginning it was not so" (Matt 19:8). Insofar as the law contains concessions to the fall, it requires repair.

This explains Matt 5:33–37, the prohibition of oaths. The presupposition of the oath is the lie. Oaths would be superfluous if all told the truth. Oaths assume that there are two types of statements, one of which demands commitment—the oath—and one of which need not—the statement without an oath. But in a world turned back to the beginning, human beings would invariably be committed to every statement; and if they were so committed, the superstition of the oath would be redundant. So forbidding swearing is like prohibiting divorce. Both set forth an Edenic standard that mends a temporal limitation in the torah.

That the coming of the kingdom impinges upon the law is explicit in Matt 11:12–13 = Luke 16:16 (Q): "From the days of John the Baptist until now the kingdom of heaven has suffered violence, and the violent take it by force. For all the prophets and the law prophesied until John came." Here Jesus distinguishes between the time of the law and the prophets on the one hand and the time of the kingdom on the other. This means that the time of the law has, in some sense, been superseded.

Probably related to such eschatological expectation is Jesus' emphasis on internal states, on the heart (see *mind*). He seeks to shift attention from murder to anger, from adultery to lust (Matt 5:21–30). He wants reflection upon the *light* within, or the lack thereof (Matt 6:22–23 = Luke 11:34–35 [Q]), for he believes that what is inside defiles (Mark 7:15; cf. Matt 7:15–20; 12:33–35 = Luke 6:43–45 [Q]). Now Jer 31:31–34 famously prophesies the interiorization of the law: "I will put my law within them, and I will write it upon their hearts; and I will be their God and they shall be my people." A new covenant will be established, and the torah will then be engraved internally (cf. Ezek 36:26–27). In accord with this, for Jesus God's kingdom has come, so the law must become effective even within one's heart. It does not surprise that the author of Hebrews and Justin Martyr find the fulfillment of Jer 31:31–34 in what Jesus wrought (Heb 8:8–12; 10:16–17; Justin Martyr, *Dialogue with Trypho* 11.3), nor that the wording of the Lord's Supper common to Luke and Paul alludes to Jeremiah's "new covenant" (Luke 22:20; 1 Cor 11:25).

Jesus' rhetoric. Several formal features mark Jesus' teaching. He obviously likes parables; the Synoptics contain dozens. He is also fond of antithetical parallelism (e.g., Matt 6:22–23 = Luke 11:33–34 [Q]; Matt 6:24 = Luke 16:13 [Q]; Matt 7:24–27 = Luke 6:47–49 [Q]; Mark 2:19–20; 3:28–29; 7:15; 8:35), rhetorical questions (e.g., Matt 5:46 = Luke 6:32 [Q]; Matt 7:9–11 = Luke 11:11–13 [Q]; Matt 24:45 = Luke 12:42 [Q]; Mark 2:8–9; 3:4, 23, 33; 4:21), prefatory *"amen"* (e.g., Matt 5:18, 26; 8:10; 10:15; 11:11; Mark 3:28; 8:12; 9:1, 41), passive constructions (e.g., Matt 6:9 = Luke 11:2 [Q]; Matt 7:7 = Luke 11:9 [Q]; Matt 10:26 = Luke 12:2 [Q]; Mark 4:24; 9:31, 45, 47), hyperbole (e.g., Matt 7:3–5 = Luke 6:41–42 [Q]; Matt 10:37 = Luke 14:26 [Q]; Matt 17:20 = Luke 17:6 [Q]; Mark 4:8, 31–32; 9:42–48; 10:25), and aphoristic formulations (e.g., Matt 10:24–25 = Luke 6:40 [Q]; Matt 10:39 = Luke 17:33 [Q]; Matt 10:40 = Luke 10:16 [Q]; Mark 2:27; 7:15; 10:15). Perhaps the most striking formal feature of all is the constant use of the unexpected or seemingly paradoxical. Examples include Matt 5:3–4, 6, 11–12 = Luke 6:20–23 (Q) (being poor, hungry, in mourning, and reviled are made out to be good things); Matt 11:25 = Luke 10:21 (Q) (revelation is not for the learned but for babes); Matt 13:33 = Luke 13:21 (Q) (the kingdom is like corrupting leaven); Matt 19:30 = Luke 13:30 (Q) (the last will be first, the first last); Matt 22:1–14 = Luke 14:15–24 (Q) (wedding invitations go to riffraff); Mark 2:17 (Jesus calls not the righteous but sinners); 7:15 (things going in do not defile); 8:35 (saving life will lose it, losing life will save it); 9:12–13 (eschatological Elijah failed in his ministry of reconciliation); 10:45 (the Son of Man came not to be served but to serve; contrast Dan 7:14); Matt 13:24–30 (the farmer ignores weeds until the harvest); Luke 10:25–37 (a Samaritan is the hero); 16:1–8 (Jesus commends a dishonest character). The unexpected is well suited to a message that has so much to say about eschatological reversal, which will turn the world upside down.

The Deeds of Jesus

Ministry to the marginal. Jesus ministers to individuals with little social status. In Mark, he heals demoniacs, paralytics, a leper, blind men. It is the same in Q (Matt 11:2–6 = Luke 7:18–23), in which Jesus blesses the poor, those in mourning, the thirsty, and the persecuted (Matt 5:3–4, 6, 11–12 = Luke 6:20–23) and announces that the humble will be exalted (Matt 23:12 = Luke 14:11). In Matthew, Jesus appeals to those who are weary and carrying heavy burdens (11:28) and correlates eschatological reward and punishment with people's treatment of the hungry, the thirsty, strangers, the naked, the sick, and the imprisoned (25:31–46). In Luke, Jesus takes the side of *poor* Lazarus, not the rich man (16:19–31), and he depicts Samaritans, traditionally enemies of Jews, in a good light (10:29–37; 17:11–19).

Even when one takes into account that healers necessarily minister to the sick, that the well have no need of a physician, one comes away with the impression that Jesus has a special interest in those on the margins of society. Yet one must also admit that Q has him healing the son or servant of a centurion, a man with great authority, without demanding any change

of life (Matt 8:5–13 = Luke 7:1–10 [Q]), that Mark has him calling a rich man to discipleship (10:17–31, although here there is a demand to abandon wealth), that Matthew has Jesus giving advice to those who can afford to give alms (6:1–4), and that Luke has him eating with a well-to-do tax collector, Zacchaeus (19:1–10), and being supported by "Joanna, the wife of Herod's steward Chuza," who must have been prosperous (8:3).

So the tradition does not depict Jesus as engaging only those in the same socioeconomic circumstances. He seeks rather to be catholic in his ministry and affections. This is, after all, the implication of the commandment to love one's enemies (Matt 5:44 = Luke 6:27, 35 [Q]). This imperative is a way of saying that one should selflessly serve all, for if love encompasses enemies, clearly it encompasses all. It is no coincidence that it is a follower of Jesus who composes both 1 Cor 13, the great paean to love, and Gal 3, which puts Jew and Gentile, male and female, slave and free on an equal footing before God. There is already a universalizing impulse with Jesus.

Moral model. Jesus is presented not just as a teacher; he is also the chief actor in a series of stories. One of the main purposes of those stories is to correlate his deeds with his words; that is, the gospel genre, which is biographical, gives us a Jesus who not only speaks the divine norm but lives it. He praises the meek (Matt 5:5) and then embodies meekness (Matt 11:29; 21:5). He enjoins mercy (Matt 5:7) and then shows mercy (Matt 9:27; 15:22; 20:30). He calls for self-denial in the face of evil (Luke 6:27–36) and does not resist the evils done to him (Luke 22:51, 63–65). And on it goes. Implicit in all this is an *imitatio Christi*, which was so important to the early church (Rom 15:1–7; Heb 12:1–4; 13:12–13; 1 Pet 2:21; 3:17–18; 1 John 2:6). "I have set you an example, that you also should do as I have done to you" (John 13:15) stands over the entire tradition. No doubt this theme has its origin in the fact that Jesus struck his contemporaries not just as a novel teacher but as a man of integrity, who lived what he spoke and so could be thought of as the best illustration of his own speech.

Miracles. However one explains the fact, whether one appeals primarily to divine intervention or to parapsychology or to the psychosomatic phenomena of mass psychology, Jesus was certainly known as a miracle worker during his own life. One guesses that the hope of being healed or of beholding miracles brought much if not most of his audience to him. His opponents themselves conceded his abilities when they offered that he was in league with Beelzebul, that he cast out demons by demons (Matt 12:27 = Luke 11:19 [Q]; Mark 3:22–27; cf. John 7:20; 8:48; 10:20). As this polemic implies, many if not most of his miracles were exorcisms.

Although Jesus was a miracle worker, this obviously does not guarantee the authenticity of any particular miracle story; and as they stand, many of the stories are highly symbolic. The transfiguration narrative in Mark 9:2–8 makes Jesus like the Moses of Exod 34 (v. 30: "When Aaron and all the Israelites saw Moses, the skin of his face was shining") and so confirms him as the prophet foretold in Deut 18:15, 18, the one Israel should listen to. The feeding of five thousand in Mark 6:32–44 and John 6:1–15 not only foreshadows the Last Supper but strongly recalls the miracle of 2 Kgs 4:42–44 and so makes Jesus like Elisha. The story of the widow of Nain in Luke 7:11–17 makes Jesus rather like Elijah because it is clearly modeled upon 1 Kgs 17:8–24: in both cases a healer approaches a city gate; in both a widow's son has died; in both the healer brings the son back to life; and in both the phrase "gave him to his mother" occurs.

Most of the miracles are healings of people and so display Jesus' compassion. There are also, however, the so-called nature miracles—the stilling of the storm (Mark 4:35–41), the walking on the water (Mark 6:45–52; John 6:16–21), the feedings of the five thousand and four thousand (Mark 6:32–44; 8:1–9; John 6:1–15),

the cursing of the fig tree (Mark 11:12–14), the coin in the fish's mouth (Matt 17:24–27), Peter's catch of fish (Luke 5:1–11), and the turning of water into wine at the wedding at Cana (John 2:1–12). Some of these miracles, like the healing and exorcism stories, serve the needs of others. Yet as a whole they seem designed less to demonstrate Jesus' compassion than to show his numinous powers. He is a channel of an otherworldly force; he is the presence of another world; he has abilities no one else has. "Who then is this, that even the wind and the sea obey him?" (Mark 4:41).

The tradition interprets the miracles of Jesus as signs of eschatological fulfillment, and this was no doubt the interpretation of Jesus himself. For the way Matt 11:2–6 = Luke 7:18–23 (Q) correlates Jesus' miracles with prophecies of Isaiah, see p. 246. Matthew 12:27 = Luke 11:20 (Q) holds something similar. If Jesus casts out demons by the finger of God, then the kingdom of God has come. The defeat of Satan's realm is what happens in the latter days; so if Satan's realm is now being conquered, the latter days have arrived.

Self-Conception

Jesus alone was the focus of early Christian theology, and this was not a post-Easter development. That Jesus was arrested, not the disciples, shows that he was from the beginning the center of the new movement. This is confirmed by the title on the *cross*: Pilate charges Jesus alone with being "the King of the Jews" (Mark 15:25; John 19:19).

Prophet. According to the Synoptics, people regarded Jesus as a prophet: Mark 6:14–16; 8:28; Luke 7:16. The title also appears on the lips of Jesus himself in Mark 6:4 ("Prophets are not without honor, except in their hometown, and among their own kin, and in their own house") and Luke 13:33 ("It is impossible for a prophet to be killed outside of Jerusalem"). Jesus, like John the Baptist, evidently considered himself some sort of prophet.

Beyond this generality, Matt 11:2–6 = Luke 7:18–23 (Q) associates his ministry with Isa 61:1–2 (see pp. 241–42). The Beatitudes do the same thing. The blessing of the poor echoes Isa 61:1 ("The spirit of the Lord GOD is upon me, because the LORD has anointed me; he has sent me to bring good news to the oppressed"), and "Blessed are those who mourn, for they will be comforted" (Matt 5:4) alludes to Isa 61:2 ("to comfort all who mourn"). Further, the word about the reviled and persecuted has thematic parallels in Isa 61:3 and 10. So the Beatitudes, like Matt 11:2–6 = Luke 7:18–23 (Q), make Jesus' ministry the realization of Isaiah's prophecy: he is the anointed herald who brings good news (cf. Luke 4:16–21).

In addition to taking on the role of the prophet of Isaiah 61, there is a good chance that Jesus, like the early church (cf. Acts 3:22), reckoned himself the prophet like Moses of Deut 18:15, 18 in the time of a new exodus. In Matt 12:28 = Luke 11:20 (Q), Jesus alludes to Exod 8:19 in claiming that he casts out demons by the finger of God, so in this respect at least he is like the miracle-working Moses. In revising Lev 19 (see pp. 241–42) and reversing the commandment to love parents (Matt 10:37 = Luke 14:26 [Q]), Jesus daringly sets his own words over against those of the first lawgiver. Matthew 5:21–22 and 27–28 do the same thing. He also characterizes his own generation with language originally descriptive of Moses' generation (cf. Matt 12:38–42 = Luke 11:29–30 [Q] with Deut 1:35). And then there are the words of institution in Mark 14:24, where Jesus, in a *passover* context, speaks of "my blood of the covenant." The phrase functions partly as an allusion to Exod 24:8: "Moses took the blood and dashed it on the people, and said, 'See the blood of the covenant that the LORD has made with you in accordance with all these words.' " Finally, if behind the various versions of the feedings of the five thousand and four thousand lies a meal with a large crowd in a deserted place, a meal that was intended to be an eschatological symbol,

an anticipation of the messianic feast, perhaps Jesus was—like some of the sign prophets Josephus reports on (*Antiquities of the Jews* 18.85–87; 20.97–99, 188)—deliberately recalling memories of Moses and the exodus.

Mark 6:15 and 8:28 assign to some the opinion that Jesus might be Elijah, whom many expected to herald the end (cf. already Mal 4:5). The comparison would have been natural. Jesus was a prophet in northern Israel, purported to have worked many miracles, including raising the dead (cf. 1 Kgs 17:17–24). He also called (see *call*) disciples to follow him and abandon their livelihoods, the memory of which came to be written up in stories that imitate Elijah's call of Elisha (1 Kgs 19:19–21). There are, however, no sayings in which Jesus implies that he might be Elijah. Mark 9:13, like Matt 11:10 = Luke 7:27 (Q), rather has Jesus identify the eschatological Elijah with the Baptist (cf. Luke 1:17). Did Jesus regard both John and himself as Elijah-like prophets?

The Son of Man. This is the title Jesus uses most often in the Gospels. Traditionally Christians have taken it to complement another title, "the Son of God"; it indicates Jesus' true humanity. This understanding occurs as early as the second century. Modern scholars, however, tend to adopt other interpretations of the title. Some suppose that "the Son of Man" was a known messianic title that Jesus used of himself or of another yet to come. Others have contended that "the Son of Man" goes back to an Aramaic idiom that meant something like "one"; it was an indirect way of talking about oneself, of speaking of the particular by way of the general (cf. our "One must do one's duty"). This proposal makes good sense of several sayings (e.g., Mark 2:28: "The Son of Man is lord even of the sabbath").

The Aramaic specialists, however, remain divided over the linguistic issues surrounding "the son of man" in first-century Aramaic. Further, even if the phrase was common and functioned like a pronoun, one can always take an everyday expression and do something interesting with it (cf. the use of "I am" in John). This is not an idle point, given that Jesus was innovative in the linguistic sphere (e.g., in his use of "Amen" at the beginning of sentences).

Some sayings clearly link "the Son of Man" with Dan 7; see, e.g., Mark 13:26 ("Then they will see 'the Son of Man coming in clouds' with great power and glory") and 14:62 ("You will see the Son of man . . . coming with the clouds of heaven"). Especially important is Matt 10:32–33 = Luke 12:8–9, which surely goes back to Jesus. This Q saying echoes Dan 7 in that it concerns the last judgment, has as its central figure the Son of Man (Daniel speaks of "one like a son of man," 7:13 Mg), depicts that figure as being "before" the divine court, sets the stage with angels, and speaks to a situation of persecution. This then is evidence that Jesus associated "the Son of Man" and so his own ministry with Daniel's vision of the judgment, that he indeed identified himself or the group whose leader he was with Daniel's exalted figure.

Messiah (see *anointed*). What did Jesus make of the promises to David? Mark 12:35–37 (on David's son and Lord) does not help, for even if it preserves an argument from Jesus, the point has been lost. Also less than helpful are Mark 8:27–30 (the confession at Caesarea Philippi) and 14:53–65 (the Jewish trial in which Jesus acknowledges his messiahship). For aside from how much history lies behind these stories (see p. 252 for 14:53–65), in both Jesus does not comment directly on the title "Messiah"; at best he qualifies it (contrast Matt 16:13–20). The very fact that "Messiah" is so rare in the Gospels but so common in the Epistles has suggested to many that the title marks a post-Easter interpretation of Jesus.

Nonetheless, if Jesus thought of himself as destined to be Israel's eschatological, Davidic king, we might not expect him to speak openly about it in view of the potential dangers and misunderstanding (cf. John 6:15). Furthermore, the Romans did indeed execute him as a "king" (Mark 15:26), and since they surely did not invent this charge out of nothing, somebody must have perceived Jesus as a messianic figure (cf. the entry to Jerusalem and see p. 251). Certain items in the tradition suggest this was not a false perception. If Jesus identified himself with the eschatological prophet of Isa 61:1–2, he would have thought of himself as an anointed one, for that figure declares, "The LORD has anointed me." Again, if either Matt 19:28 = Luke 22:28–30 (Q) (Jesus stands outside of and above the twelve who sit on thrones in the kingdom) or Mark 10:35–40 (disciples sit at Jesus' right and left in the kingdom) contains authentic material, Jesus must have thought himself to be king. The same result follows if he spoke of rebuilding the temple (see p. 251), for 2 Sam 7:4–17 foresees a descendant of David who will build God's house, and this was an eschatological prophecy in first-century Judaism, as the Dead Sea Scrolls show (4QFlorilegium). The Targum on Zech 6:12 bestows upon the temple builder of 2 Sam 7 the title "Messiah."

Disciples

The Twelve. Because he was a teacher, Jesus had disciples. Not all agree, however, that he gathered a select group of twelve. Doubt comes from the fact that they show up only once in Q (Matt 19:28 = Luke 22:28–30). Yet "the twelve" is already a fixed expression in 1 Cor 15:5, which guarantees its antiquity. Furthermore, Judas, who was, according to the Gospels, chosen by Jesus himself, was known as "one of the twelve" (Mark 14:10, 43). The community probably would not have invented something so potentially offensive and for which it had to create explanations (see Matt 26:25; Luke 22:3; John 6:64, 70–71; 13:11, 27; 17:12). It is also notable that, to judge from Paul and Acts, the Twelve did not play much of a role in the early church, which makes their post-Easter creation less plausible.

In selecting a group of twelve from amongst his followers, Jesus' intent was probably the creation of a prophetic and eschatological symbol: the twelve disciples represented the twelve tribes of Israel (cf. 1QM 2:1–3). Jesus presumably shared the expectation, widely attested, of the eschatological restoration of the twelve lost, or rather hidden, tribes (Hos 11:11; 2 Macc 1:27; 2:18; Bar 4:37; 5:5; *1 En.* 57:1). The Synoptic tradition itself invites us to connect the number twelve with eschatology. Matthew 19:28 = Luke 22:28–30 (Q) promises Jesus' followers that they will "rule over" or "judge" the twelve tribes of Israel, which assumes that those tribes will soon return to the land, an expectation that is probably also present in Matt 8:11–12 = Luke 13:28–29 (Q); the "many" who assemble "from east and west" are likely scattered Jews.

Itinerants. If the Twelve functioned as an eschatological symbol of Israel's renewal, they also served, along with other followers, to spread Jesus' message. This is likely why we have reliable information about Jesus in the first place. Pre-Easter itinerants, according to Matt 10:7 = Luke 10:9 (Q), were instructed to proclaim the kingdom of God and its imminence. Although we do not learn beyond that what specifically they were to say, their message cannot have differed from that of Jesus. Certainly their other activities were in imitation of his, for their purpose was to enlarge his influence. This is why he could say: "Whoever welcomes you welcomes me; and whoever welcomes me welcomes the one who sent me" (Matt 10:40 = Luke 10:16 [Q]; cf. Mark 9:36–37; John 5:23; 12:44–50; 13:20). So their proclamation of the kingdom must have been his proclamation. It follows that if Jesus, in addressing crowds, used parables to communicate his message and made moral demands in the face of the end, then his disciples used those same parables and moral demands. That is, the materials in the Jesus tradition that originally had a missionary setting were not spoken by Jesus alone but also by the group associated with him. So we may speak of the pre-Easter Jesus tradition.

Much of the original tradition must have once functioned, not as public proclamation, but as advice and encouragement for these itinerants in particular. The missionary discourse in Matt 9:37–38; 10:7–16 = Luke 10:2–16 (Q; cf. Mark 6:6–13), the counsel on care in Matt 6:25–34 = Luke 12:22–31 (Q), the Lord's Prayer in Matt 6:9–13 = Luke 11:2–4 (Q), and the exhortation to faithfulness in Matt 10:26–33 = Luke 12:2–12 (Q) are all likely examples of complexes that Jesus composed as guidance for those he called to "fish for people" (Mark 1:17; cf. the call stories in Mark 1:16–20; 2:13–14; Matt 8:18–22 = Luke 9:57–60 [Q]; Luke 9:61–62). Only later did these complexes get turned into general exhortations for all believers.

Women. The traditional image of Jesus wandering around Galilee with twelve male disciples is mistaken. Not only were the Twelve presumably part of a larger group, but Mark tells us that when Jesus was crucified, some women looked on from a distance, among them "Mary Magdalene, Mary the mother of James the younger and of Joses, and Salome" (15:40–41). Luke 8:1–3, which in several particulars derives from non-Markan tradition, adds that Jesus "went on through cities and villages, proclaiming and bringing the good news of the kingdom of God. The twelve were with him, as well as some women who had been cured of evil spirits and infirmities: Mary, called Magdalene, from whom seven demons had gone out, and Joanna, the wife of Herod's steward Chuza, and Susanna, and many others, who provided for them out of their resources." This text and Mark 15:40–41 stand out from the rest of the Synoptic tradition, which otherwise does not inform us that among the itinerants who followed Jesus were women. Yet despite its meager attestation in the extant sources, the existence of such a group is certain. There is no clear tendency in the tradition that tempts us to regard it as a fiction.

Mark 15:41 says that the women "ministered" to Jesus. This may mean that they offered him financial support—this is what Luke 8:3 claims—and/or served him at table (cf. Mark 1:13, 31). But Mark also says that the women "followed" Jesus, and this implies that they were, like the Twelve, "disciples." Perhaps we should be prepared to think of Mary Magdalene and the others as students of Jesus (cf. Luke 10:39, 42) and genuine coworkers.

The presence of women among Jesus' followers sheds light upon several items in the tradition. First, Matt 11:19 = Luke 7:34 (Q) and Mark 2:15–16 use a phrase that Jesus' detractors coined—"tax collectors and sinners." In Mark the context is a banquet, and in Q the charge is joined to the slur that Jesus is a "glutton and a drunkard." Given that Greco-Roman banquets featured prostitutes, it seems likely enough that the women around Jesus were slandered as such with the polemical phrase, "tax collectors and sinners." In Matt 21:31, the phrase becomes "tax collectors and prostitutes."

Second, Matt 5:27–28 demands that men not look at women with lust in their hearts. While we cannot eliminate the possibility that this warning was a sort of global counsel, sage advice directed to Galilean peasants without distinction, if Jesus' band of itinerants included women as well as men, some of whom were either unmarried or married and away from their spouses, a concrete setting for Matt 5:27–28 suggests itself. Men and women, away from their homes for weeks or months at a time, in the joint promotion of a momentous cause, might well have been attracted to one another. In such a circumstance, a warning against a man looking lustfully at a woman would have had a very specific function.

Third, there is Jesus' prohibition of divorce (Matt 5:31–32 = Luke 16:18 [Q]; Mark 10:2–9; 1 Cor 7:10–11). Perhaps he issued his rule simply because he was called upon to do so. But a complementary motivation is possible. If it was necessary, because the men and women of his company traveled together, for Jesus to address the issue of sexual temptation, then it may, for the very same reason, have been necessary to address the subject of divorce and remarriage. One way of overcoming illicit sexual desire would be to make it licit through marriage. But for any, such as Peter, who were already married, that would have required divorce. So by forbidding divorce, Jesus would be eliminating the one recourse that his married followers would have had if they wanted to turn their attraction into lawful union.

Final Days

Anticipation of death. Jesus almost certainly anticipated suffering and an untimely death. Although this is sometimes contested, especially in conjunction with skepticism concerning the formal passion predictions, the balance of the evidence favors this conclusion. Not only do the prophetic and apocalyptic traditions, which so influenced Jesus, recognize that the saints must pass through tribulation before salvation arrives, but the Baptist's martyrdom must have served as a warning. A number of sayings furthermore depict Jesus enjoining his followers to reckon seriously with the prospect of both suffering and death: Matt 10:28 = Luke 12:4–5 (Q); Matt 10:37–39 = Luke 14:25–27 (Q); Mark 8:34–35; 9:1; 10:38–39; 13:9–13. If any of these texts is authentic, then it is likely that Jesus himself expected to suffer and die before his time, for surely he would have anticipated for himself a fate similar to those around him. In line with this, the Synoptics contain a mass of material that clearly looks forward, explicitly or implicitly, to Jesus' death. While the genuineness of many of the relevant verses may justly be queried, at least Mark 10:38–39 ("The cup that I drink you will drink; and with the baptism with which I am baptized you will be baptized"); Luke 12:49–50 ("I came to bring fire to the earth, and how I wish it were already kindled! I have a baptism with which to be baptized"); and Luke 13:31–33 ("It is impossible for a prophet to be killed outside of Jerusalem") lay good claim to preserving original material.

As for how Jesus interpreted his own death, two possibilities suggest themselves. First, he probably understood it to be part and parcel of the eschatological tribulation that would herald the end. Matthew 10:34–35 = Luke 12:51–53 (Q) applies Mic 7:6 to the present, and Mic 7:6 was widely understood as a prophecy of what the rabbis called "the woe of the Messiah" (cf. *m. Sota* 9:16). In line with this, Luke 16:16 speaks of the kingdom of heaven suffering violence and seems to construe the death of the Baptist as belonging to the eschatological trial. According to Mark 9:49, everyone will go through the coming eschatological fire, and there is no reason to exclude Jesus from the generalization, as Luke 12:49–50 confirms.

The other good possibility is that Jesus construed his death as in some way salvific, although one hardly finds any theory of the atonement in the Gospels. If he composed Mark 10:45 ("The Son of Man came not to be served but to serve, and to give his life a *ransom* for many"), he seems to have drawn upon Isa 53, although the allusion has been doubted. More solid are the words of institution at the Last Supper (Mark 14:22–25; 1 Cor 11:23–25). For not only do these contain sacrificial language ("poured out for you/many"), but given Paul's familiarity with this tradition, it is hard to think that there is no basis in the life of Jesus.

Jerusalem and the temple. Jesus went to Jerusalem in either A.D. 30 or, less probably, 33 (John has him going up more than once, perhaps correctly). Whether he wanted to provoke a confrontation, or even to die, Mark 11:1–10 and John 12:12–19 have him deliberately approaching Jerusalem not on foot but on a donkey, thereby making a public claim to kingship (cf. Zech 9:9). The scenario is plausible given his exalted self-conception (see pp. 246–48) as well as the probability that he engaged in another prophetic action at the same time, turning over tables in the temple (Mark 11:11, 15–17; cf. John 2:13–17). Commentators tend to suppose that, by his disturbance in the temple, he was either symbolizing the destruction of the temple or protesting certain corrupt practices. It is unclear, however, why the two interpretations should be opposed. Protestation of abuses and an enacted parable of destruction could have gone together. In Jeremiah, Ezekiel, Mic 3, and *1 En.* 83–90, criticism of priestly corruption is joined to expectation of the temple's destruction and/or hope for a new temple. It is plausible enough that Jesus, perhaps with Zech 14:21 in mind, performed a violent act that expressed the divine displeasure and that he opposed, not the sacrificial system itself, but what he perceived to be inappropriate business proceedings, which had made the sacred secular and encouraged or confirmed thoughts of the temple's demise. Given, in any case, the nearness of the tower of Antonia with its Roman cohort and the usual custom of placing additional guards around the temple during festivals, the incident must have been relatively minor. Josephus, who records many disturbances in the temple, fails to take note.

Mark 13:2; 14:58; 15:29; Luke 19:44; John 2:19; Acts 6:14; and *Gos. Thom.* 71 attribute to Jesus a prophecy of the temple's destruction. We need not doubt their joint testimony. Not only did other Jewish prophets foretell the temple's doom (Mic 3:12; Jer 7:8–15; 9:10–11; 26:6, 18; Josephus, *Jewish War* 6.300–301), but Theodotion's translation of Dan 9:26 can be read to prophesy that the messiah will destroy the temple. Further, the Romans burned the temple, and a forecast after the event might have reflected this circumstance (cf. *Testament of Judah* 23:2; *2 Baruch* 7:1; *Apocalpyse of Abraham* 27:3). More controversial is the proposition that Jesus also spoke of a new temple being built. But the sources with this prophecy (Mark 14:58; 15:29; John 2:19; *Gos. Thom.* 71) show that Christians wrestled with its interpretation. John 2:13–22, for instance, says that people misunderstood it, and Mark 14:58 and 15:29 attribute the prophecy to false witnesses. That the forecast was unusually troublesome is manifest, which speaks against a post-Easter origin. So it appears that Jesus, like the authors of *1 En.* 90:28–29 and 11QTemple 29:8–10, anticipated both the end and renewal of Jerusalem's temple.

Arrest and interrogation. Whether or not it was the incident in the temple that eventually led to Jesus' arrest, he was taken before members of the Jerusalem Sanhedrin, although we should probably not speak of a formal trial but of a preliminary inquiry (Mark 14:53–65; John 18:13–24). We can further accept the report that he was then accused of acting and/or speaking against the temple and that the authorities, probably because they did not have the authority to execute (John 18:31), subsequently handed him over to Pilate (Mark 15:1; John 18:28). The more difficult question is whether Mark 14:62 ("'You will see the Son of Man seated at the right hand of the Power' and 'coming with the clouds of heaven'") rests upon anything Jesus said, either before or during his interrogation. The words sound like a Christian confession, and how could Jesus' followers have learned what he said to the authorities? And yet "the right hand of the Power" hardly looks like a free Christian creation, while "you will see" suggests antiquity because it was not fulfilled in any straightforward manner. It is, further, entirely likely that a charge about destroying and raising the temple came up at Jesus' interrogation, which matters because of 2 Sam 7, where the son of David builds the temple. This text held messianic meaning for ancient Jews (cf. 4QFlorilegium and the pre-Pauline confession in Rom 1:3–4). So a prophecy about the temple's destruction could have led, as it does in the Gospels, to the issue of Jesus' identity—and Jesus' identity is the content of the charge above his cross ("King of the Jews").

After Death

Burial. Roman law commonly denied burial to criminals, who often were thrown into a collective pile as food for beasts. While some have imagined that this happened to Jesus, the burial story in Mark 15:42–47 depicts the Sanhedrin in a positive light, which is against the tendency of the tradition. This is precisely why Mark and the other evangelists stress that Joseph was exceptional—he was a disciple of Jesus (Matt 27:57; John 19:38), or he was looking for the kingdom (Mark 15:43). Beyond that, the story as it stands does not illustrate Isa 53:9, as one might expect a legend to do ("they made his grave with the wicked"). According to Josephus, *Jewish War* 4.317, "the Jews are so careful about funeral rites that even malefactors who have been sentenced to crucifixion are taken down and buried before sunset" (cf. Deut 21:22–23). These words are illustrated by discovery of an ossuary containing the bones of a crucified man from pre-70 Judea. So it seems likely enough that a pious member of the Sanhedrin, perhaps acting on their behalf, sought and obtained from the Roman authorities permission to bury Jesus.

Resurrection. When the first Christians proclaimed that God had raised Jesus from the dead, they were affirming that their leader was right, his executioners wrong. They were declaring that the divine judge had overturned the sentence of Rome. How did they come to this conviction? What really happened? Until the Enlightenment, almost all Christians took the NT accounts to be historically accurate. The traditional theological explanation followed. After the Enlightenment, no one explanation has won the day. (1) Many continue to hold to the traditional account: God raised Jesus from the dead. The tomb was empty, and people saw the glorified Jesus. (2) Others say maybe the visions were real, objective. Maybe Jesus survived death and communicated to his disciples, but the story of the empty tomb is late and legendary, the creation of people who believed, on the basis of their faith alone, that the body must have disappeared. (3) Some have suggested that the accounts rest upon historical events that Jesus' followers misinterpreted. Perhaps, for instance, the tomb was empty, not because Jesus rose from the dead, but because people visited the wrong tomb, or because Joseph later moved the body to a permanent burial site (cf. John 20:2, 14–15), or because Jesus, who never really died, revived in the tomb's cool air, or because the authorities, not wanting a venerated tomb, moved the body. Early Christians then interpreted the empty tomb in terms of their religious hopes and dreams. (4) Maybe option (3) has things backward: the empty tomb is a late legend and Easter faith began with the subjective hallucinations of certain disciples. (5) There could, a few have judged, have been deliberate fraud. Perhaps the disciples stole the body (cf. Matt 28:11–15) because they wanted to be leaders of a religious movement.

Historians have not constructed and cannot construct decisive arguments for any of these positions, which raise questions beyond the reach of critical historiography. One can only sort the data and weigh some of the probabilities.

(1) The sentence, "God has raised Jesus from the dead" (Rom 10:9; 1 Cor 6:14; 15:15), must go back to the beginning of Christianity. Also ancient is the pre-Pauline formula in 1 Cor 15:5–8, which mentions appearances to, among others, Peter, the Twelve, and James—all people whom Paul knew. Clearly belief in Jesus' resurrection goes back to individuals who followed Jesus before his crucifixion.

(2) First Corinthians 15:5 refers to an appearance to the Twelve, and stories of appearances to the Twelve appear in Matt 28:16–20; Mark 16:9–20; Luke 24:36–49; and John 20:19–23. These four narratives seem to be variants of the same tradition, to which Mark 16:7 also presumably alludes ("He is going ahead of you into Galilee; there you will see him"). The texts cited all have the same outline: narrative setting, sudden appearance of Jesus, commissioning to evangelistic activity, and promise of succor; and all but John 20:19–23 mention fear or doubt (a motif John moves to the episode with Thomas). This story line is clearly primitive, and there is no reason to deem it unhistorical. There was evidently an occasion on which members of the Twelve believed that Jesus had appeared to them. Their experience brought them comfort and prodded their missionary endeavors.

Beyond that, the facts cannot be recovered, including whether the event took place in Galilee or Jerusalem.

(3) It is also hard to recover many facts regarding the other appearances—to Peter in Luke 24:34 and 1 Cor 15:5 (no details are offered); to James in 1 Cor 15:7 (again we have no details, although this may well have been a conversion experience, as James does not appear to have been among Jesus' followers before Easter); to women in Matt 28:8–10 and John 20:11–18 (Mary Magdalene and "the other Mary" in Matthew, Mary Magdalene alone in John); to two disciples on the way to Emmaus in Luke 24:13–35 (cf. Mark 16:12–13; this story is strikingly similar to portions of Tobit); to the Twelve along with Thomas in John 20:24–29 (there is no other account of this memorable story); to seven disciples by the sea in John 21 (Why have the disciples gone back to work? Is this a late variant of the first appearance to the Twelve?); to the five hundred in 1 Cor 15:6 (Is this Pentecost?); and finally to Paul (1 Cor 15:8; Acts 9:1–19; 22:6–16; 26:12–18; in his epistles Paul nowhere narrates the details of his own conversion; the closest he comes is Gal 1:11–17). The number and variety of these stories have encouraged some to speak of mass hysteria. Others, to the contrary, have urged that the diversity of witnesses, times, and places speaks against mundane explanations. A few have constructed psychological narratives to explain some of the appearances, especially those to Peter and Paul, but the mental states of the individuals involved are, it goes without saying, beyond recovery.

(4) Regarding the story of the vacated tomb, 1 Cor 15:3–8 does not mention it, and there are parallels roundly reckoned to be unhistorical—the vain search for the remains of Job's children (*Testament of Job* 39:1–40:6), the failure to find the body of the father of John the Baptist (*Protevangelium of James* 24:3), the disappearance of the corpse of the thief who asked Jesus to remember him in his kingdom (*Story of Joseph the Carpenter* 4:1), and the later legends about Mary's ascension.

Greco-Roman analogies also exist: the missing bones of Heracles (Diodorus Siculus 4.38.4–5), the failure to find Aeneas's body (Dionysius Halicarnassus, *Early History of Rome* 1.64), the disappearance of Romulus (Plutarch, *Romulus* 27.7–28.3). If Christians believed, on other grounds, that God had raised Jesus from the dead, then perhaps they freely invented the discovery of the empty tomb.

These arguments are balanced by others. First Corinthians 15 may assume an empty tomb but pass over the story of its discovery because, given the prejudices of the day, many denigrated the testimony of women (cf. Josephus, *Antiquities* 4.219; Origen, *Against Celsus* 2.55; *Sifre Deut* 190). In any case, the odds seem against the invention of a story that features women witnesses. It is telling that the tradition betrays a tendency to bring the male disciples onto the scene to confirm things (Luke 24:12, 24; John 20:2–3).

The legendary parallels are the best argument against the historicity of an empty tomb. But several of these parallels (e.g., those about the good thief and Mary's ascension) are based upon the story of Jesus' resurrection, while others are dissimilar to the Gospel accounts in that they either originated not decades but centuries after the supposed facts recorded or are indeed about purely legendary figures (e.g., the tales about Heracles, Romulus, and Job's children). One wonders, moreover, whether early Christians could have successfully proclaimed Jesus' resurrection in Jerusalem if the tomb were not empty (presuming that its location was known; see p. 252). So maybe Mary Magdalene (and other women?) did after all visit Jesus' tomb and find it empty. There is certainly nothing unbelievable about friends visiting his grave site. Later on, other followers of Jesus understood that discovery to confirm their own experiences and revived faith.

Final Remarks

Striking antitheses run throughout Jesus' teaching. On the one hand, things could not be worse. There is not peace but a sword. The kingdom of God suffers violence. The faithful are poor, hungry, oppressed. The greatest of those born among women is arrested, imprisoned, and beheaded. Families are split apart with religious conflict. And God's final, eschatological messenger is derided as in league with Satan. There is nothing ahead for him but torture and death.

On the other hand, Jesus proclaims that the blessings of the messianic age have already appeared. Satan has fallen like lightning from heaven. The devil is now bound, his house plundered. It is time to rejoice. Jesus' contemporaries are blessed because they see what prophets from old longed to witness. Miracles abound. The lame walk. The blind see. Lepers are cleansed. The poor have good news preached to them. The old world is passing away.

The tension between the two sides of Jesus' teaching has its complement and illustration in the canonical accounts of his own story, above all, in the passion and resurrection narratives. His chosen companions forsake him in his hour of need. The crowds, once full of cheers, now cruelly mock him. Pagan soldiers, after slapping and whipping him, nail Jesus to their most shameful and horrible instrument of torture. He utters a cry of despair and dies in darkness. The first has become last.

Not long thereafter, Jesus triumphantly returns to his bereft friends, having broken the bonds of death and entered into a new, heavenly existence. As if that were not enough, he has received "all authority in heaven and on earth" (Matt 28:18). The last has become first and can now comfort the distraught: "Peace be with you" (John 20:19, 21); "I am with you always, to the end of the age" (Matt 28:20). This is the happiest ending anyone could imagine.

Jesus fascinates and inspires in part because his words and story give paradigmatic expression to the extreme polarities of human existence. He speaks about and suffers what human beings fear most—rejection, alienation from family, misunderstanding, loneliness, doubt, torturous pain. And he speaks about and enjoys what human beings hope for most—happiness, wisdom, nearness to God, victory over death. The man of sorrows, acquainted with grief, with nowhere to lay his head, the man reviled as blasphemer, drunkard, glutton, whose life ends in torture and an agonizing question, "My God, my God, why have you forsaken me?" (Mark 15:34), is also the one who knows God's parental goodness, invites all to celebrate the presence of utopia, and attains eternal life. The crucified is the resurrected.

Dale C. Allison Jr., *Jesus of Nazareth: Millenarian Prophet* (Minneapolis: Fortress Press, 1998); J. Dominic Crossan, *The Historical Jesus: The Life of a Mediterranean Jewish Peasant* (San Francisco: Harper, 1991); C. H. Dodd, *The Parables of the Kingdom*, rev. ed. (New York: Charles Scribner's Sons, 1961); J. Jeremias, *New Testament Theology: vol. 1: The Proclamation of Jesus* (London: SCM, 1971); John P. Meier, *A Marginal Jew*, 3 vols. (New York: Doubleday, 1991–2001); E. P. Sanders, *Jesus and Judaism* (London: SCM, 1985); Albert Schweitzer, *The Quest of the Historical Jesus* (Minneapolis: Fortress, 2001); Gerd Theissen and Annette Merz, *The Historical Jesus: A Comprehensive Guide* (Minneapolis: Fortress, 1998); J. Weiss, *Jesus' Proclamation of the Kingdom of God* (Philadelphia: Fortress, 1971).

DALE C. ALLISON JR.

Jonah (Sign of)   To the Jewish leaders who asked for a sign that would validate his authority, Jesus answered, "An evil and adulterous generation asks for a sign, but no sign will be given to it except the sign of the prophet Jonah" (Matt 12:38–42; 16:1–4; Mark 8:11–12; Luke 11:29–32). Only Matt 12:40, however, has these words: "For just as Jonah was three days and three nights in the belly of the sea monster, so for three days and three nights the Son of Man will be in the heart of the earth"—thereby making the circumstances of Jonah a prefiguration or type of the resurrection of Jesus.

Probably the original point of Jesus' allusion to the story of Jonah is captured by Luke, where the sign of Jonah is used (1) to parallel the preaching of Jonah and that of Jesus and (2) to contrast the repentance of the people of Nineveh with the unbelief of the Jews (Luke 11:30–32). Matthew, however, appears to have adapted this saying, finding in its reference to "three days and three nights" an irresistible analogy to the time that the body of Jesus was in the tomb. In Matthew's treatment, therefore, the circumstances that Jonah experienced are a prefiguration of the resurrection of Jesus. But even with this sign, the Jews would not believe (Matt 28:11–15; Luke 16:31).

The parallels between Jonah and Jesus, of course, do not exactly fit at every point. Unlike Jesus, Jonah did not die. Moreover, the correspondence is not exact between "three days and three nights" with respect to Jonah and "after three days" (in Mark) or "on the third day" (in Matthew and Luke) with respect to Jesus (cf. also "after three days" in Matt 27:63 and "until the third day" in Matt 27:64). But Matthew was evidently not concerned with such matters.

What was significant for Matthew was not only the correspondences between these two preachers and their respective audiences but also the divinely intended similarity between Jonah and Jesus in being returned to life after three days. And so for Matthew, the "sign of Jonah" to unrepentant Jews is the "resurrection of Jesus"—a sign that the "evil and adulterous generation" of that day (and ours today) would come to know through the preaching of the church.

Simon Chow, *The Sign of Jonah Reconsidered: A Study of Its Meaning in the Gospel Traditions*, CBNT 27 (Stockholm: Almqvist & Wiksell, 1995); Richard A. Edwards, *The Sign of Jonah in the Theology of the Evangelists and Q*, SBT[2] 18 (London: SCM, 1971).

RICHARD N. LONGENECKER

Joy, Joyful, Joyous, Enjoy, Glad, Gladness, Rejoice   There is no substantial difference in meaning among these words. This is demonstrated by the fact that in both Testaments they sometimes appear in parallel constructions: "So the ransomed of the LORD shall return, and come to Zion with singing; everlasting joy shall be upon their heads; they shall obtain joy and gladness, and sorrow and sighing shall flee away" (Isa 51:11; cf. Isa 35:10). "This is the day that the LORD has made; let us rejoice and be glad in it" (Ps 118:24). "You will have joy and gladness, and many will rejoice at his birth" (Luke 1:14).

Humans characteristically experience joy under happy circumstances. These circumstances are by no means always what we would call religious. In the Bible there are many causes of joy, such as great feasts (Isa 22:13), the birth of a child (Luke 1:14; cf. 1 Sam 2:1), triumph over an enemy (Judg 16:23; 2 Sam 1:20; etc.). Sometimes these are used as metaphors for the joy that comes from God: "You have multiplied the nation, you have increased its joy; they rejoice before you as with joy at the harvest, as people exult when dividing plunder" (Isa 9:3). There can be, however, no firm distinction between religious and nonreligious joy. For the righteous, all joy comes in the end from God.

Joy is a primary human response to the presence and activity of God in the world. "In your presence there is fullness of joy; in your right hand are pleasures forevermore" (Ps 16:11). Such language is repeated throughout the psalms of Israel and in Scripture as a whole. In the NT joy is "in the Lord" (Phil 4:4 and other instances). It comes from the presence of the Holy Spirit: "The fruit of the Spirit is love, joy, peace . . ." (Gal 5:22). We look to God to bring us joy: "Satisfy us in the morning with your steadfast love, so that we may rejoice and be glad all our days" (Ps 90:14). When we are rescued from trouble and perceive God's love, joy is the result: "I will exult and rejoice in your steadfast love, because you have seen my affliction" (Ps 31:7). Especially when God recovers the lost, there must be joy. The father in Jesus' great parable reminds the older son: "But we had to celebrate and

rejoice, because this brother of yours was dead and has come to life; he was lost and has been found" (Luke 15:32; cf. vv. 6, 9). The one who cannot rejoice at such times knows nothing of God.

It is not only the righteous who experience joy, however. Joy is a nearly universal human experience. The wicked, for their part, also rejoice. The difference is that the righteous rejoice in God, while the wicked characteristically rejoice in the discomfiture of the righteous: "Do not let my treacherous enemies rejoice over me" (Ps 35:19; the righteous may also display that latter tendency; see, for example, Ps 58:10). So universal is the experience of joy that it can even be said poetically that all nature rejoices. At creation, for example, "the morning stars sang together and all the heavenly beings shouted for joy" (Job 38:7; cf. Ps 65:13).

Joy inevitably finds expression. Joy leads to rejoicing. When the righteous rejoice, they **praise** the goodness and favor of God. Indeed, in Greek, the word usually rendered "joy," *chara*, is closely related philologically not only to the verb "rejoice," *chairo*, as in English, but also to the words "grace," *charis*, and the verb "to give thanks," *eucharisteo*. Though there is no similar philological connection in English, it is apparent even in translation that praise is an expression of our joy before God. Even a quick glance at a concordance will show that words of joy appear particularly frequently in psalms of praise: "But may all who seek you rejoice and be glad in you; may those who love your salvation say continually, 'Great is the LORD!'" (Ps 40:16 and many examples). To praise or to *glorify* God is also to rejoice, and vice versa. The two are very nearly the same, as in the famous line from the Westminster Shorter Catechism, "The chief end of man is to glorify God and enjoy him forever." In Scripture, there is actually an *obligation* to rejoice: "Rejoice during your festival, you and your sons and your daughters, your male and female slaves" (Deut 16:14; cf. v. 11).

There are, of course, many circumstances in life that are anything but happy. The Bible, even in its emphasis on joy, never denies the painful reality of sorrow. Some of the most beautiful verses in Scripture remind us, however, that sorrow is never the last word for the faithful: "May those who sow in tears reap with shouts of joy" (Ps 126:5). "Weeping may linger for the night, but joy comes with the morning" (Ps 30:5). The faithful can anticipate joy because they trust that God can and will give comfort. See, for example, Isa 51:3 ("For the LORD will comfort Zion; he will comfort all her waste places, and will make her wilderness like Eden, her desert like the garden of the LORD; joy and gladness will be found in her, thanksgiving and the voice of song") and many other examples. Joy is thus related not only to praise but to faith (see *believe*).

It might seem that such faith is useless, because death ends all things human, especially joy. The Christian *hope*, however, is in resurrection. It is not surprising that a primary response to the resurrection of Jesus Christ is joy. "[Jesus] showed them his hands and his side. Then the disciples rejoiced when they saw the Lord" (John 20:20; cf. Matt 28:8). Christians may rejoice because they hope to share in the resurrection (1 Pet 4:13).

It is not only individual believers who may look forward with joy, however. Already in the OT, there is hope that the future will hold joy for the people of God as a whole. When God saves the people, "Then shall the young women rejoice in the dance, and the young men and the old shall be merry. I will turn their mourning into joy, I will comfort them, and give them gladness for sorrow" (Jer 31:13). In the NT the hope of the resurrection and the joy it brings have a cosmic scope. Looking forward, the seer of Patmos declares, "Let us rejoice and exult and give him the glory, for the marriage of the Lamb has come" (Rev 19:7). Joy in the NT is an eschatological reality.

Because of this hope, joy is freed from the tyranny of present circumstances. There can be joy not only in happy circumstances but amid suffering of every kind, even amid persecution (Matt 5:12),

and trials (Jas 1:2). Because of the resurrection, our suffering can be seen in a new light: "But rejoice insofar as you are sharing Christ's sufferings, so that you may also be glad and shout for joy when his glory is revealed" (1 Pet 4:13; Acts 5:41).

Until that glory is revealed, the word to the Christian is simple: "Rejoice in the Lord always; again I will say, Rejoice" (Phil 4:4).

———

STEPHEN FARRIS

Judge, Judgment, Condemn, Condemnation, Punish, Punishment

Three pairs of terms that describe a judicial sequence in which a party is tried, found guilty, and punished (see *sin*). The terms have other meanings as well, and they also overlap: e.g., "judge" can also mean "condemn," and "judgment" can mean "condemnation."

Judge, Judgment

The word "judge" can be either a noun designating an official or a verb signifying the findings of a judge. It is used both ways in the Bible. The noun "judgment" can signify either statutes, especially those of God, or the rulings of a judge. In the case of God, judgment may fall within time or at the end of time.

Old Testament. The two primary Hebrew verbs translated "judge" by NRSV are *shaphat* (e.g., Gen 16:5; 18:25; 19:9), which means "govern, act as a lawgiver, judge," and *din* (e.g., Gen 49:16; Prov 31:9; Ps 50:4, 6; cf. the same root in Aramaic), which means "judge, exercise judgment, punish, or even vindicate" (i.e., judge to be innocent). The most common nouns are *shophet* and *dayyan*, which are derived from the verbs. The idea that a ruler or lawgiver can also be a judge may seem strange to moderns accustomed to separation of the powers in a state, but in the ancient Near East the king was typically the lawgiver. An excellent example is Hammurabi, the king of the First Babylonian Dynasty in the eighteenth century B.C. Shortly before his death he issued a compilation of laws, but he also heard cases of injustice and appeals from lower judges. The same was true of kings in the Old Testament, including David (2 Sam 15:2) and Solomon (1 Kgs 3:16–28). Ideally the king would judge with perfect impartiality (Isa 11:3). The lawgiver Moses, though not a king obviously, was also said to have heard cases—so many, in fact, that his father-in-law advised him to set up lower courts to hear cases of lesser import (Exod 18:13–23). Of course, the ultimate king/judge in the OT was God: "For the LORD is our judge; the LORD is our ruler; the LORD is our king; he will save us" (Isa 33:22).

The noun *shophet* was also used to designate the "judges" in the book of Judges and elsewhere. These judges fell into two categories. The first consisted of charismatic military heroes, on whom the spirit or charisma of God fell, enabling them to fight (e.g., Samson in Judg 15:14–15; cf. 6:14; 11:29). The second category was persons who heard cases, like the prophetess Deborah (Judg 4:4) and the priest Samuel (1 Sam 7:15). Terms for "judgment" include *mishpat* ("judgment, justice, rectitude, ordinance"; cf. Exod 28:15, 29), *shephot* ("judgment, act of judgment"; cf. 2 Chr 20:9), and *shephet* ("act of judgment"; cf. Exod 6:6; 12:12). Job 11:10 uses the verb *qahal* ("assemble") in the Hiphil or causative stem in the sense of "assemble for judgment," and Isa 28:7 employs the term *peliliya* ("umpire, decision") in the sense of priests' rendering a decision or judgment. Of these terms, the most frequently used was *mishpat*, which could be used interchangeably with other legal terms (cf. Deut 6:1–2, 17): *mitzwah* ("commandment"), *hoq* ("statute"), and *ʿedah* ("testimony").

The OT assigns a number of contexts for judging. Exodus 21:22 presupposes the existence of judges to hear cases, and Deut 16:18 prescribes their appointment. The OT was concerned that they judge rightly (Deut 1:16) and accept no bribes (Deut 16:19). Exodus 21:12–14, Num 35:9–34, and Deut 19:1–13 direct the establishment of cities of refuge, where

persons accused of murder could go for a trial. Also, Lev 13 assigns priests the responsibility of diagnosing leprosy and other skin diseases and of judging people "clean" or "unclean."

It is possible to piece together how court trials might have functioned. Deuteronomy 1:16–17 directs judges to hear both (or all?) parties, residents or aliens, and to judge fairly, that is, without being swayed by intimidation or bribe. Psalm 109:6 seems to allude to the plaintiff's standing to the right of the defendant as they faced the judge(s). At least two witnesses were required to convict someone (Num 35:30; Deut 17:6; 19:15). The Danielic narrative Susanna shows Daniel cross-examining witnesses (vv. 45–59), and Deut 19:15–21 not only allows for it in civil suits but stipulates that false witnesses should receive the penalty that would fall to the defendant if convicted.

In other situations, people could bring questions to a temple, where a priest or a prophet would consult God and then give an instruction (*torah*). If the same or a similar question arose again, the official could appeal to the instruction as a precedent or judgment (*mishpat*). Collectively, these laws could be called statutes and ordinances (Deut 4:1) as well as commandments, precepts, and statutes (Ps 119:10–15; see *law*).

Since God was the source of these judgments, God could be conceived of as a judge (e.g., Gen 16:5; 18:25; 31:53; Ps 75:7; 1 Chr 12:17; Hab 1:12; Mal 3:5). At times, a beleaguered person would wish or cry out for God to judge between contending persons (1 Sam 24:12). Others longed for God to judge the wicked (Ps 7:9–11) or the nations (Ps 67:4; Isa 2:4; Mic 4:3). Job simply wished for God to judge him innocent (23:7). Ultimately OT people wanted to be sure that God judged righteously or fairly (Ps 7:11; Jer 11:20).

The OT also spoke of God's final judgment of the world and its kingdoms. God will set a time to judge the whole world (Ps 75:2). God will put down the exalted and lift up the fallen (75:7). All the wicked of the earth will feel its full effects (75:8). Various OT authors refer to that day as the *day of the Lord,* the day when God would punish all of God's enemies. The prophet Amos declared that the day of the Lord the people were anticipating would be a day of "darkness, not light" (5:18) for those whom God punished. What they failed to understand was that their conduct warranted God's punishing Israel first! Later prophetic books also referred to God's future judgment with phrases like "on that day," "in those days," "at that time," "behold, days are coming," and "afterwards" or "after this." Later prophets, particularly those that flourished during and after the exile in Babylon (586–539), expected Gentile world powers to feel the brunt of God's judgment (Ezek 25–32; Joel 3; Obad 8–16; Isa 63), though Israel would not be exempt (Zech 12:2; 14:1–3). In some ways the crowning depiction of God as judge, however, is the portrayal of God as one Ancient of Days (NRSV, Ancient One) (Dan 7:9–14), who would sit in judgment of the terrifying fourth beast (the Greek empire), overthrow it, and return rulership to God's own people ("the people of the holy ones of the Most High," 7:27).

"Messianic" passages in the OT important to Christianity include Isa 9:2–7 and 11:1–5. The first celebrates the birth or coronation of a crown prince, while the second hopes that the king will govern properly. It hopes or predicts that the king "shall not judge by what his eyes see" (11:3b). Rather, it hopes that he will be guided by righteousness in judging cases when powerful people press unjust claims against the "poor" and "meek."

Some intertestamental literature envisions God as the end-time judge (e.g., *1 En.* 90:20–35; 97:1–10) or God's surrogate as judge (e.g., the "Righteous One" in *1 En.* 38:1–6; the "Elect One" in *1 En.* 45:3–6; 49:1–54:6; 55:3–4; the messiah in *2 Baruch* 40:3; 72:1–5). Perhaps the clearest texts portraying the messiah as judge are *Pss. Sol.* 17:21–44; 18:7–9. Those verses envision God's raising up a new son of David, the messiah, to judge

both Israel (vv. 26–8, 30b) and the nations (vv. 29–30a) and to rule as king (vv. 31–43).

New Testament. Overwhelmingly the NT uses the verb *krino* ("separate, distinguish, select, prefer, judge, think, decide, purpose") to signify the act of judging, both by humans (e.g., Matt 7:1, 2; Luke 6:37; 7:43) and by God (e.g., Rom 2:12; Rev 20:12–13) or Christ (e.g., Acts 17:31). In Paul's writings especially it means "pass judgment" (Rom 2:1; 14:3, 4, 13; 1 Cor 4:5). The NT employs the noun *krites* (judge, critic) to signify one who judges, whether an ordinary human (Luke 12:14; 18:2; Acts 24:10; 1 Cor 4:3), the judges of premonarchic Israel (Acts 13:20), Jesus (Acts 10:42), or God (Rom 2:16; 3:6; 1 Cor 5:13; 2 Tim 4:1; Heb 10:30; Jas 5:9). In one place Paul even asserts that "the saints will judge the world" and the angels (1 Cor 6:2–3). The NT also uses several secondary terms. These include the noun *dikastes* ("regent, judge, arbitrator") as a synonym of "ruler" in Acts 7:27, 35 (quoting Exod 2:14) and the verbs *anakrino* ("question, examine, judge, discern") in 1 Cor 4:3–4 (cf. 2:15, where the verb is translated "discern") and *diakrino* ("pass judgment, judge correctly") in 1 Cor 11:31. Once (1 Tim 1:12) the NT employs *hegeomai* ("lead, guide, think, consider, regard") and once (Jas 3:1) the phrase *krima lambano* ("receive a verdict") in the sense of judge.

Of particular note in the NT is its emphasis on the "day of judgment" (*krisis*). In Matthew, Jesus warns about that day when things would be more tolerable for the people of Sodom and Gomorrah than for towns that rejected his disciples (10:15), for Tyre than for cities that did not repent upon hearing Jesus' preaching (11:22, 24; cf. Luke 10:14), for the people of Nineveh and the queen of the South than for Jesus' own generation (Matt 12:41–42; cf. Luke 11:31–32). Even believers would give an account of their conduct (Matt 12:36; cf. 1 Pet 4:17). Various passages emphasize judgment on the godless (Heb 10:27; 2 Pet 2:4–6, 9; 3:7; Jude 15), especially Babylon in the book of Revelation (17:1; 18:10, 20) and on fallen angels (2 Pet 2:4; Jude 6). The eschatological judgment is certain (Heb 9:27) and will be eternal (Heb 6:2). Most important, judgment will fall on Satan, the ruler of the world (John 16:11; cf. 12:31).

The *bema* or judgment seat is mentioned thirteen times, eleven in reference to a specific platform or place of judgment ("tribunal"): where Jesus was tried (Matt 27:19; John 19:13); where Herod Agrippa I died while making a speech (Acts 12:21, 23); where Paul stood trial before Gallio in Corinth (Acts 18:12, 16–17); where Sosthenes was beaten (Acts 18:17); and where Paul faced trial before Festus at Caesarea (Acts 25:6, 10, 17). The other two references are to the judgment seat of God (Rom 14:10) or Christ (2 Cor 5:10).

The Gospel of John exhibits an apparent but not genuine inconsistency in its presentation of divine judgment. In John 5, Jesus says that God has turned over judgment to him (v. 30), the Son (v. 22), who is the *Son of God* (v. 25) and the *Son of Man* (v. 27). In 8:16, Jesus asserts his unity with God, so that Jesus and God judge, not Jesus alone. That verse coheres well with the larger perspective of John 5:22–30, which also stresses that Jesus does not act in isolation from God. Jesus' coming brings judgment, positive on those who believe, negative on those who do not (9:39–40). His impending death would be the judgment on the world (12:31), that is, it would illuminate godlessness, showing how horrific it could be.

Condemn, Condemnation

These two terms make clear that judging may result in a guilty verdict. They also point ahead to the need for God to punish guilt in a morally construed universe.

Old Testament. The most frequent word for "condemn" is *rasha͏ʿ* (Exod 22:9; 1 Kgs 8:32; Job 9:20, 29; 10:2; 15:6; 34:17, 29; 40:8; Ps 34:21–22, 94:21; Prov 12:2; 17:15), which most often means "be wicked, act wickedly," but can have the causal (Hiphil) meaning "condemn as guilty" in civil (Exod 22:9), ethical (1 Kgs 8:32; Ps 34:21–2), or religious (Job 10:2) contexts. The meaning "condemn as

guilty" is an extended meaning, but it shows the connection between wicked behavior and condemnation. In two other cases (Ps 109:31; 141:6), however, NRSV translates as "condemn" the verb *shaphat*, which means "judge, govern," and particularly "judge righteously." In both of these verses, the wicked are in the process of condemning the righteous, who appeal to God for help. NRSV also translates the nominal form of the word as "condemnation" in Prov 19:29.

New Testament. The NT employs four verbs translated "condemn" in the NRSV: *krino* (Luke 6:37; John 3:17, 18; 8:26; 16:11; Acts 13:27; Rom 2:1, 27; 3:7; 14:22; 1 Cor 11:32; Col 2:16; 2 Thess 2:12), which means "judge, decide, condemn" as a legal technical term; *katakrino* (Matt 12:41, 42; 27:3; Mark 14:64; 16:16; Luke 11:31, 32; John 8:10, 11; Rom 8:3, 34; 14:23; 2 Cor 7:3; Heb 11:7; 2 Pet 2:6), which means "condemn," sometimes in connection with terms like "death" or "destruction"; *kataginosko* (1 John 3:20, 21), which means "condemn, convict"; and *katadikazo* (Matt 12:7, 37; Luke 6:37; Jas 5:6), which means "condemn, find or pronounce guilty." Further, the NRSV translates four nouns as "condemnation": *krisis* (John 5:29; Jas 5:12; Jude 9), which may designate a judgment that goes against a person, particularly the judgment of God or the messiah as judge on the last day; *katakrisis* (2 Cor 3:9), which means "judgment against" and necessarily involves condemnation; *krima* (Mark 12:40; Luke 20:47; 23:40; Rom 3:8; 1 Cor 11:34; 1 Tim 3:6; 5:12; 2 Pet 2:3; Jude 4), which designates "lawsuit, decision, judgment, judicial verdict"; and *katakrima* (Rom 5:16, 18; 8:1), which means "punishment, doom" rather than "condemnation" per se.

Punish, Punishment

The third pair of terms in the legal sequence that proceeds from judge/judgment to condemn/condemnation to the consequences. As seen above, however, the distinction between condemnation and punishment is not precise.

Old Testament. The Hebrew verb most frequently translated "punish" is *paqad* ("attend to, visit, muster, appoint"), which appears at least twenty-five times in Jeremiah alone, all in connection with God's punishing humans for their sinfulness. The meaning "punish" seems to be a derived meaning. God could "visit" people for good or for harm, but often such a visit was designed to recompense people for their sins (cf. Exod 32:34; Ps 89:32; Isa 10:12; 13:11; 24:21; 26:21; Jer 30:20; Hos 1:4). In such cases it is properly translated "punish."

NRSV translates other terms "punish" as well: *yasar*, which means "discipline, admonish, chasten, or *correct*," but also designates recompense for sins (cf. Lev 26:18, 28); *yakah*, which means "decide, adjudge, convict, or reprove," but can be administered by humans with a rod or God by means of a human "rod" (cf. 2 Sam 7:14); *naqam*, which means "avenge" (cf. Exod 21:20), but can be used of God's recompensing Israel for defiling the land of Canaan (Lev 18:25); *ʿanash*, which refers to fining a guilty party or more generally to punishment (Prov 21:11); and *shith*, which means to "put, set, constitute, or take a stand," but can be used to mean take a stand against or punish (Num 12:11). A pair of terms designates giving (*nathan*, cf. Ezek 7:3, 4, 8, 9) or withholding (*hasak*, cf. Ezra 9:13) punishment. Another term, *shub*, means "turn, return, or repent," but can also mean "turn back on" or "punish" (Hos 2:13); and *ʿanah* typically means "answer, respond, testify," but can be used to mean "respond with punishment" (1 Kgs 8:25; 11:39; 2 Chr 6:26; Isa 64:12).

The OT often portrays God as threatening to punish people (Exod 32:34; 1 Sam 3:13; Ps 89:32). That punishment may occur at a future time signified by the phrase "on that day" (Isa 24:21–22; 26:1, 14, 21; 27:1). God may use natural calamities to punish people (Amos 3:6) or human agencies (Isa 10:5–19). Both are problematic and require further discussion. It is possible to overstate the extent to which the OT understands calamities as God's punishment. While Amos 3:6 seems to say that all disasters are sent by God as punishment (3:2), it is not always

clear that is what the text means. In Amos 4, God declares that God had sent famine (4:6), drought (4:7–8), blight, mildew and locusts (4:9), disease (4:10), and political reversals if not military destruction (4:11). Still, the prophet does not directly connect them to sin as punishment. Perhaps one should read these calamities as simply events from which Israel could and should have learned but did not (she was not self-sufficient), rather than as punishment for past misdeeds or warnings against future ones.

God's use of armies to punish Israel was fraught with such moral difficulties that the texts themselves addressed the issue. Isaiah announced that God would employ the Assyrians to punish Israel (1:7–9; 5:26–30; 7:17; 8:5–8; 10:5–11; cf. Hos 10:1–8), but Assyria's haughtiness was legendary (Isa 36:1–22), calling forth God's repudiation (Isa 37:21–29). Moreover, her pride led to excesses in warfare that demanded punishment (Isa 10:12–19; cf. Nah 2 and 3). Possibly the prophet Habakkuk had God's use of Assyria in mind when he predicted that God would send the Babylonians to punish wickedness (Hab 1:5–11), and he questioned the justice of doing that (1:12–17). In any case, the book of Jeremiah proclaimed that God would use Babylon to punish Judah (Jer 6:22–23; 8:10; 21:1–10; 22:24–27; 25:1–14, etc.), and the exilic contributor to the book of Isaiah made exactly that point (Isa 42:22).

Yet the Judeans surely could object that they had at least tried to worship God (the temple, after all, was still standing) and were in no case guilty of the excesses of the Babylonians (Hab 1:6–11). She had indeed suffered double what she deserved (Isa 40:2). So God had to punish the Babylonians (Isa 43:14–21), and did so by means of the Persian army under Cyrus the Great (Isa 44:24–45:8), thus liberating the exiles to return home (Isa 48:20).

The symbol for Medo-Persia in Dan 8 was the ram with two horns, the longer representing Persia. It charged in all directions, the other nations being powerless to stop it. Only the dreadful fourth kingdom, the Greeks (Dan 7:7–8, 23–25;

8:5–7), could subdue it, and much of the book of Daniel was devoted to describing its excesses and its fall before God. In some ways, then, the book of Daniel offers the OT's last word on the subject of imperial armies: they were not part of God's doings and would all be punished directly by God.

New Testament. The NT employs several verbs for "punish." They include *kolazo*, which means "punish" or "cut off" (Acts 4:21; cf. 2 Pet 2:9, where it is translated as a noun). The nominal form *kolasis*, which can also mean "retribution," appears in Matt 25:46 and 1 John 4:18. Other verbs are *timoreo* (Acts 22:5, where it too is translated as a noun; cf. *timoria* in Heb 10:29) and *hypopiazo*, which literally means to "give someone a black eye" (see Paul's statement that he punishes his body in 1 Cor 9:27). Once NRSV translates the verb *ekdikeo*, which can also mean "avenge," as "punish" (2 Cor 10:6), showing the close connection between the concepts, and twice it translates nominal forms of the word as "punishment" (2 Cor 7:11; 1 Pet 2:14). It also translates *epitimia*, which can mean "reproof" or "rebuke," as "punishment" (2 Cor 2:6).

To a lesser extent than the OT, the NT also thought in terms of God's use of civil authorities as a vehicle for punishment. Paul argues that authority per se was instituted by God, that rulers do not oppose those who are doing good, and that such authority could be God's servant in executing wrath on wrongdoers (Rom 13:1–4). While this statement is less than a full-fledged endorsement of all that governments do, it does articulate a high estimation of government. One wonders if Paul revised his thinking when he was tried by the Roman government. Regardless, the book of Revelation looked forward eagerly to the fall of the Roman Empire (Rev 13:1–10; 17:1–18:24), which it deemed guilty of persecuting the church (17:6; 18:24).

The new emphasis of the NT was the idea of eternal punishment. Twice it employs the noun *dike* in phrases that speak of punishment resulting in eternal destruction (2 Thess 1:9) or accompanied by eternal fire (Jude 7, 23). Similar ideas appear in the teachings of Jesus (Mark 3:29, in connection with the unpardonable sin) and the book of Revelation (cf. the lake of fire into which the "beast" and his "prophet" were thrown in 19:20; cf. also the second death of those not registered in the book of life according to 20:14–15). To be sure, the NT speaks more often of eternal life, and at times the opposite might simply be death, but in the texts cited here the idea seems to have been eternal punishment meted out to sinners.

G. B. Caird, *New Testament Theology* (Oxford: Clarendon Press, 1994), 77–87; Walther Eichrodt, *Theology of the Old Testament* (Philadelphia: Westminster Press, 1961), 1:457–71; Claus Westermann, *Elements of Old Testament Theology* (Atlanta: John Knox Press, 1982), 118–37.

PAUL L. REDDITT

Just, Justice, Justification, Justify, Righteous, Righteousness

"The LORD of hosts is exalted by justice (*mishpat*), and the Holy God shows himself holy by righteousness (*tsedaqah*)" (Isa 5:16). "Let justice (*mishpat*) roll down like waters, and righteousness (*tsedaqah*) like an ever-flowing stream" (Amos 5:24). God "himself is righteous (*dikaion*) and . . . he justifies (*dikaiounta*) the one who has faith in Jesus" (Rom 3:26). The massive contribution to biblical theology from a single Hebrew root (*tsadaq*) and a single Greek stem (*dikai-*) is often masked in English by the variety of terms employed from both the Latin *justitia* ("justice, just, justification") and Anglo-Saxon "rightwise" ("righteous, righteousness"). There are also other closely related themes involving "justice" and "judgment," (see *judge*), and "right" (see **upright**). Catholic Bibles generally have preferred words from the Latin; hence "the justice of God" (Rom 1:17; 3:5, 21, etc.). NRSV has "justification" as a term only six times in the NT (RSV three), "justify" only five times in the OT (RSV six). Some would limit justification to Rom 4:25 and 5:18 (Greek *dikaiosis*) and 5:18 (*dikaioma*), though NRSV uses "justification" also at Rom 5:21; 2 Cor 3:9; Gal 2:21, plus the verb "justify" thirty-three times in the NT. To get the effect of the more than 500 occurrences in the OT and 225 in the NT where terms from these two roots are found (and Hebrew *tsadaq*-words are rendered in the Greek OT by *dikaio*-terms about 90 percent of the time), one needs to resort in English to "righteousness/justification language," and to treat "righteousness" and "justification" together.

In biblical thought, God is constantly and consistently presented as righteous/just: "The Rock . . . all his ways are just. A faithful God . . . just and upright" (Deut 32:4). "The Righteous One" is praised (Isa 24:16). The Psalms vibrate with the thought "You are righteous" (119:137–38; cf. 7:9; 11:7; 116:5; 129:4). God says, in a sort of self-definition, "I am the LORD; I act with steadfast love, justice, and righteousness in the earth" (Jer 9:24). "I the LORD speak the truth (*tsedeq*), I declare what is right" (Isa 45:19). This took the form in Israel of giving righteous judgment (Ps 9:4; Isa 58:2) and, for the sake of righteousness, teaching (*torah*) (Isa 42:21) and "righteous ordinances" (Ps 119:7). Those outside Israel could be moved to confess, in light of what God does, "The LORD is in the right" (Exod 9:27, Pharaoh), but Jeremiah also realized, "You will be in the right, O LORD, when I lay charges against you" (Jer 12:1). Such emphases continue in the NT. God is the "righteous judge" (2 Tim 4:8) and "righteous Father" (John 17:25).

The God of the Bible also calls for righteousness/justice on the part of people in their relations with one another. Admission to God's community, both civic and cultic, means doing what is right. Psalm 15:1–5 and Ezek 18:5–9 provide long lists of how one who is righteous lives, with regard to idols, women, debtors, the poor. The king particularly is to be righteous and give just judgments (Pss 45:4, 7; 72:1–2, 7; 18:20–24; Prov 31:8–9). Individuals may be identified as righteous: Noah

(Gen 6:9, 7:1; 2 Pet 2:5); Lot (2 Pet 2:6–8); Joseph (Matt 1:19); Zechariah and Elizabeth (Luke 1:6); Simeon (Luke 2:25). Noah, Daniel (or Danel), and Job are mentioned at Ezek 14:14 as figures whose righteousness could, in a land that sins, at best save only their own lives, and no one else (righteousness is neither transferable nor cumulative, Ezek 33:12–13). Judah had to say of Tamar, in a famous case, "You are righteous, not I" (Gen 38:26 NRSV, "more in the right than I"). In Israel this meant keeping God's will expressed in torah (Ps 119:1, 7, etc.; Isa 51:7; Ezek 18:19–22). The aim was for words that are righteous, not crooked (Prov 8:8), and right conduct in society. God looked for justice (*mishpat*) but alas "found bloodshed (*mispah*); righteousness (*tsedaqah*) but heard a cry (*tseʿaqah*)" from the oppressed, Isaiah charged (Isa 5:7). Oppression of the righteous continued to be singled out as a sin of a rich, unjust society (Jas 5:6; Amos 2:6; 5:12).

God's nature (righteous) and ethical will (righteous conduct) are intertwined. "The LORD is our righteousness" (Jer 23:6); "I have called you in righteousness" (Isa 42:6), so "Keep justice and do righteousness" (Isa 56:1) (NRSV, "Maintain justice, and do what is right). That the relationships involved often assume a legal or law court setting—in litigation, you're "in the right" or "in the wrong"—implies a "forensic" sense, pertaining to the forum, the site of court cases. For example, Deut 16:18–20 condemns justifying the wicked or condemning the righteous (cf. Prov 17:15; Exod 23:6–8); and Isa 5:23 condemns acquitting the guilty for a bribe. On the other hand, to give back at night the cloak a poor person has pledged for a loan "will be to your credit (*tsedaqah*) before the LORD" (Deut 24:13). Inevitably, God appears as judge, one who is righteous (Pss 7:7–11; 96:13). In procedures of the day the Lord might be engaged in lawsuits with Israel, bringing charges against the people (Jer 2:4–13; Mic 6:1–8; and they against God; cf. Jer 12:1, above). In much of the OT period there was not yet any expectation of a resurrection for the righteous, let alone the unrighteous (perhaps first in Dan 12:2; Isa 25:6–10), or of a "last judgment." Therefore judgment of the wicked and unrighteous and reward of the righteous, when all get their due, were expected in this life and in this world. But all too often the wicked seemed to flourish and the righteous suffered, contrary to what should justly be (Ps 92:12–15; Job). The exile especially raised such questions. The matter of "theodicy" runs through Scripture: that God needs to account for why things work out as they do, if the Lord is righteous and all-powerful; so that, as the psalmist put it, "you are justified in your sentence and blameless when you pass judgment" (51:4; Rom 3:4). The issue continues in the NT: Will God "grant justice to his chosen ones, who cry to him day and night?" (Luke 18:7). How can Jesus receive sinners? How can a righteous God justify the ungodly? (Rom 4:5). The wording seems deliberately to contradict Exod 23:7, where God says, "I will not acquit the guilty." God, justify yourself!

Most striking is the way in which God's righteousness at times seems to save, a gracious activity where *tsadaq*-terms mean, or parallel, "deliverance," "salvation," and "victory." Some see this in Judg 5:11, "the triumphs of the LORD"; more clearly in 1 Sam 12:7, which speaks of "all the saving deeds of the LORD" during the exodus, the conquest of the land, and under the judges; cf. Isa 1:27, "Zion shall be redeemed by justice, and those in her who repent, by righteousness"; most clearly in Deutero-Isaiah: "I will bring near my deliverance (*tsidqathi*) . . . and my salvation will not tarry" (46:13; similarly in 51:5, 6, 8 "deliverance forever," "my salvation to all generations"). One's hope is to be able to say, "[God] has clothed me with the garments of salvation, . . . with the robe of righteousness" (61:10). The "righteous God" is a Savior (Isa 45:21). The picture of vindication (or God as "vindicator") in Isa 58:8 is coupled with such fruits as loosing the bonds of injustice, letting the oppressed go free, and sharing with the hungry, poor, and naked (58:6–7).

Some have sought to relate these various aspects of righteousness to "covenant": God's saving righteousness rescues Israel from slavery and, in the stipulations in the covenant (e.g., at Sinai), calls for righteousness. But *tsadaq* terms do not occur in the Ten Commandments; admonitions like Deut 6:18, "Do what is right (*hayyashar*) and good in the sight of the LORD," are rather general, in comparison with what the prophets say. Nehemiah 9:6–37 begins as a confession of faith about what God has done, from Abraham on, including the Sinai covenant, but then it becomes a confession of sin, about Israel's disobedience; cf. also Dan 9:11–18. All in all, it is not as easy as one might expect to relate "righteousness" to "covenant." The most significant verse for NT use, Abram "believed the LORD, and the LORD reckoned it to him as righteousness" (Gen 15:6), comes before the making of the covenant in Gen 15:12–21 or Gen 17, let alone that at Sinai. Paul was able to make much of the fact that the righteousness reckoned to Abraham was by promise, through faith, prior to the institution of circumcision, so that Abraham might be the father of all who believe (Rom 4:9–25; Gal 3:6–9). God justifies "the circumcised on the ground of faith and the uncircumcised through the same faith" (Rom 3:30).

Even though "justification" as a term is not common in the OT in English, the elements were there for what Paul will later develop in the NT. People try to justify themselves (Job 32:2; 40:8). How God works, or does not, needs to be justified (the theodicy question). Righteousness/ justification comes through divine promise and faith, both as human response (see *believe*) and as God's faithfulness to the promise. And *grace* abounds, which will abound all the more in Christ (Rom 5:17, 20). One may see "justification events" in OT history: call by grace (*choose*; Gen 12:2–3); amid failures and judgment, the hope of new beginnings (Hosea, e.g., 2:14–15); and in the Psalms, hope for individuals who, as righteous people, know God's nature and who look to God for vindication (17:1–5), for they know God's mighty deeds (Pss 77:11–18; 40:9–10, "your saving help [*tsidqatheka*]"). At times the insight emerged that God alone can execute righteousness (in Ps 99:4 the Lord is the "Mighty King"; Isa 61:11); no mortal is righteous (Ps 143:1–2). Righteousness became part of the hope for a future messianic king called "The LORD is our righteousness" (Isa 11:4–5; Jer 23:5–6).

In the NT, righteousness/justification is used far more *about* the meaning of the coming of Jesus Christ, especially his death and resurrection, than in the teachings of Jesus of Nazareth. He did talk about the goodness of God in sending sun and rain "on the righteous and on the unrighteous" (Matt 5:45) and criticized the overwhelming percentage of "righteous persons who need no repentance" (Luke 15:7; cf. 18:9, "who trusted in themselves that they were righteous and regarded others with contempt"). Woe to people who "on the outside look righteous to others, but inside . . . are full of hypocrisy and lawlessness" (Matt 23:28). Jesus was, on this evidence, a prophet preaching judgment, like John the Baptist, in a long line of envoys sent by Wisdom/God (Luke 7:35 par. Matt 11:9). His mission, positively, was to call "not . . . righteous persons but sinners" (Mark 2:17 par.; Matt 9:13; Luke 5:32 adds "to repentance"). During his ministry this took the form of open table fellowship (Mark 2:16; Luke 15:2). In the parable at Luke 18:9–14 it is the tax collector, a sinner who threw himself on God's mercy, not the Pharisee, who goes home "justified" ("accounted righteous"; the parable at Luke 18:1–8 about a judge provides a forensic context). Jesus' good news was the announcement that God's reign was breaking in.

In Matthew, Jesus' baptism by John is described as a step "to fulfill all righteousness" (3:15), the Baptizer having come "in the way of righteousness" (21:32). The implication is that righteousness has a history, in which the two proclaimers stand. Now the promise is made that those "who hunger and thirst for righteousness" are "blessed" and "will be filled" (5:6). Why? Because "the kingdom of heaven has come near" (3:2; 4:17). People can strive, above all else, "for the kingdom of God and his [or its] righteousness" (6:33), a gift (cf. 5:3, 10; 5:6 "will be filled [by God]"). But the ethical side of righteousness is present. In Matt 6:1 it is "piety" (*dikaiosyne*), taking the form of almsgiving (cf. 2 Cor. 9:9–10); in 5:10 it is what disciples are persecuted for; and in 5:20 Jesus calls for righteousness that exceeds that of the scribes and Pharisees. Some would see moral conduct in all six Matthean references; others, eschatological gift and salvation history in all six. Given the dual tracks in the OT, Matthean usage seems likely to include both, as presented above.

Not so much during his ministry, in the Gospels, but after the resurrection (in Acts and the Epistles), Jesus came to be viewed as "the righteous one." At Matt 27:19, Pilate's wife calls him "innocent" (Greek *dikaios*; cf. 27:24 with its textual variants, NRSV Mg, "this righteous blood" or "this righteous man's blood"). In Luke 23:47, the centurion affirms that Jesus was "innocent" (or "righteous"). The fuller title comes to the fore in speeches in Acts: "the Holy and Righteous One" was rejected (3:14); Saul was chosen "to see the Righteous One and to hear his own voice" on Damascus Road (22:14); the history of persecution included the martyrdom of prophets "who foretold the coming of the Righteous One" (7:52; cf. 1 Pet 1:10–11). The reference is to prophets like Isaiah (chap. 53, especially v. 11, "The righteous one, my servant, shall make many righteous, and he shall bear their iniquities"; cf. also Wis 2:12–20, about "the righteous man," who is God's "child" [or servant]). The title turns up also at 1 John 2:1, "Jesus Christ the righteous" is "the atoning sacrifice for our sins" and "an advocate with the Father," as well as at 1 Pet 3:18, "Christ also suffered for sins once for all, the righteous for the unrighteous." While the OT sometimes speaks of some figure like "the Servant" in Isaiah as "the righteous one," it must be asked further whether in the NT something said about God in the OT is being applied to Christ.

The catalyst for application of OT "righteousness/justification" themes was the need, in earliest Christianity, to explain and find significance in the death of Jesus and God's intervention, raising him to life and lordship. For Jewish Christians, materials lay at hand in the OT (and Judaism) about (saving) righteousness, though "righteousness" was also a well-known theme in the Greco-Roman world. Justice or *dikaiosyne* was one of the four cardinal virtues. For justice as a deity or force in the world, see Acts 28:4. One could even speak, as Plato does, of the just man martyred for a cause. Besides 1 Pet 3:18, examples of such statements in (Jewish) Christianity include "Christ Jesus, who became for us wisdom from God, and righteousness" (1 Cor 1:30) and, with regard to effects on Christ, "He was revealed in flesh, vindicated (or justified) in spirit" (1 Tim 3:16, which goes on to speak of the risen Christ's being "seen by angels," proclaimed, believed in, and "taken up in glory"). Other instances trace the meaning for believers: "for our sake [God] made him to be sin [or a sin offering] who knew no sin, so that in him we might become the righteousness of God" (2 Cor 5:21). The link applying to us the benefits of Christ's death, namely justification and sanctification, is response in faith to the message about Jesus and then baptism into Christ: "you were washed, you were sanctified, you were justified in the name of the Lord Jesus and in the Spirit of our God" (1 Cor 6:11). Romans 4:25 sees the results of Christ's death ("for our trespasses") and resurrection as "our justification" ("acquittal by resurrection"). The most detailed summary comes in Rom 3:24–26. It involves Day-of-Atonement imagery. All who have sinned "are now justified by [God's] grace as a gift, through the redemption that is in Christ Jesus, whom God put forward as a sacrifice of atonement by his blood, effective through faith. [God] did this to show his righteousness, because in his divine forbearance he had passed

over the sins previously committed." All of these passages likely contain formulations developed before the time when Paul (or the other writers of the epistles where they occur) cited them. They testify to a common Christian view on the meaning of the death of the Righteous One that justifies baptized believers. Each serves as climax of a section (e.g., Rom 4:25) or is foundational for further theological development in its new context. At Rom 3:26, for example, Paul goes on in the seminal statement, quoted above at the outset of this article, that all this serves to prove that God is "righteous" and "rightwises" the person who believes in Jesus (cf. NRSV). There is nothing in the context here to encourage the reading "who has the faith of Jesus" (3:26, NRSV Mg). How Jesus believed is not the topic, but how Christ's atoning death applies to sinners who cannot be justified in God's sight by deeds prescribed in the law. Paul's example of having faith and how this translates into righteousness is Abraham, not Jesus (Rom 4:3, 10–12).

Under "righteousness/justification," Paul could bring his entire gospel together, touching on salvation from God and human conduct, the forensic and now eschatological, as well as the ethical aspects. With regard to courts (the forensic aspect), Paul says, "I am not aware of anything against myself, but I am not thereby acquitted (*dedikaiomai*). It is the Lord who judges me" (1 Cor 4:4). With regard to conduct, we live lives that are "pure, upright (*dikaios*), and blameless" (1 Thess 2:10). With regard to the history of God's redeeming righteousness, in a contrast between the Sinai covenant and the new covenant, Moses and Christ, one can speak of a "ministry of condemnation" (RSV a "dispensation") that had a glory of its own and "the ministry (dispensation) of justification" that proceeds from God's own righteousness, from the Spirit and life (2 Cor 3:9, in the context of the entire chapter). This way of expressing the gospel has far greater resonance with the OT than "reconciliation" (a much less frequent term in the Bible, usually piggybacking on righteousness/ justification, Rom 5:8–12; 2 Cor 5:18–21) or "Christ" or "in Christ" (hardly major OT themes). There are far more Pauline and NT usages of righteousness/justification, in number of references, than "covenant," "church," "sacraments," or even our terms like "salvation history." It allies with, and sometimes provides the foundation for, expressions like "redemption" (Rom 3:24; 1 Cor 1:30), grace (Rom 3:24, "as a gift"), the cross (Rom 3:25, "blood"), and even Spirit (2 Cor 3; Rom 8:10–11, 30, 33). Eventually, as rootage in the OT became less pertinent for Christians in the Greco-Roman world, the verb "save" sometimes replaced "justify," even while all the traditional Pauline themes were preserved, as at Eph 2:8, "by grace you have been saved by faith, and this is not your own doing; it is the gift of God" (see *save*).

In the process of deepening the meaning of righteousness/justification since Christ, Paul was guided by certain texts in OT Scripture. Genesis 15:6 has been noted. It had a considerable history of interpretation. For example, Neh 9:8: God "found his heart faithful." According to 1 Macc 2:52, Abraham was found faithful when tested by being asked to sacrifice Isaac (Genesis 22; cf. Sir 44:19–21). This line of interpretation was followed in Jas 2:21–25 (see below); cf. also Heb 6:13–15 and 11:17–19. To this, Paul replied, in effect, that "being reckoned righteous" came in Abram's case in Gen 15, before he was circumcised (Gen 17; see Rom 4:10), before any tests or works, when he simply trusted God "who justifies the ungodly" (Rom 4:3–5, Paul's most stark assertion, justification of the impious, not "the righteous"). Not only the role of faith is at stake but also the universal nature of this example, for Gentiles as well as Jews, before Abram was involved in any covenant.

The other formative text was Hab 2:4, "Look at the proud! Their spirit is not right in them, but the righteous live by their faith" (or "faithfulness," NRSV Mg). Paul employs the verse, which had many textual variants and interpretations, to make the point at Gal 3:11, "No one is justified before God by the law; for 'The one who is righteous will live by faith'" (or, NRSV Mg, "The one who is righteous by faith will live"). The variant word orders open up the possibilities both of how one becomes righteous and how one lives, in each case, "by faith." The contrast here is between faith and (deeds of the) law. Romans 1:17 employs Hab 2:4 to buttress the thesis that it is "through faith for faith" that "the righteousness of God is revealed." Hebrews 10:38 cites the Habakkuk verse, along with Hab 2:3, to stress not "shrinking back" (Hab 2:4b, "My soul takes no pleasure in anyone who shrinks back"), so that "we are . . . among those who have faith and so are saved." Habakkuk 2:4 is thus used to stress faith and the resulting life of faith.

To be noted also from the OT is the phrase "the righteousness of God" (Rom 1:17; 3:21–22; 2 Cor 5:21; Jas 1:20), "the justice of God" (Rom 3:5), "the righteousness that comes from God" (Rom 10:3; Phil 3:10), among other examples, perhaps a technical term going back to Deut 33:21, "the justice of the LORD," but hardly fixed in meaning ("from God"? an attribute of God? saving righteousness or demanding justice?). The apocalyptic aspects—righteousness is "revealed" (*apokalyptetai*, Rom 1:17), along with God's wrath, at the "last day"—cannot be overlooked, however (Rom 1:18; 5:9–10, 8:31–39; 1 Thess 1:9–10; 5:9).

Righteousness/justification includes future fulfillment (Rom 3:30; Gal 5:5) as well as a certain realization in the present (Rom 3:24–25), based as it is on Christ's work for us once and for all in the past; compare the use of the verb "save" in Rom 5:9–10 ("we will be saved"); 1 Cor 15:2 and 1:18 ("are being saved"); and Rom 8:24 ("in hope we were saved"), respectively.

In three different situations Paul discusses righteousness/justification in some depth. At Phil 3:2–21 he takes up two kinds of righteousness on the basis of his own autobiographical experience, in order to warn readers about "enemies of the cross of Christ" who may soon threaten the house churches in Philippi. The one kind of righteousness is that of one's "own that comes from the law" (v. 9). For Jews, the relationship with God may originally have been by election into the covenant for the nation, but staying in this relationship for the individual had become a matter of performing deeds prescribed by the law. The other kind of righteousness "comes through faith in Christ" (3:9, not, as in NRSV Mg, "the faith of Christ," for even Phil 2:6–8 has not told us how Jesus believed). This "faith righteousness" holds for Gentiles and Jews. It applies both to getting into the right relationship with God and to staying in that relationship, that is, how one lives. The end of 3:9 is to be connected with v. 10, "righteousness from God that depends on faith to know Christ" (NRSV has, unhelpfully, added "I want" to know Christ). Paul has experienced both kinds of righteousness in his lifetime. As Saul of Tarsus he knew circumcision, law, and righteousness under it. This he does not denigrate (3:5–7, a list of credentials) but contrasts with what had proven better, gaining Christ and resurrection, through God's kind of righteousness. But he cautions (3:12–21) that (even!) he and other believers have not as yet obtained the goal and final transformation. The picture here is of the justified believer still engaged in the struggle with the forces of this world, not yet at the "heavenly city" (*politeuma*, 3:20).

In Galatians Paul argues polemically, from Scripture. Here the example of Abraham (Gen 15:6) and the role of faith (Hab 2:4) enter into his presentation on righteousness/justification (3:6–10). So do Gen 12:3 (cf. 18:18) and 12:7: "the promises were made to Abraham and to his offspring," offspring being a singular noun that Paul, in accord with exegesis of the day, takes literally and applies to Christ (Gal 3:8, 16). Paul brings in as well Deut 27:26 ("Cursed is everyone who does not . . . obey all the things written in the book of the law," Gal 3:10); and Deut 21:23 (Gal 3:13), plus the Sarah/Hagar

story in Gen 16 (Gal 4:21–31). Also involved in the case he presents for justification by faith is chronology: the law at Sinai came 430 years after the covenant of promise with Abraham (3:17–18) and does not supersede it. But experience in Christianity by the Galatians is not overlooked (3:2–5). They have received the Spirit in connection with believing the message about Christ crucified that they heard, and Paul adds some personal and apostolic history (1:11–2:21).

At the heart of the dispute in Galatia is "the truth of the gospel" (2:5, 14), over righteousness/justification. Does justification, getting right with God, come about through Christ's death or via covenant law, including circumcision (2:21; 5:2–6); by "works of the law or faith in Christ" (2:16)? Righteousness/ justification and related matters had earlier been under dispute among Jewish followers of Jesus, in Jerusalem (1:18–2:10) and Antioch (2:11–14. How do the law and what it demands, the keys in Jewish and some Jewish-Christian thought, apply to Gentiles? The proposition in 2:16, "We know that a person is justified (or reckoned as righteous, NRSV Mg) . . . through faith in Jesus Christ. And we have come to believe in Christ Jesus, so that we might be justified by faith in Christ . . . because no one will be justified by the works of the law" (cf. Ps 143:2), is not just Paul's opinion. Note the "we." It is a Jewish-Christian assertion, in which Peter and others joined, even though they did not always draw out all the implications in practice (Gal 2:13–14). This declaration of freedom (cf. 5:1, 13) the rest of Galatians seeks to support.

In Romans, Paul presents his gospel more systematically (though not "systematic theology," even though this epistle became the basis for Melanchthon's *Loci* and Calvin's *Institutes of the Christian Religion*). It is presented scripturally (that meant for Paul the Hebrew Scriptures in their Greek forms), and so his manifesto might be termed an exercise in biblical theology. It is less polemical than Galatians (barbs against the law at Sinai, like

Gal 3:19–20, are ameliorated; see Rom 7:7–14: "the law is holy, and the commandment is holy and just and good" [v. 11]), though it may be written in light of conflict in Rome (14:1–15:13, the "strong" and the "weak"). It remains personal (15:14–32).

The theme announced at the outset of Romans in discussing the gospel is "the righteousness of God" (1:17). In the face of sin that dominates Gentiles and Jews alike, though in different manifestations (1:18–3:20), the conclusion is that "'no human being will be justified in [God's] sight' by deeds prescribed by the law." But now there is available for all, in Christ, apart from law, the righteousness of God, providing justification for all who believe. Romans 3:21–31, which sets forth this good news, is the most concentrated biblical statement on righteousness/justification; hence it has frequently been alluded to above. Abraham's example in chapter 4 leads into what the life of the justified is like (chaps. 5–8). The two kinds of righteousness, faith righteousness and that from law (10:5–13), are prominent in the discussion of "Israel after the flesh" (chaps. 9–11). The life that justified Christians are to lead is spelled out in chapters 12–15: the implications from being "rightwised," life in God's kingdom that means "righteousness and peace and joy in the Holy Spirit" (14:17). Compare also, for Pauline principles, Gal 5:6, "the only thing that counts is faith working [or made effective, NRSV Mg] through love"; Phil 1:11, "the harvest [or fruit] of righteousness that comes through Jesus Christ," illustrated in Gal 5:22 by "the fruit of the Spirit" in contrast to the "works of the flesh" (5:19–21); and 2 Cor 9:10, the righteousness or benevolence of the person who gives generously to the poor. In ethics and belief, "biblical thought" has sometimes meant the theology of Romans as guide and organizing principle.

The other NT writings add little theologically to the heights attained in these three letters on righteousness/justification, though they do reflect the pervasiveness of many OT aspects of *tsadaq* terms and adaptation of *dikaio* language in the Greco-Roman world. As noted, Ephesians preserves faith and grace, but not justification, in speaking of salvation at 2:8. It loses the future aspect in Paul's tension about justification as present and yet to come but does put emphasis on "the new self, created according to the likeness of God in true righteousness and holiness" (through baptism as new creation, or new creatures, 4:24; cf. 1 Cor 6:11). Hence the ethical exhortation to those with "the breastplate of righteousness" (6:14; in Isa 59:17 God's armor) to live with "all that is good and right and true" as fruit (5:9). The Pastoral Epistles (recall 1 Tim 3:16, Christ "justified/vindicated") set forth (in Titus 3:5) how God "saved us, not because of any works of righteousness that we had done, but according to his mercy, through the water of rebirth and renewal by the Holy Spirit." The reference to baptism again (cf. Rom 6:1–11) leads to what some term "baptismal justification": "whoever has died is freed (*dedikaiotai*) from sin" (Rom 6:7 NRSV). The outcome is "that, having been justified by [God's] grace, we might become heirs according to the hope of eternal life" (Titus 3:7). Future eschatology continues: The Lord, "the righteous judge," will bestow "the crown of righteousness" at the last day (2 Tim 4:8). Scripture serves for "training in righteousness" (2 Tim 3:16).

James, who knows the phrase "the righteousness of God" (1:20, human anger does not produce it), writing in the interest of a practical ethics, has pursued in 2:14–26 the view that Gen 15:6 is to be interpreted by Gen 22 (see above). James does this in an effort to correct a misunderstanding by some of the idea that "faith alone" justifies (the phrase, which does not occur in Paul, appears in 2:24), and faith understood in a very limited way. The points James wants to make, that faith should not be merely intellectual belief (2:19) and should not be idle and inert, were matters on which Paul had spoken adequately. Faith is knowing

Christ, trusting God, indeed obeying ("the obedience of faith," Rom 1:5; 16:26), and something that works itself out in love for others (Gal 5:6). James's attempt at a correction has probably done more harm than good over the years, though misunderstandings of Paul have not been uncommon.

If James relates to the Pauline orbit as a reaction to exaggerated Paulinism, other NT books stand in a more positive relationship theologically to righteousness/justification as set forth in Paul or to what was termed above common or apostolic (Jewish) Christian use of the terms. Luke-Acts provides a large body of evidence (fifty-six examples of *dikaio* words, second most in the NT after Paul) in a two-volume work where Paul was featured (Acts 13–28). This is a "Lukan version" of Paul, who is usually not regarded by Luke as an apostle. There is little evidence that Luke knew or grasped the depths of what Paul wrote on righteousness/justification. References especially in Luke 1–2 to "righteous people," akin to OT usage, have been noted above, as have some examples using the terms that Luke shares with Mark (e.g., Luke 5:32; 15:2) or with Matthew (Luke 7:35). Terminology about unrighteousness (*adikia*) often appears (NRSV: "dishonest," "unjust," "wicked") as in Luke 16:8–11; 18:6,11; Acts 1:18; 8:23. Acts 24:15 has Paul speak of "a resurrection of both the righteous and the unrighteous." Luke continues to speak in Acts of persons like Cornelius who are "upright" (10:22) and do "what is right (*dikaiosynen*)" (10:35). In a phrase at Acts 24:25, referring to Paul's discussion with Felix and Drusilla of "justice, self-control, and the coming judgment," Luke may reflect both his Greco-Roman setting and biblical heritage, for the first two items can suggest Hellenistic virtues. Note also Luke 23:47 (Jesus is "innocent," *dikaios*; the two thieves are "condemned justly" [23:41]); and the subsequent use of "Righteous One" for Christ in Acts (3:14, etc.). Jesus, in Luke, dies a martyr's death, like Stephen in Acts (compare Luke 23:34, 46 with Acts

7:59–60), and Luke-Acts scarcely connects Jesus' death on the cross with atonement "for our sins" (at best, Acts 20:29). This is because, in Luke-Acts, God has always been the forgiving Father (Luke 15:11–32; 7:36–50).

All these points have made many interpreters cautious about reading the two main passages on justification/righteousness in Luke-Acts in an overly Pauline way. Acts 13:39 provides the one instance where Paul uses the verb that could be translated "all who believe are justified from all things from which ye could not be justified by the law of Moses" (KJV). NRSV has, however, "set free from all those sins from which you could not be freed by the law of Moses." The context, in a sermon in the synagogue at Pisidian Antioch, is "the forgiveness of sins" (13:38), a favorite Lukan theme, though not one that Paul's letters stress. Some term 13:39 "partial justification," involving belief (faith) for what the law could not accomplish. The other example, the parable at Luke 18:9–14, has already been noted, about the "justified" publican. Since Acts reflects so little of Paul's doctrine of righteousness/justification, it is hard to claim that Luke 18 is reading in a Pauline view. Some would see in 18:9–14 a contrast between pride and repentance, not works and faith. But precisely because the parable is not specifically Pauline, it can be taken as a foreshadowing, a generic form, of what early Christianity and Paul more precisely developed. Compare also how Jesus' table fellowship with sinners leads to the implications that Paul drew at Gal 2:12–14 about eating with Gentiles and not compelling them to live like kosher Jews.

The Johannine literature usually functions in the NT, along with Paul, as a major theological source. This is scarcely so with righteousness/justification. The book of Revelation, to begin with material most akin to the OT, presents God and judgment as just (16:5, 7) and Christ as judging in righteousness (19:11). God's judgments have been revealed (15:4). The righteous are to do right (22:11). There is much on avenging (*ekdikein*, 6:10; 19:2) and harm (*adikein*), little on "saving righteousness." God as righteous has already been noted for John (17:25) and 1 John (1:9). Thrice in 1 John, Jesus is called righteous (2:1, 29; 3:7). The first refers to his work of atonement and advocacy for sinners (2:1–2). The second and third references are to how those who do right are "born of him" and are righteous, "as he is righteous." They "do righteousness." The Fourth Gospel presents Jesus as, among other things, a judge, judging justly (5:30; 7:24, 18), whose appearance among people causes division (Greek *krisis*, "judgment," a forensic situation). One major passage reflects how this will continue through the Paraclete whom Jesus will send (16:8–11): "he will prove the world wrong about sin and righteousness and judgment: about sin, because they do not believe in me; about righteousness, because I am going to the Father and you will see me no longer; about judgment, because the ruler of this world has been condemned." Sin is failure to believe in Jesus, who will be vindicated in going to the Father. The world is judged. This brief vision is a cosmic court scene, far beyond debates over law and works, which John has treated in other ways.

Hebrews says that its readers need skill "in the word of righteousness" (5:13). That means both teachings about Christ and moral imperatives. God's Son, with righteous scepter, "loved righteousness" (1:9 = Ps 45:6–7). He is "the one who is coming" (10:37; cf. 9:28, "a second time"). Meanwhile, everyone who is righteous is to live by faith (10:38–39; Hab 2:4, above), aware of the cloud of witnesses (12:1) through the ages (listed in chap. 11), whose "approval as righteous" is sometimes mentioned (11:4; cf. 11:7, 33, "administered justice"; "spirits of the righteous made perfect," 12:23). One cannot always pin down these allusive phrases the way one can in Paul, with his fuller, clearer presentation, but the theme of righteousness/justification appears with nuances of its own from the theology of this book that is so different from other NT writings.

First Peter reflects common, early Christianity in 3:18 (above), akin to which is 2:24, Christ "bore our sins . . . on the cross, so that . . . we might live for righteousness." Christians may have to suffer, however, "for righteousness' sake" (KJV), which NRSV interprets ethically, "for doing what is right" (3:14; cf. Matt 5:10–11). What may sound threatening, that judgment looms even over "the household of God"—"If it is hard for the righteous to be saved, what will become of the ungodly and the sinners?" (4:17–18 = Prov 11:31)—can be a note of comfort when it is realized that the God "who judges justly" is the one to whom "the shepherd and guardian" of our souls, Jesus, entrusted himself (2:23–25). In spite of (possible) suffering at the hands of the authorities (3:13–16; 4:12), 1 Peter affirms the role of the Roman emperor and governors as human institutions to punish (*ekdikesin*) evildoers and "to praise those who do right" (what is good) (2:14).

Second Peter is noteworthy for expanding the phrase "the righteousness of God" (1:1) to include "our Savior Jesus Christ." In this way an expression going back to the ancient passage in Judg 5:11 has become christological in what may be the last book in the NT to be written. And to the vision of Isa 65:17 and 66:22 about "new heavens and a new earth," the phrase has been added, "where righteousness is at home," a vision of justice as well as *shalom* (3:13).

Eliezar Berkovits, "The Biblical Meaning of Justice," *Judaism* 18 (1969): 188–209; John H. P. Reumann, *Righteousness in the New Testament: Justification in the Lutheran-Catholic Dialogue*, with responses by J. A. Fitzmyer and J. D. Quinn (Philadelphia: Fortress Press, 1982); Mark A. Seifrid, *Christ Our Righteousness: Paul's Theology of Justification* (Grand Rapids: Eerdmans, 2000); Moshe Weinfeld, *Social Justice in Ancient Israel and in the Ancient Near East* (Minneapolis: Augsburg Fortress Press, 1995).

JOHN REUMANN

Kill, Murder A great deal of killing is recorded in the Bible, but within the record one finds evidence for a remarkable sense of uneasiness about the taking of life. The intimate association of God with *life* that prevails throughout Scripture ("I have no pleasure in the death of anyone, says the Lord GOD. Turn, then, and live," Ezek 18:32) was projected back to the time of creation. Before the flood, there was no killing for food. All creatures were to eat the plants of the earth (Gen 1:29–30). The same ideal was projected into the ideal future, when everything will be in keeping with God's will. There will be peace among the animals, the lion will eat straw like an ox, and "they will not hurt or destroy on all my holy mountain" (Isa 11:6–9).

In the meantime, however, after the flood and before the eschaton, God permits the killing of animals for food, but murder—the illegal killing of people—is forbidden, with a fearsome penalty: "Whoever sheds the blood of a human, by a human shall that person's blood be shed" (Gen 9:3–6). *Blood* was understood to be literally the life of humans and animals. The Israelite was reminded that to kill an animal for food was by divine permission—not something that could be done arbitrarily or randomly—by special regulations for the treatment of the animal's blood. When the animal was a sacrifice, the blood was caught in a bowl and poured out on the altar—giving the life back to God as a reminder that all life belongs to God (Lev 17:10–14; Deut 12:27). Blood was not to be eaten; it was not food, but life. The blood of nonsacrificial animals was to be poured on to the ground so that it might sink into the earth (Deut 12:16, 24).

God permitted and sometimes ordered the killing of human beings, in *war* and as punishment for certain crimes considered to be destructive of the very fabric of the Israelite community. These were offenses against human life (murder and kidnapping to sell into slavery), against the integrity of the *family*, and against the unique character of the Israelite religion, such as idolatry (Greenberg). It should be noted that, unlike other ancient and modern cultures, Israel did not consider any crimes involving property worthy of the death penalty.

The commandment familiarly translated "You shall not kill" (Exod 20:13; Deut 5:17) is more accurately rendered "You shall not murder" in the NRSV, for the verb *ratsah* is never used of the killing of animals or of people in warfare, and occurs only once in the OT with reference to an execution (Num 35:30). In all other cases it denotes homicide, if not always first-degree murder (Childs).

In the Sermon on the Mount, Jesus assumed that the motives for murder are anger and hatred, so he expanded the commandment beyond forbidding the physical act of taking a life. He made *reconciliation* an essential requirement for the lives of those who would follow him (Matt 5:21–26). John's emphasis on love as an essential Christian virtue led him to equate those who hate brother or sister with murderers (1 John 3:15).

The early Christians did not have to make decisions about capital punishment, for the Roman government held that power (Rom 13:4). The issue of whether a Christian could participate in warfare seems not to have arisen within the church until after the NT period. The NT writers saw no need to do more than to quote the commandment, "You shall not murder" (Rom 13:9; Jas 2:11; cf. 1 Pet 4:15; for Jesus' citation: Matt 19:18; Mark 10:19; Luke 18:20), and to include it in lists of the worst sins (Matt 15:19; Mark 7:21; Rom 1:29; Rev 21:8; 22:15).

Brevard S. Childs, *The Book of Exodus: A Critical, Theological Commentary*, OTL (Philadelphia: Westminster Press, 1974), 419–21; J. Greenberg, "Crimes and Punishments," *IDB* 1:737–41; Walter Harrelson, *The Ten Commandments and Human Rights* (Philadelphia: Fortress Press, 1980), 107–22.

DONALD E. GOWAN

King *see* **Anoint**

Kingdom of God, Kingdom of Heaven

The term plays a central role in the teachings of Jesus, but occurs surprisingly seldom elsewhere in the Bible. It is rare in the OT and the intertestamental literature. Most of its occurrences are in the Synoptic Gospels. Other NT authors use it occasionally, but without developing its meaning (in John, only 3:3, 5; elsewhere about twenty-six times). This article will thus focus on Jesus' use of the term in the Synoptics, after establishing an OT background against which to compare his teachings.

The kingship of God in the Old Testament

Both Testaments call God "king" and speak of his "kingdom," but there is a significant discontinuity in their uses of the terms. The OT frequently refers to Yahweh as king, but seldom speaks of his kingdom, and only twice actually uses the term "kingdom of Yahweh" (1 Chr 28:5, with *malkuth*; 2 Chr 13:8, with *mamleketh*). Jesus used "kingdom of God/heaven" as one of his favorite expressions, but called God "king" only once (Matt 5:35) and seldom compared God to a king (Matt 18:23–34; 22:1–13; cf. Luke 19:12).

Yahweh is sometimes affirmed to be specifically Israel's king, just as the high gods of the other ancient Near Eastern nations were considered to be their supreme kings. But often Yahweh's comprehensive kingship over all the world was acclaimed in Israel. Although Ps 33 does not use the noun *melek* or the verb *malak*, it clearly expresses this double understanding of kingship. "The earth is full of the steadfast love of the LORD" (v. 5), the Creator (vv. 6–7, 9, 15a). All the earth, that is, all its inhabitants, must fear God (v. 8), for the nations and peoples cannot resist him (v. 10), and he knows everything done by humankind (*bᵉne haʾadam*; vv. 13–15). But he has a special relationship with one nation, not named, but obviously Israel, "the people whom he has chosen as his heritage" (v. 12).

This special relationship with Israel, generally appealed to in the sense that a king should be the protector of his people, appears, for example, in Num 23:21; Deut 33:5; Jer 8:19 (cf. Exod 15:18). Elsewhere, the future manifestation of Yahweh's kingship specifically for Israel's benefit is promised (Obad 21, "kingdom"; Mic 4:7; Zeph 3:15; Isa 24:23; 33:22; 41:21; 43:15; 44:6; 52:7, "reign"). All these promises refer to the need for physical security and blessing for Israel as a nation, in the midst of other nations.

The books of Judges and Samuel record Israel's memory that before the time of David some insisted that the kingship of Yahweh precluded having an earthly king. So Gideon refused the offer of kingship, saying, "I will not rule over you, and my son will not rule over you; the LORD will rule over you" (Judg 8:23). Later, when the Philistine threat led many in the individual tribes to advocate a unified government (kingship, 1 Sam 8:4–5, 19–20), Samuel at first claimed that to accept a human king was to reject the kingship of Yahweh (1 Sam 8:6–18) but eventually took the responsibility of anointing first Saul (1 Sam 10:1), then David (1 Sam 16:13). From that point on, the relationship between divine and human kingship was understood in Israel as it was in the other nations: a human being served as the earthly ruler under the supreme sovereignty of the high god (cf. 1 Chr 17:14; 28:5).

Yahweh's universal kingship is celebrated frequently in the Psalms. In the group of YHWH (or *ᵉlohim*) *malak* Psalms ("the Lord [or God] is king"), it is clear that he is in a unique sense the God of Israel, but the emphasis is on his sovereignty over all the nations and all creation (Pss 93:1b; 95:4–5). So his choice is the "pride of Jacob" (Ps 47:4), and he is "great in Zion" (Ps 99:2), but he is "king of all the earth," "king over the nations" (Ps 47:7–8). He established the world and is from everlasting (Ps 93:1–2). He is "a great King above all gods" (Ps 95:3; cf. 96:4–5; 97:7), and is judge of the peoples (Ps 96:10, 13; cf. 98:9). The Psalter twice refers to God's "kingdom." It "rules over all" in Ps 103:19, and all God's works testify to the glory of his kingdom, which endures forever, in Ps 145:10–13.

To speak of one's god as "king" was natural in the ancient Near East, since the greatest concentration of power at the human level was to be found in the courts of kings, and that institution was then projected into heaven and magnified. The best functions of government—providing for security and prosperity—were also the functions one hoped would be more perfectly provided by one's god. Israel shared this common outlook by calling Yahweh king, but the emphasis on universal sovereignty just documented from the Psalms may provide a possible explanation for the paucity of references to God's "kingdom." Normally a kingdom is a locality with boundaries, as when the word is used of Israel or Moab, and it may have seemed to be too limiting a word for authors who emphasized the universality of Yahweh's reign. In the Chronicles references mentioned above, Yahweh's kingdom is localized in Israel (and in Judah in Obad 21), but Jer 10:7, 10 calls him "King of the nations," Isa 37:16 says he is God of all the kingdoms of the earth, and Zech 14:9 looks forward to the time when he will become king over all the earth.

These were remarkable claims to be made for the God of a tiny nation (in the preexilic period) and a tinier ethnic group within a great empire (after 587 B.C.). The book of Daniel, which uses the word "kingdom" in the most significant way theologically in the OT, does so in clear recognition that the claim needed to be reaffirmed and somehow justified. All power seemed to reside in the great empires of Babylon, the Medes and Persians, and the Greeks, but this book tells of exploits of Daniel within the court of Nebuchadnezzar that persuaded even the great king that "truly, your God is God of gods and Lord of kings" (Dan 2:47), whose "kingdom is an everlasting kingdom (4:3, 34). Daniel knew kingdoms as world empires, and claimed for his God an undying world empire (2:44; 7:27).

The kingdom of God/heaven in the New Testament

"King" and "kingdom" are completely political terms, referring, as used in the OT and Judaism of Jesus' time, to the governments of nations. (The intertestamental literature can be passed over for the purposes of this article, since the occasional uses of "kingdom" remain fully in continuity with the OT.) Jesus, living under Roman rule, thus took a considerable risk when he chose "kingdom of God" as one of the key elements of his teaching. (Matthew's preference for "kingdom of heaven" involves no differences in meaning, "heaven" being a common Jewish substitute for the name of God. Cf. Matt 18:4 and 19:23 with Mark 10:15 and 10:23.) Although Jesus avoided the word "king," as noted above, he was finally executed on the charge of having claimed to be king of the Jews (see *anoint; Jesus*). He made a radical, nonpolitical definition of "kingdom," but that was one of the aspects of his teaching that was poorly understood, and not only by Pilate (John 18:33–38). Pilate condemned Jesus to death as "King of the Jews" (John 19:19) and clearly did not know what to make of "my kingdom is not from this world" (John 18:36).

Although Jesus defined what he meant by "kingdom of God" at considerable length, he also spoke of "secrets" (or "mysteries," NRSV Mg) of the kingdom (e.g., Matt 13:11), and a full understanding of his teaching seems to remain beyond human apprehension to this day. Through much of Christian history the kingdom was simply identified with the *church*, but scholarship has shown that the NT does not identify the two (for the relationship, see Bauckham). The importance and difficulty of the term have led to the production of an extensive literature and a wide variety of interpretations. A brief dictionary article cannot explain and evaluate all of the options, so the intent of this article will be to present in a systematic way what Jesus said about the kingdom, with a few references to the conflicting theories that have not yet been completely reconciled.

Although OT authors insisted that God presently rules over all the nations and everything in the world, as noted above, they knew that this truth was not evident in real life, so they offered promises that it would be manifested in God's good time. Jesus announced that the time had come: "The time is fulfilled, and the kingdom of God has come near [or "is at hand," *engiken*]; repent and believe in the good news" (Mark 1:15; cf. Matt 4:17; and Matt 3:2 for the similar message of John the Baptist). But the OT understanding of God's manifest rule—peace among the nations and in nature itself—did not come true, and Jesus made no claims concerning those subjects. So the interpretation of *engiken* in this text and the time elements in Jesus' sayings about the kingdom have become subjects of great concern for scholars.

The "apocalyptic" reading of Jesus' sayings claims that he consistently spoke of the kingdom as near at hand, but not yet present. "Realized eschatology," on the other hand, insists that although Jesus did speak at times of the future, his central message was that the kingdom *had* truly come, with his presence (Dodd, 40–41). Many scholars at present attempt to hold together both the present and future aspects of Jesus' teaching, saying that the kingdom did break into history with the coming of Jesus, but that it will be fully consummated only in the time to come (e.g., Ladd, 89–92). This article will simply call attention to the present and future elements in Jesus' sayings.

Kingship or kingdom? Although *basileia* can mean "kingship," "royal power/sovereignty," and "kingdom" (a realm), many scholars have insisted that Jesus referred only to God's kingship or sovereignty, not to a realm. This would resolve the problem created by the nonevidence of any visible "kingdom of God" on earth (if the church is ruled out). Several of Jesus' sayings do not fit well with the ideas of kingship and sovereignty, how-

ever. He spoke of "entering" the kingdom (Matt 5:20; 7:21; 18:3; 21:31; 23:13; Mark 9:47; 10:23–25), and even of trying to take it by force (Matt 11:12; Luke 16:16). Sitting at table with Abraham, Isaac, and Jacob scarcely fits well with "in the *kingship* of heaven" (Matt 8:11). There are other texts that read most naturally if Jesus was speaking of a realm of some sort, and if they are to make sense to us, presumably they must be taken as referring to a future consummation.

The kingdom in the imminent future. In the Lord's Prayer Jesus taught his disciples to pray for the coming of the kingdom: "Your kingdom come" (Matt 6:9; Luke 11:2). Other texts clearly speak of the kingdom as something that is yet to come, although that will be soon, for example, "There are some standing here who will not taste death until they see that the kingdom of God has come with power" (Mark 9:1; Luke 9:27), and "Truly I tell you, I will never again drink of the fruit of the vine until that day when I drink it new in the kingdom of God" (Mark 14:25; Luke 22:16, 18). C. H. Dodd justified his realized eschatology interpretation by saying the kingdom *had* come with Jesus' presence, and these texts refer to one's future participation in it (Dodd, 43).

The presence of the kingdom. The most striking passage that affirms the immediate presence of the kingdom tells of the healing of a blind and mute demoniac. When the Pharisees claimed Jesus must have used the power of Beelzebul, he responded, "But if it is by the Spirit of God that I cast out demons, then the kingdom of God has come to you" (Matt 12:28; Luke 11:20). There has been debate over whether "has come" (*ephthasen*) means "near" or "present," but other uses support "present" (2 Cor 10:14; Phil 3:16). Another passage has Jesus directly speaking of the kingdom in the present tense. Some Pharisees asked him when it was coming, and he answered, "The kingdom of God is not coming with things that can be observed; nor will they say, 'Look, here it is!' or 'There it is!' For, in fact the kingdom of God is among you" (Luke 17:20–21). The phrase *entos hymon* is sometimes read "within you," but it seems doubtful that Jesus would have said that to Pharisees.

The apparently contradictory texts cited in these two sections are held together by scholars who claim that Jesus said a new reality (which he called the kingdom of God) had come into the world with his presence and that those who could recognize and accept it could then participate in it. But he knew that there was more to be done in order for "your kingdom come; your will be done, on earth as it is in heaven" to be fulfilled, and he expected that to come after his death. "Here indeed is the revelation of a new truth: that the Kingdom of God can actually come into the world, creating children who enjoy its blessings without effecting the eschatological judgment. . . . The Kingdom that is present but hidden in the world will yet be manifested in glory" (Ladd, 95).

Citizenship in the kingdom. Jesus devoted more attention to the qualifications necessary for citizenship in the kingdom of God than he did to describing it. In order to summarize them, they may be grouped as follows:

1. Righteousness: Worthy of the kingdom are those who do and teach the commandments (Matt 5:19); whose righteousness exceeds that of the Pharisees (Matt 5:20); who do the will of the Father (Matt 7:21); who are obedient (Matt 21:31); who avoid any cause of sin (Mark 9:47); and who practice forgiveness (Matt 18:23–35). Except possibly for Matt 5:20, any Jewish teacher might have said the same. If these qualifications sound contrary to Paul's teaching about being saved by grace alone, note that three of his few references to the kingdom associate it with righteousness (Rom 14:17; 1 Cor 6:9; Gal 5:21).

2. Reversal of fortune: "Blessed are the poor in spirit" (Matt 5:3), or simply "the poor" (Luke 6:20). "Blessed are those who are persecuted for righteousness' sake" (Matt 5:10). "Truly I tell you, unless you change and become like children, you will never enter the kingdom of heaven. Whoever becomes humble like this child is the greatest in the kingdom of heaven" (Matt 18:3–4; cf. 19:14; Mark 10:14–15; Luke 18:16–17). Children were virtual nonpersons in Oriental societies, and these sayings are among Jesus' most extreme ways of insisting on the reversal of status in the kingdom (see *family*). His sayings concerning the rich are of the same type, for conventional wisdom associated prosperity with righteousness: "It will be hard for a rich person to enter the kingdom of heaven" (Matt 19:23–24; Mark 10:23–25; Luke 18:24–25).

3. Willingness to risk everything: "Then Peter said, 'Look, we have left our homes and followed you.' And he said to them, 'Truly I tell you, there is no one who has left house or wife or brothers or parents or children, for the sake of the kingdom of God, who will not get back very much more in this age, and in the age to come eternal life" (Luke 18:28–30; cf. 9:60–62). Two parables concerning the value of the kingdom involve risk as well. In order to gain the treasure in the field and the pearl of great value, one sells everything one has (Matt 13:44–46).

4. Radical change: John uses the term only twice, but in a key passage. Elsewhere, "eternal life" takes the place of "kingdom of God" for John. Jesus said to Nicodemus, "Very truly, I tell you, no one can see the kingdom of God without being born from above [or "anew"]" (John 3:3; "born of water and spirit" in 3:5).

Jesus thus used "kingdom of God" to identify a new community that was beginning to come into existence around him, into which those rejected by other communities were welcomed. The welcoming required a willingness to accept a new and better way of life, and offered the power to change. The definition of this kingdom challenged the legitimacy of other kingdoms, but only tacitly. Jesus had little to say about Rome or about Jewish hopes for a renewed Davidic monarchy. His kingdom was presently insignificant, but he believed it would overcome the world.

The mystery of the kingdom. This article began with a reference to the failure of Jesus' contemporaries to understand his radically new use of the word "kingdom." The kingdom of God he proclaimed was nothing like any kingdom they knew. After the resurrection, the disciples still hoped for the kind of manifestation of the kingship of God that the OT promised, for they asked the risen Christ, "Lord, is this the time when you will restore the kingdom to Israel?" (Acts 1:6). Jesus had assured them that the secret (or mystery) of the kingdom would be revealed to them alone, but evidently it had not happened yet. His reference to the secret (or secrets) occurs in connection with his teaching by means of parables, which clearly puzzled his listeners and which keep scholars busy to this day: "To you has been given the secret of the kingdom of God, but for those outside, everything comes in parables; in order that 'they may indeed look, but not perceive, and may indeed listen, but not understand; so that they may not turn again and be forgiven'" (Mark 4:11–12; paraphrasing Isa 6:9–10). The very explanation of Jesus' reason for using parables introduces a mystery, for he alluded to a passage from Isaiah that insisted judgment was inevitable, and yet Jesus' message was called the "good news" (gospel; Mark 1:15; Luke 4:43; 8:1). This may be a comment on the fact that during his lifetime Jesus failed. He did not become an acclaimed leader but was executed as a failed revolutionary. His teachings were indeed subversive and revolutionary, but only his death and resurrection began to make clear what kind of revolution he would initiate, and that was the secret of the kingdom.

1. It was a nonpolitical kingdom, so it was unlike any previously known. Jesus did not talk about a change in government, so *for the time being* his work did not affect earthly kingdoms. "Give to the emperor [Caesar] the things that are the emperor's, and to God the things that are God's" (Mark 12:17).

2. Although the kingship of God was a universal belief, Jesus emphasized that God does not rule as earthly kings do. In his parable of the king and the debtor (Matt 18:23–35) he spoke of the rather unlikely case where a king was willing to forgive an enormous debt—but only until he found that the debtor had failed to learn the lesson of forgiveness. In the parable of the landowner and the workers (Matt 20:1–16) he described an employer who cared not what his workers *deserved* but paid them all alike, simply because that was what he wanted to do. Jesus introduced a king in the parable of the banquet (Matt 22:1–14) who insisted that his son's wedding *must* be celebrated, whether others cared or not. And the last two parables are concluded with somewhat cryptic comments: "So the last will be first, and the first will be last." "For many are called, but few are chosen."

3. As noted above, this overturning of what had been normal and expected led to the acceptance by Jesus of the least in society: tax collectors and prostitutes (Matt 21:31), lepers, women and children, and the demand of *repentance* (turning around and going the other way) of everyone (Mark 1:15). For the overturning he offered made possible a life of righteousness in a community created without regard to former status.

4. That community was insignificant in Jesus' lifetime, as he acknowledged, but he promised that the day would come when it would be vindicated by God. Aspects of this appear in the parables of the mustard seed, the yeast (Matt 13:31–33), and the seed growing secretly (Mark 4:26–29). So faith is required, for there is little evidence that Jesus' redefinition is true. The parable of the sower and the seed comments on the uncertainty of it all (Matt 13:18–23; Mark 4:3–20; Luke 8:4–15), and the parable of the bridesmaids emphasizes that the day is indeed coming, so one must make one's life ready (Matt 25:1–13).

5. In the meantime, the world will not look much different in spite of the presence of the kingdom—still largely secret, although many enjoy its blessings. The world is like a wheat field infested with

weeds, and they will grow together until the day of judgment, when the difference between those who have accepted the kingdom and those who have rejected it will be made manifest (Matt 13:24–30).

Richard Bauckham, "Kingdom and Church according to Jesus and Paul," *HBT* 18 (1996): 1–26; C. H. Dodd, *The Parables of the Kingdom* (London: Collins, 1961); George Raymond Beasley-Murray, *Jesus and the Kingdom of God* (Grand Rapids: Eerdmans, 1986); George Eldon Ladd, *A Theology of the New Testament*, rev. ed. (Grand Rapids: Eerdmans, 1993); W. Willis, ed., *The Kingdom of God in 20th-Century Interpretation* (Peabody, Mass.: Hendrickson, 1987).

DONALD E. GOWAN

Know, Knowledge, Perceive, Understand, Understanding, Insight
These terms are part of the "wisdom vocabulary" of the Bible.

Old Testament. In the OT "know" and "knowledge" (most commonly) and "understand" (occasionally) are used to translate forms of the Hebrew root *yadaᶜ* and its derivatives. "Understand" and "understanding" more frequently translate the root *biyn* and its noun forms (*biynah* and *tebunah*), but NRSV also uses "understand" where Hebrew uses *shemaᶜ* (hear) to refer to comprehension of a foreign language (e.g., Gen 11:7; Deut 28:49; 2 Kgs 18:26 = Isa 36:11). Occasionally "understand" also represents forms of the Hebrew root *sakal*, when it is synonymous with *yadaᶜ* (as in Isa 41:20) or with *biyn* (as in Deut 32:29). Elsewhere NRSV translates forms of *sakal* and *biyn* as "prudent," "insight," and "discretion" (see *wisdom*). "Perceive" is an alternate English term used to translate both *biyn* (e.g., Job 9:11; 23:8; Ps 94:7; Prov 24:12) and *yadaᶜ* (2 Sam 19:6; Isa 43:19).

In many cases the Hebrew *yadaᶜ* has approximately the same range of meaning as the English word "know," denoting (a) various types of mental activity, (b) existential or personal experiences with events, persons, places, and so forth,

(c) feelings of empathy and assurance, and (d) skill or ability, requiring the translator to render *yadaᶜ* in some texts as "know how to" (e.g., Exod 36:1; Isa 50:4; Jer 1:6; 4:22; Job 32:22). In several Hebrew texts *yadaᶜ* is also used as a euphemism for sexual intercourse (what English may call "carnal knowledge").

Verbs of hearing and seeing are often parallel to know, indicating that knowledge comes first of all from the senses, but *yadaᶜ* can also connote discernment (making a distinction between one thing and another), as in Jonah 4:11 ("know their right hand from their left") or Deut 1:39 ("know right from wrong"). When an internalized form of knowing is intended, the Hebrew sometimes refers to knowing "in the heart" or in the *mind* (as in Deut 8:5; Josh 23:14). But feelings of certainty (having confidence that something will happen or has happened) are often expressed by "know" alone (as in Deut 31:29; Judg 17:13; 6:37; Job 5:24–25; 9:28; 10:13; 30:23; Ps 20:6; Eccl 3:12, 14).

To "know" can connote firsthand experience with places (as in Num 14:31, "they shall know the land that you have despised"); with events (as in Judg 3:2, to "know war"); or with God's activity in history (in either a negative sense, as in Num 14:34, "you shall know my displeasure," and Ezek 25:14, "they shall know my vengeance," or in a positive sense as in Mic 6:5, "that you may know the saving acts of the LORD"). "Know" can also refer to empathy derived from personal experience, as in Exod 23:9, "you know the heart of an alien, for you were aliens in the land of Egypt."

When the object of "know" is a person, the meaning can vary from a superficial acquaintance (as in Gen 29:5, "Do you know Laban son of Nahor?") to intimate and/or carnal knowledge. Sometimes the Hebrew text adds other words that make it obvious that "know" is being used as a euphemism for sexual intercourse. Thus, for instance Num 31:17, 18, 35 supplements the phrase "know a man" with the explanatory phrase "by sleeping with him." And sometimes the context makes it clear that "know" means carnal knowledge (as in Gen 4:1, 17, 25, when the birth of a child immediately follows). However, the original text is often ambiguous, leaving the reader or translator to decide what kind of knowledge is meant. Thus when the Hebrew text of 1 Kgs 1:4 says merely that "the king did not know her," the NRSV removes all ambiguity by adding the word "sexually." In some passages NRSV retains the euphemistic quality of the original by translating *yada*ᶜ as "know" (e.g., Gen 24:16), but in other texts the translators render the same Hebrew word as "lie with" (Gen 38:26) or "slept with" (Judges 11:39; 21:12). The variability in NRSV becomes most perplexing in the parallel accounts of Gen 19:4–11 and Judg 19:22–26, when the exact same Hebrew word (*yada*ᶜ) is translated "know" and "known" in Gen 19:5, 8 but as "have intercourse" in Judges 19:22 and as "raped" in Judg 19:25. Although the stories themselves are extremely similar, the translator's choice of words gives the account in Judges a more highly charged emotional tone than the euphemistic use of "know" conveys in Gen 19.

In Wisdom literature knowledge (*da*ᶜ*ath* or *de*ᶜ*ah*) is roughly synonymous with wisdom (Prov 30:3; Eccl 1:18; 7:12; Dan 2:21) and instruction (Prov 1:7; 2:6, 10; 8:10; 19:27; 23:12) or is the result (the outcome) of instruction (Prov 21:11). Knowledge (like wisdom) is the opposite of *folly* (Prov 14:18; 15:2, 14) and involves not merely thinking but putting thoughts into practice. In Proverbs the attitude of awe and respect for God known as "the *fear* of the LORD" is said to be "the beginning of knowledge" (Prov 1:7) and hating knowledge is equated with not choosing the fear of the Lord (1:29).

Old Testament texts use the relational aspects of the words "know" and "knowledge" to talk about the essential relationship between God and humankind. Humans are "known" by God and are expected to "know" God in return. To know the Lord is an existential rather than an intellectual exercise and requires that

one both recognize the power and the purposes of God and align oneself with them. In Jer 4:22 knowing Yahweh is synonymous with "knowing how to do good" and opposite to "skilled in doing evil." To know the Lord means to judge equitably on behalf of the poor and needy (Jer 22:16). People show that they do not know the Lord when "they proceed from evil to evil" (Jer 9:3); their refusal to know the Lord manifests itself in "oppression upon oppression, deceit upon deceit" (Jer 9:6).

God's activity in creation and in human history is the primary source of humanity's knowledge of God. Yahweh's various interventions in human history are done so that you (or they) shall "know that I am the LORD" (e.g., Exod 6:7; 7:5, 17; 14:4, 18; 16:6, 12; 29:46, and more than fifty times in Ezekiel). "Knowledge of God" can be acquired either directly, from a person's own experience of God's actions (2 Kgs 5:15) or in a mediated fashion, through the testimony of other witnesses to God's self-revelation (Isa 40:21). The Lord's self-revelation has both salvific (Exod 6:7) and judgmental (Ps 9:16) aspects and requires an appropriate response in either case.

As evidence to support the charge that there is "no knowledge of God in the land" Hosea testifies that "swearing, lying, and murder, and stealing and adultery break out; bloodshed follows bloodshed" (4:1–2). Such "lack of knowledge" will lead to the destruction of God's people (Hos 4:6) because what God wants is "steadfast love and not sacrifice, the knowledge of God rather than burnt offerings" (Hos 6:6).

Hosea draws on the euphemistic uses of "know" to label the idolatry of Israel "whoredom" ("knowing" other gods instead of "knowing" only the Lord). In other prophetic texts the term "without knowledge" is virtually synonymous with the practice of idolatry (e.g., Jer 10:14; 14:18; 51:17). In contrast, the well-known prophetic hope for the future pictures an offshoot of Israel manifesting "the spirit of wisdom and understanding, the spirit of counsel and might, the spirit of knowledge and the fear of the LORD" (Isa 11:2).

New Testament. The Greek words most often translated "know" (*eido, ginosko, epiginosko, epistamai*) and "knowledge" (*gnosis, epignosis*) have roughly the same semantic range in the NT as they do in Hebrew and English. Occasionally NRSV also translates *ginosko* and *eido* as "understand" or "perceive." In other places, "understand," "understanding," and "perceive" translate a variety of Greek originals such as *syniemi, synesis, noieo* (most frequently) and (less frequently) *epistamai, epistemon, logizomai, katalambano, gnorizo, nous, blepo,* and *dianoia* as well as words meaning "hard to understand" (*dysnoetos*) and "without understanding" (*asynetos*). "Make known" translates *exegeomai* (John 1:18).

In many cases *ginosko* and *eido* seem virtually interchangeable. The English reader can see no difference at all between the two words translated "know" in John 21:17 ("Lord, you know [*eido*] everything; you know [*ginosko*] that I love you"), nor between "He did not want anyone to know (*ginosko*) it" (Mark 9:30) and "He did not know (*eido*) what to say" (Mark 9:6). Either word can be used to describe conclusions drawn by logic, as in Matt 24:32–33 (*ginosko*) and John 3:2 (*eido*), as well as feelings of certainty, as in "How will I know (*ginosko*) that this is so?" (Luke 1:18) and "I know (*eido*) that he will rise again" (John 11:24).

Either word can mean to "recognize," as in John 10:4, 27, where a parallel is drawn between sheep who "know" (*eido*) their owner's voice and Jesus, who says, "I know (*ginosko*) them, and they follow me." "Know," connoting recognition, can also translate *epiginosko*, as in "You will know them by their fruits" (Matt 7:16, 20).

In the story of Peter's denial of Jesus (Matt 26:70, 72; Mark 14:68, 71; Luke 22:57, 60), know (*eido*) is used to mean both the comprehension of a statement ("I do not know what you are talking about") and personal acquaintance with Jesus ("I do not know the man"). Like *yada^c* in the OT, *ginosko* can connote skill,

knowing how to do something, as in "You know how (*ginosko*) to interpret the appearance of the sky" (Matt 16:3).

Sometimes NRSV uses "understand" to translate *ginosko* and *eido* (apparently for the sake of variety in the English text), as in Rom 7:15; 10:19; 1 Cor 2:14 (*ginosko*); and 1 Cor 2:12; 11:3; 13:2 (*eido*). The Greek *syniemi* (implying a mental "putting together") is usually rendered "understand." All four passages that quote versions of Isa 6:9 (Matt 13:14; Mark 4:12; Luke 8:10; Acts 28:26) use *syniemi* in this way. "Perceive" is used for *eido* in three of those four passages (Matt 13:14; Mark 4:12; Acts 28:26), but in the parallel texts of Matt 13:13 and Luke 8:10 "perceive" is also used where the Greek word is *blepo*. Thus NRSV obscures the variations in the Greek texts by using identical English words even when the Greek words differ.

All the words translated "know" (*ginosko, epiginosko,* and *eido*) can be used to describe personal relationships between God and humankind. They are used somewhat interchangeably, as in 1 Cor 13:12, "Now I know (*ginosko*) only in part; then I will know (*epiginosko*) fully," or in John 1:10 (*ginosko*) and 1:31 (*eido*). When Heb 8:11 quotes Jer 31:34 (where the Hebrew uses only *yada^c*), the first "know" comes from *eido*, and the second comes from *ginosko*; and in Gal 4:8–9 NRSV translates both *eido* in verse 8 and *ginosko* in verse 9 as "know God." The noun forms translated "knowledge" (*gnosis, epignosis*) can be used to connote either experiential or intellectual knowledge.

Sometimes the NT uses the phrases "know God" and "knowledge of God" in ways that are very similar to the OT. God's activity in creation and human history is the primary source of humanity's knowledge (*gnosis, epignosis*) of God (Rom 1:19–20), and knowing God is assumed to include both experiencing and responding in appropriate ways to God's activity in the world. Thus Titus 1:16 says, "They profess to know (*eido*) God, but they deny him by their actions" (and see 1 Thess 4:5), while 1 John asserts, "Now by this we may be sure that we know (*ginosko*) him, if we obey his commandments" (2:3–4), and "Whoever does not love does not know (*ginosko*) God" (4:8). Also, as in OT texts, not to know God is equated with idolatry (Gal 4:8).

While some passages seem to speak of a hidden knowledge granted only to a select group (such as Matt 13:11 and Luke 9:10), Paul claims that "what can be known about God is plain" to all (Rom 1:19). Thus Paul rails against those who are merely aware of God in a dispassionate, intellectual manner and do "not honor him as God or give thanks to him" (Rom 1:21). If the "wisdom of the world" consists of mere intellectual knowledge about God, then it is no better than what the OT calls folly (Rom 1:22; 1 Cor 1:18–25). This is the kind of knowledge (*gnosis*) that "puffs up" in contrast to love, which "builds up" (1 Cor 8:1). People are "puffed up" by knowledge they think they have gained for themsleves, but Paul is sure that the world cannot come to "know God" through this kind of wisdom (1 Cor 1:21). The kind of wisdom that enables us to know God actually comes from being "known by God" (Gal 4:9). "Anyone who loves God is known by him" (1 Cor 8:3). True knowledge of God is based on God's own self-revelatory activity and has a giftlike quality. It needs only to be accepted and appropriated. But failure to do so is blameworthy and will inevitably manifest itself in blameworthy behavior (Rom 1:28–32).

Although 1 Tim 6:20 cautions the recipient against "what is falsely called knowledge (*gnosis*)," Paul seems quite comfortable using the words *gnosis* (e.g., Rom 11:33; 2 Cor 10:5) and *epignosis* (e.g., Eph 4:13; Col 1:9–10) to refer to the knowledge of God. But the Gospel of John seems to avoid these noun forms, perhaps to avoid confusion with the specialized ways the concept of knowledge was used by the gnostics (or their precursors). Instead John uses various verbal forms meaning "know," "knowing," and "make known" to emphasize the revelatory necessity of coming to know God through Jesus Christ: "No one has ever seen God. It is God the only Son, who is close to the Father's heart, who has made him known (*exegeomai*)" (John 1:18). John quotes Jesus as saying, "If you know me, you will know my Father also. From now on you do know him and have seen him. . . . Whoever has seen me has seen the Father" (John 14:7, 9), and "Even though you do not believe me, believe the works, so that you may know and understand that the Father is in me and I am in the Father" (John 10:38).

Thus, while there is continuity between the OT and NT uses of "know" and "knowledge" in theological formulations, it is clear that the concept has been differently shaped and molded by the NT authors' need to address a different (and often non-Jewish) audience and by their perception that knowledge of God in its fullest sense depended on God's new self-revelatory act in Jesus Christ. Their goal was not merely to acquire knowledge about God but "to know the love of Christ that surpasses knowledge" (Eph 3:19).

KATHLEEN ANNE FARMER

Labor   *see* **Work**

Lamb   *see* **Animals**

Land   Next to God's self-revelation and God's *covenant law* relationship to Israel, land is central in Israel's faith. "Land" occurs 1,961 times in NRSV, including Apocrypha (another 165 times for plural, "lands"), but only 44 are in the NT. Overwhelmingly, "land" translates Heb. *ʾeretz*, often with the definite article, *haʾaretz*. But *ʾeretz*, the fourth most frequent noun in the OT, occurs in Hebrew Scripture 2,504 times; it is also translated "earth" and "ground." While *ʾeretz* may denote the cosmos, most frequently it refers to land, in the sense of geographical regions or politically governed areas, and soil or ground. The dominant NT Greek term for land is *ge* (252 times), most often translated "earth," as in Matt 5:5 and Rev 21:1.

Land has many dimensions of significance. Habel presents six land ideologies: as the source of wealth, as a conditional grant, as family lots, as Yahweh's inheritance, as Sabbath bound, and as a host country for immigrants. Land is the place and means of God's abundant *blessings* to Israel; harvest festivals and Israel's worship are oriented to land (Pss 104; 105; 135; 147). The land promised to Israel is distinguished environmentally from Egypt in that it is a hilly land, which God tends by sending rain from the heavens (Deut 11:10–12). But the most important features of land for Israel are that God the Lord owns the land (cf. Ps 24:1) and God promises the land of Canaan to Israel, as *his* possession—"the land is mine" (Lev 25:23)! Faith and stewardship, fundamental responses in Israel's covenant relationship to God—hence self-identity—are thus intrinsically tied to the land.

That *God owns the land* is a fundamental conviction of the OT. The Holiness Code (Lev 17–26) puts it sharply: "The land shall not be sold in perpetuity, for the land is mine; with me you are but aliens and tenants. Throughout the land that you hold, you shall provide for the redemption of the land" (25:23–24). Before and after these verses are important provisions governing Israel's stewardship of the land. This includes observing the *Sabbath* with no toil on the land, the sabbatical year of rest for the land, as well as the jubilee year, in which "you shall return, every one of you, to your property" (v. 13). Land was thus allocated to family units, described in detail in the land allocation in Josh 13–21; it was to remain with that family line from generation to generation. Hence, if a kin person falls into debt, the land is to be redeemed by the next of kin (Lev 25:25–34); in sale of land, cheating is condemned (vv. 14–17). In the jubilee year this land returns to the original family. Such radical land laws starkly remind the people that the land is a gift, a trust from God the owner. If Israel disobeys God's covenant law or serves other gods, they "shall perish quickly from the good land that he has given you" (Josh 23:16). Nor shall Israel ever presume that God's favor to them depends on their intrinsic goodness or their own power and might (Deut 7–8).

Given this theology of the land, removing the neighbors' or the ancient landmarks (Deut 19:14; 27:17; Prov 22:28; 23:10), coveting neighbors' fields (Mic 2:1–2; Isa 5:8), or plotting acquisition of adjoining or desirable plots (as Ahab and Jezebel did for Naboth's, 1 Kgs 21:1–26) are strongly condemned, subject to severe punishment. Israel's loss of the land through exile culminates such punishment, warranted by these sins (Amos) and idolatries (Hosea, Isaiah).

Through deliverance from slavery, God graced Israel with the freedom of the Sabbath (Exod 20:2, 8–11; Deut 5:12–15), in which nature and time conjoined in holy celebration. With promise fulfilled, Israel became an agrarian society, and their holiest festivals, forming calendar time, were linked to the fruits of the land. First, Passover celebrated deliverance from Egypt's bondage, the first stage in fulfillment of God's *promise* to Abraham that his descendants would inherit the land. Second, fifty days after Passover, Israel observed the seven-day feast of Weeks, a harvest festival remembering deliverance from bondage and rejoicing, in which the firstfruits of harvest were brought before the Lord (Exod 23:16, 19; 34:21–22, 26; Deut 16:8–12; Lev 23:9–22). The priest's waving the sheaf before the Lord dramatically affirmed God as owner of the harvest. In later Jewish thought the giving of the law was linked to this festival of rejoicing (Pss 1; 19:7–10; 119). In the NT the Pentecost gift of the Holy Spirit continues this celebration of God's goodness. The third great feast, known as the feast of Ingathering, Booths, or Tabernacles, also seven days, falls at the end of the harvest season and is marked also by rejoicing and celebration of social solidarity and economic leveling in the community (Exod 23:16b; 34:22b; Deut 16:13–15). At this feast on the sabbatical year "you shall read this law before all Israel in their hearing" in order that all the people may "hear and learn to fear the LORD your God . . . as long as you live in the land" (Deut 31:10–13).

Of great theological significance is the combining of Israel's historical *redemption* and nature, the land, in the Sabbath, sabbatical, jubilee, and these triple feasts of celebration. Redeemed by God's mighty deeds in history *and* living as God's people in God's land, Israel experienced its identity as God's people via both time and nature.

The second important feature of Israel's land experience centered on *promise* and *fulfillment,* a theme that unifies Genesis–Joshua. God's threefold promise to Abraham (great nation, great name, and blessing to all peoples), is founded on and intertwined with Abraham leaving his home country and going "to the land that I will show to you" (Gen 12:1–3). The entire patriarchal narrative is oriented to the testing and reaffirming of this promise. Likewise, Exodus–Deuteronomy narrates Israel's deliverance from Egypt, God's establishing of covenant and law, and Israel's testing in the wilderness, all in anticipation of entering into the promised land. Joshua fulfills the promises and narrates the means of Israel's possession of the land. The land is indeed God's gift to them: "I sent the hornet [elsewhere, angel of the Lord] ahead of you, which drove out before you the two kings of the Amorites; it was not by your sword or by your bow. I gave you a land on which you had not labored, and towns that you had not built, and you live in them; you eat the fruit of vineyards and oliveyards that you did not plant" (Josh 24:12–13).

Often the promise of the land is connected to the promise of many descendants (Gen 17:1–8; 22:17) and is interwoven with blessing upon Israel (28:13–15). The Abrahamic covenantal promises are complemented by the conditional Mosaic (Exod 19:5–6) and Davidic (2 Sam 7:11–29; Ps 132) covenants. But the land aspect of the Abrahamic covenant is also condi-

tional (1 Kgs 9:4–9; 2 Chr 7:19–22). The prophets not only warn but predict loss of the land because of the nation's idolatries and military dependence (Isa 2:6–10; Jer 7; 31:32; Hos 1; 8:1). Exile from the land is God's punishment (reflected also in Pss 74; 126; 137). But beyond the exile, hope rises in the prophetic announcement that Israel will be restored to its land (Hos 1:10–11; Jer 23:3; 33:7–11; Ezek 28:25–26; 36–37; Joel 3; Zech 2:6–12; 8:2–8; 10:8–12). The majestic declaration of a new era initiated by the sovereign, holy, redeemer Lord God of the universe in Isa 40–66 celebrates this "new thing" (43:19) about to happen, grounded in the condition of Israel fulfilling its role to be the Lord's servant of justice to the nations (42:1–9; 49:5–6, "that my salvation may reach to the end of the earth"), which mission will entail suffering (chap. 53).

This fulfillment motif joins the Testaments, since Jesus interprets his own mission as fulfilling the role of the servant (see *peace,* as well as Luke 4:16–21 quoting Isa 61:1–2a and 58:6). With Jesus declared as God's Son (Mark 1:9–11, echoing Ps 2:7) commissioned to fulfill the servant's mission (baptismal voice echoing Isa 42:1), a most astounding shift occurs: in Jesus' proclamation of the dawning kingdom of God, land is *not* a factor in covenant promise and fulfillment. In the Gospels, especially Mark, "entering into the kingdom of God" (Mark 9:1, 43, 45, 47; 10:15, 23–25) likely echoes the exact phrase in the LXX of the OT oft-recurring phrase of "entering into the land of promise" (Exod 23:23–33; 33:1–3; Deut 1:8; 4:1; 6:18; 16:20). But the kingdom of God is not associated with any specific territorial piece of land. Jesus' promise that the meek "will inherit the earth" (Matt 5:5) shifts "land" to "earth," universalizing the scope (cf. Acts 1:6–8, "my witnesses . . . to the ends of the earth"). Even Paul, when affirming God's faithfulness to Israel (Rom 9–11) uses *ge* only in sense of "all the earth" (9:17; 10:18; cf. 9:28). Rather, God's promise to Abraham now fulfilled in Jesus Christ is understood as inheriting the *world* (Rom

4:13; cf. 1 Cor 3:21–23); Paul also speaks of a "new creation" in Christ (2 Cor 5:17). The whole earth is now the landscape of God's salvation for all people, worldwide. The Revelator foresees a "new heavens and new earth," for the former things have passed away (Rev 21). Brueggemann's view (170–80) that key NT theological symbols ("kingdom of God" in Synoptics, "eternal life" in John, "inheritance" in Paul, "homeland" in Hebrews, and "crucifixion/resurrection" as core symbol) included land dimensions is not convincing (see, rather, Davies).

This striking difference between the Testaments begs explanation. True, the Christian movement was centered in urban areas, and NT literature comes from A.D. 55–90, when Christians were more separated from Judaism. But the reason lies deeper. Isaiah's messianic vision foresaw the knowledge of God covering the earth as the waters cover the sea (11:9). A similar universalizing of God's salvation occurs often in OT Scripture (Ps 67; Isa 49:6; 52:10). This universal vision rooted in the OT messianic hope (Rom 10:18 quotes Ps 19:4!) finds fulfillment in the gospel of Jesus Christ, new wine that could not be contained within territorial land notions. Being "aliens and exiles" (1 Pet 2:11) appears normative for Christians in the late first century (cf. Heb 11:13–16). In *The Epistle to Diognetus* (2d–3d century) Christians are described as essentially landless, despite their living in many lands: "They dwell in their own fatherlands, but as if sojourners in them; they share all things as citizens, and suffer all things as strangers. Every foreign country is their fatherland, and every fatherland is a foreign country" (v. 5).

Walter Brueggemann, *The Land* (Philadelphia: Fortress Press, 1977); W. D. Davies, *The Gospel and the Land* (Berkeley: University of California Press, 1974); Norman C. Habel, *The Land Is Mine* (Minneapolis: Fortress Press: 1995); Theodore Hiebert, *The Yahwist's Landscape* (Oxford: Oxford University Press, 1996); Elmer Martens, *God's Design: A Focus on Old Testament The-*

ology (Grand Rapids: Baker, 1981); Christopher J. H. Wright, *God's People in God's Land* (Grand Rapids: Eerdmans, 1990).

WILLARD M. SWARTLEY

Laugh, Mock, Deride, Derision, Scorn

These words, which form a closely related family, could be used in combinations for effect, or singly. Either way, the distinctions among them are slim, and NRSV uses English translations interchangeably in many cases. Generally the terms are negative in connotation, as if laughter in the Bible was generally at someone's expense.

NRSV translates three Hebrew words "laugh." By far the most common is the word *sahaq*, which means "laugh," "mock," or "deride." Eliphaz, for example, promises Job that if he will repent, God will pardon him. Then he would be able to laugh at destruction and famine (Job 5:22). Similarly, the psalmist promises that righteous people will laugh at evildoers who did not take refuge in God (Ps 52:6–7; cf. Ps 59:8). In these cases the word carries a note of sarcasm, as it does also when Dame Wisdom says to simpletons that ignore her: "I also will laugh at your calamity" (Prov 1:26). Another word with a similar meaning is *la'ag*, which means "laugh to scorn" (Job 22:19; cf. Job 9:23) or "deride" (cf. Pss 2:4; 59:8). The third word is *tsahaq* and its derivatives; its basic meaning is "laugh outright." It too can carry a note of scorn. In the narratives about the birth of Isaac (whose name means "laughter"), however, it carries the gentler connotation of laughing in amusement (Gen 17–18 and 21:6). In the NT, bystanders attempt to "laugh down" (*katagelao*) Jesus when he announces that the daughter of Jairus is only sleeping (Mark 5:40 and par.), whereas Jas 4:9 simply uses a less emphatic word for "laugh" (*gelao*).

The observation that "laugh" often carried a negative connotation is borne out by further uses of two of those terms. NRSV translates the word *la'ag* ("laugh at") as "mock" (cf. Job 11:3; 21:3; Ps 22:7;

Prov 17:5), as "deride" or "derision" (Pss 2:4; 59:8; Ezek 36:4), and as "scorn" (Job 22:19; Pss 44:13; 123:4; Prov 30:17). It also translates *sahaq* as "derision" (Jer 48:39) and "scorn" (2 Chr 30:10). Ezekiel 23:32 uses the two terms as synonyms. In the allegory of the sisters Oholah and Oholibah (symbols for Samaria and Jerusalem respectively), God warns Oholibah that she will be scorned (*la'ag*) and ridiculed (*sahaq*) like a prostitute.

Besides *la'ag* ("laugh at") NRSV translates five different Hebrew words as "mock," including *lits* (Prov 14:9; 19:28; Hab 2:6), *hathal* (Judg 16:10, 13, 15; 1 Kgs 18:27), *'anag* (Isa 57:4), and *qalas* (Ezek 22:5). The fifth word is *haraph* (Ezek 5:14), which typically means "reproach" or even "taunt" (Ps 102:8). In the narrative of the destruction of Sennacherib's army (2 Kgs 19:4, 16, 22, 23; Isa 37:23, 24), it appears in the taunting speech of the Babylonian general and carries the similar translation "mock." It also is translated "mockery" (Ezek 5:15; 16:57; Joel 2:17, 19). The NT uses the word *empaizo*, often translated "ridicule," in connection with the actions of the crowd at the crucifixion (cf. Matt 20:19; 27:31, 41; Mark 10:34; 15:20, 31; Luke 18:32; 22:63; 23:11, 36). Paul uses the term *mukterizo* (treat with contempt) in Gal 6:7.

Besides *la'ag* and *sahaq*, Hebrew terms mentioned earlier in this article that are translated "deride" and "derision" include *qeles* (Ps 79:4), *lits* (Ps 119:51), *sahaq* (Jer 48:39), and *haraph* (Ps 44:13; Jer 29:18). Three additional Hebrew words require attention. The first is the participle *meholal* (Ps 102:8), which might be translated: "those deriding me." Among its many meanings, the term may designate one who boasts, but it can mean "make a fool of," as it does here. A second unusual term is *rahab* in the prayer of Hannah (1 Sam 2:1). With the preposition employed in the verse, the word normally would mean "grow large against." So, Hannah anticipates responding to her enemies with a "big mouth." The third word is *shimtsah* (Exod 32:25), which is similar to a rare word meaning "whisper." One gains the

impression here that the word depicts the enemies of Israel whispering behind the backs of the Israelites, that is, gossiping and speaking derisively. In the NT the people at the crucifixion were said to "deride" Jesus. The Greek word means "slander" or "blaspheme."

Hebrew terms mentioned earlier in this article that are translated "scorn" include *haraph* (Judg 5:18; Ps 22:6; 31:11; 39:8; 71:13; 89:41; 109:25; 119:22; Jer 6:10; and Mic 6:16), *qalas* (Ezek 16:31), *lits* (Job 16:20; Prov 3:34), *sahaq* (2 Chr 30:10), and *tsahaq* (Ezek 23:32). Two other terms warrant mentioning here: *bazah*, which also may be translated "despise," and *madon*, which generally means "strife" or "contention." In the NT, Paul commends the Galatians for not "despising" or "scorning" (*ethenesate*) him for a physical condition of his that might have led to them to reject him with contempt (Gal 4:14).

PAUL L. REDDITT

Law, Command, Commandment, Ordinance, Statute

Words and meaning. The primary word that is translated as "law" in the standard English versions of the Bible is Hebrew *torah*, which properly means "instruction," or "guidance." That the noun *torah* could apply to forms of advice or instruction of a far wider variety than that implied by specifically legal rulings is evidenced by the fact that both prophets and counselors could offer *torah*, showing that it could be at the level of guidance or advice for living more generally. That God could be the author of instructions through the mediation of a prophet connects the word closely with the idea of "oracle, prophetic message."

The word did not originally mean "law" in the sense of court ruling or judicial decision, nor was it even originally used to describe a "decree" or "constitutional ruling" in the sense of a tribal or royal decree imposed on members of a tribe or nation. So the decision in English versions of the Bible to translate the term, usually but not consistently, as "law" is the result of a complex and extensive linguistic and historical process. The first stage in this development occurred with widespread translation of Hebrew *torah* in the Greek (LXX) translation of the OT by the word *nomos* ("law"), which led, in turn, to the translation in the later Latin versions by the word *lex* ("law"). Although these words carried legal overtones, and were intended to convey a measure of understanding that the rulings and instructions given in the OT through Moses expressed the "laws" of God for all humankind throughout all ages, this was clearly only one aspect of the choice of so important a term. It has consequently been an important feature of the interpretation of the OT as a book of law that this unique and highly distinctive word *torah* should be understood in light of its own special context. As a result many scholars have advocated the use of the transliteration of the Hebrew as "Torah," to show that it expresses a wider range of meaning than does the more familiar English "law."

The OT contains several other words for "law." The most significant of these is the word *mishpat*, which stands closest to describing the ruling, or legal principle, which was upheld by a court of law. It is derived from a verb meaning "to judge" and so properly means "verdict, decision." It describes the verdict arrived at by a popular assembly of a community, when acting as a court of law. Such a decision then established a precedent that could be applied in other similar cases, or even to establish a principle (for instance, concerning the admissibility of evidence) that could be applied widely. This word is closest to what is familiarly understood to be law in a juridical sense, and it is certainly used in this way in the OT. However, it is widely translated in KJV, and later EVV, as "judgment," and in its OT setting it has acquired a broad meaning as "custom, tradition," covering the popular habits and manner of life of a community. Although it has a close legal reference, it is not an exclusively legal term and has

sometimes posed problems for translators (as, for instance, in Isa 42:4).

Other words also are used in the OT to describe the ruling of a person of authority, such as a king or military commander, who could issue a "decree" (Heb. *hoq, huqqah*). Similar is the word for "commandment, ruling," which was an authoritative pronouncement made by a family head or other person of authority. A key passage of the OT's understanding of law (Heb. *torah*) is found in Deut 4:44–45, where the law (Heb. *torah*) that Moses set before Israel is said to comprise decrees, statutes, and ordinances. These were first spoken to the people (Deut 4:44), and subsequently written down (cf. Deut 31:9). It was evidently a matter of importance to the book of Deuteronomy that the "law," which Moses communicated to Israel, comprised instructions and guidance covering very large areas of life, roughly equivalent to the constitution of a small modern state. This pronouncement also shows that all categories of law and popular custom were subject to the authority of the law Moses gave. These included legal rules for dealing with criminal offences and administrative procedures for the organization of legal affairs, as well as rules of worship, commercial transactions, and family and domestic affairs. The contents of the book of Deuteronomy amply illustrate this feature.

Forms and categories of law. From the various terms in use in OT times, it is evident that the comprehensive description of its instructions as *torah* was the end result of a growing concern to set under one heading rules dealing with all areas of social and political life. These included family, religious, and military activities, besides specifically legal proceedings. The roots of all these rulings can be traced back to a period when authority was primarily exercised by chiefs and elders within the larger community. With the passage of time and the introduction of kingship, there emerged semiprofessional judges and officials (Deut 16:18–20). These were authorized to uphold justice with the aim of ensuring consistency and fairness in settling disputes and criminal cases (Deut 16:20). It is these rulings that come closest to the modern-day understanding of law, where agreed court procedures are applied to deal with criminal offences. The oldest collection of such laws in the OT is to be found in Exod 20:22–23:19, often described as "the book of the covenant." The Hebrew title for these laws is *mishpatim* (EVV "judgments").

For criminal cases in which it proved difficult to reach a clear verdict, for lack of evidence or because the evidence proved unsatisfactory, the priests of nearby sanctuaries could be called in to help reach a verdict (Deut 17:8–13). Their knowledge of the community, access to a long tradition of such problems, and, as a last resort, the use of the sacred lot could help to settle such cases. It was a matter of importance to avoid long-running grievances that could lead to feuds and personal vendettas. For this reason the decision made by such priests was absolute and final. Refusal to accept their decision carried the death penalty (Deut 17:12–13). Priests also made rulings regarding the duties of worship and the appropriate times and manner of their fulfillment. In this way they also became responsible for "laws" of a special kind, which could nevertheless overlap with more narrowly legal proceedings. Examples of such laws are to be found in the handbook of sacrificial practice set out in Lev 1:1–7:38.

It should not occasion surprise that we find this intermixing of religious and civil laws in the OT, since religious observance formed a foundational feature of all social activity. As a consequence, infringements of religious practice could carry severe penalties, not excluding the death penalty (cf. Deut 13:1–18; Josh 7:1–26; etc.). In such instances the assumption was that God's honor had been called in question and the holiness of the whole community had been threatened. Laws and rulings relevant to matters of justice and criminal activity are frequently intermixed with other matters of a more narrowly religious

nature. This overlapping of religious (ritual) obligations and those directly relating to civil duties and the punishment of criminal actions is a marked feature of the lists of "laws" that the OT contains. "Law" in ancient Israel was never a wholly secular affair, as is the case in most modern societies. A noticeable example of this feature is the long collection of rulings in Lev 17–26, in which the underlying goal of all of them is that the entire community of Israel should be "holy" (Lev 19:2; 22:31–33). As a result, this entire collection of laws is usually called the Holiness Code. Such overlapping of religious and social duties led to confusion and differences of interpretation among later Jews in deciding where the greater obligation lay when the demands of holiness came into conflict with more social and compassionate demands.

A further prominent category of instruction in the OT concerns commands or advisory exhortations where right and desirable conduct is commended, but no specific penalty for failing to adhere to it is set out. Usually described as admonitions rather than laws, they frequently deal with issues where a legal requirement was involved. The book of Proverbs is understandably largely comprised of such admonitions, but they also appear in significant ways interspersed in other more directly legal rulings. Most significant among these is the admonition "to love one's neighbor as oneself" set out in Lev 19:17–18, which occurs in a situation where legal obligations concerning a neighbor are spelled out. The citation of this by Jesus as the second of the two "great commandments" (Matt 22:39) elevates it to a position of unique importance among all the laws of the OT. Such admonitory advice, frequently found in Deuteronomy interspersed among more obvious legal rulings, shows that law required a commitment of heart as well as mind.

These admonitions are not strictly laws in any legal sense, since they carry no penalties and are recognized as largely unenforceable. They have, however, remained among the most influential and enduring features of the legislative literature of the OT, precisely because they seek to write "the law" in the hearts and consciences of individuals (cf. Jer 31:31–34).

The Ten Commandments. The Ten Commandments of Exod 20:1–17 (= Deut 5:6–21) are set out as admonitory rules of this kind and are notable because they do not include specific punishments, even though they deal with matters, for example, homicide, where legal procedures against crimes were expected to be used. Opinions have differed widely among scholars whether this short list of "commandments" should be regarded as laws in the narrower sense or are properly to be classed as admonitions of the kind noted above. In a widely adopted interpretation, they have been held to represent a particular category of law (called "apodictic," or "declaratory" law), which stood apart from and originated prior to the rulings of the legal system. Presenting a short summary of primary duties placed special emphasis on them as fundamental guidelines covering a wide expanse of religious and moral obligation. Both in Judaism and Christianity they have undoubtedly been a major influence and have drawn forth extensive discussion concerning their primary purpose in their biblical setting. This has focused on two features: (1) they are formulated in this highly distinctive "command" pattern; (2) they are authorized directly by God, who declares them through a human spokesperson. By including as religious duties the rejection of all forms of idolatry and the observance of the Sabbath (cf. Deut 13:12–16; Num 15:32–36) they raise questions concerning the wisdom of applying civil punishments for purely religious offences. The OT itself shows that these commands proved difficult to implement (see Neh 13:15–22) in cases where they were not obeyed.

In contrast, two of these commandments (honoring parents and rejecting covetousness) one could not reasonably have expected to be enforced by applying civil punishments. The offence would have been impossible to prove in light of the OT's own rules of evidence. However, some of these commandments, for example, homicide and theft, cover offences where criminal action could be expected in a court of law if they were broken. Such features have encouraged some scholars to seek to define each of them very narrowly, so as to show that they dealt with problems in which customary legal procedures may have been weak or ineffective. In the opposite direction, rather different interpretations of some of them have been proposed in order to demonstrate that they all originally referred to offences where failure to observe them carried a major penalty of exclusion from the community, or even death. Other suggestions have been that they simply outlawed bad and unacceptable conduct, in a manner comparable to that of curses (cf. Deut 27:15–26).

However, none of these attempts to give to these Ten Commandments a special range of meaning is necessary, once it is recognized that they are essentially headings, or topical summaries, listing those areas of life where human conduct was intended to be shaped and enriched by adherence to the demands of living as a community of God's people. They are to be understood, not apart from the other laws that the OT sets out, but as useful summaries and guidelines showing where a God-given order and responsibility exists for every human being.

Deuteronomy and the development of law. We have already noted the importance of Deut 4:44 for its definition of what constitutes *torah* (Greek *nomos*; English "law"). There it is said to comprise "decrees, statutes, and ordinances." The contents of Deuteronomy fully bear out its purpose of expressing a comprehensive body of rulings dealing with legal, religious, and wider political obligations. It contains pronouncements applying to the administration of justice, a collection of directions regarding obligations for regular worship, besides a host of rules covering commercial transactions, slavery, the appointment of a king, and protection of the environment. Its evident intention to be comprehensive and inclusive is in agreement with its claim that *torah* covers all areas of social and political life. Deuteronomy evidently owes many of its features to a familiarity with far older Mesopotamian law collections. It aims, by making total loyalty to the Lord God its foundational demand, to set out a way of life for every member of the people of God, past, present, and future.

Certainly the evident concern of Deuteronomy to show that *torah* provides guidance for Israelites wherever they are, or whenever they happen to live, implies that it presents a "covenant law." This makes it a "manual of guidance" for those members of Israel who are shown to be (cf. Deut 5:1–3) in *covenant* with the Lord God. In this way its rulings and instructions make it closely comparable to the conditions and stipulations that were included as part of international treaties or covenants negotiated between nations. Many scholars have discerned in the book an influence from familiarity with such treaties. Israel is a people who are in covenant (= treaty) with the Lord God. As these treaties often made a total and absolute demand of allegiance upon its signatories, Deuteronomy, by its emphasis that commitment to the Lord God was similarly total and absolute, placed God above all human authorities. The origins of Peter's assertion that "we must obey God rather than any human authority" (Acts 5:29; 4:13–22), is to be found here.

The understanding of law shapes the structure and purpose of the entire book of Deuteronomy, and, from this, extends the claims of *torah* to cover all five books of the Pentateuch. Together these books constitute Israel's *torah* and form the foundation of the entire OT. Moreover, the Pentateuch's emphasis upon *torah* as the law of the covenant between Israel and the Lord God ensures that it controls the understanding of all the remaining books of the OT. The entire OT can therefore be held to represent a literature of "covenant law."

The law in the Prophets. With the first five books of the OT classified as Torah, the second part of the canon, in its Hebrew form, is broadly classified as Prophecy, more formally defined as the Former Prophets (Joshua–Judges, 1 and 2 Samuel, 1 and 2 Kings) and the Latter Prophets (Isaiah, Jeremiah, Ezekiel, the Book of the Twelve).

The primary concern of Deuteronomy to present a comprehensive book of *torah* was evidently the end result of a long process. The extended nature of this process, witnessed by the many different subunits, or collections, within the Pentateuch, focuses attention on its relationship to the Prophets. The wealth of information about Israel's conduct and wayward religious loyalty provided by the many great prophets sheds much further light on the development and effectiveness of Israel's legal administration. How well did it actually work?

At times the sharp condemnation of whole series of crimes and wrongdoing, as in Hos 4:2, suggests that the prophet was familiar with lists of commandments, closely comparable to those of the Ten Commandments. Yet the prophet's rebuke of the prevalence of such serious crimes indicates both a popular indifference to even quite basic laws and the ineffectiveness of the legal administration to counter this. Unfortunately far too little is known about familiarity among the people of ancient Israel generally with the laws that are traced back to Moses. Lists of laws from an even earlier period were composed in ancient Mesopotamia, beginning in ancient Sumeria, but the existence of good laws does not demonstrate that they were widely respected and enforced. Overall the picture given to us by the prophets is that a whole range of social, economic, and political uncertainties led to widespread violence and exploitation. This supports the contention that the portrayal of violence and lawlessness in ancient Israel given by the great prophets is likely to have been close to the mark— at least in particular periods of weak central government. However, it tells us little about popular familiarity with lists of laws. The general accusation against Israel made in Elijah's prayer to God sums up the message of the prophets as a whole: "The Israelites have forsaken your covenant" (1 Kgs 19:10). How the prophets reacted to this is well summarized in the review of their message in 2 Kgs 17:13: "Yet the LORD warned Israel and Judah by every prophet and every seer, saying, 'Turn from your evil ways and keep my commandments and my statutes, in accordance with all the law that I commanded your ancestors and that I sent to you by my servants the prophets.'"

Overall the rebukes of the prophets regarding the prevalence of lawlessness and widespread violence in ancient Israel show well why the development of well-made and justly administered laws was so central a need for ancient Israel. The prophetic strictures do not demonstrate that the average Israelite did not know right from wrong, but they show very well that, as with other ancient societies, the task of building up fair and justly applied laws proved a complex and difficult task. Much of the importance of what the OT has contributed in this direction lies in the strength and firmness of the prophetic claim that only when there exists respect for a just and righteous God can there be a just and righteous social order.

The Holiness Code and the postexilic development of Israel's laws. If the book of Deuteronomy has provided the most central and foundational written record of law in ancient Israel, then the Holiness Code of Lev 17–26 and the wider inclusion of priestly and ritual laws in the books of Exodus, Leviticus, and Numbers are also significant features. As in the case of Deuteronomy, so also with these laws their origin and authority are traced back to the person of Moses. This is not simply the result of a desire to find a human personal authority for them, but rather illustrates the centrality of the claim that all Israel's laws were part of its covenant heritage as a people of the Lord God. The authority of the law is also the authority of the covenant and ultimately the authority of God.

The collection of laws in Lev 17–26 provides a helpful example of the complex way in which laws were composed, modified, and administered, first in ancient Israel, and then more broadly in Jewish society. These ten chapters cover several of the areas of activity and social life already covered in Deuteronomy. They do so, however, from a rather different standpoint, and they look to priests, rather than an order of judges, to see that they are adhered to. Many of the topics dealt with are concerned with right and proper forms of sacrifice, the observance of religious festivals, and sexual relationships within the larger kinship structures of the extended family. At times they are similar in form to the Ten Commandments (cf. Lev 19:2–37) and cover similar social problems. At other times they are content with affirming strong admonitions, of which the most memorable and influential is that of Lev 19:18: "You shall love your neighbor as yourself." Overall their primary significance is not that they exemplify a different range of moral insights from the book of Deuteronomy, nor that they can be traced to a different period of Israel's history. Rather it lies in the different way in which their appeal to respect for God as the ultimate authority ("You shall not profane my holy name," Lev 22:32; cf. Exod 20:7) is set out from the appeal to Israel's covenant with the Lord God in Deuteronomy.

Opinions have differed as to whether this particular group of laws at one time formed a separate and self-contained book that could be learned and taught. More relevant is the fact that it shows the way in which the priests and Levites of ancient Israel were directly involved in legal and moral affairs, alongside the elders and judges of a community. Often their areas of concern overlapped, particularly regarding sexual ethics.

Several of the same issues reappear further in the extensive literary compilation of laws and rules regarding worship and its duties that form the main subject of the books of Exodus–Numbers. Priests, elders, and officially appointed judges were all involved in promoting respect for the law in ancient Israel, and this has carried over into later (postbiblical) Jewish life. In many instances, infringements of the order of worship are declared to have carried the most extreme of punishments. In these cases, it is God who acts as Prosecutor, Judge, and Executioner, as in the case of the priests who offered unholy fire (Num 16:28–40).

Since a literal obedience to many of the rules laid down for regular worship at the one approved sanctuary—the temple of Jerusalem—proved impossible for a large number of Jews, a very complex body of compensatory activities of prayer and devotion was developed. Worship was often confined to the home or to local assemblies of Jewish adults, at which the singing of psalms and the offering of prayers of contrition provided an "inward" counterpart to the "outward" presentation of sacrifices. Already therefore, well before the earliest Christian era, a practical distinction had begun to emerge between the "moral" laws of social righteousness and the "ritual" laws pertaining to worship in the temple.

Old Testament law in the Wisdom writings and Psalms. The book of Proverbs contains a large collection of sayings, instructions, and admonitions that are traced back to the teaching of King Solomon. The same is true of the book of Ecclesiastes, although most scholars regard this attribution of authorship as a carefully chosen literary fiction or stylistic device. An even more extensive collection of this class of instruction is found in the OT Apocrypha in the book of Ecclesiasticus, whose author was Ben Sira, writing in the early second century B.C. The particular relevance of these books for the study of biblical law and legal practice lies in their sharp focus on matters of conduct, lifestyle, and other factors that promote a healthy and law-abiding social order. Although these writings do not set out laws in any formal sense, they offer an abundance of comments on criminal behavior, on the difficulty of getting redress by the victims of such conduct through the legal system, and more generally on the psychological and social factors that lead to criminal lifestyles. In general the sharp-witted observers who collected and wrote down these admonitions and comments provide a wealth of insight to show that good laws do not necessarily, by themselves, lead to a law-abiding society. Good administration and careful scrutiny of the sometimes pernicious influence of wealth and family connections serve to highlight the problems that the legal systems of antiquity faced. The numerous appeals throughout the Bible to a fundamental concern for justice, truth, and compassion, rooted in a regard for every fellow citizen as a creature of God, show that respect for law was central to the fear of God.

All these books (usually described as Wisdom writings) also help to show that new problems faced the Jews of OT times after the breakup of the first kingdom of Judah in 587 B.C. From that time onwards, all Jews found themselves living under the restraints of foreign government (first that of Persia, and later those of Greece and Rome). Moreover, increasing numbers of Jewish citizens were living in small communities in the midst of Gentile neighbors. The authority of local Jewish courts was often limited, and the need was paramount to submit to the often irksome legal impositions of local Gentile authorities. The book of Esther well illustrates these problems and their dangers. In general, respect for the law was largely dependent on local Jewish leadership, with only limited support from the larger regional or national community. This uncertain political situation highlighted the importance of commitment to God's revealed law as a part of the covenant loyalty, which was the spiritual heritage of every Jew. It also served to show why the Jewish way of life was held in high regard among Gentiles in late Hellenistic times. This was a feature that later formed a vital part of the success story of the rise and spread of Christianity, when it built upon the foundations of the OT teaching regarding law.

In the book of Psalms a quite distinctive affirmation of joy and thanksgiving for the existence of the torah is found in certain compositions (especially Pss 19:7–13; 119:1–176). Described as Torah psalms, these affirmations of praise to God for the gift of the law appear to have little to do with the administration of law in the strict juridical sense but are rather teaching documents, aimed at promoting a careful study of the law and adherence to its demands. Quite striking in regard to Psalm 119 is that, in commending the law as the gift of God for a happy and rewarding way of life, it does not single out any specific precept or ruling as illustration of its merits. It simply presents the law as a single comprehensive written work, which it commends as a necessary form of guidance for the pursuit of the good life.

The law in the New Testament. The central new feature that Jesus brought to the understanding and interpretation of the Mosaic law of the OT is to be found in the Sermon on the Mount (Matt 5:1–7:29). Like Moses, Jesus delivered the new law upon a mountain, and in a great many respects he modifies, extends, and in some cases sharply revises the law given by Moses. The central claim of Jesus' new law is to represent the fulfillment of the earlier law (so Matt 5:17–20). Extensive discussion has arisen over what is implied by this claim, since it is evident that the earliest Christian church was comprised at first of Jews only and later of a large Gentile (non-Jewish) following. Understandably many, perhaps most, Jewish followers of Jesus in the early period maintained without questioning their formal obedience to the accepted requirements of the Jewish law. These included many demands of personal hygiene and dietary practice, especially regarding the eating of meat. With ever-growing numbers of Gentiles becoming members of the Christian community, the necessity for such adherence to former Jewish practices, which were regarded as Jewish customs rather than universal laws, was questioned. It became a matter of dissension and was a primary factor in bringing about the division of Jews from Christians. Central among such issues was the practice of *circumcision.* This had already proved to be contentious when Gentile men had sought to convert to Judaism. In general, the consensus had been against allowing uncircumcised men to become full members of the Jewish community, classing them simply as adherents, or "God-fearers." Their inclusion as members of the Christian community was therefore a matter that led to disagreements between Jewish and Gentile Christians.

The overall character and intention of the new "law of Christ" was to simplify and categorize the demands of God's law by establishing clear and firm priorities. Central to this concern was the affirmation that the entire law must be focused upon the two supreme commandments (Luke 10:25–28). Accordingly love and compassion are to take priority over vengeance and punishment; saving life is to take priority over formal, ritual demands; and racist and sectarian distinctions are wholly repudiated (cf. Luke 10:29–37). In general the physical and ritual demands of holiness are set aside in order to give priority to the nurturing of inner attitudes fostering love and compassion (cf. Mark 7:14–23). The summarizing demand of the Sermon on the Mount, "Be perfect, therefore, as your heavenly Father is perfect" (Matt 5:48), both replaces and revises the older demand of the OT's Holiness Code that Israel should be a "holy" nation. Evidently the mixed ritual demands associated with the idea of holiness were too confused and restrictive for the teaching of Jesus to be grasped in its full universal context.

Even though certain important contrasts are made in the teaching of Jesus between the requirements of the old law and the new (see Matt 5:21–48), the overall tenor of the Sermon on the Mount lies in its establishing firm priorities for the most important issues and the setting aside of lesser commitments in the interests of a larger and more all-embracing ethic of compassion and love. Inwardness and consistency of intent are given priority over external and purely ritual concerns.

The distinction between the ritual demands of the OT law and its parallel ethical requirements are also extensively explored in the Epistle to the Hebrews, where the necessity for making such a distinction is upheld. This is achieved through a complex series of arguments, exploring both some of the intricacies of Jewish (rabbinic) interpretation and also the insights of Hellenistic (Platonic) philosophy. Overall, however, through such a line of argument, there is a robust defense of the Christian dismissal of the purely ritual and cultic features of the Mosaic law. These features are held to express only types and shadows of a more inward and lasting spiritual reality.

By far the most extensive exploration of the meaning of the Mosaic laws of the OT is carried out by the apostle Paul, chiefly in two major letters to Gentile churches. The first of these, the Epistle to the Romans, reaches across the divide between Jews and Gentiles, by arguing forcibly that even the peoples who do not possess the written law of Moses know inwardly through the natural order of the world, the law of God (Rom 1:18–32). So the distinction between a "Jewish" law and a "Gentile" law is set aside by the argument that there is ultimately only one true law of God, which is made evident through the created world, and was revealed through Moses to the Jewish people first. This law, nevertheless, is written on the heart of every human being and its reality is attested by the promptings of *conscience* (Rom 2:12–16). More searchingly, and more controversially, Paul proceeds to explore the deep psychological and spiritual dilemmas that knowledge of this law brings to each individual (Rom 2:17–7:25). The breadth and uncompromising nature of the law show that, in its full extent, every human being fails to fulfill its demands. Only faith in

Jesus Christ as the one true victor over sin can offer deliverance from the consequent threat of death.

The second of Paul's letters that deals extensively with the relationship of Christians to the law revealed in the OT is that written to the Christians of Galatia. Underlying this epistle is the question whether it was necessary for Christians, especially Gentile Christians, to obey the whole range of requirements of the traditional Jewish Law. Although the central issue concerned the rite of circumcision, other factors included dietary laws, festival observance, and, overall, the meticulous regulation of daily life. Even several of the most prominent early Jewish Christian leaders, including Peter the apostle and Barnabas, had agreed to adherence to this traditional system. It represented law, not in the juridical sense of obeying the civil and criminal laws of the community generally, but in the distinctive religious sense of adherence to a wide-ranging and complex set of rules governing daily conduct. For Paul, law can never bring the justified and secure relationship with God that constitutes humankind's redemption; only the grace of God, made evident in the atoning death of Christ, can achieve that (Gal 2:15–21). So Christ is the end of the law, not in the sense that the Christian lives without law, since the Sermon on the Mount shows that not to be the case. Rather, law was given as humankind's guide and mentor so that we might be driven to Christ and thereby receive the fulfillment of the *promise* made to Abraham (Gal 3:1–29).

Hans Jochen Boecker, *Law and the Administration of Justice in the Old Testament and the Ancient Near East* (Minneapolis: Augsburg Publishing House, 1980); Walter Harrelson, *The Ten Commandments and Human Rights* (Philadelphia: Fortress Press, 1980); Dale Patrick, *Old Testament Law* (Atlanta: John Knox Press, 1985); Stephen Westerholm, *Israel's Law and the Church's Faith: Paul and His Recent Interpreters* (Grand Rapids: Eerdmans, 1988).

RONALD E. CLEMENTS

Laying on of Hands
The practice of laying on hands is associated in both Testaments with the belief that certain individuals possess a power that can be transmitted to others by touch. In the OT it sometimes serves instead as a mark of identification of one kind or another. For example, the worshiper (or the priest) was to lay his hand on the head of a sacrificial animal (Lev 1:4; 8:22; etc.) to mark it as *his* gift, brought to the Lord (de Vaux, 416). The consecration of the Levites for service before the Lord also called for the Israelites to lay hands on their heads, by analogy to the bringing of an offering into God's presence (Num 8:9–13). In the case of one who blasphemed the holy name, the witnesses were to lay their hands on his head (Lev 24:14). This may have been a way to identify the guilty party, but may also involve a sense of power—transferring the pollution his act had produced back upon him.

There was one ritual that clearly involved the transfer of guilt. On the Day of Atonement, Aaron was to lay both hands upon the head of the scapegoat, to put upon it all of Israel's sins, but this animal was not sacrificed. It was sent away into the wilderness (Lev 16:21).

The other practices involving the laying on of hands include the power of *blessing*, of being chosen for a special work, and of healing. Jacob blessed Ephraim and Manasseh with his hands on their heads, and the blessing was more than kind words; it determined their futures (Gen 48:13–20). When children were brought to Jesus to be blessed, he laid his hands upon them (Matt 19:13–15; Mark 10:16). The seer in Rev 1:17 even sensed the right hand of the risen Christ upon him as he received a blessing. The gift of the Holy Spirit as a result of prayer and laying on of hands may also be included as one of the blessings associated with this practice (Acts 8:17; 19:6; and cf. 8:18–19).

The power to carry out Moses' special work was transferred from him to Joshua as Moses laid his hands on him (Num 27:18, 23; Deut 34:9). In a temporary way, King Joash shared the prophetic power of Elisha when the latter laid his hands on the king's hands (2 Kgs 13:16). The NT church may have been following the example of Moses (or perhaps of Num 8:9–13) by laying hands on those chosen to do the Lord's work (Acts 6:6; 13:3; 1 Tim 4:14; 2 Tim 1:6). Those responsible for the commissioning did not claim to be transferring their own power, however; for the act was an acknowledgment that the Holy Spirit had chosen those who were to take on new responsibility. The author of the letter to the Hebrews includes laying on hands as one of the six foundations of the church, along with repentance, faith, baptism, resurrection, and judgment (6:1–2), but does not explain what that rite meant to his community.

In one OT case the touch of hands is involved in a significant way in healing. Elisha lay on a dead child, mouth upon mouth, eyes upon eyes, and hands upon hands; and clearly it was thought that his prophetic power was transferred to the child, restoring him to life (2 Kgs 4:32–35). Many of Jesus' healing acts involved the touch of his hands. He healed the deaf and speechless man (Mark 7:32), the blind man (Mark 8:23–25), and the woman who could not stand up straight (Luke 13:13) by laying hands on them, and Jairus assumed Jesus could heal his daughter in the same way (Matt 9:18; Mark 5:23). Summaries of his healing acts also speak of laying on hands (Mark 6:5; Luke 4:40). Two of the healings in Acts are described this way (9:12, 17; 28:8), and there are other cases of healing by touch (3:7; 9:41). But when James offered advice concerning healing in the church, he did not assume that the elders possessed power they could transmit by laying on hands. They are told only to pray and anoint with oil (Jas 5:14–15).

Ordination in the church continues to use the NT practice of laying on hands as a way of commissioning those called to a special work. In keeping with NT usage, it represents the community's acknowledgment that this person has been chosen by the Holy Spirit, but in some traditions the sense of transfer of authority, as from Moses to Joshua, is also present.

Roland de Vaux, O.P., *Ancient Israel: Its Life and Institutions* (New York: McGraw-Hill, 1961), 416–18, 448–49, 452.

DONALD E. GOWAN

Leviathan   *see* **Animals**

Liberty   *see* **Free**

Lie, Lying, Liar   *see* **True**

Life, Live (*see also* **Eternal Life**)
The Bible is principally concerned with life—physical life, spiritual life, eternal life—and looks on life as being the most important feature of human existence, whether temporal or eternal. "Life" connotes the totality of God's relations with humanity, the quality of existence that God desires for all human beings, and the nature of relationships that God wants to bring about between humans whom he has created and redeemed. The Bible also speaks of God's dealing with sin, his defeat of death, and the redemption of his people from sin and **death**. But the essential message of the Bible, as found in Ezek 18:23, is this: "Have I any pleasure in the death of the wicked, says the Lord GOD, and not rather that they should turn from their ways and live?" (or as proclaimed by Jesus in John 10:10: "I came that they may have life, and have it abundantly").

Life in the Old Testament
The Hebrew word *hayyim* (which is plural in form, but as an abstract noun means simply "life") and its verb *hayah* ("to live," "to have life," "to live prosperously") have to do not only with physical life, as opposed to nonexistence and death, but also, more importantly, connote relationship with God, obedience to his will, and beneficial existence within the realm of divine grace. On the purely physical level, all animate beings have life and live (ani-

mals as well as humans). On the transcendental level, however, only humans are the possessors of life that has self-knowledge, potentialities, and the ability to be self-critical; that makes value judgments, expresses orientations, and enters into spiritual relationships. The Hebrew noun *nephesh* ("*soul*," "living being," or "creature"), which originally meant a light breath and so was taken to be the characteristic sign of life, is often used as a synonym for *hayyim*, with occasionally *yomim* ("days"; 1 Kgs 3:11; 2 Chr 1:11; Job 7:16; Ps 61:6; 91:16), *basar* ("flesh"; Gen 6:13, 17; 9:11; Deut 5:26; Ps 136:25), and once even 'etsem ("bone"; Job 7:15) being so used as well.

In the Old Testament generally. "The most significant aspect of the Hebrew understanding of 'life,'" as David Hill has pointed out, is "its dependence on God. Wherever there is life, it is God's gift" (*Greek Words,* 168). That God is the ultimate source for all human life is stated at the very beginning of the creation account of Gen 2: "In the day that the LORD God made the earth and the heavens . . . the LORD God formed man from the dust of the ground, and breathed into his nostrils the breath of life; and the man became a living being (*nephesh hayah*)" (vv. 4b and 7). And this created vitality is considered throughout the OT as the supreme good of human existence, which is never to be trivialized, relativized, or subsumed under some supposedly greater good. Though the statement is attributed to Satan in dialogue with God, it is nonetheless true: "All that people have they will give to save their lives" (Job 2:4). Throughout the OT, in fact, the prolongation of physical life to a ripe old age is regarded as a special grace (Gen 15:15; 25:8; 35:29; Job 42:17; Ps 128:1–6). It is at times even asserted that long life is the principal reward for keeping God's commands (Deut 5:16; 16:20; 30:19) or for pursuing divine wisdom (Prov 3:16; 9:10–11; 10:27; 24:14).

But the implanting of physical life at creation, while important, is not the major focus in the OT story of human existence. Rather, what sets the OT narrative off from all other ancient accounts of human life are the convictions that (1) God is the Lord of both life and death (Deut 32:39; Job 12:10; Ezek 18:4), and (2) God controls human destiny and has "the book of life" (Exod 32:32; Ps 69:28; Isa 4:3; Mal 3:16). Or as the psalmist has so eloquently stated in his praise of God: "With you is the fountain of life" (Ps 36:9). Furthermore, there was a consciousness among many godly Israelites that (1) life is more than mere physical existence, being not only created but also sustained, directed, and brought to fulfillment by God (Deut 8:3; Prov 19:23), and (2) somehow fellowship with God cannot be broken, even by death, for God has established an eternal covenant with his people (Ps 16:10–11; Prov 12:28). So God's people were to live in response to God's goodness and grace by being obedient to God's word, that is, to his instructions or torah.

The message of Moses. Thus Moses set before Israel "life and prosperity," on the one hand, and "death and adversity," on the other (Deut 30:15), and urged the people to "choose life" by "loving the LORD your God, walking in his ways, and observing his commandments, decrees, and ordinances" (Deut 30:16–20; cf. Lev 18:2–5). For, as Moses stated in his final exhortations, "This is no trifling matter for you, but rather your very life" (Deut 32:47). And so the refrain throughout the OT is this: "One does not live by bread alone, but by every word that comes from the mouth of the LORD" (Deut 8:3; cf. Amos 8:11).

The prophecy of Ezekiel. The prophet Ezekiel in particular highlights this understanding of human life lived in relation to God, thereby freeing it from dependence on all material, external support and relating it principally to "a word" from God's mouth (2:1; 3:17; et passim) or, as more often phrased, "the word of the LORD" (3:16; 6:1; 7:1; 12:1, 8, 17, 21; 13:1; 14:12; 15:1; 16:1; et passim). As Gerhard von Rad points out, the prophecy of Ezekiel contains "the culmination of the relationship between the

natural process of life and the Word of God," and, as von Rad goes on to insist, "The theological deduction from this belief is obviously that Israel is to understand elemental life quite radically in terms of grace" (*TDOT* 2.845).

Life in the New Testament

The Greek noun *zoe* ("life") and its verb *zao* ("to live") parallel the uses of the Hebrew noun *hayyim* and verb *hayah*. The Greek term *bios* is also at times equivalent to *hayyim* and *zoe* (1 John 2:16), though most often it is used with reference to the duration of one's earthly existence (i.e., "lifetime"; Luke 8:14; 1 Tim 2:2; 2 Tim 2:4; 1 Pet 4:2–3), or the means of sustaining one's physical life (e.g., "wealth"; Mark 12:44 and par. Luke 21:4; Luke 15:12, 30; possibly also Luke 8:43, as in some manuscripts). The Greek noun *psyche* ("soul," "breath of life," "life principle") is also equivalent in some of its uses to *hayyim* and *zoe*, though more frequently to the Hebrew *nephesh* as a synonym for natural life, both in its external, physical features and in its inner, personal, and spiritual aspects. And the noun *sarx* ("flesh"), like its Hebrew counterpart *basar*, while usually referring simply to the material body, is sometimes used synonymously with *psyche* to signify the human person in his or her mortal condition. Furthermore, going beyond the OT uses of *nephesh* and *basar*, both *psyche* and *sarx* appear in the NT as ethical adjectives—that is, *psychikos* and *sarkikos* or *sarkinos*—to denote (1) for *psychikos*, a characterization or feature that is purely natural, as opposed to what is supernatural and given by God (1 Cor 2:12; 15:44; Jas 3:15), and (2) for *sarkikos* and *sarkinos*, an orientation that belongs to the earthly order of things (Rom 15:27; 1 Cor 9:11), with such an orientation often represented as being opposed to the direction given by God through his Holy Spirit (Rom 7:14; 1 Cor 3:1, 3 [twice]; 2 Cor 10:4; Heb 7:16; 1 Pet 2:11).

In the New Testament generally. As with *hayyim* and *nephesh* in the OT, the terms *zoe* ("life") and *psyche* ("soul") in the NT can be used synonymously to mean physical, organic life (Mark 8:35; Luke 12:15, 20; et passim) and to refer to the natural existence of both humans and animals (1 Cor 15:45, where *psyche zosa,* "a living being," refers to Adam, and Rev 16:3, where *pasa psyche zoes,* "every living thing," refers to all animate creatures). Such life expresses created vitality, is sustained by physical nourishment, incorporates latent potentialities, and at its best is characterized as being in good health (Mark 5:23, et passim). But this earthly life is also mortal, perishable, "of the dust," mere "flesh and blood" (1 Cor 15:42–54), limited in its duration (Jas 4:14, "a mist that appears for a little while and then vanishes"), dysfunctional and sinful in its desires (Jas 4:1–3), "held in slavery by the fear of death" (Heb 2:15), and finally suffers a natural death (Phil 1:20; 2 Tim 4:6).

But human life, though sustained by physical nourishment and the wealth needed to provide that nourishment, cannot be assured by only such earthly matters. Rather, it depends ultimately on God and the power he gives through his Spirit (Rev 11:11), that is, on the "spirit of life" (*pneuma zoes*), which is not just the created vitality of life represented by the terms *nephesh* in the OT and *psyche* in the NT, but the gift of God "who gives breath to the people on [the earth] and spirit to those who walk in it" (Isa 42:5). Only God truly possesses life in himself (John 5:26; 6:57), lives eternally (Rev 4:9–10; 10:6; 15:7), and is immortal (1 Tim 6:16). He makes alive through his Spirit, and so his Spirit is called "life giving" (John 6:63; 1 Cor 15:45). Furthermore, God is the lord of life and death (Luke 12:20; 2 Cor 1:9; Jas 4:15) and the judge of both the living and the dead (Acts 10:42; 2 Tim 4:1; 1 Pet 4:5).

Human life in the NT, therefore, is absolutely dependent on God, who has life in himself and is the source of all life, and on the continued support and activity of God, who by his Spirit causes his will to be worked out in the lives of those he has created. Life takes its meaning not from its "longevity" or its "wealth," which are features of the term *bios,* but from God who is its creator, sustainer,

lord, and judge. So, as Rudolf Bultmann aptly states matters from a NT perspective: "Man, and specifically the believer, is not to live his life for himself, but for God, for the *kurios.* If he tries to live for himself, he lives for sin and death. His life stands under the question of its whence and whither" (*TDNT* 2.863).

The paradox of life in Jesus' teaching and ministry. One of the paradoxes of Jesus' teaching can be found at six places in the Gospels, which suggests something of its importance. Twice it is recorded in the parallel passages of Matt 10:39 and Luke 17:33 that when Jesus taught about discipleship he said: "Those who try to make their life secure will lose it, but those who lose their life will find it." Three times it is recorded, in the parallel passages of Matt 16:25; Mark 8:35; and Luke 9:24, that when facing his own death on the cross Jesus said, "Those who want to save their life will lose it, and those who lose their life for my sake [and for the sake of the gospel] will find [or save] it." And once when speaking about the coming "glorification" of the "Son of Man" on the cross, Jesus is reported in John 12:25 as saying, "Those who love their life lose it, and those who hate their life in this world will keep it for eternal life."

Such teaching is quite radical. For while it recognizes the validity of human existence, it calls on people to give up reliance on and merely protecting their own lives (following, rather, the example of Jesus in being faithful to his mission in proclaiming and bringing about the kingdom of God). In effect, as Xavier Leon-Dufour points out, Jesus was teaching his disciples that "one has to be able to put one's very existence at risk, rather than want to save it in betraying the cause of the gospel mission" (*Life and Death,* 35), or, as Leon-Dufour later summarizes this teaching of Jesus: "The human present is 'ecstasy,' a continued going-out of oneself. Therefore, I acknowledge that my life is not so much mine as his; it is an endless gift" (ibid., 41).

More particularly, however, the greatest paradox of Jesus' ministry is that while he came so that people "may have life and have it abundantly" (John 10:10), he effected this life through his own death (as well as, of course, his resurrection). The Synoptic Gospels tell us that the disciples were mystified by Jesus' speaking about his approaching death at Jerusalem (Mark 8:31; 9:31; 10:33–34; and pars.). How could the Messiah suffer and die? He was to conquer the enemies of Israel, overthrow the rule of the pagan Romans, and set up the everlasting throne of David. Surely the Messiah would go to Jerusalem for other purposes than to die! And this has been a common reaction of people throughout the past two millennia and today.

But the death of Jesus is not presented in the NT as an interlude in the story of God's greater work, the establishment of his kingdom. Rather, together with his resurrection, Jesus' death is at the heart of God's saving work, for it was the basis and means for the establishment of a new kind of life called *eternal life*. This new reality of the kingdom of God and this new type of life could only, it seems, be established at the cost of the death of God's Son, which was "a ransom for many" (Matt 20:28; Mark 10:45), with his blood being "the blood of the new covenant, which is poured out for many for the forgiveness of sins" (Matt 26:28).

Resurrection life in Paul. At many places in his letters Paul uses the noun *zoe* to mean physical life, whose antithesis is physical death (Rom 8:38; 1 Cor 3:22; Phil 1:20), even at times to signify simply his own "lifetime" (1 Cor 15:19; cf. 1 Tim 4:8). In line with OT declarations, which he often quotes in support, he proclaims that God is "the living God" (Rom 9:26; 2 Cor 3:3; 6:16; 1 Thess 1:9), who is not only the source of life but also the one "who gives life to the dead and calls into existence the things that do not exist" (Rom 4:17). Furthermore, Paul uses "eternal life" (*zoe aionios*) most often in an eschatological sense for the reward or blessing that God will bestow on the righteous in the future (Rom 2:7; 5:21; 6:22; Gal 6:8).

Nonetheless, while "life" and "eternal life" are in Paul's letters predominantly blessings bestowed by God on his people in the future, the apostle also uses "life" in the absolute sense as being the present possession of believers in Jesus (Rom 6:4, 11, 13; 8:2–10). It is, in fact, the content of his proclamation. So he commends his Philippian converts for "holding fast to the word of life" (Phil 2:16), which "word of life" in the context of his Philippian correspondence, as well as the apostle's letters generally, has to do with resurrection life. Paul's essential message focused on the resurrection life given by God through the death and resurrection of Jesus, the ministry of the Spirit, and human responses of faith. Or as David Hill has aptly characterized Paul's message of life: "By participating in the death and resurrection of Christ the man of faith receives the transformation of life now, in humility and hope, and also the entry into the life which is eternal" (*Greek Words,* 191).

Life and eternal life in the Gospels. The term "life" (*zoe*) appears fifteen times in the Synoptic Gospels, with the adjective "eternal" (*aionios*) being added in eight of these occurrences. "Life" and "eternal life" are often used equivalently (as, for example, in the rich man's question, "Teacher, what good deed must I do to have eternal life?" and Jesus' response: "If you wish to enter into life, keep the commandments"; Matt 19:16–17). The expression "eternal life," in particular, frequently refers to future, eschatological blessings, that is, the inheritance promised to the righteous in "the Age to Come" of Jewish expectation (Matt 19:29; 25:46; Mark 10:30; Luke 18:30). And the two terms are used at times interchangeably with the expression "the kingdom of God" or in Matthew's Gospel, "the kingdom of heaven" (Matt 19:23–29; Mark 9:43–47; 10:17–30; Luke 18:24–30).

More prominence, however, is given to the absolute use of "life" (*zoe*) and the expression "eternal life" (*zoe aionios*) in the Fourth Gospel than in the Synoptic Gospels, as can be seen from the statistics alone; "life" appears nineteen times and "eternal life" eighteen times, for a total of thirty-seven times, in John's Gospel. In addition, the verb "to live" (*zao*) appears in John seventeen times. The theme of life is introduced quite early in the Fourth Gospel with the statement "In him was life, and the life was the light of all people" (1:4); and it comes to dramatic conclusion with the statement of the evangelist's purpose for writing: "These are written so that you may come to believe that Jesus is the Messiah, the Son of God, and that through believing you may have life in his name" (20:31). Throughout the Fourth Gospel, there regularly recurs this theme of "life" and "eternal life"; for example, in (1) the promise of Jesus to those who would follow him: "I came that they may have life, and have it abundantly" (10:10); (2) many of the "I am" sayings of Jesus: "I am the bread of life" (6:35, 48); "I am the light of the world. Whoever follows me will never walk in darkness but will have the light of life" (8:12); "I am the resurrection and the life" (11:25); "I am the way, and the truth, and the life" (14:6); and (3) the most oft-quoted verse of John's Gospel: "For God so loved the world that he gave his one and only Son, so that everyone who believes in him may not perish but may have eternal life" (3:16). And this same emphasis on "life" and "eternal life" is found also in the other writings attributed to John, with these terms appearing eleven times in the three short Johannine epistles and fifteen times in the Johannine apocalypse.

In the Fourth Gospel, as in the Synoptic Gospels, "life" (*zoe*) is used most often, in concert with "eternal life" (*zoe aionios*), to connote a quality of life, that is, a personal relationship with God and the quality of the life of the Age to Come, not merely human existence (as with the term *psyche*) or the duration of one's human existence or its means of physical support (as with the term *bios*). What distinguishes the Fourth Gospel from the Synoptic Gospels in its use of "life" and "eternal life," however, is, first of all, its more "realized" emphasis in highlighting the present actualization of the life of the Age to Come (3:15, 36; 5:24, 40; 6:40,

47, 54; 10:28; 11:25; 17:3; 20:31), without denying that such actualizations will come to full culmination in the future. In illustration of his thesis that "in many ways John is the best example in the NT of realized eschatology," Raymond Brown has observed: "For the Synoptics 'eternal life' is something that one receives at the final judgment or in a future age (Mark x 30; Matt xviii 8–9), but for John it is a present possibility for men [i.e., 'people,' citing John 5:24]" (AB 1:cxviii). Furthermore, John's Gospel is to be distinguished from the Synoptic Gospels in its more explicit statements that true life has its source in God alone (5:26; 6:57), its more intense focus on Jesus as the possessor and mediator of this divine life (1:4; 5:26, 40; 6:33, 35, 48, 53, 63, 68; 8:12; 10:10, 28; 11:25; 14:6; 17:2–3; 20:31), and its express calls for a believing response to the person and work of Jesus in order to receive this new life (3:36; 5:24, 40; 6:35, 40, 47, 53–54, 68; 8:12; 11:25; 20:31).

The Gospel of John, however, differs from 1 John and the Johannine apocalypse in this: whereas the Gospel speaks most often of "life" and "eternal life" as present possessions, without denying a future fulfillment, 1 John and the Apocalypse, while also recognizing the believer's present possession (1 John 1:2; 5:11–12), have more of an emphasis on the future possession of life and its benefits (Rev 2:7, 10; 21:6–7; 22:14). This is probably, as C. F. D. Moule has repeatedly argued, because John's Gospel has an "extremely individualistic message" and an evangelistic purpose ("to bring outsiders within the fold of the believers"), which call for a message of response in the present, whereas 1 John and the Apocalypse are directed to communities of Christian believers who need warning and hope for the future, and so require a message of judgment and blessing in the future (*Birth of the New Testament*, 93–96; see also *NovT* 5 [1962]: 171–90; *JTS* 15 [1964]: 10; *Phenomenon of the New Testament*, 103). But however that may be, no more all-encompassing term appears in either the Synoptic Gospels or the Johannine writings, or for that matter throughout the OT and the NT, than that of "life," to connote the totality of God's relations with humanity, the quality of existence God desires for all human beings, and the nature of relationships God wants to bring about between humans whom God has created and redeemed.

Raymond Brown, *The Gospel according to John (I–XII)*, AB (Garden City, N.Y.: Doubleday, 1966); David Hill, *Greek Words and Hebrew Meanings: Studies in the Semantics of Soteriological Terms* (Cambridge: Cambridge University Press, 1967), 163–201; Xavier Leon-Dufour, *Life and Death in the New Testament: The Teachings of Jesus and Paul*, trans. T. Prendergast (San Francisco: Harper & Row, 1986); Richard N. Longenecker, ed., *Life in the Face of Death: The Resurrection Message of the New Testament* (Grand Rapids: Eerdmans, 1998); C. F. D. Moule, *The Birth of the New Testament* (London: Black, 1962, 1966²); idem, "The Individualism of the Fourth Gospel," *NovT* 5 (1962): 171–90; idem, "The Influence of Circumstances on the Use of Eschatological Terms," *JTS* 15 (1964): 1–15; idem, *The Phenomenon of the New Testament* (London: SCM, 1967); Gerhard von Rad, Georg Bertram, and Rudolf Bultmann, "zao, zoe," *TDNT* 2:832–75.

RICHARD N. LONGENECKER

Light, Dark, Darkness

Light: Hebrew mostly ʾor; Greek *phos*. Dark, Darkness: Hebrew *hoshek, ophel, ʾaphelah, ʿaraphel*; Greek *skotos, skotia*.

While the word "light" is often used literally in the Bible, it is also frequently used figuratively. In some passages, it is difficult to determine which use is intended, and it is entirely possible that some biblical writers would not have made the distinction.

Like most other religious traditions, the Bible associates "light" with God, the presence of God, the work of God, and humans who do the will of God. Where God is, there is "light." "Light" is used in the Bible as a sign of God's presence in the world, offering life and order to creation.

The first words of God in the Bible are "Let there be light" (Gen 1:3). God created light and "God saw that the light was good" (1:4a). God separated light from darkness and "called the light Day, and the darkness he called Night" (1:4b–5). Thus God's first act of creation established life and order and separated life and order from death and chaos.

"Light" characterizes the relationship of God with humans (Conzelmann, 319). "God is light," John affirms (1 John 1:5), "and in him there is no darkness at all." John's two-pronged affirmation asserts first that God is the source of life and order, and second that death and chaos cannot come from God. God's "light" is the source of guidance for humans. God's word is a "lamp" and a "light" that illuminates human life (Ps 119:105).

The psalmist describes God as being "wrapped in light as with a garment" (104:2) and affirms that in God's light, "we see light" (36:9). And so the prayer is uttered: "Let the light of your face shine on us, O LORD!" (Ps 4:6; see also Num 6:25; Pss 31:16; 44:3; 80:7). "Light dawns for the righteous" (Ps 97:11), so the psalmist can declare, "The LORD is my light and my salvation; whom shall I fear?" (27:1).

Light is an important symbol for salvation and deliverance in the OT. Conversely, darkness is understood as a way of thinking about the absence of divine deliverance (Mic 7:8–9; 2 Sam 22:29; Ps 18:28; Isa 9:2; 42:16). Exodus 10:21–23 describes the ninth plague as a plague of darkness against Egypt, "but all the Israelites had light where they lived." This contrast between darkness and light is a contrast between the impotence of the sun god of Egypt and the power of the God of Israel to save, a contrast between destruction and deliverance (Brueggemann, 766). That God works to deliver and to destroy is affirmed in Isa 45:7, where God declares through the prophet, "I form light and create darkness, I make weal (or well-being; Heb. *shalom*) and create woe; I the LORD do all these things."

Before God created light, "the earth was a formless void and darkness covered the face of the deep" (Gen 1:2). Darkness symbolizes death (Isa 5:30; 47:5; Ps 143:3; Job 17:13) and can be thought of as being the result of disobedience to God's will (Deut 28:29; Ps 35:6).

While the Israelites looked with longing for the great day of the Lord, when God will deliver the people of God, Amos warned that the day of the Lord would not be a bright day filled with light but a day of darkness and gloom (5:18–20). And yet Zechariah held on to a hope that the great day of the Lord would inaugurate an age when there would be "continuous day," when even "at evening time there shall be light" (Zech 14:7; cf. Isa 60:19–20).

Use of the contrasting images of light and darkness continued during the intertestamental period. This contrast is especially clear in the Dead Sea Scrolls from Qumran, where light and darkness are symbolic of good and evil. In the Qumran scroll known as the Community Rule, there are children of light and children of darkness. (See 1QS 1, 3.) The Qumran community viewed the final battle as a war between the children of light and the children of darkness. This battle is described in the Qumran War Scroll (1QM).

A similar contrast between light and darkness is apparent in the NT. Picking up the same wording as is found in the Dead Sea Scrolls, Paul assures his Thessalonian readers that they "are not in darkness," but are instead "all children of light and children of the day" (1 Thess 5:4–5). Paul further develops a light/darkness contrast in 2 Corinthians. He asserts that "Satan disguises himself as an angel of light" (11:14) and describes Satan or Beliar (6:15) as "the god of this world" (4:4). Paul asserts that this "god of this world has blinded the minds of the unbelievers, to keep them from seeing the light of the gospel of the glory of Christ, who is the image of God" (4:4). In contrast to "the god of this world," the God who created light at the time of creation "has shone in our hearts to give the light of the knowledge of the glory of God in the face of Jesus Christ" (4:6).

Paul's mention of Jesus Christ signals the key point of development in the NT regarding the idea of "light." When "light" is used figuratively in the NT, it is often used in reference to Jesus. This is especially true of the Johannine writings, where themes of light and darkness are most fully developed. "God is light and in him is no darkness at all" (1 John 1:5). Yet Jesus declares, "I am the light of the world" (John 8:12; 9:5; see also 12:46). It was through Jesus that God's light came into the world (John 1:1–5; 3:19). God is light, and God's light shines into the world through Jesus.

In Matt 5:14, Jesus declares that those who follow him are "the light of the world." God is light, and Jesus is the light of God in the world, so Jesus' followers are supposed to shine with the light of God that is in the world. Eschatological punishment is described in Matthew's Gospel as "outer darkness" (8:12; 22:13; 25:30).

Although NT writers often used light imagery in reference to Jesus, some NT passages continue the OT practice of using light imagery with God. For example, in language that has echoes of Ps 104:2, 1 Tim 6:16 declares that God "dwells in unapproachable light." James 1:17, speaking of God as the source of "every perfect gift," refers to God as "the Father of lights, with whom there is no variation or shadow due to change."

In the Revelation, John builds on the prophets' eschatological hope for the day when there will be no more darkness and light will prevail. John declares that in the New Jerusalem sun and moon will no longer be needed for "God is its light, and its lamp is the Lamb" (21:23). By this light of God "the nations will walk" (21:24; see also 22:5).

_____

Elizabeth Achtemeier, "Jesus Christ, the Light of the World: The Biblical Understanding of Light and Darkness," *Int* 17 (1963): 439–49; Walter Brueggemann, *The Book of Exodus, NIB* 1; Hans Georg Conzelmann, "*phos*," *TDNT* 9:310–58.

JAMES A. DURLESSER

Likeness   *see* **Image**

Look   *see* **See**

Lord   NRSV uses the word "lord" in the OT usually for the Hebrew noun ʾ*adon;* in the NT the NRSV renders with "lord" almost exclusively the Greek *kyrios* (except Acts 4:24 and Rev 6:10 where *despotes* is translated "Sovereign Lord"). In both Testaments the word is used both denoting mastery or rule over persons or things that are part of the secular world and as a divine attribute speaking of God as ruler.

The secular use of "Lord." OT and NT exhibit little difference in the secular usage of the word "lord." The lord is, by definition, distinguished from the servant or slave who is under the lord's power. "A disciple is not above the teacher, nor a slave above the master" (Matt 10:24, where "master" translates *kyrios*). As in Matt 24:10, NRSV frequently renders the Hebrew ʾ*adon* and the Greek *kyrios* not with "lord" but with "master" or a similar term more adapted to contemporary usage. Abraham's servant who is sent out to secure a wife for Isaac refers to Abraham as "my master (ʾ*adoni*) Abraham" (Gen 24:12, 27), who has become a wealthy man having many "male and female slaves" (24:35). In the parable of the unmerciful servant NRSV preserves the contrast between the "lord" and his "slaves" (Matt 18:23–35), but often it chooses the less harsh "master" to denote the same relationship, as in Col 4:1, "Masters, treat your slaves justly and fairly" (cf. Eph 6:5, 9). Lordship can extend over nonhuman objects also. Joseph is the lord of the land of Egypt (Gen 45:8), and a certain Shemer is the owner (ʾ*adon*) of a hill that is to become Samaria (1 Kgs 16:24). The NT speaks of the owner (*kyrios*) of a vineyard (Mark 12:9) and the master (*kyrios*) of a house (Mark 13:35).

The words ʾ*adon* and *kyrios* are employed as polite forms of address. Frequent in the OT is the address to a king "my lord the king" (e.g., 1 Sam 24:8). In the NT the word *kyrios* appears when a person is addressed with a sense of respect. NRSV captures this meaning by translating with "sir": the son calls his father "sir" (Matt 21:30), Greeks approach Philip with the same address (John 12:21), and the chief priests and Pharisees appeal to Pilate as "sir" (Matt 27:62–63). In the Gospels and in Acts Jesus is often addressed in the same way. NRSV translates the Greek address *kyrie* either with "sir" (Mark 7:29; John 4:11, 15, 19, 49; 5:7; 6:34; 8:11; 9:36; 20:15) or, much more frequently, with "Lord" (e.g., Matt 15:22, 25, 27; Luke 7:6; 19:8). The choice of different words in NRSV to render the address *kyrie* to Jesus is due to the difficulty of deciding whether the intent is no more than a polite and respectful greeting or an application of the christological title "Lord" (see below). A precise and definite determination is in most cases difficult to achieve. It is entirely possible that the question whether we are meant to hear in a specific case merely a polite greeting or a confessionally determined title cannot be resolved, because the connotations were already inseparable to those who transmitted the tradition.

Lord as title/name for God. The word "Lord" (ʾ*adon*) is used as a title of the God of Israel in very early OT documents. The song of Moses places the name Yahweh and the title Lord (ʾ*adonai*) in conjunction (Exod 15:17; NRSV renders with the repeated "O LORD," adopting a secondary text variant), and Exod 23:17 uses the phrase "the Lord GOD" (*haʾadon yhwh*). The title "Lord" for Yahweh is often used to emphasize the unlimited sovereignty of Israel's God over the whole earth and over all other gods: Yahweh is "the Lord of all the earth" (Josh 3:13; cf. Ps 97:5; Zech 6:5); "the LORD (*yhwh*) is great, our Lord (ʾ*adonenu*) is above all gods" (Ps 135:5); "the LORD (*yhwh*) . . . is God of gods and Lord of lords (ʾ*adone haʾadonim*)" (Deut 10:17; similar, Ps 136:1–3). Approximately with the beginning of the Hellenistic age (death of Alexander the Great in 323 B.C.) there occurs an increasing tendency in

Judaism to avoid the use of the name Yahweh and to substitute in the reading of OT texts the pronunciation of the tetragram *yhwh* with the title "Lord" (*ʾadonai*) (see **God**). The OT concept of Yahweh as creator of heaven and earth, as the ruler of world history, including nations not knowing Yahweh's name, as the divine authority beyond all gods, and as the sovereign over the ultimate destiny of all things—this inheritance of OT faith was cast into the embracing word "Lord" so that it ceased to be merely a description of God and became synonymous with God's name indicating the essence of the divine being.

It has been taken for granted that translations of the OT into Greek translated the Hebrew tetragram with *kyrios*, "Lord." The oldest complete codices of OT and NT, from the fourth and fifth centuries A.D., show that this was indeed uniformly accepted Christian tradition at the time the manuscripts were written. But relatively recently investigations have shown that in Greek translations of the OT produced by Jews for Greek-speaking Jews before the time of the NT, the letters of the divine name Yahweh were not translated but were inserted into the Greek text with Hebrew script. This discovery cast doubt on the common assumption that, at the time our NT authors wrote, the rendition of *yhwh* by *kyrios* in Greek translations had been standard practice. On the other hand, it is certain that Greek-speaking Jews of NT times knew of the rendition of the tetragram with the Greek *kyrios* and that Palestinian Jews were familiar with addressing God as "Lord," either in Aramaic or in Hebrew (see J. A. Fitzmyer, 1979 and 1998). It is also certain that many NT authors spoke of God as Lord (*kyrios*) not only in quotes from the OT but also in independent turns of phrases that disclose their own linguistic practices. In the Synoptic Gospels Jesus talks of God almost exclusively as Father (see **abba**). But even Jesus' speech, as the Synoptics present it, includes an occasional reference to God as Lord. The invocation

of God in Matt 11:25 begins with the words "Father, Lord of heaven and earth," and the discourse on the end time contains the statement "if the Lord had not cut short those days," where the Lord is identical with the Creator who is mentioned in the preceding verse (Mark 13:19–20). In Matthew's language God has spoken as "the Lord through the prophet" (Matt 1:22), and in Luke's narrative the parents of John the Baptist have lived a life "according to all the commandments and regulations of the Lord" (Luke 1:6). Matthew 1:22 and Luke 1:6 are here quoted only as examples of a linguistic pattern that permeates those Gospels as a whole. Paul is very familiar with the use of the title "Lord" for God. He had an OT text before him in which the divine name Yahweh was translated as "Lord" (*kyrios*), a fact that is evidenced in many of his OT quotations, for example, in Rom 4:8, where the person is called blessed "against whom the Lord will not reckon sin," quoting Ps 32:2, "Happy are those to whom the LORD (*yhwh*) imputes no iniquity."

Jesus Christ the Lord. The letters of Paul show that the title "Lord" was applied to Jesus, remembered as a person of history. The Jesus tradition that Paul knows and hands on contains specific instructions that are remembered as commands of the Lord. The prohibition of divorce and the regulation that preachers of the gospel should be supported by the congregations are remembered as teachings of the Lord (1 Cor 7:10; 9:14). First Thessalonians 4:15 refers to a lost saying of Jesus as the "word of the Lord." James is mentioned by Paul as "the Lord's brother" (Gal 1:19), and without names a group of "the brothers of the Lord" is placed alongside the other apostles (1 Cor 9:5).

The picture in the Gospels is, in part, in agreement with the language of Paul. Addresses of the earthly Jesus by a variety of people were mentioned above; the use of the word "lord" in these contexts remains often ambiguous. But, aside from these instances, some Gospels employ the term "lord" freely in contexts that indicate the evangelist's own preference. Writing in narratives about Jesus, Luke calls him "Lord" about fifteen times, from the infancy narratives (1:43; 2:11) to the notice of the empty tomb (24:34). In Luke's view, the use of the title "Lord" to identify the earthly Jesus does not stand in conflict with traditions, preserved in Acts, that connect the lordship of Jesus with the act of God in Jesus' resurrection and ascension, an act through which God "made him both Lord and Messiah" (Acts 2:32–36; cf. 4:33; 9:27). Similar to Luke is the language of the Gospel of John, although it is far less readily employed than in Luke. Outside the use of the title "Lord" in the resurrection narratives of the Fourth Gospel (20:2, 13, 18, 20, 25; 21:7, 12), John tells of the "Lord" in accounts of incidents in Jesus' life (4:1 Mg; 6:23; 11:2). Quite different is the tradition in Mark and in Matthew. They do not speak of Jesus as Lord during their accounts of his activity and teaching prior to the last days in Jerusalem. Only then, Matthew and Mark report about two scenes in which Jesus refers to himself as "Lord." Mark 11:3 and Matt 21:3 tell of Jesus' instruction to two disciples to secure a donkey (Matt: two animals) because "the Lord needs it (them)." The dispute about whether the messiah is David's son or David's Lord (Mark 12:35–37; Matt 22:41–46) is answered with reference to Ps 110:1, a verse that in the NT became one of the most widely used OT echoes with christological intentions. The question of the messiah's relation to David contains the implication that the Christ is David's Lord, a conclusion that is attributed to Jesus. Surveying the traditions of the NT as a whole, one can note that two different concepts stand side by side. In Mark and Matthew we find no identification of Jesus with the titular use of "Lord," with the exceptions mentioned above, while in Luke, John, and Paul the earthly Jesus is called "Lord" in the sense of a christological title of distinction.

The simplest, and most basic, Christian confession is the sentence "Jesus is Lord." It is understood in Paul's congregations that "no one can say 'Jesus is Lord' except by the Holy Spirit" (1 Cor 12:3). The confession that Jesus is Lord arises out of the event of the resurrection. Already pre-Pauline statements talk of the resurrection and exaltation of Jesus as the act of God through which Jesus was installed into the status of Lord. Philippians 2:9–11, an early Christian hymn quoted by Paul, adopts the model of the ceremony of installation used for Oriental kings to celebrate the exaltation of Jesus, who had humbled himself, taking on himself the status of a slave. The enthronement of Jesus is done by God, who confers on him a new name after which the entire creation pays homage to him by prostrating themselves before him and acknowledging the throne name given to the new ruler. In this enthronement the name given to the master of the universe is the title "Lord."

A different piece of pre-Pauline tradition is found in Rom 1:3–4, which tells of the gospel of God's Son "who was descended from David according to the flesh and was declared to be Son of God with power according to the spirit of holiness by resurrection from the dead, Jesus Christ our Lord." The first stage of Jesus' life is, in this tradition, superseded by a second stage in which resurrection marks the transition to sonship of God, which is the ground for the confession "Jesus Christ our Lord." Romans 10:9 states that the power of salvation is at work "if you confess with your lips that Jesus is Lord and believe in your heart that God raised him from the dead." In this statement, the public confession and the internal faith are put together in a way that identifies the confession "Jesus is Lord" with the faith in God who raised Jesus from the dead.

Often the installation of Jesus as Lord through his resurrection is expressed through a reference to the christologically understood Ps 110:1. The psalm's sentence "The LORD says to my lord, 'Sit at my right hand until I make your enemies your footstool'" is interpreted to mean the placing of Jesus at God's right hand.

After quoting Ps 110:1, Acts 2:36 continues, "God has made him [i.e., Jesus whom God raised up, 2:32] both Lord and Messiah." To sit at the right hand of God is nothing other than the status of lordship, even when the title Lord is not expressly used, and this sitting at God's right hand is consistently connected with God's raising of Jesus from the dead: "It is Christ Jesus, who died, yes, who was raised, who is at the right hand of God" (Rom 8:34). "God put his power to work in Christ when he raised him from the dead and seated him at his right hand in the heavenly places, far above all rule and authority and power and dominion, and above every name that is named, not only in this age but also in the age to come" (Eph 1:20–21). Hebrews 1:3–4 says of the Son of God, "When he had made purification of sins, he sat down at the right hand of the Majesty on high, having become as much superior to angels as the name he has inherited is more excellent than theirs."

Jesus the Lord is expected as the future one whose coming will complete God's work of redemption. "The Lord comes," and "the coming of the Lord" are repeated phrases in Paul's letters (1 Cor 4:5; 11:26; 15:23; 1 Thess 2:19; 3:13; 4:15; 5:23). The formation of the title "Lord" in its application to the risen Christ is linked to the expectation of his coming. The prayer "Our Lord, come" (1 Cor 16:22) translates in the NRSV an Aramaic phrase preserved in its Aramaic wording in the Greek text. The Aramaic prayer, *maranatha*, can be spelled in different ways and can be rendered either as a request, "Our Lord, come," or as a statement, "Our Lord has come." The very end of the book of Revelation contains the same phrase, "Amen. Come, Lord Jesus" (Rev 22:20), and here the verb has the form of a petition. The Aramaic prayer *maranatha* is also found at the end of the eucharistic prayer in the *Didache* (*Did* 10:1–6), an early-second-century work of the Apostolic Fathers. The connection of the petition "Our Lord, come" to the celebration of the Lord's Supper is also evident in the tradition of its institution that Paul has handed on in 1 Cor 11:23–26, where we have the concluding remark that the eating of the bread and the drinking of the cup is a proclamation of the Lord's death "until he comes." Very early, then, Aramaic-speaking Palestinian Christians assembled to share the Lord's Supper, and in this celebration the risen Christ was called "our Lord" whose coming was implored. As the coming Lord, the risen Christ, seated at the right hand of God, is going to judge the world, participating in God's prerogative. Paul counts himself among those who will be judged by the Lord (1 Cor 4:4), as all Christians are subject to being judged by him (1 Cor 11:32). The "day of the Lord" (1 Cor 1:8; 2 Cor 1:14) is approaching. God's Son from heaven "rescues us from the wrath that is coming" (1 Thess 1:10), but that does not exclude that Christian believers will receive their rewards and suffer their losses (1 Cor 3:14–15). Even a wrongdoer whom Paul expels from the Christian community and so suffers "destruction of the flesh" remains answerable to the Lord in whose day he will be saved (1 Cor 5:5).

The Christian community—and each individual within it—is called to serve the Lord (Rom 12:11). The lordship of Jesus Christ, whom God made victor over all powers inimical to God's purpose, is the motif and dynamic that inspires the ethics of the Christian congregations. Often, therefore, exhortations to faithful living are combined with the appeal to act "in the Lord." The primary reason for conduct becoming a Christian is to "render service with enthusiasm, as to the Lord and not to men and women" (Eph 6:7). All members of the Christian community are called, each in their own way, to serve their Lord: wives are to be subject to their husbands "as is fitting in the Lord" (Col 3:18); children are to obey their parents as their "acceptable duty in the Lord" (Col 3:20); slaves are to obey their masters "fearing the Lord" (Col 3:22); the conduct of all is determined by the challenge "Whatever you do, in word or deed, do everything in the name of the Lord Jesus, giving thanks to God the Father through him" (Col 3: 17).

Very often the titles "Lord" and "Christ" (see **anoint**) are combined in Paul's letters, especially in the frequent phrase "our Lord Jesus Christ" (e.g., Rom 5:1, 11, 21). As Lord, the risen Christ is exalted to the position of God, the victor over powers in conflict with God, accomplishing God's work of reconciliation and redemption, judging on behalf of God, and inspiring service in those who have God's Spirit. As Christ, Jesus is the man who steps into the place of a sinful humanity, who becomes sin for us (2 Cor 5:21), a curse under the condemnation of the law (Gal 3:13), the one destined to die on the cross (Rom 5:6, 8; 1 Cor 1:23; 2:2). The two titles must never be severed one from the other. Only the one who bears condemnation is, by God's judgment and power, the Lord who shares God's rule.

Joseph Fitzmyer, "New Testament *Kyrios* and *Maranatha* and Their Aramaic Background," in *To Advance the Gospel: New Testament Studies*, 2d ed. (Grand Rapids: Eerdmans, 1998), 218–35; Joseph Fitzmyer, "The Semitic Background of the New Testament *Kyrios*-Title," in *A Wandering Aramean: Collected Aramaic Essays* (Missoula, Mont.: Scholars Press, 1979), 115–42; Larry Hurtado, *One God, One Lord: Early Christian Devotion and Ancient Jewish Monotheism*, 2d ed. (Edinburgh: T. & T. Clark, 1998).

ULRICH W. MAUSER

Love

Love in the Old Testament

The central word for love in the Hebrew Bible is ʾahab. Love usually requires some form of action, but the word is rooted in emotion and affection. The act of love is often described with words of desire and pleasure. Love prompts one to desire (Ps 34:12–13) or cleave to another person (Deut 11:22; Prov 18:24), to pursue (Jer 2:25) the object of love, to take pleasure in (1 Sam 16:21; 18:20), or to be knit to another (1 Sam 18:1), suggesting union.

The meaning of "love" in Hebrew is broad, ranging from romance, including a sexual relationship (Gen 24:67), to community ethics, as in loving one's neighbor (Lev 19:18). Love usually describes an interpersonal relationship between the sexes (Jacob and Rachel, Gen 29:18), companions (David and Jonathan, 1 Sam 20:17; 2 Sam 1:26), or between God and humans (Exod 20:6; Hos 3:1). Less often humans are described as loving objects such as food (Gen 27:4) or even sleep (Isa 56:10). Other Hebrew words signifying love include *raham* (**"mercy"**), *hesed* (**"steadfast love"**), *hashaq* ("to cling," Deut 7:7; NRSV: "set his heart on"), and *dod* ("beloved," especially in the Song of Songs). The LXX translates the Hebrew ʾahab with the various forms of the Greek *agapao*, which narrows in meaning, excluding the sexual background of the Hebrew term. Sexual desire is conveyed in Greek by *eros*, a word absent from the NT.

Love and marriage. Love describes the sexual attraction between a man and a woman within the context of marriage. Isaac loved Rebekah (Gen 24:67) and Jacob loved Rachel (29:18, 20, 30), signaling their marriage. The Preacher offers advice, "Enjoy life with the wife whom you love" (Eccl 9:9). Proverbs 5:18–20 underscores the desire and sexual emotion in love. The teacher encourages the pupil to "rejoice in the wife of your youth, a lovely deer," whose breasts satisfy, and whose love "intoxicates." The intoxication of love is immediate and often all-consuming. Its passion can entice, overpower, and persuade. When Samson refuses to share the secret of a riddle with his Philistine wife, she coaxes the secret out of him with an accusation, "You hate me; you do not really love me" (Judg 14:16). The language of love and hate in this context is a contrast between marriage and divorce, in which the declaration of *hate* for a wife signals the act of divorce by a husband (see the statement of Samson's father-in-law, Judg 15:2).

Love need not be associated with marriage. It can convey the raw emotion of sexual desire and the passion of romance.

The Song of Songs celebrates the power of love "as better than wine" (Song 1:2; 4:10), again suggesting its intoxicating effects. It makes the lovers faint (2:5). The woman describes her male partner as "beloved" or "darling" (*dod,* 2:8, 17; 7:11, 13; 8:14), a term of sexual endearment. He is beautiful and lovely (1:16), the object of her desire, resulting in a passionate ecstasy that forces her into the city at night in search of her beloved (3:1–5; 5:2–6:3). But such desire is dangerous. The female repeatedly warns her friends of the power of love, cautioning them, "do not stir up or awaken love until it is ready" (2:7; 3:5; 8:4). She describes the passion of love as fierce, beyond the measurement of wealth (8:7). It is able to compete with the cosmic forces of fire and even the mythological flood waters (8:7). The strength of love even surpasses death itself, it is "passion fierce as the grave" (8:6).

The story of Amnon's rape of Tamar (2 Sam 13) illustrates the dark side of the desire at the heart of love. The story opens with the statement that "Amnon fell in love with her" (v. 1). His passion for Tamar is sexual to the point where it becomes physically overwhelming. He becomes sick and is bedridden, requiring the care of Tamar, whom he forces to have intercourse with him ("Come, lie with me," v. 11). The story illustrates the violence of love and its volatile nature. Love can overwhelm the human will, creating interpersonal and social violence. Amnon's love for Tamar drives him to rape her. And once the violence was completed, his volatile love is transformed into its opposition, hate in the form of a "loathing . . . even greater than the lust he had felt for her" (v. 15). And to complete the social violation of Tamar, when King David was informed of the rape, he "would not punish his son Amnon, because he loved him, for he was his firstborn" (v. 21).

Love's passion becomes a theological motif in the prophetic tradition. The prophet Hosea describes the Israelites' rejection of God as an illicit love affair. Israel, like the prophet's prostitute wife, Gomer, pursues lovers for the immediacy of pleasure and the resulting money (Hos 2:7, 10, 12, 13). The Israelites love idols, lewdness, sexual orgies (Hos 4:18), the prostitute's pay (Hos 9:1), and even the act of oppression (Hos 12:7). And as a result, they are transformed into the object of their desire (Hos 9:10). The book of Hosea uses the sexual background of the illicit love affair to probe the divine response to the Israelites' religious unfaithfulness as though God were the offended lover. The deity commands the prophet, "Go, love a woman who has a lover and is an adulteress, just as the LORD loves the people of Israel, though they turn to other gods and love raisin cakes" (Hos 3:1). The passion of love allows the prophet to probe the emotion of God and the intimacy between the deity and the Israelites. God desires the intimacy of love, promising to "allure [Israel] into the wilderness . . . and speak tenderly to her" (Hos 2:14). God and the Israelites are bound together in the wilderness with bands of love (Hos 11:4). But the unfaithfulness of the people so enrages the deity that love is transformed into hate. At Gilgal, God states, "I came to hate them" (Hos 9:15). Yet divine hate cannot be the last word in the relationship. The passion of love resurfaces, prompting God to purge anger, and, instead, to love Israel freely (Hos 14:4).

The book of Jeremiah expands the marriage tradition of Hosea to describe the relationship of the Israelites and God as a bride and groom. God states, "I remember the devotion of your youth, your love as a bride, how you followed me in the wilderness" (Jer 2:2). But, as in the book of Hosea, the people become vulnerable to the volatility of love's passion, prostituting themselves in the land (Jer 3:1–5) and loving false prophecy (Jer 5:31). The book of Jeremiah explores the same themes of love and hate in the character of God. And as in the book of Hosea, the love of God prevails. God proclaims, "I have loved you with an everlasting love; therefore I have continued my faithfulness (steadfast love) to you" (Jer 31:3). The book of Jeremiah also goes beyond

Hosea in exploring the intimacy between prophet and deity with images of love. The book of Hosea explored the prophet's passion in love through his marriage to a prostitute, which then provided analogy to the passion of God for the Israelites. The passion of love between the prophet Hosea and God was not explored directly. The book of Jeremiah does not state that God loves the prophet or that the prophet loves God, yet imagery of love is central. The prophet Jeremiah becomes overpowered directly by the passion of God. The lament of the prophet is filled with the sexual imagery of love, "O LORD, you have enticed me, and I was enticed; you have overpowered me, and you have prevailed" (Jer 20:7). But within the broader context of Israel's infidelity, the enticement of God is experienced as social violence and not as the ecstasy of the Song of Songs. The prophet becomes the object of social ridicule. "Everyone mocks me," he states, leading to the outburst, "I must shout, 'Violence and destruction!'" (Jer 20:7–8). Yet the passion of God is unrelenting within the prophet: "If I say, 'I will not mention him, or speak any more in his name,' then within me there is something like a burning fire shut up in my bones; I am weary with holding it in, and I cannot" (Jer 20:9). Emotion similar to that of the prophet Jeremiah is voiced through the language of love in the Psalms. The psalmist declares, "I love you, O LORD" (Ps 18:1), and encourages the fellow worshiper to share the affection: "Love the LORD, all you his saints" (Ps 31:23).

Love and community. Love also describes ethical actions between humans and in the larger community. The emotional content of love remains—it is an attitude and outlook that prompts action—but the sexual connotations fade. The student in the book of Proverbs is encouraged to love wisdom and discipline (Prov 12:1). Wisdom requires the love of oneself (Prov 19:8). It also demands love between friends, which must be constant, not fickle (Prov 17:17). And the one who loves

wisdom will pursue acts of righteousness, resulting in God's love (Prov 15:9). Personified wisdom declares, "I love those who love me" (Prov 8:17). The prophets and the Psalms echo the teaching of Proverbs. The psalmists repeatedly declare that God loves justice (Ps 33:5; 37:28; 99:4). The prophet Amos encourages his audience to "hate evil and love good," requiring the establishment of justice at the city gate (Amos 5:15). The prophet Micah takes the call to love even further. It is not simply the establishment of justice, but the love of kindness itself (i.e., steadfast love, Mic 6:8). The Priestly legislation formulates the teaching of Proverbs and the prophets into a law that envisions an ideal society: "You shall love your neighbor as yourself" (Lev 19:18). The command to love includes both fellow citizens and the resident alien: "You shall love the alien as yourself" (Lev 19:34).

The book of Deuteronomy provides extensive theological reflection on the role of love in community and in covenant with God. God is the source of love in humans. The Israelites are able to love God because the Lord circumcised their hearts and the hearts of their descendants (Deut 30:6). The election of the Israelites to be the people of God and the divine act of their salvation from Egypt are rooted in the love of God for their ancestors (Deut 4:37; 10:15). God's love finds expression in the revelation of law, which establishes covenant. The Israelites are commanded to obey the law of Torah as an expression of their love for God. The *Shema*^c commands the Israelites, "You shall love the LORD your God with all your heart, and with your soul, and with all your might" (Deut 6:4), indicating that the love of God is internalized in the will of humans. And as a result, love is not simply a law to be fulfilled through actions that lack proper motivation. Love is affection, stemming from the heart of humans, which finds expression in obedience to the Torah (Deut 7:9, 13; 11:1, 13, 22; 19:9; 30:16). When heart and actions reflect the harmony of love, they prompt even more love from God (Deut 7:13).

The meditation on the law of God in Ps 119 shares the theology of the book of Deuteronomy. The psalmist repeatedly declares, "Oh, how I love your law!" (Ps 119:97, see also vv. 47, 48, 113, 119, 127, 159, 163). Again, the love of law goes beyond legalistic observance. It is the object of meditation and the source of life for the psalmist.

Love in the New Testament

In classical and Hellenistic Greek the passionate and sexual dimension of Hebrew ʾahab is conveyed by the word eros. Eros is love that intoxicates, seeking satisfaction wherever it may be found. Eros could also be spiritualized into a form of ecstasy. Plato already describes eros as creative inspiration (Symposium 200). And the Neoplatonist Plotinus understands eros as a form of sublime mysticism. It is love that transcends the human senses and rationality (Enneades III, 5). The translators of the LXX avoided the word eros in translating the Hebrew ʾahab, even though the Hebrew conveyed a broad range of sexual and emotional forms of love. They chose instead the Greek agapao to emphasize choice, selection, and action in the meaning of love, rather than the impulsive desire of eros. The New Testament is based on the LXX translation. As a result, the more passionate and volatile meaning of love in the Hebrew Bible, summarized under the heading Love and marriage, gives way to an exploration of agape, a love that emphasizes choice, distinction, and free decision. Yet the passion continues in the idealization of love as suffering, especially in martyrdom.

Love and suffering. The connecting of love and suffering is implicit in the lament of Jeremiah noted above (Jer 20), but it is not explicitly developed. The same is true in the teaching of Deuteronomy, where testing is part of love (Deut 13:3). Suffering as an aspect of love becomes more prominent in rabbinic teaching. The experience of suffering is understood by the rabbis as loving chastisements that the godly person must endure in order to grow in the love of God (Mekilta Exod 20:23; b. Berakhot, 5b). Suffering can even be a way of earning God's love (Lev Rabbah 32). Rabbinic tradition surrounding Rabbi Akiba demonstrates the idealization of love as suffering to the point of martyrdom. Rabbi Akiba taught that the highest fulfillment of the command to love in the Shemaᶜ (Deut 6:4) was martyrdom (b. Berakhot, 61b). The intimate relationship between love and suffering finds expression in the following teaching: "Concerning those who are humiliated without humiliating others, who listen to insults without replying, who fulfill the commandments out of love and rejoice in chastisements, the Scripture says that those who love Him are as the sun rising in its glory" (b. Shabbat, 88b).

The idealizing of suffering in rabbinic teaching is also central to the presentation of Jesus in the New Testament. The Gospel of Mark provides illustration. Jesus is revealed as the "beloved" son in his baptism (Mark 1:11). The message is repeated to the disciples of Jesus during the experience of the transfiguration (Mark 9:7). The voluntary passion of Jesus provides the content of what it means to be the beloved son. The parable of the vineyard provides the interpretation (Mark 12:1–12). After the master sends many servants to inquire of his vineyard, all of whom suffer in their role of messenger, he finally sends his "beloved son" (v. 6), who also suffers to the point of death. The ideal of love and suffering reaches a high point in the Gospel of John. John 3:16 provides the foundation for understanding the relationship between love and suffering. The self-giving love of God is stated in the following manner: "For God so loved the world that he gave his only Son." John 15 contains a mystical reflection on the web of self-giving love from God through Jesus to disciples. The teaching reaches a crescendo in verses 12–13: "This is my commandment, that you love one another as I have loved you. No one has greater love than this, to lay down one's life for one's friends."

Love and community. The teachings on love and community in the Hebrew Bible are central to the teaching of Jesus. When asked what is the greatest commandment (Mark 12:28; Matt 22:34–40), Jesus responds by quoting the *Shemaᶜ* (Deut 6:4), namely to love God with all of one's heart, soul, and mind. The second greatest commandment is the love of neighbor (Lev 19:18). "On these two commandments," states Jesus, "hang all the law and the prophets." Jesus reinforces other teachings on love from the Hebrew Bible. He underscores the incompatibility of love and hate, as well as the exclusive claims of love, when he states that no person can serve two masters, for he or she will love the one and hate the other (Matt 6:24). Jesus also underscores the mutuality of love. The woman who was forgiven by Jesus of many sins was able to love much, as compared to the one who was forgiven little (Luke 7:47). An innovation in the teaching of love by Jesus may be his requirement to love both neighbor and enemy (Matt 5:44; Luke 6:32–36). The love of enemy is also implicit in the rabbinic teaching about love and humiliation (cf. above). If anything, the teaching of Jesus makes the teaching more explicit. Jesus concludes that the love of enemy is a form of godly perfection.

Love is also central to the theology of the apostle Paul. The love of God in Christ is at the core of the Christian experience. The self-giving love of God is proven, according to Paul, in the voluntary death of Christ for humans (Rom 5:8), which ushers in a new quality of human life, empowered by God's love (1 Cor 8:3). And, as a result, Paul proclaims that nothing can separate the Christian from the love of Christ, including persecution and death (Rom 8:31–39). The love of God in humans is a fruit of the Spirit of God in the new age of humanity (Gal 5:22). It fulfills the law (Rom 13:8–10). It becomes the central virtue for Christians, the glue that holds all other values together. Love is even the greatest virtue of the triad faith, hope, and love (1 Cor 13:13). Even martyrdom without love is nothing, according to Paul (1 Cor 13:1–3).

The Pauline vision of community as knit together in God's love reaches near mythical proportions in the Gospel of John and in the letters of John. At the Last Supper Jesus gives his disciples a new commandment, that they love one another as Jesus has loved them (John 13:34). In his high-priestly prayer Jesus calls forth the love of God toward him into his disciples. The result is a unity among God, Christ, and disciples, "so that the love with which you have loved me may be in them, and I in them" (John 17:26). First John 4 provides the resulting vision of community in which love casts out fear. Its members are bold in the day of judgment, and they cast out all fear in their community, thus attaining the perfection of love.

Victor Paul Furnish, *The Love Command in the New Testament* (Nashville: Abingdon Press, 1972); Norman H. Snaith, *Distinctive Ideas of the Old Testament* (London: Epworth Press, 1944), 131–42.

THOMAS B. DOZEMAN

Lowly *see* Pride

Lust *see* Desire

Magi The word is represented (not translated) by "wise men" in NRSV (Matt 2:1, 7, 16), with a note offering the alternative "astrologers," and pointing out that the Greek word is *magi* (actually *magoi*). The same word occurs in the singular in Acts 13:6, 8, where NRSV and most translations read "magician." While Bar-Jesus/Elymas in Acts is denounced as a thoroughly reprehensible character, the magi in Matthew are presented as the first to acknowledge Jesus as king of the Jews.

The magi are not described in Matthew as kings or as being wise; neither are they said to have numbered three. Since there were three gifts, it has been assumed there must have been three givers. They were not identified as kings until after the time of Constantine (fourth century A.D.), and the earliest reference to their wisdom is in the work of Venerable

Bede (eighth century A.D.). By this time a tremendous body of legend had grown up around the mysterious figures, including names for them, none of which has any foundation in ancient records.

The word *magi* originally denoted one of the tribes of the Medes, who served the Zoroastrian religion as priests (Herodotus I.101, 132). They also gained an early reputation as interpreters of dreams (Herodotus I.107; VII.19). Their reputation spread into the Hellenistic world, where the word came to have almost contradictory meanings. It might still refer to the priests of Persia, with positive associations but was frequently used as a derogatory term for anyone claiming magical powers (as in Acts 13). Philo of Alexandria in the first century A.D. writes of "associations of men of the highest excellence. Among the Persians there is the order of the Magi, who silently make research into the facts of nature to gain knowledge of the truth and through visions clearer than speech, give and receive the revelations of divine excellency" (*Every Good Man Is Free*, 74; cf. *The Special Laws* III.100). Elsewhere he also uses the word in its negative sense, however, with reference to charlatans (*The Special Laws* III.93).

Since Matthew identified these magi as coming from the East, it seems likely that he intended to identify them with the Persian priests and to distinguish them from magicians such as the Elymas of Acts 13. Since he tells us nothing more, everything else that might be said about them is speculation. Some modern translations call them astrologers, since they took a star to be the sign a king had been born to the Jews (e.g., NEB, REB; cf. TEV and CEV's note). That they were wise men (KJV, RSV, NRSV) was a relatively late deduction in Christian history, as noted above. The value of their gifts must have led to the assumption they were kings. Since so little is known about them, NAB and NIV may be wise in simply using the word "Magi."

Arthur Darby Nock, Note XIV, "Paul and the Magus," in *The Beginnings of Christian-*

ity, part 1, *The Acts of the Apostles*, ed. F. J. Foakes Jackson and Kirsopp Lake (London: Macmillan 1933), 5:164–82; Richard C. Trexler, *The Journey of the Magi: Meanings in History of a Christian Story* (Princeton: Princeton University Press, 1997).

DONALD E. GOWAN

Male   *see* Man and Woman

Man and Woman, Male and Female

These words occur thousands of times in the Bible, but relatively few times in overtly theological contexts. The most important passages, however, have broad implications for much that Scripture says about men and women. The English language does not serve us well in dealing with the biblical terminology, because there is no literal way to translate ʾadam. The Hebrew ʾish and ʾishshah and the Greek aner and gyne can be directly translated "man" and "woman," and the Hebrew zakar and neqebah and the Greek arsen and thelus mean "male" and "female." The Greek anthropos can mean either a human being or specifically a man, as "man" was formerly used in English to designate both a male and humanity in general. But the Hebrew ʾadam denotes humanity or the human race, and an individual man would be designated a "son of ʾadam" (e.g., Ps 8:4; Ezek 2:1, NRSV Mg). The use of ʾadam in the first key text, Gen 1:27, is clear enough, but matters become more complicated in Gen 2 and 3.

At the beginning, when human beings were created, according to Gen 1:26–28, they were marked by four characteristics: they were made in the *image* of God, they were male and female, they were to be fruitful and multiply and fill the earth, and they were to subdue it and have dominion over every living thing. "Male and female" scarcely distinguishes *humans* from other animals, but the sexuality of animals is not mentioned (vv. 24–25). In the story of creation it seems to be taken for granted that being male and female is important for humans in a way that it is not for the animals. The parallelism of lines in v. 27, "in the image of God he created him; male and female he created them," makes the remarkable suggestion that to be male and female somehow makes us like God. Since there is not a hint elsewhere in the Bible of the idea that God might be androgynous, interpreters focus on relationship—between men and women and between humans and God—as the most likely way to understand the parallelism (for brief comments on Karl Barth's extensive discussion: Jewett, 43–48). It remains important to note that for Gen 1:27 the first point in defining what it means to be human is that we are male and female (cf. Gen 5:2: "Male and female he created them, and he blessed them and named them 'Humankind' [i.e., ʾadam] when they were created").

The second account of creation, in Gen 2, takes another way of emphasizing the male-female relationship as essential to human nature. In Gen 2:7 God created "the human" (haʾadam; not "man" as in NRSV), with no reference being made to sexuality. As the story progresses, it becomes clear that this is not the human race, as in Gen 1, but a single individual, unlike any "human" we know, however. This being is alone (v. 18), without the kind of relationships necessary for life to be good. God then set out to make "a helper as his partner," as NRSV renders words that have often been misunderstood. KJV's accurate translation, "an help meet [i.e., appropriate] for him," became distorted to "helpmate," and it has been assumed that "help" made the woman inferior to the man. When the OT uses this word (ʿezer), however, it refers to one with superior power able to meet a serious need. So fifteen of its twenty-one occurrences refer to God, and the others, except for Gen 2:18, indicate the inadequacy of human help. The woman God makes is thus depicted as more than a "partner"; she is one able to deliver the human from solitude. She will be kenegdo, which can be translated several ways, but perhaps "corresponding to him" is more appropriate than KJV's "meet for," or RSV's "fit

for"; that is, not identical but essential. These two chapters of Genesis thus found two very different ways to claim that thinking about our humanness begins with our sexuality. That is not so remarkable, but it is remarkable that authors writing in and for a patriarchal culture make no claim for male supremacy—and that those who received these texts did not alter them to make them agree with prevailing ideas. According to Gen 3, some of the prevailing ideas were not God's intention but the result of sin, so the three chapters stand as a remarkable challenge to the understanding of the sexes that prevailed in the culture for which they were written.

The human in Gen 2 has nothing to do with the creation of woman. It occurs while he is in a coma; when he awakes he recognizes that this being makes him whole, so to speak: "This at last is bone of my bones and flesh of my flesh" (2:23). God has made a woman (ʾishshah, v. 22), and so now the words "man" (ʾish) and "woman" appear for the first time. For Israelites, the relationship of marriage was such a fundamental part of life that "man and woman" immediately leads to a reflection not relevant to Adam and Eve, for they had no parents: "Therefore a man leaves his father and mother and clings to his wife, and they become one flesh" (2:24). The actual marriage custom was for the wife to leave her family and join her husband's, so this is a psychological rather than a sociological comment on the power of the attraction that draws a man to a woman. The nakedness of verse 25 is an explicit reference to their sexual relations (as "naked" is used in the OT), and in the ideal relationship as God intended it, there would be nothing to cause shame.

The woman plays a remarkable role in Gen 3, one mostly misunderstood because of sexist bias. The claim that the serpent began with the weaker party and though her was able to entice the man to sin (already found in 1 Tim 2:14) is not a good fit to the way the story is told. The author felt no need to explain why the serpent addressed the woman; she can serve as well as the man. It is she who demonstrates reasoning powers, making a judgment as to what is good; she has been called the world's first theologian. The man does nothing, asks no questions, makes no protest. When the woman says, "Here, eat this," he eats it. Then when God asks questions, the man cannot take responsibility, and neither can she (3:1–13). They are still equal.

The conclusion of the story brings readers into the real world, where there is enmity between animals and humans, childbirth is painful, and men rule over women and struggle to gain enough to feed their families and then die. The author is saying that none of this— including the male supremacy of his (or her) own time—was God's intention for us but is the result of our own choice.

Both Testaments show evidence of tensions between the traditional supremacy of men in society and the subversive ideal that men and women are different but equal. An article dealing on theology needs to focus on the latter, for male-dominated societies are simply the "way things are," and scarcely the result of a revelation of the divine will. The many studies of the place of women in ancient Israel, Judaism, and the early church reveal both the general prevalence of patriarchal systems and exceptions that showed women were not always completely without rights, with the emphasis depending on the attitude of the writer of the study. That the basic structure of society, with reference to the relative status of men and women, was seldom questioned in Israel is revealed by the eschatological passages in the prophetic books, which do not speak of hoped-for changes in the male-female relationship. This makes one text stand out because of the breadth of its hopes, Joel 2:28–29: "Then afterward I will pour out my spirit on all flesh; your sons and your daughters shall prophesy, your old men shall dream dreams, and your young men shall see visions. Even on the male and female slaves, in those days, I will pour out my spirit." For God's spirit to be poured out

so that both sons and daughters and even male and female slaves would prophesy would mean that all would have equal, direct access to God.

When Peter quoted Joel on the day of Pentecost, he said nothing of male-female equality (indeed, his address begins "Men (*andres*) of Judea"; Acts 2:14–21). He used the text to account for an outpouring of the Spirit, but already the example of Jesus had produced a community in which men and women met together (Acts 1:14). Most of Jesus' challenges to the assumptions about female inferiority came by example rather than teaching. In contrast to the practice of other teachers of his time, who took only male students, Jesus had women disciples (Luke 8:1–3). He would freely discuss serious matters even with a strange woman (John 4:1–30). His most explicit comment on the appropriateness of teaching women came when Martha protested his teaching of her sister when there was housework to do: "There is need of only one thing. Mary has chosen the better part, which will not be taken away from her" (Luke 10:38–42).

Although NT authors do not appeal to Jesus' actions or teachings in this regard, it seems likely that the presence of women in leadership roles in the early church was largely due to his influence (see Acts 18:2, 18, 26; Rom 16:1, 3, 6, 12, 15; 1 Cor 16:19; Phil 4:2–3). Paul in effect declared Joel's hope to have been fulfilled beyond expectations: "There is no longer Jew or Greek, there is no longer slave or free, there is no longer male or female; for all of you are one in Christ Jesus" (Gal 3:28). From his other writings it is clear that he did not mean by "one" that male-female distinctions had somehow been spiritually erased. He had a great deal to say about marriage in 1 Cor 7 and about unacceptable sexual relations in several passages (see *immorality*). He also addressed problems created in certain churches by the freedom that some women seem to have been abusing. These situations produced the texts that have been regularly appealed to by those who believe leadership in the church (or at least the preaching ministry) should be limited to men (1 Cor 11:2–16; 14:34–36). The opportunities afforded to women in the first generation or two were soon limited as the church was influenced by its environment, and most scholars attribute 1 Tim 2:8–15 to a disciple of Paul who reflected the church's reversion to more restrictions on women's freedom.

Marriage is discussed more explicitly in the NT than in the OT, where it is largely taken for granted (see *family*). The so-called *Haustafeln*, little lists of instructions for families, do not seek to overturn the order of things that was customary in the Hellenistic communities where the church was thriving, so the father's place as head of the household is upheld (Eph 5:21–6:9; Col 3:18–4:1; 1 Pet 3:1–7; cf. Titus 2:1–10). The "theologizing" of marriage in Eph 5:21–33 deserves attention in this article, however. At first reading the text reinforces the subordination of wife to husband by comparing the marriage relationship with that of the church to Christ. This leads to a remarkably high view of the husband-wife relationship, however, which raises serious questions about taking "be subject" in its usual way. The passage begins "Be subject to one another" (v. 21), which scarcely permits any sort of serious inequality. The different roles of the sexes are defined as subjection for the wife and love for the husband, and that love is defined at some length as self-giving, like the love that led Christ to die for the church (vv. 25–27). Husbands are to love their wives as they love themselves, which challenges the idea that they might think of their wives as inferior in any way (vv. 28–33). And finally, as if realizing that what had been said raised serious questions about "Wives, be subject to your husbands," the paragraph ends with "and a wife should respect her husband."

"But within the limits set by his contemporary world, he attempted to show that a woman is neither primarily passive, nor weaker than nor inferior to man. He describes the union between husband and wife as a give and take, an exchange of offering and receiving, seeking and finding, tension and fulfillment. 'Subordinate yourselves to one another!' Unless he and she are different there cannot be meaningful unity, but only boring sameness, stifling identity, abstract egalitarianism. Unless they demonstrate together to one another and all others what it means to be truly human, they do not live up to the creation of man in 'God's image' as 'male and female' (Gen 1:27). They are true mates and a convincing pair inasmuch as each one of them is active and passive, imaginative and yielding, preceding and following, in carrying out their special responsibilities for one another" (Barth, 650).

As the OT began with a definition of humanity that took the male-female relationship to be primary, so the NT in this passage exalts marriage (in its ideal form) so as to make it an appropriate analogy for the relationship between Christ and the church. Sexuality, which can be grossly distorted and abused, can also be idealized in Scripture so as to speak of the best that God intends.

Markus Barth, *Ephesians: Translation and Commentary on Chapters 4–6*, AB (Garden City, N.Y.: Doubleday & Co., 1974), 655–753; Paul K. Jewett, *Man as Male and Female* (Grand Rapids: Eerdmans, 1975); Samuel Terrien, *Till the Heart Sings: A Biblical Theology of Manhood and Womanhood* (Philadelphia: Fortress Press, 1985); Phyllis Trible, *God and the Rhetoric of Sexuality* (Philadelphia: Fortress Press, 1978).

DONALD E. GOWAN

Maranatha A transliteration of two Aramaic words, found in 1 Cor 16:22 and *Didache* 10:6. NRSV translates the expression as "Our Lord, come!" and cites the original word in a footnote, but there are other possible translations. If it is divided *maran ʾatha ʾ* it could mean "Our Lord has come," although the imperative is also possible. The division *maranaʾ thaʾ* must be read as an imperative. This uncertainty leads to three possible meanings: (1) "Our Lord, come!" as a petition for Christ's return; (2) "Our Lord has come," that is, into the world in human flesh; and (3) "Our Lord has come," that is, to be present in the Eucharist. There is no evidence to support the second meaning. The fact that the *Didache* cites it in the context of a description of the Lord's Supper has led many scholars to claim the early church used it as a liturgical term in the Eucharist, with either the first or third meaning.

More important theologically than the translation and use of the expression is the evidence that the Aramaic word *mar* "Lord" was used very early in Christian history with reference to Jesus (see *Lord*). Paul used this Aramaic term in a letter to the church at Corinth and did not translate it. This must indicate that *maranatha* was regularly used in the worship even of Greek-speaking churches (as the *Didache* reference also indicates). The use of a foreign word can be accounted for only by the assumption that it was taken from the liturgy of the earliest Palestinian churches (1 Corinthians is usually dated ca. A.D. 52–55). There is evidence that LORD (*ʾdonai* in Hebrew; *mar* in Aramaic; *kyrios* in Greek) was used as a substitute for the divine name YHWH in first century Judaism. When Christians began to call Jesus "Lord," they were thus making a striking claim for his relationship with God the Father (cf. Phil 2:9–11), and the occurrence of *maranatha* reveals that this claim was being made very early.

Joseph A. Fitzmyer, S.J., "The Semitic Background of the New Testament *Kyrios*-Title," in *A Wandering Aramean: Collected Aramaic Essays*, SBLMS 25 (Missoula, Mont.: Scholars Press, 1979), 115–42; and "New Testament *Kyrios* and *Maranatha* and Their Aramaic Background," in *To Advance the Gospel: New Testament Studies* (New York: Crossroad 1981), 85–101.

DONALD E. GOWAN

Marriage, Marry, Husband, Wife, Bride, Bridegroom, Adultery

Marital terminology is employed in the Bible to describe the legal, physical, and spiritual union of a man and woman who covenant to live together. It is also employed in startling metaphorical ways to depict God's covenant relationship with Israel and Jesus' relationship to both the kingdom of God and the church.

Marital terminology in the Old Testament

The OT has no word for marriage. Instead, a man is usually described as "taking" a woman "for a wife" and "ruling" over her, or a woman is "given" to a man "for a wife" by her father. (The NRSV conveys this in terms of the taking of a woman "in marriage," or simply indicates that a man "married" a woman.) A woman can also be described as "becoming" a man's wife. In the OT world, as in all ancient cultures, women were understood to be acquired by men in marriage. In several instances, the verb *baʿal* is also employed to describe this transaction. This verb, which can be translated "to take a wife" or "to marry" also means "to rule over" or "to become master." Moreover, while the Hebrew word *ʾish* (primarily "man" and secondarily "husband") is most commonly used to designate the male partner in marriage (just as *ʾishsha*, "woman" or "wife," designates the female partner), other Hebrew words for "husband" include *baʿal* ("master," e.g., 2 Sam 11:26; Prov 31:11, 23, 28) and *ʾadon* ("lord," Gen 18:12). This terminology reflects the OT's emphasis on the husband's rights and authority within the marriage relationship, a given in ancient patriarchal cultures. It should not be supposed, however, that wives were regarded as chattel or possessions of their husbands. (The tenth commandment is often cited in support of this erroneous view; Exod 20:17.) Recent scholarship suggests that the husband's rights and authority were tied to the land that was the source of the family household's survival. As Carol Meyers notes, "marriage arrangements involved female mobility and male stability"; a woman left her own household upon marriage and became a member of her husband's household. The particular parcel of land upon which they lived was transmitted along patrilineal lines, and the man's knowledge and experience in management of it was crucial for the household's continued subsistence. However, the wife's role within the family unit was by no means inconsequential. As the remarkable job description of the "capable" wife in Prov 31:10–31 attests, she performed productive and managerial tasks that were essential to the existence and survival of the whole household. Thus economic interests and property rights were integral to the institution of marriage.

Knowledge of marriage in the OT world is limited, for the OT provides no systematic legal discussion of marriage. It must be gleaned from a handful of legal statements that deal with marriage or divorce and from scattered narrative portrayals of marriage that are often at odds with the legal references. An ideal is stated in the opening chapters of Genesis: "Therefore a man leaves his father and his mother and clings to his wife, and they become one flesh" (2:24). But the narratives that follow often present a different picture. Typically it is the woman who leaves her household, rather than the man, and polygamy is practiced by venerable patriarchs such as Abraham, Jacob, and Esau and by kings such as David, Solomon, and Rehoboam. However, polygamy appears primarily in connection with men of distinction, who are wealthy or in prominent positions of leadership. No woman is depicted with more than one husband. In both ancient Israel and early Judaism, monogamy appears to have been the norm.

For the most part, marriages depicted in the OT were not a matter of individual decision and choice, least of all for women. Customarily they were arranged by parents, though in many instances it is apparent that children were not without voice or influence in the matter. This practice, standard in ancient cultures, reflects the fact that marriage was more than a union between two individuals. It was a matter of importance for whole households. In fact, marriage partners were often selected from the larger kinship group or clan (*mishpahah*). Marriage between cousins, for example, was a favored arrangement (Gen. 24:4; 28:2). This practice of marriage within the larger kinship group, called endogamy, safeguarded the family's property and religious ethos, and also ensured a marriage partner's familiarity with the skills and strategies needed by the family household to subsist on its particular parcel of land. However, exogamy, marriage outside the larger kinship group, even to foreigners, is also illustrated in OT narratives (e.g., Joseph, Moses, Esther). In the postexilic period, Ezra and Nehemiah rail against exogamy as a threat to the nation's religious integrity (Ezra 9–10; Neh 13:23–28). Nonetheless, both endogamy and exogamy are practiced in the world depicted in the OT narratives.

The custom of "levirate marriage" also appears in the OT. According to this custom, detailed in Deut 25:5–10, a widow of a man who died childless would cohabit with a brother of the deceased (the Hebrew *levir* means "brother-in-law") in order to raise up an heir who would continue his name. The custom also provided security for the widow by providing a new attachment to the family into which she had married. The stories of Judah and Tamar (Gen 38) and of Ruth and Boaz (Ruth 2–4) both reflect the custom of levirate marriage, while providing variations on the theme, for neither Judah nor Boaz is a brother of the deceased husband: Judah is rather Tamar's father-in-law, and Boaz is a distant kinsman. The custom of levirate marriage continued into the NT era, for it is reflected in the Sadducees' question to Jesus about the resurrection in Mark 12:18–27.

The words "bridegroom" and "bride" convey the Hebrew words *hathan* and *kallah* respectively. However, *hathan* can also designate a man in relationship to his father-in-law, as well as in relationship to a woman to whom he is betrothed. In these instances it is translated as "son-in-law" rather than as "bridegroom." Similarly *kallah* can designate a woman in relationship to her husband's father or mother (as "daughter-in-law"), as well as in relationship to her husband-to-be. These double meanings reflect the extended family structure of ancient Israel: when a woman married, she joined her husband's household, in which her husband's father exercised authority. Thus her new status was defined by both her relationship to her husband and her relationship to the head of the extended family and his wife.

When the words "bride and bridegroom" (*kallah* and *hathan*) appear together in the OT, specific individuals are never in view. The paired terms function instead as a symbol of great human joy. Thus the "voice of the bride and bridegroom" connotes great rejoicing, and its absence connotes destruction and mourning (e.g., Isa 62:5; Jer 7:34; 16:9; 25:10; see also Rev 18:23). A further use of *kallah* appears in the Song of Songs, where "bride" is a term of endearment or affection (Song 4:8–12; 5:1) rather than a marital designation.

The OT presupposes the reality of divorce (Deut 24:1–4) but does not specifically prohibit it (though it is strongly condemned in Mal 2:16). Adultery (*nі̉uphim* in Hebrew), however, was regarded as a serious sin, but it had a limited definition: it connoted sexual relations between a married or betrothed woman and any man other than her husband. It was thus committed only against a husband, never against a wife. The woman's marital status was the critical factor. Adultery was a grave offense, for it undermined the family, the foundational unit of society, and was a serious threat to paternity, inheritance, and economic interests. It also undermined personal integrity (an emphasis characteristic of the book of Proverbs; e.g., Prov 2:12–22; 5:1–14) and was an offense against the God who ordained marriage (Gen 39:9). For all of these reasons, adultery was strictly forbidden in the Ten Commandments (Exod 20:14; Deut 5:18), and the dangerous "adulteress" (literally, a "foreign" or "strange woman") was a major preoccupation of Israel's sages (Prov 2:16–19;

5:3–8, 20; 6:24–26, 29, 32; 7:5–27; 30:20). Adultery carried the penalty of death (Lev 20:10; Deut 22:22). Although the OT does not contain any narrative in which the death penalty is actually applied, the threat of execution is reflected in John 7:53–8:11, and thus persists well into the first century A.D.

Clearly, the OT presents faithfulness as the divine will for marital relationships. This ideal finds clearest expression in Gen 2:24, a programmatic statement in which loyalty to one's parents is subordinated to loyalty to one's spouse. While the OT depiction of marriage is largely pragmatic, marriage is not merely a human institution. The opening chapters of Genesis affirm its role in the created order and God's ordination of it. Indeed marriage can be described as a holy covenant (Prov 2:17; Ezek 16:8), to which God is a witness (Mal 2:14; Gen 31:50).

The marriage bond was thus well suited as a metaphor for God's own covenant relationship with Israel, and adultery as a metaphor for apostasy to other gods. While the Torah hints at this when it describes Yahweh as a "jealous" God (Exod 20:5; 34:14; Deut 4:24; 5:9; 6:15), Israel's prophets fully develop the metaphor, making of it a theological lens for understanding God's abiding faithfulness to the covenant people (see *love*). The prophet Hosea was the first to advance the metaphor, making bold use of it to convey an understanding of the past, present, and future relationships between Yahweh (specifically identified as ʾish or "husband" in 2:16) and Israel (Yahweh's ʾishsha or "wife," v. 19). His reflections on the turbulent history of this relationship are poignant, for they are intertwined with his own painful experience of marriage to Gomer, a faithless wife. Indeed God commissions Hosea to make his own life a symbolic enactment of the divine love for Israel. Thus Hosea's own marriage is disrupted by Gomer's adultery (Hos 1:2), just as God's marriage is disrupted by Israel's unfaithfulness— in particular, by its apostasy, its acceptance of other gods. Indeed Hosea's own personal trauma provides vivid illustration of the pain, anger, and struggle that Israel's unfaithfulness evokes in the heart of God. God no longer recognizes Israel as wife and announces her judgment in the form of military defeat and destruction (2:2–13). Nevertheless, behind the wrath of God is a love that will not let Israel go. The divine love includes discipline, for impending judgment will take Israel back into the wilderness, where Yahweh and Israel first pledged themselves in covenantal relationship. But therein lies the promise of a new beginning and a new marriage between God and Israel in the future. Yahweh will woo his estranged wife, forgive her transgressions, and betroth her once again, reestablishing their covenantal relationship (2:14–20).

Hosea's use of marital and sexual imagery influenced later prophets such as Jeremiah, Ezekiel, and Second and Third Isaiah, all of whom provide further depictions of Yahweh as the faithful yet aggrieved husband of Israel (or Jerusalem/Zion), a faithless and adulterous wife (e.g., Jer 2:2, 20–37; 3:1–4; 5:7–9; 9:2; 13:20–27; 31:32; Isa 50:1; 54:5–7; 61:10; 62:4–5; Ezek 16; 23). In fact, references to adultery in the OT are concentrated in the prophetic literature. Often the metaphor evolved in brutal ways, for in the eyes of the prophets Israel's "adultery," its religious transgression, justified savage punishment. The threat of cruel punishment is intimated in Hosea (2:1–13) but becomes explicit in later prophetic reflection (e.g., Jer 13:20–27). The prophet Ezekiel in particular provides disturbing images of God as an outraged and menacing husband, who delivers up his whoring wife (Jerusalem in Ezek 16, and both Jerusalem and Samaria in Ezek 23) to rape, mutilation, and murder. Indeed Ezek 16 and 23 are among the most violent chapters in the OT, using very crude language, but the metaphorical violence corresponds to the real terror and suffering experienced by Judeans with the fall of Jerusalem.

The use of the marital metaphor to describe God's covenantal bond with Israel is thus deeply problematic. It powerfully conveys God's faithfulness, compassion, and vulnerability. But in casting God as faithful husband and Israel or Jerusalem as adulterous wife, it also suggests divinization of men and demonization of women. Furthermore, it justifies violence as a means of restoring broken relationships, and presents troubling images of God as an abusive husband. Consequently, the metaphor cannot be employed uncritically in contemporary theological reflection.

Marital terminology in the New Testament

The NT presumes much of the OT discussion of marriage. Thus the most important statement of Jesus on the subject (Mark 10:3–9) reaffirms the divine will for fidelity in marriage articulated in Gen 2:24. Moreover, in the NT, as in the OT, marital terminology and imagery are used in both literal and metaphorical ways. Following the lead of OT prophets such as Hosea, Jeremiah, and Ezekiel, who found the marital bond well suited as a metaphor for God's covenantal relationship with Israel, NT authors employed it to describe Jesus Christ's relationship to the church. Marital imagery also appears in association with the present and future "kingdom" or "rule of God" inaugurated in his messianic ministry.

Marital terminology in the NT, as in the OT, reflects the patriarchal culture out of which it emerges. Thus, the Greek verb *gameo* ("to marry") is used primarily with reference to the act of a man who *takes* a woman in marriage; and the verb *gamizo* ("to give in marriage") usually describes the action of a father who *gives* a daughter in marriage (e.g., Luke 17:27). Passive constructions of the verbs *gameo, gamizo,* and *gamisko* are usually employed to speak of a woman as being "married" or "given in marriage," though active forms of *gameo* can be used with reference to both sexes.

Much of the marital terminology in the NT bears varied nuances. The Greek noun *gamos* refers primarily to a "wedding," and even to a "marriage feast" (John 2:1; Matt 22:2). Secondarily it refers to "marriage" (Heb 13:4; Rev 19:7). The Greek word *aner* conveys both "man" and "husband," and the Greek word *gyne* conveys both "woman" and "wife" (just as the Hebrew *>ish* and *>ishsha* refer to both man/husband and woman/wife). Most of the NT references to a "bridegroom" (*nymphos* in Greek) are christological in nature, that is, references to Jesus Christ. The word "bride" (*nymphe*) appears less frequently, and in one instance denotes a "daughter-in-law" (Matt 10:35; Luke 12:53), just as the Hebrew term *kallah* can denote a woman both as "bride" in reference to her husband and also as "daughter-in-law" in reference to her husband's parents.

Literal use of marital terminology. Distinctive emphases with respect to marriage can be noted in various parts of the NT canon. In the Gospels, Jesus reaffirms the divine will for fidelity in marriage articulated in Gen 2:24 but provides a more rigorous position on divorce, eliminating the possibility of divorce conceded to the Jews by Moses because of their "hardness of heart" (Mark 10:1–12; Matt 5:31–32; 19:1–12; Luke 16:8). Indeed those who divorce and marry another or who marry a divorced person are said to commit adultery (*moichao*). Scholars continue to debate the meaning of the one exception to the rule added in Matt 5:32 and 19:9, which allows for divorce in the case of *porneia* ("unchastity," or perhaps "incestuous marriage"). While in the OT only the man could initiate divorce (and both Matthew and Luke reflect this assumption), Mark's version of this teaching assumes that women too might initiate divorce and thus stand guilty of adultery. Roman law allowed women to initiate divorce, though Jewish law did not. Mark thus explicitly reflects legal realities prevailing outside Palestine.

In the Gospels' presentation, Jesus clearly endorses marriage as a normal state of affairs. He chooses and acknowledges an alternative way of life, that of celibacy (Matt 19:10–12), but he does not

urge it on his followers. However, he sounds a profoundly countercultural note when he subordinates family loyalty to loyalty to the gospel (Mark 3:31–35 and par.). The Gospel of Luke even reflects an ascetic tendency when it explicitly includes "wife" among the family members whom a disciple may be required to "hate," or "love less" than the gospel (cf. Luke 14:26; Matt 10:37–38). The Gospels also note that marriage is an institution for the present age rather than the future, for in the age to come those who rise from the dead "neither marry nor are given in marriage, but are like angels in heaven" (Mark 12:25 and par.).

The apostle Paul's references to marriage are concentrated in 1 Cor 7, in which he deals with questions about sexuality that have emerged in the Corinthian church. Because the end of the world is fast approaching, he advises the Corinthian Christians to remain in the state in which they find themselves: it is best for the unmarried and the widowed to remain unmarried and for married Christians not to divorce, unless it be the will of the unbelieving partner. Clearly celibacy has practical advantages in Paul's view, for it frees one for "unhindered devotion to the Lord" (7:35). Indeed he repeatedly states his preference for celibacy over marriage and his wish that all were single like him. However, he also acknowledges that celibacy is a charism, a spiritual gift, and that gifts differ (7:7). By implication marriage is a gift as well. Thus Paul assures those who marry that they do not sin. In fact, he recommends marriage as a means of sexual containment and self-control: "it is better to marry than to be aflame with passion" (7:9).

While not a ringing endorsement of marriage, Paul's discussion of it is noteworthy in several respects. For one thing, Paul takes pains to address husbands and wives in evenhanded fashion, emphasizing the mutuality of sexual relations within marriage, and he never mentions procreation. He further acknowledges the holiness of marriage, noting that its sanctifying power embraces one's children and even an unbelieving spouse. Thus, on the authority of Jesus' prohibition of divorce (7:10), Paul urges the married not to separate, unless it be the will of an unbelieving spouse. Though the widower is not addressed, Paul states that the widow is free to remarry (albeit "only in the Lord,"), but is "more blessed if she remains as she is" (7:39–40). Remarkably Paul argues for options in Christian living: both marriage and singleness can be holy ways of life.

Paul's reflections on sexuality (and secondarily marriage) in 1 Cor 7 were clearly influenced by his conviction that the end of the world was fast approaching. "The impending crisis" was at hand (7:26). Its failure to appear had a significant impact on discussion of marriage in later NT epistles, which struggled to articulate the shape of continued Christian existence in the world amidst the structures of society. The NT "household codes" in particular reflect the tensions experienced in early Christian communities as they tried to negotiate distinctive Christian identity on the one hand and affirm common cultural values on the other, for the sake of both their well-being and their witness. Five such codes appear in the NT (Eph 5:21–6:9; Col 3:18–4:1; 1 Tim 2–3; Titus 2:1–10; 1 Pet 2:18–3:12), all of which consist of instructions to various members of the household (husbands and wives, parents and children, masters and slaves). The codes draw on a standard pattern of ethical instruction among both Jews and Greeks and reflect values of patriarchal Greco-Roman culture. Thus in each of the codes wives are exhorted to "be subject" (*hypotasso*) to their husbands (Eph 5:22; Col 3:18; 1 Pet 3:1; 1 Tim 2:11; Titus 2:4–5), who ruled over the Greco-Roman household on the basis of their alleged intellectual and physical superiority to women and slaves (1 Pet 3:7). Husbands, in turn, are urged to "love" (Eph 5:25; Col 3:19) or "show consideration" (1 Pet 3:7) for their wives. While the codes are not adopted uncritically by the NT authors, and theological modification of them can be discerned (e.g., Eph 5:21,

25), they nonetheless reflect accommodation to patriarchal cultural views. The egalitarian vision of life in the household of God articulated in Gal 3:28 and the parity and mutuality in marriage reflected to some extent in 1 Cor 7 are nowhere in view in the codes (though see 1 Cor 11:2–6, where Paul does assert gender hierarchy). The burden of alleviating tensions between the Christian community and Greco-Roman culture falls on wives and slaves, who are urged to conform to societal expectations.

However, it should also be noted that the Ephesian household code provides the NT's most elevated statement on marriage. At its conclusion, the author reaffirms the divine ordination of marriage, quoting Gen 2:24. Then, grasping at metaphors, he suggests that the "great mystery" at the heart of a marriage is a profound one that mirrors the very mystery of the love that exists between Christ and the church (Eph 5:31–32).

Figurative use of marital terminology. In the NT, marriage is used figuratively in association with the kingdom of God and is further employed to describe Jesus Christ's relationship to the church. In the Gospels, for example, Jesus' teaching takes up the notion of a messianic wedding and marriage feast to convey the arrival of the kingdom of God in his life and ministry, death and resurrection, and second coming for final judgment. Thus in Matt 22:1–10 and Luke 14:16–24 the kingdom of heaven is compared to a king who gave a wedding banquet for his "son." Those who foolishly refuse the invitation to the banquet leave the door open for others to come in. In the parable of Ten Bridesmaids (Matt 25:1–12), Jesus urges disciples to be prepared for his second coming. In these parables Jesus is patently the "son" for whom the wedding banquet is given and the "bridegroom" who is delayed in coming. He is also the "bridegroom" whose presence precludes fasting until the time when he is "taken away" by the events of his passion (Mark 2:18–20). Though Israel is identified as God's bride in the OT use of the marital metaphor, no "bride" is identified in the Gospel parables. Disciples take the role of "guests."

Marital imagery is of particular note in the Gospel of John, in which the inaugural event of Jesus' public ministry takes place at a wedding in Cana (John 2:1–12). On this occasion Jesus produces vast quantities of choice wine. Messianic implications are again conveyed, for in the OT abundance of wine was an image of the joy of the messianic last days and of the arrival of God's new age (Amos 9:13–14; Joel 3:18; Jer 31:12; 33:6; Isa 25:6–10). In the next chapter, John the Baptist clarifies his own subordinate relationship to Jesus as that of best man, or "friend of the bridegroom" who "rejoices greatly at the bridegroom's voice" (3:29–30), and the scene that follows (John 4) reprises a familiar OT theme: boy meets girl at a well (Gen 24:10–61; 29:1–20; Exod 2:16–22). Sandra Schneiders makes a compelling case that the Samaritan woman whom Jesus meets at a well plays a representative role in John's Gospel, and that her irregular marital history evokes the religious infidelity of the Samaritan people, their worship of false gods. In sum, the story evokes the OT prophets' use of the marital metaphor, and the entire dialogue between Jesus and the Samaritan woman becomes "the 'wooing' of Samaria to full covenant fidelity in the New Israel by Jesus, the New Bridegroom."

Elsewhere in the NT, bridal imagery appears in explicit association with the church, along with an emphasis on bridal purity. In 2 Cor 11:2–3, Paul speaks of himself as the father of the bride (i.e., the church at Corinth), who longs to keep her pure and undefiled and present her "as a chaste virgin to Christ" (11:2) upon his second coming. Just as in the prophetic literature Israel's adultery/apostasy threatened her marriage with Yahweh, the "purity" of the Corinthian church is threatened by the acceptance of false teachings.

The most striking ecclesiological use of the marital metaphor appears in Eph 5, in which Christ's relationship to the church becomes a model for human marriage.

Thus wives are exhorted to be subject to their husbands as the church is subject to Christ. Husbands in turn are exhorted to love their wives "as Christ loved the church and gave himself up for her, in order to make her holy by cleansing her with the washing of water by the word, so as to present the church to himself in splendor, without a spot or wrinkle or anything of the kind—yes, so that she may be holy and without blemish" (5:25–27). While arresting, the analogy is problematic in many respects. As the prophetic use of the marital metaphor identified the husband with God, so the NT use of the marital metaphor identifies the husband with Christ. In both cases, the identification subtly promotes the divinization of men. Moreover, the wife/church is a passive member of the union, while the husband/Christ is active in love, as "savior." Indeed, the relationship between Christ and the church is hardly a relationship between equals. Ephesians thus provides christological validation of the subordinate position of the wife in marriage and an impossibly divine standard for the husband's behavior (see **man and woman**).

Bridal imagery makes a final appearance in the closing chapters of the book of Revelation (19:7–8; 21:2, 9–11; 22:17), in which the marriage of the Lamb becomes a metaphor for the union of Christ as bridegroom and the church as bride. Following the destruction of evil female figures (Jezebel and the great whore of Babylon), the pure "bride of the Lamb" appears as a central symbol in the vision of God's heavenly realm, as the new Jerusalem appears "coming down out of heaven from God, prepared as a bride adorned for her husband" (21:2). Here the people of God are represented as a city, and the expectation of a new Jerusalem merges with the image of the church as Christ's bride. While in the Synoptic Gospels the wedding days are associated with the days of Jesus' earthly ministry, in Revelation they are associated with final fulfillment, with the arrival of God's new heaven and new earth.

Adultery in the NT. The NT presumes the continuing validity of the OT's prohibition of adultery, explicitly citing the sixth commandment (Exod 20:13; Deut 5:17) six times (Matt 5:27; 19:18; Mark 10:19; Luke 18:20; Rom 13:9; Jas 2:11). "Adultery" (*moicheia*) also appears in two of the traditional "vice lists" (Mark 7:20–23; Matt 15:19–21; Gal 5:9), and adulterers (*moichoi*) are numbered among those who will not inherit the kingdom of God (1 Cor 6:9). Jesus' rigorous prohibition of divorce asserts that those who divorce and remarry "commit adultery" (*moichao*; Mark 10:11–12; Matt 5:31–32; 19:9; Luke 16:18). Indeed, Jesus is presented as radicalizing the concept of adultery in the Sermon on the Mount, by expanding the commandment to forbid even the lustful gaze directed toward someone else's spouse (Matt 5:27–28). In so doing, the Gospel of Matthew calls attention to the wholeness of life to which God calls disciples. More than correct behavior is in view: Matthew is interested in the orientation of the whole self— including actions, feelings, desires, the workings of the imagination—toward love of God and love of neighbor.

Like the OT, the NT also employs the concept of adultery in figurative ways to convey infidelity to God (e.g., Jas 4:4). Those who reject Jesus, God's own son, are excoriated as an "adulterous generation" (Matt 12:39; 16:4; Mark 8:38). Adultery is also associated with the acceptance of false teaching (Rev 2:20–22). In sum, the NT's figurative use of adultery conveys the seriousness of spurning the love of God in Christ.

Carol Meyers, *Discovering Eve: Ancient Israelite Women in Context* (New York: Oxford University Press, 1988); Carolyn Osiek and David L. Balch, *Families in the New Testament World: Households and House Churches* (Louisville, Ky.: Westminster John Knox Press, 1997); Leo G. Perdue, Joseph Blenkinsopp, John J. Collins, and Carol Meyers, *Families in Ancient Israel* (Louisville, Ky.: Westminster John Knox Press, 1997); Sandra Schneiders, chap. 7, "A Case Study: Feminist Interpretation of John 4:1–42," in *The Revelatory Text: Interpreting the New Testament as Sacred Scripture* (San Francisco: HarperSanFrancisco, 1991), 180–99; Renita J. Weems, *Battered Love: Marriage, Sex, and Violence in the Hebrew Prophets* (Minneapolis: Fortress Press, 1995).

FRANCES TAYLOR GENCH

Marvel, Marvelous *see* Sign

Mediator

Except for Job 33:23, where the translation can be questioned, "mediator" does not occur in the OT. There is no word in biblical Hebrew with precisely this meaning. Postbiblical Hebrew had to create a word to serve the purpose. At Job 9:33 the LXX uses *mesites*, "mediator," but this suggestion is not followed in our English translations (NRSV has "umpire").

It is clear, however, that the mediator idea is present in the narratives about Moses. He mediates between God and Israel in the exodus (Exod 12), in the giving of the law (Exod 19–20), and in other communications. He also mediates between Israel and God. When Aaron casts a golden calf, God tells Moses that he will destroy Israel and create a new people from Moses. Moses implores the Lord not to forget his promises to Abraham, Isaac, and Jacob, and the Lord relents (Exod 32:7–14). Later in the same chapter Moses tells the people, "You have sinned a great sin. But now I will go up to the LORD; perhaps I can make atonement for your sin." In his speech to God, the mediator says, "But now, if you will only forgive their sin—but if not, blot me out of the book you have written" (Exod 32:30, 32). The motif of Moses as mediator appears in later Jewish writings, for example, *Assumption of Moses* 1:14: "Accordingly he designed and devised me, and he prepared me before the foundation of the world, that I should be the mediator of his covenant" (see also 3:12).

Alongside the emphasis on Moses as mediator, there developed a tradition that angels also served as mediators in the giving of the law, as reflected in Gal 3:19: "it was ordained through angels by a mediator" (see also Acts 7:53; Heb 2:2). The idea of angelic mediation was extended to include other circumstances. The tradition that the archangel Michael was Israel's special protector (Dan 12:1) is probably reflected in *Testament of Dan* 6:2: "Draw near to God and to the angel that intercedes for you, for he is a mediator between God and men for the peace of Israel."

The letter to the Hebrews presents Jesus as the mediator who surpasses Moses. After contrasting the Levitical priesthood (mediated through Moses) with Jesus' high priesthood "after the order of *Melchizedek*" (Heb 7:17), the author declares, "But Jesus has now obtained a more excellent ministry, and to that degree he is the mediator of a better covenant, which has been enacted through better promises" (8:6). Scriptural support for this "better covenant" is found in Jeremiah's promise of a new covenant (Jer 31:31–34, quoted at length in Heb 8:8–12). In the next chapter of Hebrews the author contrasts the Aaronic sacrifices with that of the new high priest, Jesus: "he entered once for all into the Holy Place, not with the blood of goats and calves, but with his own blood, thus obtaining eternal redemption" (9:12). He adds: "For this reason he is the mediator of a new covenant, so that those who are called may receive the promised eternal inheritance, because a death has occurred that redeems them from the transgressions under the first covenant" (9:15). The motif recurs in 12:24, "Jesus, the mediator of a new covenant."

In 1 Tim 2:5 we read, "For there is one God; there is also one mediator between God and humankind, Christ Jesus, himself human, who gave himself a ransom for all." Noteworthy here is the insistence that there is only one mediator. Is the author protesting against the belief that one or more angels serve in this capacity? Is he denying Moses' mediatorship? No clue is given. All emphasis lies on Jesus' atoning role.

DOUGLAS R. A. HARE

Meek   *see* **Pride**

Meeting, Tent of   *see* **Presence**

Melchizedek   The name Melchizedek (*malki-tsedeq*) occurs in the OT only at Gen 14:18 and Ps 110:4. It appears to be an ancient theophoric name of Canaanite origin, meaning "my king is Zedek." Philo, Josephus, and the author of Hebrews all understand it to mean "king of righteousness."

In the enigmatic episode narrated in Gen 14:18–20, Melchizedek is introduced in v. 18 as the king of Salem, and further identified as "*priest* of God *most high* (*El Elyon*)." His sudden appearance occurs in the wake of several battles and as part of their denouement. Previously an alliance comprising King Chedorlaomer of Elam and three other kings had routed a coalition of five kings in an engagement near the Dead Sea (the Valley of Siddim), seizing "all the goods of Sodom and Gomorrah, and all their provisions" as spoils of war (14:8–11). As part of this process Abram's nephew Lot and his goods had also been taken (14:12). When Abram was informed of this situation, he raised a force and succeeded in driving the invading coalition from the region, capturing all the booty and liberating his nephew (14:13–16). Upon Abram's return, the king of Sodom went out to meet him (14:17); at this point King Melchizedek of Salem appears with bread and wine (14:18) and proceeds to bless Abram by God Most High. This blessing explicitly credits God Most High, "maker of heaven and earth," with delivering to Abram victory over his enemies. In response Abram gives "one tenth of everything" to Melchizedek (14:19–20). The use of the epithet "maker of heaven and earth" for "God Most High" in Melchizedek's blessing (14:19) indicates that Abram and Melchizedek are devoted to the same Lord (see 14:22; cf. Ps 78:35, where the Most High God is a synonym for Yahweh; cf. 1 QapGen 21:20; 4QPrNab). The text allows Abram's acknowledgment of Melchizedek's superiority to stand without comment and is silent regarding the clear implication that already in Abram's time there was present in Jerusalem a ruler who was both king and priest.

Apart from Gen 14:18–20, Melchizedek appears elsewhere in the OT only at Ps 110:4, where ostensibly David is told by the Lord: "You are a priest forever according to the order of Melchizedek" (unless *malki-tsedeq* here is taken not as a name but interpreted along with the NRSV Mg to this verse to mean "a rightful king by my edict"). Evidently the oracle contained in Ps 110:4 names Melchizedek precisely because of the combination of royal and priestly functions in his person as specified by the Genesis passage. That Melchizedek was the king of Salem, that is to say, Jerusalem (cf. Ps 76:2; Josephus, *Antiquities of the Jews* 1:180), is equally significant insofar as Melchizedek serves as a precedent from patriarchal times for the combinations of royal and priestly power precisely in the ruler of Jerusalem.

In Hasmonean times Ps 110:4 was taken as providing warrant for the joining of priestly and royal functions in one ruler (1 Macc 14:41; *As. Mos.* 6:1). It substantiated the notion of an everlasting priesthood (*T. Levi* 8:3), on occasion in combination with Melchizedek's status as a priest of the Most High God in Genesis (*Jub.* 32:1). Josephus refers to Hyrcanus as "high priest of the Most High God" (*Antiquities* 16:163). In a fragmentary first-century B.C. text from Cave 11 at Qumran (11Q13), Melchizedek proclaims liberty to the captives (see Isa 61:1) in the context of the eschatological jubilee (see Lev 25:13; Deut 15:2). He oversees the final judgment in which the holy ones of God are atoned for, while Belial and his lot are condemned. Melchizedek is characterized as the messenger and anointed prince (see Dan 9:25); but there is no explicit reference to his priestly status.

While Ps 110:1 is cited or alluded to by a variety of NT writings, Hebrews is the only Christian writing prior to Justin Martyr to mention Melchizedek and cite Ps 110:4. For Hebrews, Melchizedek is not only a priest but a high priest (cf. 1 Macc 14:41; Philo, *De Abrahamo* 235 calls Melchizedek a "great priest"; cf. Heb 4:14). After noting Jesus' status as "a high priest forever according to the order of Melchizedek" in Heb 6:20 (previously mentioned at 5:6 and 5:10), the author of Hebrews in chapter 7 provides exegetical observations on Gen 14 and spells out the implications of Ps 110:4 for Christ. Hebrews is interested not in Melchizedek per se but in the way he prefigures the everlasting high priesthood of Christ. In agreement with the psalm's declaration that Melchizedek's priesthood lasts forever is the fact that nowhere in the biblical text is there a reference to Melchizedek's parentage, genealogy, birth, or death (Heb 7:3). With respect to this unqualified duration of his priesthood, Melchizedek resembles the Son of God as a transcendent figure. Moreover, the surprising fact that according to the biblical account the patriarch Abraham (the name used in Hebrews) paid a tithe to Melchizedek allows Hebrews to assert the latter's superiority both to Abraham and by implication to his descendants (7:4–10). Thus the mortal, Levitical priests who normally receive tithes in this instance pay them through their most illustrious ancestor to an exalted priestly figure with no connection to their lineage. Having advanced the fundamental implications of the Genesis account with respect to the figure of Melchizedek, the author of Hebrews can now draw out the implications of the priesthood according to the order of Melchizedek found in the psalm.

Since the Levitical priesthood through Aaron was unable to attain perfection, and the law that was received under it was weak and ineffectual (7:11, 18), a need existed for a priest of a different order along with an accompanying change in the law (7:11–12). For the author of Hebrews the very existence of the statement in Ps 110:4 pointed to this problem with the Levitical priesthood. Extrapolating from the details of the verse in light of the wider biblical context, the author finds a clear allusion to another priesthood that is marked "not through a legal requirement concerning physical descent, but through the power of an indestructible life" (7:16). Only Christ suitably resembles Melchizedek (7:15), which is to say that only he can be a member of his order, not so much because he is not a Levite but descends from Judah (7:14), although this fact is pertinent, but principally by virtue of his eternal status, which is confirmed by his exaltation. Thus it emerges that Ps 110:4 in fact can be taken as scriptural confirmation of Christ's status. The advent of a this new priesthood based on the "power of an indestructible life" means not only the passing of the former priestly system but also the abrogation of the law in favor of a "better hope" (7:18–19). Christ is further differentiated in his role as a priest according to the order of Melchizedek by the oath formula in the first part of Ps 110:4, cited for the first time in Heb 7:21. While the Levitical priests were not confirmed by an oath, God has sworn concerning the eternal priesthood of Jesus who now becomes "the guarantee of a better covenant" in place of the law (7:20–22). Christ's transcendent status ensures the effectiveness of his intercession, in contrast to the temporally limited priests of the old covenant (7:23–25). As high priest he is "holy, blameless, undefiled, separated from sinners, and exalted above the heavens" (7:26). Thus his sacrifice was once for all (7:27), because the oath "appoints a Son who has been made perfect forever" (7:28), according to the order of Melchizedek.

Harold W. Attridge, *The Epistle to the Hebrews: A Commentary on the Epistle to the Hebrews*, ed. H. Koester, Hermeneia (Philadelphia: Fortress, 1989); M. Delcor, "Melchizedek from Genesis to the Qumran Texts and the Epistle to the Hebrews," *JSJ* 2 (1971): 115–35; Paul J. Kobelski, *Melchizedek and Melchiresa'*, CBQMS 10 (Washington, D.C.: Catholic Biblical Association of America, 1981).

CHRISTOPHER R. MATTHEWS

Memory, Memorial   see **Remember**

Mercy, Merciful   In English, "mercy" typically refers to compassionate treatment of those in need, who may not be deserving of it. In translations of Scripture the word is associated with a group of terms denoting compassion. Several words convey the meaning of mercy, including *hamal* (*"pity"*), *naham* ("console"), *hanan/hanun* (*"grace"*), *hesed* (*"steadfast love"*), and *hus* ("pity"). In Greek, mercy is rendered as *sympatheo* ("sympathy"), *plysplanchnos* and *splanchnizomai* (*"compassion"*), *makrothymia* ("patience"), and *charis* ("grace"). The most common words for mercy are in Greek *eleos* ("mercy") and in Hebrew the verb *raham* ("to show mercy") and the adjective *rehum* ("merciful").

In the Old Testament. The language of emotion is often tied to physical anatomy in the Hebrew Bible. Anger, for example, is a "hot nose" (see *patience*). The root meaning of "mercy" derives from the noun *rehem*, meaning "womb" or the abdomen in general. The organ of the womb and its intimate role in giving birth gives rise to a metaphorical use, signifying intimate attachment and strong emotion toward another. When Joseph sees Benjamin in Egypt after many years of separation, he "hurried out [of the room], because he was overcome with affection [*nikmeru rahamaw*, lit. "his bowels did yearn" KJV] for his brother, and he was about to weep" (Gen 43:30). When the two women appear before Solomon, each claiming an infant as her own, the real mother is willing to give up her child "because compassion for her son burned within her [*nikmeru rahameyha*]," as compared to the other woman, who advocated the slaughter of the child (1 Kgs 3:26). Mercy is "being overcome with affection" and "burning with compassion." It is the opposite of cruelty. Proverbs 12:10 states, "The righteous know the needs of their animals, but the mercy of the wicked is cruel." The metaphor takes on metaphysical connotations when the power of death and Sheol over sinners is expressed as "the womb forgets them" (Job 24:20).

The imagery of the womb as the source of birth, and its metaphorical development as an affection for another, are applied to God in the prophetic tradition. The prophet Hosea forges the tradition, describing the relationship between God and Israel as a marriage on analogy to his own marriage to the prostitute Gomer. The context of marriage provides the setting for the emotional language of mercy. Divine judgment against Israel is symbolized by the absence of mercy, in the naming of Hosea and Gomer's daughter, "No-Mercy" (Hos 1:6–7; 2:23; NRSV Mg "Not pitied"). Yet the affection of mercy prevails, and God envisions a future reconciliation with Israel: "I will take you for my wife in righteousness and in justice, in steadfast love, and in mercy" (Hos 2:19).

The book of Isaiah adds to the emotional language of mercy with its roots in the imagery of birth. The judgment of Israel, leading to the loss of their land, involves emotional conflict within God. Even though God created and formed Israel, the deity "will not have compassion on them . . . and will show them no favor," because of their worship of other gods (Isa 27:11). But judgment cannot be the last word between mother and child. And in the end the pathos of mercy returns: "Can a woman forget her nursing child, or show no compassion for the child of her womb?" (Isa 49:15). So it is with God, states the prophet, with regard to Israel and Zion. The prophet Jeremiah builds on the words of Isaiah: "Is Ephraim my dear son? Is he the child I delight in? As often as I speak against him, I still remember him. Therefore I am deeply moved for him; I will surely have mercy on him, says the LORD" (Jer 31:20). The psalmist echoes the same familial imagery, shifting the metaphor of God from mother to father: "As a father has compassion for his children, so the LORD has compassion for those who fear him" (Ps 103:13).

The mercy of God becomes the basis for future hope in the prophetic tradition. The restoration of the fortunes of Jacob will be an act of divine mercy (Ezek 39:25). The return of the Israelites to their land will arise out of the mercy of God (Jer 42:12). Divine mercy and future hope are also intimately related in the visions of the prophet Zechariah (Zech 1:12, 16; 3:9; 10:6). The conclusion to the book of Micah encapsulates the role of mercy in prophetic vision of a future salvation: "Who is a God like you, pardoning iniquity? . . . He does not retain his anger forever, because he delights in showing clemency. He will again have compassion upon us" (Mic 7:18–19).

The metaphorical language of mercy becomes one of the foundational characteristics of God, a divine attribute first revealed to Moses at Mount Sinai: "the LORD, the LORD, a God merciful and gracious, slow to anger, and abounding in steadfast love and faithfulness" (Exod 34:6; see also Pss 111:4; 112:4; 145:8; Joel 2:13; Jonah 4:2; etc.). The emotion and affection of mercy is one of the characteristics that enables God to forgive sin, allowing the covenant with Israel to continue even after it is broken. Mercy is not indulgence, saying sin does not matter. Mercy found Israel condemned as guilty, then, for some reason that only God understands, set free. The book of Deuteronomy provides interpretation of divine mercy. God is able to displace anger (Deut 13:17), to remain with Israel rather than abandon them, to resist destroying them, to remember the covenant of the ancestors (Deut 4:31; 13:17), and to bring the people back from exile (Deut 30:3). Mercy may even prompt God to change his mind and reverse the course of action against Israel (Joel 2:13–14) or even against the nations (Jonah 4:2). And for these reasons calling upon the mercy of God becomes a resource for prayer: "Have mercy on me, O God, according to your steadfast love; according to your abundant mercy blot out my transgressions (Ps 51:1; see also 25:6; 40:11; 145:8–9, etc.; for a narrative context see Gen 43:14).

In the New Testament. The verb *eleeo* and the noun *eleos* denote an emotional experience arising from the affliction of another person. In the Synoptic tradition Jesus is often called upon to be merciful to a person in affliction, recalling the language of the Psalms (see Ps 51:1). The blind beggar Bartimaeus son of Timaeus (Mark 10:47–48), two blind men (Matt 9:27; Luke 18:38), the Canaanite woman and her daughter (Matt 15:22), the man with the son (Matt 17:15), and the ten lepers (Luke 17:13) entreat Jesus for mercy. In each case they request an act of healing from blindness or disease. Jesus grants their wish on the basis of their faith, which was demonstrated in the request itself. Jesus also describes the exorcism of the Gerasene demoniac as an act of divine mercy (Mark 5:19). And once the call for mercy is placed in an eschatological setting, in the story of the rich man and Lazarus. The rich man, who dies and descends into hell, calls to Abraham in heaven, "Have mercy on me," requesting a glass of water. Abraham responds that mercy is no longer possible for the rich man, implying that he did not show mercy to the poor man in his life (Luke 16:19–25). The story recalls the beatitude of Jesus in Matthew, "Blessed are the merciful, for they will receive mercy" (Matt 5:7).

In addition to the miracle stories, the motif of mercy is used in the Synoptic Gospels to explore the ethical requirements of humans and to underscore the tension between ethics and the law. Matthew in particular explores the tension between mercy and law in two stories of conflict between Jesus and the Pharisees. When Jesus is criticized for eating with sinners, he quotes Hos 6:6 to his opponents: "I desire mercy, not sacrifice" (Matt 9:13), implying that God's affection for humans is greater than the laws regulating eating and thus separating persons. Hosea 6:6 is quoted a second time by Jesus in a conflict over picking grain on the Sabbath (Matt 12:7). Divine mercy in this instance is the presence of Jesus on earth, which is greater than the Sabbath command against work. The ethics of mercy for humans is that they love their enemies (Luke 6:35), show compassion to the outcast (the good Samaritan, Luke 10:25–37), give mercy to

others in the same way that they received it from God (the story of the unjust slave, Matt 18:23–35).

The ethical and theological issues surrounding mercy in the Gospel tradition continue in the rest of the New Testament literature. God's mercy is celebrated as the source of salvation for Christians, including their new birth in Christ (Eph 2:4). Mercy also provides Christians with a continued living hope (2 Cor 4:1; 1 Pet 1:3). Christians find mercy at the throne of Jesus, according to the writer of Hebrews (Heb 4:16). Paul celebrates the power of God's mercy to heal Epaphroditus (Phil 2:27), recalling the miracle stories of Jesus. He also describes the ethics of mercy, encouraging the Christians at Rome in the power of God's mercy to be transformed in their relationship, thus demonstrating what is "good and acceptable and perfect" (Rom 12:1–2).

Paul also takes up the reflection on divine mercy and future hope from the prophetic tradition. In Rom 9–11 he speculates on divine mercy and the future of the Israelite people. Paul quotes the attributes of God from Exod 34:6, in which the mercy of God is revealed. The future, he concludes, does not depend on human will, "but on God who shows mercy" (Rom 9:16). The mercy of God is hope-filled, according to Paul, creating a mystery regarding the future salvation of Israel (Rom 11:25–36). The author of James is more pragmatic is his reflection on mercy and the end time. He advises his fellow Christians, "For judgment will be without mercy to anyone who has shown no mercy; mercy triumphs over judgment" (Jas 2:13).

THOMAS B. DOZEMAN

Messiah *see* **Anoint**

Might, Mighty *see* **Power**

Mind, Heart, Think, Thought, Hardening of the Heart "Heart" usually renders Hebrew *leb/lebab* or

Greek *kardia*, which refer anatomically to the heart but sometimes translate other words that more often appear as "*soul*," "kidneys," or "stomach." "Mind" in the OT also usually renders *leb/lebab*. In the NT "mind" sometimes represents *kardia* but more often *nous, phronema,* or related words, which refer more explicitly to thinking.

The locus of feelings. As in English, the heart can refer to the locus of strong emotions, with more or less emphasis on the way these are felt physically. Job's heart threatens to burst unless he expresses himself (Job 32:19; cf. 37:1). The heart can melt like wax, shake with fear, cry out for someone in pain, reel, burn, desire, love, be faint, grieve, rejoice (Deut 20:8; 28:47, 65, 67; 1 Sam 1:8; 2 Chr 1:11; Pss 22:14; cf. 38:8, 10; 39:3; 55:4; Isa 1:5; 7:2; 13:7; 15:5; 21:4; Jer 4:19; Luke 24:32; Rom 1:24). The heart prompts people to act (Exod 25:2; 35:5, 21–22, 26, 29; 36:2). It goes out to someone, loves, ensnares, gets captivated (Judg 5:9; 16:15; 2 Sam 15:6, 13; 19:14; Eccl 7:26). Being the man after God's heart means being the one God set God's heart on and chose (1 Sam 13:14).

The heart can refer to what we would call the conscience as the locus of guilt feelings (2 Sam 24:10; Job 27:6; 1 John 3:19–21); *leb* is rendered "conscience" in 1 Sam 25:31.

The inner person. Like soul or spirit, the heart can suggest the inner person more generally. We must guard our heart, because everything else flows from there (Pss 10:17; 57:7; Prov 4:23; Matt 6:19–21). God's spirit dwells in our hearts (2 Cor 1:22; Rom 5:5; Gal 4:6; cf. Eph 3:17). If the heart is peaceful and joyful, this can overcome outer deficiencies and make the person healthy—and vice versa (Job 23:16; Prov 14:30 [NRSV: "mind"]; 15:13, 15; 17:22). The Israelites know the heart of a stranger—know how that feels inside (Exod 23:9). Transgression speaks to the wicked deep in their hearts (Ps 36:1). Tamar is not to take her rape to heart, and David is not to take to heart the murder of his son the rapist (2 Sam 13:20, 33)—not to let it get to them, we might say.

Nabal's heart died within him, and he became like a stone (1 Sam 25:37; he died ten days later). God was grieved to his heart by human wickedness (Gen 6:6). God promises that his heart will be in the temple—that is, God in person will be there (1 Kgs 9:3). David's heart would be one with people who supported him (1 Chr 12:17).

In Paul, the mind similarly stands for the inmost self with inclinations different from those of the outer person (Rom 7:22–25). Its calling is to focus on the Spirit's priorities (Rom 8:5–7). The renewing of the mind is thus key to personal transformation (Rom 12:2). But the mind can also be contrasted with the spirit (1 Cor 14:14–19).

One speaks in one's heart—to oneself. Sometimes this means thinking things rather than saying them aloud (e.g., Gen 8:21; Mark 2:6). Sometimes it means really believing them, and thus acting as if we do (Pss 10:6, 11, 13; 14:1). If people are of one heart (Acts 4:32), they really are one. To despise or know or forgive or trust or be upright or pure or godless in or from the heart is to do or be those things truly or deeply (Deut 8:5; 2 Sam 6:16; 1 Kgs 3:6; Job 36:13; Ps 28:7; Prov 31:11; Matt 5:8; 18:35; Acts 2:37). Thus people are to seek, love, serve, obey, follow, turn to, and walk before God with all their heart and soul (Deut 4:29; 6:5; 10:12; 30:2, 10; 1 Kgs 8:23; 14:8; Matt 22:37; cf. 1 Sam 2:1). To that end, the heart needs to be circumcised; that is, every obstacle to the preceding virtues needs to be removed (Lev 26:41; Deut 10:16; 30:6; Jer 4:4; Rom 2:29).

As standing for the inner person, the heart can be semidistinguished from the rest of the person (Ps 27:8; Song 5:2; 1 Thess 2:17; Jas 1:26). While the heart can be wide open (2 Cor 6:11), it is inherently inaccessible and private (Ps 64:6; Prov 14:10; 1 Cor 14:25). But God has access to it (Jer 17:9–10; Prov 15:11; 1 Sam 16:7; 17:28; Ps 44:21; Rom 8:27). Reference to the heart thus often links with reference to coherence between the outward appearance and the heart, coherence that may be actual or desired or threatened (e.g., Lev

19:17; Job 31:27; Pss 15:2–3; 24:4; 28:3; 40:10; 44:18; 55:21; Song 8:6; Isa 29:13; Jer 32:40; Matt 5:27; 15:8; Mark 11:23; Rom 10:10; 2 Cor 5:12). In God's case too, it can seem that the purpose in the heart is different from what appears outwardly (Job 10:13). We need to be upright and pure in heart as well as outwardly (Ps 73:1); "upright" is a particularly frequent epithet for the heart. Integrity of heart implies real integrity and contrasts with perverseness of heart, inner perverseness that can contrast with a person's outward profession (Ps 101:2–5). People can have a double heart, and need to be of one heart (1 Chr 28:9; 29:9, 19; Pss 12:2; 86:11–12; Jer 32:39; Ezek 11:19; Eph 6:5)—so that their whole being acknowledges God rather than being divided.

Heart and mind. When distinguished from the mind, the heart will refer to the inner being (Matt 22:37; Phil 4:7; Rev 2:23). More often the heart actually refers to what we would call the mind (e.g., 1 Sam 2:35; 9:19; 2 Sam 14:1; 1 Kgs 10:2; Neh 6:8; Job 9:4; 15:12; Ps 90:12; Matt 13:15). Thus NRSV sometimes translates *leb/lebab* and *kardia* as "mind," though sometimes it renders "heart" even when the reference is to thinking.

The heart or mind is like a tablet on which things can be written (Prov 3:3; Jer 17:1; Rom 2:15). The gospel message is like seed sown in the heart (Matt 13:19). Israelites have God's word in their hearts and need to keep them there and take them to heart, and not let things slip from their mind (Deut 4:9; 6:6; 30:14; 32:46; cf. Job 22:22; Ps 119:11). But if they fail to do that, God will write his teaching anew on their hearts (Jer 31:33) or minds (Heb 8:10; 10:16). There are things the heart cannot conceive (1 Cor 2:9), but God has shone into our hearts (2 Cor 4:6) and enlightened the eyes of our heart (Eph 1:18).

The heart or mind can suggest the attitude one takes to God or to other people. Believers are to be humble-minded (1 Pet 3:8) and one-minded (Phil 2:2; 4:2), having the mind Jesus had (Phil 2:5). By nature people may be enemies in mind (Col 1:21). The heart can be overconfident

or proud (2 Kgs 14:10; 2 Chr 25:19; 32:25–26), or penitent (2 Kgs 22:19), or generous and God-directed (1 Chr 29:18; cf. Ezra 6:22; 7:27).

The heart or mind can refer to the intentions, bad or good (e.g., Gen 6:5; 8:21; 20:5–6; 1 Chr 12:38; 2 Chr 29:10; Prov 6:18; Eccl 8:11; 11:9; Isa 63:4; 1 Cor 4:5; Heb 4:12). The thoughts of Yahweh's heart stand forever (Ps 33:11). God has acted in accordance with his heart (2 Sam 7:21; 1 Chr 17:19). Job should direct his heart rightly (Job 11:13). Arrogant hearts plan great achievements (Isa 9:9) but God scatters the proud with the intentions of their hearts (Luke 1:51).

"Change the mind" can render a Hebrew expression suggesting that the mind "turns" (Exod 14:5). Yahweh "turned another mind" for Saul (1 Sam 10:9). Jerusalem's mind changes so as to acknowledge its rebellion (Lam 1:20). Yahweh's mind changes about punishing Ephraim (Hos 11:8). But more often "change the mind" represents Hebrew *naham* or Greek *metamelo* "regret, relent, give up." This can be negative (Exod 13:17; Num 23:19; 1 Sam 15:29; Ps 110:4; Ezek 24:14; Heb 7:21), but it is usually positive, in connection with human beings (Job 42:6; Jer 8:6; 31:19; Matt 21:32) and more often with God (Exod 32:12, 14; 1 Sam 15:11, 35; 2 Sam 24:16; 1 Chr 21:15; Jer 18:8, 10; 26:3, 13, 19; 42:10; Joel 2:13–14; Amos 7:3, 6; Jonah 3:9–10; 4:2).

Expressions such as "keep in mind" and "be mindful of" sometimes render *zakar*, which is more often translated *"remember"* (e.g., 2 Sam 14:11; 19:19; Pss 25:6; 77:11; 78:42). Elsewhere an expression that more literally means "keep in mind" stands in parallelism with *zakar* (e.g., Ps 8:4; Jer 3:16). Conversely "I have passed out of mind" is literally "I have been forgotten from mind"—that is, put out of mind (Ps 31:12). Remembering and forgetting are seen as deliberate actions. Keeping (retaining) God's commands is also the opposite of forgetting them (Prov 3:1; cf. 4:4, 21).

"Thinking" in the OT usually involves the ordinary word "say"; thinking is speaking to oneself (e.g., Gen 20:11; Exod 2:14). Sometimes "thinking" refers to how things look to people—how they "see" things (e.g., Gen 20:10) or how things are "in their eyes" (e.g., Num 36:6; Jer 40:4–5) or how things "seem" to them (*dokeo*), which tends to be different from how things really are (e.g., Matt 6:7; 22:42; 26:53; Mark 6:49; 1 Cor 7:40 is therefore ironic). In this sense God never "thinks" (see below).

Sometimes "thinking" refers to what people "intend," stressing the link between thought and action (e.g., Isa 10:7; Jer 23:27; Matt 9:4). The noun "thought" often denotes deliberation or intention that issues in action (Hebrew *mahashabah*, Greek *enthumesis, dialogismos, logismos, noema*; e.g., Ps 56:5; Prov 12:5; 15:26; Isa 59:7; Jer 4:14; Mark 7:21; Jas 2:4). Before the flood, the intentions of humanity were all bad (Gen 6:5). Yahweh discerns human plans and intentions and knows they are mere breath (Pss 94:11; 139:2; 1 Chr 28:9; Heb 4:12). Jesus knows the thoughts people are having that will issue in accusation and plotting (Matt 9:4; 12:25). David prays that Yahweh may always keep right purposes and intentions in people's minds (1 Chr 29:18). Yahweh frustrates the intentions of the wicked (Job 5:12; NRSV "devices"). Intentions need not to be led astray but captured for Christ (2 Cor 10:5; 11:3; cf. 1 Pet 4:1). Yahweh does "think," in the sense of having intentions, and does so spectacularly, though people may find Yahweh's thoughts or intentions unintelligible (e.g., Pss 40:5; 92:5; 139:17; Isa 55:6–9; Mic 4:12). Yahweh frustrates the nations' intentions, but Yahweh's intentions stand permanently (Ps 33:10–11; *"plan"* and "thought" both represent this word).

When it is hard to tell whether "heart" refers to feelings, thoughts, attitudes, or intentions, it is perhaps best to assume it refers to the inner person in general (e.g., Deut 4:9; 8:2; 17:17; 29:18; 30:17; Josh 24:23; Judg 5:15–16; 1 Sam 10:9).

Hardening of the heart. Scripture assumes that God can influence the human mind, for example, by putting insight there (e.g., Deut 29:4; 1 Kgs 3:9, 12; 10:24; 2 Chr 9:23; Neh 7:5; Luke 24:45) or keeping people generous in heart and directing their hearts to God (1 Chr 29:18) or turning a king's heart to the Judeans and putting it into his heart to glorify the temple (Ezra 6:22; 7:27). God also promises a new, soft, fleshlike heart to replace a stone one (Ezek 11:19; 36:26). God opens Lydia's heart to listen to Paul (Acts 16:14). At the same time Scripture assumes that we have the capacity and responsibility to get the right kind of heart (Ezek 18:31; cf. Prov 2:2, 10).

The hardening of (e.g.) Pharaoh's heart or mind similarly refers to the stiffening of his resolve. The expression comes in several forms: (a) God intends to harden Pharaoh's resolve or dull Israel's mind (Exod 4:21; 14:4, 17; Isa 6:10). These expressions affirm God's initiating sovereignty in events. (b) Pharaoh's heart is hardened (Exod 7:13, 14, 22)—more literally "is hard," as the verb is not passive. This expression draws attention to the bare phenomenon of strange resistance. (c) The NT verb *is* passive (Matt 13:15; Mark 6:52; 8:17; 2 Cor 3:14–15). Is the concealed subject God or Satan (see 2 Cor 4:4)? But the expression draws further attention to the mystery of human sinfulness. (d) People harden their own hearts (Exod 8:15, 32; 9:34; cf. Ps 95:8; Heb 3:8). This form of expression affirms human responsibility. (e) God hardens the heart (Exod 9:12; 10:1, 20, 27; 11:10; Job 17:4; Ps 105:25; Isa 63:17; John 12:40). This expression affirms God's sovereignty in the midst of events.

Scripture does not seek to resolve the tension between these different expressions, implying that each conveys an aspect of reality. Human decision making may reflect an interaction between divine intention and human reflection.

Rudolf Bultmann, *Theology of the New Testament* (New York: Charles Scribners' Sons, 1951), 1:211–26; Brevard S. Childs, *The Book of Exodus: A Critical, Theological Commentary*, OTL (Philadelphia: Westminster Press, 1974), 170–75; Donald E. Gowan,

Theology in Exodus: Biblical Theology in the Form of a Commentary (Louisville, Ky.: Westminster John Knox Press, 1994), 131–40; Hans Walter Wolff, *Anthropology of the Old Testament* (Philadelphia: Fortress Press, 1974), 40–58.

JOHN GOLDINGAY

Minister, Ministry, Priest, Deacon, Elder

"Ministers" and "ministry" in the OT most commonly refer to the office and roles of the priests who served at the tabernacle (Exod 28:35, 43; 29:30; 30:20; etc.) or the temple (1 Kgs 8:11; 2 Chr 5:14; 13:10; 23:6; 29:11; Neh 10:36, 39; Joel 1:9; 2:17). In Ezekiel's vision, the descendants of Zadok are to continue the priestly ministry in the restored temple (Ezek 40:46; 42:14; 43:19; 44:11; etc.).

In the NT the Greek term *diakonos*, which in ordinary usage refers to a servant, is often rendered "minister," but only in certain passages does it refer to a recognized office of "deacon" (e.g., 1 Tim 3:8, 12). The cognate term *diakonia* has a basic meaning of service and is usually rendered "ministry." The associated verb *diakoneo* is a common word and can be used for services of any kind, although it often is used in the sense of "to wait at table" (Luke 17:8; Acts 6:2). This basic sense of service and the particular image of service at table is used at Luke 22:26–27 to characterize the attitude and duty of Christian ministers after the model of Jesus. In this scene the disciples of Jesus are instructed that they are to lead by serving, since Jesus is among them as "one who serves." Indeed, the entire mission of Jesus can be summed up in the notion of service: "The Son of Man came not to be served but to serve" (Mark 10:45 and par.). Several other Greek nouns such as *leitourgos* ("minister," Rom 15:16) and *hyperetes* (usually translated "servant"; see Luke 1:2; 1 Cor 4:1) along with their various cognates can be used in ways synonymous to *diakonos* and its cognates.

In the Gospels the verb *diakoneo* is rendered with various English translations. After the ordeal of the temptation, angels "wait on [Jesus]" (Mark 1:13 and par.); Simon Peter's mother-in-law, after being cured of a fever, "serves" Jesus and his initial group of disciples (Mark 1:31 and par.); Martha complains that she has been left alone to "do all the work" (Luke 10:40); a master in a saying "serves" his slaves (Luke 12:37); a slave in another saying "serves" his master's supper (Luke 17:8); those condemned in the parable of the last judgment ask when they "did not take care of" the Lord (Matt 25:44); the women who followed Jesus "provided" for him (Mark 15:41 and par.; Luke 8:3). All of these usages inform the concept of ministry as service in the Gospels, in which those found in the role of minister follow the pattern that has been established by Jesus (Luke 22:26–27). According to John 12:26, those who "minister" to Jesus (NRSV "serve") "follow" him in discipleship. As his servants they will be with him, and as such they will be honored by the Father.

The word *diakonia* occurs only once in the Gospels, not in the positive sense of "ministry," but as a way of describing the "many tasks" that distract Martha (Luke 10:40). In Acts, Judas is referred to as one who had been allotted a share in the apostolic ministry (Acts 1:17) and now is to be succeeded in it by Matthias (1:25). The *apostles* thus comprise a very special group of ministers who, at least in Luke's perspective, are limited to the Twelve and serve primarily by their proclamation of the gospel and witness to the validity of the church's claims about Jesus. Paul describes his own work as apostle to the Gentiles as a ministry, and broadly characterizes his role and that of his coworkers as a ministry in which as servants of God they persevere through all circumstances (2 Cor 6:3–10). In this case Acts quite properly characterizes Paul's entire career as "a ministry," which he "received from the Lord Jesus, to testify to the good news of God's grace" (Acts 20:24; cf. 21:19). Paul's ministry or vocation is comparable to that of the OT prophets insofar as his call to be an apostle can be described as having been determined before his birth (Gal 1:15). Apart from the comprehensive sense in which *diakonia* can stand for the sum total of Paul's apostolic work, it can also be used more specifically to refer to distinct activities or tasks, such as the collection for the poor in Jerusalem (Rom 15:25; cf. 2 Cor 8:19–20). This more restricted sense of *diakonia* is also found at Acts 12:25, where it is translated "mission." Of course the most notable example of this kind in the NT is the particular ministry that is established in Acts 6:1–6 to ensure the proper daily distribution of food to widows.

In 1 Cor 12, Paul discusses the "varieties of services" (*diakoniai*, v. 5) that are found in the body of Christ under the rubric of "spiritual *gifts*." Here we learn that "God has appointed in the church first apostles, second prophets, third teachers" as well as "forms of assistance" and "forms of leadership" (1 Cor 12:28). But in this passage Paul's discussion centers on prophecy and tongues, and we do not learn how the other forms of ministry are envisaged to function on a day-to-day basis. In Rom 12 Paul can distinguish ministry (*diakonia*) from other gifts such as prophecy, teaching, and leadership (vv. 6–8). In Eph 4, like Rom 12, references to miraculous gifts are absent and the focus is on apostles, prophets, evangelists, and pastors and teachers as those who "equip the saints for the work of ministry" (vv. 11–12), which in agreement with 1 Cor 12 means "building up the body of Christ." Thus *diakonia* can both stand for particular types of service and act as a generic term encompassing all acts of Christian ministry.

The image of the Christian minister as a pastor resonates with a long biblical tradition that reflects on leadership and guidance under the image of the shepherd. God appears as a shepherd in Ps 23 and claims this role in Ezek 34:11–16 over against those shepherds of Israel who have failed in their duties (Ezek 34:1–10). God promises to establish his servant David as the one shepherd over Israel (Ezek 34:23–24; 37:24). This OT image has its obvious analogues in the NT parable

of the Lost Sheep (Luke 15:4–7) and especially in the discourse of Jesus on the good shepherd (John 10:1–18), among other texts (Matt 2:6; Mark 6:34; Heb 13:20; 1 Pet 2:25; Rev 7:17). At the end of the Fourth Gospel the risen Jesus instructs Peter to "tend [that is, shepherd] my sheep" (John 21:16). The pastor in the NT is among the various recognized ministers who serve to equip other believers for the work of ministry (Eph 4:11–12). In Luke's account of Paul's farewell speech to the Ephesian elders, Paul charges these leaders to keep watch over themselves and "over all the flock, of which the Holy Spirit has made you overseers, to shepherd the church of God" (Acts 20:28). At 1 Pet 5:2 elders are exhorted "to tend (shepherd) the flock of God" in their charge, in expectation of a crown of glory at the appearance of "the chief shepherd" (5:4). Thus both Acts and 1 Peter refer to the shepherding duties of elders (*presbyteroi*) who are "overseers" (*episkopoi*, "bishops," Acts 20:28) who "oversee" (*episkopeo*, 1 Pet 5:2) the flock. Bishops are singled out for greetings, together with deacons, in the salutation of Philippians (1:1), but no information is provided with respect to their functions. That a ministerial office is involved (cf. Acts 1:20) eventually becomes clear in 1 Tim 3:1, where the bishop's duties are spelled out (3:2–7; cf. Titus 1:7–9). Christ, of course, remains the exemplar that all such ministers are to imitate, since he is "the shepherd and guardian (*episkopos*)" in 1 Pet 2:25.

As was mentioned above, in the OT priests are the ones who are frequently referred to as "ministers" in connection with their various roles in seeing to it that the daily cultic requirements associated with the temple are properly carried out. In an earlier period priests had also held certain oracular responsibilities. In addition they fulfilled obligations with respect to instruction in the law, although this duty was eventually taken over by scribes. Apart from Zechariah, the father of John the Baptist in Luke 1, priests do not play much of a role in the Gospels. While the word for priest (*hiereus*) occurs only 31 times in the NT, that for high priest (*archiereus*) is found 122 times in the Gospels, Acts, and Hebrews. In the Gospels and Acts it is a matter of naming the opposition to Jesus among the priestly aristocracy. In Hebrews, by contrast, Christ emerges as the high priest "according to the order of *Melchizedek*," whose atoning service has done away with the need for the earthly cult and the law that came with it.

Otherwise, the most positive reference to the priestly role is found in the account of the announcement of the birth of John the Baptist to his father Zechariah, during the time of his service as a priest at the temple (Luke 1:5–23). Jesus does not identify himself with priests or draw on priestly associations to describe the tasks of his disciples. While Jesus can highlight the shortcomings of priests as in the parable of the Good Samaritan (Luke 10:31–32), elsewhere his injunctions to lepers to show themselves to a priest (Mark 1:44 and par.; Luke 17:14) indicate a respect for their function in accordance with the law (Lev 13:49). In the dispute about plucking grain on the Sabbath (Mark 2:23–28 and par.), however, priestly privilege is shown to have its limits. Although Acts represents the early church in Jerusalem as frequenting the temple, there is no development of a priestly role within the Christian community. Nevertheless priests are not excluded from membership in the church, which they are said to join in great numbers (Acts 6:7).

Paul does not use the word for priest and only refers obliquely to their role once, at 1 Cor 9:13, as part of his discussion of compensation for those who proclaim the gospel. Hebrews makes more references to priests than any other NT book. Especially in Heb 7 the Levitical priesthood is shown to have been superseded by the high priesthood of Christ, who following in the eternal order of Melchizedek has replaced its imperfect and fleshly service with his enduring sacrifice that need not be repeated. The Apocalypse, however, twice refers to

Christian believers as a kingdom and priests serving God (Rev 1:6; 5:10) under the influence of Exod 19:6. Those who share in the first resurrection "will be priests of God and of Christ" during the millennial reign (20:6). In 1 Pet 2:5 believers are to allow themselves to be built into a "holy priesthood" that offers "spiritual sacrifices" to God. Thus the imagery of the OT priesthood survives to characterize the access of believers to God through Christ, even if in the NT a ministerial office of priests is absent. Already in *1 Clement* 40–41 the author reflects on the ministerial order of the Christian community after the OT model of the high priest, priests, and Levites over against commandments for the laity.

Although deacons are mentioned along with bishops in Phil 1:1, nothing further is said about them in the letter. At Rom 16:1 Paul identifies Phoebe as a deacon of the church at Cenchrae. Whether she holds an office is uncertain; nevertheless her function as a minister is not in doubt. In her case ministry includes being a benefactor (16:2). Paul employs the noun for "service" or "ministry" in Rom 12:7 twice in his phrase "ministry, in ministering," which occurs among other generic references to ministerial gifts. Deacons are often supposed to have their origin from the ordaining action of the apostles in the account of the tension between the Hebrews and the Hellenists in Acts 6:1–7. Yet this account does not use the noun *diakonos* (nor does the word occur elsewhere in Acts). Several cognate words do appear, however, which provided impetus for an ecclesiastical "memory" of the institution of the office of deacon in this passage. In 6:1 *diakonia* refers to the "aid" or "distribution" of food to widows (cf. 11:29). The same word also appears in 6:4, where it refers to the apostles' "serving the word." Finally the verb *diakoneo* appears in 6:2 in the phrase "wait on tables." But it is only in 1 Tim 3:8–13 that we find a concentrated focus on deacons as members of the church who hold a particular office. But as in the case of the office of bishop treated immediately before the deacons in the same text, what is set out is not a list of the duties of deacons but rather the personal qualifications they must meet even to be considered for appointment.

While a threefold ministry of bishops, elders, and deacons eventually becomes the most recognized pattern for the organization of church offices, the NT exhibits a greater variety. Acts pictures the church in Jerusalem at the time of the apostolic council as under the guidance of the apostles (in Acts equivalent to the Twelve) and a group of elders (Acts 15:4, 6, 22, 23; 16:4; cf. 11:30). At Acts 21:18 the apostles are no longer mentioned, while the elders appear with James the Lord's brother at their head. Elders also play a role in Ephesus, as previously noted (Acts 20:17), and Paul and Barnabas are described as appointing elders in each church during their mission that originated out of the church at Antioch (Acts 14:23). It is commonly thought that the body of elders found in synagogues (see, e.g., Luke 7:3–4) in the Greco-Roman world afforded Christians groups with their main precedent for this type of local leadership. Indeed, in the Synoptic tradition, it is the elders together with the chief priests and the scribes (Mark 8:31; 11:27; 14:43, 53; 15:1) who form the coalition that opposes Jesus. Matthew not only has parallels for the Markan references just cited but adds to them in the passion account (Matt 26:3; 27:3, 12, 20, 41; 28:12), perhaps reflecting the continuing Jewish influence on his community. In Luke's Gospel, however, Mark's references to elders are paralleled in only three places (Luke 9:22; 20:1; 22:52 [cf. Mark 14:43]), and there are no parallels to Matthew's expanded references in the passion account. Yet in Acts, elders reappear as opponents first of the apostles (Acts 4:5, 8, 23; 6:12) and later of Paul (23:14; 24:1; 25:15). That Christian groups would have adopted a leadership style prevalent among their Jewish forebears is not surprising. Even so, the precise duties of Christian elders and the requirements for joining their ranks are spelled out only in some of the later NT documents. Elders who "rule well," particularly those who are engaged in "*preaching* and teaching," are entitled to double compensation according to 1 Tim 5:17. The verb that is used here for "ruling" (*proistemi*) appears elsewhere in 1 Timothy with reference to the qualifications for the offices of bishop (3:4, 5) and deacon (3:12). The same verb is employed at Rom 12:8 and 1 Thess 5:12 in generic references to those who hold positions of leadership but with no further specificity with regard to an "office." In the latter passage those who "have charge of you in the Lord" are further described as "those who labor among you" and "admonish you"; such persons are to be esteemed highly (5:13). Additional references to leaders, using yet another verb (*hegeomai*), apart from any identification with elders or bishops, occur in Hebrews (13:7, 17, 24). The same word appears at Acts 15:22 to describe Barsabbas and Silas as "leaders among the brothers," who appear to be distinguished from the elders who along with the apostles appoint them.

The epistle to Titus attests the procedure of appointing "elders in every town" based on a Pauline warrant (1:5), which is reminiscent of the pattern portrayed by Acts. Peter is represented in 1 Pet 5:1 as an elder who exhorts other elders in their pastoral duties (5:2–5) as previously mentioned. In the local community represented by the epistle of James, the elders appear in a ministry that consists in praying over the sick and anointing them with oil in the name of the Lord (Jas 5:14); forgiveness of sins is closely associated with this action (5:15). The writer of 2 and 3 John employs the simple self-designation "the elder." In the Apocalypse, twenty-four elders surround the throne of God in the company that offers unceasing praise in heaven (Rev 4:4, 10; 5:5, 6, 8, 11, 14; 7:11, 13; 11:16; 14:3; 19:4).

The information presented above suggests a certain fluidity in the application of specific titles to the most prominent of Christian leaders. In his letter to the Philippians Paul addresses the local believers together with their bishops and deacons (1:1). When he is portrayed as speaking to the leaders of the Ephesian church in Acts 20:17–35, however, it is the elders who are addressed, who can also be termed "bishops" (NRSV "overseers") in 20:28. The association of elders with the responsibility of "oversight" (*episkopeo*) also appears in 1 Pet 5:1–2, as previously noted. Moreover, after the instruction to Titus to "appoint elders in every town" (1:5), the qualifications of these elders is spelled out in detail with respect to the attributes required of a bishop as God's steward (1:7–9). The epistles of Ignatius of Antioch show that, at least during his time and in certain of the areas in which he traveled, a pattern of a single bishop at the head of a Christian community with whom was associated a council of elders was emerging. It may be that bishops emerged from these presbyterial bodies as the most prominent of their members.

R. Alastair Campbell, *The Elders: Seniority within Earliest Christianity*, SNTW (Edinburgh: T. & T. Clark, 1994); Hans von Campenhausen, *Ecclesiastical Authority and Spiritual Power in the Church of the First Three Centuries*, trans. J. A. Baker (Stanford, Calif.: Stanford University Press, 1969); Alan Richardson, *An Introduction to the Theology of the New Testament* (New York: Harper & Bros., 1958), 312–36.

CHRISTOPHER R. MATTHEWS

Miracle *see* **Sign**

Mock *see* **Laugh**

Moses *see* **Covenant; Law**

Most High This adjective with superlative force is derived from a noun meaning "height," and is used generally to refer to that which is "uppermost" (e.g., a basket in Gen 40:17). The word is used primarily as a divine epithet ("the exalted one") or name and translates ʿElyon (Hebrew, with Aramaic variants in Daniel). The Greek translation *hypsistos* appears in the NT. In the OT it became a popular name for Israel's God, but almost exclusively in poetic literature (e.g., Ps 9:2; 21:7). In the NT it is used as a name for God (Luke 1:35; Acts 7:48), and Jesus is referred to as the "Son of the Most High [God]" (Mark 5:7; Luke 1:32). "Most High" is even more commonly used in apocryphal and pseudepigraphical literature (e.g., Sir 7:9; 3 Macc 6:2), as well as the Dead Sea Scrolls. Its common usage in Daniel and intertestamental literature suggests that God was understood in terms more exalted and removed from the life of the world. This could be a reason for the reticence of the NT, where the language occurs only nine times (all in Luke/Acts except Mark 5:7; Heb 7:1).

"Elyon" may be rooted in the name El Elyon, "God Most High," and probably reflects the use of the name El for the high god in Canaanite religion. El is also the common Semitic name for the deity and becomes a generic appellative for Israel's God as well. Other El compounds (e.g., El Roi; El Shaddai [see *power*]) have their counterparts in West Semitic literature; they are probably understood as local manifestations of El. The use of El Elyon by Melchizedek in Gen 14:18–19 (cf. Ps 78:35) may be one such reference, designating the name of the God worshiped in pre-Davidic Jerusalem. That El names are common in Gen 12–50 may reflect the language for God most prominent in the pre-Mosaic era. The use of the name Yahweh in these same narratives probably entails a claim that Yahweh is El (see Gen 16:13). In Gen 14 El Elyon is explicitly identified with Yahweh (14:22). "Most High" is commonly used with the name Yahweh elsewhere (e.g., Ps 7:17; 47:2; 83:18).

"Most High" is used in association with several different contexts and themes. Generally, the use of a superlative places stress on the incomparability of Yahweh in relation to other gods. The name is especially linked to God's creative activity (Gen 14:19; 2 Sam 22:14; cf. Ps 87:5) and to God's worldwide rule (Pss 47:2; 83:18; 97:9; Lam 3:35–38; Dan 4:17, 25, 32;

5:18, 21; cf. Acts 7:48–50), including the gods of other peoples (Pss 82:6; 97:9; cf. Isa 14:14). Even the pagan king Nebuchadnezzar acknowledges Israel's God in these terms (Dan 3:26; 4:2)! In Deut 32:8–9 Yahweh is placed in relation to Israel and Most High to other peoples. When used of God in association with redemptive activity, the context may use creational (Gen 14:20; Ps 18:13) and royal/Zion motifs (Pss 18:13; 21:7; 46:4; 87:5; the word is used for the Davidic king, Ps 89:27, and for the temple, 2 Chr 7:21). In a related vein, "Most High" is also used when reference is made to God's comprehensive knowledge (Num 24:16; Ps 73:11; cf. Ps 107:11). This usage suggests that the epithet was especially applicable when more universal claims were being made for Israel's incomparable God.

In view of such universal divine activity, "Most High" is predominantly used in contexts of worship, whether praise (Pss 9:2; 47:2; 92:1; Dan 4:34) or lament (Pss 7:17; 57:2; 77:10), as well as oaths (Gen 14:22) and vows (Ps 50:14). Indeed, "Most High" is used most often in the Psalms and may be especially associated with temple worship.

TERENCE E. FRETHEIM

Mother   see Family

Murder   see Kill

Mystery   The only OT word translated "mystery" or "mysteries" in the NRSV is a Persian loanword that appears nine times in the Aramaic portion of the book of Daniel (2:18, 19, 27, 28, 29, 30, 47 [2×]; 4:9). In each case, it refers to a dream of Nebuchadnezzar, king of Babylon, that only Daniel is able to interpret. At first glance, it would appear that this meaning of "mystery" has no direct connection to NT usages of the Greek *mysterion,* except perhaps those in the book of Revelation (see 1:20; 10:7; 17:5, 7), which like the book of Daniel is apocalyptic literature.

This may indeed be the case; however, it is interesting that King Nebuchadnezzar's dream, according to Daniel, indicates that "the God of heaven will set up a kingdom that shall never be destroyed" (Dan 2:44). In this regard, it is worthy of note that the only use of *mysterion* in the Gospels (NRSV "secret[s]" in Matt 13:11; Mark 4:11; Luke 8:10; see "mystery" or "mysteries" in NRSV notes to those verses) is in the parable of the Sower, which has to do with "the kingdom of heaven" or the *"kingdom of God."* In this case, of course, the "mystery" is not a dream to be discerned or deciphered. Rather, it is a reality that remains undisclosed even to those to whom it is publicly proclaimed. The mystery is that the enduring, royal power of God is being enacted and embodied for all people in the servant ministry of Jesus.

The word "kingdom," with which "mystery" is associated in both Daniel and the Gospels, connotes sovereignty and power. So it is not surprising to find that the apostle Paul mentions "the mystery of God" in 1 Cor 2:1 in the midst of his discussion of the "power of God" (1 Cor 1:18; see "power" or "powerful" also in 1:24; 1:26; 2:5). Paul's discussion in 1 Cor 1:18–2:5 also features the concept of wisdom (see 1:19–22, 24–27, 30; 2:1, 4–5). The "mystery" of God's power and wisdom is that it was and is enacted and embodied not by an internationally recognized wise man or king in impressive feats of rhetorical or military prowess but rather by an unknown peasant named Jesus, and quintessentially on the cross (see 1:18, 23; 2:2). There is continuity, Paul suggests, between the divine wisdom and power revealed in Jesus and his own ministry (2:1–4), as well as that of the Corinthians (1:26–31). The "mystery" is that God's wisdom and power continue to be revealed and embodied in the church, the members of which are "servants of Christ and stewards of God's mysteries" (1 Cor 4:1). While "mysteries" may involve matters ordinarily beyond intellectual grasp (see 1 Cor 13:2; 14:2; 15:51), the comprehension of such "mysteries" is subordinate to the practice of love (1 Cor 13).

In a real sense, the "mystery" for Paul is Christ himself (Col 2:2; 4:3), especially Christ as experienced in and among the believing community, which includes the Gentiles (Col 1:26–27). This dimension of meaning is also present in Ephesians, which probably represents a development of Paul's thought. In any case, the first mention of "mystery" is in the context of God's intent to "gather up all things in him [Christ], things in heaven and things on earth" (Eph 1:9). As Eph 3:3–6 makes clear, this "mystery" means specifically that "the Gentiles have become fellow heirs" (3:6). In essence, God's world-encompassing work in Christ constitutes "the mystery of the gospel" (Eph 6:19; see Rom 16:25). Another Pauline usage of the term is in Rom 11:25, where the issue also involves the matter of Gentile inclusion (see also 2 Thess 2:7).

In the two usages of "mystery" in 1 Tim 3:9, 16, the word has become nearly synonymous with the content of the proclamation about Jesus. As suggested above, the four occurrences in Rev 1:20; 10:7; and 17:5, 7 are reminiscent of the book of Daniel. The "mystery of God [that] will be fulfilled" (10:7) clearly involves the ultimate establishment of God's kingdom (see Rev 11:15; 12:10–12; 15:3–4; 19:6–8); and in a convergence with the understanding of mystery in Paul and Ephesians, this will finally mean "the healing of the nations" (Rev 22:3).

J. CLINTON MCCANN

Name   As in English usage, in the Bible most names are simply convenient labels to identify people and places and to distinguish them from others. This is so with the first names in the OT (Gen 2:11–14). Names thus designate and draw attention to individuals in their individuality, as is the case in Western culture, where addressing someone by name and remembering his or her name has special significance. To list names is thus to indi-

cate the presence of the concrete individuals to whom the labels attach: see the lists of names in (e.g.) Gen 46. To call people by name implies knowing them as individuals (John 10:3). When we know people, their names then sum up for us their individual personalities and characteristics. Thus Joseph stands firm "by the hands of the Mighty One of Jacob, by the name of the Shepherd, the Rock of Israel" (Gen 49:24). The name stands for the person. Conversely, to say that Yahweh's name is "Passionate One" (Exod 34:14; NRSV "Jealous") is to say that this is Yahweh's character. Strictly, "Passionate One" is not Yahweh's name but is the character of the person who bears the actual name "Yahweh."

Because the name thus stands for the person, speaking or blessing or ministering in a person's name (e.g., Exod 5:23; 18:5, 19; Matt 7:22; Mark 9:37–41) means speaking as that person's representative, with their authority, and being treated accordingly. Similarly, praying in someone's name means praying in accordance with their character (e.g., John 16:23–26). Saying that Yahweh's name is "in" Yahweh's aide implies that Yahweh in person is embodied in that aide (Exod 23:21). If a person's name is made known, the person is made known (e.g., Exod 9:16). To know God's name makes it possible to trust God (Ps 9:10). If a person's name is improperly linked to something, the person is linked with it (Exod 20:7; cf. blaspheming the name in a curse, Lev 24:11, 16). If a person's name is mentioned, the person is mentioned and is thereby present (Exod 20:24). If a person's name is invoked, the person is invoked (Exod 23:13; cf. swearing in someone's name, e.g., Lev 19:12). To carry people's names is to draw attention to the people themselves (Exod 28:29–30). To call by name is to call someone in person (Exod 31:2). To know by name is to know in person (Exod 33:12, 17). For Yahweh to proclaim the name "Yahweh" is to get as near as is feasible to Yahweh's becoming present in person (Exod 33:19; 34:5). For Yahweh to put that name in a place is to come to live there in person (e.g., Deut 12:5, 11, 21; cf., e.g., 2 Sam 7:13), so that one can speak to God as present there (Deut 26:2–4). To revere the name is to revere the person, and to profane the name is to profane the person (Lev 18:21; 19:12; 20:3; 21:6; Deut 28:58). To put Yahweh's name on people is to put Yahweh in person there and thus to convey Yahweh's blessing (Num 6:27). Yahweh's name can protect because it stands for Yahweh in person (Ps 20:1, 7; cf. Ps 54:1, 6). Thanking God's name is equivalent to thanking God; keeping God's name in mind or putting it out of mind is doing that to God (Ps 44:8, 20).

To be called by someone's name is to be identified with them in person and identified as theirs (e.g., Jer 7:10–14; 14:9; 15:16; 25:29). To be baptized in someone's name has similar implications (Matt 28:19; Acts 2:38; 8:16; 10:48; 19:5). Hallowing or glorifying someone's name implies hallowing or glorifying the person (Matt 6:9; John 12:28). Believing in someone's name means believing in the person (John 2:23). Calling on someone's name (e.g., Gen 4:26; 12:8; 13:4; Ps 80:18) means appealing to them in person. Knowing someone's name opens up the possibility of gaining their attention because it carries the connotation of knowing the person, because you are able to address them by name.

Eliminating a people's name from under heaven is to eliminate the people themselves (Deut 9:14; cf. Job 18:17; Ps 83:4; Isa 14:22). Making people's names perish implies making their memory perish (Deut 7:24). Conversely, to remember someone's name after he or she dies is to remember the person (Jer 11:19). To keep the name in being is to keep the person in being (Isa 56:5; 66:22). The name thus stands for memory (Prov 10:7; Isa 56:5). Conversely, to kill someone's descendants is to wipe out the person's name (1 Sam 24:21). Keeping someone's name in being if the person dies childless seems to refer to having a title to the person's land (Deut 25:6–7; Ruth 4:5, 10).

Naming someone can be a sign of authority, for example, of God over humanity (Gen 5:2), of Enoch over his city (4:17), of a mother or a father over children (4:25–26; 5:3, 29), and of owners over wells (26:18). But the fact that Hagar gives God a name (16:13) suggests that this connotation does not always apply. Giving someone a name can be a way of recognizing a person's significance in his or her own right and/or his or her significance for the name-giver. It is a matter of dispute what connotation applies in (e.g.) Gen 2:20, 23; 3:20.

Significance given to names. It is sometimes said that there is a deep meaning inherent in names in a society such as Israel's, but there is little evidence of this as a general point in OT or NT. As is the case in Western cultures, individual biblical names may once have had an inherent meaning, but in most cases there is no indication that people were aware of that original meaning. This is so (e.g.) with Sarai and Sarah, which both mean "princess," and Laban, which might have marked Laban as a moon worshiper. Such names parallel English names such as "Patrick," whose original meaning neither the givers nor the bearers of the name are aware of.

But occasionally the names people are given do have an intrinsic meaning that in their story is related to their destiny, their significance in God's purpose, their parents' hopes for them, the circumstances of their birth, or their character. Thus "Ishmael" means "God hears," because God responded to his mother's affliction (Gen 16:11). "Isaac" means "he laughs/plays," a recurrent motif in his story. It is significant that the one person whose name Jesus asks is a man afflicted with many demons, who is thus called "Legion" (Mark 5:9).

Adam's name resembles the word for ground (*'adamah*), from which he was formed, which he must serve, and to which he must return (Gen 2:7; 3:19, 23), though Genesis does not make this point explicit. It is the naming of Eve as the "mother of all living" that actually introduces the idea that names can sometimes have meaning (Gen 3:20), and Eve's name also shows how this commonly involves new connotations being given to names on the basis of paronomasia; it is exceptional for the names in themselves to have meaning. "Eve" (*hawwah*) does not *mean* "mother of all living," but it looks something like the Hebrew word for "living" (*hayyah* in the feminine), and it can thus be given that connotation. "Noah" looks as if it links with words for "rest," but in origin it likely has other connections, and in any case Lamech explains the name by referring to the verb *naham* ("comfort"), not the verb *nuah* ("rest"). It is unlikely that Nabal's parents meant to designate him as a "fool" (there are several other roots that look the same as *nabal*; only one means "fool"), but his wife finds a nice irony in the fact that the name can be understood that way (1 Sam 25:25). "Israel" means "God strives" or "God rules," but it can suggest to Jacob's opponent the idea that "he strives with God" (Gen 32:28). The name "Jesus" does not mean "he will save his people from their sins" (Matt 1:21), but "Yahweh is salvation." Similarly there are likely no intrinsic links between names such as Cain, Babel, Abraham, and Moses and the significance these names are given. When Jacob's opponent asks Jacob his name (Gen 32:27), the point may be that in his case his name can be understood to express his character, like Nabal's. Yet when Jacob is then given the new name Israel, this does not mean it actually replaces the name Jacob, which continues to be his usual name. Later, Simon's name is supplemented by the name Rock (Peter), suggesting his significance for the church; it is not wholly replaced by this new name (Matt 16:18).

Similarly, the prophets sometimes give people artificial names that have direct meaning but may not be names that are used in everyday life, such as "God-is-with-us," "Spoil-speeds-prey-hastens," "The-mighty-God-is-a-wonderful-counselor-and-the-eternal-father-is-a-prince-of-peace," "There-is-no-kingdom-there" (Isa 7:14; 8:3; 9:6; 34:12); "God-sows," "Not-pitied," and "Not-my-people" (Hos 1). Likewise, when Jesus is also given the name "God-is-with-us" (Matt 1:23), this does not mean it is a name he is actually called.

Similar principles apply to some divine names, crucially the name Yahweh. When Moses asks after God's name (Exod 3:13), that is a way of asking after God's identity. Similarly Jesus makes known God's name—that is, God's nature (John 17:6, 26). Before eventually giving Moses the name Yahweh (Exod 3:15), God answers the question behind the question by talking about the divine identity. As happens with the explanation of many human names, this does not involve explaining a meaning inherent in the actual name Yahweh. Exodus does not show any knowledge of what that name in itself means, if it ever had a meaning in itself. What happens is that the form of the name generates ideas on the significance of the person. In this case, the name resembles a form of the verb "to be" and suggests the idea that Yahweh is "the one who has been/is/will be there, being and doing whatever is needed in different contexts." In addition, Exodus identifies Yahweh with the God of Abraham, Isaac, and Jacob. The implication is that Moses is being given a new revelation about this familiar God, a new revelation linked with a new name in the way just noted. As God puts it in Exod 6:3, "By my name Yahweh I did not make myself known to them." The giving of a new name suggests a new revelation of God's character as one involved in the life and destiny of a nation, which comes with the exodus. Admittedly Genesis often speaks as if the name Yahweh was known to the ancestors. This functions as a way of making the theological point that the God the ancestors knew really was the same God as the one who would eventually bring the people out of Egypt, even if the exodus would bring a new revelation of that God.

The name for God that Exod 6:3 associates with the period before the exodus is El Shaddai, and we do not know what that name means (NRSV notes that "God almighty" [see *power*] is the "traditional rendering"). The point about using this distinctive "label" for God in Genesis is to draw attention to the distinctiveness of that period over against the new situation after God appears to Moses. Elsewhere the OT asserts (e.g.) that God's name is *Yahweh tseba^coth* (NRSV "the LORD of hosts"; e.g., Jer 31:35; 51:19, 57); perhaps it is significant that this is also an enigmatic expression.

In Gen 32:29, Jacob's wrestling opponent refuses to reveal his name. As the name indicates the person, the opponent may be declining to give away himself. The divine aide in Judg 13 gives the same refusal, explaining that the name is extraordinary or impenetrable. Apparently it is possible to know God's name but not the name of God's representatives.

Names as suggesting reputation. In Gen 11 people want to make a name for themselves, which God resists, but God then promises to make Abram's name great (Gen 12:2). A good name is better than riches or precious perfume (Prov 22:1; Eccl 7:1). Slandering someone involves bringing a bad name on them (Deut 22:14, 19). By the exodus God made a name for God's self (e.g., Jer 32:20; Dan 9:15), and Israel was supposed to be "a people, a name, a praise, and a glory" for Yahweh (Jer 13:11). "For the sake of your/my name" implies "for the sake of your/my reputation/glory" (e.g., Pss 23:3; 25:11; 31:3; Ezek 20:9, 14, 22, 44; 36:21–22). "In my name" (John 14:13–14; 15:16) has similar implications.

James Barr, "The Symbolism of Names in the Old Testament," *BJRL* 52 (1969): 11–29; Donald E. Gowan, *Theology in Exodus: Biblical Theology in the Form of a Commentary* (Louisville, Ky.: Westminster John Knox Press, 1994), 76–97; Johannes Pedersen, *Israel: Its Life and Culture* (London: Geofferey Cumberlege, 1926), I–II.245–59.

JOHN GOLDINGAY

Nations   One of the most widely used words in the OT is "nations." Beginning with the book of Genesis, the OT provides a comprehensive view of how humanity developed into "nations." Non-Israelite countries became known as *goyim* "nations," and Israelites called themselves *^cam, ^cammim* "people." The authors and editors of the biblical text depict all the nations not only experiencing divine *judgment* and chastisement (e.g., Joel 3:2; Amos 1–2) but also living under the promise of divine salvation and redemption (see Isa 2:1–4; Mic 4:1–5; Zech 8:20–23).

The first part of Genesis (chaps. 1–11) focuses on the creation of the world, inclusive of human beings. The development of human beings from families into nations begins in Gen 5, which outlines Adam and Eve's descendants to Noah and his family. Genesis 10 lists the generations that descended from Noah and concludes with the phrase "These are the families of Noah's sons, according to their genealogies, in their nations; and from these the nations spread abroad on the earth after the flood" (v. 32). Genesis 11:10–32 develops this genealogy further until one hears about Abram (v. 27), to whom a divine promise is given in the second part of Genesis (chaps. 12–50): "I will make of you a great nation" (Gen 12:2). The promise is repeated to Abraham's son Isaac and Isaac's son Jacob/Israel. As for Abraham's other son, Ishmael, the same divine promise is also extended: "As for Ishmael, I have heard you; I will bless him and make him fruitful and exceedingly numerous; he shall be the father of twelve princes, and I will make him a great nation" (Gen 17:20). Promise is not confined to Abraham's descendants, for Gen 12:3 concludes, "and in you all the families of the earth shall be blessed." When it is repeated to Abraham in Gen 22:18, the wording is slightly different: "and by your offspring shall all the nations of the earth gain blessing for themselves." Israel thus found God's concern for all the nations at the very beginning of their history.

Thus, the first part of Genesis draws attention to the nations of the earth, and the second part narrows this focus to the implied designation of these nations as Israelites and non-Israelites. Both sets of nations share a divine origin and a human ancestral lineage (through Noah). Through Abraham and Sarah, Isaac and Rebekah, and Jacob, Rachel, Leah, Bilhah, and Zilpah and all their descendants, the nation Israel evolves, and through the leadership of Moses it becomes a "holy nation" (Exod 19:6) among the other nations. Not until the time of David and Solomon, however, does Israel become a powerful political nation led by these two kings, the first of whom is specifically chosen by God and anointed by Samuel (see 1 Sam 16:1–13), and whose descendant and son, Solomon, is the last king to reign over Israel as a united kingdom (see 1 Kgs 2:1–4). Prior to Israel's becoming a great and strong nation, those nations more powerful than Israel included "the Hittites, the Girgashites, the Amorites, the Canaanites, the Perizzites, the Hivites, and the Jebusites—seven nations" that God promised to clear out of the land of Canaan that God had promised to give to Israel (see Deut 4:38; 7:1).

Throughout its history, Israel had to endure the oppression and threat of other nations. Living in Egypt, the Israelites had to endure the oppressive treatment of Pharaoh and his taskmasters (Exod 1:8–22). In the promised land their identity was severely threatened by the Philistines. Later on, the two great nations that posed a threat to Israel were Assyria and Babylon. Eventually the northern kingdom (Israel) succumbed to the Assyrians, and the southern kingdom (Judah) to the Babylonians. In both instances Israel's prophets warned the people about the threat of these two nations, and in both instances these two nations and their successful defeat of the two kingdoms were seen as part of God's divine plan of justice to chastise the Israelites and Judahites for their apostasy, idolatry, and resultant social injustices occurring among their own people (see, e.g., Isa 5:8–30; 8:1–15; 10:5–11; Jer 1:14–16; 21:1–10).

In the writings of the prophets, both Israel as a nation and the other nations figure predominantly. As a nation, Israel has infuriated God by its infidelity to *covenant* and Torah (see, e.g., Isa 1:2–31; Jer 2:1–3:5; 11:1–23; Ezek 7:1–27; Hos 4:1–19; 8:1–9:17; Mic 2:1–3:12; Zeph 1:2–13). Its religious and political leaders stand condemned; its people guilty of social injustices against their own will receive their "just deserts." Furthermore, through the prophet Ezekiel, God forewarns that this "chosen people" (see Deut 7:7–11) will become an "example" for other nations: "You shall be a mockery and a taunt, a warning and a horror, to the nations around you, when I execute judgments on you in anger and fury, and with furious punishments—I, the LORD, have spoken" (Ezek 5:15). Furthermore, God's "chosen people" will be scattered among the nations as part of their chastisement: "And they shall know that I am the LORD, when I disperse them among the nations and scatter them through the countries" (Ezek 12:15). Thus a people holy to the Lord will be brought low and will be made to realize that even though they are a people most loved by their God, they are not above God's justice. And neither are the nations who seem not to take heed of the lesson being taught to them through Israel. Rather, they take advantage of Israel in its humiliated and powerless state. The God of Israel is also God of the nations, and just as Israel experienced God's judgment, so do the nations (Isa 10:5–19; Jer 46–51; cf. Ezek 25–32).

Neither Israel nor the other nations are a people without God's hope. Jeremiah is a prophet sent to be "a prophet to the nations" (Jer 1:5, 10), to whom he often delivers a harsh but graced word of truth. God's servant will bring forth justice to the nations (Isa 42:1) and will be a light to the nations (Isa 42:6). Together with Israel, the nations will experience *shalom*, a divine gift that God will establish, and all will abide in security and freedom. Israel will receive a new divine covenant (Jer 31:31–34), will be called "blessed" (NRSV "happy") by the nations (Mal 3:12), and will be both a sign (Jer 4:1–2a) and a blessing for them (Isa 19:24–25), and thus bring to fulfillment the promise made to Abraham (Gen 12:2–3).

In the Psalms, the psalmist recalls many of the events in the history of Israel and the other nations, as heard in the writings of the prophets, while reinforcing the idea that God is king over the nations (Pss 22:28; 47:8), a God who judges the people with equity and guides the nations upon the earth (Ps 67:4). All nations belong to God (Ps 80:8) to whom their homage is due (Ps 22:27).

In the NT, Jesus instructs his disciples that the good news is to be proclaimed to all nations (Mark 13:10), that they are to make disciples of all nations (Matt 28:19), and that "repentance and forgiveness of sins is to be proclaimed in his name to all nations, beginning from Jerusalem" (Luke 24:47; see **Gentiles**). Finally, the book of Revelation captures many of the sentiments of the prophets but also speaks of a vision of divine healing for all the nations: "On either side of the river is the tree of life with its twelve kinds of fruit, producing its fruit each month; and the leaves of the tree are for the healing of the nations" (Rev 22:2).

Norman K. Gottwald, *All the Nations of the Earth: Israelite Prophecy and International Relations in the Ancient Near East* (New York: Harper & Row, 1964); Joachim Jeremias, *Jesus' Promise to the Nations*, SBT 24 (London: SCM Press, 1958).

CAROL J. DEMPSEY

Neighbor The Hebrew word for "neighbor" is *re*a*c*, a derivative of the verb *ra*c*ah*, which means "to associate with." Having the nuance of relationship, a "neighbor" could be another person (Gen 11:3), a friend (2 Sam 13:3), an enemy (1 Sam 28:17), a lover (Jer 3:1), or a spouse (Jer 3:20).

In the OT, a "neighbor" is a virtuous person who provides needed goods (Exod 11:2), shares food (Exod 12:4), and safeguards another's property (Exod 22:7). Various laws protect a neighbor. Specifically, neighbors are not to be vic-

tims of false witness (Exod 20:16); their houses, wife, male and female slave, ox, donkey, and other possessions are not to be coveted (Exod 20:17). One is not to defraud a neighbor (Lev 19:13), render unjust judgment against a neighbor (Lev 19:15), or cheat a neighbor (Lev 25:14). If someone makes a loan to a neighbor, then that person is not to go into the neighbor's house to take the pledge (Deut 24:10). Anyone who strikes down a neighbor in secret will be cursed (Deut 27:24). Although one is not to hate one's neighbor, one can reprove a neighbor (Lev 19:17). A neighbor is to be loved as one loves one's self (Lev 19:18). A needy neighbor is to be treated with exceptional generosity (Deut 15:7–11). One is also not to withhold help when a neighbor is in need of assistance (Deut 22:3).

In the Prophets, because of the infidelity and waywardness of the Israelites, social havoc is reported; neighbor turns on neighbor: "The people will be oppressed, everyone by another and everyone by a neighbor; the youth will be insolent to the elder, and the base to the honorable" (Isa 3:5). In Isa 19:2, God is portrayed as the one causing division against neighbors. This division is part of the divine **judgment** against the ferocious nation, Egypt: "I will stir up Egyptians against Egyptians, and they will fight, one against the other, neighbor against neighbor, city against city, kingdom against kingdom" (Isa 19:2). A similar fate is Judah's destiny: "See, I am laying down before this people stumbling blocks against which they shall stumble; parents and children together, neighbor and friend shall perish" (Jer 6:21). Elsewhere, in Jeremiah, neighbors are not to be trusted (Jer 9:4) and are to learn laments to bewail the Israelites' sorry state of affairs (Jer 9:20). Division among neighbors is foreshadowed by the poet Zechariah, who captures the divine rage felt against the "inhabitants of the earth" upon whom God will no longer have pity: "I will cause them, every one, to fall each into the hand of a neighbor, and each into the hand of the king; and they shall devastate the earth, and I will deliver no one from their hand" (Zech 11:6; cf 14:13).

"Neighbor" is used extensively throughout the Writings. God is the cause of a person's painful loneliness: "You have caused friend and neighbor to shun me; my companions are in darkness" (Ps 88:18). The writer of Proverbs admonishes one to be generous to a neighbor in need (Prov 3:28), to cause no harm to a neighbor (Prov 3:29), and to be judicious in setting oneself "right" with a neighbor when discretion has not been exercised wisely (Prov 6:1–3). With respect to legal matters, one should not be a witness against a neighbor without cause; nor should one deceive a neighbor (Prov 24:28) or hastily bring a neighbor to court (Prov 25:8). Cases against neighbors are to be argued directly (Prov 25:9). As for socializing with neighbors, one should exercise a certain restraint, implying that too much familiarity could breed contempt between neighbors (Prov 25:17). Thus, in all dealings with a neighbor one is to remain wise, generous, virtuous, and astute.

Ben Sirach offers additional wisdom. He advocates that one say nothing to a neighbor unless one has an appropriate response (Sir 5:12). He also warns against getting angry at a neighbor for every injury incurred and frowns upon resorting to acts of insolence (Sir 10:6). When trouble arises in a relationship, one should question the neighbor first before making accusations or issuing threats (Sir 19:14–17). A neighbor is worthy of trust and forgiveness (Sir 22:23; 28:2). Furthermore, one must be generous toward a neighbor (Sir 29:2) and refrain from reproaching one during a time of merrymaking (Sir 31:31). Thus, a neighbor is to be treated with care and respect, discretion and kindness.

In the NT, Matthew makes four references to a "neighbor." In two instances the word occurs in the context of the Sermon on the Mount (Matt 5:1–7:29). In Matt 5:43–48, Matthew presents Jesus instructing his disciples on love. The lesson opens with Jesus making an appeal to the Law: "You have heard that it was said, 'You shall love your neighbor and hate your enemy'" (v. 43; cf. Lev 19:18). While love of one's neighbor is held up as an important concept, Jesus takes the concept further and extends it to one's enemies. This becomes a new challenge for his disciples: "But I say to you, Love your enemies and pray for those who persecute you" (v. 44). Thus for Jesus, love of one's neighbors and enemies are equally important, and both reflect godliness. In Matt 7:1–5, Jesus' teaching concerns judging others. Here Jesus warns that one should be consciously self-reflective before judging one's neighbor (cf. Luke 6:42). In two other instances, Matthew depicts Jesus appealing to Lev 19:18, to provide a teaching about riches (Matt 19:16–22, specifically v. 19) and an instruction on the two greatest commandments (Matt 22:34–40). Here Jesus suggests to a Pharisee that the love of God is intimately connected to the love of one's neighbor and vice versa (cf. Mark 12:31). Mark adds that the love of God and neighbor is "much more important than all whole burnt offerings and sacrifices" (Mark 12:33). In Luke's Gospel, Luke features Jesus conversing with a lawyer who wants to know what he must do to inherit eternal life. Again Jesus is depicted appealing to Lev 19:18 and stressing love of God, love of self, and love of neighbor (Luke 10:27). When the lawyer inquires further as to who is his neighbor, Jesus answers the question through the parable of the Good Samaritan, whose love for his unknown neighbor surpassed that of a priest and a Levite who did nothing to help the one beaten by robbers and left to die. It was the Samaritan, not the keepers of the law, who showed great love by caring for the injured one. Thus Luke stresses that it is good to know about the law of love, but it is better to do it and live, for the neighbor is anyone in need of loving help.

Paul also offers a teaching on the love of one's neighbor (Rom 13:8–10). For Paul, the love of another is the fulfillment of the law. He takes four of the commandments found in the Decalogue, alludes to others, and simplifies everything, stating that all the commandments can be summed up in a word: "Love your neighbor as yourself" (v. 9). He elucidates on this statement by explaining what it means to love a neighbor, "Love does no wrong to a neighbor," and then draws the obvious conclusion stated earlier: "therefore, love is the fulfilling of the law" (v. 10). Paul expands this notion of love and neighbor further in Rom 15:2, where he states that "each of us must please our neighbor for the purpose of building up the neighbor." Finally, in Gal 5:2–15, Paul reflects on the nature of Christian freedom. For Paul, freedom and the law are interconnected, and both reach their fulfillment through love of one's neighbor (v. 14).

In the Catholic Epistles, "neighbor" appears twice in the letter of James. In 2:1–13, James issues to his brothers and sisters a warning against performing acts of favoritism, particularly toward those who have wealth and status. He emphasizes that God has chosen the poor to be rich in faith and heirs of the kingdom. In this context, he informs his listeners that they would do well if they would "really fulfill the royal law according to the scripture, 'You shall love your neighbor as yourself' " (v. 8) and concludes by stating that "mercy triumphs over judgment" (v. 13). Like those preachers before him, James views love of neighbor as central to the law and its fulfillment.

In 4:11–12, James reflects on a theme he discussed earlier: judgment. In this passage he warns his listeners against passing judgment against another. In v. 12 he makes a bold statement, followed by an equally bold rhetorical question, both of which communicate his point directly and succinctly: "There is one lawgiver and judge who is able to save and to destroy. So who, then, are you to judge your neighbor?"

In summary, both the OT and the NT stress "right relationship" with one's neighbor. This right relationship is to be grounded in and flow from the virtue of love, which, when love is authentic, brings the law to fulfillment.

———

CAROL J. DEMPSEY

New, Old, Renew, Refresh

In the OT the adjective "new" (Hebrew *hadash*) carries the sense of something that is novel or recently developed, something newly manufactured, such as the new ropes in Judg 15:13; 16:11–12. In Num 28:26 only the new grain is to be offered at the offering of first fruits. New carts (1 Sam 6:7; 2 Sam 6:3), new houses (Deut 20:5), or new garments (1 Kgs 11:29–30) are some of the items described by this adjective.

The adjective may provide a contrast with that which is old. This may imply that what is new replaces something old, and on occasion renders the old obsolete. This would describe the situation in Isa 42:9, where new things stand in contrast with the former things, and Jer 31:31, in which Jeremiah speaks of a new *covenant* to replace the old one. This same implicit sense can be found in Ezek 11:19, in which a new *spirit* is given to the people. See also Isa 65:17 and 66:22 referring to a new *heaven* and a new earth. It may, however, simply refer to something that is next in a sequence, as in Exod 1:8, when a new king came to the throne in Egypt.

The adjective "new" also describes the new moon (Hebrew *hodesh*), new growth (Hebrew *deshe'*), or new wine (Hebrew *tirosh*). In these examples the English adjective does not render a separate word but expresses a semantic element in the Hebrew term itself. The adjective identifies an early stage within a natural cyclical process. In the case of new wine, the adjective refers more to a preliminary stage in a noncyclical process.

"New life" is how NRSV renders a Hebrew noun, *mihyah*, in Ezra 9:9. The noun itself speaks of the preservation of life, an opportunity for a new start to one's life.

In the NT the adjective "new" renders two different Greek words, *neos* and *kainos.* The former is used only four times, while the latter is clearly the primary and frequent term. Matthew 9:17 renders *neos* as "new" (wine), that is, young or immature wine, but it clearly is a synonym for the other adjective *kainos,* since Matt 26:29 uses *kainos* to describe the wine that is new. In Acts 2:13 the new wine renders a Greek noun (*gleukos*), paralleling the Hebrew noun *tirosh.*

More abstract items such as new teaching (Mark 1:27), new covenant (Luke 22:20), new commandment (John 13:34), and a new self (Col 3:10) all emphasize the replacement of what was old with something new and by implication better. This sense also applies to the new material order—a new creation, a new heaven and a new earth (2 Cor 5:17; 2 Pet 3:13).

It is clear that the adjective "new" as used in NRSV can refer to something immature, something freshly made, such as a new tomb (Matt 27:60) or a new garment (Mark 2:21–22), as well as to something that replaces some former item.

Something not previously available seems to be the sense of "new" in Heb 10:20. In this case the Greek term is *prosphatos.* To bring to new birth, on the other hand, is a rendering of the verb *anagennao* in 1 Pet 1:3.

The antonym, "old," appears in a number of semantic contexts. Most often the term appears in the NRSV in references to the ages of individuals. In these many cases the word "old" is necessary to the English expression but is not marked in the Hebrew or Greek text.

As an adjective, the word "old" in the OT renders the Hebrew root *zaken.* Its focus is clearly on longevity. An alternative expression, which indicates that a person has reached a good old age, describes that person as essentially having gray hair; it is the Hebrew word *seb* (see Judg 8:32; Ruth 4:15; Ps 92:14 for some examples). On three occasions NRSV uses "old" to render the adjective *gadol,* normally meaning "great" (see 1 Sam 5:9; 2 Chr 15:13; 31:15). This suggests that the focus is on status rather than on age, since

it is set in contrast to *qaton,* "small," or in these contexts "young."

Very frequent are references to "days of old." Here the reference is to times past. Two main expressions are found in the Hebrew text: *miqqedem* (meaning "from before," as in 2 Kgs 19:25) and expressions using *'olam* ("age," "long duration"). See Gen 6:4 for a typical example. Two minor expressions are similar: *ri'shonoth,* "(former) things of old," as in Isa 43:18, emphasizing a previous situation now to be replaced, and *rahoq,* having to do with distant past time (Isa 25:1).

In the NT, "old things" may render the Greek adjective *archaios,* used with inanimate objects (2 Cor 5:17), while "old age" is how *geras* is translated (Luke 1:36). This latter is drawn from the verb *geroo,* as in John 21:18, and seems to apply to persons or animate objects. However, the most common adjective is *palaios,* as in Matt 9:16–17 and elsewhere. This adjective can describe inanimate objects but also refer to one's old or former self (Eph 4:22; Col 3:9). When the reference is to an old man, the Greek text has the word *presbyteros* (Acts 2:17 for example), in other versions usually rendered as "elder."

The verb "renew" appears only ten times in the OT in NRSV. There are five examples in which it so renders the verb *hadash,* and four when it translates the verb *halaph.* In the latter it addresses the issue of change for the better (Isa 40:31; 41:1); in the former, it indicates something fresh without any necessary evaluation as to its being better (e.g., 1 Sam 11:14). Of the seven NT uses of this verb, all but one recall the two adjectives, *neos* and *kainos.* One exception of note is the reference in Matt 19:28, where renewal of all things in the kingdom refers to their "rebirth."

The verb "refresh" carries the sense of being sustained or supported (Gen 18:5), while in Exod 23:12; 31:17 and 2 Sam 16:14 the Hebrew verb is derived from the noun *nephesh,* and so refers to a revival of one's physical and mental well-being (see also Prov 25:13). In the NT the sense is usually that of giving physical relief

(Rom 15:32; 1 Cor 16:18) or reviving a person's mental state, cheering them up.

R. A. Harrisville, "The Concept of Newness in the New Testament," *JBL* 74 (1955): 69–79.
GRAHAM S. OGDEN

New Covenant   *see* Covenant

Noah In spite of Noah's prominence in Gen 6–9, he and the story of the flood are seldom alluded to in the rest of the OT. The Genesis account uses the tradition of a worldwide flood that was well known in the ancient Near East in order to make some important theological points: Yahweh is master of the entire cosmos and can use all of nature for his purposes, he stands in judgment of human sin but is the savior of the righteous, he is patient with sinful humanity now, recognizing their frailties (Gen 8:21), and he guarantees that now the normal processes of nature can be depended on (Gen 8:22; 9:8–17). These themes are developed in other ways in the OT, usually without explicit reference to Noah and the flood. Noah is mentioned in two other places. In Isa 54:9–10 the prophet assures the Jewish exiles in Babylonia that God's compassion for them involves a divine oath as solemn as the one that promised there would never be another worldwide flood, and he speaks of a covenant of peace with them. Ezekiel cites Noah, Daniel, and Job as exemplary cases of righteousness (Ezek 14:14, 20), assuming the exiles would know that Noah had a reputation superior to almost any other character in their history (Gen 6:9).

Noah reappears as an example of righteousness in Heb 11:7 ("the righteousness that is in accordance with faith") and in 2 Pet 2:5; but the theme of judgment that pervaded the flood story appears more prominently in the NT, as the Last Judgment is compared with the time of Noah (Matt 24:37–38; Luke 17:26–27; 1 Pet 3:20). In the later Christian use of Scripture, the ark, by which God saved his people, became a favorite symbol of the church.

In Jewish thought the covenant of Gen 9 took on special importance, since it included all of humanity, not just the descendants of Abraham. So it provided a way of thinking about the relationship of the Gentiles to God.

DONALD E. GOWAN

Numbers Numbers were frequently used symbolically in the Bible as a way of making theological statements or religious affirmations.

One. The number one is fundamental to the belief in the singleness, wholeness, and uniqueness of God. Deuteronomy 6:4, known as the Shema (meaning "hear," "listen to," "obey"), after the first word of the verse in Hebrew, affirms the oneness, wholeness, and uniqueness of God. See NRSV footnotes for the various ways in which the verse can be translated.

In the Gospel of John, the number one is used to affirm the unity of Jesus with God (10:30). God is whole and undivided. And Jesus is whole and undivided with God. Similarly, the church needs to be one. That is, the church needs to be whole and undivided (John 17:11, 21; Eph 4:4–6).

Three. In the Bible, the number three is frequently used as a sacred number or a number of completeness. Ritual purification with *water* was to take place on the third day and on the seventh day (Num 19:12; 31:19). Three feasts were to be observed each year (Exod 23:14): the festival of Unleavened Bread, the festival of Harvest (the festival of Weeks or *Pentecost*), and the festival of Ingathering (the festival of Booths) (Exod 23:14–17; Deut 16:1–17). Thus the declaration is made that "three times in a year" all males were to "appear before the Lord [your] GOD" (Exod 23:17; Deut 16:16). The hymn of the *seraphs* in Isa 6:3 begins with the threefold affirmation of the holiness of God: "Holy, holy, holy is the LORD of hosts" (see also Rev 4:8). In this way, the hymn affirms that God is completely holy.

While some ancient religions had triads of deities, the Bible affirms the oneness of God (Deut 6:4). Instead of recognizing a triad of deities, the Bible occasionally uses the number "three" to suggest God's presence or work. Genesis 18:2 tells of Abraham being visited by "three men." The implication is that Abraham is being visited by God, although the exact identity of the three men is difficult to determine. Several times in the Bible, "three days" is viewed as the time period within which the work of God will take place (Exod 19:11; Josh 1:11; 2 Kgs 20:5; Jonah 1:17). This can be seen especially in the expectation of Jesus' resurrection after three days (Mark 8:31; 1 Cor 15:4). Although the NT contains the roots of the doctrine of the Trinity, it does not speak of "one God in three persons," which is a later formulation.

Four. The number four is used in the Bible primarily with reference to creation and to parts of the world. There are the four branches of the river that flowed from Eden (Gen 2:10), "the four corners of the earth" (Isa 11:12; Rev 7:1), and the four winds (of heaven) (Jer 49:36; Dan 7:2; Zech 2:6; Rev 7:1). The same association of the number four with creation can be seen in Rev 21:15–16, where in his vision of the new creation John sees the New Jerusalem as being "foursquare."

The prophets and seers frequently thought in groups of four (Jer 15:1–3; Ezek 14:21; Zech 1:18–21; 6:1–8; Rev 6:1–8). Notice especially the frequency of references to the "four living creatures" in visions of the throne of God (Ezek 1; 10; Rev 4–6; 15:7; 19:4).

Seven. The sum of three and four, the number seven is used in the Bible to suggest ideas of perfection, completeness, and wholeness. In Gen 2:2–3, the seventh day of creation designated the completion and wholeness of God's creative work, while in Revelation the seventh item in several different series denoted the completion and wholeness of God's designs (the seventh seal, 8:1; the seventh trumpet, 11:15–19; the seventh bowl, 16:17). The seven churches of Rev 1–3 are suggestive of the whole church.

The symbolic use of the number seven appears frequently in the religion of ancient Israel. The festival of Unleavened Bread and the festival of Ingathering (the festival of Tabernacles) were both seven days in duration. The festival of Harvest (the festival of Weeks or Pentecost) was calculated on a square of seven (seven weeks of seven days; see Deut 16:9). The year of jubilee (Lev 25:8–12) was similarly calculated on a square of seven ("seven weeks [or Sabbaths] of years" or "seven times seven years" [Lev 25:8]). Ritual purification with water took place on the third day and on the seventh day (Num 19:12; 31:19). Priests were to sprinkle blood from sacrifices seven times (Lev 4:6, 17; 14:7; 16:14; Num 19:4). In some cases, ritual impurity lasted for seven days (Lev 15:19, 28; Num 19:11, 14, 16). The prophet Elisha instructed Naaman to "wash in the Jordan seven times" in order to be healed of leprosy (2 Kgs 5:10).

Complete or limitless punishment and vengeance were described through the use of "seven" and "seventy-sevenfold" (Gen 4:24; Lev 26:18; Prov 6:31). Similarly, as a way of expressing complete or limitless forgiveness, Jesus taught his disciples that they should be willing to forgive "not seven times, but . . . seventy-seven times" (or "seventy times seven," NRSV Mg) (Matt 18:22; see also Luke 17:4).

Seven could be *doubled* as a way of suggesting complete completeness. Matthew constructed Jesus' genealogy around a pattern of *three* fourteens (1:17), perhaps building on the idea that David's name in Hebrew has a numerical value of fourteen (*daleth* = 4, *waw* = 6, *daleth* = 4).

Twelve. The product of three times four, the number twelve is another number (see above on seven) that was used to indicate wholeness or completeness. The notions of the twelve tribes of Israel and the twelve disciples of Jesus probably emerged from ideas of completeness or wholeness.

Revelation 4:4 speaks of twenty-four thrones upon which twenty-four elders are seated. The idea of the twenty-four elders (twelve plus twelve) is suggestive of all of Israel and the entire church. In his vision of the New Jerusalem in Rev 21,

John sees twelve gates in the city wall. These twelve gates are associated with the twelve tribes of Israel (vv. 9–13; see also Ezek 48:30–35). Similarly the wall had twelve foundation stones. The twelve foundation stones are associated with the twelve disciples (v. 14). The twelve gates and the twelve foundation stones are suggestive of the wholeness of the people of God and of the completeness of the New Jerusalem. The dimensions of the city are foursquare, "its length the same as its width," at twelve thousand stadia (Rev 21:16; NRSV's "fifteen hundred miles" obscures the use of the symbolic number twelve thousand), and the city walls at one hundred forty-four cubits (21:17; twelve squared) reinforce the point that the city is complete and perfect.

Forty. A multiple of four, the number forty was frequently used in the Bible as a way of expressing a lengthy period of time. Forty seems to have been thought of as the length of a generation, as indicated by the traditions of the forty years in the wilderness (Exod 16:35; Deut 2:7; 8:2; 29:5; Josh 5:6; Neh 9:21; Ps 95:10; Amos 2:10; 5:25). During the forty years in the wilderness, the entire exodus generation was believed to have died, so that a new generation could enter Canaan. Judges 3:11; 8:28; 13:1; 1 Sam 4:18 all seem to use the number "forty" as a round number denoting a generation.

Eighty years (forty times two) was viewed as the desired life expectancy of a human (Ps 90:10; see also 2 Sam 19:34–35). One hundred twenty years (forty times three) was considered the longest time that a person could live (Gen 6:3), and this was Moses' age when he died (Deut 34:7).

David, Solomon, and Joash are all said to have reigned for forty years (2 Sam 5:4; 2 Kgs 2:11; 11:42; 1 Chr 29:27; 2 Chr 9:30; 2 Chr 24:1). Besides suggesting that these three kings reigned for an entire generation, the forty-year reigns also suggest that their reigns enjoyed a special blessing from God. Saul's age at the time of his accession to the throne and the duration of his reign are missing in the Hebrew text of 1 Sam 13:1 and the verse does not

appear at all in the Septuagint. Acts 13:21 says that Saul reigned for forty years, but the textual tradition of 1 Samuel was reluctant to allow Saul to reign for a period of time that might suggest that his reign enjoyed God's blessing (Pope, "Number," 565).

Frequently in the Bible, forty days is viewed as an adequate period of time, or perhaps the longest period of time possible, for discipline, fasting, and penitence (Gen 7:4, 12, 17; 8:6; Exod 24:18; 34:28; Deut 9:9, 11, 18, 25; 1 Kgs 19:8; Ezek 4:6; 29:11–13; Jonah 3:4; Matt 4:2; Mark 1:13; Luke 4:2; Acts 1:3). People could receive forty lashes "but not more" (Deut 25:3; see also 2 Cor 11:24).

Six hundred sixty-six. The "mark" or "the name of the beast (see *animal*) or the number of its name" in Rev 13:16–17. This number, John says, "is the number of a person" (13:18).

In antiquity, the letters of the Hebrew and Greek alphabets were frequently used as numbers. People would add together the numerical value of the letters of their name to arrive at "the number of [their] name" (Rev 13:17).

Numerous possibilities have been suggested for the identity of the person whose name or number was 666. Most likely, however, the person whose number was 666 was the Roman emperor Nero (reigned A.D. 54–68). In Hebrew, the alphabet from which the symbolic number 666 was probably derived, the name Nero Caesar is spelled N R W N Q S R (the Hebrew alphabet has no vowels, only consonants). The letters of Nero's name in Hebrew and their numerical values are as follows:

N	R	W	N	Q	S	R
50 +	200 +	6 +	50 +	100 +	60 +	200 = 666

As we have seen, the number seven symbolizes completeness, wholeness, and perfection. Six is one less than seven. Consequently, six suggests imperfection and incompleteness. By saying that the emperor Nero's name and number was 666, John was declaring that the emperor

Nero was incomplete and imperfect. The emperor was not 777.

One hundred forty-four thousand. A multiple of twelve (twelve squared times 1000, or twelve times 12,000). Just as the number twelve suggests completeness and wholeness, 144,000 represents "complete completion" or "whole wholeness." The number is used in Rev 7:1–8; 14:1–5 to refer to the servants of God who have been marked with the seal of God. By describing the number of the sealed of God as "one hundred forty-four thousand" John was affirming that the church was going to be complete and that the multitude of the "redeemed from the earth" (14:3) would be whole.

Marvin H. Pope, "Seven, Seventh, Seventy," *IDB* 4:294–95; Marvin H. Pope, "Number, Numbering, Numbers," *IDB* 3:561–67.

JAMES A. DURLESSER

Oath, Swear In the biblical world the oath was either a solemn *vow* by which people promised their faithfulness, the certainty of their actions, and the like or a self-imposed *curse* uttered to give assurance that a statement was true. The OT expresses oaths frequently through use of the verbal root *shaba^c*. It is also common to enhance the statement of obligation by making reference to God as the guarantor of the oath (Keller, *TLOT* 3:1294). Hence, oaths take several recognizable forms through which ancient Israelites placed themselves under the Lord's potential punishment ("May the LORD do thus and so to me, and more as well if . . ."; Ruth 1:17; 2 Sam 3:35) or enhanced the force of the statement ("As the LORD lives . . ."; Judg 8:19; 1 Sam 14:39, 45; 26:10, 16). To swear an oath was to bind oneself to an irrevocable pledge. Therefore, it is not surprising that oaths were sworn sometimes at sanctuaries or sacred places (Gen 26:28–31; Hos 4:15). The level of commitment in oaths is indicated by the accompaniment of symbolic acts such as raising the hands (Gen 14:22 [Hebrew]; Rev 10:5–6). Hence when Ps 144:8 speaks of

right hands that are false, it refers to those who swear oaths with no intention to abide by them. Abraham requires his servant to place his hand under his thigh when swearing an oath, probably to acknowledge its seriousness by linking it with procreation (Gen 24:2–9). These gestures have their counterpart in modern, Western society in swearing on the Bible or promising by God that a statement is true (Pope, *IBD* 3:576).

Scripture recognizes two ways in which an oath may be sworn inappropriately. First, it was reprehensible to utter an oath with no commitment behind it (Jer 5:2; 7:9). This was particularly offensive since the oath was spoken in the name of the Lord. Deuteronomy 6:13 reveals the essence of the problem by placing as parallels, swearing in the name of the Lord and fearing and serving him (Keller, *TLOT* 3:1296). To swear by a deity was to declare allegiance. Hence, to swear falsely was to make a disingenuous declaration of piety. The Third Commandment may be understood in this context ("You shall not make wrongful use of the name of LORD your God"; Exod 20:7; Deut 5:11). The second type of false oath is one that invokes the name of a foreign deity (Jer 5:7). Such an oath was problematic for reasons already stated, namely, that such an oath was an inherent declaration of faithfulness to the deity named in the utterance.

The virtual absence of references to swearing oaths in the Wisdom material is striking. This is due most likely to wisdom's cautious view of the matter. Sirach 23:9 counsels, "Do not accustom your mouth to oaths, nor habitually utter the name of the Holy One" (cf. Eccl 9:2). Such views are pronounced in the wisdom strains of the NT. The admonition of Jas 5:12, "Do not swear, either by heaven or by earth or by any other oath," is quite forceful. It has a close parallel in Matt 5:33–37, in which Jesus refutes the conventional idea of not swearing falsely by stating that one should not swear at all, either by heaven, or by the earth, or by Jerusalem. Matthew 23:16–23 does not so much renounce the practice of swearing oaths as it refutes the pharisaical ranking of oaths and making some lesser oaths more binding. This teaching highlights again the seriousness of the oath and the caution with which it should be used.

Despite the NT emphasis on not swearing, it remained an important part of the NT world, as it continues to be used in contemporary society. Peter's denial of Jesus illustrates the role of the oath and the related curse. When confronted with his association with Jesus, Peter first offers a simple negation (Matt 26:70). On the second occasion he makes his statement more emphatic with an oath (Matt 26:72). Finally, he swears an oath again and utters a curse (Matt 26:74). The oath and curse give greater weight to Peter's abnegation and also invite harm to come upon him if he is untruthful. So while the story shows the continuing import of swearing an oath or imposing a curse, it also provides support for the sages' warning against swearing falsely.

S. Blank, "The Curse, Blasphemy, the Spell, and the Oath," *HUCA* 23 (1950–51):73–95; C. A. Keller, "*shbʿ* 'to swear,'" *TLOT* 3:1292–97; M. H. Pope, "Oaths," *IDB* 3:575–77.

JEROME F. D. CREACH

Offense   *see* **Sin**

Offer, Offering   *see* **Sacrifice**

Old   *see* **New**

One   *see* **Numbers**

One Hundred Forty-Four Thousand   *see* **Numbers**

Oppress, Oppressor, Oppression   *see* **Slave**

Oracle   *see* **Prophet**

Ordinance   *see* **Law**

Orphan   *see* **Alien**

Paradise   *see* **Heaven**

Pardon   *see* **Forgive**

Passover   Both Old and New Testaments anchor the theology of Passover in the memory of Israel's exodus from Egypt, specifically to the liminal or threshold experience of living within the pregnant pause between the reality of bondage and the promise of freedom. The OT associates this liminal period with eating the Passover meal "at twilight" (Exod 12:6), literally, "between the two evenings." As such it looks to the tensive interval between the end of Israel's slavery in Egypt and the beginning of its freedom in Canaan as the seminal moment of preparation for God's wondrous act of redemption. The NT associates this liminal period primarily with Jesus' passion, especially with the fraught interval between Jesus' death and resurrection. In this respect, the NT portrays Passover as a seminal moment of decision for both Jesus and his disciples. When Passover arrives, Jesus prepares to "depart from this world and go to the Father" (John 13:1); Jesus' disciples and followers, in turn, prepare to live amid present trials in the confident expectation that God's abiding promise of redemption will not be thwarted. For Jesus and his followers, as for their forebears in Egypt, Passover is the vigil of preparation for living in the assured but always precarious intersection between fear and hope, bondage and freedom, death and life.

Pentateuchal references support the understanding that Passover and the feast of Unleavened Bread were originally two distinct celebrations (Exod 12–13; 23:15; 34:18; Lev 23:4–8; Num 9:1–14; 28:16–25; 33:3; Deut 16:1–8). The former is usually associated with the spring rituals of the presettlement period, when shepherds sacrificed an animal in the hope of securing the successful movement of their flock to summer pasture. The latter likely originated in settled communities, when farmers offered the first of their grains in the hope of realizing a successful harvest. When and how the two rituals came to be joined is a matter of considerable debate, but two matters are clear: (1) both were linked in Israel's memory with the historical experience of the exodus from Egypt (Exod 12–13); and (2) both evolved from domestic celebrations, most likely at local altars, that focused on the concerns of individual families and tribes, to celebrations at a central sanctuary, principally the temple in Jerusalem, that addressed the hopes and aspirations of the nation (Deut 16:1–8).

Of the Pentateuchal texts, Exod 12, a composite text of multiple sources, presents the most complete and theologically formative account of the Passover. In its final form, this text locates Passover between God's announcement of the tenth plague on the Egyptians (Exod 11:1–10), the penultimate step in Israel's deliverance from slavery, and the subsequent enactment of this plague (Exod 12:29–32), through which God completes Israel's rescue. The salient details of what occurs within this moment of dramatic narrative pause are as follows: On the tenth day of the month Nisan (March–April), Israelite families are to select a one-year-old unblemished male lamb for the Passover sacrifice. The lamb is to be slaughtered on the fourteenth day of the month, specifically "at twilight" (12:6). The blood from this lamb is to be placed on the doorposts of the houses as a sign that the Lord will "pass over" (*pasah*; 12:13, 23) the Israelite homes and execute the plague only on the Egyptians. The family is to eat the meat of the lamb, roasted over the fire, with unleavened bread and bitter herbs, and as they eat they are to be dressed for the journey ahead, with loins girded, sandals on their feet, and their staffs in hand. This meal is to be observed as a "perpetual ordinance." In years to come, when the children ask what this observance means, they are to be taught that "it is the passover sacrifice (*zebah pesah*) to the LORD, for he passed over (*pasah*) the houses of

the Israelites in Egypt, when he struck down the Egyptians but spared our houses" (12:26). The composite text couples these various renditions of Passover instructions (12:1–13, 21–28, 40–51) with instructions governing the festival of Unleavened Bread (12:15–20; cf. 13:1–10), which stipulate that from the evening of the fourteenth day until the evening of the twenty-first day of the month, that is, for seven days, the Israelites must eat nothing leavened. The chapter concludes with the announcement that the Israelites did as they were commanded, and on "that very day"—a narrative marker now obliquely inclusive of the whole of the Passover-Unleavened celebration—"the LORD brought the Israelites out of the land of Egypt, company by company" (12:51; cf. vv. 28–29).

The remaining references to Passover in the OT both affirm its abiding importance and provide a link to postbiblical and early rabbinic references that extend the trajectory of Passover's place in the community of faith. Joshua 5:10–12 reports the first celebration of Passover in the promised land, at Gilgal. Once the temple in Jerusalem is established as Israel's central sanctuary, Passover emerges as a major national celebration that articulates and revivifies Israel's memory of God's saving acts on its behalf. Toward this end, both Hezekiah (2 Chr 30:1–27) and Josiah (2 Kgs 23:21-23; 2 Chr 35:1–19) are reported to have spearheaded reform movements that included instructions to give special attention to the celebration of Passover.

When Jerusalem is destroyed (586 B.C.) and all of Israel's hopes and aspirations are seemingly swallowed up by exile to Babylon, Ezekiel envisions the restoration of a purified temple, which resounds once more with the rituals of faith that define and sustain Israel's covenant relationship with God. The first of the celebrations to be reinstated, Ezekiel says, will be the Passover (Ezek 45:21–25). With the return from exile, Ezekiel's vision for the future becomes palpable and real. Ezra reports that when the temple's reconstruction and dedication was complete, the first joyous response of the people of Israel was the celebration of the Passover on the fourteenth day of the month, followed by the weeklong festival of Unleavened Bread (Ezra 6:19–22). A variety of post-biblical (e.g., *Jub* 49:1–23; 11QT 17:6–17; Wis 18; Philo, *De Specialibus Legibus* II:27–28; Josephus, *Jewish War* 6.9.3) and rabbinic texts (e.g., *m. Pesahim.* 10:1–9) extend this trajectory of Passover's importance. Of these, the text in *Jubilees* 49 may be singled out for its eschatological dimension. The admonition that faithful observance of Passover ushers in the jubilee of jubilees, when both Israel and its land will be purified from sin "from that time and forever" (*Jub* 50:5–6), anticipates Christian connections of the Passover with the expectation of the *parousia*.

The New Testament recognizes the distinction between Passover and Unleavened Bread (e.g., Acts 12:3; 20:6), but the majority of its references use the word "Passover" (*to pascha*) to refer to both festivals (e.g., Matt 26:1; Luke 22:1; John 2:23; 11:55; 12:1; 13:1). As one of the major pilgrimage festivals observed in Jerusalem (along with Pentecost and Tabernacles), Passover provides the setting for a number of different episodes in the life and ministry of Jesus: teaching the elders in Jerusalem (at age twelve), who were "amazed at his understanding" (Luke 2:41–52); cleansing the temple of merchants and money changers (John 2:13–16); feeding the multitudes by the Sea of Galilee (John 6:1–15); and the anointing in Bethany by Mary (John 12:1–8; cf. Matt 26:6–13; Mark 14:3–9; Luke 7:36–50).

Of all the events in Jesus' life, none is more critically connected to Passover than the days of his passion. All of the Gospels set the last days of Jesus' life against the backdrop of the Passover in Jerusalem, but they do so in different ways and with different emphases. The Synoptics describe the last meal Jesus ate with his disciples on the night before he was crucified as a Passover meal, specifically a meal shared on the first evening of Passover (Matt 26:17–35; Mark 14:12–31; Luke 22:7–38). While we may assume that this meal comprised the traditional Passover condiments—lamb, unleavened bread, bitter herbs—associated with the memory of Israel's exodus from Egypt, the Synoptics portray Jesus, like his Jewish forebears, extending the Passover's trajectory to the new circumstances of his day. The bread he breaks and blesses for his disciples now foreshadows the sacrifice of his body, broken for their salvation. The wine he pours out for them now anticipates the "blood of the new covenant," shed for the forgiveness of sins. In Luke's account of the Last Supper, the bread/body and the wine/blood are specifically linked to an eschatological banquet in which Jesus and his disciples will one day celebrate the realization of the kingdom of God (Luke 22:16, 18). Jesus' invitation to share this Passover meal is a summons to participate *now* in the *future* redemption that his death and resurrection will secure.

The Gospel of John offers a different chronology for the last days of Jesus' life and an additional emphasis within the Passover's trajectory. Jesus' last meal with the disciples occurs "before the festival of the Passover" (13:1). Jesus' trial before Pilate, crucifixion, death, and burial take place on the "Jewish day of Preparation" (John 19:31, 42), that is, on the day when the Passover lambs would be slaughtered (19:14). John thus portrays Jesus as the paschal lamb who will be sacrificed for the sins of the world.

Outside the Gospels, there is evidence of a typology that identifies Jesus with the paschal lamb (e.g., Rev 5:6, 9; 12:11) and that may well have its origins in Jesus' own teaching. As part of this trajectory, Paul urges the church for which Christ sacrifices himself as the paschal lamb to extend his ministry to the world by becoming the "unleavened bread of sincerity and truth," uncorrupted by the "leaven" of "malice and evil" (1 Cor 5:8). In a similar vein, 1 Pet 1:13–21 admonishes the baptized, for whom the blood of Christ has been shed like "a lamb without blemish" (v. 19), to "love one another" (v. 22), for such love bears witness to the love that both redeems them and summons them as agents of the good news.

The theological thread that stitches together the variegated tapestry of Scripture's Passover traditions may be discerned in the ancient admonition that it is be observed "at twilight" or "between the two evenings" (Exod 12:6). With this admonition, which lingers over every Passover celebration from Egypt to Jerusalem, those who step into the memory of God's promised redemption submit themselves to the summons to live faithfully in the interim between now and then, between what is and what will be. Between the two evenings, Jesus' Jewish forebears hunkered down in the reality of Egyptian slavery and waited for the dawning of a new day, a new journey, and an urgent but seemingly impossible deliverance into freedom. Between Jesus' passion and his resurrection, his followers yielded in unequal measures of fear and hope to the silence of death, only to discover that Passover's promise of redemption could not ultimately be nullified by nails on a cross. Between slavery and freedom, between death and redemption, Scripture's "old" and "new" summons is to the long journey of waiting, waiting for the fulfillment of a promise already set in motion by the celebration of Passover.

J. Jeremias, *The Eucharistic Words of Jesus* (New York: Charles Scribner's Sons, 1966); T. Mann, "Passover: The Time of Our Lives," *Int* 50 (1996): 240–50; A. Saldarini, *Jesus and Passover* (New York: Paulist Press, 1984); J. Segal, *The Hebrew Passover from Earliest Times to A.D. 70* (London: Oxford University Press, 1963); N. Theiss, "The Passover Feast of the New Covenant," *Int* 48 (1994): 17–35.

SAMUEL E. BALENTINE

Patience, Patient

The Hebrew phrase, *ʾerek ʾappayim*, means "patience," but it is usually translated "slow to anger" in English. The Hebrew translates literally, "long of nose," with the nose or nostrils often representing anger. Thus to be "long of nose" is to put off anger, hence "to be patient." Patience is a central characteristic of God in the Hebrew Bible. It is also a divine gift to humans, which must be cultivated in social interaction.

The patience of God is revealed to Moses at Mount Sinai in Exod 34:6. The context provides its central meaning. The Israelites have rejected the divine covenant by building and worshiping the golden calf (Exod 32:1–6). The divine response to the event is based on a strict sense of justice. The rejection of God by the Israelites prompts divine wrath. God's "nose is hot" (Exod 32:10), and the deity wishes to destroy the Israelite nation and to create a new people with Moses. Moses intercedes to defer the punishment (Exod 33), to which God finally agrees, prompting a new revelation into the character of Yahweh (Exod 34:6). A central feature of the divine character is patience. God becomes "long of nose," translated "slow to anger" in the NRSV. Other characteristics that accompany the patience of God in the new revelation include *grace, mercy,* and *steadfast love.* The patience of God defers the punishment of the Israelites, allowing the story to continue. The Israelites proceed in their wilderness journey rather than being destroyed at Mount Sinai.

The patience of God underscores the ability of the deity to change the course of events. The role of Moses in the story of the golden calf underscores the central place of intercessory prayer in fostering divine patience. Such prayer has the power to persuade God to change the future by withholding *wrath.* The new revelation of God as "slow to anger," "gracious," "merciful," and "steadfast in love" becomes the basis for future intercessory prayers (Num 14:18; Joel 2:13; Nah 1:3; Pss 86:15; 103:8; 145:8), which seek to persuade God to change the course of events by withholding wrath. Patience even becomes the foundation for

God to withhold wrath against the nations of the world, rather than limiting this quality to the Israelite people (Jonah 4:2).

Patience is also a human ideal in the Hebrew Bible. A person who is "slow to anger" is wise and possesses understanding, as compared to the fool, who is quick of temper (Prov 14:29). Patience is better than the strength of war (Prov 16:32) and is more persuasive in times of war than threats: "With patience a ruler may be persuaded, and a soft tongue can break bones" (Prov 25:15). And finally patience is better than to be proud in spirit (Eccl 7:8).

The Hebrew, *qawah*, meaning "to wait," can also indicate patience on the part of a worshiper who has not yet received a divine response to prayer (Ps 40:1). Patience in this instance is endurance.

The Septuagint translates the Hebrew expression "slow to anger" with the Greek *makrothymia*, meaning "patience," "steadfastness," and even "endurance." The NT employs the word to describe the patience of God. Second Peter 3:9 characterizes the delay of wrath on the day of the Lord as divine patience, allowing for human repentance. The parable of the master who forgives the debt of his slave (Matt 18:23–35) is also a characterization of God as patient.

The patience of God also becomes the model for Christians. Human patience is a divine gift, according to the apostle Paul (Gal 5:22), which Christians must cultivate in their interactions with each other (Col 3:12; 2 Tim 4:2). Patience is associated with kindness (1 Cor 13:4), meekness and lowliness (Eph 4:2; Col 3:12), and delayed judgment (1 Thess 5:14).

The quality of perseverance, *hypomone*, may also be associated with patience, as in the psalmist's determination to wait for God (Ps 40:1). In the NT, Christians are called upon to endure or have patience during the present time of tribulation. The author of Hebrews encourages Christians to endure "so that when you have done the will of God, you may receive what was promised" (Heb 10:36). The present time of trials, according to

the author of James, will test the faith of Christians in order to produce "endurance," making them "mature and complete, lacking in nothing" (Jas 1:4).

THOMAS B. DOZEMAN

Peace　"Peace" translates the OT Hebrew *shalom* and the NT Greek *eirene*. Both are deeply interwoven into the central theological purposes of both Testaments. Shalom occurs more than 200 times and *eirene* about 100 times (once NRSV translates *siopa* as "peace," Mark 5:39). *Shalom* is iridescent in meaning, connoting total well-being. *Shalom* may denote (material) prosperity (Pss 37:11; 72:1–7; 128:5–6; 147:14; Isa 66:12; Zech 8:12), ethical relations among humans (Zech 8:19), or eschatological (messianic) hope that brings peace among nations (Isa 9:2–7; Zech 9:9–11; cf. Isa 2:2–4; Mic 5:4–5). *Shalom* cannot be understood apart from Israel's understanding of Yahweh-war that establishes and maintains creation order against chaos (see *war*; Exod 14:14; Pss 29; 68; 89:6–18; Ollenburger). Though war is not an antonym of *shalom* (2 Sam 11:7—David asks Uriah about the *shalom* of the war), *shalom* is usually absence of war, often by negotiated peace treaties between nations (Deut 20:10–12; Josh 9:15; 10:1, 4; Judg 4:17; 1 Sam 7:14; 1 Kgs 5:12). *Shalom* is also tranquility or quietness of spirit (Ps 119:165). Its cognate, *shalem*, is best translated "health." *Shalom* is paired with healing (Jer 8:15; 14:19; 33:6–9; Isa 53:5; 57:19); Jesus' healing brings *eirene*-peace (Mark 5:24–34; Acts 10:36, 38). In Psalms *shalom* is "health" (38:3). "Shalom be with you" is a common greeting (Judg 6:24; 19:20; 1 Sam 25:6; 2 Sam 18:28; Pss 122:6; 125:5; 127:5; 128:6). Seeking and pursuing peace is a moral imperative for God's people (Ps 34:14).

The much-loved Moses/Aaronic benediction begins with "The LORD bless you and keep you" and ends with "the LORD . . . give you peace (*shalom*)" (Num 6:24–26). Yahweh is self-designated as *shalom* (Judg 6:24; cf. Yahweh-*rapha*ʾ, healer in Exod 15:26). God ultimately is the source of peace (Isa 52:7; 60:17; 66:12). God promises a "covenant of peace" with the faithful (Isa 54:10; Ezek 34:25; 37:26; Mal 2:5–6), for "the effect of righteousness will be peace" (Isa 32:17); "righteousness and peace will kiss each other" (Ps 85:10). Peace is associated with God's steadfast love and faithfulness, the fruit of salvation (Ps 85:7–13).

While the base meaning of *shalom* is "well being" or "wholeness," three main dimensions of meaning occur in the Hebrew Bible. For von Rad, *shalom* denotes material, physical well-being within a social context, thus characterizing human relations. Eisenbeis concurs that *shalom* designates "wholeness" and "intactness" of life, but its primary use describes some aspect of relationship with God and is theological, closely associated with **salvation**. Westermann concurs that *shalom* denotes wholeness and well-being but views *shalom* as a state or condition, rather than relationship. Gerlemann concludes that *shalom* refers to both state and relationship (Yoder in Yoder/Swartley, 1992: 3–9; 2001:1–8).

A second scholarly perspective (Schmid and Steck) argues that *shalom* denotes a correct order of life; the notion of **creation** order binds together the various uses of *shalom* into a unified whole. War, not an antithesis to *shalom* (2 Sam 11:7), may be divine judgment to restore the *shalom* of the creation order. Whatever blocks Yahweh's order for the world, materially or relationally, is the foe and antithesis of *shalom*. In Jerusalem's cult the king was authorized to administer and defend the *shalom* of God's order against injustice and oppression.

Yoder proposes also a moral quality in *shalom*. It stands against oppression, deceit, fraud, and all actions that violate the divine order for human life. *Shalom* contrasts to deceit (Ps 34:13–14; 37:37; Jer 9:4–9), denotes innocence from moral wrongdoing (Gen 44:17; 1 Kgs 5:12), and is paired with **justice** (*mishpat*; Isa 59:18; Zech 8:16–19) and righteousness (*tsede-*

qah; Ps 72:7; Isa 54:13; 48:18 [NRSV: "prosperity" and "success"]; 60:17).

Hanson holds that *shalom* underwent shifts in understanding through Israel's history. In early Yahwism it was understood "as something other than a human achievement. It was a condition of life, received by those allowing themselves to be drawn into a pattern of community manifested by the God who delivered Hebrew slaves from their bondage" (Hanson, 347). The wars of the kings, waged mostly not "in the name of God's order of righteousness and peace but rather in the name of an imperialistic ideology" (351), competed against *shalom*, which the prophet Isaiah identified with quiet trust in God (Isa 8:1–5; 30:15). Israel's royal ideology threatened the early Yahwistic and Isaiah's view of *shalom*. The prophets criticized this threat.

Forged out of the exilic crisis, Second Isaiah affirms new visions and understandings of *shalom* (52:7–10). Not only is God's order of *shalom* now seen in cosmic proportion, but Israel's vocation is defined as one of agent and witness, even in suffering (53:5 "whole" is *shalom*). Finally, in Isa 56–66 this cosmic vision extends to "a renewal of creation to its divinely intended wholeness" (Hanson, 359). But in postexilic Israel, internal community strife and exclusivist views toward neighbors subverted this vision of *shalom*. Differing essentially from the prophetic messianic hope of "beating swords into plowshares" (Isa 2:4; Mic 4:3), an apocalyptic view developed that deferred *shalom* beyond history's horizon. In much of Israel's apocalyptic, Yahweh's order of *shalom* "ceases to be taken up as the community's earthly vocation, but is awaited as a divine act which inflicts stinging defeat on outsiders even as it imbues the insiders with paradisiacal blessing" (Hanson, 361).

Eirene in secular Greek sources is comparatively narrow in meaning. It simply contrasts to war, and often describes the time of tranquility and prosperity that follows victory in war. But in addition to *eirene* describing the sociopolitical condition, it may denote virtue as well. Klassen (*ABD*, 207) proposes two paths to such peace in Greek literature, one whereby such virtue is achieved heroically in war and another, unheroic means through work that produces peace and justice.

When *eirene* is used in classical Greek literature, it is not always clear whether the term refers to a sociopolitical condition or to the Greek goddess Eirene. Historians Herodotus (1:87) and Thucydides (2:61.1) speak of peace as a desirable sociopolitical condition, for humanitarian and political reasons. Euripides, however, recognizing that the spear-raging Hellas would destroy herself, calls people to turn to the goddess Eirene. A statue of Eirene was erected on the *agora* in Athens in 375 B.C., and thereafter the annual celebration of the peace treaty between Sparta and Athens in 375 B.C. began with an offering to Eirene. Even with this visibility Eirene never emerged beyond minor goddess status in Greco-Roman culture. Dinkler cites H. Fuchs, "Although she is peace, she is not the one that brings peace" (in Yoder/Swartley 1992, 175; 2001, 86).

Complementing this emergence of Eirene as a significant minor deity in the Greek-speaking East, in the Latin West Augustus introduced the Pax cult into Roman imperial politics. The older Roman Concordia cult was now nicely balanced with a Pax cult. The former was directed to internal policy; the latter toward imperial policy. Through this relationship, *eirene* as Pax Romana became a power pacifying foreign nations to enable harmony to continue at home. The erection of the Altar of Peace to Augustus on the field of Mars in Rome in 9 B.C. is telling. The location discloses the means of Pax Romana: wars to subjugate the nations. Vespasian's Peace Temple, built A.D. 75, celebrates Rome's victory over the Jews, depicted on the famous arch.

The Pax Romana was considered an ideal world of prosperity and order with a worldwide Greco-Roman language and culture. These features superficially accord with the Hebrew notion of *shalom*. But the Pax Romana was maintained by subjugating peoples who suffered oppression in Rome's "golden age" of prosperity—features that oppose and mock *shalom* (Wengst).

In NT usage peace (*eirene*) carries meaning derived from OT *shalom*, because the LXX consistently translated *shalom* with *eirene*. But Dinkler contends that we cannot know the precise degree of influence that the classical Greek use of *eirene* had upon the NT writers. He rightly holds that the NT use of *eirene* is best understood by the OT *shalom*.

The semantic field of peace puts these terms into relationship with other key theological concepts. Key OT coemphases for *shalom* are creation, covenant, steadfast love, faithfulness, salvation, and God's reign (see above for texts). *Shalom* is indeed a gift, but its maintenance in human life depends upon human response to God's order that values and acts in accord with the divine moral order for human society. For *eirene*, occuring 100 times and in all NT books except 1 John, the co-terms are kingdom of God (Matt 5:9), justice/justification and righteousness (Rom 3:21–26; 5:1–11), reconciliation (Rom 5:11; Col 1:20; Eph 2:14–17), joy (Rom 14:17; Gal 5:22), faith and salvation (Rom 5:1, 6–11; Eph 6:15–17), love (Rom 5:1, 8; Gal 5:22), and wholeness in body and spirit (1 Thess 5:23).

Jesus and the Gospels. NT peace language accrues meaning against the context of social and political conflict, as well as human alienation from God (Swartley, 1996). The passion account narrates conflict between Jesus and the political powers, but in all four Gospels Jesus refuses vengeance and models nonviolence (Desjardins, 20–22). Jesus' call to discipleship sets up conflict between peoples, so that Jesus says, "Do not think I have come to bring peace to the earth; I have not come to bring peace but a sword" (Matt 10:34–36; Luke 12:51, "division" for "sword").

Paul's theology of atonement links peace to conflict, battle, and victory. Specific texts like Luke 10:1–20; Rom 16:20; and Eph 6:10–18 are exemplary and foundational. Jesus' victory over the powers (Col 2:12–15; 1 Cor 15:24–27; Rom 8:37–39; Eph 6:10–20) is an essential aspect, even precondition, for God's peacemaking among humans, in relation to God's self and fellow humans. It is important, therefore, to treat *eirene* in the broader conceptual perspective, via semantic field relations and conceptual associations, though word-occurrences are important and control the scope. Pervasive NT emphases on nonretaliation toward evil and love of the enemy (Matt 5:38–48 and par. Luke 6:27–36; Rom 12:17–21; 1 Thess 5:15; 1 Pet 2:21–23; 3:9–17) are the ethical components that break the spiral of human violence and make peace possible. The parable of the Good Samaritan (Luke 10:27–36) and Jesus' encounter with the Samaritan woman (John 4) depict the peace gospel. The Golden Rule captures the essence of peacemaking: "in everything do to others as you would have them do to you" (Matt 7:12).

In the Synoptics, "kingdom of God" and "gospel" are interrelated to *eirene.* The Sermon on the Mount links the kingdom of God to peace in the seventh beatitude, by identifying peacemakers (*eirenopoioi*) as the children ("sons") of God (5:9), using here an image from Israel's royal tradition. This call to peacemaking is fleshed out in the six antitheses (supertheses) in Matt 5:21–48, especially in the first (reconcile with brother or sister), fifth (do not resist evil with evil), and sixth (love your enemies). In this peacemaking, humans press toward the goal of God's perfect (*teleios* = complete) love.

Mark witnesses to Jesus' teaching his disciples in a sustained pattern the way of peacemaking as essential to "entering the kingdom of God" (8:27–10:45), with distinctive use of the verbal form *ereneuete* in 9:50. Jesus' strong admonition to "be at peace with one another" contrasts to the disciples' vying for greatness in the coming kingdom; rivalry that foments strife opposes peace. The admonition follows a puzzling command, "Have salt in yourselves" (9:50), which, echoing the salted offering to covenant with God (Lev 2:13),

suggests that the disciples are to give themselves as salted offerings for Jesus' peace covenant with them (cf. Rom 12:1–2). Becoming as "a little child" to enter the kingdom (Luke 10:15; Matt 18:4) also models humble peacemaking as a mark of the true disciple.

Luke accentuates these three related themes: announcing the gospel, the kingdom, and peace. While Mark uses "gospel" only as a noun, Luke uses the verb *euangelizesthai*, "to announce the gospel," and thus witnesses Jesus' understanding of his mission in light of the gospel-kingdom-peace proclamation of Isa 52:7. Luke uses *eirene* fourteen times in the Gospel and seven times in Acts. The texts that link gospel and kingdom are 4:43; 8:1; 16:16; Acts 8:12. Those linking gospel and peace are 2:10, 14, which heralds the keynote theme of the messianic age, "Peace on earth." Zechariah's Benedictus concludes with assurance that the baby born to Mary will "guide our feet into the way of peace" (Luke 1:79). With these assurances, Simeon praises God and says, "Master, now you are dismissing your servant in peace" (2:29). Acts 10:36 sums up Jesus' ministry as "preaching the good news of peace." Luke 10:1–12 is important in linking peace and kingdom. The message that the seventy take to the people is introduced by a greeting of peace (*shalom/eirene*): "Peace be to this house" (v. 5). The one who receives the gospel is called "a son or child of peace" (v. 6). This echoes Jesus' beatitude "Blessed are the peacemakers, for they will be called the children of God" (Matt 5:9; cf. 5:48). The gospel-peace message is further defined as "the kingdom of God" come to them (vv. 9, 11), whether or not they accept it. Jesus' statement in Luke 10:18, "I watched Satan fall from heaven like a flash of lightning," declares the victory of God's kingdom-peace-gospel proclaimed by Jesus. The gospel is God's reign of peace; it shall be victorious and embrace all peoples.

Peace (*eirene*) is one of Luke's journey narrative emphases in his distinctive central section. The narrative begins by Jesus rebuking his disciples for desiring to destroy enemy Samaritans (9:51–55). Then the early and last narratives in the section (10:1ff.; 19:28ff.) are laced with Luke's peace accent. The word occurs three times in 10:5–6, including the phrase "son of peace," and twice again in 19:28–42. The disciples following Jesus to his triumphal entry into Jerusalem praise God, announcing, "Peace in heaven, and glory in the highest heaven" (19:38). But the mood shifts at the Pharisees' unbelief, and Jesus weeps over Jerusalem for its coming judgment, saying, "If you, even you, had only recognized on this day the things that make for peace!" (19:42). Certainly these uses of *eirene* carry forward Luke's narrative intentions, with 19:38 as antiphonal response to the angelic choir in 2:14 heralding Jesus' birth as "glory in heaven" and "peace on earth." Though rejected by Jerusalem, Jesus in resurrected power appears to and greets his disciples, "Peace be with you" (24:36).

In John, Jesus' abiding gift is peace (*eirene*), twice in his farewell address (14:27; 16:33) and three times in his postresurrection appearances ("Peace be with you" in 20:19, 21, 26). The gift of peace contrasts to what the world gives; it frees from fear: "do not let your hearts be troubled, and do not let them be afraid" (14:27). In 16:33, the promised peace is in Jesus, whereas in the world there is persecution. Understood within the larger conflictive ethos of the Gospel, peace is God's eschatological gift that Jesus instills into his community abiding in his love (13:34–35; 15:9–13; cf. 1 John 4:7–16). The postresurrection triple greeting assures the despairing disciples that the Jesus who promised abiding peace is here, in glorified form, and will empower them with the promised Holy Spirit for mission in the world (21:21–23).

Pauline (and deutero-Pauline) writings. *Eirene* occurs forty-four times in Pauline writings: Romans, ten (1:7; 2:10; 3:17; 5:1; 8:6; 14:17, 19; 15:13, 33; 16:20); Ephesians, eight (1:2; 2:14, 15, 17[2×]; 4:3; 6:15, 23); four each in 1 Corinthians (1:3; 7:15; 14:33; 16:11) and the Pastorals (1 Tim 1:2; 2 Tim

1:2; 2:22; Titus 1:4); three each in Galatians (1:3; 5:22; 6:16), Colossians (1:2, 20; 3:15), Philippians (1:2; 4:7, 9), 1 Thessalonians (1:1; 5:3, 23), and 2 Thessalonians (1:2; 3:16[2x]); twice in 2 Corinthians (1:2; 13:11); and once in Philemon (1:3).

A most distinctive phrase is "God of peace," occurring six times: Rom 15:33; 16:20; 2 Cor 13:11; Phil 4:9; 1 Thess 5:23; 2 Thess 3:16. These benedictions together with Paul's salutations of "grace and peace" are not merely cultural but convey blessing emanating from the gospel (Mauser, 106–8); they show the extent to which peace functioned as formational ethos in early Christian communities. Paul claims peace as reality through Christ; his opponents promise false peace and foment dissensions, deceive believers, and serve their own bellies (Rom 16:17–20; 1 Thess 5:3; cf. Phil 3:17–21; 1 Cor 6:12–20).

Romans 5:1–11 and Eph 2:14–17 are central texts in Paul's peace theology (Mauser, 112–21, 151–65; Dinkler, 1992: 176–85; 2001: 90–105). Peace with God (Rom 5:1) is through justification by faith. The pronouncement stands in the wider context of God's wrath against sin (Rom 1:18ff.), the primacy of faith (chaps. 3–4), and human disobedience (5:12–6:23). In Ephesians Paul sums up Jesus' mission by joining two key Isaiah peace texts. Jesus comes "preaching peace" (*euangelizesthai eirene*), echoing Isaiah's *mebasser shalom* (52:7). Likewise the phrase "peace to those far and near" denotes Isaiah's universal vision (42:6; 49:6; 52:10; and here 57:19). For Paul, this peace phrase fits beautifully his own experience of God's expanding kingdom gospel of peace: Gentiles, those far, and Jews, those near, have been made one in and through the peace of Christ. Jesus Christ breaks down the dividers, destroys the enmity, creates one new humanity, and thus makes peace.

Reconciliation is the outcome of God's peacemaking event through Jesus Christ, incarnating God's love for enemies. "All this is from God, who reconciled us to himself through Christ, and has given us the ministry of reconciliation: that is, in

Christ was God reconciling the world to himself, not counting their trespasses against them" (2 Cor 5:18–19). The cosmic goal of God's salvation in Jesus Christ is to reconcile all things to God's self "by making peace through the blood of his cross" (Col 1:20). God's peacemaking is anchored fully in the cross of Jesus Christ, who disarmed the powers (Col 2:15), forgave sins (Col 1:13–14; Eph 1:7), and united formerly alienated parties, Jews and Gentiles, in common access to God.

Peace with God bears fruit in life in the Spirit (Gal 5:22–23; Rom 6:8; 8:9–11; Mauser, 121–25). "To set the mind on the Spirit is life and peace" contrasts to setting the mind on the flesh, which is death (Rom 8:6); similarly the "works of the flesh" (Gal 5:19) stand opposed to the "fruit of the Spirit," which is "love, joy, peace, patience, kindness, generosity, faithfulness, gentleness, and self-control" (Gal 5:22–23). Believers are called to peace (1 Cor 7:15), and as members of one body are to make "every effort to maintain the unity of the Spirit in the bond of peace" (Eph 4:3–6). Thus, "let the peace of Christ rule in your hearts, to which indeed you were called in the one body" (Col 3:15). Further, the peace of God is power that "will guard your hearts and your minds in Christ Jesus" (Phil 4:7). Peace also characterizes living for the service of God (Rom 12–15 and parallel thought in 1–2 Corinthians). Further, believers are admonished to be at peace with one another and to seek/pursue peace (Rom 12:18; 1 Thess 5:13; 2 Cor 13:11; 2 Tim 2:22; Heb 12:14; cf. Ps 34:14). Peace is thus both a gift and a virtue to strive toward, for believers know that the cross of Christ makes such possible.

Hebrews, James, and Peter. Jesus, the priest resembling Melchizedek, rules over the city of peace (Jerus-salom): "His name, in the first place, means, 'king of righteousness'; next he is also king of Salem, that is, 'king of peace'" (Heb 7:2). This high priest suffered in the flesh (5:7–10); so the discipline believers experience "yields the peaceful fruit of righteousness" (12:11). Believers are called to

"pursue peace with everyone" (12:14). A "God of peace" benediction (13:20–21) climaxes the epistle.

James contrasts "pure . . . peaceable" wisdom to "earthly, unspiritual, devilish" wisdom (3:15, 17) and then (3:18) echoes and complements Isa 32:17, reversing the order between peace and justice: "a harvest of righteousness (justice) is sown in peace for [by, RSV] those who make peace." Peacemaking is the way to peace and contrasts to conflicts, disputes, and war (4:1–4; cf. Rev 6:4, where war takes peace from the earth).

First Peter develops at length a nonretaliation ethic that appeals to Jesus as model in enduring suffering, calling believers to "follow in his steps " (2:21). Psalm 34:12–15 is quoted to authorize turning from evil to doing good, and to "seek peace and pursue it" (3:11). The epistle concludes characteristically, "Peace to all of you who are in Christ" (5:14).

Michel Desjardins, *Peace, Violence, and the New Testament* (Sheffield: Sheffield Academic Press, 1997); Victor Paul Furnish, "War and Peace in the New Testament," *Int* 38 (1984): 363–83; Paul D. Hanson, "War and Peace in Hebrew Scripture," *Int* 38 (1984): 341–62; Joseph P. Healey and William Klassen, "Peace," *ABD* 5:206–13; William Klassen, *Love of Enemies: The Way to Peace* (Philadelphia: Fortress, 1984); Ulrich Mauser, *The Gospel of Peace* (Louisville, Ky.: Westminster/John Knox, 1992); Ben C. Ollenburger, "Peace and God's Action against Chaos in the Old Testament," in *The Church's Peace Witness*, ed. Marlin E. Miller and Barbara Nelson Gingerich (Grand Rapids: Eerdmans, 1994), 70–88; Willard M. Swartley, "War and Peace in the New Testament," in *Aufstieg und Niedergang der römischen Welt*, ed. H. Temporini and W. Haase, II.26.3 (1996): 2298–2410; Klaus Wengst, *Pax Romana and the Peace of Jesus Christ* (Philadelphia: Fortress Press, 1987); Perry B. Yoder, *Shalom: The Bible's Word for Salvation, Justice, and Peace* (Newton, Kans.: Faith and Life Press, 1987; Nappanee, Ind.: Evangel Press, 1998); Perry B. Yoder and Willard M. Swartley, eds., *The Meaning of Peace: Biblical Studies*, SPS 2 (Louisville, Ky.: Westminster/John

Knox Press, 1992; rev. ed., Elkhart, Ind.: Institute of Mennonite Studies, 2001): key articles in this collection of twelve trans. from German are: Claus Westermann, "Peace (*Shalom*) in the Old Testament," (1992): 16–48; (2001): 37–70; J. Kremer, "Peace—God's Gift: Theological Considerations," (1992): 133–47; (2001): 21–36; and Erich Dinkler, "*Eirene*—The Early Christian Concept of Peace," (1992): 164–212; (2001): 71–120.

WILLARD M. SWARTLEY

Pentecost　Pentecost was the biblical feast of Weeks, so called because it occurred fifty days (Greek *pentekonta*, "fifty") after Passover (i.e., seven weeks plus one day). In the Hebrew Bible, the feast of Weeks celebrated the firstfruits of the coming summer wheat harvest; it was one of the three great pilgrimage festivals (Exod 34:22; Num 28:26; Deut 16:10, 16; 2 Chr 8:13). Israelites offered the first of their harvest to the Lord and ceased from work that day, showing their dependence on God's provision. The image probably lies behind Paul's mention of the *spirit* as the firstfruits of believers' end-time inheritance (Rom 8:23). Jewish tradition came to associate the festival with covenant renewal and eventually with God's gift of the law (which some have associated with the gift of the Spirit in Acts 2:33, 38).

When Christians today think of Pentecost, they usually think of the gift of the Spirit to the church in Acts 2. When Jesus promised the Spirit to his disciples shortly before this time (Acts 1:4–5, 8), they would have understood his promise in the light of biblical prophecies about God restoring Israel in the end time (Isa 44:2–3; Ezek 36:24–28; 37:14; Joel 2:28–3:1). Presumably they also recognized the traditional association of the Spirit with prophecy (Joel 2:28) to empower Israel as witnesses in the end time (Isa 42:1; 44:3, 8). The disciples naturally associated his promise with the end time (Acts 1:6), though misunderstanding that the kingdom comes in two phases because the Messiah comes twice (1:7).

This idea of the future kingdom (see *kingdom of God*) breaking into the present age probably pervades the entire Pentecost narrative that follows (Acts 2). It likely appears in the signs at Pentecost (2:2–4). First, the wind (Acts 2:2) probably recalls Ezekiel's prophecy about the Spirit restoring and raising God's people in the end time (Ezek 37:5–10, 14). The *fire* (Acts 2:3) likewise may proleptically suggest end-time judgment (cf. Isa 66:15–16; Zeph 1:18; Mal 3:2; Luke 3:9, 16–17). Peter's speech also associates tongues (2:4; see *gifts*) with the end time. The Spirit-given tongues function in this narrative as a fulfillment of Joel's prophecy about the Spirit empowering God's people to prophesy (2:16–18; notice the connection between "this" in 2:6 and in 2:16). The point seems to be that if the disciples can praise God in languages they do not know, by the Spirit's inspiration, they can also witness (presumably in languages they do know) across cultural barriers by the Spirit's inspiration (1:8). In view of this, it is not surprising that in Acts, the prophetic "word of the Lord" usually refers to the gospel message.

Further, the nations in a proleptic sense hear this gospel on Pentecost; Diaspora Jews present for the festival recognize the various languages (2:5–13). Because the list of nations in Acts 2:9–11 covers the same territory found in the table of nations in Gen 10, many scholars see in the Pentecost experience of tongues a symbolic reversal of the divine division of nations accomplished at the tower of Babel (Gen 11).

Peter's speech uses the phenomenon of tongues (2:16–17) to demonstrate that the end time has arrived in some sense, hence the time of salvation for all who call on the Lord's name (2:21). Whereas Joel 2:32, which he quotes, speaks of the divine name, Peter argues that Jesus is the true bearer of this name and must be called on in baptism for salvation (2:38). In 2:39, having finished expounding salvation through Jesus' name, Peter resumes the quotation from Joel 2:32. Luke applies the language of the "gift," "promise," and "baptizing" in the Spirit interchangeably, as also "receiving" the Spirit and, in this instance, being "filled" with the Spirit (1:4–5, 8; 2:4, 38–39).

Luke's account of Jesus' gift of the Spirit to the church emphasizes some of his major themes, such as Jesus' exaltation, prophetically inspired speech, and witnessing across cultural boundaries. Although the relation to John's account of the Spirit's coming (John 20:19–23) is debated, the presence there of peace, joy, and commissioning suggests that that account climaxes John's promise of the Spirit (14:26–27; 15:26–27; 16:22). Thus both Luke and John present their respective "receptions" of the Spirit in ways that climax the promises about the Spirit that they record. Some suggest that on a historical level disciples experienced the Spirit on both occasions, but more fully in the account described by Luke. If so, John and Luke have each emphasized the event in ways that fit their consistent emphases about the Spirit in their narratives.

Craig S. Keener, *The Spirit in the Gospels and Acts: Divine Purity and Power* (Peabody, Mass.: Hendrickson, 1997); Max Turner, *Power from on High: The Spirit in Israel's Restoration and Witness in Luke-Acts* (Sheffield: Sheffield Academic Press, 1996).

CRAIG S. KEENER

People of God
The terms "people of God" and "people of the Lord" do not appear very often in Scripture, but they represent a theological concept that is prominent throughout the Bible. The concept more often appears in the form "my people" or "his people," and occasionally as "your people" (e.g., Exod 32:11–12). The ordinariness of the word "people" in English somewhat obscures the importance of the Hebrew and Greek words it translates: ʿam and laos. The Hebrew word ʿam denotes initially relationship through the male lineage, beginning with the father's household and extending eventually to the whole nation of Israel. Israel was thus thought of as a family, and

the word ʿam tended to distinguish them from the "nations" (*goyim*). The few texts that speak of Israel as a nation (*goy*) will thus be seen to have special importance. The LXX translators chose the archaic and poetic Greek word *laos* to represent ʿam, perhaps because they recognized the special sense of ʿam as a term for Israel's status as the people of God. The NT writers were clearly influenced by the LXX in their similar uses of *laos*.

The Old Testament

Israel as the family of God. Even though the Israelites knew their numbers had increased over the years by the addition of people with no claim to have descended from Abraham, Isaac, and Jacob (e.g., Uriah the Hittite bore a Yahwistic name, 2 Sam 11:3; cf. Exod 12:38), they thought of themselves as an extended family. The book of Exodus begins with a list of the sons of Israel (Jacob's other name, Gen 32:28; 35:10), and from that point on we read of the people of Israel, that is, Jacob's family. But soon they become the people of Yahweh (Exod 3:7), and God uses explicit family language in Exod 4:22: "Israel is my firstborn son." Israelites did not think of themselves as having a natural or "biological" relationship with God. This relationship was the result of adoption, a free choice made by God at a given point in history to claim a people for his special possession by setting them free from Pharaoh's ownership (see *adopt*; *choose*). So the refrain "Let my people go" runs throughout the account of the plagues (Exod 5:1; 7:16; 8:1, 20; 9:1, 13; 10:3). The understanding of one's people as one's family accounts for the concept of God as Father, which appears in Deut 14:1; Ps 103:13; Isa 1:2; 43:6; 50:1; 63:16; Hos 11:1; Mal 2:10 (see *family*).

Israel as an adopted son. The OT authors knew Israel had done nothing to deserve a unique status as the people of God. Deuteronomy frequently comments on that status with words of wonder: "For what other great nation has a god so near to it as the LORD our God is whenever we call to him?" (Deut 4:7). "But the LORD has taken you and brought you out of the iron-smelter, out of Egypt, to become a people of his very own possession, as you are now" (4:20; cf. 4:33–34). The frequently asked question "Why Israel?" had already occurred, and Deuteronomy insists the choice was entirely due to God's grace: "It was not because you were more numerous than any other people that the LORD set his heart on you and chose you—for you were the fewest of all peoples. It was because the LORD loved you and kept the oath that he swore to your ancestors, that the LORD has brought you out with a mighty hand, and redeemed you from the house of slavery, from the hand of Pharaoh king of Egypt" (7:7–8). Israel accounted for its existence as a unique people, then, by appealing to an unexplainable quality in God—love, which does not depend on anything lovable in the one loved (cf. Deut 4:37; see *grace; love*).

"*I will be your God, and you shall be my people.*" God's way of establishing and maintaining this relationship was to offer a *covenant* to Israel, which called for faithfulness on both sides. God was, of course, solely responsible for its initiation, at Mount Sinai. God described the special role this would create for Israel at the beginning of the covenant-making ceremony: "You have seen what I did to the Egyptians, and how I bore you on eagle's wings and brought you to myself. Now therefore, if you obey my voice and keep my covenant, you shall be my treasured possession out of all the peoples. Indeed, the whole earth is mine, but you shall be for me a priestly kingdom and a holy nation" (Exod 19:4–6a). After reminding them that he had already taken redemptive action on their behalf (cf. Exod 6:6–7), God described Israel's uniqueness in three ways: "my treasured possession out of all the peoples," "a priestly kingdom," and "a holy nation." This is one of the few places where Israel is called a nation rather than a people, and the term "holy nation" appears only here. *Holy* is clearly used in its basic sense of being set apart for God. The

terms used here have been widely discussed, especially "priestly kingdom" (or kingdom of priests). Since the priests had been chosen by God and set apart for a special work, this term probably carries a meaning similar to "treasured possession" and "holy nation." Each of them refers to Israel's special relationship to God and to its distinctive character as compared with the other nations.

On God's side, the promises associated with the covenant included the gift of the land (Exod 6:8), blessing (Deut 26:15), and care for his people in every vicissitude. He promised to be their deliverer (Ps 3:8), savior (Ps 28:9; Hab 3:13), redeemer (Ps 111:9), strengthener (Ps 29:11), a refuge and stronghold (Joel 3:16). On Israel's side, obedience to God's voice (Exod 19:5), to his statutes and ordinances, was essential (Lev 26:3–12; Deut 26:17–19). The central part of this obedience involved the fact that this was an exclusive relationship. To be God's people, his treasured possession, meant for Israel to acknowledge no god but Yahweh: "To you it was shown so that you would acknowledge that the LORD is God; there is no other besides him" (Deut 4:35). "So acknowledge today and take to heart that the LORD is God in heaven above and on the earth beneath; there is no other" (Deut 4:39). Directly associated with the demand to serve Yahweh alone was the prohibition of idolatry, attempting to represent God by anything in the created world, and Deut 4:15–20 emphasizes that this was a part of being "a people of his very own possession."

Failure. According to Lev 26, the relationship could be severely damaged if Israel refused to be obedient, and the damage is described as a series of terrible curses (cf. the parallel in Deut 28). But the text insists that God remains faithful under all circumstances and promises that repentance will lead to a restoration of the covenant promises (vv. 40–45). The prophets did not speak in conditional terms, as Leviticus and Deuteronomy did; for they claimed the relationship had been broken, not just damaged. But they still spoke of Israel as God's people. The earliest of the canonical prophets, Amos, spoke of judgment rather than privilege as the result of Israel's unique status: "You only have I known of all the families of the earth; therefore I will punish you for all your iniquities" (Amos 3:2). Israel had been given more than any other; so Israel's responsibilities were heavier. Amos spoke of the death of Israel, at the same time reminding them that they had been the chosen people: "The end has come upon my people Israel" (Amos 8:2). Other prophets spoke of the wrath of the God who had chosen them in love; this was their way of accounting for the disasters that had befallen and would befall their people (e.g., Isa 5:25). They sensed both anger and lament in the God who still spoke of "my people" (Isa 1:2b–3; Mic 6:3; cf. Jer 9:6–7).

Hopes. Although everything had gone wrong and neither the northern (since 722 B.C.) nor the southern kingdom (after 587) existed, Jeremiah and Ezekiel insisted that God's intention to have a people of his own could not be thwarted by anything. The possibility lay in the character of God alone: "It is not for your sake, O house of Israel, that I am about to act, but for the sake of my holy name. . . . you shall be my people, and I will be your God" (Ezek 36:22, 28). A new covenant would, someday, make obedience possible: "I will put my law within them, and I will write it on their hearts; and I will be their God, and they shall be my people" (Jer 31:33). Promises to the Babylonian exiles insisted that they were still God's people, in spite of all the evidence to the contrary: "For the LORD has comforted his people, and will have compassion on his suffering ones" (Isa 49:13b; cf. vv. 14–16).

Those promises sometimes looked forward to a position for Israel superior to the other nations (e.g., Isa 49:22–23; and see Deut 26:19), but some prophets extended the implications of monotheism so as to project a time when other nations would also be called the people of the Lord. Early in the postexilic period, Zechariah added to his promise of the restoration of Jewish exiles the remarkable thought: "Many nations shall join themselves to the LORD on that day, and shall be my people; and I will dwell in your midst" (Zech 2:11). Even more remarkable, and unparalled in the OT, is the prediction (probably also postexilic in date) that one day Israel and the old enemies, Egypt and Assyria, will be equals: "On that day Israel will be the third with Egypt and Assyria, a blessing in the midst of the earth, whom the Lord of hosts has blessed, saying, 'Blessed be Egypt my people, and Assyria the work of my hands, and Israel my heritage'" (Isa 19:24–25). The prophet dared to use the words that once played a key role in Yahweh's battle against Egypt (in Exodus) and looked forward to a day when God would also call Egypt "my people." The term itself thus reflects the ambivalent attitude toward the nations in the OT. (See *nations*.) On the one hand, "my people" means chosen by the one God for special privileges and responsibilities, but the belief that there is only one God sometimes led to the conviction that the nations would not be excluded from God's future beneficent activity.

The New Testament
The NT extends the concept of people of God beyond its identification with the Jewish people. Originally it had denoted family relationships and was extended to include the nation of Israel by the fiction that all who worshiped Yahweh were descendants of Abraham, Isaac, and Jacob. A few OT texts looked forward to the time when other nations might be called people of God, and the NT authors (convinced that the time had come) cited favorable OT references to the nations as they argued that the gospel of Jesus Christ was intended for everyone. They used *laos* like *'am*, to refer to God's people, and *ethne* like *goyim*, to refer to the nations—and now to individual non-Jews (translated in English versions "*Gentiles*," a term derived from a Latin word referring to family). The usage of *laos* was complicated, however, by the

appearance of a community composed of Jews and Gentiles, distinct from the Jews of the synagogue. Several theological uses of *laos* can thus be identified.

Israel as God's people. There is continuity of two kinds with the OT, as the NT authors spoke of the people of God. The first is continuity both of terminology and of subject: "people" referring to Israel of the past or to Jews of the present. Israel as the people of God is distinguished from the Gentiles in the traditional way in the song of Simeon: "a light for revelation to the Gentiles and for glory to your people Israel" (Luke 2:32), but the reference already includes Gentiles in the blessing expected from the coming of Jesus. The song of Zechariah also speaks of the Jews of his time as God's people (Luke 1:68, 77), and Matthew offers "for he will save his people from their sins" as the explanation of Jesus' name (Matt 1:21). Even authors who are intent on identifying the church as a new people of God still speak of Israel as God's people. The author of Hebrews describes Moses as "choosing rather to share ill-treatment with the people of God than to enjoy the fleeting pleasures of sin" (Heb 11:25). And Paul, in an extended passage to be discussed later, wrote, "I ask, then, has God rejected his people? By no means! I myself am an Israelite, a descendant of Abraham, a member of the tribe of Benjamin. God has not rejected his people, whom he foreknew" (Rom 11:1–2).

The church identified with Israel. The second form of continuity is of terminology but with a change of subject. Often OT texts that originally referred to Israel are cited, taking it for granted that they now refer to the church, without showing any need to justify it or considering the issues that raises. In 2 Cor 6:16–18 Paul's advocacy of purity in the church is bolstered with quotations from Lev 26:12 (cf. Ezek 37:27), Isa 52:11, and Isa 43:6. "Since we have these promises" (7:1), he says of these OT texts, assuming they were addressed to Corinthian Christians as well as to ancient Israel. When the author

of Hebrews issued a stern warning against willful sins in the Christian community, the OT quote, "The Lord will judge his people" (Deut 32:36; Heb 10:30), could be cited without any need to justify applying it to them.

These uses of the OT were the result of a major shift in the understanding of the identity of the people of God, which involved serious issues for the first-century church. The texts just cited reflect decisions already made, the kind of conclusion assumed by Titus 2:14, where the church is called people of God without any reference to the OT: "He it is who gave himself for us that he might redeem us from all iniquity and purify for himself a people of his own who are zealous for good deeds."

The church as a new people of God. Explicit discontinuity from the OT and contemporary Judaism appears when an author claims that a new people of God has come into being with the appearance of a religious community composed of Jews and Gentiles, and separated from the synagogues. Two factors were involved in the separation: the refusal of most Jews to accept Jesus as Messiah, and the decision to accept Gentiles into the Christian community without requiring circumcision and adherence to the whole law of Moses. James the brother of Jesus explicitly attributed the admission of Gentiles to an act of God: "Simeon has related how God first looked favorably on the Gentiles, to take from among them a people for his name" (Acts 15:14). Paul found in Hos 1:10 and 2:23 evidence of God's intention to make his people of those who had been called "not my people," applying the texts to the Gentiles, rather than to Israel, as Hosea had done (Rom 9:25–26). These claims left a big question largely undiscussed, except for Rom 9–11 (for which, see the next section). Did this mean the Jews of the synagogue were no longer the people of God? Had all the promises to Israel been transferred to the church? The NT writers answer the second question in the affirmative but are not so clear about whether the transfer meant that all had been taken away from the Jews. Except for Paul, they tend to speak of the positive side of the matter, rejoicing in the appearance of this new community, the church. This unquestioning use of OT material as addressed to the church appears in 1 Pet 2:9–10, which alludes to Exod 19:6 and Hos 1:10; 2:23: "But you are a chosen race, a royal priesthood, a holy nation, God's own people, in order than you may proclaim the mighty acts of him who called you out of darkness into his marvelous light. Once you were not a people, but now you are God's people; once you had not received mercy, but now you have received mercy." The church has now received the promises once made to Israel, making it a unique community on earth, Peter claimed, and this has come about because Christians have received "a new birth into a living hope through the resurrection of Jesus Christ from the dead" (1 Pet 1:3).

The author of Hebrews makes a more explicit contrast between Judaism and Christianity than most NT authors, since the sacrifice of Christ is taken to be the final, sufficient, and complete sacrifice, which the temple cult only foreshadowed (e.g., Heb 9:11–14). So this author takes Christianity to be the new covenant predicted in Jer 31:31–34 (Heb 8:8–12; 9:15; 10:11–18), and does say that "in speaking of a 'new covenant,' he has made the first one obsolete" (8:13).

A similar claim appears in Paul's statement, "For it is we who are the circumcision, who worship in the Spirit of God and boast in Christ Jesus" (Phil 3:3). James even addressed Christians as "the twelve tribes in the Dispersion" (James 1:1). Once Paul speaks of the Israel of God (Gal 6:16), and many take this to be a reference to the church, although the context is not completely explicit. Since elsewhere by Israel he means Judaism, this may be a prayer for those who have not yet accepted Christ (cf. Rom 10:1). In the post-NT period, however, the church claimed to be the new Israel, a term never used in the NT, and insisted that unbe-lieving Jews had forfeited all right to be called God's people.

Two peoples of God? The church's claim to have superseded the Jews as the people of God, as the new Israel, has led to a terrible history of misunderstanding, suspicion, and persecution. Nothing in Scripture could justify those results, but the claim that the church has received the promises God originally addressed to Israel is certainly present throughout the NT. One can only guess what those authors would have written if they could have foreseen the miserable history of Jews and Christians that ensued; but they expected Christ to return soon, so they did not anticipate any such problems. Those who believed in Christ as their savior, both Jews and Gentiles, needed to assure themselves that Jesus really did give them access to the saving activity of God, which he had promised to Israel. So they needed to claim that they were the continuation of the historic "people of God," and that led them to use language that suggests (and did promote) supersessionism. Part of that language (the valid part) affirmed the truth of what Christians had received through faith in Jesus Christ. Another part reflects disappointment, failure to understand, and the defensiveness that resulted when large numbers of Jews refused to believe that Jesus was the Messiah.

For Paul the division between Jews who accepted Jesus and those who did not was a serious issue, and he worried over it at length in Rom 9–11. He was writing to Gentile Christians and emphasized that he is Jewish, and that both he and God remain faithful to the Jewish people (Rom 9:2–3, 6; 10:1; 11:1–2). His reasoning is difficult to follow and may not always be consistent, for finally he admits the ultimate answer is a mystery (Rom 11:33–36). It is clear, however, that in spite of his failures in the synagogues he did not think of the church as a Gentile institution, a "new Israel." He emphasized the primacy of the historic Israel as the recipient of God's gracious promises, which will not fail (9:4–5; 11:29). The people of

God—Israel—is compared with a cultivated olive tree onto which God has grafted wild branches—Gentiles. This is Paul's way of correcting an apparent tendency toward superior feelings on the part of his readers (11:13–24). He expected all Israel eventually to be saved (11:26), but he also did not imagine an extended period of time during which synagogue and church would exist side by side. For Paul there was one people of God, Israel, to whom Gentiles had been joined, and from whom (temporarily, he believed) some Jews had become estranged. The amount of space devoted to the subject in Romans, the complexity of the discussion, and the final appeal to mystery show that there was no simple and obvious answer for Paul, and this should caution the church against providing its own simple answers.

Brevard S. Childs, *Biblical Theology of the Old and New Testaments* (Minneapolis: Fortress Press, 1993), 413–51; W. D. Davies, "Paul and the People of Israel," in *Jewish and Pauline Studies* (Philadelphia: Fortress Press, 1984), 123–52; E. A. Speiser, "'People' and 'Nation' of Israel," *JBL* 79 (1960): 157–63.

DONALD E. GOWAN

Perceive, Perception   *see* **Know**

Perfect, Perfection   The common sense meanings of "perfect" and "perfection" in English stress the absence of error or defect. In contrast, these words, in translations of either the OT or the NT, bear meanings that stress certain positive qualities. In the OT, the most typical Hebrew word so translated bears a root meaning of completeness or wholeness. In the NT, the most frequent word so translated signifies reaching a goal or having matured.

The Hebrew root (*tamam*) signifies completeness or wholeness. One can have complete or perfect knowledge (Job 36:4). Similarly, a person can be entirely just (Job 12:4; NRSV "just and blameless").

Noah was totally righteous (Gen 6:9). In each of these three cases, the notion of completeness is linked with some other positive quality, suggesting that to be perfect is to be totally knowledgeable, just, or righteous. People are not, however, normally whole or "perfect" without some other quality.

Animals, in contrast, can simply be *tamam*. An animal that is acceptable for a sacrifice is to be "blameless," without bodily defect: "When anyone offers a sacrifice . . . it (the animal) must be perfect; there shall be no blemish in it" (Lev 22:21). The word translated "perfect" here is otherwise translated with the phrase "without blemish" (e.g., Lev 3:1, 6).

It is not surprising that the deity—and things associated with God—are perceived as perfect. "His way is perfect" (2 Sam 22:31; Ps 18:30); "the law of the LORD is perfect" (Ps 19:7). Here again, the text surely means that the *torah* or instruction is complete. Such a complete *torah* would include everything of importance. In such texts, the notion of completeness can function without an associated quality like justice or knowledge (cf., however, Deut 32:4, a text in which the parallel poetic lines link "perfect" to "just"). Zion, the deity's dwelling place, is the "perfection of beauty" (Ps 50:2; Lam 2:15).

In the NT, the word *teleios*, sometimes translated "perfection" can also mean "mature." As with the OT, the NT affirms the perfection of the deity. However, unlike the OT, that perfection becomes something that humans are admonished to emulate: "Be perfect, therefore, as your heavenly Father is perfect" (Matt 5:48).

A number of NT texts offer perfection as a goal of the life of maturing faith. "Therefore, let us go on toward perfection" (Heb 6:1). Some early Christians clearly believed that perfection could be attained: "Whoever obeys his word, truly in this person the love of God has reached perfection" (1 John 2:5). "Anyone who makes no mistakes in speaking is perfect" (Jas 3:2).

Of all the biblical books, Hebrews offers the most extensive reflection about perfection. The argument begins with

Jesus, who is sometimes described with passive verbs. He was made perfect, that is, "although he was a Son, he learned obedience through what he suffered; and having been made perfect, he became the source of eternal salvation for all who obey him" (Heb 5:8–9; cf. Heb 7:28, "a Son who has been made perfect forever"). Elsewhere in the book the reader learns that Jesus' death was a definitive sacrifice: "he has perfected for all time those who are sanctified" (10:14). That onetime act enables the author of Hebrews to admonish his audience, "Let us run with perseverance the race that is set before us, looking to Jesus the pioneer and perfecter of our faith" (Heb 12:1–2). This highly nuanced view of perfection focuses on the perfection wrought by Christ though his sacrificial death. As a result, Hebrews offers fewer admonitions to its readers to be perfect, since Christ's death was unrepeatable (cf. Heb 6:1, "let us go on toward perfection," though the alternate translation, "let us go on toward maturity," is preferable).

DAVID L. PETERSEN

Perish   *see* **Death**

Persecute, Persecution, Persecutor   *see* **Suffer**

Pit   *see* **Grave**

Pity   The Hebrew words *hus* and *hamal* are frequently translated "pity" in English. Both terms represent a positive quality of concern and shared suffering between persons, or of God to humans. Infrequently the meaning is extended to include an inanimate object (Jonah 4:10), but this is likely for the purpose of satire. In the Hebrew Bible the emotion of "pity" is never isolated from action. Thus pity, as sympathy, is a motivation for action. The NRSV translation of Ezek 20:17 illustrates the inherent relationship between emotion and action by translating *hus* with the English "spare" in the divine speech:

"my eye spared them (i.e., pitied them), and I did not destroy them."

The vast majority of the instances of *hus* and *hamal* occur in negative statements, stressing the withholding of pity in the context of judgment. The book of Deuteronomy employs the word *hus* in legal contexts to underscore the need for punishment, even if the community is in sympathy with the accused. The extreme demands of the "ban," ordering the killing of all humans, requires that the Israelites show "no pity" (Deut 7:16). The execution of a family member because of apostasy also demands "no pity" (Deut 19:13). The negative commands to withhold pity presuppose the opposite, namely, the desire to withhold the punishment out of sympathy.

The desire of humans to withhold punishment evident in the laws of Deuteronomy is also applied to God in the prophetic tradition. The natural tendency of God to pity humans is the basis for the prayer of deliverance. The prophet Joel calls the priests to intercede for the people during a time of disaster with the words, "Spare (*hus*) your people, O LORD" (Joel 2:17). More frequently the prophets employ the negative formulation to underscore the divine determination to execute judgment regardless of any tendency to sympathize with the Israelites. God declares judgment against Judah and Jerusalem in Ezek 5:11: "my eye will not spare (*hamal*), and I will have no pity (*hus*)." Jeremiah 13:14 employs similar language in an oracle about the cup of wrath, while also showing the broader relationship between pity and *mercy*, when God states, "I will not pity (*hamal*) or spare (*hus*) or have compassion (*raham*) when I destroy them."

The Hebrew *nud* explores the relationship between sympathy, pity, and grieving. The psalmist illustrates, "I am in despair. I looked for pity (*nud*), but there was none; and for comforters (*naham*), but I found none" (Ps 69:20). The same word pair, *nud* and *naham*, appears in Isa 51:19, where the NRSV translates "who will grieve (*nud*) with you?" and "who will comfort (*naham*) you?"

The Greek *splanchnizomai* is often translated "pity" in the NT. The verb is derived from the noun, *splanchnon*, meaning inner organs, which were considered the seat of feelings. The father who intercedes to Jesus for his epileptic son reflects the liturgical use from Joel 2:17, saying, "Have pity on us and help us" (Mark 9:22). The parables of the Good Samaritan (Luke 10:29–37) and the master who forgives the debt of a slave (Matt 18:23–35) illustrate the positive content of pity and its close relationship with action. The good Samaritan rescued the man on the road because "he was moved with pity" for him (Luke 10:33). And likewise the master initially forgave the debt of his slave out of pity (Matt 18:27).

THOMAS B. DOZEMAN

Plan, Purpose, Will of God

The several Hebrew roots that are translated "plan" or "purpose" in the OT are used in relation to both human and divine decision making and action. Of particular interest and importance is a text like Ps 33:10–11, which juxtaposes human and divine plans: "The LORD brings the counsel [from the root *ya'ats*, often translated as "plan"] of the nations to nothing; he frustrates the plans [from the root *hashab*] of the peoples. The counsel of the LORD stands forever, the thoughts [the same root as "plan" above] of his heart to all generations." Other texts also suggest that the divine purpose will ultimately prevail (see Isa 14:24–27; 46:10–11; 55:11; Ps 146:4; Prov 19:21).

This does not mean, however, that God's will goes unopposed. In fact, God and God's purpose are regularly opposed, not only by "the nations" and "the peoples" (see Ps 2:1–3), but also by God's own people. As Isa 30:1 puts it: "Oh, rebellious children, says the LORD, who carry out a plan [the root *ya'ats*], but not mine."

In the broadest sense, what God purposes or wills is communicated clearly in Jer 9:24, by way of the verb NRSV translates "delight" (*haphats*), but which it sometimes translates "purpose" (see Isa 44:28; 48:14; 55:11): "I act with steadfast love, justice, and righteousness in the earth, for in these things I delight, says the LORD" (Jer 9:24).

While the loving God wills justice and righteousness (and peace, which results from justice and righteousness; see Isa 32:16–17; Ps 72:1–7), the actual course of events is affected by human cooperation or the lack thereof. Another striking example is Jer 18:1–17. On the one hand, it is clear that God, the divine potter, has a design or plan in mind for Israel and the nations. The final product, however, will depend upon human responsiveness. If a nation "turns from its evil," God says, "I will change my mind about the disaster that I intended to bring on it" (Jer 18:8).

As for Israel, the divine warning is this: "Look, I am a potter shaping evil against you and devising a plan [Hebrew root *hashab*] against you. Turn now, all of you from your evil way, and amend your ways and your doings" (Jer 18:11). But God's ultimate plan for justice and righteousness is thwarted by the people's own "plans." As they respond to the divine warning: "It is no use! We will follow our own plans [Hebrew root *hashab*], and each of us will act according to the stubbornness of our evil will" (Jer 18:12). Hence in this situation what God ultimately wills is *not* done. In essence, the people's own "plans" force God to resort to God's "plan B," the "disaster" (Jer 18:8) that could have been averted by human cooperation with God's purposes. See also Exod 32:14, where God "changed his mind about the disaster that he had planned [Hebrew *dibber*, literally "spoken"] to bring on his people" (and see *determine*).

As suggested above, alongside the recognition that human response affects God's plan or purpose for the world, Scripture also maintains that God's purpose will ultimately prevail. In the NT, of course, God's plan for the world involves Jesus Christ (see Acts 2:23; 4:27–28); and as in the OT, God's ultimate purpose reveals God's fundamental character. As Jas 5:11 puts it, "you have seen the purpose [Greek *telos*] of the Lord, how the Lord is compassionate and merciful" (see also 2 Tim 1:9).

God's gracious plan or purpose, enacted through Jesus Christ, has the whole world in view (see Eph 1:10–11; 3:9–11); and of course, it involves the gathering of persons to be God's own people. Not coincidentally, the word NRSV translates "plan" in Eph 1:10; 3:9 is *oikonomia*, "economy," literally "law of the household." God's ultimate plan, purpose, or "economy" is to gather a "household" (Eph 2:19) that includes both Jew and Gentile and that is nothing short of "one new humanity" (Eph 2:15). This "one new humanity" is the ultimate expression of "peace" (Eph 2:14, 15, 17), which in turn is the fullest expression of God's purpose for the world (see above).

The bringing together of Jew and Gentile is also a central feature of Paul's letter to the Romans, where, not surprisingly, the concept of God's purpose appears in conjunction with the vocabulary of predestination (Rom 8:28) and election (Rom 9:11; see also *choose*).

Bertil Albrektson, *History and the Gods: An Essay on the Idea of Historical Events as Divine Manifestations in the Ancient Near East and in Israel*, ConBOT 1 (Lund: CWK Gleerup, 1967), 68–97); G. B. Caird, *New Testament Theology* (Oxford: Clarendon Press, 1995), 40–51.

J. CLINTON MCCANN

Poor, Rich, Wealth Generally understood as that which pertains to one lacking material goods, "poor" is an economic and social concept as well as a political one. A person who is "poor" can be lacking in financial resources, social status, honor, or power, or any combination of these attributes. Those who are poor are often the objects of oppression and victims of injustice. Considered to be just as vulnerable as the widow and the orphan (see *alien*), the poor are favored by God and protected by Jewish law.

Historically and socially, in ancient Israel most of the people lived on small farms and had just enough means to provide for their own families. The poor among them were those who could not afford to provide for their own food and shelter and who had no resources to barter for it. They depended on the goodwill of others to help them survive. In the eighth century B.C., social and economic power shifted from the small landowners and farmers to the wealthy and those in political power, who became richer and more powerful at the expense of those who had fewer resources and less power. Hence a basic two-tier social structure developed: the rich and the poor, the powerful and the powerless. For Israel's prophets, the oppression and injustice that followed was intolerable, especially since the Israelites themselves were once few in number and wanting in military prowess. Yet they were loved and chosen by God, who freed them from unjust Egyptian oppression, only to have some of them turn on their own and do to one another what had once been done to them. In both the OT and the NT, poverty is not a virtue, but care for the poor is a constitutive dimension of both Torah and the gospel.

In the Pentateuch "the poor" generally refers to those with little or no economic means. God's law informed the Israelite community of their responsibilities toward the poor and the poor's basic rights. Those who lent money to the poor could not exact interest from them (Exod 22:25), nor were they to be treated any differently from anyone else in legal matters. In other words, the poor were not to be given special consideration in lawsuits. *Justice* was to be done fairly, regardless of one's means or lack thereof (Exod 23:3, 6; cf. Lev 19:15). The fallow year for the land was to be an opportunity for the poor to gather food for themselves, along with the wild animals (Exod 23:11), and they were entitled to glean on a regular basis (Lev 19:10; 23:22). Atonement offerings were to be the same for the rich and the poor alike (Exod 30:15) or whatever the poor could afford (Lev 14:21). A just wage was to be paid to the poor and needy laborers daily and before sunset (Deut 24:14–15), and if a garment from a poor person was given as a pledge, then that garment had to be returned by sundown (Deut 24:12). Last, because poverty was always going to be part of the fabric of life, the Israelites were obligated to be forever generous: "Since there will never cease to be some in need on the earth, I therefore command you, 'Open your hand to the poor and needy neighbor in your land'" (Deut 15:11). The poor were not to be considered "outcasts" of the society; they were to be accepted as "neighbors."

In the Former Prophets, the poor are mentioned twice in Hannah's prayer. For Hannah, God has power over one's lot: "The LORD makes poor and makes rich; he brings low, he also exalts" (1 Sam 2:7). For Israel, God was Lord of both creation and history. Hannah develops this initial thought in the following verse, where she proclaims that the ones whom God exalts are the poor whom God raises from the dust to seat them with princes (1 Sam 2:8). The text suggests a divine preferential option for the poor in God's desire to recognize the intrinsic goodness of all humanity despite their social and economic status. In 1 Sam 18:23, one learns that David himself is "poor" both economically and with respect to status; it seems that he cannot offer a marriage present to Saul in exchange for his daughter Michal, whom David is to wed. And thus, Saul makes an alternative agreement with his intended son-in-law (1 Sam 18:20–25). Later on, the story about a poor man becomes Nathan's indictment parable that instructs David on how he had wronged Uriah the Hittite when he took Uriah's wife as his own (2 Sam 12:1–15, esp. v. 4). Thus, the poor find favor with God, are raised up by God to become great leaders, and serve as fonts of wisdom for prophets who hold others accountable to God and God's ways.

Elsewhere in the writings of the Prophets, the poor are exploited and oppressed by those in the Israelite community who are more powerful—socially, economically, and politically. The prophets, who have the responsibility of making known God's words and ways to the people and holding them accountable to covenant and Torah, express passionate vehemence against such unjust actions. Isaiah bluntly indicts the leaders of his people: "The LORD enters into judgment with the elders and princes of his people: It is you who have devoured the vineyard; the spoil of the poor is in your houses" (Isa 3:14; cf. 32:7; Ezek 18:12; 22:12; Jer 2:34). With a biting rhetorical question, he calls them to task: "What do you mean by crushing my people, by grinding the face of the poor? says the Lord GOD of hosts" (Isa 3:15). In a poignant prayer, the prophet praises God for God's great care of the poor and reveals God's *compassion*, especially for those most vulnerable: "For you have been a refuge to the poor, a refuge to the needy in their distress, a shelter from the rainstorm and a shade from the heat" (Isa 25:4; cf. 41:17). Proper worship of God is not, according to Isaiah, the mere offering of grains and animals or fasts; it is care for those in need—an expression of love that brings the law and the worship of God to their fullness (see Isa 58:6–9). As a prophet, Isaiah also offers a vision of hope for the poor—for those among the Israelites who are powerless. In time a new leader—God's servant—will emerge who will act with justice on behalf of the poor (Isa 11:4).

With a spirit of mourning and lamentation, Jeremiah takes pity on the wretched condition of his community. He knows how far astray they have gone from right relationship with their God and with one another; he sees the pain and suffering that has been inflicted upon them because of their injustices, and he suffers their sin, their pain of divine judgment and chastisement, and their feeling of being abandoned by their God (see Jer 6:26; 8:19, 21–22; 9:1). As God's servant, he endures the pain of the oppressed.

Like Isaiah, Amos exposes the injustices that people in positions of power do to the poor—the powerless who are trampled, cheated, and bartered (Amos 2:7; 4:1; 5:11; 8:4–6; see also Hab 3:14). Zechariah holds up for his listeners the obligations of Torah: "do not oppress the widow, the orphan, the alien, or the poor; and do not devise evil in your hearts against one another" (Zech 7:10). For Zechariah, right deed and right intention are equally important.

The Writings reveal that the poor—the powerless—suffer in the time of Job (Job 20:19; 24:4, 9, 14). In an argument of self-defense, Job acknowledges his justice toward the poor: "I delivered the poor who cried, and the orphan who had no helper" (Job 29:12). For Job, the situation of the poor troubled him deeply, to the point of grieving him to the core of his being: "Did I not weep for those whose day was hard? Was not my soul grieved for the poor?" (Job 30:25). Job's attitude toward the poor reveals him as a righteous and compassionate person of godly virtue (see also Job 31:16, 19).

Throughout the Psalter, God is portrayed as a refuge for the poor, who listens to their cries and groans and acts on their behalf (see, e.g., Pss 12:5; 14:6; 22:26; 34:6; 70:5; 72:2, 4, 12; 113:7; 132:15; 140:12). The book of Proverbs offers extensive wisdom with regard to the grace and esteem that belong to the poor although they are poor, and also sheds light on how some within the community viewed the poor. The poor are often disliked by their neighbors (Prov 14:20) and are left friendless because of their poverty (Prov 19:4). Some are hated even by their kin, and among the friends they do have they are sometimes shunned (Prov 19:7). For the writer of Proverbs there is a link between how one treats the poor and one's attitude toward God: "Those who oppress the poor insult their Maker, but those who are kind to the needy honor him" (Prov 14:31; cf. 17:5; 19:17). Throughout Proverbs, contrasts are established between the poor and the rich. These contrasts value the integrity of the poor despite their lack of wealth (Prov 19:1; 28:6, 8, 11). The greatest wisdom and

knowledge that this Wisdom writer imparts to listeners down through the ages is this: "The rich and the poor have this in common: the LORD is the maker of them all" (Prov 22:2).

Ben Sirach picks up Proverbs' theme of the rich and the poor and offers additional comparisons and contrasts that teach wise lessons, while acknowledging the virtue and real power of the poor, regardless of their lack of wealth, status, and position of power (see, e.g., Sir 10:30; 30:14). Theologically Ben Sirach makes an astute point: God "will not show partiality to the poor; but he will listen to the prayer of one who is wronged" (Sir 35:16).

In the NT, the poor have an important place in Jesus' preaching and teaching. Jesus' first beatitude of the Sermon on the Mount praises the "poor in spirit" and proclaims that the kingdom of heaven is theirs (Matt 5:3; cf. Luke 6:20). The poor have the good news brought to them. This implies that they are not only a part of Jesus' mission and ministry but also are given a message of hope that will be fulfilled on their behalf (Matt 11:5). They will be freed from oppression just as the blind see, the lame walk, the lepers are cleansed, the deaf hear, and the dead are raised (cf. Luke 7:22). Matthew's narrative about the anointing at Bethany in Matt 26:6–13—which describes a woman anointing Jesus' head with expensive ointment, the disciples' objection to the use of such a costly ointment in favor of the money being given to the poor, and Jesus' response that the poor will always be with them but he will not—sheds light on the social climate of the first century A.D. The total alleviation of poverty will never happen, but it can be relieved. The disciples' concern that the money for the ointment could have been given to the poor shows that they have consciousness of a desire for a life centered on fidelity to Torah. But Jesus' response highlights his hospitality of heart and his ability to receive a gift that, in fact, foreshadows his own burial. Hospitality of heart surpasses the juridical adherence to Torah (cf. Mark 14:5; John 12:8).

In Luke's Gospel, Luke depicts Jesus standing in the synagogue and reading from the scroll of the prophet Isaiah (see Isa 61:1–2). Here Jesus makes a statement to those leaders and people assembled before him: he is the one anointed by God, gifted with the Spirit of God, who walks in the tradition of the prophets, and whose mission is one of liberation aimed at the poor, whether the poor be those who are oppressed by others or the oppressors themselves who are in need of God's justice and compassion to release them from the captivity of their own sin (Luke 4:18–19). The author of Proverbs had reminded listeners and readers that "the poor and the oppressed have this in common: the LORD gives light to the eyes of both" (Prov 29:13). Furthermore, those who will dine in the reign of God at the eschatological banquet will be the poor, the crippled, the lame, and the blind (Luke 14:13)—those who would be deemed worthless by society because of their poverty and infirmities.

In keeping with one of the themes of the Wisdom writings of the OT, Luke also draws a comparison between the rich and the poor in his parable about the rich man and the poor man Lazarus (Luke 16:19–31). The rich man could have relieved the suffering of Lazarus, but he chose not to do so. When both men died, Lazarus was carried away by angels to be with Abraham and was, presumably, relieved of his misery. The rich man, on the other hand, went to Hades, where in death he experienced great suffering after having lived a wonderful life without any concern for the needs of his neighbor. Luke's lesson teaches that indeed the poor are justified by God and if they are not relieved of their suffering in this life, then they will be in the next.

Three times in his second letter to the Corinthians Paul mentions the poor: first, in reference to being servants of God who are willing to endure anything for the preaching of the Gospel (2 Cor 6:1–10); second, in relation to Jesus, who "became poor, so that by his poverty you might become rich" (2 Cor 8:9); and third, in 2 Cor 9:9, where he equates giving to the poor with godliness and righteousness. It should be noted that Jesus was not economically poor; his father was a carpenter—a tradesman. Jesus chose to leave family, friends, home, and property to embrace a life of itinerant preaching, teaching, and healing.

In the Pastoral Epistles, James warns against making distinctions between the poor and the rich and reminds his audience that God has chosen the poor to be rich in faith (see Jas 2:1–13). Finally, the book of Revelation makes clear the folly of the distinctions made between rich and the poor and points up the ironic reality of those who are rich and thus see themselves in need of nothing. Their shortsightedness and their self-reliant attitude are indeed their poverty (Rev 3:17).

In contrast to the poor, and yet often mentioned with the poor, are the rich and the wealthy. In the OT, one who was considered rich or wealthy usually possessed much property, for example, livestock, silver, gold, children, wives (see Gen 13:2; 2 Sam 12:2).

In the ancient word, economic poverty was not considered a virtue, whereas riches and wealth were often a sign of God's *blessing* and must be acknowledged as a gift from God. When the Israelites are about to enter the promised land, Moses reminds them that all they have experienced thus far and all that they are about to inherit is because of God's power: "Do not say to yourself, 'My power and the might of my own hand have gotten me this wealth.' But remember the LORD your God, for it is he who gives you power to get wealth, so that he may confirm his covenant that he swore to your ancestors, as he is doing today" (Deut 8:17–18).

The Chronicler's version of Solomon's dream and his request reinforce the notion of wealth as a blessing from God (2 Chr 1:7–13). When Solomon goes in to pray before God, he asks God to give him wisdom and knowledge for the sake of the people whom he has been giving the task of governing (v. 10). Pleased by Solomon's selfless request, God grants him these two gifts along with riches, *possessions*, and honor (v. 12). Furthermore, Isaiah proclaims that those who remain faithful to God will be given by God the wealth of the nations (Isa 45:14; 60:5, 11; 61:6; 66:12).

Perhaps the best lesson on the relationship between the terms "poor," "rich," and "wealth" is found in Matt 27:57–61, the story about Jesus' burial. After Jesus had been crucified, one of his disciples, Joseph of Arimathea—a rich man—approached Pilate, asked for Jesus' body, received it, wrapped it in clean linen cloth, laid it in a new tomb that he had hewn in the rock, sealed up the tomb, and then departed. What is significant in this story is that among Jesus' followers were the wealthy—the rich—whom Jesus embraced as disciples and who embraced Jesus as their teacher (cf. Luke 8:2–3). Because of his means, Joseph of Arimathea was able to provide for Jesus' dead body clean linen and a new tomb. Although Jesus had experienced the kind of death afforded to criminals, Joseph now extended to Jesus the kind of burial that was suitable for a righteous person. A man of poverty in life, Jesus received a gracious resting place in death for his body. Joseph provided for the one who at that moment in time was perhaps the poorest of all humanity—the one despised and deemed abandoned by his God. But for Joseph, Jesus was his teacher and his friend, and he loved him even in death.

In summary, what matters is not what one has or how much one possesses but one's ability to realize that all is gift, meant to be shared with grace and generosity.

H. L. Bosman, I. G. P. Gous, I. J. J. Spangenberg, eds., *Plutocrats and Paupers: Wealth and Poverty in the Old Testament* (Pretoria: van Schaik, 1991); Martin Hengel, *Property and Riches in the Early Church* (Philadelphia: Fortress Press, 1974).

CAROL J. DEMPSEY

Possess, Possessions, Rob, Steal

The four words "possess," "possessions," "rob," "steal" are rich in meaning and widespread in use throughout the OT and the NT. As a series of words with an apparent contrast embedded among them, "possess" and "possessions" for the most part pertain to land and goods; "rob" and "steal" refer to the loss of the *land* and goods, and more specifically, to the law and the transgression of it.

In the OT "possess" is used often in reference to the land that God has promised to give to the Israelites. In Gen 15:1–21, God's *promise* of land is announced to Abraham: "Then he said to him, 'I am the LORD who brought you from Ur of the Chaldeans, to give you this land to possess'" (Gen 15:7). After Abraham poses a question to God that indirectly asks for some sort of confirmation, God makes a *covenant* with Abraham to assure him that indeed the land will be his to possess (cf. Gen 17:1–18). This same promise of land is also given to Moses: "But I have said to you: You shall *inherit* their land, and I will give it to you to possess, a land flowing with milk and honey. I am the LORD your God; I have separated you from the peoples" (Lev 20:24; cf. Deut 30:5).

A slight turn of events occurs in Num 14:20–24. Here the biblical writer depicts God informing Moses that those who have tested God and have not obeyed God's voice will not see the land promised to their ancestors, except for Caleb, God's servant who has followed God wholeheartedly. He will enter the land (Num 14:24). Entrance into and possession of the land is contingent upon trusting in God and following God's ways and precepts. This point is reinforced in Deut 5:31, 33 and 1 Chr 28:8. In truth, the land is not theirs, but God's: "The land shall not be sold in perpetuity, for the land is mine; with me you are but aliens and tenants" (Lev 25:23).

When the Israelites eventually possess the land, certain tasks and responsibilities will be required of them: they are to set apart three cities for dealing with crimes (Deut 19:1–13); they are to give the Levites towns to live in (Num 35:2); they must not remove their neighbor's boundary marker on the property that will be allotted to them (Deut 19:14); they are to make certain acts of restitution and perform certain rituals if a body is found lying in the open country on the land (Deut 21:1–9); they may charge a foreigner interest on a loan but not another Israelite (Deut 23:20); they are to blot out the remembrance of Amalek from under heaven (Deut 25:19); they are to make an offering of firstfruits and tithes to the priest and retell their story in the presence of their God (Deut 26:1–11); and they are to obey all of God's commandments while walking in God's ways, which in turn will provide them with additional blessings, inclusive of numerous descendants and a long life in the land (Deut 30:16; 32:47). Disobedience, though, will lead to curses, hardships (Deut 28:15–68), and eventual expulsion from the land (Deut 28:63).

The books of Joshua and Judges outline how the Israelites are to possess the land (Josh 1:11; 17:18; 23:5; Judg 18:9). Unfortunately, since any land that one might "possess" is ordinarily already occupied by someone else (in this case, the Canaanites), the verb *yarash* is translated both "possess" and "dispossess" (as in Deut 7:17; 9:1; 11:23; 12:2; etc.).

In the Prophets, "possess" also refers to land. In Isa 34:1–17, the prophet communicates God's enraged state concerning the nations, in particular the Edomites, whose land will be turned over to the wild animals, who will possess it from one generation to the next. In Isa 57:13, the poet proclaims that whoever takes refuge in God will possess the land and inherit God's holy mountain. After Israel loses its land, God promises to restore it to them but only when the people become righteous once again (Isa 60:21; cf. Ezek 36:12). Ezekiel questions the people as to whether they are worthy to possess the land, since they as a community are riddled with transgressions (Ezek 33:25–26). Obadiah speaks of the house of Jacob taking possession of all those who had dispossessed Jacob (Obad 19–20). Thus, the nations who claimed Israel's land as their own—when the land was God's and given to Israel as a gift—will be stripped of their coveted possession.

In the Writings and deuterocanonical books, "possess" is used in relation to the land (Ps 25:13), in addition to its use with the cities of Judah (Ps 69:35), the temple (Judith 9:13), wisdom (Wis 8:21; cf. Ezra 7:25), and counsel (Sir 25:4).

In the OT "possessions" generally refers to movable property and land (see, e.g., Gen 26:14; 36:7; Deut 18:8; 1 Chr 7:28; 2 Chr 21:3; 32:29; 35:7; Eccl 2:7). In the NT "possessions" is equivalent to goods as well. Being caught up in one's possessions as opposed to being single-hearted can be an impediment to discipleship and a cause of grief (Matt 19:21–22; cf. Luke 12:15, 33; 14:33).

Violations of the right to own possessions are robbery and stealing. The verb *gazal* is sometimes translated "rob" in the OT, since its basic sense is violent, "to seize." Isaiah inveighs against those who make "iniquitous decrees" and write "oppressive statutes" to rob the poor, make widows their spoil, and orphans their prey (Isa 10:1–2). The sages warned, "Do not rob the poor because they are poor, or crush the afflicted at the gate" (Prov 22:22), and Jeremiah challenged the king himself, "Execute justice in the morning, and deliver from the hand of the oppressor anyone who has been robbed" (Jer 21:12).

Torah strictly forbids stealing (usually *ganab*; Exod 20:15; Lev 19:11, 13; Deut 5:19). Stealing is a crime exposed by the prophets (Jer 7:9). The Gospels portray Jesus reiterating the Decalogue that prohibits stealing (Matt 19:18; cf. Mark 10:19; Luke 18:20), and Paul points out the Romans' hypocrisy: they preach against stealing and yet commit the offense themselves (Rom 2:21). For the sake of this community, Paul also reiterates the Decalogue, which includes "You shall not steal" (Rom 13:9; cf. Exod 20:15). Thus the NT upholds the OT's insistence on the right to own private property.

CAROL J. DEMPSEY

Power, Might, Mighty, Almighty

The English word "power" derives by way of Old French from the Latin *potens,* "to be able." The locus of power can be institutions or processes as well as persons. The ingredients of capability depend upon the task to be accomplished: to propel a machine, to organize a society, to confront opposition, to shape minds, to motivate. The English noun *might* derives from Anglo-Saxon, also with the meaning "to be able," though shading toward physical strength, energy, preponderant force.

Old Testament

The NRSV uses "power" to translate a half dozen Hebrew words, most of which have a root meaning of strength or energy. The upshot is that the word "power" in the NRSV OT has a narrower range of meanings than the word bears in English and isn't found where we might expect it. The Hebrew words translated "might" and "mighty" are a closer match to the English.

A full-fledged doctrine of divine power in Hebrew Scripture would have to range beyond passages with key words. One can discern the idea of God's power as potentiality in a few passages. When Sarah laughs at the announcement of a pregnancy, the Lord retorts, "Is anything too wonderful (or too hard) for the LORD?" (Gen 18:14). Job confesses, after hearing the voice from the whirlwind, "I know that you can do all things, and that no purpose of yours can be thwarted" (Job 42:2). These passages articulate a belief running through the biblical narrative that God is capable of delivering on what he promises.

It also should be noted that "power" is not used for aspects of God's exercise of governance. For example, God's issuing of commandments and rules of law is not described as exercise of power. This deficiency is partially overcome in lists of divine attributes that associate power and kingdom (e.g., 1 Chr 29:10–19).

The divine epithet "Almighty" (Gen 17:1; 35:11; Exod 6:3, etc.), needs explanation. To the modern reader this term probably suggests the idea of omnipotence. The Hebrew word translated "Almighty" is *shaddai;* its conceptual meaning is unknown. It was the name for a deity in the Canaanite pantheon or perhaps the epithet for the patriarch of the pantheon, El. Like a number of other such names, it was applied to the God of Israel. The Greek translators of Hebrew Scripture assumed that *shaddai* was descriptive, though they were uncertain as to what it meant. In the course of time, the convention developed of translating it "omnipotent," "almighty." No conceptual weight should be placed on this rendering. On the other hand, the designation "the Mighty One of Jacob" (Gen 49:24; Ps 132:2, 5; Isa 49:26; 60:16) is an accurate rendering of *ʾabir Yaʿacob.*

"Power" and "might" are ascribed to humans and to natural elements. Reuben is said to be Jacob's "might," excelling in rank and "power" (Gen 49:3). "Might" is ascribed to Samson (Judg 16:30) and Gideon (Judg 6:12), and the king is once called "mighty one" (Ps 45:3). The seas through which the Israelites passed were "mighty waters" (Exod 15:10; Isa 43:16).

While humans do have some control over their lives, Deuteronomy reminds Israel that it is not to say, "My power and the might of my own hand have gotten me this wealth" (8:17). It is the Lord who supplies the power (8:18) and determines the outcome.

Because Hebrew words bear the idea of strength, they are applied to the Lord chiefly in contexts where the Lord displays his control of humans and natural elements. The Lord tells the Pharaoh, "This is why I have let you live: to show you my power, and to make my name resound through all the earth" (Exod 9:16). The song of the sea (Exod 15:1–18) is a celebration of the Lord's power. The exodus is recalled frequently as a display of great power (e.g., Deut 4:37; 2 Kgs 17:36; Neh 1:10). "Might" and "mighty" are also used frequently of the exodus (e.g., Deut 5:15; 7:8).

The Lord's power and might are celebrated often in psalms of praise (e.g., Pss

66:3; 145:4); his prowess in protecting Israel from its enemies is uppermost. Hence, psalms of lament plead for God's display of power (e.g., Pss 79:11; 80:2; Isa 63:15).

God's constructive work tends not to attract the words "power" and "might" (except Deut 8:18). This pattern can be observed in creation texts as well. Genesis 1 renders the creating of the cosmos in the acts of speaking, separating, and blessing, all exercises of awesome power, yet neither term is mentioned. Psalm 33 praises God for his creation and rule of human affairs through his word, but the adjectives used to describe this word are "upright," "faithful" (v. 4)—terms for moral probity, not efficacy. "Power" and "might" do make an appearance in some creation texts. Some echo the myth of a primeval battle between God and chaotic powers (e.g., Ps 89:5–19; Job 26:2–14; cf. Isa 51:9–11). Job 9:4–10 depicts God's power in the destructive events of nature. Other creation texts do associate power with the creation of the heavens and earth without any reference to conflict (Isa 40:26; Pss 68:34; 147:4–5); in each case, the power of God in creation assures the availability of power to faint and powerless humans or Israel.

The sanctuary is the location for the display of God's power in Pss 24:7–10; 63:2; 68:35. The domain created by ritual is of a different order from creation and history, but its representations mediate the knowledge of the God who exercises sovereignty over space and time.

In the OT, there are several references to God's Spirit taking control of individuals. When Saul hears of the plight of Jabesh-gilead, the spirit came upon him "with power" (Hebrew: "rushed upon" him; 1 Sam 11:6). Micah describes his empowerment to prophesy judgment in similar terms (3:8). Jeremiah complains that he was overpowered (20:7).

Finally we should note that Isaiah's messianic prophecy in 9:2–7 bestows the name "Mighty God" on the coming Davidic ruler (v. 6). Evidently the names are descriptive of the ruler. It is rather shocking to have "God" applied to this human. This figure will have the might or prowess of a deity, being God's representative on earth. "Might" is one of a series of attributes (v. 2) bestowed on the messianic figure depicted in Isa 11:1–5. He will exercise the power of judgment by his word (v. 4).

New Testament

There is a Greek root that corresponds to the Latin *potens* and the English *power*. The noun is *dynamis*, preserved in the English words "dynamic," "dynamite," "dynamo." It is translated "ability" in Matt 25:15 and "meaning" in 1 Cor 14:11; otherwise, the word "power" is in the translation. The verb *dynamai* means "to be able"; it occurs very frequently in the NT, but since the word "power" is not used in the translation, it falls outside our investigation. Another verb, *dynamoo*, means "to strengthen." The Greek noun *kratos* is also translated "power" in a few NT passages (Eph 1:19; Col 1:11; etc.), as well as "might" (Acts 19:20) and "dominion" (1 Tim 6:16; Rev 1:6).

The Gospels. We can divide the occurrences of the word "power" in the Gospels into a few categories. In Mark 12:24 and Matt 22:29, Jesus ascribes power to God in the sense of what God is capable of. Otherwise the Synoptics follow the Hebrew in using the term for displays of extraordinary efficacy. We meet the expression "deeds of power" in Matt 11:20–23; 13:54, 58; Mark 6:2, 5; Luke 10:13; 19:37. Jesus passes on this capability to his disciples/apostles (Luke 10:19; cf. Mark 9:39). Jesus experiences the flow of power into the woman who touches him secretly (Mark 5:30; Luke 8:46; cf. 6:19). Despite John's representation of Jesus as the incarnate Son of God who controls the exchanges and events that make up his story, the Gospel does not employ the expression "deeds of power"; in its place is the term "sign" (3:2; 7:13; etc.).

In eschatological sayings, divine power includes the position of sovereignty and overwhelming force; the reign of God is to be established to the exclusion of all other political realms. The Synoptic Gospels speak of the Son of Man coming with power and glory (Mark 13:26; Matt 24:30; Luke 21:27). Mark 9:1 speaks of the kingdom "coming with power." Jesus testified before the Sanhedrin that they would see the "Son of Man seated at the right hand of Power" (Matt 26:64; Mark 14:62; cf. Luke 22:69). John 5:27 is probably a reformulation of a Synoptic saying with another Greek word (*exousia*) within the framework of realized eschatology.

In Luke and Acts various figures receive the Spirit, who gives them power. John the Baptist receives the power of Elijah (Luke 1:17). Mary is overshadowed by "the power of the Most High" (1:35). Jesus returned to Galilee "filled with the power of the Spirit" (4:14; cf. Mark 1:12). The disciples must wait "until you have been clothed with power" before they can go out as apostles (Luke 24:49; cf. Acts 1:8). After Pentecost the apostles exhibit this power in healing and preaching (Acts 4:33; 6:8, etc.).

We need to bring in one other term, *authority*, defined as "the power to command, enforce obedience, make decisions." The Greek is *exousia*. The source of authority may be formal, traditional, or, as in Jesus' case, charismatic. Jesus is said to have spoken and acted "with authority" (Matt 7:29; Luke 4:32; Mark 1:27). He claimed the authority to forgive sins (Matt 9:6; Mark 2:10; Luke 5:24) and conveyed that authority to his disciples (Matt 16:19; 18:18; John 20:22–23). In Matthew's account of the resurrection, Jesus claims to have received "all authority" and then commissions his disciples to an evangelistic mission to all nations (28:18–20).

Pauline letters. The Pauline corpus uses the word "power" frequently and distinctively. About half of the occurrences in the NRSV translation of the NT are found here, and they always have theological import. A few are simply a continuation of Jewish usage (Rom 1:20; 9:17, quoting Exod 9:16).

God's power is demonstrated in the resurrection of Christ; believers can look forward to the exercise of such power in their resurrection (1 Cor 6:14; 2 Cor 13:4; Phil 3:10).

Christ himself is the power of God. This is stated as the thesis of Romans (Rom 1:16). Other places include 1 Cor 1:24–25, which occurs in a passage describing Paul's preaching: "For Christ [sent me] to proclaim the gospel, and not with eloquent wisdom, so that the cross of Christ might not be emptied of its power" (1:17). Here power is the *rhetorical power* of the gospel message, contrasted to human rhetorical power, eloquent wisdom, which has proven false by its incapacity to know God. In the crucifixion and resurrection of Christ, humans exercised their ultimate power, and God's power proved greater by raising Jesus from the dead. Now the cross, sign of weakness, becomes the manifestation of God's power and wisdom (1:18). This message communicates power to those who believe (1:26–31).

The truth of this gospel is demonstrated by its communication of power. First Corinthians 2:4–5 associates the work of the Spirit with power; God must intervene in the heart of the hearer to empower reception in faith (so also 1 Thess 1:5). Paul characterizes the paradox of his preaching as by "truthful speech and the power of God" (2 Cor 6:7; cf. 1 Thess 2:1–12). While the power Paul is speaking of is often rhetorical, a few passages might be taken to refer to miracles (e.g., Rom 15:18–19; 1 Cor 12:28).

Finally, there are benedictions in Paul's letters that request that God or the Holy Spirit convey power to his addressees (Rom 15:13; Eph 3:16; Col 1:11; 2 Thess 1:11).

Before we leave Paul, we should note that Paul uses the word "power" for autonomous or rebellious potencies in the creaturely world (Rom 8:38; 1 Cor 15:56; Eph 1:21; 6:12). Death, by the way, is designated as one of these powers in Rom 8:38; 1 Cor 15:26, 54–55. The NRSV translates Gal 3:22 as follows: "the scripture has imprisoned all things under the power of sin," though there is no Greek word for power here; the RSV translation, "the scripture consigned all things to sin," is to be preferred.

General Epistles. The prologue of Hebrews ascribes to the Son the power belonging to the Creator (1:3). Otherwise, "power" is applied to Christ only to explain how he acceded to the priesthood (7:16). Power here is a life-giving force. His life force was able to shatter the "power of death" held by the devil (2:14). Faith itself is said to bestow power (11:11, 34).

The Petrine letters speak of the power of God working providentially in the lives of believers for their salvation (1 Pet 1:5; 2 Pet 1:3). Second Peter 1:16 also speaks of the eschatological power of Christ. Both letters use the term "power" of supernatural beings (1 Pet 3:22; cf. 2 Pet 2:11).

The word power appears fairly frequently in the Revelation to John. It is one of the standard attributes of God for which God and the Lamb are praised (4:11; 5:12; 7:12; 12:10; 19:1). At the seventh and last trumpet blast, the twenty-four elders break into praise of God for finally drawing on his power to reign (11:17). God's adversaries have a hierarchy of power of their own (13:2; 17:13).

————

DALE PATRICK

Praise   As part of the general vocabulary of prayer (see **bless; pray; thank**), the OT uses a variety of related terms to convey the ideas of "praise" and "give thanks," for example, *samah*, "rejoice," *ranan*, "rejoice" (see *joy*), *shir*, "*sing*," *gadal*, "exalt," and *zamar*, "sing, praise." The range of this vocabulary is a reminder that praise offered to God is fundamentally a rich and full-hearted expression of inestimable joy; no single term is completely adequate for all that one wants to say. Two particular groups of words are especially revealing of the form and purpose of Hebraic praise: (1) *yadah* (Hiphil), "give thanks, laud, praise," and its noun *todah*, "thanksgiving"; and (2) *halal* (Piel), "praise," and its noun *tehillah*, "praise." To these a third group of terms, *barak*,

"bless," and *berakah*, "blessing," may be added, for in important respects they provide the generative center of ancient Israel's practice of praise.

Claus Westermann has demonstrated that "the most original and immediate form of praise, the simple and joyous response to a definite act of God which has just been experienced," is found in the *baruk* sentence, "Blessed be the Lord who . . ." (Westermann, *Praise and Lament*, 88). Of the fourteen occurrences of this sentence in the Old Testament, Exod. 18:10 may be singled out as an illustration of two characteristics that are fundamental to praise: praise is offered *to God* ("Blessed be the LORD") and is *grounded in reasons* ("who has delivered you from the Egyptians . . ."). Other occurrences of the *baruk* sentence confirm that while the reasons for praising God may vary, they are never omitted. Typically such praise emerges spontaneously from everyday life experiences (cf. Gen 24:27; 1 Sam 25:39; 1 Kgs 1:48). The *baruk* sentence, however, gradually evolves into a more liturgical response in which the reasons for praising God are both less personal and less concrete. David's prayer in 1 Chr 29:10 is a case in point: "Blessed are you, O LORD, the God of our ancestor Israel, forever and ever" (cf. 1 Kgs 8:15, 56). The setting of this prayer is cultic, a formal gathering of "all the assembly" in Jerusalem; the praise is generic and only loosely connected to any specific act of God.

The nexus of shifting reasons for praising God is apposite when considering the two primary words for praise: *yadah* and *halal*. Both verbs and their noun derivatives invite special attention to the Psalter, the Hebrew name for which is *tehillim*, "Praises." Approximately 60 percent of the occurrences of *yadah* (Hiphil), "give thanks, laud, praise," and *todah*, "thanksgiving," and two-thirds of the occurrences of *halal* (Piel), "praise," and the noun *tehillah*, "praise," are in the Psalms (the psalmic tradition is also substantially represented in texts from Qumran called *Hodayot* [IQH; 4QH], "Thanksgiving Hymns"). The structure of psalms employing these two clusters of words is fundamentally the same: an introductory summons or announcement of intent to praise God; a grounding of this praise in reasons and motivations; and a concluding statement of praise. Within this common structure, several important differences, often difficult to discern in English translations, are important to note: (a) Although there is considerable overlap in meaning between these terms, *yadah* and *todah* highlight the dimension of *thanksgiving; halal* and *tehillim* are more generally regarded as terms for *praise*. (b) The declaration of intent at the beginning and the concluding statement at the end of psalms of praise (psalms of thanksgiving) are typically voluntary and singular, for example, "I will give thanks (*'odah*) to the LORD with my whole heart" (Pss 9:1; 111:1; 138:1). Psalms of praise that use *halal* almost always begin with a summons addressed to the community in imperative form, for example, "Praise (*halelu*), O servants of the LORD; praise (*halelu*) the name of the LORD" (Ps 113:1; cf. Pss 117:1; 135:1–3). (c) The reasons for offering thanksgiving in *yadah* prayers are typically expressed with verbs in the Hebrew perfect (past tense in English) that describe *what God has done*. Such reasons often recall times of affliction, distress, or uncertainty when a person sought God's presence in a prayer of lament and now gratefully acknowledges that God has heard and intervened. The transition from lament to thanksgiving is signaled by the word *ki* ("because, for, that"): "Blessed be (*baruk*) the LORD, for (*ki*) he has heard the sound of my pleadings . . . and with my song I give thanks to him (*'ahodennu*; Ps 28:6–7); " I will extol you (*'aromimekah*), O LORD, for (*ki*) you have drawn me up, and did not let my foes rejoice over me" (Ps 30:1); "I thank you (*'odekah*) that (*ki*) that you have answered me and have become my salvation" (Ps 118:21). *Halal* prayers typically use participial verbs (often translated with past tense verbs introduced by the relative pronoun "who") that anchor the reasons for praising to *who God is*, that is,

to the characteristics of God that are permanent and thus always worthy of praise, regardless of one's present circumstances: "Praise (*halelu*) the LORD, O my soul . . . who made heaven and earth . . . who keeps faith forever; who executes justice for the oppressed, who gives food to the hungry" (Ps 146:1, 6–7). Not infrequently the summons almost eclipses the reasons for praise. Psalm 148, for example, comprises two elaborate summonses, the first calling forth praise "from the heavens" (vv. 1–4), "for (ki) he commanded and they were created" (v. 5), the second praise "from the earth" (vv. 7–12), "for (*ki*) his name alone is exalted" (v. 13). On other occasions, the summons to praise seems such a preoccupying impulse, the joy that evokes it so indescribable, that any listing of reasons would be redundant. Psalm 150, the prayer that concludes the Psalter, ultimately defines its theological objective with a single summons, "Praise the LORD" (*halelu yah*), a summons repeated thirteen times with breathtaking rapidity.

The NT also uses a variety of terms to express the general idea "praise" (e.g., *aineo, epaineo, homologeo, halleluouia*), but the dominant cluster of words derives from the root *chairo*, "rejoice," especially *eucharisteo*, "be thankful." The Synoptic Gospels record relatively few prayers of praise for Jesus (cf. Matt 11:25; Luke 10:21), although there is sufficient reason to believe that he and his disciples followed the traditional Jewish practice of offering thanks before meals (at Emmaus, Luke 24:30; in the miraculous feedings of the multitudes, Matt 14:13–21; Mark 6:30–44; Luke 9:10–17; cf. John 6:1–13; and esp. before and after the Last Supper, Matt 26:26–30; Mark 14:22–26; Luke 22:17–19). Luke's Gospel calls special attention to the OT's models for Mary's praise in the Magnificat (Luke 1:46–55; cf. 1 Sam 2:1–10), Zechariah's Benedictus (Luke 1:67–79; cf. Pss 18:1–3; 92:10–11; 132:17–18), and often describes people offering praise (*doxazo*) in response to God's saving work on their behalf (Luke 2:20; 5:25–26; 7:16; 13:13; 18:43; 23:47).

Thanksgiving and praise are especially prominent in Paul. His letters to the churches typically contain introductory thanksgivings (e.g., Rom 1:8; 1 Cor 1:4; Phil 1:3; Col 1:3) and benedictory blessings (e.g., Rom 16:25–27; 1 Cor 16:23; Phil 4:23; Col 4:18). Like Jesus and his disciples, Paul embraces the Jewish custom of saying grace before meals (Rom 14:16; 1 Cor 10:30). First Timothy 4:3–5 (Deutero-Pauline?) makes an explicit connection between giving thanks for food and praising God for the gifts of creation. Paul's instructions for celebrating the Lord's Supper presuppose Jesus' custom of giving thanks before meals (1 Cor 11:23–26) and lay the foundation for the custom, beginning in the second century, of referring to this meal as the Eucharist (*eucharistia*; cf. *Didache* 9:1, 5; Ignatius, *Philadelphians* 4:1; Smyrnaeans 7:1; 8:1; Justin, *Apology* 66:1). Paul cites a variety of reasons for praise (e.g., the gift of grace, 2 Cor 4:15; the inheritance of God's saints, Col 1:12; the gift of tongues, 1 Cor 14:18; the faith and hope of the church, 1 Thess 1:2), each one of which buttresses his admonition to "give thanks in all circumstances, for this is the will of God in Christ Jesus" (1 Thess 5:18; cf. Col 3:15–17; 4:2). Above all else, the genesis of Paul's praise was the saving work of God in Christ (Phil 3:1, 7–11; 4:1, 4); his goal was to proclaim this good news until the praise of God became universal (2 Cor 4:15).

The reverberation of praise throughout the world is nowhere more evocatively sounded than in the eschatological vision of the book of Revelation, Scripture's last canonical word. With a vision that echoes the cosmic crescendo of Ps 150 (see above), Scripture's last word envisions a time when not only the earth but also the heavens resound with the praise of God. With a threefold "Holy, holy, holy" in praise of the One "who was and is and is to come" (Rev 4:8; cf. Isa 6:3), the winged creatures of heaven proclaim the praise that now characterizes creation's response to God's uncontested and everlasting reign: "You are worthy, our Lord and God, to receive glory and honor and power, for [*hoti*] you created all things" (Rev 4:11). And with a succession of hymnic acclamations, they give voice to a "new song" that fills the cosmos with an unending chorus of praise (Rev 5:8–12; 7:10; 11:15–18; 15:3–4; 19:1–8). The only response envisioned, the only word that is authentic and true, is "*amen*" (Rev 1:6–7; 3:14; 5:14; 7:12; 19:4; 22:20–21), which is always the most fitting way to endorse the lingering promise that God is indeed "enthroned on the praises of Israel" (Ps 22:3).

S. E. Balentine, *Prayer in the Hebrew Bible: The Drama of Divine-Human Dialogue* (Minneapolis: Fortress Press, 1993); O. Cullmann, *Prayer in the New Testament* (Minneapolis: Fortress Press, 1995); P. T. O'Brien, *Introductory Thanksgivings in the Letters of Paul* (Leiden: Brill, 1977); P. Miller, *They Cried to the Lord: The Form and Function of Biblical Prayer* (Minneapolis: Fortress Press, 1994); P. Schubert, *Form and Function of the Pauline Thanksgivings* (Berlin: Walter de Gruyter, 1939); C. Westermann, *Praise and Lament in the Psalms* (Atlanta: John Knox, 1981).

SAMUEL E. BALENTINE

Pray, Prayer, Intercede Both Old and New Testaments depict prayer as a dialogue between God and humans in which both parties are mutually invested. Two fundamental convictions generate and sustain this dialogue: (1) the Creator of the world is desirous of and responsive to the concerns of human beings; and (2) the contributions of human beings to this dialogue are of vital importance, not only for nurturing the relationship with God, but also for preserving and when necessary repairing the world in accordance with God's creational design. In short, prayer puts into words a belief embedded deep with Judaism and Christianity: once God made the radical decision to create human beings in the divine image and to entrust them with the stewardship of the world, the relationship between heaven and earth could never be sustained by monologue. On the other side of Gen 1, nothing short of the give and take of dialogue that creates intimate, responsible divine-human partnership could ever fulfill God's highest hopes and expectations for the world.

In its broadest sense, prayer comprises both word and deed, both verbal discourse and performative act. The recorded prayers of the Bible preserve the special language that constitutes the words people offer to God. Along with these words, the Bible also describes a number of nonverbal ways by which people communicate with God, including sacrifice, dance, and bodily gestures and postures, such as standing (e.g., 1 Kgs 8:22; Matt 6:5), lifting the hands (e.g., Pss 28:2; 143:6), and bending the knee (e.g., Ezra 9:5; Dan 6:10; Luke 22:41; Acts 7:60). Thus one may speak praise and thanksgiving and also enact it, through rituals of eating, anointing with oil, and putting on festal garments (e.g., Pss 30:11–12; 66:13–17; 116:12–14). One may voice lamentation and mourning and also embody it, through symbolic acts of weeping, fasting, putting dust on the head, and tearing the garments (e.g., Josh 7:6; Joel 2:12–13; Dan 9:3–4; Ezra 9:3, 5; Neh 1:4). One may verbalize prayers of intercession on behalf of others and, in the supreme act of compassion, persons may lay down their lives for another (Isa 53:12; cf. Job 29:12–20). The close connection between verbalization and enactment, between articulating the innermost joys and sorrows of the heart and bodying them forth in palpable ways underscores the notion that prayer is fundamentally an active way of partnering with God, not a passive one.

Historical and sociological data support the general understanding that prayer in ancient Israel developed in accordance with the shifting contexts of both individual piety and institutional religion. In the prestate period the family and the local community provide the social setting for a personal piety in which prayer is a natural and spontaneous response to everyday situations in life. Such prayers typically require no for-

mal cultic setting and no liturgical specialist: when a child is born, a parent gives thanks to God; when a child is sick or injured, a parent prays for healing. With the emergence of the monarchy and the establishment of the central cult in Jerusalem, prayer becomes more formulaic. Prescribed rituals orient individual concerns toward corporate issues that affect the nation's well-being: the community prays for the king's victory in battle (e.g., Pss 20; 21); the king's provision of justice (e.g., Pss 72; 110); and the nation's deliverance from its enemies (e.g., Pss 44; 74; 79; 83). With the dissolution of the monarchy in the exilic and postexilic periods, the cult loses its institutional base, and the survival of all religious behavior, including prayer, depends on its adaptability.

Drawing upon important aspects of personal piety and cultic ritual, the prayers of early Judaism (ca. 250 B.C. to A.D. 200) may be categorized as both spontaneous and statutory. Various prayer texts, though fragmentary, have been recovered from Qumran, suggesting that the posttemple community recited prayers each morning and evening (4Q503), each day of the week (4Q504–506), and on special festival days like the Day of Atonement (4Q507–509). In the synagogue, the fixed liturgy of public prayers included the *Amidah* or Prayer of Eighteen Benedictions (*shemoneh ʿesreh*) and the *shemaʿ* (Deut 6:4–9). In the home, prayers of a more informal nature were offered at the beginning and ending of the Sabbath, before and after meals, and before tasks for which a special sense of God's presence was desired. This interplay between personal piety and official religion suggests that during much of the biblical period ancient Israel recognized and nurtured a genetic connection between extemporized and conventional modes of praying. It may be plausibly argued that prescribed prayers *grew out of* and *standardized* the religious impulses of everyday life, impulses that in turn drew new and renewing energy from the liturgies inviting their repetition.

The vocabulary of prayer in the Old Testament. The vocabulary of prayer in the OT varies, in accord with its different forms, settings, and degrees of formality and informality. A number of technical expressions may be prefaced to or included within a verbal address to distinguish it clearly as prayer, especially the following: (1) The verb *hithpallel* ("pray") and its noun derivative *tephillah* ("prayer") are the most generic terms. Both come from the root *palal*, which means "to intervene" or "to impose." In the context of prayer, these words convey the idea of placing some situation before God that requires assessment and intervention. A wide range of situations may be addressed in such prayers: a "prayer (*tephillah*) of David" implores God to respond to the need for justice (Ps 17:1–3); Hezekiah "prayed" (*wayyithpallel*) for healing (2 Kgs 20:1–3); Jonah prayed (*wayyithpallel*) to secure his own deliverance (Jonah 2:1) and to protest the deliverance of the Ninevites (Jonah 4:2). (2) The verb *ʿathar*, variously translated as "entreat," "make supplication," or simply "pray," conveys the idea of intercession. Whether the entreaty is for oneself (e.g., Job 22:27; 33:26; 2 Chr 33:13, 19) or on behalf of another (e.g., Gen 25:21; Exod 8:4–5, 24–26; 9:28; 10:17–18; 2 Sam 24:25), such prayers suggest not only that God *can* meet a specific need but also that God *should* do so. (3) The verbal forms of *hanan*, together with the noun derivative *tehinnah*, also belong to the semantic field of "intercession" but typically carry the more focused meaning of imploring God "to be gracious" and "to show mercy." The expectation that God will respond positively rests on the conviction that it is God's nature to be gracious (*hannun*; Exod 33:19; 34:6–7; cf. Pss 103:8; 116:5). The plea "be gracious to me" is especially frequent in the Psalms (e.g., Pss 4:1; 6:2; 9:13; 25:16; 26:11; 27:7; 30:10; 31:9; 41:4, 10; 51:1; 56:1; 86:16).

In addition to these technical terms, a number of more general expressions frequently serve as identifiers of prayers, for example, "call on the name of the Lord" (*qarah beshem yhwh*), verbs meaning "ask" or "seek" (*biqqesh, shaʾal, darash*), and verbs meaning "cry out" (*tsaʿaq/zaʿaq*). Of these, the quite common verb "say" (*ʾamar*) deserves special mention. A large number of recorded prayers, particularly in prose narratives, is introduced with the statement "And X said to God" (e.g., Gen 17:18; 24:12; 32:9; Num 14:13; 16:22; Judg 6:39; 1 Sam 7:6; 2 Sam 15:31; 1 Kgs 3:6; 2 Kgs 6:20; Amos 7:2, 5; Ezra 9:6; 2 Chr 20:6). Such language depicts prayer as conversational dialogue, not unlike that which is shared routinely between persons of equal stature. In this respect Old Testament prayers affirm a fundamental theological understanding of the intimacy, indeed the near equality, that human beings may rely upon in their relationship with God. Divine-human dialogues are distinguished from intra-human conversations by the weighty nature of the issues that are "discussed." Conversational prayers typically emerge out of some crisis situation that, if unaddressed, threatens to destabilize or subvert one's trust in God (see the discussion of prose prayers below).

A distinction may be drawn between prose prayers and those that adopt the more formulaic language of poetry. The largest collection of poetic prayers occur in the Psalms, where formulaic language provides models for praying that are appropriate for repeated use by a variety of persons in both personal and corporate contexts of worship. Two basic types of prayers dominate: lament and praise. Lament prayers are more numerous than any other single type, comprising roughly one-third of the Psalter (e.g., Pss 3, 13, 22, 42–43, 44, 69, 79, 88, 130). The typical pattern of these prayers—invocation, petition, affirmation/hope of God's response—provides a rhetorical and substantive means for both articulating and coping with the brokenness and loss that so often strikes life unawares. Prayers of *praise* and *thanksgiving* are also well attested in the Psalter (e.g., Pss 8, 30, 33, 66, 100, 113, 138, 146–150). Their standard pattern—summons to praise, reasons/motivations for praise, concluding summons to praise—suggests that praise remains connected, in both form and content, to lament. When people in distress call out in lamentation to God, God hears and responds. The natural response, the "reason" for praying, is to offer heartfelt gratitude and adoration to God. As the psalmist puts it, "You have turned my mourning into dancing . . . so that my soul may praise you and not be silent" (Ps 30:11–12).

In addition to psalmic prayers, the OT records approximately 100 prose prayers. In contrast with the conventional, patterned rhetoric of the Psalms, prose prayers are integrated into the specifics of a narrative context; their meaning is directly connected to what precedes and follows them in a clearly defined situation. They are especially frequent in Genesis–Kings, where narrative is the primary literary style. Some are quite brief, comprising little more than a simple petition for something concrete and practical (e.g., information, a child, healing) and an answer (Gen 15:2, 3, 8; Judg 13:8; 2 Sam 15:31; 2 Kgs 6:17, 18, 20). Others are more elaborate, with petitions of a more abstract nature (e.g., for blessing, remembrance, hearing), which are buttressed by reasons why God should respond positively (2 Sam 7:18–29; 1 Kgs 8:22–61; 2 Kgs 19:15–19).

Prose prayers serve a variety of literary and theological functions within narrative contexts. They provide insights into the character of the participants—both human and divine—in the narrative. The prayers of Elijah (1 Kgs 17:17–24), Solomon (1 Kgs 3:4–15), and Hezekiah (2 Kgs 20:2–3), for example, confirm their exemplary piety; in the words of the woman whose child was healed by Elijah's prayers, "Now I know that you are a man of God, and that the word of the LORD in your mouth is truth" (1 Kgs 17:24). By contrast, the prayer of Jacob (Gen 32:9–12), which is but one of several strategies he employs to secure his safety, and the prayer of Jonah (Jonah 4:2; cf. 2:2–9 [poetic]), which angrily protests

God's mercy for the Ninevites, provide a subtle caricature of piety more professed than real. Postexilic prayers of penitence (Ezra 9:6–15; Neh 1:5–11; 9:6–37; Dan 9:4–19) are in effect doxologies in praise of the God who can be trusted to forgive, as the repeating refrain in these prayers puts it, "the great and awesome God who keeps covenant and steadfast love with those who love him and keep his commandments" (Neh 1:5). A number of prose prayers contain a petition for divine justice (Gen 18:22–33; Exod 32:11–14; Num 11:11–15; 14:13–19; Josh 7:7–9; 1 Kgs 17:17–19). Located at the critical narrative juncture between some crisis that jeopardizes trust in God and its subsequent resolution, these texts depict prayer as an important and effective means for addressing issues of theodicy.

The last mentioned prayers for justice invite further reflection on those occasions when prayer becomes a potent vehicle for human intercession with the deity. The biblical tradition links intercessory prayer with the role of the prophet, especially Jeremiah (7:16; 11:14; 14:11–12), Ezekiel (9:8; 11:13), and Amos (7:1–6; 8:1–3), while at the same time tracing the prophetic antecedent to Abraham (Gen 18:22–33; 20:7, 17), Moses (e.g., Exod 5:22–23; 14:10–15; 32:11–14; Num 11:2; 12:13; 14:13–19; 16:22; 21:7; Deut 9:20, 25–29), and Samuel (1 Sam 7:5, 8–10; 12:19–25). The role of the intercessor is to stand in between God and some situation on earth and to pray on behalf of others. The situations are varied: persons may be sick and need God's healing; persons may have sinned and need God's forgiveness; persons may suffer and be abused and need God's justice. The common thread is that intercession not only calls God's attention to need but also summons God to respond positively to that need.

Most striking of all are intercessions that call upon God to alter or even reverse decisions that would appear to be justified. Abraham questions God's decision to punish the wicked cities of Sodom and Gomorrah and pleads that the innocent be spared; God accepts Abraham's questions and responds affirmatively to his intervention (Gen 18:22–33). In the aftermath of the golden calf idolatry, Moses asks God to turn away from wrath and reverse the decision to withdraw the covenant; in response, "the LORD changed his mind about the disaster that he planned to bring on his people" (Exod 32:11–14). Not every such intercession receives a positive response (cf. God's repeated refusal to hear Jeremiah's pleas for Israel; Jer 7:16; 11:14; 14:11–12), for prayer is genuine dialogue, and even in its most importunate forms its leverage is that of persuasion, not control or manipulation. Even so, the conviction that every divine decision will be tempered by God's abiding mercy sustains the hope that God is never unmoved by earnest intercession.

Prayer in the New Testament. The NT also uses a variety of specific and general terms for prayer. The most common are *proseuchomai*, "pray," and its noun form *proseuche*, "prayer," terms used in the LXX to translate the Hebrew words *hithpallel* and *tephillah* respectively. Both words are used with respect to prayer addressed to God or to Jesus, and both sustain the OT understanding that prayer is at heart dialogue, not monologue. The relationship the NT envisions between God and pray-er is indeed more personal and intimate, for Jesus taught his followers to address God with childlike trust as "Father" (*pater*: Matt 6:6–9; Luke 11:2; cf. *abba*: Rom 8:15; Gal 4:6) (see *abba*). Other terms, often found in common, intrapersonal contexts, take on more specific connotations when employed in the vocabulary of prayer: verbs for "ask" or "seek" (*aiteo, deomai, erotao*); verbs meaning "cry out" or "shout" (*boao, krazo*); and verbs for "praise" and "give thanks" (*aineo, eucharisteo*). Still other expressions refer to bodily gestures (*gonypeteo*, "kneel"; *proskyneo*, "prostrate oneself"), sometimes metaphorically, as in the verb *krouo*, "knock (at the door)," which describes a way of beseeching God.

In general, all these terms are used in ways which confirm that the NT draws deeply on the OT's rich legacy of prayer. Praise, thanksgiving, lament, petition, and intercession remain prominent in the dialogue with God that Jesus models and invites from his followers. Jesus gives thanks to God (Matt 11:25–27 and par. Luke 10:21–22; John 11:41–42) and laments to God (Matt 27:46 and par. Mark 15:34 [Ps 22:1]; Luke 23:46 [Ps 31:5]). He petitions God (principally in the Lord's Prayer; see below) and teaches his followers to do the same, for "everyone who asks receives, and everyone who searches finds" (Matt 7:8; Mark 11:24; Luke 11:10; cf. 1 John 5:14–15). He intercedes with his Father on behalf of his followers (John 17:1–26; see below) and promises, through his servant Paul, that in his absence the Holy Spirit will continue to intercede for them, even when they themselves do not have the words (Rom 8:15, 26; Gal 4:6). In the assurance of this promise, Paul exhorts congregations to become communities of intercession; with him they should pray for the success of his mission (e.g., Rom 15:30–32; Col 4:3; 2 Thess 3:1), for the healing of the sick (Acts 9:40; 28:8), for spiritual growth (e.g., Eph 1:16–17; Phil 1:9), for help in times of peril (Acts 12:5; Phil 1:19; Heb 13:18), and for the civil authorities (1 Tim 2:1–2).

For all its indebtedness to the OT, however, the NT's portrait of prayer has its own distinctive perspectives. Three of these may be singled out for special attention.

1. In contrast with the OT, which preserves the words of more than 250 prose and psalmic prayers, the NT contains relatively few recorded prayers: the prayers of Jesus (Matt 11:25–27 and par. Luke 10:21–22; Matt 26:39 and par. Mark 14:36 and Luke 22:42; Matt 27:46 and par. Mark 15:34; Luke 23:34, 46; John 11:41–42; 12:27–28; 17:1–26); the prayer of Peter and the assembly (Acts 1:24–25); the prayers of Peter and John in their Jerusalem prison (Acts 4:24–30); and the prayer of Stephen at his stoning (Acts 7:59–60). Prayer is prominent in Paul's letters to the churches, especially in the introductory thanksgivings (e.g., Rom 1:7–8; 1 Cor 1:3–4; 2 Cor 1:2; Gal 1:3; Phil

1:2–3; Col 1:2) and the benedictory blessings (e.g., Rom 16:25–27; 1 Cor 16:23; 2 Cor 13:13; Gal 6:18; Eph 6:23; Phil 4:23; Col 4:18), but otherwise the actual words of Paul's prayers are not recorded.

The infrequency of recorded prayers is likely a difference without a distinction, for the Gospels, particularly Luke, make it clear that Jesus prayed at the critical junctures of his life: at baptism (Luke 3:21); the choosing of the disciples (Luke 6:12); the transfiguration (Luke 9:28–29); in Gethsemane (Luke 22:32, 41–42); and at the crucifixion (Luke 23:46). Luke's Gospel elaborates on the critical role of prayer with two parables of Jesus, Luke 11:5–8 and 18:1–8, the latter of which connects persistent prayer with the abiding concern for justice for the disadvantaged and the oppressed. Acts depicts Jesus' followers as "constantly devoting themselves to prayer" (Acts 1:14; cf. 1:24; 6:6; 9:11; 10:9; 12:5; 13:3; 14:23; 16:25; 22:17). They were to "pray without ceasing" (1 Thess 5:17; cf. Rom 12:12; Eph 6:18; Col 4:2). They were to infuse every dimension of their lives with prayer. In suffering and in joy, in sickness and in health, the church was to live by the truth bequeathed by its forebear Elijah: "they should pray" and "pray for one another" because "the prayer of the righteous is powerful and effective" (Jas 5:13–16).

2. The OT offers very little instruction on when or how to pray (cf. Job 8:5–6; 11:13–15; 22:23–27). The NT often addresses this issue. In the Sermon on the Mount, Jesus cautions against impious and pretentious prayer (Matt 6:5–8); what one asks must be pleasing to God and in accord with God's will (Matt 7:11). Prayer must be offered in faith (Matt 21:22), not doubt (cf. Jas 1:5). Prayers that are selfish or abusive of others, prayers that feign love of God while harboring ill will towards others are invalid; they bear witness only to the sin of the pray-er (1 Pet 3:7; Jas 4:3; cf. Matt 5:23–24; Mark 11:25).

The NT anchors its instructions to the prayers of Jesus himself. Two "model" prayers exemplify what Jesus expects from his followers. Luke reports that in response to the disciples' request— "Lord, teach us to pray" (Luke 11:1)— Jesus offered the example we call the Lord's Prayer (Luke 11:2–4 and par. Matt 6:9–13). The differences between the two versions of this prayer, for all their critical importance, are not as crucial as the fundamental theological truth that together they proclaim. They both join praise and petition in a simple and spontaneous form, which is rooted in Jewish antecedents (cf. the Prayer of Eighteen Benedictions). More significantly, they both begin with two (or three) petitions that tune the heart first and foremost to God's will ("hallowed be your name," "your kingdom come," "your will be done"), which in turn invite and inform three (or four) petitions that address human needs within the context of God's purposive plan for the world ("give us each day our daily bread," "forgive us our sins/debts," "do not bring us to the time of trial," "rescue us from the evil one"). The discipline of praying and, more important, living in a way that commits one, in accordance with God's will, to the well-being of others is further exemplified in John 17:1–26. Conventionally described as the "high priestly prayer," these words compose Jesus' farewell instruction before the betrayal that leads to his death. He models a prayer that begins with his own needs (vv. 1–8) but does not end there. Jesus is more concerned about the immediate welfare of his disciples, who in the aftermath of his death will suffer persecution and may be tempted to lose heart (vv. 9–19). But Jesus is still more concerned for the long-term future of the church (vv. 20–26). His abiding prayer is that those who will yet come to believe will know and exemplify the unity between Father and Son, which is a mirror of the mutuality and reciprocity between heaven and earth, upon which "the foundation of the world" depends (v. 24). It is of no small consequence that Jesus imparts his vision for the future of the world by teaching his disciples how to pray.

3. The OT contains a rich tradition of lament prayers. In addition to the lament

psalms, the practice of addressing hard, often accusing, questions to God is modeled by Isaiah (e.g., Isa 63:7–64:12), Jeremiah (esp. Jer 11:18–23; 12:1–6; 15:10–21; 17:14–18; 18:18–23; 20:7–13, 14–18), Joel (Joel 1–2), Habakkuk (Hab 1:12–17), and Job (e.g., Job 3:3–26; 6:1–20; 10:18–22; 13:20–14:22; 19:7–20; 30:16–31). On occasion, lament prayers give vent to a desire for vengeance against the enemy (e.g., Pss 58; 109; 137), which, though strongly expressed, is entrusted to God. Apart from Jesus' lament from the cross (see esp. the quotation of Ps 22:1 in Matt 27:46; Mark 15:34), the New Testament preserves very little of Israel's lament tradition. Moreover, the New Testament characteristically reshapes the prayer for judgment against one's enemies with a "theology of the cross" (Miller, *They Cried to the Lord*, 321–24). Jesus teaches his followers to pray for the forgiveness of their enemies (Matt 5:44 and par. Luke 6:28). Jesus' model prayer, *"Your* kingdom come, *your* will be done," is concretized in Gethsemane by his submission to oppression, suffering, even death as God's will: "My Father, if it is possible, let this cup pass from me; yet not what I want but what you want" (Matt 26:39; cf. Mark 14:36; Luke 22:42). Stephen images Jesus' example in his own last words (Acts 7:60). Paul prays for deliverance from his affliction but learns that trouble and suffering are seeded with the power of Christ that dwells within him: "My grace is sufficient for you, for power is made perfect in weakness" (2 Cor 12:9). Having learned that enduring "weaknesses, insults, hardships, persecutions, and calamities *for the sake of Christ"* (2 Cor 12:10) is the way of imaging Christ, Paul exhorts the Christian community not only to "be patient in suffering, persevere in prayer" but also to "bless those who persecute you; bless and do not curse them" (Rom 12:12, 14).

In sum, Scripture recommends prayer as a primary means of engaging God in an ongoing dialogue for the sake of *personal* well-being, *corporate* stability, and ultimately the redemption of the *world*

that God designed to be "very good." The hopes, expectations, and promises of such prayer are nowhere more clearly voiced than in the petition of Jesus: "Your will be done, *on earth as it is in heaven"* (Matt 6:10). Paul's discernment that "creation waits with eager longing for the revealing of the children of God" (Rom 8:19) surely raises the stakes for the prayers of the people of God. And yet, against every counsel of despair, there remains God's invitation to pray: "I was ready to be sought out by those who did not ask, to be found by those who did not seek me. I said 'Here I am, here I am,' to a nation that did not call on my name" (Isa 65:1). Perhaps this abiding invitation explains in part why the book of Revelation, Scripture's last canonical word, so frequently punctuates its eschatological vision with the liturgical asseverative "Amen" (Rev 1:6, 7; 3:14; 5:14; 7:12; 19:4; 22:20, 21), which typically confirms everything that has preceded should be treated as prayer.

S. E. Balentine, *Prayer in the Hebrew Bible: The Drama of Divine-Human Dialogue* (Minneapolis: Fortress Press, 1993); O. Cullmann, *Prayer in the New Testament* (Minneapolis: Fortress Press, 1995); M. Greenberg, *Biblical Prose Prayer As a Window to the Popular Religion of Ancient Israel* (Berkeley, Los Angeles: University of California Press, 1983); J. Jeremias, *The Prayers of Jesus* (London: SCM, 1967); J. Koenig, *Rediscovering New Testament Prayer* (San Francisco: Harper & Row, 1992); P. Miller, *They Cried to the Lord: The Form and Theology of Biblical Prayer* (Minneapolis: Fortress, 1994); G. P. Wiles, *Paul's Intercessory Prayers: The Significance of the Intercessory Prayers in the Letters of Paul* (Cambridge: Cambridge University Press, 1974).

SAMUEL E. BALENTINE

Preach, Preaching, Teach, Teacher, Teaching

In general one may distinguish the task of preaching from that of teaching in the NT with the observation that the former is focused on the proclamation of the *Gospel* of God's salvation in

Christ to nonbelievers, while the latter refers to the instruction of the faithful in the spiritual and practical knowledge that characterizes Christian life. Thus Paul can refer to his initial proclamation to those who formed churches in various regions (e.g., 1 Cor 2:1–5) in the course of his subsequent instruction of these communities on numerous topics of belief and practice (e.g., 1 Cor 7–15).

In the Gospels the verb *kerysso* ("to preach, proclaim") is first used of John the Baptist, who appears "proclaiming a baptism of repentance for the forgiveness of sins" (Mark 1:4; Luke 3:3) and that "the kingdom of heaven is at hand" (Matt 3:2 Mg). John also preaches about the one coming after him who would baptize with the Holy Spirit (Mark 1:7 and par.). Jesus begins his ministry by "proclaiming the good news of God" (Mark 1:14) as well as a message regarding repentance and the coming kingdom (Mark 1:15 and par.). All three Synoptic Gospels use *kerysso* to refer to the preaching of Jesus and certain others (e.g., the disciples at Mark 6:12). That the verb *euangelizo* ("to preach the gospel") can be used as a synonym for *kerysso* emerges from a comparison of Mark and Luke. In Luke 4:43, which parallels Mark 1:38, Luke replaces Mark's "proclaim the message" (*kerysso*) with "proclaim the good news" (*euangelizo*). But in the next verse, Luke 4:44 retains the verb used in Mark's reference to "proclaiming the message" (*kerysso*) in Mark 1:39. These two verbs also appear together in Luke's paradigmatic account of Jesus' appearance in the synagogue at Nazareth. Jesus quotes Isaiah to define his own commission "to bring good news to the poor" (*euangelizo*), "to proclaim (*kerysso*) release to the captives" (Luke 4:18; Isa 61:1), and "to proclaim (*kerysso*) the year of the Lord's favor" (Luke 4:19; Isa 61:2). In all, *euangelizo* occurs ten times in Luke and fifteen time in Acts, usually to denote "preaching the gospel" by Jesus (Luke 4:43; 7:22; 8:1; 16:16; 20:1) or the apostles and others in Acts (Acts 5:42; 8:4, 12, 25, 35, 40; 11:20; 13:32; etc.). Elsewhere in the Gospels it is found only at Matt

11:5, which parallels Luke 7:22 and is part of the sayings source Q. Although it does not occur in the Gospels, *katangello* ("to proclaim, preach") is used by Paul to refer to preaching (1 Cor 2:1; 9:14; Phil 1:17–18; cf. Col 1:28), and the verb also appears in Acts with this meaning (Acts 4:2; 13:5, 38; 15:36; etc.).

Only in a few places do references to preaching or proclamation in the OT approximate the usage found in the NT. The use of *basar* ("bring good news") and *qara* ("proclaim") in Isa 61:1–2 is the closest parallel and has not only been influential in Luke 4 but also is significant for the NT use of "gospel" in general. The reference at Lev 25:10 to the jubilee and the injunction to "proclaim liberty" is a significant parallel to both Isaiah and Luke. In a number of texts Jeremiah is directed by the Lord to "proclaim" certain words (Jer 3:12; 7:2; 11:6; 19:2), and Jonah is instructed to proclaim the Lord's message to Nineveh (Jonah 3:2). Elsewhere festivals (Lev 23:2) and fasts (1 Kgs 21:9; 2 Chr 20:3; Ezra 8:21) are proclaimed, but not a particular message from God.

In the OT the primary verbs translated "to teach" in English are *lamad* and *yarah*. God is often the teacher, either directly or indirectly (Exod 4:12, 15; Lev 10:11; 1 Kgs 8:36; Job 36:22; Pss 25:4–5, 9; 27:11; 119:12, 33; Isa 2:3; 48:17; Mic 4:2). The law is written for the instruction of Israel (Exod 24:12), and Moses is the teacher of Israel par excellence (Deut 4:1, 5, 14; 5:31; 6:1; etc.). Priests are entrusted with the teaching of the law (Deut 33:10; cf. 2 Kgs 17:27–28; Ezra 7:10; Ezek 44:23). Various others such as Samuel (1 Sam 12:23) or a father (Prov 4:4, 11) may be singled out as teachers.

The Greek word for teacher (*didaskalos*) is used fifty times in the Gospels and ten times elsewhere in the NT. In the Gospels it is frequently used in direct address to Jesus by his disciples (Mark 4:38; 9:38; 10:35; 13:1; Luke 21:7), various petitioners (Mark 9:17 and par.; 10:17 and par.; Luke 12:13), opponents (Matt 22:36 and par.; Mark 12:14, 19 and par.; Luke

19:39; 20:39; John 8:4), and others (Mark 12:32; Luke 7:40; 11:45). Jesus employs it as a self-reference at Mark 14:14 and par. (cf. John 13:13–14), and others refer to Jesus indirectly as "teacher" (Matt 9:11; 17:24; Mark 5:35 and par.). The Fourth Gospel especially underlines the equivalency of "rabbi" with "teacher" (John 1:38; 3:2; cf. Matt 23:7, 10; 26:25; Mark 9:5; 11:21; 14:45 and par.; John 1:49; 4:31; 6:25; 9:2; 11:8; 20:16). Both terms are also used in direct address of John the Baptist (Luke 3:12: teacher; John 3:26: rabbi), who like Jesus has an associated group of disciples. At Luke 2:46, the portrayal of the boy Jesus among the teachers in the temple foreshadows his own teaching role.

If a distinction can be made between preaching and teaching in the case of early Christians after the time of Jesus (i.e., preaching to the unconverted, teaching believers), this differentiation does not seem to hold for Jesus himself. For example, in Matt 11:1 after instructing (*diatasso*) his disciples (see the content of Matt 10), Jesus is said to teach (*didasko*) and preach (*kerysso*) his message in a setting in which the auditors presumably hear him for the first time (Matt 11:1). It is not the "preaching" (*kerygma*) of Jesus that elicits surprise (in the Gospels the word is only used of Jonah's preaching: Matt 12:41; Luke 11:32); rather it is his "teaching" (*didache*) that causes amazement (Matt 7:28–29; 22:33; Mark 1:22 and par.; 1:27; 11:18). Jesus' typical activity is frequently summarized with reference to his teaching. The synagogue often provides the context for Jesus' teaching during his ministry (Matt 4:23; 9:35; Mark 1:21; 6:2 and par.; Luke 4:15; 6:6; 13:10; John 6:59). In addition, the temple serves as a significant setting, especially before the passion (Matt 21:23; Mark 11:17–18; 12:35; 14:49 and par.; Luke 19:47–48; 21:37; John 7:14, 28; 8:20; 18:20). But Jesus is also found teaching in a great variety of other settings: beside the sea (Mark 2:13; 6:34), from a boat (Mark 4:1–2 and par.; Luke 5:3), on a mountain (Matt 5:2); and his task is an itinerant one as he proceeds from village to village (Mark 6:6 and par.),

throughout Galilee (Matt 4:23; 11:1), beyond the Jordan (Mark 10:1), and on the way to Jerusalem (Luke 13:22). Because teaching is fundamental to Jesus' activity, it is significant that he also sends his disciples out to teach (see Mark 6:6b–7 with 6:30; Matt 10:5; Luke 9:2). As in the case of Jesus' activity, what the disciples do can be also described in seemingly synonymous terms as preaching (*kerysso*, 6:12) or teaching (*didasko*, 6:30). In the Fourth Gospel, Jesus stresses that his teaching is not his own but comes from God (John 7:16–17). When Jesus is arrested, the high priest questions him about his disciples and his teaching (18:19; cf. Luke 23:5).

At Mark 4:2 it is noted that "[Jesus] began to teach them many things in parables," and most of the rest of the chapter contains examples of the parables themselves. It is important to note that in many cases the content of Jesus' teaching, which of course is abundant in the Gospels, can be introduced without explicit reference in terms of the vocabulary of teaching. The Sermon on the Plain in Luke 6:20–49, for example, is introduced simply by "he said" (v. 20), and the parable of the Wicked Tenants in Mark 12:1–11 by "he began to speak" (v. 1). Although Mark explicitly includes the passion predictions of 8:31 and 9:31 as something taught by Jesus to his disciples, the parallels to these verses in Matthew (16:21; 17:22–23) and Luke (9:22; 9:43–44) make no reference to teaching.

An important role in teaching is played by the Holy *Spirit*, which in time of persecution will teach Christians what to say before their examiners (Luke 12:12; cf. 21:12–15). In the Fourth Gospel Jesus promises his disciples that the Holy Spirit (Advocate) will teach them everything and also remind them of everything Jesus said (John 14:26). In 1 John 2:27 the anointing that believers have received precludes the need for human teachers, since it teaches about all things.

Acts makes only one explicit reference to teachers (13:1); those of the church at Antioch. But the people of Jerusalem are said to devote themselves to the apostles' teaching (2:42), which soon fills the city (5:28). Upon Paul's confrontation with a magician, the proconsul Sergius Paulus is "astonished at the teaching of the Lord" (13:12). In Athens Paul gains an audience for his "new teaching" (17:12).

Paul refers to the teaching received by the Romans (Rom 6:17; 16:17) and discusses teaching in connection with the problem of speaking in tongues at Corinth (1 Cor 14:6, 26). In 1 Cor 12:28 teachers are listed third, after apostles and prophets, among the various ministries given by the Spirit (12:4–7). In the list at Eph 4:11 "pastors and teachers" are closely associated, with the former term drawing on the image of the shepherd tending the flock to indicate the detailed attention such *ministers* are called to in fulfilling their roles. Although Paul does not use the word "teacher" to describe his own activity (and stresses that he was not taught the gospel in Gal 1:12), the Pastoral Epistles characterize him as a "herald," an "apostle," and a "teacher" (1 Tim 2:7; 2 Tim 1:11). The word herald (*keryx*; elsewhere in the NT only of Noah at 2 Pet 2:5) aptly describes Paul's preaching (*kerysso*) of the gospel (Gal 2:2; 1 Thess 2:9), Christ crucified (1 Cor 1:23; cf. 2 Cor 1:19; 4:5), and the word of faith (Rom 10:8). God saves those who believe through the foolishness of the proclamation (*kerygma*, 1 Cor 1:21), which is backed up by the Spirit and power (2:4). Preaching and faith are in vain apart from the resurrection of Christ (15:14). Those who have not heard the gospel cannot believe unless someone proclaims the good news to them (Rom 10:14–15). Patient teaching (*didache*) is urged at 2 Tim 4:2 in light of a coming time when people will not accept "sound doctrine" (*didaskalia*) but engage teachers suited to their own desires (4:3; cf. Titus 1:11; Heb 13:9; Rev 2:14, 20). In order to avoid such problems, faithful people are to be sought out who can teach others well (2 Tim 2:2). The author of the epistle to the Hebrews scolds readers who should already be teachers but instead need someone to teach them the basics of the oracles of God (Heb 5:12). In contrast, the epistle of James warns that not many should become teachers, since those who teach will be judged with greater strictness (3:1). The elder in 2 John cautions against going beyond the teaching of Christ or receiving anyone who does not hold to it (vv. 9–11).

Floyd V. Filson, "The Christian Teacher in the First Century," *JBL* 60 (1941): 317–28; V. P. Furnish, "Prophets, Apostles, and Preachers: A Study of the Biblical Concept of Preaching," *Int* 17 (1963): 48–60.

CHRISTOPHER R. MATTHEWS

Predestine *see* Determine

Presence, Face, Countenance, Appearance, Pillar of Cloud, Ark of the Covenant, Tent of Meeting, Tabernacle, Temple, Sanctuary

"Presence" is the comprehensive term; "face" and "countenance" are alternative translations of the same Hebrew word. Appearance is a deliberate act of becoming present, the pillar of cloud a physical manifestation of God's presence, the ark of the covenant a portable shrine signifying God's invisible presence, the tent of meeting/tabernacle another portable shrine, a temple a stationary shrine, and "sanctuary" a general word covering these various types of shrine. The word presence derives from the Latin *praesens*, "being before." In common usage, it means two or more persons being together in time and space. In theological discourse, it bears a specific meaning of humans (or other creatures) being aware of God's attention.

Old Testament

"Presence" in the NRSV translates (with a few exceptions) the Hebrew *panim*, which literally means "face," "countenance," but which is used in so many combinations that its literal meaning is no longer primary. The NRSV renders *panim* "presence" only in passages in which even the metaphorical use of face would seem odd or forced (Exod 18:12; 33:14; Ps 16:11).

Face and countenance. The theological meaning of *panim* has dynamics of its own. That God has a face is not disputed in Hebrew Scripture, but humans were not allowed to see it or depict it. Moses is told that he could see God's back (Exod 33:23; also 33:18–19), but not God's face (33:20). This is the same Moses who is said to have conversed with God "face to face" (Exod 33:11).

The people saw even less than Moses, according to Deut 4:15, "Since you saw no form," which offers that as the reason Israel is prohibited the use of idols in its worship (4:16–18). Without images, God's face cannot be represented. So what can the commendable "seeking God's face" (2 Chr 7:14; Ps 27:8; Hos 5:15) mean? Perhaps "presence" distills the meaning of such passages.

"Countenance" is face considered in terms of the mood it projects. When the text says, let God's *panim* "shine" on one, it means a facial expression projecting benevolence and approval (Num 6:26; Pss 44:3, 89:15).

Numerous passages speak of the Lord hiding his face from Israel or an individual (e.g., Pss 10:11; Isa 8:17; Ezek 39:23). Psalm 51:11 pleads with God to "not cast me away from your presence." Other passages use the language of distance, for example, "Do not be far from me" (Ps 22:11; cf. v. 1). How can the omnipresent God be absent? Affirmations of God's filling heaven and earth (Isa 66:1; Jer 23:24; etc.) or being impossible to hide from (Ps 139:7–12; Amos 9:1–4) confirm that ancient Israelites knew of God's omnipresence. To reconcile the contradiction, we must regard God's universal presence as compatible with his deliberate absence or inaccessibility; this is not just a matter of human consciousness but of God's will. Perhaps we can compare it to a meeting of estranged persons—presence sometimes communicates distance and coldness in another.

Appearance. Some narratives depict God as *appearing* (from the Hebrew verb, "to cause to see") to individuals or the community. The expression "the Lord appeared to so and so" is frequent in the Pentateuch (Gen 12:7; 17:1; 35:9; Exod 3:2; Lev 9:23; Num 14:10; Deut 31:15; Judg 6:12; 13:3; 1 Kgs 3:5). Genesis accounts do not describe what patriarchs saw; what God says is the point, and that is quoted. The appearance to Moses is graphic, yet words are even more important. In appearances to the whole people, God's glory is visible in a cloud; words are not communicated (Exod 16:10; 24:15–18). In Judges, God appears as an angel. With appearances in dreams (see **reveal**), we have passed to another type of experience. In the book of Daniel, symbolic figures appear (Dan 5:5; 7:5; 8:1).

The appearance of God to humans belongs to a certain period of biblical history—when natural and supernatural were not sharply differentiated. As the biblical narrative proceeds, differentiation begins to influence representation, divine communication begins to take place in an altered state of consciousness, and the word "appear" disappears. However, the idea that God deliberately makes his presence visible and audible remains; these are extraordinary events, to select people for specific purposes.

The patriarchs built altars at the sites of appearances. "Altar" translates the Hebrew *mizbeah*, formed on the root meaning "to sacrifice." Appearance produces memory that gives legitimacy to an altar. "In every place where I cause my name to be remembered I will come to you and bless you" (Exod 20:24b; e.g., Gen 12:7; 26:23–25; 28:10–22; Judg 6:11–24).

Sanctuary. The Hebrew word most often behind the NRSV "sanctuary" is *miqdash*, based on the root meaning "holy." It is sometimes applied to open-air altars (e.g., Josh 24:26), or identified with "high places" (Isa 16:12, Amos 7:9) or the wilderness tabernacle (e.g., Exod 28:8) or the Jerusalem temple (e.g., 1 Chr 22:19); hence, it is a general term for a sacred place; it is even used of the promised land as a whole (Exod 15:17; Ps 114:2).

"High places" were open-air precincts with altars (e.g., Lev 26:30; Num 33:52; 1 Kgs 3:2). Evidently it was common to erect "pillars" (standing stones) and "sacred poles" (called *ʾasherah/ʾasheroth*, the name of Baal's consort) in the sacred precincts; since pillars and poles had suspect associations, they were prohibited in Deuteronomy (16:21, 22). High places themselves became suspect (Hos 10:8; Jer 7:31), and Josiah destroyed them in his reform (2 Kgs 23:8–20).

Sanctuaries located in towns and countryside were sanctified by the Lord, places where Israelites had access to God near their homes; the slaughter of domestic animals for food was performed there. However, the ritual practices of these places were under the influence of popular piety and therefore eclectic.

Pillar of cloud. During the exodus, Israel's religious life lacked fixed places of **worship** and **sacrifice**. They were a people on the move, and their sacred places and objects had to move with them. A mysterious "pillar of cloud" accompanied them throughout their journey. "The LORD went in front of them in a pillar of cloud by day, to lead them along the way, and in a pillar of fire by night, to give them light, so that they might travel by day and by night" (Exod 13:21). When the Egyptian army caught up with them, the pillar of cloud moved (14:19b), coming between army and escaping slaves (v. 20). After this decisive intervention, we read of the pillar of cloud only sporadically (Exod 33:9–10; Num 12:5). There is no suggestion that the same cloud descended on Mount Sinai. The pillar of cloud was both visible manifestation of the Lord's guidance and protection and medium of revelation to Moses. Nehemiah 9:12, 19 recall its role as guide, Ps 99:7 its role in revelation.

Ark. The "ark of the covenant" (Hebrew *ʾaron*) is first introduced in God's revelation of the sanctuary. It was a chest carried by poles to be placed in the tabernacle, representing the throne or footstool of the invisible God (Exod 25:10–22; constructed in 37:1–9). It is often called the ark of the "covenant" or "testimony" because the tablets containing the Ten Commandments were deposited in it (Deut 10:1–5; Exod 25:16; 40:20).

As the most sacred object in the tabernacle, it was hid from human sight, to be used annually in the atonement ritual (Lev 16:11–16). When the tent was disassembled and in transit, the ark led the march (Num 10:33–36). From the language associated with the march, we can surmise that it was a palladium of Israelites in battle. The ark performs a military function in the conquest. First, it stopped the flow of the Jordan while the Israelites forded (Josh 3:7–11); it then was marched around Jericho (Josh 6). It doesn't participate in any other battle, though it is mentioned in Josh 8:33; Judg 20:27.

The ark was in Shiloh when Samuel was a boy (1 Sam 3:3). In battle at Aphek (1 Sam 4) it was captured by Philistines, to whom it caused such trouble that they devised a scheme for returning it (1 Sam 6). It remained at Kiriath-jearim until David brought it, with some difficulty, to Jerusalem (2 Sam 6). David housed it in a tent throughout his reign because the Lord through Nathan rejected the plan of a permanent house (2 Sam 7:1–7). David kept it out of the battle with his rebellious son (2 Sam 15:24–25), and it never went out to battle again. Its military days were preserved in the divine epithet, "The LORD of hosts who is enthroned on the cherubim" (1 Sam 4:4; 2 Sam 6:2; 2 Kgs 19:15 = Isa 37:16). The ark itself remained in Solomon's temple (1 Kgs 8:3–9). Ritual tours of the temple grounds, or perhaps the city (Pss 24; 132) may have taken place.

Tent of meeting and tabernacle. In the wilderness there was a portable sanctuary, alternately named the "tent of meeting" (Hebrew *ʾohel moʿed*) and the "tabernacle" (Hebrew *mishkan*). The plans were revealed to Moses in Exod 25–31. It was a large tent divided into two rooms with an altar in front. The tabernacle was located in the center of the encampment, with the tribe of priests and Levites settled around it and the other tribes fanning out from it.

Before construction of the tabernacle, we read of a "tent of meeting" (Exod 33:7–11), which appears to be small (33:9). It was stationed outside the camp. It was not a place of sacrifice and was not associated with priests; rather, it was a place for receiving oracles, accessible only to Moses, guarded by Joshua (but cf. Exod 38:8). This oracle sanctuary plays a role only in one other narrative, Num 12:4–5, 10.

The tabernacle is frequently called the tent of meeting (Exod 27:21, etc.); a tradition about an oracle tent in the wilderness has been absorbed into a timeless, ideal portable sanctuary. Indeed, the tabernacle absorbs the ark and the pillar of cloud as well (see Exod 40:34–38). It is itself a prototype of the Jerusalem temple.

Temple. Constructing the temple is recounted twice, 1 Kgs 5–6; 8 and 1 Chr 29; 2 Chr 2–7. According to 1 Kings, Solomon takes full initiative to construct the temple as a part of the royal quarter in Jerusalem. He purchased supplies from Tyre and employed Phoenician artisans. It should surprise no one that much symbolism in the temple had Phoenician-Canaanite analogues. The ark stood where the statue of the god would have stood. The overall layout resembled the tabernacle, but twice the size. According to Chronicles, David took the initiative, preparing everything for construction and organizing the rights and duties of cultic personnel.

The meaning of the temple is articulated in the dedication story. When the ark was carried into its place, the "house" was filled with a cloud (1 Kgs 8:4–10). Solomon delivered the dedication prayer: "The LORD has said that he would dwell (*shakan*) in thick darkness. I have built you an exalted house, a place for you to rest in forever" (8:12–13). The temple is where the Lord "tabernacles" among his people. Solomon acknowledges the paradox of the omnipresent God dwelling in one place (8:27), and pleads that he will keep his eyes and ears trained on this place where his name is located (8:18–29). Thus, the text juxtaposes two different ideas: that the Lord dwells in the temple and the name dwells there while the Lord keeps watch over it from heaven.

The temple was a sign of election. The Lord chose to dwell in this place, on Zion, the "mountain" within the *city* of Jerusalem (Ps 68:16; cf. Pss 76:2; 78:68). The choice of Jerusalem was closely associated with the choice of the Davidic dynasty (1 Kgs 11:13, 32; Ps 132). When Sennacherib was besieging the city, the Lord responded to the king's plea for deliverance, "I will defend this city to save it, for my own sake and for the sake of my servant David" (2 Kgs 19:34).

Solomon's words planted seeds for a later time. The temple immediately rose to the status of premier sanctuary in the kingdom. The ark contributed to its prestige, as did its royal patronage. However, it had to compete with other sanctuaries, which had deeper associations with Israel's sacred past.

When Solomon died, about three-fourths of his kingdom seceded. The northern kingdom established two royal sanctuaries, at Bethel and Dan, on the southern and northern borders. According to 1 Kgs 12:26–28, Jeroboam built these to supplant Jerusalem. There are no descriptions of these temples except for the images of golden calves (12:28–29). Jeroboam is purported to have said, "Here are your gods, O Israel, who brought you up out of the land of Egypt" (12:28). The citation is rather tendentious, for Jeroboam's temples were clearly dedicated to the Lord. His golden calves probably were meant to be pedestals for the Lord, much like the ark in Jerusalem. Unlike the ark, though, they were condemned by prophets (1 Kgs 13; Hos 13:2; 10:5).

During the divided monarchy (ca. 931–722 B.C.), Bethel and Dan retained their primacy in the northern kingdom while Jerusalem retained its in Judah. Other temples were built: Ahab built one in Samaria (1 Kgs 16:31–33), but it never attained the status of Bethel and Dan.

When Assyria conquered the northern kingdom, Jerusalem had no serious rival. Josiah found the sanctuary in Bethel still in operation, and destroyed it (2 Kgs 23:15–17) along with local sanctuaries in towns (2 Kgs 23:19–20).

Destruction of "high places" was a general policy of Josiah, who was following mandates of the book of Mosaic law. According to this law, found in the temple during restoration and validated by the prophetess Huldah (2 Kgs 22:8–20), the Jerusalem temple was the only place for sacrifice. Josiah put an end to heterodox religious practices in the temple and the city of Jerusalem and destroyed the local sanctuaries in the countryside (2 Kgs 23:4–14). The temple in Jerusalem had reached its zenith; no other place could rival it among worshipers of the Lord. Solomon's words about the Lord's dwelling in the temple became an exclusive claim.

But just at its apotheosis, the temple was challenged by prophets, particularly Jeremiah. According to Jer 7:1–15, the people of Judah were basing their hopes on "the temple of the Lord" (v. 4); the temple had become a "robbers' den" (v. 11)—a place of sanctuary for people whose daily lives were filled with violations of God's commandments (vv. 9–10). The Lord is free to abandon the temple, as the Lord did Shiloh (vv. 12–15). One cannot manipulate God by ritual and special pleading (cf. 7:16–26). Jeremiah's is a climax of the prophetic critique of false piety and manipulative ritual (see Isa 1:12–17; Amos 5:21–15; Hos 6:4–6; Mic 6:6–8). Some prophets carried on this critique after the exile, opposing rebuilding the temple (Isa 65–66).

The temple was destroyed along with the city of Jerusalem in 587 B.C. by the Babylonians. During the next seventy years the Jews learned to live without it. Mosaic law and nonsacrificial ritual took the place in piety once occupied by sacrifice and formal ritual. Ezekiel 40–48 articulated hopes for restoration of kingdom and temple. When Cyrus of Persia took sovereignty over Babylon, he permitted exiled peoples to return to their homelands. The Jews were promised funds to rebuild their temple (Ezra 1:2–4; 6:3–5). After delays and obstructions, it was finished in 515 B.C. It probably had the same dimensions and layout as Solomon's temple, but the *Holy of Holies* was left empty.

The Jerusalem temple acquired a different role and valence in postexilic Judaism. There was no longer a state for which it was the royal sanctuary. Judaism had become international—dispersed communities in Egypt, Mesopotamia, and elsewhere. Jerusalem became a temple city of great symbolic significance but little practical import for Diaspora Jews.

One other expression of God's presence deserves our attention. Isaiah announces that a young woman is pregnant with a child who will be named *Immanuel*, "God (is) with us" (Isa 7:14). The name is probably derived from a popular slogan, for Amos exhorts the people, "Seek good and not evil, that you may live; and so the LORD, the God of hosts, will be with you, just as you have said" (Amos 5:14). One could construe the concluding clause as "you frequently say." The Isaianic prophecy is cryptic: the mother is unnamed, and the child's name seems to contradict the message of judgment delivered to Ahaz (7:17). Though the child is not a messiah, only a sign and a timetable of Isaiah's oracle, his portentous name gravitates to the messianic prophecy in Isa 9:2–7, in which a child is born who receives four symbolic names. The endless reign of this royal figure who establishes peace, justice, and righteousness among his subjects certainly fits the hope expressed in "God is with us."

New Testament

The NT evidence is paradoxical. The word "presence" in the theological sense is rare in the NRSV, and there is no specific Greek term behind it, yet the reader would say that God is uniquely present in Jesus Christ. There is a Greek term, *parousia*, which does bear the meaning of presence, but it is used in the NT with that sense only of Paul and his coworkers (1 Cor 16:17; 2 Cor 10:10; Phil 2:12). When it refers to Christ, it refers to his return (Matt 24:3 and sixteen other times), translated in NRSV as "coming."

The word "face" (Greek *prosopon*) is used in symbolic expressions now and then, some of which are translated "presence," for example, Luke 2:31; Acts 2:28 (OT in Greek translation). Indeed, the symbolic use of "face" seems to be a Septuagintism (cf. Matt 18:10; Heb 9:24). The same word is translated "appearance" in Matt 16:3 and par. Luke 12:56.

The Gospels. At the very outset of the Gospel of Matthew, an angel tells Joseph that the Immanuel passage (Isa 7:14) is fulfilled in Jesus (Matt 1:23). We are to read the story of Jesus as God is with us. John 1:14 says something similar: "The word became flesh and lived among us." The Greek word rendered "lived" is *eskenosen*, a form of *skenoo*, to "tabernacle"—alluding to the Lord's mode of presence in the wilderness.

The NRSV translation of John 8:38 and 17:5 speaks of Jesus being in God's presence. In 8:38, Jesus claims to "declare what I have seen in the Father's presence," and in 17:5 he requests, "Father, glorify me in your own presence with the glory that I had in your presence before the world existed." Both of these passages refer to Jesus' state of being before the incarnation; the second asks that this state be reinstated, in crucifixion and exaltation. The John passages actually lack any Greek word for presence. A similar idea, though, is found in Heb 9:24, which speaks of the exalted state of Christ as "appear[ing] in the presence (Greek *prosopon*) of God on our behalf."

The ark and tent are mentioned in the NT only in typological connections (Heb 8:2; 9:1–10; Rev 15:5; 21:3), but the temple was a living institution at the time of Jesus and the apostles, so it is named frequently in the Gospels and Acts as the scene of particular encounters; occasionally its theological import is addressed. There are two Greek terms translated "temple" in the NRSV, *hieron* and *naos*. Although they have different nuances (*naos* means the shrine containing the image of a deity, as in Acts 17:24; 19:24), they are equivalent when applied to the Jerusalem temple.

The Synoptic Gospels differ from John on how frequently Jesus participated in temple worship. John has him visit the temple regularly throughout his ministry (2:14; 5:14; 7:14; 8:20, 59; 10:23; 11:56; 18:20). According to the Synoptics, Jesus' movement is restricted to Galilee and the road to Jerusalem until he spends a week in Jerusalem teaching in the temple just before his crucifixion.

John 4 makes a programmatic statement about the temple. In a conversation with a Samaritan woman at Jacob's well, Jesus declares: "The hour is coming when you will worship the Father neither on this mountain [Gerizim] nor in Jerusalem . . . [but] in spirit and truth" (4:21, 23). Even Jerusalem's time is passing, because the Messiah brings a different, nonspatial form of worship. The spiritual God is not located in space but is wherever people receive God in their hearts and minds (4:21–24).

The cleansing of the temple plays a similar programmatic role in the Synoptics. At the beginning of Jesus' Jerusalem ministry he disrupted the "business" of the temple, quoting two OT prophecies to explain his action: "Is it not written, 'My house shall be called a house of prayer for all the nations'? But you have made it a den of robbers" (Mark 11:17; cf. Matt 21:13; Luke 19:46). Jesus is performing a prophetic symbolic act to demonstrate God's displeasure with the actual temple practice.

We have other indications that Jesus demoted the importance of the sacrificial cult. Jesus agreed with a friendly scribe that to recognize and love God with one's whole being and to love one's neighbor equally to oneself are "much more important than all whole burnt offerings and sacrifices" (Mark 12:33; cf. also Matt 12:7). His claim of authority to forgive sins (Mark 2:1–12; Matt 9:2–8; Luke 5:17–26) and nullify Sabbath prohibitions also demotes the temple (see esp. Matt 12:5–6).

Jesus predicts the destruction of the temple at the beginning of the Synoptic apocalypse (Matt 24:1–3; Mark 13:1–4; Luke 21:5–7; also 19:42–44). While destruction is not presented as God's judgment for the abuses cited in the cleansing, the earlier condemnation belongs theologically with the sentence. In the Sanhedrin trial, witnesses report that Jesus said: "I will destroy this temple that is made with hands, and in three days I will build another, not made with hands" (Mark 14:58; cf. Matt 26:61). Mark terms this false witness (Mark 14:57, 59–60). The high priest must have taken the saying to be messianic in implication, because that is his next question (Mark 14:61).

John locates the cleansing of the temple early in Jesus' ministry, to characterize Jesus' entire ministry, and combines it with the saying about destroying the temple. John's version of the pronouncement is bland: "Stop making my Father's house a marketplace!" (2:16). The temple authorities ask for a "sign," and Jesus says, "Destroy this temple, and in three days I will raise it up" (vv. 18–19). The subject of the first clause has changed, and the saying is referred by the narrator to the "temple of his body," agreeing with John's spiritualization of the temple.

The visit of Nicodemus following the cleansing of the temple may be designed to present Jesus' alternative to the religion of the marketplace. Echoing baptismal tradition, Jesus says a person can enter God's *kingdom* only by being born of water and the Spirit (3:5). A person must come into being again, empowered by God, given a heart and mind for heavenly things (3:6–7), as mysterious and unpredictable as the wind (3:8).

Pauline letters. Although Acts reports that Paul frequented the temple when he visited Jerusalem (21:26–30; 22:17; etc.), in his letters he only once uses either Greek word to refer to the Jerusalem temple. He speaks of temple service in 1 Cor 9:13 as a precedent for ministerial compensation. Otherwise, the word is applied to believers (1 Cor 3:16–17; 6:19; 2 Cor 6:16). Paul has completely spiritualized the concept of temple; the dwelling of God in the temple has become the residence of the Holy Spirit in the believer. Ephesians 2:21–22 applies the term to the community.

Paul uses the word "face" in some interesting theological statements. In 1 Cor 13:12 he contrasts our present life with eschatological life: "For now we see in a mirror, dimly, but then we will see face to face. Now I know only in part; then I will know fully, even as I have been fully known." In 2 Cor 3:7–4:6, Paul constructs an allegory on the story of Moses' shining face, concluding "[God] has shown in our hearts to give the light of the knowledge of the glory of God in the face of Jesus Christ" (4:6). The face of Christ is how God communicates himself to the inwardly illuminated.

General Epistles. Hebrews 9 and the Revelation to John transfer the sanctuary to heaven by different routes, but their convergence is noteworthy. Hebrews 9 is part of a section that allegorizes priesthood, covenant, sanctuary, and sacrifice. The general thesis is that "we have . . . a high priest, one who is seated at the right hand of the throne of the Majesty in the heavens, a minister in the sanctuary and the true tent that the Lord, and not any mortal, has set up" (Heb 8:1–2). The institutions of the Pentateuch, including priesthood and tabernacle, are types, shadows or copies of heavenly, eternal reality. Warrant for this allegory is the Lord's instruction to Moses: "See that you make everything according to the pattern that was shown you on the mountain" (Exod 25:40, cited in Heb 8:5).

Hebrews 9 rehearses the design of the tabernacle and its paraphernalia. The author, however, is concerned not with the meaning of objects but with the purification rituals performed by priests. These rituals are mere shadows of the purification performed by Christ with his own blood, which purifies the conscience of believers (9:14) once and for all. The surprise here is that the conscience, not the heavenly sanctuary, is purified by Christ's sacrifice; there is a hint, though, that Christ removed an objective stain left by sin.

The Revelation to John describes the world as existing on two planes, earthly and heavenly. Heavenly reality is hidden from mortal sight, but the destiny of all things is decided there. John is admitted, by revelation, to this supernatural realm

(4:1–2), and the rest of the book surveys the world and its future from the divine perspective. There is temporal sequence, but past, present, and future are collapsed, and sequences are repeated. Something analogous happens to imagery: the work is a collage of OT images, and the interpreter can become lost in allusions. The supernatural world is both a political and a religious reality, so God is on a throne engaged in warfare with worldly powers. Indeed, the throne room is like a command center, with angels going and returning from assignments (14:15–17; 15:5–8; 16:1, 17). At the same time, the throne room is a temple. It is first so named in 7:15, where martyrs in white robes (in 6:9 they are under the altar, in 7:15 before the throne) worship perpetually in the (heavenly) temple. In 11:1–2 there is a reference to the earthly temple. The temple mentioned in 11:19 is the heavenly inner sanctuary with the ark; it will become visible to the world at the last judgment.

One of the great surprises of the book of Revelation comes in 21:22: "I saw no temple in the city (the New Jerusalem), for its temple is the Lord God Almighty and the Lamb." We expect the heavenly temple to be eternal and therefore located in the center of the city (as it is in Ezek 40–48). John's vision is of the dissolution of the division of sacred and profane, the heavenly and the earthly, the physical and the spiritual.

Ronald E. Clements, *God and Temple: The Idea of the Divine Presence in Ancient Israel* (Philadelphia: Fortress Press, 1965); Marie Joseph Congar, *The Mystery of the Temple; or The Manner of God's Presence to His Creatures from Genesis to the Apocalypse* (Westminster, Md.: Newman Press, 1962); M. Haran, "The Divine Presence in the Israelite Cult and the Cultic Institutions," *Biblica* 50 (1969): 251–67; C. R. Koester, *The Dwelling of God: The Tabernacle in the Old Testament, Intertestamental Jewish Literature, and the New Testament*, CBQMS 22 (Washington: Catholic Biblical Association, 1989).

DALE PATRICK

Pride, Proud, Boast, Meek, Meekness, Lowly, Lowliness, Humble, Humility This cluster of words refers both to an internal disposition of the character and to external status. These realities are interrelated. Those of low social status, the *poor* and lowly, are more likely to be humble. Conversely, the rich and powerful may more easily be tempted into pride. Some readers of Scripture may be tempted always to spiritualize these matters, reading these words only as moral characteristics. Such readings would tend to obscure the near revolutionary aspect of God's treatment of the proud on the one hand and of the lowly on the other. It would be possible, however, to err in the opposite direction and to read these words only in their social and economic contexts. This also would be a misreading; certain attitudes and characteristics are appropriate to those who trust God, among them, meekness, lowliness, and humility. We begin with the words "pride" and "proud." In our time, "pride" is for the most part a positive word, though we still recognize that it can be excessive or misplaced. In the NT, pride is also used positively in a number of verses. Paul speaks of his pride in the Corinthians (2 Cor 7:4). There is even "the confidence and the pride that belong to hope" (Heb 3:6). More often, pride is one of many sins the follower of Jesus must avoid: "adultery, avarice, wickedness, deceit, licentiousness, envy, slander, pride, folly" (Mark 7:22). In the OT, "pride" and "proud" are primarily used negatively. The best-known example might be the familiar proverb, "Pride goes before destruction, and a haughty spirit before a fall" (Prov 16:18). The parallel structure of that verse helps us define the nature of pride. To be proud is to have a "haughty spirit." Other instances of parallelism further amplify the meaning of the word: pride is linked with contempt (Ps 31:18), loftiness, arrogance, and haughtiness (Jer 48:29), and arrogance of heart (Isa 9:9).

Pride is not, however, merely a matter of thinking too highly of oneself. It is not a matter of thinking wrongly. It is also a wrong disposition of the heart (see *mind*), that is to say, a flawed orientation of the person. Much evil flows from this orientation. The proud characteristically leave God out of account: "In the pride of their countenance the wicked say, 'God will not seek it out'; all their thoughts are, 'There is no God'" (Ps 10:4). Sometimes pride appears to refer to a misplaced or an inflated confidence. To be proud of something is to place confidence in it. The wicked place their confidence in their own strength, their position, or their wealth and are sure that none of this can be taken away from them. "Your proud heart has deceived you, you that live in the clefts of the rock, whose dwelling is in the heights. You say in your heart, 'Who will bring me down to the ground?'" (Obad 3). Clearly it is the wealthy who are most likely to be tempted to place their trust in these things. The poor or the lowly, by contrast, have nothing in which they may place their trust, except the Lord. Nor need they fear being brought low. As John Bunyan, the author of the classic *A Pilgrim's Progress*, wrote, "Those who are down need fear no fall."

In this respect, pride is similar to "boasting." Sometimes the word "boast" refers, as in common contemporary English, to the practice of bragging about one's own accomplishments or status or of vaunting oneself over others. Hence we read Paul's injunction to Gentile Christians not to hold themselves above the people of Israel: "Do not boast over the branches" (Rom 11:18). To boast in something also means to place that something first in one's heart. It may even mean to place ultimate trust in it. This implication of the word can be clearly seen in Rom 2:17: "But if you call yourself a Jew and rely on the law and boast of your relation to God . . ." The classic statement of this sort, however, is Jer 9:23–24, quoted by Paul in 1 Cor 1:31. "Thus says the LORD: Do not let the wise boast in their wisdom, do not let the mighty boast in their might, do not let the wealthy boast in their wealth; but let those who

boast boast in this, that they understand and know me, that I am the LORD." This sounds very much like one of the few verses in the OT in which pride has a positive connotation: "Some take pride in chariots, and some in horses, but our pride is in the name of the LORD our God" (Ps 20:7). We might also think of Hab 2:4,"Look at the proud! Their spirit is not right in them, but the righteous live by their faith." (This verse, as quoted by Paul in Rom 1:17, was read with considerable spiritual profit by Martin Luther.) Pride, it appears, is the opposite of living by faith.

The confidence of the proud is a delusion. In time God will bring low the proud. "The haughty eyes of people shall be brought low, and the pride of everyone shall be humbled. . . . For the LORD of hosts has a day against all that is proud and lofty, against all that is lifted up and high" (Isa 2:11–12; cf. Isa 2:17). Note that it is the "lofty" and those "lifted up and high," that is, those of high social status, who are proud. Where the word "humble" is a verb, it sometimes refers, as in Isa 2, to the work of God in bringing low the proud. See in this connection Isa 5:15: "People are bowed down, everyone is brought low, and the eyes of the haughty are humbled." Sometimes the divine humbling is not only a punishment but a blessing, painful though it may be. Moses reminds the children of Israel that God "fed you in the wilderness with manna that your ancestors did not know, to humble you and to test you, and in the end to do you good" (Deut 8:16; cf. Ps 119:71).

There is a more frequent use of the verb "to humble." It is possible for humans to humble themselves and thus avert the anger of God. See, for example, 2 Chr 32:26, "Then Hezekiah humbled himself for the pride of his heart, both he and the inhabitants of Jerusalem, so that the wrath of the LORD did not come upon them," and many other examples. Some, however, such as the wicked King Amon of Judah, refused to humble themselves (2 Chr 33:23). Their guilt is the greater. It may be that we face a choice: either we humble ourselves, or God humbles us instead.

It is not only that God brings low those who refuse to humble themselves, however. Some of our texts, particularly in the NT, speak rather of a reversal in the order of things, bringing low the proud and powerful and lifting up the humble: "All who exalt themselves will be humbled, and all who humble themselves will be exalted" (Matt 23:12; cf. Luke 14:11; 18:14; and Mary's Magnificat, Luke 1:46b–55).

We may suppose that pride is only an individual tendency. Among the OT prophets, however, pride is frequently represented as a corporate, indeed a national reality. We read of the pride of Babylon (Isa 13:19), Assyria (Zech 10:11), Philistia (Zech 9:6), Egypt (Ezek 32:12), Sodom (apparently here a symbol of wealth and indifference to the poor rather than of sexual depravity; Ezek 16:49, 56), and even Moab (Isa 16:6; Jer 48:29). These are powerful nations, proud in that they rejoice in their power and greatness and suppose that they can do whatever they wish without rendering account to God. God's people too can be led into a national pride that forgets that the only true security lies in a dependence on God. We dare not suppose that this kind of pride is a phenomenon of the biblical period only.

This kind of pride may be encouraged and named patriotism, but the line between patriotism and biblical "pride" is a fine one. Moreover, social entities are capable of catching up the selflessness of individuals in the name of the much greater selfishness and pride of the corporate entity. (This insight found classic expression in Reinhold Niebuhr's *Moral Man and Immoral Society*.) God will not forever endure such pride. Just as God humbles individual pride, so also will God bring low social and national pride. "I will punish the world for its evil, and the wicked for their iniquity; I will put an end to the pride of the arrogant, and lay low the insolence of tyrants" (Isa 13:11). These verses that speak of the pride of powerful nations must surely be sobering reading for those of us who live in the wealthy nations of the West.

In the NT, however, the "lowly" are clearly those of low degree in society, the equivalent of the poor. Mary's lovely hymn of praise, the Magnificat, is very helpful in understanding our complex of words. Because of the parallelism in this hymn, both synonymous and antithetical, we can see both what the lowly are and what they are not. In the first place, the lowly are the opposite of the powerful. "He has brought down the powerful from their thrones, and lifted up the lowly" (Luke 1:52). Similarly, it is widely agreed, Mary's own "lowliness" (Luke 1:48), which is looked upon with favor by the Lord, is not the virtue of humility, but her low social and economic status. She is one with the hungry, with those who are filled with good things. The opposite of the lowly is not only the powerful but also the rich who are sent away empty (v. 53). But note that the rich and powerful are also those who are "proud in the imagination of their hearts." Once again, social status and the disposition of the character overlap. The lowly are also likely those of low social status in Rom 12:16, "Do not be haughty, but associate with the lowly," and Jas 1:9, "Let the believer who is lowly boast in being raised up."

At Jas 4:6, however, NRSV renders the same Greek adjective as in Jas 1:9 by the English, "humble": "God opposes the proud, but gives grace to the humble." It appears that in the NT, NRSV normally reserves the adjective "humble" for the internal disposition rather than low social status, as in 1 Pet 3:8: "Finally, all of you, have unity of spirit, sympathy, love for one another, a tender heart, and a humble mind" (cf. 1 Pet 5:5–6; Matt 18:4; Acts 20:19). The related noun is "humility." To display this humility is a Christian duty. See, for example, Phil 2:3: "Do nothing from selfish ambition or conceit, but in humility regard others as better than yourselves." See also Eph 4:2; Col 2:23; 3:12; and 1 Pet 5:5. Jesus himself is the model of humility: "Take my yoke upon you, and learn from me; for I am gentle and humble in heart" (Matt 11:29; cf. 2 Cor 10:1; Phil 2:8).

"Meek" and "meekness" appear to be near synonyms of "humble" and "humility" and likewise refer to disposition rather than social status. NRSV uses the adjective "meek" only in the familiar beatitude, "Blessed are the meek, for they will inherit the earth" (Matt 5:5). Nevertheless the Greek adjective behind that phrase also appears in Matt 11:29, there translated "gentle," where it is parallel to "humble." Note that this beatitude does not appear in Luke. Luke appears to be more interested in social status, "Blessed are you poor," while Matthew writes of disposition, "Blessed are the poor in spirit," and, in a similar vein, "Blessed are the meek." Where the related noun "meekness" is found in the NT, the internal disposition also seems to be in view. See 2 Cor 10:1, where meekness appears in parallel to gentleness, and Col 3:12, where the word appears in a series with such words as compassion, kindness, humility, and patience.

In the culmination of all things, the humble will find blessing: "I will leave in the midst of you a people humble and lowly. They shall seek refuge in the name of the LORD" (Zeph 3:12). These words appear to refer to a disposition of the national character of Israel, rather than to status in society. God will even condescend to be present with a humbled people: "For thus says the high and lofty one who inhabits eternity, whose name is Holy: I dwell in the high and holy place, and also with those who are contrite and humble in spirit, to revive the spirit of the humble, and to revive the heart of the contrite" (Isa 57:15).

At the very heart of the gospel is even more amazing good news, however. It is not simply the case that if we humble ourselves, God will join us in our humility. Such a demand would lay an impossible burden on us. One of the earliest Christian hymns declares, however, that Christ Jesus "humbled himself (literally, emptied himself) and became obedient to the point of death—even death on a cross" (Phil 2:8). The incarnation is the manifestation of the humility of God. This humility was made known to us, not once we ourselves had achieved humility, but "while we still were sinners" (Rom 5:8). That is to say, the divine self-humbling came first. In response, we are told, "Let the same mind be in you that was in Christ Jesus" (Phil 2:5).

We cannot expect that our society will receive the Bible's teaching concerning pride and humility gladly. If we speak too strongly of individual humility, some will object that we are threatening the self-esteem of others. If we warn of the dangers of national pride, hyperpatriots may accuse us of a lack of patriotism or even, at worst, of treason. But in this as in all things, the word that is both command and promise comes to us, "Do not be conformed to this world, but be transformed by the renewing of your minds" (Rom 12:2).

STEPHEN FARRIS

Priest *see* **Minister**

Profane *see* **Clean**

Promise, Ancestors There is no Hebrew word that corresponds to the English word "promise." Where translators use "promise," they have been led to do so by the context, for the Hebrew verb is likely to be simply "say." Another verb, the word for "taking an oath," is often used in contexts where promises are made, however. Since oaths between human beings were usually made by invoking the authority of a deity as guarantor of the oath, in the case of a divine oath God could appeal to no other superior authority. In making a promise therefore, God simply gives a command, for example, Gen 1:28, that all humankind should reproduce to fill the earth. Alternatively God may use an established form of words for swearing an oath, as in making a promise to Abraham concerning his descendants (Gen 12:1–3; cf. Gen 15:1–21). Here the action of fire, passing between the parts of dismembered animals, is a form of enacted oath, declaring the binding nature of what is promised. Since God's promise to Abraham, Isaac, and Jacob plays such a prominent role in the OT, "ancestors" (Hebrew: "fathers") has been cross-referenced to this article. In the NT, *epangello* and related forms are good equivalents to our word "promise."

The promise to humankind. The command given on the sixth day of creation that the first human couple should "be fruitful and increase, fill the earth and subdue it, and have dominion over . . . every living thing that moves upon the earth" (Gen 1:28) is effectively a promise that human beings are privileged to exercise authority over the entire animal kingdom. It confers a unique status on the first human couple, but also contains an element of future expectation, since the dominion and filling of the earth will be achieved only in years to come. In creating human beings "in God's *image*" (Gen 1:26), God placed human beings in an order of life only a little lower than God, crowned with glory and honor (so Ps 8:5), which implies a future promise, as well as conferring a present status. Implicit in this primeval command to the first human couple therefore is the notion of a divine order that pervades all creation and will bring about a future realm of wholeness and well-being.

The fulfillment of this primeval command for the increase and spread of the human race (Gen 6:1) is subsequently threatened by the violence and disorder of human relationships (Gen 6:5–7). As a punishment for this disorder and violence, destruction by a great flood is brought upon the whole earth. Noah, a righteous and blameless man, together with his family, is saved to fulfill the original command and to repopulate the earth (Gen 6:9–9:28). God reaffirms the right of Noah's descendants to rule over the animal kingdom by allowing animals, along with plants, to be killed for food (Gen 9:2–3). As the nations spread out to fill the earth in accordance with God's command (Gen 10:1–32), the promise of blessing for all creatures is further qualified as a result of the continuing violence of human actions. Further limitation of its scope occurs when human beings exceed their God-given authority by building a great tower (Gen 11:1–9). The confusion of languages that then follows creates yet another barrier between nations through yet more failure to achieve peace and wholeness.

Throughout this account of the primeval beginnings of humankind, the initial command to the first couple to reproduce to become many nations is interpreted as a fundamental promise that remains valid through the disasters that occur, and it survives to become a central theme of the Bible. As the story of humankind unfolds, God's promise of increase and blessing is both fulfilled and challenged. The thwarting of God's original primeval promise calls for a plan of redemption through which the goal of worldwide blessing is postponed for a future age. It is no longer a state of blessing that exists for the world but is tied to the promise of redemption in an age to come.

The promise to Abraham. After the setbacks and disappointments of humanity's primeval age in Gen 1–11, the new era of salvation begins in Gen 12:1–3 with the calling of Abraham and God's making a threefold promise to him. He is to leave his Mesopotamian homeland to go to a new land, where his descendants will become a great nation. There his descendants will achieve such greatness that "all the families of the earth shall be blessed" (Gen 12:3). God's promise is that these descendants will grow into a nation, take possession of the land through which Abraham was passing, and attain a reputation among all peoples as exemplars of divine blessing. This promise is reaffirmed and further amplified in Gen 15:1–21, when it is ratified by a strange and solemn ceremony that carries the force of a solemn oath. There is also added the significant warning that Abraham's descendants must first become slaves in a foreign land, before returning to the land promised to Abraham (Gen 15:13–16). This reference to the events that are told in the book of Exodus ties the promise made to Abraham to an experience of deliverance from slavery. This deliverance (exodus) is inseparably linked to a new promise made to Moses concerning the nature of the nation that will come into being as Abraham's heirs. In this fashion the story of God's primeval promise begins to take on a more fully defined character as it introduces the people of Israel as the servants of its fulfillment.

A further account in Gen 17:1–8 of God's promise to Abraham describes it as "an everlasting *covenant*" (Gen 17:7, 13, 19) and links it with the command to *circumcise* all male children from eight days old (Gen 17:9–14, 23–27). This birth rite is a sign of the covenant made with Abraham and includes all male children, including those of slaves. This further account of the promise to Abraham couples it with a change of name (from Abram to Abraham, Gen 17:5) and enlarges the promise of future greatness beyond the confines of the nation Israel: "You shall be the ancestor of a multitude of nations" (Gen 17:4). It further expands the promise to Sarah, giving assurance that "kings of peoples shall come from her" (Gen 17:16), which reinforces the scope of the promise.

The promise to Abraham and Sarah then remains the central theme of the book of Genesis, as its story unfolds. Initially it focuses on the plight of the slave wife Hagar and the birth of her son Ishmael (Gen 16:1–16). The birth of a son, Isaac, to Sarah, even when she was past the age of childbearing (Gen 18:1–15), and a threat to her by Abimelech, king of Gerar, brought on by Abraham's fear and deceit (Gen 20:1–18), continue the story. Such events show how God's promise was fulfilled in spite of human weakness. God's overriding purpose is maintained in the face of human faithlessness. The climax occurs when Isaac's very life is threatened by his father Abraham in a

mistaken desire to please God by offering his son as a sacrifice (Gen 22:1–20). The fulfillment of promise hangs on a narrow thread of faith. This incident is central to understanding the nature of God's promise, since it brings into sharpest focus the centrality of faith as the indispensable human response. Faith is essential, since without it the path to blessing cannot remain open.

The story of the search for Rebekah to be a suitable bride for Isaac (Gen 24:1–67), and the birth to her of twin sons, Jacob and Esau (Gen 25:23–26) continues the story of how the patriarchal promise was fulfilled (Gen 26:23–25). After Abraham's death (Gen 25:7–8) Jacob's name is changed to Israel when he wrestles with an angelic visitor (Gen 32:28), thereby introducing us to the name of the family, and eventually nation, through which the promise is to take effect. When Jacob becomes father to twelve sons, one of them, Joseph, is sold as a slave in Egypt, where he unexpectedly comes to fame and fortune (Gen 37:1–41:57). As a consequence the entire family, including Jacob, is brought to Egypt, thereby setting the scene for the next step in the rise of Israel as a nation through which the promise is to be fulfilled. The note of challenge reemerges when the descendants of Jacob's family are forced into slavery, giving reality to the warning made to Abraham that, before the promise made to him can be fulfilled, his descendants must become slaves in Egypt.

The promise to Moses (Exodus–Deuteronomy). In Egypt, Jacob's descendants fulfill the first part of the promise to Abraham when they increase so greatly in number that they become a great nation (Exod 1:7; cf. Deut 26:5). Yet this growth is scarcely a blessing, since it arouses a fear of them among the Egyptians, which brings about their enforced slavery. Exodus 3:1–22 recounts how God, who had earlier addressed Abraham, Isaac, and Jacob, now reveals a new name to Moses as the Lord (Hebrew *YHWH*; Exod 3:14–15). This revelation also brings a warning that the promised land is already inhabited by other peoples, who must first be conquered. Once again the theme of promise is maintained, and more closely defined, but at the same time new difficulties and obstacles appear in its path.

Mere growth in numbers, however, is not sufficient to form Hebrew slaves into a nation. For this to occur, a covenant is required between the Lord God and Israel (Exod 19:1–24:11), which takes place on Mount Sinai. By keeping the terms of this covenant, Israel will be unique among the nations and will become "a priestly kingdom and a holy nation" (Exod 19:6). The promise to Abraham as the ancestor of many nations has now narrowed to focus on Israel as the one nation to whom is entrusted the sacred law of God. However, fear of the risks and dangers attendant on entering the land (Num 14:1–4) lead to a forty-year delay wandering in the desert of Sinai.

The promise in the Former Prophets. The central theme of the six books that make up the Former Prophets of the Hebrew canon (Joshua, Judges, 1 and 2 Samuel, 1 and 2 Kings) is the story of how the land was finally conquered as a result of unique demonstrations of the power of God (Joshua–Judges). It continues, however, to recount how this land was subsequently lost as a consequence of Israel's failure to keep the covenant made with God on Mount Sinai (1 Samuel–2 Kings). All six books belong together and tell a connected story, even though they themselves make clear that they have been composed from a variety of sources. The central focus is on the message of God's promise to Israel as a nation that it will become great and will have dominion over many nations. This time, however, a new figure stands as the central mediator of this promise. As the persons of Abraham and Moses have dominated the Pentateuch, now a new figure occupies center stage. This is King David, whose story brings to the fore the institution of kingship. The exercise of royal authority is highlighted as a potential means of blessing through which God's promise may be fulfilled (cf. Lam 4:20). The story

of Israel's kingship proves, however, to be a story of failure and disappointment. How this came about is basic to Israel's history, since, like the comparable story of Israel's wilderness years, it is a story of both triumph and disaster. After the earliest chapters in Josh 1–12 have recounted the triumphant winning of the land in fulfillment of God's promise to Moses, the book of Judges adds a note of warning by showing how easily and quickly Israel could turn away from wholehearted allegiance to the Lord as God.

The hinge point of the entire story is set on the record of how David rose to become Israel's king, replacing the ineffective Saul, who had first introduced the office of kingship to the nation (1 Sam 15–2 Sam 6). The climax of David's achievement is reached with God's promise to him through the prophet Nathan: "Your house and your kingdom shall be made sure forever before me; your throne shall be established forever" (2 Sam 7:16). This theme of divine promise fulfilled for Israel through the kingly leadership of David is made a cause of celebration in a number of psalms (so especially Pss 2:1–11; 72:1–20; 89:1–37; 132:1–18). A prominent feature is the claim that David would be great among the kings of the earth (Ps 72:8–11), thereby fulfilling the promise made to Abraham's wife Sarah (Gen 17:16). The narrative accounts of David's achievements (2 Sam 8:1–18) serve to support the contention that it was through him, in the period of his military triumphs, that the promise to Abraham and his descendants received its fullest measure of fulfillment.

However, all such celebration of David and the honor that he brought to Israel among other nations proved premature and short-lived. His successor, Solomon, came to be regarded by many as an upstart and a troublesome tyrant, and his oppressive rule opened again the wounds that had scarcely been healed by the civil war occasioned by David's replacement of the first king, Saul. After Solomon's death the united kingdom fell apart, with the repudiation by the majority of Israel's tribes of the claim that God had conferred on the Davidic dynasty the right to rule over Israel "forever" (1 Kgs 12:16–17). This promise now remained the central point at issue in the situation when Israel was split into two separate kingdoms.

The remaining chapters of the books of 1 and 2 Kings tell the story of how, after the death of Solomon and the division of the nation, no king like David emerged to rule over either Judah or Israel. Not until the reign of King Josiah was one found who briefly sought to restore the unity of the nation under the rule of the Davidic royal house (2 Kgs 23:25). This attempt proved short-lived with Josiah's untimely death (2 Kgs 23:28–30). The promise of royal dignity and power declared in Isa 32:1–8 probably reflects this king's brief time of glory. After this the surviving remnants of Judah continued into decline in the face of Babylonian control, until eventually the last ruler of the Davidic dynasty was deposed from his throne in Jerusalem in 587 B.C. (2 Kgs 25:1–7). The promise of God to David, the illustrious royal ancestor, appeared to have reached a full end, save for the uncertain hope that the surviving branch of the royal house, which had been exiled in Babylon in 598 B.C. (2 Kgs 24:8–12), might one day return to Jerusalem's throne (cf. 2 Kgs 25:27–30).

The promise in the Latter Prophets. The story of the rise and fall of the first kingdom of Israel contained in the Former Prophets reappears from several different perspectives in the writings of the Latter Prophets. This part of the Hebrew canon is made up of four great books: Isaiah, Jeremiah, Ezekiel, and the Book of the Twelve (taken as a single book). They relate, for the most part, to the period covered by the Former Prophets but offer several important fresh insights into the manner in which the theme of the divine promise to Israel was interpreted. Central is the theme of God's promise to David of kingship over Israel, but these prophets reveal more of how this promise was received and interpreted in the face of the disastrous interventions of the imperialist powers Assyria and Babylon. Moreover, by continuing the story further, beyond the final removal of the last Davidic king from his throne in Jerusalem in 587 B.C., these prophets bring to light an important transition. From being a promise relating to the contemporary political situation, it was transformed into a hope for a future new order in which God's promise to David would continue to be a prominent feature. Out of this promise the Bible's "messianic hope" emerged.

In Isaiah the promise to the royal dynasty of David is most sharply set in the forefront of the prophet's message. That this promise could not be realized without a response of faith on the part of each reigning king is the central feature of the message to King Ahaz (Isa 6:1–8:8). When faced with a threat to remove him from his throne, Ahaz meekly resorted to seeking support from the mighty ruler of Assyria (Isa 7:1–8:18), thereby initiating a political path that quickly brought disaster to both Israel and Judah (Isa 7:17; 8:5–8). Isaiah asserted that, without faith, God's promise to the royal ancestor could not be fulfilled: "If you do not stand firm in faith, you shall not stand at all" (Isa 7:9). This remained a consistent warning from the prophet, whose book reflects this central theme again when King Ahaz's successor, Hezekiah, sought an alliance with Egypt for defense against Assyria (Isa 28:14–22; 30:1–9; 31:1–3). In the prophet's eyes this demonstrated yet again that a king of the chosen line of David had placed his trust in human alliances, rather than in the Lord God of Israel who alone was the one true support and guardian of Judah's royal dynasty.

The word of promise addressed to the royal house of David reappears in Amos (Amos 9:9–15) and Hosea (Hos 3:5), although uncertainty is frequently expressed concerning the time of origin of these prophecies. Awareness of the failure attaching to the later rulers of the Davidic royal house is expressed forcibly by the prophet Jeremiah (21:1–22:30), by whom only the ill-fated Josiah is accorded any praise (Jer 22:15; Josiah was

King Jehoiakim's father). Hope that the Davidic line would eventually return to rule over a restored Israel is expressed in Jer 23:5–6; 33:14–26, and the same message is echoed in the book of Ezekiel (Ezek 37:24–27).

By far the strongest assurances concerning an eventual return to authority of the royal house of Judah are those found in the book of Isaiah (Isa 4:2; 11:1–5; 55:1–5), but what form this restoration would take is left undefined. At first these reaffirmations of the ancient promise made to the royal ancestor David suggest a restoration of kingship, but the expectations of this appear quickly to have faded. The imperial Persian rule that extended to Judah precluded any such possibility but did not rule out that the surviving branch of Judah's royal family could exercise leadership in some other way. The political realities are left in uncertainty, but hopes for a time centered on the royal prince Zerubbabel (Ezra 4:1–3; 5:2; Zech 4:1–10). The assurance of Isa 55:1–5 reaffirms the validity and authority of God's unbreakable promise to David but leaves the manner of its fulfillment unclear and indeterminate. The avoidance of the title "king" in Isa 11:1–5 (cf. also Isa 4:1) and the fact that promises concerning Jerusalem's future headship over the nations are reasserted without a kingly figure present (cf. Isa 2:2–4; 60:1–22; Mic 5:2–5) reflect the changed political background of political life in Judah after the catastrophic events of 587 B.C. These upheavals had made necessary a more radical rethinking of God's promise to David and the government of Israel.

In any case such a message had never been exclusively focused on the institution of kingship and the royal dynasty of David since the nation had divided into two after Solomon's death. It therefore comes as no surprise that, after Judah's collapse in the mid–sixth century B.C., the survivors' hopes, as voiced by prophets, looked back to the very foundations of the tradition concerning Abraham. Recollection that Israel was the offspring of Abraham (Isa 41:8) and that the Lord God of Israel was the God of Abraham (cf. Gen 26:24; 28:13; 31:42, 53; Ps 47:10; 1 Chr 29:18; 2 Chr 30:6) echoes the foundation promise made to this patriarch (see Isa 51:2). The remembrance of Israel's origin out of slavery in Egypt, made possible by the all-powerful hand of God, brought hope of a second exodus by which the nation could begin again (see Isa 51:9–11). In this way God's promises made to the great ancestral figures of Israel, Abraham, Moses, and David all continued to find a new place as providing a groundwork of hope in the writings of the Latter Prophets.

The promise of God in the Psalms. One of the most remarkable and enduring features of this transition, from the idea of a divine promise made to a reigning royal dynasty to one in which some future offspring of this dynasty would arise to deliver Israel, is to be found in the Psalter. The book of Psalms contains many hymns of celebration and praise that laud the greatness of David and the line of kings descended from him (esp. Pss 2:1–11; 21:1–13; 72:1–20; 89:1–37; 132:1–18). Similar psalms hymn the praise of Jerusalem as an impregnable fortress, which will withstand the assaults of all the enemies of God's people (Pss 46; 48; 84). Other psalms celebrate the rule of God over all the earth as a veritable "kingdom of God" (Pss 93:1–5; 96:10–13; 99:1–5; 145:1–13; 149:1–9). In their origin these implied that God's rule in the present was maintained through Jerusalem, its temple, and its royal family. In preserving these psalms for a later age, however, the OT turns the focus into the more distant future, seeing in these beautiful compositions an assurance that God's promise is for a future age, when the disappointments and failures that had brought Israel so low would be swept aside in a new era of salvation. God's promise was opened out into a much larger and richer vision of the future than the original psalm compositions had anticipated. In their own very distinctive way, therefore, these psalms also came to be regarded as prophecies concerning God's promises, first to Israel, and then to the world.

The New Testament: The fulfillment of the promise. In turning from the OT to the NT the reader is immediately faced with a fundamental change of perspective. This major shift brings the Bible's message from one of promise to one of fulfillment. In Jesus of Nazareth, all that had been promised to Abraham, to Moses, and to David is declared to have been fulfilled. More fundamentally still, the NT writings declare that, through Jesus of Nazareth, the promise implicit at the beginning of creation, that all the world would receive blessing and all humankind experience the wholeness of life intended from the beginning, was fulfilled.

The primary evidence from which the NT demonstrates this assurance, that all the promises of God revealed in the OT have been realized through the life, death, and resurrection of Jesus, is by showing how the life and deeds of Jesus had been foretold in words of prophecy. At a primary level this is accomplished by relating specific prophecies directly to particular events and circumstances in the life of Jesus. Matthew's Gospel is full of such instances, beginning with the manner of Jesus' birth from the virgin Mary (Matt 1:23; cf. Isa 7:14) and the location of that birth in Bethlehem (Matt 2:6; cf. Mic 5:2). The incident of "the slaughter of the innocents," which took place when King Herod commanded that all children of two years old and under in the vicinity of Bethlehem (Matt 2:16–18) were to be killed, is linked to a prophecy given through Jeremiah (Jer 31:15). This example is especially instructive, since the fulfillment implies a new, and somewhat different, context from that originally envisaged by the OT prophet.

These examples are instructive in showing that it is not through a narrowly literal fulfillment of relatively incidental aspects of OT prophecy but through the more comprehensive conviction that all prophecy, and in fact the entire revelation of God made in the OT, was a preparation

for the fullness of revelation now made known in Jesus. All that had gone before, in the promises made to Abraham, to Moses, and to David, was provisional and incomplete. Only when the age of fulfillment had brought to humankind the whole picture of the purpose of God could the significance of each of its intermediate steps be made clear. The end sheds new light on the beginning. This is a central feature of the assertion made in 1 Pet 1:10–12 that the words of all the prophets of the OT are to be understood as pointing forward to the new era of salvation that had been brought through the life and work of Jesus. As a result, prophecies from widely separate, and frequently historically very different, periods and situations of the OT are brought together and given a much fuller meaning in the NT. Moreover, passages that do not derive from the books that are specifically designated as those of the prophets—in particular the promises of greatness for the royal dynasty of David expressed in several psalms—are taken up to become part of this prophetic inheritance of the OT.

A related, if differently expressed, assertion that the promises of God given in the OT have received their fulfillment in Jesus is set forth in the Epistle to the Hebrews. This letter, which is essentially an essay in biblical interpretation, shows how the entire organization, purpose, and rituals of the ancient Jewish temple worship and priesthood were an anticipation and promise of the salvation brought through Jesus. An old order had been decisively swept aside and a new order brought to realization, in which all humankind could find access to the one true God.

Another theme, that through Jesus all the ancient promises of God implicit in the act of creation have been brought to fulfillment, is expressed in the letter to the Ephesians: "With all wisdom and insight he [God] has made known to us the mystery of his will, according to his good pleasure that he set forth in Christ, as a plan for the fullness of time, to gather up all things in him, things in heaven and things on earth" (Eph 1:8–10). This same theme, that God's work through Jesus marks the fulfillment of the promise of creation, is also set out in visionary form in the book of Revelation. In Rev 21:1–2 the promises of a new heaven and a new earth (cf. Isa 65:17) and of the building of a new Jerusalem (cf. Isa 54:11–17; Ezek 40:1–47:3) are seen as about to achieve their realization through the saving work of Christ. This remarkable vision is put together from a large number of sayings and pictorial images drawn from many parts of the OT. It is designed, however, to show that all these promises are brought to one supreme fulfillment through the work of Jesus for all humankind. The message is triumphantly described in summary form in Rev 21:4: "He [God] will wipe away every tear from their eyes. Death will be no more; mourning and crying and pain will be no more, for the first things have passed away" (Rev 21:4; cf. Isa 35:10). With this glorious assertion, the idea of divine promise passes into history, for all such promises will have come to their realization and fulfillment.

Donald E. Gowan, "Promise," chap. 5 in *Theology in Exodus: Biblical Theology in the Form of a Commentary* (Louisville: Westminster John Knox Press, 1994), 98–125; Claus Westermann, *The Promise to the Fathers: Studies on the Patriarchal Narratives* (Philadelphia: Fortress Press, 1980).

RONALD E. CLEMENTS

Prophet, Prophesy, Inspire, Oracle

The English noun "prophet" and its related verb "prophesy" are derived from the Greek *prophetes* and *propheteuein*. The related terms "inspire" and "oracle" convey certain aspects of prophetic activity; however, both have greater significance as explanatory concepts than as biblical key words.

The root meaning of *propheteuin*, to "proclaim beforehand," suggests that the Hellenistic world regarded prophecy primarily as prediction of the future. The Hebrew noun *nabiʾ* is always translated as "prophet" in NRSV, and to some extent it has acquired the connotation of prediction by virtue of the NT's emphasis on the fulfillment of OT prophecy. But in the OT, other activities besides prediction are at one time or other associated with the OT phenomenon of prophecy. Because the announcement of impending events was always subordinated to the proclamation of the sovereignty of God, with the corresponding demand for proper worship and conduct, prophecy is often characterized as "forthtelling," as opposed to the predictive activity of "foretelling."

Both OT and NT also present prophecy as the disclosure of God's clearly discernible purpose in history. Through his servants the prophets, Yahweh has always made his word known to the kingdoms of Israel and Judah; thus there can and should be no surprise about their respective fates. Because Israel and Judah refused to heed the warnings of the prophets, Yahweh acted in accordance with the prophetic announcement of judgment. The major proponents of this theme are Deuteronomy and the books of Samuel and Kings, but it is also implicit in the editorial superscriptions of each of the prophetic books. The NT contributes to this theme by interpreting the ministry of Jesus Christ as the fulfillment of the prophets.

However, the problem of "true and false" prophecy in the OT and NT complicates the theological usage of these terms. Both Testaments express anxiety over the need to determine the validity of prophecy. While the NT resolves the problem by rejecting the messenger (hence the designation *pseudoprophetes*), the OT rejected the messages by characterizing them as lies and deceptions. Even so, it was recognized that God could be at work in these deceptive words (see 1 Kgs 22). In the OT, if not in the NT, the very ambiguity of prophecy serves a theological purpose, in that it calls the reader to contemplate the mystery of Yahweh's sovereignty.

The etymology of *nabiʾ* and its related verbs remains a matter of some discussion. For much of the last century, the noun was explained as either a passive or active form of the Akkadian *nabu*, to call or name. According to this etymology, a prophet is either "one who is called," with the emphasis on the prophet's being commissioned by God for a special task, or "one who proclaims," with the emphasis on the prophet's message. But neither explanation has been entirely satisfactory. Call narratives are not attested for every prophet, and some prophetic activity does not involve the proclamation of the *word* of God (e.g., Elisha, Saul). More recently, it has been suggested that the Hebrew *nabiʾ* connotes the human activity of calling on the name of God. The *nabiʾ* is thus "one who invokes" God's presence.

The latter explanation is comprehensive enough to accommodate the wide variety of phenomena associated with the OT *nebiʾim*. In early narratives, prophecy does not necessarily involve the delivery of an articulate message, but it is always associated with the presence of Yahweh's spirit. When Saul begins to prophesy, that is, to fall into an ecstatic trance, he becomes "a different person" and is thereby equipped to serve the tribes of Israel as their king (1 Sam 10:6). Narratives about the prophet Elisha are primarily concerned with his miracles (2 Kgs 4–5), and other early narratives that involve the proclamation of a divine word revolve around the presence of divine assistance, for example, in battle (1 Kgs 20). Finally, the use of the noun *nabiʾ* in nonprophetic contexts is consistent with this understanding of the prophet's role. For example, in the designation of Abraham as a *nabiʾ*, what is implied is precisely his ability to invoke the healing presence of God in another's behalf (Gen 20:7).

Whatever the word's etymology may be, the divine freedom to respond, or not, and to speak truthfully, or not, made the work of the *nabiʾ* one of the central mysteries of Israelite religion. The related verb, "to act as a prophet," commonly understood to refer to ecstatic states (see especially 1 Sam 10:9–16) and occasion-

ally translated by NRSV "to rave" (1 Sam 18:10; 1 Kgs 18:29; cf. 2 Kgs 9:11; Hos 9:7–9), suggests that the phenomenon was never entirely under human control. In some of the early narratives, prophesying indicated God's intervention to control the outcome of human events (1 Sam 19:18–24). Even as prophecy came to be associated with the proclamation of a reasonably articulate message, the ambiguity remained. It remained unclear whether the word was truly from Yahweh or from the prophet's imagination (Ezek 13; Jer 23:16, 21). Even if the message was false, that did not necessarily mean that Yahweh had nothing to do with it. In 1 Kgs 22, for example, Yahweh intentionally deceives the prophets by means of a "lying spirit" in order to have Ahab killed in battle. The use of deceit is not an isolated occurrence: Yahweh declares that he has used this strategy against Israel (Hos 6:5; 12:10), and an unnamed prophet of Bethel uses deceit in order to test the obedience of the man of God from Judah (1 Kgs 13:11–25). At the same time that Ezekiel condemns prophets for speaking out of their own imaginations, he can claim that God is the source of these lying visions (Ezek 14:9–10). This ambivalence regarding the prophetic message persists from the beginning of the classical prophetic period until after the exile. Amos rejects the designation of prophet (Amos 7:14), while other eighth-century prophets speak in blistering terms about their lies (Isa 9:15; 28:7; 29:10; Mic 3:5, 6, 11). Jeremiah recounts the failure of institutional mechanisms to differentiate between the truthfulness of Jeremiah's message and that of the other prophets, particularly Hananiah. Only with the demise of prophecy does the ambivalence cease. In the postexilic book of Zechariah, prophets themselves will be ashamed of their role; like Amos, they will protest that they are not prophets (Zech 13:2–6).

Nowhere in this diverse testimony to the positive and negative impact of prophecy on public and private life is there a consistent approach to the problem of true and false prophecy. Prophets who speak out of their own imaginations are not called false prophets, and even their lies may further the divine purpose. One much-discussed attempt to resolve the problem of true and false prophecy is Deut 18:15–22, which provides for the sending of prophets like Moses who will speak Yahweh's words. The section concludes with the exchange, "'How can we recognize a word that the LORD has not spoken?' If a prophet speaks in the name of the LORD but the thing does not take place or prove true, it is a word that the LORD has not spoken" (18:21–22).

Deuteronomy's solution hardly accounts for the preservation of many prophecies that were never fulfilled but which nevertheless were considered truthful proclamations of the word of God. Perhaps a more theologically sound approach to the problem of prophecy is found in the account of Jeremiah's trial for announcing the destruction of Jerusalem (Jer 26). As the elders consider executing him for his treasonous words against the city, they evaluate the precedent of Micah's announcement of the destruction of Jerusalem to King Hezekiah. They point out that neither the word of judgment nor the fate of the city was a fait accompli; what mattered was that Hezekiah sought God's favor and thereby averted the disaster. Even though Micah's prophecy was not fulfilled, his announcement of judgment and the king's response became a model for subsequent responses to difficult messages purporting to be from God. This particular narrative suggests that, whether a prophecy came true or not, its intended outcome was repentance and return to Yahweh (cf. Jonah).

Standing in tension with this apparent ambivalence toward prophetic utterances is the emergence of a prophetic theology of history. The basis of this theology is the Deuteronomistic idea that Yahweh would send prophets like Moses who would proclaim God's word to the people. Accordingly, in Samuel–Kings, the prophets Samuel (1 Sam 3:20), Nathan (2 Samuel 7), and Ahijah (1 Kgs 11:29)

inaugurate new eras in Israel's history, while numerous other prophets announce judgment on kings who fail to abide by the covenant. Key events are thus summed up by the formula "thus X happened according to the word of the LORD, which he spoke by his servants the prophets" (1 Kgs 14:18; 2 Kgs 14:25; 17:23; 21:10–15; 24:2). The formula does not appear all that often, and it obscures some of the other roles played by prophets in Samuel–Kings (e.g., Nathan as secular court adviser, 1 Kgs 1:8, 10, 33, 34, 38). Nevertheless, the summary formulas appear often enough to establish a pattern of prophecy and fulfillment in the history of Israel and Judah. Deuteronomy is not alone in this schematic presentation of the message of the prophets; comparable viewpoints are evident in Jeremiah, Zech 1:1–6, and Dan 9. But all of these are late; and for Daniel, the prophecy of Jeremiah has already acquired the status of an authoritative writing. Thus one may conclude that the pattern of prophecy was evident only in retrospect.

The theological consequence of this development is profound: the actions of a deity who proclaims his intentions through his servants the prophets are no longer inscrutable or deceptive, as in the earlier narratives. Rather, this deity is now portrayed as not only a just but also a long-suffering and patient God who constantly calls his people back to him and executes judgment only when there is no other alternative. The problem with prophecy is thus no longer its ambiguous status as truth but rather the perennial failure of the people to accept it as God's word.

The NT reflects the same tensions regarding the nature and value of prophecy. As in the OT, the contemporaneous experience of prophecy in the church presents a host of problems, while retrospective narratives allow for the development of coherent narratives that give shape and meaning to the Christian life.

There were prophets in the early church (Matt 7:22; 10:41; Acts 11:27; 13:1; 15:32; 19:6; 21:9–10). Paul prizes prophecy as a spiritual *gift* (1 Cor 14); indeed, it is one of the gifts that is to be eagerly sought, since it builds up the church through its "encouragement and consolation" (1 Cor 14:3, 12; cf. Eph 2:20). The Spirit was no respecter of persons; hence women as well as men prophesied, at least in the church at Corinth (1 Cor 11:5). Paul does not say exactly how prophecy builds up the church, but he does say that it works to convict the heart and can lead unbelievers to testify to the presence of God (1 Cor 14:24–25). In the Revelation to John, which is explictly called a prophecy, a predictive survey of what is to happen in the last days is a significant element of the message. But in Revelation, these predictions serve primarily as exhortations to remain faithful to God in the face of persecution. As in the OT, then, prophecy exhorts believers to remain faithful to God, and predictive elements are subordinated to that purpose.

The presence of prophecy in the churches was initially welcomed as a sign of the last days (Acts 2:17; cf. Joel 2:28–32); however, it appears to have become a problem early on. The Gospels contain warnings against false prophets (Matt 7:15; 24:11, 24). Second Peter compares false prophecies in the OT with false *teachings* in the church (2 Pet 1:19–2:3), and the pagan prophet Balaam (see Num 22–24) becomes a warning against false teaching and divination (2 Pet 2:16; Jude 11). Church officials sought to control prophecy by controlling the types of people who were allowed to speak; hence the relatively frequent use of the term *pseudoprophetes* in the NT (eleven times). While women are not explicitly called either prophets or false prophets, they did exercise the spiritual gift of prophecy (1 Cor 11:5; Acts 21:9) and were among the first to be silenced. For example, 1 Cor 14:34b–36, the prohibition against women speaking in church, interrupts a general discussion of the regulation of prophecy. If, as it is widely believed, this is a post-Pauline interpretation, it is likely that it specifically targeted women's prophetic utterances.

Despite its ambivalence toward prophets in its midst, the church embraced the OT prophets as a testimony to God's work of salvation in Jesus Christ. The pattern of prophecy and fulfillment is most clearly evident in the Gospels of Matthew and Luke, which interpret nearly every aspect of Jesus' birth, life, and death as a fulfillment of prophecy. Indeed, all of Scripture—and most important, prophecy—provided the narrative into which the story of Christ and the church was fitted. Although the era of the law and the prophets ended with John, their testimony had not been abrogated (Matt 5:17–19; 7:12; 22:40; John 1:45; 6:45). While Jesus is certainly more than a prophet (Luke 9:19–20), the people regard him as one (Matt 21:11, 46; Luke 7:16, 26; 24:19; John 4:19). He shares the destiny of Israel's prophets as he faces dishonor (Luke 4:24), rejection, and death (Matt 5:12; 23:29–39; Luke 6:23, 26; 11:47, 49, 50; 13:28, 33–34; 16:29–31; 18:31).

In conclusion, the words of living prophets remained uncertain and in need of testing and discernment, while the written words of prophets long past had established a pattern for discerning the work of God in the present. In this context, it is interesting to note that the word "inspire" (Greek *theopneustos*) is used only in 2 Tim 3:16 and only of Scripture (Greek *graphe*; see *write*). While Hellenistic mantic practices may lie behind the use of this word, the author of Timothy uses it to describe not contemporary prophetic activity but rather the reliability of Scripture, written testimonies that have been preserved from the past. Because Scripture is "God-breathed," it is a reliable source of teaching and instruction in the godly life. The author of 2 Timothy appears to have derived this understanding of the authority of Scripture from Hellenistic Jewish thought (Philo, *De Vita Mosis* II.188; 2 Esd 14).

A. Graeme Auld, "Prophets through the Looking Glass," JSOT 27 (1983): 3–23; Daniel Fleming, "The Etymological Origins of the Hebrew *nabiʾ*: The One Who Invokes God," *CBQ* 55 (1993): 217–24; D. Hill, *New Testament Prophecy* (Atlanta: John Knox Press, 1979); Michael E. Stone, "Excursus on Inspiration," in *Fourth Ezra: A Commentary on the Book of Fourth Ezra*, Hermeneia (Minneapolis: Fortress, 1990), 119–21.

MARGARET S. ODELL

Prudent   *see* **Wise**

Punish, Punishment   *see* **Judge**

Pure, Purify, Purity   *see* **Clean**

Purpose   *see* **Plan**

Rahab   *see* **Animals**

Rainbow   *see* **Noah**

Raise, Raise Up   *see* **Resurrection**

Ransom   *see* **Redeem**

Rebel, Rebellion, Rebellious
see **Sin**

Rebuke   *see* **Correct**

Recompense   *see* **Reward**

Reconcile, Reconciliation   These terms are not common in NRSV, but their significance is greater than a simple word count would reveal. The verb "reconcile" appears once in a passage from the Hebrew Bible. In the Apocrypha and NT, both verb and noun appear, translating the Greek verb *katallasso* and related nouns and verbs.

As often with theological vocabulary, the meaning of these terms is grounded in their normal social usage, as found, for example, in 1 Sam 29:4. Here, the Philistine commanders are afraid that David, though purportedly their ally, will betray them in battle with his own people since it would be an opportunity for him to reconcile himself with Saul. Reconciliation, in this context, is a public transition from

enmity to friendship, made possible through a decisive action by one of the previously opposed parties.

Similarly the basic meaning of the Greek word group in question is "changing an enemy into a friend." As used in the Apocrypha, however, it means more specifically the *"restoration* of a broken friendship." Sirach is interested in the limits of reconciliation with a friend whose trust one has abused. Some things can be overcome by friendship, others not: "If you open your mouth against your friend, do not worry, for reconciliation is possible. But as for reviling, arrogance, disclosure of secrets, or a treacherous blow—in these cases any friend will take to flight" (Sir 22:22; cf. 27:21).

In the NT, too, we find a reference to reconciliation between human beings when the people of Tyre and Sidon seek to come to terms with Herod (Acts 12:20). Reconciliation also has a religious dimension, however, even in purely human matters. Stephen speaks of how Moses tried to act as reconciler between two quarreling Israelites, a kind of forecast of his future role with the people as a whole (Acts 7:26). Paul specifies that Christian women, if separated from their husbands, should either remain single or "be reconciled to" the spouse (1 Cor 7:10–11).

In 2 and 3 Maccabees we find a shift toward focusing on God's willingness to be reconciled with the people, despite their failures. The distress of Jerusalem and its people under Antiochus Epiphanes is explained as a consequence of God's temporary wrath at their sins; its reversal is explained by God's willingness to be reconciled (2 Macc 5:15–20). Reference to God's willingness to be reconciled is therefore an assertion of hope at moments of near despair (2 Macc 7:33); and appropriately it appears as part of the address to God in prayer (2 Macc 1:5, 8:29; 3 Macc 5:13).

The usage here represents a certain shift from the more purely social references treated above, in that it is not the offender (as in Sirach) or the disadvantaged party (as in 1 Samuel) who seeks reconciliation. Rather, it is God, the offended party and also the more powerful. Those who appeal to God for help are confident because they perceive this willingness to be reconciled as integral to God's being.

In the NT, this word group, understood in precisely this way, is an important way of speaking about God's work in Christ, most notably in 2 Cor 5:16–21. Here Paul tells us that "in Christ God was reconciling the world to himself, not counting their trespasses against them" (5:19). The faithful are "in Christ" and have therefore become "a new creation" (5:17). It is precisely the transition to being "in Christ," a part of the community of the saints, that marks the transition from enmity to friendship with God.

God has sought this reconciliation even to the point of making Christ, "who knew no sin," himself to be "sin" so that we by a process of exchange might be categorized as "righteousness" (5:21; "sin" here might better have been translated "sinfulness," to make the parallelism with "righteousness" clearer). In other words, God's great gesture of willingness to reconcile is to have his Chosen One share the alienation of those who had become enemies in order to provide a bridge for them to be treated again as friends.

The reconciliation between humanity and God, though in principle fully accomplished in Christ, must be further realized in human community; to that end, this reconciliation has been entrusted to Paul and, by extension, to the faithful at large. Paul asserts twice that God has "given us" the ministry and message of reconciliation (5:18–19). This necessarily shapes all Christian ministry, for those given this ministry can no longer regard any one "from a human point of view" (5:16).

Paul insists that this reconciliation is entirely at God's initiative, without human prompting. Even though we were God's enemies, God reconciled us "through the death of his Son" (Rom 5:10). Paul goes on to assert the even greater importance of Christ's resurrected life in this respect. Christ's death effected the reconciliation, but salvation comes about through Christ's life. This double bond is so strong that we can now "boast in God through our Lord Jesus Christ" (5:11), implying the most intimate possible connection of friendship with God.

This link between the cross and reconciliation reappears in Colossians, which Paul may or may not have written. Colossians describes this as part of a process by which Christ is both the *firstborn* of creation and the firstborn from the dead (1:15–20). In the family language of the time, this status makes him the senior member and principal authority in both categories, that is to say, in both the Present Age and the Age to Come. Parallel to (and reinforcing) this claim, Christ is also "the *image* of the invisible God" and "the head of the body, the church" (1:15, 18). In a sense Christ already reconciles all creation with God in his very person.

The ongoing process of reconciliation, in Colossians, means converting all enmity into friendship and therefore involves "all things, whether on earth or in heaven" (1:20). The phrase includes intermediate supernatural beings as well as humanity and, presumably, the material world. In some sense, it is all becoming "the body, the church" through the process of reconciliation. The role of Christ's death here lies in God's "making peace through the blood of the cross." The reconciling act is God's doing and at great cost.

The idea that God makes peace through the *blood* of the cross is further expanded in Ephesians, probably written by a later disciple of Paul. The peace in question here is not simply peace between God and the creation but peace within the creation as well. Reconciliation with God implies that we experience reconciliation with the rest of creation too. In particular, according to Ephesians, there is reconciliation between Jews and Gentiles (2:15–16). The author explains this in terms of the abolition of the law, that is to say, of those religious observances that separate the two groups and of the hostility that results from their separation. All ethnic antagonisms must now be laid aside, for both groups now constitute a "new humanity," recalling the "new creation" of 2 Cor 5:17 and the cosmic thinking of Col 1:15–20.

Matthew's Jesus makes a related point about the theological implications of reconciliation in the Sermon on the Mount. If you are about to offer sacrifice and remember that "your brother or sister has something against you," you must go and "first be reconciled" and only then offer your gift (5:23–24). In other words, there is no friendship with God that also allows us to maintain enmity with others. This is parallel to Matthew's teaching on *forgiveness* in the way it links relationship to God with relationship to neighbor.

Reconciliation, of course, is a two-sided affair. This is implicit in Paul's appeal, "We entreat you on behalf of Christ, be reconciled to God" (2 Cor 5:20). The whole purpose of Christ's reconciling death is to present the faithful as "holy and blameless and irreproachable before" God (Col 1:22). While God initiates the process of reconciliation and makes the necessary public gesture in allowing Christ to become "sinfulness" for us so that we might become God's "righteousness," the reconciliation truly takes effect only as it is accepted and enacted by both parties. This means that the human side can also reject it, at least for the time being.

The earliest Christians were painfully aware that acceptance of their good news was less than universal among people of their day, Jewish and Gentile alike. Paul, accordingly, theorizes a possible historical dimension in the process of reconciliation. In Rom 11:15, he suggests that God is actually using the gospel's relative failure to win recognition among other Jews as an opportunity to bring about the reconciliation of "the world." In context, he has in mind specifically the Gentiles, but it is not difficult to see how Colossians could extend this to include a cosmic dimension. In either case, a historical process is implied—one in which Paul

and the other faithful are the servants of a reconciliation that moves in constantly, though not smoothly, widening circles.

Reconciliation is a much larger theme in the Scriptures than this survey of linguistic usage can fully convey, but a thematic study is outside the scope of this work. Anyone who is familiar with the biblical story as a whole will hear echoes of it everywhere. God's anger at Israel's unfaithfulness is again and again voiced in the context of God's desire to renew the relationship of friendship and love. This is nowhere more evident than in Hosea's pursuit of reconciliation with his wife Gomer, even if the vocabulary of reconciliation does not appear there (Hos 1–3).

Again, in John's Gospel Jesus declares of his forthcoming crucifixion and return to the Father: "And I, when I am lifted up from the earth, will draw all people [NRSV Mg, all things] to myself" (12:32). Taken with a characteristic passage like the well-known John 3:16, this too expresses the theme of reconciliation, even if the precise terminology does not appear.

Reconciliation then is a way of speaking about the end goal of the scriptural story. Even if the terminology is rare in the Scriptures of Israel, it represents something central in them—God's determined and unflagging effort to restore a relationship of friendship with the creation, not least the human creation, despite our own tendency to sabotage it. God does this not only by direct action but by enlisting human cooperation, as in the work of the prophets.

In the NT, God's search for reconciliation culminates in the ministry of Jesus, including the costly gift of Jesus' death. The NT writers are not specific about how the crucifixion brings about reconciliation. There is at least the hint, however, in Col 1:18 that it has to do with Christ's becoming the "firstborn from the dead," thereby inaugurating the new reality of the Age to Come.

The process thus begun moves outward through the ministry of apostles like Paul and ultimately of the whole community of the faithful. The lives of the faithful are shaped by the ministry and message of reconciliation and so become the principal medium for including new persons in the process of living into the Age to Come.

Vincent Taylor, *Forgiveness and Reconciliation* (London: Macmillan, 1941).

L. WILLIAM COUNTRYMAN

Redeem, Redeemer, Redemption, Ransom, Vindicate

The words in this article all have to do with restoration of lost status. In modern Christian parlance, they have become rather generalized, so that the term "redeemer," for instance, is barely distinguished from "savior" or "messiah." In the centuries when the Scriptures were being written, however, they were more distinct and specific, for reasons pertaining to the history and culture of the times. "Vindicate," which will be dealt with separately at the end of the article, has its home primarily in the courts. "Redeem," "ransom," and related terms have a more complex social basis.

Redeem/ransom

Old Testament. Social mobility tended to be low in ancient Mediterranean cultures. The individual's place in society was determined by membership in a particular household. The household, in turn, inherited its social standing along with its property. Individuals and families could fall out of their inherited status through incurring debt, losing property, being taken prisoner in war, being sold into slavery, or experiencing adverse judgment in a court. In each case, return to the earlier, preferable status was very difficult.

The redeemer was a person of wealth or influence who intervened on behalf of the person in trouble. In Israelite usage, the next of kin, if able to perform the task, had a certain obligation to assume this role. Indeed the Hebrew *goʾel*, usually translated "redeemer," often means simply "next of kin." The story of Ruth offers a good example. Boaz is willing and able to serve as redeemer of the land of his deceased male relative Elimelech, but he is not first in line to do so. Accordingly, he must negotiate with the next of kin, who waives his prerogative in the matter (4:1–12). In this way, Boaz becomes the redeemer. He not only keeps the land within the larger kinship group but, by marrying Ruth, also undertakes to restore a line of descent to Elimelech. (Another example of redemption of family land can be found in Jer 32:6–15.)

The Torah makes detailed provisions for the redemption of land and people. These have a theological basis in the conviction that God has called all of Israel equally to be a chosen people and given them the land of Canaan. Accordingly, every clan has its allotted land, which it can never permanently alienate. In addition, all Israelites are, by fundamental definition, free persons. The institution of the jubilee, even though it may have been an ideal more than actual practice, serves to guarantee this equality by returning every family's land to it and by restoring freedom to Israelite slaves (Lev 25:8–55).

Since each household has a permanent relationship to its agricultural property, even if the property is sold, the next of kin has a permanent right to buy it back (Lev 25:25). Houses in villages are reckoned with agricultural property in this respect; the right of redemption for urban property, on the other hand, is limited to one year. Since the tribe of Levi, however, is understood to have been allotted only urban property at the conquest of Canaan, they have an ongoing right of redemption for their urban property (25:32–34). Strict limits are also placed on Israelites' holding of other Israelites as *slaves* (Lev 25:39–43). And if Israelites become slaves of resident aliens, the redeemer has the right and responsibility to redeem them (25:47–55). The laws of redemption, then, have a theological basis in the special relationship between God, the people, and the land.

There is also another dimension to the language of redemption as a way of speaking about the intricacies of the relationship between God and Israel, and the two do not coexist easily. In this dimension, God is not the sponsor of redemption, but the one from whom certain beings must be redeemed. Indeed, one major context for the language of redemption is the law of the firstborn in Exod 13. Every firstborn male, human or animal, belongs to God. If it is a clean animal, it must be sacrificed (13:11–12). If it is an animal from one of the species not fit for sacrifice, it must be redeemed with a sheep or else have its neck broken (13:13). The human firstborn must be redeemed (Exod 13:13–16). The same law is reiterated in Exod 34:19–20. It reappears in Num 18:15–18, though here a money payment is allowed for the redemption of human firstborn and those of unclean animals. (A point of confusion arises in Num 8:14–19, where the tribe of Levi appears to be substituted for all Israelite firstborn.) The point in every case is that what belongs to the sphere of the holy cannot be put to ordinary human use without some kind of compensation, whether a monetary payment or the substitution of an animal appropriate for sacrifice.

"Ransom" covers a range of rights and obligations similar to "redemption," but its use in NRSV typically reflects the Hebrew word *kopher* rather than *ga'al*. *Kopher* applies specifically to compensation paid for the restoration of living beings to their former status. "Ransom" is also used as equivalent to "redemption," in the case of the firstborn, as a way of obtaining their "secularization" so that they can live and function in the profane world rather than the sacred sphere (Lev 27:27).

There are also situations in which ransom or redemption is specifically forbidden, particularly the case of a person who is under a curse or ban or, as NRSV translates, "*devoted* to destruction" (Lev 27:29). The most notable (albeit atypical) instance of such a person is Jonathan, who unwittingly violates his father's oath by tasting some honey during a long day's pursuit of the Philistines (1 Sam 14:24–46). In this story, the people do ransom Jonathan, though this appears to be in violation of Torah.

Another group included under the ban is composed of murderers, who must be executed, and those who have fled to cities of refuge because of having committed involuntary homicide. Ransoming them is specifically forbidden (Num 35:31–32). Their status is complicated by the necessity of resolving the pollution of *blood* that the slaying has produced. The murderer's own blood purges the pollution of this offense, while the death of the high priest somehow acts as an equivalent to ransom for those who have killed someone unintentionally (Num 35:22–28).

The ritual obligation of ransoming the firstborn offered a metaphor for speaking about the larger relationship between God and humanity. Psalm 49:7–9 speaks of every life as belonging to God and asserts that the ransom is too great for any human being to pay. All must eventually die. In a sudden shift of metaphor, however, the psalmist goes on to say, "But God will ransom my soul from the power of Sheol" (v. 15). This sort of shift is a good reminder that the language of ransom may be used in a metaphorical way, with God playing more than one possible role in the metaphor. As we move from a ritual context to more independent theological use of the language of redemption, we should be cautious of efforts, however traditional they may be, to make the language of scriptural texts more precise than it really is.

In many contexts, God unambiguously takes on the role of redeemer. Indeed, God is particularly known to Israel as the one who redeemed them from slavery in Egypt. References to this foundational event are scattered widely through the Scriptures of Israel (e.g., Exod 15:13; Deut 7:8; 2 Sam 7:23; Mic 6:4). Second Isaiah gives redemption new significance as a theme. God repeatedly speaks as Israel's redeemer, ransoming Israel from captivity in Babylon (e.g., 43:14; 44:6; 49:7). God promises to give other, greater nations as Israel's ransom, apparently evoking the idea of substitution, as in the ransoming of the firstborn (43:3). The promise of redemption appears, albeit less frequently, in other prophets as well (e.g., Jer 15:21; Mic 4:10). Hosea, however, fears that the people will only spurn it (7:13).

God acts as redeemer for individuals as well. Joseph speaks of God as "the angel who has redeemed" him (Gen 48:15–16). And David describes God as having done the same for him (2 Sam 4:9). Job too seems to refer to God in this role: "I know that my Redeemer lives, and that at the last he will stand upon the earth" (19:25). This claim is in marked contrast to the speeches of his friends, who imply that God will redeem Job only if he follows their advice (5:20; 33:28).

Pleas for redemption are common in the Psalms (e.g., 25:22; 69:18). God will help the faithful by redeeming them from oppression and violence (72:14; 119:134). The psalmist expresses confidence that God will provide a level of help and protection not to be found among human beings (e.g., 34:22; 74:2). God becomes, in a sense, the ultimate next of kin (*go'el*) for the people (e.g., Ps 78:35; Isa 41:14; Jer 50:34).

There is a strong link between God's role as redeemer and God's demand that the people too must observe the demands of justice among themselves. Proverbs 23:11 admonishes the powerful person who is tempted to steal the property of orphans that "their redeemer is strong; he will plead their cause against you." And Isaiah declares that "Zion shall be redeemed by justice, and those in her who repent, by righteousness" (1:27).

Throughout the Scriptures of Israel, the theological understanding of redemption remains close to its basic social meaning. The redemption that God will bring about is the restoration of lost status here and now. God redeems by bringing the people out of captivity, slavery, poverty, and landlessness and restoring them to their former condition.

New Testament. In the NT, God shares the work of redemption with Jesus. And the image of redemption itself comes to be focused more on eschatology. This is

not, however, a simple either/or opposition. Zechariah, in Luke's infancy narratives, celebrates God, in traditional terms, "because he has looked favorably on his people and redeemed them" (1:68; cf. 2:38). But Luke's Jesus, with reference to the signs of the end, speaks in more eschatological terms: "Now when these things begin to take place, stand up and raise your heads, because your redemption is drawing near" (21:28).

In the NT, redemption language reflects both the next-of-kin-as-redeemer complex and the custom of redeeming the firstborn. It finds its particular home in the Pauline tradition, where its reference is both broader than in the OT (including Gentiles as well as Israelites) and more specifically eschatological. Paul speaks of redemption in terms of being translated from the status of slaves to that of children of the household. In both Rom 8:23 and Gal 4:5, he parallels it with the metaphor of *adoption*. In both texts, there is a sense that adoption replaces a profoundly disadvantaged prior status.

According to Romans, the whole creation has been "subjected to futility," but only in the hope that it "will be set free from its bondage to decay" (8:20–21). Humanity participates in this bondage; and our adoption liberates us from it, thus constituting "the redemption of our bodies" (v. 23). It is perhaps easiest to understand this line of thought by connecting it with Paul's argument in favor of bodily resurrection in 1 Cor 15. The body is included within redemption because it is a necessary component of the human being. The essence of redemption here is to be brought from slave to free status.

The Galatians text is more complex and difficult. Paul maintains, in this letter, that "Christ redeemed us [i.e., Jewish Christians] from the curse of the law by becoming a curse for us" (Gal 3:13). While the text does not refer specifically to the redemption of the firstborn, it seems to echo the basic pattern of that rite: Christ redeems by substituting himself for the original victim. Yet there are also significant differences here. For one, Paul seems to be arguing for a violation of the Torah's prohibition against redeeming those under a curse. For another, Paul insists that God is the prime mover of this redemption (4:4–5). Is God then paying a debt to liberate what already belongs to God? We must again caution ourselves (as above in relation to Ps 49) against overliteralizing the metaphorical use of "redemption."

It seems that Paul regards all experience of life before Jesus, whether Jewish or Gentile, as in some sense a state of slavery from which humanity needs to be redeemed or ransomed. In Galatians, he is arguing against what he sees as an overvaluation of Jewish status on the part of some Gentile converts to the gospel, and accordingly he shapes his argument particularly to relativize the status of the Torah. He does not even treat the Torah as having been given directly by God, but rather by angelic beings (3:19–20). Accordingly it represents a kind of enslavement to the "elemental spirits of the world" (4:3). It is from these spirits, whether in their Israelite or their Gentile manifestation, that humanity needs to be redeemed.

The language of redemption also appears in Hebrews, which emphasizes that it takes place through Jesus' blood or death (Heb 9:12, 15). Given this author's great interest in sacrificial cultus, one might expect a reference here to the redemption of the firstborn, but in fact the author is using other rites, particularly those of the Day of Atonement, as the theological model. Redemption language seems to be used only rather generally. The result of redemption, once again, is to restore us to a higher status. In Hebrews, it serves to "purify our conscience from dead works to worship the living God" (9:14). That is, it counteracts the alienating effects of human sin and allows us once again to worship God as true members of the community of faith.

In the Pauline tradition, the authors of Colossians (1:14) and Ephesians (e.g., 1:7, 14) use the language of redemption allusively rather than working out any detailed account of who must be paid what to effect redemption or who (God or Christ) is acting as redeemer. It is enough to say that redemption delivers us from our earlier transgressions and comes about through the work of Christ. It is parallel to the redemption of Israel from Egypt in that it creates a people for God (Eph 1:14).

Redemption language is used alongside other ways of speaking about the transformation wrought by the work of Jesus. Like Hebrews, the letter to Titus parallels it with purification language (2:14). Perhaps Revelation has a similar point in mind when it describes the redeemed as those "who have not defiled themselves with women" (14:4), though the passage is not clear. Paul in Romans pairs it with justification (see *just*) (3:24).

Vindication

Vindication terminology is in many ways parallel to redemption language. NRSV, for example, offers "Vindicator" as a translational alternative to "Redeemer" in Job 19:25. It differs in that its context is more that of the courts. Indeed, two of the Hebrew verbs translated "vindicate" in NRSV (*din; shaphat*) are more commonly translated "judge." When translated "vindicate," they are being used to say that the judge has found in favor of the plaintiff. Another verb (*tsadaq*) makes the same point. It can also be translated "found innocent." Its Greek counterpart (*dikaioo*) is often translated "justify."

In this case, it is not the next of kin but the judge in the court of law who restores the needy person to his or her former status. The psalmists and the author of Job appeal repeatedly to God as the ultimate vindicator (e.g., Job 6:29; 13:18; Pss 26:1; 54:1). "The LORD works vindication and justice for all who are oppressed" (Ps 103:6).

Vindication may become known through events, such as the political destruction of one's foes (e.g., Isa 34:8; Jer 46:10). God as vindicator may be not only the judge who renders the verdict of "innocent" but also the warrior who exacts vengeance on the wrongdoer (e.g., Isa 63:1). The restoration of normal rainfall after a drought may also be seen as a sign of God's work of vindication (Joel 2:23).

In 4 Maccabees, on the other hand, it is the endurance of human martyrs that vindicates Israel. The constancy of a mother and her seven sons, even under torture, proves the philosophical superiority of the faith of Israel and defeats the cruelty of the Greek emperor (15:29; 17:10).

In the NT, vindication language appears only in an unusual saying about Wisdom that occurs, in slightly different forms, in Matthew and Luke. Jesus notes the comparison made between him and the ascetic John the Baptist and the criticism directed against him as "a glutton and a drunkard, a friend of tax collectors and sinners," and then responds by saying, "Yet wisdom is vindicated by her deeds" (Matt 11:18–19), or in Luke's version, "by all her children" (7:33–35). It appears that in Matthew's version Jesus is himself being identified with Wisdom. In Luke's, he may be one of her children, along with John. In either case, Wisdom's vindication is a divine act, evident either through her victory in court and deeds of power or through the number and success of her children.

Powerful as the language of redemption, ransom, and vindication is in the Bible, it is perhaps better to think of it as bringing theological metaphors into play rather than as embodying a theological concept. The reality of redemption as a social institution in ancient Israel was the foundation of the rest. Given the importance of the go'el, redemption or ransom was a ready metaphor for evoking God's committed, ongoing care for Israel. God buys the people back from slavery, vindicates them against their legal oppressors, brings them back from exile, and treats them as kin.

At the same time, the relationship between Israel and God could be thought of as ownership by God, expressed particularly in God's ownership of the firstborn. In this case, what belongs to God could be reclaimed for ordinary life only by paying a ransom. This distinct aspect of redemption incidentally contributes an element to later Western *atonement* theory because it recognizes the possibility of the substitution of one victim for another. For the firstborn of unclean animals, the Israelites are allowed to substitute the sacrifice of a sheep or other clean animal. For their own firstborn, they are commanded to do so. A similar thought appears in God's offer, in Isa 43:3, to substitute Egypt or Ethiopia or Seba as a ransom for the people of Israel. As an expression of generosity on the part of the redeemer, this is moving. As an element in atonement theory, it only leads to unnecessary confusion.

The theological metaphor of ransom or redemption, properly understood, focuses less on who pays what to whom than on the intervention of the next of kin and the restoration of status that results. The metaphor of vindication is somewhat more precise, from a theological perspective, since God can pretty generally be assigned the role of judge and, at times, of avenger. To insist on a similarly precise and detailed assignment of roles with regard to redemption results in considerable confusion.

Robert L. Hubbard Jr., "The Divine Redeemer: Toward a Biblical Theology of Redemption," in *Reading the Hebrew Bible for a New Millennium: Form, Concept, and Theological Perspectives*, vol. 1, *Theological and Hermeneutical Studies*, ed. W. Kim et al., Studies in Antiquity and Christianity (Harrisburg, Pa.: Trinity Press, 2000), 188–204; I. H. Marshall, "The Development of the Concept of Redemption in the New Testament," in *Reconciliation and Hope*, ed. R. Banks (Grand Rapids: Eerdmans, 1974), 153–69.

L. WILLIAM COUNTRYMAN

Refresh *see* **New**

Rejoice *see* **Joy**

Remember, Remembrance, Forget, Memory, Memorial The Hebrew verb *zakar* and the Greek verb *mnemoneuo*, along with several words derived from them, are used frequently in Scripture. Not only do human beings remember, but also God remembers or is requested to remember. This suggests that, in contrast to contemporary understandings of memory and remembering, the Scriptural concept is much broader and richer than merely the cognitive recalling of the past. As Allen Verhey succinctly puts it, "In Scripture, . . . memory is typically constitutive of identity and determinative of conduct" (667). This conclusion applies to both human and divine remembering.

From a canonical perspective, it is significant that God's remembering is featured in the opening chapters of the Bible. In Gen 8:1, "God remembered Noah and all the wild animals and all the domestic animals that were with him in the ark." The intent is not to suggest that God had ever forgotten Noah and the animals, but to assert that God will act toward Noah and the animals in the way that God had promised to act. In other words, the point is not God's cognitive capacity, but rather God's *character*. God will be faithful.

In this regard, the conclusion to the flood story portrays God proclaiming, "I will remember my covenant that is between me and you [Noah and his descendants, that is, humanity] and every living creature of all flesh" (Gen 9:15; see also v. 16). God has promised, in essence, to be in an everlasting relationship (see "everlasting covenant" in v. 16) with humankind, all creatures, and according to verse 13, with the earth itself! At the heart of this relationship is God's promise never again to destroy, and this promise comes *after* God has discovered that "the inclination of the human heart is evil from youth" (Gen 8:21; cf. Gen 6:5). In short, God promises to be eternally gracious and loving, faithfully maintaining the relationship among God, humanity, the creatures, and the creation, even when God's human partners demonstrate their inclination to be and to do evil. Everything that follows in the Bible is governed by this promise, which

God will faithfully "remember"—that is, the Bible will reveal that God's character and characteristic activity involve gracious love for the world (see Exod 6:5; Lev 26:42, 45; Deut 9:27; Ezek 16:60; Luke 1:72–73).

Even when the scope of the narrative narrows to Abraham and his descendants, the content and context of the story demonstrate that God's intent to bless Abraham ultimately aims at effecting a blessing for "all the families of the earth" (Gen 12:3). So when God remembers Abraham (see Gen 19:29), this is in keeping with God's characteristic activity of faithful love for the world.

Not surprisingly, the beginning of the exodus from Egypt is described in part by noting that "God remembered his covenant with Abraham, Isaac, and Jacob" (Exod 2:24; see also 32:13). Again, the point is not that God had forgotten Abraham and his descendants, but rather that the exodus inaugurates a new episode in God's faithful dealing with the world. As Terence Fretheim points out, the exodus represents nothing less than the fulfillment of God's creational purposes (12–14).

It is appropriate, therefore, that when Israel worshiped God, the celebration of their deliverance from Egypt (Ps 105:37–42) culminated with the affirmation that God "remembered his holy promise, and Abraham, his servant" (v. 42). The celebration of other divine deliverances (see Ps 106:43) culminates in a similar affirmation, in which it is explicitly clear that God's remembering is essentially a matter of God's character: "For their sake he remembered his covenant, and showed compassion according to the abundance of his steadfast love" (Ps 106:45). The Hebrew word *hesed* ("**steadfast love**") especially recalls God's self-revelation to Moses (Exod 34:6–7) and serves as a succinct summary of God's character. In Exod 34:6, *hesed* is parallel to "faithfulness," so it is not surprising that Ps 98:3 proclaims that God "has remembered his steadfast love and faithfulness to the house of Israel." Psalm

98 is another celebration of deliverance, involving not only "the house of Israel" but also "all the earth" (v. 4), which appropriately greets the God whose presence effects world-encompassing justice and righteousness (vv. 7–9). All this is entirely consistent with what God says God will remember in Gen 9:15–16.

In situations where God's justice and righteousness do not prevail, the appropriate prayer is for God to remember. Because of the responsibility entrusted by God to humankind, frequently what God wills for the world is *not* done (see **plan; determine**). In these instances, it is not the case that God has forgotten what God wills or forgotten God's love for the world, although this may appear to be the case.

Hence, the psalmists sometimes ask why God has forgotten them or their suffering (Pss 13:1; 44:24); and their plea is, for instance, "Do not forget the life of your poor forever" (Ps 74:19). The issue is not God's mental recollection but rather God's character and the enactment of God's will in the world; this is indicated by the fact that the psalmist can say in almost the same breath (Pss 9 and 10 were originally a single poem): "For he who avenges blood is mindful of [or "remembers," Hebrew *zakar*] them; he does not forget the cry of the afflicted" (Ps 9:12). "Rise up, O LORD; O God, lift up your hand; do not forget the oppressed" (Ps 10:12).

In a prayer for help that is found outside the book of Psalms, Hannah prays, "If only you will look on the misery of your servant, and remember me, and not forget your servant . . ." (1 Sam 1:11). In her situation of barrenness—one in which God's will for life is not manifest—Hannah's prayer for God to "remember me" and "not forget" is an emphatic plea for the fulfillment of God's creational purposes in a particular situation.

Within the book of Psalms, the more usual request is simply for God to "remember me" (25:7; 106:4), or "Remember your congregation" (74:2), or "Remember Mount Zion" (74:2; see also 74:18, 22).

Psalm 25:7 is particularly instructive: "Do not remember the sins of my youth or my transgressions; according to your steadfast love remember me, for your goodness' sake, O LORD!" The double request, "Do not remember" (see also Ps 79:8) and "Remember me," amounts to a request for God to be loving and *gracious*—that is, for God's character and characteristic activity to be manifest in the psalmist's life and in the world. In essence, the psalmists' prayers for God to remember find their functional equivalent in what Jesus would later teach his disciples to pray: "Your will be done, on earth as it is in heaven" (Matt 6:10).

Just as God's remembering is fundamentally about the divine character and will for the world, so is human remembering. It is significant that the first scriptural call for the people to remember is written into the story of the exodus from Egypt, a prototypical demonstration of God's fundamental character and activity. The call is to "remember this day on which you came out of Egypt, out of the house of slavery" (Exod 13:3), and the remembrance is to be formalized as a ritual to be observed "at its proper time from year to year" (Exod 13:10)—the feast of **Passover** or Unleavened Bread.

The point of this "day of remembrance" (Exod 12:14) is not simply to recall and honor the past. Rather, the goal is to shape the present and the future. The observance is to include the following (Exod 13:8): "You shall tell your child on that day, 'It is because of what the LORD did for me when I came out of Egypt.'" In short, the goal of this "day of remembrance" is not primarily *information* about the past, but rather the *formation* of future generations of the faithful. Every generation is to derive its identity from the life-giving will and work of God.

The centrality of remembering is especially evident in the book of Deuteronomy, which means "second law." The book itself is an exercise in remembrance; it retells major portions of the story found in Exodus–Numbers (Deut 1–11) and offers a reformulation of the covenant stipulations (Deut 12–26). The book is presented as the testimony of Moses to the wilderness generation and the new generation that is poised to enter the land of promise. In terms of cognitive recall, the new generation has no access to the past. But they too are called to remember it nonetheless; that is, they are called to claim the identity of their ancestors or, more to the point, to claim the identity shaped by the God of exodus and Sinai.

So they are called to "remember that you were a slave in the land of Egypt" (Deut 5:15; see also 15:15; 16:12; 24:18, 22), to "remember what the LORD your God did to Pharoah and to all Egypt" (7:18; see also 16:3), and to "remember the long way that the LORD your God has led you these forty years in the wilderness" (8:2; see also 9:7; 25:17). In effect, they are called to remember the whole sequence of deliverance and divine guidance, so that they will be prepared "today" (see Deut 30:15, 16, 19) to "choose life" (Deut 30:19), which is the essence of God's will for the world.

Not surprisingly, the book of Deuteronomy demonstrates the same educational concern that was evident in the ritual of the feast of Unleavened Bread/Passover—namely, that children be told the sequence of God's saving activity, beginning with the liberation from slavery in Egypt and continuing with the gift of the land (Deut 6:20–25). All this constitutes what it means to "not forget the LORD" (Deut 6:12).

In a real sense, worship is an act of remembrance. In both praise and prayer, the psalmists remember God and God's work (see Pss 77:11; 105:5; 119:55; 143:5). In addition, certain stipulated offerings involve remembering. Psalms 38 and 70 include in their titles the phrase "for the memorial offering" (see Isa 66:3). The description of the "sin offering" in Lev 5:11–13 mentions a "memorial portion" (v. 12), as does the description of "the grain offering" in Lev 6:14–18 (see v. 15). In view of the descriptions of "grain offerings of remembrance" (v. 15) in Num 5:11–31, the function of the "memorial portion" (Num

5:26) may have been to recall the wrong committed; but it may also have served to call attention to the character of the God being worshiped—that is, a gracious God whose willingness to forgive makes atonement possible (see Lev 5:13).

Other offerings (see Num 31:54), objects (see Zech 6:14), and practices also served a memorial function. In the first version of the Ten Commandments, the people are told, "Remember the sabbath day, and keep it holy." The accompanying rationale is based upon Gen 2:1–4, the conclusion of the creation account where God rests. Thus, to remember the Sabbath means to be like God, in this case, by one's distinctive inactivity. The Deuteronomic version of the commandment changes "Remember" to "Observe," and the accompanying rational cites exodus rather than creation. Nonetheless, remembrance is still involved; for the people are enjoined to "remember that you were a slave in the land of Egypt, and the LORD your God brought you out from there" (Deut 5:15).

Even the way people dressed was designed for remembrance. For instance, the priestly vestments for Aaron and his sons included two "shoulder-pieces," consisting of "stones of remembrance" engraved with the names of the twelve children of Israel (Exod 28:12). Perhaps the primary purpose was to (re)present the people before God in worship, but at least secondarily the stipulation itself also served to proclaim to the people themselves their identity as God's children. Moreover, the clothing of every Israelite was designed for remembrance. The "fringes on the corners of their garments" (Num 15:38) were so that they would "remember all the commandments of the LORD and do them" (Num 15:39). As Num 15:40–41 makes clear, the issue is both behavior and identity, both the people's and God's. The people's obedience is to render them "holy to your God" (v. 40), the God "who brought you out of the land of Egypt" (v. 41).

The people's crossing of the Jordan River into the promised land, an event clearly analogous to the crossing of the sea during the exodus from Egypt (see Josh 3:14–17; cf. Exod 14:21–29), was accompanied by the setting up of twelve stones, one for each tribe. These stones were meant to be "to the Israelites a memorial forever" (Josh 4:7). Recalling the Unleavened Bread/Passover ritual (see Exod 13:8) and the educational thrust of the book of Deuteronomy (see Deut 6:20–25), the account of the setting up of the stones includes the admonition to the Israelites to tell their children about the meaning of the stones (Josh 4:6–7). As usual in Scripture, memory is as much about the present and future as it is about the past.

In what seems at first glance to be a contradiction to the above admonitions for the people to remember God and God's works, Isa 43:18 says, "Do not remember the former things, or consider the things of old." But the contradiction is more apparent than real. This admonition is the prelude to the announcement that God is "about to do a new thing" (Isa 43:19), which will make "the former things" pale in comparison. Actually, the book of Isaiah discerns a continuity between "the former things" and God's "new thing," inasmuch as the return from exile announced in Isa 40–55 is portrayed as a new exodus. It is not surprising, therefore, that this same portion of the book of Isaiah also invites the people to "remember the former things of old" (46:9). This invitation immediately precedes an affirmation of God's character and activity (vv. 9–11). Again, as is typical in Scripture, remembering is fundamentally about identity and conduct. Indeed a major goal of the book of Isaiah is to offer the people of God a new identity as God's servant (41:8–9; 42:9; 43:10; 49:6; 52:13; 53:11; see esp. 44:21, which links this identity with remembering), "a light to the nations" (42:6; 49:6), based upon the "new thing" that God is doing.

Several hundred years later, some first-century-A.D. Jews were convinced that God had continued and was continuing to do new things in and through

Jesus of Nazareth. In the new covenant or NT, remembering continued to play an important role. The notice in Matt 26:75 that "Peter remembered what Jesus had said" is significant. Not only was it a transformative moment for Peter, but it also describes what happened generally among the followers of Jesus—that is, they remembered what Jesus had said, and it made all the difference in the world, in terms of their identity and activity.

In the Gospel of Luke, the women at the empty tomb are told to remember what Jesus had told them (24:6); and they "remembered his word" (24:8), becoming the first witnesses to the resurrection (24:9). In the Gospel of John, Jesus tells the disciples that the role of the Holy Spirit will be to "remind you of all that I have said to you" (14:26). As in the OT, remembrance means not simply mental recall but believing (John 2:22; see also 12:16; 16:4), which in turn means life (see John 20:30–31).

Remembering Jesus' words means, in essence, being like Jesus and doing what Jesus did (see Acts 20:35). Thus, preserving and passing on the story of Jesus, including his words and his works, was vital in the early church (see Rom 15:15; 1 Cor 15:1–5; 2 Tim 2:8; Rev 3:3). Indeed, the central act of Christian worship, the common meal, which according to both Paul and the Gospels was instituted by Jesus himself, is for the purpose of "remembrance" (Luke 22:19; 1 Cor 11:24–25). To be sure, the meal is a reminder of Jesus' suffering and death; but for those who participate it is also an enactment of how the earthly Jesus ate. Sharing the bread and sharing the cup is an actual practice of the grace that impelled Jesus to eat with all people. In short, those who eat together in remembrance of Christ will share a distinctive identity and practice. Remembrance shapes the present; and according to Paul, it also shapes the future: those who "eat this bread and drink the cup . . . proclaim the Lord's death until he comes" (1 Cor 11:26). As always in Scripture, memory transforms the present and engenders hope in God's future.

Brevard S. Childs, *Memory and Tradition in Israel*, SBT 37 (London: SCM Press, 1962); Terence Fretheim, *Exodus* (Atlanta: John Knox Press, 1991); Allen Verhey, "Remember, Remembrance," *ABD* 5:667–69.

J. CLINTON MCCANN

Remnant The English word "remnant" derives from the Latin "to remain, be left over." It translates a number of Hebrew nouns derived from three roots: *sha'ar* and *yathar*, with "to remain, be left" as their basic meaning, and *palat*, "to escape, survive." These words are used in various nontheological contexts (e.g., Neh 7:72; Gen 32:8).

Old Testament. The theological concept of remnant develops from "survivors," those who remain to carry on after a disaster. Although "remnant" is our key word, the idea is often conveyed in passages translated "to be left," and so forth, in the NRSV. Some of our best examples from biblical narratives lack "remnant." Genesis 7:23 summarizes the effects of the flood thus: "[God] blotted out every living thing. . . . Only Noah was left, and those that were with him." The occupants of the ark constitute a remnant that will repopulate the world.

Genesis 45:7 does have the key word. Joseph gives theological instruction to his brothers: "God sent me before you to preserve for you a remnant on earth, and to keep alive for you many survivors." He articulates the theology of remnant nicely, though the family actually survived intact.

Elijah at Mount Horeb became a paradigm of the remnant idea, though the key word is absent. When asked why he came, Elijah replies that Israel has forsaken the Lord, "and I alone am left" (1 Kgs 19:10, 14). The Lord commissions Elijah to inaugurate judgment, but assures Elijah that "I will leave seven thousand in Israel, all the knees that have not bowed to Baal" (19:18). God will bring destruction on his

people in judgment but deliver a faithful few to bear responsibility for fulfilling the purpose of Israel's election.

"Remnant" does not necessarily bear a positive or hopeful connotation: it can be used of utter disaster, as in "only a remnant" (2 Sam 14:7; Isa 14:22; cf. Deut 28:62; Isa 30:17). The prophet Amos uses "remnant" mostly in this negative way, for example, "The city that marched out a thousand shall have a hundred left" (5:3). Surviving a devastating military attack may not be the end of judgment: "and those who are left I will kill with the sword; not one of them shall flee away, not one of them shall escape" (Amos 9:1).

Amos does offer a glimmer of hope: to support the exhortation, "hate evil and love good, and establish justice in the gate," he offers possible divine clemency: "it may be that the LORD, the God of hosts, will be gracious to a remnant of Joseph" (5:15). "Remnant" here borders on a positive theological meaning: God in his freedom *may* reverse himself and maintain a people on earth (cf. v. 14). Amos 9:9–10 also hints at a future for the people of God dispersed among the nations, although it may have the opposite meaning. The book of Amos was collected and preserved for survivors—to forge them into a remnant in the positive theological sense. The book concludes with promises of salvation (9:11–15); to receive these promises, readers must acknowledge the truth of Amos's words of judgment on their people.

Isaiah too can use "remnant" as a measure of disaster (e.g., 30:17; cf. 17:3–6). However, Isaiah is most known for references to remnant as a sign of hope. How important this was to him is indicated by the naming of his son Shear-jashub, "a remnant shall return" (7:3 NRSV Mg). The verb, *yashub*, could mean "return" to the land from exile (so Isa 11:11–12), but could equally well mean "repent" (so Isa 10:20–23). Isaiah elsewhere speaks of cool confidence in the Lord as a "stone" to which the faithful can cling as the country passes through desperate times (28:16–17; cf. 30:15–17; 1:21–31).

During the Assyrian siege of Jerusalem, Hezekiah requested Isaiah to "lift up your prayer for the remnant that is left" (Isa 37:4). Isaiah responded with several oracles of salvation, one of which runs, "The surviving remnant of the house of Judah shall again take root downward . . . for from Jerusalem a remnant shall go out" (37:31–32). The people of the Lord will survive the catastrophe and repopulate the land. After the withdrawal, the people of the city celebrated when Isaiah thought they should mourn (22:1–4, 12–14). Isaiah 1:8–9 would fit this situation well: "If the LORD of hosts had not left us a few survivors, we would have been like Sodom."

The book of Isaiah is a collection not only of the prophet's words, but of reflections and expansions by his disciples and their disciples. A number of the references to "remnant" in the book grow from seeds Isaiah planted: Isa 10:20–22 and 11:11–16 grow from "A remnant will return"; 4:3 and 6:13b develop "holy" remnant.

In the latter part of Isaiah, Judean exiles in Babylon are addressed as "all the remnant of the house of Israel" (46:3), foreshadowing identification of the postexilic community as "remnant." In Isa 49:19–21, Zion is a bereaved wife who discovers she is a mother: "I was left all alone—where then have these come from?" (v. 21).

Micah, Joel, Obadiah, and Zephaniah all address promises to the remnant. The survivors of judgment will be gathered into a sheepfold (Mic 2:12). The lame, scattered, and afflicted will be preserved as a remnant ruled by God from Zion (4:6–7). Micah ends with praise for God's forgiveness of the remnant (7:18). Joel 2:32 and Obad 17 address Jerusalemites as survivors. Obadiah 17; Zeph 2:7, 9; and Mic 5:7–8 promise a reversal of power vis-à-vis neighbors, ending the period of vulnerability and constriction.

Like Amos and Isaiah, Jeremiah and Ezekiel employ "remnant" to describe the severity of divine punishment. "Death shall be preferred to life by all the remnant" (Jer 8:3). "Any who are left . . . shall

die of famine" (Ezek 6:12; cf. 17:21). As exile followed exile, those who remained were told that their time would come (Jer 24:8–9; 44:11–12). Earlier, when Judah's fate still hung in the balance, Jeremiah was told to "glean thoroughly as a vine the remnant of Israel" (6:9). Jeremiah's reply (v. 10) indicates his task was to convert those who would listen. Though he found no takers, he later holds out hope for a remnant in the future (23:3–4). In the Little Book of Comfort (Jer 30–31), the Lord encourages the people to "sing aloud with gladness for Jacob, . . . and say, 'Save, O LORD, your people, the remnant of Israel'" (31:7), involving the people in the decision for a future.

Ezekiel twice pleads for the remnant of the people (9:8; 11:13). The first answer is God's determination to carry it through (9:9–10); the second sees dispersion among the nations as a time of purgation (11:16–21). In 37:1–14, the "remnant" has been reduced to dry bones that must be raised to life.

In the postexilic period, "remnant" could be applied to all Jews everywhere, but most texts refer to those living in and around Jerusalem (Hag 1:12, 14; 2:2; Neh 1:2, 3). Zechariah 8:5 and 11–12 promise a national revival in the midst of hopelessness.

The theological use of "remnant" belongs to prophets, who were called to communicate God's message of judgment and salvation. It entered the common language of the people during the exile as they adopted the prophetic interpretation of their experience. Ezra's prayer shows how it found its place: "After all that has come upon us for our evil deeds, . . . seeing that you, our God, . . . have given us such a remnant as this, shall we break your commandments again?" (Ezra 9:13). The remnant looks upon its very existence as divine grace and strives not to repeat the sins of the past.

The reader may have the impression that the remnant surviving judgment is the loyal and righteous, while those who die are sinners. This reward and punishment scheme may well fit 1 Kgs 19:18, but not all our passages. Amos 5:15 does not promise that individuals who reform will survive while others perish, but that Israel collectively may have a remnant. Isaiah envisages judgment as purgation (Isa 1:21–31; 28:14–22; cf. 8:11–15), but the actual survivors of Sennacherib's invasion were hardly regarded as a righteous remnant (1:8–9; 22:1–4, 12–14).

Although the concept of remnant originated as a measure of disaster and basis of hope for restoration, it could be appropriated by sectarian movements claiming that the mass of the people and its leaders have defected and compromised and that their fellowship alone adheres to the Lord and his law. One can detect such a mindset scattered through Isa 56–66 with the designation "my servants" (e.g., Isa 65:13–16). Zephaniah 3:12 may have a particular group—"the humble and lowly"—in mind. Some texts from Qumran indicate that "remnant" had been appropriated to characterize the community as true Israel (e.g., 1QM 14:8f.; 1QH 6:8, 32; 7:22).

New Testament. The Greek translation of the Hebrew Bible (LXX) rendered *sha'ar* and *yathar* in their various forms by Greek words deriving from *leipein*. Most of these forms appear in the NT, but only twice do they bear the weight of "remnant" (Rom 9:27; 11:5). In Rom 9–11, Paul uses "remnant" only once in his own words (11:5); the other references are OT quotations (9:27; 11:3, 4). Romans 11:1–6 begins with the question "Has God rejected his people?" No, right up to the present, God has remained faithful to a remnant. The remnant of Paul's time is Jewish people, like himself (11:1), who have accepted Christ.

Why does Paul ask about the rejection of Jews? The truth of the gospel depends upon God fulfilling his promises to his own *people* (Rom 9:6). Paul argues that it is God's way to elect some and reject others by hardening their hearts (9:7–23). The resistance of the majority of Paul's fellow Jews is God's hardening (9:24–10:4). At the same time, God has incorporated Gentiles into his people

(9:25–26; 11:17–24). Paul cannot accept the conclusion that the people of God consists only of Jews and Gentiles who have accepted the salvation offered to his people Israel "because the gifts of God and the call of God are irrevocable" (11:29). Israel's "hardening" is only temporary; it is a part of God's plan to open the people of God to Gentiles, so that Jews and Gentiles alike receive God's mercy and grace (11:11–16, 25–32).

Paul uses "remnant," thus, only to analyze the present. In the end, the whole Jewish people will receive the grace God has offered Jew and Gentile alike. God's gracious will is too inclusive to be restricted to a remnant. Paul's struggle with remnant theology tells us why "remnant" was not used elsewhere in the NT. Paul's call to "proclaim [Christ] among the Gentiles" (Gal 1:16) moves in the opposite direction from the idea of a remnant. The gospel opens up the people of God; the church is to be a "new people" (Gal 5:6–26). The fact that the church debated including Gentiles without circumcising them suggests Jesus had left no teachings on this issue. However, Jesus' message, as depicted in the Gospels, moved in the direction of inclusivity. The early church simply expanded Jesus' inclusivity.

J. C. Campbell, "God's People and the Remnant," *SJT* 3 (1950): 78–85; Roland de Vaux, "The Remnant of Israel According to the Prophets," in de Vaux, *The Bible and the Ancient Near East* (Garden City, N.Y.: Doubleday, 1971), 15–30.

DALE PATRICK

Renew *see* **New**

Repent, Repentance, Turn, Return The Hebrew word used to denote repentance is *shub*, which means literally "to turn, turn around, return." Metaphorically, thinking of life as a *way* on which one walks, *shub* then was used to indicate reversing one's course, changing allegiance, giving up one way of life for another. This is the biblical sense of "repent"; so although the "turning" likely involves regret and remorse for past allegiances and actions, it is far more than that. In the NT, "repent" and "repentance" always translates *metanoeo* and *metanoia*, which originally meant to change one's *mind*, without the life-changing sense of *shub*. The NT writers used the words as *shub* was used in the OT, however. They also used *strepho* and *epistrepho*, which have the same sense of "turning."

Repentance in the Old Testament. Deuteronomy 30 and Ezek 18 contain two classic statements of the typical OT view of human opportunity and responsibility. Two ways lie before us, and we have the freedom and ability to choose the way of obedience to God's will, or the way of disobedience—the way of life—the way of death. Life and death, in these texts, are umbrella terms that include all that is good, on the one hand, and all that is bad, on the other. The choices we make are not irrevocable. It is possible to turn, from life to death, and from death to life (Deut 30:10, 17; Ezek 18:21–32), and the latter possibility is afforded by God's willingness to *forgive*: "For I have no pleasure in the death of anyone, says the Lord GOD. Turn, then, and live" (Ezek 18:32). Having made the wrong choice need not inevitably determine the future, for it is possible to turn, turn around, repent; and God makes a new future possible by forgiveness.

The writers of the OT were fully aware that wrong choices tend to be typical, so they occasionally wrote of turning away from God (e.g., Judg 8:33 [NRSV: "relapsed"]; Isa 53:6; Hos 3:1; 7:16), but they most often wrote of the need to turn to God, thus to repent, as we understand the word. Usually, repentance is considered the necessary human decision in order to receive forgiveness, but there are significant exceptions. Forgiveness is possible only because God makes it so, and that becomes strikingly clear in the account of the sin of the golden calf in Exod 32–34. The people deserve to die because of their apostasy, and they never repent. Moses intercedes for them, but finally it is only the character of God that makes forgiveness possible (Exod 33:19; 34:6–7).

The way of "life" is possible only because God has chosen it for us and continues to desire it for us, no matter what we have done. But the OT writers knew we have the power to reject it—the evidence for that is overwhelming—and they believed God has also given us the ability to recognize what is wrong, to desire to do better, and to choose obedience. All this they denoted by *shub*. Translators can use "repent" for *shub* when it is not followed by a prepositional phrase, for example, "Zion shall be redeemed by justice, and those in her who repent, by righteousness" (Isa 1:27). In English, one cannot "repent from" or "repent to," however, so "turn" and "return" are often used. Negatively, repenting means turning from one's evil (or wicked) ways or from sin (e.g., 1 Kgs 8:35; 13:33; 2 Chr 7:14), or simply from one's "ways" (Ezek 18:23). Positively, it means turning or returning to the Lord (e.g., Neh 1:9; Ps 51:13; Isa 55:7). The turning can be mutual, in the later prophets: "Return to me, says the LORD of hosts, and I will return to you, says the LORD of hosts" (Zech 1:3; Mal 3:7).

Since Israelites believed their God desired good for them, misfortune told them they must be on the wrong way, so much that is said about repentance in the OT is connected with national disasters: "You have struck them, but they felt no anguish; you have consumed them, but they refused to take correction. They have made their faces harder than rock; they have refused to turn back [*shub*]" (Jer 5:3). "Come, let us return [*shub*] to the LORD; for it is he who has torn, and he will heal us; he has struck down, and he will bind us up" (Hos 6:1; cf. Ps 78:34; 1 Sam 7:3–4; Amos 4:6–11; Zech 1:6). The book of Joel provides evidence that times of national repentance were called for, by prophets and priests, involving fasting and other outward signs of mourning (Joel 2:12–17; cf. Isa 63:7–64:12). The message of hope associated with those appeals for divine help came from God's own self-description in Exod 34:6–7: "Return to the LORD, your God, for he is gracious and merciful, slow to anger, and abounding in steadfast love, and relents from punishing" (Joel 2:13).

Outward signs of repentance may be misleading, however, representing only regret or remorse and not a true intent to change. So the call to repent is in Joel and elsewhere qualified by "with all your heart" (2:12; and v. 13: "rend your hearts and not your clothing"; cf. Deut 30:10; 1 Sam 7:3; 1 Kgs 8:48; Jer 24:7). Although these references to repentance are often plural, referring to the nation as a guilty party, of course it is only individuals who have hearts and can actually choose to turn, so the singular will be used as well when referring to the plight of Israel. Ezekiel's emphasis was strongly individual, since he wrote in the Babylonian exile, when there was no more nation. He responded to the cynicism of exiles who claimed they were being punished only for the sins of their ancestors, so they called God unjust (Ezek 18:1–2, 25). His answer began with an overly individualistic claim that one suffers only for one's own sins, but the point of the chapter is that the future is open for everyone, and that God passionately desires them to acknowledge their sinfulness, that they may be forgiven, and live. "Get yourselves a new heart and a new spirit!" Ezekiel says here; it is what they need (18:31). But he knew that true change was not in fact humanly possible apart from divine intervention, so later he promised that the new heart and spirit would be a divine gift (36:26; cf. Jer 24:7; 31:31–34). Ezekiel then seems to speak of repentance (using his own language, without *shub*) as the result of, rather than the prerequisite for forgiveness (36:31; 16:61–63).

Ritual played a role in assuring Israelites that their sins could be forgiven, but repentance was understood to be necessary before sacrifice could be effective. Note Lev 5:5: "When you realize your guilt in any of these, you shall confess the sin that you have committed." After the destruction of the second temple in A.D. 70, the rabbis focused on repentance, which was sufficient even without sacrifice, as the way to forgiveness provided by God. They referred to texts such as 1 Sam 15:22, "to obey is better than sacrifice," but they were building on emphases that already had appeared in the intertestamental literature (e.g., Tobit 13:6; Wis 11:23; Sir 4:26; 5:7; 17:24–26; Pr Man 7, 13; in the Qumran documents: 1QH 2.9; 6.6; 14.24; 1QS 10.20).

Older translations used "repent" for the Niphal of *naham*, with God as the subject, thus introducing the unnecessary question of God's repentance. "Repent" in English always carries the connotation of having done something wrong, and *naham* is never used that way with God as subject. It is appropriately translated by NRSV, in passages such as Exod 32:14; Jer 26:13; Joel 2:13; Amos 7:3, 6; and Jonah 3:9–10 as "change his mind," or "relent." It almost always refers to God's willingness to change his original intent to punish, and is thus an aspect of the grace of God.

Repentance in the New Testament. The OT's use of "turn" to signify repentance is preserved in the NT's occasional use of *strepho* and *epistrepho* in that sense. The acceptance of Jesus Christ as savior is several times described this way in Acts; for example, "The hand of the Lord was with them, and a great number became believers and turned to the Lord" (Acts 11:21; cf. 9:35; 15:19; 26:20). That turning away from wrong, hence repentance, was involved is indicated by "from these worthless things" (Acts 14:15), "from the power of Satan" (Acts 26:18), and "from idols" (1 Thess 1:9).

More often, *metanoeo*, "repent," and *metanoia*, "repentance," are used. The Synoptic Gospels indicate that "repent" was a key word in the messages of both John the Baptist and Jesus. They spoke not of conversion to a new belief, as in Acts, but of the need for their fellow Jews to return to faithful obedience to the will of God, as the prophets had spoken to Israel (e.g., Matt 3:2, 8, 11; 4:17 and par.; Luke 5:32). John made it clear that repentance had to be more than remorse; it required a changed life (Luke 3:10–14). Both he and Jesus proclaimed messages filled with a new urgency, since they were convinced the kingdom of God was at hand, and citizenship in the kingdom required repentance (e.g., Luke 13:3, 5). Luke summarized the gospel that was to be preached after Jesus' ascension in this way: "repentance and forgiveness of sins is to be proclaimed in his name to all nations, beginning from Jerusalem" (Luke 24:47).

The Gospel according to John and the letters of John say nothing of repentance but focus instead on believing (e.g., John 3:3–19; 5:22–30). Paul mentions repentance a few times (Rom 2:4; 2 Cor 7:9–10; 12:21), but as a human responsibility normally thought to precede forgiveness, it did not fit well with his emphasis that one cannot be saved by works (cf. Rom 5:6–11). In the life of the early church, believing in the gospel, on the part of converts, typically led to repentance (which must have been public) and baptism for the forgiveness of sins (Acts 2:28; 19:1–7). The fact that Christians continued to sin, in spite of the new life they had received, made it evident that repentance would be a necessary part of the Christian life (e.g., 2 Cor 7:9–10; 12:21; 2 Tim 2:25; 2 Pet 3:9; Rev 2:5, 16; 3:3, 19). The author of Hebrews judged full-fledged apostasy, however, to be beyond the power of repentance to be redeemed (Heb 6:1–8).

The balance between human responsibility and divine grace, found already in the OT, is maintained in the NT. Decision is called for, as if people really have the power to change: "Repent therefore, and turn to God so that your sins may be wiped out" (Acts 3:19; cf. 8:22; 17:30; 26:20). Forgiveness, and thus true change, is possible only because it is the work of God, however: "Then God has given even to the Gentiles the repentance that leads to life" (Acts 11:18; cf. 3:26; 5:31). "Do you not realize that God's kindness is meant to lead you to repentance?" (Rom 2:4).

J. D. Choi, *Jesus' Teachings on Repentance* (Binghamton, NY: Global Publishing, 2000); W. L. Holladay, *The Root* shubh *in the Old Testament* (Leiden: Brill, 1958).

DONALD E. GOWAN

Reprove   *see* **Correct**

Rescue   *see* **Save**

Rest   "Rest," occurring 364 times in NRSV and translating more than forty Hebrew and Greek words, often connotes cessation from something or enjoyment of peace and quiet, either in spirit or place. Primary Hebrew words are: nominal, *menuhah* (fifteen times) and verbal, *nuah* (ca. fifty times). Numerous uses denote remnant or remainder (Hebrew *she'ar*; Greek *loipos*; 2 Chr 9:29; Rev 2:24). Most important theologically is **Sabbath** rest (*shabbathon*, nine verbal uses), with Gen 2:2 as paradigmatic, "God rested on the seventh day." For this reason humans are commanded to rest on the seventh day (Exod 16:30; 20:11; 23:12; Lev 25:5). The OT practices of seventh-year sabbatical and fiftieth-year jubilee extend this Sabbath rest. All these dimensions of rest are intended to *re-create* one physically and spiritually, and thus bring enjoyment of God's gift of *shalom* (see **peace**). Similarly, "rest" may be used to denote refreshment given by the Lord (Gen 18:4) or bestowal of blessing (1 Cor 16:18; 2 Cor 7:13; Phlm 20).

Rest also denotes cessation from war: rest from enemies and freedom to enjoy the land promised to Abraham and descendants (Deut 12:10; 25:19; Josh 1:13; 11:23; 21:44; 2 Sam 7:11; 1 Chr 22:18).

Using "rest" in ways related to Sabbath and peaceful living, Jesus welcomes the weary and heavy laden, promising rest (Matt 11:29), a qualitative feature of salvation. Rest is also a gift promised to those who find Wisdom, granted by the Lord (Sir 6:28; 51:27).

Hebrews 3:7–4:11 expounds the promised rest granted to believers through the coming of Jesus Christ, to those who "today...hear his voice" (3:15; 4:3). *Believers* are exhorted to "make every effort to enter that rest, so that no one may fall through . . . disobedience" (4:11). But Hebrews also anticipates a rest to come, specified as reaching the divinely promised consummation of life with God in "the heavenly Jerusalem" (Heb 12:22), a heavenly country (11:16), and the city "whose architect and builder is God" (11:10). In Revelation, rest is promised by the Spirit as the final reward for faithfulness to the end: "they will rest from their labors, for their deeds follow them" (Rev 14:13).

Rest is sometimes a synonym for trust, as in Ps 37:7 (NRSV, "be still") and, negatively, Isa 31:1 (NRSV, of those who "do not look to the Holy One of Israel"). The poetic parallel is prominent in the great Isaiah text: "In returning and rest you shall be saved; in quietness and in trust shall be your strength" (30:15). Failure to rest in this sense is reason for denial of God's promised rest (safety) in the land and through salvation in Christ (Ps 95:11; Heb 3:11).

Rest may also connote *relief* from difficult experiences, as in 2 Thess 1:7 (Greek, *anesin*; RSV, "rest"; NRSV, "relief"; cf. 2 Cor 2:13; 7:5). "Resting place" designates one's burial place or final abode (Gen 8:9; Ruth 3:1). "Rest" in "my heart is glad, my soul rejoices, and my body rests secure" (Ps 16:9) connotes health and safety from Sheol (v. 10) and enjoyment of presence with God forevermore (v. 11). Used metaphorically, this notion of rest may designate the Lord's resting in Zion (1 Chr 28:2; Ps 132:8–14; Isa 66:1). Similarly "resting upon" is used for God's spirit coming upon the elders of Israel (Num 11:25f.), abiding with the Messiah (Isa 11:2), or resting upon the believers when reviled for the name of Christ (1 Pet 4:14).

Marva Dawn, *Keeping the Sabbath Wholly: Ceasing, Resting, Embracing, Feasting* (Grand Rapids: Eerdmans, 1989).
WILLARD M. SWARTLEY

Restore In general, this English word expresses or describes a change of a state of being that by extension also includes a change in one's health or well-being. In the NRSV "restore" is one of the many ways the Hebrew word *shub* is translated. The basic meaning of this Hebrew word is to turn back or return. This term is commonly used to describe apostasy or turning away from God (Num 14:43) as well as a penitential return to God (Hos 6:1). The Hiphil or causative form of the Hebrew verb is correctly rendered in English as "restore." Some person, human or other than human, causes or brings about a return to a former good or preferable state.

Since God is viewed as the one ultimately responsible for the fate of human beings, the phrase "restore the fortunes" occurs very frequently (Hos 6:11; Joel 3:1; Amos 9:14; etc.). God even promised to restore the fortunes of non-Israelites, for example, Moabites (Jer 48:47); Ammonites (Jer 49:6); Sodomites and Samaritans (Ezek 16:53)! As Job reflected: "The LORD gave, and the LORD has taken away; blessed be the name of the LORD" (Job 1:21). God restored the kingdom to Manasseh after first sending him into exile (2 Chr 33:13), and God restored the exiles to their land (Jer 42:12) with the accompanying blessings (Jer 29:14; 30:3, 18; 31:23; 32:44; 33:7, 11, 26).

Since family is one of the two central social institutions in the ancient world, family integrity is a cherished value. Abimelech restores Abraham's wife to him, and Abraham's family is reconstituted (Gen 20:7, 14). Knowing how precious Joseph is to his father, Jacob, Joseph's brother Reuben schemes to spare his life and restore Joseph to Jacob (Gen 37:22). Thieves must restore what they have stolen (Lev 6:4; 2 Sam 12:6) and a righteous person will be recognized by his willingness to do precisely that (1 Sam 12:3).

Failed health or loss of life is an undesirable change of state. God withers the hand of Jeroboam that threatens a man of God but restores it at that man's intercession (1 Kgs 13:6). God, Israel's healer

(Exod 15:26), restores health and heals wounds (Jer 30:17). God also restores the dead to life (2 Kgs 8:1, 5). Whether concerning an individual or the nation, a repeated prayer in the Bible is "Restore us, O God!" (Ps 51:12; 80:3, 7, 19; Lam 5:21). Of the 120 occurrences of "restore" in the NRSV, just 16 of those appear in the New Testament. Half of these translate the Greek word *apokathistemi*, whose essential meaning is to restore to a former good or preferable state. Jesus announced that Elijah will accomplish this restoration when he returns (Matt 17:11 and par. Mark 9:12). Prior to Jesus' returning to his Father, the disciples asked Jesus if the kingdom would soon be restored to Israel (Acts 1:6). Sometimes the word has a very simple meaning of returning to loved friends (Heb 13:19). Restoring sight (Mark 8:25) and a hand to healthy usefulness (Mark 3:5 and par. Matt 12:13 and Luke 6:10) are key elements in Jesus' healing ministry, "restoring" meaning to life.

In two instances the NRSV reports "restore (saltiness)" when the Greek literally says something else. Luke asks, "How can it [salt] be seasoned?" (Luke 14:34) while Matthew asks, "How can the salt be salted?" (Matt 5:13). Salt never loses its saltiness, but it does lose its ability to sustain a fire in the earth oven that burns dung for fuel (1 Kgs 14:10). "Restore" is correct in these passages so long as the scenario of fire is kept in mind.

Finally, the NRSV translates two other Greek words by restore: *katarizo*, to "arrange for something to happen" (Gal 6:1; 1 Thess 3:10; 1 Pet 5:10); and *anakainizo*, to "renew" (Heb 6:4–6).

John J. Pilch, "Salt of the Earth," in *The Cultural Dictionary of the Bible* (Collegeville, Minn.: Liturgical Press, 1999), 4–5.

JOHN J. PILCH

Resurrection, Raise Up The Greco-Roman world accepted "the *immortality* of the soul" and "the transmigration of souls," but never "the rising" or "resurrection of the dead." There may be occasional stories in various Greek and Roman writings about somebody miraculously restoring to life again someone who had died, but these incidents were never used in support of a doctrine of resurrection.

In the religion of Israel, however, based on convictions regarding the justice of God and the eternality of his covenant, there was a consciousness among the spiritually sensitive regarding God's continued concern for the dead—and hopes were expressed for his "raising up" the nation Israel and people generally at the eschatological end of history. These convictions and hopes were developed in many ways in Second Temple Judaism, with belief in a general resurrection becoming firmly entrenched during the latter part of this period—particularly within Pharisaism and early rabbinic theology. The writers of the NT also built on these convictions and hopes. The new and crucial fact for the earliest Christians, however, was resurrection as evidence that Jesus of Nazareth was "the Christ" (i.e., Messiah), for God had vindicated him and his ministry by raising him from the dead (Acts 2:22–36). So the resurrection—both that of Jesus and that of people in the eschatological future—became the cornerstone of Christian hope and proclamation (cf. 1 Cor 15:12–19).

Our English word "resurrection" translates the Greek noun *anastasis*—with the prefix *ana*, which may mean "up" or "again," connected to the noun *stasis*, which here means "existence," "continuance," or "standing," signifying either a rising *up* of someone who has been in a reclining position or a coming to life *again* of someone who has died. In its basic sense "resurrection" denotes restoration to "existence" or "life" after a period of decline, oppression, or obscurity (as with the nation or a group of people) or after an interval in the realm of the dead (as with a person or people). Our English expression "raise up" translates the Hebrew verb *qum* and the Greek verbs *anistemi* and *egeiro*. The noun *anastasis* (or *exanastasis*) and the verbs *anistemi* and *egeiro* appear throughout the NT for both the resurrection of Christ and the resurrection of people in the eschatological future.

On being "raised up" in the Old Testament. There are stories in the OT of people being brought back to life after their deaths (see 1 Kgs 17:17–24; 2 Kgs 4:18–37; 13:20–21). But these are not, strictly speaking, resurrection accounts, but rather miracle stories about resuscitation, revivification, or reanimation. For these people were restored to their former lives, not to a new life or to the life of the new eschatological order, and so (evidently) they had to die again. There are also stories of certain righteous individuals who were taken up by God into heaven without (apparently) dying (cf. Gen 5:22–24; 2 Kgs 2:1–12). But again, these are not resurrection accounts, but stories of translation into God's presence without dying.

The imagery of being "raised up" by God is used primarily in the OT for the restoration of the nation in the eschatological future. In Isa 44:21–26, for example, God is portrayed as declaring that he has not forgotten the nation Israel, and, in particular, as saying of Jerusalem, "It shall be inhabited," and of the cities of Judah, "They shall be rebuilt, and I will raise up their ruins" (v. 26). In Isa 49:6 the eschatological Servant's mission will include the task "to raise up the tribes of Jacob and to restore the survivors of Israel." In Hos 6:2 there is the prophet's assurance to his people: "After two days he will revive us; on the third day he will raise us up, that we may live before him." In Amos 9:11, included within God's promises regarding the nation's eschatological future, are these words: "On that day I will raise up the booth of David that is fallen, and repair its breaches, and raise up its ruins, and rebuild it as in the days of old." And throughout the prophecy of Ezekiel such a "raising up" of the nation is graphically portrayed by various dramatic actions and symbolic figures—particularly by the vision of the valley of dry bones in chapter 37 and the visions of restoration in chapters 40–48.

Hope based on divine justice and God's covenant. Among the righteous, however, there was also hope that God would somehow sustain relations with his people even after their deaths. It was a hope based on their convictions about divine justice and the fulfillment of God's covenant. Thus Job could declare: "I know that my Redeemer lives, and that at the last he will stand upon the earth; and after my skin has been thus destroyed, then in my flesh I shall see God" (Job 19:25). David exclaimed: "My heart is glad, and my soul rejoices; my body also rests secure. For you do not give me up to Sheol, or let your faithful one see the Pit" (Ps 16:9–10).

Likewise the Korahites are credited with proclaiming: "God will ransom my soul from the power of Sheol, for he will receive me" (Ps 49:15). And in what Gerhard von Rad has called a "remarkably plain expression" and "purist formulation" of the conviction that "fellowship initiated by God cannot be destroyed" (*TDNT* 2:848), Asaph's words of praise to God are framed as follows: "I am continually with you; you hold my right hand. You guide me with your counsel, and afterward you will receive me with honor. Whom have I in heaven but you? And there is nothing on earth that I desire other than you. My flesh and my heart may fail, but God is the strength of my heart and my portion forever" (Ps 73:23–26).

Among the later prophets, such individualist convictions about God's justice and the eternality of his covenant were developed to apply to the life of the nation, as in the words of Isaiah: "Your dead shall live, their corpses shall rise. O dwellers in the dust, awake and sing for joy! For your dew is a radiant dew, and the earth will give birth to those long dead" (Isa 26:19; cf. Ezek 37:1–14; Hos 6:1–2). Furthermore, these basic convictions began to be developed in ways that not only had national but also universal significance, as in Daniel's prophecy: "At that time Michael, the great prince, the protector of your people shall arise. There shall be a time of anguish, such as has never occurred since nations first came into existence. But at that time your people shall be delivered, everyone who is found written in the book. Many of those who sleep in the dust of the earth shall awake, some to everlasting life, and some to shame and everlasting contempt" (12:1–2).

Developing expectations within Second Temple Judaism. Expectations regarding the future state of the dead were in flux during the period of Second Temple Judaism (ca. 200 B.C.–A.D. 120). Immortality doctrines were rampant, with some clothed in resurrection language, others in astral imagery, others in phraseology that paralleled ideas about reincarnation and the transmigration of souls, and still others in distinctly Grecian anthropological forms of expression. Yet hopes for "the resurrection of the dead" also came more and more into prominence during this time.

First Enoch 22:1–14, for example, which is the major pre-Maccabean passage on Sheol, contains allusions to "the spirits/souls of the righteous," who will experience a resurrection (v. 9), and to "sinners," who lived prosperously and without punishment during their lives, being raised so as to receive the judgment that they escaped in life (vv. 10–11). It is explicitly said, however, that thoroughly wicked and despicable people (i.e., "sinners and perfect criminals") will not rise (v. 13). And while the resurrection of "the righteous" in verse 9 may be seen in purely spiritual terms and that of "sinners" in verses 10–11 is described as a "retribution of their spirits," the fact that elsewhere in "The Book of the Watchers" (*1 En.* 6–36) the righteous are said to be destined to eat of the tree of life (25:4–6) and to enjoy abundant life in the messianic kingdom on a purified earth (10:16–22), with Jerusalem and the temple as its center (25:5), suggests that some type of physical resurrection is in view.

Likewise the dream visions of *1 En.* 83–90, which probably were composed sometime about 165–161 B.C., come to a climax in 90:28–42 in a vision of all those sheep [i.e., the righteous within Israel] that have been destroyed and dispersed, and all the beasts of the field and the birds of the sky, being "gathered together" at the end of history into a "new house" (v. 33)—with, then, the birth of "a snow-white cow" and all the righteous "transformed" into "snow-white cows" (vv. 37–38). The vision suggests a resurrection and gathering of righteous Jews into an earthly messianic kingdom, with some type of transformation of the righteous then taking place. And it implies that Gentiles who have survived the judgment will be brought in and transformed as well (see 89:10–27, 42–43, 49, 55–58, 65–68; 90:2–19). But though the vision of 90:28–42 is powerful in its imagery and dramatic in its hope, its content is exceedingly difficult to unpack.

Explicit statements regarding the resurrection of the dead, however, are to be found in 2 Maccabees, which was probably written in the last decade of the second century B.C. Such statements appear particularly in 7:1–41 (the martyrdom of the seven brothers and their mother), 12:43–45 (the action of Judas Maccabeus on behalf of certain of his fallen soldiers, which he did "bearing in mind the resurrection"), and 14:37–46 (the martyrdom of Razis, an elder and esteemed patriot of Jerusalem). And a text from cave 4 of Qumran on "The Messiah of Heaven and Earth," which is catalogued as *4Q521*, also includes a reference to belief in the resurrection of the dead among the Dead Sea covenanters: "then he [the Messiah] will heal the sick, resurrect the dead."

Resurrection statements are to be found, as well, in the Parables of Enoch, or *1 En.* 37–71, which most scholars view today as a Jewish composition of the middle or late first century A.D. For example, *1 En.* 51:1–5 begins: "In those days, the earth will give back all that has been entrusted to it, and Sheol will return all the deposits which she had received, and hell will give back all that which it owes"; while 61:5 speaks of "those who have been destroyed in the desert, those who have been devoured by the wild beasts, and those who have been eaten by the fish of the sea" as those who will "all return and find hope in the day of the Elect One—for there is no one who perishes before the Lord of Spirits, and no one who should perish." And 62:14–16 says of "the righteous and elect ones": "The Lord of the Spirits will abide over them; they shall eat and rest and rise with that Son of Man forever and ever. The righteous and elect ones shall rise from the earth and shall cease being of downcast face. They shall wear the garments of glory. These garments of yours shall become the garments of life from the Lord of the Spirits. Neither shall your garments wear out, nor your glory come to an end before the Lord of the Spirits."

Likewise in 2 Esdras, which was written about A.D. 100, the ultimate hope of the author is in God's resurrection of the dead, as set out in 7:32–38: "The earth will give up those who are asleep in it, . . . and the chambers [i.e., Sheol/Hades] shall give up the souls that have been committed to them. The Most High shall be revealed on the seat of judgment" and judgment of both the righteous and the wicked will take place; and "the nations that have been raised from the dead" will be similarly judged. Thus the author's final words to the people in 14:35: "After death the judgment will come, when we shall live again; and then the names of the righteous shall become manifest, and the deeds of the ungodly shall be disclosed."

In 2 Baruch, written during the first or second decade of the second century A.D., there is a much more focused depiction of the resurrection of the dead than found in 2 Esdras, particularly with respect to the nature of the resurrection body. For while in the earlier portions of 2 Baruch there are numerous statements of a somewhat general nature regarding the final fate of both the righteous and the wicked, with these statements often including allusions to the resurrection of the dead (e.g., 14:12–13; 30:1–4 of the righteous; 30:5; 36:11 of the wicked), in 50:1–51:16 a resurrection doctrine is spelled out in quite explicit detail in answer to the question that is posed to God in 49:1–3: "In what shape will the living live in your day? Or how will remain their splendor which will be after that? Will they, perhaps, take again this present form, and will they put on the chained members which are in evil and by which evils are accomplished? Or will you perhaps change these things which have been in the world, as also the world itself?" So in 50:1–4 the resurrection of dead persons is set forth in terms of their revivification or reanimation, as seen earlier in 2 Macc 7:1–41. The purpose of this "not changing anything in their form" is stated as being so as "to show those who live that the dead are living again, and that those who went away have come back" (v. 3)—in other words, so that the living and the dead might be able to recognize one another (v. 4). Yet in 51:1–16 there is also an emphasis on the transformation of both the righteous and the wicked dead, with the righteous taking on "the splendor of angels" and becoming "equal to the stars" (vv. 5, 10) and the wicked changed into "horrible shapes" (v. 5). The reason given for these transformations is so that resurrected bodies might be suited to their places of final destination: the righteous "so that they may acquire and receive the undying world which is promised to them" (v. 3) and the wicked so that they will "waste away even more" (v. 5).

And Book 4 of the Sibylline Oracles— whose Jewish authorship is fairly well established, whose provenance is to be located in Syria or Palestine, and whose date is usually assigned to the latter part of the first century A.D.—presupposes a similar doctrine of the resurrection of the dead as found in 2 Esdras 7:32–38 and 2 Bar. 50:1–51:16. This is most clearly evidenced in lines 175–91, with the following statements and lines being most significant for our purposes here: "God himself will again fashion the bones and ashes of men, and he will raise up mortals again as they were before" . . . (lines 181–82). "But as many as are pious, they will live on earth again, when God gives spirit and life and favor to these pious ones. Then they will all see themselves beholding the delightful and pleasant light of the sun. O most blessed, whatever man will live to that time" (lines 187–91).

The resurrection of Jesus. While in Judaism it was understood that both the nation corporately and righteous people individually would suffer—with hope that both the nation and the dead would somehow be "raised up" or "resurrected" in the eschatological future—there was hardly any expectation that the messiah would suffer death or need to be resurrected from the dead. Only in 2 Esdras 7:28–32, written sometime about A.D. 100, is there any reference in Second Temple Jewish writings to the death of the messiah or any suggestion of his resurrection. Jewish hopes for the future were expressed, at least in the great majority of cases, without any thought of the messiah's death and resurrection.

But Jesus is portrayed in all four canonical Gospels as repeatedly speaking about both his coming death at Jerusalem and his resurrection three days afterwards (Mark 8:31 and par.; 9:31 and par.; 10:33–34 and par.; cf. Mark 9:9 and par. Matt 17:9; Mark 14:58 and par. Matt 26:61 and John 2:19–22; Mark 15:29 and par. Matt 27:40; see also Matt 12:40; see *Jonah*). And all four evangelists focus on Jesus' death and resurrection as being the most crucial and significant features of his ministry—not only in the concluding chapters of their respective Gospels, but also by way of anticipation in all that they set out earlier. The resurrection of Jesus is, in fact, the high point in the Christology of the four NT Gospels. For God's resurrection of Jesus from the dead vindicates all that Jesus believed, said, and did, and so it is the definitive answer to the cross.

The resurrection of Jesus, which was an intrinsically eschatological event, was the impetus for the christological thinking of the early church and the content of much of its preaching. But it is also the proper beginning for any distinctly Christian eschatology and the foreshadowing of the coming resurrection of the dead. Its message is that the eschatological glory that Jesus received through resurrection and ascension will be shared by believers in Jesus as well—that the future belongs to those who commit themselves to Jesus, death notwithstanding.

The salvation that God accomplished through the ministry of Jesus—that is, the establishment of the kingdom in human hearts and in the world—has been accomplished by the cross. Its full experience, however, is promised and assured by God's resurrection of Jesus from the dead. For that reason the resurrection of Jesus produced in the disciples—and should produce in believers—a distinct note of great joy (Matt 28:8; Luke 24:52).

The resurrection of the dead in the New Testament. As in the OT, there are also stories in the NT of people being brought back to life after death (cf. Mark 5:35–43; John 11:30–44; Acts 9:36–42; as well as the amazing report in Matt 27:52–53). But as with the similar OT instances, these are not, strictly speaking, resurrection accounts but miracle stories about the resuscitation, revivification, or reanimation of people who were restored to their former lives and had (evidently) to die again. The proclamation of Jesus' resurrection, however, has to do with the defeat of death and the inauguration of the Messianic Age—while the promise of a future general resurrection has to do with the completion of the salvation that God effected through the redemptive work of Jesus.

God's resurrection of Jesus, together with the implications of this momentous event for the eschatological resurrection of the dead, is the central affirmation of the Christian message throughout the Acts of the Apostles. The mandate given by Jesus to his followers was to be "my witnesses" (1:8), and that mandate is further explicated in that first chapter as being "witnesses to his resurrection" (1:22). The preaching of Peter in chapters 2–3 focuses on God having raised Jesus from the dead, to which events the apostles were commissioned the accredited "witnesses" (2:24, 32; 3:15, 26). The accounts of the trials of Peter and John before the Jerusalem authorities in chap. 4–5 begin with the council's accusation that the apostles were "proclaiming that in Jesus there is the resurrection of the dead" (4:2) and end with the apostolic statement: "The God of our ancestors raised up Jesus, whom you had killed by hanging him on a tree. . . . And we are witnesses to these things" (5:30–32). Paul's own conversion resulted from being confronted by the resurrected, ascended, and heavenly Jesus (9:3–5). Peter's preaching to the Roman centurion Cornelius had as its high point the proclamation that "God raised him [Jesus] on the third day and allowed him to appear, not to all the people but to us who were chosen by God as witnesses" (10:40–41). Paul's preaching in the synagogue at Antioch of Pisidia had as its major content the resurrection of Jesus from the dead (13:32–37), and his message to the Athenians is summarized as "good news about Jesus and the resurrection" (17:18). Furthermore, Paul in his defenses before Jewish and Roman courts in chapters 22–26 is presented as declaring that the central issue for which he was being tried was "the hope of the resurrection of the dead" (23:6).

The importance of the resurrection in Acts is rivaled only by the significance of the death of the Messiah within the divine purpose, alongside which it often appears. The author of Acts wants his readers always to keep in view the nexus between Jesus' death and Jesus' resurrection. But while always emphasizing the importance of the death of Christ in the divine program of redemption, Luke in writing Acts must also be seen to have been particularly concerned to present the apostolic response to Jesus' resurrection and its redemptive implications—a concern not just with giving a *narrative about* the apostle's witness to Jesus as having been resurrected from the dead by God, but also with itself presenting *a witness to* that resurrection and its sig-

nificance for the realization of God's redemptive purposes.

Three types of resurrection life can be distinguished in Paul's letters. First, there is the past bodily resurrection of Christ *from* the grave *to* immortality: "We know that Christ, being raised from the dead, will never die again" (Rom 6:9). Second, there is the present spiritual resurrection of believers with Christ, which is *from* slavery to sin *to* newness of life: "When you were buried with him in baptism, you were also raised with him," in order that you might "no longer be enslaved to sin" but live a new life (Col 2:12; Rom 6:4, 6, 13, 17). Third, there is the future bodily resurrection of believers *from* the dead *to* immortality: "The dead will be raised imperishable" (1 Cor 15:52). Resurrection signifies the raising of persons from the dead to a new and permanent life in the presence of God. Such a definition applies first of all to the resurrection of Christ. But it also applies to both the present spiritual resurrection and the future bodily resurrection of believers.

Resurrection in the NT is never spoken of as a present process, but always as a past event with significant future implications—that is, present tense verbs are never found in the NT with respect to resurrection, but always aorist passive, perfect passive, or future passive verbs. Thus, when speaking about the resurrection of Christ, Paul says in 1 Cor 15 that he "has been raised from the dead, the first fruits of those who have died" (v. 20, using the perfect passive tense for Christ's resurrection a total of seven times in that chapter). When speaking about the spiritual resurrection of believers with Christ, he says: "When you were buried with him [Christ Jesus] in baptism, you were also raised with him through faith in the power of God, who raised him from the dead" (Col 2:12; cf. Rom 6:4, 13, using the aorist passive tense). And when speaking about the future resurrection of believers from the dead, he says, "the dead will be raised imperishable, and we will be changed" (1 Cor 15:52, using the future tense).

In the final analysis, resurrection has to do with three matters. First, resurrection in its most elementary sense denotes *resuscitation, revivification,* or *reanimation.* That is how it appears in most of the writings of Second Temple Judaism, how it is used in many NT passages (see, e.g., Mark 5:41–42; John 5:28–29; Heb 11:35; Rev 20:5), and what is at least minimally involved in all of Paul's statements regarding bodily resurrection (see 1 Cor 15, passim). Second, resurrection has to do with *transformation,* since "flesh and blood cannot inherit the kingdom of God" (1 Cor 15:50). It is a transformation or change that results in immortality and is coincident with resurrection—in fact, it is part of the resurrection event itself. Third, and most important, true resurrection involves *exaltation.* This is what took place with respect to Jesus but will also take place with respect to believers in Christ. For there will be the resurrection of believers from the dead (resuscitation) in newness of life (transformation) into the presence of Christ (exaltation).

The logic of the NT's resurrection message leads to viewing "the resurrection of the dead" as a resurrection of believers in Christ, both in their present and in their future eschatological lives (John 6:39–40, 44, 54; Rom 8:11; 1 Cor 15:52). Yet there is also an insistence throughout the NT of a double resurrection—that is, a "first resurrection" for "those who have done good, to the resurrection of life," and a further resurrection before the "great white throne" of God "for those who have done evil, to the resurrection of condemnation" (John 5:28–29; 2 Cor 5:10; Rev 20:4–6, 11–15). Or in the words of Dan 12:2, which seems to have been the basic biblical text on which all apocalyptic writers, whether Jewish or Christian, based their teachings: "Many of those who sleep in the dust of the earth shall awake, some to everlasting life, and some to shame and everlasting contempt."

Murray J. Harris, *Raised Immortal: Resurrection and Immortality in the New Testament* (London: Marshall, Morgan & Scott, 1983; Grand Rapids: Eerdmans, 1985); Richard N. Longenecker, ed., *Life in the Face of Death: The Resurrection Message of the New Testament* (Grand Rapids: Eerdmans, 1998); Robert Martin-Achard, *From Death to Life: A Study of the Development of the Doctrine of the Resurrection in the Old Testament,* trans. J. P. Smith (Edinburgh and London: Oliver & Boyd, 1960); George W. E. Nickelsburg Jr., *Resurrection, Immortality, and Eternal Life in Intertestamental Judaism* (Cambridge: Harvard University Press, 1972; London: Oxford University Press, 1992); Pheme Perkins, *Resurrection: New Testament Witness and Contemporary Reflection* (Garden City, N.Y.: Doubleday, 1984).

RICHARD N. LONGENECKER

Return   *see* **Repent**

Reveal, Revelation, Dream The OT verb *galah,* "to uncover, open," has the theological connotation of divine revelation or disclosure in only one-sixth of its occurrences (28 of 180). Like the NT verb *apokalypto, galah* signifies the disclosure of that which is hidden from human perception. In ordinary usage, concealment is valued, while exposure (*galah*) is discouraged. One who discloses secrets is scorned (Prov 11:13; 20:19; 25:9); even a fugitive's whereabouts ought not to be disclosed (Isa 16:3). The use of *galah* in the expression "uncover nakedness" in Lev 18 and 20 reflects an analogous concern *not* to expose oneself outside of properly defined sexual relationships (cf. also Exod 20:26; Ezek 16; 23; Isa 47:2, 3). In all of these instances, the verb signifies the disclosure of that which is ordinarily concealed, and a somewhat pejorative connotation is attached to the idea of uncovering or revealing these secret things. In theological usage, the pejorative connotation disappears; however, the verb continues to signify the disclosure of secret or hidden things. A distinction that is often made in systematic theology is useful here: because the disclosure involves things that are ordinarily hidden from view, *galah* is concerned with special, not natural, revelation.

There is no sense in which human beings can infer divine knowledge on the basis of their own perceptions.

In some forms of the verb, *galah* implies human transformation, since revelation involves opening (*galah*) the eyes or ears of someone so that the divine disclosure can be understood (Num 22:31; 1 Sam 9:15; cf. nontheological usage in 1 Sam 20:2, 12, 13; 22:8, 17). The verb is thus semantically comparable to other expressions for God's appearing, particularly the passive form of the verb "to see" (i.e., God was seen, or appeared); in fact, the two expressions are interchangeable in Gen 35:1, 7. The human reception of divine revelation requires divine assistance (i.e., opening ears or eyes; see *hear* and *see*), while its opposite involves human dullness, which God also imparts (see Isa 6:10). Revelation is itself salvific, since it implies divine presence and accessibility. The content of the revelation can be God (Gen 35:7), God's will as expressed in the law (Deut 29:29), or salvation itself (Ps 98:2; Isa 53:1; 56:1). In the NT, revelation continues to disclose that which is hidden from ordinary human perception. God's work has been kept secret from the beginning, but in Jesus, God's plan of salvation is being revealed. There is an already/not yet character to this revelation: Jesus reveals God to his followers, but creation still waits with eager longing for the full revelation of God's work.

The sparse number of occurrences of *galah* in its theological sense prevents any firm conclusions regarding its social and literary contexts. In some contexts, revelation confirms old loyalties or singles out particular individuals for significant roles. The use of the verb in ordinary situations suggests why this is so. Disclosures are confidences that are made to close, trusted allies (1 Sam 20:2, 12, 13; 1 Sam 22:8, 17). In theological contexts, at least in the early literature, revelation is comparable to calling or preferment, since God's self-disclosure is only to particular individuals, and not to the nation as a whole. God reveals himself to Jacob in a reaffirmation of the covenant (Gen 35:7). Divine self-disclosure also inaugurates priestly and royal dynasties (1 Sam 2:27; 3:21; 2 Sam 7:27). The term appears not to be significant in the prophetic literature. Although the pagan prophet Balaam uses the verb to describe his experience of revelation (Num 24:4, 16), it appears elsewhere only with Samuel (1 Sam 9:15). The programmatic statement about God's revelation to the prophets in Amos 3:7 is probably a Deuteronomistic gloss.

The frequent occurrence of *galah* in Job suggests that it was associated with the Wisdom tradition. Things that are revealed cannot be known through ordinary perception—the foundations of the deep or the gates of death (Job 12:22; 38:17; cf. 2 Sam 22:16 = Ps 18:15). Revelation also is concerned with things that human beings should be able to see and understand but do not. Job 33:12–16 describes God's use of visions and dreams to prick the conscience and lead to repentance, while Job 36:10, 15 suggests that God uses suffering and adversity to "open (*galah*) the eyes." The implication is that human beings remain perversely blind to the consequences of their own actions and require divine revelation in order to see them.

The association of *galah* with wisdom is also evident in Dan 2, where, as in Job, wisdom is divinely revealed knowledge. In Dan 2, Nebuchadnezzar's dream of a great statue discloses himself to himself: the source of his power, his place in human history, and his final downfall. The irony is that even this dream must be interpreted to him. His magicians and diviners admit that "no one on earth" can reveal his dream or its interpretation to him (Dan 2:10, 11), and Daniel concurs: only God in heaven can reveal these mysteries (2:22, 28). Daniel interprets the dream for Nebuchadnezzar so that he may understand the "thoughts of [his] mind" (2:30). In Daniel, then, the true meaning of human and earthly affairs can be understood only through divine revelation.

Wisdom influence may also be reflected in the few texts that use the verb in connection with the revelation of God's torah (Ps 119:18; Deut 29:29). The disclosure is by no means complete, since certain "secret things" remain beyond human reach. But the "revealed things" of the torah are a source of joy and life (Ps 119:18).

Like the verb *galah*, dreams appear to be less important in prophecy than in Wisdom contexts. God uses dreams to disclose information about present and future situations (Gen 20:3, 6; 31:10), and Joseph's ability to interpret dreams is often understood as a Wisdom motif (Gen 37; 41). A few texts do associate dreams with prophecy (Num 12:6; Joel 2:28); however, the Deuteronomistic tradition rejects dreams as one of many divinatory techniques that are prone to deception and lies (Deut 13:1–3; Jer 23:25, 28, 32).

In Second and Third Isaiah, the conception of the revelation of secret or hidden things remains a significant element; here, however, it begins to deepen into a theology of history. Although the suffering of the exiles has led them to conclude that God is either absent or impotent to do anything about their situation, Second Isaiah proclaims that God's salvation will soon be revealed (Isa 40:5; see also 56:1). There will no longer be any doubt about God's power to save Israel, because all nations will see God's glory. An essential part of the disclosure is that God has been present with them all along, in exactly that which had implied God's absence (Isa 53:1). This idea of divine power—hidden to the world but nevertheless steadily working toward the realization of God's purpose in history—becomes a prominent theme in the NT.

The Greek verb *apokalypto*, "uncover, reveal," is found in the Gospels, primarily Matthew and Luke, the Pauline and Pastoral letters, and the Revelation to John. Although the term is commonly used to designate the genre of apocalyptic literature, revelation is not restricted to apocalyptic but pervades the NT discussion of God's work of salvation through Christ Jesus. In some texts God is the source of the revelation (Matt 16:17), while in others Jesus is the means whereby God is made known (Matt 11:27). What has been hidden for long ages is now finally revealed in Christ (1 Cor 2:10; Eph 3:5). In many occurrences, the content of revelation is God's character (Rom 1:17–18) and God's gracious presence through the work of Jesus Christ (Matt 11:25–27 and par. Luke 10:21–22; 17:30). Even as the believers thank God for what has been revealed to them, they nevertheless await the full and final revelation at Christ's second coming (Rom 8:18–19; 1 Pet 1:5, 7, 13; 4:13; 5:1).

Because revelation continues to refer to the disclosure of a secret, it can function as election and preferment, as in the OT. The revelation of the kingdom has bypassed the wise and created a new community of God's elect (Matt 11:25; 1 Cor 2:10). In addition, Paul uses his own experience of the revelation of Christ to legitimate his calling as an apostle (Gal 1:16) and to justify his actions with respect to the Jerusalem leadership (Gal 2:2).

Although visions are a frequent characteristic of apocalyptic literature, dreams are of little significance in the NT outside of Matthew, where dreams foil human plans. Joseph is persuaded in a dream not to divorce Mary (Matt 1:20), and Herod's plan to kill Jesus is doubly thwarted, as the wise men are warned in a dream not to return to Herod (Matt 2:12) and an angel warns Joseph to flee to Egypt (2:13–15). Tragically, the dream of Pilate's wife does nothing to avert Jesus' death (Matt 27:19). Matthew's use of dreams is consistent with the concept of revelation in that they reveal that which is hidden from ordinary human perception.

Jean-Marie Husser, *Dreams and Dream Narratives in the Biblical World*, Biblical Seminar 63 (Sheffield: Sheffield Academic Press, 1999); H. Wheeler Robinson, *Inspiration and Revelation in the Old Testament* (Oxford: Clarendon Press, 1946).

MARGARET S. ODELL

Reward, Recompense Two closely related concepts, whose basic idea is that "one reaps what one sows." The words most frequently translated "reward" were *sakar* and *misthos* (Hebrew and Greek respectively for "wages"; cf. Prov 11:18 and Matt 5:46). The root *sakar* meant "hire," and two nouns derived from it meant "wages" or "reward for work well done." A glance at other words so translated is instructive. The Hebrew root *gamal* meant "deal fully or adequately with, benefit." Hence a worker earned his wages; a good deed reaped a reward. Figuratively speaking, a reward was the "fruit" of a laborer's work, so in places the Hebrew word *peri* ("fruit") is translated "reward" (e.g., Ps 58:11). Elsewhere (2 Sam 22:21; Ps 18:24) the verb *shub* ("return") seems to mean "recompense." In other words, what one did "returns" to reward a person. The root *pa'al* was used in poetry to mean "make" or "do." It was the equivalent of the more prosaic root *'asah*. NRSV translates noun forms of both as "wages" and the derivative *pe'ullah* (Isa 40:10; 61:8; 62:11) as "recompense." In the last of those examples (Isa 62:11), the word *sakar* (translated "reward") stands in parallelism as a synonym.

Old Testament. The OT spoke of rewards for proper ethical conduct. Two antithetical proverbs will illustrate this point. Proverbs 13:21 reads: "Misfortune pursues sinners, but prosperity rewards (*shallem*; cf. *shalom*: "peace, completeness") the righteous." This proverb seems to say that righteous people will profit in every way. A second verse, Prov 11:18, speaks more guardedly: "The wicked earn no real gain (*pa'al*, often translated "reward"), but those who sow in righteousness get a true reward (*seker*)." This second proverb distinguishes between trivial (material) and real (spiritual) gains or rewards, apparently aware that righteous people did not always prosper materially. Proverbs 11:17 acknowledges that sometimes the reward is strictly personal: "Those who are kind reward themselves."

At times "recompense" too can be expressed as the appropriate "wages" one

has earned. Jeremiah asks: "Is evil a recompense (*yeshullam*, "earned wage") for good?" (18:20). The implied answer is negative. Jeremiah feels unfairly treated by his enemies, who have tried to harm him for delivering his prophetic message. Various other texts view recompense negatively. Hosea 9:7, for instance, uses *shillum* ("recompense") in synonymous parallelism with *piqqudah* ("punishment"), interpreting an attack of the Assyrians as God's punishment of Israel for its sinfulness. Similarly Deut 32:35 uses *shillem* in parallelism with vengeance (*naqam*) (see *avenge*), and Jer 51:56 calls the Lord "a God of recompense," that is, the one who would punish Babylon for its wanton destructiveness. In all these cases, however, the anticipated punishment was appropriate for the work done.

The books of Job and Ecclesiastes, however, challenge any easy assumption that individuals always receive what they deserve. In Job 15:31, Eliphaz the Temanite opines that emptiness will be the recompense (*temurah*, "exchange," from a root meaning change) for those who do not trust in God. Eliphaz calls Job a windbag, one who has abandoned the fear of the Lord (15:2–4). Job knows otherwise, of course. He was guilty of nothing that warranted the run of misfortune that had struck him (Job 1 and 2). The problem, therefore, lay with Eliphaz's theory of retribution. That theory found its most thorough refutation in Ezek 18, where the prophet argued that individuals reap only what they sow and not the results of other people's actions. That chapter constitutes an attack on a view of collective responsibility that would allow people to blame their misfortune on the sins of their families and neighbors. The author of Ecclesiastes also addressed the concept of retribution. As he saw it, all humans, good and bad, meet the same fate, death (9:2); and he questioned whether "the righteous and the wise and their deeds are in the hand of God" (9:1). Such pessimism was not, however, the final word of the Hebrew Bible. A just God would not leave deeds unrecompensed. If recompense does not always come in this life, biblical writers wondered whether it would come in the next life. In the Hebrew Bible, Dan 12:2–3, 13 offers the clearest expression that extreme cases will be settled by the resurrection. In deuterocanonical books, 2 Macc 12:43–45 expects the resurrection of the righteous (and prayers for the dead to that effect), and 2 Esd 2:23 (probably written by a Christian) also anticipates the resurrection.

New Testament. This development came to full expression in the NT, which teaches that individuals will receive recompense for the way they lead their lives. In Rev 22:12, for example, Jesus promises to return to earth, bringing his reward (*misthos*, "wages") with him to repay everyone according to their works. Similarly, Col 3:24 concludes a household code with the general promise that those who perform their household tasks faithfully "will receive the inheritance [heaven] as their reward" (*antapodosis*, "repayment"). In the Sermon on the Mount, Jesus tells his disciples to rejoice when other people revile, persecute, and slander them, "for your reward (*misthos*) is great in heaven" (Matt 5:12). Speaking of people who practice their piety before others (Matt 6:1), sound a trumpet before giving alms (6:2), pray where people will see them (6:5), and look dismal while fasting (6:15), he says that "they have received their reward." That is, they wish to be seen and praised on earth for their good deeds, and such praise will be their reward. They will, however, receive no heavenly reward, because they were not acting for heaven's sake. Jesus uses a different word (the verb *apodidomi*, "render, reward, recompense") to speak of God's reward (6:4, 6, 18). The word can have the meaning to pay back, as in paying back a debt (Matt 5:26; 18:25) or repaying an advance (Luke 10:35), so it is rich in the connotation of justice. The term *misthos* appears twice in Matt 10:41, where Jesus says that "whoever welcomes a prophet" or "a righteous person" will receive the reward of a prophet or a righteous person: eternal life. It appears again in the

next verse, where Jesus says that people who offer a simple service (give someone a cup of water) in the name of a disciple also will not lose their reward. These two verses point to the generosity of God in giving believers even more than their deeds deserve. That is not to say that Jesus and the authors of the NT would not recognize virtue for its own sake, but that the writers were convinced that Jesus had promised believers their virtue would receive an even higher reward.

G. de Ru, "The Concept of Reward in the Teaching of Jesus," *NovT* 8 (1966): 202–22.
PAUL L. REDDITT

Rich   *see* **Poor**

Right   *see* **Upright**

Righteous, Righteousness   *see* **Just**

Rob, Robber   *see* **Possessions**

Sabbath   Israel's Scriptures anchor the Sabbath day in the theology of creation, specifically in God's primordial designation of "the seventh day" as "holy" (Gen 2:2–3). As the first and only part of God's creation to receive this attribute, this day embodies both a revelation and a commission that defines God's hopes and expectations for a world created to be "very good."

The revelation and the commission are most clearly expressed in the two principal versions of the Decalogue (Exod 20:1–17; Deut 5:6–21), both of which understand Sabbath observance (commandment 4) as the linchpin that holds together Israel's covenantal commitments to love God absolutely (commandments 1–3) and to live in the world in full accordance with this love (commandments 5–10). The Exodus Decalogue grounds the commission to "remember" the Sabbath day (*yom hashabbath*) and "keep it holy" in the revelation that to do so images God's own commitment to the rhythms of work and rest on which creation depends (Exod 20:8–11; cf. 23:12). In Exodus, fidelity to this commandment is actualized through worship in the tabernacle, the design and construction of which is explicitly tied to God's instructions concerning the Sabbath day (Exod 31:12-17; 35:2–3). Sabbath keeping, including the rituals of worship that keep it alive and vital, is an act of "creation keeping," without which the world cannot realize its full potential (Fretheim, *Exodus*, 230). The Decalogue in Deuteronomy grounds the commission to "observe/keep" the Sabbath day and "keep it holy" in the revelation that to do so sustains God's own commitment to redeem the world through acts of liberating compassion (Deut 5:12–15). Upon this Sabbath commandment, Deuteronomy builds a "sabbatical principle," which extends the trajectory of the commission explicitly to the sphere of economic justice (Miller, *Deuteronomy*, 138). If Israel is to image God faithfully, it must remember its redemption from bondage in Egypt and enact the abiding promise of God's redemption on behalf of the poor, the enslaved, and the powerless, wherever they may be found (cf. Deut 15:1–18). In sum, the observance of the Sabbath day is envisioned as an act of *worship* that issues forth in concrete deeds of *justice*, both of which are essential for the sustenance of the world God has created.

The Sabbath's importance for worship of God that is inextricably coupled to enactments of justice in the world is a critical concern of both Israel's prophets and its priests. The prophets uphold Sabbath observance as the criterion for devotion to God, even as they steadfastly warn against all worship that does not issue forth in righteous living outside the sanctuary (Amos 8:3–6; Isa 1:10–17; 56:2, 4, 6; 58:13; Jer 17:21, 22, 24, 27; Ezek 22:26; 45:17; 46:1, 3, 4, 12). Ezekiel, a prophet deeply rooted in the priestly tradition, explicitly ties Israel's fall (to the Babylonians in 586 B.C.) to the profanation of the Sabbath (Ezek 20:12, 13, 16, 20–21, 24), which is the punishment envisioned in Exod 31:15 and 35:2 (cf. Num 15:32–35).

The priests incorporate the Sabbath day into the regularized rhythms of sacred observances built into the calendar (Lev 23:3; Num 28:9; cf. Exod 23:12; 34:21). The priestly calendar is comprised of multiple seven-day festivals, including three sacred observances to be observed in the seventh month of the year, which is the yearly analogue to the weekly sabbath day. From the priests' perspective, each of these ritual observances inculcates a summons to be ever attentive to the ethical requirements that always attach to life in the presence of God. This perspective is foundational in the Holiness Code (Lev 17–27; see esp. Lev 26:2), perhaps most clearly so in its provisions for sabbatical years and jubilee years (Lev 25–26) that extend God's promise of redemption not only to people who may have fallen into debt but also to the land, which is also entitled "to observe a sabbath to the Lord" (Lev 25:2).

Postexilic and intertestamental texts ascribe special significance to Sabbath observance, which along with circumcision emerges as a principal criterion for measuring fidelity to the covenant. Much attention is devoted to clarifying strict prohibitions of work that defile the Sabbath (e.g., Neh 13:15–22), and in various intertestamental texts (e.g., *Jub* 2:17–33; CD 10:14–11:18; *m. Shabbat.* 7:2) the list of proscribed behaviors becomes increasingly more specific and more comprehensive. The presumption of joy and celebration that attaches to Sabbath observance remains, nevertheless, persistent and strong. In the home the Sabbath day of rest was to be celebrated with a good meal and the happy fellowship of family and friends; in the temple it was to be announced with three blasts of the trumpet, which signaled the appointed time for sacrifices, Scripture reading, and rituals that welcome the beginning of a new week as the promise of yet another opportunity for a new beginning with God (e.g., *Jub* 2:21, 31; *b. Shabbat* 119a; *m. Sukkah* 5:5).

The NT embraces Jewish teachings on the Sabbath (*sabbaton*), even as it adds its distinctive perspectives. The presumption of the Sabbath's sanctity, the prohibitions of work it customarily entails, and its abiding invitation to worship that may never be severed from the imperatives of compassion and justice remain foundational for Jesus and his disciples (e.g., Mark 1:21; 6:2; Luke 4:16–21 and par.; 23:56). Within the context of these presumptions, each of the Gospels records instances of serious debate between Jesus and Jewish authorities concerning Sabbath observance, particularly on the question of what work could or could not be done. Of six such instances, five deal with the question of healing on the Sabbath (Mark 3:1–6 and par.; Luke 13:10–17; 14:1–6; John 5:1–9; 9:1–41) and one deals with the issue of plucking ears of grain on the Sabbath (Mark 2:23–26 and par.). In each case, as a general rule, Jesus teaches that Sabbath observance does not exempt one from the responsibility to bring healing where life is infirm and to bring sustenance where life is threatened. Drawing upon an OT precedent (1 Sam 21:2–7), Jesus articulates the principle that underlies his actions: "the sabbath was made for humankind, and not humankind for the sabbath" (Mark 2:27). On this point, Jesus adheres closely to the teachings of his Jewish forebears, who also recognized that observance of the Sabbath was necessarily superseded by the commandment to save life when it was threatened (e.g., *Tanhuma* 245a; *m. Shabbat* 16:1–7; 18:3). Jesus' teaching echoes that of the rabbis, who affirmed that "the Sabbath is given over to you [the Jews] and not you to the Sabbath" (*Midrash on Exod* 31:12; cf. *Exod Rabbah* 25:11; *Deut Rabbah* 1:21).

Jesus' claim that "the Son of Man is lord even of the sabbath" (Mark 2:28; Matt 12:8; Luke 6:5) places him in acute opposition to the Jewish leaders of his day. With this assertion Jesus disputed the claims of Jewish law to be able to define Sabbath, insisting instead that the God whom he served and embodied, not any human authority (or any religious institution), determines Sabbath's ulti-

mate claim on humankind (cf. Paul's assertion that Christ's death frees Gentile converts from Jewish laws regulating the Sabbath; Gal 4:10; Col 2:16). In this respect, Jesus effectively reclaims a basic affirmation of Hebrew Scriptures: God ordained the Sabbath as a blessing that leaves no part of a world created to be "very good" outside its reach (Gen 2:1–3).

There remains one aspect of Sabbath theology that evocatively lingers in the testimony of both canons of Scripture. In its account of the ultimate realization of God's creational purposes, the book of Isaiah envisions a new heaven and a new earth, where "from sabbath to sabbath, all flesh shall come to worship before me" (Isa 66:23). This vision reverberates in the promise of Heb 4:9: "a sabbath rest (*sabbatismos*) still remains for the people of God." This vision, yet unattained but inviolably real, lies at the heart of the hope that if those to whom the promise has been vouchsafed should faithfully observe but two Sabbaths, the messiah would come (R. Simeon ben Yohai in *b. Shabbat* 118b).

N.-E. Andreasen, *The Old Testament Sabbath* (Missoula, Mont.: Society of Biblical Literature, 1972); S. Bacchiocchi, *The Sabbath in the New Testament* (Berrien Springs, Mich.: Andrews University, 1985); T. Fretheim, *Exodus*, Interpretation, A Bible Commentary for Teaching and Preaching (Louisville, Ky.: John Knox, 1991); P. Miller, *Deuteronomy*, Interpretation, A Bible Commentary for Teaching and Preaching (Louisville, Ky.: John Knox, 1990).

SAMUEL E. BALENTINE

Sacred *see* **Holy**

Sacrifice, Offer, Offering The words that focus this entry invite reflection on the rituals of sacrifice in the OT and their appropriation in the NT. Consonant with the objectives of this wordbook, the emphasis will be on the *theological* importance of sacrifice—as may be discerned from the final canonical form of both Old and New Testaments—not on the myriad of theoretical explanations, as instructive as they are, concerning its pre-biblical history, originating impulses, and evolutionary development. Within the OT the theological lens directs attention first to the Pentateuch—especially to the Priestly traditions in Leviticus and Numbers, which provide the foundational perspective for the Israelite sacrificial system—and beyond the Torah to the prophetic literature, which offers substantive critique of this system. The NT offers nothing comparable to the precise sacrificial instructions of Israel's priests, primarily because its witness concerns the new emphases announced by Jesus. Nonetheless, close attention to the language and imagery, especially in the letter to the Hebrews, confirms that for all its important distinctives, the NT understanding of Christian life remains anchored to the theological legacy of Israel's sacrificial system.

Old Testament. The Priestly tradition places its most extensive discussion of sacrifices—Lev 1–7 (cf. Num 28–29)—at the epicenter of the foundational revelation at Sinai (Exod 19–Num 10) that constitutes Israel as a covenant people. The mandate that undergirds and defines this covenant relationship is set forth in Exod 19:6: "you shall be for me a priestly kingdom and a holy nation." Towards this end, the Priestly tradition reports that God gave instructions for building the tabernacle (Exod 25–31), which upon its completion (Exod 35–40) becomes the only place in all creation that is filled with the "glory of the Lord" (Exod 40:35). On the heels of this report, Lev 1:1 announces that God summoned Moses from this newly erected sacred space and gave him the instructions for sacrifice that follow in Lev 1–7. When these instructions are completed, and when the priests are ordained for their ministry at the sacrificial altar (Lev 8–9), the "glory of the LORD" appears to "all the people" (Lev 9:23). Now the people's dramatic journey toward becoming the priestly kingdom and the holy nation that God has called them to be is ready to begin. As startling

as it may be to modern sensibilities, which are largely so untuned to Priestly theology, these instructions for sacrifice are the invitation to enter into the most immediate and intimate presence of God that is available in all the cosmos.

Before outlining the specifics of the sacrifices described in Lev 1–7, two general comments about Priestly terminology are in order. First, the distinctive Priestly word for "offering" is the noun *qorban* (e.g., Lev 1:2), which derives from the verb "to come near" or "to approach" (*qarab*). In cultic contexts the verbal act has to do with "drawing near" to God for the purpose of making a presentation or offering. The term *qorban* is inclusive of a variety of offerings and sacrifices, but common to all is the basic meaning of "gift," that is, a presentation that pleases and delights the recipient. Priestly theology understands "sacrifice" not as something that is grudgingly *given up*, as we moderns might say, but rather as something that is happily *given to* (or *for*). Donors do not give up something they would prefer to withhold for themselves; they offer a gift celebrating the intimate communion that is their delight and God's. Second, the basic Priestly term for "sacrifice" is *zabah*, "to slaughter." In cultic contexts *zabah* assumes the technical meaning of slaughtering or sacrificing animals at the altar, the Hebrew noun for which, *mizbeah*, comes from the same verb and means literally "the place of slaughter." This terminology brings into focus a basic distinction between "most holy" sacrifices that are offered wholly or in part (animals and grains by incineration; liquids by dispersion) at the altar—the "burnt offering," the "well-being offering," the "grain offering," the "sin offering," and the "guilt offering" (see below)—and other "holy" offerings, which, although sometimes presented at the altar, are not slaughtered or burned, for example, tithes, firstfruits, wave-offerings (KJV), and heave-offerings (KJV; NRSV renders the last two as "elevation offering" [Lev 7:30] and "offering" [Lev 7:32]).

Leviticus 1–7 describes the "gifts" (*qorban*) of sacrifice and how they are to be brought to God in two series of instructions. The first (Lev 1:1–6:7) deals with five major offerings, each presented from the perspective of the donor. The first three are voluntary offerings: burnt offerings (*ʿolah*) from the herd (bull or ox; 1:3–9), the flock (sheep or goat; 1:10–13), or birds (doves or pigeons; 1:14–17); grain offerings (*minhah*) of uncooked wheat (2:1–3), cooked wheat (2:4–10), and natural barley (2:14–16); and well-being offerings (*shelamim*) from the herd (3:1–5) or the flock (3:6–16). All three offerings envision a spontaneous movement toward God, the impulse for which is joy and celebration, not duty. The last two in the list are required expiatory gifts: the sin offering (*hattaʾth*; 4:1–5:13) of an unblemished bull, goat, or sheep, required for "atonement" and "forgiveness" (4:20) whenever anyone sins "unintentionally" by violating one of God's prohibitive commandments; and the guilt (or reparation) offering (*ʾasham*; 5:14–6:7) of an unblemished ram "convertible into silver by the sanctuary shekel," plus a one-fifth penalty payment (5:14–16), which is required to restore something sacred (cf. 5:14: "holy things of the LORD") that has been unintentionally diminished or violated by a "bad faith" deed. In both of the required offerings, the donor's motivation is the yearning for forgiveness and restoration. The second series (Lev 6:8–7:36) presents the same offerings, now from the perspective of the priests who must administer the ritual process.

The ritual process for the sacrifice of animals comprises seven basic steps, outlined initially with reference to the burnt offering (Lev 1:3–9; the procedure for grain offerings [2:1–16] differs slightly). Laypersons and priests share the ritual responsibilities. Laypersons (1) select and present the animal at the sanctuary, (2) lay hands on it to indicate that it belongs to them and that they desire it to be acceptable on their behalf, and (3) ritually slaughter the animal. The priests are responsible for (4) presenting the blood at the sacred altar; (5) stoking the fire, arranging the wood, and placing the animal parts on the fire; (6) burning the animal, literally "turning it into smoke" (*hiqtir*); and (7) disposing of the remains (cf. 4:11–12, 21; 6:8–11; 7:11–18). These seven steps recall and ritually reenact God's seven-day process of creating the world. As such, they invite the whole congregation, laity and priests alike, to participate with God in the mutual task of celebrating, sustaining, and when necessary repairing the "very good" world (Gen 1:31) of God's primordial design.

The prophets offer another perspective on the efficacy of Israel's sacrificial system. Ever attentive to the moral and ethical requirements of the covenant relationship with God, the prophets persistently criticize priestly rituals for their neglect of the weightier matters of social justice (e.g., Isa 1:1–17; Jer 7:1–14; Amos 2:6–16; Mic 3:9–12; cf. Pss 40:6–8; 50:8–15; 51:18–19; Prov 15:8; 21:3). Similar criticisms are incorporated in the NT (e.g., Matt 9:13; 12:7, both of which quote Hos 6:6). Moreover, Pauline theology places clear and strong emphasis on the surpassing efficacy of faith, which seems effectively to reduce, if not altogether eliminate, the importance of Mosaic law (e.g., Gal 3; see further below). For these and other reasons, many Christians find it easier to identify with the prophetic critique of the sacrificial system than with the priestly concern to sustain it.

Upon closer inspection of Priestly theology, however, it is clear that it never endorses a separation between the requirements for ritual purity and ethical behavior; on this matter, the priests and the prophets are of one mind. The book of Leviticus itself, which offers the most concentrated collection of Priestly writings in the OT, is case in point. Following the detailed instructions for sacrifice (chaps. 1–7) and the ordination of the priests who will oversee the ritual procedures (chaps. 8–10), Leviticus shifts from its concern with ritual obedience *inside* the sanctuary to the corresponding requirements to distinguish between the "unclean and the clean" (10:10) in matters of everyday life *outside* the sanctuary, especially the customs and practices of the home and the table (chaps. 11–15). These instructions are subsequently coupled to a still more expansive corpus (the so-called Holiness Code in chaps. 17–27) that details the requirements for conduct in a wide array of ethical matters, for example, sexual behavior, love of neighbor, and financial destitution. In between these two sets of prescriptions (chaps. 11–15; 17–27), Lev 16 describes the rituals for the Day of Atonement, which address both ritual and moral transgressions (see 16:16) and provide the promise of forgiveness that restores the sanctuary (16:11–19) and the people (16:20–22) to right relationship with God. In effect, the Priestly emphasis on moral and ethical integrity in all aspects of life not only responds to prophetic concerns about social justice; it also calls for the implementation of measures that potentially resolve them.

Postbiblical Jewish and Hellenistic texts confirm that Israel's sacrificial practices evoked ongoing discussion and refinement. Apocryphal and pseudepigraphical works continued to endorse compliance with the ancient Priestly instructions (e.g., *Jub* 3:26–31; 6:1–3; 14:6–16; 1 Macc 4:36–61; 2 Macc 1:18–36). Hellenistic authors like Philo used allegorical methods to interpret sacrifice as a spiritual process of soul renovation (e.g., *De Vita Mosis* 2:106–8). Rabbinic Judaism also saw the need for reinterpretation, for once the temple was destroyed and sacrifice was no longer possible, the rabbis recognized that the synagogue might support an equivalent substitute piety defined by repentance, prayer, and Torah study (e.g., *m. Yoma* 8:8; *b. Menahot* 110a; *b. Berakhot* 26a–b). Such texts indicate that by the time the NT begins to take shape, the role of sacrifice in the rituals that bind together God and humankind was already the subject of serious and faithful reflection.

New Testament. The basic verb for "to slaughter, sacrifice" in the NT is *thyo,*

from which come the nouns *thysia,* "sacrifice, offering," and *thysiasterion,* "altar." The distribution of these words draws attention to the letter to the Hebrews (e.g., fifteen of the twenty-eight occurrences of *thysia* are found here); they are comparatively infrequent elsewhere (e.g., *thyo* only once in Matthew, Mark, and John). Other words associated with specific sacrifices or sacrificial procedures provide additional references (e.g., *holokautoma,* "whole burnt offering" in Mark 12:33; *prosphora,* "offering" in Rom 15:16; Eph 5:2; Heb 10:10) but do not substantially alter the primary conclusion: the letter to the Hebrews offers the NT's most extensive treatment of Israel's sacrificial practices. Although sacrificial terminology is decidedly less frequent in the NT, a survey of its many and varied allusions to sacrifice and related imagery indicates that it draws deeply upon the OT, even as it appropriates its witness in distinctive ways.

A clear indication of the NT's debt to ancient Israel's Priestly tradition is the appropriation of sacrificial imagery in the Gospels to frame and inform the account of Jesus' life and ministry. It was a priest named Zechariah, a descendant of Aaron, who was officiating in the temple when the angel Gabriel revealed to him that the son his wife was to bear, John, would prepare the way for the Messiah (Luke 1:8–25). The same Gabriel subsequently revealed to Mary that she would bear a son who was to be called Jesus (Luke 1:26–38), and when his birth became reality, she and Joseph dutifully brought him to the temple, where "they offered a sacrifice (*thysian*) according to what is stated in the law of the Lord" (Luke 2:24). Although the Gospels never report that Jesus himself offered sacrifices in the temple, they provide ample evidence that his life and teaching remained tuned to their importance. On several occasions, including the Sermon on the Mount, Jesus' words assume the validity of sacrificial practices (cf. Matt 5:23–24; Mark 1:44; Luke 17:14). On other occasions, Jesus acknowledges the efficacy of sacrifice, but like Israel's prophets he stresses the overriding importance of the requirement to demonstrate love and mercy to others (Matt 9:13; 12:7 [both cite Hos 6:6]; Mark 12:33). In the same manner Jesus rebukes the Pharisees for a myopic fixation on ritual fidelity at the expense of social justice (Matt 23:13–24; Luke 11:42) and worshipers for turning the temple's rituals into a marketplace of commercial transactions (Matt 21:12–13; Mark 11:15–19; Luke 19:45–48; cf. John 2:13–17). Here too Jesus' rejection of rituals that subvert worship's abiding summons to ethical behavior stands squarely within the tradition of the prophetic critique of Israel's cult (Isa 56:7; Jer 7:5–12). The accounts of Jesus' last days on earth, like those reporting his birth, are also set against a backdrop of sacrificial imagery. Mark 10:45 speaks of Jesus' life and death as a "ransom for many" (see *redeem*), imagery deeply rooted in Isaiah's description of the "suffering servant," whose death was to be a "sin offering" on behalf of many (Isa 53:4–12). Jesus' "last supper," which each of the Gospels associate with *Passover* and the killing of the paschal lamb, is richly imbued with sacrificial imagery, exemplified best perhaps in Matthew's rendering of Jesus' offering of the cup: "this is my blood of the covenant, which is poured out for many for the forgiveness of sins" (Matt 26:28; cf. Mark 14:24; Luke 22:20).

The Pauline corpus shows a certain double-mindedness concerning the efficacy of the sacrificial system. On the one hand, Paul was not only familiar with Jewish sacrificial practices, he also presented offerings himself (Acts 21:26 [cf. Num 6:13–21]; 24:16–18), conducting himself "as a Jew . . . under the law" as part of his missionary strategy to "win those under the law" (1 Cor 9:20). Paul defines his ministry with priestly, often sacrificial, imagery: he ministers "in the priestly service of the gospel of God" (Rom 15:16); the gospel he preaches is analogous to the sweet "fragrance" (*euodia*) and "aroma" (*osme*) of incense offerings (2 Cor 2:14–16); he understands his

life and his death as a "libation over the sacrifice and the offering of your faith" (*epi te thysia kai leitourgia*; Phil 2:17). From the same priestly stock of imagery, he appeals to his listeners to present themselves as "a living sacrifice (*thysian zosan*), holy and acceptable to God" (Rom 12:1); the mandate is to give oneself up to others in love, which is "a fragrant offering and sacrifice (*prosphoran kai thysian*) to God" (Eph 5:2). The model for living sacrificially comes from Jesus, who offered himself as the paschal lamb (1 Cor 5:7), and whose invitation to share the cup and the bread henceforth defines a partnership (*koinonia*) with God and with all humanity that in Christian theology surpasses anything the sacrificial system can offer (1 Cor 10:14–22).

On the other hand, Paul was keenly aware that sacrificial practices were vulnerable to corruption through pagan influences. Like the golden calf that threatened Israel's covenantal relationship at Sinai, sacrifices may be offered to idols (Acts 7:35–49; cf. Exod 32:1–6). When he saw pagan altars dedicated "to an unknown God" in Athens, Paul denounced those who bowed before them as idolaters. Did they not know that "the God who made the world and everything in it . . . does not live in shrines made by human hands, nor is he served by human hands" (Acts 17:24–25)? The problem was evidently acute in Corinth, where the question of whether it was permissible to eat meat sacrificed to idols threatened the harmony of the fellowship. While some in Corinth boasted of sophisticated knowledge that insulated them against the dangers of idolatry, Paul warned that it was not knowledge but love, especially as manifest in the responsibility not to become a stumbling block to others, that must guide their conscience (1 Cor 8:1–13). Toward this end, he urged his listeners to "flee from the worship of idols" (1 Cor 10:14) and commit themselves to "do everything for the glory of God" (1 Cor 10:31).

In terms of both its language and imagery the letter to the Hebrews offers the most sustained discussion of Israel's sacrificial system in the NT. The Aaronic priesthood is the model for understanding the work and ministry of Jesus (Heb 4:14–5:10). Jesus is the "great high priest" (4:14), whose "gifts and sacrifices [*thysias*] for sins" (5:1), now transformed by his sacrificial death on the cross, enable his followers to "approach the throne of grace with boldness, so that we may obtain mercy" (4:16). Jesus' priestly mediation is modeled on the rituals of the Day of Atonement (Heb 9:1–10; cf. Lev 16). Christ, the high priest, enters into the Holy Place, and with the unblemished blood of his unique redemption he purifies "our conscience from dead works to worship the living God!" (9:14). Through this "more excellent ministry" (8:6), Christ removes the burden of sin and opens the door to the new covenant promised by God in Jer 31:31–34 (Heb 8:6–13; 9:15).

Not to be overlooked in Hebrews is the clear and certain affirmation that Christ's priestly ministry surpasses its Aaronic model. Aaron offered "the blood of goats and calves"; Christ offered his own blood (9:12). It was necessary for Aaron to offer sacrifices repeatedly, for their efficacy was limited (9:25), and it was ultimately "impossible for the blood of bulls and goats to take away sins" (10:4); but through the offering of his blood, Christ bears the sins of the world "once for all" (7:27; 9:12, 26; 10:10). Aaron's rituals allowed him entry into an earthly sanctuary, "a mere copy of the true one"; Christ's death led him "into heaven itself, now to appear in the presence of God on our behalf" (9:24). For all these critically important distinctives, however, the portrait of Christ's ministry in Hebrews remains anchored to the abiding witness, hope, and expectation bequeathed by ancient Israel's priests and prophets. As a result, when Christ offers a new covenant that no longer requires the old sacrificial system (Heb 10:18), he stands alongside his Jewish forebears, who long ago had discerned that sacrifices and offerings ought never

be equated with the sum total of what God desires (10:5–10; cf. Ps 50:8–15; Isa 1:10–17; Jer 7:21–26).

Whereas Hebrews focuses on the priestly ministry of Christ, 1 Peter addresses the *ministry* of priesthood that belongs to the Christian community. The recipients of the letter are "exiles" and "resident aliens" scattered throughout Asia Minor (1 Pet 1:1, 17; 2:11). Because their minority status had caused them to question their identity, the author of this letter urges these Christians to reconsider their position by calling attention to their rich heritage as a *people of God*. As descendants of those born from "imperishable seed" (1:23), they are Sarah's "daughters" (3:6), thus members of God's "chosen" people (2:9). Because they have been redeemed by the blood of Christ (cf. 1:2), they are summoned to a life of holiness that sustains the hopes and aspirations of their ancestors in Israel: "for it is written, 'You shall be holy, for I am holy'" (1:16; cf. Lev 11:44; 19:2). The most freighted metaphor for their identity and vocation is none other than the lingering summons God first issued to their forebears at Sinai. They are to become "a royal priesthood, a holy nation" (2:9; cf. Exod 19:6).

God's ancient summons from Sinai abides, ever inviting the community of faith to the path mapped out by the ministries of both Aaron and Jesus. As George Herbert (1593–1633), the English rector and poet, discerned, even those whose "doctrine [is] tuned by Christ" are invited to come to God as "Aaron's dressed": "Holiness on the head, Light and perfections on the breast, Harmonious bells below, raising the dead To lead them unto life and rest. . . . Thus are true Aaron's dressed. . . . So holy in my head, Perfect and light in my dear breast, My doctrine tuned by Christ (who is not dead, But lives in me while I do rest), Come people; Aaron's dressed (G. Herbert, "Aaron," *The Complete Poems*, ed. J. Tobin, 164).

G. Anderson, *Sacrifices and Offerings in Ancient Israel: Studies in Their Social and*

Political Importance (Atlanta: Scholars Press, 1987); S. E. Balentine, *The Torah's Vision of Worship* (Minneapolis: Fortress Press, 1999); Markus Barth, *Was Christ's Death a Sacrifice?* SJT Occasional Papers 9 (Edinburgh: Oliver & Boyd, 1961); H.-J. Kraus, *Worship In Israel: A Cultic History of the Old Testament* (Oxford: Basil Blackwell; Richmond: John Knox, 1965); R. Nelson, *Raising Up a Faithful Priest: Community and Priesthood in Biblical Theology* (Louisville, Ky.: Westminster John Knox, 1993); J. Tobin, ed., *George Herbert: The Complete English Poems* (New York: Penguin, 1991).

SAMUEL E. BALENTINE

Saint   *see* Holy

Salvation   *see* Save

Sanctify, Sanctification   *see* Holy

Sanctuary   *see* Holy; Presence

Satan, Adversary, Devil, Enemy

"Adversary" and "enemy" can be used generically as descriptors of hostile human beings. Even "devil" can, in lower case, refer to a lesser evil spirit, that is, a demon. For this article, however, these three terms are considered in their function as synonyms for Satan.

Surely ancient Israel was well acquainted with the mythologies of its ancient Near Eastern neighbors, including their beliefs in evil deities and a ruler of the netherworld. However, whether because of a revulsion against polytheism going back to Sinai or even to the very beginnings of Israel, or because of the austere and radical monotheism of the final editors of the Hebrew Bible, very little pluralism of deity or demonology remains there. True, as early as the famous "Let *us*" of Gen 1:26 we get hints that a heavenly court surrounded God. Some prophets actually claim to have stood in the council and overheard the proceedings (1 Kgs 22:19–23; Isa 6:1–13; Jer 23:18), but no member of that divine community rises to the status of individual identity until the very end of the

Hebrew canon. Whether growing out of the struggle with neighbors or received as an independent prophetic insight, biblical faith is monistic, not dualistic. *God* is one and God is *good*. Evil and Satan come from somewhere else.

Fourteen of the seventeen mentions of Satan in the OT of the NRSV occur in Job 1–2, the dramatic narrative of the testing of the world's most righteous man, agreed to by YHWH and "the satan" at a meeting of the heavenly council. In these chapters the word "satan" is a title given to one member of God's court whose function is that of the prosecutor (investigator and attorney rolled into one). In other words, in Job the satan actually works for God; in no way is he king of the evil spiritual powers.

Satan is mentioned only three other times in the NRSV. (Contra KJV, NRSV properly translates the Hebrew *satan* as "an accuser" in Ps 109:6.) In the postexilic prophetic text Zech 3:1–2, the satan plays the same role as the accuser in Job 1–2. The Lord rebukes the satan for falsely accusing the high priest Joshua, who plays a part in the prophet's vision of the reconstruction of Jerusalem after the exile. Only in 1 Chr 21:1 does Satan appear in the OT as a proper name (without an article): "Satan stood up against Israel, and incited David to count the people of Israel." David fails this test, because the census violates God's will. The failure results in a deadly plague that ends only with David's intervention. This singular mention of an independent personality with the proper name Satan is particularly interesting, because the parallel passage in the earlier text of 2 Sam 24:1 reads, "Again the anger of the LORD was kindled against Israel, and he incited David against them, saying, 'Go, count the people of Israel and Judah.'" Perhaps the Chronicler found unseemly the hint in his source of a punitive, even demonic side to God. That side can also be glimpsed in other texts in which YHWH is called "adversary" (e.g., Num 22:22–35; Job 31:35), or "enemy" (e.g., Isa 63:10; Lam 2:4, 5), or even, famously, the one who makes "weal" and "woe" alike (Isa 45:7). For whatever reason, the Chronicler separates God from God's "shadow" side and introduces for the first time an "antigod," Satan, who could lead the people into sin and death.

This is none other than the Satan whom the NT writers knew, and knew also as the devil, and less commonly as the adversary (1 Tim 5:14–15; 1 Pet 5:8) and the enemy (Matt 13:39; Luke 10:19). In the NT Satan has other names, too, such as "the tempter" (Matt 4:3), "the evil one" (Matt 6:13), "Beelzebul" (Luke 11:15–19 and par.; Matt 10:25). Several of these are drawn together in Rev 12:9–12: "great dragon . . . ancient serpent . . . deceiver . . . accuser." (Throughout the Bible a demon is always a lesser evil spirit; see the separate discussion under the heading of *evil*.)

Many theories have been advanced to explain the dramatic appearance of Satan as the leading demonic figure in the NT. We have to assume first of all that Jesus, Paul, and the Gospel writers drew on a current of thought running in the Judaism of their days. The flowering of Satan is not evident in the OT Apocrypha, however, most of which predates the earliest NT writings. On the other hand, Satan has a major role to play in the sectarian documents of Qumran and to some extent in the older pseudepigraphic Jewish apocalypses, all of which were written near the turn of the era. What happened? Did a leader of the fallen angels emerge from the already extant but suppressed Israelite mythology of earlier periods? Did the radically dualistic religion of Zoroaster—with its nearly evenly matched good and evil gods— influence Jewish thought during the Persian period? Or did the push toward a satanology in sectarian Judaism and early Christianity come from Hellenistic-gnostic sources with their typically sharp dichotomy between the good world of spirit and the corrupt world of matter and flesh? No definitive answer to the source of the NT Satan has as yet been offered.

In the Synoptic Gospels, Satan first appears in the story of the temptation in the wilderness where he quotes Scripture in the well-known dialogue with Jesus (Matt 4:1–11; Mark 1:13; in the Lukan version, 4:1–13, "Satan" is completely displaced by "the devil"). The fact that Jesus proved to be stronger than Satan in this contest of wills sets the stage for the assessment of Satan that eventually prevails. Initially, however, as the Gospels unfold, it becomes evident that the narrators believe that Satan interferes in human lives, testing people as he tested Job (Luke 22:31) and causing physical as well as mental illness (Luke 13:16). At Satan's prompting, people engage in evil deeds: He leads Ananias into fatal sin (Acts 5:3), and his entry into Judas leads him to betray his master (Luke 22:3; John 13:27).

Jesus too speaks of Satan. In some of his teachings Jesus links Satan with demons (e.g., Matt 12:22–32; Mark 3:20–27; Luke 11:14–23). In Luke 10:18 Jesus makes the visionary statement, "I watched Satan fall from heaven like a flash of lightning." In its immediate context, this saying marks the triumph of the reign of God, manifested in the success of the seventy apostles whom Jesus had commissioned to preach and heal, over the "power of the enemy," that is, the power of Satan to accuse and do harm. It may also anticipate the apocalyptic motif of the expulsion of Satan from heaven by divine warriors (Rev 12:7–12).

Perhaps the most famous use of the term "Satan" on the lips of Jesus is his rebuke to Peter, "Get behind me, Satan" (Matt 16:23; Mark 8:33)—a remark surely intended metaphorically, yet without force if Jesus had had no concept of an actual spiritual power by that name.

In short, the narrators of the Gospels and Jesus himself seem to have had a lively sense of an evil spiritual being who stood at the head of all demonic powers and who was able to enter into human hearts and to challenge the influence of God there. At the same time, the reader of the Gospels is left with the sense that Satan, though a spiritual reality in the mind of the early church, does not rise to the level of an evil god whose power is in near balance with that of the good God Almighty. He gives evil a persona, he causes illness and suffering, and he links the evil that appears in human hearts with the cosmic principalities and powers of evil. However, his capacity to direct a human heart is not greater than the capacity of that heart to redirect itself to the good. There is a real spiritual struggle, but the outcome of that struggle is not foregone in favor of the evil one. It is noteworthy that in the Gethsemane narrative, the most powerful spiritual struggle recounted in the Gospels, Satan plays no role at all.

Paul never sets forth a developed view of Satan, and his use of the term occurs mostly in nontheological discussions. He sees Satan primarily as an enemy of the community of believers, against whose divisive designs vigilance is necessary (2 Cor 2:11). Not surprisingly, then, he mentions Satan frequently in the context of moral instruction (e.g., Rom 16:20). (The allusion to handing someone over to Satan in 1 Cor 5:3–5 and 1 Tim 1:20 may simply mean expulsion from the church.) In 1 Cor 7:5 Satan takes charge if one does not exert self-control. But that is in fact Paul's point: Satan's wiles can be overcome by a holy will. Only in 2 Thess 2:9 is Satan tied into Paul's apocalyptic vision of evil escalating as the end approaches.

In the book of Revelation, Satan (often known by other names) rises to cosmic status, along with the general projection of the spiritual powers of good and evil onto the large screen of the final titanic struggle. His role culminates in Rev 20:1–7. The millennial reign of the saints with Christ begins with the binding of "the dragon, that ancient serpent, who is the Devil and Satan" (v. 2). The thousand-year kingdom ends when Satan is unbound (v. 7). Only then is the final battle joined and he, Death, and Hades are cast into the lake of fire from which there is no return (vv. 10, 14; compare Matt 25:41).

The term "devil," used only four times in the OT of the KJV, is altogether absorbed into demons in the NRSV OT. In contrast, the devil (*diabolos*) is mentioned thirty-six times in the NT (many more times in KJV, which often translates *daimon* as "devil" as well). He is an entity superior to mere demons and often paired or equated with Satan himself. (Beelzebul, who is Satan in Matt 12:24; Mark 3:22; Luke 11:14–23, but not the devil, has, nevertheless, the title "the ruler of the demons.") As noted, many uses occur in the temptation in the wilderness stories. In Revelation, the cliche "the Devil and Satan" suggests that the seer of Patmos equated the two beings as well.

In summary, though not an unimportant feature of NT thought, Satan (or the devil, or any of his other manifestations) is not a reality meant to haunt every human moment. Evil and sin, Yes. They are much more real and serious matters than a bad fallen angel, who personified evil in ancient folklore. One might throw an inkwell at the devil, as Luther did, but mentally and spiritually healthy believers are invited to walk on the path of love and peace in the company of the Comforter sent from God. God offers to believers the strength and wisdom necessary to confront the evil within and without, so that no one can ever resignedly claim, "The devil made me do it!"

W. SIBLEY TOWNER

Save, Salvation, Savior, Deliver, Deliverance, Deliverer, Rescue

In many treatments of (biblical) theology, "salvation" looms large. Under it other themes are often arranged, making it an umbrella term. "Salvation history" as an overarching structure ran through many articles in Richardson's *Theological Word Book of the Bible* (1950). "Jesus saves" is a common slogan (even though no NT verse puts it quite that way). The passive voice is often preferred with "save" in the NT: "Believe on the name of the Lord Jesus, and you will be saved" (by God; Acts 16:31). In Rom 10:13 Paul quotes Joel 2:32, "Everyone who calls on the name of the Lord will be saved," and couples that with belief from the heart, confession that "Jesus is Lord," and so justification, 10:9–10. In 1 Pet 3:21 it is baptism, into Christ, that now saves you. Such an emphasis on salvation is based on a number of Hebrew and Greek terms and often includes closely related terms in English, like "deliver" and "rescue" (see also *redeem, reconcile, free,* and *just*). Convenient outlines include "salvation from (sin, death, law, the flesh)" and "salvation for (service)"; or "recipients, agents of salvation, its nature, and the mediators of salvation" (so O'Collins in *ABD*). But the idea of salvation history as a continuum from creation, through Israel's history (including the several covenants), to a climax in Christ and a future consummation has always been plagued by the objection that history does not save or redeem (God does) and by questions about the connection, increasingly under discussion, of how the faith-interpreted biblical accounts and testimony to events relate to "actual history" as attested from archaeological artifacts and extrabiblical sources. Hence (perhaps as a consequence) some have moved in recent years to emphasize "literary narrative" or "story" and a world of readers not necessarily connected with past "history." To this extent, "salvation" as history may not play the role in biblical interpretation it once did.

Still useful, however, because its implications run through many passages, is attention to the terms rendered by NRSV and other English translations into the theme words being examined in this article. They include, in Hebrew, the root *yasha*ᶜ, "save" (354 times in the OT, often with God as subject), from which the nouns for "salvation" derive (especially *yᵉshuᶜa* and *hoshiaᶜ*, regularly God's salvation, e.g., Isa 19:20), as well as proper names like Elisha, Joshua, and Hosea, all suggesting "[God] saves." Other, related terms are *natsal*, "take away, protect from (danger)," "deliver," especially in the form *hitstsil*; *gaʾal*, "buy back, redeem"; and, among others, *padah*, "redeem, ransom," and *palat*, "bring to safety, rescue."

Much has been made of the first root, *yashaᶜ*, meaning originally "be wide, spacious" and hence a broad area where one can live and develop without hindance or constraints. In Greek the root *sozo* is the most frequently used one: "preserve, rescue from danger, save." Derived forms from it are the noun *soteria* (English "soteriology"), and the term *soter* ("deliverer, savior"), which was sometimes used in the world of the day as a title of honor for a physician, benefactor, or ruler, like Ptolemy I Soter, a Macedonian king who ruled in Egypt after Alexander the Great. Also occurring in the NT, but much less frequently (16 times, compared with 106 for *sozo*) is *rhyomai*, meaning "rescue (from danger), save, deliver." Links to such terminology are sometimes more direct than we might expect, as when Matt 1:21 gives theological significance to the name "Jesus" (= Hebrew "Joshua"), through the comment of an angel, "He will save his people from their sins" (*sosei* = Hebrew verb *yashaᶜ*), or the cry of the people as Jesus entered Jerusalem, "Hosanna" (Mark 11:9 and par. Matt 21:9; John 12:13), "Save us, we pray" (cf. Ps 118:25 for the Hebrew *hosiʾanna*).

These various terms had everyday uses in life quite apart from, though never in Israel separated completely from, the God of Israel. Groups could help each other in battle (2 Sam 10:11, "help," a sense short of "deliver"; Josh 10:6, "save us, and help us"). One could come to the defense of women (Exod 2:17) or help a person who is without power (Job 26:2). Deliverance might be from all sorts of people and situations and come in various forms and ways. Often the situation was in a battle, and so the sense then became "victory." First Samuel 14:45 provides a good example: Jonathan "accomplished this great victory (*hayeshuᶜa*) in Israel" (cf. Pss 18:50, "great triumphs"; 44:4, "victories" [given by God]). But theologically the starting point, to understand biblical thought, must be with God as deliverer and savior, God who works directly or indirectly, sometimes through earthly agents.

The Lord is the one who saved Israel, par excellence in the exodus from Egypt (Exod 14:30). The God who saw "the misery of my people" under their taskmasters there said, "I have come down to deliver them from the Egyptians" (Exod 3:8). Moses may complain at one point, "You have done nothing at all to deliver your people" (Exod 5:23), but eventually the people "see the deliverance" that the Lord, as divine warrior, accomplishes (14:13), and they sang "he has become my salvation" (15:2).

Such experiences continued from Israel's God. The people prayed that "he may come among us and save us from the power of our enemies" (1 Sam 4:3), from the Philistines (1 Sam 7:8). He is the one "who saves you from all your calamities and your distresses" (1 Sam 10:19). The verbs "save" and "deliver" are more frequent in OT treatments of the time of the judges and in 1 Samuel than with reference to the exodus. The common confession, borne out in these and other experiences, was that God is Israel's Savior (Ps 106:21); the deliverer to whom one could appeal (Pss 3:7–8; 18:2; 40:17; 70:5; 144:2), a "strong deliverer" (Ps 140:7). The ideal was that the people "trusted" and God "delivered" them (Ps 22:4); the frequent testimony was "He has delivered me from every trouble" (54:7; 56:13, from death; 86:13, from Sheol; from distress, 107:6). This experience, that God saves, was recalled regularly, at Passover for the events in Egypt (Exod 12:21–23) and in worship, where Pss 105; 136 recited past history and Ps 107 told more generally what the redeeemed experience. The petition "Save us" (v. 47) is the conclusion to the story of the "mighty doings of the LORD" (v. 2) in Ps 106. Both individual and community appear in the request, "Help me when you deliver them" (v. 4). "The LORD lives who saves Israel" (1 Sam 14:39) was probably a common way of speaking; and "save us, O God of our salvation" (1 Chr 16:35) a frequent plea.

While God alone is the one who saves directly in holy war accounts, as of the exodus, often the deliverer God worked through leaders charismatically appointed, like the judges ("saviors who saved them from the hands of their enemies," Neh 9:27). Gideon was told by the angel of the Lord, "Go in this might of yours and deliver Israel from the hand of Midian" (Judg 6:14, cf. 6:15, 36–37; 7:7). Similarly with Othniel (Judg 3:9), Tola (Judg 10:1), Samson (Judg 13:5), and others. On one disastrous occasion the ark of the covenant was rushed into battle so that "[God] may come among us and save us from the power of our enemies" (1 Sam 4:3), but it was captured. In the accounts of this period, people pray for divine rescue (1 Sam 7:8). The seer Samuel still championed the old idea of God as deliverer (1 Sam 7:3), but eventually the king came to be looked upon as the servant through whom God would deliver Israel (David, 2 Sam 3:18; Saul, 1 Sam 9:16). David becomes the one through whom God "will save my people Israel" (2 Sam 3:18; 2 Sam 8:6, 14, like 1 Sam 19:5, report the victories God gives the king). The phrase continued in use: "the LORD gave Israel a savior" (2 Kgs 13:5, echoing Judg 3:9, here perhaps with reference to Jereboam II, unless some unnamed figure is meant). But during the Assyrian siege of Jerusalem, the hope in that dire situation was for the Lord "to deliver us" (2 Kgs 18:30–35), and God did (19:35).

The fall of Jerusalem in 586 B.C. dealt a blow to the theology of God as deliverer, one who worked through his anointed king for the salvation of the nation. The Davidic house ceased to rule. The holy city was captured, Zion humbled, the temple destroyed. But the view of God as Savior found new life eventually in the presentations to the exiles by the prophet Isaiah of Babylon. To the people who had become "a prey with no one to rescue" them (Isa 42:22), with the God of Israel, the Savior, now regarded as "a God who hides himself" (45:15), this prophet announced that their "righteous God" and "Savior" (45:21) was going to act and deliver and restore Israel. They "cannot deliver themselves" (47:14), but the Lord will "bring near my deliverance swiftly"

(51:5), a deliverance never to be ended (51:6), "salvation to all generations" (51:8). The expectations are well-known: God will lead a new exodus back across the wilderness (40:3–11; 43:15–21), employing as God's servant a new anointed agent, Cyrus (45:1–7). Zion/Jerusalem will see the refugee exiles returning (52:1–2, 7–12), and "all the ends of the earth shall see the salvation of our God" (52:10).

Not always noted in Second Isaiah, amid the polemic against idols (in Babylon, 40:18–20; 44:9–20; 46:6–7), is a new basis for the message that the prophet brings about God as savior. The old appeal to God's victory at the exodus, which had sustained the view of Yahweh as Deliverer/Savior, since 586 no longer carried the conviction it once did. Surrounded by Babylonian stories of creation and of how Marduk had become king, prophet and people now present and affirm the basis for their hopes about God's imminent action to lie, not in the victory over Pharaoh, but in the victory that their God (not Marduk) had won in the creation battle against the forces of chaos. This imagery fuses with phrases reflecting the exodus to provide a basis for what is expected to occur (cf. 42:5–13, the mighty warrior; 43:16–19, a way in the sea, a way in the wilderness; 51:9–11, victory over Rahab and "the dragon"). It amounts to "creative redemption," a combination of the two categories, or "redemptive (re)creation." The watchword is "Soon my salvation will come, and my deliverance be revealed" (56:1). From the Deuteronomist, material can also be cited for an emphasis on God's power to save (e.g., Deut 20:4; 23:14; 12:10; 25:19, rest in the land). But the Priestly account of creation (Gen 1) does not employ such language.

At least a remnant returned to the land around Jerusalem and built a second temple, but found the deliverance far from what had been expected. Despair was not ended by the end of the exile. The hopes expressed in Zech 2:8–13, for example, about the apple of God's eye, were dashed. Talk of rescue and salvation moved more and more to the future, to a day when God would act, "on that day," the *day of the Lord*. The denouement would be beyond history (Dan 12:2–3; Isa 26:19, resurrection). Apocalyptic images had to carry the idea of a broad, wide, secure place of *shalom* for the people of God, because the present world was a place where "no one could rescue from its power" (this beast or that, the current tyrant overlord, Dan 8:4). Accompanying this further shift from older views of God as the one who saves or will save was an awareness that suffering is involved in the life of God's people, as with the servant figure for Israel in Isa 53. There was also a continuing shift from the nation to a remnant to the individual, expressed in the statements that each is afflicted by the sour grapes he or she has eaten, not what the prior generation has done (Jer 31:29; Ezek 18:2–4). The language of psalms like 88:1–3 became more precious for such individuals: "O LORD, God of my salvation, . . . my soul is full of troubles." The formula "There is no deliverer," which ran through Israel's history (Judg 18:28; Isa 5:29, "no one can rescue"; Isa 42:22; Hos 5:14; Mic 5:8; Pss 7:2; 50:22; Job 5:4 and elsewhere, usually of God!), became tragically true. Some retreated into apocalyptic hopes; some went with the powers and forces of the age; some, like the Maccabees, took up, in the warrior tradition, a struggle for power, seeking a national expression of deliverance.

For the NT, a factor of some importance was the prevalence of "savior" language in religions of the Greco-Roman world and in the Hellenistic and Roman "ruler cult." "Deliverer, preserver, savior" were titles used, for example, of Zeus, Serapis/Isis, and Asclepius. As noted above, "Soter" was used of Ptolemaic rulers, along with "Benefactor" (*Euergetes*). Augustus Caesar was called "a savior for us" (inscription at Priene in Asia Minor, 9 B.C.) and "savior of the world." There were expectations of a Golden Age coming (Virgil, Fourth Eclogue, a new age or *saeculum*). For some, the result was optimism about human (and divine) progress, for others, pessimism over what existence was like. Yet statues of benefactors and savior-gods dotted many a city. What proves to be a paucity of language about salvation in at least the earlier books of the NT has sometimes been explained as a reluctance to employ such pagan terminology. When such terms do appear, they may be in opposition to pagan claims of the day.

"Savior" and "deliverer" seem not to be terms used by Jesus or even of him till the christological assertions after Easter. To speak of *God* as savior, as in Mary's Magnificat (Luke 1:47, God my Savior) reflects typical OT piety (cf. 1 Sam 2:1–10 as model for the poetry), as does "a horn of salvation" (NRSV "a mighty savior") in Luke 1:69 (cf. Ps 18:2, of God; Ps 132:17, of David). To affirm of Jesus in John 4:42, "This is truly the Savior of the world," goes beyond what a Samaritan woman, let alone a Jew, in Jesus' lifetime would likely have said. In the OT, no messianic king is given such a title. It may reflect language about Caesar and stand in opposition to such a claim for the emperor. Luke 2:11, "a Savior, who is the Messiah, the Lord," brings together a series of titles in the angelic praise of the Christ child, in Luke implied from 1:69, but not a title likely heard during Jesus' earthly ministry. "Deliverer" does not occur in the Gospels. Matthew 1:21 ("Jesus" = "save his people," the only place in the Gospels where "from their sins" occurs with "save") has been noted. Where Zech 9:9 had "triumphant and victorious" to describe Israel's coming king (in the Greek OT "righteous and saving"), Matthew omits it at 21:5. All in all, the Gospels make little more of Jesus as savior than they do of just(ice)/righteous(ness) for his ministry (see *just*).

More pertinent to the "historical Jesus" may be the declaration made often at the end of a miracle story, which could be translated,"Your faith has saved you" (Mark 5:34; 10:52, par.). But already in the KJV the phrase was rendered "made thee whole" (NRSV "made you well"; Matt 9:21; Luke 8:36, "healed"; Luke 13:16, "set free"). This is a reflection of the sense of wholeness in life, in the Hebrew and Greek terms, of life as a spacious place, marked by well-being. The taunt to Jesus on the cross, "He saved others; he cannot save himself " (Mark 15:31 and par. Matt. 27:42; Luke 23:35), is typical of what was said to pious Israelites (cf. Ps 22:7–8; Dan 6:16; Wis 2:18–20).

True to the pessimism of the day are the questions "Will only a few be saved?" (Luke 13:23) and "Then who can be saved?" (Mark 10:26 and par. Matt 19:25; Luke 18:26). Jesus' answer to the first question (unique to Luke) comes in terms of material shared with Matthew (Luke 13:23–30 = Matt 25:10–12; 7:22–23; 8:11–12) that is mainly pessimistic. Many will try to enter "the narrow door" but "will not be able." They will claim that they ate and drank with Jesus but are dismissed as "evildoers" (Ps 6:8). They will be "thrown out" of the kingdom. The one bright spot is that people will come from the four corners of the world to "eat in the kingdom of God." The tag line about the first being last and vice versa (Luke 13:30 and par. Matt 19:30; Mark 10:31) rounds out this piece that bodes well for Gentiles but not Jews who claim to be under God's reign. The other question occurs in the context of how hard it will be for those with wealth to enter the kingdom. It produces the answer, "For mortals it is impossible, but not for God; for God, all things are possible" (Mark 10:27). Jesus appears here as one who preaches God as the possibility for salvation, in a world where riches or status are obstacles to entry into the kingdom, a (or the) term in the Gospels for "salvation" (see *kingdom of God*). Yet the possiblity of a wealthy tax collector being saved is affirmed in the story of Jesus and Zacchaeus (Luke 19:1–10). The repentance of Zacchaeus is shown by his giving half of his possessions to the poor and paying back fourfold anything he has taken by fraud from someone; this leads to the declaration, "Today salvation has come to this house" (19:9, part of Luke's interest in people rich and people poor and the right use of wealth; see *poor*) and the otherwise unparalleled statement about Jesus' mission, "The Son of Man came to seek out and to save the lost" (19:10; cf. chap. 15 on "the lost"). It is of a piece with Luke's scene of Jesus at the start of his public ministry (4:16–30). Here Isa 61:1–2; 58:6 are quoted, about "release" (to captives) and the oppressed going free (in Greek, *aphesis* is the operative term, not "salvation"). The term is used in Luke not politically but for the forgiveness of sins (1:77, along with "knowledge of salvation"; 3:3; 24:47; Acts 5:31; 10:43; 13:38; 26:18; see *forgive*). It is akin to Jesus' prayer that disciples are to use, "Forgive us our sins/debts" (Luke 11:4 and par. Matt 6:12).

Thus direct connection of Jesus with salvation/deliverance is rare in the Gospels. It occurs mostly in Luke. There is surprisingly little in John; see, however, 3:17; 5:34; 12:47. But salvation is spoken of more in Paul. Terms like "savior" appear especially in the Pastoral Epistles and other later NT documents.

For Paul, the continuity of salvation for believers is seen as past event, present experience, and future hope (Rom 8:24, "we were saved"; 1 Cor 15:2, "you are being saved"; Rom 5:9–10, "will we be saved"). This balanced continuity must be kept in mind as a corrective to the surprise sometimes expressed that so many Pauline references are eschatological, about a day and time to come. This aspect about what is yet to be is a reflection in part of the apocalyptic outlook in the later parts of the OT and of the fact that Jesus' announcement of the kingdom and his resurrection, plus the giving of the Spirit, were thought to have set in motion the "last times." There is also the obvious fact that "salvation" was not yet complete. Paul's oldest extant letter includes, in a summary of the apostle's message, Jesus' resurrection and that he "rescues us from the wrath that is coming" (1 Thess 1:10). Similar is a phrase at Gal 1:4, Christ "gave himself for our sins to set us free from the present evil age." That assumes a new age to come that, for believers, already overlaps the world or

age that is passing away (1 Cor 7:31; cf. 1 Cor 10:11; "forever and ever" at Gal 1:5 is literally "the ages of the ages").

God's plan, according to Paul, was "to save those who believe" (1 Cor 1:21). Paul saw his own ministry as an effort to save some Gentiles and some Jews (1 Cor 9:22; Rom 11:14). He spoke so that people might be saved (1 Thess 2:16). On occasion—an important one, at Rom 1:16—he can put his gospel in terms of "the power of God for salvation," adding as to recipients, "to everyone who has faith," Jew first and also Greek. As he spells out this power of God to save, in terms of righteousness/justification (1:17), salvation extends to all who believe and confess the risen Lord Jesus (10:9–13). Paul's larger hope for "Israel after the flesh" is that "all Israel will be saved" (11:26), though whether that means every last Jew or a representative portion (like the "full number of the Gentiles," 11:25) remains debated. It is all part of what Paul himself calls a "mystery," involving words from the LXX version of Isa 59:20–21 (cf. 27:9): "Out of Zion will come the Deliverer," banishing ungodliness from Jacob and effecting "my covenant with them, when I take away their sins" (vv. 26–27). The picture reverses the OT notion of an eschatological pilgrimage of the nations *to* Mount Zion in Jerusalem (Isa 2:2–3 = Mic 4:1–2; Isa 56: 6–7; 60:3–14; Zech 14:16–17) in favor of a Deliverer (Christ or God) coming *out of* Zion to Diaspora Israel (scattered among the nations). Some see the Second Coming here, but quite likely the proclamation of the gospel Paul has presented in Romans is involved. Paul can talk hopefully because of his own continuing experiences with rescue through God (2 Cor 1:10). The only time Paul (apart from the Pastoral Epistles) speaks of Christ as savior is at Phil 3:20. This is a future expectation about the one who will "transform the body of our humiliation (or humble bodies)" to be "conformed to the body of his glory" (v. 21). The title here, like "Lord" (Phil 2:11), belongs to Christ and his "commonwealth" or city-state (empire), not to

Caesar. Ephesians at 1:13 refers once to "the gospel of your salvation" and at 5:23 to Christ as "head of the church, the body of which he is the Savior" (cf. 5:25).

"Savior" came into much greater prominence in the Pastoral Epistles. It is used of God at 1 Tim 1:1; 2:3; 4:10; Titus 1:3; 2:10; and 3:4: "God our Savior." These six examples are very much a continuation of that primary OT use about the Lord as one who saves, even if 1 Tim 4:10 may stretch the horizon in speaking of "the living God, who is the Savior of all people, especially of those who believe," the object of their hope. In four cases Christ is spoken of as "Savior": 2 Tim 1:10 says his "appearing . . . abolished death and brought life and immortality to light through the gospel." The others are in Titus 1:4; 3:6; 2:13; the last one extends Christology to the ultimate if read as in the NRSV text, "our great God and Savior, Jesus Christ"; the alternative in NRSV margin is to take it as "the great God and our Savior." These usages seem influenced by, and a response to, claims for savior-gods and the imperial cult in the Roman world, where the Emperor saves. Such language also appears in 2 Peter (1:1, 11; 2:20; 3:2, 18; note 3:15, "regard the patience of our Lord as salvation") and Jude (vv. 3 and 25). James is in line with OT thought in referring to the "one lawgiver and judge [God] who is able to save and to destroy" (4:12). Prayer will "save [heal] the sick" (5:15); bringing a sinner back from wandering will save his soul (make whole his life, 5:20). James also speaks of "the word" (implanted in baptism) as having "the power to save your souls" (1:21).

For all its high Christology and emphasis on the work of Christ for persons in a world of darkness and sinning, the Fourth Gospel, we have seen, has little in the way of salvation/deliverance terminology. John 4:42 has been noted; similar is 1 John 4:14, "the Father has sent his Son as Savior of the world." The Johannine imagery is of darkness, pierced now by *light*; death confronted by one who is *life*. But Paul's emphasis on "faith" is paralleled by use of the verb "believe," specifically believing

in Christ. Revelation affirms the old biblical truth, "Salvation belongs to our God" (Rev 7:10), salvation that has now come effectively into battle against Satan (12:10). The doxology at the end runs appropriately, "Salvation and glory and power to our God" (19:1).

Gerald G. O'Collins, "Salvation," *ABD* 5:907–14; Robert A. Guelich, ed., *What Is Salvation?* Ex Auditu 5 (Allison Park, Pa.: Pickwick Publication, 1989); Alan Richardson, *A Theological Wordbook of the Bible* (New York: Macmillan, 1955).

JOHN REUMANN

Scorn *see* **Laugh**

Scripture(s) *see* **Write**

Seal "Seal" translates primarily the verbs *hatham* (Hebrew and Aramaic) and *sphragizo* (Greek) and their nominal derivatives. In secular use these terms refer to marking documents or other objects as authentic, or granting official status (Jer 32:10–11, 14, 44), by pressing a signet (usually a ring or cylinder) into clay. A few occurrences have the sense of closing for security's sake, for example, in Dan 8:26, where "seal" translates the Hebrew root *satham*. It may also apply to Matt 27:66, which speaks of Jesus' tomb being made secure "by sealing the stone." The noun forms refer either to a signet (used to make the defining mark) or the image it produced (Gen 38:18, 25; 41:42; 1 Kgs 21:8; Esth 8:8; Sir 38:27).

As a biblical metaphor, the term is used principally in three ways:

1. Several NT texts speak of God identifying the faithful with a seal. Revelation 7:2–3 is particularly graphic. It reports that an angel held "the seal of the living God" (v. 2) and went out to mark God's servants (v. 3; cf. Rev 13:16–17). Most theological use is clearly figurative, but it still carries the sense of being marked. John 6:27 says God "has set his seal" on Jesus. Paul defends his ministry by saying that God's seal is upon it (2 Cor 1:22).

2. In Eph 4:30 "seal" expresses God's protection of the believer who is "marked . . . for the day of redemption." This line (and later baptismal theology) is informed by the practice of sealing up legal documents to prevent damage or scribal alteration. Hence the believer is said to be protected, sealed, by God until the eschaton.

3. Three prominent texts refer to sealing documents in a way that has theological implications. Isaiah 8:16 says the prophet orders his prophecy to be sealed among his disciples to preserve it unaltered until the prediction comes to pass. Daniel 8:26 speaks of sealing a document so its secrets would be hidden until the time of fulfillment, a common notion in apocalyptic literature. Revelation 5:1 is often thought to have the same sense, but its meaning is more difficult. The reference to seven seals is probably an implicit declaration that the document is like a legal text that is verified by the seal of witnesses. The fact that only the Lamb (Jesus) is worthy to open the seals perhaps indicates the scroll has the authority of a testimony or will that can be unsealed only by the beneficiary. The emphasis is not so much on its secrecy, as in Dan 8:26, as on its reliability and authority. The seven seals are evidence of its trustworthiness.

David Aune, *Revelation 1–5*, WBC 52 (Dallas: Word Books, 1997); G. R. Beasley-Murray, *The Book of Revelation*, NCB (Grand Rapids: Eerdmans, 1978).

JEROME F. D. CREACH

Secret   When used theologically, the language of secrecy or hiddenness communicates the transcendence of God. On the one hand, the OT recognizes that the God of Israel is "a God who hides (Hebrew *sathar*) himself" (Isa 45:15); on the other hand, God proclaims just a few verses later that "I did not speak in secret (Hebrew *sathar*)" (Isa 45:19; see 48:16). In other words, as both OT and NT affirm, the God who transcends human experi-

ence and capability has chosen ultimately to reveal the divine self and the divine will to humankind.

To be sure, not everyone gets the message when God speaks. Some persons are convinced that human experience is all that there is. Thus, there is no transcendent being or dimension to which human behavior is accountable. But in response to those who think that they "can hide in secret places so that I cannot see them" (Jer 23:24; see also Ps 10:7–11; Isa 29:15), God asks, "Do I not fill heaven and earth?" (Jer 23:24). In short, God's transcendence does not mean that God is not also immanent. The divine hiddenness or secrecy does not mean that secrets can be hidden from God or that God does not care about the daily workings of human life in the world.

If God's purposes are not evident to all, God has at least revealed them to the prophets. The issue in Jer 23, cited above, is false prophecy. Against those who prophesied falsely and thought they would not be accountable—that is, who thought they could "hide in secret places" (Jer 23:24)—Jeremiah claims to have stood in "the council of the LORD" (Jer 23:18; see 23:22) and to have seen and heard God's word, which he then faithfully delivered. The Hebrew word translated "council" is *sod*, and the image suggests that Jeremiah has somehow stood in the heavenly council and thus has had personal access to the secrets of the transcendent God. In Amos 3:7, which appears to generalize upon the phenomenon of genuine prophecy, the word *sod* is translated "secret": "Surely the Lord GOD does nothing, without revealing his secret to his servants the prophets." The hidden God is not content to remain hidden. The divine "secret" or purpose will be shared with humankind (see also Dan 2:22).

In the NT, what remains "hidden" (see Matt 11:25, which recalls Isa 29:14) cannot be attributed to the lack of public proclamation. The "secret(s) of the kingdom" (Matt 13:11; Mark 4:11; Luke 8:10; Greek *mysterion*; see **mystery**) is not something that has been intentionally hidden (see

Matt 10:26–27; John 18:20). Rather, it is the reality that the transcendent God is incarnationally at work in the servant ministry of Jesus of Nazareth. The so-called wise and intelligent of the world—that is, those convinced of their own sufficiency and importance—simply cannot discern this "secret" or "mystery."

The logic of this kind of "secret" underlies Jesus' admonition to his followers to give alms and to pray and to fast "in secret" (Matt 6:4, 6, 18). The point of piety is not to appear important in the eyes of others, but rather to submit the self to God. Just as misdeeds done "in secret places" (Jer 23:24; see also Rom 2:16; 1 Cor 14:25) will not escape God's attention, neither will good deeds done "in secret" (see also 1 Tim 5:25). In any case, the admonitions of Matt 6:4, 6, 18 should be heard in conjunction with Matt 5:14–15, which suggests that "good works" are not to be "hid," but rather are like light that is to "shine before others, so that they see your good works and give glory to your Father in heaven."

Although it has the NT specifically in view, the following conclusion applies to the whole Bible (*TDNT* 3:977): "The concept of the hidden does not lead in the NT to esotericism. It leads to world mission."

Albrecht Oepke, "*Krupto,*" *TDNT* 3:957–1000.

J. CLINTON MCCANN

See, Eye, Look, Sight, Vision

The human eye and the capacity to see are gifts of God's creation (Ps 94:9; Prov 20:12; see also Exod 4:11; Prov 29:13), and it is God who restores sight to the blind (Ps 146:8). The latter blessing marks the return of God's favor to his people (Isa 29:18; 35:5; 42:7) and in the NT the grace and power of Jesus' ministry (Matt 15:31).

Though the idols worshiped by pagan nations cannot see (Pss 115:5; 135:16; Dan 5:23; Rev 9:20), and though doers of evil may be under the illusion that not even God sees their actions (Pss 10:11; 64:5; 94:7; Isa 29:15; 47:10; Ezek 8:12), the "eyes

of the LORD range throughout the entire earth" (2 Chr 16:9; Prov 15:3; see also Zech 4:10), and nothing is hidden from their view (Sir 39:19; Heb 4:13). All human activity is subject to his scrutiny (Job 34:21; Prov 5:21), even that which is concealed from the eyes of other people (Matt 6:4). People may be deceived by outward appearances (Matt 6:1; 23:27–28), but God looks at the heart (1 Sam 16:7; Jer 20:12). Though God may be pictured as having to "come down" from his heavenly dwelling to see the puny efforts of mortals (Gen 11:5; see also 18:21), he is more commonly portrayed as seeing from heaven all they do (Pss 14:2; 33:13–15). What he sees is at times "good" or "right" in God's "sight" (Deut 6:18; 12:25, 28; 2 Cor 8:21; also "acceptable," 1 Tim 2:3; or "pleasing," 1 Tim 5:4; Heb 13:21); at other times, it is, in his "sight," "corrupt," "evil," or "displeasing" (Gen 6:11; 38:10; Num 32:13, etc.). Some, indeed, "find favor" or are "precious" in God's "sight" (Gen 6:8; Exod 33:12; Isa 43:4). To say that God's "eye" is "on" someone (or something) is, most frequently, to speak of his providential care (Deut 11:12; Judg 18:6; Ezra 5:5; Pss 33:18; 34:15; Sir 34:19); at other times, however, God's resolve to punish is intended (Amos 9:4, 8; see also Ezek 5:11; 7:4, etc.). Conversely, divine judgment may be indicated by God's refusal to "look at" (or his "hiding his eyes" from) the prayers and sacrifices of his people (Isa 1:15; Amos 5:22). In the assurance that God sees their needs, the afflicted and oppressed may find consolation (Gen 29:32; Exod 2:25; 3:9; 1 Sam 9:16; Pss 10:14; 102:19–20; Lam 3:59), though Job, in his distress, wished that God would turn away from him his all-seeing gaze (Job 7:19). Pleas that God will "see" or "look at" (and act to meet) the needs of those who cry to him are common in petitionary prayers (2 Kgs 19:16; Ps 80:14; Lam 1:9; 2:20; Dan 9:18).

People who "look" (or "lift up their eyes") to God for help are assured of his aid (Pss 34:5; 123:1–2; 145:15; Isa 17:7; Mic 7:7). Isaiah, on the other hand, condemns his people for "looking" elsewhere than to God for guidance and support (Isa 22:11; 31:1). To be invited to "look at" some object or phenomenon in nature is to be asked, not simply to make it a matter of physical observation, but also to consider what it may have to say to human beings (Matt 6:26; Luke 21:29–31). The distinction becomes important when it is claimed that certain people (generally Israel, or Jesus' own disciples) "see" (physically) without (really) "seeing" (or recognizing the true implications of what they see). Many texts insist that the people of Israel had "seen" (with their "own eyes") God's marvelous activity on their behalf (Deut 6:22; 10:21; 11:7; Josh 23:3; 24:7; Judg 2:7, etc.); but a frequent complaint faults them with remaining rebellious or unbelieving in spite of all that they had seen (Num 14:22; Ps 95:9), and Deut 29:2–4 points out that God had not given his people "eyes to see" in spite of all that "[their] eyes" had seen (see also Isa 6:10; Jer 5:21; Ezek 12:2; Rom 11:8). Jesus' disciples betrayed a similar obtuseness (Mark 8:18).

That God himself cannot be seen is noted in a number of texts (e.g., John 1:18; 6:46; 1 John 4:12, 20). Sometimes this is attributed to his own divine nature (Heb 11:27; see also Deut 4:12; 1 Tim 6:16). At other times the irreverence or peril of attempting to look upon God is stressed (Exod 3:6; 19:21; 33:20). Nonetheless, in a number of OT texts God is said to appear to human beings in a form that they *can* see—though the peril of their doing so remains a persistent theme (Gen 16:13; 32:30; Num 14:14; Judg 13:22; see also Judg 6:22). In Exod 24:10–11; Ps 84:7, NRSV takes the original text to refer to people "seeing" God, even though the textual tradition shows that scribes reworked the text to avoid direct statements of that kind. The Lord is at times said to be seen in prophetic visions (1 Kgs 22:19; Isa 6:1, 5; see also Ezek 1:28; Dan 7:9–10); but, though much may be said about the awesomeness of the scene, great reserve is shown in portraying God himself. In the NT, particularly in the Johannine writings, the point is made that though God (or the Father) cannot be seen, he is so present in the person of his Son that those who see him see God (John 12:45; 14:7, 9; 15:24; see also 1:18). The "glory" seen by those in the company of the Son (John 1:14) is, of course, the glory of God (11:40)—the very glory seen centuries earlier by Isaiah (John 12:41; see also 8:56).

If God himself cannot be seen, people may at least see, in the course of history, his deliverance (Exod 14:13), salvation (Isa 52:10; Luke 2:30; 3:6), victory (2 Chr 20:17; Ps 98:3), glory (Exod 16:7; Isa 35:2; 40:5; 66:18), and judgment (Ezek 20:48). Frequently it is in Israel's eyes that God's marvelous works are said to be done, though at times what God does for his people is said to be visible to "the ends of the earth" (Ps 98:3; Isa 52:10; Mic 7:15–16), and Israel is said to be the means by which God makes himself known to other peoples (Ezek 20:9; 36:23; 38:23). When others see the appropriate behavior of God's people, this in itself may lead them to glorify God (Matt 5:16; 1 Pet 2:12; see also 3:2).

At times God is said to "open" people's eyes, enabling them to see some aspect of spiritual reality normally unseen by mortals (Num 22:23! and 31; 2 Kgs 6:17; see also 1 Chr 21:16); elsewhere the heavens themselves are said to "open" to make possible such vision (Ezek 1:1; Matt 3:16). Revelatory visions in the OT are particularly associated with the prophets (Num 12:6); indeed, the entirety of the revelation granted to a prophet may be summed up as "the vision" that the prophet "saw" (Isa 1:1; Obad 1:1; Nah 1:1; see also Amos 1:1; Mic 1:1; Hab 1:1). Elaborate and complex visions play a prominent role in Ezekiel and especially in the books of Daniel and Zechariah, where an intermediary figure is frequently required to interpret the significance of what is seen (Dan 7:16; 8:15–16; 10:10–21; Zech 1:9, 19, etc.). In the NT, revelatory visions are referred to most frequently in Acts (9:10, 12; 10:3; 11:5; 16:9; 18:9; 26:19; see also 2:17; 7:55–56; 23:11). The terms rendered "vision" in the OT and the NT simply denote an "appearance" or "sight"; the unusual content of what is seen becomes apparent from the context, not from the words themselves.

Present limitations of sight will one day be removed. Already Job had some adumbration of a day in which he would see God (Job 19:26–27; see also Isa 30:20). The NT notes that purity of heart, or holiness, is required of those who will "see God" (Matt 5:8; Heb 12:14); those who will "see" his kingdom must be "born from above" (John 3:3; or "born anew," NRSV Mg). Jesus prayed that those who believe in him may one day be with him and "see [his] glory" (John 17:24). They will, indeed, be "like him" when they "see him as he is" (1 John 3:2; see also Rev 22:4). In the meantime, those who do not now see him may still love him (1 Pet 1:8) as they live "by faith, not by sight" (2 Cor 5:7). All that they now see is the reflected glory of the Lord (1 Cor 13:12; 2 Cor 3:18); indeed, their life would not be one of "hope" if they could already see what they hope for (Rom 8:24–25). The Johannine Christ pronounces a special blessing on those believe in him even though they have not seen him (John 20:29).

Johannes Lindblom, *Prophecy in Ancient Israel* (Oxford: Basil Blackwell, 1962), 122–48.

STEPHEN WESTERHOLM

Seraph (plural Seraphim) Prominent in Isaiah's vision of the presence of the Lord (Isa 6) were the seraphim, heavenly creatures who appear only here in the Bible. As to their appearance, we know only that they had six wings. Only two were used for flight. They covered their faces with two, presumably so as not to look directly upon the glory of God. With the other two they covered their feet, perhaps a euphemism for their bodies (cf. Isa 7:20). They spoke Hebrew, for Isaiah understood their hymn and the assurance of forgiveness one of them offered him (vv. 3, 7). Only then did Isaiah hear the voice of the Lord. Seraphim

are thus depicted as servants of God in heaven who praise him and carry out his gracious will.

The word *seraph* appears with a different meaning elsewhere in the OT. The verbal form, which occurs frequently, means "burn," but one cannot be certain whether this means Isaiah's seraphim had a fiery appearance. The noun, in its other occurrences, always refers to a serpent (Num 21:6, 8; Deut 8:15; Isa 14:29; 30:6). One should be cautious in drawing conclusions from this about the appearance of the beings in Isa 6, although there are depictions of winged serpents in Egyptian art. But how did Isaiah know these beings were to be called seraphim? The verb and the other uses of the noun are the only clues we have.

Like the *cherubim, angels,* and the heavenly host, seraphim represent Israel's belief that there is another realm of creation, normally invisible to us, a realm where the joy of God's presence is continually experienced and where God's will is faithfully done. It is the belief that would be expanded at length, after the OT period, in speculations about heaven.

DONALD E. GOWAN

Serve, Servant, Service The Hebrew verb translated as "serve" in the NRSV (*'abad*) primarily means to work or to do work for another person (God: Deut 6:13; or human: Gen 29:18) or in a place dedicated to God (in the tabernacle: Num 4:37; or the temple: 1 Chr 6:10). Such an activity, termed "service," is therefore something done by lower status persons for those who control their existence. As a rule, service entails a hierarchical relation of superior to subject. The subject may be either paid, payment symbolizing subjection, or unpaid, as slave or forced laborer (corvée, tax payment by labor). In either case the "worker" providing some service stands in a relationship of social inferior to a social superior. All service is "servile," regardless of whether the servant is slave or free, in bondage or paid.

With regard to God, such service is worship and fulfillment of required rituals (Exod 31:10). In the Christian dispensation, the service that believers owed to God is to be exercised through "slave service" (the literal meaning of the Greek, *douleuo*) to one's neighbor, which is also service to Christ (Rom 12; Gal 5:13). Slavery is treated in a separate article, but for the moment it should be noted that while servants were often indeed slaves, slavery in antiquity was not at all like New World slavery of the seventeenth to nineteenth century. It is anachronistic to impose contemporary interpretations on the terms servant/slave in the Bible.

Of the varieties of servanthood to individuals mentioned in the OT, a few are especially noteworthy. All the subjects of a king—including his family—refer to themselves as servants of the king (2 Sam 13:24; 1 Kgs 1:17, though Bathsheba's status seems to have changed when she became the queen-mother: 1 Kgs 2:19–22). The king could be viewed as a servant of his people (1 Kgs 12:7), and at times in Israel's history he was a servant of other kings (2 Kgs 24:1). The characteristic that identifies a servant is behavior appropriate toward someone who controls his or her existence. While Solomon is certainly not a servant of Bathsheba, her request to him on behalf of Adonijah certainly reflects the well-known control mothers wield over [even adult] sons [including kings!] in ancient Near Eastern culture (1 Kgs 2:19–22; see Prov 31:1–9). Small wonder that the self-designation "your servant" occurs frequently in a variety of contexts: in relationship to God (1 Sam 3:10), by subjects to the monarch (1 Kgs 3:20), by a host to guests (Gen 19:2), and very often in prayers (Pss 31:16; 69:17; 86:2, 5, 16).

Since all theology is rooted in human experience, which is always culturally conditioned, it is no surprise that Yahweh God, who is perceived in ancient biblical culture as Lord, expects proper service from his "servants" (Mal 1:6). Moreover, God is Lord of lords, hence a lord in any other capacity is a servant of God (Deut 10:17; Ps 136:3; Dan 2:47; Rev 19:16; the title "Lord of lords" is extended to the Lamb in Rev 17:14).

The tradition, however, singles out some special few whom God personally designated as "my servant." The promise God made to Isaac (blessing and descendants) was for the sake of his father, "my servant Abraham" (Gen 26:24), who is patriarch and head of the clan. Moses, "my servant" the national leader, quite clearly enjoys a special relationship with God (Num 12:7–8). Similarly God rewards Caleb "my servant" for his fidelity when the others had faltered (Num 14:24). God pledges to save Israel through "my servant David" (2 Sam 3:18). Even the king of Babylon, Nebuchadnezzar, is called "my servant" by God (Jer 25:9). Others who identify themselves to God as "your servant" include Samson (Judges 15:18), Elijah (1 Kgs 18:36), and even Israel (Isa 63:17). To be servant of the one and only God not only honors Yahweh but is an honorable role for each servant too.

Four poems in Second Isaiah (42:1–4; 49:1–6; 50:4–9; 52:13–53:12) describe a figure who is to come soon in order to establish the reign of God. It is God who speaks in the first poem (42:1–4) presenting an unidentified servant, spirit-endowed just like a prophet, who will exercise sensitive service to the nations and not just to Israel. In the second poem (49:1–6), the servant speaks, presenting himself as a cultural hero (mastery of speech is one way of demonstrating manliness in Middle Eastern cultures) whose natural gifts served to further God's purposes. The servant is identified as the nation, Israel (49:3), yet this servant is to assist in rescuing Israel! Scholars have not resolved this problem, but all note that the servant becomes a light to the nations so that God's rescue may extend to the ends of the earth.

Once more in the third song (50:4–9) the servant affirms his honorable masculinity by repeating his linguistic competence. Going beyond this, the servant further enhances his admirable manly reputation by asserting how he can bear shameful physical punishment without crying or shrieking. God helps him and thus turns this potentially shameful experience into an expression of honorable manliness.

In the final song (52:13–53:12), God speaks again (52:13–15) but unidentified bystanders also chime in (53:1–12). God's statement completely reverses customary Mediterranean values: the servant appears shamed and disgraced, yet God has exalted him exceedingly! How can this be? What does this mean? This servant suffers for others, yet by his shame others are healed, made whole! Scholars note how exceptional this is in Israel's ideology. It is not the servant's preaching that is effective so much as it is the suffering he endures, which has resulted from the rejection of his message. This is an extraordinary new dimension to the concept of servanthood. Suffering innocently seems to be the principal service of this servant. Very likely, this servant is not a historical figure of the past or present (e.g., Second Isaiah himself), nor of the future (a king/prophet/"Messiah" yet to come). He is rather an ideal figure embodying the best of Israel's hopes, and the image becomes a model for others.

The Gospels present Jesus after the pattern of this servant (especially 52:13–5:12). Quite likely the evangelists were influenced by the Septuagint, which in Isa 42:1; 49:6; 52:13 rendered the Hebrew word for slave as child (*pais*). The Gospels portray Jesus as obedient son (child)/servant (Matt 12:17–21, citing Isa 42:1). Sirach 3:6–7 (LXX) sheds some light on this substitution: "Whoever fears the Lord honors his father, and serves his parents as masters." Master (*despotes*) is a title for God in the Septuagint (Sir 23:1; 34:29), and serve (*douleuein*) is literally "slave service" (see above). Recall that all God talk is based on culturally specific human experience (see *family*). It is clear then that the notion of a son who respects his father (and mother) as a servant/slave respects and serves his master is the context in which God would be perceived in this culture: namely, as a father/

master. The word "child" thus clearly carries the overtone of servant. At his baptism (Mark 3:17 and par.) and transfiguration (Mark 9:12 and par.), Jesus is identified as an obedient son/servant. In Mark 10:45, Jesus alludes to Isa 53 as he identifies himself as one who came to serve and "to give his life as ransom for many." Luke 22:37 reports an explicit segment from Isa 53:12 to explain how it is possible to view Jesus as a shameful criminal. In writing the story of Jesus' passion and shameful death, the evangelists drew heavily on Isaiah's Servant Songs and on the psalms of a suffering just or innocent man (especially Pss 22 and 69) who ultimately gains victory and vindication. This gave believers a context in which Jesus' passion could be situated, understood, and appreciated as a mystery that was finally fully disclosed. Other allusions to Isa 53, joined with specific references to Jesus as servant of God, can be found in Acts 3:13, 26; 4:27–30. Jesus indeed was fully son/servant of God.

The Greek word *diakonos* and its related terms is variously translated in the NRSV. It occurs just six times in the OT and identifies servants of the king (e.g, Esth 1:10; 4 Macc 9:17, where servants is translated "lackeys") and a foolish son (Prov 10:4 LXX). In the NT that Greek word occurs twenty-nine times, seven of which are in the phrase "servant of Christ." Four times it is translated "*minister*" (2 Cor 3:6; 11:23; Eph 6:21; Col 4:7) and four times "deacon" (Rom 16:1, though a note presents "minister"; Phil 1:1, where it also occurs with slaves [*douloi*] translated as servants; 1 Tim 3:8, 12: in vv. 10 and 13 the verb is rendered "serve as deacons"). Linguistically the Greek word belongs to the subdomain of the semantic field "help, care for" and properly means "to serve," or "render service."

The translations "minister" and "deacon" require special attention because while these words do indeed connote service, the modern usage of these words could lead to anachronistic interpretations. For the average person, the word "deacon" calls to mind the story in Acts

6:1–6. Greek-speaking widows of the house of Israel felt that they were neglected. The complaint was brought to the apostles, who advised the group to select seven men of their own company to address the needs of the widows. These seven are customarily termed "deacons," though that word (*diakonos*) is not used in this passage nor anywhere in Acts. The noun *diakonia* occurs eight times in Acts and twice in this passage.

A closer look at the passage highlights the nature of this new "daily service" (*diakonia*, Acts 6:1, translated by the NRSV as "daily distribution") and the requisite qualifications for performing this service. This service stands in relationship with "serving the word" performed by the apostles (Acts 6:4). The community is to select from its number "seven men of good standing, full of the Spirit and of wisdom" (Acts 6:3). Goodwill, a generous heart, a spirit of self-sacrifice are not mentioned, nor would they alone qualify. The candidates for this service must be honorable and recognized as such ("good standing"). This is not surprising in a culture whose core value is honor, reputation. Further, they must be Spirit-filled, much like the prophets, and possess wisdom. The fact that these qualifications far surpass what is needed for "waiting on tables" (Acts 6:2) suggests their task was different from and more than that. The relationship of their service to that of the apostles may be less a contrast than one of complementarity. But most important, these servants (for that is what the word basically means) do not volunteer or appoint themselves. Nor does the community appoint them. They are selected by the community from the community, but appointed by the apostles. This is very official. Thus, if the translator or interpreter chooses to call this activity ministry, it is clearly something very different from the contemporary understanding of ministry.

Paul describes himself and his associates as servants (*diakonoi*) and their activity as service (*diakonia*) in a variety of ways: ministers of a new covenant (2 Cor 3:6); ministry of reconciliation (2 Cor 5:18); servants of God (2 Cor 6:4, though the activity in v. 3 is translated "ministry"); minister of Christ (2 Cor 11:23); servant of the gospel (Eph 3:7); servant of the church by God's commission (Col 1:25). When Paul sends Timothy and Erastus, two of his helpers (literally, servants to Paul) into Macedonia we may be glimpsing a continuation of the process initiated by the Twelve with the seven Greek-speaking Hebrew men who served the needs of Greek-speaking widows. In other words, ministry in a formal sense is developing.

These comments about ministry notwithstanding, Jesus' challenge to service touches all members of the community. To leaders he said: "The greatest among you must become like the youngest, and the leader like one who serves" (Luke 22:26). This and similar Gospel advice gave rise to the popular contemporary notion of "servant leadership" that may well be a special gift from God (Rom 12:4–8; 4:11–13). But all believers are exhorted to follow the example of Jesus' service (John 13:12–27) and extend that kind of service to one another (Gal 5:13).

Sigmund Mowinckel, *He That Cometh* (Nashville: Abingdon Press, 1959), 187–260.

JOHN J. PILCH

Seven *see* **Numbers**

Shaddai *see* **Power**

Shame, Dishonor Biblical scholars who make use of the insights and methods of social anthropology identify the societies in which the OT and NT arose as "honor/shame" societies. In such societies, social approbation or honor was a primary incentive to certain behaviors, and disapprobation or shame an extraordinarily strong deterrent. (Given the preoccupation with prestige, status, and reputation in contemporary Western society, the distinction from our own time implied by this label must surely be a matter of degree only.) This is to say not only that people living in those societies were motivated by a desire to gain honor and avoid shame but that honor and shame are socially determined realities. Honor and shame are easily internalized and the latter in particular generates strong feelings. Shame and its near synonym, dishonor, denote both a social and an internal reality. In contemporary English we most frequently speak of the feeling of shame. (This is much less the case with respect to dishonor.) When the Bible uses the words "shame" or "dishonor," however, it is usually referring to the external and social aspects of the reality. The words "shame" and "dishonor" are usually best understood as the equivalent of "public disgrace." See, for example, the characteristic Hebrew synonymous parallelism in Ps 71:13, "Let my accusers be put to shame and consumed; let those who seek to hurt me be covered with scorn and disgrace."

In some cases, shame has no particular ethical content. It means "humiliation" in the sense of being publicly brought low. See, for example, Neh 1:3, where the word simply describes the downtrodden state of the inhabitants of ruined Jerusalem. Often, however, evil or foolish actions and attitudes lead to shame, especially in Proverbs (Prov 18:13; 19:26; 25:10; 28:7). God may even be brought into disrepute, at least metaphorically, by our unlawful behavior (Rom 2:23).

God preserves the righteous from shame: "To you they cried, and were saved; in you they trusted, and were not put to shame" (Ps 22:5; see also Rom 10:11). The Psalms are filled with appeals to God to save from shame (Ps 25:2–3 and many examples). By contrast, God may put the wicked to shame, "Fill their faces with shame. . . . Let them be put to shame and dismayed forever; let them perish in disgrace" (Ps 83:16–17). The parallelism in that verse clearly demonstrates the fundamental meaning of the word. The assumption in all this appears to be that God's justice operates through the honor/shame system.

Nevertheless God's justice must never be completely identified with the system that produces shame and dishonor or identifies certain acts as shameful. Neither social realities nor personal feelings are ultimate. For one thing, the concept of what is shameful can and does change. This is doubtless more apparent in our rapidly changing times than in the biblical period. The Bible knows, moreover, that it is possible for God's people to experience shame not only despite their righteousness but because of it: "It is for your sake that I have borne reproach, that shame has covered my face" (Ps 69:7). This was, above all, the experience of Jesus, "the pioneer and perfecter of our faith, who for the sake of the joy that was set before him endured the cross, disregarding its shame" (Heb 12:2).

This radically relativizes the concept of shame. God works through the system of shame and dishonor but is not limited by it. Indeed, in Jesus Christ and in the calling of the church, God actively subverts and reverses it. "But God chose what is foolish in the world to shame the wise; God chose what is weak in the world to shame the strong" (1 Cor 1:27).

STEPHEN FARRIS

Sheep, Shepherd   see **Animals**

Sheol   see **Grave**

Sick, Sickness   see **Heal**

Sight   see **See**

Sign, Wonder, Miracle, Astonish, Amaze, Marvel   A "sign" (in NRSV usually for Hebrew ʾoth, Greek semeion) is something visible that points to a reality beyond itself. A rainbow is the sign of the covenant God made with Noah (Gen 9:12, 13, 17); circumcision is the sign of God's covenant with Abraham (Gen 17:11; Rom 4:11). A heap of stones served as a sign, or visible reminder, of how God had enabled Israel to cross the Jordan

River (Josh 4:5–7). Prophets themselves served as signs when they appeared or behaved in a way that symbolized coming events (Isa 8:18; 20:3–4; Ezek 4:3; 12:6, 11; 24:24, 27). Recipients of a divine message were at times given assurance of the reliability of its content and bearer by a sign, sometimes of their own specification (Judg 6:17; Isa 7:11), and generally involving the performance of some miracle (Exod 4:8–9, 28, 30) or the foretelling of some future event, itself at times miraculous (Exod 3:12; 1 Sam 10:1–7; 1 Kgs 13:3; 2 Kgs 19:29; 20:8–11; Isa 7:14–17; Jer 44:29–30). Miraculous signs were expected in the ministry of an apostle (2 Cor 12:12; see also Acts 2:43; 5:12; Rom 15:19) and were done by Stephen (Acts 6:8) and Philip (Acts 8:6, 13) as well; God thus confirmed the truth of their message (Acts 14:3; Heb 2:4). The signs performed by Jesus and related in John's Gospel (2:11; 3:2; 4:54, etc.) were intended to lead to faith in Jesus as the Christ, the Son of God (20:30–31). The plagues by which God brought about the deliverance of Israel from slavery in Egypt were also signs of his power (Exod 10:1–2). They are recalled in texts that celebrate God's goodness to his people and encourage their obedience and trust in him (Deut 4:34; 6:22; 7:19; 11:3; Josh 24:17; Pss 105:27; 135:9, etc.).

In the OT, "wonder(s)" in NRSV usually stands for (the plural of) Hebrew *mopheth*, "sign," "token," or a form of the word group *pala*, suggesting something different, extraordinary, or marvelous; in the NT it renders Greek *terata* (plural), "portents," "wonders." God "alone does great wonders" (Ps 136:4; see also Exod 15:11; Judg 13:19; Ps 77:14). In the OT, God's "wonders" frequently refer to his marvelous deeds in rescuing Israel from Egypt (Exod 3:20; Neh 9:10; Pss 77:11; 78:32); these mighty acts were, indeed, both "signs *and* wonders"—acts that were filled with significance *and* that inspired awe (Exod 7:3; Deut 4:34; 7:19, etc.). In the NT, the term occurs in the same combination, generally referring to the miraculous deeds—both significant and wondrous—

of Christ or his apostles (Acts 2:22, 43; 4:30; 5:12; Rom 15:19; 2 Cor 12:12; Heb 2:4). NRSV uses "miracles," less frequently, for the same Hebrew words sometimes rendered "wonders" (1 Chr 16:12; Pss 78:11, 43; 105:5, 27). Other renderings of these terms include "marvels" (Exod 34:10; Ps 78:12), "marvelous works" (1 Chr 16:24; Ps 96:3; see also Ps 118:23), or "marvelous things" (Ps 98:1; Mic 7:15), and "miracles" for Greek *dynameis*, "mighty deeds" (Acts 8:13; 19:11; 1 Cor 12:10).

Though we often think of the miraculous as that which defies the "laws" of "nature," such a notion is foreign to biblical thought and not implied in any of these terms (signs, wonders, miracles). Of course it was recognized that the raising of the dead (for example) was no normal event; it stood out—and attracted wonder—precisely because it was an extraordinary divine act. But God's sovereignty over his creation is as operative in the growth of grass and the coming of night as it is in the raising of the dead (Ps 104:14, 20). And though in most cases it is unusual events that draw attention to the (always operating) divine rule and are therefore designated "signs" and "wonders," Ps 65:8 uses "signs" for phenomena that are recurrent within the created order, and Ps 136:4 celebrates the "wonders" by which the universe was created.

That people respond to the miraculous with astonishment and amazement is surely predictable (Matt 8:27; 9:33; 15:31; Mark 5:42; Luke 5:9; John 5:20; 7:21; Acts 3:10–11; 8:13). One would expect faith to follow as well—not only because this would seem a natural response to the witnessing of an extraordinary event, but also because the events themselves are sometimes said to be brought about in order that the Lord may become known (Exod 10:1–2) or in order that he may confirm the word of his servants (Acts 14:3; Heb 2:4). John in particular stresses that Jesus' signs were meant to bring people to faith. That faith sometimes follows miraculous events is certainly indicated in a number of texts—but it is often faith of a kind that proves neither deep nor lasting. Frequently, the occurrence of "signs and wonders" serves only to demonstrate the stubbornness of those who refuse to believe in spite of what they have seen. Significantly, the Jesus of the Synoptics explicitly refuses requests to perform "signs." Finally, a number of texts note that "signs and wonders" themselves may be deceptive. Each of these points warrants reflection.

In John's Gospel, Jesus' miracles are typically called "signs." Though the Gospel contains fewer accounts of miracles than do the Synoptics, more is made of the significance of those that are related. A Sabbath healing leads to a lengthy discussion of the authority of God's Son (John 5). The feeding of the five thousand (6:1–14) is followed by a controversy over Jesus as the "bread from heaven" (6:25–71). In the story of the raising of Lazarus, it is insisted that Jesus himself is "the resurrection and the life" (11:25). The "signs" are thus meant to lead to insight and faith (2:11; 4:53–54; 20:30–31). John indicates, however, that people both did and did *not* "see" the signs (compare John 6:2, 26); that is, they saw and were attracted by extraordinary acts of power, and some even came to a measure of faith (2:23; 3:2; 6:14; 7:31; 12:18); but they did not grasp the significance of the "signs" with true insight or persevering faith (2:23–25; 6:26). Jesus laments a faith that is dependent on seeing "signs and wonders" (4:48). He challenges those who request a "sign" from him to further insight rather than meeting their requests on their own terms (2:18–22; 6:30–40). And he pronounces blessed those who believe without the benefit of seeing what Jesus' contemporaries had seen (20:29)—though few of them truly believed (12:37; see also 11:47; 15:24).

The latter note is struck in the Synoptic Gospels as well: the sight of Jesus' mighty works did not lead people to repentance and faith (Matt 11:20–24). The same is said repeatedly of Moses' generation: though they witnessed unprecedented displays of God's power in "signs and wonders," their persistent rebellion

and unbelief in spite of what they had seen led to their destruction in the wilderness (Num 14:11, 22–23; Deut 34:11; Neh 9:17; Ps 78:32, 42–43).

In the Synoptic Gospels, Jesus persistently refuses requests that he perform a sign that would demonstrate his divine commission (see also Luke 23:8; 1 Cor 1:22). In places, the refusal is made absolutely (Mark 8:11–12). Elsewhere the only sign given is that of the prophet *Jonah*, whose emergence from the belly of a sea monster parallels Jesus' coming death and resurrection (Matt 12:38–40; see also 16:1–4; Luke 11:29–30). The request itself indicates the evilness of the "generation" that makes it (Matt 12:39; 16:4; Luke 11:29); its stubborn unbelief in spite of the manifest presence of God's kingdom, its insistence on spelling out the terms that have to be met before it is prepared to acknowledge what God is doing. We may compare these accounts with that in which Jesus refuses to declare the source of his own authority to those who would not acknowledge the divine authority of John the Baptist's ministry (Matt 21:23–27).

Finally, it should be noted that "signs and wonders" are not in themselves a reliable indicator that those who perform them are authorized by God. Some of the signs performed by Moses and Aaron were reproduced by Egyptian magicians (Exod 7:11–12, 22; 8:7). Deuteronomy warns against the possibility that prophets may give omens or portents that prove true, then attempt to lead Israel to worship other gods (13:1–4). Jesus speaks of a day when false prophets will deceive many by the "great signs" they perform (Matt 24:24; Mark 13:22; see also 2 Thess 2:9–10). Signs are performed by those opposed to God in the book of Revelation as well—and prove deceptive for many (13:13–14; 16:14; 19:20). God's own sovereignty over nature and history is not brought into question by these false displays of the miraculous: Deuteronomy sees in them God's own testing of his people's loyalty (13:3), and 2 Thessalonians sees them as a divine tool leading to the judgment of those who refuse to believe the truth (2 Thess 2:9–12). The upshot is that those who perform astonishing deeds are not to be blindly followed but to be tested for their conformity to known truth.

STEPHEN WESTERHOLM

Simple   *see* **Folly**

Sin, Sinner, Iniquity, Rebel-(lion), Transgress(ion), Guilt(y), Wicked(ness), Wrong(doing), Trespass, Fault, Offense   The many English words dealt with in this article correspond to the large vocabulary of sin in the Hebrew Bible. One author estimated that about fifty words in the OT should be included in a full study of its teachings about sin. The NT authors tended to prefer a single term, forms of *hamartia*, and this article will not deal with other words that occur occasionally. As to the OT, it will be necessary here to focus on the words used the most often: *hata²*, *ᶜawon*, *pashaᶜ*, *²asham*, and *rashaᶜ*. There is nothing like exact correspondence with the English words listed above. For example, *hata²* is translated "sin, fault, offense," *ᶜawon* "sin, fault, guilt, and iniquity," *pashaᶜ* "iniquity, offense, rebel, transgress, and trespass," and *rashaᶜ* "iniquity, wicked, and wrong." Although some differences in meaning will be identified, OT authors could use several of the words interchangeably when they wished. Sometimes they needed to pile up words: "For our transgressions (*peshaᶜ*) before you are many, and our sins (*hattaᵖth*) testify against us. Our transgressions (*peshaᶜ*) indeed are with us, and we know our iniquities (*ᶜawon*); transgressing (*pashaᶜ*) and denying the LORD, and turning away from following our God, talking oppression and revolt, conceiving lying words and uttering them from the heart" (Isa 59:12–13). See also Isa 1:4, where "sin," "iniquity," "evil," "corruptly," "forsaken," "despised," and "estranged" are used in a single sentence.

The word used most often, *hata²*, literally means "to miss" or "go astray," as in Judg 20:16; Job 5:24; Prov 8:36. This meaning may account for the puzzling verse in Isa 65:20, which as translated in RSV speaks of a one-hundred-year-old sinner in the New Jerusalem: "and the sinner a hundred years old shall be accursed." It seems more likely that *hoteᵖ* here refers to missing, failing to reach 100 years, as in NEB and NRSV: "and one who falls short of a hundred will be considered accursed." Used of human behavior, the word refers to going astray from, falling short of what is right. The Greek word *hamartia* has the same literal meaning. The word *ᶜawon*, often translated "iniquity" (e.g., Exod 20:5; Lev 16:22), is used to refer to a sinful act, to the guilt incurred because of that act, and also to the punishment that it deserves. For example, NRSV sometimes interprets "bear one's iniquity" in the last sense, translating it "subject to punishment" as in Lev 5:1, 17. That the word could be used in this broad way suggests the authors sensed a certain inevitability about the effects of sin. A stronger word than *hata²* is *pashaᶜ*, for it denotes more than going astray; it refers to deliberate disobedience or rebellion and is often translated "transgression." "Guilt" is the rather specific meaning of *²asham*. Among the most common words referring to sin, *rashaᶜ* denotes the quality of the act and the character of the sinner, namely "wickedness."

Sin cannot be explained, and the biblical authors do not try to explain it. They report hundreds of sins, they condemn sin, and they have much to say about God's ways of dealing with sin. But it remains one of the greatest absurdities of human experience. "Sin is the opposite of righteousness, but these two conceptions cannot be set up as equal quantities. Only the righteous act can be termed an action in the proper sense of the word, because it has the characteristics of the normal. A sinful act is, properly speaking, no action, but a caricature. Sin is the negative, that which preys upon the positive forces of life" (Pedersen, I-II.411). The "caricature," or the "impossible possibility," as it has been called, appears very early in the OT. The first thing human beings do, in a world where "God saw everything that he had made, and indeed, it was very good" (Gen 1:31), is commit a sin, by disobeying the one prohibition he had given them (Gen 2:17; 3:6). In human relationships, most sins cause harm of some sort to the one sinned against, but there is more to sin than that, as we see already here. The author of Gen 3 speaks of the harm done to the sinner, but first deals with another aspect: sin insults, perverts, and destroys good relationships (Gen 3:7, 10). The account of the first sin in the Bible, although it does not use words for sin, contains profound insights into that truth.

God clearly intended a close and harmonious relationship with the human beings he had created in his own *image* (Gen 1:26–27). The relationship between creature and creator required them to *trust* that the creator knew what was good for them, and the shaking of trust led to the first sin. "Did God [really] say . . . ?" (Gen 3:1), and the woman was led by that question to use her intelligence to consider the fruit of the tree freely, without regard to what God had said, and to use her freedom to decide for herself (Gen 3:6). Lack of trust then made it possible for desire, for dissatisfaction with having *anything* prohibited, perhaps even for envy of God, to begin working. The initial result was a gain of some sort, the still-debated knowledge of good and evil, but good relationships were disrupted by that forever. The ability to take an act *over against* God revealed Adam and Eve to themselves as individuals who can potentially act over against one another, and so a threat was introduced into their experience. Their nakedness had caused them no shame when their relationship was perfect (Gen 2:25), but now they needed defenses—clothes being the first line of defense (and God knows that now they need them, Gen 3:21). Since they can act over against God, why would he not act the same way toward them, they reason, and so now they are

afraid of him (Gen 3:10). And this initial alienation from one another and from God leads to alienation from nature (v. 15), and between husband and wife (v. 16), and between people and the source of their livelihood (vv. 17–19). Finally, they learned that "the wages of sin is death" (vv. 19, 22–23; Rom 6:23).

Adam and Eve could do no physical harm to God; the first sin destroyed a relationship. Genesis moves immediately to the common physical effects of sin with the story of Cain's murder of Abel in chapter 4, where the word *hatta'th* first appears (v. 7), and appears almost in a personification, crouching at the door. For Cain, it was envy of his brother and anger at God that motivated him to a violent act, so two more insights into the inner human processes that lead to sin have now been introduced. God attempted to persuade Cain that there is a better way, but note that he did not bother to respond to God. Cain was angry with God, so he killed his brother; a classic example of the nonsense that is sin. And he is a figure representing the human race, as his parents are. We recapitulate in our own decisions Adam and Eve's failure to trust and their desire to be more than we can rightfully be. (The first-century-A.D. apocalypse, *2 Bar.* 54:19, says, "Each of us has become our own Adam.") So also, like Cain, we have the opportunity to deal with disappointments without envy and anger, but regularly fail. God's effort to reason with Cain, to assure him that there is a better option, already reflects Scripture's insistence that we are responsible for our sins, as Paul argued at length in Rom 1–3. Then, when Cain learned that he would be punished for murder, he introduced a second of the primary sin words, *'awon*. Since it can mean both "guilt" and "punishment," those who want to give him the benefit of the doubt make 4:13 a confession: "My guilt is greater than I can bear." What we know of Cain's character suggests instead that he is whining: "My punishment is greater than I can bear" (so NRSV).

Any human act that does harm is sin, including to a limited extent, in OT law, harm to things in nature (trees, Deut 20:19–20; birds, Deut 22:6–7). God's aim for the world is that "they will not hurt or destroy on all my holy mountain" (Isa 11:9). This means that any harm done is a sin against God, as Joseph said of the temptation to commit adultery: "How then could I do this great wickedness, and sin against God?" (Gen 39:9).

Genesis moves rapidly and without explanation to speak of the universality of sin: "The LORD saw that the wickedness of humankind was great in the earth, and that every inclination of the thoughts of their hearts was only evil continually" (Gen 6:5). Apocalyptic writers much later elaborated on Gen 6:1–4 in order to explain the presence of evil on earth (e.g., *1 En.* 6–16), rather than taking Gen 3 as an account of the fall, as Christian writers did, but there is no use of this passage elsewhere in Scripture. The flood, God himself acknowledges, did not solve the problem: "I will never again curse the ground because of humankind, for the inclination of the human heart is evil from youth" (Gen 8:21). There is no effort made to explain how that could be, in the good world God created, but it is a fact. Later Jewish thought focused on the word *yetser* "inclination" in this verse and found a way to justify God and acknowledge human responsibility for sin. The rabbis said the *yetser* was part of God's good creation, and it included desire, ambition, and envy, intended for good purposes, for without them we would neither build nor marry nor raise a family nor engage in commerce (*Genesis Rabbah* 9.7). But when they are not kept under control, they lead to sin. This line of thought is not developed in the Bible, however.

The heart (see *mind*), on the other hand, is identified as the source of sin in both Testaments. The OT writers spoke of making decisions with the heart, and although we have the ability to determine what is right, according to Deut 30:14, in truth, "The heart is devious above all else; it is perverse—who can understand it?" (Jer 17:9). "For it is from within, from the human heart, that evil intentions come" (Mark 7:21).

Temptation, it is true, appears to originate in something outside of us. Eve saw the fruit, and it was a delight to the eyes. Even so, she might not have begun her train of thought if there had not been someone else to raise the question. Paul almost excuses himself as he describes the struggle within him between temptation and the desire to do good: "But sin, seizing an opportunity in the commandment ["You shall not covet"], produced in me all kinds of covetousness. . . . Now if I do what I do not want, it is no longer I that do it, but sin that dwells within me" (Rom 7:8, 20). He knows he is responsible, however (cf. Rom 3:20), and chapters 6 and 7 of Romans take the inner struggle with the utmost seriousness. Although *flesh* is not inherently evil, as the concept is used in the NT, Paul is inclined to use that word when he speaks of our inability to obey, as Jeremiah spoke of the heart in Jer 17:9.

George Caird has described the various aspects of sin in terms of four things God has done to correct it, and these will provide a useful way to summarize some of Scripture's teachings: "Justification, consecration, reconciliation, and redemption imply a guilt to be cancelled, a stain to be erased, an enmity to be dispelled, and a servitude to be abolished" (Caird 87).

Enmity, requiring *reconciliation*, appeared early in Genesis. It involves uncertainty about whether God can be trusted (or a conclusion that God cannot be: "The LORD will not do good, nor will he do harm" [Zeph 1:12]) and anger, we have already seen. It leads to the conclusion we can do as well as God, or likely better (see *pride*), and our relationship is thus gravely distorted (never broken on God's side). Israel's awareness that choices of this kind can lead only to disaster was founded on their understanding of the uniqueness of Yahweh and thus of their relationship to him. The first four commandments summarize it. "You shall have no other gods before me" (Exod 20:3). "I the LORD your God am a *jealous* God" (Exod 20:5). Elsewhere, "The LORD is our God, the LORD alone" (Deut 6:4), and "You shall be holy, for I the LORD your God am holy" (Lev 19:2, and often). Sin thus involves far more than doing harm to others. Everything that pertains to Israel's relationship with Yahweh must be done in accordance with God's will, and this forms the basis for prohibitions of idolatry and identifying ritual sins. The latter can be corrected by the means of *atonement* God has provided, as described especially in Lev 1–7. Paul speaks bluntly of sin as enmity in Rom 5:8–10: "But God proves his love for us in that while we were sinners Christ died for us. . . . For if while we were enemies, we were reconciled to God through the death of his Son . . ." (for hatred of Christ and of God, see John 15:18–27).

Guilt is in part the sentence declaring that we are wrong, and in part our awareness of it. The classic statement is that of Judas: "I have sinned by betraying innocent blood" (Matt 27:4). The sense of guilt is expressed frequently in the Psalms of lament. The great penitential Ps 51 contains an especially powerful statement: "For I know my transgressions (*pesha^c*), and my sin (*hatta[>]th*) is ever before me. Against you, you alone, have I sinned (*hata[>]*), and done what is evil in your sight, so that you are justified in your sentence and blameless when you pass judgment. Indeed, I was born guilty (*^cawon*), a sinner (*hata[>]*) when my mother conceived me" (vv. 3–5; cf. Ezra 9:6–15). Although Ps 51:5 has been used in the development of the doctrine of original sin in Christian theology, the idea that everyone bears the guilt that incurred from the sin of Adam and Eve, passed on by procreation from generation to generation, does not appear in the OT. The psalmist was here simply expressing in vivid poetic terms the depth of his guilt feelings. It was Paul's use of *Adam* as the antitype of Christ in Rom 5:12–21 that contributed most to the doctrine of original sin.

The word "guilt" appears with the greatest frequency in English translations with an objective meaning, however, referring to the *[>]asham*, the guilt offering (Lev 5:14–6:7). This was one of the means of atonement God provided in order to assure the repentant sinner that forgiveness was possible (see *sacrifice*).

Stain refers to the sense of uncleanness that typically accompanies feelings of guilt. "Purge me with hyssop and I shall be clean; wash me, and I shall be whiter than snow" (Ps 51:7). "Wash yourselves; make yourselves clean; remove the evil of your doings from before my eyes" (Isa 1:16). This language describes an inner feeling and does not refer to the ritual cleanness that was an important part of Israelite religion. That was not associated with sin and guilt (see *clean*). But the sense of having "transgressed" in some way seems instinctively to be associated with dirtiness in most people. Comparable to that is shame and self-loathing (Ezek 16:54, 61–64; 20:43; 39:26) and the crushed and depressed spirit (Isa 57:15; 66:2). So forgiveness in the OT can be described as cleansing: "I will cleanse them from all the guilt (*^cawon*) of their sin (*hata[>]*) against me, and I will forgive all the guilt of their sin and rebellion (*pesha^c*) against me" (Jer 33:8; cf. Ezek 36:24–25, 29; 37:23).

Although the early church showed no interest in ritual cleanness, the instinctive association of sin with pollution and forgiveness with cleansing appears in the NT. Peter said of Gentile believers that God has cleansed their hearts by faith (Acts 15:9), and 2 Pet 1:9 speaks of the "cleansing of past sins." The use of *blood* as a ritual cleansing agent in Judaism led John to speak of the blood of Christ in that way: "The blood of Jesus his Son cleanses us from all sin. . . . If we confess our sins, he who is faithful and just will forgive us our sins and cleanse us from all unrighteousness" (1 John 1:7, 9).

Servitude is a prominent theme in the NT, but the OT does not normally speak of sin in this way. *Slavery* remained a physical threat, and the words for salvation (see *save*) and *redemption* were used almost exclusively for deliverance from physical distress. One interesting exception is Ps 130:8, "It is he who will redeem Israel from all its iniquities (*'awon*)," the only time "redeem" is used in this way. For the NT, however, salvation means healing and forgiveness. In Luke 8:48 "made you well" translates *sozo*, the same word translated "saved," with reference to forgiveness, in Luke 7:50. Matthew took care to explain Jesus' name (Joshua in Hebrew; Jeshua in Aramaic = "Yahweh saves") as "he will save his people from their sins" (Matt 1:21). This imagery depicts sin as a power to which we are inescapably enslaved, unless faith in Jesus Christ gives us *freedom*. The theme of slavery to sin is especially prominent in the writings of Paul. He writes of sin's "dominion" in Rom 6:12–14, and of being slaves of sin in 6:20. Freedom means being enslaved to God (v. 22), for we will inevitably have a master, like it or not, and the choice is between sin and the righteousness of God. Commentators debate whether Rom 7 describes Paul's agonies of *conscience* before his conversion, or afterward, for it is true that "slavery under sin" (Rom 7:14) has not yet been fully broken in any Christian life (7:24–25). There is no despair in Paul, however, "for all who are led by the Spirit of God are children of God. For you did not receive a spirit of slavery to fall back into fear, but you have received a spirit of adoption" (Rom 8:14–15).

For discussions of the sin against the Holy Spirit, called the unforgivable sin, see the articles on *forgive* and *Spirit*. For articles on other words associated with sin, see *abomination, blaspheme, desire, folly, hate, hypocrisy, idolatry, immorality, kill, marriage, possessions, pride, true, violence*, and *war*. See also *evil, Satan, tempt*. For the remedies for sin, see *atone, forgive, grace, heal, justify, mercy, reconcile, redeem, repent, restore, sacrifice*, and *save*.

G. B. Caird, *New Testament Theology* (Oxford: Clarendon Press, 1994), 74–117; Walther Eichrodt, *Theology of the Old Testa-*

ment (Philadelphia: Westminster Press, 1967), 2:380–443; Johannes Pedersen, *Israel: Its Life and Culture* (London: Oxford University Press, 1926), I-II.411–37; C. Ryder Smith, *The Bible Doctrine of Sin and of the Ways of God with Sinners* (London: Epworth Press, 1953).

DONALD E. GOWAN

Sinai   *see* **Covenant**

Sing, Song   Music is not mentioned very often in the NT, but it appears very frequently in the OT. Singing and instrumental music were natural human responses or accompaniments to a great variety of situations (*IDB* 3:457–63), but their theological importance is to be found in the association of music with the *praise* of God. Singing seems, in fact, to be the natural form that praise took in Israel. The intimate association between the sense of the presence of God and singing is expressed in a striking way in Exod 15:2 (echoed in Isa 12:2): "The LORD is my strength and my song (NRSV Mg), and he has become my salvation." The three most common terms for singing in the OT are *shir*, a general word for song; *gamar*, which is associated with the playing of musical instruments (Pss 71:22; 98:5; 144:9; 147:7) but is regularly translated "sing praises" in NRSV; and *ranan*, a joyful cry, translated "sing for joy" or "sing aloud." In Ps 95:1 it is parallel to "joyful noise." Israelite worship on festive occasions seems to have been rather boisterous. The music of Ps 33:3 was to be accompanied by "loud shouts" (also Pss 27:6; 47:6; 89:15), namely, the *teru'ah*, which could be in other settings a battle cry (e.g., Amos 1:14; 2:2) or an acclamation of the presence of the ark of the covenant (e.g., Josh 6:5, 20; 1 Sam 4:6; 2 Sam 6:15). The singing probably bore little resemblance to Western melody, but the occurrences of these words are always in contexts of rejoicing, with a minor exception to be noted later.

The language of *worship* in ancient Israel may have made no sharp distinctions among what we would call rhythmic speech, chanting, and singing, for Moses and David are said to have recited or spoken (*dibber*) their "songs" (Deut 31:30; 32:44; 2 Sam 22:1), and Hannah's prayer, which we would be inclined to group with other OT songs, is not so designated (1 Sam 2:1). But clearly, occasions of triumph, thanksgiving, and rejoicing instinctively led the Israelites to lift up their voices in the magnificent poetry of the OT songs. The words noted above appear especially frequently in the Psalms, in calls to the congregation to sing to the Lord, or in statements of the psalmist's intention to sing.

That song rather than speech was the usual way to praise God is indicated by the references to musical instruments. Psalm 150 is almost entirely a list of the available instruments. Psalms 33:2–3 and 71:22 speak of song accompanied by lyre and harp, Ps 81:2 adds the tambourine, and Ps 98:5–6 adds trumpets and horn (cf. 1 Chr 13:8; 15:28; 25:6; 2 Chr 5:13; Pss 144:9; 147:7).

God's mighty and gracious acts and all of God's praiseworthy attributes are cited as reasons that led the Israelites to break forth in song. The list is long but is worth citing, partly because of its length. God's acts include triumph (Exod 15:1, 21), victory (Ps 98:1), wonderful works (1 Chr 16:9; Pss 92:4; 105:2; cf. Ps 9:11), salvation (1 Chr 16:23; Pss 95:1; 96:2; Isa 38:20; Jer 31:7), judging the earth (1 Chron 16:33; Pss 67:4; 96:12–13), dealing bountifully (Ps 13:6), deliverance (Ps 51:14; Jer 20:13), help (Ps 63:7), rescue (Ps 71:23), doing gloriously (Isa 12:5), redeeming (Isa 44:23), comforting and having compassion (Isa 49:13). God's attributes include righteousness (Pss 7:17; 145:7), power/might/strength (Pss 21:13; 59:16–17; 81:1), faithfulness (Pss 71:22; 89:1), steadfast love (Pss 59:16–17; 89:1; Jer 33:11), loyalty and justice (Ps 101:1), goodness (Pss 135:3; 145:7; Jer 33:11), graciousness (Pss 135:3; 147:1), glory (Ps 138:5), greatness (Isa 12:6), and majesty (Isa 24:14).

A few of the laments in the Psalter are identified as "songs" in their superscrip-

tions (see Pss 83; 88; 120; 129; 130), but these are minor exceptions to the general practice of using *shir* to refer to a song of praise.

Occasionally a "new song" was called for, an idea that has not yet been adequately explained. The contents of the songs so designated are not significantly different from others, and they do not show evidence of responding to some unique, new event of salvation (except perhaps for Ps 40:3). They tend to emphasize something quite stable: God's work as Lord of creation (Pss 33:6–7; 96:11–12; 98:7–8; 144:5–7, 13–14; Isa 42:10). God's lordship over the nations is a second prominent theme (Pss 33:8–10, 13–17; 96:3, 10; 98:2; 144:7b, 11; 149:7–9; Isa 42:13), and it may be that the idea of his "coming to judge the earth" influenced the call for a new song (Pss 96:13; 98:9; 149:9).

The singers imagined themselves testifying to the nations concerning Yahweh's greatness (Pss 18:49; 57:9; 108:3). Even the nations were sometimes called upon to join in singing Yahweh's praise (Pss 67:4; 68:32; Isa 42:11; "all the earth," Ps 66:4). In their exuberance, Israelites called upon all of creation to join in a great chorus of praise: "Then shall all the trees of the forest sing for joy" (Ps 96:12). "Let the floods clap their hands; let the hills sing together for joy" (Ps 98:8). "The meadows clothe themselves with flocks, the valleys deck themselves with grain, they shout and sing together with joy" (Ps 65:13). "Sing for joy, O heavens, and exult, O earth; break forth, O mountains, into singing!" (Isa 49:13; cf. Isa 44:23; Jer 51:48).

A special use of "song" appears in Deut 31:19, where the song of Moses is declared to be a "witness" against Israel when they disobey the Lord in the future. This song was thus the Lord's revealed word, rather than the usual response of the people to the Lord.

The NT contains relatively few songs but mentions singing in several significant places. Luke records poetry like that of the OT in what are now called the songs of Mary and Zechariah, but he introduces them with "said" rather than "sang" (Luke 1:46, 67). The accounts of the Last Supper in Matthew and Mark contain an important reference to the use of the Psalms in the home celebration of *Passover*: "When they had sung the hymn, they went out to the Mount of Olives" (Matt 26:30; Mark 14:26). This was most likely Pss 113–118, which the Mishnah (*Pesahim* 4.6–7; codified ca. A.D. 190) prescribes for singing at the conclusion of the Passover meal.

We know little about singing in early synagogue worship, but it is likely that the Psalms were used during this period, since early Christian worship largely followed the synagogue pattern, and a few NT texts refer to singing. Worship, according to Eph 5:19 and Col 3:16, should include psalms and hymns and spiritual songs. James counseled prayer for the suffering and singing praise for the cheerful (Jas 5:13). Paul and Silas spontaneously sang hymns at midnight while in prison (Acts 16:25). These hints that the joyful singing of Israel reappeared in early Christian worship are reinforced by the relative prominence of music in Revelation. The central message of the book—that despite all the suffering on earth God's victory was certain—was conveyed in a striking way by scenes of joyful song in heaven, interrupting the accounts of terrible devastation on earth: "Without ceasing they sing, 'Holy, holy, holy, the Lord God the Almighty, who was and is and is to come'" (Rev 4:8b). "They cast their crowns before the throne, singing, 'You are worthy, our Lord and God, to receive glory and honor and power, for you created all things, and by your will they existed and were created'" (Rev 4:10b–11). For Revelation, the term "new song" was fully appropriate, for it celebrated the final victory of Christ over the powers of evil: "They sing a new song: 'You are worthy to take the scroll and to open its seals, for you were slaughtered and by your blood you ransomed for God saints from every tribe and language and people and nation; you have made them to be a kingdom and priests serving our God, and they will reign on earth'" (Rev 5:9; cf. 14:3). The OT's celebration of God's greatness in song is brought together with eschatological celebration of Christ's victory in 15:3–4, which introduces a hymn called the song of Moses and the song of the Lamb.

J. H. Eaton, "Music's Place in Worship: A Contribution from the Psalms," *OtSt* 23 (1984): 85–107; A. Sendrey, *Music in Ancient Israel* (London: Vision Press, 1969); E. Werner, "Music," *IDB* 3:457–69.

DONALD E. GOWAN

Sister   *see* **Family**

Six Hundred Sixty-Six   *see* **Numbers**

Slave, Slavery, Bond, Bondage, Oppression   From a linguistic perspective, the words "slave, slavery" are a subdomain of the semantic field "status." The Hebrew word for slave (*ʿebed*) derives from the verb meaning "to work." The Greek noun *doulos* is a subdomain of the semantic field "control, rule" and describes someone who is completely controlled by something or someone. The related Greek verb, *douleuo*, is a subdomain of two semantic fields: help, care for (one sense of work), serve; and serve another as slave (another sense of work). "Bondman" in the NRSV is frequently a synonym for slave (e.g., 2 Kgs 9:8; 14:26). It also describes a prisoner (Ps 69:33, in bonds), someone restrained by chains (Luke 8:29), or a person "enslaved" to a serious illness or powerful spirit (Luke 13:16).

"Oppression" occurs only in the OT of the NRSV, translating the Hebrew *lahats*. The Septuagint renders this Hebrew word *lahats* by *thlipsis* (trouble that inflicts distress; oppression, affliction, tribulation), a word that occurs more than forty times in the NT, especially in Paul (Rom 5:3 "suffering"; 8:35 "hardship"; 1 Cor 7:28 "distress"; 2 Cor 1:4 "affliction"; 2 Cor 8:13 "pressure"; 1 Thess 1:6 "persecution"). Notice the varied English renditions of the same Greek word. This survey highlights the fact that in most cases oppression refers to that aspect of slave/slavery that reflects depriving another of freedom, hence control, though not necessarily slavery itself.

The commonalities of Hebrew and Greek words and their counterparts confirm the general definition of slavery proposed by experts. Institutionally, slavery is an act of dishonor (social death—self or other inflicted) consisting of depriving a person of freedom of decision and action, by means of force or enforced solidarity, with a view to the social utility of the enslaving agent. Slavery involves one person holding ownership rights over another/others. Perhaps more precisely from another perspective, slavery is voluntary or involuntary servitude to an individual, the state, or temple that involves reduction of legal and social status to the impersonal level of property. The institution of slavery most likely came into existence toward the conclusion of the fourth millennium, but in each country it developed and evolved differently. Indeed within the same country, slavery changed over the course of time.

The Old Testament. It must, however, be emphasized at the outset that slavery in the ancient world had practically nothing in common with slavery familiar from New World practice and experience of the eighteenth and nineteenth centuries. It would distort the interpretation of the Bible to impose such an understanding on its books. The differences between slavery in the New World and the ancient world, especially in the first century, are significant. Regarding slavery in the ancient world, racial factors played no role. One of the chief sources of slaves was prisoners of war (1 Macc 3:41). Men, boys, and even women were killed, but young girls were spared and taken as wives by their captors (Num 31:9–18). Slaves were encouraged to be educated, and some were even better educated than their owners. Many slaves were entrusted with very sensitive and highly responsible social functions (e.g., Joseph,

Gen 39–40). Slaves were able to own property, including other slaves. Their religious and cultural traditions were the same as those of the freeborn. For example, male household slaves had to be circumcised (Gen 17:12–14). They were also associated with the family in ritual meals (Exod 12:44; Deut 12:12; 16:11–15). There were no prohibitions against slaves assembling in public. The majority of urban and domestic slaves could realistically look forward to being freed by the age of thirty.

Besides war, there were other sources of slaves. It was always possible to purchase slaves (Ezek 27:13), either to become working members of the household (Gen 39:4) or as concubines (Gen 30:1–13). Inability of someone to repay a debt would cause the creditor to take that person (and/or his family) into slavery (Deut 15:12; Isa 50:1). Sometimes, a debtor could sell himself into slavery to repay the debt (Lev 25:39–55). In this latter instance, however, a distinctive characteristic of slavery in Israel comes to the fore. Israelites forced into these circumstances shall be hired servants or bonded laborers, but they may not serve as slaves (v. 39). The reason is that they are now slaves of Yahweh, liberated from slavery in Egypt (Deut 15:15). To make them slaves of another person would be a challenge to the honor of Yahweh their master. This is why kidnaping for slavery was considered a capital offense (Exod 21:16; Deut 24:7) and is very likely the sense of the commandment: "You shall not steal," that is, "kidnap a fellow Israelite for the purpose of enslaving him" (Exod 20:15).

While slaves in Israel had the legal status of property, just as in other contemporary Middle Eastern societies, the Torah provided some protection. If one beat a slave to death, an unspecified punishment was levied (Exod 21:20). On the other hand, if a master maimed a slave permanently, that slave would have to be set free (Exod 21:26–27). Slaves were also entitled to the Sabbath rest (Exod 23:12). Hebrew slaves had still other protection. Their bondage could not last longer than six years (Exod 21:2; Deut 15:12). Moreover, the released slave was to be provided for "liberally" from the flock, the threshing floor, and the winepress (Deut 15:14). The reason once again is that Israelites were once slaves but had been redeemed by God. They ought to imitate in their relationships with their slaves the behavior of Yahweh, their gracious emancipator (redeemer), toward them.

Nevertheless, the status of a slave was always one of dependence and submission. This is especially evident when compared with kinship relations. As one might expect as an outcome of war, an Israelite male who took to wife a woman captured in war had absolute rights in his choice. In the circum-Mediterranean culture where marriages are typically arranged by families, the female captive's family had no say in this matter, nor in fact did the woman! Thus the master-slave relationship superseded that of family ties (Deut 21:10–14). But if the male decided she was not a satisfactory partner, he had to free her. She could not be sold again into slavery, because the male had shamed her (v. 14), that is, rendered her unacceptable and undesirable to another male (see Num 31:17–18).

In addition, when the master provided a male slave with a wife, the wife and children remained with the master if the slave accepted his freedom when offered (Exod 21:4). Slaves were indeed property from the legal point of view. The case was similar for females with regard to their slaves. The relationship between the mistresses Rachel and Leah and their slaves Bilhah and Zilpah completely negated the mother-child relationship between these slaves and the sons they bore (Gen 30:9–13). Rachel's response to the birth of Bilhah's son, "God has judged me, and has also heard my voice and given me a son" (Gen 30:6, emphasis added), illustrates this well.

Slaves could gain freedom in a number of ways. A member of the clan could redeem them (Exod 21:8; Lev 25:48), or the slave could purchase his or her own freedom (Lev 25:49). As already noted, if

a master did permanent physical harm to a slave (e.g., causing loss of an eye or a tooth), that slave would have to be liberated (Exod 21:26). Since a master would be reluctant to lose a slave on these grounds, the law served as a means for curtailing physical abuse of slaves. Of course the six-year limitation on slavery applied only to Hebrew slaves, not to foreigners (Lev 25:45–46). While the jubilee year (every forty-nine or fifty years) granted freedom to all Israelite slaves, there is no evidence the jubilee was ever observed. Moreover, given the typical life expectancy in the ancient Near East, perhaps very few would have benefited from this stipulation.

The New Testament. For the NT period, it is important to keep in mind that there existed significant differences among three different Mediterranean traditions that might have some bearing on the NT. A considerate reader would have to take into account these varying philosophical frameworks, which might serve as the appropriate context in which to read the documents. In general, Greeks considered a slave as inferior by nature. His or her good fortune would be to have a Greek master. Romans regarded slaves to be like things, yet they seemed to view slavery as a process for integrating people into society, since many slaves could look forward to Roman citizenship when set free. This was a frequent occurrence.

The Greeks and Romans actually—and independently—transformed slavery into something quite novel in world history. They managed to establish an institutionalized system of slave labor to work in the rural and the urban areas. This was already in place by the second century B.C. and helps us to understand the cultural contributions of both these civilizations. Culture requires leisure, which slave labor provided for others who could create and support culture.

The slaves mentioned in the NT are very likely those who were born into slavery. Greek and Roman law recognized as slaves those born to mothers in slavery. Records indicate that this provided a sufficient supply of slaves to meet society's needs at the time. Others (as in the Judaic tradition) sold themselves into slavery as a way to improve their life. Some of the benefits included the possibility of attaining a better job or of climbing the social ladder. As Scott Bartchy has pointed out, Erastus, the city treasurer of Corinth mentioned in 1 Cor 16:23, very likely sold himself to the city (as a slave) in order to attain that job (Bartchy, 60–61). At the age of forty, he would be emancipated and then, in his new position as freedman and Roman citizen, would be elected to the position of local Roman administrator (*aedile*). Inscriptional evidence about such an Erastus indicates that as *aedile*, an official in charge of buildings, roads, sanitation, public games, and the like, he paved the street in front of the main theater. Thus what might seem contradictory in modern Western eyes (a slave holding such a high position and moving up in status upon gaining freedom), actually made Erastus a socially very prominent member of the Corinthian congregation.

The honor accruing to the title "slave of God" in the OT continues to echo in NT documents. In Titus (1:1), Paul is designated "slave of God" (NRSV Mg). Paul transforms that phrase when he calls himself a "slave of Christ" (Rom 1:1). He also applies the honorific to Timothy (Phil 1:1). They stand of a long line of honorable slaves of God: Abraham, Moses, David, Elijah (see *servant*).

It is well known that the NT says nothing of the origins of slavery, nor does it seek to justify it. Neither does the NT explicitly condemn it. In fact, slaves appear as typical figures in Jesus' preaching (Matt 6:24; 13:24–30; etc.), and Jesus exhorted his followers to serve one another in such a capacity (Matt 20:26–27). However, Matthew's Jesus told an interesting parable of relevance to this discussion of slavery (Matt 18:23–34). Though Athens outlawed it in 594/593 B.C., most other places, including Palestine, endorsed the enslavement of debtors by creditors. In this parable, the slave owed the king an astronomical sum of talents. Since he could not pay it, the king ordered him to be sold along with his wife and children and all his possessions in order to settle the debt. But at his plea for understanding, the king forgave the slave and released him. In his turn, the pardoned slave encountered a fellow slave who owed him a significant amount but far less than the pardoned slave owed the king. This slave too was unable to pay and begged for patience. The pardoned slave turned a deaf ear and instead had his debtor imprisoned. When the king learned of this, the king reversed his decision, imprisoned the forgiven slave, and directed that he be tortured until the debt was satisfied. The "new" context of "forgiveness" in which this parable is set (vv. 21–22, 35) blunts the ugliness of enslavement because of the inability to repay a debt. Jesus' audience would have gasped in awe at the mercy of the king but turned away in revulsion at the behavior of the forgiven slave.

Luke's version of the prayer that Jesus taught to his disciples reinforces the lesson. "And forgive us our sins, for we ourselves forgive everyone indebted to us" (Luke 11:4). The petitioner boldly proclaims forgoing the "privilege" of casting debtors into slavery in order to receive divine pardon for sins which are actions that shame God and require divine vengeance.

The heart of Paul's advice to slaves in 1 Cor 7:21–24 is to remind them they "were bought with a price." They were *redeemed* or set free, and this entails a new obligation to a new patron. These redeemed people are now "slaves of Christ" (7:22). If this is their new condition, they should not become "slaves of human masters" either by self-sale into debt bondage or by becoming enslaved to human expectations, aspirations, ideas. Similarly, the author of 1 Peter (2:16) exhorts converts to the *way* to live as free people, yet as "slaves of God."

Thus in the Bible, no one is ever really "free" but rather always a slave of someone. Israel accepted with gratitude its new status as "slaves of God." Paul suggests the same for Christians. The slave "called in the Lord" is now a "freed person belonging to the Lord" (1 Cor 7:22). In the Greco-Roman world, the phrase "freed person" entailed the legal obligations (*paramone* in Greek) of a freed slave to his former owner. By granting freedom, the former master has become a patron, and in his new status, the former slave serves as a client by showing lifelong willingness to be of service, to offer assistance, and to fulfill moral duty. These are the duties of believers as slaves of God.

S. Scott Bartchy, MALLON CHRESAI: *First-Century Slaves and the Interpretation of 1 Corinthians*, SBLDS 11 (Missoula, Mont., 1973); K. R. Bradley, *Slaves and Masters in the Roman Empire: A Study in Social Control* (Oxford: Oxford University Press, 1987); Gregory C. Chirichigno, *Debt-Slavery in Israel and the Ancient Near East*, JSOTSup 141 (Sheffield: Sheffield Academic Press, 1993); Dale B. Martin, "Slavery and the Ancient Jewish Family," in *The Jewish Family in Antiquity*, ed. Shaze J. D. Cohen, Brown Judaic Studies 289 (Atlanta: Scholars Press, 1994), 113–29; Willard B. Swartley, *Slavery, Sabbath, War, and Women* (Scottdale, Pa.: Herald Press, 1983), 31–64.
JOHN J. PILCH

Son   *see* Family

Son of David
The OT uses this phrase in its literal sense to refer to a man begotten by David, most notably Solomon (2 Chr 1:1; 13:8; 35:3; Prov 1:1; Eccl 1:1). Eventually it was used of any descendant of David, as in Matt 1:20, where Joseph is addressed by an angel as "son of David." Elsewhere in the NT the phrase refers to the messiah, as in Matt 22:42, where the Pharisees say that the messiah is the son of David. In the opening line of Matthew Jesus is identified as "the Messiah, the son of David" (Matt 1:1).

While the expectation of the Messiah was not as pervasive in first-century Judaism as Christians often assume (see *anoint*), wherever there is talk of an ideal future king, it is regularly assumed that he will be a descendant of David. The *Psalms of Solomon*, a Pharisaic writing of the first century B.C., refers to "the son of David" in this way (17:21). Although "the son of David" does not appear with this sense in any OT passage, the messianic interpretation lies ready to hand wherever reference is made to a future "David," as in Ezek 34:23: "I will set up over them one shepherd, my servant David, and he shall feed them . . . and be their shepherd" (see also 37:24; Jer 23:5; 33:15).

In Matt 12:23 the crowds who have just witnessed an impressive miracle ask, "Can this be the Son of David?" There is little evidence that first-century Jews expected the royal deliverer to perform healings. It was believed that he would possess extraordinary powers, however, and consequently this is not a historically incredible question.

The blind Bartimaeus of Mark 10:46–52 twice calls Jesus "Son of David." Mark makes no attempt to explain why this beggar would address Jesus in this way (Mark 8:30 demands secrecy concerning Jesus' messianic identity), but literarily it prepares for the cry of the crowd escorting Jesus into Jerusalem, "Blessed is the coming kingdom of our ancestor David!" (11:10).

Luke 18:38–39 preserves the repeated "Son of David" of the blind man. Matthew doubles the incident; in each case two blind men address Jesus in this way (9:27; 20:30–31). He retains a reference to David at the triumphal entry: "Hosanna to the Son of David!" (21:9). This acclamation is repeated by children in the temple (21:15). Still more striking is Matthew's attribution of the phrase to a Gentile woman in the region of Tyre and Sidon (15:22). Matthew seems to suggest thereby that the crowd's question concerning Jesus' messiahship (12:23) has spread far and wide. Kingsbury points out that, although Matthew uses "Son of David" more often than Mark and Luke, it does not serve as a confessional title. It is used not by disciples but by "no-accounts," blind men, a

Gentile woman, and children, "in order to underline the guilt that devolves upon Israel for not receiving its Messiah" (Kingsbury, 100, 103).

"Son of David" does not appear in the rest of the NT. It is implied, however, in those texts that speak of Jesus' or the Messiah's descent from David (John 7:42; Rom 1:3; 2 Tim 2:8; Rev 22:16). Revelation 5:5 refers to Jesus as "the Root of David."

The reason for the infrequent use of the phrase may be seen in an important Synoptic passage. In Mark 12:35, at the conclusion of a long series of disputes in the temple, Jesus poses a question to his religious opponents: "How can the scribes say that the Messiah is the Son of David?" After quoting Ps 110:1, he continues, "David himself calls him Lord, so how can he be his son?" (see also Matt 22:41–46; Luke 20:41–44). For the Gospel writers the point seems to be that "the Son of David," perhaps because of its nationalistic and militaristic connotations, is an unsatisfactory title for Jesus, the Son of God.

J. D. Kingsbury, *Matthew: Structure, Christology, Kingdom* (Minneapolis: Fortress Press, 1975).

DOUGLAS R. A. HARE

Son of God

Son of God In the OT the plural "sons of God" occurs in Gen 6:2, 4 and Job 1:6; 2:1; 38:7 with reference to heavenly beings. The singular "son of God" in Dan 3:25 probably has the same meaning. The Israelites are called "sons of God" in Deut 14:1 (compare "my sons . . . my daughters" in Isa 43:6). Israel as a whole is referred to by God as "my son" in Exod 4:23 and Hos 11:1 (cited in Matt 2:15; see *adopt*). In Wis 2:18 "son of God" is used of the righteous man, but there is no definite article. Nowhere in the OT or Apocrypha do we find "*the* Son of God."

In Ps 2:7 God addresses Zion's king, "You are my son; today I have begotten you" (quoted in Acts 13:33; Heb 1:5). Also of special interest to the NT is Nathan's prophecy in 2 Sam 7:14 con-

cerning David's offspring, "I will be a father to him, and he shall be a son to me" (see Heb 1:5). This motif appears also in Ps 89:26–27. Neither Solomon nor any of his successors is referred to as "son of God," however. This was probably in reaction to the custom of the surrounding nations of assigning semidivine status to their kings by means of this epithet, often implying physical descent.

The same reluctance to use "son of God" of the messiah is seen in Jewish writings of the time of Jesus, perhaps because the Roman emperor was so designated. In 2 Esdras (late first century A.D.) God refers to the messianic rescuer as "my son" (2 Esdr 13:32, 37, 52). In one of the Qumran fragments "the son of God" appears, but because of the poor state of the text it is disputed whether the reference is to the messiah or to a foreign oppressor. Nevertheless, one fragment associates 2 Sam 7 with "the shoot of David," suggesting that it was possible for some of Jesus' contemporaries to think of the messiah as "son of God." It is unlikely that divine status was implied. "Son of God" probably referred to role rather than nature.

It is impossible to determine when the title "the Son of God" was first applied to Jesus. This must have happened before Paul's conversion, that is, no more than five years after Jesus' death. It may have emerged from post-Easter study of passages in the Scriptures pertaining to the messiah, such as Ps 2:7 and 2 Sam 7:14. Some would maintain that its origin lies in the filial consciousness of Jesus, as reflected in his unusual use of *Abba* in addressing God (Mark 14:36), the Q saying concerning the mutual knowledge of the Father and the Son (Matt 11:27 = Luke 10:22), and the experience of the voice from heaven at his baptism and transfiguration (Mark 1:11; 9:7). Other scholars maintain than none of these can be confirmed except for *Abba*, and that this is not enough to prove that Jesus claimed to be God's son in a unique sense. The earliest NT use of the phrase may be in Rom 1:3–4, probably a pre-Pauline formula:

"who was descended from David according to the flesh and was declared to be Son of God with power according to the spirit of holiness by resurrection from the dead." It is not clear whether this statement presents Jesus as first becoming Son of God at the resurrection (see Acts 2:36) or whether "with power" indicates that he had been Son of God but was now empowered to fulfill the role.

Paul's Letters. The messianic role of the Son of God seems to be implied in 1 Thess 1:10, "to wait for his Son from heaven" (cf. Phil 3:20). For Paul, however, "the Son of God" and "Son" have less to do with Jesus' messianic status than with his relationship to God. Wherever "Son" is used, "Father" is implied. Characteristic of Paul is the phrase "the God and Father of our Lord Jesus Christ" (Rom 15:6; 2 Cor 1:3; see also 2 Cor 11:31; Eph 1:3; Col 1:3), which implies Jesus' unique status as "Son."

The apostle uses "Son" and "the Son of God" in a variety of ways. Most important is the association of "Son" with Jesus' saving death, as in Rom 8:32, "He who did not withhold his own Son, but gave him up for all of us," and Gal 2:20, "the Son of God, who loved me and gave himself for me" (see also Rom 5:10). Paul may feel that Son language is particularly appropriate here as a reminder that Jesus' sacrifice is an expression of God's love, not merely a human offering to an angry god.

The Father-Son correlation also underlies the statements about the sending of the Son in Rom 8:3, "by sending his own Son in the likeness of sinful flesh, and to deal with sin, he condemned sin in the flesh," and Gal 4:4, "when the fullness of time had come, God sent his Son." These statements may point to the Son's origin in heaven but need not do so; the verb "send" is used of God sending prophets.

Since the resurrected Son now has a heavenly residence, Paul can use "Son" and "Spirit" interchangeably, as in Gal 4:6, "God has sent the Spirit of his Son into our hearts" (cf. "Spirit of Christ" in Rom 8:9). It is this spiritual presence of the exalted Jesus that permits Paul to say, "God is faithful; by him you were called into the fellowship of his Son" (1 Cor 1:9).

Despite the exalted status Paul ascribes to the Son, there is one passage in which the apostle explicitly subordinates the Son to the Father: "Then comes the end, when he hands over the kingdom to God the Father. . . . When all things are subjected to him, then the Son himself will also be subjected to the one who put all things in subjection under him, so that God may be all in all" (1 Cor 15:24, 28). Paul refers to believers as "sons of God" (Rom 8:14; Gal 3:26; NRSV "children of God").

Synoptic Gospels. For Matthew, Mark, and Luke "the Son of God" is the most important christological title; it is affirmed by God's own voice at the baptism (Matt 3:17; Mark 1:11; Luke 3:22) and the transfiguration (Matt 17:5; Mark 9:7; Luke 9:35). In Mark the baptismal voice constitutes Jesus' call to serve as the Messiah (compare Acts 10:38). Matthew and Luke present Jesus as Messiah from birth (Matt 2:2–6; Luke 1:32; 35, 2:11). In all three Gospels demons recognize Jesus as the Son of God (Matt 8:29, Mark 3:11, 5:7, Luke 4:41, 8:28). That "Son of God" is a synonym for "Messiah" is made clear in the high priest's question, "Are you the Messiah, the Son of the Blessed One?" (Mark 14:61; cf. Matt 26:63, Luke 22:67, 70). In Matthew's version of Peter's confession, the two terms appear together: "You are the Messiah, the Son of the living God" (Matt 16:16; see also Acts 9:20,22). Consequently, the centurion's confession following Jesus' death, "Truly this man was God's Son" (Mark 15:39; cf. Matt 27:54), should be understood as an acknowledgment of Jesus' messiahship.

In the temptation narrative common to Matthew and Luke, the devil acknowledges Jesus' messianic status: "If you are the Son of God . . ." (Matt 4:3, 6; Luke 4:3, 9). The three temptations are best understood in relation to Jesus' messianic calling.

It is disputed whether "the Son of God" is for Matthew merely a synonym for "Messiah" or whether it ascribes divine status to Jesus. In Matt 14:33, after Jesus walks on the water, "those in the boat worshiped him, saying, 'Truly you are the Son of God.'" This anticipates the resurrection scene, when the eleven disciples worship the risen Jesus and are told to baptize "in the name of the Father and of the Son and of the Holy Spirit" (Matt 28:17, 19). The worship of the risen Jesus and the inclusion of the Son between Father and Holy Spirit in the baptismal formula suggest that, for Matthew, Jesus does have divine status.

Hebrews. This writing opens with a lofty statement about the Son, "whom he appointed heir of all things, through whom he also created the worlds. He is the reflection of God's glory and the exact imprint of God's very being, and he sustains all things by his powerful word" (Heb 1:2–3a). This affirmation of Jesus' heavenly origin and status is balanced by words that establish the real humanity of the Son: "In the days of his flesh, Jesus offered up prayers and supplications, with loud cries and tears, to the one who was able to save him from death. . . . Although he was a Son, he learned obedience through what he suffered" (Heb 5:7–8).

John. The view that "the Son of God" designates the messiah is found also in John, both at the beginning (1:34, 41) and at the end (20:31), and in the confessions of Nathaniel (1:49) and Martha (11:27). The author finds this traditional view true but by no means adequate. For John "the Son of God" speaks primarily not of an office (messiah) but of a relationship. This relationship did not begin at Jesus' baptism (Mark) or at his birth (Matthew and Luke) but is eternal. In the Prologue he declares that the Word, who was in the beginning with God and was God (John 1:1), became flesh and lived among us (1:14). In the conclusion of the Prologue he is bold to name this incarnate Word "God": "No one has ever seen God; *monogenes theos* [literally,' the only begotten God'], who is in the bosom of the Father, he has interpreted him" (John 1:18, my trans.). The best manuscripts have *theos*; other scribes avoided

the audacity of this statement by substituting "Son" for "God").

Because the Father-Son relationship is central in John's theology, the most frequent way of naming God is "the Father" or "my Father" (more than 100 occurrences). In John 5:17, in response to the charge that he is not observing the Sabbath, Jesus says, "My Father is still working, and I also am working." Jesus' opponents then seek to kill him because he was "calling God his own Father, thereby making himself equal to God." After Jesus declares, "The Father and I are one," his enemies take up stones to punish his blasphemy, "because you, though only a human being, are making yourself God" (John 10:30–33; Jesus publicly claims the title "God's Son" in v. 36). A major motif of the Father-Son relationship employs the verb "send." Very frequent is the phrase "the Father who sent me" (e.g., John 5:37). The prophets are also "sent" (John 1:33), but in the case of the Son, the mutual indwelling of Father and Son (John 10:38; 14:10–11) makes this a very different kind of sending. Jesus is more than a messenger from God; he is the human face of God: "Whoever has seen me has seen the Father" (John 14:9).

This language, of course, is metaphorical: what Jesus reveals is the Father's love. Quite correctly John 3:16 is regarded as the key to the Fourth Gospel: "For God so loved the world that he gave his only Son." The giving may refer to the incarnation, but it is more likely a reference to Jesus' saving death. Nevertheless, the following clause, "so that everyone who believes in him" refers to faith in the incarnation of the Father's love in Jesus.

———

DOUGLAS R. A. HARE

Son of Man In NRSV, the phrase "the Son of Man" (with or without capitals) is found only in the NT. In other English versions of the OT, the phrase is used to render the Hebrew *ben ᵓadam*, which often appears as a poetic synonym for *ᵓadam*, *ᵓish*, or *ᵓenosh*, "man," as in Ps 8:4, "what is man (*’enosh*) that you are mindful of him, the son of man (*ben ’adam*) that you care for him?" (NIV; see **human**). A special use is found in Ezekiel, where it occurs frequently as God's way of addressing the prophet, as in 2:1, "Son of man, stand up on your feet and I will speak to you" (NIV; NRSV has "O mortal"). Since the Hebrew definite article is never used with the phrase, it does not have the force of a name or title.

The same is true of Dan 7:13, the instance that is of greatest interest to NT writers. In this Aramaic passage the phrase *bar ’enosh*, lacking the Aramaic equivalent of a definite article, is correctly translated without any capital letters: "one like a son of man" (NIV) or "one like a human being" (NRSV, REB; KJV "one like the Son of man" is erroneous).

In the NT "the Son of Man" (with capital letters) translates the Greek phrase *ho huios tou anthropou*, which literally means "the son of the man" or possibly "the son of humanity" (taking the second Greek article as generic). Outside the Gospels, where it occurs approximately eighty times, it appears only in Acts 7:56. The use of "the Son of Man" by NRSV in Rev 1:13; 14:14 is inappropriate, since the Greek articles are missing; much to be preferred is NIV, "like a son of man," in quotation marks, with a footnote indicating the allusion to Dan 7:13.

Because of the two definite articles the phrase appears to be a name or title for Jesus, and yet, with the single exception of Acts 7:56, it is not used by others as a way of referring to Jesus or confessing faith in Jesus (Luke 24:7 and John 12:34 are not clear exceptions). It finds no place in the missionary speeches of Acts or in the letters of Paul. It is often claimed that "the son of the man" would be of little use in the Gentile mission because it is "barbaric Greek," but it is surely no more so than "the Christ," *ho christos*, which to uninitiated Greek ears would mean "the one smeared with oil." It must have been necessary for Paul to explain the meaning of *Christos* to his Gentile hearers. He could have done the same with "the Son

of Man," had he found it a useful tool for communicating the meaning of Jesus.

The phrase is also absent from the Apostolic Fathers. Ignatius uses a shortened version, omitting the articles, in a statement that seems to contrast Jesus' two states as Son of God and son of man (*To the Ephesians* 20:2). This was a natural development once the doctrine of the incarnation was accepted. From Ignatius to the modern period "the Son of Man" was taken as a way of referring to the humanity of the incarnate Son of God.

In the eighteenth century a very different understanding of the phrase was proposed by scholars who studied Jewish apocalyptic literature. In *1 En.* 37–71, the Parables of Enoch, the phrase designates a heavenly judge. Most scholars accepted the hypothesis that "the Son of Man" was current in Jesus' day as the title for a heavenly Messiah.

Since many of the Son of Man sayings in the Gospels refer to Jesus' earthly life (e.g., Matt 8:20 = Luke 9:58) or his death (Mark 8:31 and par.), it was necessary to explain how the title of a heavenly redeemer could be used in this way. The most widely accepted proposal was that of Rudolf Bultmann (*Theology*, 1:30). He divided the Son of Man sayings into three groups: those referring to (1) the coming Son of Man (e.g., Mark 13:26); (2) the earthly Son of Man (e.g., Matt 11:19 = Luke 7:34); (3) the suffering Son of Man (Mark 8:31). He then proposed that, since "the Son of Man" originally referred to a heavenly figure, only those in the first group can be attributed to Jesus. In these authentic sayings Jesus was not suggesting that he himself would fulfill this heavenly role. In Mark 8:38, Bultmann argued, there is clear proof that Jesus distinguished himself from the Son of Man: "Those who are ashamed of me . . . of them the Son of Man will be ashamed when he comes." The earthly and suffering sayings were created by later Christians who were not aware of the apocalyptic meaning of the term.

Bultmann's view predominated in the twentieth century, but in the last decades serious objections were raised. First, apart from the Parables of Enoch there is no firm evidence that "the Son of Man" was used as an apocalyptic title, and the date of this part of 1 Enoch is uncertain (it is the only section not found in the Dead Sea Scrolls). Moreover, even here the phrase is not clearly a fixed title.

Second, there is a linguistic problem. It is difficult to see how the Aramaic phrase could be used as a title. Either with or without the Aramaic equivalent of the definite article, bar ᵓenash(a) meant simply "someone," "anyone," "a man." Geza Vermes (Aramaic Approach) claimed that in some rabbinic statements the phrase served as a self-reference, "this man," the equivalent of "I" and nothing more.

Vermes's proposal has been criticized by other Aramaic experts. They argue that there is no first-century evidence in support of his hypothesis, and that whatever the exact form of the Aramaic expression, it must have sounded like a name or title to those who translated it into the Greek phrase with its two articles.

Consequently many scholars still support Bultmann's hypothesis that for Jesus the phrase was an apocalyptic title; he prophesied the imminent arrival of the Son of Man who would preside at the last judgment. It was only after his resurrection that his followers came to believe that Jesus himself would return as the Son of Man. The earliest Christology was consequently a "Son of Man Christology."

Clearly both sides of this ongoing debate must resort to conjecture. Some scholars have declared the Son of Man problem insoluble, barring new evidence proving either that bar ᵓenasha was used as an apocalyptic title or that it was a circumlocution for "I," or both. A few scholars have indeed argued that Jesus used the phrase in both ways; his audience heard him say only "I," but he himself was using it as a disguised messianic title. Again, this conjecture cannot be substantiated.

In the effort to discover the meaning of "the Son of Man," all we really have to go on is the way the phrase is used in the NT. When it occurs in apocalyptic sayings, it certainly has the appearance of a known title referring to a heavenly figure, as in Mark 13:26, "Then they will see 'the Son of Man coming in clouds' with great power and glory," where there is a clear allusion to Dan 7:13. On the other hand, this appearance may be deceptive, because in each of the Synoptic Gospels this supposed apocalyptic use is preceded by nonapocalyptic Son of Man sayings that prepare the reader to regard the phrase simply as Jesus' peculiar way of referring to himself.

Accordingly, while the evidence presented by Vermes is not wholly convincing, it accords with the way the phrase functions in the Gospels. When Jesus declares in Mark 2:10, "But so that you may know that the Son of Man has authority on earth to forgive sins," the narrative audience makes no response to his use of the phrase. The context makes it clear that Jesus is referring to himself by the phrase, but it does not suggest to anyone that Jesus claims to be the messiah, heavenly or earthly. This is true of every passage in which "the Son of Man" occurs in all the Gospels. Even though Jesus may seem to be speaking of someone else, the reader assumes that Jesus is referring to himself. As Bultmann conceded, the Synoptic authors do not treat the term as an apocalyptic title. This is indicated also by the fact that Matthew and Luke can substitute "I" for "the Son of Man" and vice versa (compare Matt 5:11 with Luke 6:22; Matt 10:32–33 with Luke 12:8–9; Matt 16:13 with Mark 8:27; Luke 9:18).

Another hypothesis concerning the original meaning of "the Son of Man" as used by Jesus deserves mention. T. W. Manson argued that Jesus' understanding of the phrase derived from Dan 7:27, where it is explained that the "one like a son of man" represents "the people of the holy ones of the Most High." Accordingly, "the Son of Man" in Jesus' teaching stands for Israel's holy remnant; the term points to a corporate body, not an individual. "His mission is to create the Son of Man, the Kingdom of the saints of the

Most High. . . . Finally, when it becomes apparent that not even the disciples are ready to rise to the demands of the ideal, he stands alone, embodying in his own person the perfect human response to the regal claims of God" (*Teaching of Jesus,* 227–28). Although the majority of scholars rejected this hypothesis, it has been revived recently in various forms (e.g., W. Wink, *The Human Being*).

Still other hypotheses have been proposed. According to M. Casey, *bar ʾenasha* was an idiom used only for general statements, in which a speaker could include himself indirectly but not exclusively (*Son of Man*). R. Bauckham has proposed that in Jesus' use *bar ʾenasha* had its normal meaning of "a man" or "someone." Jesus left it to his hearers to infer that he was speaking of himself (Bauckham, 23–33).

John's Son of Man sayings display little overlap with the Synoptic sayings. John 3:14, "so must the Son of Man be lifted up," is perhaps an echo of the passion announcement in Mark 9:31, "The Son of Man is to be betrayed into human hands, and they will kill him." John 12:23, "The hour has come for the Son of Man to be glorified," seems to reflect Mark 14:41, recast in John's particular vocabulary. Despite the fact that there are no apocalyptic sayings, many scholars believe that John builds on the tradition that "the Son of Man" designated a heavenly redeemer. Others associate John's use with Gnosticism. Still others propose that in this Gospel "the Son of Man" refers to the unique humanity of the incarnate Logos.

Richard Bauckham, "The Son of Man: 'A Man in My Position' or 'Someone'?" *JSNT* 23 (1983): 23–33; Rudolf Bultmann, *Theology of the New Testament* (New York: Charles Scribner's Sons, 1951), 1:30; P. Maurice Casey, *Son of Man: The Interpretation and Influence of Daniel 7* (London: SPCK, 1979); Douglas R. A. Hare, *The Son of Man Tradition* (Minneapolis: Fortress Press, 1990); T. W. Manson, *The Teaching of Jesus* (Cambridge: Cambridge University Press, 1931); Geza Vermes, "The Use of *bar nash/bar nasha* in Jewish Aramaic," in *An Aramaic Approach to*

the Gospels and Acts, by Matthew Black, 3d ed. (Oxford: Clarendon Press, 1967), 310–28; Walter Wink, *The Human Being: Jesus and the Enigma of the Son of the Man* (Minneapolis: Fortress Press, 2002).

DOUGLAS R. A. HARE

Soul   "Soul" usually represents Hebrew *nephesh* or Greek *psyche*. These words can also be translated "person" or "life."

Soul as the inner person separable from the body. In Scripture a human person comprises an outer being and an inner being, both indispensable to the person as a whole. The English word "soul" often denotes the inner person, conceived of as independent of the body. This is a rare usage in Scripture, though Scripture does speak of our soul going down to Sheol/Hades when our body is put in the tomb (e.g., Pss 89:48; 94:17; Acts 2:27). John sees the martyrs' souls under the altar (Rev 6:9; cf. 20:4). Yahweh can kill both soul and body (Isa 10:18). There is one who can kill body but not soul, but both can perish in hell (Matt 10:28). Jesus is our souls' shepherd and guardian (1 Pet 2:25). The gospel can save our souls (Jas 1:21; 1 Pet 1:9). Restoring someone to the truth saves the person's soul (Jas 5:20). Nevertheless, Scripture is inclined to see the soul as more intrinsically connected with the body than Western thinking does.

Soul as the inner being of the whole person. In English "soul" can mean the inner being or heart or deeply felt emotions ("she bared her soul," "soul music," "soul food"). The word *nephesh* can thus have a similar meaning to *leb* ("heart"; see **mind**). The first occurrences of the word in Scripture (Gen 34:3, 8) relate how Shechem's soul was drawn to Dinah— that is, he fell in love with her (cf. Song 1:7; 3:1–4). God's soul hates Israel's festivals (Isa 1:14; cf. Ps 11:5). We are to seek, love, serve, obey, and turn to God with soul as well as heart and might (e.g., Deut 4:29; 6:5; 10:12; 11:13; 30:2, 10; Matt 22:37). God restores Israel with heart and soul (Jer 32:41). We are to put God's words in our heart and soul (Deut 11:18). It is in our hearts and souls that we acknowledge what God has done (Josh 23:14). Hannah pours out her soul before God (1 Sam 1:15; cf. Ps 42:4). Our leaders watch over our souls (Heb 13:17). We lift our souls not to false gods but to Yahweh (e.g., Pss 24:4; 25:1). Jonathan's soul is bound to David's (1 Sam 18:1). People can be one in soul (Acts 4:32). The soul desires (1 Kgs 11:37; cf. Prov 21:10; Isa 26:8–9; Rev 18:14) and delights (Isa 42:1; Matt 12:18). It is possible to be bitter in soul (e.g., Job 3:20; 7:11; 10:1; 21:25; 27:2) or grieved in soul (Job 30:25; cf. Ps 31:9) or forlorn (Ps 35:12) or cast down (Pss 42:5, 6, 11; 43:5) or pierced (Luke 2:35) or strengthened (Acts 14:22) or purified (1 Pet 1:22) or troubled (John 12:37; cf. also Pss 77:2; 107:5; 123:4; 131:2; Song 5:6; 2 Pet 2:8). One's soul can be struck with terror (Ps 6:3) or weep (Jer 13:17) or lose peace (Lam 3:17) or be mindful (Lam 3:20). Knowledge is pleasant to one's soul or is life to it (Prov 2:10; 3:22; cf. 24:14). Pleasant words are sweetness to the soul and health to the body (Prov 16:24).

"Soul" is used in parallelism with "heart" (e.g., Prov 24:12) or linked with spirit and body (1 Thess 5:23). "I languish" when my bones shake with terror and my soul shakes with terror (Ps 6:2–3). God's word can divide soul and spirit (Heb 4:12). John prays for good health alongside it being well with your soul (3 John 2). The *flesh* desires war against the soul (1 Pet 2:11).

Occasionally "soul" translates *kabod*, which usually means "glory" but here recalls *kabed*, "liver" (Pss 7:5; 16:9; 30:12; 57:8; 108:1). In Prov 23:16 it translates *kelayoth*, "kidneys." In Isa 16:11 it translates *meʿim*, "insides."

Soul as the whole person. In English "soul" can mean person or self ("the ship went down with all souls"). So in the classic description of human origins in Gen 2, God makes a human from dirt and breathes living breath into him so that he becomes "a living soul/person" (NRSV "living being"). The soul or person thus comprises physical body plus divine breath. Psalm 84:2 suggests an alternative

formulation: the soul longs and faints for Yahweh's courts, which is spelled out as implying that the heart and flesh sing for joy. Deborah urges her soul to "march on with might" (Judg 5:21). Abner says, "As your soul lives . . ." (1 Sam 17:55; cf. 2 Sam 11:11); NRSV elsewhere translates the same phrase "as you yourself live" (1 Sam 20:3; 25:26). Our whole being waits for God (Ps 33:20) or boasts in God (Ps 34:2) or listens for God to promise our deliverance (Ps 35:3) or rejoices in God (35:9; Luke 1:46) or longs and thirsts for God (e.g., Ps 42:1, 2) or takes refuge in God (Ps 57:1) or obeys God (Ps 119:129, 167) or is bowed down (Ps 57:6) or waits (Pss 62:1, 5; 130:5, 6) or feasts (Ps 63:5) or clings (Ps 63:8) or blesses (e.g., Ps 103:1–2) or trembles (Isa 15:4) or finds rest (Ps 116:7; Jer 6:16; Matt 11:29) or sins (Mic 6:7) or is full of troubles (Ps 88:3). By fasting I humble my self (Ps 69:10). God gladdens our soul (Ps 86:4; cf. 94:19; Prov 23:16) or strengthens it (Ps 138:3). Cold water is welcome to a thirsty soul (Prov 25:25). I speak to my self (Luke 12:19). Our hope anchors the whole self (Heb 6:19). God's soul does not rejoice in people who shrink back (Heb 10:38). The wicked entice unsteady souls (2 Pet 2:14).

The idea of the soul as thirsty or feasting may link with the fact that *nephesh* sometimes means appetite or gullet or desire (e.g., Eccl 6:7, 9).

Soul as the life of the person. In the OT *nephesh* sometimes denotes "*life*," a meaning harder to parallel for "soul" in English. When Rachel was dying, "her soul was departing" (Gen 35:18). Jonathan loved David as he loved his own soul (1 Sam 18:1, 3)—i.e., life (20:17, where NRSV has "life"; cf. 1 Kgs 1:29; 17:21–22). Job's soul is poured out within him (literally, "upon him")—his life is running out (Job 30:16). God's teaching renews life (Ps 19:7). God gives us our lives (Jer 38:16), delivers our lives (e.g., Pss 22:20; 33:19; 56:13; 71:23; 74:19) or restores our lives (Ps 23:3 Mg).

Johannes Pedersen, *Israel: Its Life and Culture* (London: Geoffrey Cumberlege, 1926), I–II.99–181; Bo Reicke, "Body and Soul in the New Testament," *ST* 19 (1965): 200–212; Hans Walter Wolff, *Anthropology of the Old Testament* (Philadelphia: Fortress Press, 1974), 10–25.

JOHN GOLDINGAY

Spirit, Holy Spirit, Advocate, Breath, Wind

This article first explores the use of the term "spirit," especially with reference to the divine Spirit, in the Hebrew Bible, and then turns to various questions raised by the NT evidence (the Spirit marking God's eschatological people; baptism in the Spirit, including both the arguments that it involves regeneration and the arguments that it involves divine empowerment for mission; and the Spirit's role in Christian life and ministry). Because early Christian writers theologically developed earlier biblical teachings about the Spirit at greater length, this article focuses more on the NT evidence. Although we have arranged the early Christian evidence in ways that fit the article with minimal overlap, one could have arranged the themes in various other ways.

Spirit in the Hebrew Bible

The Hebrew term most often translated "spirit" has an extensive range of potential meaning, requiring dependence on the context to interpret it in any given instance. Thus translators typically render the Hebrew term *ruah* by the English terms "spirit," "wind," or "breath," depending on the context. The term often carries only one of these English senses, such as "wind" (2 Kgs 3:17; Job 1:19; Ps 55:8). Other passages may play on more than one of these senses (e.g., Isa 25:4; 32:15); occasionally, all these nuances of the Hebrew term may be present (possibly in Ezek 37:1–14).

The meaning of God's spirit in the Hebrew Bible. The Hebrew Bible speaks often of God's spirit. In part, the terminology may reflect God working directly through the wind (Exod 10:13, 19; 14:21; Num 11:31; 1 Kgs 18:45; Ps 104:4; Jonah 1:4; 4:8; Ps 148:8), including poetic descriptions of judgment (Ps 48:7; Isa 11:4; 17:13; Jer 4:11–12; 13:24; 18:17; 22:22; 49:32, 36; Ezek 13:11, 13; 17:10), which could be poetically envisaged at times as God's own breath (Exod 15:8, 10; Job 4:9; Isa 40:7; Hos 13:15).

Such an image would prove relevant to an ancient audience. Ancient Near Eastern cultures typically viewed the gods of storm as among the most powerful and important; the biblical prophets, however, protested that idols lacked even breath, whereas YHWH directly controlled the winds (Jer 10:13–14; 51:16–17; Amos 4:13; Hab 2:19). God's breath formed creation (Ps 33:6, where it parallels his word; cf. Gen 1:2–26); his breath continues to exert power over creation, exhibited in acts that include slaying the monster of the sea (Job 26:12–14). In pagan tradition, Baal, the Canaanite storm god, had also engaged primeval chaos in the hostile sea. In the Bible, God's *ruah* was active in calming the chaotic waters at creation (Gen 1:2), as well as after the flood (Gen 8:1), though biblical writers often envision God's conquest of the sea monster historically in the parting of the sea (Job 26:12–13; Pss 74:14; 89:9–10; Isa 51:9) or prophetically in the future (Isa 27:1). Like Baal, YHWH could be described poetically as riding on the wind (2 Sam 22:11; Pss 18:10; 104:3). The Lord might come to people in the windy part of the day (Gen 3:8) or in a theophany presaged by wind (Ezek 1:4)—though he would not always be found in the wind (1 Kgs 19:11). When God acted on behalf of his servants, however, this activity could be compared with dramatic cosmic upheavals caused by his breath (2 Sam 22:16; Ps 18:15).

Probably more important for understanding this term, however, is the analogy with the human spirit or breath of life (cf. also 1 Cor 2:11). In ancient Israelite anthropology, humans, like all living creatures (Gen 6:17; 7:15, 22; Num 16:22), had the *ruah* of life in them. Some texts use it to depict the incorporeal part of life (Isa 31:3; more negatively, *ruah* can represent that which is as empty as air or wind—Job 6:26; 30:15; Prov 11:29; Eccl 2:11, 17, 26; Isa 26:18; 41:29; Jer 5:13; Hos 8:7; 12:1; Mic 2:11). Just as blood represented life in one sense (Gen 9:4; Lev 17:11, 14; Deut 12:23), so the continuing of human breath represented life. A spirit was a person's life force or vitality or strength (e.g., Pss 142:3; 143:4). Thus, a spirit that had grown weak with age or exhaustion could be revived by nourishment or encouraging news (Gen 45:27; Judg 15:19; 1 Sam 30:12; Isa 38:16). Likewise physical or emotional weakness or terrifying or astonishing news could also weaken this vigor, leading to fainting (Josh 2:11; 5:1; 1 Kgs 10:5; Job 17:1; Pss 76:12; 77:3; 143:7; Prov 15:4, 13; 17:22; 18:14; Isa 7:2; 19:3; 61:3; 65:14).

More specifically, a person's spirit could function as a seat of emotion that could be disturbed (Gen 41:8; Exod 6:9; 1 Sam 1:15; Job 7:11; Isa 54:6; Dan 2:1, 3). Sometimes it signified a person's desire or will, parallel with analogous general terms like heart or soul (Exod 35:21; Ps 77:6; Isa 26:9); it thus embraced one's moral condition (Pss 32:2; 51:10; 78:8; Prov 16:18–19; 29:23; Dan 5:20) and must be controlled (Prov 16:32; 25:28). The term could refer to an attitude (Num 5:14, 30; 14:24; Judg 8:3; 1 Kgs 21:5) or mode of behavior (Hos 4:12; 5:4). (Sometimes in both secular and canonical Greek it meant something like "attitude" or "ethos," e.g., Rom 8:15; 11:8; 1 Cor 2:12; 2 Cor 4:13; 7:1, 13; Phil 1:27; 2 Tim 4:22; Phlm 25.) Early Christians also used the regular Greek terms for interior life, including *pneuma*, usually translated "spirit" (e.g., Rom 1:9; 1 Cor 5:5; 7:34; 14:2, 14–16; 16:18; Gal 6:18; Phil 4:23; 1 Thess 5:23; Heb 4:12; Jas 2:26; possibly 1 Cor 14:32). First Corinthians 5:3–4 and Col 2:5 employ a regular epistolary formula ("present in spirit") compensating for distance.

Thus God's spirit in the Hebrew Bible might refer to God's "self" (cf. Gen 6:3) or to an aspect of his personality, as people's "spirits" might refer to themselves or to an aspect of their personality. Indeed, for some ancient Israelite expositors, the human spirit might refer to an aspect of God's image in people. God's spirit was the source for the breath of life in people (cf. Job 27:3; 32:8; 33:4; esp. Gen 2:7, though it does not employ the term *ruah*). Although God's spirit gave life to all creatures, Israelites never understood this in a pantheistic sense; God withdrew the *ruah* from his creatures and they died; he sent his *ruah* on them and they lived again (Ps 104:29–30; Job 34:14–15). Likewise the human spirit was clearly mortal (Job 7:7; Pss 78:39; 146:4; Eccl 3:19, 21; 12:7; Isa 57:16; Lam 4:20) and existed only when God created it (Zech 12:1) and sustained it (Job 10:12). God was nearest those, in fact, who had a broken spirit, recognizing their own frailty (Isa 57:15; 66:2; Pss 34:18; 51:17); life depended on God and ended when he chose (Isa 42:5). Further, the God who gave and took life sovereignly discerned all spirits, knowing what was in each heart (Num 16:22; 27:16, 18). God could stir people's spirits to do his good works (Ezra 1:5; Hag 1:14); he could also stir the spirit of some people to become unwitting agents of good for others (2 Chr 36:22; Ezra 1:1), to become unwitting agents of judgment against others (1 Chr 5:26; 2 Chr 21:16; Jer 51:1, 11), or to become its unwitting recipients (Deut 2:30). He could also send a spirit on evildoers that led them further in the path of destruction (1 Kgs 22:22–23; 2 Kgs 19:7; Isa 29:10; 37:7).

The activity of God's spirit in the Hebrew Bible. All living creatures had the *ruah* of life in them (Gen 6:17; 7:15, 22); although the Hebrew uses a different term (*nephesh*) for God's breath in humans, this animation may reflect something of God's image in people. Yet the divine Spirit could involve something more dramatic than this as well. Biblical narratives portray even pagan kings as recognizing that some bear the divine Spirit in a special way, such as Joseph (Gen 41:38) and (probably developing the Joseph story) Daniel (Dan 4:8–9, 18; 5:11–14; 6:3). Likewise, though no place in creation could be devoid of God's spirit or presence (Ps

139:7–8), God was with some of his servants in a special way.

Some writers could also speak of God's presence with Israel in the wilderness as his spirit marking them out as his people in a special way (Neh 9:20; Isa 63:10–11, 14), though they rebelled against his spirit there (Ps 106:33; Isa 63:10; cf. Neh 9:30). God would impart his spirit again in the promised new exodus to come (Ezek 39:29; Hag 2:5). These images become very prominent in NT apologetic.

Thus God empowered people with aspects of his own character or presence to accomplish work for him. This could include artistic skills (Exod 28:3; 31:3), other kinds of expertise (Job 32:8; Prov 1:23; cf. Dan 5:12), or supernatural strength (Judg 14:6, 19; 15:14; perhaps 1 Sam 11:6–7). God often empowered people with his spirit for leadership (Num 27:18; Deut 34:9; 1 Sam 11:6–7; 16:13–14). Judges, which tells of leaders that God raised up for Israel before the monarchy, reports this empowerment especially frequently (Judg 3:10; 6:34; 11:29; probably 13:25). God's spirit, not human power, would enable David's descendant to help the exiles (Zech 4:6). It is thus not surprising to find the promise of God's provision of such attributes for the ultimate Davidic ruler, who would be empowered to judge with equity (Isa 11:1–5). God also places his spirit on Israel to bring his justice to the nations (Isa 42:1; 44:3; 59:21); because Israel fails this servant mission (Isa 42:18–19), God raises a remnant or person within Israel to fulfill this mission (49:5–7; 52:13–53:12).

Some Israelites expected that the Spirit could relocate people (as later in Acts 8:39–40). Although those who feared that God's spirit would carry Elijah away proved mistaken in one sense (1 Kgs 18:12; 2 Kgs 2:16—but cf. the whirlwind in 2 Kgs 2:11), God's spirit did move Ezekiel from one place to another, at least in a visionary sense (Ezek 3:12, 14, 24; 8:3; 11:1, 24; 37:1; 43:5), and stood him on his feet (Ezek 2:2; 3:24).

Perhaps most significantly, God's breath or spirit in people moved them to recognize God's own purposes (by knowing his spirit or heart) and speak for him in prophecy (Num 11:17, 25–29; 1 Sam 10:6, 10; 2 Chron 15:1; 20:14; 24:20; Neh 9:30; Isa 61:1; Ezek 11:5, in addition to Ezekiel's visions above; Joel 2:28; Zech 7:12). Sometimes prophets apparently even prophesied to themselves (2 Sam 23:2–3; Hos 1:2; Jer 25:15; 27:2), an activity which could also be attributed to the Spirit (2 Sam 23:2). When the verity of a prophecy was in dispute, parties to the dispute could argue which side spoke by God's spirit and which side by a deceiving spirit from the Lord (1 Kgs 22:23–24; 2 Chr 18:22–23). Thus a prophet speaking by his own spirit would prophesy falsely (Ezek 13:3; cf. Jer 14:14; 23:16; Mic 2:11; 3:7–8; Zech 13:2). God's spirit could also inspire other forms of speech, including an appropriate royal acclamation (1 Chr 12:18) and presumably the language of worship that came through prophesying (1 Chr 25:1–3; 2 Chr 29:30).

God could spread the activity of his spirit through those most obedient to him. Thus, for example, prophetic activity was rare in the period of Samuel's childhood (1 Sam 3:1) but more common in his later years (1 Sam 10:5, 10), probably because Samuel was mentoring prophets (1 Sam 19:20). Elijah and Elisha also provided opportunity for younger prophets to grow in prophetic sensitivity with some supervision (2 Kgs 2:3, 5, 7; 4:1, 38; 6:1). Moses recognized that the Spirit that was on him (Num 11:17, 25) was God's own spirit (Num 11:29), but that the activity of God's spirit in him could be shared with others (Num 11:17, 25; Deut 34:9). God and Elijah permit Elisha to inherit a "double portion" (the normal inheritance share for the firstborn) of God's spirit on Elijah (2 Kgs 2:9, 15). When God's spirit was very active in a place, it could likewise affect those who were present (1 Sam 19:20, 23). God's spirit could work through people regardless of their own moral commitments (Num 24:2; 1 Sam 19:20, 23), though it could also be withdrawn in response to continuing disobedience (cf. Judg 16:20).

Hostile or harmful "spirits." God could send a "bad" or harmful spirit as an attitude of conflict between two parties (Judg 9:23), a fear or direction that leads to destruction (2 Kgs 19:7), or dangerous madness (1 Sam 16:15–16; 18:10; 19:9). The picture of God sending a bad spirit on Saul (1 Sam 16:15–16) contrasts with God endowing others with his spirit for leadership (1 Sam 16:13–14). Although Israelites recognized that God's spirit could produce a different (albeit equally socially abnormal) kind of frenzy or madness (2 Kgs 9:11), they recognized that this disturbing spirit from the Lord was unhelpful (1 Sam 16:15). (Anthropological studies reveal that a wide range of traditional cultures personify the forces understood to be behind such possession behavior; it is plausible that Israelites would understand this spirit similarly.) By contrast, the music of David, now guided by God's spirit, could calm Saul (1 Sam 16:16, 23). Just as surrounding cultures could use music to induce ecstasy or a possession trance, Israelites could associate it with inspiration (1 Sam 10:5; 2 Kgs 3:15) and presumably surmised that music could counter bad inspiration. Song and prophecy blend freely in some texts (cf., e.g., Pss 12:5; 46:10; 91:14), and it is probably no coincidence that most of the writings of the preexilic prophets are in poetic form (cf. Hab 3:1).

But just as deities of other cultures could send deceiving spirits (like Greek Morpheus's activity in dreams), Israel's God could also send spirits from his heavenly court on such missions (1 Kgs 22:21–23; 2 Chr 18:20–22; cf. the spirit in Job 4:15–16). Micaiah's vision of the heavenly court in 1 Kgs 22 reflects the sort of heavenly assembly envisioned by the Canaanites for their pantheon, but Israelites would view its members in angelic rather than divine terms (cf., e.g., Job 1:6; Ps 89:7; Jer 23:18, 22); "spirits" came to be understood in this manner (Zech 7:12). While ancient Israel probably presupposed some malevolent spirits as their neighbors did (see Lev 17:7; Deut 32:17; Ps 106:37; especially in view of cog-

nate terms in Akkadian), spirits like those that segments of early Judaism and Christianity called "demons," the Hebrew Bible pays little attention to these spirits, perhaps as part of its emphasis on God's oneness. For example, whereas many Levitical rituals and purity rules resemble those found in Hittite and other settings, they lack the explicitly prophylactic purpose of warding off demons found in the latter. Still, the biblical prophets' emphasis on God's sovereignty would place even these spirits under God's ultimate control. By the NT period (and even more a few centuries later) Jewish demonology was far more developed. Jews sometimes borrowed the Greek term *daimon* to describe malevolent spirits (although *daimones* in Greek could include benevolent ones as well).

The Spirit in Early Christian Thought and Experience

The pervasive early Christian experience of the Spirit led early Christian writers to develop their understanding of God's spirit in more dramatic ways than, though often along the same contours as in, writings of the Hebrew Bible. Early Christians saw God's spirit marking out their community the way that God's spirit had marked Israel in the wilderness (note exodus language in Rom 8:14–15, 23; Eph 1:13–14; see Isa 63:10–14).

The Spirit's activity also marked out the coming of the new age, hence demonstrating that the Messiah had come. The prophets had associated the coming of the Spirit with the future era of restoration (e.g., Isa 44:3; 59:21; 61:1; Ezek 36:27; 37:14; 39:29; Joel 2:28–29), and many Jews believed that the Spirit was no longer as active prophetically as in the OT, until the Messiah would come (cf. Sir 36:14–16; *t. Sotah* 13:3; for nuancing, see Keener, 13–19). Early Christians also associated the Spirit with the coming resurrection and kingdom (Rom 8:10–11; 1 Pet 4:6; perhaps Rev 11:11), though they also contended that the Spirit had already begun the end-time works (Rom 1:4; 8:23; 14:17; 1 Tim 3:16; 1 Pet 3:18). Jesus taught that the kingdom that would come in future glory was already present in a hidden way (Mark 4:26–32; Matt 13:33). This teaching became foundational in the thought of many of his followers; such an understanding was natural for Jews who believed that the messianic king who was yet to come had already come once, and that he himself had experienced the resurrection that still awaited the rest of God's people (1 Cor 15:20, 23).

Some early Christians understood the Spirit as a foretaste of the coming world (cf. Heb 6:4–5). Thus Paul could speak of the Spirit as the "down payment" of believers' future inheritance (2 Cor 1:22; 5:5; Eph 1:13–14; cf. Eph 4:30). Likewise, the Spirit's activity in one's life could encourage their future hope (Rom 15:13; Gal 5:5; 6:8). In the same way, believers had the Spirit as the "first fruits" of their final redemption (Rom 8:23); "first fruits" were the actual beginning of harvest. Whereas no one could know by oneself the glorious future God had prepared for those who love him (1 Cor 2:9), God had revealed it to them by his spirit (1 Cor 2:10). It is possible that early Christians experienced some of this foretaste of the kingdom by the Spirit in worship, which they often connected with the agency of the Spirit (John 4:23–24; 1 Cor 12:10–11; Phil 3:3; cf. Eph 6:18; Jude 20), a natural connection in view of OT tradition noted above. This connection might also be implicit in Revelation's portrayal of heaven as a temple (Rev 4:5–6; 6:9; 7:15; 8:3–5; 11:19; 13:6; 14:15; 15:2, 5), which John entered by the Spirit (1:10). After John was caught up in the Spirit on the Lord's day (1:10; cf. 4:2; 17:3; 21:10; Ezek 2:2; 3:12, 14, 24; 8:3; 11:1, 24; 37:1), he experienced scenes of intense worship (Rev 4:8–11; 5:9–14; 7:10–12; 15:3–4; 19:1–7).

The Spirit as an eschatological foretaste also seems to pervade the description of the Spirit's coming on *Pentecost*. As Jesus discussed the kingdom and the soon coming of the Spirit (Acts 1:3–5), his disciples asked the obvious question: when would he restore the kingdom to Israel (1:6)? He replied that they did not need to know the final eschatological time (1:7), but that the Spirit and their eschatological work of witness was imminent (1:8; see Isa 43:10, 12; 44:3, 8). It is possible that the wind (Acts 2:2; cf. Ezek 37:5–10, 14), fire (Acts 2:3; cf. Isa 66:15; Lk 3:9, 16–17), and tongues (Acts 2:4; cf. 2:16–17) are all signs of the inbreaking kingdom, as is the proleptic witness to the nations (2:5–13; cf. 2:17, 39; Matt 24:14). Peter breaks off his Joel quote at Joel 2:32 in Acts 2:21, then expounds that final line, and resumes the quotation in 2:39. The intervening exposition claims that the salvation of the last days is now available to all who call on Jesus (2:21, 38; see Keener, 190–213).

The coming of the Spirit indicates that the eschatological era, hence the Messiah, had come. Matthew indicates that the Spirit marks out Jesus as the called servant (Matt 12:18). That Jesus does his signs, including his exorcisms, by God's spirit, indicates that the eschatological kingdom had already invaded the present (12:28; probably Matthew's reasonable interpretation of "God's finger," Luke 11:20). Thus when Jesus' critics accuse him of exorcising demons by Satan, Jesus warns that they are so obstinate that they are in danger of speaking not only against him, but against God's spirit who demonstrably empowers him (Matt 12:31; cf. Heb 10:29; Mark 3:29; Luke 12:10). (In this context, blasphemy against the Spirit refers to hard-heartedly rejecting even the Spirit's clear proof of Jesus' identity.)

The presence of the Spirit (and attendant ethical markers expected to follow from this) constitutes the essential assurance to believers that they are set apart for eternal life (Rom 8:9, 16; Gal 4:6; 1 John 3:24; 5:7–8; Jude 19–20). For early Christians, the reality of whose faith was regularly challenged by outsiders, the Spirit was a living and vital evidence of their relationship with God, not simply a doctrine unrelated to their lives. Their experience of the Spirit was often dramatic, though there is no evidence that everyone experienced every aspect of this in the same manner (e.g., Acts 2:17; 19:6; Rom 8:15, 26–27; 1 Cor 12:1–4; Gal 4:6; Rev 17:3; 21:10).

Many Christians apparently expected the biblical Spirit of prophecy (which they clearly recognized; see, e.g., Heb 3:7; 9:8; 10:15; 1 Pet 1:11; 2 Pet 1:21) to be now available to all believers to enable them to experience God's voice and intimacy with him (relevant, e.g., to persecuted Johannine Christians: John 16:13–15; cf. 10:14–15; 14:16–17, 26; 15:15). Paul characteristically uses this experience to identify God's saved people (Rom 2:29; 7:6; 8:16), and Luke applies it especially to cross-cultural evangelism (Acts 8:29; 10:19–20; 11:12; 16:6–10).

Baptism in the Holy Spirit. New Testament writers developed the OT image of God pouring out his spirit like *water* on God's thirsty people (Prov 1:23; Isa 32:15; 44:3; Ezek 36:25–27; 39:29; Joel 2:28–29; Zech 12:10). This image possibly evoked water's use in rituals (Exod 25:29; Num 28:7), but portraying spirit or soul as water is also simply good Hebrew idiom (cf. 1 Sam 1:15; Job 30:16; Pss 42:4; 62:8; Isa 29:10; Lam 2:11–12, 19). Sometimes the NT refers to God "pouring" the Spirit (Acts 2:17–18, 33; 10:45; Rom 5:5; Titus 3:5–6); likewise, it develops this water image with the language of "baptizing in the Spirit" (Matt 3:11; Mark 1:8; Luke 3:16; John 1:33; Acts 1:5; 2:38; 10:47; 11:16; 1 Cor 12:13).

Various NT writers emphasize different aspects of the Spirit's work. For example, although Luke includes some other perspectives, he focuses on prophetic empowerment for proclaiming the good news of Christ across cultural boundaries (Acts 1:8; see below). The Fourth Gospel emphasizes both the Spirit purifying believers (see below) and the prophetic Spirit (the Spirit providing a fuller revelation of Jesus and empowerment to testify for him; 14:16–17, 26; 15:26–27; 16:7–15; 20:21–23).

Mark's application of "baptism in the Spirit" language (in material followed by Matthew and Luke) is relevant. Mark mentions the Spirit by name only six times in his Gospel, once with reference to the inspiration in ancient Israel (Mark 12:36), once with reference to empowerment to testify for Christ when arraigned for one's testimony (13:11), and once when warning against blasphemy against the Spirit (Mark 3:29). But Mark mentions the Spirit three times in his compact introduction, which provides an interpretive grid for the rest of his Gospel. Here John proclaims the Spirit-baptizer (1:8). Then Jesus at his baptism receives the Spirit (1:10), making him not only the baptizer in the Spirit but also the model for the Spirit-baptized life. Finally, Mark shows us what the model looks like. The Spirit drives Jesus into the wilderness for conflict with the devil (1:12–13), which sets the stage for the rest of the Gospel: Jesus strikes at Satan by healing, exorcising, and challenging injustice; Satan attacks Jesus through his own agents; and finally Jesus triumphs in the resurrection. Mark thus warns the church that the Spirit-baptized life follows Jesus' model, a model of conflict with evil (Keener, 49–90).

The Spirit of purification in John's Gospel. Because "baptism" in the Spirit is a water metaphor, John probably implies the pervasive contrast between the Spirit and water much more often than he mentions it. Although John also emphasizes the Spirit teaching and revealing (as also in the Dead Sea Scrolls and many Jewish traditions we have grouped generally under the prophetic Spirit), we focus here on John's fairly distinctive emphasis on the Spirit purifying God's people.

Although early Judaism especially developed the earlier biblical image of the Spirit empowering God's servants prophetically, at least the Essenes also drew on the biblical image of the Spirit's involvement in purification of the heart (Ezek 36:25–27; 1QS 3.7; 4.21; cf. 1 Cor 6:11; 12:13). This image may be implicit in the Baptist's phrase "baptized in the Holy Spirit" and the early Christian emphasis on the Spirit's empowerment for the Christian life (e.g., Rom 8:2–17; Gal 5:16–25), but it appears most fully in John's running contrast between the Spirit and Jewish ritual purity.

As in the other Gospels, the Baptist proclaims that the coming one would baptize in the Spirit, something greater than John's baptism in water (John 1:31–33). Yet all forms of traditional ritual purity matter less than cleansing by the Spirit (2:6, 9; 3:25–26, 30). Jesus also offers the water of life superior to the water of Jacob's well sacred to the Samaritans (4:14) and genuine experience better than the empty promise of a sort of healing shrine at one Jerusalem pool (5:7–8). (This last instance is important for John's overall plot; John contrasts one man Jesus healed at a pool, who betrays him in 5:14–16, with another healed at a pool who remains faithful to him in 9:38.)

In Jesus' conversation with Nicodemus, John may contrast Jesus' gift of the Spirit with Jewish proselyte baptism (or on some views, John's baptism). If some later Jewish sources reflect ideas in this period, some Jewish teachers claimed that (at least as far as legal status) proselyte (convert) baptism made a person like a new child. Birth from above (3:3) means being born from water and the Spirit (3:5); the Greek construction there might be translated, as Calvin and some other exegetes contend, "the water of the Spirit" (cf. similarly possibly "the Spirit of truth" in 4:23–24). If so (and this is debated), Jesus speaks of a spiritual rather than physical proselyte baptism, a conversion depicted as a baptism in the Spirit. But in contrast to later Jewish teachers' merely forensic image, John here speaks of an ontological change (cf. 3:6; 6:63), the beginning of eschatological life (3:16; see comments below on early Christian views of life in the Spirit; 1 John 2:29; 3:9; 4:7; 5:1, 4, 18; Gal 4:29; Titus 3:5; 1 Pet 1:3, 23).

That John uses water as a metaphor for the Spirit is clear in John 7:37–39. A key for understanding John's use of water, the passage carefully fits its context and prefigures Jesus' climactic crucifixion. Priests drew water from the pool of Siloam during the feast of Tabernacles (7:2) and poured it out in the temple, intending thereby to prefigure eschato-logical water from the temple. Public Scripture reading on the last day of the festival probably spoke of this end-time hope (Zech 14:8, 16; Ezek 47:1–12; *t. Sukkah* 3:3–10). Jewish people often called the temple the navel, or belly, of the world (e.g., *Jub* 8:12, 19; the Greeks described Delphi similarly). The exact punctuation of 7:37–38 in Greek is unclear (the water might come not from the believer's belly, as in the NRSV Mg, but from Jesus'), but 7:39 in any case suggests that Jesus is the ultimate source of the water that believers receive from him. Jesus is the foundation of God's new temple and the source of the water of life (cf. also Rev 22:1). John, who revels in word-plays and narrative symbolism more than our other Gospel writers do, thus reports Jesus "glorified" on the cross giving water and "his spirit" (John 19:30, 34).

Receiving the Spirit at conversion. Scholars from various theological traditions today debate whether "*baptism* in the Holy Spirit," when applied to believers' experience, refers to conversion (usually viewed either as expressed in verbal confession of faith, in baptism, or in both) or to an event in one's life after conversion (usually compared in various traditions with confirmation, sanctification, or empowerment for service). It appears that early Christians, from whose writings theologians claim to support these various views, also applied the image in different ways.

Despite some debate, it seems that first-century Judaism immersed Gentile converts to purify them from their old Gentile ways (see Keener, 62–65). Those who see baptism in the Spirit as at least sometimes subsequent to conversion may appeal to the immersion component of Jewish baptism, contrasting this with a less overwhelming experience of the Spirit at conversion (but cf. 1 Cor 12:13, which joins baptism and drinking). Those who identify baptism in the Spirit with conversion may appeal to an analogy with the conversion component of Jewish proselyte baptism; baptism was used for conversion. Jewish traditions that developed the biblical image of the Spirit of prophecy could suggest that the image includes empowerment for mission. Essene traditions that developed the biblical image of the Spirit purifying God's people morally (Ezek 36:25–27) could suggest that the image includes conversion (though also continuing purification in 1 John 1:7, 9).

The Fourth Gospel's contrast between the Spirit and ritual purification, addressed above, suggests that believers are baptized in the Spirit at their conversion (see esp. John 3:5). Some other NT witnesses share this perspective.

The first NT voice addressing baptism in the Spirit is John the Baptist, who speaks of the greater one baptizing in the Holy Spirit and fire (Matt 3:11; Luke 3:16). (Since only God could pour out God's own Spirit in the OT, the stronger one announced in this account is probably viewed as divine; supporting this view, prophets were "servants of God," and normally only servants handled the master's feet.) The "fire" in the surrounding context is clearly judgment and evokes the harshest picture of Gehenna, or hell, held by some of John's contemporaries (Matt 3:10, 12; Luke 3:9, 17). Just as wind blew out the lighter chaff that would be gathered for destruction, so God's holy "wind" or spirit would bring destruction to the moral chaff (Job 21:18; Pss 1:4; 35:5; 83:13; Isa 17:13; 33:11; 41:15–16; Dan 2:35). John is inviting his hearers (the crowds in Luke 3:7; the hostile religious leadership in Matt 3:7) to repentance and describing the two options: those who *repent* will be like wheat gathered into the barn, baptized in the Holy Spirit (Matt 3:11–12; Luke 3:16–17). Those who do not will be like firewood or chaff, baptized in fire (Matt 3:10–12; Luke 3:9, 16–17).

In short, John urges his hearers to accept baptism in the Spirit rather than the alternative of divine judgment. For John, therefore, the coming one will baptize all the repentant in the Spirit, and the experience must include what we call conversion. This is not to say, however, that he identifies baptism in the Spirit

with an act of conversion only. John draws on earlier prophetic images of God pouring out his Spirit on his people when he would restore Israel (Isa 44:3–4; Ezek 36:24–28; Joel 2:28; 3:1). Thus for John, baptism in the Spirit presumably marks the end-time remnant of God's people and involves the entire sphere of the Spirit's work in their lives, starting with conversion but including prophetic empowerment (cf. Titus 3:5–6).

Paul also speaks of believers being "baptized" in (or "by"; the Greek term *en* is the same as in the Gospels and Acts) the Spirit into Christ's body (1 Cor 12:13). Paul elsewhere uses the language of "receiving" the Spirit to describe the initial reception of the Spirit at conversion (Rom 8:15; 1 Cor 2:12; 2 Cor 11:4; Gal 3:2, 14). This is not to suggest that Paul believes that the believer's experience with the Spirit stops at conversion (e.g., Rom 8:2–16, 23, 26; 14:17; 15:13; Gal 5:16–18; Eph 5:18; Phil 1:19). But Paul applies "receiving the Spirit" particularly to believers' initial reception of the Spirit, a description also frequent in Acts (1:8; 2:33, 38; 8:15, 17, 19; 10:47; 19:2), where context links it with being baptized in the Spirit, at least for half of the examples (see 1:5; 11:16). Paul also emphasizes the Spirit setting believers apart at conversion (1 Cor 6:11; 2 Thess 2:13; cf. 1 Pet 1:2).

Receiving the Spirit after conversion. The above description might seem to settle the debate in favor of those who argue that the NT teaches that Jesus baptizes Christians in the Spirit at conversion (or, in a slightly more nuanced view, that Christians at conversion share in the church's baptism at Pentecost). To stop with this description, however, risks missing the rich diversity of perspectives among NT authors. Even when authors make the same theological point, they often use different language to do so, and similarly may employ the same language in different ways (cf., e.g., Rom 1:5; 3:28 with Jas 2:14).

Acts provides this different perspective, perhaps because Acts not only recounts early Christian theology but describes early Christian experience. To be sure, some received the Spirit initially, immediately upon conversion (Acts 10:44; see 15:9). But most other cases are at least slightly more complex. On Pentecost, disciples who already have resurrection faith are baptized in the Spirit (2:4, 17–18, 33, 38–39 in light of 1:4–8). Because this was the first outpouring of the Spirit, the case is undoubtedly exceptional (see 1:4; 2:38), but it does illustrate that in Acts, baptism in the Spirit is not *ontologically* inseparable from resurrection faith. Scholars debate whether the disciples in Acts 19:1–7 were yet believers (most conclude that they were not) before Paul explained Christian baptism to them. The interval between their faith in Paul's message and their reception of the Spirit through Paul's laying on hands was probably not much longer than the time it took them to find water for baptism (19:5–6; perhaps they used Ephesus's usually accessible public baths). Any interval at all is longer than one might expect simply from the theological explanation in Paul's letters, but the interval here between baptism and the coming of the Spirit is brief.

After Saul encounters Jesus on the road to Tarsus, he not only obeys Jesus' instructions but also fasts for three days (apparently in penitence) before being filled with the Spirit (9:5–9, 17). Three days is not a long interval, but again it is longer than one might expect from Paul's descriptions of "receiving the Spirit" in his letters (unless Paul "receives" and "is baptized in" the Spirit earlier and is again "filled" with the Spirit at this point). Luke might view Paul's conversion as progressive, but this would still differ from Paul's usual portrayal in his letters, a portrayal with which most discussions today begin. Perhaps the gift awaited Paul's baptism, a normal pattern in Acts (2:38); but God could sovereignly vary this sequence (10:44–48).

The most problematic example for the usual paradigm is the case of the Samaritans (8:12–17). James Dunn's brilliantly argued case that Philip's ministry failed to genuinely convert the Samaritans (Dunn, 55–72) has failed to persuade most scholars; the arguments that he uses would, if applied consistently, exclude too many other converts in Acts as well. The Samaritans believed, were baptized, and accepted God's message (8:12, 14). Nevertheless, they had not received the Spirit (8:16); the apostles thought this unusual and serious enough to pray for them to receive this (8:16–17). Most scholars see this case as another exception, because the Jerusalem apostles needed to ratify the Samaritan mission. Most do not draw from it the corollary that converts (especially those on new mission fields) must receive the Spirit by apostles' laying hands on them (though this passage is the strongest argument for the confirmation position).

What we should make of the exceptions in Acts depends on our approach to Acts. If we read it as primarily a historical description of the early church's mission, we can explain the exceptions as mere historical anomalies. If, however, we read Acts as also prescribing models for the church's continuing mission, the historical description may allow that Samaria was not the final anomaly, nor Acts 10 the final exception to the normal sequence of Acts 2:38. That is, the narrative of Acts may allow some of the various models on which current theological traditions draw. To be sure, Luke uses the specific expression "baptize in the Spirit" only with reference to Pentecost and the household of Cornelius (1:5; 11:16); but these passages also speak of "receiving the Spirit" as in some instances that appear to be postconversion. Further, if we are to be particular about terminology, Paul uses the designation only once (1 Cor 12:13), and no biblical writers utilize the noun phrase "baptism of the Spirit."

How would such a conclusion match Paul's theology of conversion noted above? We should note that in Luke's theology one also receives the Spirit at conversion (Acts 2:38). The tension may be less between the two authors than between two genres: theological arguments and propositions on one hand, and narratives describing spiritual experience on the other. That is, early Christians believed that they received full access to the Spirit at conversion but may have noticed that at times some did not experience the full impact of this access at once (in the same way that Christians offered some other theological propositions that differed from yet informed their experience, e.g., Rom 6:2–11).

Luke's distinctive theological emphasis may affect his telling of the narrative, because in the majority of his references to the Spirit in his writings he emphasizes the Spirit of prophecy (probably best argued, though overstated, by Menzies). Many of Luke's texts not connected with prophetic speech in the narrow sense relate to the sort of signs performed by some biblical prophets, whose model John and Jesus to some degree followed (Luke 1:17, 76; 4:24–27; 7:26; 13:33; 24:19; Acts 3:22–23; 7:37; 10:38). Thus filling with the Spirit often provides prophetic speech (Luke 1:15, 41–42, 67; 4:18; Acts 4:25; 5:32; 7:51; 11:28; 13:2, 4) or revelation (Luke 2:25–27; Acts 5:3, 9; 7:55; 8:29; 10:19; 11:12; 15:28; 16:6–7). Luke's emphasis fits the OT relationship between the Spirit and the prophets, as well as prophetic expectation for the end time (Joel 2:28; cf. Num 11:29). It is a common emphasis throughout the NT, but Luke focuses on it almost exclusively (though not entirely—see esp. Lk 3:16; Acts 13:52).

The purpose of Spirit empowerment in Acts is Spirit-inspired, cross-cultural witness (Acts 1:8), comparable to OT prophetic speech (2:17–18). Thus it is not surprising that in the slight majority of cases where he describes initial Spirit reception, Luke emphasizes prophetic speech of some sort (19:6), sometimes as inspired praise in languages unknown to the speaker (2:4; 10:46; 19:6; relevant to his emphasis on cross-cultural witness). Some scholars thus argue that passages depicting delayed reception of the Spirit in Acts may refer only to the prophetic empowerment dimension of the Spirit, rather than to its salvific effects.

In Luke-Acts, prayer (another Lukan emphasis) often invites the coming of the Spirit (Luke 3:21–22; 11:13; Acts 1:14 with 2:1–4; 4:31; 8:15–17). Further, for Luke, initial fillings with the Spirit (e.g., Acts 2:4; 9:17) do not preclude subsequent empowerments, which he also describes as fillings (e.g., 4:8, 31; 13:9). He also describes various leaders as "full of the Spirit" (Luke 4:1; Acts 6:3, 5; 7:55; 11:24). Although Paul generally prefers a different vocabulary, his emphasis on dependence on the Spirit in every aspect of the Christian life (see most thoroughly Fee, passim) suggests that he would have been amenable to Luke's point.

The Spirit of life in the New Testament. Biblical tradition affirmed that in addition to God's spirit revealing his thoughts to his servants, God's spirit could transform behavior (1 Sam 10:6). Resurrection and restoration, like the giving of life in creation, require a restoration of breath from God (Ezek 37:5–10); this breath would be God's own spirit (Ezek 37:14), through which he had already promised to transform his people's hearts to reflect his will (Ezek 36:26–27; cf. Ezek 11:19).

To some extent the Christian "Spirit of life" (Rom 8:2) may reflect a deeper activity of the same divine spirit that provided humans with life to begin with; some Spirit texts seem to recall the first creation (John 20:22 with Gen 2:7). When transformed by the Spirit, a person is recreated in God's image in Christ as God once created Adam in his image (Rom 8:29; Eph 4:22–24; Col 3:10; cf. Rom 5:12–21; 1 Cor 15:49; 2 Cor 3:18). (The Dead Sea Scrolls also speak of God's Spirit purifying the spirits of the remnant of Israel for holy living.)

Early Christians saw their community as God's temple (1 Cor 3:16; Eph 2:18–22; 1 Pet 2:5; cf. John 4:21, 23; cf. similarly 1QS 8.5, 8–9; 9.6). At least some applied this temple image even to the individual believer, affirming that God lives within each believer (1 Cor 6:19; cf. Phil 2:13). Many also spoke of Christ living among the Christians (2 Cor 13:5; Col 1:27; 3:15–16) and in the believer (John 15:4–10;

Rom 8:10; Gal 2:20; Eph 3:17; cf. 2 Cor 13:3–5; Col 1:27–29; Phlm 6). No less typically, they speak of the Spirit dwelling in the believer (John 14:17; Rom 8:9, 11; 1 Cor 6:19; 2 Cor 1:22; 2 Tim 1:14; cf. Matt 10:20; Jas 4:5; 1 Pet 1:11). Often they present the Spirit as the primary agent of Christ indwelling believers; sometimes they speak of the indwelling Spirit and indwelling Christ interchangeably (Rom 8:9–11; Eph 3:16–17; 1 John 3:23–24; 4:13). Scholars sometimes argue for some degree of identification between Jesus and the Spirit on the experiential level (cf. perhaps 1 Cor 15:45). Thus as Moses saw the Lord's glory in Exodus, God reveals his glory in the gospel even more clearly by the Spirit (2 Cor 3:3, 6, 8, 17–18).

Old Testament texts that speak of the Spirit "upon" someone often seem to refer to empowerment for speech or ministry (e.g., Num 11:17, 25–29; 24:2; Judg 3:10; 6:34; 11:29; 14:6, 19; 15:14; 1 Sam 10:6, 10; 11:6; 16:13; 19:20, 23; 2 Kgs 2:9; 1 Chr 12:18; 2 Chr 20:14; Isa 42:1; 59:21; 61:1; Ezek 11:5). These may differ from the early Christian idea of the Spirit being "in" someone (cf. John 14:17; Rom 8:9–11; 2 Cor 1:22; though it remains possible that "upon" was simply the more common Hebrew idiom (cf. 1 Sam 18:10), not preferred by some early Christian writers like Paul. In any case, one cannot argue for a strict salvation historical distinction of the Spirit coming only "upon" in the OT, as some have (cf. Ezek 36:27), since it appears in many NT writers (Mark 1:10; Luke 1:35; 2:25; Acts 1:8; 2:17–18; 10:44–45; 11:15; 19:6; 1 Pet 4:14), and sometimes God's servants in the OT had the Spirit "in" them (Gen 41:38; Num 27:18; Dan 4:8, 9, 18; 5:14; cf. 1 Pet 1:11). Old Testament writers occasionally speak of being "filled with the spirit" (Exod 31:3; 35:31; Deut 34:9; Mic 3:8), language that recurs in the NT most frequently in Luke-Acts (Luke 1:15, 41, 67; Acts 2:4; 4:8, 31; 9:17; 13:9, 52; also Eph 5:18), partly by linguistic preference (cf. Luke 4:28; 5:12, 26; 6:11; Acts 5:3; 13:45; 19:28, 29). (For "full" of the Spirit, see Luke 4:1; Acts 6:3, 5; 7:55; 11:24.)

In contrast to those who insist that God's Spirit works only through the human spirit (Rom 8:16), the Holy Spirit clearly renews the mind as well (Rom 8:5–6, 9; cf. Rom 12:2; Eph 4:23; also 1 Cor 12:10–11; 14:13–14, where interpretation with the mind as well as tongues from the human spirit are gifts of the Spirit). Nor are Paul's "Spirit ethics" divorced from practical material issues like how believers should use their economic resources (Gal 6:6–10).

The Spirit clearly affected believers' behavior. While Paul viewed believers as dead to sin in Christ (in terms of their status and destiny; Rom 6:2–7) and expected them to internalize this perspective (Rom 6:11), it was the Spirit who dynamically enabled them to think in these terms and live this new way (Rom 8:5–6, 13–14). (The "mind of the Spirit" here thus fills the role that many Jewish teachers would have allotted to study of Scripture and philosophers to reason.) Those who committed sexual sin defiled themselves as vessels of God's Holy Spirit (1 Cor 6:16–19; 1 Thess 4:8).

In his extant letters, Paul addresses the Spirit in relation to behavior perhaps most fully in Gal 5:16–6:1. This letter emphasizes that righteousness (and membership in God's people) comes not by human ability to perform works of the law (which would favor those raised under the law), but by dependence on God's own power (cf. 2:15–21). Elsewhere it contrasts the ways of the Spirit (God's personal involvement and enabling) with those of the flesh (usually meaning human effort without divine aid; 3:3; 4:29; 5:16–17; 6:8; cf. Rom 8:4–9, 13; Phil 3:3; 1 Tim 3:16). He argues that works of the law did not provide them the Spirit (Gal 3:2, 5), hence that the moral leading of the Spirit replaces the need for the more limited written law (Gal 5:18, 23; cf. 5:14; 6:2; Rom 2:29; 7:6; 8:2; 2 Cor 3:3, 6, 8, 17–18; Ezek 36:27). In contrast to some Jewish traditions that linked acquisition of the Spirit with piety, Paul regularly emphasizes that the Spirit is God's gift (Gal 3:2–5, 14; 4:6; Rom 5:5; 1 Cor 6:19; 2 Cor 11:4).

Thus in Gal 5:16–18 Paul points out that one must choose between the life of the Spirit (led directly by God) and of the flesh (run by one's own desires and inclinations; 5:17); these lifestyles are so contrary that if one walks by the Spirit, one emphatically will not fulfill fleshly passions (5:16). (Biblical and subsequent Jewish tradition spoke of "walking" in God's commandments; here, however, walking by the Spirit that inspired the law obviates the need for following a written law that would limit sin less fully.)

Paul then adapts the standard rhetorical forms of vice (5:19–21) and virtue lists to describe the opposite behavior of flesh and Spirit. If one has only one's own strength to fulfill religion, the best one can do remains sin (5:19–21). But the Spirit, not human effort, produces God's character in his people, changing their character or nature so it bears different "fruit" (5:22–23; cf. Matt 7:16–18; Luke 6:44; John 15:2–4). In context, love is the most important element of this fruit (Gal 5:13–15), expressed also in humility (5:26; 6:1). Indeed, most of the fruit Paul lists here appear elsewhere in his writings in the context of relationships. Elsewhere in Pauline literature the Spirit produces love (Rom 15:30; 2 Cor 13:14; Eph 3:16–17; 4:3–4, 30–32; Phil 2:1; Col 1:8; perhaps Rom 5:5) as well as joy and peace (Rom 14:17; 1 Thess 1:6) and submission to one another (Eph 5:18–21).

As in Acts (above), the Spirit in Pauline literature enables ministry (cf. 2 Cor 6:6; 2 Tim 1:14; also 1 Pet 1:12). The Spirit causes God's agents to speak his own message, like earlier prophets (Matt 10:20; Mark 13:11; Luke 12:12; Eph 6:17; 1 Thess 1:5–6; 2:13; 1 Tim 4:1; cf. Acts 21:11; Rev 2:7, 11, 17, 29; 3:6, 13, 22; 14:13; 19:10). For Paul, the message of Christ verifies that it is genuinely God's Spirit who is speaking (1 Cor 12:3; cf. 2 Cor 11:4; 12:18; 1 John 4:1–3). Rhetoricians "demonstrated" arguments with proofs, but Paul's greatest demonstration was the Spirit, who gave power during his preaching in weakness the humanly "weak" message of the cross (1 Cor 2:4). As had happened with earlier prophets, so now the Spirit provided knowledge of God's will (1 Cor 7:40) and revelations (1 Cor 2:10–14; Eph 3:5; Rev 1:10; 4:2; 17:3; 21:10; 22:17). All believers are to exercise or be gifts of the Spirit to Christ's body; Paul heavily emphasizes this ministry activity of the Spirit among all believers (see at much greater length *gifts*).

The Spirit as a person. The Hebrew Bible rarely provided hints that would allow one to distinguish God's spirit from himself in any ontological sense (one might at most advance Isa 48:16, but even here the Lord and the Lord's spirit may simply reflect Hebrew parallelism); early Christian writers often continued the same general use of God's spirit. In some cases, however, they distinguished the Spirit from the Father as they distinguished the Son from the Father. Gordon Fee has demonstrated the proto-Trinitarian formula in some of the earliest NT writings (e.g., 1 Cor 12:4–6; 2 Cor 13:14; Eph 4:4–6; see Fee, *Presence*, 839–42, for other examples). Later writings are even more explicit (e.g., Matt 28:19; John 14:16, 26).

Jewish wisdom tradition may have aided this process by sometimes personifying *wisdom* as the Spirit, as well as personifying it as the Word or Torah. Among NT writings, the Fourth Gospel articulates most clearly the Spirit's distinct personality as "another Advocate" who will carry on Jesus' mission (John 14:16–17, 26; 16:7–15). To be sure, we should not read too much personality into John's use of the male pronoun "he" here: whereas *pneuma* is neuter in Greek, requiring the neuter pronoun in most of the NT, *parakletos* is masculine, and "he" is used only with this masculine noun. (In the same way, Hebrew uses the feminine pronoun for *ruah*, since "spirit" in Hebrew is a feminine term.) The description of the Paraclete's function, however, is a personal description that consistently parallels that of Jesus elsewhere in the Gospel. The Paraclete convicts the world of sin and judgment (16:8–9, 11) as Jesus does (3:19–20; 8:46; 12:31); he also functions in Jesus' place when he goes to the Father (14:16; 16:10).

The Paraclete's connection with Jesus continues elsewhere in the Gospel. The Paraclete provides fresh revelation (John 16:12–15), but this revelation remains consistent with the original Jesus proclaimed by Johannine tradition (14:26; 1 John 4:1–6). Some also find forensic functions in the image of the Paraclete: against the implied backdrop of God judging the world (12:48), *parakletos* may derive the legal sense of "advocate" (as in 1 John 2:1); the Spirit also functions as prosecutor of the world (John 16:8–11) and witness (15:26). That is, God is judge, defender, prosecutor, and witness: the outcome is decided.

Thus it is clear that at least by the end of the first century and probably earlier, some Christians recognized the Spirit as a distinct divine person, not just an impersonal force.

Conclusion

Although various biblical writers emphasize diverse activities of God's Spirit, some common themes are important. Whereas humanity is weak in itself, God empowers his servants to accomplish his works by his spirit. Their works represent service for God, include purity of living and, in individual cases, leadership, miracles, and especially hearing and speaking the divine message. In the NT, dependence on God's spirit characterizes the regular life of faith as a supernatural experience throughout.

James D. G. Dunn, *Baptism in the Holy Spirit: A Re-examination of the New Testament Teaching on the Gift of the Spirit in Relation to Pentecostalism Today* (Philadelphia: Westminster; London: SCM, 1970); Gordon D. Fee, *God's Empowering Presence: The Holy Spirit in the Letters of Paul* (Peabody, Mass.: Hendrickson, 1994); Gordon D. Fee, *Gospel and Spirit: Issues in New Testament Hermeneutics* (Peabody, Mass.: Hendrickson, 1991); Marie E. Isaacs, *The Concept of Spirit: A Study of Pneuma in Hellenistic Judaism and Its Bearing on the New Testament*, Heythrop Monographs 1 (London: Heythrop College, 1976); Craig S. Keener, *The Spirit in the Gospels and Acts: Divine Purity and Power* (Peabody, Mass.: Hendrickson, 1997); Robert P. Menzies, *The Development of Early Christian Pneumatology with Special Reference to Luke-Acts*, JSNTSup 54 (Sheffield: Sheffield Academic Press, 1991); Max Turner, *Power from on High: The Spirit in Israel's Restoration and Witness in Luke-Acts* (Sheffield: Sheffield Academic Press, 1996).

CRAIG S. KEENER

Statute   *see* Law

Steadfast Love   Steadfast love is conveyed in Hebrew by the word *hesed*, a central theological term occurring 245 times in the Hebrew Bible. The Hebrew *hesed* carries a range of meanings to describe human relationships as well as the character of God. English translations vary widely depending on context, including the words "loyalty," "kindness," and "faithful love" in addition to "steadfast love." Also no single word in Greek conveys the meaning of *hesed*. The LXX translates the Hebrew most often as *eleos* (*"mercy"*), but also as *charis* (*"grace"*), and *dikaios* (*"justice"*), and even *doxa* ("glory"). The NT follows the LXX, rendering the Hebrew *hesed* most frequently as *eleos*.

Steadfast love between humans is often described in Hebrew with the phrase, "to make *hesed* with someone." The NRSV provides different translations to render the meaning of the phrase. When Lot is rescued from the city of Sodom, he states to the divine messengers who rescued him in Gen 19:19, "Your servant has found favor with you, and you have shown me great kindness (*hesed*) in saving my life." Abimelech states to Abraham in Gen 21:23, "Now therefore swear to me here by God that you will not deal falsely with me or with my offspring . . . but as I have dealt loyally (*hesed*) with you, you will deal with me." The two translations indicate the range of meaning of steadfast love. On the one hand, *hesed* signifies "kindness" as an act of spontaneous favor or grace, as in the statement of Lot. The spontaneity of steadfast love is underscored in the study of K. D. Sakenfeld. The story of Abimelech and Abraham indicates that steadfast love can also mean "loyalty" within the context of making an oath or establishing a covenant. The covenant context of steadfast love was first underscored in the study of N. Glueck.

Whether the situation is legal or spontaneous, steadfast love between humans always indicates an interpersonal relationship. The relationship may be between friends (David and Jonathan, 1 Sam 20:8), relatives (Isaac and Laban, Gen 24:49), a husband and wife (Abraham and Sarah, Gen 20:13), or even between a king and subjects (Saul and the population of Jabesh-gilead, 2 Sam 2:5). Steadfast love is not simply an attitude of one person toward another, but implies some form of action. The messengers save Lot's life (Gen 19:19). Ruth seeks out her older relative Boaz for marriage, rather than a younger man (Ruth 3:10). The people of Jabesh-gilead bury Saul (2 Sam 2:5). Acts of steadfast love are described as "good deeds" (Neh 13:14; Ruth 3:10) and as "doing justice." The famous passage from Mic 6:8 illustrates the close relationship between steadfast love, good deeds, and justice: "He has told you, O mortal, what is good; and what does the LORD require of you but to do justice (*mishpat*), and to love kindness (*hesed*), and to walk humbly with your God?"

An act of steadfast love calls forth a similar response from the one who receives it, and the resulting relationship is enduring. The harlot Rahab shows steadfast love to the spies in rescuing them from discovery, calling forth a similar response of the spies toward her and her family (Josh 2:12–14). David asks Jonathan for an act of steadfast love, prompting the same action from Jonathan toward David (1 Sam 20:8–14). The mutuality of steadfast love between David and Jonathan, moreover, is permanent. Jonathan asks David in 1 Sam 20:15, "Never cut off your faithful love (*hesed*) from my house." The servant of Abraham seeking a wife for Isaac states to Laban in Gen 24:49, "Now then, if you will deal loyally (*hesed*) and truly (*'emeth*, "**true**") with my master, tell me; and if not tell me, so that I may turn either to the right hand or to the left." The linking of steadfast love and truth underscores permanence and certainty. The participants are secure in the relationship (see also Gen 47:29; Josh 2:14). Proverbs 3:3 encourages the wise person to interrelate steadfast love and truth (translated in the NRSV as "loyalty and faithfulness"). The two qualities are essential to a good plan (Prov 14:22), they atone for iniquity (Prov 16:6), and they have the power to preserve the king and the realm (Prov 20:28).

Steadfast love becomes a central description of God in the Hebrew Bible. The steadfast love of God is revealed to Moses in Exod 34:6–7. The context provides definition. God and the Israelites enter into a covenant at Mount Sinai in Exod 19–24. And as a result, the Israelites become the personal possession of God in exchange for exclusive allegiance to the deity. When Moses ascends the mountain to receive the documents containing the conditions of the covenant, the Israelites worship the golden calf, thus nullifying the covenant (Exod 32). God wishes to destroy the Israelite nation for breach of covenant and create a new people from Moses. Moses successfully intercedes for the continued existence of the people, prompting a new revelation into the character of God as a deity who is merciful (*rahum*, "mercy"), gracious (*hanun*, "grace"), and filled with steadfast love. The context for the revelation of the divine character indicates that, as in human relations, the steadfast love of God is both legal and spontaneous. The legal implication of steadfast love is that it signifies the continuation of covenant. But steadfast love also goes beyond law and encompasses a spontaneous act of *love* and forgiveness. Exodus 34:7 states that keeping steadfast love is "forgiving iniquity and transgression and sin." The steadfast love of God, moreover, like its human counterpart, is linked with the

Hebrew word *ʾemeth* ("truth," translated in the NRSV as "faithfulness"), indicating its permanent quality. Steadfast love is the preferred term to describe divine love as compared to the more general term in Hebrew, *ʾahab* ("love").

The permanent quality of God's steadfast love becomes a resource for prayer. It is able to change the course of events in history. Moses calls upon the steadfast love of God in seeking the Israelites' forgiveness after their failure to enter the promised land (Num 14:19). The prophet Joel encourages the priests to pray to God during the terrible Day of the Lord, because the spontaneous character of God's steadfast love may prompt the deity to change the course of punishment (Joel 2:13). The mutuality of steadfast love in human relationships also continues between God and humans. Lack of steadfast love in humans engenders judgment from God (Hos 4:1). But, the psalmist states, "steadfast love surrounds those who trust in the LORD" (Ps 32:10). Such persons take on the quality of steadfast love, becoming characterized as "the faithful ones" (*hasidim*, Ps 4:3; 12:1, etc.).

The steadfast love of God is represented as divine mercy (*eleos*) in the NT, blurring somewhat its distinctive role in the Hebrew Bible. The following uses of *eleos* are in keeping with the OT concept. The course of salvation history in the birth story of Jesus flows from God's *eleos*, according to the Gospel of Luke. In the Magnificat, Mary proclaims that "[God's] mercy is for those who fear him" (Luke 1:50; see Ps 102:17) and that God helps his servant Israel by remembering mercy (Luke 1:54; see Ps 97:3). Also Zechariah, the father of John the Baptist, proclaims that God "has shown the mercy promised to our ancestors, and has remembered his holy covenant" (Luke 1:72; see Ps 105:8). And steadfast love remains a source for prayer in the stories of Jesus. Repeatedly humans entreat Jesus for healing by pleading for mercy (Mark 5:19; 10:47; Luke 18:38; Matt 15:22). The Good Samaritan in the Gospel of Luke demonstrates steadfast love in rescuing a fellow human being (Luke 10:25–37). The parable of the Unmerciful Slave in Matt 18:23–35 demonstrates the necessary mutuality of steadfast love, in that the sin of the slave was his inability to reciprocate acts of steadfast love to his follow slaves. And the apostle Paul underscores the need for steadfast love to become part of the character of the godly person, identifying compassion as one of the divine gifts to humans (Rom 12:8).

Nelson Glueck, *Hesed in the Bible*, Eng. trans. (Cincinnati: Hebrew Union College, 1967); Robin Routledge, "*Hesed* as Obligation: a Re-Examination," *TynBul* 46 (1995): 179–96; Katherine D. Sakenfeld, *Faithfulness in Action: Loyalty in Biblical Perspective* (Philadelphia: Fortress Press, 1985); Katherine D. Sakenfeld, *The Meaning of Hesed in the Bible* (Missoula, Mont.: Scholars Press, 1978).

THOMAS B. DOZEMAN

Steal *see* **Possessions**

Stranger *see* **Alien**

Stumble, Stumbling Block In the OT, "stumble" is normally a translation of *kashal*, and "stumbling block" represents *mikshol*. In the NT the few occurrences of these terms usually translate forms of *proskopto*. The words are usually metaphorical, but the literal meaning appears in Ps 105:37; Isa 5:27; 63:13; Jer 31:9; and John 11:9, 10. There are a good many passages that sound literal, but the metaphorical overtones may be more important, such as "When my enemies turned back, they stumbled and perished before you" (Ps 9:3), and "Do not rejoice when your enemies fall, and do not let your heart be glad when they stumble" (Prov 24:17). Usually the metaphorical sense is obvious, as in Ps 119:165: "Great peace have those who love your law; nothing can make them stumble." The idea of falling over something as a general symbol for disaster appears most often in connection with the threats of enemies (e.g., Lev 26:37; Prov 24:11; Isa 8:15), the destiny of enemies (e.g., Pss 9:3; 27:2; Isa 31:3; Jer 20:11), or sin as the cause of one's trouble (e.g., Jer 18:15; Hos 5:5; 1 Pet 2:8).

"Stumbling block" represents a single word in Hebrew and in Greek, denoting anything over which one stumbles. Tyndale introduced the English term in his translation of the NT in 1526, and it has been retained in most translations. The most interesting use of the Hebrew word is the only literal one, in Lev 19:14: "You shall not revile [or curse] the deaf or put a stumbling block before the blind." Why was the likelihood of anyone doing either of those strong enough to lead to such a prohibition? Answer: Neither the deaf nor the blind would be able to identify the culprit. This reveals the lawgiver's awareness of the power of a certain kind of temptation: mean acts that one can get away with. Elsewhere the stumbling block may be placed by God as a means of judgment (Jer 6:21; Ezek 3:20), or it may be the sin (idols) that leads to judgment (Ezek 7:19; 14:3, 4, 7; 44:12). The NT warns against using one's Christian freedom in a way that would become a stumbling block to others, that is, tempting them to violate their consciences (Rom 14:13; 1 Cor 8:9). The term is also used of an obstacle to belief (the cross; 1 Cor 1:23; Gal 5:11 ["offense" in NRSV]).

DONALD E. GOWAN

Suffer, Suffering, Affliction, Persecution, Tribulation, Trouble, Woe

When human life proceeds as expected, according to plan, or even with pleasant surprises, it is generally experienced and described as well-being. When anything goes wrong with that scenario, it is a misfortune. Human beings are familiar with many misfortunes: war, death, divorce, loss of a job or one's home or one's health, and so on. All misfortunes entail suffering, which invariably includes pain, distress, and tribulation among other things. Someone described suffering as the pain of life, suggesting that pain is central to the experience of suffering. The words "pain" and "suffering" are frequently paired. Human beings do not assign entirely private meanings to their suffering. Rather, the meaning assigned by any individual to a personal (or communal) experience of suffering is one that is available in that individual's culture or subculture. Moreover, these meanings themselves change over time, because human understanding and interpretations change over time.

For those who do not believe in God, suffering is just there. The only problem is what to do about it or how to get rid of it, if at all possible. Suffering is a theological problem primarily for those who believe in a provident, good God. For these, an entirely different set of problems and questions arise. If God is good, how can the deity allow this to happen? More specifically, how could God allow this to happen to me/us, who are so faithful in love and service? Why do the wicked seem to escape all suffering? Opinions about these and similar questions in the Bible vary because they reflect shifts in understanding over two thousand years in circum-Mediterranean culture.

Those fluctuating and evolving understandings are manifest not only in the variety of words that express suffering but also in the nuances imposed on these words. In the following instances in which the NRSV uses "suffering," the actual Hebrew word means "pain" (Ezek 18:19), "trouble" (Judg 10:16), "distress" (Neh 9:27). Sometimes the Hebrew word for suffering is lacking but the context allows it (Ps 60:3, Hebrew v. 5). Clearly a purely linguistic approach to understanding suffering in the Bible will be unsatisfactory. It will be more appropriate to attend to the social system from which all language derives its meaning. To this end we adopt a cultural and historical approach.

Cultural perspectives. According to a now classic model for comparing values across cultures, circum-Mediterranean traditional cultures in general tend to adopt an attitude of being subservient to nature. Peasant populations certainly knew they could not master or control nature (e.g., Mark 4:1–9), though they did learn how to live in harmony with it (e.g., Mark 2:22). Pain and suffering were considered part and parcel of a defective universe and defective nature (Gen 3). Thus it was believed that no one could master, control, or eliminate pain. Everyone accepted in practice Aristotle's view that pain was felt not by the body but rather by the sentient soul, which is coterminous with the body. Since no one can deal with the soul, there was no way to eliminate pain. The most one could hope for was alleviation of pain (Mark 15:23). Stoics encouraged heroic endurance of suffering and pain. Jesus exhorted followers to "take up the cross" and follow him (Mark 8:34). To endure acute suffering without shrieking was a mark of manliness (Isa 53:7; Mark 15:25–39).

This perspective lasted from antiquity until the mid–seventeenth century, when Descartes proposed that suffering and pain were good, since they gave clues about ills in the body that could then be attended to and perhaps remedied. Leibniz argued further that suffering and pain were the sign of the perfect order of nature. The universe was not flawed. Pain and suffering, like hunger and thirst, are part of the inviolable laws of nature. With these insights, it was now possible to work at effectively eliminating pain. Indeed, according to the classic model for comparing values across cultures mentioned above, contemporary Western cultures are absolutely convinced human beings can indeed control nature and eliminate pain. Of course, what made sense objectively no longer made sense subjectively, especially when pain begins to surpass tolerable limits. With this framework we can now review the biblical material.

Old Testament. In the preexilic period the dominant view was that suffering is the result of human behavior that shames God ("sin"). The etiological legend in Gen 3 clearly indicates that suffering

entered the world because of the disobedience of God's first creatures. God punished each actor in the story with some form of suffering. This was not part of God's original plan. The story also reflects a typical Mediterranean cultural value, namely, unwillingness to admit a mistake or a bad choice. It is not so much a denial of the choice as a denial that it really was a "free choice." Blaming another, passing the buck, is typical. The man blames the woman; the woman blames the serpent, who has accomplished what it set out to do.

Another view of suffering derives from the all-embracing consequences of the couple's disobedience. All nature is affected, as are all the couple's descendants. God was perceived to "visit the iniquity of the parents upon the children and the children's children, to the third and the fourth generation" (Exod 34:7; see also Exod 20:5–6; Num 14:18; Deut 5:9). God is thus directly responsible for human suffering. In the Mediterranean cultural context, God is obliged to do this. It is the only way God can satisfy his honor for the shame inflicted by disobedient creatures. God thereby regains his honor (the Bible commonly uses the word "glory"). Leviticus 26 relates how God will bless obedience but punish disobedience by vigorously pursuing vengeance for slighted honor and sending suffering unless and until they repent. Sometimes God even appears to act unreasonably in sending suffering (Exod 4:11). The dominant perspective is corporate; the focus is on the whole tribal people, Israel, and the preexilic prophets were eloquent in detailing the shortcomings of their society that would surely bring punishment and suffering from God.

The experience of the Babylonian exile posed a strong challenge to earlier "simplistic" notions. It was inconceivable that God's people should suffer more than their enemies. More important, why should this generation suffer for the sins of earlier generations? A sense of the individual and individual responsibility came to the fore, especially in Isaiah, Jeremiah, Ezekiel, and Job. It is important to realize that this is not individualism as understood and experienced in the West, where each person stands on his or her own two feet quite independently. Individuals in circum-Mediterranean cultures are collectivistic personalities. Such persons depend upon and derive their identity from the group: family, village, and so on. Their behavior is guided by group opinion more than by independent "free choice." Jeremiah declared that the old proverb, "The parents have eaten sour grapes, and the children's teeth are set on edge," would no longer hold true. "But all shall die for their own sins; the teeth of everyone who eats sour grapes shall be set on edge" (Jer 31:29–30; the NRSV obliterates the singulars "every one," "his own sin," "each man," "his teeth" in its inclusive translation). Ezekiel is even more blunt, for this statement is a direct word of the Lord: "it is only the person who sins that shall die" (Ezek 18:4, 20).

Job offers perhaps the best review of the problem of suffering and the reflections offered by earlier tradition. In a sense, Job expects the "law of retribution" to operate in his case. He is a good and devout person (see Job 29–31) who has never displeased God (as God asserts in Job 1:8). Why does God not treat him appropriately? His interlocutors for the most part repeat the law of retribution to him. If he is suffering like this, then he must be guilty, and his best option is to admit it honestly. God's answer (Job 38–41) to Job's appeal is hardly satisfying. In fact, it is no answer at all, except to remind Job that human beings are quite limited in their abilities to understand the complexities of life, including suffering, which has been described as "the pain of living." Thanks to the epilogue, the reader learns that Job's "friends" were wrong and recognizes that Job has indeed suffered innocently as he has insisted all along (Job 42:7–9).

One other important consideration about the book of Job is that it echoes the cultural value previously noted in Gen 3.

Job is innocent; he is not the cause of his suffering. But now neither is God the cause of his suffering. It is rather Satan (mentioned only three times in the OT: 1 Chr 21; Zech 3; and here); that is, Job's suffering is someone else's doing, someone else's fault (the woman's fault, the serpent's fault—but not *my* fault!). This reasoning is culturally predictable, whether appropriate to the situation or not.

Second Isaiah (chaps. 40–55) repeats the point that Judah's behavior brought upon it deserved punishment and suffering (42:18–22, 24, 25; 43:24b; 47:6). The Servant Songs, however, recall and refine another idea. Already the Deuteronomist indicated that suffering might have some benefit for the one who suffers or dies for others (Deut 8:1–6). God uses suffering to humble, to test loyalty (v. 2). God uses suffering to teach lessons: "one does not live by bread alone" (v. 3). As a father physically disciplines his son (Prov 13:24; 19:18; 22:15; 23:13–14; 29:15, 17), so does God send physical suffering for the same purpose (Deut 8:5; cf. Heb 12:5–11). Sometimes, God elects to bring good out of evil (Gen 50:15–20). Second Isaiah makes the same point in the Servant Poems. The suffering of Israel works for the good of others (Isa 53:4–5, 10–12).

New Testament. In the NT, the word "suffer" describes people "gripped" by an illness (Luke 4:38, literally, "gripped by a fever," though elsewhere the word *pathein*, "to suffer," occurs). Jesus' Israelite compatriots were faithful heirs of their tradition. They continued to believe that God blesses the righteous and punishes sinners and/or their children (see John 9:2). If this punishment did not occur in this world, it would surely occur in the world to come (Matt 25:46). Yet Jesus proposes that those who suffer and seem to be receiving divine punishment at the present actually are the truly honorable ones (Matt 5:3–12).

For the most part, however, the word "suffer" is associated with Jesus' passion and death. That event posed the greatest challenge to his followers after his death. Here was a good and blameless person who not only suffered insults and other challenges to his reputation during life but was physically tortured and suffered intensely during his arrest and execution. How and why would God allow this? When God raised Jesus very shortly after his death, it became clear that God had actually been pleased with Jesus' life. While that fact was not slow to sink in, a fuller understanding of the meaning of Jesus' suffering remained to be developed.

The risen Jesus himself explained that his suffering and death was God's will and plan: "Was it not *necessary* that the Messiah *should suffer* these things and then enter into his glory?" (Luke 24:26). The note of necessity occurs also in the passion predictions placed on Jesus' lips by later tradition (Mark 8:31 and par. Matt 16:21; Luke 9:21). This was a constant motif in early Christian preaching (Acts 3:18) and was part of the bedrock of the early Christian creeds. Quite often in the NT when used of Jesus, "to suffer" meant "to suffer death," and it was all God's will ("in accordance with the scriptures" 1 Cor 15:3–5; "foretold through all the prophets" Acts 3:18).

The Synoptics drew parallels between Jesus' life and that of the Servant described by Second Isaiah (esp. Isa 53: compare Matt 8:16–17 with Isa 53:4; Luke 22:37; Mark 15:28 with Isa 53:12; Mark 9:12 with Isa 53:3; Mark 10:45; 14:24 with Isa 53:11; Matt 20:28; Mark 14:24 with Isa 53:10–11). This helped believers to make sense of Jesus' suffering and death. They interpreted it as test of his loyalty imposed by the Father. Jesus of course remained faithful to the very end.

It was Paul who drew out the further implications, namely, that the suffering and death of Jesus proved his great attachment to God and his own friends (this is what love means: 2 Cor 5:14; Gal 2:20; Rom 5:5; 8:35, 37). His suffering and death were collectivistic events, with benefits for others attached or related to him (this is what "vicarious" means). By it, all might be redeemed, reconciled with God, freed from sin and its consequences, indeed freed from all the cosmic powers

of evil. More than this, Paul argues that the pattern of Jesus' death resulting in new, risen life is the model for all believers. Human suffering is a participation in the passion and suffering of Jesus (2 Cor 4:7–11) and through it, accepted in faith, believers also assure themselves a share in his glory (Rom 8:17). The sufferings of the present are far surpassed by the glory to come (Phil 3:8, 10; Rom 8:18). As Christ suffered and died for others, so ought his followers be willing to suffer and die for others (Matt 16:24–25; 1 John 3:16).

Two words did not figure prominently in this discussion: "woe" and "persecution." The Hebrew noun for "woe" occurs only in Ezek 2:10. All the other occurrences are the interjection expressing grief and despair (e.g., Isa 6:5) or a denunciation (e.g., Num 21:19; Jer 13:27). The word appears as a substantive in Prov 23:29: "Who has woe?" (v. 30: "those who linger late over wine, those who keep trying mixed wines"—leading to suffering of a different sort). The Greek word is also an interjection denoting pain or displeasure (e.g., Matt 18:17), but it is also used as noun denoting intense hardship or distress (Rev 9:12; 11:14). In this latter case, the emphasis is on the intensity of the suffering.

Finally, the Hebrew word translated as "persecute" in the Hebrew Bible (e.g., Ps 119:84, 86, 150, 161) basically carries the idea of pursuing or chasing someone with hostile intent (e.g., Lev 26:7–8; Deut 28:22 of various misfortunes). All such experiences bring a wide variety of suffering in their wake. Jeremiah recounts his experience of persecution in his memoirs (sometimes called "confessions": 11:18–12:6; 15:10–21; 17:14–18; 18:18–23; 20:7–13, 15–18). The Psalms of lament both communal (Pss 12; 44; 74; etc.) and of collectivistic individuals (Pss 3; 4; 22; 31; etc.) report the suffering that comes from persecution. The followers of Jesus are persecuted for fidelity to the gospel (Matt 5:10–12; 10:13), but Jesus remains the model of faithful endurance (Luke 22:34–46). Persecution is a test, a share in the suffering of Christ, and a blessing (1 Pet 4:12–19).

In the final analysis, the Bible offers no single answer to questions about the origin or meaning of suffering. Many instances of human suffering simply admit of no explanation. For Christians, the resurrection of Jesus, in which all share through baptism, is the only consolation (2 Tim 3:10–12; 1 Pet 5:10; Rev 2:10).

J. Christiaan Beker, *Suffering and Hope: The Biblical Vision and the Human Predicament* (Philadelphia: Fortress Press, 1987); Terence E. Fretheim, *The Suffering of God: An Old Testament Perspective* (Philadelphia: Fortress Press, 1984); E. S. Gerstenberger and W. Schrage, *Suffering* (Nashville: Abingdon Press, 1980).

JOHN J. PILCH

Swear *see* **Oath**

Tabernacle *see* **Presence**

Teach, Teacher, Teaching *see* **Preach**

Temple *see* **Presence**

Tempt, Temptation When the NRSV translators eliminated the word "temptation" from its best-known NT use in the Lord's Prayer ("and lead us not into temptation," Matt 6:13; Luke 11:4), they may have borne in mind the adage of another NT writer, the author of the Epistle of James, who said: "No one, when tempted, should say, 'I am being tempted by God'; for God cannot be tempted by evil and he himself tempts no one" (Jas 1:13: a remark that is part of the longest essay on temptation in the NT, Jas 1:12–16). In spite of our modern conviction that all beings have a shadow side, contemporary theology does not think it appropriate to depict *God* as a tempter.

The shift is not simply theological, however, for it also reflects the changing semantics of the English words. The first dictionary definition of "tempt"—"to induce or persuade by enticement or allurement, as to do something unwise, wrong, or immoral"—seems to outweigh by far the ever more infrequent meaning "to invite" (as in "May I tempt you with this piece of chocolate cake?"), not to mention the meaning that was lively in the days of King James but is now listed as obsolete, "to try or test." For us, temptation is a pejorative notion. It is generally involved with evil and even with the Tempter himself, who is **Satan**.

This double shift—theological appropriateness and English meaning—has led to a dramatic drop in the frequency of terms clustering around "tempt" from seventy-three occurrences in the KJV to just fifteen in the NRSV, all forms of the Greek *peirao* (though notes offer "tempt" as an alternative to the preferred "test" in several other instances, including the Lord's Prayer). Furthermore, in the NRSV "temptation" is banished from the OT altogether, mostly in favor of "test" and "testing." In five of the fourteen NT occurrences, Satan or the Tempter is the subject (the parallel accounts of Jesus tempted by Satan in the wilderness: Matt 4:1, 3; Mark 1:13; Luke 4:2; also in Paul's instructions concerning marriage, 1 Cor 7:5, as well as in 1 Thess 3:5). In the other instances (Gal 6:1; 1 Tim 6:9, and the sustained discussion in Jas 1:12–16) temptation to sin comes from joining others in the work of the flesh, from riches, or from one's own desire.

The much larger role played by the words "tempt" and "temptation" in older English versions depends upon their willingness to render with these terms Hebrew words and other occurrences of forms of the Greek *peirao* that have more to do with "testing" than with incitement to do evil. In the KJV we read, for example, that God "tempted" Abraham to sacrifice his son Isaac on Mount Moriah (Gen 22:1), a situation that the NRSV construes not as an incitement to do evil, but as a "test" of trust. In ten other cases, the KJV renders the same Hebrew word used in this verse, *nasah*, with "tempt." All of these occur in passages in which the Israelites are accused of "tempting" God.

Sometimes the KJV renders the noun derived from *nasah* with "temptation"

(Deut 4:34; 7:19; 29:3; Ps 95:8). All of these refer to the "temptations" of Israel in the wilderness after the exodus from Egypt (see also Heb 3:8: "Harden not your hearts, as in the provocation, in the day of temptation in the wilderness," KJV). In the NRSV this entire motif becomes the theme of "testing" in the wilderness, a construal of the Hebrew and Greek that is surely more intelligible than the earlier one.

W. SIBLEY TOWNER

Tent of Meeting *see* **Presence**

Testify, Testimony, Witness One testifies (or gives testimony, or bears witness; Hebrew ʿedh, "witness," and related terms; Greek martys and related terms) to what one knows to be true. In most instances, personal observation provides the basis for the knowledge to which one testifies; in some cases in the NT, one testifies to that of which one has come to assurance through faith.

In ancient Israel, the evidence of witnesses provided the basis on which legal action was taken (note the special provisions made where no witnesses were available in Num 5:11–31; Deut 21:1–9). In capital cases, more than one witness was required to establish guilt (Num 35:30; Deut 17:6); the principle is applied generally in Deut 19:15. The natural concern that witnesses speak truthfully is given added urgency by the realization that God is the overseer of justice: earthly judges act on God's behalf (Deut 1:16–17), and God can be expected to intervene to restore justice when it has been perverted on earth (Ps 82). The divine stake in earthly justice is apparent not only in the prohibition of "false witness" in the Decalogue (Exod 20:16; Deut 5:20) and the laws for punishment of those who bear false testimony (Deut 19:16–21), but also in the insistence in Proverbs that the Lord "hates" lying witnesses (Prov 6:19) and that disaster awaits them (19:5, 9; 21:28; see also 12:17; 24:28; 25:18). False witnesses are a com-

mon complaint of psalmists, who cry out to God to intervene and vindicate the innocent (Ps 27:12; 35:11). On the other hand, those who have witnessed wrongdoing but who fail to come forward when testimony is called for also incur guilt (Lev 5:1). Apart from their role in legal proceedings, witnesses were summoned to attest to commercial transactions as well (Jer 32:10, 12, 25; cf. Ruth 4:9–11).

God, in whose presence all life is lived, was frequently invoked as a witness (and judge of the guilty) when solemn commitments were made. This is of course the point whenever an oath is taken in God's name (e.g., Ruth 1:17) but is explicit elsewhere as well (Gen 31:50; Jer 42:5). In non-Israelite cultures, a variety of deities could be summoned to witness solemn engagements. Possibly such a custom is echoed in texts like Deut 4:26; 30:19; 31:28, where "heaven and earth" are rhetorically invested with the capacity to testify that Israel has been given due warning of the consequences of disobedience: as parts of creation, they are pictured as sharing the Creator's concern over the unfaithfulness of his creatures (note Isa 1:2–3). In other texts, stones and altars are designated witnesses (Gen 31:48, 52; Josh 22:27, 28, 34; 24:27; 1 Sam 6:18; Isa 19:20). In some cases the point may be simply that they serve as visible reminders of commitments that have been made or of what the Lord has done; but at times, stones and altars, as inanimate but enduring objects, are pictured as able to provide "witness" at some future date against those who prove false to their solemn undertakings. The song of Moses (Deut 31:19, 21; 32:46) and other texts (Deut 31:26; Isa 8:16; 30:8) that foretell Israel's rebelliousness and punishment are also envisaged as "witnesses" in this sense. But prophets, above all, bore testimony to the guilt of God's people (see 2 Chr 24:19; Amos 3:13; also Ps 50:7, which was presumably spoken by a prophet attached to the sanctuary to crowds who gathered there) and of others, as witnessed by God (Jer 29:23; Mic 1:2; Mal 2:14).

In Isa 43:9–13 (see also 44:8–9) the prophet pictures a gathering of the nations in order that the claims of their gods to divinity may be tested against those of the Lord. Witnesses are summoned to attest to the power of the would-be gods to foretell the future. Against any such claims the people of Israel, as the Lord's witnesses, can attest that the Lord not only declared in advance what would happen but also brought about Israel's salvation. Thus the Lord alone is shown to be God and Savior.

In the NT many of the same senses appear. False witness—a sin that tells of the corruption of the heart (Matt 15:19)—is brought against both Jesus and Stephen (Matt 26:59–62; Acts 6:13). The OT law that charges of wrongdoing must be established by the testimony of two or three witnesses (see Heb 10:28) is cited or alluded to in reminders of the seriousness with which any such charges must be treated (Matt 18:16; 2 Cor 13:1, where the observations of Paul on more than one occasion are thought to meet the requirement; 1 Tim 5:19). God is summoned as the witness to the truth of various claims (Rom 1:9; 2 Cor 1:23; Phil 1:8; 1 Thess 2:5, 10). Testimony is frequently given about the conduct or character of certain people by those who know them (Rom 10:2; 2 Cor 8:3; Col 4:13; etc.); but it is noted that Jesus, who knew the hearts of others, needed no such testimony (John 2:25).

In the Synoptic Gospels, a leper whom Jesus had cured was to appear before a priest as a witness of Jesus' power to heal and, perhaps, of his attention to this detail of the law (Matt 8:4). The disciples whom Jesus sent out to spread the gospel of the kingdom were told to shake from their feet the dust of a place where they had not been received: it would serve as a testimony (or evidence) against that place (Mark 6:11). They could expect to be put on trial but should use such occasions as an opportunity to bear witness (Matt 10:18). The gospel itself must be preached in all the world for a witness to the nations (Matt 24:14).

In Acts, those who had been with Jesus from the beginning of his ministry were commissioned as his witnesses (Acts 1:8; see Luke 24:48). They could testify of all that he had done (Acts 10:39) and, most important, of his resurrection (1:22; 2:32; 3:15; 4:33; 13:31; cf. 1 Cor 15:15). Paul too was to bear witness to the Christ who had appeared to him (Acts 22:15; 26:16); much of the narrative of Acts is a record of his faithfulness in fulfilling this commission (18:5; 20:21, 24; 23:11; 26:22; 28:23). The truth to which these "witnesses" bore testimony was not confined to events that they had seen but included convictions of which their faith gave them assurance: the messiahship of Jesus (18:5), his role as judge of all (10:42), the forgiveness of sins that is available in Christ (5:31–32), the kingdom of God (28:23), and the need for salvation from a corrupt generation (Acts 2:40). God, whose goodness is always to be witnessed in the bounty of creation (Acts 14:17), now added his confirming witness to the testimony of the apostles by granting them the power to do signs and wonders (Acts 14:3; cf. 5:32; Heb 2:4).

A central theme in John's Gospel is that the Son of God came to earth to bear witness to the truth (John 18:37; see also 3:32; 7:7). To the truth of Christ's witness John the Baptist himself bore witness, testifying that Christ is the "light" of the world, the preexistent one, the one who baptizes with the Spirit, and the Son of God (1:7–8, 15, 32–33, 34; 3:26; 5:33–35). Greater than his witness was that of the works done by Jesus at his Father's behest (5:36; 10:25); the Scriptures, too, bear witness to Christ (5:39). But the supreme witness to Christ is that of the Father himself: a divinely granted assurance of the heart, granted to those who believe in Christ, that he was indeed sent by the Father and carried out the Father's will (5:32, 37; 8:18; see also 1 John 5:9–10; Rom 8:16). Though any testimony that Christ might be thought to bear to himself independently of his Father would of necessity be false (John 5:31), he in fact does nothing apart from the Father, whose testimony validates the truth of what Christ says (8:13–19). Those who believed in Christ were themselves to bear witness to him; their testimony would be aided by the Spirit, whom Christ would send to be in them (John 4:39; 15:26–27; in the "we" who give testimony according to John 3:11, Jesus associates himself with the witness of his followers). The gospel itself preserves the testimony of one such disciple, whose witness is trustworthy (John 19:35; 21:24).

First John speaks of the unified testimony to Christ borne by the Spirit, the water, and the blood (5:6–8). The references to "water" and "blood" underline the importance to Christian faith of Christ's empowerment by the Spirit as attested at his baptism and of his real, physical death. The testimony of the "Spirit" refers to the convicting power granted by the Spirit to the church's proclamation about Christ.

The book of Revelation is the testimony of John to the word of God that he received; but that divine word is itself the testimony of Jesus Christ to what, in God's plan, must shortly take place (Rev 1:1–2; see also 22:16, 20). Jesus Christ is himself the "faithful witness," not only in what he testifies about God's plan, but also in his faithful fulfillment of his Father's commission during his life on earth (1:5; 3:14). Those followers of Jesus who remain true to him are commended for their faithful witness (2:13). Since such faithfulness led at times to death, the word for "witness" (Greek *martys*; hence English "martyr") came more and more to be used of those whose witness cost them their lives (2:13; 6:9; 17:6; 20:4; see also Acts 22:20).

A. A. Trites, *The New Testament Concept of Witness*, SNTSMS 31 (Cambridge: Cambridge University Press, 1977).
STEPHEN WESTERHOLM

Thank, Thanksgiving In the OT "thank" and "thanksgiving" translate various forms of the Hebrew root *yadah*. The terms refer to the act of expressing gratitude or to the statement of gratitude

itself. However, the notion of gratefulness, as the word is commonly used in English, does not capture fully the theological implications of the Hebrew. Indeed Claus Westermann argues rightly that the verb *yadah* means "to *praise*," since it has the specific connotation of worship as response to salvation (Pss 35:17–18; 52:9; Westermann, *Praise and Lament*, 25–30). The nuances of *yadah* can be best understood in relation to *halal*, from which comes the common expression "*hallelujah*" ("praise the Lord"; see 1 Chr 6:4, 35; 23:30; 25:3; 29:13; 2 Chr 5:13; 31:2; Ezra 3:11; Neh 12:24, 46; *TLOT* 2:502–8). The latter (*halal*) offers praise for some inherent feature of the one being lauded (Gen 49:8; Ps 49:17), while the former (*yahah*) pays homage as a reaction to a particular experience with the one being praised (Gen 29:35).

The words "thank" and "thanksgiving" are highly concentrated in the Psalms (fifty-four times). The most common contexts are statements that thank the Lord for particular benefits (Pss 57:9–10; 140:12–13) and imperatives that call the worshiper to laud God for his goodness (Pss 107:1; 118:1, 19, 29). In some occurrences of this terminology, the words denote the thanksgiving offering, a type of sacrifice given by an individual to acknowledge divine favor (Lev 7:12, 13, 15; 22:29; Jer 17:26; 33:11; Amos 4:5; 3 Macc 1:9). This offering was closely related to the votive gift because it was voluntary and it followed an experience of divine deliverance (Lev 7:16–17; Num 6:21; see *vow*). The sacrifice of thanksgiving was also parallel to the freewill offering, given in response to good fortune (Exod 35:27–29; 36:3; Deut 12:17; 16:10; 23:23). In fact, these various ritual gifts may be simply variegated expressions of the same sacrifice, prompted by the worshiper's favorable circumstances (*TLOT* 2:506–507; Gaster, "Sacrifices and Offerings," *IDB* 4:149).

An important development in the use of the thanksgiving terminology is the notion that a prayer or song (see *sing*) of thanks could be given in place of the thanksgiving offering. This is particularly evident in the Psalter. Psalm 28:7b states, "*With my song* I give thanks to him." Similarly Ps 50:23a says, "Those who bring thanksgiving *as their sacrifice* honor me." In the second example, thanksgiving translates the Hebrew *todah*, a designation for a particular type of song. Israelites in the Diaspora or in remote regions of Palestine, for whom the temple was either destroyed or inaccessible, utilized the song of thanksgiving as a surrogate for sacrifices of well-being. As Jonah 2:9 indicates, it was a vehicle that gave them access to the divine, just as a gift on the altar did. However, this does not mean that sacrifice was replaced by the thanksgiving song. Burnt offerings would continue into the Common Era, until the temple was destroyed in A.D. 70 (1 Macc 4:56). What this delineation of the song of thanksgiving indicates, rather, is that the *todah* was treated *like a sacrifice*, sung with awareness of God's presence in the temple. So, for example, the song was directed toward Jerusalem when offered by worshipers removed from the holy place (Ps 138:2). The thanksgiving song became an essential part of worship in the temple itself. Nehemiah 12:8 identifies a company of Levites in charge of the *todah*. Also 1 Chr 25:3 declares that Jeduthun "prophesied with the lyre in thanksgiving and praise." These references indicate that the thanksgiving song became a kind of institution. It stood alongside sacrifice as an essential part of the worshiper's experience that linked the believer with God.

Several OT texts make the striking statement that those in the realm of the dead do not give thanks to God (Isa 38:18; Pss 6:5; 30:9; 88:11). These declarations are addressed to God as part of a request for God to act, to maintain the pray-er. But such statements are important theologically for what they say about the nature of life in relation to God, namely, that life in fullness and humility is characterized by thanksgiving. This is most clear in Sir 17:28: "From the dead, as from one who does not exist, thanksgiving has ceased; those who are alive and well sing the Lord's praises." The implication is similar to that formally stated in the Shorter and Larger Catechisms, "Man's chief end is to glorify God."

The NT use of "thanks" differs from that of the OT in that it does not have the same cultic overtones, or at least such implications are not immediately obvious in most texts. The Greek, *eucharisteo* does not indicate a prayer that has sacrificial significance. Nevertheless *eucharisteo* has continuity with Hebrew *yadah* in that it expresses thanks to God for particular benefits and is an essential element of prayer (John 6:11, 23). Revelation has close parallels to OT in the form of address to God (Rev 4:9; 11:17).

The two most important theological uses of the terminology in NT are as follows: first, *eucharisteo* appears in prayers of thanks for food (Mark 8:6; John 6:11, 23). This is prominent in accounts of the Lord's Supper (Matt 26:27; Mark 14:23; Luke 22:17, 19; 1 Cor 11:24). In such mealtime prayers *eucharisteo* seems to be almost interchangeable with *eulogeo*, meaning "**bless**" (equivalent to Hebrew *barak*). This is evident in the alternation of the two terms in Mark 6:41; 8:6. However, the two parallel words should not be taken as allusions to the Eucharist wherever they appear. Rather, they reflect, and the use in the story of the supper reflects, the Jewish regulation that food and drink should always receive a blessing (*b. Berakhot* 35a; see Conzelmann, *TDNT* 9:411–12).

Second, Paul uses the language of thanksgiving in a distinct section of his letters that comes after the salutation (1 Cor 1:4; 1 Thess 1:2; 2:13). He typically expresses thanks to God for the church being addressed, some feature of their faith or particular acts of support for his ministry. Letters often considered Deutero-Pauline follow the same pattern (Eph 1:16; Col 1:12).

It is also important to notice that the NT assumes many of the OT's theological implications of the word "thanks," even though the frequency of such use is small. Romans 1:21 (using *eucharisteo*) clearly connects giving thanks with the creature's proper orientation to the creator. Similarly, Heb 12:28 identifies giving thanks as proper worship, in recognition of the gift of God's grace. Revelation 11:17 also carries the notion that the created order has a correct stance before God when it gives thanks. Furthermore, in the Hebrews example, the word translated "thanks" is *charis*, the term otherwise translated "grace" (Heb 12:15). The variant meaning is understandable in that grace is something freely offered. Likewise, thanksgiving by nature cannot be offered begrudgingly. An awareness of God's goodness that produces a free expression of gratitude is at the heart of the biblical notion of giving thanks.

H. Conzelmann, "eucharisteo," *TDNT* 9:407–15; T. H. Gaster, "Sacrifices," *IDB* 4:147–59; Claus Westermann, *Praise and Lament in the Psalms* (Atlanta: John Knox Press, 1965); Claus Westermann, "*ydh* to praise," *TLOT* 2:502–8.

JEROME F. D. CREACH

Think, Thought   see Mind

Thousand   see Numbers

Three   see Numbers

Time, Age, Day, End, Eternal, Everlasting, Forever, Hour, Year

This article deals with the vocabulary of terms in the Bible, as compared with the words used in English.

Time. NRSV renders several different Hebrew nouns and phrases by the word "time." The Hebrew noun "day," in singular or plural form, can be so rendered, as in expressions like "her time to give birth" (Gen 25:24) or the "time of harvest" (Prov 25:13). A certain occasion may be conveyed by the noun "day" as in Num 3:1, "the time when the LORD spoke with Moses." Plural forms of the noun "day" are more frequent in expressions such as "in the course of time," literally "from the end of days" (Gen 4:3; 26:8).

Future time, the "time to come," is expressed in phrases like "at the end of the days" (Deut 31:29), while a broader sense is carried by the phrase "for all time" (literally, "all the days") in Deut 18:5; Jer 33:18. That future time may appear as soon as tomorrow (Josh 4:6) or at some less-defined future moment as in Judg 11:4 ("after a time"). The phrase "A time is coming . . ." can be found in 1 Sam 2:31, though this phrase would normally be translated more literally as "the days are coming," as happens in Jer 51:47. This general sense of time may also be expressed in Hebrew as years rather than days as in Hab 3:2: "in our own time."

Fixed moments of time are indicated by the Hebrew noun *mo‘ed*. In Gen 18:14; 21:2; Ps 75:2; Hab 2:3 "set time" and "appointed time" are how NRSV renders it, while in Dan 12:7 it occurs in the phrase "time, two times, and half a time."

The most common Hebrew noun used in the context of particular time or event is *‘eth* (Gen 38:1; 2 Sam 11:1; 1 Kgs 19:2; 20:6). Ezra 10:13 uses it to refer to an occasion of heavy rain, and Job 27:10 translated the phrase *b‘kol-‘eth* as "at all times." However, it is the "time poem" in Eccl 3:1–8, in which the noun appears twenty-nine times, that provides most examples. There it is used in parallel to the noun "season." *‘Eth* can refer to an "acceptable time" (Ps 69:13), while "the time of the end" is a phrase met in Dan 12:9. On the other hand, a specific occasion, "this time," is how NRSV handles the Hebrew phrase *pa‘am hazzoth* (e.g., Exod 8:32), similar to "at one time" in 1 Chr 11:11.

The phrase "for all time" in the sense of "forever" is the way NRSV translates Hebrew *‘ad-‘olam* on one occasion in 1 Sam 1:22, and *l‘dor wador* in Ps 77:8. In this latter example it is literally "to generation and generation."

"For some time," in the sense of previously, renders *’ethmol* in 2 Sam 5:2 while "time past" renders the phrase *me’az* in 2 Sam 15:34. Present time in the phrase "from this time on and forevermore" (Pss 113:2; 115:18; 121:8; Isa 9:7) is literally "from now and until . . ."

On a number of occasions English expression requires the use of the noun "time" when no specific Hebrew term is present in the text: Gen 22:15, "a second (time)"; 1 Kgs 18:29, "the (time) of the offering"; Ezek 16:47, "very little (time)."

In the Greek NT two basic nouns are used to express time. One is *chronos*, which can refer to length of time; the second is *kairos*, which expresses moments of time or fixed times. However, *chronos* can also refer to specific times as in Luke 1:57 ("the time came for Elizabeth to give birth"). NRSV's rendering of Matt 2:7 illustrates well this feature of *chronos* when it speaks of "the exact time" that the star signaling Jesus' birth appeared. Speaking of the length of time he had been with them, Jesus uses *chronos* in John 14:9 (similarly, Acts 1:21).

A set or appointed time agreed upon by two parties translates *kairos* in 1 Cor 7:5. It also is used frequently to refer to the approaching time of God's kingdom (Matt 8:29; Mark 1:15; John 7:6). It may be used of harvest time (Matt 21:34) and of the present period of time (Rom 8:18) and refers to the time of Jesus' return in 1 Tim 6:15. It speaks of a future, "in due time," in 1 Pet 5:6. As in the OT, so in the NT, "time" can be used in parallel with the word "day" (Matt 10:19; 11:25; 12:1; 2 Cor 6:2). In Heb 12:10 a "short time" is literally "few days." It is also NRSV's way of translating the adverb *brachy* (Acts 5:34).

Phrases in NRSV using "time" that do not have a Greek equivalent are "time of trial" (Mark 14:38), where the phrase is literally "temptation." "At the same time" in the sense of "together" renders the adverb *hama*, while "at one time" with a sense of the same occasion is found in 1 Cor 15:6. "Time" in the phrase "at the time of the deportation" in Matt 1:11 is indicated by the preposition *epi*. Another adverb, *tote*, meaning "at that time" is so rendered in Matt 4:17; 16:21; Mark 13:21. Additionally the adverb "already" (*ede*) becomes in Matt 14:24 "by this time."

Age. The majority of uses of the word "age" occur in phrases relating to a person's actual age in years (e.g., Lev 27:3,

"60 years of age") in which the noun translates a Hebrew noun for "year." The noun "days" as in Gen 18:11, "advanced in age" (literally "gone in days"), also can be used in these circumstances. There is also the phrase "old age" (e.g., Gen 21:2— "in his old age"), which renders the Hebrew adjective *zaqen*, "old" or "aged."

Those references to "age" as a period of time, such as the phrase "from age to age" (Isa 60:15), may be parallel to the Hebrew noun *ʿolam*, often rendered as "for ever." Here the phrase is literally "(from) generation to generation." An eschatological sense is found in the phrase "the end of the age." In Matthew's Gospel this has a future sense, of a coming age that will mark the end of the world or the end of time (see 13:39, 40, 49; 24:3; 28:20). In Heb 9:26 the same phrase appears, but it has reference back to the time of Christ's coming into the world to fulfill his mission. Similar ideas are contained in the references in 1 Cor 10:11 and Heb 6:5. One interesting rendering of "age" is found in Ezek 16:8, where "the age for love" is the way NRSV expresses the phrase "your time (is) a time of love."

In the NT, these extended periods of time, whether the present age or the age to come, are represented by the noun *aionos* (Matt 12:32; 13:39–40; Luke 16:8; 1 Cor 1:20; Eph 1:21). NRSV renders all of these occurrences by the noun "age" or "ages." This present age is considered to be a time of evil according to 2 Cor 4:4 (where *aionos* is translated "world") and Gal 1:4. In Mark 10:30 "the present age" renders the phrase *toutos kairos*. See also Luke 18:30, where it is rendered more literally as "this time." Paul speaks of the future age as already present in Jesus Christ (1 Cor 10:11), a view found also in Heb 6:5; 9:26. The division of world history into a present and a future age rests upon an apocalyptic expectation that Christ will inaugurate a new age. Being of a certain age, or mature, is literally "to have an age" (*elikian echei*), as in John 9:21, 23, or beyond a certain age (*para kairon elikian*), as in Heb 11:11. In these few examples, "age" refers to a span of life.

Day. When used literally, a "day" refers to the period of time between sunset of one day and sunset the following day (Gen 1:5). This method of counting time continued into the NT. As a result, the Last Supper, Jesus' trial and crucifixion all took place on the same day. The noun "day" can also refer specifically to the hours of daylight (Mark 4:27; 5:5; John 9:4). A full "day" then can be divided such that one can speak independently of the night as well as the morning, evening, and noon. The psalmist can speak of the cycle or rhythm within nature as the sun rises each morning as evidence of God's power in the phrase "day to day pours forth speech" (Ps 19:2). Here "day" represents the sun's regular morning appearance.

"To this day" is a phrase by which a writer refers to a past situation that persists up to the time of writing. See Gen 22:14; 26:33; 32:32; Exod 10:6; Matt 27:8; 28:15; and so on.

"Days" may describe a specific period of time related to an individual life. Genesis 26:18 speaks of the famine that occurred in the "days of Abraham." The book of Ruth is set in "the days when the judges ruled" (Ruth 1:1). References back to a situation in the past also use the plural "days," as in Judg 21:25. Mention of specific kings of Judah and Israel and their time on the throne is expressed as their "days" (Zeph 1:1). Hebrews 5:7 refers to the time of Jesus' earthly life with the phrase "in the days of his flesh."

When used figuratively, "day" can refer to an event or occasion, often linked closely with salvation. The exodus is described in Deut 16:3 as "the day of your departure from the land of Egypt." In Ps 18:18 the psalmist speaks of the time of his troubles as the "day of my calamity." In Rom 13:11–13 Paul speaks of the former time, the time before faith in Christ, as the night that preceded the "day" of salvation. That "day" or moment is near. (See also *Day of the Lord*.) This NT conception builds on that of the OT as expressed in Joel 2:31 in which the "day of the LORD" is characterized as "great and terrible." See also Zeph 1:8–9.

The "day," as a figure for the spiritual state of those who belong to Christ, allows Paul to speak of them as "children of the day" and "children of light" (1 Thess 5:5–8), in contrast to others who are "of the night." Believers thus belong to "the day" created by the *light* of the gospel, and so they must live accordingly.

Extended periods of time are indicated by the phrase "day after day" as in Gen 39:10; Judg 16:16; 2 Sam 13:37; Matt 26:55; Luke 22:53. Similarly, the phrase "day by day" (2 Chr 30:21; Ezra 6:9; Acts 2:47; 2 Cor 4:16) emphasizes constant daily activity. "From day to day" (Num 30:14) also indicates action that is regular or constant.

End. The noun "end" has a number of senses, some geographical ("from one end of the earth to the other"), some referring to objects ("the end of the pole"), some referring to the destruction of nations, as Deut 32:20, or an individual's death (Num 23:10). "End" may also indicate purpose, such as "to that/this end" (Eph 6:18; 2 Thess 1:11).

Temporal references are perhaps the most common, however. "End" in such contexts refers to the culmination of a period of time, such as the "end" of a number of days or years (Gen 8:6, "at the end of forty days"), the "end" of seven years of plenty (Gen 41:53). In Matthew there are several references to "the end of the age," carrying an eschatological sense—13:39, 40, 49; 24:3, 14. In 28:20 it is clear that this refers to the eternal presence of Christ with his followers. The eternal nature of God is reflected in the confession in Ps 102:27, "your years have no end."

Adverbial phrases such as "to the end" meaning the end of time can be found in Ps 119:33, 112; John 13:1; Heb 3:14. A focus in Daniel is on the end time (Dan 2:28; 11:27, 35, 40; 12:4, 9, 13, etc.), a time when God will bring judgment on those who oppose him and rescue for those who are faithful. Less specific time is noted in the phrase "in the end" as in Ps 112:8; Prov 5:4; 16:25.

In Rev 21:6 and 22:13 the "end" appears in the phrase "Alpha and Omega, the beginning and the end" in which case the "end" represents the temporal as well as the natural consummation of Christ's person and power.

Forever. NRSV uses this adverb some 359 times. For the most part it translates the Hebrew noun *ʿolam* or the Greek *aionos.* (NRSV renders *ʿolam* as "eternal" on only four occasions.) The basic sense of the words is "duration" or "age" as a period of time.

In the OT the noun is prefixed by prepositions "to" or "until" that turn it into the adverb "for ever" as in Gen 3:22 or 13:15. In other settings it serves as an adjective describing a commandment, literally "a statute of duration" (Lev 10:9) or "a covenant forever" (Lev 24:8; Num 18:19). Using the adverb "forever" to emphasize an action is one way that NRSV handles a compound verb. An example is in 2 Sam 14:14, in which a person is "banished forever." In Jer 15:14 "forever" is added to the text to convey the emphasis present in the Hebrew text.

Less frequently the Hebrew phrase "all the days" is rendered in NRSV as "forever" as in 1 Kgs 11:39; 2 Chron 10:7. Similarly, the phrase *lanetsah* in 2 Sam 2:26; Job 14:20; 23:7; 36:7; Ps 77:8. In Amos 1:11 *netsah,* "for ever," is used in parallel to "perpetually." The basic sense of the Hebrew is of something that endures for a long time. Also the adverb "continuously" (*tamid*) is rendered as "forever" in Ps 40:11. In NT the Greek phrase is literally "to the ages" (*eis ton aiona*) and translated as "for ever" in Luke 1:33, 55; John 6:51, 58; Rom 9:5; etc.). The phrase does not appear in Matthew or Mark in NRSV. The compound phrase "forever and ever" appears in Eph 3:21; 1 Tim 1:17; Rev 19:3. In Rom 11:10 "forever" is the way it translates the phrase, literally, "through everything." The adverb "always" (*pantote*) is also rendered "forever" in 1 Thess 4:17.

Eternal. This adjective appears only four times in OT (Gen 49:26; Eccl 12:5; Jer 20:11; Hab 3:6), each time as the rendering for the Hebrew word *ʿolam,* otherwise translated as "everlasting." It is

parallel to "everlasting" in Hab 3:6. It may describe mountains (Gen 49:26; Hab 3:6), a home (Eccl 12:5), or "dishonor" (Jer 20:11). In the NT the word is used seventy times and renders two different Greek terms, the majority term is *aionios.* The alternative term, *aidios,* appears only twice (Rom 1:20; Jude 1:6). There seems to be no essential semantic difference between these terms. Both can be applied to divine attributes such as God's power and glory. Although the adjective "eternal" may describe the Christian's inheritance, the gospel, God's purposes and the like, the primary use is with the noun "life" (forty-four times). Within the Johannine corpus, "eternal" is used only with this noun (see ***eternal life***). It is also the corpus within which the majority of occurrences are found (twenty-three times).

Everlasting. Examples of this term in NRSV are confined to the OT; none appear in the NT. However, the Hebrew term that underlies the word "everlasting" is essentially the same as that rendered "eternal"; that is to say, the Hebrew word *ʿolam* may be rendered as "eternal" or "everlasting." There is one example of the phrase *lanetsah,* literally "to perpetuity," in Ps 9:6. Additionally, NRSV in Ps 76:4 speaks of "everlasting mountains," a rendering based on the LXX text and following the example in Gen 49:26—"eternal mountains" (*horay-ʿad*) parallel to the "everlasting hills" (*gibʿoth ʿolam*).

"Everlasting" may describe hills and mountains (Deut 33:15; Ps 76:4; Hab 3:6), God's covenant with God's people (Gen 9:16; 17:7, 13, 19; 2 Sam 23:5; Isa 55:3; 61:8; Jer 32:40; Ezek 16:60; etc.), Yahweh as a rock (Isa 24:5), Israel's statutes and laws (Lev 16:34), even joy (Isa 35:10; 51:11; 61:7). Apart from the Psalms, the majority of examples of this adjective appear in Isaiah (sixteen times), many of them describing Yahweh (Isa 40:28; 60:19) and his covenant with his people.

Adverbial uses in the temporal phrase "from everlasting to everlasting" are frequent (1 Chr 16:36; Neh 9:5; Pss 41:13; 90:2; 103:17; 106:48). It is applied almost exclusively to Yahweh who predates creation and who will postdate its culmination. The phrase occurs in a context of praise or blessing him for his steadfast love. It is a fixed phrase used as a doxology that concludes the first and fourth books in the Psalms (41:13 and 106:48) and may be said to open the fourth book as well (90:2). Books Two (72:19) and Three (89:52) conclude with a doxology that praises Yahweh "forever." The Hebrew word in each case is also ʿolam.

Hour. The word occurs some seventy times, but only in NT. Of these, two-thirds are in the Gospels. With two exceptions (Matt 6:27; Luke 12:25) the Greek noun used is *hora*. It can refer to a moment of time or a period of time. Most occurrences refer to a moment of time. The "hour" may indicate the time of day (Matt 14:15; 24:36 Acts 3:1; 1 Cor 4:11; 15:30; etc.) or the moment of an action such as betrayal (Matt 26:45; Mark 14:41). In John's Gospel most references are to Jesus' final moments in the expressions "my hour has not yet come" (2:4), "the hour is coming" (4:21; 5:25, 28; 16:2; etc.), or "the hour has come . . ."(12:23). Periods of time from "half an hour" (Rev 8:1) to "twelve hours" (John 11:9) are covered by this term. The two unusual examples noted above are based on NRSV's rendering of an ambiguous text. The Greek noun *pechys* can mean an hour or a day, as well as a cubit, a measurement of length. The two references, Matt 6:27 and Luke 12:25, are identical. NRSV chooses to render as time duration ("add a single hour to your span of life") rather than as measurement of length.

Year(s). Both periods of time and a given age are indicated by this term. To identify periods of time, such as "seven years" (Gen 29:27), "forty years" (Exod 16:35), or any other number of years, is perhaps the most common context in which this noun is used. It also is used to note specific years within a cycle such as sabbatical years (Lev 26:34, 43), the year of jubilee (Lev 27:23), the year of remission (Deut 31:10). A formally similar expression, "the year of their punishment" (Jer 11:23), suggests a judgment that falls upon the people at some point during a given year rather than the entire year itself. The historical books of the OT ring with references to events occurring in a given year, such as Sennacherib's attack against Judah "in the fourteenth year of King Hezekiah" (2 Kgs 18:13).

The other prominent use of the noun "year" is in statements about a person's age or the age of an object. "When Abram was ninety-nine years old . . ." (Gen 17:1), "After Noah was five hundred years old . . ." (Gen 5:32) are two examples of the many in which this noun appears giving a person's age in years. Leviticus 23:12–19 speaks of animals to be offered for sacrifice as being lambs "a year old." Related to this usage is the expression "old and full of years" with reference to a death of a person in old age (Gen 25:8) The full expression is a way of speaking about a person's long life.

It is also used adverbially in phrases like "from year to year," or "year by year" to express frequency. Two different Hebrew phrases are rendered in this manner, the one using the noun "year" (*shanah* *bᵉshanah*) and the other using a compound form with the noun "day" (*miyyamim* *yᵉmimah*). These are translated as "year by year" and "from year to year" respectively, though in Judg 11:40 the rendering of this latter is "every year."

A figurative use in Joel 2:25 is noted in which the noun "years" refers not so much to the time itself as to what happened during that time. They are described as "the years that the swarming locust has eaten." It refers to the crops that grew during the years of the locust plague.

Similar features are noted in the NT. Periods of time are noted: Luke 13:16 notes that a woman had been bound by Satan "for eighteen long years"; John 5:5 refers to the man who had been ill "for thirty-eight years." Time during which something happens is expressed as "last year" in 2 Cor 8:10. A reference to the "year of the Lord's favor" in Luke 4:19, quoting Isa 61:1–2, represents the more general sense in which an event takes place during a given year. Here "year" focuses on the arrival of a specific moment in time. It is similar to Ezek 22:4, "You have brought your day near, the appointed time of your years has come." A person's age is expressed in years as "two years old" (Matt 2:16) and "forty years old" (Acts 4:22). The adverbial phrase "year after year" (Heb 9:25; 10:1, 3) marks a frequentative sense. Similarly "year by year" indicates regularity and constancy (Deut 15:20; 1 Kgs 5:11; Esth 9:21).

James Barr, *Biblical Words for Time*, SBT 33 (London: SCM Press, 1962); Gershon Brin, *The Concept of Time in the Bible and the Dead Sea Scrolls*, STDJ 39 (Leiden: Brill, 2001); J. R. Wilch, *Time and Event: An Exegetical Study of the Use of* 'eth *in the Old Testament in Comparison to Other Temporal Expressions in Clarification of the Concept of Time* (Leiden: Brill, 1969).

GRAHAM S. OGDEN

Transfigure This verb appears only twice in NRSV, both in the Synoptic narrative known as the transfiguration (Matt 17:1–8 and Mark 9:2–8; Luke 9:28–36 uses a different verb). Jesus takes Peter, James, and John up a high mountain, "and he was transfigured before them, and his face shone like the sun, and his clothes became dazzling white" (Matt 17:2).

Except for a few poetic instances (e.g., Julia Ward Howe, "The Battle Hymn of the Republic," stanza 5, "With a glory in his bosom that transfigures you and me"), the verb hardly ever occurs in English literature and conversation, being reserved for references to this biblical narrative.

Early English translations, including KJV, were undoubtedly influenced in their choice of the word by the use of *transfiguro* in the Latin Vulgate and by the ecclesiastical feast of the Transfiguration.

The Greek verb employed in Matt 17:2 and Mark 9:2 is *metamorphoomai*, "transform" (from which "metamorphosis" is derived). In pagan religion this verb was used both of the change that gods underwent in order to become visible to humans and of the changes experienced by humans by means of mystical practices. Perhaps for this reason Luke omits the verb, fearing that it would be misunderstood by Gentile readers. He writes instead that "the appearance of his face changed" (Luke 9:29). The background of "transfigured" in Matthew and Mark is to be found not in pagan religion but in Jewish eschatology.

Daniel 12:3 promises that at the resurrection "those who are wise shall shine like the brightness of the sky, and those who lead many to righteousness, like the stars forever and ever." This motif is repeated in 2 Esd 7:97: "It is shown them how their face is to shine like the sun, and how they are to be made like the light of the stars." We find it also in Matt 13:43, "Then the righteous will shine like the sun in the kingdom of their Father." This eschatological hope helps to explain the narrative of the transfiguration. The incredible brightness of Jesus' transformed appearance is an anticipation of the heavenly glory to come. It is an insufficient explanation, however, since the heavenly visitors, Moses and Elijah, are not so described. Jesus' transformation is to be understood christologically: he is presented as superior both to Moses, the mediator of the law, and to Elijah, the eschatological prophet ("Lo, I will send you the prophet Elijah before the great and terrible day of the LORD comes," Mal 4:5). The voice from heaven, like the voice at his baptism (Matt 3:17), declares that Jesus is the Messiah: "This is my Son, the Beloved; with him I am well pleased; listen to him!" (Matt 17:5; cf. Mark 9:7; Luke 9:35). In Matthew, Mark, and Luke, where the idea of incarnation is not found, "Son" refers not to Jesus' divine nature but to his divinely ordained function as Messiah (see *anoint*). The transfiguration is an anticipation of his future glory when exalted to God's right hand (Matt 22:44; 26:64).

The verb *metamorphoomai* is used by Paul with reference to the transformation of Christians: "And all of us, with unveiled faces, seeing the glory of the

Lord as though reflected in a mirror, are being transformed into the same image from one degree of glory to another" (2 Cor 3:18). Although light imagery is used ("glory"), the transformation is not visible but interior. "Transfigured" would be an inappropriate translation. The same Greek verb, used with reference to the interior, moral transformation of believers, is found in Rom 12:2.

DOUGLAS R. A. HARE

Transgress, Transgression   *see* Sin

Tree   The Bible speaks frequently of common trees of the forest and uses images of various kinds of trees in similes, metaphors, fables, and parables (Judg 9:7–21; Pss 1:3; 92:12–14; Isa 61:3; Jer 11:16–17; 17:8; Ezek 31:1–19; Matt 21:18–22; 24:32–34; Mark 11:12–14, 20–24; 13:28–31; Luke 13:6–9; 21:29–33; Rom 11:17–24).

In addition to the common trees of the forest, the Bible also talks about two mythological trees. These were the tree of *life* (Gen 2:9; 3:22, 24) and the tree of *knowledge* of *good* and *evil* (Gen 2:9, 17; and 3:3, 6, but without being named).

God created the human as a "living being" (2:7) and envisioned humans living in the garden of paradise (see *heaven*) in harmony with the will of God. The humans disobeyed the will of God, though, by eating the forbidden fruit of the tree of the knowledge of good and evil. Although there has been much debate regarding the nature of the knowledge that the humans acquired by eating the forbidden fruit, what is clear is that the knowledge they acquired was knowledge that was God's alone to possess (3:22).

Because of their disobedience, the humans were threatened with *death*. It seems from 3:22–24 that God feared that the humans might try to avoid death by eating the fruit of the tree of life. So, to prevent the humans from obtaining *immortality* by eating the fruit of the tree of life, God banished them from the garden of paradise (Fretheim, 350).

The book of Revelation envisions a tree of life in a restored garden of paradise (2:7; 22:2, 14, 19).

———

Terence E. Fretheim, *The Book of Genesis*, NIB 1; Claus Westermann, *Genesis 1–11: A Commentary* (Minneapolis: Augsburg Publishing House, 1984), 211–14, 242–48.

JAMES A. DURLESSER

Trespass, Trespasses   *see* Sin

Tribulation   *see* Suffer

Trouble   *see* Suffer

True, Truth, Deceit, Deceive, False, Falsehood, Lie, Lying, Liar   Truth and falsehood in Scripture include the difference between fact and fiction, but they involve far more than that, as God's truth becomes identified with life and the gospel.

True, Truth

Several words are translated "true" and "truth" in NRSV, but this article will focus on the Hebrew *ʾemeth* and the Greek *aletheia* (and the related words *alethes* and *alethinos*), since they reveal all that is meant by "truth" in Scripture. In English, "truth" essentially denotes factual accuracy, what is correct, not imaginary or fictional. The same ideas appear in the Bible, but the words just noted also carry a much broader and deeper meaning. Their fundamental sense concerns what is reliable and trustworthy.

What is true may indeed involve the accurate reporting of facts: "So she said to the king, 'The report was true that I heard in my own land of your accomplishments and of your wisdom'" (1 Kgs 10:6; cf. Gen 42:16; Isa 43:9). Luke claims to have researched Jesus' life with care, "so that you may know the truth concerning the things about which you have been instructed" (Luke 1:4; cf. John 10:41; Acts 26:25; 2 Cor 7:14).

For the NT writers, the facts about Jesus involve more than the reporting of events, however, for there is *truth* contained in those facts that is more than information. It is the way to life-changing power, and so "truth" became virtually equivalent to "gospel," the *meaning* of Jesus' appearance on earth. Paul wrote of "the truth of the gospel," which meant both correctness and saving power (Gal 2:5, 14). The "word of truth" is directly equated with the gospel in Eph 1:13 and Col 1:5. Throughout the NT, and especially in the later letters, "truth" means the Christian message: "This is right and acceptable in the sight of God our Savior, who desires everyone to be saved and to come to the knowledge of the truth" (1 Tim 2:4; cf. Jas 1:18; Heb 10:26; 1 Pet 1:22; and many others).

Truth involves the facts of Jesus' life and the meaning of his appearance on earth and thus becomes equivalent with God's saving power. In order for that power to be effective in the life of an individual, it must, of course, first be believed (John 8:45; Rom 1:25), and not distorted (Gal 2:14; 1 Tim 4:3; 2 Tim 2:18); and then one must live by it, for in addition to being a message, it is a way of life: "If we say that we have fellowship with him while we are walking in darkness, we lie and do not do what is true" (1 John 1:6; cf. Rom 2:8; Titus 1:1; Heb 10:26; Jas 3:14; 2 Pet 2:2).

These uses of *aletheia, alethos,* and *alethinos* are in continuity with *'emeth* in the OT. "Truth" is a synonym for the way of life God has planned for his people. "O send out your light and your truth; let them lead me" (Ps 43:3). Since God reveals himself by his word, word and truth appear together: "So the woman said to Elijah, 'Now I know that you are a man of God, and that the word of the LORD in your mouth is truth'" (1 Kgs 17:24). "The sum of your word is truth; and every one of your righteous ordinances endures forever" (Ps 119:160; cf. vv. 42–43, 142, 151; Neh 9:13; Prov 30:5). The parallel with ordinances draws attention to the forms in which OT authors believed God's truth was made known. The prophetic word and the law

have just been noted (and for law, see Rom 2:20). For the sages, who believed true wisdom comes from God, "wisdom, instruction, and understanding" were set in parallel with "truth" (Prov 23:23). As "truth" later came to denote the gospel and the Christian way of life, in the book of Daniel it once seems to denote the Jewish religion. In a vision, Daniel saw the little horn (Antiochus IV Epiphanes) "cast truth to the ground" (8:12), a symbolic way of referring to his attempt to eradicate the Jewish faith.

The word *'emeth* is also used to emphasize that Yahweh is the only God: "But Yahweh is the true God; he is the living God and the everlasting king" (Jer 10:10; cf. 2 Chr 15:3).

That truth is far more than what is rationally demonstrable is revealed by the words with which it is regularly associated. They denote the gracious attributes of God, which are then manifested as the way people ought to try to live: righteousness (Isa 48:1; 59:14), justice (Isa 59:14; Jer 5:1), uprightness (Jer 4:2; Isa 59:14), kindness and loyalty (Zech 7:9; 8:16). Unfortunately, most of these references refer to the human failure to display these attributes: to live by the truth. Wickedness is thus an opposite of truth in Prov 8:7: "My mouth will utter truth; wickedness is an abomination to my lips."

The concept of truth as God's own way that people regularly fail to apprehend became a theme that runs through the Gospel according to John. John speaks of "truth" more than any other NT writer, starting with three times in the Prologue: "The true light, which enlightens everyone, was coming into the world" (John 1:9). This light was the Word, who is now more than law or wisdom, for "the Word became flesh and lived among us, and we have seen his glory, the glory as of a father's only son, full of grace and truth. . . . grace and truth came through Jesus Christ" (John 1:14, 17). This is a clear reference to Moses' request in Exod 33:18 to see God's glory and to God's eventual "self-introduction," which includes the words "gracious" and *'emeth* (translated "faithfulness" in NRSV; Exod 34:6). The presence of God that Moses desired had become real in Jesus Christ, John affirms—"we have seen his glory"—but earlier John had to acknowledge that "he was in the world, and the world came into being through him; yet the world did not know him" (1:10; see also v. 11). Throughout the Gospel John uses "truth" as a way of developing this tension. He speaks of *testimony* and of bearing witness to Jesus' relationship to God, and the issue is whether that testimony is true. "No one accepts his [Jesus'] testimony. Whoever has accepted his testimony has certified this, that God is true" (John 3:32b–33). But Jesus acknowledged the problem with self-testimony: "If I testify about myself, my testimony is not true. There is another who testifies on my behalf, and I know that his testimony to me is true. You sent messengers to John [the Baptist], and he testified to the truth" (John 5:31–33; see also 10:41). At this point "truth" refers to facts and their meaning, but they are not facts available to observation and experiment, for they concern who Jesus really is (note John's concern for the facts in 19:35 and 21:24). Jesus continued to make the claim of uniqueness for himself, however, with "true" referring to his real identity in 7:16–18. He then spoke of God as "true," referring to God's faithfulness and reliability (7:28). A long debate over truth is recorded in 8:12–47, partly obscured by NRSV's use of "valid" to translate *alethes* and *alethinos* in verses 13, 14, 16, and 17. A key saying occurs in the midst of the debate: "If you continue in my word, you are truly my disciples; and you will know the truth, and the truth will make you free" (8:31–32). Truth, which was associated with God's word in the OT, is now identified with Jesus' word and is essentially the gospel, as elsewhere in the NT. The freedom it offers is freedom from sin (8:34). Jesus' claim, "I am the way, and the truth, and the life" (14:6), thus insisted that he was the trustworthy revelation of God and of God's way to eternal life. Pilate's brusque rejection of any talk about truth—"What is truth?" (18:38)—is thus the appropriate way for John to remind readers of his prologue: "the world did not know him" (1:10).

Deceit, Deceive, False, Falsehood, Lie, Lying, Liar

"Deceit" and "deceive" are usually translations of some form of *ramah* in the OT and *planao* in the NT. False, falsehood, and lie usually represent forms of *kazab* and *shaqar* in the OT and forms of *pseudomai* in the NT, but there are other synonyms.

Deceit, Deceive. To deceive is to mislead, usually by means of false information and hence usually by speech (Job 27:4; Pss 10:7; 17:1; 35:20; 50:19; Prov 12:17; Isa 53:9; Rom 3:13; 16:18; Eph 5:6). Deception is usually the work of an enemy but may be unintentional, and it is possible to deceive oneself. The last possibility shows that deception also involves the making of a decision, but based on something misleading. Deceit thus, in contrast to some lies and falsehood, involves an incorrect projection of the future. (Note that false witness refers to a past event.)

The Rabshakeh claimed in his speech to the inhabitants of Jerusalem that they were the potential victims of unintentional deception, which was leading to the decision to resist the Assyrian army. It was King Hezekiah and even their God, he claimed, who were misleading them, and he knew better than they (2 Kgs 18:29; 19:10; 2 Chr 32:15; Isa 36:14; 37:10).

Self-deception is of greater interest to NT writers than to those of the OT; for example, "If we say that we have no sin, we deceive ourselves (*planao*, "go astray"), and the truth is not in us" (1 John 1:8; cf. 1 Cor 3:18; Jas 1:22; but see also Obad 3 and Jer 37:9).

Most deception is ascribed to the work of enemies: "Deceit is in the mind of those who play evil, but those who counsel peace have joy" (Prov 12:20; cf. Ps 36:3). As the act of an enemy, forms of *ramah* appear in parallel with "iniquity" (Ps 32:2), "evil" (Ps 34:13; 50:19; Prov 12:20), and "oppression" (Jer 9:6). False teachers (Acts 13:10; Rom 16:18) and the devil

(Rev 18:23; 19:20; 20:3, 8, 10) are accused of deception in the NT.

The motive for some deceit is not completely clear, especially in the case of those declared to be false prophets in Jeremiah and Ezekiel. The Lord declared, "They are prophesying to you a lying vision, worthless divination, and the deceit of their own minds" (Jer 14:14). The "false prophets" (or some of them) may have sincerely believed their messages, but those who accused them at least sometimes suspected they were just producing what people wanted to hear, so deceiving not with intent to harm but for their own profit (cf. Mic 3:5). But Ezekiel claimed God was in fact the deceiver in one case, as he attempted to explain false prophecy as a part of God's judgment of exiles who still practiced idolatry (Ezek 14:9; and cf. the lying spirit in 1 Kgs 22:22–23). But Jeremiah accused God of deceiving the people by saying, "It shall be well with you" (Jer 4:10), probably referring to the messages of peace given by other prophets, and accepting that they may have come from God.

False, Falsehood, Lie, Lying, Liar. Unlike deceit, falsehood is always deliberate, or inherent if "false" refers to an object, such as an idol. These words may refer to misinformation (and like deceit are usually associated with speech), but more generally they denote what is unreliable, untrustworthy, unfaithful, and thus worthless.

In the law court, "falsehood" and "lying" were used to denote the report of a witness that something happened in the past which in fact did not happen—false witness. Fairness in court proceedings was crucial enough to the stability of a community that false witness was forbidden in one of the Ten Commandments (Exod 20:16; Deut 5:20; and cf. Exod 23:1, 7; Deut 19:18; Ps 27:12; Prov 6:19; 12:17; 14:5; 19:5; 21:28; 25:18).

With reference to the future, the words are often used of information, advice, boasts, oaths, and objects that are unreliable and thus misleading if acted on: "A false balance is an abomination to the LORD, but an accurate weight is his delight" (Prov 11:1; Hos 12:7). "Do not devise evil in your hearts against one another, and love no false oath; for all these are things that I hate, says the LORD" (Zech 8:17).

Idols are called false because depending on them for help would be completely worthless: "Everyone is stupid and without knowledge; goldsmiths are all put to shame by their idols; for their images are false, and there is no breath in them" (Jer 10:14; Hab 2:18).

"False" in the sense of untrustworthy is used to describe human disobedience to the will of God. The psalmists will ask, "Put false ways far from me; and graciously teach me your law" (Ps 119:29), and may claim, "All this has come upon us, though we have not forgotten you, or been false to your covenant" (Ps 44:17). Jeremiah, however, explained the distress of his people in this way: "This is your lot, the portion I have measured out to you, says the LORD, because you have forgotten me and trusted in lies" (Jer 13:25). God, on the other hand, can be depended on: "God is not a human being, that he should lie, or a mortal, that he should change his mind. Has he promised, and will he not do it? Has he spoken, and will he not fulfill it?" (Num 23:19; cf. 1 Sam 15:29).

The same uses of falsehood appear in the NT. The commandment against false witness is repeated (Matt 19:18; Mark 10:19; Luke 18:20), and Jesus' trial involved false witnesses (Matt 26:59–60; Mark 14:56–57; also Stephen, Acts 6:13). Christians are warned against false prophets (Matt 7:15; 24:11, 24; Mark 13:22; 2 Cor 11:13; 1 John 4:1) and apostles (Rev 2:2), and falsehood is included in lists of the worst sins (Matt 15:19; 1 Tim 1:10; Rev 21:8; 22:15). First John regularly identifies lying with unbelief (1 John 1:6; 2:4, 22; 4:20; 5:10).

In John, the devil is associated in a significant way with lying. In one of Jesus' most severe sayings he called the devil the "father of lies": "He was a murderer from the beginning and does not stand in the truth, because there is no truth in him.

When he lies, he speaks according to his own nature, for he is a liar and the father of lies" (John 8:44). It was noted above that John emphasized the identity between Jesus and truth. It is not surprising, then, that he claims the devil's own nature makes him a liar. It is significant, however, that he does not move far in the direction of dualism, for he does not develop ideas about the Lie in contrast to the Truth to the extent that he might have done.

This group of words reflects the human need for certainty and reliability of the information on which one must act, of the individuals with whom one must deal, and primarily, of God. So "truth" is taken to be one of the essential ingredients that holds together a healthy community. The writers of Scripture say that human beings are on the whole not dependable enough, and at the worst of times some were not completely sure of God. The NT's intimate association of truth with Jesus Christ was thus a powerful response to the normal uncertainties of life, with its claim that there is One on whom those who believe in him can depend.

DONALD E. GOWAN

Trust, Trustworthy *see* **Believe**

Turn *see* **Repent**

Twelve *see* **Numbers**

Unbelief *see* **Believe**

Unclean, Uncleanness *see* **Clean**

Understand, Understanding *see* **Know**

Upright, Uprightness, Right In the OT, these words usually translate the Hebrew word *yashar*, with several other words translated this way a few times. In the NT they usually represent *dikaios* or *dikaiosyne*, although there are a few occurrences of the English words as translations of seven other Greek words. This article will focus on the most common words.

The root *yashar* has the physical sense of being straight, level, or upright (meaning vertical), but it is frequently used metaphorically, and these are the uses to be considered here. Given the common idea of life as a journey, OT authors say one's *way* through life should be straight (*yashar*), not crooked. So the evil "forsake the paths of uprightness [*yashar*] to walk in the ways of darkness" (Prov 2:13); "the way of the lazy is overgrown with thorns, but the path of the upright is a level highway" (Prov 15:19; cf. Prov 4:11; 14:2; 16:17; 1 Kgs 3:6; 9:4; Isa 57:2; Mal 2:6). What is straight is better than what is crooked, and so *yashar* will be paired with *tob*, "good and right" (e.g., Deut 6:18; 12:28; Josh 9:25; Jer 26:14; 40:4, 5).

The translator will normally use "upright, uprightness" when *yashar* expresses general approval of character, whereas "right" will usually describe specific kinds of behavior. For example, you shall "Do what is right and good in the sight of the LORD" (Deut 6:18), but "Rejoice in the LORD, O you righteous! Praise befits the upright" (Ps 33:1). The Hebrew word is the same in both texts. It refers to God and his gifts in a few cases, where it is parallel with "good," "perfect," and "just" (Deut 32:4; Neh 9:13; Pss 19:8; 25:8; 33:4; 92:15; 119:137; Hos 14:9). Usually it refers to human character or behavior, where it may be parallel to "blameless" (Prov 28:10), "*innocent*" (Job 4:7), "pure" (Job 8:6), and "righteous" (Ps 94:15). The antonyms of *yashar* are "wicked" (Ps 11:2), "perverse" (Prov 3:32), and "evil" (Prov 10:29).

When *yashar* is used to describe character, it may be defined more specifically by adding "in heart," since it is with the heart (see *mind*), as Israel understood it, that one makes rational decisions. So "justice will return to the righteous, and all the upright in heart will follow it" (Ps 94:15; cf. 1 Chr 29:34; Pss 7:10; 94:15; etc.). The eye (see *see*) was also involved in making judgments, as the Hebrew language used parts of the body to denote mental, emotional, and spiritual processes. The idiom, *yashar bᵉᶜene* "right in the eyes (or sight) of . . ." is used to indicate a judgment as to what is good and proper, of the behavior of others, when God is the subject (e.g., Exod 15:26; Deut 6:18; Jer 34:15), or of one's own behavior, when used of people. Sometimes the expression is neutral and does not involve an evaluation of human judgment, as in Josh 9:25; Jer 26:14; 40:4–5, but more often it is a reminder that the human "eye" is likely to see imperfectly. "All deeds are right in the sight of the doer, but the LORD weighs the heart" (Prov 21:2; cf. 12:15). "In those days there was no king in Israel; all the people did what was right in their own eyes" (Judg 17:6; 21:25).

"Upright" (*dikaios*) is used as an evaluation of character in Acts 10:22 and Titus 1:8; 2:12. "Right," translating words from the same root, denotes just and proper behavior, always human in the NT. It describes the correct wage in Matt 20:4, proper decisions in Luke 12:57; John 7:24; Acts 4:19, and the behavior appropriate for Christians, elsewhere (e.g., Eph 6:1; 2 Pet 1:13; 1 John 2:29; Rev 22:11).

————

DONALD E. GOWAN

Vain, Vanity The English idiom "in vain" is used to translate several Hebrew and Greek words that indicate futility or worthlessness. They occur in texts that acknowledge that people's good efforts may be to no avail: "All in vain (*riq*) have I kept my heart clean and washed my hands in innocence" (Ps 73:13). "For this reason, when I could bear it no longer, I sent to find out about your faith; I was afraid that somehow the tempter had tempted you and that our labor had been in vain (*kenos*)" (1 Thess 3:5). They are also used to pass judgment on mistaken efforts or dependence on useless things: "Those who worship vain (*shawʾ*) idols forsake their true loyalty" (Jonah 2:8). The most important occurrence of the term *shawʾ* is in the commandment traditionally translated "You shall not take

the name of the LORD your God in vain; for the LORD will not hold him guiltless who takes his name in vain" (Exod 20:7; Deut 5:11). The verb literally means "lift up," and must refer to lifting up the Lord's name in speech. What kind of speech may be designated by *shawʾ* is not as clear as one would like. One is not to lift up God's name in a worthless way. This surely includes swearing a false oath by the name of the Lord, but it is probably a commandment broadly worded so as to protect the holiness of the name in any way that it might be used. So NRSV has appropriately translated the commandment "You shall not make wrongful use of the name of the LORD your God, for the LORD will not acquit anyone who misuses his name."

NRSV has retained the traditional "Vanity of vanities; all is vanity" of Ecclesiastes, even though it is not an accurate translation for our time of that book's favorite word, *hebel*. "Vanity" now usually refers to an unduly high opinion of oneself, and that has nothing to do with *hebel*, which means "breath, vapor," thus something insubstantial and transitory. The repetition of the word in Eccl 1:2 and 12:8 is the Hebrew way of expressing a superlative. For example, "holy of holies" means "the holiest place." REB offers one of the best translations of many that have been suggested: "Futility, utter futility, everything is futile." Another option is "Enigma of enigmas."

————

C. L. Seow, "Beyond Mortal Grasp: The Usage of *hebel* in Ecclesiastes," *Australian Biblical Review* 48 (2000): 1–16.
DONALD E. GOWAN

Vengeance *see* **Avenge**

Vindicate, Vindication *see* **Redeem**

Vine, Vineyard, Wine Vine: usually in Hebrew *gephen*, in Greek *ampelos*; vineyard: Hebrew *kerem*, Greek *ampelon*; wine: Hebrew *yayin*, Aramaic *hamar*,

Greek *oinos*. Hebrew used the words *soreq* (Isa 5:2; Jer 2:21) and *soreqah* (Gen 49:11), meaning "red," to refer to a particularly fine species of vine or grape.

The use of vines, vineyards, grapes, and wine as symbols in the Bible seems to have arisen from an appreciation of the importance of viticulture for the economy of ancient Israel. According to Gen 9:20, the planting of vineyards began right after the great flood. For Israelites, the vine was a treasured agricultural resource and a symbol of security and peace. Numbers 13:17–23 speaks of the vine as one of the characteristics of the land of Canaan. Similarly Deut 8:8 describes the land of Canaan as "a land of wheat and barley, of vines and fig trees and pomegranates." To sit under one's own vine and fig tree was thought to be a sign of security and a blessed life (1 Kgs 4:25; Mic 4:4; Zech 3:10).

The images of the vine, vineyard, and vinedresser were frequently employed in the OT as ways of thinking about the covenant relationship between God and Israel. Just as a vinedresser diligently cares for a vineyard, expecting a bountiful harvest, God was thought of as caring for Israel, expecting faithfulness to the covenant (Ps 80:8–19; Isa 27:2–6). Thus an agricultural resource that was characteristic of Canaan and representative of peace and security in the land became a symbol for the spiritual richness that was characteristic of Israel's relationship with God.

While the prophets adopted the analogies between the vine and Israel, they also reversed or twisted the image in order to suggest the faithlessness of Israel to the covenant, God's disappointment over Israel's repeated failure to keep the covenant, and the failure of the Israelite monarchy to uphold its worth (Isa 5:1–7; Jer 2:21; 8:13; Ezek 15; 19:10–14; Hos 9:10; 10:1; see also Ezek 17).

In the Synoptic Gospels, Jesus tells three parables that use vineyard imagery. Matthew 20:1–16 records the parable of the Workers, who were hired at different times of the day to work in the vineyard. In Matt 21:28–32, those who will enter God's kingdom are thought of as a son who at first refuses to work in his father's vineyard, but later decides to go. Matthew 21:33–46 and par. Mark 12:1–12 and Luke 20:9–19 recount the parable in which a vineyard is taken by its owner from wicked tenants and given to other tenants. The similarity in wording between Isa 5:1–7 and Matt 21:33 suggests that this parable (at least as it is recorded in Matt) is to be read in light of Isa 5 (Boring, 413).

In John 15:1–11, Jesus applies the metaphor of Israel as a vine to himself. Contrasting himself with the vine of Israel that was perceived to have become useless and unproductive (Isa 5; Ezek 15), Jesus declares himself to be the "true vine" and invites his followers to maintain a productive relationship with him.

Wine was viewed as a blessing from God (Gen 27:28; Deut 7:13), as an appropriate sacrifice (Lev 23:13; Num 28:14), and as a symbol of salvation at the end time (Joel 3:18; Amos 9:13). Building on this symbolism, Jesus turned water into wine at a wedding feast (John 2:1–12) and offered his disciples wine to drink at the Last Supper (Matt 26:26–29; Mark 14:22–25; Luke 22:14–23).

M. Eugene Boring, *The Gospel of Matthew*, *NIB* 8.

JAMES A. DURLESSER

Violence, Violent

"Violence" in the OT usually translates one of two Hebrew words, *gazal* and *hamas*. Three nouns etymologically related to *gazal* also occur (twelve uses). The basic meaning of *gazal* is "snatching something away violently." It is used for robbery (Gen 31:31; Lev 6:2; Judg 21:23; Ps 62:10; Eccl 5:8; Isa 61:8; Ezek 33:15) and denotes oppression of the poor and weak, evident from connection with "to oppress, extort" (ʿashaq) or "oppression, extortion" (ʿosheq; Lev 19:13; Deut 28:29; Jer 21:12; 22:3; Ezek 18:18; 22:29; Mic 2:2). The oppression may be linked with legal charges of injustice (Isa 10:2; Eccl 5:8).

The more significant term, *hamas*, occurs sixty-eight times (eight verbal, sixty nominal). Though much current literature speaks of God's violence in the OT, Scripture speaks differently. Rather, "The LORD . . . hates the lover of violence" (Ps 11:5). Violence describes *human* conduct; other terms are used to denote God's actions, such as destruction, *judgment*, or punishment (see also *wrath*). In two nominal uses is God *possibly* indicted: in Job's outcry (19:7) and Jeremiah's outcry (20:8, "Violence and destruction!" cf. Hab 1:2). In two verbal uses God violently shakes unripe grapes (Job 15:33) and breaks down the booth (tabernacle, Lam 2:6). Both are figurative of God's judgment. Most uses denote human violence, frequently speaking of oppression of the alien, fatherless, and widow, or shedding of blood in murder or war (Jer 22:3 includes both aspects; Gen 49:5; Judg 9:24; Ezek 45:9; Hab 2:8 17; Zeph 1:9; Ps 72:14). Often *hamas* occurs in a general sense, with these connotations.

A notable comprehensive use is "the earth was filled with violence" (Gen 6:11, 13), which motivates God's judgment to destroy humankind through the flood. The psalmist cries out for salvation from and/or protection against the violent (Pss 18:8; 25:19; 27:12; 140:4, 11; cf. 2 Sam 22:3, 49). In several instances, violence boomerangs for self-destruction (Pss 7:16; 140:11). The general use, "violent person," occurs often in Proverbs (3:31; 4:17; 10:6, 11; 13:2; 16:29; 26:6, cf. Mal 2:16). On occasion the NRSV translates *hamas* as "malicious" (Exod 23:1; Deut 19:16; Ps 35:11) or "iniquity" (Ps 55:10) or "stir up wars" (Ps 140:2). In several uses "the law" and "the holy things" have been violated (Ezek 22:26; Zeph 3:4; Hab 1:3–4). Sarah accuses Abraham of violence, "wrong (NRSV) done to me," in the face of Hagar's contempt of her (Gen 16:5). Striking is Isaiah's depiction of the Lord's servant of justice: "he had done no violence, and there was no deceit in his mouth" (53:9).

In Wisdom writings violence is antisocial and destroys community (Prov 22:22; 28:24) and falls under God's retributive justice (Ps 62:10–12; Job 20:19 [view of Job's friend, on which Job demurs, 24:2, 9]; Sir 16:13). In prophetic literature, God is on the side of the oppressed and socially weak; punishment of oppression comes through historical and natural calamities (Isa 3:14; 10:2; Mic 2:2; Ezek 22:29). God hates offerings gotten by violence (Isa 61:8; Mal 1:13). In priestly literature violence violates holiness (Lev 19:13); Yahweh's curse is on those who disobey divine law and commandments (Deut 28:29, 31).

In this range of uses several theological claims emerge: all violence is ultimately against the community and Yahweh; the righteous cry out to God for deliverance from the violent; and God is the just judge who hears the outcry of the victims and will defend them (Haag, 485–86). In Qumran's use of *hamas*, a similar range of meaning occurs, with connection especially to wealth: the Wicked Priest "collected the wealth of the men of violence" (1QpHab 8:11).

In the NT terminology for violence is limited, though what may be judged as violence is more extensive (Desjardins, 63ff.). Terms for *war* and fight are more frequent. *Bia* is used to denote use of force or violence four times in Acts (5:26; 21:35; 24:7; 27:41), but none is consequential for Christian ethics. The use of *diaseio* (Luke 3:14) in "do not extort money from anyone" (RSV, "rob no one by violence") is ethically significant since it proscribes violence by those repenting to prepare for the One coming. *Biazomai/biastes* in Matt 11:12 connects Jesus' announced kingdom with violence: "From the days of John the Baptist until now, the kingdom of heaven has suffered violence, and the violent take it by force." Clearly, the sense is not that the kingdom brings or condones violence but that the kingdom coming sets up violent reactions by those who refuse or subvert its message; it also causes Satan's fall (Luke 10:1–20). Though *violence* is not used in the passion narrative, human violence caused Jesus' death. Jesus' nonviolence exposed the violence of humans (Girard, Bailie, Alison, Williams).

Many narratives in both Testaments, including atonement language, currently are considered productive of violence in their effectual history. These include a vast range, from God's actions in judgment to stories such as Jephthah's sacrifice of his daughter (cf. Abraham's willingness to sacrifice Isaac) to the imagery of the book of Revelation. The covert violence of patriarchal culture results in misogyny; metaphors of God's relation to Israel and men's attitudes toward female bodies "batter" women (Weems). Trible points a direction in dealing with these problematic features of Scripture (1–5). Old Testament battles, whether fought by Yahweh or humans, add to the violence that permeates Scripture, which reveals God also as Yahweh-*shalom* (see *peace*).

In order to assess the violence in Judeo-Christian Scripture, René Girard's contribution is essential (also Schwager). For Girard, culture and religion universally are founded on violence and maintained through sacrificial religion, the scapegoat mechanism. Mimetic desire generates rivalry, conflict, and violence. The third party scapegoat pacifies the violence; culture also formulates law to limit bloodshed. Having developed his views studying cultural myths worldwide, Girard later came to see in Judeo-Christian Scripture a new dynamic at work. Scripture exposes victimage, and God sides with the victim. Thus Scripture, especially the Gospels, exposes the rivalrous scapegoat mechanism and reveals the potential of new creation, in and through Jesus Christ. Biblical scholars have assessed Girard's contribution in various ways (Swartley, 2000). Jesus Christ provides a new pattern for imitation that frees from rivalry and violence (Mark 8:27–10:45). Anchored in Jesus' death and resurrection-exaltation (Phil 2:5–11), imitating this Christ model leads to peace and reconciliation.

James Alison, *Raising Abel* (New York: Crossroad, 1996); Gil Bailie, *Violence Unveiled* (New York: Crossroad, 1995);

Michel Desjardins, *Peace, Violence, and the New Testament* (Sheffield: Sheffield Academic Press, 1997); René Girard, *Violence and the Sacred* (Baltimore: Johns Hopkins Press, 1977); René Girard, *I See Satan Falling Like Lightning* (Maryknoll, N.Y.: Orbis Books, 2001); H. Haag, *hamas, TDOT* 4:478–87; Raymund Schwager, *Must There Be Scapegoats?* (San Francisco: Harper & Row, 1987); Willard M. Swartley, ed., *Violence Renounced: René Girard, Biblical Studies, and Peacemaking* (Telford, Pa.: Pandora Press US, 2000); Phyllis Trible, *Texts of Terror* (Philadelphia: Fortress Press, 1984); Renita J. Weems, *Battered Love: Marriage, Sex, and Violence in the Hebrew Prophets* (Minneapolis: Fortress, 1995); James G. Williams, *The Bible, Violence, and the Sacred* (San Francisco: HarperCollins, 1991).

WILLARD M. SWARTLEY

Virgin (Birth) Like the English word, the Hebrew *bethulah* and the Greek *parthenos* normally refer, when intended literally, to a woman, usually young, who has never had sexual relations with a man. Although the Bible as a whole has a positive view of sex within marriage, there is nonetheless a strand of thought running through both Testaments that regards even marital sex as impure in comparison with the untouched purity of a virgin. This can be seen in the restriction laid upon the high priest: "He shall marry only a woman who is a virgin. A widow, or a divorced woman, or a woman who has been defiled, a prostitute, these he shall not marry" (Lev 21:13–14), because the priests "are holy to their God" (Lev 21:7).

Because of this connection between virgin and purity, it is surprising to find the expression "virgin daughter" applied to Israel's enemies: "virgin daughter Sidon" (Isa 23:12), "virgin daughter Babylon" (Isa 47:1), "virgin daughter Egypt" (Jer 46:11). We must assume that this was a poetic way of referring to nations, and hence imprecise. We should not be surprised, therefore, to find the phrase applied to sinful Israel (Jer 14:17; Lam 1:15; 2:13). The contrast between the purity of virginity and the idolatrous practice of God's people is starkly present in Jer 18:13, 15: "The virgin Israel has done a most horrible thing. . . . my people have forgotten me, they burn offerings to a delusion." Jeremiah 31, however, speaks of the future after God has restored his people, when God will address his people positively as "virgin Israel" (Jer 31:4, 21).

According to the Gospels of Matthew and Luke, Jesus was conceived by his mother Mary while she was still a virgin (Matt 1:18–25; Luke 1:26–38). In Luke the announcement of the miraculous conception is made to Mary by the angel Gabriel: "The Holy Spirit will come upon you, and the power of the Most High will overshadow you; therefore the child to be born will be holy; he will be called Son of God" (Luke 1:35). What is most striking about Luke's presentation is that this narrative of the angelic annunciation is bracketed by the announcement of the miraculous conception of John the Baptist and his subsequent birth. In John's case also an angel announces that Zechariah's barren, aging wife will conceive, but the reader is left to assume that Zechariah, although an old man (1:7, 18) is empowered to impregnate Elizabeth (as in the story of Abraham and Sarah, Gen 18:9–14). This juxtaposition enhances the status of the baby born to the virgin Mary.

In Matthew the angelic announcement is made not to Mary but to Joseph, and not before the miraculous conception but after her pregnancy has become evident. Assuming that Mary has been unfaithful to her marriage compact, Joseph is compelled to divorce her ("righteous" in Matt 1:19 probably implies his faithfulness to the law), but he resolves to save her from public disgrace by keeping the divorce private. Before this intention is fulfilled, the Lord's angel appears in a dream, saying, "Joseph, son of David, do not be afraid to take Mary as your wife, for the child conceived in her is from the Holy Spirit" (1:20). Matthew declares that this was the fulfillment of a scriptural prophecy, "Look, the virgin shall conceive and bear a son, and they shall name

him Emmanuel" (1:23). The quotation is from the Greek translation of Isa 7:14, which differs significantly from the Hebrew text, as rendered literally by NRSV: "Look, the young woman is with child and shall bear a son, and shall name him Immanuel." Here, "young woman" represents the Hebrew ʿalmah, not bethulah, "virgin." Nothing in the context of Isa 7:14 suggests that the one who is already pregnant is a virgin. Why did the LXX translators use parthenos and make the pregnancy future (Isaiah's verb is ambiguous)? Perhaps they perceived here a messianic prophecy by taking the young woman as the virgin, virgin Israel, who, by divine intervention, will bring forth the messiah. For Matthew, Mary may thus represent virgin Israel. In comparison with Luke's nativity story, however, Mary's role is not emphasized in Matthew, where Joseph is the primary actor.

It must be emphasized that this story of Jesus' miraculous conception is a Jewish story, not a pagan one. Nothing in either Matthew or Luke suggests that God impregnates Mary just as Zeus impregnates human women, who then give birth to demigods. Jesus is presented as God's Son (Matt 3:17; Luke 3:22) but not as a demigod.

In the parable of Wise and Foolish Virgins of Matt 25:1–13, NRSV prefers "bridesmaids" to the literal rendering of KJV and NIV. Paul uses "virgin" both literally (1 Cor 7:28, 34) and figuratively (2 Cor 11:2). A figurative use is probable also in Rev 14:4.

DOUGLAS R. A. HARE

Vision see See

Voice, of God see Hear

Vow The act of making a spoken promise to God, or the promise itself. The Hebrew root nadar implies a verbal pledge, as evinced by the note that "Jacob made a vow, saying . . ." (Gen 28:20).

Likewise, Num 30:2 describes a vow as that which "proceeds out of" the mouth.

"Vow" is used in two primary ways in NRSV. First, the term can have the general sense of "a solemn pledge." This usage is evident in David's promise not to rest until he finds a proper place to house the ark (Ps 132:2–5; cf. Deut 4:21). In this case, the Hebrew root nadar is paired with a term meaning swear (see **oath**). The verbal form does not have an object and so emphasizes the solemnity of the promise.

Second, and most commonly, "vow" refers to a pledge of some particular gift, such as an item for sacrifice. This use is distinct in that it often involves the employment of the verbal form of nadar along with its nominal derivative neder. Thus, behind the English expression "made a vow" in some cases is the phrase in Hebrew "vowed a vow" (Gen 28:20; 31:13; Judg 11:30, 39; 1 Sam 1:11; 2 Sam 15:8; Eccl 5:4). The noun connotes a gift offered, while the verbal form indicates the promise of its being given. In such contexts the vow is often made as a formal part of worship. Hence, some references to the vow appear alongside the mention of sacrifice (Ps 56:12–13; Jonah 1:16).

In general, the content of vows is not prescribed and, therefore, varies widely. Animal sacrifice (Lev 22:18–20) and grain offering (Num 15:1–10) are discussed as items that may fulfill a vow. The only legal issue seems to be that laws governing the acceptability of what is sacrificed apply to votive gifts as well. In some cases, a monetary equivalent could be given for what was promised. This was the case, for example, if a slave was vowed (Lev 27:2–8). Votive offerings were similar to thanksgiving and freewill offerings (see **thank**) in that they were given in response to divine favor.

Vows may be either conditional or unconditional. There are numerous examples of the former, pledges filled when God gave the requested assistance (Judg 11:30–31; 1 Sam 1:11; 2 Sam 15:8). Regardless of the circumstances under which the vow is offered, the OT emphasizes the importance of fulfilling it (Deut 23:21–23;

Eccl 5:4–5). Although there is no punishment stated for not completing the pledge, the nonfulfillment of a vow is a sin and would be a sign of dishonor. Hence, Jephthah complies with his promise to sacrifice "whoever (or whatever) comes out of the doors of my house" on his return from victory, even though his daughter is the first to exit the dwelling (Judg 11:30–34). Numbers 30 makes an exception to vows made by women. If a woman's father or husband, the head of the household to which she belongs, disapproves of a vow, it can be revoked with no negative consequences (Num 30:5).

The Nazirite vow is a special type that involved a pledge of cultic purity, abstinence from any product from the vine, and allowing the hair to grow (Num 6:1–12). This vow, which could be made by men or women, was temporary, though Samson seems to be intended as a Nazirite for life (Judg 13). In Samson's case, however, the lifelong commitment becomes almost comical since he breaks the vow at every turn. In Judg 13:5–9 he touches a dead animal, thus breaking his vow of cultic purity. Moreover, he does this while in the midst of vineyards, a subtle reference to breaking his pledge of abstinence from fruit of the vine. The Nazirite vow was concluded with a special offering of animal and grain (Num 6:13–20).

Vows are mentioned only twice in the NT (Acts 18:18; 21:23). The nature of the vow is uncertain in both cases. However, these references indicate the seriousness of the vow and the intention to fulfill them, in accordance with OT stipulations.

JEROME F. D. CREACH

War, Fight War (Hebrew milhamah; Greek polemos) in the sense of battle between armies occurs frequently in the OT (more than 150 times) and comparatively seldom in the NT. NRSV often translates man or men of war as "warrior(s)." The Heb. verb to fight (laham) occurs also about 150 times; *tsaba*ʿ, with similar meaning, occurs five times. Other Hebrew and Greek words, both nouns and verbs, occur also in both Testaments, but always in preponderance in the OT. "Wage war" or "fight" (*strateuomai*) occurs ten times in the NT, but with different meanings: the spiritual battle (2 Cor 10:3; Jas 4:1; 1 Pet 2:11) and the fight to keep the faith lifelong (1 Tim 1:18; 2 Tim 2:4). Similarly, *agonizomai* is used thrice (keeping the faith in 1 Tim 6:12; 2 Tim 4:7, and repudiating fighting with weapons, John 18:36). With all war/fight terms together, occurrences approximate 500, with another 100 in Apocryphal books. Scripture is not shy in portraying the life of God's people involved in battle (Boyd).

Three types of war may be identified in the OT: divine warfare, holy war, and wars fought by military strength of national armies. Fourth, warfare imagery is used to describe personal, spiritual battle (Ps 18:1–3; Eph 6:10–18). Yet a fifth type is the metaphorical use for keeping the faith: "I have fought the good fight" (2 Tim 4:7; cf. 1 Tim 6:12).

In the OT, God is the divine warrior who fights for Israel (Exod 15:3; Isa 42:13; Zeph 3:17; see Boyd, Lind, Wood); the human role is to trust in Yahweh's defense and victory (Exod 14:13–14; Isa 7:9; 30:1–5, 15–18; 31:1–3; Ps 33:10–21). Numerous texts portray God as the warrior who fights against chaos to establish *shalom* and maintain creation order (Pss 29; 68; 89:7–18; cf. 18:7–15 in context of vv. 1–6; 74:12–17; see *peace*); others identify God as the warrior fighting for Israel against their enemies (Exod 15:3; 17:15; Deut 33:2–3, 29; Josh 5:13–15; Ps 24:8–10); and still others combine the Lord God's fight against primeval chaos and deliverance of Israel (e.g., Isa 51:9–11; Hab 3). In many texts above, "the LORD of hosts" (*Yahweh Sabaoth*), literally, Lord of the armies, wins the victory.

The battles that receive lengthy narrative space are those in which the victory is won by divine miracle: the defeat of the Egyptians (Exod 14–15 with prelude in Exod 5–13), the crashing of Jericho's walls (Josh 6), God's victory over the Syrians through Elisha's faith (1 Kgs 6), and Jehoshaphat's victory over the Ammonites (2 Chr 20). Frequently the prophets criticize Israel for their dependence upon military alliances and weapons; they call rather for radical trust in God. Many wars fought during the monarchy fit neither the formula of divine warfare nor holy war. They are simply military battles in which Israel sometimes wins and sometimes loses. In some cases the prophets declare that God is fighting against Israel precisely because they failed to trust in God for protection and defense. Israel's defeats in war are regarded often as God's fighting against Israel, even employing nature miracles to confound Israel (Jer 21:3–9; 29:16–19; 44:11–29; cf. Isa 10:5–11; 28:1–4). The image of Zion that occurs frequently in the Psalms and Isaiah focuses specifically on God's power to defend the people, calls for complete trust in Yahweh, and repudiates human pride that boasts in one's own defense and power (Ollenburger, 1987).

"Holy war," a term introduced into OT scholarship through von Rad's influential study, is not synonymous with the broader more substantive category of "divine warfare." While numerous theories have been advanced for both the origin and meaning of "holy war" (Ollenburger in Rad, 1991), von Rad's work has been crucial in locating it within the Deuteronomist ideology stressing the cultic aspects of Israel's role in God's warfare, especially the priestly preparations and the practice of the *herem* (see Deut 20). The *herem*, which banned Israelites from reaping spoils in war but required such to be *devoted* to God as a sacrifice or a means to establish justice (Niditch, 28–77), puzzles modern readers of the text. It can best be understood within the dual context of ancient sacrificial practices in which sacrificial violence was practiced to restore peace to the community (René Girard's theory) and God's promise to give the *land* to Israel by driving out those whose practices God deemed abhorrent (Deut 18:9–14).

While the relation of "holy war" to the NT is largely one of "miscarriage," elements of "divine warfare" continue. The themes of continuity include the call to complete trust in God, exemplified by Jesus' own life and teaching; God's continuing fight against evil in the ministry of Jesus—note especially the exorcisms (Matt 12:28–30 and par.); and God's defeat of evil through Jesus' death and resurrection. In this conquest the principalities and powers were disarmed and ultimately defeated (1 Cor 2:6–8; 15:24–27; Col 2:15). Jesus' confrontation of the powers of evil ascribes the victory to God and calls the people to trust in God.

In continuity with God's fight against evil in the OT, Jesus fights against evil, especially through his healing ministry (e.g., Mark 1:32–34), and even takes prophetic action against the injustices surrounding the use of the temple (Mark 11:15–18). Both of these conflictive encounters stand clearly within the biblical prophetic tradition, but do not provide warrant for participation in military wars.

The strongest point of discontinuity is Jesus' command to love the enemy (Matt 5:43–44; Rom 12:19–21), complemented by the early church's teaching on and practice of being one new humanity in which previously hostile groups, the Jews and the Gentiles, were joined into one body of peace (Eph 2:12–22; Col 3:15). Other teachings of Jesus that permeate the NT with rootage in the OT contribute further to the Christian ethical response to war. These are nonretaliation, that is, do not repay evil for evil (Matt 5:39–41; Rom 12:17, 19–21; 1 Pet 3:9; 1 Thess 5:15); overcome evil with good (Rom 12:21); and because Christ's kingdom is not of this world, his servants do not fight (John 18:36).

Numerous texts also use language of *violence* and warfare metaphorically to denote spiritual warfare, in which the opponent is Satan. "I have come to bring a sword" (Matt 10:34) must be interpreted in the context of Luke 10:17–20; 11:21–22; Matt 11:12. Images of violence here are associated with the kingdom of God; they describe the warfare between the kingdom of God inaugurated by Jesus and the resisting stronghold of Satan (Mauser, 45).

Jesus' battle against evil is indeed a strategic aspect of his peacemaking mission. Jesus' victory over evil frees humans from its power. "The whole struggle is not against but, without abridgment and reservation, for the benefit of and on behalf of all human life, including the human adversary. The battle against Satan includes the command, 'Love your enemies and pray for those who persecute you' (Matt 5:44); in fact, love to the human enemy is the very battle line at which the victory over God's adversary is decided" (Mauser, 174).

In Pauline writings, God defeats the powers of Satan in Jesus' death and resurrection; God in Christ defeats also the principalities and the powers. The phrase "principalities and powers" comprises both spiritual (angelic and demonic) and humanly historical dimensions; the spiritual dimension works in and through political leaders and structures—as it does all of life. This double dimension of the powers, found most clearly in 1 Cor 2:6–8; Eph 6:10–18, is present in other texts as well (Eph 1:19–23; 3:9–10; 1 Pet 3:22; 1 Cor 15:24–27; and possibly Rom 13:1–2). The believers' role in the battle against evil (demons, flesh, sin, and death) is nonmilitary in nature.

Christians disagree on whether the NT allows believers to participate in wars of their nation. Specific texts have been used to justify participation. Twenty-four such texts have been appealed to, with fifteen in the Synoptic Gospels (Swartley 1983; 99–101, 250–55). Most notable are Luke 3:14 (John the Baptist accepts soldiers as disciples); Luke 22:36–38 ("Sell [your] mantle . . . buy [a sword]"); Mark 12:13–17 and par. ("give to the emperor the things that are the emporer's"; cf. Matt 17:24–27); Matt 10:34–35 and par. Luke 12:51 ("I have not come to bring peace, but a sword"); Luke 7:5–10 and par. Matt 8:5–10 (Jesus commends a soldier's faith); and Acts 10–11 (Cornelius, the first Gentile admitted to the church, received with no critical comments about his army position).

Scholarly commentary on these texts, however, does not consider them as condoning the use of violence or providing support for believers' participation in war (Furnish, 369–71; Marshall, 115–32). Holding that "the question of war is not addressed directly in the NT," Marshall points to five "indirect indications" that bear on the subject: (1) numerous references to war and strife; (2) the central role of the kingdom of God and Jesus' kingship in the Gospels' narratives; (3) Jesus' commands of nonretaliation and love of enemies; (4) the relevance of Jesus' personal behavior—is it unique because of his messianic mission, or is it a pattern for his followers in all times and places? (5) the significance of texts that discuss or reflect the state's role, the use of force, and the roles of military officials (Marshall: 115–16). Jewish revolts and Rome's retaliation were indeed part of the first-century world, and this reality punctuates the biblical narratives (Luke 13:1–3; Acts 5:36–37; Mark 13:7 and par.). Since the Gospels were written after A.D. 65–70, both Nero's blaming of the Christians for the fire of Rome and the awful sufferings of the Jews in the A.D. 66–70 war inform the narratives. Jesus' statement that there will be wars and rumors of wars does not justify war, nor does it mean his followers should not work to prevent war. These texts witness to the fact that Jesus' gospel of peace entered a world that knew war and violence. That war and violence are reflected in Jesus' language and predictions of the future does not legitimate Christian participation in war. The fact that military officials are not told to leave their service has been often cited as evidence that Jesus did not regard it as "inherently wrong to be a soldier," but we do not know whether leaving the military was an option open to them. To base an argument on this stream of evidence is hermeneutically dubious. A constructive moral proposal must rest rather on the explicit teachings of Jesus and the NT as a whole, and, via both, contemporary theological and ethical reflec-

tion discern the impact of Jesus' call to be peacemakers—through transforming enmity into friendship—upon our moral decisions and positions today. Indeed, "the starting point" must be "the New Testament's attitude to hatred, oppression, war, and all forms of violence," rather than simply an analysis of contemporary social problems (Mauser, 184).

The martial imagery and conflict between good and evil in Pauline writings is the logical extension of Jesus' confrontation of the demonic power in the Gospels. In both Jesus and Paul personal and systemic, structural aspects of evil are in view, and the battle continues for believers, in the name of Jesus. For while Christ disarmed or "depotentiated" the powers (*katargeo* in 1 Cor 15:24, 26), they are not abolished. By putting "on the whole armor of God" and standing vigilant "against the wiles of the devil" (Eph 6:11; cf. 4:14), believers maintain God's gift of salvation victory in Christ (Rom 5:1–11; Eph 2). The well-known call to Christian warfare (Eph 6:10–18) emphasizes this point. The armor is derived from Isaiah texts that earlier described God's battle against chaos and evil (11:4–5; 49:2; 59:17; cf. Wis 5:17–20). Truth, righteousness, salvation, gospel of peace, and faith are powerful in confronting and disarming the enemy. In the Christian life, the offensive and defensive blend together. Prayer and reliance on the armor of God enable one to stand against evil. But the Christian's weapons are not military or worldly: "Indeed we live as human beings, but we do not wage war according to human standards; for the weapons of our warfare are not merely human, but they have divine power to destroy strongholds. We destroy arguments and every proud obstacle raised up against the knowledge of God, and we take every thought captive to obey Christ" (2 Cor 10:3–5).

Such resistance against evil eschews messianic imperialism that subverts Jesus' refusal of violence in both his teaching and death. Spiritual warfare does not employ violence to overcome evil.

In Revelation the enthroned Son of Man (1:13) will make war "with the sword of my mouth" against Pergamum believers who do not repent (2:16; cf. 1:16) and "The Word of God" rider on the white horse makes war with a sharp sword of his mouth in righteous judgment (19:11–16). War breaks out in heaven between Michael the archangel and the dragon and his angels (12:7–10). In most uses the dragon or beast initiates war against the Lamb or the saints (11:7; 12:17; 13:7; 17:14; 19:19). Known as "the Lamb's war," the victory lies with the slain Lamb and his faithful followers (5:6–14; 11:15–18; 12:10–13; 17:14; 18–19). The entire book is punctuated with praise to God and the Lamb for sovereign victory over the dragon's and beastly empire's persecution against God's people. The Hallelujah chorus (chap. 19) is the culmination of God's victorious battle against evil, from first to new creation of the heavens and earth (chaps. 21–22).

Gregory A. Boyd, *God at War: The Bible and Spiritual Conflict* (Downers Grove, Ill.: Inter-Varsity Press, 1997); Victor Paul Furnish, "War and Peace in the NT," *Int* 38 (1984): 363–79); Paul D. Hanson, "War and Peace in Hebrew Scripture," *Int* 38 (1984): 341–62; Millard C. Lind, *Yahweh Is a Warrior* (Scottdale, Pa.: Herald Press, 1980); Tremper Longman III and Daniel G. Reid, *God Is a Warrior* (Grand Rapids: Zondervan, 1995); I. H. Marshall, "New Testament Perspectives on War," *EvQ* 57 (1985): 115–32; Ulrich Mauser, *The Gospel of Peace* (Louisville, Ky.: Westminster/John Knox, 1992); Susan Niditch, *War in the Hebrew Bible* (Oxford: Oxford University Press, 1993); Ben C. Ollenburger, "Introduction: Gerhard von Rad's Theory of Holy War," in Rad, *Holy War in Ancient Israel*, 1–34; Ben C. Ollenburger, *Zion the City of the Great King*, JSOTSup 41 (Sheffield: Sheffield Academic Press, 1987); Gerhard von Rad, *Holy War in Ancient Israel* (Grand Rapids: Eerdmans, 1991), 41–134; Willard M. Swartley, "The Bible and War," in *Slavery, Sabbath, War, and Women* (Scottdale, Pa.: Herald Press, 1983), 96–149; Willard M. Swartley, "War and Peace in the New Testament," in *Aufstieg und Niedergang der römis-*
chen Welt, ed. H. Temporini and W. Haase, II.26.3 (1996): 2298–2410; John A. Wood, *Perspectives on War in the Bible* (Macon, Ga.: Mercer University Press, 1998).

WILLARD M. SWARTLEY

Water, Drink, Fountain, Wash

Water: Hebrew *mayim*; Greek *hydor*. To wash: Hebrew *rahats*; Greek *louein*. To drink: Hebrew *shatah*; Greek *pino*.

In contrast to Mesopotamia and Egypt, which were well-watered by the Tigris and Euphrates Rivers and the Nile River respectively, the land of Israel never enjoyed an abundance of water. Rain was the primary source of water in Palestine. Dependable streams were infrequent, and the dry streambeds provided water only during the winter rainy season. The undependable nature of the water supply in the land of Israel gave rise to several similes and analogies that find expression in the Bible. See Gen 49:4; Job 6:15; also Job 3:24; Ps 22:14; Josh 7:5; Ps 58:7.

In a land where thirst was common and plant life was frequently parched, water was viewed as a gift from God that gives life to humans, animals, and plants (Isa 30:23; 44:3–4; Jer 5:24; 14:22; Ezek 34:26; Hos 6:3; Ps 104:10–13). The psalmists and prophets used water as a symbol for the blessings and salvation of God (Ps 1:3; 23:2; 36:8–9; Isa 49:10; 55:1; 58:11; Jer 17:8). One psalmist likened a longing for God during time of trial to a longing for the water of a flowing stream (Ps 42:1). Indeed, God is referred to as "the fountain of living water" (Jer 2:13; 17:13), and the fresh, living water of God's blessings is contrasted with, and is seen as preferable to, the water that has been sitting in cisterns (Jer 2:13). These notions of living water in OT contribute to the development of the idea of the water of life in the Johannine literature of the NT (John 4:7–15; 7:37–38; Rev 21:6; 22:17).

The sparse streams and the uncertainty of water in the land of Israel gave rise to an eschatological hope in which water would be in abundance. The prophet Ezekiel (47:1–12) envisioned a river flowing from "below the threshold of the temple" (v. 1). Even in the barren wilderness, "everything will live where the river goes" (v. 9). On the banks of the river, the prophet saw trees that bore fresh fruit each month because of the life-giving flow of the miraculous water from God's sanctuary. The leaves of the trees had healing qualities (v. 12; see also Zech 14:8; Joel 3:18). Similarly, John envisioned a "river of the water of life . . . flowing from the throne of God and of the Lamb" (Rev 22:1; see Gen 2:10–14 where, at the dawn of time, a river flowed from Eden; Ps 46:4). On either side of the river stood "the tree of life," which produced fruit each month and whose leaves were "for the healing of the nations" (Rev 22:2).

Besides acknowledging the life-giving quality of water, the Bible also speaks of the cleansing quality of water. In very practical ways, water cleansed people. For example, water was offered to guests so that they could wash their feet (Gen 18:4; 24:32; 43:24; Luke 7:44). But water was also used as a means of ritual cleansing in religious contexts.

In ritual cleansing, people and articles were washed in preparation for, or as a part of, a religious ceremony. This washing takes on the symbolic meaning of the purification of the person or article for some particular service to God. The book of Leviticus prescribes washing with water for the restoration of cleanness after a person or article has been unclean (Lev 11:24–25, 27–28, 32; 15:5–27; see also Deut 23:11).

Note that the ritual outlined in Lev 14 is not designed to heal a person from leprosy but to purify a person after they have recovered. This can be contrasted with 2 Kgs 5:10–14, where water functions as a curative agent.

From these literal washings in connection with ritual cleansing, it is just a small step to the development of a metaphor that refers to spiritual cleansing as washing with water (Isa 1:16; Ezek 36:24; Ps 51:2, 7; Eph 5:25–27).

Jesus came into conflict with the Pharisees on the matter of ritual cleansing. He differentiated between ritual purity and ethical purity. At issue were the washing of hands before eating and the washing of food and utensils (Mark 7:1–7).

The NT teachings on *baptism* combine the symbolism of water as an agent of cleansing and the symbolism of water as an agent of life and (re)birth. On the one hand, baptism was viewed as a ritual that symbolically cleansed people and washed away their sins (Acts 22:16; 1 Cor 6:11; Eph 5:26; Heb 10:22). On the other hand, baptism was viewed as a ritual that symbolized dying and rising with Christ and gave people a new birth (Rom 6:1–14; Col 2:12; Titus 3:5). This understanding of baptism draws on OT traditions of the great flood (1 Pet 3:20–22) and the crossing of the sea at the time of the exodus (1 Cor 10:1–2).

When the biblical writers focused on the life-giving and purifying qualities of water, they were focusing on two positive aspects of water. Water, however, can also take life away and be destructive. Images of rampaging waters were common in the myths of the ancient Near East. These deadly waters had to be vanquished by the god who was the hero in the myth, in order to bring about creation and order. Frequently the myths also spoke of a water monster that had to be vanquished (see *animals*). Remnants of these ancient Near Eastern myths abound in the Bible. The OT writers affirm that it was the God of Israel, not one of the hero gods of the myths, who vanquished the sea and the water monster and brought creation and order to chaos (Isa 51:9–10; Nah 1:4; Hab 3:8, 10, 15; Pss 74:13–15; 77:16–18; 89:9–10; 93:3–4; Job 7:12; 9:13; 26:12–13). The nature miracles in the Gospels in which Jesus subdues the waters of the sea are a continuation of these mythic traditions (Matt 8:23–27; 14:22–33; Mark 4:35–41; 6:45–52; Luke 8:22–25; John 6:16–21).

The English words "fountain" and "spring" are used to render several Hebrew words, most commonly ʿayin and maqor. The Greek word pege is rendered "spring" in 2 Pet 2:17; Rev 7:17. "Fountain" and "spring" are used in both

Testaments as symbols for the life and refreshment that come from God (Pss 36:9; 74:15; 104:10; 107:35; Isa 35:7; 41:18; Rev 7:17), and even as a way of describing God (Ps 68:26; Jer 2:13; 17:13). Jesus declares that the "living water" that he offers is "a spring of water gushing up to eternal life" (John 4:14).

"To drink" (Heb. *shatah*; Gk. *pino*) from the fountain or spring of the water of life is to receive the salvation and blessings of God (Ps 36:8–9). Those who drink water from a well, Jesus declares, will eventually be thirsty again, but those who drink the water that he offers will never thirst. Instead, because they drank the water of life, they will enjoy the benefits of "a spring of water gushing up to eternal life" (John 4:13–14).

JAMES A. DURLESSER

Way   Both Testaments speak of life as a journey. They use words meaning "road" to refer to various aspects of life: in the OT, *derek* and several synonyms; in the NT, *hodos*. The words are appropriately translated "way," because the uses of "way" in English correspond reasonably well to the uses of the biblical words. One walks through life and may choose right or wrong ways to go. "Teach me your way, O LORD, that I may walk in your truth" (Ps 86:11). Three aspects of the course of one's life may be denoted by "way":

1. Conduct: One may follow the way of righteousness (Prov 8:20; Matt 21:32; 2 Pet 2:21), of faithfulness (Ps 119:30), of truth (2 Pet 2:2), and of love (1 Cor 12:31); or on the other hand, the way of evil and perverted speech (Prov 8:13), false ways (Ps 119:29), or the ways of Balaam (2 Pet 2:15) and Cain (Jude 11). God also has his ways of acting: "The Rock, his work is perfect, and all his ways are just" (Deut 32:4; cf. Rev 15:3). Some of them are unique to God, and beyond human understanding (Isa 55:8–9; Rom 11:33).

2. The "map" or plan; the source of guidance for the good life: This is the way of wisdom (Prov 4:11) and fundamen-

tally, the way of the Lord (Pss 18:21; 27:11; 86:11; Matt 22:16).

3. The results of one's choice of how to live: "Our steps are made firm by the LORD, when he delights in our way" (Ps 37:23). Of wisdom it is said, "Her ways are ways of pleasantness" (Prov 3:17), and "Happy are those who keep my ways" (Prov 8:32). Zechariah's hope was that God would "guide our feet into the way of peace" (Luke 1:79). There is a way that leads to life and a way to death (Prov 6:23; 14:12; Jer 21:8).

Jesus said, however, that the way (NRSV: "road") to life is hard, and the gate is narrow; while the way to destruction is easy (Matt 7:13–14; Luke 13:23–24). This belongs with the more pessimistic sayings of Jesus. The word translated "hard" does not mean that the way to life is very difficult to follow, but has the sense of constricted, in parallel with the narrowness of the gate. Jesus thus spoke of the likelihood that relatively few would follow him, as in Matt 7:21: "Not everyone who says to me, 'Lord, Lord,' will enter the kingdom of heaven, but only the one who does the will of my Father in heaven," and in Matt 22:14: "For many are called, but few are chosen."

Following the right way, the way of the Lord, had been the means of access to life, but Jesus offered access to life in a new way, not through conduct, but through himself, when he told the disciples, "I am the way, and the truth, and the life" (John 14:6). The connection between truth and way reappears in John 16:13: "When the Spirit of truth comes, he will guide you into all the truth."

Although NT authors still used "way" in the sense of conduct, as noted above, the teaching that Jesus offered a new means of access to eternal life (cf. Heb 10:19–22), and thus could be called "the Way," seems to account for special uses of the term in Acts. When it is said that Apollos had been instructed in "the Way of the Lord" (Acts 18:25), that probably does not mean "Christian conduct," but a rudimentary form of the gospel, for Luke adds that he "taught accurately the things concerning Jesus." When Priscilla and Aquila gave him additional instruction in the "Way of God," he was said to have been able to show by the Scriptures "that the Messiah is Jesus" (Acts 18:28). Without further explanation, Luke calls the early Christian communities "the Way" and by it must mean the way to salvation via faith in Jesus Christ (Acts 9:2; 19:9, 23; 22:4, 14, 22).

DONALD E. GOWAN

Weak, Weakness Both "weak" and "weakness" have a variety of meanings, depending upon their OT and NT contexts. For example, both can refer to one's physical or spiritual condition, one's social, political, or economic status, or one's virtue.

In the Prophets, "weak" often refers to the powerless—to those who suffer oppression at the hands of the politically, economically, and socially strong (see, e.g., Isa 35:3; Ezek 34:4, 16; Zeph 3:16). In the Psalms, one's eyes become physically weak from crying because of some sort of oppression caused by either a sickness or one's foes, or a combination of both: "my eyes waste away because of grief; they grow weak because of all my foes" (Ps 6:7). Elsewhere in the Psalms, "weak" is associated with a sense of "powerlessness," and the psalmist acknowledges that God is a friend to the weak. God can and will do something to remedy the painful state of the weak (Pss 72:13; 82:3–4). Similarly, in the deuterocanonical texts, to be "weak" is also related to being powerless and oppressed. In a fervent prayer to God, Judith confesses: "For your strength does not depend on numbers, nor your might on the powerful. But you are the God of the lowly, helper of the oppressed, upholder of the weak, protector of the forsaken, savior of those without hope" (Jdt 9:11; cf. 16:11; Wis 2:11).

Paul challenged the usual understanding of weakness and strength, because of what he had learned about the saving power of Christ's shameful death on the cross: "For the message about the cross is foolishness to those who are perishing, but to us who are being saved it is the power of God" (1 Cor 1:18). The cross had turned upside down what humans knew of wisdom and folly, strength and weakness: "For God's foolishness is wiser than human wisdom, and God's weakness is stronger than human strength" (1 Cor 1:25; cf. v. 27). Paul found that the same paradox applied to his ministry. "We are fools for the sake of Christ, but you are wise in Christ. We are weak, but you are strong," he said with some irony, but then cited examples of his actual physical weakness (1 Cor 4:10–13; cf. 2 Cor 11:30; 13:9). He learned his personal lesson about weakness and the strength that comes only from God because of his "thorn . . . in the flesh" (2 Cor 12:7). God did not see fit to remove it from Paul but promised instead, "My grace is sufficient for you, for power is made perfect in weakness" (12:9), and since Paul obviously found in practice that this was true, he could make the otherwise nonsensical claim, "Whenever I am weak, then I am strong" (v. 10).

CAROL J. DEMPSEY

Wealth, Wealthy *see* **Poor**

White Hebrew *laben*, "be(come) white," *laban*, "white"; Aramaic *hor* (Dan 7:9); Greek *leukos*, from the root *leuk* = Latin *lux* < English "light." *Leukos* has as its primary meaning "light," "bright," "brilliant," "gleaming."

"White" garments were garments that were clean and freshly washed (Eccl 9:8). Thus the color "white" was associated with notions of purity and cleanliness, and, by extension into religious thought, holiness (Ps 51:7; Isa 1:18; see also Dan 11:35 and NRSV Mg; 12:10).

The association of the color "white" with notions of "bright," "brilliant," and "gleaming," along with the association of the color "white" with purity and holiness, inspired the use of the color "white" to describe God and things that have to do with God. In Dan 7:9, it is said of God, referred to here as "the Ancient of Days" (NRSV "an Ancient One," but see NRSV Mg), that "his clothing was white as snow, and the hair of his head like pure wool." These references to white garments and hair like pure wool highlight the purity and holiness of God and suggest that a dazzling radiance shone forth from the Ancient of Days and his throne (see also Ps 104:2). Revelation 20:11 describes God's throne as being white.

In NT, the color "white" is frequently used to describe some characteristic of Christ (Matt 17:2; Mark 9:3; Luke 9:29; esp. Rev 1:14, where the description of the Risen Christ is based on Dan 7:9). Angels (Matt 28:3; Mark 16:5; John 20:12; Acts 1:10 and probably Rev 19:14, although this might be a reference to the saints) and the saints of the church (Rev 3:4, 5, 18; 4:4; 6:11; 7:9, 13, 14) dress in white clothing.

JAMES A. DURLESSER

Wicked, Wickedness   see Sin

Widow   see Alien

Wife   see Marriage

Will, of God   see Plan

Wind   see Spirit

Wine   see Vine

Wisdom, Wise, Counsel, Advice, Instruction, Intelligent, Prudent

The books of Job, Proverbs, Ecclesiastes, Wisdom of Solomon, and Sirach have traditionally been identified as wisdom literature, but "wisdom" plays an important role throughout Scripture and takes on a special theological significance in the NT.

Old Testament

In the OT "wisdom" and "wise" are commonly used to translate forms of the Hebrew root hakam and its derivatives (hokmah and hokmoth) as well as the Aramaic cognate hakkiym (found in Daniel). Occasionally forms of sakal and biyn are also rendered as "wise" or "wisdom" (e.g., Prov 1:3; 28:7). All of these words have a wider range of meaning in Hebrew than "wisdom" and "wise" have in English. Thus NRSV uses "ability" and "skill" to translate hokmah in certain contexts where it connotes expertise in all sorts of arts, crafts, or construction (e.g., Exod 28:3; 31:3, 6; 35:25, 31; 36:1, 2; 1 Kgs 7:14; Jer 10:9). Similar performance-related overtones remain in many other uses of the terms "wisdom" and "wise." "Wisdom" in Ezek 28:4–5 refers to the ability to amass wealth through trade, and in Prov 30:24 insects and animals are said to exhibit behavior that is "exceedingly wise" when they gather food in summer or make homes in inaccessible places.

Wisdom is related to, but distinct from, *knowledge*. "The wise lay up knowledge" (Prov 10:14), but the mere possession of information does not make one wise. Rather, those who are wise know how to make effective use of what they know. They are able to apply their knowledge in concrete situations and to anticipate the consequences of their actions (Prov 14:8). Understanding (sometimes translated "discernment") is thus an essential ingredient in wisdom, and the two terms are often matched in synonymous parallelism (e.g., Prov 8:1).

The wise heed wholesome admonition (Prov 15:31) and cherish precious things (31:10). They don't wear themselves out to get rich (23:4) and they turn away or hold back wrath (29:8, 11). In both narrative and proverbial texts, wisdom is said to be one of the essential ingredients needed in order to perform leadership and judicial functions in a just and equitable manner (Deut 1:15; Prov 8:15–16). Wisdom is more likely to be found "with the humble" and "with those who take advice" than with the proud or the insolent (Prov 11:2; 13:10).

It is frequently said that the wise value other people's opinions. The Wisdom writers repeatedly emphasize the importance of paying attention to counsel, advice, and instruction (see Prov 8:33; 12:15; 13:10; 19:20; etc.). In English usage, opinions that are given or solicited before any action is taken are called counsel or advice. Opinions that are given after the fact and disagree with the actions taken are called rebuke or correction (see *correct*). Instruction can include both the sense of counsel or advice and correction. NRSV uses "counsel" to translate either the verb *ya'ats* or the nouns *'etsah* and (occasionally) *'uts*. However, NRSV also translates *'etsah* as "advice" (as in 1 Kgs 1:12; 12:8, 13, 14; 2 Chr 10:8, 13, 14; 22:5; 25:16, Ps 1:1). In 1 Kgs 12:6 both "took counsel" and "advise" translate forms of *ya'ats*.

Instruction is used to translate *torah* in narrative and prophetic texts, where it is more or less synonymous with "the word of the Lord" (as in Isa 2:3 = Mic 4:2; Isa 5:24; 30:9; Mal 2:7). However, in the Wisdom literature (and also in Jer 10:8; 17:23) "instruction" represents the Hebrew *musar* and *torah* is rendered "teaching" (see, e.g., Prov 1:8; see *preach*). In many contexts *musar* seems more or less synonymous with "rebuke" or "correction" (see Prov 10:17; 13:18; 15:5, 32).

NRSV uses "prudent" and "prudence" to translate a variety of Hebrew words that are rather fluid in meaning and move easily through the whole semantic range of wisdom, knowledge, and understanding. In English, "prudence" implies being careful, taking precautions, or approaching decisions and actions with some degree of caution. In Hebrew, *mezimmah* (translated "prudence" in Prov 1:4; 2:11; 3:21; 5:2) implies planning ahead or weighing the possible consequences of one's actions. The original language does not distinguish between the good or the bad intentions of the planner. But in English translations a person who plans ahead with good intentions can be called prudent, and a person with evil intentions can be called a "schemer" (as NRSV translates *mezimmah* in Prov 14:17).

It is difficult for an English reader to see any difference between the prudence of "a child who gathers in summer" (*maskiyl*, Prov 10:5) and that of a person who ignores an insult (*'arum*, Prov 12:16) or is "prudent in speech" (*nebon*, from *biyn*, 1 Sam 16:18). In other contexts *'aram/'ormah / 'arum* are translated "clever" (as in Prov 14:15; 22:3) or "shrewdness" (Prov 1:4), *maskiyl* is translated "wise" (as in Prov 15:24) and words derived from *biyn* are more often rendered "insight," "intelligence," or "understanding." Meaning derived from the context can explain why *maskiyl* is translated "prudent" in Amos 5:13; Prov 10:5 but does not explain why NRSV translates the same word "wise" in Pss 14:2 = 53:2 ("the LORD looks down to see if there are any who are *maskiyl*").

Variations on the Hebrew root *biyn* also lie beneath most occurrences of the words "insight," "intelligence," and "intelligent" in NRSV. In modern American usage, "intelligence" often refers to an inborn ability to use one's mental functions. When NRSV uses the word in Exod 31:3; 35:31; or 1 Kgs 7:14, "intelligence" (*tebunah*) seems to have similar connotations, implying a God-given gift allowing recipients to understand metalworking and other specialized crafts. However, the contexts in which the words translated "intelligence/intelligent" occur in Proverbs suggest that the quality referred to could be acquired with effort and determination. Thus, in Prov 8:5, personified Wisdom advises the simple (see *folly*) to "learn prudence" and "acquire intelligence" (literally, a heart/mind of *biynah*, which is elsewhere translated "insight" or "understanding"). "Intelligence" is that which allows a person to see beneath the surface of human behavior (*tebunah*, Prov 20:5 and *mebiyn*, 28:11) and to gain knowledge from being corrected (*nabon*, Prov 19:25). The wise observe that intelligent people (*tebunoth*) do not belittle others (Prov 11:12) and that "an intelligent mind" (*leb nabon*) is like "the ear of the wise" in that both seek to acquire knowledge (Prov 18:15). A country can achieve lasting order under an "intelligent (*mebiyn*) ruler" (Prov 28:2), but "the intelligent" (*neboniym*) are just as much subject to the vagaries of time and chance as anyone else (Eccl 9:11).

"Insight" is used once to translate a form of *sakal* in Job 34:35, ten times to translate *biynah* in Prov 1–9, and twice more for related forms from *biyn* in Dan 1:4, 17. In every case, insight is indistinguishable in meaning from either wisdom or understanding.

Wisdom comes ultimately from God, who "by wisdom founded the earth" (Prov 3:19). "With God are wisdom and strength; he has counsel and understanding" (Job 12:13, 16). The Lord is "wonderful in counsel and excellent in wisdom" (Isa 28:29). Thus human wisdom has a giftlike quality (Eccl 2:26). While the Wisdom teachers urge their listeners to expend a great deal of energy in order to "get wisdom" (e.g., Prov 4:5–6), they also recognize that wisdom is not entirely attainable through human efforts. Only God knows where wisdom can be found: "it is not found in the land of the living" (Job 28:13), it cannot be bought with gold or silver or exchanged for pearls or precious jewels, it is "hidden from the eyes of all living" (28:21), and only "God understands the way to it" (28:23). All human beings have to know is that "the fear of the Lord, that is wisdom; and to depart from evil is understanding" (Job 28:28).

Israel only has to follow God's instructions (*torah*) to be thought wise and discerning by the rest of the world (Deut 4:5–8). Thus "the fear of the Lord" (understood to mean a reverent respect for God and God's purposes or intentions) is understood to be "the beginning of wisdom" (Prov 9:10; Ps 111:10) and "instruction (*musar*) in wisdom" (Prov 15:33). A dedicated search for wisdom will lead the seeker to "understand the fear of the Lord and find the knowledge of God. For the Lord gives wisdom; from his mouth come knowledge and understanding" (Prov 2:5–6). To be "wise in one's own eyes" must therefore be the height of folly (see Isa 5:21; 29:14; 44:25; Jer 8:9).

In the OT human wisdom is clearly understood to be subordinate to the power of God: "No wisdom, no understanding, no counsel can avail against the Lord" (Prov 21:30). If there is a conflict between human and divine counsel, the faithful must remember that "The Lord brings the counsel of nations to nothing" (Ps 33:10), while "the counsel of the Lord stands forever" (33:11). The goal of the wise is to bring human wisdom, counsel, and instruction into alignment with their divine counterparts. Thus the prophet who speaks in Isa 11:2 assumes that the hoped-for king will have wisdom and understanding because "the spirit of the Lord shall rest on him."

The view that wisdom is a gift given by God is spelled out in narrative form in 1 Kgs 3:3–28. In a dream by night Solomon asks God for "an understanding mind to govern your people, able to discern between good and evil" (1 Kgs 3:9), and God grants him "a wise (*hakam*) and discerning (*nabon*) mind" (3:12). What it means to have such a gift is illustrated immediately afterwards when Solomon makes his highly memorable judgment in the case of the two women who claimed the same child. When the people of Israel heard of Solomon's solution, "they perceived that the wisdom of God was in him, to execute justice" (1 Kgs 3:28). A similar connection is made between wisdom and justice in Ps 37:30 ("The mouths of the righteous utter wisdom, and their tongues speak justice"). Elsewhere, in synonymous parallelism, wisdom is matched with righteousness or "uprightness" (Prov 4:11; see 10:31), and the wise are equated with the righteous (Prov 9:9; 23:24). Wisdom personified travels "in the way of righteousness, along the paths of justice" (Prov 8:20). Those who are wise understand that "the ways of the Lord are right, and the upright walk in them, but transgressors stumble in them" (Hos 14:9).

Solomon's God-given wisdom was also said to manifest itself as talent in the composition of proverbs and songs and as encyclopedic knowledge in the classification of plants and animals. In the book of Proverbs, which has been associated in tradition with the aphoristic aspects of

Solomon's wisdom, the wise are said to be those who will (among other things) "heed commandments" (Prov 10:8), "keep the law" (Prov 28:7), and "turn away from evil" (14:16).

The personification of Wisdom. In Prov 1:20–33; 8:4–36; 9:1–6, 11–12 wisdom seems to take on a life of its own. The author of these passages uses a type of figurative language called personification to make the abstract quality of wisdom speak as if it were a self-conscious entity. Since the words translated wisdom in these passages are grammatically feminine (*hokmoth* in 1:20 and 9:1 and *hokmah* in 8:1, 11, 12), the poet makes personified Wisdom speak as if she were a woman engaging in human activities. In this guise personified Wisdom cries out in 1:20–33; 8:4–21 like an OT prophet, confronting people wherever they live and work. Her speeches resemble the way the Lord speaks through the classical prophets. Since wisdom is the gift of God to humankind, rejecting what Wisdom has to offer is virtually the same as refusing to give reverence to the Lord (1:29).

In Prov 8:22–31 Wisdom claims to have been present when the Lord was creating the foundations of the universe. In early Christian debates about the nature of Christ (in the fourth century A.D.) this passage was used in arguments both for and against the position that was eventually codified in the Nicene Creed. Both sides understood Wisdom to be a distinct entity and both sides linked Christ with the "Wisdom of God" (1 Cor 1:24). But they differed regarding the meaning of the word that NRSV translates "created me" in Prov 8:22. The original Hebrew could be taken to mean God "possessed" or "created" or "begot" Wisdom. The position that was eventually held to be heresy claimed that the Son, like Wisdom, was created and was therefore subordinate to the Creator. The position declared orthodox at the Council of Nicea asserts that the Son was "begotten, not made" and thus was not subordinate but of the same substance and status as the Creator. In the context of the OT, it is much more likely that the author of Prov 8 intended for Wisdom to be understood here as a personification of a characteristic of the Lord's creative activity (as in Prov 3:19–20), rather than as a companion with a distinct identity.

The apocryphal books Sirach and Wisdom of Solomon also made use of the personification of Wisdom in order to make important points about human access to God. Sirach (ca. 190 B.C.) identified Wisdom with the Word of God (24:2), then specifically associated her with "the book of the covenant of the Most High God, the law that Moses commanded us" (24:23). Wisdom was thus the link between Scripture and God himself. In Wisdom of Solomon (ca. 100 B.C.) the emphasis is more on the association between Wisdom and the Spirit of God: "For she is a breath of the power of God, and a pure emanation of the glory of the Almighty" (7:25; cf. v. 22). As spirit, Wisdom fills the whole of creation and thus makes God accessible to all who seek her (7:27, and see the whole passage, 7:22–8:8). The Prologue to the Gospel of John (John 1:1–8) makes use of these ideas concerning the Wisdom of God in a new way, speaking of the *logos*, the Word of God who was with God and was God. Since Wisdom had been associated with the Word of God prior to the NT period, John's choice of *logos* as he uses material from the Wisdom tradition is understandable, as C. H. Dodd has demonstrated (Dodd, 274–77).

New Testament

In the NT "wisdom" and "wise" most often translate the Greek words *sophia* (wisdom) and *sophos* (wise). These words have much the same range of meaning in Greek as Hebrew *hakam* and *hokmah* and occur far more frequently in the epistles than in the Gospels. NRSV also translates *phronimos* as wise, but the contexts in which it occurs suggest that *phronimos* connotes planning ahead, as in the case of the "wise man who built his house on rock" (Matt 7:24). People who are alert and ready to cope with the fact that "the Son of Man is coming at an unexpected hour" (Matt 24:44) are called *phronimos* (translated "wise" in the parable of the Bridesmaids, Matt 25:2, 4, 8, 9 and in Matt 24:45, but "prudent" in the parallel passage of Luke 12:42). Thus we can assume that the word also has similar overtones of meaning for Matthew in the phrase "be wise as serpents" (Matt 10:16). Paul tells the Corinthians "you are wise (*phronimos*) in Christ" (1 Cor 4:10) and then uses the word again in what may be an ironic statement in 2 Cor 11:19. But when *phronimos* occurs in 1 Cor 10:15, NRSV translates it "sensible." Paul cautions the Romans against claiming "to be wiser than you are," implying that such behavior would cause division in the community (Rom 12:16; see 11:25). The related word *phronesis* is translated "wisdom" in Luke 1:17 (where the context also has to do with "getting ready") and as "insight" in Eph 1:8.

The word *magos* is translated "wise" only in the story of the three "wise men" who came to pay homage to the newborn king of the Jews (Matt 2:1, 7, 16; see *magi*). In Acts 13:6, 8 the same word is translated "magician."

The word "instruction" is used only in Rom 15:4, to translate *didaskalia*; in Eph 6:4, translating *paideia*; in 1 Tim 1:5 for *parangelia*; and in Heb 6:2 for *didache* (see **preach**). "Intelligent" is used to translate *syneton* only in Matt 11:25; Luke 10:21; and Acts 13:7. When the same word occurs in 1 Cor 1:19 (quoting Isa 29:14), NRSV translates it as "the discerning."

Like *hakam/hokmah* in the OT, *sophos* and *sophia* connote skill and ability as well as discernment (leading NRSV to use "skilled" to translate *sophos* in 1 Cor 3:10). Jesus' growth in wisdom as a child is illustrated by his exceptional ability to ask perceptive questions and give insightful answers to the teachers in the temple (Luke 2:40, 52). The people in his hometown link the "wisdom" he shows as an adult with his "deeds of power" (Matt 13:54; Mark 6:2). Since the Greek word *sophia* (wisdom) is grammatically feminine (as *hokmah* is in Hebrew), the OT concept of Wisdom personified as a woman carries naturally over

into Jesus' assertion that "wisdom is vindicated by her deeds" (Matt 11:19), or "by all her children" (Luke 7:35).

In the NT, as in the OT, wisdom (*sophia*) is assumed to be an attribute of God (see Rev 7:12). Paul prays "to the only wise God" (Rom 16:27), marvels over "the depth of the riches and wisdom and knowledge of God" (Rom 11:33), and speaks of "God's wisdom, secret and hidden" (1 Cor 2:7, see 1 Cor 1:21). It is God's plan that "through the church the wisdom of God in its rich variety might now be made known" (Eph 3:10; see Eph 1:8).

In the early church, the wisdom attributed to God was also understood to be personified in Christ. Paul speaks of Christ as "the power of God and the wisdom of God" (1 Cor 1:24) and declares that "Christ Jesus . . . became for us wisdom from God" (1 Cor 1:30). When Jesus condemns "this generation" for their hypocrisy in Luke 11:49, he quotes "the Wisdom (*sophia*) of God" as having said, "I will send them prophets and apostles, some of whom they will kill and persecute." In the parallel passage in Matt 23:34 these words are presented as Jesus' own words, leading early interpreters to assume that Jesus was to be identified with the wisdom of God (see also Rev 5:12).

The authors of the NT seem to distinguish between the kind of human wisdom that comes as a gift from God and "earthly wisdom" or "the wisdom of this world." While Paul indicates that wisdom (*sophia*) is not interchangeable with knowledge, he assumes that both are "given through the Spirit" (1 Cor 12:8) and he prays "that the God of our Lord Jesus Christ, the Father of glory, may give you a spirit of wisdom" (Eph 1:17). Paul was said to have written his letters "according to the wisdom given him" (2 Pet 3:15), and, according to Jas 1:5, anyone who is lacking in wisdom can ask God for it and it will be given. In Luke 21:15 Jesus promises to give his followers "a wisdom that none of your opponents will be able to withstand or contradict," and Acts 6:3–10 illustrates the fulfillment of that promise in Stephen, who was selected for a leadership position because he was "full of the Spirit and of wisdom" and who successfully argued against opponents who "could not withstand the wisdom and the Spirit with which he spoke."

Paul uses "wise" (*sophos*) in the ordinary, generic sense of being able to distinguish between the relative merits of one thing or another (1 Cor 6:5) and urges the Romans to be "wise in what is good" (Rom 16:19). But the majority of Paul's references to wisdom (*sophia*) are phrased as warnings to his listeners against letting their faith rest on "human wisdom" rather than on "the power of God" (1 Cor 2:5). In this context, reliance on "human wisdom" seems to entail thinking that one can attain either salvation or knowledge of God through one's own efforts. Paul is convinced that both salvation and knowledge of God come as gifts from God (a similar point seems to be made in Matt 11:25 and its parallel in Luke 10:21, when Jesus thanks the Father for having "hidden these things from the wise and intelligent" and "revealed them to infants").

In his letters to the Corinthians Paul argues that those who claim to be wise in the ways that the world calls wisdom are foolish in the eyes of God (1 Cor 1:20–25; 3:19). God has chosen to reveal God's self through the cross of Christ (which, according to ordinary human standards of judgment, seems to be a foolish thing to do), so that no one can boast that they have acquired knowledge of God through their own wisdom (1 Cor 1:18–31). Those who think their wisdom qualifies them for election into God's service are simply fooling themselves, as the composition of the Corinthian community indicates (1 Cor 1:26). God has chosen what seems to be "foolish" or "weak" or "low and despised" in the eyes of the world, so that "no one might boast" unless they "boast in the Lord" (1 Cor 1:29, 31). When it comes to boasting, Paul says he is willing to boast only on the fact that he has not depended on "earthly wisdom" but on "the grace of God" (2 Cor 1:12).

In a similar way, Paul declares that his proclamation of the gospel does not depend on "plausible words of wisdom" for its effectiveness but on "a demonstration of the Spirit and of power" (1 Cor 2:4). The content of Paul's preaching can be called wisdom as long as it is understood that "it is not a wisdom of this age" but "God's wisdom" that "God has revealed to us through the Spirit" (1 Cor 2:6–10).

James 3:15–17 elaborates further on Paul's distinction between earthly wisdom and "wisdom from above," tying specific human behaviors to each. Earthly wisdom (the kind that "does not come down from above") is "unspiritual" and produces "envy and selfish ambition" leading to "disorder and wickedness of every kind. But the wisdom (*sophia*) from above is first pure, then peaceable, gentle, willing to yield, full of mercy and good fruits, without a trace of partiality or hypocrisy."

C. H. Dodd, *The Interpretation of the Fourth Gospel* (Cambridge: Cambridge University Press, 1960); Roland E. Murphy, O.Carm., *The Tree of Life: An Exploration of Biblical Wisdom Literature*, AB Reference Library (New York: Doubleday, 1990); Rebecca D. Pentz, "Jesus as Sophia," *RefJ* 38 (Dec. 1988): 17–22; Leo G. Perdue, *Wisdom and Creation: The Theology of Wisdom Literature* (Nashville: Abingdon Press, 1994); Ben Witherington III, *Jesus the Sage: The Pilgrimage of Wisdom* (Minneapolis: Fortress Press, 1994).

KATHLEEN ANNE FARMER

Witness   *see* **Testify**

Woe   *see* **Suffer**

Woman   *see* **Man and Woman**

Wonder   *see* **Sign**

Word   The translation generally used for Hebrew *dabar* and Greek *logos* and *rhema*, "word," connotes both spoken utterances and things or events in both the OT and NT. When the Hebrew term is used of spoken utterances, it can have a range of meanings, among them word, speech, command, promise. NRSV expresses these nuances in some contexts (e.g., "promise," Ps 105:42; "false charge," Exod 23:7; "report," Deut 1:22, 25). At times, NRSV's translation obscures the use of the noun; for example, "The LORD did according to the word of Moses" becomes "The LORD did as Moses asked" (Exod 8:13, 31). NRSV does, however, underscore the theological importance of such expressions as the "word of the Lord" or the "words" of the prophets by translating these expressions literally, in both the OT and in the NT.

While it is often observed that the use of *dabar* in the OT reflects a primitive conception of the inherent efficacy of speech, there is little evidence to support that claim. Such claims are often based on observations concerning the power of the spoken word in curses and blessings (Gen 27) or the power of the divine word to accomplish its purpose (Isa 55:10–11). But the latter theological conception is relatively late, and critical discussions of curses and blessings rarely take either their narrative or sociopolitical function into account. Meanwhile, this emphasis on the quasimagical efficacy of speech often is made at the expense of the OT's preoccupation with the need for integrity in human speaking. Words bind individuals together in social relationships, strengthen commitments, and regulate community life in legal proceedings. As such, words do indeed have considerable power. But such power is not inherent in the words themselves; rather, it resides in the integrity of the speakers and in their willingness and intention to live in accordance with their words. This concern with the integrity of the speaker directly contributes to the OT's testimony concerning the word of God.

The Psalms provide a useful window into the social and theological contexts of human and divine words. In psalms of complaint, petitioners express human vulnerability to the effects of words. When words are deceitful, false, or filled with evil plans, the petitioner's own life is threatened (Pss 35:20; 36:3; 52:4; 59:12; 64:3, 109:3). Human beings are capable of plotting "deadly thing(s)" (41:8), devising "evil purpose(s)" (64:5) and "deeds of iniquity" (65:3). By contrast, because God's word is reliable and upright (33:4), it is extolled as a source of life and light (Ps 119, throughout). Thus, although there are some few texts that imply the creative efficacy of the divine word (33:6; 107:20; 147:15, 18, 19), the primary emphasis in the Psalms is on the integrity of the speaker. God's word can be trusted, because God is known to act in accordance with his word (105:8, 42).

Thus, just as words cement and characterize human social relationships, so also do words formalize the covenantal relationship between Yahweh and Israel. The formula, "this is the word/thing that the LORD commanded," is found at both the beginning and end of specific legislation (Exod 16:16, 32; 35:1, 4; Lev 8:5; 9:6; 17:2; Num 30:1; 36:6) and may have contributed to the later conception of the "ten words," or Decalogue (Exod 34:27–28; Deut 4:13). The current narrative form of the Sinai traditions revolves around words that the Lord speaks and the people accept (Exod 19:6, 7, 8, 9; 24:3, 7, 8; 34:1). In Deuteronomy, the word replaces all other modes of divine disclosure: "You heard the sound of words but saw no form; there was only a voice" (Deut 4:12). Human mediators give speech to the divine voice: Moses stands between the Lord and the people at Mount Horeb to proclaim the commandments (5:5). The authority of these words in the life of Israel is indicated by their being written down on stone tablets (Deut 5:22; 9:10; 10:2) and subsequently in a book (Deut 31:24). While Deuteronomy can certainly imagine other "things" (*debarim*) inhabiting the divine realm, the revealed "things" belong to Israel, in the forms of words or commandments that are to be closely guarded, transmitted to future generations, and observed (Deut 29:29; cf. also 6:6; 11:18; 12:28; 17:19).

In Deuteronomy, then, the "word" does not have the connotation of divine power but rather of the articulation of the divine will. As such, the people must accept it; indeed, even though the "word" may be in their hearts to do it (30:14), the whole thrust of Deuteronomy is to conform the hearts of Israel to the will of Yahweh (cf. 17:8–11; 27:26, 58; 29:9). The word in Deuteronomy is thus hardly a magically effective word that accomplishes the divine will; rather, it is, as Bultmann has observed, a summons to which the people must respond. In the future, the Lord will send prophets "like Moses" (18:18) who will continue to speak God's words. The formulaic expression "the word of the LORD" thus comes to be uniquely associated with the prophets. In Deuteronomy, the prophetic word has a comparable function to the word announced by Moses: it is an announcement of the divine will, to which the people must respond.

Legal contexts of weighing charges (*dabar*) and determining the outcome of a case (*dabar*) also contribute to theological usage (Exod 18:19, 22, 26; 23:8; cf. Deut 16:19; 19:4, 15; 22:14, 17, 20, 26). In situations where contentiousness arises between Yahweh and the people, Moses speaks Yahweh's words, which typically settle the case in his favor (Num 11:23–24; 12:6; 14:39; 16:31). Comparable announcements of the "word of the Lord" appear in pre-Deuteronomistic narrative traditions (Gen 15:1; 2 Sam 7:4; 24:11; 1 Kgs 13:20). The frequent occurrence of the prophetic formula, "Hear the word of the LORD," may therefore have its roots in legal controversies and thus reflect a prophetic declaration of Yahweh's testimony or charge against Israel. In Hosea, for example, the formula introduces a controversy that has been identified as a covenant lawsuit (Hos 4:1); the usage in other prophets is similar (cf. Amos 4:1; 5:1; 7:16; Jer 2:4; 7:2; 11:2; 9:20; 17:20; 19:3; 44:24, 26). Certainly the absence of the formula from oracles against the foreign nations would suggest that the "word of the Lord" is spoken within the context of the covenant, from one covenant partner to another.

To conclude: although it has been a regular feature of critical discussions to suggest that the word of God has quasi-magical powers, it is more likely that the power of the word of God resides elsewhere. The historical narratives of Kings do assert that the word of God guides and shapes the course of history (1 Kgs 16:7, 34; 17:2, 8; 18:1, 31; 21:17); thus it cannot be denied that the conception of the power of the word of God exists. However, when Second Isaiah proclaims, "The grass withers, the flower fades, but the word of our God remains forever" (Isa 40:8), the emphasis is not on the inherent efficacy of the word but on the integrity of the speaker. In contrast to human beings, who are no more constant than grass that withers and fades, the word of God endures forever. This is not because of the words' inherent power, but because it is in God's character to act in accordance with his covenant promise to Israel.

The NT use of *logos* and *rhema* is consistent with the OT usage. In the Gospel of Matthew, the primary emphasis is on the demand for obedience to the words of Jesus, which have **authority** to confer life to all who receive them (Matt 13:19–23; 24:35). Jesus' words establish the rules for the community (7:24, 26). Moreover, it is of utmost importance that those who hear Jesus' words also do them: "Not everyone who says, 'Lord, Lord,' will enter the kingdom of heaven, but only the one who does the will of my Father in heaven" (Matt 7:21). Matthew's usage thus reflects the OT emphasis on covenantal obedience.

Although the Lukan parallels to Matthew continue to emphasize the importance of both hearing and doing the word of God (Luke 6:47; 8:21), Luke's primary theme is the proclamation of the word of God (Luke 5:1). By linking this proclamation to the fulfillment of OT prophecy, Luke suggests that the word testifies to the reliability of God, who keeps covenant with his people (cf. Luke 1–2). The angels proclaim a new "word" to Zechariah and Mary, which is a fulfillment of the promises to the ancestors (1:20, 29); Jesus announces that the "word" of the prophet has been fulfilled (4:21); and crowds gather to hear the word of God (5:1). It is in Acts, however, that Luke's theological conception is most fully articulated; in fact, in some sixty-five occurrences of *logos* and the fourteen occurrences of *rhema* in Acts, only a handful are *not* theologically significant. In most instances, the "word" refers to the proclamation of the gospel, the precise content of which is illustrated in 2:22–36. In this sermon as in others, the apostles proclaim God's faithfulness to Israel despite its habitual rebellion (cf. also 10:36, 37). The proclamation of the word of God is the central activity of the apostles Peter and Paul, as well as of those who are scattered from Jerusalem. The Holy Spirit opens up new areas for the proclamation of the word (or not, 16:6); alternatively, the Spirit confirms its reception (8:14; 10:44). Because the proclamation of the word leads to belief (4:4; 8:14), the word is not simply the message, but also the power of God for salvation. In this sense, Acts speaks of the word "increasing" (6:7; 11:1; 13:49; 19:20). Interestingly, upon Paul's final arrest, *rhema* and *logos* cease to be used in Acts.

For Paul, "word" connotes divine commands (Rom 13:8–10; Gal 5:14) and also, more importantly, the will of God as it is articulated in his promise to Israel (Rom 9:6, 9) and the gospel (1 Thess 1:6, 8; Phil 2:16; Gal 6:6). As in Acts, this "word" is not merely a message about God but the power to bring about salvation (1 Thess 2:13). The connotation of "word" as divine power begins to disappear in the disputed Pauline epistles, where "word" continues to refer to the gospel (2 Tim 2:9; Titus 1:3) even as it acquires the connotation of sound doctrine (2 Tim 1:13; Titus 1:9).

The Gospel of John presents a special case in its use of *logos* in the Prologue (1:1–18); however, it remains uncertain the extent to which OT conceptions of the word of God have contributed to this concept. It is likely that the concept of *logos* in 1:1–18 is more closely related to the Stoic philosophical conception of Logos as world reason and Jewish speculation concerning personified *Wisdom*

(Prov 8:22–31; Wis 7:22–8:8; Sir 24:2–23). Elsewhere in the Gospel, Jesus' words function in much the same way that they do in the Synoptics. Jesus' word is the word of God (3:34; 17:8), because God speaks through him (14:10). The words of Jesus are thus the source of eternal life (5:24; 6:63, 68; 8:51), which is made available through the intimate fellowship of God, Jesus, and the believers (8:31; 14:23). The word that Jesus proclaims is a summons, a call to decision. Those who reject Jesus' words reject God; thus they face certain judgment. John's explanation for the rejection of the words of Jesus is more sharply dualistic than that given in the OT. Moreover, the life-giving character of Jesus' words seems more deeply mystical; nevertheless, the Gospel's understanding of the covenantal and life-giving dimensions of a divine word that requires a human response remains deeply rooted in the OT conception of the word.

Bertil Albrektson, *History and the Gods: An Essay on the Idea of Historical Events as Divine Manifestations in the Ancient Near East and in Israel*, ConBOT 1 (Lund: CWK Gleerup, 1967), 53–67; Rudolf Bultmann, "The Concept of the Word of God in the New Testament," in *Faith and Understanding*, vol. 1, ed. Robert W. Funk, trans. Louise Pettibone Smith (New York: Harper & Row, 1969), 286–312; Anthony Thiselton, "Supposed Power of Words in the Biblical Writings," *JTS* n.s. 25 (1974): 283–99.

MARGARET S. ODELL

Work, Labor

In the NRSV the words "work" and "labor" sometimes translate the same Hebrew word (e.g., verb: ʿabad, "to work" or "to serve") but more often translate a variety of other Hebrew nouns and verbs. For example, "Israel saw the great work [literally, the great or mighty hand] that the LORD did against the Egyptians" (Exod 14:31). Or "Six days you shall labor [literally, work] and do all your work [literally, occupation, work] (Exod 20:9). This latter phrase, "do work," is a common expression and describes God's creative activity in Genesis: "And on the seventh day God finished the work that he had done" (Gen 2:2). "Labor" is particularly interesting since, in addition to work, the English word also describes the birth process, which Hebrew expresses with the term *yalad*, "to bear, bring forward, beget" (Gen 35:16; 38:28). Any attempt to understand why the NRSV translators have rendered the Hebrew and Greek as they have would be futile. It is sufficient for our purposes to reflect on the occurrences of "work" and "labor" in the NRSV and present the bigger picture.

A common misunderstanding of work as a curse imposed by God on humankind as a punishment for sin (Gen 3) is still surprisingly current. Work was part of the divine plan for human beings from the very beginning. God worked (Gen 1:1–2:4a); why not God's creatures? The earthling (meaning of the Hebrew *'adam*) was given a divine imperative to "fill the earth and subdue it" and to have dominion over creation (Gen 1:28). In the Yahwist account, the earthling was placed in the garden of Eden "to till it and to keep it" (see also Sir 7:15). The soil was cursed, not the laborers (Gen 3:17). But it will now take much hard work and endless "toil" to raise crops in incredibly difficult soils. This was indeed the experience of early Israelites in the highland settings of the early Iron Age. With this tale, the sacred writer provides divine sanction for human endeavors that are difficult, demanding, seemingly futile. The earthling's partner shares in this difficulty: "I shall give you great labour in childbearing; with labour you will bear children" (Gen 3:16, REB). Women will have to work hard just as the men and will have to bear many children.

In Egypt the Israelites were set to forced labor (Exod 1:11, 14), but after the exodus God established a rhythm to work and rest. A period of work should be offset with a time for rest (Exod 20:9–10; Heb 3:7–4:11) either to honor God by imitation (Exod 20:10) or for pragmatic reasons (Exod 23:12). Given the nature of Mediterranean climate, it is hardly likely that any-

one worked from sunrise to sunset (Ps 104:19–23), except perhaps those who could work indoors. Of course all work was difficult (Sir 38:25–34), but that of the scribe (hardly two percent of the ancient population) was sweeter. In a subsistence economy, few could afford the leisure that the scribal role required (Sir 38:24) or enjoy the benefits it brought (Sir 38:34b–39:11). Still, God is recognized as the one who rewards labor (Ps 65:9–13), and without God's aid, human labor could be empty (Ps 127).

Jesus the artisan (Mark 6:3) undoubtedly apprenticed with Joseph. In late adolescence or adulthood, Jesus quite likely worked with him on the building projects of Herod Antipas in Sepphoris, about four miles away. When he sent the disciples out on mission, Jesus reminded them to rely on the hospitality of the local folk, "for the laborer deserves to be paid. Do not move about from house to house [abusing this hospitality]" (Luke 10:7–8).

John's Jesus made a startling statement, "The one who believes in me will also do the works that I do and, in fact, will do greater works than these" (John 14:12). In this case, the Greek sheds some helpful light. The Synoptics call Jesus' activities "mighty deeds" (*dynameis*) while John calls them "signs" (*semeia*). In John, Jesus himself refers to deeds as "works" (*erga*). This latter Greek word is used by the LXX in describing God's works, the greatest of which are creation or giving life and redemption or restoring meaning to life. The word used by John's Jesus is very likely an intentional allusion to these works of God. The seven works of Jesus that John reports are easily located in one or the other category. In the story of the royal official's request that Jesus heal his son, who is on the point of death, the phrase "the son lives" (NRSV legitimately translates the simple present as the future) is repeated three times (John 4:50, 51, 53). When Jesus feeds the crowd of five thousand with five barley loaves and two fishes, he performs a very obvious life-giving deed (John 6:1–14). Finally, nothing can be more obvious than restoring Lazarus—already dead and four days in the tomb—to life (John 11:1–44).

When the joy of a village wedding feast verges on collapse because the wine has run out, Jesus restores meaning to that event and to the lives of all involved by providing abundance of wine better in quality than the original stock (John 2:1–11). The man ill for thirty-eight years who waited for healing at the Sheep Gate pool (John 5:1–9) was alive to be sure, but he did not have the ability to walk. His life lacked complete meaning. Jesus' work (John 5:17) on behalf of this man restored meaning to his life. His joy was so overwhelming he failed to learn the identity of his benefactor. Sadly, for his gift of restored meaning in life, he failed to defend his benefactor, Jesus, adequately, but instead set up new conflict for him. The trance experienced by the disciples of Jesus walking on the sea presents good news that Jesus has the ability to tame nature, something peasants considered impossible. This is truly life-enriching (John 6:16–21). The case of the man blind from birth (John 9) is similar to the man at the pool (John 5). He too was alive but without sight. When Jesus restored his sight, the man not only had life but now had it "abundantly" (John 10:10). This gift gave him the courage to defend Jesus before the religious authorities. Giving life and restoring meaning to life are two works that all human beings can perform.

The apostle Paul took pride in not burdening any of his churches. He notes: "You remember our labor and toil, brothers and sisters; we worked night and day, so that we might not burden any of you while we proclaimed to you the gospel of God" (1 Thess 2:9). Consider his advice to the Thessalonians, and the motive behind the advice: "But we urge you, beloved, to do so more and more, to aspire to live quietly, to mind your own affairs, and to work with your hands, as we directed you, so that you may behave properly toward outsiders and be dependent on no one" (1 Thess 4:10–12). Paul's proclamation of the proximate coming of Jesus in

power (*parousia*) seems to have had the effect on some believers that they quit their jobs and thus had to freeload on others. His successors advise, in Paul's name: "Anyone unwilling to work should not eat. For we hear that some of you are living in idleness, mere busybodies, not doing any work. Now such persons we command and exhort in the Lord Jesus Christ to do their work quietly and to earn their own living" (2 Thess 3:10–12).

Work is not always pleasurable or fulfilling. One study reported that 80 percent of those interviewed in the modern industrial world felt they were involved in instrumental work, while only 20 percent were involved in expressive work. Instrumental work is that which provides sufficient money and time so that the worker can afford to do what she or he really wants to do in life. Only about 20 percent of workers indicated they feel blessed by doing work they love and are getting paid for it! Qoheleth offered a similar reflection on life in his day (third century B.C.). He set out to discover life's meaning and purpose (Eccl 2:3) by exploring and experiencing pleasure (2:1–11), wisdom and folly (2:12–17), and work (2:18–6:9). Reflecting on work, he observed that one cannot take its rewards to the next life (2:18–6); humans never seem to know the opportune time (3:1–4:6); your "second one" (companion, heir, etc.) may actually betray you (4:7–16); unexpected loss is always possible (5:1–6:9). His conclusion? Enjoy life and all that it offers (2:24; 3:13; 3:22), which finds an echo in Paul centuries later (Phil 4:8–9).

———

JOHN J. PILCH

Worship The word "worship" comes from the Old English "weorthscipe," that is, "worth-ship"; this suggests that originally the term referred to the action of human beings in acknowledging the status of God in appropriate ways because God is worthy of such homage. It therefore covers such activities as *praise* and *thanksgiving* and such attitudes as *fear* and reverence but also faith and love as the responses to who God is and what God does. If, however, actual usage is decisive for meaning, the term is used much more widely to include virtually all human actions toward God, including *prayer* to him, and also all that happens when a group of believers meet together, including such actions as reading Scripture, *singing*, and *preaching*. This wide sense can be justified in that whatever believers do, and perhaps particularly when they meet together for a specifically Christian gathering, they should be doing it to the glory of God (1 Pet 4:11). However, there is a danger in using the word in this way, since it can lead to the erroneous conclusion that Christian meetings are primarily or even exclusively concerned with what *human beings* do, with little or no consideration given to what *God* does in them.

From the beginning it is God who takes the initiative in the creation of the world and the people in it, in providential care of them and in communicating with them in various ways. The Bible is the story of what God does and how people respond to him, both positively and negatively. Within this framework the major part of the story is God's choice of the patriarchs and then of the descendants of Jacob to be his people. They respond to him as God with appropriate homage and there is an extensive vocabulary relating to this, including "worship," "bow down," "fear." As the story stands, right from the beginning worship included making offerings to God, generally in the form of *sacrifices* of animals (Gen 4:3–7); the rationale for sacrifice is complex and includes elements of making a gift to God, having communion with God, and canceling out the effects of sin. Since the Israelites lived in a context where many other gods were worshiped, great stress is laid on the importance of proper worship, according to the patterns laid down by God himself and canonized in Scripture (Leviticus; Numbers). Worship had to be offered in the right places; against the earlier proliferation of sites there was a centralizing

tendency that led to the temple in Jerusalem (a replacement for the earlier portable tabernacle; see *presence*) being the only legitimate site (Deut 12:5–7). There was a fixed set of administrators of the cult, drawn from the tribe of Levi. There were elaborate rules regarding the types of sacrifice to be offered and the festivals of the religious year.

Alongside this formal cult, the Psalms in particular bear witness to the growth of a more spontaneous literature of devotion that might be used by individuals or groups; most of the Psalms are addressed to Yahweh in lament, thanksgiving, and praise, but some are more instructional, addressed to the worshipers themselves.

Also alongside the cult at certain periods we have the activity of prophets who tended to be "outsiders" through whom God spoke to the people, often in criticism of the rulers, the cultic officials, and the people generally for their departures from him. More than one prophet inveighed against the maintenance of religious ritual despite moral failure in ordinary life and condemned the hypocrisy (Ps 40:6–8; Hos 8:11–14; Amos 5:21–24).

By NT times the extensive temple area was a place where the regular, prescribed sacrifices and other offerings were the focus of Jewish worship and were attended by many people who would pray there (Luke 1:10; cf. Acts 3:1). It was also a meeting place where religious teachers were active (Luke 2:46). The majority of Jews, especially when more and more lived outside Judea in the Dispersion, were too far distant from Jerusalem to be able to participate in the rituals at the temple, although they were expected to make pilgrimages up to three times annually. The practice of regular local meetings or "synagogues," eventually in buildings dedicated to this purpose, developed and was a feature of Jewish life by the time of Jesus. The center of synagogue activity was the systematic reading of the Law and other parts of Scripture, accompanied by a "sermon" based on the reading and set in a context of prayer.

Luke describes the piety of the parents of John the Baptist and Jesus and their fulfillment of their religious obligations at the temple (Luke 1–2). Jesus and his disciples normally visited the synagogues on the Sabbath (Luke 4:16), and indeed Luke 4:16–30 is the oldest surviving description of a synagogue service. They also visited the temple in Jerusalem on the occasion of religious festivals; here Jesus taught within the precincts and protested against the way in which the temple was not fulfilling its purpose as a place for prayer for all peoples (Mark 11:17). There is no mention of Jesus ever offering sacrifice or of specific "worship occasions" by his disciples. We do hear of his own personal prayers and of his teaching to his disciples about how they should pray, and this is particularly important for the emerging theology of a father/children relationship within which prayer is natural (Luke 11:1–13).

After the departure of Jesus, his disciples, who were at first based in Jerusalem, continued to use the temple as a place of meeting, and there are indications that they participated in various forms of sacrifice for some time (Acts 21:17–26); so long as they were available, they used its facilities for Christian teaching (Acts 5:12–42). Over a period of time the concept of the death of Christ as a sacrifice that rendered the temple sacrifices for sin obsolete developed; the theology of the book of Hebrews, which saw the sacrifices as foreshadowings of the sacrifice of Christ, was not an isolated or marginal development. As the center of gravity of the Christian movement tended to shift from Jerusalem and Judea to such places as Antioch and eventually Rome, and as the church became increasingly Gentile in composition, the temple played less and less part in Christian worship. After A.D. 70, temple worship was in any case impossible. Following the twofold development in Judaism of a piety based on the home and the synagogue, so too Christian piety developed at a local level, and there was no sense of a central "place of worship," such as Jerusalem was for the Jews.

The Christians then met together at first in whatever premises were suitable, usually the homes of those believers that were large enough to accommodate the group, in practice, the better-off members of the congregations. These meetings were not closed to outsiders (1 Cor 14:22–25), but there were also other occasions more specifically used for evangelism, whether indoors in homes (Acts 28:30–31) or other premises (Acts 19:9) or in the open air; the line between meetings that were more evangelistic and those that were more for converts will have been quite fuzzy. Buildings set aside for Christian purposes are not attested at this period.

Influences from the temple, the household, and the synagogue shaped the pattern of Christian meetings. The concept of the temple as a place where God himself was present in a special way, and therefore his people could have fellowship with him, is reflected in the Christian belief that the believers collectively form a temple or dwelling place of the Holy Spirit (1 Cor 3:16f.; 6:19–20). There was a consequent sense of the numinous quality of the Christian gathering with, on occasion, fear of what might happen there to sinners (Acts 5:1–11) and also a sense that those present must seek to be *holy* and blameless. Occasionally the activity of Christians is thought of as priestly service to God. In particular Paul saw his missionary activity in the conversion of the Gentiles to be part of God's people in this way (Rom 15:16), and the proclamation of the mighty deeds of God and the demonstration of loving deeds to other people were regarded as the Christian equivalent to the OT sacrifices of thanksgiving to God (Heb 13:15–16; 1 Pet 2:4–5, 9). In contrast to the OT pattern, there is no separate human priesthood in the Christian church, Christian believers collectively constituting a holy priesthood.

The influence of Jewish family piety is less easy to define, except in that the local Christian church developed the idea of being a spiritual family of brothers and sisters. It is interesting that Jesus rejects the idea that individual Christians should be dignified as "father," "rabbi," or "instructor," since this would be a usurping of the place of God or the Messiah (Matt 23:8–10). In any case Christians continued the practice of personal prayer, which was, of course, not peculiar to Judaism but found in other religions also.

As for the synagogue, this would have been the natural model for Jewish Christians (both native Jews and proselytes) to follow. Christians certainly attended synagogues and spoke about Jesus Christ in them. They may well have hoped that the members would accept their message and the synagogue would then become a Christian gathering; the fact that Christian gatherings are called "synagogues" (NRSV "assembly") in James 2:2 may indicate that this sometimes happened, or that Christians who withdrew from a Jewish synagogue set up their own group with the same name. Normally, however, Christian groups were called "churches" (*ekklesiai*), a word that combined nuances of a gathering of citizens to transact their common business and also of the people of Israel gathered together as an assembly of God's people (see *church*). Neither of these words suggests that "worship" in the narrow sense was the primary function of the meetings.

This is confirmed by the fact that the actual word "worship" (*leitourgeo*) is scarcely used to describe any part of the conduct of a Christian meeting; the exceptions are Acts 13:2 with reference to prayer and fasting and 1 Cor 14:24–25, where an outsider is moved to awe by hearing the words of a prophet.

Nevertheless, elements of worship in this sense are there. The proclamation of the mighty acts of God is a confession of his greatness, love, and power, and the line between telling other people how great God is and addressing God himself is a thin one. The descriptions of what goes on in the immediate presence of God in the heavenly scenes described in Revelation, with their reverence before God and their confessions of his greatness and wonderful deeds, may well reflect what Christians did in their earthly meetings

and in turn may have helped to shape their practices. There is a fair amount of creedal and doxological material in the NT that probably reflects the actual utterances in Christian meetings.

There is abundant evidence that prayer occupied a significant place in the lives of believers. There are few reports of the words of actual prayers in church (Acts 4:24–30), but numerous references to Christians praying, singly or in company, and Paul's letters in particular tend to commence with prayer reports in which he tells his readers what he says to God when he prays for them, and he asks them to pray for him; in 1 Tim 2:1–10 the primary place of prayer in the Christian meeting is strongly urged.

In Acts 2:42 Luke lists four items that characterized the communal life of the first Christians, and these were undoubtedly ongoing constituents of the life of Christians. In addition to "the prayers" he mentions the apostles' teaching, fellowship, and the breaking of bread. The first of these indicates that a primary aspect of Christian meetings was instruction in the new faith. The continuation of this is demonstrated in the fact of traveling teachers who instructed the congregations and in the central place of the letters sent to churches for public reading when the believers were gathered together. In the Pastoral Epistles, in particular, teaching and specifically "sound teaching" receives enormous emphasis. The reference of the second term in Acts 2:42, "fellowship," is debatable; it may refer to the sharing of possessions (Acts 2:44–45; 4:32–37), or to some kind of common religious experience (possibly eating together [Acts 2:46b], but since "breaking of *bread*" is listed separately, this is open to question). In any case, it is more concerned with relationships among the believers than between them and God. The "breaking of bread" reflects a form of words used by Paul in connection with the Lord's Supper (1 Cor 10:16). In 1 Cor 11:17–34 the Lord's Supper takes place in the context of a full meal (cf. Acts 2:46). The listing of these activities indicates that "worship" in the narrow sense was only one aspect of early Christian meetings.

Other NT evidence confirms this general impression. The most detailed account of what went on in such a meeting is found in 1 Cor 12–14. The focus here is on the problems raised by the exercise of the *gifts* of the Spirit in the meeting. Believers who could speak in tongues were taking too prominent a place in the meeting, and their activity was open to criticism in that the exercise of the gift may have edified them personally but was not edifying other believers if nobody could interpret the tongues. The possessors of some gifts were depriving others of the opportunity to exercise their gifts (a limit has to be put on the number of speakers in tongues and the prophets, 1 Cor 14:26–33), and they were despising other members of the congregation who were exercising what they regarded as inferior gifts or who had no gifts at all. From Paul's critical discussion of what was wrong in the meeting, we can gather that he believed that all believers could possess gifts of the Spirit and that there was a considerable variety of gifts, which he lists in some detail. These included the communication of wisdom and knowledge to the congregation, the ability to do mighty works such as healing (see *heal*), the reception and communication of prophetic messages from the Lord, as well as speaking in tongues. Other lists in the chapter (1 Cor 12:27–30) and in Rom 12 indicate that various forms of leadership and the capacity to help other people (pastoral care and generosity) were also regarded as divine gifts to the church. Teaching (see *preach*) and singing were also parts of the meeting (1 Cor 14:26). Granted that some of these activities, for example, pastoral care and generosity, may have been practiced apart from the meeting, it remains the case that Paul here reflects a fairly wide range of items that could form part of the meeting. What is significant is that he rates their value in terms of their potential for what he calls "edification," that is, the promotion of the good of the members

individually and as a congregation. Uninterpreted tongues don't edify, but clear prophecy and teaching do. For Paul, then, a major aim of the Christian meeting is the good that it does to the people present.

At this point it is assumed that the gifts of the Spirit were exercised by any member of the congregation. Later on there is more stress on the activity of people who have come to be known by the roles that they were able to undertake—apostles, prophets, evangelists, and pastors and teachers (Eph 4:11). We see the beginnings of the way in which the person who does a particular task comes to be known as "the prophet" or "the evangelist" or whatever, and then it becomes natural to look for somebody who is gifted by the Spirit to step into that role when there is a vacancy. However, the significant point here is that the purpose of these people is to build up the people of God ("the saints") and the body of Christ (Eph 4:12) so that they grow as Christians. Again, the proximate purpose of the church meeting is not to worship God but to benefit his people.

A much more succinct account of the matter is given in 1 Pet 4:10–11. Here Peter urges each person who has a gift to exercise it in service, and he then distinguishes two gifts, "speaking" and "serving." While "serving" might be understood as "serving God," it is more likely that it is to be understood as serving the people of God (as in 2 Cor 8:4), promoting their good through teaching and pastoral care. Nevertheless Peter concludes with the comment that the aim in all this is "so that God may be glorified through Jesus Christ." This shows that the ultimate purpose of what Christians do is to bring glory to God, in the sense that more and more people will praise him for the goodness that he has shown to them through the people empowered by his Spirit, and in that way the glory of God will increase.

Putting all this together, we can see that there is an underlying pattern. Under the old covenant the starting point was the initiative of God, who graciously delivered Israel from bondage, formed them into his people, and taught them how they should live, and they for their part responded with worship and obedience. Similarly, in the new covenant the starting point is the redemption wrought by God in Christ, the creation of the renewed Israel (now including Gentile believers), and the teaching about how believers are to live as the *people of God*. There is thus a primary movement from God to his people, expressed verbally in preaching and teaching. Then in response to God's initiative, people believe in the good news, commit themselves to their God, demonstrate their gratitude in praise and thanksgiving, and live under his direction. This twofold pattern of divine initiative and human response is reflected in the Christian meeting, which provides for God's communication to us and our response to him. Thus the Christian meeting is more than just worship in the narrow sense by believers; it is also—and surely primarily—the occasion where God meets with his people in fellowship; consequently the main thing that happens is his approach to them, giving them his gifts and teaching them his ways. Secondary to this is their response in faith, thanksgiving, and obedience.

Peter comments that the glorification of God that occurs in the activity of ministry is "through Jesus Christ" (1 Pet 4:11). This phrase qualifies all Christian activity. Prayer is offered to God through Jesus Christ, in that it is in union with him that we are able to approach God acceptably.

Robert J. Banks, *Paul's Idea of Community* (Peabody, Mass.: Hendrickson Publishers, 1994); I. H. Marshall, "How Far Did the Early Christians Worship God?" *Churchman* 99:3 (1985): 216–29; R. P. Martin, *Worship in the Early Church* (Grand Rapids: Eerdmans, 1974); David Peterson, *Engaging with God* (Downers Grove, Ill.: InterVarsity Press, 2002).

I. HOWARD MARSHALL

Wrath, Anger, Indignation   A set of
terms that translate eleven Hebrew and five Greek words so closely related that a given biblical word might be translated by two or all three of these English words. For example, the Hebrew root *zaʿam* (rendered "be indignant" or "indignation" by the lexicons and often meaning "curse") is translated "wrath" in Jer 50:25, "angry" in Prov 25:23, and "indignation" in Ps 38:3. Frequently, the terms *ʾaph* ("anger," derived from the word for nose, perhaps because of a change in color of the face or nose when one becomes angry) and *hemah* (a word for "heat" or "burning anger") are used synonymously in parallelism (e.g., Isa 63:6; Jer 32:37; 33:5; Ezek 13:13; Dan 9:16; Mic 5:15). In addition, two of these nouns could stand next to each other, with the second serving as an adjective modifying the first: for example, "in my jealous wrath" (Ezek 36:6).

Old Testament

Anger, wrath. Anger is portrayed as a human emotion. Moses' anger, for example, flared at the sight of the golden calf in the camp of Israel (Exod 32:19), with the result that he broke the tablets of stone with the commandments written on them. His behavior went without comment nevertheless. In the revolt of Korah, Moses became "very angry" (Num 16:15) at the reproach of Dathan and Abiram and prayed to God, who caused the earth to swallow the offenders. By contrast, at Meribah Moses became angry or at least impatient with the Israelites' whining about a lack of water and struck a rock rather than addressing it as God had told him. Water gushed forth (Num 20:11), but God reprimanded Moses for disobeying the commandment to speak to the rock and for the lack of trust in God that his action betrayed. For his failure, Moses would not lead the people into Canaan. The implication of these passages taken together is that the OT did not perceive human anger as sinful per se, indicated that at times anger might even be appropriate, but recognized that it could lead to disobedience and bad faith.

The OT knows nothing of an impassive God who shows no emotion. Instead, it portrays God as a being who loves and hates (Mal 1:2–3), regrets actions (Gen 6:6), and erupts in wrath. The word *haron* derives from a verb that means "burn" or "be kindled," and is used forty-one times, exclusively of God's anger. It is often coupled with the word *ʾaph* (e.g., in Exod 32:12; Num 25:4; 32:14; Josh 7:26; 1 Sam 28:18; Hos 11:9; Isa 13:9, 13). Similarly, the verb *ʾanaph*, which is related to *ʾaph*, is used fourteen times, all of God. Another word for wrath/anger is *ʿebrah*, which can mean "overflow," "arrogance," or "fury." It can be used of humans (e.g., in Gen 49:7 and Amos 1:11 in parallelism with *ʾaph*) or of God (typically translated "wrath" as in Isa 10:6; Hos 5:10; 13:11; Zeph 1:18). At times the wrath of God is described in ways that seem violent (e.g., Amos 9:1–4), prejudiced against groups of people (e.g., the poor in Jer 5:4–5b), abusive to people (children in Lam 4:4; the city of Nineveh in Nah 1:2, 8–10), abusive to the natural world, particularly the land (Isa 6:11–12), or negatively gendered (Mic 1:6–7). Such descriptions may need to be read in light of later revelation or criticized in the light of theories of justice.

Indignation. The English word "indignation" perhaps connotes less rage than the other two, but in the OT the words translated "indignation" are the same as those translated "wrath" and/or "anger." It too expresses the emotion of anger of persons against persons or God against persons. Of these words, *zaʿam* is used of God's wrath or indignation exclusively, except for Dan 11:30, where it is used of Antiochus Epiphanes, when he was forced by the Romans to withdraw from a campaign in Egypt in 167 B.C.

New Testament

Anger, wrath. The two primary terms are the stem *org-* and the word *thymos*. Generally speaking, NRSV translates *orge* as "wrath," except in the book of Revelation and in lists of such emotions where distinctions are not the point. All forms of the Greek stem *org-* except for *orge* itself are used exclusively of God's wrath, and *orge* itself often designates God's wrath (e.g., Matt 3:7; John 3:36; Rom 1:18; Eph 5:6; 1 Thess 2:16). Typically NRSV translates *thymos* as either "wrath" or "anger." It can designate divine (Rev 15:1) or human (Rev 14:8) wrath. The two sometimes are used interchangeably, though a distinction is possible. While both connote a passionate rage that flares up suddenly, NT writers prefer *thymos* for that meaning (e.g., Luke 4:28, translated "rage"). Conversely, they use *orge* rather than *thymos* in cases where the anger comes after deliberation (Jas 1:20, translated "anger").

The term *thymos* appears in connection with the wrath of humans, for example, in Paul's letters (2 Cor 12:20; Gal 5:20), in the deutero-Pauline letters Ephesians (4:31) and Colossians (3:8), in Hebrews (11:27), Luke (4:28), and Acts (19:28). *Orge* can carry that meaning too (cf. Col 3:8). The NT distinguishes different types of such anger. On the one hand, it recognizes a "righteous" anger at things that God opposes, particularly in connection with the actions of Jesus (Mark 3:5). Most often, however, the NT describes human anger as sinful. In the parable of the Prodigal Son, the elder brother became so angry (the word is the verb *orgizo*) at his father's killing the fatted calf that the son refused to participate in the celebration (Luke 15:28). His anger was not righteous, but selfish. Ephesians 4:26 recognizes that anger is a human emotion ("Be angry but do not sin"), but cautions against allowing anger to build ("do not let the sun go down on your anger"). When people nurse anger, they grant Satan entrance into their lives (Eph 4:27).

The NT speaks often of the wrath of God. Revelation uses *thymos* nine times of the wrath of God and once of the wrath of the devil (12:12). Paul uses the word in connection with divine wrath in Rom 2:8. Fifteen times he uses the term *orge* alone when he means the "wrath of God" (e.g., Rom 2:5; 4:15; 1 Thess 5:9), as did John the Baptist (Matt 3:7; Luke 3:7) and Revelation of the dragon (12:17). Often Paul uses the phrase "the day of wrath" in reference to the day of judgment (e.g., Rom 2:5). In contrast with its estimation of human wrath, the NT always views the wrath of God favorably. That is true even of God's ultimate wrath, which could result in God's destruction of the total person ("body and soul") in hell (see *grave*) (Matt 10:28; cf. also 5:21, 27–30).

Indignation. NRSV translates the word *aganakteo* as "indignant" in Mark 10:14 and Luke 13:14, but as "angry" in Matt 20:24. It translates *aganaktesis* as "indignation" in 2 Cor 7:11, the only place the word appears in the NT. It also translates *pyroo* (to burn) as "am indignant" (2 Cor 11:29). There is little apparent difference among the terms.

Walter Brueggemann, *Theology of the Old Testament: Testimony, Dispute, Advocacy* (Minneapolis: Fortress, 1997); Murdoch Dahl, *Daughter of Love* (Worthing, Sussex: Churchman Publishing, 1989); Carol J. Dempsey, *Hope amid the Ruins: The Ethics of Israel's Prophets* (St. Louis: Chalice, 2000).
PAUL L. REDDITT

Write, Book, Scripture The concept of Scripture is not evident until the NT, where *graphe* ("writing") nearly always refers to sacred writings; however, the written word is theologically significant throughout the OT and NT. For nearly every socioeconomic situation where writing plays a key role, one may find a corresponding theological usage. Writing is employed in instruction (Hos 8:12), to denote possession (Isa 8:1), and to file legal indictments and record legal transactions (Jer 17:1; Jer 32:10–11; Job 31:35). In many instances, the act of writing indicates the *authority* of the writer. In the OT, for example, only kings and high officials are depicted as writing or sending written messages (2 Sam 11:14–15; 1 Kgs 21:8, 9, 11; 2 Kgs 10:1, 6). The one exception is Jeremiah, the rejection and destruction of whose writing proves the rule (Jer 36:20–26). In Esther, writing bears such great authority that a published royal decree cannot be revoked and can be mitigated only by means of yet another decree (Esth 8:5, 8). Writing is thus easily appropriated as a

metaphor of divine authority. As writing is adapted for theological usage, it is God who instructs through writing, lays claim to Israel as a possession, sets forth legal requirements, and files legal indictments. The *seal*, or mark, of God (Exod 39:30; Ezek 9:4; Job 9:7) has its correlate in the practice of stamping objects with the name of their owners (Isa 8:1); those who are so marked belong to God. God records the names of the righteous in the book of life (Exod 32:32; Ezek 13:9; Mal 3:16; Pss 69:28; 87:6; 139:16). All of these theological appropriations of writing embody the central theological conviction of the Bible: God lays claim to the elect and exercises sovereign authority over them. Because the written word was understood to be the *word* of God, its authority continues to be evident in the NT, where it becomes the foundation of the interpretive tradition of the early church. The written word was never, however, an uncontested authority, and both Testaments demonstrate the tension between the word as written and as interpreted.

The writing of the covenant constitutes the pivotal event of the Pentateuchal narratives and signifies not only the establishment of the covenant but also its transmission and promulgation. In the Yahwistic traditions, Moses writes down the words of the covenant, which consist both of God's commands and the people's assent to them (Exod 24:4, 8). By contrast, in the Elohistic traditions, God himself writes the covenant on the two tablets, and the people are commanded to accept and observe it (Exod 31:18; 32:15–16; 34:1).

The two traditions of divine and human writing are harmonized in Deuteronomy. At Mount Horeb, God establishes the covenant by writing it on the two stone tablets (Deut 4:13; 5:22; 10:2, 4). A generation later, as the Israelites prepare to enter the land, Moses records the covenant in a "book," or scroll (Deut 31:24; cf. 28:58, 61; 29:21, 27; 30:10). In contrast with divine writing, which establishes the covenant, Moses' writing is a process of saving and transmitting what has already been received. This process of transmission becomes the responsibility of all Israel, since the people are commanded to write the words of the covenant on the doorposts of their houses and bind them on their arms and foreheads (Deut 6:4–9; 11:18–20). In so doing, the people signify their acceptance of Yahweh's sovereignty over home and person. Just as God has laid claim to Israel, so also does God's law regulate every aspect of its life.

The recording and transmission of the laws constitute a central theme in the Deuteronomist's account of the history of Israel (Joshua–Kings). Adhering to what Moses had written, Joshua renews the covenant at Mount Ebal (Josh 8:30–35). As part of the covenant renewal, Joshua inscribes the covenant on large stones, in effect creating display texts that claim Canaan for Yahweh and put the land under the obligation of the covenant (Josh 8:32–33; cf. Deut 27:2–8). When the monarchy is established, Samuel writes "in a book" all of the rights and duties of kingship, so that the king may have them constantly before him (1 Sam 10:25; cf. Deut 17:18–20). Of all of the kings of Judah and Israel, only David admonishes his son to abide by the covenant (1 Kgs 2:3). Thereafter, the book of the covenant is, presumably, lost. Josiah later finds the book of the covenant in the temple and launches his reforms based on all that had been written in it (2 Kgs 22:13; 23:3).

For the Deuteronomistic historian, then, both the act of writing and the act of heeding the written words are essential to the observance of the covenant. Writing is a conservative act, not a creative one. It allows the words to be present in a variety of media, all of which serve as witnesses to the authority of Yahweh, who first promulgated the words, and as witnesses against Israel, who continually defied the covenant. The Deuteronomistic emphasis on recording the words of God is found also in the book of Jeremiah. As in Deuteronomy, the prophet is commanded to write down all the words that God speaks to him (Jer 36:2). These words serve as testimony against Judah,

who failed to heed Jeremiah's words of warning. The function of the book of Jeremiah is thus also comparable to the curses of Deuteronomy, as God promises to punish Jerusalem according to all of the words found in his book (Jer 25:13).

Outside of Jeremiah, the prophetic literature does not exhibit any single theory of writing that would explain the preservation of the prophetic message as written text. Isaiah is commanded to write down his words as an indictment of the rebellious people (Isa 30:8); in later times, this written testimony will serve as teaching and instruction (Isa 8:16). The scroll of Ezekiel should be understood along the lines of a fixed royal decree that cannot be changed (Ezek 3:1–3). The prophets also occasionally used writing in metaphors expressing the permanency of human character and disposition. In Jeremiah, the sin of Judah is "written with an iron pen," and "engraved on . . . their hearts" (Jer 17:1). Under the new covenant, however, the law will be written on their hearts, and there will no longer be any need for instruction (Jer 31:32).

In the Hellenistic era, the concept of Scripture begins to emerge. Scriptures are ancient writings that continue to have authoritative significance, both in providing norms for daily life and in disclosing the divine purpose in history. The concept of Scripture is first evident in Dan 9, where Daniel reads "in the books" about the years of punishment allotted for Jerusalem. Daniel 9 refers to two authoritative collections of writings: the prophets, or, more specifically, the book of Jeremiah (Dan 9:2), and the Torah, or the "law of Moses" (Dan 9:11, 13). Together, the two collections explain the calamitous history of Israel. Because all of the curses that were written in the law of Moses have been poured out on Israel, the truth and hence the normativity of the Torah for daily life is confirmed. In addition, since Daniel's reading of Jeremiah suggests to him that the curses have not yet come to an end, prophecy that had originally been written for an ancient audience remains to be fulfilled in the present and immediate future. This dual emphasis on the normativity and fulfillment of Scripture is evident throughout the NT.

Nearly all of the theological uses of writing that appear in the OT are found in the NT. The book of Revelation is a virtual catalogue of these. Like Jeremiah, John is instructed to "write in a book" all that he sees (Rev 1:11, 19; 14:13; 19:9; 21:5). Those who read John's prophecy are advised to obey and observe what is written (1:3). Those who persevere are inscribed with the name of God, which signifies that they belong to God (Rev 2:17; 3:12; 7:3; cf. 17:5); they also have their names written in the book of life (13:8; 17:8; 20:15; 21:27). And, finally, the written will of God has the character of a fixed royal decree that cannot be revoked (5:2). As such, Revelation concludes with a curse on anyone who might change the words of the book (Rev 22:18–19; cf. Deut 4:2; 12:32). Elsewhere in the NT, two themes are prominent. First, the Scriptures cannot guarantee adequate interpretation on their own. Second, the Scriptures are fulfilled in the church's experience of the crucified and resurrected Messiah.

In the Matthean and Lukan temptation scenes, both Satan and Jesus acknowledge the authority of Scripture through their use of the formula "it is written" (Matt 4:4–10 and par. Luke 4:1–13); however, Jesus and Satan quote Scripture to drastically different ends. Similarly, in the Gospel of John, the Scriptures testify to Jesus, but that is not enough to lead people to him (John 5:39–47). In both instances, Scripture on its own cannot guarantee its proper interpretation. For Matthew's Jesus, one's relationship to God, which is a relationship of obedience, is necessary for an adequate understanding and use of Scripture. In the case of John, the proper understanding and Scripture is rooted in belief, which is a gift of the Holy Spirit (John 3:8).

The theme of fulfillment of Scripture is evident throughout the Gospels (Matt 2:5; 11:10; 26:24, 31; Mark 1:2; 9:12, 13; 14:21, 27; Luke 3:4; 7:27; 18:31), though Luke-Acts may be credited with the clearest articulation of this pattern. The NT emphasis on the fulfillment of Scripture is most often associated with the theme of messianic suffering, as if this were a problem in the early church that needed to be explained and justified (cf. Luke 3:4; 7:27; 18:31). Through their interpretation of the Scriptures of Judaism, the early church demonstrated that the incongruity of a suffering Messiah was in accordance with the divine plan (Luke 7:27; 18:31; 24:46; Acts 7:42; 13:29, 33). This plan had already been fully disclosed in the Scriptures, which simply awaited interpretation (Luke 24:27).

Isaac Rabinowitz, *A Witness Forever: Ancient Israel's Perception of Literature and the Resultant Hebrew Bible* (Bethesda, Md.: CDL Press, 1993).

MARGARET S. ODELL

Wrongdoing   *see* **Sin**

Year   *see* **Time**

Zeal, Zealous   *see* **Jealous**

Zion   *see* **City**